- "I always think when I'm writing a song: What's this going to sound like to me in the distant future? Am I doing something that will pin me like a butterfly to this context, or have I created something that has an essentially organic nature where you can add water to it and it comes back to life later? Will it have importance, or in ten years will it seem charitably quaint and even just muddle-headed? Timelessness is what I'm striving for."

  —Todd Rundgren, songwriter/producer/performer, page 233

- "A lot of new performers seem to think that once they have a manager all the work is done—that having management is some sort of magic bullet that will lead to success. There's a lot of work on both ends, and artists have to be prepared to pick up their piece of the whole process."

  —Dennis Colligan, partner, DSM Management, page 286

- "The most important thing to remember is that writing for film is not a part-time activity; it can't be a supplement to your other songwriting. Writing music for film is a specialized craft, and it's not learned overnight. But any songwriter with enough motivation can learn the basics."

  —Barbara Jordan, film music supervisor, page 377

1997
SONGWRITER'S
MARKET

Managing Editor, Annuals Department:
Constance J. Achabal; Supervising
Editor: Mark Garvey; Production Editor: Anne Bowling

International Standard Serial Number
0161-5971
International Standard Book Number
0-89879-745-4

Cover illustration: Celia Johnson

Attention Booksellers: This is an annual directory of F&W Publications. Return deadline for this edition is December 31, 1997.

1 9 9 7
SONG WRITER'S MARKET

WHERE & HOW TO MARKET YOUR SONGS

EDITED BY

CINDY LAUFENBERG

WRITER'S DIGEST BOOKS
CINCINNATI, OHIO

Contents

From the Editor

Just about a year ago, after enjoying a plate of Kung Pao chicken at a Chinese restaurant, I cracked open a fortune cookie. Instead of the usual vague anecdote, my fortune read: "Your love of music will be an important part of your life." The year that has followed has given me a new respect for the prophetic powers of that little cookie.

While I've had my hand in some sort of musical endeavor for as long as I can remember, this year I really immersed myself in the music world. I started by playing bass in a local band and now run an independent record label to release not only my band's material but that of other local artists. I've discovered what it's like to be in a band struggling for recognition, trying to get songs recorded and released as well as finding places to play. I've also learned what it's like to be on the other side of the fence running a record label and dealing with the time and expense of manufacturing, promoting and selling records. With this experience, I've gained a better understanding of the readers of *Songwriter's Market*, since I now find myself in the same position as any aspiring songwriter/performer trying to find an audience.

With this in mind, this edition addresses the most important thing a songwriter needs to know—how to get songs heard. Turn the page and you'll find articles focusing on alternative ways of getting songs heard other than the typical mailing of demos. John Braheny, author of *The Craft and Business of Songwriting*, has written a practical guide entitled "Getting Heard in a 'No Unsolicited Material' World." With fewer companies accepting unsolicited material, he provides advice on how to open those closed doors. The Performing Songwriter's Roundtable features three singer/songwriters who make a living writing and performing their songs—*without* the help of a record label. They offer advice on how to rely on yourself to make a living from your music.

We also have an impressive lineup of Insider Reports. Among the nine industry professionals we interviewed, producer/songwriter/performer extraordinaire Todd Rundgren talks about the creative process of writing songs; Academy Award-nominated film composer Mark Isham discusses what it's like to work in Hollywood; and David McPherson, A&R director at Jive Records, offers his view of the R&B and rap markets and where they're heading. Look to these and the six other Insider Reports for insight and advice on how the music industry works and what to look out for.

We've added a new feature to the book this year, a geographic index listing companies by state. You'll also notice many listings now provide e-mail and website addresses, and we've added a "Websites of Interest" page to help you start exploring opportunities on the Internet. Plus we've updated each listing, as well as added more than 475 companies new to this edition.

With a little talent and a whole lot of motivation, you can find an audience for your music, and the 1997 *Songwriter's Market* can help you get started. Be sure to let me know what you like, dislike, or would like to see in future editions of *Songwriter's Market*. And pay attention to those fortune cookies.

Cindy Laufenberg
wdigest@aol.com

How to Get the Most Out of *Songwriter's Market*

The hardest task for you, the aspiring songwriter, is deciding where and to whom to submit your music. You're reading this book in the hope of finding information on good potential markets for your work. You may be seeking a publisher who will pitch your music, a record company that will offer you a recording contract, or a chamber music group or theater company to produce and perform your music live. *Songwriter's Market* is designed to help you make those submission decisions. Read the articles, Insider Report interviews and section introductions for an overview of the industry. With careful research you can target your submissions and move toward achieving your goals.

WHERE DO YOU START?

It's easiest to move from the very general to the very specific. The book is divided into Markets and Resources. The Resources section contains listings and information on organizations, workshops, contests and publications to help you learn more about the music industry and the craft of songwriting. The Markets section contains all the markets seeking new material and is the part of the book you will need to concentrate on for submissions.

Markets is further divided into sections corresponding to specific segments of the industry. This is of particular help to composers of music for the theater and concert hall, who can find prospective markets in the Play Producers & Publishers and Classical Performing Arts sections, respectively. Composers of audiovisual (film and TV) and commercial music will also find a section of the book, Advertising, AV and Commercial Music Firms, devoted to these possibilities.

THE GENERAL MARKETS

If you don't fall into these specific areas, you will need to do a little more work to target markets. Questions you need to ask are: Who am I writing this music for? Are these songs that I have written for an act I now belong to? Am I a songwriter hoping to have my music accepted and recorded by an artist?

If you fall into the first category, writing songs for an existing group or for yourself as a solo artist, you're probably trying to advance the career of your act. If you're seeking a recording contract, the Record Companies section will be the place to start. Look also at the Record Producers section. Independent record producers are constantly on the lookout for up-and-coming artists. They may also have strong connections with record companies looking for acts, and will pass your demo on or recommend the act to a record company. And if your act doesn't yet have representation, your demo submission may be included as part of a promotional kit sent to a prospective manager listed in the Managers and Booking Agents section.

If you are a songwriter seeking to have your songs recorded by other artists, you may submit to some of these same markets, but for different reasons. The Record Producers section contains mostly independent producers who work regularly with particular artists, rather than working fulltime for one record company. Because they work closely with a limited number of clients, they may be the place to send songs written with a specific act in mind. The independent producer is often responsible for picking cuts for a recording project. The Managers and Booking Agents section may be useful for the same reason. Many personal managers are constantly seeking new song material for the acts they represent, and a good song sent at the right time can mean a valuable cut for the songwriter.

The primary market for songwriters not writing with particular artists in mind will be found in the Music Publishers section. Music publishers are the jacks-of-all-trade in the industry, having knowledge about and keeping abreast of developments in all other segments of the music business. They act as the first line of contact between the songwriter and the music industry.

If you're uncertain about which markets will have the most interest in your material, review the introductory explanations at the beginning of each section. They will aid in explaining the various functions of each segment of the music industry, and will help you narrow your list of possible submissions.

NOW WHAT?

You've identified the market categories you're thinking about sending demos to. The next step is to research each section to find the individual markets that will be most interested in your work.

Most users of *Songwriter's Market* should check three items in the listings: location of the company, the type of music they're interested in hearing, and their submission policy. Each of these items should be considered carefully when deciding which markets to submit to.

If it's important to send your work to a company close to your home for more opportunities for face-to-face contact, location should be checked first. Each section contains listings from all over the U.S. as well as the rest of the world. Check the Geographic Index at the back of the book for listings of companies by state.

Your music isn't going to be appropriate for submission to all companies. Most music industry firms have specific music interests and needs, and you want to be sure your submissions are being seen and heard by companies who have a genuine interest in them. To find this information turn to the Category Indexes located at the end of the Music Publishers, Record Companies, Record Producers and Managers and Booking Agents sections. Locate the category of music that best describes the material you write, and refer to the companies listed under those categories. (Keep in mind that these are general categories. Some companies may not be listed in the Category Index because they either accept all types of music or the music they are looking for doesn't fit into any of the general categories.) When you've located a listing, go to the Music subheading. It will contain, in **bold** type, a more detailed list of the styles of music a company is seeking. Here is an example from a listing in the Record Companies section:

Music: Mostly **heavy metal/hard rock** and **alternative guitar-based rock;** also **dance** and **pop**.

Pay close attention to the types of music described. For instance, if the music you write fits the category of "rock," there can be many variations on that style. Our sample above is interested in hard rock, another listing may be looking for country rock, and another, soft rock. These are three very different styles of music, but they all fall under the same general category. The Category Index is there to help you narrow down the listings within a certain music genre; it is up to you to narrow them down even further to fit the type of music you write. The music styles in each listing are in descending order of importance; if your particular specialty is country music, you may want to search out those listings that list country as their first priority as your primary targets for submissions. Going back to our sample Music subhead again, see the emphasis on rock, but also the interest in dance/pop.

You will also want to check and see if a listing has an editorial comment, see the sample below, which will be marked by a bullet (●).

● Note that Canyon Records is a very specialized label, and only wants to receive submissions by Native American artists.

Editorial comments give you additional information such as special submission requirements, any awards a company may have won, and other details that will help you narrow down which companies to submit to. They will also let you know if a company is listed in other sections of the book.

Finally, when you've placed the listings geographically and identified their music preferences, read the How to Contact subheading. As shown in the example below, it will give you pertinent information about what to send as part of a demo submission, how to go about sending it and when you can expect to hear back from them.

How to Contact: Submit demo tape by mail. Unsolicited submissions are OK. "Telephoning A&R Director prior to submission is recommended." Prefers cassette, DAT or VHS videocassette with 3 songs and lyric sheet. SASE. Reports in 3-4 weeks.

This market accepts unsolicited submissions, but not all of the markets listed in *Songwriter's Market* do, so it's important to read this information carefully. Most companies have carefully considered their submission policy, and packages that do not follow their directions are returned or discarded without evaluation. Follow the instructions: it will impress upon the market your seriousness about getting your work heard.

You've now identified markets you feel will have the most interest in your work. Read the complete listing carefully before proceeding. Many of the listings have individualized information important for the submitting songwriter. Then, it's time for you to begin preparing your demo submission package to get your work before the people in the industry. For further information on that process, turn to Getting Started.

Getting Started

To exist and thrive in the competitive music industry without being overwhelmed is perhaps the biggest challenge facing songwriters. Those who not only survive but also succeed have taken the time before entering the market to learn as much as they can about the inner workings of the music industry.

Newcomers to the music business can educate themselves about the industry through experience or education. Experience, while valuable, can be time-consuming and costly. Education can be just as effective, and less painful. Many sources exist to help you educate yourself about the intricacies of the industry *before* you jump in. Reading, studying and learning to use the information contained in sourcebooks such as *Songwriter's Market* expand your knowledge of the music industry and how it works, and help you market yourself and your work professionally and effectively.

IMPROVING YOUR CRAFT

Unfortunately, no magic formula can guarantee success in the music business. If you want to make it in this competitive business, you must begin by believing in yourself and your talent. As a songwriter, you must develop your own personal vision and stick with it. Why do you write songs? Is it because you want to make a lot of money, or because you love the process? Is every song you write an attempt to become famous, or a labor of love? Successful songwriters believe they have a talent that deserves to be heard, whether by two or two thousand people. Songwriting is a craft, like woodworking or painting. A lot of talent is involved, of course, but with time and practice the craft can be improved and eventually mastered.

While working on songs, learn all you can about the writing process. Look for support and feedback wherever you can. A great place to start is a local songwriting organization, which can offer friendly advice, support from other writers, and a place to meet collaborators. (For more information on songwriting organizations in your area, see the Organizations section on page 444.) Many organizations offer song critique sessions, which will help you identify strengths and weaknesses in your material and give you guidance to help improve your craft. Take any criticism you receive in a constructive manner, and use it to improve your writing style. The feedback you receive will help you write better songs, create connections within the industry and continue your education not only in the craft of songwriting but in the business as well.

THE STRUCTURE OF THE MUSIC BUSINESS

The music business in the United States revolves around three major hubs: New York, Nashville and Los Angeles. Power is concentrated in those areas because that's where most record companies, publishers, songwriters and performers are. A lot of people trying to break into the music business, in whatever capacity, move to one of those three cities to be close to the people and companies they want to contact. From time to time a regional music scene will heat up in a non-hub city such as Austin, Chicago or Seattle. When this happens, songwriters and performers in that city experience a kind of musical Renaissance complete with better-paying gigs, a creatively charged atmosphere and intensified interest from major labels.

All this is not to say that a successful career cannot be nurtured from any city in the country, however. It can be, especially if you are a songwriter. By moving to a major music hub, you may be closer physically to the major companies, but you'll also encounter more competition than you would back home. Stay where you're comfortable; it's probably easier (and more cost-effective) to conquer the music scene where you are than it is in Los Angeles or Nashville. There are many smaller, independent companies located in cities across the country. Most international careers are started on a local level, and some may find a local career more satisfying, in its own way, than the constant striving to gain the attention of the major companies.

Any company, whether major or independent, relies on the buying public. Their support, in the form of money spent on records, concert tickets and other kinds of musical entertainment, keeps the music industry in business. Because of that, record companies, publishers and producers are eager to give the public what they want. To stay one step ahead of public tastes, record companies hire people who have a knack for spotting musical talent and anticipating trends, and put them in charge of finding and developing new talent. These talent scouts are called A&R representatives. "A&R" stands for "artist and repertoire," which simply means they are responsible for discovering new talent and matching songs to particular artists. The person responsible for the recording artist's product—the record—is called the producer. The producer's job is to develop the artist's work and come out of the studio with a good-sounding, saleable product that represents the artist in the best possible manner. His duties sometimes include choosing songs for a particular project, so record producers are also great contacts for songwriters.

Producers and A&R reps are aided in their search for talent by the music publisher. A publisher works as a songwriter's advocate who, for a percentage of the profits (typically 50% of all earnings from a particular song), attempts to find commercially profitable uses for the songs he represents. A successful publisher stays in contact with several A&R reps, trying to find out what upcoming projects are looking for new material, and whether any songs he represents will be appropriate.

When a song is recorded and subsequently released to the public, the recording artist, songwriter, record company, producer and publisher all stand to profit. Recording artists earn a negotiated royalty from a record company based on the number of records sold. Producers are usually paid either a negotiated royalty based on sales or a flat fee at the time of recording. Publishers and songwriters earn mechanical royalties (money a record company pays a publisher based on record sales) and performance royalties, which are based on radio airplay and live performances.

As you can see, the people you need to make contact with are publishers, A&R reps and producers. Managers can also be added to that list—most are looking for material for the acts they represent. Getting your material to these professionals and establishing relationships with as many people in the industry as you can should be your main goal as a songwriter. The more people who hear your songs, the better your chances of getting them recorded.

Any method of getting your songs heard, published, recorded and released is the best way if it works for you. *Songwriter's Market* lists music publishers, record companies, producers and managers (as well as advertising firms, play producers and classical performing arts organizations) along with specifications on how to submit your material to each. If you can't find a certain person or company you're interested in, there are other sources of information you can try. The *Recording Industry Sourcebook*, an annual directory published by Cardinal Business Media, lists record companies, music publishers, producers and managers, as well as attorneys, publicity firms, media, manufacturers, distributors and recording studios around the United States. Trade publications such as *Billboard* or *Cash Box*, available at most local libraries and bookstores, are great sources for up-to-date information. These periodicals list new companies as well as the artists, labels, producers and publishers for each song on the charts. Album covers, CD booklets and cassette j-cards can be valuable sources of information, providing the name of the record company, publisher, producer and usually the manager of an artist or group. Use your imagination in your research and be creative—any contacts you make in the industry can only help your career as a songwriter.

SUBMITTING YOUR SONGS

When it comes to presenting your material, the tool of the music industry is a demonstration recording—a demo. Cassette tapes have been the standard in the music industry for decades because they're so convenient. Songwriters use demos to present their songs, and musicians use them to showcase their performance skills. Demos are submitted to various professionals in the industry, either by mail or in person.

Demo quality

The production quality of demos can vary widely, but even simple guitar/vocal or piano/vocal demos must sound clean, with the instrument in tune and lyrics sung clearly. Many songwriters are investing in home recording equipment such as four- or eight-track recorders, keyboards and drum machines, so they can record their demos themselves. Other writers prefer to book studio time, hire musicians, and get professional input from an engineer or producer. Demo services are also available to record your demo for a fee. It's up to you to decide what you can afford and feel most comfortable with, and what you think best represents your song. Once a master recording is made of your song, you're ready to make cassette copies and start pitching your song to the contacts you've researched.

Some markets indicate that you may send a videocassette of your act in performance or a group performing your songs, instead of the standard cassette demo. Most of the companies listed in *Songwriter's Market* have indicated that a videocassette is not required, but have indicated the format of their VCR should you decide to send one. Be aware that television systems vary widely from country to country, so if you're sending a video to a foreign listing check with them for the system they're using. For example, a VHS format tape recorded using the U.S. system (called NTSC) will not play back on a standard British VCR (using the PAL system), even if the recording formats are the same. It is possible to transfer a video from one system to another, but the expense in both time and money may outweigh its usefulness. Systems for some countries include: NTSC—U.S., Canada and Japan; PAL—United Kingdom, Australia and Germany; and SECAM—France.

Submitting by mail

When submitting material to companies listed in this book:
- Read the listing carefully and submit exactly what a company asks for and exactly how it asks that it be submitted. It's always a good idea to call first, just in case a company has changed its submission policy.
- Listen to each demo before sending to make sure the quality is satisfactory.
- Enclose a brief, typed cover letter to introduce yourself. Indicate what songs you are sending and why you are sending them. If you're a songwriter pitching songs to a particular artist, state that in the letter. If you're an artist/songwriter looking for a recording deal, you should say so. Have specific goals.
- Include typed lyric sheets or lead sheets if requested. Make sure your name, address and phone number appear on each sheet.
- Neatly label each tape with your name, address and phone number along with

the names of the songs in the sequence in which they appear on the tape.
- If the company returns material (many do not; be sure to read each listing carefully), include a SASE for the return. Your return envelope to countries other than your own should contain a self-addressed envelope (SAE) and International Reply Coupon (IRC), available at your local post office. Be sure the return envelope is large enough to accommodate your material, and include sufficient postage for the weight of the package.
- Wrap the package neatly and write (or type on a shipping label) the company's address and your return address so they are clearly visible. Your package is the first impression a company has of you and your songs, so neatness is important.
- Mail first class. Stamp or write "First Class Mail" on the package and on the SASE you enclose. Don't send by registered or certified mail unless the company specifically requests it.
- Keep records of the dates, songs, and companies you submit to.

If you are writing to inquire about a company's needs or to request permission to submit (many companies ask you to do this first), your query letter should be typed, brief and pleasant. Explain the type of material you have and ask for their needs and submission policy.

To expedite a reply, you should enclose a self-addressed, stamped postcard requesting the information you are seeking. Your typed questions (see the Sample Reply Postcard) should be direct and easy to answer. Place the company's name and address in the upper left hand space on the front of the postcard so you'll know which company you queried. Keep a record of the queries you send for future reference.

SAMPLE REPLY POSTCARD

I would like to hear:
____ "Name of Song"   ____ "Name of Song"   ____ "Name of Song"

I prefer:
____ cassette ____ DAT ____ videocassette

With:
____ lyric sheet ____ lead sheet ____ either ____ both
____ I am not looking for material at this time, try me later.
____ I am not interested.

_____
Name   Title

It's acceptable to submit your songs to more than one person at a time (this is called simultaneous submission). The one exception to this is when a publisher, artist or other industry professional asks if he may put a song of yours "on hold." This means he intends to record it, and doesn't want you to give the song to anyone else. Your song may be returned to you without ever having been recorded, even if it's been on hold for months. Or, your song may be recorded but the artist or producer decides to leave it off the album. If either of these things happens, you're free to pitch your song to other people again. (You can protect yourself from having a song on hold indefinitely. Establish a deadline for the person who asks for the hold, i.e., "You can put my song on hold for *X* number of months." Or modify the hold to specify that you will pitch the song to other people, but you will not sign a deal without allowing the person who has the song on hold to make you an offer.) When someone publishes your song and you sign a contract, you grant that publisher exclusive rights to your song and you may not pitch it to other publishers. You can, however, pitch it to any artists or producers interested in recording the song without publishing it themselves.

If a market doesn't respond within several weeks after you've sent your demo, don't despair. As long as your demo is in the possession of a market, there is a chance that someone is reviewing it. That opportunity ends when your demo is returned to you. If after a reasonable amount of time you still haven't received word on your submission (check the reporting time each company states in its listing), following up with a friendly letter or phone call giving detailed information about your submission is a good idea. Many companies do not return submissions, so don't expect a company that states "Does not return material" to send your materials back to you.

Submitting in person

Planning a trip to one of the major music hubs will give you insight into how the music industry functions. Whether you decide to visit New York, Nashville or Los Angeles, have some specific goals in mind and set up appointments to make the most of your time there. It will be difficult to get in to see some industry professionals as many of them are extremely busy and may not feel meeting out-of-town writers is a high priority. Other people are more open to, and even encourage, face-to-face meetings. They may feel that if you take the time to travel to where they are, and you're organized enough to schedule meetings beforehand, you're more professional than many aspiring songwriters who blindly submit inappropriate songs through the mail. (For listings of companies by state, see the Geographic Index at the back of the book.)

Take several cassette copies and lyric sheets of each of your songs. More than one of the companies you visit may ask that you leave a copy to review and perhaps play for other professionals in the company. There's also a good chance that the person you have an appointment with will have to cancel (expect that occasionally) but wants you to leave a copy of the songs so he can listen and contact you later. Never give someone the last or only copy of your material—if it is not returned to you, all the hard work and money that went into making that demo will be lost.

Another good place to meet industry professionals face-to-face is at seminars such as the yearly South by Southwest Music and Media Conference in Austin, the National Academy of Songwriters' annual Songwriters Expo, or the Nashville Songwriters Association's Spring Symposium, to name a few (see the Workshops and Conferences section of this book for further ideas). Many of these conferences feature demo listening sessions, where industry professionals sit down and listen to demos submitted by songwriters attending the seminars.

Many good songs have been rejected simply because they just weren't what the particular publisher or record company was looking for at the time, so don't take rejection personally. Realize that if a few people don't like your songs, it doesn't mean they're not good. However, if there seems to be a consensus about your work—for instance, the feel of a song isn't right or the lyrics need work—give the advice serious thought. Listen attentively to what the reviewers say and use their criticism constructively to improve your songs.

Getting Heard in a "No Unsolicited Material" World

BY JOHN BRAHENY

Once you've written that great song or completed your writer/artist masters or demos, you face the prospect of getting heard by the music industry. You take off your creative songwriter hat and put on your marketing hat. For some of you, this is an exciting challenge. For others, it runs a close second to major surgery. Like anything else, though, it gets much less daunting when you have some practical information. Let's start by understanding the barriers you may encounter when trying to get through the doors of the music industry.

WHY IS IT SO HARD TO GET IN?

To be able to deal with this problem effectively, we need to look at it from the point of view of the publishers, producers, record company A&R representatives and managers who are your most prominent "targets." They have two major concerns: finding great talent/songs in the most time- and cost-efficient way possible, and protecting themselves from lawsuits.

In the first case, if they have an open-door policy, most companies are deluged with tapes. Even with "no unsolicited material" policies, they're still deluged with solicited tapes (those referred by other writers or industry people they respect). The biggest problem for those with open-door policies, particularly producers and record companies looking for songs for specific projects, is that most of the songs they receive are totally inappropriate for their needs. Usually this is because writers who are sending in tapes haven't taken the time to research the project (more about this later). Consequently, those listening to tapes already know that more than 90 percent of their time will be wasted. Pretty bad odds for someone who may have only one or two assistants who can screen tapes.

Time is another barrier keeping industry professionals from listening to unsolicited tapes. Music publishers who don't have a particular project in mind but are just looking for great songs or writer/artists for development will have a broader scope of material they're seeking. It may take more time to evaluate the songs they receive because they're listening for more than whether the song will work for a current project. They're also looking for artists who have potential for future success that they can work with and develop.

The legal barrier is also a formidable door-closer, as most companies' legal departments advise them against accepting unsolicited material in fear of potential copyright infringement suits. A key factor in determining infringement is proof of "access." In other words, if a copyright infringement suit goes to court, the prosecution has to prove that the accused had the opportunity to hear the material. Proving that someone at the company opened the package containing your tape is, of course, proof of access. You

---

JOHN BRAHENY is executive vice president of Wynnward Music Enterprises, former co-founder/ director of the Los Angeles Songwriters Showcase, and author of The Craft and Business of Songwriting, published by Writer's Digest Books.

may wonder, can't an infringement lawsuit result from solicited material? Of course it can, but the odds are much lower because industry people already know that most infringement suits are brought by writers who are not seriously pursuing a career as a songwriter. Since a suit has to be dealt with by the company's legal department, it uses up valuable time and resources.

Is this fear of lawsuits why many companies ask you to have an attorney submit a demo tape for you? No. Certainly, your attorney could document the publisher's "access" to your tape. But most industry pros do not believe that submission of a tape by someone with a law degree guarantees its artistic and commercial quality. Not that there aren't entertainment attorneys whose musical tastes are respected, but it isn't the law degree that insures it. So why is it they ask you to do it? After pursuing this question for years and asking a lot of questions of a lot of industry people, I've come to one conclusion: they want to know you're serious. On countless occasions I've heard industry people say, "I don't accept unsolicited material but if someone is really worth hearing, they'll find a way to get to me or I'll hear about them." This is sort of a "survival of the fittest" philosophy that, like it or not, has some merit. They figure if you're serious enough to pay a couple hundred dollars an hour to have an attorney shop your tape, you're serious enough for them to listen to.

GETTING THROUGH THE DOOR

Showing the industry you're serious is the key. One of the most important things you need to do is research. Become aware of the industry people involved in your style of music. Read the credits on the recordings of your favorite artists—find out who produced them, who wrote and published the songs, the record label and possibly even the record company A&R representative who works with that artist. If the A&R rep's name isn't on the package, call the record company's artist relations department or A&R coordinator and get his name. You can also get the phone and fax numbers of the artist's producer and manager. You should also study the artist in order to "cast" the right song so you can be reasonably confident it will be appropriate. Casting involves knowing the artist's style and, if it's an established artist, being familiar with the artist's most successful recordings. Know the vocal range. Artists will often have a special place in their range that highlights the uniqueness of their vocal sound or style. It's referred to as their "sweet spot;" give them something in that place to enhance their style. Try to determine what it is that makes the artist's music successful and make sure you have that quality in your writing. Is his attitude positive, negative or spiritual? Does he sing about lost love or hopeful love? Are they victim songs, songs of strength, rebellion, sarcasm, cynicism or alienation? Look as much for the absence of these as you do for their presence.

Another thing to remember in casting is that it may be a couple of years before an artist's next album is released, so if you copy the current production style your demo may sound dated. Try to imagine how you'd like to hear the artist develop and produce your demo accordingly. This is tricky, but creative. Whenever possible, try to find out from the artist's producer, manager or record company if there's a change in the artist's direction. If you're pitching for a new artist, get information from those same sources or find a tip sheet.

If you're pitching yourself to record companies as a self-contained artist or group, it's more complex. The same no-unsolicited-material policies exist here. You're much better off if you have some performing experience. All the better if you've got good reviews, have been on the road and are used to traveling. Record companies want a band or performer to have been field-tested, if not test-marketed regionally with some success. If they're going to risk (in the case of major labels) at least a quarter of a million dollars to record and market you nationally, they want to know you can handle it.

In this situation, too, you need to research the names of companies, producers, managers and A&R reps who know how to market the artists and groups in your musical style. You need to know their names and who they've worked with. Read the trade magazines such as *Billboard, Hits, Radio and Records, Cash Box, The Hollywood Reporter* (especially if you're interested in film music) and any industry trades that relate to your own musical style. Call the biggest newsstand in town to find these publications. If they don't carry them, call your local library. If they don't have them, gather a group of other songwriters to formally petition the library to subscribe. They may not be getting the music trades because they don't think anyone is interested. Most are weekly magazines and they're very expensive ($250-$300 per year), but if you feel you're ready to begin your assault on the industry, they're one of your best investments.

Trade magazines can provide valuable information such as what records are on the charts in every genre of music and who performed, wrote, produced, published, released and distributed them. For those who want to write songs for others to record, the charts can tell you whether or not an artist records "outside" songs. Are the songs written by the artist and/or the producer? If so, you have a pretty good idea, though not a certainty, that sending songs to this artist is a waste of time. Those few songs you see on the *Billboard* Hot 100 charts with writer names that differ from the artist and producer names are the ones to analyze for casting purposes. You'll find more of these opportunities on the country and R&B charts. This information gives you a savvy-sounding opener for your industry calls. Here's an example: In *Billboard* you see Bonnie Raitt's name on the charts with a new single. You don't have any of her CDs yet (you'll buy them today) but you've heard her on the radio and think you might have something for her. You've also read an article in which she talks about the songs on her new project, where she got them, who wrote them and about working with her producer, Don Was. You've also seen his name listed as producer under the song title on the chart and noticed that a different name appeared there as writer, so you know she's open to "outside" songs. You also learn she's on Capitol Records. So you call Capitol and ask for the A&R coordinator. "Hi! This is so-and-so at This and That Music. Will Don Was be producing Bonnie Raitt's next album? Do you have a number for him? Who's doing A&R on the project?" Get each name down quick. If you ask them to spell it for you, you're already another step away from credibility with them. They figure if you're the pro you seem to be, you'll already be familiar with the names. (Look to directories such as the *A&R Registry* to help you out—see sidebar for more resources.)

Once you have the name of the A&R person at Capitol or someone in Don Was's office, call directly and ask about the musical direction of Bonnie's next album and how to go about submitting songs for it. It's a good idea to ask if there's a code you should use on the package. They often use a personal code so their secretaries or mail room personnel know that it's actually been "solicited."

All the trades publish special focus issues which will contain a treasure of information on specialized areas of the industry such as children's music, classical, heavy metal, alternative, folk, music publishing, Latin, Celtic and film music. They may focus on cities and countries that are emerging as music centers such as Minneapolis, Seattle, Atlanta, Ireland, etc. You'll get information on the movers and shakers in those genres or places, the record labels, publishers, producers, managers, radio stations, booking agents and artists, along with stories about who signed whom and their career strategies.

Following music industry trends is also important. Industry legend Russ Regan, now CEO of Quality Records, gave me a great bit of advice once. He not only looks at what's on the charts now but what isn't there. Looking at it that way, we shouldn't have been surprised a few years ago when, on a chart full of drum machines and sterile, sequenced tracks, an acoustic-based record called "Fast Car" by a new artist named Tracy Chapman broke through like a breath of fresh air. It's the business of the trades to help the industry predict and follow trends.

Technology is also a predictor of trends, and you can find some useful information in the trades about how new technology will affect the industry. For example, *Billboard*'s SoundScan technology revolutionized the industry by providing accurate retail sales and airplay information, and proved country music was selling much more than was thought. Transmission of music over the Internet has opened a new avenue for exposing and selling music, though monitoring these performances has presented the performing rights organizations with a new challenge. The Internet now provides up-to-date research information from the performing rights organizations, making their catalogs accessible to anyone with a modem. There are now several Internet services available for exposing and selling independent recordings to the online audience, among them Kaleidospace (http://kspace.com) and Internet Underground Music Archive (http://www.iuma.com). Browsing the music related websites on the Internet will turn up many more (see the Websites of Interest section on page 490 for more information). These are all developments you can stay abreast of by regularly reading the trades.

Think of your local record store as a research center. It usually has a list of current hits in your favorite style. Familiarize yourself with them and find the albums in the record bins. Many stores have listening posts where you can spend some time listening to new releases and reading the CD covers for information on the artists. Some stores even have information kiosks where you can bring up artist information on a monitor and look up past albums, reviews, etc. If you have an Internet connection, look to see if the artist has a website you can contact. You can also look at an Internet directory under "music" and find websites for record companies too.

MAKING THE CALLS

If you know up front that industry people are deluged by calls from writers and artists who haven't done their homework, you have a distinct advantage if you put in the research time before you call. It lets you call with a certain amount of confidence in your voice. Don't come off as arrogant, but do project confidence. If you can let them know you're serious and have done your research, the "gatekeepers" will be afraid to shut you down too quickly because, for all they know, you may be someone important to their boss. The boss is also more likely to take you seriously. Don't beg for a chance to be heard! This is very unprofessional. Though you may not actually say it, the subtext of your conversation should be, "I have great songs that I know are appropriate for this artist. They deserve to be heard."

No matter who you're trying to get to, be nice to assistants and secretaries. Treat them with respect. There's a better than average chance that they are the ones who will initially be listening to your tape. In fact, you may acknowledge that possibility ahead of time by asking for their opinion on your songs. Also, by the next time you call, they may be the boss and the relationship you developed on the phone gets you into their office. If you're serious enough to want a career in songwriting, you need to think years ahead and build bridges now.

Always request permission to submit tapes or CDs. For the reasons outlined at the beginning of this article, you must get permission to submit your demo. You can do this by phone but you may not have much time to "sell" yourself. A short fax can be more efficient. Include any information that may set you off from everyone else; reviews or favorable critiques of your songs or performances, sales figures on your CDs or tapes, a short history of your career, other songs held or recorded, and evidence that you've done your research on the artist or company.

FOLLOW UP!

If you do get through the door, consider it a great accomplishment but only the first of a series. Don't figure that all you have to do now is wait for them to call you back and tell you how great your song is. Know that they're very busy and you may have to remind them that they have your tape. After calling to make sure they've received it, always ask them to give you a date or time frame to check back. You might say, "Look, I know you guys are busy and I don't want to make a pest of myself so I'd appreciate it if you could give me some guideline about when to check back." That way, when you do call back you don't feel like a pest because you can say, "You suggested I call back in a couple of weeks." Don't be shy about calling back several times. Nobody in the music business will ever fault you for persistence. Though it will be frustrating, don't let it affect your professional attitude on the phone.

OTHER AVENUES

If you plan to pitch your songs directly to record companies, managers, producers and artists, you're being a publisher. You'll get through their doors easier if you have your own company, logo and letterhead. Don't choose a name for your company that reflects your own (JoJac for Joe Jackson) or it will be obvious to them that you're a "hip-pocket" publisher (a writer only representing your own material) rather than a company that has invested in a writer it believes in. If you decide to pitch your songs to publishers, don't send them on your publishing letterhead. They'll wonder why another publisher is sending them a song. You can also send your letterhead packages to record companies, producers and managers. Managers should not be overlooked since, as "captain" of the artist's team, they are usually very close to the decision process on selection of songs, direction of the artist, choice of producers, etc. and may not be deluged as are record company A&R reps and producers.

Make sure you keep a tape and lyric sheets with you at all times. You never know when you'll get an unexpected opportunity to give it to someone. That someone could be the artist's hairdresser, limo driver, recording engineer, road manager, friend or anyone else who has access to the artist or the artist's official "team." You can even offer them a sales incentive of a percentage of the income on whatever song any of those people are responsible for helping you place. Note that I said income, not a percentage of the publishing, which implies a percentage of ownership of the copyright. I'm talking about about a cut in or participation in a percentage of the publisher's share of the income for that particular recording. The income can be mechanical (on sales of CDs, tapes, etc.), performance (from ASCAP, BMI or SESAC for airplay) or a combination.

Other good sources of information and contacts are local or national songwriter organizations and events. Most organizations have regularly scheduled events in which they invite music industry professionals to speak and listen to tapes. Familiarize yourselves with those guests, their histories and current needs. The personal contact has much more impact than a cold call. Support those organizations with your membership and volunteer time and you'll often find yourselves surrounded by opportunities. Organization newsletters also frequently provide valuable information about industry events of interest to songwriters such as the annual Songwriters Expo in Los Angeles, Nashville Songwriters Association International's yearly seminars and many others.

Always remember that this is a people business. As in most other businesses, maintaining your personal relationships, networking for new contacts, taking advantage of your memberships in organizations that can put you in touch with the industry, doing favors for your colleagues, researching the trade magazines and being ready to immediately take advantage of opportunities are all things that could contribute to your success.

RESOURCES

These sources can help you begin gathering information on the music industry. Research them carefully to help you contact those within the industry who can get your songs recorded.

Doing Research

Recording Industry Sourcebook, published by Cardinal Business Media
(800) 233-9604
More than 10,000 listings in 55 categories. Listings include names, titles, phone, fax, styles of music and whether unsolicited material is accepted.

Annual Talent/Personal Managers Guide, published by Performance Publications
(817) 338-9444
This comprehensive cross-referenced directory lists artists, their personal managers, booking agents and record companies.

Nashville 415/Country Music Sourcebook
(800) 223-7524
A comprehensive resource of business-to-business listings for the Nashville area and country music genre.

SRS Publishing
(800)377-7411
This company, headed by former Arista Records A&R rep Ritch Esra, publishes the *A&R Registry*, a comprehensive listing of record company A&R reps including their stylistic focus, direct phone numbers and names of their assistants. They also publish the *Music Publisher Registry* and *Film and TV Music Guide*, updated every two months.

Pitching Your Songs

The National Academy Of Songwriters (NAS)
(213) 463-7178
The recent merger of two national organizations, the Los Angeles Songwriters Showcase and NAS, has created the largest U.S songwriters organization, offering two weekly mail-in pitch opportunities. Members can pitch songs to different publishers, producers and record company A&R representatives every week in person or by mail. All styles.

TAXI
(800) 458-2111
An innovative tip-sheet/independent A&R service. Members receive listings every two weeks by major and independent labels and publishers, film and TV music supervisors looking for writers, writer/artists and bands. All submissions pre-screened and critiqued by industry pros. All styles.

For more information, see the Organizations, Workshops and Conferences, and Publications of Interest sections at the back of this book.

Film composers must develop a distinct style

When composer and jazz trumpet player Mark Isham accepted a deal to write the score for Disney's *Never Cry Wolf* in 1982, he had no idea composing for film would become the mainstay of his musical career.

Mark Isham

photo: William Claxton

"I had never considered film as a career opportunity," says Isham, who at the time was struggling to get a solo jazz career off the ground. "I must have known that there were people who wrote music for film, but I never thought that would be something I would pursue. I was aware enough to realize that this was an opportunity I shouldn't ignore. I thought, hey, I can get paid for writing instrumental music, and get paid to have it recorded at a high quality, and I suddenly sort of got with the program."

Fifteen years and 39 films later, Isham has established himself as one of the most sought-after film composers in Hollywood. His credits include scores for *Little Man Tate*, *Quiz Show*, *Time Cop*, *Nell* and *Losing Isaiah*. His classical score for Robert Redford's *A River Runs Through It* received a 1993 Academy Award nomination for best original score and a Grammy Award nomination for best instrumental composition for a motion picture.

Writing scores for film is a collaborative creative process, Isham says, which is why talented composers without the ability to hear and translate the direction of others may not find much work.

"Over 50 percent of the gig has nothing to do with music," he says. "It has to do with the art of communication . . . and ultimately [composers] are creating something that has to fall into the vision of another. That's a tricky line; directors are hiring you because you're an expert in your field, and they want you to create your own thing, but it has to fit within certain boundaries. You have to be able to duplicate what this person is saying to you, to understand what it is they really want. Ultimately, you're not finished until the director says you're finished."

Scoring for film is a "very, very competitive field," but those who come in with an established musical style have an edge, Isham says. "I think there's a gradient scale of composers—at one end you have the guys who might work at a production house, who can knock off a string quartet and an acid jazz group, but you really don't know who they are. They don't have a point of view. At the other end you have individual artists. The successful film composers are the people who begin with a distinct style. They have a point of view, but they broaden their vocabulary enough so they can be available for a wider spectrum of styles, because there's a broad spectrum of film out there. Personally, I think it's more important to be weighted on the side of individuality than it is to be weighted on the side of eclectic, broad vocabulary because no one's going to remember who you are."

In a field that attracts contenders from all walks of the music industry—composers, orchestrators, songwriters—"you just have to keep looking for that vehicle that will allow your point of view to be seen by others," says Isham, who counts trumpet player Miles Davis and pianist Keith Jarrett as contributors to his style. "That's where the persistence enters in—you just have to keep pushing until you get that theater piece or commercial that allows you to just say 'here I am.' "

For Isham, it was a circuitous path to success. He grew up in New York City and San Francisco, in what he describes as a "very rich and somewhat classical upbringing." Encouraged by his mother, a professional violin player, and his father, a professor of humanities, Isham studied piano, violin and trumpet from an early age.

"Having grown up in a classical household was good, because by the time I started looking at music on my own—I wanted to know about jazz and rock and roll and electronic music, all the hip stuff—I had already gotten some of the classical stuff out of the way. So that was one of the main contributions to my success as a film composer, my education."

Isham's first professional experience included stints with the San Francisco Symphony and a summer opera company. He moved on to play for a period in the Beach Boys' horn section ("probably the least interesting musical phenomenon in the universe," he says), and with Van Morrison, who at the time was experimenting with electronic and ambient music. A writer for the magazine *Venice* observed Isham's film scores reflect nearly every jazz decade: from the 1920s and '30s with *Mrs. Parker and the Vicious Circle*, to the '50s with *Quiz Show*, to modern jazz with *Romeo Is Bleeding*.

"Every film allows one to sort of put on different musical personalities," Isham says. "So for film composers, it's great, because most directors say 'we want something brand new,' and it's that spirit that keeps me interested. You're allowed to develop a unique musical personality for each film, and indulge it."

During this period of steady production for film, Isham has nurtured a career as a solo jazz artist, recording with Columbia, Virgin and Windham Hill Records. In addition, he has made guest appearances on albums for the Rolling Stones, Bruce Springsteen, Willie Nelson and Kenny Loggins, among others. Isham says his solo career offers him artistic independence, which he calls a necessary complement to his work for film.

"All the rumors are true about Hollywood," he says. "It is warfare here among the directors, producers and studio bosses. Everyone's got an opinion as a film is being made, and you have to sort out whose are the important opinions. Sometimes it's the producer's wife or the studio boss's boyfriend. It can be that diverse and bizarre and hidden, these instructions coming out of nowhere. That is one of the major skills of operating in Hollywood as a composer, learning how to handle all of that."

—*Anne Bowling*

The Business of Songwriting

The more you know about how the music industry functions, the less likely you'll be to make a mistake dealing with contracts and agreements. Signing a contract without knowing exactly what you're agreeing to can ruin a career you've worked years to build. Becoming familiar with standard industry practices will help you learn what to look for and what to avoid.

COPYRIGHT

When you create a song and put it down in fixed form, it becomes a property you own and is automatically protected by copyright. This protection lasts for your lifetime (or the lifetime of the last surviving author, if you co-wrote the song) plus 50 years. When you prepare demos, place notification of copyright on all copies of your song—the lyric sheets, lead sheets and cassette labels. The notice is simply the word "copyright" or the symbol © followed by the year the song was created (or published) and your name: © 1997 by John L. Public.

For the best protection, you may want to consider registering your copyright with the Library of Congress. Although a song is copyrighted whether or not it is registered, registering a song establishes a public record of your copyright and could prove useful in any future litigation involving the song. Registration also entitles you to a potentially greater settlement in a copyright infringement suit. To register your song, request government form PA from the Copyright Office. Call the 24-hour hotline at (202)707-9100 and leave your name and address on the recorder. Once you receive a form, you can photocopy it if you want to register more than one song. It is possible to register groups of songs for one fee, but you cannot add future songs to that particular collection.

Once you receive the PA form, you will be required to return it, along with a registration fee and a tape or lead sheet of your song, to the Register of Copyrights, Copyright Office, Library of Congress, Washington DC 20559. It may take as long as four months to receive your certificate of registration from the Copyright Office, but your songs are protected from the date of creation, and the date of registration will reflect the date you applied for registration. If you need additional information about registering your songs, call the Copyright Office's Public Information Office at (202)707-3000 or visit their website at http://lcweb.loc.gov/copyright.

Don't be afraid to play your songs for people or worry about creating a song that might be similar to someone else's. True copyright infringement is rarer than most people think. First of all, a title cannot be copyrighted, nor can an idea or a chord progression. Only specific, fixed melodies and lyrics can be copyrighted. Second, a successful infringement suit would have to prove that another songwriter had access to the completed song and that he deliberately copied it, which is difficult to do and not really worthwhile unless the song is a huge hit. Song theft sometimes does happen, but not often enough for you to become paranoid. If you ever feel that one of your songs has been stolen—that someone has unlawfully infringed on your copyright—you must prove that you created the work. Copyright registration is the best proof of a date of creation. You *must* have your copyright registered in order to file a copyright infringement lawsuit. One way writers prove a work is original is to keep their rough drafts and revisions of songs, either on paper or on tape, if they record different versions of the song as they go along.

CONTRACTS

You will encounter several types of contracts as you deal with the business end of songwriting. You may sign a legal agreement between you and a co-writer establishing percentages of the writer's royalties each of you will receive, what you will do if a third party (e.g., a recording artist) wishes to change your song and receive credit as a co-writer, and other things. As long as the issues at stake are simple, and co-writers respect each other and discuss their business philosophy in advance of writing a song, they can write up an agreement without the aid of a lawyer. In other situations—when a publisher, producer or record company wants to do business with you—you should always have any contract reviewed by a knowledgeable entertainment attorney.

Single song contracts

The most common type of contract you may encounter at first will be the single song contract. A music publisher offers this type of contract when he wants to sign one or more of your songs, but he doesn't want to hire you as a staff writer. You assign your rights to a particular song to the publisher for an agreed-upon number of years (usually the life of the copyright).

Every single song contract should contain this basic information: the publisher's name, the writer's name, the song's title, the date and the purpose of the agreement. The songwriter also declares that the song is an original work and he is the creator of the work. The contract must specify the royalties the songwriter will earn from various uses of the song. These include performance, mechanical, print and synchronization royalties, as well as an agreement as to what will be paid for any uses of the song not specifically set forth in the contract.

The songwriter should receive no less than 50% of the income his song generates. That means that whatever the song earns in royalties, the publisher and songwriter should split 50/50. The songwriter's half is called the "writer's share" and the publisher's half is called the "publisher's share." If there is more than one songwriter, the songwriters split the writer's share. Sometimes songwriters will negotiate for a percentage of the publisher's share; that is, a co-publishing agreement. This usually happens only if the songwriter already has a successful track record.

Other issues a contract should address include whether or not an advance will be paid to the songwriter and how much it will be; when royalties will be paid (quarterly or semiannually); who will pay for demos—the publisher, songwriter or both; how lawsuits against copyright infringement will be handled, including the cost of such lawsuits; whether the publisher has the right to sell the song to another publisher without the songwriter's consent; and whether the publisher has the right to make changes in a song, or approve of changes written by someone else, without the songwriter's consent. In addition, the songwriter should have the right to audit the publisher's books if the songwriter deems it necessary and gives the publisher reasonable notice.

Songwriters should also negotiate for a reversion clause. This calls for the rights to the song to revert to the songwriter if some provision of the contract is not met. The most common type of reversion clause covers the failure to secure a commercial release of a song within a specified period of time (usually one or two years). If nothing happens with the song, the rights will revert back to the songwriter, who can then give the song to a more active publisher if he so chooses. Some publishers will agree to this, figuring that if they don't get some action on the song in the first year, they're not likely to ever get any action on it. Other publishers are reluctant to agree to this clause.

They may invest a lot of time and money in a song, re-demoing it and pitching it to a number of artists; they may be actively looking for ways to exploit the song. If a producer puts a song on hold for a while and goes into a lengthy recording project, by the time the record company (or artist or producer) decides which songs to release as singles, a year can easily go by. That's why it's so important to have a good working relationship with your publisher. You need to trust that he has your best interests in mind. If a song really is on hold you can give him more time and/or know that if your song is recorded but ultimately not released by the artist, it's not your publisher's fault and he'll work just as hard to get another artist to record the song. (For more information on music publishers, see the Music Publishers section introduction on page 37.)

While there is no such thing as a "standard" contract, The Songwriters Guild of America (SGA) has drawn up a Popular Songwriter's Contract which it believes to be the best minimum songwriter contract available. The Guild will send a copy of the contract at no charge to any interested songwriter upon request (include a self-addressed stamped envelope). SGA will also review free of charge any contract offered to its members, checking it for fairness and completeness.

The following list, taken from a Songwriters Guild of America publication entitled "10 Basic Points Your Contract Should Include," points out the basic features of an acceptable songwriting contract:

1. **Work for Hire.** When you receive a contract covering just one composition, you should make sure the phrases "employment for hire" and "exclusive writer agreement" are not included. Also, there should be no options for future songs.
2. **Performing Rights Affiliation.** If you previously signed publishing contracts, you should be affiliated with either ASCAP, BMI or SESAC. All performance royalties must be received directly by you from your performing rights organization and this should be written into your contract.
3. **Reversion Clause.** The contract should include a provision that if the publisher does not secure a release of a commercial sound recording within a specified time (one year, two years, etc.), the contract can be terminated by you.
4. **Changes in the Composition.** If the contract includes a provision that the publisher can change the title, lyrics or music, this should be amended so that only with your consent can such changes be made.
5. **Royalty Provisions.** You should receive fifty percent (50%) of all publisher's income on all licenses issued. If the publisher prints and sells his own sheet music, your royalty should be ten percent (10%) of the wholesale selling price. The royalty should not be stated in the contract as a flat rate ($.05, $.07, etc.).
6. **Negotiable Deductions.** Ideally, demos and all other expenses of publication should be paid 100% by the publisher. The only allowable fee is for the Harry Fox Agency collection fee, whereby the writer pays one half of the amount charged to the publisher for mechanical rights. The current rate charged by the Harry Fox Agency is 3.5%.
7. **Royalty Statements and Audit Provision.** Once the song is recorded, you are entitled to receive royalty statements at least once every six months. In addition, an audit provision with no time restriction should be included in every contract.
8. **Writer's Credit.** The publisher should make sure that you receive proper credit on all uses of the composition.
9. **Arbitration.** In order to avoid large legal fees in case of a dispute with your publisher, the contract should include an arbitration clause.
10. **Future Uses.** Any use not specifically covered by the contract should be retained by the writer to be negotiated as it comes up.

For a thorough discussion of the somewhat complicated subject of contracts, see these two books published by Writer's Digest Books: *The Craft and Business of Songwriting*, by John Braheny and *Music Publishing: A Songwriter's Guide*, by Randy Poe.

THE RIPOFFS

As in any business, the music industry has its share of dishonest, greedy people who try to unfairly exploit the talents and aspirations of others. Most of them use similar methods of attack which you can learn to identify and avoid. "Song sharks," as they're called, prey on beginners—those writers who are unfamiliar with ethical industry standards. Song sharks will take any songs—quality doesn't count. They're not concerned with future royalties, since they get their money upfront from songwriters who think they're getting a great deal.

Here are some guidelines to help you recognize these "song sharks":

- Never pay to have your music "reviewed" by a company that may be interested in publishing, producing or recording it. Reviewing material—free of charge—is the practice of reputable companies looking for hits for their artists or recording projects.
- Never pay to have your songs published. A reputable company interested in your songs assumes the responsibility and cost of promoting them. That company invests in your material because it expects a profit once the songs are recorded and released.
- Never pay a fee to have a publisher make a demo of your songs. Some publishers may take demo expenses out of your future royalties, but you should never pay upfront for demo costs for a song that is signed to a publisher.
- Never pay to have your lyrics or poems set to music. "Music mills"—for a price—may use the same melody for hundreds of lyrics and poems, whether it sounds good or not. Publishers recognize one of these melodies as soon as they hear it.
- Avoid CD compilation deals where a record company asks you to pay a fee to be included on a CD. They ask you to supply a master recording (along with a check for an amount of $500 or more), and they include your song on a CD to be sent to radio stations, producers, etc. First of all, the company is making a lot of money on this. The cost of mastering, pressing and mailing the CD is going to be a lot less than the amount of money they take in from the artists they solicit. Second, radio stations and other industry professionals just don't listen to these things to find new artists. Besides, would you want your material to be buried on a CD with 15-20 other acts? It would be better to spend the money making a quality demo or putting out a CD on your own. It's one thing if a record company puts out a compilation of the artists they've signed as a promotional item—it's another when they ask you to pay to be included.
- Read all contracts carefully before signing and don't sign any contract you're unsure about or that you don't fully understand. Don't assume any contract is better than no contract at all. It is well worth paying an attorney for the time it takes him to review a contract if you can avoid a bad situation that may cost you thousands of dollars in royalties if your song becomes a hit.
- Don't pay a company to pair you with a collaborator. A better way is to contact songwriting organizations that offer collaboration services to their members.
- Don't sell your songs outright. It's unethical for anyone to offer such a proposition.
- If you are asked by a record company or some other type of company to pay expenses upfront, be careful. A record producer may charge you a fee upfront to produce your record, or a small indie label may ask you to pay recording

costs and they will finance mastering, pressing and promotional costs. Each situation is different, and it's up to you to decide whether or not it will be beneficial. Talk to other artists who have signed similar contracts before signing one yourself. Research the company and its track record by finding out what types of product they have released, and what kind of distribution they have. Visit their website on the Internet, if they have one. Beware of any company that won't let you know what it has done in the past. If it has had successes and good working relationships with other writers and artists, it should be happy to brag about them.

- Before participating in a songwriting contest, read the rules carefully. Be sure that what you're giving up in the way of entry fees, etc., is not greater than what you stand to gain by winning the contest. See the Contests and Awards section introduction on page 474 for more advice on this.
- There is a version of the age-old chain letter scheme with a special twist just for songwriters. The letter names five songwriters whose tapes you are supposed to buy. You then add your name to the letter and mail it to five more songwriters who, in turn, are supposed to purchase your tape. Besides the fact that such chain letters or "pyramid" schemes generally fail, the five "amateur" songwriters named in the letter are known song sharks. Don't fall for it.
- Verify any situation about an individual or company if you have any doubts at all. Contact the performing rights society with which it is affiliated. Check with the Better Business Bureau in the town where it is located or the state's attorney general's office. Contact professional organizations you're a member of and inquire about the reputation of the company.

RECORD KEEPING

As your songwriting career continues to grow, you should keep a ledger or notebook containing all financial transactions relating to your songwriting. It should include a list of income from royalty checks as well as expenses incurred as a result of your songwriting business: cost of tapes, demo sessions, office supplies, postage, traveling expenses, dues to organizations, class and workshop fees and any publications you purchase pertaining to songwriting. It's also advisable to open a checking account exclusively for your songwriting activities, not only to make record keeping easier, but to establish your identity as a business for tax purposes.

Any royalties you receive will not reflect taxes or any other mandatory deductions. It is the songwriter's responsibility to keep track of income and file the appropriate tax forms. Contact the IRS or an accountant who serves music industry clients for specific information.

INTERNATIONAL MARKETS

Everyone talks about the world getting smaller, and it's true. Modern communication technology has brought us to the point where information can be transmitted around the globe instantly. No business has enjoyed the fruits of this progress more than the music industry. American music is heard in virtually every country in the world, and having a hit song in other countries as well as in the United States can greatly increase a songwriter's royalty earnings.

Each year there has been a steady increase in the number of international companies listed in *Songwriter's Market*. While these listings may be a bit more challenging to deal with than domestic companies, they offer additional avenues for songwriters looking for places to place their songs. To find international listings, see the Geographical Index at the back of the book.

Performing Songwriter Roundtable: Making a Living Without a Record Deal

For many performing songwriters, getting a record deal seems like the only way to make a living through music. But it's quite possible to succeed without support from a record company, as the three singer/songwriters gathered here can attest.

Roger Day has been performing in coffeehouses and on college campuses for more than ten years, carving out a solid niche for himself on the college circuit. A finalist at the 1992 Kerrville New Folk Festival, the Nashville-based singer/songwriter has released two CDs as well as scoring an award-winning play, *Light in Love*.

Jana Stanfield has released five CDs, tours extensively, and works as a motivational speaker. Her song "If I Had Only Known," recorded by Reba McEntire, sold over three million copies. Based in Nashville, Jana is also the author of *A Musician's Guide to Outrageous Success*, to be published by Writer's Digest Books in 1997.

John Tirro landed his first publishing deal only four months after arriving in Nashville, and has been a staff writer at Hayes Street Music for the past six years. He just had his first top 40 single, "Look At Me Now," recorded by Bryan White, and released his first CD, *Americana Rag*.

These talented performing songwriters are making a living doing what they love to do—writing and performing—without the help of a record label. They enjoy the freedom of writing their own songs, performing live and selling their own CDs and cassettes. They're shining examples of what anyone can do with talent, motivation and a little marketing savvy. Roger Day, Jana Stanfield and John Tirro may not be household names, but if making a living through your music is your goal, they show that it certainly can be done.

How did you get started in songwriting? At what point did you decide to pursue songwriting and performing as a fulltime career?

Roger Day: I started writing songs when I was in high school and continued writing throughout college. I began playing out in clubs three nights a week, and started having the idea that I might be able to make a living doing music. Back then, it was all cover tunes and fraternity gigs—performing has always been the main motivation. My writing has come along because I've been performing. If I hadn't been performing I don't know that I would have been motivated to write as much. Somewhere along the line the motivation to write became as strong as the motivation to perform.

Jana Stanfield: I wrote a couple of songs when I was a television news reporter. I wasn't thinking of myself as a songwriter—I wanted to be a recording artist. When I arrived in Nashville, it became clear that if I was writing songs, I would have a better chance of getting a record deal. In Nashville singer/songwriters have a lot more clout than someone who just sings. So I started writing songs to help me get a record deal, not realizing that songwriting was my true calling. I didn't ever decide I wanted to be a songwriter for a living—I wanted to write songs and record them and have them heard. Songwriting to me is a way of expressing my own ideas to the world and that's what I wanted to do, more than wanting to be a professional songwriter. I decided to devote myself fulltime to my career when I got fired from a job on Music Row. For four years I worked an office job promoting records. On the side, I was writing songs and trying to get a record deal. I was working less and less, and I finally cut my hours so much that they didn't need me anymore. So I lost my job, and that was at roughly the same time that I was turned down by all the major record labels for a record deal. I spent a year soul-searching and working freelance television jobs while I tried to figure out what I was going to do.

John Tirro: I grew up in a musical family—my Dad was the Dean of the Music School at Yale—so I was always around music. I got a music degree from Yale myself. I moved to Nashville after I graduated from college and started playing writer's nights at the Bluebird Cafe. I was also knocking on every door in town. It was more of a decision by default than anything. Although I had this theoretical education I didn't have a whole lot of skills. I could write songs, that's about it. I came to town thinking I'd go into production or perhaps be a session piano player. But being a writer was the one job where, at least in Nashville, somebody offered me a paycheck to do it.

How did you educate yourself in the music business when you started?

Roger Day: I started reading books about it. The best advice I've ever gotten comes from an ASCAP writer's workshop I went to. One of the moderators said there is no school you can go to to learn how to be a songwriter—the only way you're going to do it is to spend money. Think of it as your tuition. You're going to spend money doing demo tapes, putting together packages, getting the equipment to record. And you're going to make mistakes. As long as you have the attitude that the money you spend is like your tuition, you can handle it. It's really helped me as far as being an independent artist—every time I do a project I start spending more and more money, and I think, why don't I put this money in the bank and use it for when I might not be able to play music anymore. But instead I keep investing it back into putting more product out and I realize that every piece of product I put out is getting better and better.

Jana Stanfield: My education started when I was a reporter in Albuquerque. One of the things I did to learn about the industry was to get the Nashville Network. I would watch the Ralph Emery Show, and they always had songwriters and performers on there. I watched that show as often as I could, trying to get some glimpse into the music world. When I got to Nashville, my education came from working in the music business and from going to songwriter nights and starting to get to know other writers.

John Tirro: I would go to the music section of every bookstore in town. I was very glad to find *Songwriter's Market* because although Nashville is a very open town compared to other music towns, it's still hard to get in the door. Everybody's got a receptionist designed to keep you out, and books like that help you find out who might be interested in hearing from you before you bother them. I also joined NSAI and went to their meetings; periodically they'd have publishers come in and talk. I got my hands on any information I could find. I went to all the writer's nights I could stand. You gradually find a circle of friends, and they teach you more than you could ever learn from anyone else.

How did you begin marketing yourself as an artist?

Roger Day: Getting some product together was a good first step. I was able to show people, this is what I do, and this is the art I can create. I also got an agent, and he's great at the marketing end of things. I figured out about three years ago that if I did the college circuit I could work. I didn't really go into this with a grand scheme that I was going to play colleges. In fact, I went through a period of time where I didn't want anything to do with colleges because I thought it was the kiss of death for an artist. And to a certain extent that's true, to my knowledge I don't have any major record labels looking at me. And what makes you successful in that circuit isn't necessarily going to make you successful working at Sony Tree in Nashville. But I kind of stumbled into it—I had been playing a lot of colleges and one of the student activity directors told me to send a tape to the NACA (the National Association of Campus Activities). I did and was selected to showcase, and this year I'm playing in about 20 different states at about 80 colleges. I realize that I'm doing better than most people I know with publishing deals, and even some people with record deals, because I've been able to maintain total artistic independence and it has given me the financial resources to do independent projects. My hope is that I can use this as a stepping stone. I've played a lot, have been able to put out some CDs and have a lot of experience.

Jana Stanfield: My philosophy is different from a lot of other people's. A lot of people think the only way to market your songs is to send them to publishing companies and to try to get a recording artist to record one of them. I believe that any performance of your songs is important and very valuable, whether you're performing your songs, a local band is recording them or a local recording artist puts one of your songs on a self-produced album. The most important place to start is with your friends and family. That is the beginning of your fan base. Instead of spending all your time trying to get some record company or publishing company or recording artist to notice you, focus your energy on the people who already like your music. It's also important to start recording your music, and making your tapes available to people who would like to take them home and listen to them, whether it's your child's teacher or a music executive.

John Tirro: Early on, I was making tons of tapes and sending them to everybody that *Songwriter's Market* said would take them. A few people did get back to me—I got some really nice rejection letters—but what ended up being the most helpful was when I got to Nashville and could make calls and say, could I come by and bring you stuff? And once again, *Songwriter's Market* let me know of three or four active publishers in town that were willing to accept unsolicited material. The best thing to do is to go everywhere you can and at some point you'll be at the right place at the right time.

How did you get the money together to put out your first recording?

Roger Day: I put some money that I had saved from performing into doing the cassette. One piece of advice to anyone who is doing this independently is don't spend any of the money that you make from product sales. Put it right into the bank. Over two years, I put a good bit of money back from the sale of the first couple of projects I did. I was able to fund my last project by myself. It can be a tough thing, because most people are living hand to mouth, and when they need ten bucks to eat on the way home they'll spend the 10 out of the 30 that they made from CD sales. But if you do that, it'll get frittered away pretty quickly.

Jana Stanfield: I had been recording demos for several years. Each demo cost about $300 to do, so for my first album I just used those demos. I spent another $100 to have an engineer string it all together and set the levels, and it cost only a few hundred dollars more to get the artwork done, which I had done very simply in black & white. I got a hundred cassettes and started with that.

John Tirro: Randy Travis had recorded a song of mine and although it didn't make it into his album, one of the engineers that recorded the vocals on his version of my song turned out to go to my church. Apparently he was interested in producing a project, and he offered to work as an engineer for free. It was a trade off, in exchange for production points and experience he would produce my album. That cut off the main bulk of the cost. He also knew somebody at a major studio in town, and whenever they had downtime we would go in and record. Sometimes it was late at night or on the weekend, but it kept the price down. I ended up borrowing money from family, but it looks like we might break even within the next year or so. Recording a CD has done a lot in pushing everything forward. I played shows every couple of weeks in Nashville and people were asking if I had a recording, and I finally decided to make one. Having a CD or tape allows people to have something to show their friends to convince them that they ought to come and hear you.

How do you market your merchandise at your shows?

Roger Day: I have a table set up. I travel with a portable CD player, so if somebody wants to listen to the CD before buying it they can. I keep one copy of the CD from my first and second releases open on the table so people can look at the graphics and see if they like it.

Jana Stanfield: At my shows, I have a table set up. I always ask for a long table that I can spread my music out on and that people can gather around without feeling crowded. And I tell people about the merchandise from the stage when I'm performing, which is very important.

John Tirro: Usually somebody at the door sells them for me. I've got kind of a cushy situation in that I mostly play at the Bluebird Cafe, and I know the folks there. They're happy to have my CDs by the door and take the money for me so I don't have to stand there and make people uncomfortable. I can just be their entertainer!

Do you sell your merchandise at outlets other than your live shows?

Roger Day: I found that mail order wasn't real effective—I didn't sell enough to cover the cost of sending out the packages. But I have about 1,200 people on my mailing list. I'm real hopeful that the Internet is going to make it easier to contact people on my mailing list. I'm going to be selling my cassettes and CDs on a website, but that's not quite set up yet. We'll see if that will be a big market for independent writers or not.

Jana Stanfield: I don't have distribution, but my records are in a few record stores, such as a record store in my hometown of Clovis, New Mexico, and at Tower Records in Nashville. I also do mail order and advertise in *Performing Songwriter* magazine. I send out a newsletter, and when I'm going to a certain area I'll send out cards to that town to let people know that I'm coming and where I'm going to play. I also have a homepage with National Online Music Alliance. I believe that the best way of getting the word out is through word of mouth. And the Internet is a great place for people to talk and tell other people that they've discovered music they like. Once their friends hear about this music, there's a place on the Internet where they can go and listen to samples and buy albums right there, all within a few minutes.

John Tirro: Tower Records has a local section here in Nashville, and I sell my tapes and CDs there. I've got an online page and have not yet seen that be profitable—but it's been fun. I've gotten a lot of nice comments from people, but I think people are still reluctant to do business over the Internet.

How important is the mailing list?

Roger Day: It's something I'm fairly ambivalent about. I've got 1,200 people on my mailing list, and two thirds of those never come to my shows. It can get expensive, so you have to cultivate your list very carefully. But having a mailing list does enable me to keep track of people.

Jana Stanfield: The mailing list is essential; I cannot stress enough how important that mailing list is. Because for every person who buys one of your albums, that person can be a permanent friend, fan, buyer, customer—whatever you want to call it. It's important to let them know when you have a new album out and when you're coming back to town.

John Tirro: The mailing list is key. Especially once you get to the point where you're being paid to play, because you can play anywhere and have a full house, or at least an enthusiastic audience. It's not terribly expensive, especially if you've got a computer and can do some of the layout yourself. I might get a cluster of gigs together and send out a flyer with three or four shows on it. And it gradually grows, which is the nice thing about it. If you're playing a club that only holds a couple hundred people, once you have more than a couple hundred people on your mailing list, it gets pretty easy to have a packed house every time.

How do you deal with booking and management? Do you have any advice for dealing with agents and managers?

Roger Day: Since I'm marketing for the college market, I book almost all my gigs through NACA. I booked myself for two years and was moderately successful. But I had the hope that if I got enough of a client base I could go to an agent and say, I'm already playing 30 schools. Will you take over and get me some other gigs? That was my bait to get an agent and it's paid off in a big way. A lot of people play music to avoid having anything to do with business. But I find that the people who are willing to take the business bull by the horns and educate themselves tend to find the right relationships. Artists need to understand that if they can make somebody some money, that's really the bottom line. And the way you do that is to say, I've been able to book myself at this level and get these gigs, what can you do for me?

Jana Stanfield: I do a large portion of the booking myself, and I work with a bureau in Texas where they do some of my booking. My best advice is to always be professional and on time. Ask what a prospective manager or agent expects of you upfront. Always keep a good relationship and a good clean line of communication with them.

How did you begin touring? Did you start in your hometown and branch out from there?

Roger Day: Basically, there are two phases of my career. The first was when I was first out of college, and was part of a duo, and we didn't even have a press kit or demo tape. I just would call up some place and say, "I'm Roger Day, I'm a friend of so and so . . . will you pay us $1,000 to come play?" When I started as a solo act, I got a listing of schools in the states of Tennessee, Kentucky and Alabama and sent them all press kits. I found out I got a lot of bookings because I was charging so little. I was good enough, I got a good enough response for what I was doing and was able to build on that. That's how I got my foot in the door.

Jana Stanfield: I started with places that were within driving distance. I started in my hometown of Clovis, New Mexico. I had a little bit of name recognition there, and had lots of family and friends. So I would go there and play and the next thing you know I'm playing an hour away in Muleshoe, Texas . . . then Lubbock . . . and it just grew from there. Now I have a lot of work in Texas, New Mexico and Colorado just from going to visit family and friends and getting jobs wherever I could while I was in the area.

What's the best way to start getting booked into clubs?

Roger Day: If you're looking to start playing your own material, find someplace to play and play it consistently. Let people know where you're going to be. It doesn't necessarily have to be a high traffic area, just a place where you can invite people. That's one of the weaknesses of playing the college circuit—I don't have a consistent club gig. On occasion I'll play the Bluebird Cafe and people will show up, but I'm not a constant presence in Nashville, or any other town for that matter.

Jana Stanfield: I believe it's good to start with your friends and family. Instead of going to a town where you don't know anybody, go to a town where you know people and set up a concert either at someone's house, someone's barn, the VFW hall, whatever you can do. From that you'll get leads from the audience. They might say, could you come to my town and do something like this? I also believe it's better to start in small places and pack them than to start in large places that are empty.

John Tirro: Here in Nashville they hold auditions for writer's nights, and then they grade your performance. And you move up the ranks, at least at the Bluebird. You start playing writer's nights doing three songs on a Sunday, then maybe you have a show of your own for 20 minutes, then you play in the round for a couple hours with three other writers, then finally you end up headlining.

At what point would you say you finally felt successful? How would you define success?

Roger Day: Everybody has a different level of success. I felt successful when my wife could work part-time and raise two kids. In the last couple of years playing the college circuit, I've been doing enough repeat business that I realize it's not suddenly going to dry up in one season. I used to live in fear that next semester nobody's going to want to hire me and I'm not going to have anything to fall back on. But now I've got an extensive list of schools that will book me any particular semester. More philosophically, a couple years ago I realized that I didn't need anyone's permission to play music, and I think when I look back on my life, that will be the moment that I became successful playing music. Most people get into music thinking they're going to be a big star. That's part of their motivation, that they're going to be on the cover of *Rolling Stone* or whatever their ambition is. If you come from a middle-class educational background like many people, you're used to somebody telling you this is what you've got to do to make an A in this course, to graduate with honors, get into graduate school or whatever it is you're doing. People get into the music industry and they're expecting that same kind of affirmation, that somebody's going to tell them how to do it. It took me about eight years to realize this is my choice and these are my mistakes, and I have total ownership over this.

Jana Stanfield: I have had jobs since I was in high school. So when I lost my Music Row job and began making my living with my music I felt like a huge success because I had gone a year without having a real job. That was a miracle to me! Now I'm very confident that I can make my own living this way. My definition of success is being able to make your living doing what you love. Or even to make a life that includes doing what you love. There are some people who work a regular job and they do music on the side and that makes them very happy, so I think either way you can have success. People after my shows will come up to me and say, I hope you're a big success someday. And I smile at them and say, "I already am! I'm doing what I love."

John Tirro: Success definitely comes in plateaus; it's like a big hurdle race. You think that at any given point you've cleared all the hurdles, and then you discover another one and each time you get past that one there's another. When someone finally records a song of yours, that's a great moment. But then you're disappointed when that song doesn't make it on their CD. And when one actually makes it on the CD, it's a great moment! And then your song gets released as a single, but maybe it doesn't do well. The ratio of what's going to work to what's not going to work is always going to be kind of low. If you pitch a really great song 10 times you might get it on hold once. Get it on hold 10 times and you might get it cut once—it just kind of goes like that.

Where do you stand on signing with a major or an indie label? If a record label came to you tomorrow and said, "We're going to offer you a deal," what would you do?

Roger Day: It would really depend on the deal. I'm making a good living, and I don't know if I would want to give that up just to follow a dream, as it were. I'd have to be convinced that they were excited about what I was doing. I would give up my independence fairly slowly. All record or publishing deals are not created equal. And that's hard to think about when you're struggling and you want so badly for somebody to tell you that you're good.

Jana Stanfield: I would consider it. I have a large profit margin on albums that I would lose if I were recording for a major label. On the other hand, they would do a lot of advertising that I don't do, get my name out there and get more people to my shows. If that happened, I would get all those people on my mailing list so that if I were only on that label for a few years, I would still have that mailing list and could go back to making my own albums and continue with my career.

John Tirro: This is something I've wrestled with, and if you asked me two years ago when I was starting to record I might have answered differently. One great thing about doing a record is that I realized I absolutely love production and everything that goes on in the studio, but I also like being home. If a record company could find a way to do it where I could go out and hit a region for a weekend and then go home, that might be a possibility. But the traditional 300 dates a year stuff is strictly for someone else. Which I think makes me an unattractive proposition for a lot of labels, because if they're going to be working their butts off to sell records, I should be doing the same. But I'd rather be working my butt off writing songs.

Do you think where you live makes any difference?

Roger Day: It depends on what kind of music you're playing. I could be just about anywhere and do the college circuit. I don't have too much to do with the country industry here, which is what Nashville is mainly about. But it has been educational being around it all the time. I've learned tons about the business and met a lot of people who are good solid writers. But I think if you're living, say, in Cincinnati and you're out playing once a week and you're getting a good buzz about what you're doing, that's important. Everybody's interested in getting distribution all over the world, and we forget that sometimes it's good just to have some friends that will come and see you play on a Wednesday night and listen to what you do for a couple of hours and buy your CD. Don't underestimate that.

Jana Stanfield: If a person wants to have their songs recorded by major artists, it's important to move to a music center. These days publishers and artists won't take unsolicited cassettes of new songs from songwriters. If you're known in town you can have your songs listened to; if you want them recorded by major artists, it's important to move to a music center. If you can sing your own songs and start making your own albums you can live anywhere you want and still make a good living with your songs.

What are some lessons you've learned over the past few years as a performing songwriter?

Roger Day: I once signed an ill-advised artist development deal. It was a very dumb thing to do, and I did it because someone more or less said, "I'm going to make you a big star." I had dollar signs going on and off in my eyes, and I ignored advice from people that was real sound. I lost two years of my life, but in some ways it was the most important thing that happened because it was a big lesson. I've learned to make sure lawyers look over any documents that you sign, which I didn't do. You need to ask yourself some questions—can this person really get you a deal? Who does this person know; what is their background, their experience? What have they done lately?

Jana Stanfield: The biggest lesson I've learned is it's easy to ignore the people who love our music and think they don't count. Because we want somebody "really important" to discover our music, we overlook those people who really care about us and think our music is special. I've learned to shift my focus back to the people who really appreciate what I do instead of putting all my time and energy into people who couldn't care less about the music I do. Trying to get your songs discovered or trying to get discovered as a recording artist is like putting money in a slot machine. Yes, you might hit the jackpot, but I don't believe it's the best use of time and energy. You can play the slots in Las Vegas to make your financial dreams come true or you can work hard. I say, work hard! When you start making your own albums you've got a fan base, you've got people who love what you do, you've got people who buy your records, you've got people who want your autograph, you've got all those things you thought only a major label could give you. But you can give it to yourself, and you can really enjoy your life that way.

John Tirro: One of the early lessons I learned is that anybody that you're having a meeting with this morning is probably having lunch with someone you met with yesterday, especially if you're in Nashville. It's not that different from any other area in life. Be nice to people.

How does it feel to be able to make a living through your music?

Roger Day: It's a great feeling. I've been pinching myself lately. I'm 32 years old and have been doing this for 10 years. I'm actually making some money doing it; I'm selling CDs and I'm able to have an effect on people's lives through my music. I'm doing what I want to do! And I think, how did I get to this point, how can I sustain this and how can I just appreciate this for what it is? That's the trick. If you were working at a law firm making the kind of money I'm making you'd be real depressed and think your life is a failure. But after having not made anything for years, or just enough, now to actually be making a living doing this is such an incredible feeling. It's like I'm one of the lucky few. Persevere, if this is what you want to do, and when it comes down that you can actually pay the bills, relish it. If you can pay your bills and can still have some money at the end of the month, and you can do that consistently, then you can be fine, as long as you can avoid big debt and live within your means.

Jana Stanfield: After all the rejection I had from the major labels. . . . it's not that the major labels were rejecting me, they were saying, this is not what we're looking for today. But it felt the same as rejection. After all of that, and after feeling my music had no value, it was so wonderful to make those hundred cassettes. Every time someone handed me $10, they were saying, "I appreciate what you do, here, take this and go make more." It has been so freeing to be able to play whatever music I like. And to be able to make my living 10 and 15 dollars at a time, from people who appreciate my music, is the most wonderful thing I've ever experienced in the whole world.

John Tirro: It's really the best. It's a nebulous sort of profession, and it's hard to know whether you're doing well at any given point. Once you've got a song out on the radio that's doing great, it's going to be a year before you're going to see any money. The kudos don't necessarily come at the time that you've done something well. You have to develop some sort of mechanism to remember when you were doing things right, when things were working and put them together properly. But if you can deal with that, it's absolutely great to be paid to do what you love.

Do you have any advice for someone wanting to do what you're doing?

Roger Day: I think a good way to put it is from something I read in a Joseph Campbell book: don't seek spiritual enlightenment unless you're seeking it as a man whose head is on fire seeks water. It doesn't make sense to play music just to be rewarded—you don't get brownie points just because you have the courage to play music. People will admire you and say you've got guts to do it. But there's no financial reward for it so, if you're going to do it, don't play around. Really do it. If you're going to make mistakes, make big mistakes! Just jump into it. I have a sneaking suspicion that the important thing in all of this is not music, but more of a personal, spiritual development that people go through. When you're playing music you can't hide behind your job. In that sense, you have life stripped down to its pure essence. That's what you're doing and it's a scary thing to do, so don't do it and think you have to do it in sort of an accepted, middle class way. You're going to end up getting your butt kicked real hard if you think there's somebody who's going to promise you a certain kind of lifestyle, who's going to have all the answers, because nobody does. One day you'll wake up and you'll say, wow, this is really cool, I've learned this and this and this, and you'll realize it has nothing to do with music!

Jana Stanfield: My best advice is to keep writing. If you sing your songs keep singing them, and sing your own demos as much as possible. If you're trying to pitch something to someone like Reba McEntire, then of course it's good to try and get somebody who sounds like Reba to sing your demo, or if you want to pitch it to George Strait or Garth Brooks or Madonna or Whitney Houston, get someone who sounds like them. At the same time, continue singing your own songs and start moving toward making your own albums and making them available to the friends and family who like what you do so you can have a very successful music career whether anyone records your songs or not.

John Tirro: To paraphrase Rilke in *Letters to a Young Poet*—basically ask yourself, if you were denied to write, would you have to stop living? I think that's a little melodramatic, but I also think it's true. If you don't feel like you have to do this, do something else. If you think you do have to do this, don't waste your time doing anything else, because we need your creativity.

Music Industry Trend Report

The past year in the music industry was fairly lackluster in terms of sales, with the dollar value of domestic shipments in 1995 at $12.3 billion, up only 2.1% over last year. While this represents a positive dollar growth, it is nowhere near the 20% increase that was seen the year before. One factor in this small increase seems to be greater competition from other forms of entertainment such as online services and computer games. Another is an unhealthy retail environment, with discount electronics stores such as Best Buy and Circuit City selling $16.98 list price CDs for as low as $9.99, leading to declining profit margins for music specialty stores.

The CD continues to outsell the cassette, with 65% of all music sales coming from the purchase of CDs. The popularity of the cassette single is on the decline, but CD single sales are increasing. Vinyl made an impressive showing last year, with sales increasing by a whopping 41%. This is mostly the result of major labels offering many of their new releases on vinyl as well as CD and cassette.

MUSIC TRENDS

According to the Recording Industry Association of America, rock is currently the dominating music genre in terms of sales and airplay. Running the gamut from soft rock to punk and heavy metal, rock captured 33.5% of the market last year, with country music coming in next with 16.7%. In the rock/pop category, more women than ever before ruled the charts, with Alanis Morissette's Grammy-award winning, number one album *Jagged Little Pill* leading the way. Natalie Merchant, Joan Osborne, Sophie B. Hawkins, Melissa Etheridge, Brandy, Mariah Carey, Madonna, Whitney Houston and the late Selena all saw their latest albums hit either the gold or platinum mark. It was also a good year for debut artists, as Silverchair, Bush, The Presidents of the United States of America and the above-mentioned Joan Osborne and Alanis Morissette all saw their debut albums make impressive showings on the *Billboard* 200.

In the other top-selling category, country reached a sales plateau but the country music industry itself expanded, with more labels and artists coming out of Nashville than ever before. Music publishers continued to make their presence known in Nashville, with the opening of several new publishing offices on Music Row, including BMI's new headquarters. The use of country videos as promotional tools has been a hot topic in Nashville of late. Questioning the actual effect they have on sales, country labels have been cutting back on producing videos for their artists, putting the money into marketing and promotion instead. What effect this will have on country video outlets such as CMT and TNN remains to be seen.

Although it commands only a small portion of the market, contemporary Christian music began receiving mainstream media attention in the past year. Chart activity and increasing sales figures were behind the decision to add Contemporary Christian and gospel music to SoundScan, which tracks sales at the retail level and is the method *Billboard* magazine uses to compile its charts. Several Christian acts began to cross over to the mainstream charts as well, including Jars of Clay, who had a hit on both the Christian and modern rock charts.

Independent labels continued to show their muscle on the charts over the past year, with indie distributors commanding 19.2% of the total market share in 1995, up from 15.5% the year before. That puts them in the No. 2 slot behind distribution giant WEA, which controls 21.6% of the market. Several independent companies had top ten releases in past year, including Walt Disney Records' soundtracks to *The Lion King* and *Pocahontas*; Epitaph Records' *Smash*, by the Offspring, still on the charts after two years; Death Row Records' *Dogg Food*, by Tha Dogg Pound; and Ruthless Records' *E. 1999 Eternal*, by Bone Thugs-N-Harmony. Indie record sales increased in almost every category, including classical, jazz, rap and modern rock.

MUSIC FORMATS

The enhanced CD was probably the biggest news in the past year, cementing the commitment of the music industry to new multimedia products. These CDs provide visual as well as audio information; when played in a standard CD player, they play audio only. But when played in a CD-ROM drive, they offer videos, graphics, song lyrics, interviews, games, pictures and links to websites on the Internet—sort of an audiovisual version of album liner notes. All major labels and many independent labels released enhanced CDs over the past year (Sony and Philips market theirs under the name CD EXTRA). One of the first was Sarah McLaughlin's *The Freedom Sessions*, released on Arista Records, which sold over a quarter of a million copies. Hundreds of these multimedia CDs are already on store shelves, some at regular list price (with the multimedia portion listed as a "bonus") and others with a slightly higher price tag. Just about every major label has an inhouse multimedia department, and many independents have started their own imprints to deal exclusively with enhanced CDs, proving that the enhanced CD is more than just a passing trend.

MUSIC ONLINE

The proliferation of music sites on the Internet continues to grow at a dizzying rate, offering new artists a myriad of opportunities to get their music heard. Sites such as the Independent Underground Music Archive, Kaliedospace and others (see our Websites of Interest page on page 490 for more information) provide forums for artists to place a song (usually for a fee) onto the site along with information, photos and graphics about their music. Consumers searching the web can read about the artists, listen to samples of their music and even buy cassettes and CDs without leaving their homes. Many record company A&R personnel use online sites to find out more about bands they've heard about and are interested in working with. Many record companies now have their own webpages to use as promotional tools for upcoming releases. For a small indie record label, using the Internet is an inexpensive way to get the word out to a worldwide audience about their artists. Online sites can also help artists find out more about record labels they may be interested in submitting to—the sites usually convey what kind of artists a label is looking for, what kind of music they work with, the label's submission policy and even offer snippets of music and videos from artists on that label. Unsigned artists are able to set up their own personal webpages on the Internet to promote their music to an audience that is almost unlimited in scope.

CHANGES IN LEGISLATION

Along with the increase in the use of online services comes the need to protect the rights of songwriters and performers whose music can be accessed via the Internet. Hence the Performance Right in Sound Recordings Act, which was passed by Congress this past year. Signaling a significant victory for the songwriter, the law grants intellectual-property protection to songwriters, artists and record labels for the digital transmission of their works. This will generate new income for songwriters whose copyrighted works can be uploaded or downloaded on online services.

Other bills have been introduced in Congress, and as of press time have yet to be passed. One of them, the Fairness in Musical Licensing Act, would change the licensing fee structure for bars and restaurants who use prerecorded music as background music in their establishments. Songwriter advocates feel the passage of this bill would be detrimental to songwriters and music publishers, because it would exempt many restaurant and bar owners from paying royalties for background music and make it harder to enforce the collection of royalties. The performing rights organizations are currently working towards a non-legislation solution to this problem; they have already reached a compromise with the National Licensed Beverage Association, but are still working with the National Restaurant Association to come up with a solution.

Another bill directly affecting a songwriter's income is the Copyright Extension Bill, which will extend the copyright term of a song by 20 years. It would change from the current life plus 50 years to life plus 70 years, thus insuring income for a writer's future generations. Most European countries have already increased their copyright terms to life plus 70, so passage of this bill will bring the United States up to par with the rest of the world in copyright protection. There is no organized opposition to this bill, and it's likely to be passed in the very near future.

KEEPING UP WITH CURRENT TRENDS

With all the advances in technology, new avenues for songwriters to get their work heard are opening up to songwriters practically every day. It's important to keep up with these changes so you can utilize them throughout your songwriting career. Reading music industry trade magazines is a good idea, since they offer updated information on a regular basis about changes in legislation, technology and trends. Attending workshops and conferences can help you learn about the best and newest ways to market yourself and your music. And don't forget about national and local songwriting organizations; they can provide valuable information through newsletters and bulletins that let you know what's going on in the industry and how it affects you.

IMPORTANT INFORMATION ON MARKET LISTINGS

● Although every listing in *Songwriter's Market* is updated, verified or researched prior to publication, some changes are bound to occur between publication and the time you contact any listing.

● Listings are based on interviews and questionnaires. They are not advertisements, nor are markets reported here necessarily endorsed by the editor.

● Companies that appeared in the 1996 edition of *Songwriter's Market*, but do not appear this year, are listed in the General Index at the back of the book along with a code explaining why they do not appear in this edition.

● A word of warning. Don't pay to have your song published and/or recorded or to have your lyrics—or a poem—set to music. Read "Ripoffs" in The Business of Songwriting section to learn how to recognize and protect yourself from the "song shark."

● Songwriter's Market *reserves the right to exclude any listing which does not meet its requirements.*

KEY TO SYMBOLS AND ABBREVIATIONS

* new listing in all sections and indexes
SASE—self-addressed, stamped envelope
SAE—self-addressed envelope
IRC—International Reply Coupon, for use in countries other than your own.

(For definitions of terms and abbreviations relating specifically to the music industry, see the Glossary in the back of the book.)

The Markets

Music Publishers

Finding songs and getting them recorded—that's the main function of a music publisher. Working as an advocate for you and your songs, a music publisher serves as a song plugger, administrator, networking resource and more. The knowledge and personal contacts a music publisher can provide may be the most valuable resources available for a songwriter just starting in the music business.

Music publishers attempt to derive income from a song through recordings, use in TV and film soundtracks and other areas. While this is their primary function, music publishers also handle administrative tasks such as copyrighting songs, collecting royalties for the songwriter, negotiating and issuing synchronization licenses for use of music in films, arranging and administering foreign rights, and producing new demos of the music submitted to them. In a small, independent publishing company, one or two people may provide all of these services. Larger publishing companies are more likely to be divided into the following departments: Creative (or Professional), Copyright, Licensing, Legal Affairs, Royalty, Accounting and Foreign.

The Creative department is responsible for finding talented writers and signing them to the company. Once a writer is signed, it is up to the Creative department to develop and nurture the writer so he will write songs that will create income for the company. Staff members help put writers together to form collaborative teams. And, perhaps most important, the Creative department is responsible for getting songs recorded by other artists and used in film and other media that will expose the song to the public. The head of the Creative department, usually called the professional manager, is charged with locating talented writers for the company. Once a writer is signed, the professional manager arranges for a demo to be made of the writer's songs. Even though a writer may already have recorded his own demo, the publisher will often re-demo the songs using established studio musicians in an effort to produce the highest-quality demo possible.

Once a demo is produced, the professional manager begins shopping the song to various outlets. He may try to get the song recorded by a top artist on his or her next album or get the song used in an upcoming film. The professional manager uses all the contacts and leads he has to get the writer's songs recorded by as many artists as possible. Therefore, he must be able to deal efficiently and effectively with people in other segments of the music industry, including A&R personnel, producers, distributors, managers and lawyers. Through these contacts, he can find out what artists are looking for new material, and who may be interested in recording one of the writer's songs. The professional manager and those working with him must have extensive knowledge of all segments of the music industry.

After a writer's songs are recorded, the other departments at the publishing company come into play. The Licensing and Copyright departments are responsible for issuing any licenses for use of the writer's songs in film or TV, and for filing various forms with the copyright office. The Legal Affairs department works with the Professional department in negotiating contracts with its writers. The Royalty and Accounting departments are responsible for ensuring the writer is receiving the proper royalty rate as specified in the contract, and that statements are mailed to the writer promptly. Finally, the Foreign department's role is to oversee any publishing activities outside of the United States, and to make sure a writer is being paid for any uses of his material in foreign countries.

LOCATING A MUSIC PUBLISHER

How do you go about finding a music publisher that will work well for you? First, you must find out what kind of music a publisher handles. If a particular publisher works mostly with alternative music and you're a country songwriter, the contacts he has within the industry will hardly be beneficial to you. You must find a publisher suited to the type of music you write. Each listing in this section details the type of music that publisher is most interested in; the music types appear in boldface to make them easier to locate. You will also want to refer to the Category Index at the end of this section, which lists companies by the type of music they work with.

Do your research!

It's important to study the market and do research to identify which companies to submit to. Are you targeting a specific artist to sing your songs? If so, you must find out if that artist even considers outside material. Who was the publisher of the artist's latest release? Such information can be found in any issue of *Billboard*, the weekly magazine that covers the music industry and publishes charts of the best selling records each week. If there is an artist you are interested in and they have a recent hit on the *Billboard* charts, the publishing company they are signed with will be listed in the "Hot 100 A-Z" index. If an artist isn't currently charting in *Billboard*, check the liner notes of a recent release, which will list the name of the artist's publisher. Once you've located the name of the publishing company, you can attempt to get songs to the artist through the publisher. Carefully choosing which publishers will work best for the material you write may take time, but it will only increase your chances of getting your songs heard. "Shotgunning" your demo packages (sending out many packages without regard for music preference or submission policy) not only is a waste of time and money, but it may also label you as an unprofessional songwriter with no regard for the workings and policies of the music business.

Once you've found some companies that may be interested in your work, find out what songs have been successfully handled by those publishers. Most publishers are happy to provide you with this information in order to attract high-quality material. Ask the publisher for the names of some of their staff writers, and give them a call. Ask them their opinion of how the publisher works. Keep in mind as you're researching music publishers how you get along with them personally. If you can't work with a publisher on a personal level, chances are your material won't be represented as you would like it to be. A publisher can become your most valuable contact to all other segments of the music industry, so it's important to find someone you can trust and feel comfortable with.

Also consider the size of the publishing company. The publishing affiliates of the major music conglomerates are huge, handling catalogs of thousands of songs by hundreds of songwriters. Unless you are an established songwriter, your songs probably won't receive enough attention from such large companies. Smaller, independent publishers offer several advantages. First, independent music publishers are located all over the country, making it easier for you to work face-to-face rather than by mail or phone. Smaller companies usually aren't affiliated with a particular record company, and are therefore able to pitch your songs to many different labels and acts. Independent music publishers are usually interested in a smaller range of music, allowing you to target your submissions more accurately. The most obvious advantage to working with a smaller publisher is the personal attention they can bring to you and your songs. With a smaller roster of artists to work with, the independent music publisher is able to concentrate more time and effort on each particular project.

PUBLISHING CONTRACTS

Once you've located a publisher you like and he's interested in shopping your work, it's time to consider the publishing contract—an agreement in which a songwriter grants certain rights to a publisher for one or more songs. The contract specifies any advances offered to the writer, the rights that will be transferred to the publisher, the royalties a songwriter is to receive and the length of time the contract is valid. When a contract is signed, a publisher will ask for a 50-50 split with the writer. This is standard industry practice; the publisher is taking that 50% to cover the overhead costs of running his business and for the work he's doing to get your songs recorded. It is always a good idea to have a publishing contract (or any music business contract) reviewed by a competent entertainment lawyer. There is no "standard" publishing contract, and each company offers different provisions for their writers. Make sure you ask questions about anything you don't understand, especially if you're new in the business. Songwriter organizations such as the Songwriters Guild of America provide contract review services, and can help you learn about music business language and what constitutes a fair music publishing contract

When signing a contract, it's important to be aware of the music industry's unethical practitioners. The "song shark," as he's called, makes his living by asking a songwriter to pay to have a song published. The shark will ask for money to demo a song and promote it to radio stations; he may also ask for more than the standard 50% publisher's share or ask you to give up all rights to a song in order to have it published. Although none of these practices is illegal, it's certainly not ethical, and no successful publisher uses these methods. *Songwriter's Market* works to list only honest companies interested in hearing new material. (For more on "song sharks," see The Business of Songwriting on page 18.)

SUBMITTING MATERIAL TO A PUBLISHER

When submitting material to a publisher, always keep in mind that a professional, courteous manner goes a long way in making a good impression. When you submit a demo through the mail, make sure your package is neat and meets the particular needs of the publisher. Review each publisher's submission policy carefully, and follow it to the letter. Disregarding this information will only make you look like an amateur in the eyes of the company you're submitting to. (For more detailed information on submitting your material, see Getting Started on page 5.)

Listings of companies in countries other than the U.S. feature the name of the country in bold type. You will find an alphabetical list of these companies at the back of the book, along with an index of publishers by state.

INSIDER REPORT

The independent publisher: mentor and much more

"A music publishing company is one of the last places where you can find a person who will creatively develop writers and writer/artists and help them get ready for their careers," says Arthur Braun, president of Centium Entertainment. Braun entered the music industry in the early 1970s as a songwriter and song plugger, but quickly found out he was more interested in the work of the publisher. In 1974, he joined Dick James Music, where he served as president for 15 years. "I worked in London, New York, Los Angeles and established the Nashville office from scratch. We signed and developed some top writers and artists." Among those writer/artists are Elton John, Bernie Taupin, Tears for Fears, the Troggs and the Hollies.

Arthur Braun

In 1994, Braun established Centium Entertainment, "primarily an independent publishing company," notes Braun, but also "a little dance label." Braun describes the role of the independent publisher as being a mentor to songwriters. "One of the great things about going with an independent publisher is that you get personal attention. We give direct feedback and help songwriters develop their craft, something many companies in this industry have lost sight of."

As a publisher, Braun points out that "the song is still, and always has been, the most important item. We put a lot of emphasis on song structure and the quality of lyrics and melodies. Many songwriters have pitfalls in their writing they cannot recognize themselves; they repeat a lot of the same habits. A good publisher can break those bad habits and change the way a songwriter writes forever. Once we identify a writer's weak points, we might even get the writer involved with a collaborator who can strengthen those spots."

Another important function of the independent publisher, says Braun, is to aggressively tap the many outlets available for a writer's songs. As well as cuts by recording artists, these include motion pictures, television, theater, advertising and sheet music. Recognizing what he calls "the explosion of world music becoming mainstream," Braun also reaches out internationally by listening to songs of writer/artists from all over the world. "Living in America we are isolated and very reluctant to play foreign material on the radio, but I see this changing. The international market is a great breeding ground for getting a songwriter launched. If a song is not quite right for the American market, we might find another territory around the world where we can get a local artist to record it. We've had hits in other countries that have never been heard by the American public."

INSIDER REPORT, *Braun*

As the next century approaches and new technology is introduced, Braun sees the publisher taking on additional responsibilities. "We have a lot of new technology out there that will require special licensing. The publisher is going to be very important in working with the performing rights societies and on behalf of the songwriter to make sure every new technology has some kind of licensing standard and songwriters will get royalties for their work."

When reviewing demo submissions, Braun looks for originality, a strong chorus and wide-ranging appeal. "I want to hear new ways of saying the same old things. The feelings and emotions that the audience goes through don't change; it's the way the songwriter presents those feelings that makes them different and makes a song stand out. Musically, I look for a song that reaches out, a song that is extremely infectious and melodic. I also like a strong chorus and a song that is not pegged in a particular music style. That allows it to be used in many different outlets and cross into a lot of different markets."

One common mistake Braun sees songwriters make is not paying enough attention to lyrics. "Songwriters tend to be very repetitive without building characterization or keeping focus on what the thought is and wrapping it up in the end. In 100 new songs, this will be the case in 99 of them."

When Braun hears a song he likes, he contacts the writer by phone or mail. "I ask for additional material to see if the writer is prolific and consistent. I also try to find out if the writer is motivated enough to keep up with the rigors of what really is a fulltime job and a serious craft. That's something I need to know ahead of time before I devote the time, effort and money to promoting the writer's songs. You'd be surprised at how many people don't follow up with me."

Songwriters who do follow up with Braun may be offered one of two kinds of agreements. "One type of contract," says Braun, "requires the writer to write exclusively for us for a specified term. That writer has to be really good and consistent at all times. More often, we might like a particular song and want to work it right away within an individual, single-song contract."

Braun advises songwriters that "every single thing in a contract is negotiable. There may be a 'standard' company contract, but that does not mean you have to live with it." He also warns songwriters not to be taken in by companies asking for money. "Make sure that if you're offered an agreement you don't have to pay anything. If a company asks you for money, run!"

For songwriters who don't live in a music center, Braun suggests they "try every possible outlet there is and regularly submit material to publishers in New York, Nashville, Los Angeles and Toronto. Send a neat package containing a demo of one or two songs, lyric sheets and a self-addressed stamped envelope." Braun also suggests getting involved with local and national songwriter associations. "Many of these groups bring in people from the music centers. That gives you a chance to network and learn what's going on in the industry."

As his best piece of advice, Braun tells beginners to "listen to a lot of material, especially the work of songwriters like Elton John, Bernie Taupin, Sting and Phil Collins. Be open to criticism. Experiment and never give up. Those who give up will not make it. But many times through perseverance, you'll stumble upon someone, somewhere who wants to record your song and it will become a hit."

—Barbara Kuroff

*A.A.A. AUDIO MANAGEMENT, 2310 Hamilton Ave., Cleveland OH 44114. (216)781-1101. Fax: (216)241-5720. Director of Operations: Anthony Rolando. Music publisher. Estab. 1993. Publishes 5 songs/year; publishes 2 new songwriters/year. Hires staff songwriters. Pays standard royalty.
How to Contact: Submit demo tape by mail. Unsolicited submissions are OK. Prefers cassette, VHS videocassette or CD with 3 songs and lyric and lead sheet. SASE. Reports in 2-3 weeks.
Music: All types. "Good melody lines, period!" Published "Tribute to Rock and Roll Hall of Fame," written and recorded by Barak Galil on Whoopy-De-Doo Records (rock).

ABALONE PUBLISHING, 26068 Regency Club Ct., Suite 7, Warren MI 48089-4125. Music Director: Jack Timmons. Music publisher and record company (L.A. Records). Estab. 1984. Publishes 20-30 songs/year; publishes 20-30 new songwriters/year. Hires staff songwriters. Pays standard royalty.
Affiliate(s): BGM Publishing, AL-KY Music, Bubba Music (BMI).
   • Abalone's record label, L.A. Records, is listed in the Record Companies section.
How to Contact: Submit demo tape by mail. Unsolicited submissions are OK. Prefers cassette with 1-5 songs and lyric sheet. "Include cover letter describing your goals." SASE. Reports in 1 month.
Music: Mostly **rock**, **pop** and **alternative**; also **dance**, **pop/rock** and **country**. Published "Shive" (by Al Long), recorded by The Lords (rock); *Taboo* (by S. Stevens), recorded by Harry Carrike (pop); and *Love Junkie* (by K. Simmons), recorded by Slut (alternative), all on L.A. Records.
Tips: "Write what you feel, however, don't stray too far from the trends that are currently popular. Lyrical content should depict a definite story line and paint an accurate picture in the listener's mind."

ACCENT PUBLISHING CO., Dept. SM, 3955 Folk-Ream Rd., Springfield OH 45502. President/Owner: Dave Jordan. Music publisher, record company (Dove Song Records). Estab. 1989. Publishes 6-8 songs/year; publishes 4 new songwriters/year. Pays standard royalty.
How to Contact: Write first and obtain permission to submit. Prefers cassette (or VHS videocassette) with 2 songs and lyric or lead sheet. SASE. Reports in 6-8 weeks.
Music: Mostly **country**, **gospel** and **R&B**; also **pop** and **soft rock**. Published "A Mothers Love" (by Joy Jordan) and "Hold On" (by C. Turner), both recorded by Renewed; and *Some Sunday Morning* (by J. Jordan), all on Dove Song Records.
Tips: "Write with feeling, have a catchy title and hook. Be willing to re-write until the song is good! Send a well-recorded demo."

AIM HIGH MUSIC COMPANY (ASCAP), 1300 Division St. Suite #200, Nashville TN 37203. (615)242-4722. (800)767-4984. Fax: (615)242-1177. E-mail: www.platinumr@aol.com. Producer: Robert Metzgar. Music publisher and record company (Platinum Plus Records). Estab. 1971. Publishes 250 songs/year; publishes 5-6 new songwriters/year. Hires staff writers. "Our company pays 100% to all songwriters."
Affiliate(s): Bobby & Billy Music (BMI), Billy Ray Music (BMI), Club Platinum Music (BMI).
   • See the listings for Platinum Plus Records in the Record Companies section, Capitol Management and Talent in the Managers and Booking Agents section and Capitol Ad, Management and Talent Group in the Record Producers section.
How to Contact: Submit demo tape by mail. Unsolicited submissions are OK. Prefers cassette or VHS videocassette with 5-10 songs and lyric sheet. "I like to get to know songwriters personally prior to recording their songs." Does not return material. Reports in 3-4 weeks.
Music: Mostly **country**, **traditional country** and **pop country**; also **gospel**, **southern gospel** and **contemporary Christian**. Published *Honky Tonk Christmas* (by Bob Douglass), recorded by George Jones on MCA Records; *My Miss America* (by Bob Douglass), recorded by Carters on Curb Records; and "There By Now" (by T. Tucker), recorded by Le Clerc on Capitol Records.
Tips: "Please let us determine which songs you've written are commercial first and then get them formally recorded as demos."

*ALADDIN MUSIC GROUP (BMI), P.O. Box 121626, Nashville TN 37212. (615)726-3556. Executive Director: N. James. Music publisher. Estab. 1996. Publishes 20 songs/year; publishes 5 new songwriters/year. Hires staff writers. Pays standard royalty.

 THE ASTERISK before a listing indicates that the listing is new in this edition. New markets are often the most receptive to unsolicited submissions.

How to Contact: Submit demo tape by mail. Unsolicited submissions are OK. Prefers cassette with 2 songs and lyric sheet. SASE. Reports in 1 month.
Music: Mostly **country, rock** and **alternative**; also **blues, gospel** and **contemporary**. Published "Old Folks Know," written and recorded by Christian Ramsey (country); "The Greatest Mistake of My Life" (by David Smith), recorded by Mary Aldrich (contemporary); and *Do Ya Want To Do It*, written and recorded by Jay S. Kay (alternative).
Tips: "Listen and study current trends and try to write advanced versions of those trends. Screen your material very carefully and only submit what you feel is honestly your best. We are looking for quality A-side material with something said in a unique way; for songs and writers with a different edge or approach. Not only do we hope to supply even more material to the major record companies, but we are also looking for songs for possible placement in movies, soundtracks and television programming."

ALEXANDER SR. MUSIC (BMI), P.O. Box 8684, Youngstown OH 44507. (216)782-5031. Fax: (216)782-5955. E-mail: bp814@yfn.ysu.edu. A&R: LaVerne Chambers. Music publisher, record company (LRG Records), music consulting and promotional services and record producer. Estab. 1992. Publishes 12-22 songs/year; publishes 2-4 new songwriters/year. Pays standard royalty.
How to Contact: Write first and obtain permission to submit. Prefers cassette with 4 songs and lyric sheet. "We will accept finished masters (cassette or CD) for review." SASE. Reports in 1 month. "No phone calls or faxes please."
Music: Mostly **contemporary jazz**, **urban Christian** and **black gospel**; also **R&B**. Published *Shattered Dreams*, *Maybe Tomorrow* and *No Greater Love*, all written and recorded by Darryl Alexander on LRG Records (jazz).
Tips: "Submit your best songs and follow submission guidelines. Finished masters open up additional possibilities. Lead sheets may be requested for material we are interested in. Must have SASE if you wish to have cassette returned."

ALEXIS (ASCAP), P.O. Box 532, Malibu CA 90265. (213)463-5998. President: Lee Magid. Music publisher, record company, personal management firm, and record and video producer. Member AIMP. Estab. 1950. Publishes 50 songs/year; publishes 20-50 new songwriters/year. Pays standard royalty.
Affiliate(s): Marvelle (BMI), Lou-Lee (BMI), D.R. Music (ASCAP) and Gabal (SESAC).
How to Contact: Submit a demo tape—unsolicited submissions are OK. Prefers cassette (or VHS videocassette of writer/artist if available) with 1-3 songs and lyric sheet. "Try to make demo as clear as possible—guitar or piano should be sufficient. A full rhythm and vocal demo is always better." Does not return material. Reports in 6 weeks "if interested."
Music: Mostly **R&B**, **jazz**, **MOR**, **pop** and **gospel**; also **blues, church/religious, country, dance-oriented, folk** and **Latin**. Published *Jesus Is Just Alright* (by Reynolds), recorded by D.C. Talk on Forefront Records (pop); "Let's Pretend," written and recorded by ZAD on Grass Roots Records (R&B); and *Stand Your Ground* (by Hawkins, Joubert and Diggs), recorded by Tramaine Hawkins on Columbia Records (gospel R&B).
Tips: "Try to create a good demo, vocally and musically. A good home-recorded tape will do."

ALJONI MUSIC CO. (BMI), 8017 International Village Dr., Jacksonville FL 32211. (904)765-8276. Creative Manager: Ronnie Hall. Director/Producer: Al Hall, Jr. Rap Representative/Producer: Al Money. Music publisher, record producer (Hallways to Fame Productions). Estab. 1971. Publishes 4-8 songs/year; publishes 1-2 new songwriters/year. Pays negotiated royalty.
Affiliate(s): Hallmarque Musical Works Ltd. (ASCAP).
● Aljoni Music's record label, Hallway International Records, is listed in the Record Companies section.
How to Contact: Submit demo tape by mail. Unsolicited submissions are OK. Prefers cassette (or VHS videocassette) with no more than 3 songs and lead sheet. Does not return material. Reports in 6-8 weeks.
Music: Mostly **rap, dance/R&B** and **jazz**. Published "It's Shaped Like An Upside Down Valentine" (by Cosmos Hall), recorded by Da Hood; "Big Kids' Stuff" (by Jarr/Hall/Ryan 3), recorded by Mista Big Stuff (rap/R&B); and "We Are The Jacksonville Jaguars" (by Al Hall, Jr./Juanita Hall/Ron "Cos" Hall/Al Money), recorded by Big Al & Friends (sports song), all on 1st Coast Posse Records.

*AL-KY MUSIC (BMI), 6472 Seven Mile, South Lyon MI 48178. Phone/fax: (810)486-0505. Producer: J.D. Dudick. Music publisher, record company (Ruffcut Productions), record producer. Estab. 1994. Publishes 10-15 songs/year; publishes 3-5 new songwriters/year. Pays standard royalty.
● See the listings for Ruffcut Productions in the Record Companies section and J.D. Dudick in the Record Producers section.
How to Contact: Submit demo tape by mail. Unsolicited submissions are OK. Prefers cassette with 3 songs and lyric sheet. Does not return material. Reports in 2 months.
Music: Mostly **modern rock, young country** and **alternative**; also **dance, pop** and **blues**. Published *Changes (by Chris Pierce)*, recorded by "Q" (rock); *Itchin*, written and recorded by Laya, both on

Ruffcut Records; and *Dreams Die Hard* (by Bil-Tol), recorded by Cidyzoo on Vehicle Garage Records.

ALL ROCK MUSIC, P.O. Box 2296, Rotterdam 3000 CG **Holland**. Phone: (31) 186-604266. Fax: (32) 1862-604366. President: Cees Klop. Music publisher, record company (Collector Records) and record producer. Estab. 1967. Publishes 50-60 songs/year; publishes several new songwriters/year. Pays standard royalty.
Affiliate(s): All Rock Music (England) and All Rock Music (Belgium).
• See the listing for Collector Records in the Record Producers section.
How to Contact: Submit demo tape by mail. Unsolicited submissions are OK. Prefers cassette. SAE and IRC. Reports in 1-2 months.
Music: Mostly **'50s rock**, **rockabilly** and **country rock**; also **piano boogie woogie**. Published *Henpecked Daddy*, written and recorded by Ralph Johnson on Collector Records; *Pianorepairmen*, written and recorded by EricJan Oberbeek; and *Grand Hotel*, written and recorded by Rockin' Vincent, both on Down South Records.

ALLEGED IGUANA MUSIC (SOCAN), 44 Archdekin Dr., Brampton, Ontario L6V 1Y4 **Canada**. President: Randall Cousins. Music publisher and record producer (Randall Cousins Productions). Estab. 1984. Publishes 80 songs/year.
Affiliate(s): Secret Agency (SOCAN) and AAA Aardvark Music (SOCAN).
How to Contact: Write first and obtain permission to submit a tape. Prefers cassette with 2 songs and lyric sheet. Does not return material. Reports in 8 weeks.
Music: Mostly **country**, **country-rock** and **A/C**; also **pop** and **rock**. Published *Some Rivers Run Dry* (by David Weltman), recorded by Diane Raeside; *Easy For You To Say*, written and recorded by Mark LaForme; and *Corners* (by Di Fronzo-Nollette), recorded by Ericka, all on Roto Noto Records.

ALLEGHENY MUSIC WORKS, 306 Cypress Ave., Johnstown PA 15902. (814)535-3373. Managing Director: Al Rita. Music publisher, record company (Allegheny Records). Estab. 1991. Pays standard royalty.
Affiliate(s): Allegheny Music Works Publishing (ASCAP) and Tuned on Music (BMI).
• See their listing in the Record Companies section.
How to Contact: Submit demo tape by mail. Unsolicited submissions are OK. Prefers cassette with 3 songs and lyric or lead sheet. SASE. Reports in 2-4 weeks.
Music: Mostly **country**; also **pop**, **A/C**, **R&B** and **inspirational**. Published "Heart Full of Lovin" (by Jess Caudillo), recorded by Tim Hall on Spotlight Stars; "If God Don't Like Country Music" (by Thomas Lenartz/Bill Dewberry), recorded by Tom Woodard on Pharaoh International Records; and "Doggone" (by Jeanne C. Nalbach), recorded by Dinah Lewis on Allegheny Records.
Tips: "We would like to receive more material written for female artists. Currently, we are getting in on average ten 'male' songs to one 'female' song."

ALLISONGS INC. (BMI, ASCAP), 1603 Horton Ave., Nashville TN 37212. (615)292-9899. President: Jim Allison. Music publisher, record company (ARIA Records), record producer (Jim Allison). Estab. 1985. Publishes 50 songs/year. Pays standard royalty.
Affiliate(s): Jim's Allisongs (BMI), d.c. Radio-Active Music (ASCAP) and Annie Green Eyes Music (BMI).
• Reba McEntire's "What Am I Gonna Do About You," published by AlliSongs, Inc., was included on her triple-platinum album, *Greatest Hits*.
How to Contact: Submit demo tape by mail. Unsolicited submissions are OK. Send chrome cassette and lyric sheet. Does not return material. Reports in 1 month only if interested.
Music: Mostly **country**. Published "What Am I Gonna Do About You" (by Allison/Simon/Gilmore), recorded by Reba McEntire on MCA Records (country); "Preservation of the Wild Life" (by Allison/Young), recorded by Earl Thomas Conley on RCA Records (country); and "Cowboys Don't Cry" (by Allison/Simon/Gilmore/Raymond), recorded by Daren Norwood on Giant Records (country).
Tips: "Send your best—we will contact you if interested."

ALPHA MUSIC INC. (BMI), 747 Chestnut Ridge Rd., Chestnut Ridge NY 10977. (914)356-0800. Fax: (914)356-0895. E-mail: trfemail@aol.com. Contact: Michael Nurko. Music publisher. Estab. 1931. Pays standard royalty.

LISTINGS OF COMPANIES in countries other than the U.S. have the name of the country in boldface type.

Affiliate(s): Dorian Music Corp. (ASCAP), TRF Music Inc.
How to Contact: Submit demo tape by mail. Unsolicited submissions are OK. Prefers audio cassette. Does not return material. Reports in 2-4 months.
Music: All categories, mainly **instrumental** and **acoustic**; also **theme music** for television and film. "Have published over 50,000 titles since 1931."

AMIRON MUSIC (ASCAP), Dept. SM, 20531 Plummer St., Chatsworth CA 91311. (818)998-0443. Manager: A. Sullivan. Music publisher, record company, record producer and manager. Estab. 1970. Publishes 2-4 songs/year; publishes 1-2 new songwriters/year. Pays standard royalty.
Affiliate(s): Aztex Productions and Copan Music (BMI).
• See the listing for AKO Production in the Record Producers section.
How to Contact: Prefers cassette (or Beta or VHS videocassette) with any number songs and lyric sheet. SASE. Reports in 10 weeks.
Music: Easy listening, MOR, progressive, R&B, rock and **top 40/pop**. Published "Let's Work It Out" (by F. Cruz), recorded by Gangs Back; and "Try Me," written and recorded by Sana Christian, all on AKO Records (pop). Also "Boys Take Your Mind Off Things" (by G. Litvak), recorded by Staunton on Les Disques Records (pop).
Tips: "Send songs with good story-lyrics."

ANTELOPE PUBLISHING INC., P.O. Box 55, Rowayton CT 06853. President: Tony LaVorgna. Music publisher. Estab. 1982. Publishes 5-10 new songs/year; publishes 3-5 new songwriters/year. Pays standard royalty.
How to Contact: Submit demo tape by mail. Unsolicited submissions are OK. Prefers cassette with lead sheet. Does not return material. Reports in 2 weeks "only if interested."
Music: Only **acoustic jazz** and **MOR vocal**. Published *Nightcrawler*, written and recorded by Tony LaVorgna on Just N Time Records; *Dance Samba*, written and recorded by Dan Wall on Antelope Records; and *The Train*, written and recorded by Alice Schweitzer on Alto Sound Records.

AQUARIUS PUBLISHING, Servitengasse 24, Vienna A-1090 **Austria**. (+43)1-707-37-10. Fax:(+43)1-707-84-22. Owner: Peter Jordan. Music publisher and record company (World Int'l Records). Estab. 1987. Publishes 100-200 songs/year; publishes 10 new songwriters/year.
How to Contact: Submit demo tape by mail. Unsolicited submissions are OK. Prefers cassette with up to 10 songs. "Lyric sheets not important; send photo of artist." Does not return material. Reports in 2-4 weeks.
Music: Mostly **country, pop** and **rock/ballads**; also **folk, instrumental** and **commercial**. Published *If God Don't Like Country Music* (by T. Lenartz/W. Dewberry), recorded by Tom Woodward; *Gone, Gone, Gone Travellin' Man*, written and recorded by Carroll Baker; and *Don't Do The Crime* (by F.B. Whitley), recorded by Toni Whitley, all on WIR Records.

ARYLIS CORPORATION (SOCAN), 301-1042 Nelson St., Vancouver, British Columbia V6E 1H8 **Canada**. (604)669-7531. Vice President/A&R: Machiko Yamane. Music publisher, record company, record producer and distributor. Estab. 1990. Works with performers who produce their own recordings. Pays variable royalty.
How to Contact: Submit demo tape by mail. Unsolicited submissions are OK. Prefers cassette. "Send cassette by air mail only (no couriers please). Value for customs must be less than $10." Does not return material. Reports in 2 months. "We call only if interested. Artists should call after 1 month."
Music: Mostly **easy listening, A/C** and **light jazz**. Published *Lavender*, written and recorded by Christopher on Arylis Records (A/C).
Tips: "We are looking primarily for artists who produce their own recordings, including covers. Instrumental, or vocal."

AUDIO IMAGES TWO THOUSAND MUSIC PUBLISHING (BMI), P.O. Box 250806, Holly Hill FL 32125-0806. (904)238-3820. Contact: D.L. Carter, submissions department. Music publisher. Estab. 1995. Pays standard royalty.
Affiliates: Sun Queen Publishing (ASCAP).
How to Contact: Write first and obtain permission to submit. "No phone calls, please." Does not return material. Reports in 4-6 weeks.
Music: Mostly **MOR, country** and **contemporary Christian**; also **gospel**. Published "Santa Claus Can't Get Down My Chimney" (by Bill Barber), recorded by Ana Cristina Randolph; "Don't Let The Christmas Lights Go Out Tonight" (by Robert L. Speegle), recorded by Tom Walker; and "Speak Lord" (by James D. Barnett), recorded by The Sunshine Singers, all on BJ's Records.

AUDIO MUSIC PUBLISHERS (ASCAP), 449 N. Vista St., Los Angeles CA 90036. (213)653-0693. E-mail: unclelenny@aol.com. Contact: Ben Weisman. Music publisher, record company and

record producer (The Weisman Production Group). Estab. 1962. Publishes 25 songs/year; publishes 10-15 new songwriters/year. Pays standard royalty.
- See the listing for Weisman Production Group in the Record Producers section.
How to Contact: Submit a demo tape by mail. Unsolicited submissions are OK. "No permission needed." Prefers cassette with 3-10 songs and lyric sheet. "We do not return unsolicited material without SASE. Don't query first; just send tape." Reports in 4-6 weeks.
Music: Mostly **pop**, **R&B**, **rap**, **dance**, **funk**, **soul** and **rock (all types)**.

AUM CIRCLE PUBLISHING, Otto-Seeling-Promenade 2-4, Fuerth 90762 **Germany**. (0911)773795. Fax: (0911)747305. Owner: Blazek Dalibor. Music publisher, record company (5233) and recording studio. Estab. 1993. Publishes 68 songs/year; publishes 15 new songwriters/year. Hires staff songwriters.
How to Contact: Submit demo tape by mail. Unsolicited submissions are OK. Does not return material. Reports in 1 month.
Music: Mostly **independent rock/pop**, **rock/pop mainstream** and **industrial**; also **grunge** and **funk rock**. Published *Day by Day* (by Paret Chvaszcik), recorded by Heaven Blue; *Mad World* (by Kailerch), recorded by The Frontlets; and *Panorama*, written and recorded by Peter Gluck.
Tips: "We are looking for high quality material, very straight songs, absolutely no techno!"

AXBAR PRODUCTIONS (BMI), Box 12353, San Antonio TX 78212. (210)829-1909. Business Manager: Joe Scates. Music publisher, record company, record producer and record distributors. Estab. 1978. Publishes 30 songs/year; publishes 10-12 new songwriters/year. Pays standard royalty.
Affiliate(s): Axe Handle Music (ASCAP), Scates and Blanton (BMI).
- See the listing for TMC Productions in the Record Producers section.
How to Contact: Write or call first to obtain permission to submit demo. Prefers cassette (or VHS videocassette) with 1-5 songs and lyric sheet. SASE. Reports as soon as possible, but "we hold the better songs for more detailed study."
Music: Mostly **country**; also **country crossover**, **comedy**, **blues**, **MOR** and **rock (soft)**. Published "My Foolish Pride" and "Loving You Ain't Easy" (by Rusty Lawrence); and "Sweet Judy Blue Eyes" (by George Chambers).
Tips: "Send only your best efforts. We have plenty of album cuts and flip sides. We need hit songs."

BABY RAQUEL MUSIC, 15 Gloria Lane, Fairfield NJ 07004. (201)575-7460. President: Mark S. Berry. Music publisher. Estab. 1984. Publishes 5-10 songs/year; publishes 1-2 new songwriters/year. Pays standard royalty.
Affiliate(s): Raquels Songs (BMI).
- Baby Raquel's affiliated record label, Sonic Group, Ltd., is listed in the Record Companies section.
How to Contact: Submit a demo tape by mail. Unsolicited submissions are OK. Prefers cassette with 1-3 songs and lyric sheet. Does not return material. Reports in 2 months.
Music: Mostly **alternative**, **dance** and **rock**. Published *Say Goodbye* (by M. Berry, M. Sukowski), recorded by Indecent Obsession on MCA Records (rock); *I Feel Love* (by M. Smith, M. Berry), recorded by Fan Club on Epic Records (pop/dance); and *Crazy for You* (by M. Berry), recorded by White Heat on Sony/Canada Records (rock). Other artists include Elvis Manson, Spirit Pushers, Michelin Slave, and Faceplate.

BAD HABITS MUSIC PUBLISHING, P.O. Box 111, London W13 0ZH **England**. (+44)81 991 1516. Fax: (+44)81 566 7215. Managing Director: John S. Rushton. Music publisher, record company (Bad Habits) and record producer. Estab. 1991. Hires staff songwriters. Royalty varies depending upon type of contract.
Affiliate(s): Great Life Music Publishing (ASCAP), BHMP (America) (BMI).
How to Contact: Submit demo tape by mail. Unsolicited submissions are OK. Prefers cassette (or VHS or Beta videocassette) with 3 songs. "Include what the writer lyricist wants to do, brief details/aspirations." SAE and IRC. Reports in 4-5 weeks.
Music: Mostly **pop/rock/dance**, **soul** and **jazz**; also **classical/opera**, **soundtracks/shows** and **New Age**. Published "B.J. Merry Christmas," written and recorded by B.J. (reggae); "You Take My Love" (by J. Greenscape), recorded by Gerri Ellen, both on Bad Habits Records; and *Dido and Aeneas* (by Purcell/Van Rhijn), recorded by various artists on Musica Eclectica Records (techno opera).
Tips: "Know your market, and make sure you have created for that market."

BAGATELLE MUSIC PUBLISHING CO. (BMI), P.O. Box 925929, Houston TX 77292. (713)680-2160 or (800)845-6865. President: Byron Benton. Music publisher, record company and record producer. Publishes 40 songs/year; publishes 2 new songwriters/year. Pays standard royalty.
Affiliate(s): Floyd Tillman Publishing Co.
- See the listing for Bagatelle Record Co. in the Record Companies section.

How to Contact: Submit demo tape by mail. Unsolicited submissions are OK. Prefers cassette (or videocassette) with any number of songs and lyric sheet. SASE.
Music: Mostly **country**; also **gospel** and **blues**. Published "Everything You Touch," written and recorded by Johnny Nelms; "This Is Real" and "Mona from Daytona," written and recorded by Floyd Tillman, all on Bagatelle Records.

*BAHOOMBA MUSIC (ASCAP), 847A Second Ave., Suite 294, New York NY 10017. Phone/fax: (718)591-4382. E-mail: bahoomba@aol.com. Owner: Robert Charles Smith. Music publisher, record company (Bahoomba), record producer. Estab. 1995. Publishes 20 songs/year; publishes 2 new songwriters/year. Pays standard royalty.
How to Contact: Submit demo tape by mail. Unsolicited submissions are OK. Prefers DAT with 3 songs. Does not return material. Reports in 1 month.
Music: Mostly **blues**. Published *Comin' From You, Small & Humble* and *Georgia Confusion* (by Bobby Charles), recorded by Rust/Charles on Bahoomba Records (blues).
Tips: "Be sure submissions are blues—not rock or jazz or pop."

BAL & BAL MUSIC PUBLISHING CO. (ASCAP), P.O. Box 369, LaCanada CA 91012-0369. (818)548-1116. President: Adrian P. Bal. Music publisher, record company (Bal Records) and record producer. Member AGAC and AIMP. Estab. 1965. Publishes 2-6 songs/year; publishes 2-4 new songwriters/year. Pays standard royalty.
Affiliate(s): Bal West Music Publishing Co. (BMI).
● See the listing for Bal Records in the Record Producers section.
How to Contact: Submit a demo tape by mail. Unsolicited submissions are OK. Prefers cassette with 3 songs and lyric sheet. SASE. Reports in 3 weeks to 5 months.
Music: Mostly **MOR**, **country**, **rock** and **gospel**; also **blues**, **church/religious**, **easy listening**, **jazz**, **R&B**, **soul** and **top 40/pop**. Published "Fragile" (by James Jackson), recorded by Kathy Simmons; and "Circles of Time," written and recorded by Paul Richards (A/C), both on Bal Records.

BARKIN' FOE THE MASTER'S BONE, 1111 Elm St., #520, Cincinnati OH 45210-2271. Office Manager: Kevin Curtis. Music publisher. Estab. 1989. Publishes 16 songs/year; publishes 2 new songwriters/year. Pays 66% royalty.
Affiliate(s): Beat Box Music (ASCAP), and Feltstar (BMI).
How to Contact: Submit demo tape by mail. Unsolicited submissions are OK. Prefers cassette (or VHS videocassette) with 3 songs. SASE. Reports in 2 weeks.
Music: Mostly **country**, **soft rock** and **pop**; also **soul**, **gospel** and **rap**. Published "I Am God" (by Donald Lawrence), "Be In Heaven Come Christmas" and "The Royal Brigade (Roll Call)" (by Kevin Curtis), all recorded by Santarr on Warner Bros. Records.
Tips: "Begin to see music as a tool of healing for all the world, and yourself as one of its master surgeons."

BARREN WOOD PUBLISHING (BMI), P.O. Box 26341, Dayton OH 45426. (513)837-4854. Fax: (513)837-2327. President: Jack Froschauer. Creative Director: Chris Tanner. Music publisher. Estab. 1992. Publishes 5-6 songs/year; publishes 3-4 new songwriters/year. Pays standard royalty.
Affiliate(s): MerryGold Music Publishing (ASCAP).
● Barren Wood Publishing's record label, Emerald City Records, is listed in the Record Companies section.
How to Contact: Submit demo tape by mail. Unsolicited submissions are OK. Prefers cassette or DAT with 1-4 songs and lyric or lead sheet. "Studio quality demo cassette please." SASE. Reports in 4-6 weeks.
Music: Mostly **country**, **A/C** and **Christian**. Published *I've Got The Lord in Me*, written and recorded by David Schafer with Stephen Seifert (gospel); *Come Out From the Storm* (by Kent Pritchard), recorded by Kent Pritchard & God's Will (rock); and "Gochee Goochee" (by Jack Froschauer), recorded by Cadillac Jack & The Reel-Time All Stars (country), all on Emerald City Records.

*BARTOW MUSIC, 324 N. Bartow St., Cartersville GA 30120. (404)386-7243. Publishing Administrator: Jack C. Hill. Producer: Tirus McClendon. Music publisher and record producer (HomeBoy, Ragtime Productions). BMI. Estab. 1988. Publishes 5 songs/year; 5 new songwriters/year. Pays standard royalty.
How to Contact: Submit a demo tape by mail. Unsolicited submissions are OK. Prefers cassette (or VHS videocassette) with 3 songs and lyric sheets. SASE. Reports in 2 months.
Music: **R&B**, **pop**, **dance** and **house**. Published "I Just Wanna Love Ya," written and recorded by Dez; "Giving You All My Love," written and recorded by Da-Break; and "Early Times" (by J. Hill), recorded by The Cravens, all on Nas-T Records.

*BAY RIDGE PUBLISHING CO. (BMI), P.O. Box 5537, Kreole Station, Moss Point MS 39563. (601)475-2098. Fax: (601)475-7484. Estab. 1974. President/Owner: Joe Mitchell.
 • See the listing for Missle Records in the Record Companies section.
How to Contact: Write first and obtain permission to submit. SASE.
Music: Mostly **country, alternative, gospel, rap, heavy metal, jazz, bluegrass, R&B, soul, MOR, blues, rock** and **pop.** Published "Doctor Doctor" and "Rose Upon a Stem," recorded by Jerry Piper; and "Have You Seen My Baby," written and recorded by Herbert Lacey on Missle Records.

*BAYLOR-ESELBY MUSIC (ASCAP), 106½ S. Urbana Ave., Urbana IL 61801. (217)384-0015. Fax: (217)355-9057. E-mail: hammerhd@prairienet.org. President: Andy Baylor. Music publisher, music producer (commercial music, jingles, etc.). Estab. 1995. Publishes 25 songs/year; publishes 2 new songwriters/year. Pays standard royalty.
How to Contact: Submit demo tape by mail. Unsolicited submissions are OK. Prefers cassette. Does not return material.
Music: Mostly **contemporary** and **rock.** Published "Achieving the Summit" (by Andy Baylor) (commercial); "Surf's Up" (by Andy Baylor/Buzzy Eselby) (commercial); and "Lou Henson Show" (by Andy Baylor) (theme show music), all recorded by Baylor-Eselby.

BEARSONGS, Box 944, Birmingham, B16 8UT **England**. Phone: 44-021-454-7020. Managing Director: Jim Simpson. Professional Manager: Clare Jepson-Homer. Music publisher and record company (Big Bear Records). Member PRS, MCPS. Publishes 25 songs/year; publishes 15-20 new songwriters/year. Pays standard royalty.
 • See the listings for Big Bear Records in the Record Companies section and Big Bear in the Record Producers section.
How to Contact: Submit demo tape by mail. Unsolicited submissions are OK. Prefers reel-to-reel or cassette. Does not return material. Reports in 3 months.
Music: **Blues** and **jazz.** Published *Blowing With Bruce* and *Cool Heights* (by Alan Barnes), recorded by Bruce Adams/Alan Barnes Quintet; and *Blues For My Baby* (by Charles Brown), recorded by King Pleasure & The Biscuit Boys, all on Big Bear Records.
Tips: "Have a real interest in jazz, blues, R&B."

*BEAVERWOOD AUDIO-VIDEO (BMI), 133 Walton Ferry, Hendersonville TN 37075. (615)824-2820. Fax: (615)824-2833. Owner: Clyde Beavers. Music publisher, record company (Kash Records, JCL Records), record producer, audio-video duplication. Estab. 1976. Pays standard royalty.
Affiliate(s): Jackpot Music (BMI).
How to Contact: Submit demo tape by mail. Unsolicited submissions are OK. Prefers cassette, DAT or videocassette with 1-5 songs. Does not return material.
Music: Mostly **gospel** and **country.** Published "Mary Had a Little Lamb," *Listen to My Story* and *I Heard His Call*, all written and recorded by Lawrence Davis on JCL Records (gospel).

EARL BEECHER PUBLISHING (BMI, ASCAP), P.O. Box 2111, Huntington Beach CA 92647. (714)842-8635. Owner: Earl Beecher. Music publisher, record company (Outstanding and Morrhythm Records) and record producer (Earl Beecher). Estab. 1968. Publishes varying number of songs/year. Pays standard royalty.
How to Contact: Submit demo tape by mail. Unsolicited submissions are OK. "Please do not call in advance." Cassettes only. SASE. Reports in several months.
Music: **Pop, ballads, rock, gospel** and **country.** Published *Hero*, written and recorded by Ed Branson (country); *This Farm*, written and recorded by Nancy Learn (country); and *Help Me Elvis* (by Doug Koempel), recorded by Memory Bros. (country), all on Morrhythm Records.
Tips: "I am interested mainly in people who want to perform their songs and release albums on one of my labels rather than to submit material to my existing artists."

BERANDOL MUSIC LTD. (BMI), 2600 John St., Unit 220, Markham ON L3R 3W3 **Canada**. (905)475-1848. A&R Director: Ralph Cruickshank. Music publisher, record company (Berandol Records), record producer and distributor. Member CMPA, CIRPA, CRIA. Estab. 1969. Publishes 20-30 songs/year; publishes 5-10 new songwriters/year. Pays standard royalty.
 • Berandol Music is also listed in the Record Companies section, and Music Box Dancer Publications is listed in the Music Print Publishers section.
How to Contact: Submit demo tape by mail. Unsolicited submissions are OK. Prefers cassette with 2-5 songs. Does not return material. Reports in 3 weeks.
Music: Mostly **instrumental, children**'s and **top 40**.
Tips: "Strong melodic choruses and original sounding music receive top consideration."

HAL BERNARD ENTERPRISES, INC., 2612 Erie Ave., P.O. Box 8385, Cincinnati OH 45208. (513)871-1500. Fax: (513)871-1510. President: Stan Hertzman. Professional Manager: Pepper Bonar.

Music publisher, record company and management firm. Publishes 12-24 songs/year; 1-2 new song-writers/year. Pays standard royalty.
- Hal Bernard Enterprises is also listed in the Record Producers section, their management firm, Umbrella Artists Management, is in the Managers and Booking Agents section, and their record label, Strugglebaby Recording Co., can be found in the Record Companies section.

Affiliate(s): Sunnyslope Music (ASCAP), Bumpershoot Music (BMI), Apple Butter Music (ASCAP), Carb Music (ASCAP), Saiko Music (ASCAP), Smorgaschord Music (ASCAP), Clifton Rayburn Music (ASCAP) and Robert Stevens Music (ASCAP).
How to Contact: Submit a demo tape by mail. Unsolicited submissions are OK. Prefers cassette with 3 songs and lyric sheet. SASE. Reports in 6 weeks.
Music: Rock, R&B and **top 40/pop**. Published "Here," "Inner Revolution" and "I See You," all written and recorded by Adrian Belew on Atlantic Records (progressive pop); and "Mattress," "Joy and Madness" and "Moaner," all recorded by psychodots on Strugglebaby Records.
Tips: "Best material should appear first on demo. Cast your demos. If you as the songwriter can't sing it—don't. Get someone who can present your song properly, use a straight rhythm track and keep it as naked as possible. If you think it still needs something else, have a string arranger, etc. help you, but still keep the *voice up* and the *lyrics clear.*"

BEST BUDDIES, INC. (BMI), Dept. SM, 2100 Eighth Ave. South, Nashville TN 37204. (615)383-7664. Contact: Review Committee. Music publisher, record company (X-cuse Me) and record producer (Best Buddies Productions). Estab. 1981. Publishes 18 songs/year. Publishes 1-2 new songwriters/year. Pays standard royalty.
Affiliate(s): Swing Set Music (ASCAP), Best Buddies Music (BMI).
How to Contact: Write first and obtain permission to submit. Must include SASE with permission letter. Prefers cassette (or VHS videocassette) with maximum 3 songs. Does not return material. Reports in 4-6 weeks. Do not call to see if tape received.
Music: Mostly **country, rock** and **pop**; also **gospel** and **R&B**. Published "Somebody Wrong is Looking Right" (by King/Burkholder), recorded by Bobby Helms; "Give Her Back Her Faith in Me" (by Ray Dean James), recorded by David Speegle (country); and "I Can't Get Over You Not Loving Me" (by Misty Efron and Bobbie Sallee), recorded by Sandy Garwood, all on Bitter Creek Records (country).
Tips: "Make a professional presentation. There are no second chances on first impressions."

BETTY JANE/JOSIE JANE MUSIC PUBLISHERS (BMI, ASCAP), 7400 N. Adams Rd., North Adams MI 49262. Phone/fax: (517)287-4421. Professional Manager: Claude E. Reed. Music publisher, record company (C.E.R. Records) and record producer. Estab. 1980. Publishes 75-100 songs/year; 10 new songwriters/year. Pays standard royalty.
How to Contact: Submit demo tape by mail. Unsolicited submissions are OK. Prefers cassette or 7½ ips reel-to-reel with 1-5 songs and lyric or lead sheets. SASE. Reports in 2-4 weeks.
Music: Mostly **gospel** and **country western**; also **pop/R&B** and **MOR**. Published *Be Like Jesus* (by Greg Brayton), recorded by Toni Walker on C.E.R. Records (gospel); *Liberated Lady*, written and recorded by James Cox (country); and *Time*, written and recorded by Joseph J. Jakresky, both on World International Records.
Tips: "Try to be original, present your music in a professional way, submit only your very best songs with accurate lyric sheets and well made demo tape. Be patient! Send SASE with a sufficient amount of postage if you want your material returned."

BIG FISH MUSIC PUBLISHING GROUP (BMI), 11927 Magnolia Blvd. #3, N. Hollywood CA 91607. (818)984-0377. CEO: Chuck Tennin. Music publisher and record producer. Estab. 1971. Publishes 10-20 songs/year; publishes 4 or 5 new songwriters/year. Pays standard royalty.
Affiliate(s): California Sun Music (ASCAP).
How to Contact: Write first and obtain permission to submit. "Please do not call." Prefers cassette with no more than 4 songs and lyric sheet. "Include a dated cover letter, include your source of referral (*Songwriter's Market*)." SASE. Reports in 2 weeks.
Music: Mostly **country**, including **country pop** and **country crossover**; **pop ballads**; also **uplifting, inspirational gospel with a message, instrumental background music for TV & films** and **novelty type songs for commercial use**. Published "Espirit E," written and recorded by Don French on ABC-TV (background music for *General Hospital*); "Let Go and Let God" (by Corinne Porter), recorded by Molly Pasutti (gospel); and "Happy Landing," written and recorded by Brawley & Woodrich, both on California Sun Records.
Tips: "Demo should be professional and high quality. Clean, simple and dynamic and must get the song across on the first listen. Good clear vocals, a nice melody, a good musical feel, good musical arrangement and strong lyrics. Looking for unique country songs for ongoing Nashville music projects and songs for a female country trio."

BIG SNOW MUSIC (BMI), P.O. Box 21323, St. Paul MN 55121. President: Mitch Viegut. Vice President and General Manager: Mark Alan. Music publisher. Estab. 1989. Publishes 30 new songs/year; publishes 4 new songwriters/year. Pays standard royalty.
 • See the listing for Mark Alan Agency in the Managers and Booking Agents section.
How to Contact: Call first and obtain permission to submit. Prefers cassette with 3 songs and lyric sheet. Does not return material. Reports in 3 months.
Music: Mostly **alternative**, **rock** and **black contemporary**. Published "Too Much Attitude" (by Eldon Fisher/Wayne Estrada/Mitch Viegut) and *Swag* (by Eldon Fisher/Wayne Estrada/Steve Kennedy), recorded by Crash Alley (rock); and *Somewhere* (by Mitch Viegut), recorded by Airkraft on Curb Records (rock).

BLACK STALLION COUNTRY PUBLISHING (BMI), Box 368, Tujunga CA 91043. (818)352-8142. Fax: (818)352-2122. President: Kenn Kingsbury. Music publisher and book publisher (*Who's Who in Country & Western Music*). Member CMA, CMF. Publishes 2 songs/year; publishes 1 new songwriter/year. Pays standard royalty.
 • See the listing for Black Stallion Country Productions in the Managers and Booking Agents section.
How to Contact: Prefers 7½ ips reel-to-reel or cassette with 2-4 songs and lyric sheet. SASE. Reports in 1 month.
Music: **Bluegrass** and **country**.
Tips: "Be professional in attitude and presentation. Submit only the material you think is better than anything being played on the radio."

BLUE HILL MUSIC/TUTCH MUSIC (BMI), 282 Route 41, Sharon CT 06069. Contact: Paul Hotchkiss. Music publisher, record company (Target Records, Kastle Records) and record producer (Red Kastle Records). Estab. 1975. Publishes 20 songs/year; publishes 1-5 new songwriters/year. Pays standard royalty.
 • Blue Hill's affiliated record label, Target Records, is listed in the Record Companies section.
How to Contact: Write first and obtain permission to submit a tape. Prefers cassette with 2 songs and lyric sheet. "Demos should be clear with vocals out in front." SASE. Reports in 2 weeks.
Music: Mostly **country** and **country/pop**; also **MOR** and **blues**. Published "Coyote Moon," written and recorded by Mike Terry on Roto Noto Records (country); *Memory of You* (by P. Hotchkiss), recorded by P.J. Price on Priceless Records (country); and "For Always" (by P. Hotchkiss/M. Terry), recorded by Mercury Bros. on KMG Records (country).

BLUE SPUR ENTERTAINMENT INC./GIT A ROPE PUBLISHING (BMI), 358 W. Hackamore, Gilbert AZ 85233-6425. (602)892-4451. Director of A&R: Esther Burch. President: Terry Olson. Music publisher. Estab. 1990. Royalty varies.
How to Contact: Write or call first and obtain permission to submit. Prefers cassette with 3-5 songs and lyric sheet. "Please send only songs protected by copyright. Please be sure submissions are cassette form and call for coded submission number to insure your material will be given our full attention." Does not return unsolicited material. Reports in 6-12 weeks.
Music: Mostly **traditional/contemporary country** and **gospel**.
Tips: "Study the market carefully, listen to the trends, attend a local songwriter's association; be committed to your craft and be persistent. Write, write and re-write!"

BOAM (ASCAP), P.O. Box 201, Smyrna GA 30081. (404)432-2454. A&R: Tom Hodges. Music publisher. Estab. 1965. Publishes 20 songs/year; publishes 4 new songwriters/year. Pays standard royalty.
Affiliate(s): Mimic Music, Stepping Stone, Skip Jack (BMI).
 • BOAM's record label, Trend Records, is listed in the Record Companies section.
How to Contact: Submit demo tape by mail. Unsolicited submissions are OK. Prefers cassette (or VHS videocassette) with 6 songs and lyric or lead sheet. SASE. Reports in 3 weeks.
Music: Mostly **country**, **R&B** and **MOR**; also **rock**, **gospel** and **folk**. Published *Hank's My Daddy Too*, written and recorded by F. Branno; *Brand New Sound* (by Hodges/LaVey), recorded by LaVey; and *You'll Be Late*, written and recorded by Helen Foster, all on Trend Records.

BONNFIRE PUBLISHING (ASCAP), P.O. Box 6429, Huntington Beach CA 92615-6429. (714)962-5618. Contact: Eva and Stan Bonn. Music publisher, record company (ESB Records) and record producer. Estab. 1987. Pays standard royalty.
Affiliate(s): Gather 'Round Music (BMI).
 • Bonnfire's record label, ESB Records, is listed in the Record Companies section.
How to Contact: Submit demo cassette by mail with lyric sheet. Unsolicited submissions OK. SASE. Reports in 1 month.

Music: Country (all forms). Published "She's Just a Dreamer" (by Jim Weaver and Bobby Caldwell), recorded by Bobby Caldwell (country); and "Toe Tappin' Country Man (by Jack Schroeder), recorded by John Swisshelm (country), both on ESB Records; and "Married Man" (by Eva Bonn, Marda Philppt, Gene Rabbai Jr.), recorded by Shella Delayn on Ranch Records (country).
Tips: "You must strive to 'compete' with the top 40 country artists who write their own material today. Your demo must be a professional tight package."

BOURNE CO. MUSIC PUBLISHERS (ASCAP), 5 W. 37th St., New York NY 10018. (212)391-4300. Fax: (212)391-4306. Contact: Professional Manager. Music publisher. Estab. 1919.
Affiliate(s): Murbo Music Publishing, Inc. (BMI).
  • See their listing in the Music Print Publishers section.
How to Contact: Write first and obtain permission to submit. Does not return material. Reports in 3 months.
Music: Mostly **pop**, **ballads** and **R&B**; also **future standards**. Published "Unforgettable" (by Irving Gordon), recorded by Natalie Cole with Nat 'King' Cole on Elektra Records (pop); and "In The Wee Small Hours of The Morning" (by Bob Hilliard/David Mann), recorded by Carly Simon and Frank Sinatra on Capitol Records (pop/AC).

DAVID BOWMAN PRODUCTIONS & W. DAVID MUSIC, (formerly W. David Music), 20 Valley View Dr., Langhorne PA 19053. (215)702-7613 or (215)322-8078. President: David Bowman. Music publisher, music library producers/music production house. Estab. 1989. Publishes 10-20 songs/year; publishes 5-10 new songwriters/year. "Pays by the job."
  • See their listing in the Advertising, AV and Commercial Music Firms section.
How to Contact: Write first and obtain permission to submit a demo. Prefers cassette. "We are looking for instrumental pieces of any length not exceeding 3 minutes for use in AV music library. Also looking for 30 and 60 second music spots for television, radio and all multimedia applications." Does not return material. Reports in 1-2 months.
Music: All types. Published "Techno," "The Streets of London" and *Looking Back*, all written and recorded by W. David Bowman on Warren Records.
Tips: "Network. Get your name and your work out there. Let everyone know what you are all about and what you are doing. Be patient, persistent and professional. What are you waiting for? Do it!"

ALLAN BRADLEY MUSIC (BMI), P.O. Box 24109, Lyndhurst OH 44124. Owner: Allan Licht. Music publisher, record company (ABL Records) and record producer. Estab. 1993. Publishes 10 songs/year; publishes 5 new songwriters/year. Pays standard royalty.
How to Contact: Submit demo tape by mail. Unsolicited submissions are OK. Prefers cassette with 3 songs and lyric sheet. "Send only unpublished works." Does not return material. Reports in 2 weeks.
Music: Mostly **A/C**, **pop** and **R&B**; also **country** and **Christian contemporary**. Published "Sherrie Ann" (by Allan Licht/Mike Cavanaugh), recorded by Mike Cavanaugh; "I Wanna Feel Your Body" (by Allan Licht), recorded by Debi Levin; and ''She's All The Woman I Need," written and recorded by Allan Licht, all on ABL Records.
Tips: "Please send only songs that have Top 10 potential. Only serious writers are encouraged to submit."

BRANCH GROUP MUSIC (SOCAN), 1067 Sherwin Rd., Winnipeg MB R3H 0T8 **Canada**. (204)694-3101. President: Gilles Paquin. Music publisher, record company (Oak Street Music) and record producer (Oak Street Music). Estab. 1987. Publishes 10 songs/year; publishes 2 new songwriters/year. Pays negotiable royalty.
Affiliate(s): Forest Group Music (SOCAN).
  • See the listing for Paquin Entertainment in the Managers and Booking Agents section.
How to Contact: Submit a demo tape by mail. Unsolicited submissions are OK. Prefers cassette or VHS videocassette with 2-3 songs and lyric and lead sheet. SAE and IRC.
Music: Mostly **children's** and **novelty**. Published "Something In My Shoe" (by Al Simmons); "Heart At Work" (by Valdy); and "No Regrets" (by Tim Jackson).

KITTY BREWSTER SONGS, "Norden," 2 Hillhead Rd., Newtonhill Stonehaven AB3 2PT **Scotland**. Phone: 01569 730962. MD: Doug Stone. Music publisher, record company (KBS Records), record producer and production company (Brewster & Stone Productions). Estab. 1989. Pays standard royalty.
How to Contact: Submit demo tape by mail. Unsolicited submissions are OK. Prefers cassette (or VHS videocassette if available) with any amount of songs and lyric or lead sheet. Does not return material. Reports in 3-4 months.
Music: Mostly **AOR, pop, R&B** and **dance**; also **country, jazz, rock** and **contemporary**. Published *Sleepin' Alone* (by R. Donald); *I Still Feel the Same* (by R. Greig/K. Mundie); and *Your Love Will Pull Me Thru* (by R. Greig), all recorded by Kitty Brewster on KBS Records (AOR).

BRONX FLASH MUSIC, INC. (ASCAP), 3151 Cahuenga Blvd. W., Los Angeles CA 90068. (213)882-6127. Fax: (213)882-8414. Contact: Creative Staff. Music publisher. Estab. 1991. Publishes 30-50 songs/year; publishes 1-2 new songwriters/year. Hires staff writers. Royalty varies depending on particular songwriter.
Affiliate(s): Kenwon Music (BMI).
How to Contact: Write first for permission to submit. Prefers cassette with maximum of 2 songs. SASE. Reports in 1 month.
Music: Mostly **pop**, **R&B** and **rock**. Published "You Are My Home" (by F. Wildhorn), recorded by Peabo Bryson/Linda Eder on Angel Records (R&B); and "What I Do Best" (by F. Wildhorn), recorded by Robin S. on Atlantic Records (R&B).
Tips: "Keep it clever. Keep it short."

THE BROTHERS ORGANISATION, 74 The Archway, Station Approach, Ranelagh Gardens, London SW6 34H **England**. (0171)610-6183. Fax: (0171)610-6232. E-mail: bros@keepcalm.demon. co.uk. Director: Ian Titchener. Music publisher and record company. Estab. 1989. Publishes 20 songs/year. "Payment decided on a contract by contract basis."
How to Contact: Submit demo tape by mail. Unsolicited submissions are OK. Prefers cassette. Does not return material. Reports in 1 month.
Music: Mostly **R&B/dance**, **rock (melodic)** and **pop**. Published "Everything" (by Smart/Ward), recorded by Smart on Brothers Records (rock/pop); "Silence" (by Titchener), recorded by 3 to the Power on Yo Bro Records (dance); and "I Don't Know" (by J. Underwood), recorded by Too Busy on Attitude Records (dance).

BUG MUSIC, INC. (BMI, ASCAP), Dept. SM, 6777 Hollywood, 9th Floor, Los Angeles CA 90028. (213)466-4352. Contact: Eddie Gomez. Music publisher. Estab. 1975. Other offices: Nashville contact Dave Durocher and London contact Paul Jordan. "We handle administration."
Affiliate(s): Bughouse (ASCAP).
How to Contact: Write first and obtain permission to submit. Prefers cassette. SASE. Reports in 1 month.
Music: All genres. Published "Almost Home" (by John Croslin), recorded by Hootie & The Blowfish on Atlantic Records (alternative); *I Know This Town* (by Cheryl Wheeler), recorded by Bette Midler on Atlantic Records (pop); and "Til I Hear It From You" (by Marshall Crenshaw), recorded by Gin Blossoms on A&M Records (pop/alternative).

BURIED TREASURE MUSIC (ASCAP), 524 Doral Country Dr., Nashville TN 37221. Executive Producer: Scott Turner. Music publisher and record producer (Aberdeen Productions). Estab. 1972. Publishes 30-50 songs/year; publishes 3-10 new songwriters/year. Pays standard royalty.
Affiliate(s): Captain Kidd Music (BMI).
How to Contact: Submit demo tape by mail. Unsolicited submissions are OK. Prefers cassette (or VHS videocassette) with 1-4 songs and lyric sheet. Reports in 3 weeks. "Always enclose SASE if answer is expected."
Music: Country and **country/pop**; also **rock**, **MOR** and **contemporary**. Published *Stardust Again* (by Nanette Malher), recorded by Arden Gatlin (A/C); *Show Me the Way* (by Tony Graham), recorded by Roy Clark on Churchill Records (country); and *Your Dreams Will Be Safe* (by Tony Graham), recorded by Byron Whitman (country).
Tips: "*Don't* send songs in envelopes that are 15″x 20″, or by registered mail. It doesn't help a bit. The post office will not accept tapes in regular business-size envelopes. Say something that's been said a thousand times before . . . only say it differently. A great song doesn't care who sings it. Songs that paint pictures have a better chance of ending up as videos. With artists only recording 10 songs every 18-24 months, the advice is . . . Patience!"

CACTUS MUSIC AND WINNEBAGO PUBLISHING (ASCAP), P.O. Box 1027, Neenah WI 54957-1027. E-mail: sowtoner@aol.com. President: Tony Ansems. Music publisher and record company (Fox Records). Estab. 1984. Publishes 5-8 songs/year; publishes 3-5 new songwriters/year. Pays standard royalty.
How to Contact: Submit demo tape by mail. Unsolicited submissions are OK. Prefers cassette with 3 songs maximum and lyric sheet. SASE. Reports in 2 months.

HOW TO GET THE MOST out of *Songwriter's Market* (at the front of this book) contains comments and suggestions to help you understand and use the information in these listings.

Music: Mostly **C&W** and **gospel**. Published *Funny* (by T.H. Pete/E. Wellman/T. Ansems), recorded by Jimmy Glass on Dynamite Records; *Waiting for the Telephone* (by Mike Kaiser/Allen Jahnke) and *Sealed With A Kiss* (by Mike Kaiser), both recorded by Sheridan's Ride on Bonzai Records.

CALIFORNIA COUNTRY MUSIC (BMI), 112 Widmar Pl., Clayton CA 94517. (510)672-8201. Owner: Edgar J. Brincat. Music publisher, record company (Roll On Records). Estab. 1985. Publishes 30 songs/year; publishes 2-4 new songwriters/year. Pays standard royalty.
Affiliate(s): Sweet Inspirations Music (ASCAP).
 • California Country's record label, Roll On Records, can be found in the Record Companies section.
How to Contact: Submit a demo tape by mail. Unsolicited submissions are OK. Prefers cassette with 3 songs and lyric sheet. Any calls will be returned collect to caller. SASE. Reports in 4-6 weeks.
Music: Mostly **MOR**, **contemporary country** and **pop**; also **R&B**, **gospel** and **light rock**. Published *For Realities Sake* (by F.L. Pittman/R. Barretta) and *Maddy* (by F.L. Pittman/M. Weeks), both recorded by Ron Banks & L.J. Reynolds on Life & Bellmark Records; and *Quarter Past Love* (by Irwin Rubinsky/Janet Fisher), recorded by Darcy Dawson on NNP Records.
Tips: "Listen to what we have to say about your product. Be as professional as possible."

CALINOH MUSIC GROUP, 608 W. Iris Dr., Nashville TN 37204. (615)292-3568. Contact: Ann Hofer or Tom Cornett. Music publisher. Estab. 1992. Publishes 50 songs/year; publishes 10 new songwriters/year. Pays standard royalty.
Affiliate(s): Little Liberty Town (ASCAP) and West Manchester Publishing (BMI).
How to Contact: Submit demo tape by mail. Unsolicited submissions are OK. Prefers cassette with 3 songs and lyric sheet. "Include SASE." Does not return material. "Writers are contacted only if we are interested in publishing their material."
Music: Mostly **country**, **gospel** and **pop**.

CAMEX MUSIC, 535 Fifth Ave., New York NY 10017. (212)682-8400. A&R Director: Alex Benedetto. Music publisher, record company and record producer. Estab. 1970. Publishes 100 songs/year; publishes 10 new songwriters/year. Query for royalty terms.
How to Contact: Submit demo tape by mail. Unsolicited submissions are OK. Prefers cassettes with 5-10 songs and lyric sheet or lead sheet. SASE. Reports in 3-6 months.
Music: Mostly **alternative rock**, **pop** and **hard rock**; also **R&B**, **MOR** and **movie themes**. Artists include Marmalade, SAM and Hallucination Station.

CASH PRODUCTIONS, INC. (BMI), 744 Joppa Farm Rd., Joppa MD 21085. (301)679-2262. President: Ernest W. Cash. Music publisher, record company (Continental Records, Inc.), national and international record distributor, artist management, record producer (Vision Music Group, Inc.) and Vision Video Production, Inc. Estab. 1987. Publishes 30-60 songs/year; publishes 10-15 new songwriters/year. Pays standard royalty.
Affiliate(s): Big K Music, Inc. (BMI), Guerriero Music (BMI) and Deb Music (BMI).
 • Cash Productions' record label, Continental Records, is listed in the Record Companies section and their management firm, Cash Productions, is listed in the Managers and Booking Agents section.
How to Contact: Call first and obtain permission to submit. Prefers cassette (VHS videocassette if available) with 3 songs and lyric sheet. SASE. Reports in 2 weeks.
Music: Mostly **country**, **gospel** and **pop**; also **R&B** and **rock**. Published *Family Ties*, *Tampa* and *Party*, all written and recorded by Short Brothers on Silver City Records (C&W).
Tips: "Do the best job you can on your work—writing, arrangement and production. Demos are very important in placing material."

CASTLE MUSIC GROUP, 50 Music Square W., Suite 201, Nashville TN 37203. (615)320-7003. Fax: (615)320-7006. Publishing Director: Petty Tresco. Music publisher, record company (Castle Records), record producer. Estab. 1969. Publishes 50 songs/year; publishes 10 new songwriters/year. Pays standard royalty.
Affiliate(s): Castle Music Group, Cat's Alley Music (ASCAP), Alley Roads Music (BMI).
How to Contact: Write or call first and obtain permission to submit. Prefers cassette with 3 songs and lyric sheet. SASE. Reports in 1 month.
Music: Mostly **country** and **R&B**; also **pop** and **gospel**. Published *Little Bit of Love*, written and recorded by Chip Koehler and Clay Benson on Castle Records (country).

CENTIUM ENTERTAINMENT, INC. (BMI), 373 S. Robertson Blvd., Beverly Hills CA 90211. (310)275-3325. Fax: (310)275-3326. President: Arthur Braun. Music publisher and record company. Estab. 1994. Publishes 15-20 songs/year; publishes 3-4 new songwriters/year. Pays negotiable royalty.

● See the interview with Centium Entertainment's president, Arthur Braun, in this section. They also have a listing in the Record Companies section.

How to Contact: Submit demo by mail. Unsolicited submissions are OK. Prefers 3 songs and lyric sheet. SASE. Reports in 3 weeks.

Music: Mostly **pop**, **rock** and **R&B**.

CHEAVORIA MUSIC CO. (BMI), 1219 Kerlin Ave., Brewton AL 36426. (205)867-2228. President: Roy Edwards. Music publisher, record company (Bolivia Records) and record producer (Known Artist Production). Estab. 1972. Publishes 20 new songwriters/year. Pays standard royalty.
Affiliate(s): Baitstring Music (ASCAP).
● Cheavoria Music's record label, Bolivia Records, is listed in the Record Companies section, and Known Artist Productions is listed in the Record Producers section.
How to Contact: Write first to get permission to submit. Prefers cassette with 3 songs and lyric sheet. Does not return material. Reports in 1 month.
Music: Mostly **R&B**, **pop** and **country**; also **good ballads**. Published "Forever and Always," written and recorded by Jim Portwood on Bolivia Records (country).

CHERIE MUSIC (BMI), 3621 Heath Lane, Mesquite TX 75150. (214)279-5858. Contact: Jimmy Fields or Silvia Harra. Music publisher and record company. Estab. 1955. Publishes approximately 100 songs/year. Pays standard 50% royalty.
● Cherie Music's record label, Jamaka Record Co., is listed in the Record Companies section.
How to Contact: Submit demo tape by mail. Unsolicited submissions are OK. Prefers cassette with up to 10 songs. SASE. Reports in approximately 2 months, "depending on how many new songs are received."
Music: Mostly **country** and **rock** (if not over produced—prefer 1950s type rock). Published "Cajun Baby Blues" and *Alive with Alan Dryman* (by Hank Williams/Jimmy Fields), recorded by Allen Dryman on Jamaka Records; and "Is The King Still Alive" (by Fields/McCoy/Kern), recorded by Johnny Harra on HIA Records.

CHESTNUT MOUND MUSIC GROUP, P.O. Box 989, Goodlettsville TN 37070. (615)851-1360 or (615)851-7755. Publishing Coordinator: Ray Lewis. Music publisher, record company (Morning Star, Cedar Hill, Harvest) and record producer. Estab. 1981. Publishes 200 songs/year; publishes 30 new songwriters/year. Pays standard royalty.
Affiliate(s): Pleasant View Music (ASCAP), Chestnut Mound Music (BMI), Indian Forest (SESAC).
How to Contact: Write or call first and obtain permission to submit. Prefers cassette with 3 songs and lyric sheet. SASE. Reports in 2-4 weeks.
Music: Mostly **Southern gospel, country gospel** and **secular country**; also **inspirational**. Published "I'll Be Living That Way" (by Carroll Roberson), recorded by Dixie Melody Boys; "Rainbow Avenue" (by Vern Sullivan), recorded by Palmetto State Quartet; and "Stand On The Word" (by Laura Colston), recorded by Kindlers, all on Morningstar Records (southern gospel).

*CHICAGO KID PRODUCTIONS (BMI), 1840 N. Kenmore #304, Los Angeles CA 90027. (213)660-6817. Fax: (213)660-4756. President: John Ryan. Music publisher, record company and record producer. Estab. 1973. Publishes 40-50 songs/year. Hires staff songwriters.
Affiliate(s): 63rd St. Music (BMI).
How to Contact: Submit demo tape by mail. Unsolicited submissions are OK. Prefers DAT with 3-5 songs. "Only first-rate material for platinum level acts, unique, compelling original bands and writers (we also make many record deals)." Does not return material.
Music: Mostly **alternative rock**, **pop** and **R&B**.

CHRISTEL MUSIC LIMITED, Fleet House, 173 Haydons Rd., Wimbledon, London SW19 8TB **England**. (0181)241-6351. Fax: (0181)241-6450. Managing Director: Dennis R. Sinnott. Music publisher. Estab. 1983. Publishes 350 songs/year; publishes 50 new songwriters/year. Pays 60/40 in favor of the writer.
How to Contact: Write first and obtain permission to submit. Prefers cassette with 4 songs and lyric sheet. SAE and IRC. Reports in 2 weeks.
Music: Mostly **mainstream pop**, **rock ballads** and **MOR**. *All music with commercial potential.* Published *The Fool You Left Behind* (by Chris O'Shaughnessy/Lea Hart), recorded by D-Rox on Masonic Records (rock); *Play Along*, written and recorded by Elaine Saffer on Pickwick Records (ballad); and *Sunshine* (by Tony McDonald), recorded by Flying Superkids on All Star Records (pop).
Tips: "If you're writing songs with a view to other artists covering them, don't spend a fortune on recording costs. These days with professional equipment, good home demos are often sufficient at

least for our needs. The important thing is to strive for clean distinct recordings. Avoid distortions and inaudible lyrics."

CHRISTMAS & HOLIDAY MUSIC (BMI), 3517 Warner Blvd., Suite 4, Burbank CA 91505. (213)849-5381. President: Justin Wilde. Music publisher. Estab. 1980. Publishes 8-12 songs/year; publishes 8-12 new songwriters/year. "All submissions must be complete songs (i.e., music and lyrics)." Pays standard royalty.
Affiliate(s): Songcastle Music (ASCAP).
How to Contact: Submit demo tape by mail. Unsolicited submissions are OK. Do not call. "First class mail only. Registered or certified mail not accepted." Prefers cassette with 3 songs and lyric sheet. "Professional demos a must." Do not send lead sheets or promotional material, bios, etc." SASE. Reports in 1-2 weeks.
Music: Strictly **Christmas music** (and a little Hanukkah) in every style imaginable: easy listening, rock, R&B, pop, blues, jazz, country, reggae, rap, children's secular or religious. *Please do not send anything that isn't Christmas.* Published "What Made the Baby Cry?" (by William J. Golay), recorded by Toby Keith on Polydor Records (country); "First Day of The Son" (by Derrick Procell), recorded by the Brooklyn Tabernacle Choir on Warner/Alliance Records (gospel); and "It Must Have Been The Mistletoe" (by Justin Wilde/Doug Konecky), recorded by Kathie Lee Gifford on Warner Bros. Records (pop).
Tips: "If a stranger can hum your melody back to you after hearing it twice, it has 'standard' potential. Couple that with a lyric filled with unique, inventive imagery, that stands on its own, even without music. Combine the two elements, and workshop the finished result thoroughly to identify weak points. Only when the song is polished to perfection, then cut a master quality demo that sounds like a record or pretty close to it. Submit positive lyrics only. Avoid negative themes like 'Blue Christmas.' "

SONNY CHRISTOPHER PUBLISHING (BMI), P.O. Box 9144, Ft. Worth TX 76147-2144. (817)595-4655. Owner: Sonny Christopher. Music publisher, record company and record producer. Estab. 1974. Publishes 20-25 new songs/year; publishes 3-5 new songwriters/year. Pays standard royalty.
How to Contact: Write first, then call and obtain permission to submit. Prefers cassette with lyric sheet. SASE (#10 or larger). Reports in 10 weeks.
Music: Mostly **country, rock** and **blues**. Published *Did They Judge Too Hard* (by Sonny Christopher), recorded by Ronny Collins on Sonshine Records.
Tips: "Be patient. I will respond as soon as I can. To the young songwriter: *never, never* quit."

CIMIRRON MUSIC (BMI), 607 Piney Point Rd., Yorktown VA 23692. (804)898-8155. E-mail: lp42285@aol.com. President: Lana Puckett. Music publisher, record company (Cimirron/Rainbird Records) and record producer. Estab. 1986. Publishes 10-20 songs/year. "Royalty depends on song and writer."
 • Cimirron Music's record label, Cimirron/Rainbird Records, is listed in the Record Companies section.
How to Contact: Call first and obtain permission to submit. Prefers cassette and lyric sheet. SASE. Reports in 8-10 weeks.
Music: Mostly **country, acoustic, folk** and **bluegrass**. Published *Cornstalk Pony* (by K. Person/Lana Puckett), recorded by Lana Puckett; *Habit I Just Can't Break* and *Farmer of Love*, written and recorded by Kim Person and Lana Puckett, all on Cimirron Records.
Tips: "Be professional in your music—make sure it can compete in the industry today."

CISUM, 708 W. Euclid, Pittsburg KS 66762. (316)231-6443. Partner: Kevin Shawn. Music publisher, record company and record producer. Estab. 1985. Publishes 100 songs/year. Pays standard royalty.
How to Contact: Write first and obtain permission to submit a tape. Prefers cassette (or VHS videocassette if available) and lyric sheet. "Unpublished, copyrighted, cassette with lyrics. Submit as many as you wish. We listen to everything, allow 3 months. When over 3 weeks please call."
Music: Mostly **novelty, country** and **rock**; also **pop, gospel** and **R&B**. Published "The World's Greatest Country Novelty Song" (by Jack Barlow); and "Every Time I See a Pig I Think of You" (by Dave Talley) and "Shade Tree Mechanic," both recorded by Poison Ivy on Antique Records.
Tips: "Good demo, great song; always put your best effort on the tape first."

 THE ASTERISK before a listing indicates that the listing is new in this edition. New markets are often the most receptive to unsolicited submissions.

CLEAR POND MUSIC (BMI), P.O. Box 16555, Santa Fe NM 87506-6555. Fax: (505)474-7344. Publisher: Susan Pond. Music publisher and record producer (Crystal Clear Productions). Estab. 1992. Publishes 10-20 songs/year; publishes 1-5 new songwriters/year. Pays standard royalty. "We use the Songwriters Guild Contract."
How to Contact: Submit demo tape by mail. Unsolicited submissions are OK. Prefers cassette with 1 song and lyric sheet. "We are only interested in a singer/songwriter/artist, no exceptions!"
Music: Mostly **hard rock**, **top 40**, **alternative** and **country** (all types). Published "Rain" (by Steve Craig), recorded by Albert Hall on Maxim Headlight Records (rock); "Back To Love Again," written and recorded by Erik Darling and Bordertown on Aztec Records (country); and "Now Is The Time," written and recorded by Lourdes on Maxim Records (alternative).
Tips: "We represent *Billboard* hit songwriters. Study music, songwriting, vocals then submit a 24/48 track demo with killer hooks. Don't expect those in the music industry to empty out their bank accounts because you have talent. We recommend having financial backing, or at the very worst, finding a job."

R.D. CLEVÈRE MUSIKVERLAG (GEMA), Postfach 2145, D-63243 Neu-Isenburg, **Germany**. Phone: (6102)51065. Fax: (6102)52696. Professional Manager: Tony Hermonez. Music publisher. Estab. 1967. Publishes 700-900 songs/year; publishes 40 new songwriters/year. Pays standard royalty.
Affiliate(s): Big Sound Music, Hot Night Music, Lizzy's Blues Music, Max Banana Music, R.D. Clevère-Cocabana-Music, R.D. Clevère-Far East & Orient-Music, and R.D. Clevère-America-Today-Music.
    ● R.D. Clevère's record label, Comma Records, is listed in the Record Companies section.
How to Contact: "Do not send advance letter(s) asking for permission to submit your song material, just send it." Prefers cassette with "no limit" on songs and lyric sheet. SAE and a minimum of two IRCs. Reports in 3 weeks.
Music: Mostly **pop**, **disco**, **rock**, **R&B**, **country** and **folk**; also **musicals** and **classic/opera**.

*COAST LINE EVENTS, INC., P.O. Box 538, Newport News VA 23607. (804)244-3501. Fax: (804)244-5317. President: Waverly W. Jones, Jr. Music publisher, record producer. Estab. 1993. Publishes 1-2 songs/year; publishes 1-2 new songwriters/year. Pays negotiable royalty.
Affiliate(s): Bay Coast Publishing (BMI).
How to Contact: Write or call first and obtain permission to submit a demo. Prefers cassette and bio with 2-5 songs and lyric sheet. SASE. Reports in 6 weeks.
Music: Mostly **R&B**, **gospel** and **jazz**. Published "Devil Meant It For" (by Chris Thomas), recorded by NCRM Choir on CBT's Records (gospel); "Dreamer's Destiny," written and recorded by Carlton Savage (jazz); and "Brown Eyes," written and recorded by Herman Fields (jazz).
Tips: "Bay Coast Publishing is interested in receiving clear, quality cassette demos with understandable lyrics. Submissions should not be overproduced. Biographical information and lyric sheet should accompany submissions."

COFFEE AND CREAM PUBLISHING COMPANY (ASCAP), Dept. SM, 1138 E. Price St., Philadelphia PA 19138. (215)842-3450. President: Bolden Abrams, Jr. Music publisher and record producer (Bolden Productions). Publishes 20 songs/year; publishes 4 new songwriters/year. Pays standard royalty.
How to Contact: Prefers cassette (or VHS videocassette) with 1-4 songs and lyric or lead sheets. Does not return material. Reports in 2 weeks "if we're interested."
Music: Mostly **dance**, **pop**, **R&B**, **gospel** and **country**. Published "You Are My Life" (by Sean Chhangur), recorded by Chuck Jackson; and "If I Let Myself Go" (by Jose Gomez/Sheree Sano), recorded by Dionne Warwick/Chuck Jackson on Ichiban Records and by Evelyn "Champagne" King on RCA/BMG Records (pop/ballad).

COLSTAL MUSIC, 3 Alison St., 5th Floor, Parkrise, Surfer's Paradise, QLD H217 **Australia**. 0755 388911. Fax: 0755 703434. Director: Bernie Stahl. Music publisher and video distributor. Estab. 1985. Pays negotiable royalty.
How to Contact: Submit demo tape by mail. Prefers cassette (or PAL videocassette if available). Does not return material.
Music: Mostly **country** and **comedy**. Published *What Have You Done for Australia* (by Colin Greatorix); *Gin Gin* (by Willy Hackett); and *Home Made Brew* (by Col Elliott), all recorded by Col Elliott on BMG Australia Records (country/comedy).

*GLENN COLTON SHOWS, 256 Sunshine Dr., Amherst NY 14228. (716)691-7928. President: Glenn Colton. Music publisher. Estab. 1991. Publishes 10-15 songs/year; publishes 1-2 new songwriters/year. Pays standard royalty.
How to Contact: Submit demo tape by mail. Unsolicited submissions are OK. Prefers cassette with 3-7 songs and lead sheet. Does not return material. Reports in 3-4 weeks.

Music: Mostly **children's**, **folk** and **country**; also **rock**. Published *Let's Save The Planet*, written and recorded by Paul Swisher (children's); *Just A Cowboy*, written and recorded by Glenn Colton (country); and *The Power of the Mind* (by Paul Swisher/Glenn Colton), recorded by Glenn Colton, all on GCS Records (rock).

Tips: "Submit material with a positive message and a strong hook that will appeal to an elementary age audience in a live setting."

*COPPERFIELD MUSIC GROUP (ASCAP, BMI), 54 Music Square E., Suite 304, Nashville TN 37203. (615)726-3100. Fax: (615)726-3172. Director of Music Publishing: Greg Becker. Music publisher, artist management. Estab. 1976. Hires staff writers.

Affiliate(s): Top Brass Music (ASCAP) and Penny Annie Music (BMI).

How to Contact: Submit demo tape by mail. Unsolicited submissions are OK. Prefers cassette, DAT, VHS videotape or CD with 3 songs and lyric sheet. "3 song maximum." SASE. Reports in 1-2 weeks.

Music: Mostly **country**, **Christian** and **pop**.

THE CORNELIUS COMPANIES (BMI, ASCAP), Dept. SM, 812 19th Ave. S., Suite 5, Nashville TN 37203. (615)321-5333. Owner/Manager: Ron Cornelius. Contact: Charlie Brown. Music publisher and record producer (Ron Cornelius). Estab. 1987. Publishes 60-80 songs/year; publishes 2-3 new songwriters/year. Occasionally hires staff writers. Pays standard royalty.

Affiliate(s): RobinSparrow Music (BMI).

How to Contact: Write first and obtain permission to submit a tape. Prefers cassette with 2-3 songs. SASE. Reports in 2 months.

Music: Mostly **country** and **pop**; also **positive country** and **gospel**. Published *Time Off for Bad Behavior* (by Bobby Keel/Larry Latimer), recorded by Confederate Railroad on Atlantic Records; "A Man's Home is His Castle," recorded by Faith Hill on Warner Bros. Records; and "Give Love Away," written and recorded by Dinah and the Desert Crusaders on Gateway Records.

CORPORATE MUSIC, 154 Grande Cote, Rosemere, Quebec J7A 1H3 **Canada**. President: Paul Levesque. Music publisher, record company (Artiste Records) and management company (Paul Levesque Management Inc.). Estab. 1971. Publishes 20 songs/year; publishes 1-2 new songwriters/year. Pays standard royalty.

Affiliate(s): Savoir Faire Music (ASCAP), Transfer Music (BMI).

How to Contact: Submit demo tape by mail. Unsolicited submissions are OK. Prefers cassette (or VHS videocassette if available) with 4 songs and lyric sheet. SAE and IRC. Reports in 2 months.

Music: Mostly **rock, pop** and **R&B (dance)**. Published "What Ya Do" and "She Got Me," both written and recorded by Haze & Shuffle on Arista Records (rock); and "Tu Pars," written and recorded by Bruno Pelletier on Artiste Records (pop).

COTTAGE BLUE MUSIC (BMI), P.O. Box 121626, Nashville TN 37212. (615)726-3556. Contact: Neal James. Music publisher, record company (Kottage Records) and record producer (Neal James Productions). Estab. 1971. Publishes 30 songs/year; publishes 3 new songwriters/year. Pays standard royalty.

Affiliate(s): James & Lee (BMI), Neal James Music (BMI) and Hidden Cove Music (ASCAP).

• Cottage Blue's record label, Kottage Records, is listed in the Record Companies section, their management firm, James Gang Management, is listed in the Managers and Booking Agents section, and Neal James Productions is listed in the Record Producers section.

How to Contact: Submit demo tape by mail. Unsolicited submissions OK. Prefers cassette with 2 songs and lyric sheet. SASE. Reports in 4 weeks.

Music: Mostly **country**, **gospel** and **rock/pop**; also **R&B** and **alternative rock**. Published "She's My Love," written and recorded by Bill Fraser on Cross Wind Records (country); "Ole Rebel Flag" (by Dannie Holbrook), recorded by Clint Miracle on Kottage Records (country); and "My Love," written and recorded by Judie Bell on MAC Records.

Tips: "Screen material carefully before submitting."

COUNTRY BREEZE MUSIC (BMI), 1715 Marty, Kansas City KS 66103. (913)384-7336. President: Ed Morgan. Music publisher and record company (Country Breeze Records, Walkin' Hat Records). Estab. 1984. Publishes 100 songs/year; publishes 25-30 new songwriters/year. Pays standard royalty.

Affiliate(s): Walkin' Hat Music (ASCAP).

• You can find a listing for Country Breeze's record label, Country Breeze Records, in the Record Companies section.

How to Contact: Submit a demo tape by mail. Unsolicited submissions are OK. Prefers cassette (or VHS videocassette) with 4-5 songs and lyric sheet. SASE. "The songwriter/artist should perform on the video as though on stage giving a sold-out performance. In other words put heart and soul into the project. Submit in strong mailing envelopes." Reports in 2 weeks.

Music: Mostly **country (all types)**, **gospel (southern country and Christian country)** and **rock (no rap or metal)**. Published "Keep on Asking" (by Larry Herman), recorded by the Floridians on Angel Star Records (gospel); "I Can't Believe I Said Goodbye" (by Ed Morgan/Ed Livermore), recorded by Tanya Poe; and "She Came Back to Kansas" (by Ray Murphy), recorded by Kyle London, both on Country Breeze Records.

Tips: "Be patient. It takes time to get songs to artists who are looking for material. We send songs worldwide, and sometimes it takes three to six months for artists or other labels to get back with us."

*COUNTRY RAINBOW MUSIC (BMI), 9 Music Square S., Suite 225, Nashville TN 37203-3203. (513)489-8944. President: Samuel D. Rogers. Music publisher. Estab. 1995. Publishes 10-12 songs/year; publishes 4-6 new songwriters/year. Pays standard royalty.

Affiliate(s): Venture South Music (ASCAP).

How to Contact: Submit demo tape by mail. Unsolicited submissions are OK. Prefers cassette with 1-3 songs and lyric sheet. SASE. Reports in 2-3 weeks.

Music: Mostly **country**, **MOR** and **bluegrass**; also **cajun**.

Tips: "Songs should be unique and well crafted (hit potential, no album fillers). Professional, ready-to-plug full demos preferred. Simple guitar/vocal or piano/vocal are okay, only if professionally performed. Crisp, clean recording on good quality tape. I like songs with clever concepts, good imagery, simple everyday words—a theme which may be cliché, but told from a different perspective."

COUNTRY SHOWCASE AMERICA (BMI), 385 Main St., Laurel MD 20707. (301)725-7713. Fax: (301)604-2676. Contact: Francis Gosman. Music publisher, record company and record producer. Estab. 1971. Publishes 9 songs/year; publishes 1 new songwriter/year. Pays standard royalty.

How to Contact: Submit demo tape by mail. Unsolicited submissions are OK. Prefers cassette with 2 songs and lyric sheet. Does not return material.

Music: Mostly **country**. Published "Queen of the Mall," "Broken Hearts" and "I Grew Up Loving You," all recorded by Johnny Anthony on CSA Records (country).

COUNTRY STAR MUSIC (ASCAP), 439 Wiley Ave., Franklin PA 16323. (814)432-4633. President: Norman Kelly. Music publisher, record company (Country Star, Process, Mersey and CSI) and record producer (Country Star Productions). Estab. 1970. Publishes 15-20 songs/year; publishes 4-6 new songwriters/year. Pays standard royalty.

Affiliate(s): Kelly Music Publications (BMI) and Process Music Publications (BMI).

- See the listings for Country Star International in the Record Companies section, Country Star Productions in the Record Producers section and Country Star Attractions in the Managers and Booking Agents section.

How to Contact: Submit demo tape by mail. Unsolicited submissions are OK. Prefers cassette with 1-4 songs and typed lyric or lead sheet. SASE. Reports in 1 week. "No SASE no return."

Music: Mostly **country** (80%); also **rock**, **gospel**, **MOR** and **R&B** (5% each). Published "The Red Heifer" (by Kelly Barbara), recorded by Bob Stamper (country); "Love Tree" (by Kelly Brown), recorded by David Lee Wayne; and "Rose of Cherokee" (by Kitty Casteel), recorded by Virge Brown, all on Country Star Records.

Tips: "Send only your best songs—ones you feel are equal to or better than current hits. Typed or printed lyrics, please."

COWBOY JUNCTION FLEA MARKET AND PUBLISHING CO. (BMI), Highway 44 West, Junction 490, Lecanto FL 34461. (904)746-4754. President: Elizabeth Thompson. Music publisher (Cowboy Junction Publishing Co.), record company (Cowboy Junction Records) and record producer. Estab. 1957. Publishes 5 songs/year. Pays standard royalty or other amount.

How to Contact: Submit demo tape (or VHS videocassette) by mail. Unsolicited submissions are OK. SASE. Reports as soon as possible.

Music: **Country**, **western**, **bluegrass** and **gospel**. Published *Orange Blossom Special*, *I Wanna Go Fishing* and *She's My Florida Lovely Lady* (by Boris Max Pastuch), recorded by Buddy Max on Cowboy Junction Records (C&W bluegrass)

Tips: "You could come to our flea market on Tuesday or Friday and present your material—or come to our Country and Western Bluegrass Music Show held any Saturday."

LOMAN CRAIG MUSIC, P.O. Box 111480, Nashville TN 37222-1480. (615)331-1219. President: Loman Craig. Vice President: Tommy Hendrick. Music publisher, record company (Bandit Records, HIS Records), record producer (Loman Craig Productions). Estab. 1979. Pays standard royalty.

Affiliate(s): Outlaw Music of Memphis (BMI), We Can Make It Music (BMI) and Doulikit Music (SESAC).

How to Contact: Submit a demo tape by mail. Unsolicited submissions are OK. Prefers cassette with 2-3 songs and lyric sheet. "Does not have to be a full production demo." SASE. Reports in 4-6 weeks.

Music: Mostly **country** and **pop**; also **bluegrass** and **gospel**.

CTV MUSIC (GREAT BRITAIN), Television Centre, St. Helier, Jersey JE1 3ZD Channel Islands **Great Britain**. (1534)68999. Fax: (1534)59446. Managing Director: Gordon De Ste. Croix. Music publisher, music for TV commercials, TV programs and corporate video productions. Estab. 1986. Pays negotiable royalty.
How to Contact: Write first and obtain permission to submit. Prefers CD or cassette. Does not return material. Reports in 2 weeks.
Music: Mostly **instrumental**, for TV commercials and programs.

*CUNNINGHAM MUSIC (BMI), Dept. SM, P.O. Box 441124, Detroit MI 48244-1124. President: Jerome Cunningham. Music publisher. Estab. 1988. Publishes 8-9 songs/year; publishes 2 new song-writers/year. Pays standard royalty.
How to Contact: Submit a demo tape by mail. Unsolicited submissions are OK. Prefers cassette (or VHS videocassette if available) with 3 songs and lyric sheet. Does not return material. Reports in 1-2 months.
Music: Mostly **R&B**, **gospel** and **jazz**; also **pop** and **rock**. Published "Soul Desire" (by Julia M. Augusta).

CUPIT MUSIC (BMI), P.O. Box 121904, Nashville TN 37212. (615)731-0100. E-mail: jyoke@edge. net. Website: http://www.edge.net/cupit. President: Jerry Cupit. Music publisher and record producer (Jerry Cupit Productions). Publishes 30 songs/year. Hires staff songwriters. Pays standard royalty.
Affiliate(s): Cupit Memaries (ASCAP).
• See the listing for Jerry Cupit Productions in the Record Producers section.
How to Contact: Write first and obtain permission to submit with SASE. Does not return material. Reports in 2-3 months.
Music: Mostly **country, southern rock** and **gospel/contemporary Christian**. Published "Don't Make Me Have to Come In There" (by Jerry Cupit), recorded by Ken Mellons on Epic Records (country); "Greatest Gift" (by D. Brewer/F. Brewer), recorded by Fox Brothers on Sierra Nashville Records (gospel); and *She Don't Do Nothin' For Me* (by J. Cupit/J. Carr/K. Mellons/G. Simmons), recorded by Hank Williams Jr. on Curb Records (country).
Tips: "Keep vocals up front on demos, study correct structure, always tie all lines to hook!"

D.S.M. PRODUCERS INC. (ASCAP), 161 W. 54th St., New York NY 10019. (212)245-0006. Producer: Suzan Bader. Music publisher, record producer and management firm (American Steel Man-agement Co.). Estab. 1979. Publishes 25 songs/year; publishes 10 new songwriters/year. "Publishes and releases 10 CDs a year for TV, feature films and radio." Pays standard royalty.
Affiliate(s): Decidedly Superior Music (BMI).
• See D.S.M.'s other listings in the Record Producers and Advertising, AV and Commercial Music Firms sections.
How to Contact: Write first and obtain permission to submit. Prefers cassette (or VHS videocassette) and lyric or lead sheet. SASE. "Include SASE or we do not review nor respond to material." Reports in 3 months.
Music: Mostly **top 40**, **R&B/dance**, **CHR** and **rock**; also **jazz**, **country** and **instrumental tracks for background music**. Published *Dance America*, *Rock America* and *Horrific!*, all written and recorded by various artists on AACL Records.
Tips: "We can only publish finished masters for many uses which earn composers a steady income. We currently publish over 400 American composers. Their music is being licensed for network TV and feature films."

DAGENE MUSIC (ASCAP), P.O. Box 410851, San Francisco CA 94141. (415)822-1530. Presi-dent: David Alston. Music publisher, record company (Cabletown Corp.) and record producer (Classic Disc Production). Estab. 1988. Hires staff songwriters. Pays standard royalty.
Affiliate(s): 1956 Music.
How to Contact: Call first and obtain permission to submit a tape. Prefers cassette with 2 songs and lyric sheet. "Be sure to obtain permission before sending any material." SASE. Reports in 1 month.
Music: Mostly **R&B/rap**, **dance** and **pop**. Published "Maxin" (by Marcus Justice/Bernard Hender-son), recorded by 2 Dominatorz on Dagene Records; "Love Don't Love Nobody" (by David Alston), recorded by Rare Essence on Cabletown Records; and "Why Can't I Be Myself," written and recorded by David Alston on E-lect-ric Recordings.
Tips: "It's what's in the groove that makes people move."

DARBONNE PUBLISHING CO. (BMI), Dept. SM, Route 3, Box 172, Haynesville LA 71038. (318)927-5253. President: Edward N. Dettenheim. Music publisher and record company (Wings Record Co.). Estab. 1987. Publishes 50 songs/year; publishes 8-10 new songwriters/year. Pays standard royalty.

How to Contact: Submit a demo tape by mail. Unsolicited submissions are OK. Prefers cassette or 7½ ips reel-to-reel with up to 12 songs and lyric sheet. Does not return material. Reports in 6 weeks.

Music: Mostly **country** and **gospel**. Published "Blanche" (by E. Dettenheim) and "It Don't Always Thunder" (by E. Dettenheim/T.J. Lynn), both recorded by T.J. Lynn on Wings Records (country); and "The Room" (by T.J. Lynn/E. Dettenheim), recorded by Kathy Shelby (country).

Tips: "The better the demo—the better your chances of interesting your listener."

DAVIS & DAVIS MUSIC (BMI), 5755 June Lane, Winston-Salem NC 27127-9707. Phone/fax: (910)764-8698. President: Angel Davis. Music publisher and artist management. Estab. 1994. Pays standard royalty.

Affiliate(s): Late Dee Music Publishing (ASCAP).

How to Contact: Submit demo tape by mail. Unsolicited submissions are OK. Prefers cassette (or VHS videocassette) with up to 5 songs and lyric sheet. "Full studio demo and copyrighted material only!" SASE. Reports in 4-6 weeks.

Music: **Country**, **contemporary Christian**, **gospel**, **blues**, **R&B**, **instrumentals**, **children's music**, **novelty** and **ballads** in all genres. Published "Don't Talk," "In My Dreams" (by Kelly Jo Keaton) and "No Time For You" (by Paul Standefer), all recorded by Cheyenne on Fearless Records.

DE LEON PUBLISHING, 2903 S. Gen Bruce Dr., Temple TX 76504. (817)773-1775. Fax (817)773-4778. Contact: Thomas Cruz. Music publisher and record company.

How to Contact: Call first and obtain permission to submit. Prefers cassette with 4 songs and lyric or lead sheet. Does not return material. Reports in 4-6 weeks.

Music: All types.

THE EDWARD DE MILES MUSIC COMPANY (BMI), 4475 Allisonville Rd., 8th Fl., Indianapolis IN 46205. (317)546-2912. Attn: Professional Manager. Music publisher, record company (Sahara Records), management, bookings and promotions. Estab. 1984. Publishes 50-75 songs/year; publishes 5 new songwriters/year. Hires staff songwriters. Pays standard royalty.

- See the listings for Edward De Miles in the Record Producers section, and Sahara Records and Filmworks Entertainment in the Record Companies section.

How to Contact: Write first and obtain permission to submit. Prefers cassette with 1-3 songs and lyric sheet. Does not return material. Reports in 1 month.

Music: Mostly **top 40 pop/rock**, **R&B/dance** and **C&W**; also **musical scores for TV, radio, films and jingles**. Published "Dance Wit Me" and "Moments," written and recorded by Steve Lynn on Sahara Records (R&B).

Tips: "Copyright all songs before submitting to us."

DEAN ENTERPRISES MUSIC GROUP, Dept. SM, P.O. Box 620, Redwood Estates CA 95044-0620. (408)353-1006. Attn: Executive Director. Music publisher, record company. Member: NARAS, Harry Fox Agency. Estab. 1989. Publishes 10-12 songs/year; publishes 5-7 new songwriters/year. Pays standard royalty.

Affiliate(s): Mikezel Music Co. (ASCAP), Teenie Deanie Music Co. (BMI) and Minotaur Records.

How to Contact: Submit demo tape by mail. Unsolicited submissions are OK. "Do not write or call for permission to submit." Prefers maximum of 4 songs on cassette or CD "with typed lyric sheets and brief letter of introduction. Material must be copyrighted and unassigned. Prefers to keep tapes on file, but will return if fully paid SASE is included. A free evaluation is given with first-class SASE and evaluation form provided by the artist." Reports in 3 weeks. "Show name, address, phone number and © sign on tape and lyric sheets."

Music: Mostly **modern country**, **country/pop**, **MOR/easy listening**, **soft/easy rock**, **top 40** and **novelty**. No instrumental, rap music, jazz, heavy metal, punk/acid rock. Published "I'll Have it Made" (by R. Tomich/M. Cordle), recorded by Claudia Delon on Top Records/Italy (A/C); "Walk Between the Raindrops" (by T. Warren), recorded by David Dancer on Cougar Records/Canada (C&W) and "I Keep Reachin' " (by D. Koempel), recorded by the The Memory Brothers on Minotaur Records.

Tips: "Present a professional package with typed lyric sheets and do not send by anything other than First Class Mail, unless so requested. Have a studio demo done with a good vocalist. Join songwriting organizations and read songwriting books; submit good quality tapes and always include a SASE if a response is requested. Do not send lyric sheets only. A song is music and lyrics. Never pay to have your song recorded, other than for demo purposes."

DELEV MUSIC COMPANY, 7231 Mansfield Ave., Philadelphia PA 19138-1620. (215)276-8861. President: W. Lloyd Lucas. Music publisher, record company (Surprize Records, Inc.), record producer and management. BMI, ASCAP, SESAC, SGA, and CMRRA. Publishes 6-10 songs/year; publishes 6-10 new songwriters/year. Pays standard royalty.

Affiliate(s): Sign of the Ram Music (ASCAP), Gemini Lady Music (SESAC), and Delev Music (BMI).
- Delev Music Company's record label, Surprize Records, is listed in the Record Companies section.

How to Contact: Submit demo tape by mail. Unsolicited submissions OK. Prefers cassette (or VHS videocassette) with 1-3 songs and lyric sheet. Send all letter size correspondence and cassette submissions to: P.O. Box 6562, Philadelphia, PA 19138-6562. Larger than letter-size to the Mansfield Avenue address. "Video must be in VHS format and as professionally done as possible. It does not necessarily have to be done at a professional video studio, but should be a very good quality production showcasing artist's performance. We will not accept certified mail." Does not return material. Reports in 1 month.

Music: R&B ballads and dance-oriented, pop ballads, crossover and country/western. Published "This I Promise You," "I'll Always Believe in You" and "We Loved and Laughed Together," all written by Danny Webb and released on Surprize Records.

Tips: "Persevere regardless if it is sent to our company or any other company. Believe in yourself and send the best songs you have to any company submitted to."

FRANK DELL MUSIC, Box 7171, Duluth MN 55807. (218)628-3003. President: Frank Dell. Music publisher, record company (Music Services and Marketing), record producer and management. Estab. 1980. Publishes 2 songs/year. Pays standard royalty.
Affiliate(s): Albindell Music (BMI).
- Frank Dell's record label, Music Services and Marketing, can be found in the Record Companies section.

How to Contact: Submit demo tape by mail. Unsolicited submissions are OK. Prefers cassette. Does not return material. Reports in 3 months.

Music: Mostly country, gospel and pop. Published *Memories*, written and recorded by Frank Dell on Country Legends Records.

DELPHA'S MUSIC PUBLISHERS (BMI), Box 329, Mulberry AR 72947. (501)997-1557. Fax: (501)997-1557. CEO: Delpha J. Rosson. Music publisher. Estab. 1989. "Publishes 1 song per agreement—no limit." Pays standard royalty.

How to Contact: Submit demo tape by mail. Unsolicited submissions are OK. Prefers cassette with 3 songs and lyric sheet. "Prefers copyrighted material." SASE. Reports in 4-6 weeks.

Music: Mostly country, pop and gospel. Published "The Liberator" (by Gibbs/Ridener), recorded by Charlie Ridener on Bolder Bluff Records.

Tips: "Make sure that your song is protected before you send it to anyone. Do not pay anyone for publishing."

DEMI MONDE RECORDS & PUBLISHING LTD., Foel Studio, Llanfair Caereinion, POWYS, **Wales**. Phone/fax: (01938)810758. Managing Director: Dave Anderson. Music publisher, record company (Demi Monde Records & Publishing Ltd.), record producer (Dave Anderson). Member MCPS. Estab. 1983. Publishes 50-70 songs/year; publishes 10-15 new songwriters/year. Pays standard royalty.
- See Demi Monde's other listings in the Record Companies and Record Producers sections.

How to Contact: Submit demo tape by mail. Unsolicited submissions are OK. Prefers cassette (or VHS videocassette) with 3-4 songs. SAE and IRC. Reports in 6 weeks.

Music: Mostly rock, R&B and pop. Published "I Feel So Lazy" (by D. Allen), recorded by Gong (rock); "Phalarn Dawn" (by E. Wynne), recorded by Ozric Tentacles (rock); and "Pioneer" (by D. Anderson), recorded by Amon Dual (rock), all on Demi Monde Records.

DENNY MUSIC GROUP, Dept. SM, 3325 Fairmont Dr., Nashville TN 37203-1004. (615)269-4847. Contact: Pandora Denny. Estab. 1983. Music publisher, record company (Dollie Record Co., Jed Record Production) and record producer. Publishes 100 songs/year; 20 new songwriters/year. Pays standard royalty.

How to Contact: Write or call first and obtain permission to submit. Prefers cassette with 3 songs and lyric sheet. SASE. Reports in 6 weeks.

Music: Mostly country, bluegrass and MOR. Published "Angel Band" and "On the Other Side" (by Wes Homner).

DINGO MUSIC, 4, Galleria Del Corso, Milan **Italy** 20122. Phone: (02)76021141. Fax: 0039/2/76021141. Managing Director: Guido Palma. Music publisher and record company (Top Records). Estab. 1977. Publishes 30-35 songs/year; publishes 5 new songwriters/year. Hires staff writers. Pays 5% royalty to artists on contract; standard royalty of 50% and 10% on printed copies.
Affiliate(s): Top Records, Kiwi, Sap, Smoking.
How to Contact: Submit demo tape by mail. Unsolicited submissions are OK. Prefers cassette with 2 songs. Reports in 1 month with International Reply Coupon enclosed.

Music: Mostly **rock, pop** and **R&B (pop)**; also **New Age** and **gospel**. Published *Raga-ragazzina* (by A. De Bernardi), recorded by Alex Nardi; *Cocktail d'amore* (by Castellari), recorded by Allessandra; and *Al Mercato dell'usato*, written and recorded by P. Luciani.

DOC PUBLISHING, 10 Luanita Lane, Newport News VA 23606. (804)930-1814. A&R: Judith Guthro. Music publisher. Estab. 1975. Publishes 30-40 songs/year; 20 new songwriters/year. Pays standard royalty.
Affiliate(s): Dream Machine (SESAC), Doc Holiday Music (ASCAP).
• See the listing for Doc Holiday Productions in the Managers and Booking Agents section.
How to Contact: Submit demo tape by mail. Unsolicited submissions are OK. SASE. Reports in 2 weeks.
Music: Mostly **country** and **cajun**. Published *Sneaky Freaky People*, written and recorded by Big Al Downing on Tug Boat Records (country); *He Didn't Give Up on Me* (by Steven Johnson), recorded by The Johnson Family on Everlasting Records (gospel); and *D'Amore* (by Don Moore), recorded by D'Amore on Mega Records (R&B).

DON DEL MUSIC (BMI), P.O. Box 321, Port Washington WI 53074. (414)284-9777. Manager: Joseph C. DeLucia. Music publisher, record company (Cha Cha Records) and music promoter (Wisconsin Singer/Songwriter Series). Pays negotiable royalty.
• Don Del Music's record label, Cha Cha Records, is listed in the Record Companies section.
How to Contact: Write first and obtain permission to submit. Prefers cassette with 4-6 songs and lyric sheet. "A simple arrangement is much better than a major production—make sure the lyrics can be heard." SASE. Reports in 3 months.
Music: Mostly **acoustic folk**.

DORÉ RECORDS (ASCAP), 1608 Argyle, Hollywood CA 90028. (213)462-6614. Fax: (213)462-6197. President: Lew Bedell. Music publisher and record company. Estab. 1960. Publishes 15 songs/year; publishes 15 new songwriters/year. Pays standard royalty.
How to Contact: Submit demo tape by mail. Unsolicited submissions are OK. Prefers cassette and lyric sheet. Does not return unsolicited material. Reports in 2 weeks.
Music: Mostly **all kinds**; also **novelty** and **comedy**. Published *Percolator* (by Bideu & Freeman), recorded by the Billy Joe and the Checkmates/The Ventures on EMI Records; and *Ten-Uh-See*, written and recorded by Steve Rumph on Doré Records.
Tips: "Currently seeking an R&B group with male lead vocals. No rap."

BUSTER DOSS MUSIC (BMI), 341 Billy Goat Hill Rd., Winchester TN 37398. (615)649-2577. Fax: (615)649-2732. President: Buster Doss. Music publisher and record company (Stardust). Estab. 1959. Publishes 500 songs/year; publishes 50 new songwriters/year. Pays standard royalty.
• See the listings for Stardust Records in the Record Companies section, and Col. Buster Doss Presents in the Record Producers and Managers and Booking Agents section.
How to Contact: Write first and obtain permission to submit. Prefers cassette with 2 songs and lyric sheet. SASE. Reports ASAP.
Music: Mostly **country**; also **rock**. Published *I Only Sing The Blues* (by Buster Doss), recorded by Joey Welz on Caprice Records (country boogie); *I Don't Love You Anymore* (by Buster Doss), recorded by Jerri Arnold; and *Any Place in Texas* (by Buster Doss), recorded by Rooster Quantrell, both on Stardust Records.

*DREAM SEEKERS PUBLISHING (BMI), 3199 Logan Dr., Newburgh IN 47630. (812)853-8980. Fax: (812)853-8883. President: Sally Sidman. Music publisher. Estab. 1993. Publishes 25-50 songs/year; publishes 15-20 new songwriters/year. Hires staff songwriters. Pays standard royalty.
Affiliate(s): Dream Builders Publishing (ASCAP).
How to Contact: Submit demo tape by mail. Unsolicited submissions are OK. Prefers cassette with 3-5 songs and lyric sheet. "If one of your songs is selected for publishing, we prefer to have it available on DAT for dubbing off copies to pitch to artist. Do not send your DAT until you have received a publishing contract." SASE. Reports in 4-6 weeks.
Music: Mostly **country** and **gospel**; also **pop**, **rock** and **R&B/dance**. Published "Starting Tonight" (by Sam Storey), recorded by Wayne Horsburgh (country) on Rotation Records; "Full Moon" (by Rebecca Dills), recorded by Karla Penner on Magna Records (country); and "An Elvis Night Before

---

● **A BULLET** introduces comments by the editor of *Songwriter's Market* indicating special information about the listing.

Christmas" (by Keith Collins), recorded by C.C. McCartney (country) on Rotation Records.
Tips: "Build your song around a strong hook line (usually the title). Use strong opening lines. Keep your lyrics conversational and contemporary. Be sure to write about something that a lot of people can identify with. Make your songs believable and try to come up with fresh angles for your lyrics. Try to find unique catchy ways to say things that people have heard hundreds of times before. Avoid long intros and don't take too long to get to the chorus. Try to find something positive to say even if the song is supposed to be sad. Uptempo commercial country with positive lyrics are easier to get cut than ballads. Try to make your demos sound as good as possible and always remember to cue the tape to the first song. We have a sister office in Hendersonville, TN and pitch directly to Nashville producers, labels and artists on a biweekly basis. We also pitch material to Los Angeles and New York. We only sign material that we feel is commercially competitive. We are extremely active in pitching our catalog. We never sign songs and then just leave them sitting on the shelf."

DRIVE MUSIC, INC. (BMI), 10351 Santa Monica Blvd., Los Angeles CA 90025. (310)553-3490. Fax: (310)553-3373. E-mail: drive@earthlink.net. President: Don Grierson. CEO: Stephen Powers. Music publisher, record company (Drive Entertainment). Estab. 1993. Publishes 25 songs/year. Hires staff songwriters. Pays negotiated royalty. "Seeks single songs for representation. Acquires catalogs, large and small."
Affiliate(s): Donunda Music (ASCAP).
  ● Drive Music's record label, Drive Entertainment, is listed in the Record Companies section.
How to Contact: Submit demo tape by mail. Unsolicited submissions are OK. Prefers 3 songs and lyric sheet. "Send regular mail only." SASE. Reports in 4 weeks.
Music: Mostly **dance**, **pop** and **rock**; also **R&B**. Published all Sharon, Lois and Bram products (children's).
Tips: "Practice your craft and never give up."

DUANE MUSIC, INC. (BMI), 382 Clarence Ave., Sunnyvale CA 94086. (408)739-6133. President: Garrie Thompson. Music publisher. Publishes 10-20 songs/year; publishes 1 new songwriter/year. Pays standard royalty.
Affiliate(s): Morhits Publishing (BMI).
  ● See their listing in the Record Producers section.
How to Contact: Submit demo tape by mail. Unsolicited submissions are OK. Prefers cassette with 1-2 songs. SASE. Reports in 4-8 weeks.
Music: Blues, **country**, **disco**, **easy listening**, **rock**, **soul** and **top 40/pop**. Published "Little Girl," recorded by The Syndicate of Sound & Ban (rock); "Warm Tender Love," recorded by Percy Sledge (soul); and "My Adorable One," recorded by Joe Simon (blues).

EARITATING MUSIC PUBLISHING (BMI), P.O. Box 1101, Gresham OR 97030. Music publisher. Estab. 1979. Publishes 40 songs/year; publishes 5 new songwriters/year. Pays individual per song contract, usually greater than 50% to writer.
How to Contact: Submit demo tape by mail. Unsolicited submissions are OK. Prefers cassette with lyric sheet. "Submissions should be copyrighted by the author. We will deal for rights if interested." Does not return material. No reply unless interested.
Music: Mostly **rock**, **contemporary Christian** and **country**; also **folk**.
Tips: "Melody is most important, lyrics second. Style and performance take a back seat to these. A good song will stand with just one voice and one instrument. Also, don't use staples on your mailers."

*EARTHSCREAM MUSIC PUBLISHING CO. (BMI), 8377 Westview Dr., Houston TX 77055. (713)464-GOLD. Contact: Jeff Johnson. Music publisher, record company and record producer. Estab. 1975. Publishes 12 songs/year; publishes 4 new songwriters/year. Pays standard royalty.
Affiliate(s): Reach For The Sky Music Pub. (ASCAP).
How to Contact: Submit demo tape by mail. Unsolicited submissions are OK. Prefers cassette (or videocassette) with 2-5 songs and lyric sheet. SASE. Reports in 2 months.
Music: New rock, **country** and **top 40/pop**. Published "Ride of a Lifetime" (by Greg New), recorded by Billy Rutherford on Earth Records; "Goodbye Sexy Carol," written and recorded by Terry Mitchell (New Age); and "Do You Remember" (by Pennington/Wells), recorded by Perfect Strangers (pop/rock) on Weeny Dog Records.

EDITIONS SCIPION, 33 rue des Jeuneurs, Paris 75002 **France**. A.D.: Bialek Robert. Music publisher, management. Estab. 1983. Publishes 40 songs/year; publishes 1 new songwriter/year. Pays standard royalty.
How to Contact: Submit demo tape by mail. Unsolicited submissions are OK. Prefers cassette. SAE and IRC. Reports in 2 weeks.

Music: Mostly **rock**.

ELECT MUSIC PUBLISHING (BMI), P.O. Box 22, Underhill VT 05489. (802)899-3787. Founder: Bobby Hackney. Music publisher and record company (LBI Records). Estab. 1980. Publishes 24 songs/year; publishes 3 new songwriters/year. Pays standard royalty.
• See the listing for Jericho Sound Lab in the Record Producers section.
How to Contact: Submit a demo tape by mail. Unsolicited submissions are OK. Prefers cassette and VHS videocassette with 3-4 songs and lyric sheet. SASE. Reports in 1 month.
Music: Mostly **reggae**, **R&B** and **rap**; also **rock**, some **jazz** and **poetry**. Published "Natural Woman" and "Guanuarty" (by B. Hackney), recorded by Lambsbread; and "African Princess," written and recorded by Mikey Dread, all on LBI Records.
Tips: "Send your best and remember, the amount of postage it took to get to the publisher is the same amount it will take to have your tape returned."

EMANDELL TUNES, 10220 Glade Ave., Chatsworth CA 91311. (818)341-2264. Fax: (818)341-1008. President/Administrator: Leroy C. Lovett, Jr. Estab. 1979. Publishes 6-12 songs/year; publishes 3-4 new songwriters. Pays standard royalty.
Affiliate(s): Ben-Lee Music (BMI), Birthright Music (ASCAP), Em-Jay Music (ASCAP), Northworth Songs, Chinwah Songs, Gertrude Music (all SESAC); LMS Print/Publishing and Nadine LTD, Music/Artist Management Company, Zurich, Switzerland, Alvert Music/BMI and Andrask Music, Australia (BMI).
How to Contact: Write or call first to get permission to submit tape. Prefers cassette (or videocassette) with 4-5 songs and lead or lyric sheet. Include bio of writer, singer or group. SASE. Reports in 6-8 weeks.
Music: **Inspirational**, **contemporary gospel** and **choral**; also **strong country** and **light top 40 gospel**. Published *Something Within* (by Paul Jackson), recorded by Texas Mass Choir on Savoy Records (gospel); "Happy/You're Good to Me" (by Askey/Mayfield), recorded by Mary J. Blige on MCA Records; and *Get Busy With It* (by James Jernigan), recorded by The Jamz Gang on Faith Records (gospel).
Tips: "Continue to write with an ear to current trends. Find a 'hook'—go back to '50s and listen to the melody."

EMF PRODUCTIONS, 1000 E. Prien Lake Rd., Suite D, Lake Charles LA 70601. (318)474-0435. President: Ed Fruge. Music publisher and record producer. Estab. 1984. Pays standard royalty.
• See their listing in the Record Companies section.
How to Contact: Submit demo tape by mail. Unsolicited submissions are OK. Prefers cassette (or VHS videocassette) with 4 songs and lyric sheet. Does not return material. Reports in 6 weeks.
Music: Mostly **R&B** and **pop**, **rock**; also **country** and **gospel**.

EMI CHRISTIAN MUSIC PUBLISHING, (formerly Star Song/EMI Christian Music Publishing), 101 Winners Circle, P.O. Box 5085, Brentwood TN 37024. Music publisher. Publishes 100 songs/year; publishes 2 new songwriters/year. Hires staff songwriters. Pays standard royalty.
Affiliate(s): Birdwing Music (ASCAP), Sparrow Song (BMI), His Eye Music (SESAC), Ariose Music (ASCAP), Straightway Music (ASCAP), Shepherd's Fold Music (BMI), Songs of Promise (SESAC), Dawn Treader Music (SESAC), Meadowgreen Music Company (ASCAP), River Oaks Music Company (BMI), Stonebrook Music Company (SESAC), Bud John Songs, Inc. (ASCAP), Bud John Music, Inc. (BMI), Bud John Tunes, Inc. (SESAC).
How to Contact: "We do not accept unsolicited submissions."
Music: Published "Concert of the Age" (by Jeffrey Benward), recorded by Phillips, Craig & Dean; "God Is In Control," written and recorded by Twila Paris, both on StarSong Records; and "Faith, Hope and Love" (by Ty Lacy), recorded by Point of Grace on Word Records.
Tips: "Come to Nashville and be a part of the fastest growing industry. It's nearly impossible to get a publisher's attention unless you know someone in the industry that is willing to help you."

EMI MUSIC PUBLISHING, 1290 Avenue of the Americas, 43rd Floor, New York NY 10019-5818. (212)492-1200. This publisher prefers not to share information.

HOW TO GET THE MOST out of *Songwriter's Market* (at the front of this book) contains comments and suggestions to help you understand and use the information in these listings.

*ENID OKLAHOMA MUSIC PUBLISHING (BMI), P.O. Box 454, Enid OK 73702. (800)481-1866. Music Publisher: James O. Brown. Music publisher. Estab. 1995. Publishes 10-15 songs/year; publishes 4 new songwriters/year. Hires staff songwriters. Pays standard royalty.
How to Contact: Submit demo tape by mail. Unsolicited submissions are OK. Prefers cassette or CD with 1-3 songs, lyric and lead sheet. SASE. Reports in 2 weeks.
Music: Mostly **country**, **western swing** and **gospel**; also **ballads**, **country/crossover** and **cajun**. Published "Cajun Ways" (by Jim O. Brown), recorded by Shane Glover (cajun); "Jesus By My Side" (by Jim O. Brown), recorded by Jennifer Lowery (country gospel); and "Love You, Love Me" (by Jim O. Brown), recorded by Dave LaBrue (ballad), all on Oklahoma Records.

ESI MUSIC GROUP (BMI), 9 Music Square S., Suite 118, Nashville TN 37203-9336. (615)297-9336. Administrator: Curt Conroy. Music publisher. Estab. 1990. Publishes 50-60 songs/year. Pays standard royalty.
How to Contact: Submit a demo tape by mail. Unsolicited submissions are OK. Prefers "good quality 3-4 song demo" and lyric sheet. "Guitar or piano-vocal OK. All envelopes must meet postal requirements for content." Does not return material. "To insure reply, include stamped, self-addressed envelope with adequate postage attached." Reports within 4-6 weeks.
Music: Mostly **"new" country**, **country rock** and **country pop**; also **country blues**. Published "Wine Over Matter," written and recorded by Pinto Bennett on MCM Records (country); "In the Wings," written and recorded by David Stewart on Wings Records; and "Cornbread Boogie," written and recorded by T. Bone Wright on Santa Fe Records.
Tips: "Research the artists you want to pitch to and match your songs to those artists. Listen carefully to current songs on the radio. This is your competition. Record the best demo that you can. Write for a list of available songwriter information that is available through our company."

EVER-OPEN-EYE MUSIC (PRS), Wern Fawr Farm, Pencoed, MID, Glam CF356NB **United Kingdom**. Phone: (0656)860041. Managing Director: M.R. Blanche. Music publisher and record company (Red-Eye Records). Member PPL and MCPS. Estab. 1980. Publishes 6 songs/year. Pays negotiable royalty.
● Ever-Open-Eye's record label, Red-Eye Records, is listed in the Record Companies section.
How to Contact: Submit demo tape by mail. Unsolicited submissions are OK. Prefers cassette (or VHS videocassette). Does not return material. Reports in 2 months.
Music: Mostly **R&B**, **gospel** and **pop**; also **swing**. Published "Breakdown Song," "Shadow of the Sun" and "Outside Looking In," all written by Finn/Jones on Red Eye Records.

DOUG FAIELLA PUBLISHING (BMI), 19153 Paver Barnes Rd., Marysville OH 43040. (513)644-8295. President: Doug Faiella. Music publisher, record company (Studio 7 Records) and recording studio. Estab. 1984. Publishes 25 songs/year; publishes 5 new songwriters/year. Pays standard royalty.
● Doug Faiella is also listed in the Record Producers section.
How to Contact: Write to obtain permission to submit a tape. Prefers cassette with 3 songs and lyric sheets. Does not return material. Reports in 4 weeks.
Music: Mostly **country**, **gospel** and **rock**.

FAMOUS MUSIC PUBLISHING COMPANIES, 10635 Santa Monica Blvd., Suite 300, Los Angeles CA 90025. (310)441-1300. Fax: (310)441-4722. President: Ira Jaffe. Senior Creative Director, Film and TV: Bob Knight. Creative Coordinator: Sarah Troy. Senior Creative Director: Bobby Carlton. Creative Driector, Urban Music: James Leach. New York office: 1633 Broadway, 11th Floor, New York NY 10019. Senior Creative Director: Ross Elliot. Senior Creative Director, Standard Catalogue: Mary Beth Roberts. Nashville office: 65 Music Square East, Nashville TN 37212. Senior Creative Director: Pat Finch. Estab. 1929. Publishes 500 songs/year. Hires staff songwriters. Pays standard royalty.
Affiliate(s): Famous Music (ASCAP) and Ensign Music (BMI).
How to Contact: Query first. Does not accept unsolicited material. Prefers cassette with 3 songs and lyric sheet. Reports in 2-3 months.
Music: Mostly **rock**, **urban**, **R&B** and **country**. Published "Human Behaviour," recorded by Bjork (alternative); "One Sweet Day," recorded by Mariah Carey and Boyz II Men; and "100% Pure Love," recorded by Crystal Waters.

FARR-AWAY MUSIC, 701 N. Graycroft, Madison TN 37115. (615)865-2639. President: Tony Farr. Music publisher. Estab. 1970.
How to Contact: Submit demo tape by mail. Unsolicited submissions are OK. Prefers cassette or videocassette with 2-3 songs and lyric sheet. Does not return material.
Music: Mostly **country**.

FAT CITY PUBLISHING, 1906 Chet Atkins Place, Suite 502, Nashville TN 37212. (615)320-7678. Fax: (615)321-5382. President: Noel Michael. Vice President: Scott Bradley. Music publisher, record company (Fat City Artists), record producer and booking agency (Fat City Artists). Estab. 1972. Publishes 25 songs/year; publishes 10 new songwriters/year. Hires staff writers. Pays standard royalty. **Affiliate(s):** Fort Forever (BMI).
● See the listings for Fat City Artists in the Record Companies and Managers and Booking Agents sections.
How to Contact: Submit demo tape by mail. Unsolicited submissions are OK. Prefers cassette (or VHS videocassette) with 4-6 songs and lyric sheet. SASE. Reports in 2 weeks.
Music: Mostly **rock**, **country** and **blues**; also **alternative**, **rockabilly** and **jazz**.
Tips: "Provide as much information and material as possible."

*FINGERPRINT SONGS, 446 Linden Ave. #2, Long Beach CA 90802. Music Paralegal: Darin Kirby. Music publisher. Estab. 1993. Publishes 3-10 songs/year; 2-3 new songwriters/year. Pays standard royalty.
Affiliates: Darin Kirby Music Publishing (BMI).
How to Contact: Submit demo tape by mail. Unsolicited submissions are OK. Prefers cassette with 1 song and lyric sheet. "Review preference is given to artists who first write before submitting a demo. We like to know who is writing and what to expect." Does not return material. Reports in 6 weeks.
Music: Mostly **A/C**, **R&B** and **pop/rock**; also **jazz**, **country** and **cajun French**. Published "Foreign Land," written and recorded by Gert Daigle on Daigle Records (country); "You're Gonna Get It" and "Can't Get Away," written and recorded by Shamah on Finger Records (rock/A/C).
Tips: "To attract our attention, besides having good songs, remember that the better you present yourself to us the better chance you have in getting published. Please write and tell your story, your plans and your reasons for wanting to get into the music industry."

FIRST RELEASE MUSIC PUBLISHING, 943 N. Madison Ave., Pasadena CA 91104. Phone/fax: (818)794-5545. President: Danny Howell. Operations Manager: Tony Jennaway. Music publisher. Publishes 30-50 songs/year. Hires staff songwriters. Pays standard royalty; co-publishing negotiable. "Very active in obtaining cover records and film and TV uses."
Affiliate(s): Fully Conscious Music, Cadillac Pink, Reggatta Music, Magnetic Publishing Ltd., Animal Logic Publishing and Blue Turtle Music.
How to Contact: "We *never* accept unsolicited tapes or phone calls—you must have referral or request." Returns all unsolicited material. Reports only if interested, but "retain personally written critique for every song I agree to accept."
Music: "We are interested in great songs and great writers. We are currently successful in all areas." Published "Power of Love" (by Tom Kimmel/Elizabeth Vidal), recorded by Sam Moore on Sony Records (R&B).
Tips: "Show up at one of my guest workshops and play me the last song you would ever play for a publisher; not the worst, the last! Educate yourself as to what writers we represent before pitching me (e.g., Sting, Lyle Lovett)."

FIRST TIME MUSIC (PUBLISHING) U.K. LTD. (PRS), Sovereign House, 12 Trewartha Road, Praa Sands, Penzance, Cornwall TR20 9ST **United Kingdom**. Phone: (01736)762826. Fax: (01736)763328. Managing Director: Roderick G. Jones. Music publisher, record company (First Time Records), record producer (Panama Music Library) and management firm (First Time Management and Production Co.). Member MCPS. Estab. 1986. Publishes 500-750 songs/year; 20-50 new songwriters/year. Hires staff writers. Pays standard royalty; "50-60% to established and up-and-coming writers with the right attitude."
Affiliate(s): Scamp Music Publishing.
● See the listings for First Time Records in the Record Companies section and First Time Management in the Managers and Booking Agents section.
How to Contact: Submit demo tape by mail. Unsolicited submissions are OK. Prefers cassette, 1⅞ ips cassette (or VHS videocassette "of professional quality") with unlimited number of songs and lyric or lead sheets, but not necessary. Reports in 4-10 weeks. SAE and IRC. "Postal costs in the U.K. are much higher than the U.S.—one IRC doesn't even cover the cost of a letter to the U.S., let alone the return of cassettes. Enclose the correct amount for return and contact as stated." Reports in 4-10 weeks.
Music: Mostly **country** and **folk**, **pop/soul/top 20/rock**, **country with an Irish/Scottish crossover**; also **gospel/Christian**. Published "Lovers Chain" (by Charlie Landsborough), recorded by Daniel O'Donnell on Ritz Records (country); "I Remember Mary" (by Pete Arnold), recorded by The Fureys on EMI Records (folk); and "Love Song to You" (by Walt Young), recorded by P.J. Proby on J'Ace Records (pop).
Tips: "Have a professional approach—present well produced demos. First impressions are important and may be the only chance you get. Remember that you as a writer/artist are in a competitive market.

As an active independent-international publisher we require good writers/artists and product. As a company we seek to work with writers. If the product is good then we generally come up with something in the way of covers. Writers are advised to join the Guild of International Songwriters and Composers in the United Kingdom."

*FLAMING STAR WEST MUSIC (BMI), P.O. Box 2400, Gardnerville NV 89410. (702)265-6825. Contact: Publishing Department. Music publisher, record company (Flaming Star Records) and record producer. Estab. 1988. Pays standard royalty.
How to Contact: Submit demo tape by mail. Unsolicited submissions are OK. Prefers cassette or DAT with 3 songs and lyric sheet. "Quality demos only. We prefer studio demos." SASE. Reports in 3-4 weeks.
Music: Mostly **country**, **rock** and **gospel**. Published *What Would You Give* (by Brian Williams); *'59 Caddy* (by N. LeDune); and *Adios Amigo* (by J. Johnson), all recorded by Ted Snyder on Flaming Star Records.

*HAROLD FLAMMER MUSIC, 49 Waring Dr., Delaware Water Gap PA 18327. (717)476-0550. Fax: (717)476-5247. Editor: Lew Kirby. Music publisher. Estab. 1917. Publishes 50 songs/year. Pays negotiable royalty.
Affiliate(s): Glory Sound, Shawnee Press, Inc.
How to Contact: Write first and obtain permission to submit a demo. Prefers cassette with lyric and/or lead sheet. SASE. Reports in 6 months.
Music: Mostly **church/liturgical**.

FLASH INTERNATIONAL (BMI), P.O. Box 580058, Houston TX 77258-0058. (713)488-1978. Fax: (713)488-4559. Owner: Renel L. Boudreaux. Music publisher, record company and record producer. Estab. 1981. Publishes 3 songs/year; publishes 1 new songwriter/year. Hires staff songwriters. Pays negotiable royalty.
How to Contact: Submit demo tape by mail. Unsolicited submissions are OK. Prefers cassette and lyric sheet. SASE. Reports in 2 weeks.
Music: Mostly **R&B**, **jazz** and **gospel**; also **rap** and **country**. Published "We Gone Party" (by C. Johnson), recorded by Conrad Johnson on GC Records (jazz).
Tips: "Must have a unique style and a good sound. Be patient, consistent and never, never give up."

FLEA CIRCUS MUSIC (ASCAP), 1820 Charles Yeargin Rd., Elberton GA 30635. Professional Manager: Dianna Kirk. Music publisher. Estab. 1991. Pays standard royalty.
How to Contact: Write first and obtain permission to submit. Prefers cassette with 3 songs and lyric sheet. SASE. Reports in 2-3 weeks.
Music: Mostly **rock**, **alternative** and **country**. Published "Blame It on Me," "Garbage Man" and "Better Off Dead," all written by Greg Timms and recorded by Cookieman.
Tips: "Always include a SASE if you want a response."

FLYING RED HORSE PUBLISHING (BMI), 2932 Dyer St., Dallas TX 75205. (214)691-5318. E-mail: jshouston@aol.com. Contact: Beverly Houston. Music publisher, record company (Remarkable Records) and record producer. Estab. 1993. Publishes 15-30 songs/year; publishes 6-10 new songwriters/year. Pays standard royalty.
How to Contact: Write first and obtain permission to submit. Prefers cassette with 3 songs and lyric sheet. SASE. Reports in 6 weeks.
Music: Mostly **children's**. Published "Stuck" (by Sheryl Cadick), on Future Perfect Records; *Everybody's Special*, written and recorded by J. Perkins; and *Dinosaur Rag* (by Beverly Houston), recorded by Dixie, both on Remarkable Records.
Tips: "Even when a song is written for children, it should still meet the criteria for a well-written song—and be pleasing to adults as well."

FOCAL POINT MUSIC PUBLISHERS (BMI), Dept. SM, 920 McArthur Blvd., Warner Robins GA 31093. (912)923-6533. Manager: Ray Melton. Music publisher and record company. Estab. 1964. Publishes 4 songs/year; publishes 1 new songwriter/year. Pays standard royalty. "Songwriters must have BMI affiliation."

MARKET CONDITIONS are constantly changing! If you're still using this book and it is 1998 or later, buy the newest edition of *Songwriter's Market* at your favorite bookstore or order directly from Writer's Digest Books.

How to Contact: Call first to get permission to send a tape. Prefers cassette with 2-4 songs and lead sheet. Prefers studio produced demos. SASE. Reports in 6 months.
Music: Mostly **country** and **gospel**; also "**old-style pop and humor**." Published *Family Reunion* (by Wayne Holcomb); *Walk Away* (by Bill Arwood); and *Long Long Time Ago* (by A. Sanford/E. Adaus), all recorded by Bill Arwood on Bob Grady Records (country).
Tips: "Try it out on your friends. Go to workshops. Belong to a songwriters group. Learn how to play an instrument to accompany your songs. Write many songs on many subjects—your chances are better that way."

MARK FOSTER MUSIC COMPANY, Box 4012, Champaign IL 61824-4012. (217)398-2760. Fax: (217)398-2791. E-mail: markfostermus@champ.il.aads.net. President: Jane C. Menkhaus. Assistant Editor: Carla Hennes. Music publisher. Estab. 1962. Publishes 20-30 songs/year; publishes 4-5 new songwriters/year. Pays 5-10% over first 3,000 copies choral music sold.
Affiliate(s): Marko Press (BMI) and Fostco Press (ASCAP).
● See their listing in the Music Print Publishers section.
How to Contact: Do not call. Write for full guidelines, unsolicited mss OK. Submit demo tape by mail. Unsolicited submissions are OK. Prefers cassette and 1 copy choral manuscript (must be legible). Include brief bio of composer/arranger if new. SASE. Reports in 5-8 weeks.
Music: Exclusively classical choral music: **sacred SATB**, **secular SATB** and **sacred and secular treble & male choir**; also **conducting books** and **Kodaly materials**. Published "I Lift Mine Eyes Unto the Hills" (by René Clausen); "Go Lovely Rose" (by Mark Henderson); and "Basil the Cat" (by Valerie Shields).
Tips: "Must be familiar with traditional/classical choral music. Go beyond boring homophonic chorale-style writing."

FOX FARM RECORDING (BMI, ASCAP), 2731 Saundersville Ferry Rd., Mt. Juliet TN 37122. (615)773-5080. President: Kent Fox. Music publisher and record producer. Publishes 20 songs/year; publishes 5 new songwriters/year.
Affiliate(s): Blueford Music (ASCAP) and Mercantile Music (BMI).
How to Contact: Submit a demo tape by mail. Unsolicited submissions are OK. Prefers cassette with 4 songs and lyric sheet. SASE. Reports in 3 months.
Music: **Country**, **bluegrass** and **contemporary Christian**.
Tips: "If your song is good enough to become a hit, it's worth investing money for a good demo: drums, bass, guitar, keyboard, fiddle, sax, vocals etc."

*FRESH ENTERTAINMENT (ASCAP), 1315 Simpson Rd., Atlanta GA 30314. (770)642-2645. Vice President of A&R: Willie W. Hunter. Music publisher and record company. Publishes 5 songs/year. Hires staff songwriters. Pays standard royalty.
Affiliate(s): !Hserf Music (ASCAP), Blair Vizzion Music (BMI), Santron Music (BMI).
● See their listing in the Record Companies section.
How to Contact: Submit demo tape by mail. Unsolicited submissions are OK. Prefers cassette or videocassette with 3 songs and lyric sheet. "Send photo if available." SASE. Reports in 1 month.
Music: Mostly **rap**, **R&B** and **pop/dance**. Artists include Kilo and Cirocco.

FRICK MUSIC PUBLISHING CO. (BMI), 404 Bluegrass Ave., Madison TN 37115. (615)865-6380. Contact: Bob Frick. Music publisher, record company (R.E.F. Records) and record producer (Bob Scott Frick). Publishes 50 songs/year; publishes 2 new songwriters/year. Pays standard royalty.
Affiliates: Sugarbakers Music (ASCAP).
● Frick Music's record label, R.E.F. Records, is listed in the Record Companies section; their booking agency, Bob Scott Frick Enterprises, is listed in the Managers and Booking Agents section; and producer Bob Scott Frick is listed in the Record Producers section.
How to Contact: Write or call first to get permission to submit. Prefers 7½ ips reel-to-reel or cassette (or videocassette) with 2-10 songs and lyric sheet. SASE. Reports in 2 weeks.
Music: Mostly **gospel**; also **country**, **rock** and **top 40/pop**. Published "I Found Jesus in Nashville" (by Lin Butler), recorded by Bob Scott Frick; and "Good Lovin'," written and recorded by Teresa Ford, both on R.E.F. Records.

FRONTLINE MUSIC GROUP, P.O. Box 28450, Santa Ana CA 92799-8450. Director of Music Publishing: Kenneth Hicks. Music publisher and record company (Frontline Records). Estab. 1987. Pays standard royalty.
Affiliates: Broken Songs (ASCAP) and Carlotta Publishing (BMI).
● See the listing for Graceland Entertainment in the Record Companies section.
How to Contact: Submit demo tape by mail. Unsolicited submissions are OK. Prefers cassette with 3 songs and lyric sheet. "Address to Broken Songs." Does not return material. Reports in 1-2 months.

Music: Mostly **pop**, **rock** and **R&B**.
Tips: "Frontline is a Christian record company. The songs we would publish should have lyrics that are wholesome and/or point to a relationship with Jesus."

FROZEN INCA MUSIC, 1800 Peachtree St., Suite 333, Atlanta GA 30309. (404)355-5580. Fax: (404)351-2786. President: Michael Rothschild. Music publisher, record company and record producer. Estab. 1981. Publishes 12 songs/year; publishes 3 new songwriters/year. Pays standard royalty.
Affiliate(s): Landslide Records.
 ● Frozen Inca's record label, Landslide, is listed in the Record Companies section.
How to Contact: Submit demo tape by mail. Unsolicited submissions are OK. Prefers cassette with 6-12 songs and lyric sheet. SASE. Reports in 1 month.
Music: Mostly **R&B**, **blues** and **rap**; also **rock**. Published *Wanted Man* (by T. Ellis/S. Grimes) and *To The Devil For A Dime* (by T. Ellis/C. Long), both recorded by Tinsley Ellis on Alligator Records (blues); and *Winning* (by R. Keller), recorded by Trammel Starks on InterSound Records (jazz).

*FUNZALO MUSIC (BMI), P.O. Box 36374, Tucson AZ 85704. (520)575-9354. Fax: (520)575-2713. E-mail: mikespoop@aol.com. President: Michael J. Lembo. Music publisher. Estab. 1976. Publishes 50-150 songs/year. Hires staff songwriters. Pays standard royalty.
Affiliate(s): Tomata-du-Plenti Music (ASCAP).
How to Contact: Submit demo tape by mail. Unsolicited submissions are OK. Prefers cassette with 3 songs and lyric sheet. Does not return material. Reports in 2 weeks.
Music: Mostly **hits**; also **rock**, **pop** and **alternative**.

FURROW MUSIC (BMI), P.O. Box 4121, Edmond OK 73083-4121. (405)348-6534. Owner/Publisher: G.H. Derrick. Music publisher, record company (Gusher Records) and record producer. Estab. 1984. Publishes 10-15 songs/year. Pays standard royalty.
How to Contact: Submit demo tape by mail. Unsolicited submissions are OK. (No phone calls prior to submission). Prefers cassette (or VHS videocassette) with 1-5 songs and lyric sheet. "One instrument and vocal is OK for demo." SASE. Reports in 1-2 weeks.
Music: Mostly **country**, **R&B** and **novelty**; also **patriotic**, **cowboy** and **Christmas**. Published "Dogs Don't Care If You're Ugly," recorded by Harvey Derrick; "Hangin' Her Dreams on The Line," recorded by Michelle Williams; and "I Caught You in The Act (of Loving Me)," recorded by Devin Derrick, all written by Harvey Derrick and released on Gusher Records (country).
Tips: "Have your song critiqued by other writers (or songwriter organizations) prior to making the demo. Only make and send demos of songs that have a universal appeal. Make sure the vocal is out front of the music. Never be so attached to a lyric or tune that you can't rewrite it. Don't forget to include your SASE."

ALAN GARY MUSIC, P.O. Box 179, Palisades Park NJ 07650. President: Alan Gary. Creative Director: Fran Levine. Creative Assistant: Harold Green. Music publisher. ASCAP, BMI. Estab. 1987. Publishes a varying number of songs/year. Pays standard royalty.
How to Contact: Submit demo tape by mail. Unsolicited submissions are OK. Prefers cassette (or VHS videocassette) with lyric sheet. SASE.
Music: Mostly **pop**, **R&B** and **dance**; also **rock**, **A/C** and **country**. Published "Liberation" (by Gary/Julian), recorded by Les Julian on Music Tree Records (A/C); "Love Your Way Out of This One" (by Gary/Rosen), recorded by Deborah Steel on Bad Cat Records (contemporary country); and "Dueling Rappers" (by Gary/Free), recorded by Prophets of Boom on You Dirty Rap! Records (rap/R&B).

GENETIC MUSIC PUBLISHING (ASCAP), 10 Church Rd., Merchantville NJ 08109. (609)662-4428. E-mail: webcore@webcom.com or dedtrooper@aol.com. Website: http://webcom.com/webcore/welcome/welcome/html or http://webcom.com/webcore/gm/genetic.html. Contact: Whey Cooler or Jade Starling. Music publisher, record company (Svengali) and record producer (Whey Cooler Production). Estab. 1982. Publishes 1-5 songs/year. Pays standard royalty.
Affiliate(s): Cooler By A Mile (ASCAP), BC Music (ASCAP) SIV Songs (ASCAP) and Baggy Music (BMI).
How to Contact: Write or call first and obtain permission to submit a tape. Prefers cassette. SASE. Reports in 3-6 weeks.
Music: Mostly **dance**, **R&B** and **pop**; also **alternative rock** and **jazz**. Published *Sexual Playground*, written and recorded by Father MC on Spoiled Brat Records (rap); *Pretty Poison's Greatest Hits* (by Starling/Cooler), recorded by Pretty Poison on Svengali Records (pop/R&B); and "Crawl" (remix) (by Starling/Cooler), recorded by Sex in Violets on FTS Records (industrial).
Tips: "If it moves you, then it'll likely move someone else. Be patient and never give up."

*GFI WEST MUSIC PUBLISHING, P.O. Box 641351, Los Angeles CA 90064. (310)281-7454. A&R: "J.C." Music publisher. Estab. 1991. Publishes 10 songs/year; 10 new songwriters/year. Pays standard royalty.

How to Contact: Submit demo tape by mail. Unsolicited submissions are OK. Prefers cassette with 1-5 songs and lyric sheet. "Submissions must be copyrighted." Does not return material. Reports in 2-3 months.
Music: Mostly **instrumentals** and **incidental music**; also **pop**, **rock** and **R&B**. Published "Crazy Motion" (by Paul McCarty/Janet Jeffrey), recorded by Janet Jeffrey for the soundtrack *Stranger in the City*; "Touch My Soul" (by Alex Varden/Kent Pearse), recorded by Alex Varden for the soundtrack *The Forest*; and "I Know" (by Janet Jeffrey), recorded by Janet J. on TBRC Records.
Tips: "Strong melodies attract my attention. I look for crossover appeal as well as songs that leave you humming the words in your head."

GIFTNESS ENTERPRISE (BMI, ASCAP), Dept. SM, 1315 Simpson Rd. NW, Suite #5, Atlanta GA 30314. (404)642-2645. Contact: New Song Department. Music publisher. Publishes 30 songs/year; publishes 15 new songwriters/year. Employs songwriters on a salary basis. Pays standard royalty.
Affiliate(s): Blair Vizzion Music (BMI) and Fresh Entertainment (ASCAP).
How to Contact: Submit demo tape by mail. Unsolicited submissions are OK. Prefers cassette with 4 songs and lyric or lead sheet. SASE. Reports in 1 month.
Music: Mostly **R&B**, **pop** and **rock**; also **country**, **gospel** and **jazz**. Published "Donkey Kong" and "Nasty Dancer" (by Taz/Kilo), recorded by Kilo on Ichiban Records (rap); and BET's "Comic View" Theme, written and recorded by Cirocco on BET (R&B).

SEYMOUR GLASS SONGS/EMI (BMI), 810 Seventh Ave., 36th Floor., New York NY 10019. (212)260-8849. Fax: (800)251-9651. Executive Vice President, Creative: Andrian Adams. Music publisher. Estab. 1991. Pays standard royalty but "there are always different deals."
How to Contact: Submit demo tape by mail. Unsolicited submissions are OK. Prefers cassette with 3 songs. Does not return material.
Music: Mostly **all types**. "Joshua Kadison is our number one writer. His own record went gold in 1994, and his songs have been cut by Joe Cocker, Smokey Robinson, The Pointer Sisters and Najee."

GLOBEART INC., 530 E. 76th St., #26H, New York NY 10021. (212)249-9220. Fax: (212)861-8130. E-mail: jpetere@ibm.net. President: Jane Peterer. Music publisher. Estab. 1989. Publishes 50 songs/year; publishes 5 new songwriters/year. Pays standard royalty.
Affiliate(s): GlobeSound Publishing (ASCAP).
How to Contact: Submit a demo tape by mail. Unsolicited submissions are OK. Prefers cassette (or videocassette) with 3-5 songs and lyric or lead sheet. SASE. Reports in 8-10 weeks.
Music: Mostly **pop/R&B**, **jazz** and **gospel**; also **country**. Published "Twice the People Do" (by Norberto Diaz), recorded by Bert Diaz (children's); "Broken Hearts," written and recorded by Ron Annunziata (R&B); and *Second to None*, written and recorded by Sam Dees on Ace Records.

GO! DISCS MUSIC (PRS), 72 Black Lion Lane, London W6 9BE **England**. (081)910-4600. Fax: (081)741-2184. Contact: Bruce Craigie. Music publisher. Estab. 1984. Uses English contracts. Pays negotiable royalty.
How to Contact: Submit demo tape by mail. Unsolicited submissions are OK. Prefers cassette (or VHS English videocassette) with 3 songs and lyric sheet. SAE and IRC. Reports in 6 weeks.
Music: Published "There She Goes" (by L. Mavers), recorded by The La's (pop); *Superglider* (by Robinson/Montiero), recorded by Drugstore (pop/alternative); and "I've Seen Everything" (by F. Reader/P. Livingston/D. Hughes/S. Douglas), recorded by The Trash Can Sinatras (pop/alternative), all on Go! Discs.
Tips: "Consider the type of company, roster and songs when submitting material."

JAY GOLD MUSIC PUBLISHING (BMI), P.O. Box 409, East Meadow NY 11554-0409. Phone/fax: (516)486-8699. President: Jay Gold. Music publisher. Estab. 1981. Publishes 25 songs/year; publishes 6 new songwriters/year. Pays standard royalty.
How to Contact: Submit a demo tape by mail. Unsolicited submissions are OK. Prefers cassette with 2 songs and lyric sheets. Does not return material. Reports ASAP. "Use only high quality chrome cassettes for submissions."
Music: Mostly **pop**, **rock** and **country**. Published "A Touch of the Heart," recorded by Eric Burdon; "All the Wrong Reasons," written and recorded by Jay Gold on Turbo Records (pop); and "Long

REMEMBER: Don't "shotgun" your demo tapes. Submit only to companies interested in the type of music you write. For more submission hints, refer to Getting Started on page 5.

Time" (by Jay Gold), recorded by Joe-Joe Bentry on Cardinal Records.
Tips: "Make the best demo you can afford. It's better to have a small publisher pushing your songs than a large one keeping them on the shelf."

*S.M. GOLD MUSIC (ASCAP), % Compositions, Inc., 36 E. 22nd St., 2nd Floor, New York NY 10010. President: Steven M. Gold. Music publisher and jingle/TV/film score producer. Publishes 20 compositions/year. "We employ freelance and staff songwriters/composers." Pays standard royalty or cash advance (buy-out).
How to Contact: Submit a demo tape by mail. Unsolicited submissions are OK. Prefers cassette with 2 songs. "Commercial composers: please send DAT." Does not return material. No calls please.
Music: All types.
Tips: "We're not looking for 'album tracks' or 'B sides.' Hits only!"

THE GOODLAND MUSIC GROUP INC., P.O. Box 24454, Nashville TN 37202. (615)269-7074. Publishing Coordinator: Wes Hall. Music publisher. Estab. 1988. Publishes 50 songs/year; 5-10 new songwriters/year. Pays standard royalty.
Affiliate(s): Goodland Publishing Company (ASCAP), Marc Isle Music (BMI) and Gulf Bay Publishing (SESAC).
How to Contact: Submit demo tape by mail. Unsolicited submissions are OK. SASE. "Request inclusion of 32¢ SASE for reply only." Reports in 2-4 weeks.
Music: Contemporary country. Published "Where Does Love Go When It's Gone?" (by Barton/ Byram), recorded by Warren Johnson on MDL Records; "Swingin' for the Fences" (by Myers/Meier) and "The Best Mistake" (by Primamore), both recorded by Daniel Glidwell on Starborn Records.

RICHARD E. GOWELL MUSIC (BMI), Dept. SM, 45 Seventh St., Auburn ME 04210. (207)784-7975. Professional Manager: Rich Gowell. Music publisher and record company (Allagash Country Records, Allagash R&B Records, Gowell Records). Estab. 1978. Publishes 10-30 songs/year; 5-10 new songwriters/year. Pays standard royalty.
Affiliate(s): Global Allagash Music Co. (ASCAP).
How to Contact: Submit a demo tape by mail. Unsolicited submissions are OK. Prefers cassette with 2-4 songs and lyric sheets. SASE. Reports in 1-2 months.
Music: Mostly **country, pop** and **R&B**. Published *Colorado Rockies* (by R. Gowell), recorded by Ace Diamond on Allagash Country Records (pop/C&W); "Fireball" (by B. Lee/L. Main), recorded by The Country Line Band on Sabre Records (country rock); and *It's Love*, written and recorded by Johnnie Mandell on Allagash Country Records (MOR/country).
Tips: "Have a great song with a professional demo and keep plugging to the right people."

GREEN MEADOWS PUBLISHING (BMI), 811 W. Fourth St., Beaver Dam KY 42320. (502)274-3169. Executive Director: Robert Bailey. Music publisher and record company. Estab. 1991. Publishes 5 songs/year; publishes 1 new songwriter/year. Pays standard royalty.
How to Contact: Write or call first to obtain permission to submit. Prefers cassette with 5 songs and lyric sheet. Does not return material. Reports in 2 months.
Music: Mostly **folk** and **gospel**. Published *Where Did Our Lovin' Go*, *Land up High*, and *Oh Kentucky*, all written and recorded by Robert Bailey on Beatle Records.

GREEN ONE MUSIC (BMI), Rockin' Chair Center Suite 102, 1033 W. State Highway 76, Branson MO 65616. (417)334-2336. Fax: (417)334-2306. President: George J. Skupien. Music publisher, recording studio. Estab. 1992. Publishes 6-12 songs/year. Pays standard royalty.
• Green One Music's record label, Green Bear Records, is listed in the Record Companies section.
How to Contact: Submit demo tape by mail. Unsolicited submissions are OK. Prefers cassette or DAT. "We prefer 2-4 songs on each tape. No more than 6." Does not return material. Reports in 2 months.
Music: Mostly **country, MOR** and **light rock**; also **American polka music, waltzes** and **comedy— fun songs.** Published "Our Last Cowboy Song" (by G. Skupien), recorded by Matthew Row'd on Green Bear Records (country); "Da Bulls, Da Bears, Da Beer" (by D. Mack/G. Skupien), recorded by The Stagemen (polka); and "In the Dog House with Daisy," written and recorded by G. Skupien, both on Briar Hill Records.
Tips: "Always put your best song first on your tapes submitted. If possible, submit a professional demo of your song. Be sure your vocal is clear!"

G-STRING PUBLISHING (BMI, SOCAN), P.O. Box 1096, Hudson, Quebec, J0P 1H0 **Canada**. (613)780-1163. Fax: (514)458-2819. Music Coordinator: Ms. Tanya Hart. Music publisher, record company (L.A. Records), record producer. Estab. 1991. Publishes 20 songs; publishes 5-10 new songwriters/year. Pays standard royalty.

• G-String's record label, L.A. Records, is listed in the Record Companies section and their management firm, M.B.H. Music Management, is listed in the Managers and Booking Agents section.

How to Contact: Submit demo tape by mail. Unsolicited submissions are OK. Prefers cassette or DAT with 3 songs and lyric sheet. SASE. Reports in 2 months.

Music: Mostly **commercial rock**, **A/C** and **dance**; also **country**. Published *Parts of Me and You*, written and recorded by Jessica Ehrenworth; *Waiting For My Yesterday* (by M. Lengies), recorded by Tommy Hayes; and *Letting Go* (by D. Jones/M. Lengies), recorded by Jessica Ehrenworth, all on L.A. Records.

Tips: "Know your craft; songs must have great lyrics and good melody, and create a strong emotional reaction. They must be under 4 minutes and must be radio friendly."

GYPSY HEART MUSIC (ASCAP), 6660 Delmonico Dr. Suite D-433, Colorado Springs CO 80919. Phone/fax: (719)260-1447. Producer/A&R: Lee Tribbey. Music publisher, record company. Estab. 1987. Publishes 45-50 songs/year; publishes 10-15 new songwriters/year. Hires staff songwriters. Pays standard royalty.

How to Contact: Call first and obtain permission to submit. Prefers cassette with 3 songs and lyric sheet. "Have demo on good quality TDK or Maxell tape. Guitar/piano and vocal are OK. It must be clear and understandable. Send only your best. If you can hear the songs playing on country radio, those are the songs we are interested in!" SASE. Reports in 4 weeks.

Music: Mostly **country-contemporary**, **bluegrass** and **country-rock**; also **Western swing** and **country-blues**. Published *Cajun Street Saturday Night*, written and recorded by Jody Adams; *Win, Place & Show* (by James Lino), recorded by Gene Garrett, and *Picking Up the Pieces* (by Marcella Fisher), all on GHM Records (country).

Tips: "Be prepared to invest all of your time, energy and some money to succeed. There really are no free lunches."

HALO INTERNATIONAL (BMI), P.O. Box 101, Sutton MA 01590. E-mail: mass38m@aol.com. Owner/Publisher: John Gagne. Music publisher, record company (MSM Records, Hālo Records, Bronco Records), record producer; artists signed to labels only. Estab. 1979. Publishes 6-8 songs/year. Pays standard royalty.

Affiliate(s): Pick the Hits Music (ASCAP), Mount Scott Music (BMI).

How to Contact: Write first and obtain permission to submit a tape. Prefers cassette with 2 songs and lyric sheets. SASE. Reports in 4-6 weeks.

Music: Mostly **soundtracks** (theater and TV themes), **contemporary country**, **traditional country** and **folk**. Working with playwrights and composers for musical and theater works with incidental music. Published *Duchess of Malfi* (by John Scott), recorded by Cliniqué Chamber Ensemble and *Stages* (by John Scott), recorded by London Fox Ensemble, both soundtracks on Hale Records; and *Cactus-Same Old School*, written and recorded by Cactus on MSM Records (country).

R.L. HAMMEL ASSOCIATES, INC., P.O. Box 531, Alexandria IN 46001-0531. Phone/fax: (317)724-3900. E-mail: rlh@lquest.net. President: Randal Hammel. Music publisher, record producer and consultant. Estab. 1974. Pays standard royalty.

Affiliates: Ladnar Music (ASCAP) and Lemmah Music (BMI).

How to Contact: Write first and obtain permission to submit a demo. Prefers cassette, DAT or VHS/8mm videocassette with 3 songs and typed lyric sheet. SASE. Reports ASAP.

Music: Mostly **pop**, **Christian** and **R&B**; also **MOR**, **rock** and **country**. Published *Lessons For Life* (by Kelly Hubbell/Jim Boedicker) and *I Just Want Jesus* (by Mark Condon), both recorded by Kelly Connor on Impact Records.

HAPPY HOUR MUSIC (BMI), 2410 Del Mar Ave., P.O. Box 1809, Rosemead CA 91770. (818)571-1214. Fax: (818)288-7461. President: Wan Seegmiller. Music publisher and record company. Estab. 1985. Publishes 5 songs/year; publishes 3 new songwriters/year.

How to Contact: Write first and obtain permission to submit a tape. Prefers cassette. SASE. Reports in 3 weeks.

Music: Mostly **jazz** and **Brazilian contemporary**. Published "The New Lambadas" (by Joãs Parahyba); "Alemão Bem Brasileiro" (by Olmir Stocker); and "Hermeto Pascoal Egrupo" (by Hermeto Pascoal and Antonio Adolfo), all on Happy Hour Records (Brazilian).

*HARBOR GOSPEL MUSIC PRODUCTION (BMI), P.O. Box 641, Findlay OH 45839. (419)422-4981. President: Paul Steinhour. Music publisher. Estab. 1990. Publishes 15-20 songs/year; publishes 2 new songwriters/year. Pays standard royalty.

How to Contact: Submit demo tape by mail. Unsolicited submissions are OK. Prefers cassette or VHS videocassette with 1-10 songs and lyric sheet. SASE. Reports in 6 weeks.

Music: Mostly **country gospel**, **southern gospel** and **Christian contemporary**. Published "My New Home" (by Paul Steinhour) and "He's Living Today" (by Patty Vansicle), both recorded by The Fishermen on Clearwater Records; and *He Still Does Miracles* (by Paul Steinhour), recorded by The Majestics on Voice One Records.
Tips: "Make sure your message is consistent and your hook line is used throughout the song."

HAVASONG MUSIC, 169 Cecil Rd., Rochester, Kent ME1 2HW **England**. (01634)815613. A&R Manager: Jim Hirst-Amos. Music publisher. Estab. 1979. Publishes 2-30 songs/year; publishes 1-2 new songwriters/year. Pays standard royalty.
How to Contact: Submit demo tape by mail. Unsolicited submissions are OK. Prefers material on vinyl or CD with 1-2 songs. SAE and IRC. Reports in 1-2 weeks.
Music: Mostly **MOR**, **pop**, **rock**, **funk** or **new wave**; also **country/rock**. Published *He Was a Dreamer*, written and recorded by Lucas Campbell on Twosome Records (country); *Drug City* (by Billy Allen), recorded by Invisible Hands on Invisible Hands Records (metal/pop); and "Line of Fire" (by P. Aspill), recorded by Sharron Lee.
Tips: "We act as independent publishers for those artists who produce and distribute their own material and can advise and help with promotion and distribution."

HAWKSBILL MUSIC (BMI), P.O. Box 1281, Orange VA 22960. (540)672-0122. President: Parke Stanley. Music publisher. Estab. 1991. Pays standard royalty.
How to Contact: Submit demo tape by mail. Unsolicited submissions are OK. Prefers cassette with 3 songs and lyric sheet. SASE. Reports in 2 weeks.
Music: Mostly **rock**, **country** and **R&B**; also **crossover** and **pop**. Published "Talkin To The Walls" (by Mike Raley); "Bourbon Copy" (by Lou Sweigmon) and "Hello Greyhound" (by the Coreys), all recorded by Scott Ryan on White Oak Records.
Tips: "Strive to say the ordinary in a fresh way! Learn techniques such as alliteration, antonyms, inner rhymes, etc. which catch the ears of hit producers and artists. This is explained in my free report, '16 Ways to Make Your Songs More Commercial.' Write and request it, include SASE. I have connections at Nashville major labels, and strong U.S. independent labels. Positive, uptempo songs have the best chance of a cut, but make sure they have good melody, not just 12-bar blues. Constantly write down hit songs from the radio and observe their structure, rhyming pattern, length, etc. It's good to time your songs and write the minutes and seconds on lyric sheets. Study hard—you can make money from your music!"

HEARTBEAT MUSIC, 282 Bruce Court, Westerville OH 43086. (614)882-5919. President: Randy Kettering. Music publisher and record company. Estab. 1987. Publishes 25-30 songs/year; publishes 5-10 new songwriters/year. Pays standard royalty.
Affiliates: RGK Heartbeat Music (ASCAP), RGK Heartlight Music (BMI).
How to Contact: Submit demo tape by mail. Unsolicited submissions are OK. Prefers cassette and lyric sheet. Does not return material. Reports in 6-8 weeks.
Music: Mostly **adult contemporary Christian**, **black gospel** and **inspirational**; also **Christian rock/pop**. Published *I'll Go* and "Feel Him Movin'," both gospel LPs written and recorded by Chris Byrd; and *Bright Glory*, written and recorded by Craig Hayes, all on Pulse Records.

HENLY MUSIC ASSOCIATES (ASCAP), 45 Perham St., W. Roxbury MA 02132. President: Bill Nelson. Music publisher, record company (Woodpecker Records) and record producer. Estab. 1987. Publishes 5 songs/year; publishes 5 new songwriters/year. Pays standard royalty.
  • Bill Nelson, Henly Music's president, is listed in the Record Producers section.
How to Contact: Submit demo tape by mail. Unsolicited submissions are OK. Prefers cassette with 4 songs and lyric sheet. SASE. Reports in 1 month.
Music: Mostly **country**, **pop** and **gospel**. Published "Kentucky Memory," by Michael Walsh and David Finnerty; "Seasons of Our Love," by Connie Makris, DJ Oklahoma and Jim Sweeney; and "All Is Well," by Pam Healy.

HEUPFERD MUSIKVERLAG GmbH, Ringwaldstr. 18, Dreieich 63303 **Germany**. Phone and fax: (06103)86970. General Manager: Christian Winkelmann. Music publisher. GEMA. Publishes 60 songs/year. Pays "royalties after GEMA distribution plan."
Affiliate(s): Song Bücherei (book series).
How to Contact: Write first and obtain permission to submit. Prefers cassette and lead sheet. SAE and IRC. Reports in 1 month.
Music: Mostly **folk**, **jazz** and **fusion**; also **New Age**, **rock** and **ethnic music**. Published "Valse Mélancolique," written and recorded by Rüdiger Oppermann (New Age); and "Rainy Sundays" (by Andy

Irvine), recorded by Andy Irvine and others, both on Wundertüte Records.

HICKORY LANE PUBLISHING AND RECORDING (SOCAN, ASCAP), P.O. Box 2275, Vancouver, British Columbia V6B 3W5 **Canada**. (604)987-3756. Fax: (604)987-0616. President: Chris Urbanski. A&R Manager: Dave Rogers. Music publisher, record company and record producer. Estab. 1988. Publishes 30 songs/year; publishes 10 new songwriters/year. Hires staff writers. Pays standard royalty.
   • See Hickory Lane's listing in the Record Producers section.
How to Contact: Submit demo tape by mail. Unsolicited submissions are OK. Prefers cassette (or VHS videocassette) with 1-6 songs. SASE. Reports in 3-4 weeks.
Music: Mostly **country** and **country rock**. Published *No Reason At All* (by Chris Michaels), *Until Now* (by Steve Mitchell/Chris Michaels), and *All Fired Up* (by Chris Michaels/Kyle Davis), all recorded by Chris Michaels on Hickory Lane Records.
Tips: "Send us a good quality sounding demo, with the vocals upfront. Be original and professional in your approach. We are looking for good songs, and so are the major record labels that we deal with."

HICKORY VALLEY MUSIC (ASCAP), 10303 Hickory Valley, Ft. Wayne IN 46835. President: Allan Straten. Music publisher, record company (Yellow Jacket Records) and record producer (Al Straten Productions). Estab. 1988. Publishes 10 songs/year; publishes 5 new songwriters/year. Pays standard royalty.
Affiliate(s): Straten's Song (BMI).
   • Hickory Valley's record label, Yellow Jacket Records, is listed in the Record Companies section.
How to Contact: Submit demo tape by mail. Unsolicited submissions are OK. Prefers cassette with 3-4 songs and lyric sheets. Use a 6×9 envelope with no staples. Does not return material.
Music: Mostly **country** and **MOR**. Published *She's My Number One Fan* (by R. Hartman/S. Grogg/ A. Straten); *She's My "X" and I Know "Y"* (by D. Crisman/S. Grogg/A. Straten); and *Kisa Marie* (by S. Grogg/A. Straten), all recorded by Tom Woodward on Pharoah Records (country).

*HIGH POCKETS PUBLISHING INC. (ASCAP, BMI), P.O. Box 622, Buffalo NY 14224. (716)643-2246. (716)677-0955. President: Nick Gugliuzza. Music publisher and record company. Estab. 1978. Publishes 15 songs/year; publishes 3 new songwriters/year. Pays standard royalty.
How to Contact: Submit demo tape by mail. Unsolicited submissions are OK. Prefers cassette with 1-3 songs. SASE. Reports in 3 weeks.
Music: Mostly **rock (all types)** and **country**. Published *Blue Moon*, written and recorded by Ben Crane (country); *Try Again*, written and recorded by Fole Dean (rock); and *Hard Luck* (by Shelly Pierrce), recorded by Dan Quinn, all on High Pockets Records.

HIGH-MINDED MOMA PUBLISHING & PRODUCTIONS (BMI), 10330 Cape Arago, Coos Bay OR 97420. Contact: Kai Moore Snyder. Music publisher and production company. Pays standard royalty.
How to Contact: Prefers 7½ ips reel-to-reel, CD or cassette with 4-8 songs and lyric sheet. SASE. Reports in 1 month.
Music: Country, MOR, rock (country), **New Age** and **top 40/pop**.

HINDS FEET MUSIC (SESAC), P.O. Box 7811, Beaumont TX 77726. (409)892-6785. President: Benny Thomas. Music publisher and record producer. Estab. 1988. Publishes 10-20 songs/year; publishes 3-4 new songwriters/year. Hires staff songwriters. Pays standard royalty.
Affiliates: Open Window Music (SESAC).
How to Contact: Submit demo tape by mail. Unsolicited submissions are OK. Prefers cassette with 3 songs. Does not return material. Reports in 6 weeks.
Music: Mostly **southern gospel**, **country gospel** and **other Christian**. Published *Rise High* (by Sterling Griffin), recorded by Billy Freed (gospel); *There is Peace* (by Hollie Thomas), recorded by Richetta Logan (contemporary Christian); and *Watch and Be Ready*, written and recorded by Benny Thomas (gospel), all on H.F. Music.

● **A BULLET** introduces comments by the editor of *Songwriter's Market* indicating special information about the listing.

HIT & RUN MUSIC PUBLISHING INC., 1841 Broadway, Suite 411, New York NY 10023. (212)956-2882. Vice President: Joey Gmerek. Creative & International Director: Michelle De Vries. Music publisher. Publishes 20-30 songs/year; publishes 2 new songwriters/year. Hires staff writers. Pays standard royalty.
Affiliate(s): Charisma Music Publishing USA Inc. Hidden Pun Music Publishing Inc. (BMI).
How to Contact: Write or call first and obtain permission to submit a tape. Prefers cassette (or VHS videocassette) with lyric sheet. Does not return material.
Music: Mostly **pop**, **rock** and **R&B**; also **dance**. Published "Falling Into You," recorded by Celine Dion on Epic Records; "Let Me Be The One," recorded by Blessid Union of Souls on EMI Records; and "Black Heaven," recorded by Maysa on Blue Thumb/MCA Records.

HIT-FABRIK MUSIKVERLAG, Mühlgasse 1, Obj. 20, Guntramsdorf A-2353 **Austria**. Phone: + +43-2236/53006. Fax: + +43-2236/53006-90. E-mail: hit.fabrik@magnet.at. Director: Franz Groihs. Music publisher, record company and record producer. Estab. 1985. Publishes 150-200 songs/year; publishes 12 new songwriters/year. Hires staff songwriters. Pays standard royalty.
How to Contact: Submit demo tape by mail. Unsolicited submissions are OK. Prefers cassette, DAT, VHS videocassette or CD with lyric sheet. Does not return submissions. Reports in 1 month.
Music: Mostly **pop**, **background music** and **esoteric music**. Published *Rhodos*, written and recorded by Michalis Dukakis on WWR Records (pop); *Clair De Lune*, written and recorded by Christian Ropez; and *Horizon*, written and recorded by Robert Wittek, both on EAR Records.

HITSBURGH MUSIC CO. (BMI), P.O. Box 1431, 233 N. Electra, Gallatin TN 37066. (615)452-0324. President/General Manager: Harold Gilbert. Music publisher. Estab. 1964. Publishes 12 songs/year. Pays standard royalty.
Affiliate(s): 7th Day Music (BMI).
How to Contact: Submit demo tape by mail. Unsolicited submissions are OK. Prefers cassette (or quality videocassette) with 2-4 songs and lead sheet. Prefers studio produced demos. SASE. Reports in 6-8 weeks.
Music: **Country gospel** and **MOR**. Published "The Last Kiss" (by H. Gilbert), recorded by Jean; "The Depth of His Love" (by Harold Gilbert), recorded by Kim Crutcher; and "I'm in a Trance," written and recorded by K'leetha Gee, all on Southern City Records.

HO-HUM MUSIC (A division of Care Free Records Group), Box 2463, Caretree AZ 85377. (602)230-4177. Vice President: Doya Fairbanks. Music publisher, record company, distributor and promotion company. Estab. 1990. Publishes 25-35 songs/year; publishes 5-6 new songwriters/year. Hires staff songwriters. Pays standard royalty.
  ● See the listings for Care Free Records Group in the Record Companies and Record Producers sections.
How to Contact: Submit demo tape by mail. Unsolicited submissions are OK. Prefers cassette (or VHS videocassette if available) with 4-6 songs. SASE. Reports in 1 month.
Music: Mostly **country**, **jazz** and **classical**; also **rock/pop, metal** and **New Age**. Published *Long Branch*, written and recorded by Ward (country); *Golden Wok*, written and recorded by Ho-Zay (rock); and *Pink Pepper*, written and recorded by Pink Pepper (pop), all on Care Free Records.

HOLTON MUSIC (BMI), P.O. Box 270262, Nashville TN 37227. (615)355-9694. Fax: (615)355-9541. President: Harvey Turner. Music publisher, record company and record producer. Estab. 1986. Publishes 50 songs/year; publishes 10 new songwriters/year. Hires staff songwriters. Pays standard royalty.
How to Contact: Submit demo tape by mail. Unsolicited submissions are OK. Prefers cassette with 3 songs and lyric sheet. Does not return material. Reports in 1 month.
Music: Mostly **country**, **Christian country** and **gospel**. Published *Rose In A Bible* (by P. Pritchett/T. Pritchett/H. Pruett/D. Anderson), recorded by Lewis Family on Daywind Records (gospel); "Golden Memories" (by P. Pritchett/D. Ingkeep/H. Turner), recorded by Dolly Dailey on Holton Records (country); and "Dancin' Fool" (by T. Pritchett/D. Dixon), recorded by T. Pritchett on ALN Records.

HOLY SPIRIT MUSIC (BMI), Box 31, Edmonton KY 42129. (502)432-3183. President: W. Junior Lawson. Music publisher. Member GMA, International Association of Gospel Music Publishers. Estab. 1973. Publishes 4 songs/year; publishes 2 new songwriters/year. Pays standard royalty.
How to Contact: Submit demo tape by mail. Unsolicited submissions OK. Prefers cassette with 2 songs and lyric sheet. SASE. Reports in 3 weeks.
Music: Mostly **Southern gospel** and **country gospel**. Published *We're Goin' To A Celebration* (by Marilyn K. Bowling), recorded by The Turners on Cooke Records; *The Love In His Eyes*, written and recorded by Julia P. Rautenberg; and *Excuses* (by Harold S. Leake), recorded by The Kingsmen on Riversong Records (all southern gospel).
Tips: Send "good clear cut tape with typed or printed copy of lyrics."

HONK MUSIC & RECORDS — MUSIKVERLAG H. GEBETSROITHER, Hormayrgasse 3/
25, Vienna A-1170 **Austria**. Phone and fax: (43)1/4864287. MD: Herbert Gebetsroither. Mailing Address: P.O. Box 118 (Zip: A-1172). Music publisher, record company (Honk Records) and record producer. Estab. 1992. Publishes 100 songs/year; publishes 2-3 new songwriters/year. Pays 60% royalty.
How to Contact: Submit demo CD by mail. Unsolicited submissions are OK. Prefers CD or VHS videocassette with 3-10 songs, lyric and lead sheet. SAE and IRC. Reports in 1-2 years.
Music: Mostly **instrumentals: lite jazz, fusion, Latin, New Age, album rock/acid and dancefloor jazz, contemporary classics**; also **R&B, country, soul, funk** and **reggae**. Published *Highway of Fame*, written and recorded by J. Honk on Honk Records.
Tips: "Send only CDs you want to get played on radio and TV in our territory. We take 80 free promotion copes from you or your label and promote it so it hopefully gets airplay. For that we both get the main royallty-money here in Austria. We also have distribution partners for your CDs but our main business is radio/TV promotion for already released CDs."

HUMANFORM PUBLISHING COMPANY, Box 158486, Nashville TN 37215. (615)373-9312. Publisher: Kevin Nairon. BMI. Music publisher. Pays standard royalty.
How to Contact: Submit demo tape by mail. Unsolicited submissions are OK. Prefers cassette with 4 songs and lyric and lead sheets. SASE. Reports in 4 weeks.
Music: Mostly **country blues** and **country**. Published "The Rain Is Falling" and "I Need Your Love" (by Kevin Nairon), recorded by Sleepy Joe on CS Records.
Tips: "Please strive for maximum quality when making your demo. Write about your own experiences in a standard blues format."

GREGG HUTCHINS MUSIC (BMI), 116 Roberta Dr., Hendersonville TN 37075. (615)264-1373. Owner: Gregg Hutchins. Music publisher. Estab. 1993. Publishes 20 songs/year. Pays standard royalty.
• Gregg Hutchins's record label, Rejoice Records, is listed in the Record Companies section.
How to Contact: Write or call first and obtain permission to submit. Prefers cassette with 1 song and lyric sheet. Does not return material. Only replies if interested.
Music: Mostly **Christian country** and **bluegrass gospel**. Published "The Last Time I Fall" (by Jim Watters/Charlie Louvin), recorded by Charlie Louvin; "Adam's Side (by Jesse Wilson), recorded by Billy Walker on Rejoice Records; and "If I Hold To His Hand" (by Keith Smith), recorded by Heritage, all on Rejoice Records.
Tips: "Use creative lyrics to describe a familiar topic; i.e., say it in a different way."

*IMMORTAL BELOVED MUSIC PUBLISHING (BMI), P.O. Box 17865, Memphis TN 38187. Phone/fax: (901)766-7515 (fax only after 11P.M. CST). E-mail: jwagnerts@aol.com. President: Jim Wagner. Music publisher, record company (Immortal Beloved Records) and record producer. Estab. 1995. Publishes 12 new songs/year; 2-3 new songwriters/year. Hires staff songwriters. Pays standard royalty.
How to Contact: Submit demo tape by mail. Unsolicited submissions are OK. Prefers cassette, videocassette or CD with 4 songs and lyric sheet. Does not return material. Reports in 1-4 months.
Music: Mostly **country, bluegrass** and **folk** or **novelty**; also **classical, instrumental** and **rock** or **MOR**. Published "I Walked Here All the Way From Memphis," "Roads Back Home" and "Old Memphis Home," all written and recorded by Jim Wagner on Immortal Beloved Records.
Tips: "Keep song(s) under 3 minutes; they must be clear with vocals out front. Send only Type II cassettes or high grade videotape. Songs must have been copyrighted and never been published or released. If you don't have a good commercial voice for your demos, find a good singer and pay them to do it! Something terrible happens when you submit a bad demo—nothing!"

INSIDE RECORDS/OK SONGS, Bisschopstraat 25, 2060 Antwerp 6 **Belgium**. (32)03-226-77-19. Fax: (32)03-226-78-05. MD: Jean Ney. Music publisher and record company. Estab. 1989. Publishes 50 songs/year; publishes 30-40 new songwriters/year. Hires staff writers. Royalty varies "depending on teamwork."
How to Contact: Submit demo tape by mail. Unsolicited submissions are OK. Prefers cassette with complete name, address, telephone and fax number. SAE and IRC. Reports in 2 months.
Music: Mostly **dance, pop** and **MOR contemporary**; also **country, reggae** and **Latin**. Published *Fiesta De Bautiza* (by Andres Manzana); *I'm Freaky* (by Maes-Predu'homme-Robinson); and *Heaven* (by KC One-King Naomi), all on Inside Records.

*INTERNATIONAL MUSIC NETWORK LIMITED, Independent House, 54 Larkshall Rd., Chingford, London E4 6PD England. +44(0)181 523 9000. Fax: +44(0)523-8888. Managing Director: Ellis Rich. Music publisher. Estab. 1987. Publishes 3-4,000 songs/year; publishes 8-10 new songwriters/year. Pays 60-75% royalty.

Affiliate(s): Collaboration Music (ASCAP), American Music Network (BMI).
How to Contact: Submit demo tape by mail. Unsolicited submissions are OK. Prefers cassette (or VHS or Beta videocassette) with 3 songs (maximum) and lyric sheet. SAE and IRC. Reports in 2 months.
Music: Mostly **dance**, **soul** and **R&B**; also **ballads**. Published "Caught In The Middle," written and recorded by Juliet Roberts on Cool Tempo Records (dance); "Im Min' Alu" (by B. Nagari), recorded by Ofra Haza on Sire Records (dance); and "Gimme Gimme," written and recorded by Ava Cherry on Radikal Records (dance).
Tips: "Don't over produce your demo. Make certain lyrics can be clearly heard. Be patient."

INTERPLANETARY MUSIC (BMI), 584 Roosevelt, Gary IN 46404. (219)886-2003. Fax: (219)886-1000. CEO: James R. Hall III. Music publisher, record company (Interplanetary Records) and record producer. Estab. 1972. Publishes 10 songs/year; publishes 4 new songwriters/year. Pays standard royalty.
How to Contact: Call first and obtain permission to submit. Prefers cassette. SASE. Reports in 5 weeks.
Music: **R&B** and **top 40/urban contemporary**. Published "In The Shade" (by J. Hall/A. Dickerson), recorded by Basic Instinct; and "GI Honeys," recorded by Juvenile, both on Interplanetary Records.
Tips: "Please submit a good quality cassette recording of your best work."

INTERSCOPE MUSIC PUBLISHING (ASCAP, BMI), 10900 Wilshire Blvd. Suite 1230, Los Angeles CA 90024. (310)443-3240. Fax: (310)443-3242. Contact: Ronny Vance. Contact: Leta Gild (310)443-2237 for rock, pop and alternative; Maani E. (310)443-2238 for rap and R&B. Music publisher. Estab. 1992.
Affiliate(s): Interscope Music (ASCAP) and Interscope Pearl Music (BMI).
How to Contact: "Will accept unsolicited material under following conditions: must be on a professional sounding or recorded demo tape and must be recommended by an industry professional such as ASCAP, BMI, manager, lawyer, etc."
Music: Mostly **urban/rap/R&B**, **alternative** and **rock/pop**. Published "Back In the Day," written and recorded by Ahmad on Giant Records (rap); "Anything" (by Brian Morgan), recorded by SWV on RCA Records (R&B); and "California Love," written and recorded by 2PAC on Interscope Records.

IRON SKILLET MUSIC, 229 Ward Circle, #A21, Brentwood TN 37027. (615)371-5065. Fax: (615)370-0353. President: Jack Schneider. Music publisher, record company (Rustic Records Inc.), record producer. Estab. 1984. Publishes 20 songs/year. Pays standard royalty.
Affiliate(s): Covered Bridge Music (BMI), Town Square Music (SESAC).
How to Contact: Submit demo tape by mail. Unsolicited submissions are OK. Prefers cassette with 3 songs and lyric sheet. SASE. Reports in 3 months.
Music: Mostly **country**. Published "Turn off the Lights," "You Make Me Feel Like Dancin'," and "Maybe This Time," all written and recorded by Holt Wilson on Rustic Records.
Tips: "Material should be attention grabbing from start to finish with good hook."

ISBA MUSIC PUBLISHING INC. (ASCAP), 2860 Blvd. De La Concorde, La Val Quebec H7E 2B4 **Canada**. (514)669-4088. Fax: (514)669-5838. Contact: Maurice Velenosi or Larry Mancini. Music publisher. Estab. 1983. Publishes 85 songs/year; publishes 20 new songwriters/year. Pays standard royalty.
Affiliate(s): Gabbro Music (BMI).
How to Contact: Write first and obtain permission to submit. Prefers cassette with 3 songs and lyric sheet. SAE and IRC. Reports in 2-4 weeks.
Music: Mostly **pop/rock**, **rap/hip hop** and **dance**; also **R&B, A/C** and **MOR**. Published *Secret Admirer* (by R. Geddes/A. Breault), recorded by DJ Ray (reggae); *Ole Ola* (by G. Diodati/F. Summer), recorded by Collage (dance); and *If You Treat My Body Right*, written and recorded by M. Dozier, all on ISBA Records.

***d.t. JACKSONGS® MUSIC PUBLISHING (ASCAP)**, P.O. Box 6771, Cleveland OH 44101. (216)942-6998. Fax: (216)341-1060. E-mail: 103246.3544@compuserve.com. Owner/President: Don Thomas Jackson. Music publisher, record company. Estab. 1995. Publishes 20-40 songs/year; 5-10 new songwriters/year. Pays standard royalty.
How to Contact: Write first and obtain permission to submit a demo. Prefers cassette with 3 songs and lyric sheets. Does not return material. Reports in 1-2 months.

THE TYPES OF MUSIC each listing is interested in are printed in boldface.

Music: Mostly **country**, **ballads** and **Christian/gospel**; also **pop**, **rock/light** and **Christmas**. Published *Forever I Will Love You* (by D.T. Jackson), recorded Lisa; *I.R.S.* (by D.T. Jackson/D.P. Jackson), recorded by Gary; and *Going Home* (by D.T. Jackson/D.P. Jackson), recorded by Larry Beaird, all on Jacksongs Records.

JACLYN MUSIC (BMI), 306 Millwood Dr., Nashville TN 37217-1604. (615)366-9999. President: Jack Lynch. Music publisher, producer, recording company (Jalyn, Nashville Bluegrass and Nashville Country) and distributor (Nashville Music Sales). Estab. 1963. Publishes 50-100 songs/year; 25-50 new songwriters/year. Pays standard royalty.
Affiliate(s): JLMG (ASCAP), Jack Lynch Music Group (parent company), Nashville Country Productions and Nashville Music Sales.
 • Jaclyn Music's record label, Jalyn Recording Co., is listed in the Record Companies section, and their production company, Nashville Country Productions, is listed in the Record Producers section.
How to Contact: Submit a demo tape by mail, or write to arrange personal interview. Unsolicited submissions are OK. Send good quality cassette recording, neat lyric sheets and SASE. Prefers 1-2 selections per tape. Reports in 1 month.
Music: Country, bluegrass, gospel and **MOR**. Published *Forever Love* (by Bill Clark), recorded by Odie Gal on NCP-19961; *I'm Wanted* (by Barbara Jackson) and *Wasted Years and Dreams* (by Shirley P. Hickcox), both recorded by Don Hendrix on NCP-19964 Records.

JANA JAE MUSIC (BMI), P.O. Box 35726, Tulsa OK 74153. (918)786-8896. E-mail: janajae@aol. com. Website: http://home.aol.com/janajae. Secretary: Kathleen Pixley. Music publisher, record company (Lark Records) and record producer (Lark Talent and Advertising). Estab. 1977. Publishes 5-10 songs/year; publishes 1-2 new songwriters/year. Pays standard royalty.
 • See the listings for Lark Records in the Record Companies section, and Lark Talent and Advertising in the Record Producers section.
How to Contact: Submit demo tape by mail. Unsolicted submissions are OK. Prefers cassette (or VHS videocassette) with 4-5 songs and lyric and lead sheet if possible. Does not return material.
Music: Country, **pop** and **instrumentals** (**classical** or **country**). Published ''Mayonnaise,'' ''Bus 'n' Ditty'' (by Steven Upfold), and ''Let the Bible Be Your Roadmap'' (by Irene Elliot), all recorded by Jana Jae on Lark Records.

JAELIUS ENTERPRISES (ASCAP, BMI), Route 2, Box 94B, Royse City TX 75189. (214)636-2600. Owner: James Cornelius. Music publisher. Publishes 3-5 songs/year; publishes 3 new songwriters/year. Pays standard royalty.
Affiliate(s): Jaelius Music (ASCAP), Hitzgalore Music (BMI), Air Rifle Music (ASCAP) and Bee Bee Gun Music (BMI).
How to Contact: Write first and obtain permission to submit. Prefers cassette. SASE. Reports in 3 weeks.
Music: Mostly **pop**, **country** and **gospel**; also **R&B**. Published ''So It Shall Be'' (by G. Penny/Lang), recorded by k.d. lang on Sire Records; *She's In Love*, written and recorded by J.J. Cale on Silvertone Records (rock); and ''The Man In Love With You'' (by Steve Dorff/Gary Harju), recorded by George Strait.
Tips: ''Today's market requires good demos. Strong lyrics are a must.''

JAMMY MUSIC PUBLISHERS LTD., The Beeches, 244 Anniesland Rd., Glasgow G13 1XA, Scotland. Phone: (041)954-1873. E-mail: 100734.2674@compuserve.com. Managing Director: John D. R. MacCalman. Music publisher and record company. PRS. Estab. 1977. Publishes 45 songs/year; publishes 2 new songwriters/year. Pays royalty ''in excess of 50%.''
How to Contact: Write first and obtain permission to submit. Does not return material. Reports in 3 months.
Music: Mostly **rock**, **pop**, **country** and **instrumental**; also **Scottish**. Published ''The Wedding Song,'' (by Bill Padley/Grant Mitchell), recorded by True Love Orchestra on BBC Records (pop); *The Old Button Box* (by D. McCrone), recorded by Foster & Allen on Stylus Records; and ''Absent Friends'' (by D. McCrone), recorded by Dominic Kirwan on Ritz Records.
Tips: ''We are now working with a small writers' roster and it's unlikely we would be able to take new writers in the future.''

JA/NEIN MUSIKVERLAG GMBH, Hallerstr. 72, D-20146 Hamburg **Germany**. Phone: (40)4102161. Fax: (040)448850. General Manager: Mary Dostal. Music publisher, record company and record producer. GEMA. Publishes 100 songs/year; publishes 20 new songwriters/year. Pays 60% royalty.

Affiliate(s): Pinorrekk Mv., Star-Club Mv., Wunderbar Mv. and Sempex Mv. (GEMA).
How to Contact: Submit demo tape by mail. Unsolicited submissions are OK. Prefers cassette (or VHS videocassette) and lyric sheet. SAE and IRC. Reports in 2-8 weeks.
Music: Mostly **rock**, **pop**, **MOR** and **blues**. Published *Krieg* (by Bernadette Hengst), recorded by Die Braut on RCA Records; *Dark Blue Blues*, (by Jay McShann), recorded by Axel Zwingenberger on Vagabond Records (boogie woogie); and *Reb Itzik's Nign* (by Alan Bern), recorded by Itzhak Perlman and Brave Old World on EMI Classics (Klezmer).
Tips: "If IRC is not included, we only react if we fall in love. Single, A-Side songs only or extraordinary ideas, please. If artist, include photo. Leave three seconds between songs. Enclose lyrics. Be fantastic!"

JASPER STONE MUSIC (ASCAP)/JSM SONGS (BMI), 10 Deepwell Farms Rd., South Salem NY 10590. President: Chris Jasper. Vice President/General Counsel: Margie Jasper. Music publisher. Estab. 1986. Publishes 20-25 songs/year. "Each contract is worked out individually and negotiated depending on terms." Pays standard royalty.
How to Contact: Submit demo tape by mail. Unsolicited submissions are OK. Prefers cassette with maximum of 3 songs and lyric sheets. SASE. Reports in 2-3 weeks.
Music: Mostly **R&B/pop**, **rap** and **rock**. Published *Deep Inside* and *Praise The Eternal*, written and recorded by Chris Jasper; and *Out Front* (by Gather Williams), recorded by Out Front, all on Gold City Records.
Tips: "Keep writing. Keep submitting tapes. Be persistent. Don't give up. Send your best songs in the best form (best production possible)."

JERJOY MUSIC (BMI), P.O. Box 1264, Peoria IL 61654-1264. (309)673-5755. Professional Manager: Jerry Hanlon. Music publisher. Estab. 1978. Publishes 4 songs/year; publishes 2 new songwriters/year. Pays standard royalty.
● Jerjoy Music's record label, Universal-Athena Records, is listed in the Record Companies section.
How to Contact: Submit a demo tape by mail. Unsolicited submissions are OK. "We do not return phone calls." Prefers cassette with 4-8 songs and lyric sheet. SASE. Reports in 2 weeks.
Music: **Country** (modern or traditional), **gospel/Christian**, **Irish music**. Published *Livin' On Dreams* (by Eddie Crew), recorded by Jerry Hanlon; *When Autumn Leaves* (by Clint Miller) and *Look for Love Again* (by Steve Warner), both recorded by Clint Miller, all on VAR Records (country).
Tips: "Compare, study and evaluate your music, to the hit songs you hear on the radio. Let your songs tell a story. Choose your lyrics carefully and make every word count. Long and drawn-out songs don't seem to make it in writing. Every word should be chosen to its best commercial value. Don't submit any song that you don't honestly feel is well constructed and strong in commercial value."

*JK JAM MUSIC, Saratoga Mall, Route 50, Saratoga NY 12866. (518)984-9020. Director of A&R: Jamie Keats. Music publisher and record producer. Estab. 1992. Pays standard royalty.
● See the listing for JK Jam Productions in the Record Producers section.
How to Contact: Write first and obtain permission to submit. Prefers cassette, bio and photo. Does not return material. Reports only if interested.
Music: Mostly **pop**, **rock** and **alternative**; also **R&B** and **dance**. Artists include Johnny Valentine, Ellis Junction, Dog, Lonnie Park and Paul Traudt.

*JODA MUSIC (BMI), P.O. Box 100, Spirit Lake IA 51360. (712)336-2859. President: John Senn. A&R Director: Wes Weller. Music publisher and record company. Estab. 1970. Publishes 10 songs/year. Pays standard royalty.
Affiliate(s): Okoboji Music (BMI).
How to Contact: Prefers cassette with no more than 4 songs and lyric sheet. "Keep demos short." SASE. Reports in 3 weeks.
Music: Mostly **light rock**, **country** and **gospel**. Published "Beer & Popcorn" (by Dave Peterson), recorded by Ralph Lundquist (country); "Change is Going to Come" (by Roger Hughes), recorded by Silver $ Band (pop); and *I Hate*, written and recorded by Curt Powell (country), all on IGL Records.

JOEY BOY PUBLISHING CO. (BMI), 3081 NW 24th St., Miami FL 33142. (305)633-7469. Director: Aldo Hernandez. Music publisher. Estab. 1985. Publishes 100-150 songs/year; publishes 12-15 new songwriters/year. Pays standard royalty.
Affiliate(s): Beam of Light (ASCAP) and Too Soon To Tell (SESAC).
● Joey Boy's record label, Joey Boy Records, can be found in the Record Companies section.
How to Contact: Write first and obtain permission to submit. Prefers cassette with no more than 3 songs and lyric sheets. "Type or print lyric sheet legibly please!" SASE. Reports in 6 weeks.

Music: Mostly **R&B** and **rap**; also **dance**, **jazz**, **comedy** and **bass**. Published *Nothing But Bass* (by B. Graham), recorded by Bass Patrol; "Funky Y-2-C" and "Summer Delight," (both by C. Mills), recorded by The Puppies on Chaos Records.
Tips: "Be true to your trade and write about the things you know."

LITTLE RICHIE JOHNSON MUSIC (BMI), 318 Horizon Vista Blvd., Belen NM 87002. (505)864-7441. Manager: Tony Palmer. Music publisher, record company (LRJ Records) and record producer (Little Richie Johnson). Estab. 1959. Publishes 50 songs/year; publishes 10 new songwriters/year. Pays standard royalty.
Affiliate(s): Little Cowboy Music (ASCAP).
● Little Richie Johnson is also listed in the Record Producers section, and LRJ Records is listed in the Record Companies section.
How to Contact: Write first and obtain permission to submit. SASE. Reports in 6 weeks.
Music: Country and **Spanish**. Published *Moonlight, Roses and the Wine* (by Jerry Jaramillo), recorded by Gabe Neoto; *Ship of Fools*, recorded by Reta Lee; and *Honky Tonk Cinderella*, written and recorded by Jerry Jaramillo, all on LRJ Records.

AL JOLSON BLACK & WHITE MUSIC (BMI), 116 17th Ave. S., Nashville TN 37203. (615)244-5656. President: Albert Jolson. Music publisher. Estab. 1981. Publishes 600 songs/year; publishes 50 new songwriters/year. Pays standard royalty.
Affiliate(s): Jolie House Music (ASCAP).
How to Contact: Submit a demo tape by mail. Unsolicited submissions are OK. Prefers cassette with 3 songs and lyric sheet. Send: Attn. Johnny Drake. SASE. Reports in 6 weeks.
Music: Mostly **country crossover**, **light rock** and **pop**. Published "Come Home to West Virginia" (by Scott Phelps), recorded by Kathy Mattea; "Ten Tiny Fingers, Ten Tiny Toes" (by David John Hanley), recorded by Kelly Dawn; and "Indiana Highway," recorded by Staggerlee, both on ASA Jolson Records (country).
Tips: "Make sure it has a strong hook. Ask yourself if it is something you would hear on the radio five times a day. Have good audible vocals on demo tape."

JON MUSIC (BMI), P.O. Box 233, Church Point LA 70525. (318)684-2176. Owner: Lee Lavergne. Music publisher, record company (Lanor Records), record producer and recording studio (Sound Center Recorders). Estab. 1960. Publishes 30-40 songs/year; publishes 3-4 new songwriters/year. Pays standard royalty.
● Jon Music's record label, Lanor Records, is listed in the Record Companies section.
How to Contact: Write or call first and obtain permission to submit. Prefers cassette with 4 songs and lyric sheet. "Use a good quality cassette and make sure the vocals are above the music." SASE. Reports in 2 weeks. ("Depends how busy we are and if I am undecided.")
Music: Mostly **country**. Published *Pictures*, written and recorded by Tommy McLain (country); *Bridges* (by D. Jones/B. Cheshire), recorded by David Jones (country); and *Hey Jolie* (by R. Naquin/V. Bruce), recorded by Vin Bruce (country), all on Lanor Records.
Tips: "Write professional hit material that's fresh and different."

JOSENA MUSIC (SESAC), P.O. Box 566, Los Altos CA 94022. President: Joe Nardone. Music publisher and producer. Estab. 1983. Publishes 30 songs/year; publishes 1-2 new songwriters/year. Hires staff songwriters. Pays standard royalty.
Affiliate(s): Reigninme Music (SESAC).
How to Contact: Write first and obtain permission to submit a tape. Prefers cassette with 3 songs and lyric sheet. Does not return material. Reports in 2 months if interested.
Music: Mostly **Christian rock/pop**, **pop** and **gospel**; also **modern rock** and **Latin Music** as well—**flamenco**, **rumba style** (Spanish) and **Spanish ballads**. Published "Coming Home" (by Dino Veloz/Joe Nardone), recorded by Joe Nardone (modern Christian rock); "Make Us One" (by Lee Kalem/Joe Nardone), recorded by Lillie Knauls (gospel); and "Go God's Way" (by Mike Palos), recorded by Joe Nardone (jazz).
Tips: "Make sure it is a hot marketable tune—get unbiased opinions on your song—would it be playable on the radio?"

REFER TO THE CATEGORY INDEX (at the end of this section) to find exactly which companies are interested in the type of music you write.

PATRICK JOSEPH MUSIC INC. (BMI), 2004 Wedgewood Ave., Nashville TN 37212. Contact: Steve Markland. Music publisher. Estab. 1988. Publishes 2 new songwriters/year. Pays standard royalty.
Affiliate(s): Patrix Jamus Music (ASCAP), Second Wave Music (ASCAP), August Wind Music (BMI), PJH Music (SESAC).
How to Contact: Write first and obtain permission to submit. Does not return material. Reports in 1-2 months.
Music: Mostly **country, pop** and **A/C**. Published "Wild Angels" (by Matraca Berg/Gary Harrison/ Harry Stinson), recorded by Martina McBride on RCA Records (country); "You Can Feel Bad" (by Matraca Berg/Tim Kreckel), recorded by Patty Loveless on MCA Records (country); and "I Can Love You Like That" (by Jennifer Kimball/Steve Diamond/Mary Beth Dairy), recorded by John Michael Montgomery on Atlantic Nashville Records (country) and by All-4-One on Atlantic Records (R&B).
Tips: "Somehow get a referral from a professional in the music industry. Start at BMI or ASCAP then join the NSAI, etc."

JUMP MUSIC, Langemunt 71, 9420 AAIGEM, **Belgium**. Phone: (053)62-73-77. General Manager: Eddy Van Mouffaert. Music publisher, record company (Jump Records) and record producer (Jump Productions). Member of SABAM S.V., Brussels. Publishes 100 songs/year; publishes 8 new songwriters/year. Pays royalty via SABAM S.V.
• See the listing for Jump Music in the Music Print Publishers section.
How to Contact: Submit demo tape by mail. Unsolicited submissions are OK. Prefers cassette. Does not return material. Reports in 2 weeks.
Music: Mostly **easy listening, disco** and **light pop**; also **instrumentals**. Published "Just A Friend" (by Eddy Govert), recorded by Sherly on Ideal Records (pop); "Go Go Go" (by H. Deschuyteneer), recorded by Rudy Silvester on Scorpion Records (Flemish); and *Won't You Stay With Me* (by Eddy Govert), recorded by Frank Valentino on Holy Hole Records (Flemish).
Tips: "Music wanted with easy, catchy melodies (very commercial songs)."

*JUST A NOTE (ASCAP, BMI), 815 Ohio Ave., Jeffersonville KY 47130-3634. (503)637-2877. General Partner: John V. Heath. Music publisher, record companies (Hillview, Estate) and record producer (MVT Productions). Estab. 1979. Publishes 35 songs/year; publishes 10-15 new songwriters/year. Works with composers and lyricists. Pays standard royalty.
Affiliate(s): Two John's Music (ASCAP).
How to Contact: Submit demo tape by mail. Unsolicited submissions are OK. Prefers cassette, 7½ ips reel-to-reel or VHS videocassette with 3 songs and lead sheet. SASE. Reports in 1 month.
Music: Mostly **pop, country, R&B** and **MOR**; also **gospel**. Published *Old Age* and *Rose*, written and recorded by Mark Gibbs on Hillview Records; and *Area Code 502*, written and recorded by Adonis, on Estate Records.

JW ONE MUSIC PUBLISHING CO. (BMI), (formerly Jimmy Walton Music Publishing Co.), P.O. Box 218146, Nashville TN 37221-8146. (615)646-0506. Executive Producer: Jimmy Walton. Project Director: S. Hardesty. Music publisher, record company (Walton Record Productions) and record producer. Estab. 1992. Publishes 50-100 songs/year; publishes 40 new songwriters/year. Pays standard royalty.
How to Contact: Submit demo tape by mail. Unsolicited submissions are OK. Prefers cassette (or VHS videocassette if available) with 1-4 songs and lyric sheet. "Lyric sheets must be clearly printed." SASE. Reports in 1-8 weeks.
Music: Mostly **country ballads, new country/uptempo, pop/MOR, comedy, R&B, lite rock** and **modern gospel**. Published "My Heart Belongs to You" (by Jimmy Walton), recorded by Barry Russell; *Happy Poor Boys*, written and recorded by Jimmy Walton; and *Down In Louisiana* (by Ken Michaels), recorded by Wade McCurdy, all on Walton Record Productions.
Tips: "Submit a clear demo with typewritten lyric sheet. Keep your songs under 3 minutes."

KANSA RECORDS CORPORATION, P.O. Box 1878, Frisco TX 75034. (214)335-8004. Secretary and Treasurer/General Manager: Kit Johnson. Music publisher, record company and record producer. Estab. 1972. Publishes 50-60 songs/year; publishes 8-10 new songwriters/year. Pays standard royalty.
Affiliates: Great Leawood Music, Inc. (ASCAP) and Twinsong Music (BMI).
How to Contact: Submit demo tape by mail. Unsolicited submissions are OK. Prefers cassette with 4 songs and lyric sheet. SASE. Reports in 1 month.
Music: Mostly **country, MOR** and **country rock**; also **R&B** (leaning to country) and **Christian**. Published *I Miss You* (by K. Francisco) and *Playin' the Part of a Fool* (by P. Petersen/J. Peterson), both recorded by Glen Bailey; and *Out of Sight/Out of Mind* (by Geoffrey Jacobs), recorded by Jimmy Dallas, all on Kansa Records.

KAUPPS & ROBERT PUBLISHING CO. (BMI), P.O. Box 5474, Stockton CA 95205. (209)948-8186. Fax: (209)942-2163. President: Nancy L. Merrihew. Music publisher, record company (Kaupp Records), manager and booking agent (Merri-Webb Productions and Most Wanted Bookings). Estab. 1990. Publishes 15-20 songs/year; publishes 5 new songwriters/year. Pays standard royalty.

● Kaupps & Robert Publishing's record label, Kaupp Records, is listed in the Record Companies section and their management firm, Merri-Webb Productions, is in the Managers and Booking Agents section.

How to Contact: Write first and obtain permission to submit. Prefers cassette (or VHS videocassette if available) with 3 songs maximum and lyric sheet. "If artist, send PR package." SASE. Reports in 3 months.

Music: Mostly **country, R&B** and **A/C rock**; also **pop, rock** and **gospel**. Published "Freedom Bound" and "Kiss A Lot of Frogs" (by N. Merrihew), recorded by by Nanci Lynn (country); and "Mountain of Hurt" (by K. Birmingham/D.J. Birmingham), recorded by Birmingham Country, all on Kaupp Records.

Tips: "Know what you want, set a goal, focus in on your goals, be open to constructive criticism, polish tunes and keep polishing."

KAREN KAYLEE MUSIC GROUP (BMI), R.D. #11 Box 360, Greensburg PA 15601. (412)836-0966. President: Karen Kaylee. Music publisher. Estab. 1989. Publishes 15-20 songs/year; publishes 3 new songwriters/year. Pays standard royalty.

How to Contact: Submit demo tape by mail. Unsolicited submissions are OK; "serious submissions only." Prefers cassette (or VHS videocassette) with 3-5 songs and lyric sheet. "No phone calls please." SASE. Reports in 1 month.

Music: Mostly **country, gospel** and **traditional country**. Published "A Woman Steps Out," written and recorded by Carlene Haggerty; "My God," written and recorded by Matt Furin; and *Heading Back to the Country*, written and recorded by Karen Kaylee, all on Ka-De Records.

Tips: "Only submit professional packages on clear tapes, recorded on one side only. Must include SASE. No phone calls, please; submit by mail only."

KEL-CRES PUBLISHING (ASCAP), 2525 E. 12th St., Cheyenne WY 82001. (307)638-9894. A&R Manager: Gary J. Kelley. Music publisher, record company (Rough Cut Records and Chey-Town Records) and record producer. Estab. 1989. Publishes 2 songs/year. Pays standard royalty.

Affiliate(s): Kelley-Kool Music (BMI).

How to Contact: Submit demo tape by mail. Unsolicited submissions are OK. Prefers cassette, CD or DAT (or VHS videocassette) with 3 songs and lyric sheets. Guitar/piano demo with "words up front" is sufficient. SASE. Reports in 2 months.

Music: Mostly **rock, '50s-'60s, country** and **rockabilly**. Published *What About You*, (by Mark Gibbs); *I Like It A Lot* (by Mark Gibbs); and *Rayann* (by Tim Anderson), all recorded by Lug Nut and the Spare Tires on Chey-Town Records.

Tips: "Keep songs simple, very few lyrics with strong repeated 'hook-line.' Can a stranger hum your tune after hearing it?"

*ROBERT KELLY ENTERTAINMENT (BMI), P.O. Box 3660, Moscow ID 83843-1915. (208)883-3027. E-mail: kell9441@uidaho.edu. Proprietor: Robert Kelly. Music publisher. Estab. 1986. Publishes 3 songs/year. Pays standard royalty.

Affiliate(s): Sun Basin Music (BMI) and Lapiz Lazule Productions.

How to Contact: Submit demo tape by mail. Unsolicited submissions are OK. Prefers cassette with any number of songs and lyric sheet. "We would also like to see the lead sheet if you have it, but it is not required." Does not return submissions. Reports in 10 weeks.

Music: Mostly **hip-hop, techno-pop** and **house**; also **rock, country** and **jazz**. Published *Sundial* (by Eric Lichter), recorded by Month of Sundays (rock); "You Must've Read My Mind," written and recorded by Jim Leary (AOR); and "Heart and Soul," written and recorded by Karen Ivonne (AOR).

Tips: "Be a virtuoso. You do not need to be complicated. Deliver with sincerity and enthusiasm."

KENO PUBLISHING (BMI), P.O. Box 4429, Austin TX 78765-4429. (512)441-2422. Fax: (512)441-7072. Owner: Keith A. Ayres. Music publisher and record company (Glitch Records). Estab. 1984. Publishes 12 songs/year; publishes 10 new songwriters/year. Pays standard royalty.

How to Contact: Write first and obtain permission to submit a tape. Prefers cassette (and/or VHS videocassette if available) with 2-3 songs and lyric or lead sheets. Does not return material.

Music: **Rock, rap, reggae** and **pop**; also **metal, R&B** and **alternative** (all types). Published "I Wrote the Note" (by George Alistair Sanger), recorded by European Sex Machine (computerized); "Here It Is" (by John Patterson), recorded by Cooly Girls (rap); and "Kick'em in the Ass" (by Los Deflectors/Keith Ayres), recorded by Ron Rogers (rock), all on Glitch Records.

*KIDSOURCE PUBLISHING (BMI), 1324 Oakton, Evanston IL 60202. (708)328-4203. Fax: (708)328-4236. Contact: Alan Goldberg. Music publisher. Estab. 1994. Publishes 12 songs/year; publishes 1-3 new songwriters/year. Pays standard royalty.
Affiliate(s): Grooveland Music (ASCAP), Hitsource Publishing (BMI).
How to Contact: Write or call first and obtain permission to submit a demo. Prefers cassette with 3 songs and lyric sheet. SASE. Reports in 1-3 months.
Music: Mostly **children's music**. Published *Songs for Safe And Secure Children* (by Bob Gibson/Rich Hudson), recorded by Bob Gibson.

KILOWATT MUSIC. P.O. Box 3751, Austin TX 78764. (512)480-8041. President: William Jones. Music publisher and record company (Lectro-Fine Records). Estab. 1984. Pays negotiable royalty.
How to Contact: Submit demo tape by mail. Unsolicited submissions are OK. Prefers cassette. Does not return material. Reports in 4-6 weeks.
Music: Mostly **blues, ballads** and **roots rock**. Published *Blue Monday Live*, written and recorded by Kathy Murray & The Kilowatts on Lectro-Fine Records (Texas R&B); "Spell It Out"/"Soul Shake," written and recorded by Kathy Murray & The Kilowatts on Atomic Jukebox Records (Texas R&B); and *Daughters of Texas*, written and recorded by various artists on Magnum Records (Texas R&B).
Tips: "Being based in Austin, Texas allows us to reach a variety of artists ready for fresh material."

KINGSPORT CREEK MUSIC PUBLISHING (BMI), P.O. Box 6085, Burbank CA 91510. Contact: Vice President. Music publisher and record company (Cowgirl Records). Estab. 1980. Pays standard royalty.
  ● Kingsport Creek's record label, Cowgirl Records, is listed in the Record Companies section.
How to Contact: Submit demo tape by mail. Unsolicited submissions are OK. Prefers cassette (or VHS videocassette) with any number of songs and lyric sheet. Does not return unsolicited material. "Include photos and bio if possible."
Music: Mostly **country** and **gospel**; also **R&B** and **MOR**. Published "Who Am I," "Golden Wedding Ring" and "Let's Give Love," all written and recorded by Melvena Kaye on Cowgirl Records.
Tips: "Videocassettes are advantageous."

*KIRCHSTEIN PUBLISHING CO. (BMI), 3830 Hwy. 78, Mt. Horeb WI 53572. (608)439-8970. Fax: (608)437-4362. President: Jim Kirchstein. Music publisher, record company (Cuca/AMC), record producer. Estab. 1960. Publishes 10 songs/year; publishes 3 new songwriters/year. Pays standard royalty.
Affiliate(s): Seven Sounds Publishing (ASCAP).
How to Contact: Write first and obtain permission to submit a demo. Prefers cassette. Does not return material. Reports in 3 weeks.
Music: Mostly **R&B, ethnic, country**; also **folk, rock**. Published *Spring* (by Banks), recorded by Birdlegs (R&B); and *In So Many Ways* (by Banks), recorded by Pauline, both on Cuca Records.

KOMMUNICATION KONCEPTS, Dept. SM, Box 2095, Philadelphia PA 19103. (215)848-8474. President: S. Deane Henderson. Music publisher and management firm. Publishes 10-15 songs/year; publishes 6 new songwriters/year. Pays standard royalty.
Affiliate(s): Lions Den (ASCAP).
How to Contact: Prefers cassette (or VHS videocassette) with 4-8 songs and lyric sheets. Does not return unsolicited material. Reports in 2 weeks.
Music: **Dance-oriented, easy listening, gospel** and **MOR**; also **R&B, rock, soul, top 40/pop, funk** and **heavy metal**. Published "Monica, Brenda and Lisa," recorded by Helen McCormick; "Hot Number" (by John Fitch), recorded by The Racers (heavy rock); and "In God's Hand" (by Verdelle C. Bryant), recorded by Verdelle & Off Spring Gospel Singers (gospel).
Tips: "We're currently looking for female and male gospel groups."

KOZKEEOZKO MUSIC (ASCAP), 928 Broadway, Suite 602, New York NY 10010. (212)505-7332. Professional Managers: Ted Lehrman and Libby Bush. Music publisher, record producer and management firm (Landslide Management). Estab. 1978. Publishes 5 songs/year; publishes 3 new songwriters/year. Pays standard royalty.
How to Contact: Write or call first and obtain permission to submit. Prefers cassette (or VHS ½″ videocassette) with 2 songs maximum and typewritten lyric sheet for each song. SASE. Reports in 6 weeks.
Music: Mostly **soul/pop, dance, pop/rock** (no heavy metal), **A/C** and **country**. Published "Ain't No Cure For You" (by Ed Chalfin and Tedd Lawson), recorded by Roger Clinton on Pyramid Records; "Ride This Wave" (by Ed Chalfin and Tedd Lawson), recorded by Carol Williams on ZYX Records; and "Music to My Eyes" (by Ed Chalfin and Tedd Lawson), recorded by Jam Box (soul) on Jam Box Records.

Tips: "Send unique, well-crafted, today songs on great demos."

KRUDE TOONZ MUSIC (ASCAP), P.O. Box 308, Lansdale PA 19446. (215)855-8628. President: G. Malack. Music publisher. Estab. 1988. Pays standard royalty.
Affiliate(s): Teeze Me Pleeze Me Music (ASCAP).
How to Contact: Submit demo tape by mail. Unsolicited submissions are OK. Prefers cassette (or VHS videocassette if available) with 3 songs, bio and picture. SASE. "Do not call."
Music: Country, ballads and **alternative**. "Anything with a great hook." Published "Tonight," "Fantasy" and "Love Or Lust" (by G. Malack), recorded by Roughhouse on CBS Records (rock).

KWAZ SONG MUSIC (SOCAN), 2305 Vista Court, Coquitlam British Columbia V3J 6W2 **Canada.** (604)202-3644. Fax: (604)469-9359. E-mail: ksmrecords@infomatch.com. Contact: David London. Music publisher and record company (KSM Records). Estab. 1991. Pays standard royalty.
  • Kwaz Song's record label, KSM Records, is listed in the Record Companies section.
How to Contact: Submit demo tape by mail. Unsolicited submissions are OK. Prefers cassette, VHS videocassette, CDs, press material with 2 songs and lyric sheet. Does not return material. Reports in 1 month.
Music: Mostly **Gothic rock, techno (all types)** and **electronic**; **experimental** and **avante-garde**. Published "Angelic" (by Chad Bishop), recorded by Idiot Stare; and "Guilt" (by Andrew Amy/David Collings), recorded by Fourthman, all on KSM Records.

*LARGO MUSIC PUBLISHING (ASCAP, BMI), 425 Park Ave., New York NY 10022. (212)756-5080. Fax: (212)207-8167. Creative Manager: Peter Oriol. Music publisher. Estab. 1980. Pays variable royalty.
Affiliate(s): Catharine Hiren Music, American Compass Music Corp., Diplomat Music Corp., Larry Shayne Enterprises (ASCAP), Largo Cargo Music (BMI).
How to Contact: Submit demo tape by mail. Unsolicited submissions are OK. Prefers cassette or CD with 4 songs and lyric sheet. "Spend money on recording well, not packaging." Does not return submissions. Reports in 2-4 weeks.
Music: Mostly **alternative rock, AOR** and **adult alternative**; "good music that transcends categories." Published "Crazy Crazy Nights," "Little Caesar" and "I'll Fight Like Hell to Hold You" (by Adam Mitchell), all recorded by KISS on Polygram Records (hard rock).
Tips: "Good songs are not enough—you must be a complete artist and writer."

LARI-JON PUBLISHING (BMI), 325 W. Walnut, Rising City NE 68658. (402)542-2336. Owner: Larry Good. Music publisher, record company (Lari-Jon Records) and record producer (Lari Jon Productions). Estab. 1967. Publishes 20 songs/year; publishes 2-3 new songwriters/year. Pays standard royalty.
  • See the listings for Lari-Jon Records in the Record Companies section, Lari-Jon Productions in the Record Producers section and Lari-Jon Promotions in the Managers and Booking Agents section.
How to Contact: Submit a demo tape by mail. Unsolicited submissions are OK. Prefers cassette with 5 songs and lyric sheet. "Be professional." SASE. Reports in 2 months.
Music: Mostly **country, Southern gospel** and **'50s rock**. Published "Glory Bound Train," written and recorded by Tom Campbell; "Nebraskaland," written and recorded by Larry Good; and *Her Favorite Song*, written and recorded by Johnny Nace, all on Lari-Jon Records.

*LAST BRAIN CELL (BMI), P.O. Box 1750, Santa Rosa Beach FL 32459. (904)864-7835. Owner: Christine R. Puccia. Music publisher. Estab. 1993. Pays standard royalty.
How to Contact: Submit demo tape by mail. Unsolicited submissions are OK. Prefers cassette with 4 songs and lyric sheet. Include résumé and picture. SASE. Reports in 1-2 weeks.
Music: Mostly **alternative, R&B** and **rock**; also **blues, gospel** and **country**. Published "No Children Here," written and recorded by Christine R. Puccia.

*LATIN AMERICAN MUSIC CO., INC., P.O. Box 1844, Cathedral Station, New York NY 10025. (212)993-5557. Fax: (212)993-5551. Contact: D. Vera. Music Publisher. Estab. 1970. Publishes 20 songs/year; publishes 5 new songwriters/year. Pays standard royalty.

HOW TO GET THE MOST out of *Songwriter's Market* (at the front of this book) contains comments and suggestions to help you understand and use the information in these listings.

Affiliates: The International Music Co.
How to Contact: Submit demo tape by mail. Unsolicited submissions are OK. Prefers cassette. Does not return material. Reports in 3 months.
Music: Mostly **Latin American**; also **reggae**. Published "Anacaona," recorded by the Cheo Feliciano; and "Que te peoli," recorded by La Lupe; both written by Tite Curet.

LAURMACK MUSIC (ASCAP), 655 Wyona St., Brooklyn NY 11207. (718)272-1200. Fax: (718)649-1280. President: Alfred McCarther. Music publisher and record company (Alcarm Records). Estab. 1981. Hires staff songwriters. Pays standard royalty.
How to Contact: Submit demo tape by mail. Unsolicited submissions are OK. Prefers cassette (or VHS videocassette) with 3 songs and lyric sheet. SASE. Reports in 3 weeks to 3 months.
Music: Mostly **R&B**, **pop**, **rap** and **hip hop**; also **jazz**, **gospel** and **country**. Published "Teach Them" (by Michael Augustus), recorded by Tony Gee (pop); and *Get Ready Devil It's Your Turn* (by James Spencer), recorded by Your Brother (rap), both on Alcarm Records.

LCS MUSIC GROUP, INC. (BMI, ASCAP, SESAC), 6301 N. O'Connor Blvd., The Studios of Las Colinas, Irving TX 75039. (214)869-0700. Contact: Publishing Assistant. Music publisher. Pays standard royalty.
Affiliate(s): Bug and Bear Music (ASCAP), Chris Christian Music (BMI), Court and Case Music (ASCAP), Home Sweet Home Music (ASCAP), Monk and Tid Music (SESAC), Preston Christian Music (BMI).
How to Contact: Submit demo tape by mail. Unsolicited submissions are OK. Prefers cassette (lyric sheet is only necessary if the words are difficult to understand). "Put all pertinent information on the tape itself, such as how to contact the writer. Do not send Express!" Does not return material. Reports in 4-6 months.
Music: Mostly **contemporary Christian** and **inspirational**. Published "Touch," written and recorded by Eric Champion on Myrrh Records; "You Were Always There" (by Joe Ninowski/Jeff Smith), recorded by Jeff Smith on Myrrh Records; and "The Me Nobody Knows" (by Vincent Grimes), recorded by Marilyn McCoo on Warner Alliance Records.
Tips: "Listen to the cutting edge of whatever style you write—don't get caught in a rut stylistically."

LILLY MUSIC PUBLISHING (SOCAN), 61 Euphrasia Dr., Toronto, Ontario M6B 3V8 **Canada**. (416)782-5768. Fax: (416)782-7170. President: Panfilo DiMatteo. Music publisher and record company (P. & N. Records). Estab. 1992. Publishes 20 songs/year; publishes 8 new songwriters/year. Pays standard royalty.
Affiliate(s): San Martino Music Publishing, Paglieta Music Publishing (CMRRA).
● Lilly Music's record label, P. & N. Records, is listed in the Record Companies section.
How to Contact: Submit demo tape by mail. Unsolicited submissions are OK. Prefers cassette (or videocassette if available) with 3 songs and lyric and lead sheets. "We will contact you only if we are interested in the material." Does not return material. Reports in 1 month.
Music: Mostly **dance**, **ballads** and **rock**; also **country**. Published *My Life* and *Tonight* (by Marco A. Gomes), recorded by Riga; and *Kinta*, written and recorded by Janet Di Matteo, all on P. & N. Records.

DORIS LINDSAY PUBLISHING (ASCAP), P.O. Box 35005, Greensboro NC 27425. (910)882-9990. President: Doris Lindsay. Music publisher and record company (Fountain Records). Estab. 1979. Publishes 20 songs/year; publishes 4 songwriters/year. Pays standard royalty.
Affiliate(s): Better Times Publishing (BMI) and Doris Lindsay Publishing (ASCAP).
● Doris Lindsay Publishing's record label, Fountain Records, is listed in the Record Companies section.
How to Contact: Submit demo tape by mail. Unsolicited submissions are OK. Prefers cassette with 2 songs. "Submit good quality demos." SASE. Reports in 2 months.
Music: Mostly **country**, **pop** and **contemporary gospel**. Published *Service Station Cowboy* (by Hoss Ryder), recorded by Ace Diamond on Sabre Records; "Amusin' Cruisin';" by Susan and Frank Rosario; and "America's Song" (by Cathy Roeder), recorded by Terry Michaels, both on Fountain Records.
Tips: "Present a good quality demo (recorded in a studio). Positive clean lyrics and up-tempo music are easiest to place."

LINEAGE PUBLISHING CO. (BMI), P.O. Box 211, East Prairie MO 63845. (314)649-2211. Professional Manager: Tommy Loomas. Staff: Alan Carter and Joe Silver. Music publisher, record producer and record company (Capstan Record Production). Pays standard royalty.
● Lineage Publishing's record label, Capstan Record Production, is listed in the Record Companies section and Staircase Promotions is listed in the Managers and Booking Agents section.

How to Contact: Submit demo tape by mail. Unsolicited submissions are OK. Prefers cassette with 2-4 songs and lyric sheet; include bio and photo if possible. SASE. Reports in 1-2 months.
Music: Country, easy listening, MOR, country rock and **top 40/pop**. Published "Let It Rain" (by Roberta Boyle), recorded by Vicarie Arcoleo on Treasure Coast Records; "Country Boy," written and recorded by Roger Lambert; and "Boot Jack Shuffle" (by Zachary Taylor), recorded by Skid Row Joe, both on Capstan Records.

LIN'S LINES (ASCAP), 156 Fifth Ave., #434, New York NY 10010. (212)691-5631. President: Linda K. Jacobson. Music publisher. Estab. 1978. Publishes 4 songs/year; publishes 4 new songwriters/year. Pays standard royalty.
How to Contact: Submit a demo tape by mail. Unsolicited submissions are OK. Prefers cassette or VHS or ¾″ videocassette with 3-5 songs and lyric or lead sheet. SASE. Reports in 6 weeks.
Music: Mostly **rock, pop** and **rap**; also **world music, R&B** and **gospel**.

LION HILL MUSIC PUBLISHING CO. (BMI), P.O. Box 110983, Nashville TN 37222-0983. (615)731-6640. Fax: (615)731-9147. Publisher: Wayne G. Leinsz. Music publisher, record company (Richway Records). Estab. 1988. Publishes 40-50 songs/year; publishes a few new songwriters/year. Pays standard royalty.
  • See the listing for Richway Records in the Record Companies section.
How to Contact: Submit demo tape by mail. Unsolicited submissions are OK. Prefers cassette with 3 songs and lead sheets. SASE. Reports in 2 weeks.
Music: Mostly **country**; also **gospel** and **bluegrass**. Published "Put Me in Prison" (by Ray Sanders/Bill Armocida), recorded by Ray Sanders; "The Bigger The Fool" (by Suzi Conn), recorded by Debbie Davis; and "Fire in the Bottle" (by Richard Madison), recorded by Bobby Atkins, all on Richway Records.

LONNY TUNES MUSIC (BMI), P.O. Box 460086, Garland TX 75046. President: Lonny Schonfeld. Music publisher, record company (Lonny Tunes Records) and record producer. Estab. 1988. Publishes 8-10 songs/year; publishes 2-3 new songwriters/year. Pays standard royalty.
  • See their listing in the Record Companies section, as well as the listing for Lonny Schonfeld
    and Associates in the Managers and Booking Agents section.
How to Contact: Submit a demo tape by mail. Unsolicited submissions are OK. Prefers cassette with 3-5 songs and lyric sheet. "Professional quality only." Does not return unsolicited submissions. Reports in 6-8 weeks.
Music: Mostly **country, children's** and **rock**; also **jazz** and **comedy**. Published "Baby With You," written and recorded by Randy Stout; "One Word Question" (by L. Schonfeld), recorded by David Wilson (pop); and *James Blonde-006.95* (by Marty Brill), recorded by various (comedy), all on Lonny Tunes Records.
Tips: "Make sure your lyrical content is contemporary. 'Old time' rhymes like moon and June will not work for us."

LOUX MUSIC CO. & DOVEHOUSE EDITIONS (ASCAP), 2 Hawley Lane, Hannacroix NY 12087-0034. (518)756-2273. Contact: Editorial Review Committee. Music publisher. Estab. 1984. Publishes 12 pieces/year; mostly individual songs, folios or educational material. Publishes 3 new songwriters/year. Pays 5% royalty.
How to Contact: Write first and obtain permission to submit a demo. Prefers manuscript and audio tape. "Write for manuscript preparation guidelines." SASE. Reports in 6 months.
Music: Mostly **music for recorder, viol, flute, violin, small chamber group**; also **pro musica** and **modern**. Published "Duetto in D Minor for Two Viols," by Christoph Schaffrath, edited by Lynn Tetenbaum and Donald Beecher; "Recorder Studios, 4," by Stephan Chandler, and "Discorsi Musicale," by Mary Mageau.

LOVEY MUSIC, INC. (BMI), P.O. Box 630755, Miami FL 33163. (305)935-4880. President: Jack Gale. Music publisher. Estab. 1981. Publishes 25 songs/year; publishes 10 new songwriters/year. Pays standard royalty.

REMEMBER: Don't "shotgun" your demo tapes. Submit only to companies interested in the type of music you write. For more submission hints, refer to Getting Started on page 5.

Affiliate(s): Cowabonga Music, Inc. (ASCAP).
  ● See the listings for Playback Records in the Record Companies section and Jack Gale in the Record Producers section.
How to Contact: Submit demo tape by mail. Unsolicited submissions are OK. Prefers cassette or VHS videocassette with 2 songs max and lyric sheets. Does not return material. Reports in 2 weeks if interested.
Music: Mostly **country crossover** and **country**. Published *Angel In Disguise* (by Scheder/Turney), recorded by Tommy Cash (country); *Second Time Around* (by Rocky Priola), recorded by Del Reeves (country); and "When They Ring Those Golden Bells," written and recorded by Charlie Louvin (country), all on Playback Records.

HAROLD LUICK & ASSOCIATES MUSIC PUBLISHER (BMI), P.O. Box B, Carlisle IA 50047. (515)989-3748. President: Harold L. Luick. Music publisher, record company, record producer and music industry consultant. Publishes 25-30 songs/year; publishes 5-10 new songwriters/year. Pays standard royalty.
How to Contact: Write or call first about your interest. Prefers cassette with 3-5 songs and lyric sheet. SASE. Reports in 1 month.
  ● Harold Luick & Associates also has a listing in the Record Producers section.
Music: Traditional country and **hard core country**. Published "Mrs. Used To Be," written and recorded by Joe E. Harris on River City Music Records (country); and "Ballad of Deadwood S.P.," written and recorded by Don Laughlin on Kajac Records (historical country).
Tips: "Being successful in the music world is not based on luck alone. It is based on being prepared, educated and knowledgeable when luck does come along . . . so if you have been unlucky in the past, maybe you have just been unprepared!"

M & T WALDOCH PUBLISHING, INC. (BMI), 4803 S. Seventh St., Milwaukee WI 53221. (414)482-2194. VP, Creative Management: Timothy J. Waldoch. Music publisher. Estab. 1990. Publishes 2-3 songs/year; publishes 2-3 new songwriters/year. Pays standard royalty.
How to Contact: Submit demo tape by mail. Unsolicited submissions are OK. Prefers cassette with 3-6 songs and lyric or lead sheet. "We prefer a studio produced demo tape." SASE. Reports in 2-3 months.
Music: Mostly **country/pop**, **rock**, **top 40 pop**; also **melodic metal**, **dance**, **R&B**. Published "It's Only Me" and "Let Peace Rule the World" (by Kenny LePrix), recorded by Brigade on SBD Records (rock).

McCARTNEY MUSIC (BMI), 1610 Division St. #103, Nashville TN 37212. (615)399-0149. Fax: (615)399-0248. E-mail: merlin@edge.net or AriesM@aol.com. Website: http://www.edge.net/mccart-ney. A&R Dept: Angie Antonecci. Music publisher. Estab. 1986. Publishes 10 songs/year; publishes 2-4 new songwriters/year. Pays standard royalty.
How to Contact: Submit demo tape by mail. Unsolicited submissions are OK. Prefers cassette or DAT with 3 songs and lyric sheet. Does not return material. Reports in 6-8 weeks.
Music: Mostly **European style pop** and **country**; also **New Age** and **instrumental**. Published "Rain Dance" (by Nethercutt/McCartney), recorded by Martin Nethercutt on Phantom Records (rock); "Cigarette in the Rain" (by Ruth McCartney/Barry Coffing), recorded by Randy Crawford on Warner Brothers Records (R&B ballad); and "Spirit Worlds," written and recorded by Martin Nethercutt on Phantom Records (AOR).
Tips: "Be specific about your style and always write your phone number on your cassette."

JIM McCOY MUSIC (BMI), Rt. 2, Box 114, Berkeley Springs WV 25411. Owners: Bertha and Jim McCoy. Music publisher, record company (Winchester Records) and record producer (Jim McCoy Productions). Estab. 1973. Publishes 20 songs/year; publishes 3-5 new songwriters/year. Pays standard royalty.
Affiliate(s): New Edition Music (BMI).
  ● See the listings for Winchester Records in the Record Companies section and Jim McCoy Productions in the Record Producers section.
How to Contact: Write first and obtain permission to submit. Prefers cassette, 7½ or 15 ips reel-to-reel (or VHS or Beta videocassette) with 6 songs. SASE. Reports in 1 month.
Music: Mostly **country**, **country/rock** and **rock**; also **bluegrass** and **gospel**. Published "I'm Getting Nowhere," written and recorded by J.B. Miller on Hilton Records; "One More Time" (by S. Howard), recorded by Carl Howard and *Touching Your Heart*, written and recorded by Jim McCoy, both on Winchester Records.

McGIBONY PUBLISHING, 203 Mission Rdg. Rd., Rossville GA 30741. (706)861-2186. Fax: (706)866-2593. Music Publisher: Richard McGibony. Music publisher, record company (R.R. & R.

Music) and record producer. Estab. 1986. Publishes 20 songs/year; publishes 10-15 new songwriters/year. Pays standard royalty.
Affiliate(s): Sounds of Aicram (BMI), R.D. Wheeler, Music Publisher.
How to Contact: Write or call first and obtain permission to submit. Prefers cassette (or VHS videocassette if available) with 2 songs and lyric sheet. "Have a clear understandable tape with legible lyric sheets." SASE. Reports in 4-6 weeks.
Music: Mostly **country, gospel** and **R&B**. Published "The Aftershock Is Shocking" (by Shoron/Corey), recorded by Billy James (country rock); "A Big Smokin' Gun" (by R. McGibony), recorded by Hilda Gonzalez, both on Trend Records; and *Legends Never Die*, recorded by Billy James on J.P. Records (country rock).
Tips: "Present a good demo. Don't just throw something together. The competition is fierce."

DANNY MACK MUSIC, 3484 Nicolette Dr., Crete IL 60417. (708)672-6457. General Manager: Col. Danny Mack. Music publisher and independent record producer. Estab. 1984. Publishes 1-8 songs/year. Pays standard royalty.
Affiliate(s): Syntony Publishing (BMI), Briarhill Records.
• Danny Mack's record label, Briarhill Records, is listed in the Record Companies section.
How to Contact: Submit demo tape by mail. Unsolicited submissions are OK. Prefers cassette or phono records with no more than 4 songs and typed lyric sheets. SASE. Reports in 3-4 weeks.
Music: Mostly **country, gospel (southern/country)** and **polka**. Published *Country Love Song* (by Jim Garrison) and *I'm Coming Home To Be with You* (by Forrest Hendrick), both recorded by Danny Mack on Briarhill Records; and *No More Rocky Roads* (by Danny Mack), recorded by Tony Ansems on Tar Heel Records.
Tips: "Patience is a virtue. Since we will return songs to writers after 24 months if we haven't got a commercial release, persistent phone calls as to the song's status is bothersome, annoying and expensive. You'll be the first to know if something is happening."

MACMAN MUSIC, INC. (ASCAP, BMI), 10 NW Sixth Ave., Portland OR 97209. (503)221-0288. Fax: (503)227-4418. Secretary: David Leiken. Music publisher and record producer. ASCAP, BMI. Estab. 1980. Publishes 8-10 songs/year; publishes 1-2 new songwriters/year. Pays "deal by deal."
Affiliate(s): Fresh Force Music, Inc.
How to Contact: Submit a demo tape by mail. Unsolicited submissions are OK. Prefers cassette with lyric sheet. Does not return material. Reports "only if we are interested."
Music: Mostly **R&B, blues/rock** and **rock**. Published *If You Were Mine* (by Larry Bell), recorded by U-Krew on Enigma/Capitol Records (rap/funk); *Corbin's Place*, written and recorded by Dennis Springer on Nastymix Records; and *I Shouted Your Name* (by Marlon McClain), recorded by Curtis Salgardo on BFE/JRS Records.

*MAGIC MESSAGE MUSIC (ASCAP), P.O. Box 9117, Truckee CA 96162. (916)587-0111. Owner: Alan Redstone. Music publisher and record company (Sureshot Records). Estab. 1979. Publishes 6 songs/year; publishes 1 new songwriter/year. Pays standard royalty.
How to Contact: Call first and obtain permission to submit. SASE. Reports in 2 weeks.
Music: Mostly **country, ballads** and **rock**. Published "Emily," "Girls" and "For Yesterday," all written and recorded by Alan Redstone on Sureshot Records (country rock).

MAJESTIC CONTROL (BMI), 221 W. 57th St., 8th Floor, New York NY 10019. (212)489-1500. CEO: Half Pint. President: Tatiana. Music publisher, promotions and public relations. Estab. 1983.
• Majestic Control's record label, Pirate Records, is listed in the Record Companies section.
How to Contact: Submit demo tape by mail. Unsolicited submissions are OK. Prefers cassette with 3 songs. SASE. Reports in 8 weeks.
Music: Mostly **rap** and **R&B**. Artists include Stik-E and the Hoods, and Kamakaze.

MAKERS MARK GOLD (ASCAP), 3033 W. Redner St., Philadelphia PA 19121. (215)236-4817. Producer: Paul Hopkins. Music publisher and record producer. Estab. 1991. Pays standard royalty.
• See the listing for Makers Mark Music Productions in the Record Producers section.
How to Contact: Submit demo tape by mail. Unsolicited submissions are OK. Prefers cassette with 2-4 songs. Does not return material. Reports in 4-6 weeks if interested.
Music: Mostly **R&B, hip hop, gospel, pop, country** and **house**. Published "Last Kiss," "When Will My Heart Beat Again" and "Top of the World" (by C. Foreman/P. Hopkins), all recorded by Rachel Scarborough on Prolific Records.
Tips: "Be very persistent in submitting your material, because you never know what song in the right hands can do. It only takes one song to make you a megastar. You could be next!"

MANNY MUSIC, INC., 2035 Pleasanton Rd., San Antonio TX 78221-1306. (210)924-2224. Fax: (210)924-3338. E-mail: tejano@icsi.net. Website: http://www.ondanet.com:1995/Manny/manny.html.

Publishing Dept.: Pete Rodriguez. Music publisher, record company (Manny Records, AMS Records). Estab. 1963. Publishes 2-3 new songwriters/year. Pays standard royalty.
Affiliate(s): Rosman Music (ASCAP), Texas Latino (SESAC), Manny Music (BMI).
• See their listing in the Record Companies section.
How to Contact: Submit demo tape by mail. Unsolicited submissions are OK. Prefers cassette and lyric sheet. "Allow three to four weeks before calling to inquire about prior submission." SASE. Reports in 12-18 weeks.
Music: Mostly **Spanish**, **Tejano** or **Tex-Mex** and **C&W**; also **Spanish gospel**, **ballads** and **tropical/ Caribbean/South American rhythms**. Published *Besame* (by Luiz Ortiz), recorded by Los Traiteros on Fonovision Records (Tex Mex); *Contigo Quiero Estar* (by Alex Montez), recorded by Pete Astudillo on EMI Records (cumbia); and *Que Me Has Hecho Tu* (by Jaime Farias), recorded by La Tropa F on Manny/WEA Records (Spanish).
Tips: "Songs should have a good storyline; good punchline; the melody must have a quality that can be expressed in different rhythms and still sound 'original'."

ROD MARTIN'S MUSIC PUBLISHING (BMI), 3585 Pinao St., Honolulu HI 96822. (808)988-4859. Director: Rod Martin. Music publisher. Estab. 1992. Publishes 20-40 songs/year. Pays standard royalty with a non-exclusive agreement.
Affiliate(s): Haku Mele (Songwriter) Records.
How to Contact: Submit demo tape by mail. Unsolicited submissions are OK. Prefers high bias cassette with 3-6 songs and lyric sheet. SASE. Reports in 3 weeks.
Music: Mostly **folk**, **pop**, **comedy**, **rock**, **blues** and **instrumentals**. Published *More Than Music . . .* an album of love songs on Haku Mele Records; "Hobo Road" and "So Long," both by Stephen Goldman.
Tips: "If you can't sing, let someone else. I offer constructive comments, not form letters. I also enjoy working to improve songs with artists interested in collaborating."

THE MATHES COMPANY, P.O. Box 22653, Nashville TN 37202. (615)252-6912. E-mail: infobox @gate.net box101010. Website: http://www.gate.net./~infobox102500. Owner: David W. Mathes. Music publisher, record company (Star Image, Heirborn, Kingdom), record producer and music industry consultant. Estab. 1962. Publishes 10-30 new songwriters/year. Pays standard royalty.
Affiliate(s): Sweet Singer Music (BMI), Sing Sweeter Music (ASCAP) and Star of David (SESAC).
• The Mathes Company is also listed in the Record Companies section, and David Mathes Productions is listed in the Record Producers section.
How to Contact: Submit a demo tape by mail. Unsolicited submissions are OK. "Registered or certified mail refused." Prefers cassette with maximum of 3 songs and lyric sheet. "Only positive country songs (not controversial, political, demeaning or sex oriented). Only gospel songs that are not rock contemporary, and no New Age music." SASE. Reports in 1 month.
Music: Mostly **gospel (country)**, **country** and **instrumental**; also **jingle ideas**. Published *My Love For You* (by DeAnna and David Mathes), recorded by Warner Mack on Sapphire Records (country); *My Ole Guitar*, written and recorded by Gene Taylor on Music of America Records (country); and *I Can't Wait To Get To Heaven* (by Cherie Mullins), recorded by The Mullins on Canadian Records.
Tips: "Have fresh ideas, current song structure, no outdated clichés. Good demos (not done by song mills)."

MCA MUSIC PUBLISHING (ASCAP), 2440 Sepulveda Blvd., Suite 100, Los Angeles CA 90064-1712. (310)235-4700. Fax: (310)235-4901. President: David Renzer. Executive Vice President: John Alexander. Music publisher. Estab. 1964. "The MCA catalog contains over 100,000 copyrights." Hires staff songwriters.
Affiliate(s): Music Corporation of America (BMI) and Musicor (SESAC).
• See the interview with Executive Vice President of Creative Services John Alexander in the 1996 *Songwriter's Market*.
How to Contact: Write first and obtain permission to submit. Prefers cassette. SASE.
Music: Mostly **popular**. Published "Livin On The Edge" (by Mark Hudson), recorded by Aerosmith on Geffen Records (rock); "Run To You" (by Allan Rich), recorded by Whitney Houston on Arista Records (pop); and "Insane In The Brain" (by D.J. Muggs), recorded by Cypress Hill on Columbia Records (rap).

MENTO MUSIC GROUP, Box 20 33 12, D-20223 Hamburg **Germany**. Branch: Eppendorfer Weg 7, D-20259, Hamburg **Germany**. General Manager: Arno H. Van Vught. Music publisher and record company. Pays standard royalty.
Affiliate(s): Auteursunie, Edition Lamplight, Edition Melodisc, Massimo Jauch Music Productions, Marathon Music.
• See the listing for Playbones Records in the Record Companies section.

How to Contact: Submit demo tape by mail. Unsolicited submissions are OK. Prefers cassette. SAE and IRC. Reports in 2 weeks.
Music: Mostly **instrumental**, **pop**, **MOR**, **country**, **background music** and **film music**. Published *Anytime and Anywhere* (by Massimo-Jauch/Raschner) and *Rodeo 93* (by Massimo-Jauch), both recorded by Stephan Massimo on EMI Records (pop); and *Fusión*, written and recorded by Jan Hengmith on Acoustic Music (flamenco).

MERRY MARILYN MUSIC PUBLISHING (BMI), 33717 View Crest Dr., Lake Elsinore CA 92532. (909)245-2763. Owner: Marilyn Hendricks. Music publisher. Estab. 1980. Publishes 10-15 songs/year; publishes 3-4 new songwriters/year. Pays standard royalty.
How to Contact: Submit demo tape by mail. Unsolicited submissions are OK. No more than 2 songs per submission. "Submit complete songs only. No lyrics without music." SASE. Reports in 1-3 months (depending on volume of submissions).
Music: Mostly **country** and **MOR**. Published "This New Life She's Living," and "Sittin' Pretty" (by J. Hendricks); and *This Old Dog* (by J. Hendricks), recorded by Don Tucker on Allgheny Records.
Tips: "Write a *great* song! Something fresh and new!"

MIGHTY TWINNS MUSIC (BMI), 9134 S. Indiana Ave., Chicago IL 60619. (312)737-4348. General Manager: Ron Scott. Music publisher and record producer. Member NMPA, Midwest Inspirational Writers Association. Estab. 1977. Publishes 4-10 songs/year; publishes 5 new songwriters/year. Pays standard royalty.
How to Contact: Submit demo tape by mail. Unsolicited submissions are OK. Prefers cassette with 2-4 songs and lyric sheet. Does not return material. Reports in 2 months.
Music: Mostly **top 40**, **R&B**, **"hot" inspirational** and **gospel**; also **children's**. Published "Steady" and "Reality" (by Chuck Chu), recorded by MTM (reggae); and "Finders Keepers" (by Betty Ober), recorded by Kookie Scott (country).
Tips: Looking for "good hot songs with hot hooks. Please have tapes cued up. *Do not write for permission!* Submit a cued up cassette and wait for our response. No materials returned without proper postage. Take the time to write and re-write to get the song in its best form; then make a good clear/audible demo."

*JODY MILLER MUSIC (BMI), P.O. Box 413, Blanchard OK 73010. Phone/fax: (405)485-3836. President: Jody Miller. Music publisher and record company (Nustar). Estab. 1981. Pays standard royalty.
Affiliate(s): Myrna Joy Music (ASCAP).
How to Contact: Prefers cassette with lyric sheet and/or lead sheet. SASE. Reports in 2 weeks.
Music: Mostly **Christian country**, **contemporary Christian** and **gospel/patriotic**; also **country**. Published *Oklahoma You're My Home* (by L. Goodson), recorded Jody Miller on Amythyst Records; "Midnight Flyer," written and recorded by Don Hayes; and "Beyond These Walls" (by Jamie Denison), recorded by Jody Miller on Nustar Records.

MONTINA MUSIC (SOCAN), Box 702, Snowdon Station, Montreal, Quebec H3X 3X8 **Canada**. Professional Manager: David P. Leonard. Music publisher. Estab. 1963. Pays standard royalty.
Affiliate(s): Sabre Music (SOCAN).
  • See the listing for Monticana Records in the Record Companies section.
How to Contact: Submit a demo tape by mail. Unsolicited submissions are OK. Prefers cassette, phonograph record (or VHS videocassette) and lyric sheet. SAE and IRC.
Music: Mostly **top 40**; also **bluegrass**, **blues**, **country**, **dance-oriented**, **easy listening**, **folk**, **gospel**, **jazz**, **MOR**, **progressive**, **R&B**, **rock** and **soul**.
Tips: "Maintain awareness of styles and trends of your peers who have succeeded professionally. Understand the markets to which you are pitching your material. Persevere at marketing your talents. Develop a network of industry contacts, first locally, then regionally and nationally."

MOON JUNE MUSIC (BMI), 4233 SW Marigold, Portland OR 97219. President: Bob Stoutenburg. Music publisher. Estab. 1971. Pays standard royalty.
How to Contact: Submit demo tape by mail. Unsolicited submissions are OK. Prefers cassette (or VHS videocassette) with 2-10 songs. Does not return material.
Music: **Country**, **Christmas** and **comedy**.

MOTEX MUSIC, Rt. 1, Box 70G, Dale TX 78616. (512)398-7519. Owner: Sandra Jones. Music publisher. Estab. 1980. Publishes 50 songs/year. Pays standard royalty.
Affiliate(s): Misty Haze Music, Clock Publishing (BMI).
  • Motex Music's record label, MCR, can be found in the Record Companies section and their management firm, Misty International, is in the Managers and Booking Agents section.

How to Contact: Submit demo tape by mail. Unsolicited submissions are OK. Prefers cassette and lyric sheet. SASE. Reports in 6 weeks.
Music: Mostly **country, gospel** and **blues**; also **rock, folk** and **Tex-Mex**. Published *You Can Always Make The Mountains Move* (by Jim Price), recorded by Kristy Holland (Christian country); and *The Devil's Not Afraid of A Dusty Bible* (by Sandra Jones), recorded Sandy Samples (gospel); both on Misty Records.
Tips: "Try something different with a positive message—no cheatin' songs, no drinkin' songs."

*MOTOR MUSIC CO. (ASCAP), 2717 Motor Ave., Los Angeles CA 90064. (310)559-5580. Fax: (310)559-5581. President: Don Sorkin. Music publisher, manager. Estab. 1976. Publishes 12-20 songs/years; publishes 2 new songwriters/year. Pays standard royalty.
Affiliate(s): Outgoing Music Co. (BMI).
How to Contact: Write or call first and obtain permission to submit a demo. Prefers cassette with 3 songs and lyric sheet. "If a group or single artist, send a photo." Does not return material. Reports in 1 week.
Music: Mostly **pop** and **R&B**.

MUSIC IN THE RIGHT KEYS PUBLISHING COMPANY (BMI), 9108 Arthur Ave., Crystal Lake IL 60014. (815)477-2072. President: Bert Swanson. Music publisher. Estab. 1985. Publishes 200-500 songs/year; publishes 50-100 new songwriters/year. Pays standard royalty.
Affiliate(s): High 'n Low Notes (ASCAP).
How to Contact: Submit a demo tape (professionally made) by mail. Unsolicited submissions are OK. Prefers cassette with 3-10 songs and lyric sheets. SASE. Reports in 2 months.
Music: Mostly **country, gospel, R&B, blues** and **MOR**. Published *When The World Turns to God*, recorded by Toni Murillo on C.E.R. Records; *Love Can Say Hello* (by Bert Swanson), recorded by Vivanco-Vargas on Goldband Records; and *Catch A Rising Star* (by Harry Ectert), recorded by Dawn Jennings on All Star Records.
Tips: "Always submit a good demo for presentation. The better the demo, the better your chances for placement. Remember, Music In The Right Keys will listen to your melodies; all that I ask of you is to send me good demos please."

THE MUSIC ROOM PUBLISHING GROUP, P.O. Box 219, Redondo Beach CA 90277. (310)316-4551. President/Owner: John Reed. Music publisher and record producer. Estab. 1982. Pays standard royalty.
Affiliate(s): MRP (BMI), Music Room Productions.
How to Contact: Submit demo tape by mail. Unsolicited submissions are OK. Prefers cassette with 3 songs and lyric sheet. SASE. Reports in 2-3 weeks.
Music: Mostly **pop/rock/R&B** and **crossover**.

*MUSIKVERLAG K. URBANEK, Hadikg 1789, A-1440 Wien **Austria**. (+43)1894-8398. Contact: Mr. K. Urbanek. Music publisher. Estab. 1988. Pays standard royalty.
How to Contact: Write or call first and obtain permission to submit. Prefers cassette with lead sheet. SAE and IRC. Reports in 2 months.
Music: Mostly **instrumental** and **choir music in middle grade difficulties**.

*MUSIKVERLAG ROSSORI, Hietzinger Hptstr 94, Vienna A-1130 **Austria**. (01)8762400. Fax: (01)876240090. Manager: Mario Rossori. Music publisher and management agency. Estab. 1990. Publishes 100 songs/year; publishes 10 new songwriters/year. Pays standard royalty.
How to Contact: Submit demo tape by mail. Unsolicited submissions are OK. Does not return material. Reports in 2 months.
Music: Mostly **pop, dance** and **rock**. Published *Lucy's Eyes* (by Christel Straub), recorded by Papermoon on BMG Records (pop).

MYKO MUSIC (BMI), 1324 S. Avenida Polar, C208, Tucson AZ 85710. (602)885-5931. President: James M. Gasper. Music publisher, record company (Ariana Records) and record producer (Future 1 Productions). Estab. 1980. Publishes 4 songs/year; 2 new songwriters/year. Pays negotiable royalty.
How to Contact: Submit demo tape by mail. Unsolicited submissions are OK. Prefers cassette (or ½" VHS videocassette) with 3 songs and lyric sheet. SASE. Reports in 2 months.
Music: **Top 40, AOR, ambient** and **atmospheric electronic**. Published *Dancing Animals* (by J. Gasper), recorded by Scuba Tails (New Age); *Never Be Rich*, written and recorded by Tom Privett

THE TYPES OF MUSIC each listing is interested in are printed in boldface.

(rock); and *Climb The Mountain*, written and recorded by JTiom (atmospheric pop), all on Ariana Records.
Tips: "When working within a fixed budget remember, all the production in the world is not going to help if the song's not there. You have to start with the song."

CHUCK MYMIT MUSIC PRODUCTIONS (BMI), 9840 64th Ave., Flushing NY 11374. A&R: Chuck Mymit. Music publisher and record producer (Chuck Mymit Music Productions). Estab. 1978. Publishes 3-5 songs/year; publishes 2-4 new songwriters/year. Pays standard royalty.
Affiliate(s): Viz Music (BMI) and Tore Music (BMI).
How to Contact: Submit demo tape by mail. Unsolicited submissions are OK. Prefers cassette or VHS videocassette with 3-5 songs and lyric and lead sheets. "Bio and picture would be helpful." Does not return material but will contact if interested.
Music: Mostly **pop**, **rock** and **R&B**. Published "Just Say Goodbye" and "Never Is A Long Time," written and recorded by Chuck Mymit (A/C) on CMR Records; and "Lover Man" (by Kim Bui/Chuck Mymit), recorded by Kim Bui on Atlantic Records (R&B).

NAMAX MUSIC PUBLISHING (BMI), P.O. Box 24162, Richmond VA 23224. Music publisher. Estab. 1989. Publishes 2-4 songs/year; publishes 2 new songwriters/year. Pays standard royalty.
How to Contact: Submit demo tape by mail. Unsolicited submissions are OK. Prefers cassette with 2 songs and lyric sheet. "No phone calls please." Does not return material. Reports in 6-8 weeks.
Music: Mostly **R&B** and **pop/top 40**; also **contemporary gospel**. Published "Love Affair" (by D. Trebor/B. Tenan), recorded by Destiny on Xaman Records (R&B).
Tips: "Namax is looking for great songs with a strong hook. Our background is R&B music—do not send us country."

NASHVILLE SOUND MUSIC PUBLISHING CO. (SOCAN), P.O. Box 728, Peterborough, Ontario K9J 6Z8 **Canada**. (705)742-2381. President: Andrew Wilson Jr. Music publisher. Estab. 1985. Publishes 10 songs/year; publishes 5 new songwriters/year. Pays standard royalty.
Affiliate(s): Northern Sound Music Publishing Co. (SOCAN).
How to Contact: Submit demo tape by mail. Unsolicited submissions are OK. Prefers cassette with 2-4 songs and lyric sheet. "Please send only material you do not want returned. We have an open door policy." Reports in 3 weeks.
Music: Mostly **country**, **country/pop** and **crossover country**. Published "Slip Of The Heart" (by Steve Console), recorded by Bob Bates; "Let An Old Race Horse Run" (by Ron Simons), recorded by Tommy Cash; and "Fallin' Out of Love Can Break Your Heart" (by Andrew Wilson, Jr./Joseph Pickering, Jr.), recorded by Mark Poncy, all on Playback Records.
Tips: "Learn how to re-write a song to make it stronger. Develop strong hooks and great story line."

NATIONAL TALENT (BMI), P.O. Box 14, Whitehall MI 49461. (616)894-9208. 1-800-530-9255. President: Sharon Leigh. Vice President: Jay Ronn. Music publisher and record company (United Country). Estab. 1985. Publishes 7-8 songs/year. Pays standard royalty.
Affiliate(s): House of Shar (BMI).
How to Contact: Submit demo tape by mail. Unsolicited submissions are OK. Prefers cassette with 1-10 songs and lyric sheet. SASE. Reports in 1 month.
Music: **Country** and **gospel**. Published "Mistletoe" (by Prohaska), recorded by Jay Ronn; "Blue Days" (by Duncan), recorded by Lexi Hamilton; and "I Believe in Country" (by Koone), recorded by Bobbie G. Rice, all on United Records.

NAUTICAL MUSIC CO. (BMI), Box 120675, Nashville TN 37212. (615)883-9161. Owner: Ray McGinnis. Music publisher and record company (Orbit Records). Estab. 1965. Publishes 25 songs/year; 10 new songwriters/year. Pays standard royalty.
● Nautical Music's record label, Orbit Records, can be found in the Record Companies section.
How to Contact: Submit demo tape by mail. Unsolicited submissions are OK. Prefers cassette with 4 songs and lyric sheets. SASE. Reports in 6-8 weeks.
Music: Mostly **country ballads** and **country rock**. Published *Falling*, *Bad Reputation* and *Burning Love* (by Alan Warren), recorded by Bo Jest (rock), all on Orbit Records.
Tips: "The trend is back to traditional country music with songs that tell a story."

NEBO RIDGE PUBLISHING COMPANY (ASCAP), P.O. Box 194 or 457, New Hope AL 35760. President: Walker Ikard. Manager: Jim Lewis. Music publisher, promotions firm, record producer, record company (Nebo Record Company), management firm (Nebo Management) and booking agency (Nebo Booking Agency). Estab. 1985. Pays standard royalty.
How to Contact: Submit demo tape by mail. Unsolicited submissions are OK. Prefers cassette with 1 song and lyric sheet. Does not return unsolicited material. Reports as soon as possible.

Music: Mostly **modern** and **traditional country**, **modern** and **traditional gospel**, **country/rock**, **rock and roll**, **pop**, **MOR** and **bluegrass**. Published *Lay It On Me* (by Jack Jones), recorded by John Hill (country); *It Hurts So Much* (by Linda Hart), recorded by Joyce Boyd (country); and "In Way Too Deep" (by Sally Bend), recorded by Ann Rose (gospel), all on Nebo Records.

Tips: "Send a personal bio in written form, on a cassette 'talk' tape or VHS video. Also, we will need a few full-length photos. Tell us all about your personal goals and yourself. Finally, a SASE with the proper postage must be included. We need several female singers for our Nebo Record label. Female singers should send a personal bio, a few full-length photos, and a demo cassette tape for a review."

NERVOUS PUBLISHING, 7-11 Minerva Rd., London, NW10 6HJ **England**. Phone: +44(181)963-0352. E-mail: 100613.3456@compuserve.com. Website: http://196-72-60-96/www/nervousrecords. Managing Director: Roy Williams. Music publisher, record company (Nervous Records) and record producer. MCPS, PRS and Phonographic Performance Ltd. Estab. 1979. Publishes 100 songs/year; publishes 25 new songwriters/year. Pays standard royalty; royalties paid directly to US songwriters.

• Nervous Publishing's record label, Nervous Records, is listed in the Record Companies section.

How to Contact: Submit demo tape by mail. Unsolicited submissions are OK. Prefers cassette with 3-10 songs and lyric sheet. "Include letter giving your age and mentioning any previously published material." SAE and IRC. Reports in 2 weeks.

Music: Mostly **psychobilly**, **rockabilly** and **rock** (impossibly fast music—ex.: Stray Cats but twice as fast); also **blues**, **country**, **R&B** and **rock** (50s style). Published *I Just Flipped*, written and recorded by Darrel Higham on Fury Records; "Wreck It Up" (by Aalto), recorded by Housewreckers on Goofin' Records; and *This Is It* (by Plummer), recorded by The Firebirds on Pollytone Records.

Tips: "Submit *no* rap, soul, funk—we want *rockabilly*."

A NEW RAP JAM PUBLISHING, P.O. Box 683, Lima OH 45802. (419)228-0691 and (419)222-3163. President: James Milligan. Music publisher, record company (New Experience/Grand Slam Records). Estab. 1989. Publishes 30 songs/year; publishes 2-3 new songwriters/year. Hires staff songwriters. Pays standard royalty.

Affiliate(s): Party House Publishing (BMI), Creative Star Management.

• A New Rap Jam Publishing's record label, New Experience/Grand Slam Records, is listed in the Record Companies section.

How to Contact: Write or call first and obtain permission to submit. Prefers cassette with 3-5 songs and lyric or lead sheet. SASE. Reports in 1 month.

Music: Mostly **R&B**, **pop** and **rock/rap**; also **contemporary**, **gospel**, **country** and **soul**. Published *Sara's Smile* (by Daryl Hall and John Oates), recorded by James Junior (ballad); and *Call On The Name Of Jesus* (by Carl Mulligan), recorded by James Junior (gospel), both on Pump It Up Records; and *Come See About Me* (by T.M.C.), recorded by James Junior featuring T.M.C. on N.E.R. Records (gospel).

Tips: "Establish music industry contacts, write and keep writing and most of all believe in yourself. Use a good recording studio but be very professional. And if there is interest we will contact you."

NEWCREATURE MUSIC (BMI), P.O. Box 1444, Hendersonville TN 37077-1444. President: Bill Anderson, Jr. Professional Manager: G.L. Score. Music publisher, record company, record producer (Landmark Communications Group) and radio and TV syndicator. Publishes 25 songs/year; publishes 2 new songwriters/year. Pays standard royalty.

Affiliate(s): Mary Megan Music (ASCAP).

• See the listing for Landmark Communications Group in the Record Producers section.

How to Contact: Submit demo tape by mail. Unsolicited submissions are OK. Prefers cassette (or videocassette) with 4-10 songs and lyric sheet. SASE. Reports in 4-6 weeks.

Music: **Country**, **gospel**, **jazz**, **R&B**, **rock** and **top 40/pop**. Published *Glory* and *Popcorn, Peanuts and Jesus* (by Harry Yates), both recorded by Joanne Cash Yates on Angel Too Records (gospel); and *Were You Thinkin' Of Me*, written and recorded by Jack Mosley on Landmark Records (country).

NON-STOP MUSIC PUBLISHING, 915 W. 100 South, Salt Lake City UT 84104. (801)531-0060. Fax: (801)531-0346. Vice President: Michael L. Dowdle. Music publisher. Estab. 1990. Publishes 50-100 songs/year; 3-4 new songwriters/year. Pays standard royalty.

LISTINGS OF COMPANIES in countries other than the U.S. have the name of the country in boldface type.

Affiliate(s): Non-Stop Outrageous Publishing, Inc. (ASCAP), Non-Stop International Publishing, Inc. (BMI) and Airus International Publishing.
How to Contact: Write first and obtain permission to submit. SASE. Reports in 3 months.
Music: Mostly **pop**, **R&B** and **country**; also **jazz** and **New Age**. Published *Emerald Mist* and *Wishing Well*, written and recorded by Sam Cardon; and *A Brighter Day*, written and recorded by Mike Dondle, all on Airus Records.

NSP MUSIC PUBLISHING INC. (ASCAP), 345 Sprucewood Rd., Lake Mary FL 32746-5917. (407)321-3702. Fax: (407)321-2361. President, A&R: Vito Fera. Office Manager, A&R: Rhonda Fera. Music publisher, record company (S.P.I.N. Records), record producer (Vito Fera Productions). Estab. 1980. Publishes 10 songs/year; publishes 3 new songwriters/year. Hires staff writers "on agreement terms." Pays standard royalty.
Affiliate(s): Fera Music Publishing (BMI).
• See the listing for Vito Fera Productions in the Record Producers section.
How to Contact: Submit demo tape by mail. Unsolicited submissions are OK. Prefers cassette (or VHS videocassette) with 3 songs maximum and lyric sheet. "Package song material carefully. Always label (name, address and phone) both cassette and lyric sheet. Copyright songs. If you need assistance or advice on submission procedures or packaging, please contact us." SASE. Reports in 1-2 months.
Music: Mostly **modern jazz**, **instrumentals**, **R&B**, **kid's music** and **Christian music**. Published "The Magic Is Hot" for the Orlando Magic games on WESH TV Channel 2, recorded by Vito Fera and The Falcon Neighbors on S.P.I.N. Records; *Reindeer Rock*, kid's Christmas songs by various artists; and "Momenti Con Te Signore," performed by Salvatore Cristiano on S.P.I.N. Records.
Tips: "Carefully follow each music publisher's review instructions. Always include lyrics and a SASE for reply. A professional package and music production will help your songs stand out amongst the crowd. Always deliver exciting new music to the music industry. Use short intros and 'quality' vocalists to record your demo. Supply us with your best songs, commercial styling and catchy lyrics but not too personal. As you write, try to imagine a major artist singing your song. If you can't, rewrite it! If you are submitting yourself or band as the 'Artist or Act,' please specify your intentions. Finally, read every available songwriting book, music business manual and publication on the subject and inquire about songwriting organizations."

OH MY GOSH MUSIC (BMI), 5146 Hill Dr., Memphis TN 38109. (901)789-5296. Owner: Gerald McDade. Music publisher and record producer (Home Town Productions). Estab. 1985. Publishes 1-6 songs/year; publishes 1-6 new songwriters/year. Pays standard royalty.
How to Contact: Write first and obtain permission to submit. Prefers cassette (or VHS videocassette if available) with 2-4 songs and lyric sheet. Does not return material. Reports in 2-4 months.
Music: Mostly **traditional country**, **country rock** and **rockabilly**; also **gospel**. Published "Get Right or Get Left," written and recorded by Janice Murry (C/W); "Hands Off" (by G. McDade), recorded by Jumpin Jerry McDade (country rock); and "Slow Down" (by B. Roberts), recorded by Bobby Lee (country rock), all on Hometown Records.

OKISHER MUSIC (BMI), P.O. Box 20814, Oklahoma City OK 73156. (405)755-0315. President: Mickey Sherman. Music publisher, record company (Seeds Records, Okart Records, Homa Records and Okie Dokie Records), record producer and management firm (Mickey Sherman's Talent Management). Estab. 1973. Member OCMA. Publishes 10-15 songs/year; publishes 2-3 new songwriters/year. Pays standard royalty.
• See the listing for Mickey Sherman Artist Management in the Managers and Booking Agents section.
How to Contact: Submit demo tape by mail. Unsolicited submissions OK. Prefers 7½ ips reel-to-reel or cassette (or VHS videocassette) with 1-3 songs and lyric sheet. "Don't let the song get buried in the videocassette productions; a bio in front of performance helps. Enclose press kit or other background information." Does not return material. Reports in 3 months.
Music: Mostly **blues**, **country** and **ballads**; also **easy listening**, **jazz**, **MOR**, **R&B** and **soul**. Published "Bending A Reed," written and recorded by Jan Jo on Seeds Records; "Fiddles of Ft. Worth," written and recorded by Benny Kubiak on Homa Records (country); and "My New Connection" (by Mickey Sherman), recorded by Jan Jo on Seeds Records (rock).
Tips: "Have a 'hook' in the lyrics. Use good quality tape/lyric sheet and clean recording on demos."

OLD SLOWPOKE MUSIC (BMI), P.O. Box 52681, Tulsa OK 74152. (918)742-8087. E-mail: cherryst@msn.com. President: Rodney Young. Music publisher, record producer. Estab. 1977. Publishes 24-36 songs/year; publishes 2-3 new songwriters/year. Pays standard royalty.
How to Contact: Write first and obtain permission to submit. Prefers cassette with 4 songs and lyric sheet. SASE. Reports in 6-8 weeks.

Music: Mostly **rock**, **country** and **R&B**; also **jazz**. Published *Land of the Living*, written and recorded by Richard Elkerton; *Moments of Love*, written and recorded by George Carroll; and *Creole Woman*, written and recorded by Brad Absher, all on CSR Records.
Tips: "SASE must be sent or demo will be destroyed after 30 days."

OMNI 2000, INC., 413 Cooper St., Camden NJ 08102. (609)963-6400. President: Michael Nise. Music publisher, record company (Power Up-Sutra), recording studio (Power House) and production company. Publishes 10 songs/year; publishes 5 new songwriters/year. Pays standard royalty.
  ● See their listing in the Record Producers section and the listing for Master-Trak Enterprises in the Record Companies section.
How to Contact: Submit demo tape by mail. Unsolicited submissions are OK. Prefers cassette (or videocassette) with 3 songs. Send Attention: Michael Nise. SASE a must. Reports in 1-2 months.
Music: **Dance**, **R&B**, **country rock** and **pop**, all with pop crossover potential; also **children's**, **church/religious**, **easy listening**, **folk**, **gospel** and **jazz**.
Tips: "Submit only well-produced demos."

ONE HOT NOTE MUSIC INC./BLACK ROSE PRODUCTIONS, P.O. Box 216, Cold Spring Harbor NY 11724. (516)367-8544. Fax: (516)692-4709. A&R: Barbara Bauer. Music publisher and record company (Reiter Records Ltd.). Estab. 1989. Publishes 200 songs/year; publishes 10 new songwriters/year. "We take 100% of publishing but can be negotiated based upon track history of composer."
How to Contact: Submit demo tape by mail. Unsolicited submissions are OK. Prefers cassette. Does not return material.
Music: Mostly **pop**, **rock** and **jazz**; also **dance**, **country** and **rap**. Published "Be My Baby," written and recorded by T.C. Kross on Reiter Records; "Ready or Not" (by Lange/Bastianelli), recorded by Yolanda Yan on Cinepoly Records and by Camille Nivens on BMG Records.
Tips: "Make the song as well produced and recorded as you can."

*ONTRAX COMPANIES (ASCAP), P.O. Box 769, Crown Point IN 46307. (219)736-5815. Contact: Professional Manager. Music publisher, record company (Lennistic Records) and record producer. Estab. 1991. Publishes 30 songs/year; 7 new songwriters/year. Pays standard royalty.
How to Contact: Submit demo tape by mail. Unsolicited submissions are OK. Prefers cassette, DAT with 4-6 songs and lyric sheet. "Tapes should be mailed in as small a package as possible, preferrably in a 4×7 bubble mailer. Please include typed lyric sheet. All items must be labeled and bear the proper copyright notice. If you require a reply, please include a stamped, self-addressed card with your submissions. We listen to all submissions in the order they arrive. No phone calls please." Does not return submissions. Reports in 6 weeks.
Music: Mostly **pop/rock**, **country** and **crossover country**. Published *All Along*, written and recorded by Don Joseph on Lennistic Records; *Days and Nights*, written and recorded by D. Drasich on Canyonsongs Records; and "Better Be Good To Me" (by David Gulyas), recorded by 39th Avenue on Kinghead Records.
Tips: "Keep yourself abreast of the changes in the music business and adapt. Submit the highest quality demos possible and always strive to be improving your craft. There are extremely talented individuals (musically) who will never make a living at music because they give up or make excuses for not persisting. Rejection is a songwriter's constant companion so learn to deal with it."

OPERATION PERFECTION (BMI), 6245 Bristol Pkwy., Suite 206, Culver City CA 90230. Contact: Larry McGee. Vice-President: Darryl McCorkle. Music publisher. Estab. 1976. Publishes 15 songs/year; publishes 1-2 new songwriters/year. Pays standard royalty.
  ● See the listings for Intrigue Production in the Record Producers section, Boogie Band Records in the Record Companies section and LMP Management in the Managers and Booking Agents section.
How to Contact: Write first and obtain permission to submit. Prefers cassette (or VHS videocassette) with 1-4 songs and lyric sheet. "Please only send professional quality material!" SASE. Reports in 2 months.
Music: **Rock**, **rap**, **pop**, **MOR/adult contemporary** and **R&B**. Published "Jazzy Lady" (by Alan Walker), recorded by Wali Ali; "Holding You Close" (by Joe Caccamise), recorded by A.Vis; and *Can't Say No* (by Alan Walker), recorded by Denise Parker, all on Top Ten Records.

ORCHID PUBLISHING (BMI), Bouquet-Orchid Enterprises, P.O. Box 1335, Norcross GA 30091. (770)798-7999. President: Bill Bohannon. Music publisher, record company, record producer (Bouquet-Orchid Enterprises) and artist management. Member CMA, AFM. Publishes 10-12 songs/year; publishes 3 new songwriters/year. Pays standard royalty.
  ● Orchid Publishing's record label, Bouquet Records, is listed in the Record Companies section.

How to Contact: Submit demo tape by mail. Unsolicited submissions OK. Prefers cassette with 3-5 songs and lyric sheet. "Send biographical information if possible—even a photo helps." SASE. Reports in 1 month.
Music: Religious ("Amy Grant, etc., contemporary gospel"); **country** ("Garth Brooks, Trisha Year-wood type material"); and **top 100/pop** ("Bryan Adams, Whitney Houston type material"). Published *Blue As Your Eyes*, written and recorded by Adam Day; "Spare My Feelings" (by Clayton Russ), recorded by Terri Palmer; and "Trying to Get By" (by Tom Sparks), recorded by Bandoleers, all on Bouquet Records.

*ORDERLOTTSA MUSIC (BMI), 441 E. Belvedere Ave., Baltimore MD 21212. (410)377-2270. President: Jeff Order. Music publisher and record producer (Jeff Order/Order Productions). Estab. 1986. Publishes 20 songs/year. Works with composers and lyricists. Pays standard royalty.
   • See the listing for Order Records in the Record Companies section.
How to Contact: Submit demo tape by mail. Unsolicited submissions are OK. Prefers cassette with 3 songs. SASE. Reports in 1 month.
Music: Only **contemporary instrumental music**. Published *Unconquered Lions*, written and recorded by Uprising (reggae); *Keepers of the Light* and *Of Ancient Wisdom*, written and recorded by Jeff Order on Order Records (instrumental New Age).
Tips: "Submit high-quality, well-recorded and produced material. Original styles and sounds. Don't waste our time or yours copying the music of mainstream artists."

OTTO PUBLISHING CO. (ASCAP), P.O. Box 16540, Plantation FL 33318. (305)741-7766. President: Frank X. Loconto. Music publisher, record company (FXL Records) and record producer (Loconto Productions). Estab. 1978. Publishes 25 songs/year; publishes 1-5 new songwriters/year. Pays standard royalty.
Affiliate(s): Betty Brown Music Co. (BMI), Clara Church Music Co. (SESAC), True Friends Music (BMI).
   • See the listings for Loconto Productions in the Record Companies and Record Producers sections.
How to Contact: Submit demo tape by mail. Unsolicited submissions are OK. Prefers cassette with 1-4 songs and lyric sheet. SASE. Reports in 1 month.
Music: Mostly **country**, **MOR**, **religious** and **gospel**. Published *He's Got All Power*, written and recorded by Joseph Ford (gospel); and *Spacey's Wonderings* (by Frank X. Loconto), recorded by Cherise Wyneken (children's), all on FXL Records.
Tips: "The more you write the better you get. If you are a good writer, it will happen."

OYSTER BAY MUSIC, P.O. Box 81550, Cleveland OH 44181-0550. President: Daniel L. Bischoff. Music publisher and management firm (Daniel Bischoff Management). Pays standard royalty.
Affiliate(s): Long Island Music (ASCAP).
How to Contact: Submit demo tape by mail. Unsolicited submissions are OK. Prefers cassette or VHS tape and lyrics. SASE. Reports in 2 weeks.
Music: Country, **bluegrass**, **R&B**, **rap** and **pop**. Published "Childhood Days" (by Pat Wilson); *Tennessee Chick* (by Hulen Wilson); and "Waitin for the Phone to Ring" (by Derek Sparkman), all recorded by North Coast Bluegrass on NCB Records.

PADRINO MUSIC PUBLISHING (BMI,SESAC), P.O. Box 102, Bishop TX 78343. (512)584-3735. Fax: (512)584-3803. Proprietor: Jesus Gonzales Solis. Music publisher. Estab. 1993. Publishes 4 songs/year. Pays standard royalty. "Padrino Music is owned by Jesus Gonzales Solis, who is at this time the sole composer, publishing his own music."
How to Contact: Submit demo tape by mail. Unsolicited submissions are OK. Prefers cassette with lead sheet. SASE. Reports in 2 weeks.
Music: Mostly **Spanish rancheras**, **Latin ballads** and **cumbias**. Published *Quiero Saber Lo*, *Sabes De Mi*, "Caliente Dulce Amor" and "Quiero Besarte los Labios" (by Solis), recorded by La Sombra on Fonovisa Records.
Tips: "Write what you feel; no matter how outrageous, there is a purpose to everything that is written. Never give up if you believe in yourself, your time will come. Be persistent."

 THE ASTERISK before a listing indicates that the listing is new in this edition. New markets are often the most receptive to unsolicited submissions.

J. S. PALUCH COMPANY, INC./WORLD LIBRARY PUBLICATIONS (SESAC), 3825 N. Willow Rd., P.O. Box 2703, Schiller Park IL 60176-0703. Managing Editor: Laura Dankler. Music Editors: Nicholas T. Freund, Ron Rendek, Thomas Strickland. Music publisher. Estab. 1913. Publishes 50 or more songs/year; publishes varying number of new songwriters/year; recordings. "Pays prorated 5% for text or music alone; 10% for both."
How to Contact: Submit demo tape and/or manuscript by mail—unsolicited submissions are OK. Prefers cassette with any number of songs, lyric sheet and lead sheet. SASE. Reports in 3 months.
Music: Sacred music, hymns, choral settings, descants, psalm settings, masses; also **children's sacred music**. Published *Veni, Creator Spiritus* (by Carl Johensen); *Three Psalms* (by Mike Hay); and *Navidad, Navidad* (by Lorenzo Florian), all recorded by William Ferris Chorale on WLP (sacred).
Tips: "Make your manuscript as legible as possible, with clear ideas regarding tempo, etc. Base the text upon scripture."

PANCHATANTRA MUSIC ENTERPRISES, P.O. Box 91012, Nashville TN 37209-1012. President: Ben Reed Williams. Music publisher, record producer, promotion/public relations, personal management. Estab. 1968. Publishes 3-6 songs/year. Pays standard royalty.
Affiliates: Hickory Hollow Music, Steeple Music (BMI) and Lancaster Music (SESAC).
How to Contact: Write to obtain permission to submit a demo. Prefers cassette (or VHS videocassette) with 3 songs and lyric or lead sheet. "Enclosed SASE with *correct* postage will assure return of material we are not interested in publishing." SASE.
Music: Mostly **country, folk** and **blues**; also **bluegrass, A/C-pop** and **black gospel**. Published "A Bird With Broken Wings Can't Fly" (by Benny R. Williams), recorded by The Carter Family on Columbia Records (folk); "I've Got a Conscience (And You've Got a Wife)" (by Benny R. Williams/Paul Gasper), recorded by Lonnie Lynn Lacour on Rhinestone Rooster Records (country); and "Hey, Mr. Landlord" (by Benny R. Williams/Eugene "Texas" Ray), recorded by Eugene "Texas" Ray on Nashville Sound Records (blues).
Tips: "Give us something to listen to that doesn't sound like a repetition of the same old thing. What's needed is a lyric that has *meat* instead of *vanilla* and a melody that serves as a perfect vehicle to get the message delivered."

PARADISE PUBLICATIONS (BMI), P.O. Box 9084, Wichita Falls TX 76310. (817)691-1777. President: Leah Galligar. Music publisher, record company (Paradise Records) and record producer. Estab. 1992. Publishes 3-4 new songwriters/year. Pays standard royalty.
How to Contact: Write first and obtain permission to submit a demo. Prefers cassette with 4-5 songs and lyric sheet. SASE. Reports in 2 months.
Music: Mostly **cowboy songs, cowboy music** and **Western influence**. Published "Night on the Trail," written and recorded by D.L. Chance; "Cowgirl's Prayer" and "Howl At the Moon Saloon," written and recorded by Sharon Chance, all on Paradise Records (cowboy).
Tips: "We are interested in *cowboy* and *western music only.*"

PARRAVANO MUSIC, 17 Woodbine St., Cranston RI 02910. (401)785-2677. Owner: Amy Parravano. Music publisher, record company (Peridot Records), record producer (Peridot Productions). Estab. 1986. Publishes 5 songs/year. Pays standard royalty.
• See the listings for Peridot Productions in the Record Producers section and Peridot Records in the Record Companies section.
How to Contact: Submit demo tape by mail. Unsolicited submissions are OK. Prefers cassette with 3-4 songs and lyric sheet. Lead sheets are optional. SASE. Reports in 6 months.
Music: Mostly **country, gospel** and **folk**; also **MOR, children's, country/blues** and **novelty**. Published "All Night Long," "One Last Try" and "After All This Time" (by Mike Di Sano), recorded by Joe Kempf on BJD Records, Peridot Records and Stardust Records, respectively.
Tips: "Make sure lyrics tell a story to your listener."

*PAS MAL PUBLISHING SARL, 283 FBG St. Antoine, Paris 75020 **France**. (33)1 43485151. Fax: (33)1 43485753 Managing Director: Jammes Patrick. Music publisher. Estab. 1990. Publishes 5-10 songs/year. Works with composers and lyricists. Pays 60% royalty.
How to Contact: Submit demo tape by mail. Unsolicited submissions are OK. Prefers cassette (or PAL videocassette). Does not return material. Reports in 6 months.
Music: Mostly **new industrial** and **metal**. Published *Skinflowers*, "Only Heaven" and "Kissing the Sun," (by F. Treichler, A. Monod, U. Hiestand, R. Mosimann), all recorded by The Young Gods on Interscope Records (rock).

PECOS VALLEY MUSIC (BMI), 2709 W. Pine Lodge, Roswell NM 88201. (505)622-0244. President: Ray Willmon. Music publisher. Estab. 1989. Publishes 15-20 songs/year; publishes 4-5 new songwriters/year. Pays standard royalty.
• Pecos Valley's record label, SunCountry Records, is listed in the Record Companies section.

How to Contact: Submit demo tape by mail. Unsolicited submissions are OK. "No phone calls please." Prefers cassette or CD (or VHS videocassette if available) with 1-2 songs and lyric sheet. SASE. Reports in 4-6 weeks.
Music: Country. Published "Gone Also" (by Ron Reem), "Someday" and "No One" (by Don McKinny), all recorded by Don McKinny on SunCountry Records.
Tips: "Listen to what's playing on radio and TV and write with these in mind. Use proper song format (AAAA, ABAB, AABA, etc.)"

PEERMUSIC (ASCAP, BMI), 8159 Hollywood Blvd., Los Angeles CA 90069. (213)656-0364. Fax: (213)656-3298. Assistant to the Head of Talent Acquisitions: Nicole Bahuchet. Music publisher and artist development promotional label. Estab. 1928. Publishes 600 songs/year (worldwide); publishes 1-2 new songwriters/year. Hires staff songwriters. Royalty standard, but negotiable.
Affiliate(s): Peer Southern Organization (ASCAP) and Peer International Corporation (BMI).
How to Contact: "We do NOT accept unsolicited submissions. We only accept material through agents, attorneys and managers." Prefers cassette and lyric sheet. Does not return material. Reports in 6 weeks.
Music: Mostly **pop**, **rock** and **R&B**. Published "Run to You" (by Jud Friedman/Allan Rich), recorded by Whitney Houston on Arista Records (pop); "Can't Cry Hard Enough" (by Williams/Williams/Etzioni), recorded by The Williams Brothers on Warner Bros. Records (rock); and "I'm Gonna Get You" (by A. Scott/Bizarre, Inc./Toni C.), recorded by Bizarre, Inc. on Columbia Records (pop).

PEGASUS MUSIC, P.O. Box 127, Otorohanga 2564, **New Zealand**. Professional Manager: Errol Peters. Music publisher and record company. Estab. 1981. Publishes 20-30 songs/year; publishes 5 new songwriters/year. Pays standard royalty.
How to Contact: Submit demo tape by mail. Unsolicited submissions are OK. Prefers cassette with 3-5 songs and lyric sheet. SAE and IRC. Reports in 1 month.
Music: Mostly **country**; also **bluegrass**, **easy listening** and **top 40/pop**. Published *Make It Easy On Me* (by Ginny Peters), recorded by Josie K. on Trend Records; *If This Is Love* (by Ginny Peters), recorded by Laurie and Sharon Gleeson on L&S Records; and *I Love You, You, You*, written and recorded by Jim Perkins on Pegasus Records.
Tips: "Get to the meat of the subject without too many words. Less is better."

PEN COB PUBLISHING INC. (BMI), 5660 E. Virginia Beach Blvd., Norfolk VA 23502. (804)455-8454. Fax: (804)461-4669. A&R: Tres Swann. Music publisher. Estab. 1991. Publishes 100 songs/year; publishes 6 new songwriters/year. Pays standard royalty.
   • See the listings for Trumpeter Records in the Record Companies section and Sirocco Productions in the Managers and Booking Agents section.
How to Contact: Write or call first to obtain permission to submit. Prefers cassette (or VHS videocassette). SASE. Reports in 6-8 weeks.
Music: Mostly **alternative/progressive**, **rock (heavy)** and **country**. Published "Cambio," recorded by Big Stoner Creek; and *Flow*, recorded by Egypt, all on Trumpeter Records.

JUSTIN PETERS MUSIC (BMI), 3609 Donna Kay Dr., Nashville TN 37211. (615)331-6056. Fax: (615)831-0991. President: Justin Peters. Music publisher. Estab. 1981.
How to Contact: Prefers cassette with 3 songs and lyric sheet. Does not return unsolicited material. "Place code 1005 on each envelope submission."
Music: Published "Saved By Love," recorded by Amy Grant on A&M Records; "Love Still Changing Hearts," recorded by Imperials on Starsong Records; and "Wipe a Tear," recorded by Russ Taff and Olanda Daper on Word Records, all written by Justin Peters.
Tips: "Learn your craft and submit quality work."

PHAJA MUSIC, a division of Mega-Star Music, P.O. Box 1427, Bayshore NY 11706. (212)713-5229. General Manager: Barry Yearwood. Music publisher, record producer (Barry Yearwood) and management firm (Yearwood Management). Estab. 1984. Publishes 4 songs/year; publishes 4 new songwriters/year. Pays standard royalty.
How to Contact: Submit demo tape by mail. Unsolicited submissions are OK. Prefers cassette with 4 songs. SASE. Reports in 1 month.

REFER TO THE CATEGORY INDEX (at the end of this section) to find exactly which companies are interested in the type of music you write.

Music: Mostly **dance** and **R&B**; also **pop**. Published "Black Puddin'," recorded by SWV on RCA Records. Other artists include Paul Mitchel and James Colino.

PHILIPPOPOLIS MUSIC (BMI), 12027 Califa St., North Hollywood CA 91607. President: Milcho Leviev. Music publisher. Member GEMA, NARAS. Estab. 1975. Publishes 3-5 songs/year; publishes 1-2 new songwriters/year. Pays standard royalty.
How to Contact: Submit demo tape by mail. Unsolicited submissions are OK. Prefers cassette with 1-3 songs. Prefers studio produced demos. Does not return material. Reports in 1 month.
Music: **Jazz** and **classical fusion**. Published *Sixteen Bars, Happy Stuff* and *Studious Improv*, all written and recorded by Milcho Leviev on BMU Records (jazz).
Tips: "Consider music as an art form."

PINE ISLAND MUSIC, 9430 Live Oak Place, Ft. Lauderdale FL 33324. (305)472-7757. (Between April 15 and October 15, 4250 Marine Dr., #2335, Chicago, IL 60613. (312)525-5273.) President/A&R: Jack P. Bluestein. Music publisher and booking agency. Estab. 1974. Publishes 50-75 songs/year; publishes 10-20 new songwriters/year. Pays standard royalty.
Affiliate(s): Lantana Music/Quadrant Records (BMI).
How to Contact: Submit demo tape by mail. Unsolicited submissions are OK. Prefers cassette with 3 songs and lyric or lead sheet. SASE. Reports in 2 months.
Music: Mostly **beautiful music**, **soft rock**, **country** and **soft pop**; also **movie themes**, **movie background** and **innovative country** and **pop**.

PLANET DALLAS RECORDING STUDIOS (BMI, ASCAP), P.O. Box 191447, Dallas TX 75219. (214)521-2216. Music publisher, record producer (Rick Rooney) and recording studio. Estab. 1985. Publishes 20 songs/year; 2-3 new songwriters/year. Pays standard royalty.
Affiliate(s): Stoli Music (BMI) and Planet Mothership Music (ASCAP).
  • See their listing in the Record Producers section.
How to Contact: Call first and obtain permission to submit. Prefers cassette with 1-3 songs and lyric sheet. SASE for reply. Reports in 6-8 weeks.
Music: Mostly **modern rock**. Published "This Property is Condemned" (by P. Sugg), recorded by Maria McKee on Geffen Records (pop); *Ozone* (by various), recorded by MC 500 Ft. Jesus on Nettwerk/IRS Records; and *Scattered Remains/Poet*, written and recorded by the Blue Johnnies on Ganglion Records.

PLATINUM BOULEVARD PUBLISHING (BMI), 525 E. Moana Lane, Reno NV 89502. (702)827-4424. President: Lawrence Davis. Music publisher. Estab. 1984. Publishes 12 songs/year; publishes 1 new songwriter/year. Pays standard royalty.
  • See their listing in the Record Companies section.
How to Contact: Submit a demo tape by mail. Unsolicited submissions are OK. Prefers cassette (or VHS videocassette), with unlimited songs and lyric or lead sheets. Does not return material. "We report only if interested."
Music: Mostly **rock**, **country** and **R&B**; also **jazz** and **New Age**. Published *Crazy Thing*, *Take My Heart* and *Lonely Lovers*, all written and recorded by Lawrence Davis on Platinum Boulevard Records.

*PLATINUM GOLD MUSIC (ASCAP), 9200 Sunset Blvd., #1220, Los Angeles CA 90069. (310)275-7329. Fax: (310)275-7371. Managers: Steve Cohen and David Cook. Music publisher. Estab. 1981.
How to Contact: Write or call first and obtain permission to submit a demo. Prefers cassette with no more than 4 songs. Does not return material. Reports in 1-4 weeks.
Music: Mostly **R&B**, **pop** and **rap**; also **country** and **rock**. Published *Misunderstanding* (by Steven Russell), recorded by The Whispers on Capitol Records (R&B); *My Music* (by R. Warren/R. Benford/J. Harreld), recorded by Troop on Atlantic Records (R&B); and *Come To Me* (by L.A. McNeil), recorded by Michael Cooper on Warner Bros. Records (R&B).
Tips: "Strong hook, great lyric and melody. Have a good quality demo."

POLLARD SOUND WORLD (BMI), 1615 Pine Tree Rd., Longview TX 75604. (903)297-2096. Owner: John Pollard. Music publisher, recording studio and music store. Estab. 1979. Publishes 2-20 songs/year; publishes 1-5 new songwriters/year. Pays standard royalty.
How to Contact: Write or call first and obtain permission to submit a demo. Prefers cassette with 1 or 2 songs and lead sheet or chord chart. Does not return material. Reports in 1-2 weeks.
Music: Mostly **Southern rock**, **blues** and **country**; also **gospel** and **easy rock**. Published "It Ain't Easy" (easy rock) and "I'm Your Man" (country), (by John Pollard/Mike Willbanks), recorded by Southern Pride; and *Dangerous* (by John Pollard/Alan Fox), recorded by J.A. Band (rock), all on Pollard Sound World Records.

POLLYBYRD PUBLICATIONS LIMITED (ASCAP, BMI, SESAC), P.O. Box 8442, Universal CA 91608. (818)505-0488. Fax: (818)506-8534. Branch office: 333 Proctor St., Carson City NV 89703. (818)884-1946. Fax: (818)882-6755. Professional Manager: Maxx Diamond. Music publisher. Estab. 1979. Publishes 100 songs/year; publishes 25-40 new songwriters/year. Hires staff writers. Pays standard royalty.
Affiliate(s): Kellijai Music (ASCAP), Pollyann Music (ASCAP), Ja'Nikki Songs (BMI), Velma Songs International (BMI), Lonnvanness Songs (SESAC), PPL Music (ASCAP), Zettitalia Music, Zett Two Music (ASCAP) and Butternut Music (BMI).
 • See the listings for MCI Entertainment Group in the Record Companies section and Sa'mall Management in the Managers and Booking Agents section.
How to Contact: Submit demo tape by mail. Unsolicited submissions are OK. Prefers cassette or VHS videocassette with 4 songs and lyric and lead sheet. SASE. Reports in 6 weeks.
Music: Published *A Song for Lillie* (by Suzutte Cuseo), recorded by Condottiere on Credence Records (classical/New Age); *Homeless* (by Jaeson St. James), recorded by Buddy Wright on Bouvier Sony Records (blues); and *Why Are You Here* (by Ken Allen), recorded by Big Daddy and the Blazers on Houston Blues Records (blues).
Tips: "Make those decisions—are you really a songwriter? Are you prepared to starve for your craft? Do you believe in delayed gratification? Are you commercial or do you write only for yourself? Can you take rejection? Do you want to be the best? If so, contact us—if not, keep your day job."

POLYGRAM MUSIC PUBLISHING, 825 Eighth Ave., 27th Floor, New York NY 10019. (212)333-8300. This publisher prefers not to share information.

PORTAGE MUSIC (BMI), 16634 Gannon W., Rosemount MN 55068. (612)432-5737. President: Larry LaPole. Music publisher. Publishes 5-20 songs/year. Pays standard royalty.
How to Contact: Submit demo tape by mail. Unsolicited submissions are OK. Prefers cassette with 3 songs and lyric sheet. Does not return material. Reports in 2 months.
Music: Mostly **country** and **country rock**. Published "King of the Surf," "My Woodie" and "A-Bone" (by L. Lapole), all recorded by Trashmen.
Tips: "Keep songs short, simple and upbeat with positive theme."

*POWER VOLTAGE MUSIC (BMI), P.O. Box 808, Daytona Beach FL 32115-0808. Branch: P.O. Box 45 Church Street Station, New York NY 10008. (212)388-2767. President: Russ Mate. Vice President: Mike Fass. Music publisher, record company (Power Voltage Records). Estab. 1984. Publishes 50 songs/year; 20 new songwriters/year. Pays standard royalty.
Affiliates: Digital Dawn Music (ASCAP).
How to Contact: Submit demo tape by mail. Unsolicited submissions are OK. Prefers cassette with 3-6 songs and lyric sheet. "Send only high quality tapes. Have songs listed on tape, in order of play. Include name and phone numbers of songwriter(s), as well as band contact or artist/songwriter representative." Does not return submissions. Reports in 2-6 weeks.
Music: Mostly **rock (all types)** and **dance (most types)**; also **instrumental (all types)**. Published *Walk Away*, written and recorded by Johnny Woods (rock); *Take Me Down*, written and recorded by Eddie Testa (rock); and *The One Narrow Door* (by Gary Hensley), recorded by Neon Fire (rock), all on Power Voltage Records.
Tips: "We primarily publish and work with songwriters who write material for bands they perform with. We release promotional samplers that are sent to the industry only on a monthly basis. We are an ambitious company and are signing a lot of new writers and songs. Keep aware of current trends, but stay away from formula writing and never try to purposely write a hit."

PPI/PETER PAN INDUSTRIES, 88 St. Francis St., Newark NJ 07105. (201)344-4214. Director of A&R: Marianne Eggleston. Music publisher, record and video company (Compose Records, Parade Video, JA Records, Power Music, Peter Pan Music) and record producer (Dunn Pearson, Jr., Niney the Observer). Estab. 1928. Publishes over 100 songs/year. Hires staff songwriters. Pays standard royalty "based on negotiation."
Affiliate(s): Tifton Publishing, Compose Pubishing, Observer International, Discover International, Rego Irish-Colleen, Aurophon Classics.
 • See PPI's listing in the Record Companies section.
How to Contact: Submit a demo tape by mail. Unsolicited submissions are OK. Prefers cassette with completed full length recording only. "No longer accepting one or two songs because there are too many producers submitting material." Please include name, address and phone numbers on all materials, along with picture, bio and contact information." SASE. Reports in 6 months.
Music: Mostly **reggae, oldies, children's—audio**, **R&B** and **jazzy**; also **exercise—video**, **audio book on cassette** and **classical**. Published "Where Do Trolls Come From" (by Barry Hirschberg), recorded by various artists on Peter Pan Records; and "Johnny Clark," written by Niney the Observer on J.A. Records (reggae).

Tips: "Submit materials professionally packaged with typewritten correspondence."

PREJIPPIE MUSIC GROUP (BMI), Box 312897, Penobscot Station, Detroit MI 48231. Partner: Bruce Henderson. Music publisher, record company (PMG Records) and record producer (PMG Productions). Estab. 1990. Publishes 50-75 songs/year; publishes 2-3 new songwriters/year. Hires staff writers. Pays standard royalty.
 • See the listings for PMG Records in the Record Companies section and Prejippie Music Group in the Record Producers section.
How to Contact: Submit demo tape by mail. Unsolicited submissions are OK. Prefers cassette with 3-4 songs and lyric sheet. "No phone calls please." SASE. Reports in 3 months.
Music: Mostly **techno/house**, **funk/rock** and **dance**; also **alternative rock** and **experimental**. Published "You Enjoy the Girl" and "Lolita," written and recorded by Bourgeoisie Paper Jam (funk/rock); and "Windsong," written and recorded by Tony Webb, (jazz) all on PMG Records (techno/alternative).
Tips: "Think your arrangements through carefully. Always have a strong hook (whether vocal-oriented or instrumental)."

PRESCRIPTION COMPANY (BMI), % D.F. Gasman, 5 Slocum Ave., Port Washington NY 11050. (516)767-1929. President: David F. Gasman. Vice President of Finance: Robert Murphy. Music publisher and record producer. Pays standard royalty.
 • See Prescription Company's listing in the Record Producers section.
How to Contact: Call or write first about your interest. Prefers cassette with any number of songs and lyric sheet. "Send all submissions with SASE (or no returns)." Reports in 1 month.
Music: **Bluegrass**, **blues**, **children's** and **country**, **dance-oriented**; also **easy listening**, **folk**, **jazz**, **MOR**, **progressive**, **R&B**, **rock**, **soul** and **top 40/pop**. Published "You Came In," "Rock 'n' Roll Blues" and "Seasons" (by D.F. Gasman), all recorded by Medicine Mike on Prescription Records.
Tips: "Songs should be good and written to last. Forget fads—we want songs that'll sound as good in 10 years as they do today. Organization, communication and exploration of form are as essential as message (and sincerity matters, too)."

*PRETTY SHAYNA MUSIC (BMI), 2461 Santa Monica Blvd., #C331, Santa Monica CA 90404. (310)450-3677. Fax: (310)452-3268. Professional Manager: Stephanie Perom. Music publisher, management company (Perom International). Estab. 1994. Pays standard royalty.
Affiliate(s): Forever Shayna Music (ASCAP).
 • See the listing for Perom International in the Managers and Booking Agents section.
How to Contact: Submit demo tape by mail. Unsolicited submissions are OK. Prefers cassette with 2 songs and lyric sheet. SASE. Reports in 8-12 weeks.
Music: Mostly **pop**, **dance** and **R&B**; also **pop-rock** and **Christmas**.
Tips: "Simple demos are OK, but be certain vocal presentation is the best it can be. Short intros to songs. Always have address and phone number on cassette. Please include lyric sheets."

PRIMAL VISIONS MUSIC (BMI), 3701 Inglewood Ave., Suite 133, Redondo Beach CA 90278. (310)214-0370. President: Jeffrey Howard. Music publisher, record company (Primal Records) and record producer. Estab. 1985. Publishes 6 songs/year; publishes 2 new songwriters/year. Pays standard royalty.
How to Contact: Call or write first for permission to submit. Prefers cassette, DAT or CD with 3-5 songs and lyric sheet. SASE. Reports in 6-8 weeks.
Music: Mostly **rock**, **alternative** and **pop**; also **New Age**, **world beat** and **rhythm/percussion music**. Published *Locked In A Box*; *Mirror, Mirror*; and *Nightmares*, all written and recorded by Jeffrey Howard on Primal Records (rock).

PRITCHETT PUBLICATIONS (BMI), P.O. Box 725, Daytona Beach FL 32114-0725. (904)252-4848. Vice President: Charles Vickers. Music publisher and record company (King of Kings Record Co.). (Main office in California.) Estab. 1975. Publishes 21 songs/year; publishes 12 new songwriters/year.
Affiliate(s): Alison Music (ASCAP), Charles H. Vickers (BMI).
 • Pritchett's record label, Pickwick/Mecca/Internation Records, is listed in the Record Companies section.
How to Contact: Write first and obtain permission to submit. Prefers cassette with 6 songs and lyric or lead sheet. Does not return material.
Music: **Gospel**, **rock-disco** and **country**. Published *Have You Heard of the Holy City*, *Christ is Mine* and *Every Feeling I Have Comes From God*, all written and recorded by Charles Vickers on King of Kings Records (gospel).

*PROMO, Avenue Massenet 16, 1190 Brussels **Belgium**. Phone/Fax: (32)2-3442559. President: Hascher Francois. Music publisher, record producer. Estab. 1986. Publishes 50 songs/year; publishes 2-3 new songwriters/year. Works with composers and lyricists. Pays standard royalty.
How to Contact: Submit demo tape by mail. Unsolicited submissions are OK. Prefers cassette and lyric sheet. SAE and IRC. Reports in 2 months.
Music: Mostly **rock** and **blues**; also **French songs**. Published *Obsession* (by F. Sterckx), recorded by M.C. Michael (French); *Marylin's Busstop* (by J. Lauwers), recorded by John Lauwers Band (rock); and *Dreammaker* (by T. Frantzis), recorded by Tuner (rock), all on Krazy Kobra Rekords.
Tips: "Make real music—no sampling. Melodious, if possible."

PROSPECTOR THREE D PUBLISHING (BMI), 4003 Turnberry Cir., Houston TX 77025. (713)665-4676. Fax: (713)665-5576. Consultant-Owners: Dave or Peggy Davidson. Music publisher, record producer and management company. Estab. 1989. Publishes 2 or 3 new songwriters/year. Pays standard royalty.
How to Contact: Submit demo tape by mail. Unsolicited submissions are OK. (No replies unless interested in songs or singer.) Prefers cassette (or VHS videocassette if available) with 4 songs and lyric sheet. Does not return material.
Music: Mostly **country, country/Christian** and **pop**; also **blues, pop rock** and **bluegrass**. Published *And Then Some*, written and recorded by Joe Kirkpatrick; *Becky Wrote the Book*, written and recorded by Harry Fish, both on MC Records; and *La De Ly*, written and recorded by Karon Teague on TNT Records.
Tips: "Great songs to break the career of a new unknown artist are hard to find. Keep improving on your writing skills and let me hear them—if I can use them, I'll respond."

PURPLE HAZE MUSIC (BMI), P.O. Box 1243, Beckley WV 25802. President: Richard L. Petry. (304)252-4836. A&R: Carol Lee. Music publisher. Estab. 1968. Publishes 50 songs/year; publishes 5-10 new songwriters/year. Pays standard royalty.
• See the listing for Scene Productions in the Record Companies section.
How to Contact: Submit demo tape by mail. Unsolicited submissions are OK. Prefers cassette with 3-4 songs and lyric sheet. "Submit typed lyrics (in capital letters) and a separate lyric sheet for each song." SASE. Reports in 1-2 months.
Music: Country, rock and **R&B**. Published "My Old Friend," written and recorded by Chuck Paul on Rising Sun Records; and "Home Sweet W.V.," written and recorded by Dave Runyon on Country Bridge Records.
Tips: "A publisher can't always return phone calls to new writers so always call back. Always include SASE for some kind of reply!"

QUARK, INC., P.O. Box 7320, New York NY 10150-7320. (212)838-6775. E-mail: quarkent@aol.com. Manager: Curtis Urbina. Music publisher, record company (Quark Records), record producer (Curtis Urbina). Estab. 1986. Publishes 12 songs/year; 2 new songwriters/year. Pays standard royalty.
Affiliate(s): Quarkette Music (BMI) and Freedurb Music (ASCAP).
How to Contact: Write first and obtain permission to submit. Prefers cassette with 2 songs. SASE. Reports in 3 months.
Music: New Age (instrumentals) and **storytelling** (all kinds—spoken word).
Tips: "Research—know what style of music or stories we release. If you have no clue, give us a call and we will tell you."

R. J. MUSIC, 10A Margaret Rd., Barnet, Herts. EN4 9NP **United Kingdom**. Phone: (01)440-9788. Managing Directors: Roger James and Susana Boyce. Music publisher and management firm (Roger James Management). PRS. Pays negotiable royalty (up to 50%).
• R.J. Music's management firm, Roger James Management, is listed in the Managers and Booking Agents section.
How to Contact: Prefers cassette with 1 song and lyric or lead sheet. "Will return cassettes, but only with correct *full* postage!"
Music: Mostly **MOR, blues, country** and **rock**; also **chart material**. "No disco or rap!"

R.T.L. MUSIC, %Stewart House, Hillbottom Rd., Highwycombe, Buckinghamshire **United Kingdom** HP124HJ. Phone: (01630)647374. Fax: (01630)647612. Art Director: Ron Lee. Music publisher, record company (Le Matt Music) and record producer. Estab. 1971. Publishes approximately 30 songs/year. Pays standard royalty.
Affiliate(s): Lee Music, Ltd., Swoop Records, Grenouille Records, Check Records, Zarg Records, Pogo Records, Ltd., R.T.F.M., Value for Money Productions, Lee Sound Productions, Le Matt Distributors, Hoppy Productions.
• R.T.L.'s record label, Le Matt Music, can be found in the Record Companies section, and R.T.F.M. is listed in the Music Print Publishers section.

How to Contact: Submit demo tape by mail. Unsolicited submissions are OK. Prefers CD, cassette or DAT (also VHS 625/PAL system videocassette) with 1-3 songs and lyric and lead sheets; include still photos and bios. "Make sure name and address are on CD or cassette." SAE and IRC. Reports in 6 weeks.
Music: All types. Published *Eat 'Em Up*, *99* and *I'm A Rep* (by Bob Bowman), recorded by The Chromatics on Grenouille Records (country).

*RACHEL MARIE MUSIC LTD. (ASCAP), P.O. Box 1351, Island Heights NJ 08732. (908)270-4970. E-mail: gospundrg@aol.com. Contact: Publishing Dept. Music publisher, record company (Antiphon International), record producer. Estab. 1991. Publishes 16 songs/year; publishes 2-3 new songwriters/year. Pays standard royalty.
• Rachel Marie Music's record label, Antiphon International, is listed in the Record Companies section.
How to Contact: Submit demo tape by mail. Unsolicited submissions are OK. Prefers cassette with 3 songs and lyric sheet. "Send SASE for reply." Does not return submissions. Reports in 4-8 weeks.
Music: Mostly **gospel/rock**, **alternative** and **blues/rock**; also **Christian/rock** and **gospel/blues/rock**. Published *The Promise* (by J.D. Kucharik), recorded by Dream Child (gospel/rock); *Silently Cryin'*, written and recorded by Dean Mathias (Christian/pop); and *5000 Times* (by Loftus/Dingerdissen/Wilbur), recorded by Destination Goat (alternative), all on Antiphon Records.
Tips: "Music has to come from the heart. Writing, and the recording (even rough demos) should reflect the mood and the feeling for which it was intended. Draw the listener in!"

RADIANT MUSIC, 1445 Boonville Ave., Springfield MO 65802-1894. (417)862-2781, ext. 4130. Fax: (417)862-0416. National Secretary: Dan Crace. Music publisher. Estab. 1956. Pays negotiable royalty.
How to Contact: Submit demo tape by mail. Unsolicited submissions are OK. Prefers cassette with 3 songs and lyric sheet and lead sheet. SASE. Reports in 6 months.
Music: Mostly **evangelical choral**, **praise** and **worship choruses**. Published "Til He Comes" (by Carter/Bills), recorded by Imperials on Impact Records; "A Healing Stream" (by Steve Phifer), recorded by Steve Brock; and "The Lord Is On My Side" (by Nate Carter), recorded by Big John Hall.

RANA INTERNATIONAL & AFFILIATES, INC., P.O. Box 934273, Margate FL 33442-8034. Fax: (954)427-1819. CEO: Giuseppe Nudo. President: Raffaele A. Nudo. Vice President: Teodor Zuccarelli. Music publisher, management firm and record company. Estab. 1990. Publishes 5-7 songs/year; publishes 2-4 new songwriters/year. Pays standard royalty.
Affiliate(s): Big Z Productions (ASCAP) and Chrismarie Records.
• See their listing in the Managers and Booking Agents section, and the listing for Chrismarie Records in the Record Companies section.
How to Contact: Submit demo tape by mail. Unsolicited submissions are OK. Prefers cassette (or VHS videocassette) with 3-4 songs and lyric sheet. "Include SASE." Does not return material. Reports in 12-16 weeks.
Music: Mostly **pop**, **rock** and **ballads**; also **country**, **R&B** and **new music**. Published "Dream On," written and recorded by Niko; "Anita," written and recorded by Adamos; and "Glass of Wine," written and recorded by Festa, all on Chrismarie Records.
Tips: "Music should never overshadow the lyrics. Stay positive and have faith in your talent. All submissions must include name, phone number, etc. on all items."

RAVING CLERIC MUSIC PUBLISHING/EUROEXPORT ENTERTAINMENT, P.O. Box 4735, Austin TX 78765-4735. (512)452-2701. Fax: (512)452-0815. E-mail: rcmrecords@aol.com. President: L.A. Evans. Music publisher, record company (RCM Productions), record producer, artist management and development. Estab. 1985. Publishes 5-10 songs/year; publishes 6-8 new songwriters/year. Pays standard royalty.
Affiliate(s): Tripoli Inferno Music Publishing (BMI).
How to Contact: Write first and obtain permission to submit. Prefers cassette with 3 songs maximum and lyric sheet. "Submissions of more than 3 songs will not be listened to." Does not return material. Reports in 4-6 weeks.
Music: Mostly **rock**, **pop** and **R&B**. Published *Is It Hot?* (by Bernard/Rose/St. George); *Blue Ballet* and *Faster Than the Speed of Love* (by Epp/Van Hofwegen), all recorded by Tracy Mitchell on RCM Records.
Tips: "Unsolicited material is not accepted."

REN MAUR MUSIC CORP. (BMI), 521 Fifth Ave., New York NY 10175. (212)757-3638. President: Rena L. Feeney. Music publisher and record company. Member AGAC and NARAS. Publishes 6-8 songs/year. Pays varying royalty.

Affiliate(s): R.R. Music (ASCAP).
- Ren Maur Music's record label, Factory Beat Records, is listed in the Record Companies section.

How to Contact: Submit demo tape by mail. Unsolicited submissions are OK. Prefers cassette with 2-4 songs and lead sheet. SASE. Reports in 1 month.

Music: R&B, rock, soul and **top 40/pop**. Published *It's Our World*, *Rise Up* and *Naughty Girl* (by Billy Nichols), all recorded by Lucia Rena on Factory Beat Records.

Tips: "Send lead sheets and a good, almost finished cassette ready for producing or remixing."

RENT-A-SONG, 4433 Petit, Encino CA 91436. (818)906-0618. Publishing representative: Bradford Bell. Music publisher and record producer. Estab. 1980. Publishes 50 songs/year; publishes 1-2 new songwriters/year. Hires staff songwriters. Pays standard royalty.

Affiliate(s): Lease-A-Tune (ASCAP) and Dennis Lambert Music (BMI).

How to Contact: Write first and obtain permission to submit. Prefers cassette with 2 songs and lyric sheet. Does not return material. Reports in 2 weeks.

Music: Mostly **R&B, pop** and **rock**. Published *Finish What You Started* (by Annie Roboff), recorded by Lea Salonga on Atlantic Records (pop); *Upside* (by Pam Reswick/Steve Werfel), recorded by Girlfriend on BMG Records (dance); and *Thru My Daddy's Eyes* (by Annie Roboff), recorded by Fleetwood Mac on Warner Bros. Records (pop).

Tips: "Send only top quality, competitive hit songs."

RHYTHMS PRODUCTIONS (ASCAP), P.O. Box 34485, Los Angeles CA 90034. President: Ruth White. Music and multimedia publisher. Member NARAS. Publishes 4 titles/year. Pays negotiable royalty.

Affiliate(s): Tom Thumb Music.

How to Contact: Submit tape with letter outlining background in educational children's music. SASE. Reports in 2 months.

Music: "We're only interested in **children's songs** and interactive programs that have educational value. Our materials are sold in schools and homes, so artists/writers with an 'edutainment' background would be most likely to understand our requirements." Published "Professor Whatzit®" series including "Adventures of Professor Whatzit & Carmine Cat"(cassette series for children) and "Musical Math."

RIDGE MUSIC CORP. (BMI, ASCAP), 38 Laurel Ledge Court, Stamford CT 06903. President/General Manager: Paul Tannen. Music publisher and manager. Estab. 1961. Member CMA. Publishes 12 songs/year. Pays standard royalty.

Affiliate(s): Tannen Music Inc. and Deshufflin, Inc.

How to Contact: Submit demo tape by mail. Unsolicited submissions OK. Prefers cassette with 3 songs and lyric sheet. SASE. Reports in 2 months.

Music: Country, rock, top 40/pop and **jazz**.

RISING STAR RECORDS AND PUBLISHERS, 52 Executive Park S., #5203, Atlanta GA 30329. (404)636-2050. E-mail: ristar@mindspring.com. President: Barbara Taylor. Music publisher, record producer, record distributor and record company. Estab. 1987. Publishes 40-50 songs/year; publishes 5 new songwriters/year. Pays standard royalty.

Affiliate(s): New Rising Star Music Publications (ASCAP), Ristar Music Publications (BMI).
- See Rising Star's listing in the Record Companies section.

How to Contact: Submit demo tape by mail. Unsolicited submissions are OK. Prefers cassette with 3 songs and press kit. SASE. Reports in 1-2 months.

Music: Mostly **New Age, Celtic** and **classical**. Published *Lady of the Lake*, written and recorded by William Bowden; *One Day*, written and recorded by Gerald L. Stacy; and *In Memorium*, written and recorded by Martin Wenberg, all on Rising Star Records.

Tips: "We specialize in instrumental music, but accept Celtic and New Age vocals. We are most interested in individual New Age songs for concept compilations (Seashore Solitude, Forest Cathedrals, etc.) and distribution of 'complete' releases (CD and cassette, bar code) by individual artists and small independent labels."

RIVERHAWK MUSIC (BMI), 327 Highway 17 N., Surfside Beach SC 29575. (803)238-1633. President: Arthur W. Byman. Music publisher, record company (Peregrine Records) and record producer. Estab. 1994. Publishes 10 songs/year; publishes 3 new songwriters/year. Pays standard royalty.

How to Contact: Submit demo tape by mail. Unsolicited submissions are OK. Prefers cassette with 3 songs and lyric sheet. "Follow submission outlines exactly. Be neat." Does not return material. Reports in 4-6 weeks.

Music: Mostly **MOR, country** and **A/C**; also **cowboy-type western** and **comedy**. Published *Just One Time* (by A. Byman/J. Carothers), recorded by Art Byman on Americatone Records; "Evil Eyes" (by

A. Byman), recorded by Debbie Atwater and Midnite Run on Gold Rush Records; and "Starlight" (by A. Byman), recorded by Marie Clark on Magenta Records.

*RNR PUBLISHING (ASCAP), 212 N. 12th St., Philadelphia PA 19107. (215)977-7779. Fax: (215)569-4939. E-mail: rage@netaxs.com. President: Vincent Kershner. Music publisher and record producer. Estab. 1990. Publishes 10 new songwriters/year. Hires staff songwriters. Pays variable royalties.
How to Contact: Submit demo tape by mail. Unsolicited submissions are OK. Prefers cassette or DAT and lyric sheet. SASE. Reports in 4-6 weeks.
 • See the listings for Rage-N-Records in the Record Companies section and Ivory Productions in the Record Producers section.
Music: Mostly **commercial rock**, **AAA**, **A/C** and **R&B**; also **blues**. Published "Smack Dab" (by Ron Doroba/Mike Sanfosso/Bill Currier), recorded by Slideways; "Can't Love Yourself," written and recorded by Stevie LaRocca; and "Shelter," written and recorded by Billy Freeze, all on Ikon Records.

*ROB-LEE MUSIC (ASCAP), P.O. Box 1130, Tallevast FL 34270. Vice Presidents: Rodney Russen, Eric Russen, Bob Francis. Music publisher, record company (Castle Records, Rock Island Records and Jade Records), record producer and manager. Estab. 1965. Publishes 18-36 songs/year; publishes 6 new songwriters/year. Pays standard royalty.
Affiliate(s): Heavy Weather Music (ASCAP).
 • Rob-Lee Music's record label, All Star Promotions, is listed in the Record Companies section.
How to Contact: Submit a demo tape by mail. Unsolicited submissions OK. Prefers cassette (or VHS videocassette) with 4-8 songs and lyric sheet. Does not return unsolicited material. Reports in 4 weeks.
Music: Dance-oriented, **easy listening**, **MOR**, **R&B**, **rock**, **soul**, **top 40/pop** and **funk**. Published "I Feel Like Runnin' " and *Murray Woods and Tangled Blue,* written and recorded by Murray Woods on Castle Records (blues); and "Pile Driver" (by D. Isley), recorded by The Big Cheese on Jade Records (rock).
Tips: "Submit full arrangements, not just vocals and acoustic guitar!"

ROCKER MUSIC/HAPPY MAN MUSIC (BMI, ASCAP), P.O. Box 73, 4501 Spring Creek Rd., Bonita Springs, FL 33923-6637. (813)947-6978. Executive Producer: Dick O'Bitts. Estab. 1960. Music publisher, record company (Happy Man Records, Condor Records and Air Corp Records), record producer (Rainbow Collections Ltd.) and management firm (Gemini Complex). Publishes 25-30 songs/year; publishes 8-10 new songwriters/year. Pays standard royalty.
 • Rocker Music's record label, Happy Man Records, is listed in the Record Companies section.
How to Contact: Submit demo tape by mail. Unsolicited submissions are OK. Prefers cassette (or VHS videocassette) with 4 songs and lyric or lead sheet. SASE. Do not call. "You don't need consent to send material." Reports in 1 month.
Music: Country, **rock**, **pop**, **gospel**, **Christian** and **off-the-wall**. Published *Take That Chance* and *Yours For the Takin'* (by Ken Cowden), recorded by Overdue (rock); and *A Prayer That Has Been Answered,* recorded by Challengers, all on Happy Man Records.

ROCKFORD MUSIC CO. (BMI,ASCAP), 150 West End Ave., Suite 6-D, New York NY 10023. Manager: Danny Darrow. Music publisher, record company (Mighty Records), record and video tape producer. Publishes 1-3 songs/year; publishes 1-3 new songwriters/year. Pays standard royalty.
 • Rockford's record label, Mighty Records, is listed in the Record Companies section and Danny Darrow is listed in the Record Producers section.
Affiliate(s): Corporate Music Publishing Company (ASCAP) and Stateside Music Company (BMI).
How to Contact: Submit demo tape by mail. Unsolicited submissions are OK. Prefers cassette with 3 songs and lyric sheet. "SASE a must!" Reports in 1-2 weeks. *"Positively no phone calls."*
Music: Mostly **MOR** and **top 40/pop**; also **adult pop**, **country**, **adult rock**, **dance-oriented**, **easy listening**, **folk** and **jazz**. Published *Corporate Lady* (by Michael Greer), recorded by Danny Darrow (MOR); *Impulse* and *Let There Be Peace,* written and recorded by Danny Darrow, all on Mighty Records.
Tips: "Listen to top 40 and write current lyrics and music."

 • **A BULLET** introduces comments by the editor of *Songwriter's Market* indicating special information about the listing.

RONDOR MUSIC INTERNATIONAL, 360 N. La Cienega, Los Angeles CA 90048. (310)289-3500. Fax: (310)289-4000. Senior Vice President Creative: Brenda Andrews. Music publisher. Estab. 1965. Hires staff writers. Royalty amount depends on deal.
Affiliates: Almo Music Corp. (ASCAP) and Irving Music, Inc. (BMI).
How to Contact: Submit demo tape by mail. Unsolicited submissions are OK. Prefers cassette with 3 songs and lyric sheet. "Send DATs if possible, discography if applicable." SASE. Reports in 3-6 weeks.
Music: A/C, **R&B** and **rock**. Published "Before You Walk Out of My Life" (by Andrea Martin), recorded by Monica; "I Want to Come Over," written and recorded by Melissa Etheridge; and "Hook" (by John Popper), recorded by Blues Traveler.
Tips: "Give only your best, be original."

ROOTS MUSIC (BMI), Box 282, 885 Broadway, Bayonne NJ 07002. President: Robert Bowden. Music publisher, record company (Nucleus Records) and record producer (Robert Bowden). Estab. 1979. Publishes 2 songs/year; publishes 1 new songwriter/year. Pays standard royalty.
● Robert Bowden, Roots Music's president, has a listing in the Record Producers section, and his record label, Nucleus Records, is listed in the Record Companies section.
How to Contact: Write first and obtain permission to submit or to arrange a personal interview. Prefers cassette (or VHS videocassette) with 3 songs and lyric sheet; include photo and bio. "I only want inspired songs written by talented writers." SASE. Reports in 1 month.
Music: Mostly **country** and **pop**; also **church/religious**, **classical**, **folk**, **MOR**, **progressive**, **rock** (**soft, mellow**) and **top 40**. Published "Henrey C," and "Will You Be Missed Tonight," (by Bowden) and "Always" (by M. Sission), all recorded by Marco Sission on Nucleus Records (country).

ROSE HILL GROUP, 1326 Midland Ave., Syracuse NY 13205. (315)475-2936. A&R Director: V. Taft. Music publisher. Estab. 1979. Publishes 1-15 songs/year; publishes 1-5 new songwriters/year. Pays standard royalty.
Affiliate(s): Katch Nazar Music (ASCAP) and Bleecker Street Music (BMI).
How to Contact: Submit demo tape by mail. Unsolicited submissions are OK. Prefers cassette. "Please include typed lyric sheet. No promotional material please." SASE. Reports in 2-4 weeks.
Music: Mostly **pop/rock**, **pop/dance** and **contemporary country**. Published "Love Cake" and "Take A Chance" (by R. Ajemian), recorded by A-Jay on Sunday Records; and *Paula Goodvibes* (by G. Davidson), recorded by Smitty on Cherry Records.
Tips: "Write a simple, memorable melody with a convincing, real story."

RUSTRON MUSIC PUBLISHERS (ASCAP, BMI), 1156 Park Lane, West Palm Beach FL 33417-5957. (407)-686-1354. E-mail: p008647b@pbfreenet.seflin.lib.fl.us. Professional Managers: Rusty Gordon, Ron Caruso and Davilyn Whims. Music publisher and record producer (Rustron Music Productions). Estab. 1972. Publishes 100-150 songs/year; publishes 10-20 new songwriters/year. Pays standard royalty.
Affiliate(s): Whimsong (ASCAP).
● See the listing for Rustron Music Productions in the Record Companies, Record Producers and Managers and Booking Agents sections.
How to Contact: Submit demo tape by mail. Unsolicited submissions are OK. Prefers cassette with 1-3 songs and lyric or lead sheet. "Clearly label your tape and container. Include cover letter." SASE required for all correspondence. Reports in 4 months.
Music: Mostly **pop** (ballads, blues, theatrical, cabaret), **progressive country** and **folk/rock**; also **R&B** and **New Age** instrumental fusions with classical, jazz, pop themes and women's music. Published "Natural Love" (by Victor Paul Bersok), recorded by Jayne Margo-Reby (pop/rock fusion); "For Better or For Worse" (by Star Smiley), recorded by Star Smiley, both on Rustron Records; and "Empty House" (by Gary Barth), recorded by Gary Jess on GBR Records (New Age fusion).
Tips: "Write strong hooks. Keep song length 3½ minutes or less. Avoid predictability—create original lyric themes. Tell a story. Compose definitive melody. Tune in to the trends and fusions indicative of the 90s."

JOSHUA RYAN MUSIC (BMI), 1761 Gregory Jarvis Dr., El Paso TX 79936-5050. (915)855-0168. Fax: (915)541-1182. Owner: John A. Portillo. Music publisher, record company (DOL European Int'l Records) and record producer. Estab. 1991. Publishes 60 songs/year; publishes 5 new songwriters/year. Pays standard royalty.
Affiliates: Sol Musica (BMI) and Beowulf Music International (SESAC).
How to Contact: Submit demo tape by mail. Unsolicited submissions are OK. Prefers cassette with 4 songs and lyric sheet. "Be as thorough as possible when submitting." SASE. Reports in 3 weeks.
Music: Mostly **pop/top 40**, **rock** and **R&B**; also **A/C**, **Latin/pop** and **dance**. Published *Volver A La Tierra* (by Jose Sandoval), recorded by Vicki Carr on Sony Records (ballads); *Skydancer* (by Joshua

Ryan), recorded by Amy Lomeli (pop/rock); and *Voices In The Wind* (by Carlos Portillo), recorded by Malcria II (rock), both on D.E.I. Records.
Tips: "The writer needs to work, refine and complete the song before submitting it. Make the best demo affordable, always submitting the best songs with a good strong hook and memorable melodies."

S.M.C.L. PRODUCTIONS, INC., P.O. Box 84, Boucherville, Quebec J4B 5E6 **Canada**. (514)641-2266. President: Christian Lefort. Music publisher and record company. CAPAC. Estab. 1968. Publishes 25 songs/year. Pays standard royalty.
Affiliate(s): A.Q.E.M. Ltee, Bag Enrg., C.F. Music, Big Bazaar Music, Sunrise Music, Stage One Music, L.M.S. Ltee, ITT Music, Machine Music, Dynamite Music, Danava Music, Coincidence Music, Music and Music, Cinemusic Inc., Cinafilm, Editions La Fete Inc., Groupe Concept Musique, Editions Dorimen, C.C.H. Music (PRO/SDE) and Lavagot Music.
How to Contact: Write first to get permission to submit a tape. Prefers cassette with 4-12 songs and lead sheet. SAE and IRC. Reports in 2-3 months.
Music: Dance, **easy listening** and **MOR**; also **top 40/pop** and **TV and movie soundtracks**. Published *Always and Forever* (by Maurice Jarre/Nathalie Carien), recorded by N. Carsen on BMG Records (ballad); *Au Noy De La Passion*, written and recorded by Alex Stanke on Select Records; and many soundtracks of French-Canadian TV series like: Shadow of the Wolf (Maurice Jarre); The Breakthrough (Oswaldo Montes); Bethune (Alan Reeves); The First Circle (Gabriel Yared).

SABTECA MUSIC CO. (ASCAP), Box 10286, Oakland CA 94610. (415)465-2805. A&R: Sean Herring. President: Duane Herring. Music publisher and record company (Sabteca Record Co., Andre-Romare). Estab. 1980. Publishes 8-10 songs/year; 1-2 new songwriters/year. Pays standard royalty.
  • See the listing for Sabteca Record Co. in the Record Companies section.
Affiliate(s): Toyiabe Publishing (BMI).
How to Contact: Write first and obtain permission to submit a tape. Prefers cassette with 2 songs and lyric sheet. SASE. Reports in 8 weeks.
Music: Mostly **R&B**, **pop** and **country**. Published "Sacrifice," "One Hundred Pounds of Love" and "One Day Man" (by Duane Herring/Tom Roller), all recorded by Johnny B on Sabteca Records.

SADDLESTONE PUBLISHING (SOCAN, BMI), 264 "H" St., Box 8110-21, Blaine WA 98230. Canada Address: 6260-130 St., Surrey British Columbia V3X 1R6 **Canada**. (604)572-4232. Fax: (604)572-4252. President: Rex Howard. Music publisher, record company (Saddlestone) and record producer (Silver Bow Productions). Estab. 1988. Publishes 100 songs/year; publishes 12-30 new songwriters/year. Pays standard royalty.
Affiliate(s): Silver Bow Publishing (SOCAN, ASCAP).
  • See the listing for Saddlestone Records in the Record Companies section, Silver Bow Productions in the Record Producers section and Silver Bow Management in the Managers and Booking Agents Section.
How to Contact: Submit demo tape by mail. Unsolicited submissions are OK. Prefers cassette with 3 songs and lyric sheet. "Make sure vocal is clear." SASE. Reports in 3 months.
Music: Mostly **country**, **rock** and **pop**; also **gospel** and **R&B**. Published "Page of a Poet" (by Billy O'Hara), recorded by Debbie Davis on Richway Records (country); *She's Something* (by James Earl Wilson), recorded Razzy Bailey on BMG Records (crossover); and *Read Between the Lies* (by Frank Turner), recorded by Debbie Davis on Sabre.
Tips: "Submit clear demos, good hooks and avoid long intros or instrumentals. Have a good singer do vocals."

SAMUEL THREE PRODUCTIONS (BMI), 4056 Shady Valley Dr., Arlington TX 76013. (817)274-5530. President: Samuel Egnot. Music publisher and record company (Alpha Recording Co.). Estab. 1992. Publishes 12 songs/year; publishes 7 new songwriters/year. Pays standard royalty.
  • See the listing for Alpha Recording Co. in the Record Companies section.
How to Contact: Submit demo tape by mail. Unsolicited submissions are OK. Prefers cassette with lead sheet. SASE. Reports in 2 months.
Music: Mostly **country**, **country-gospel** and **gospel**; also **southern gospel**. Published "Now That You're Gone" (by Sam Egnot), recorded by Sam Younger; "Jesus Loves You and Me" (by Sam

---

HOW TO GET THE MOST out of *Songwriter's Market* (at the front of this book) contains comments and suggestions to help you understand and use the information in these listings.

Egnot), recorded by Samuel Three; and "I've Fallen Again," written and recorded by Sami McLemore, all on Alpha Recording Co. Records.
Tips: "Be aggressive in getting your demos out. Don't stop at one turndown, send to another and another till you feel it's going to receive recognition. If it's good to you, ask for perhaps another musical group to consider redoing your material."

*SCI-FI MUSIC (SOCAN), P.O. Box 941, N.D.G., Montreal Quebec H4A 3S3 **Canada**. (514)487-8953. President: Gary Moffet (formerly guitarist/composer with April Wine). Music publisher. Estab. 1984. Publishes 10 songs/year; publishes 2 new songwriters/year. Pays standard royalty.
  • See the listing for Gary Moffet in the Record Producers section.
How to Contact: Submit demo tape by mail. Unsolicited submissions are OK. Submit cassette with 3-10 songs and lyric sheet. Does not return material. Reports in 1 month.
Music: Mostly **rock** and **pop**.

TIM SCOTT MUSIC GROUP (BMI), 622 State St., Room 36, Springfield MA 01109. (413)746-4604. E-mail: tsmg@aol.com. President: Timothy Scott. Music publisher. Estab. 1993. Publishes 20-50 songs/year. Hires staff writers. Pays standard royalty.
Affiliates: Tim Scott Music (ASCAP).
  • Tim Scott's record label, Keeping It Simple and Safe, is listed in the Record Companies section.
How to Contact: Submit demo tape by mail. Unsolicited submissions are OK. Prefers cassette with 3-5 songs and lyric sheet. SASE. Reports in 2 months.
Music: Mostly **R&B** and **pop**; also **country**, **rock** and **gospel**. Published "What About Me" (by Tim Scott), recorded by Sweet Tooth on Southend Essex Records; "Forever Yours" (by Tim Scott), recorded by Loveworld and *Everything I Do* (by Tim Scott), recorded by S.E.D., both on Nightowl Records.

SCRUTCHINGS MUSIC (BMI), 429 Homestead St., Akron OH 44306. (216)773-8529. Owner/President: Walter E. L. Scrutchings. Music publisher. Estab. 1980. Publishes 35 songs/year; publishes 10-20 new songwriters/year. Hires staff songwriters. Pays standard royalty.
How to Contact: Submit demo tape by mail. Unsolicited submissions are OK. Prefers cassette (or videocassette if available) with 2 songs, lyric and lead sheet. Does not return material. Reports in 3-4 weeks.
Music: Mostly **gospel**, **contemporary** and **traditional**. Published "The Joy He Brings" (by R. Hinton), recorded by Akron City Mass; "God Has the Power" (by W. Scrutchings), recorded by Gospel Music Workshop Mass on Savoy Records (gospel); and "My Testimony" (by A. Cobb), recorded by Akron City Family Mass Choir on Scrutchings Music (gospel).
Tips: "Music must be clear and uplifting in message."

*SEA DREAM MUSIC, 236 Sebert Rd., Forest Gate, London E7 0NP **United Kingdom**. Phone: (0181)534-8500. Senior Partner: Simon Law. PRS. Music publisher and record company (Plankton Records, Embryo Arts of Belgium, Gutta of Sweden). Estab. 1976. Publishes 50 songs/year; publishes 2 new songwriters/year. Pays 66⅔% royalty.
  • See their listing in the Music Print Publishers section, as well as listings for Plankton Records in the Record Companies section and Sandcastle Productions in the Managers and Booking Agents section.
Affiliate(s): Scarf Music Publishing, Really Free Music, Ernvik Musik (Sweden), Chain of Love Music, Crimson Flame.
How to Contact: Write first and obtain permission to submit. Prefers cassette with 3 songs and lyric sheet. "Technical information about the recording is useful, as are the songwriter's expectations of the company—i.e., what they want us to do for them." SAE and IRC. Reports in 3 months.
Music: Mostly **funk/rock**, **rock** and **blues**. Published *Slow Burning Candle* (by Simon Law), recorded by Fresh Claim (rock); *Dreamscape* (by Stuart Elwin), recorded by Asylum (pop); and *Put It on the Front Page* (by Derek Llewellyn), recorded by Newshounds (children's), all on Plankton Records.
Tips: "We are specifically interested in material with a Christian bias to the lyrics."

*SECOND CITY PUBLISHING, P.O. Box 187, Golden City MO 64748. (417)537-8776. Contact: Sandy Williams or Mike Brandon. Music publisher. Pays standard royalty.
How to Contact: Write or call first and obtain permission to submit a demo. Prefers cassette and lyric sheet. Does not return material.
Music: Mostly **country**, **rock** and **R&B**. Published *Where Are You Now, Fly* and *Paint My Cadillac Black, Joe* (by Mike Brandon), both recorded by Solace on Weeping Onion Records (rock).
Tips: "Make sure your lyrics are contemporary. Submit clean, professional demos. Be open to constructive criticism."

SEGAL'S PUBLICATIONS (BMI), 16 Grace Rd., Newton MA 02159. (617)969-6196. Contact: Charles Segal. Music publisher and record producer (Segal's Productions). Estab. 1963. Publishes 80 songs/year; publishes 6 new songwriters/year. Pays standard royalty.
Affilate(s): Charles Segal's Publications (BMI) and Charles Segal's Music (SESAC).
• See the listing for Segal's Productions in the Record Producers section.
How to Contact: Submit demo tape by mail. Unsolicited submissions are OK. Prefers cassette (or VHS videocassette) with 3 songs and lyric or lead sheet. Does not return material. Reports in 4 months.
Music: Mostly **rock**, **pop** and **country**; also **R&B, MOR** and **children's songs**. Published "A Time to Care" (by Brilliant/Segal), recorded by Rosemary Wills (MOR); "Go to Bed" (by Colleen Segal), recorded Susan Stark (MOR); and "Only In Dreams" (by Chas. Segal), recorded by Rosemary Wills (MOR), all on Spin Records.
Tips: "Besides making a good demo cassette, include a lead sheet of music—words, melody line and chords."

SELLWOOD PUBLISHING (BMI), 170 N. Maple, Fresno CA 93702. (209)255-1717. Owner: Stan Anderson. Music publisher, record company (TRAC Record Co.) and record producer. Estab. 1972. Publishes 10 songs/year; publishes 3 new songwriters/year. Pays standard royalty.
• Sellwood Publishing's record label, TRAC Record Co., is listed in the Record Companies and Record Producers sections.
How to Contact: Submit demo tape—unsolicited submissions are OK. Prefers cassette (or VHS videocassette) with 2 songs and lyric sheet. SASE. Reports in 3 weeks. Submit studio quality demos.
Music: Mostly **traditional country** and **country**. Published *Grandpa's Old Piano* (by Ray Richmond), recorded by Jessica James; *Kick Me When I'm Down*; and *They Play Country Music in Heaven*, both written and recorded by Jimmy Walker, all country on TRAC Records.

SHA-LA MUSIC, INC. (BMI), 137 Legion Place, Hillsdale NJ 07642. (201)664-1995. Fax: (201)664-1349. President: Robert Allen. Music publisher. Estab. 1987. Publishes 10 songs/year; publishes 1-4 new songwriters/year. Pays standard royalty.
Affiliate(s): By The Numbers Music (ASCAP).
How to Contact: Submit demo tape by mail. Unsolicited submissions are OK. Prefers cassette with 3 songs and lyric sheet. "Keep package neat to make a good impression." SASE. Reports in 6 weeks.
Music: Mostly **R&B, pop** and **dance**; also **rock** and **A/C**. Published "What If" (by T. Fletcher), recorded by Shotgun Symphony on CJ Records; *Society Did It* (by Jessie Thomas), recorded by the Discontent; and *Good Karma*, written and recorded by Monte Farber, both on Sha-La Records.
Tips: "Keep in mind what kind of artist you want to record your song. The more focused on a market or genre, the better for the songwriter."

SHAOLIN MUSIC (ASCAP), P.O. Box 58547, Salt Lake City UT 84158. (801)595-1123. President: Richard O'Connor. Vice President, A&R: Don Dela Vega. Music publisher, record company (Shaolin Film and Records) and record producer (Richard O'Connor). Estab. 1984. Pays standard royalty.
• Shaolin Music's record label, Shaolin Film and Records, is listed in the Record Companies section.
How to Contact: Submit demo tape by mail. Unsolicited submissions are OK. Prefers cassette with 3-4 songs and lyric sheet. Include bio and press kit. Does not return material. Reports in 6 weeks.
Music: Mostly **rock, hard rock** and **pop**; also **soundtracks**. Published *Peace of Mind* and *Black of Night* (by T. Coyote), recorded by American Zen (rock); and *Tai Chi Magic*, written and recorded by Zhen Shen-Lang, all on Shaolin Film and Records.
Tips: "Utilize our criticisms. We almost always give a constructive criticism. Learn to improve, not react."

SHU'BABY MONTEZ MUSIC, 1447 N. 55th St., Philadelphia PA 19131. (215)473-5527. President: Leroy Schuler. Music publisher. Estab. 1986. Publishes 25 songs/year; publishes 10 new songwriters/year. Pays standard royalty.
How to Contact: Write first and obtain permission to submit. Prefers cassette with 3 songs and lyric sheet. SASE. Reports in 5 weeks.
Music: Mostly **R&B, pop** and **hip-hop**. Published *Free Style* (K. Chaney/V. Butler/Shu' Baby), recorded by Shu' Baby on Urban Logic (R&B); "Love Came Callin' " (by C. Washington/Shu' Baby), recorded by Vicki Woodlyn on Phoenix Voice (R&B); and "Nod Your Head to This" (by Rockin' Rodney Moore), recorded by B.O.B. (R&B) on Urban Logic Records (rap).

SIEGEL MUSIC COMPANIES, Friedastr 22, 81479, Munich **Germany**. Phone: +49-89-7498070. Fax: +49-89-7498077. Managing Director: Joachim Neubauer. Music publisher, record company, (Jupiter Records and 69-Records) and record producer. Estab. 1948. GEMA. Publishes 1,500 songs/year; publishes 50 new songwriters/year. Hires staff songwriters. Pays 60% according to the rules of GEMA.

Affiliate(s): Sounds of Jupiter, Inc. (USA), Step Five (Brazil), Gobian Music (ASCAP), Symphonie House Music (ASCAP), Krok 12 (Čech Republic).
How to Contact: Submit demo tape by mail. Unsolicited submissions are OK. Prefers cassette (or VHS videocassette, but not necessary). SAE and IRC. Reports in 6 weeks.
Music: Mostly **pop**, **disco** and **MOR**; also **"hard and heavy" rock**, **country** and **soul**. Published *Max, Don't Have Sex With Your Ex* (by Brandes/Gaude/O'Flynn), recorded by E-rotic on Intercord Records (dance); *Sing It to You* (by Knole/Mersmann), recorded by Lavinia Jones on Virgin Records (dance); and *Hemingway Hideaway* (by R. Siegel/T.T. Kermit), recorded by Bellamy Brothers on Jupiter Records (country).

SILICON MUSIC PUBLISHING CO. (BMI), Ridgewood Park Estates, 222 Tulane St., Garland TX 75043. President: Gene Summers. Vice President: Deanna L. Summers. Public Relations: Steve Summers. Music publisher and record company (Domino Records, Ltd. and Front Row Records). Estab. 1965. Publishes 10-20 songs/year; publishes 2-3 new songwriters/year. Pays standard royalty.
How to Contact: Submit demo tape by mail. Unsolicited submissions are OK. Prefers cassette with 1-2 songs. Does not return material. "We are usually slow in answering due to overseas tours."
Music: Mostly **rockabilly** and **'50s material**; also **old-time blues/country** and **MOR**. Published *My Yearbook* (by Dea Summers) and *Fancy Dan* (by James McClung), both recorded by Gene Summers on Sundaze Records; and *Goodbye Priscilla* (by Dea Summers/Ben Shaw/Dave Saxton), recorded by Gene Summers on Home Cooking Records.
Tips: "We are very interested in '50s rock and rockabilly *original masters* for release through overseas affiliates. If you are the owner of any '50s masters, contact us first! We have releases in Holland, Switzerland, England, Belgium, France, Sweden, Norway and Australia. We have the market if you have the tapes!"

SILVER BLUE MUSIC/OCEANS BLUE MUSIC, 5370 Vanalden Ave., Tarzana CA 91356. (818)345-2558. Music publisher. Estab. 1971. Publishes 25 songs/year. Pays standard royalty.
How to Contact: Submit demo tape by mail. Unsolicited submissions are OK. Prefers cassette with lead sheet. Does not return material.
Music: Mostly **pop** and **R&B**; also **rap**. Published "After the Lovin" (by Bernstead/Adams), recorded by Englebert Humperdinck.

SILVER THUNDER MUSIC GROUP, P.O. Box 41335, Nashville TN 37204. (615)391-5035. President: Rusty Budde. Music publisher, record producer (Rusty Budde Productions). Estab. 1985. Publishes 200 songs/year. Publishes 5-10 new songwriters/year. Hires staff songwriters. Pays standard royalty.
How to Contact: Write to obtain permission to submit. Prefers cassette (or VHS videocassette if available). Does not return material.
Music: Mostly **country**, **pop** and **R&B**. Published *Rock N Cowboys*, written and recorded by Jeff Samules on STR Records; *This Ain't the Real Thing* (by Rusty Budde), recorded by Les Taylor on CBS Records; and "Feel Again" (by Rusty Budde/Shara Johnson), recorded by Shara Johnson on Warner Bros. Records.
Tips: "Send clear, clean recording on cassette with lyric sheets."

SILVERHILL MUSIC (BMI), P.O. Box 39439, Los Angeles CA 90039. (213)663-8073. Fax: (213)669-1470. A&R: Diana Collette. Music publisher and record company. Estab. 1975. Pays standard royalty "in most cases."
Affiliate(s): Silver Ridge Music (ASCAP).
How to Contact: Submit demo tape by mail. Unsolicited submissions are OK. Prefers cassette. Does not return material. Reports in 2 months.
Music: Mostly **country, bluegrass** and **children's**; also **alternative** and **death metal**. Published *Gonna Get There Soon* (by M. Adcock); *Melting Point* and *Champagne Break*, both written and recorded by Eddie Adcock.

SIMPLY GRAND MUSIC, INC. (ASCAP, BMI), P.O. Box 41981, Memphis TN 38174-1981. (901)272-7039. President: Linda Lucchesi. Music publisher. Estab. 1965. Pays standard royalty.

LISTINGS OF COMPANIES in countries other than the U.S. have the name of the country in boldface type.

Affiliate(s): Memphis Town Music, Inc. (ASCAP) and Beckie Publishing Co. (BMI).
How to Contact: Write or call first and obtain permission to submit. Prefers cassette with 1-3 songs and lyric sheet. SASE. Reports in 4-6 weeks. "Please do not send demos by certified or registered mail."
Music: Mostly **pop** and **soul**; also **country** and **soft rock**.
Tips: "We are the publishing home of 'Wooly Bully'."

SISKATUNE MUSIC PUBLISHING CO., 285 Chestnut St., West Hempstead NY 11552. (516)489-0738. Fax: (516)565-9425. E-mail: platear1@aol.com. President: Mike Siskind. Vice President Creative Affairs: Rick Olarsch. Music publisher. Estab. 1981. Publishes 20 songs/year; publishes 10 new songwriters/year. Pays standard royalty.
• Siskatune's management firm, Platinum Ears Ltd., is listed in the Managers and Booking Agents section.
How to Contact: Write first to obtain permission to submit. Prefers cassette with a maximum of 3 songs and lyric sheet. "Send any and all pertinent information." SASE. Reports in 2-3 months. "No phone calls."
Music: **R&B** and **country**; also **dance** and **ballads**. Published "The Ballad of Romeo Spaghetti & Billy Moon" (by Georgi Smith/John C. Thomas), recorded by Georgi Smith on Red Hand Records (jazz/rock); "Should Have Been Lovers" (by Tod Stewart); and "Wild Horse from Waycross" (by Michael Ellis), recorded Georgi Smith on Red Hand Records (country).
Tips: "Send three songs maximum. Think songs that are coverable. Please don't check if we got the package unless it's been three months and you haven't heard from us. It is essential that demo is more than piano/vocal or guitar/vocal, as we send out those demos. Also include lyric sheets."

SIZEMORE MUSIC (BMI), P.O. Box 23275, Nashville TN 37202. (615)385-1662. Fax: (904)799-9958. Contact: Gary Sizemore. Music publisher, record company (The Gas Co.) and record producer (Gary Sizemore). Estab. 1960. Publishes 5 songs/year; 1 new songwriter/year. Pays standard royalty.
How to Contact: Submit a demo tape by mail. Unsolicited submissions are OK. Prefers cassette (or VHS videocassette) with lyric sheets. Does not return material. Reports in 2 weeks.
Music: Mostly **soul** and **R&B**; also **blues**, **pop** and **country**. Published "Liquor and Wine" and "The Wind," written and recorded by K. Shackleford on Heart Records (country); and "She's Tuff" (by Jerry McCain), recorded by The Fabulous Thunderbirds on Chrysalis Records (blues).

SLANTED CIRCLE MUSIC (BMI), 15114 Campbell Lane, Dale City VA 22193. (703)670-8092. A&R Dept.: Pete Lawrence. Music publisher and record producer. Estab. 1993. Publishes 15 songs/year; publishes 10 new songwriters/year. Pays standard royalty.
How to Contact: Submit demo tape by mail. Unsolicited submissions are OK. Prefers cassette or DAT with 2 songs and lyric sheet. "Only fully produced band demos." SASE. Reports in 3 weeks.
Music: Mostly **go cat rockabilly**; also **Chicago blues**, **Christian pop** and **contemporary jazz**. *Absolutely no country!* Published "Full Size Woman," written and recorded by Larry LaVey; "If You Get to Know Him" (by LaVey/Voyles), recorded by Larry LaVey and Kim Clennan; and "Another Empty Table For Two" (by LaVey/Kingery), recorded by Teri Schaeffer, all on Trend Records.
Tips: "Have a good clear demo made and use the best tape when pitching material. A demo should sound authentic to the style the publisher wants. Research the style before sending."

SLEEPING GIANT MUSIC INTERNATIONAL LTD., 34 Great James St., London WC1N 3HB United Kingdom. (071)405-3786. Fax: (071)405-5245. A&R Director: Ian Taylor King. Music publisher, record company and record producer. Pays varying royalty.
How to Contact: Submit demo tape by mail. Unsolicited submissions are OK. Prefers cassette (or VHS videocassette if available) with 4 songs and lyric sheet. SAE and IRC.
Music: **All types**. Published "World Is So Small," recorded by Francesco Bruno and Richie Havens; "Till the Next Somewhere," recorded by Dee Dee Bridgewater and Ray Charles; and "Shades," recorded by George Williams, all on Prestige Records Ltd.

*SMOKEY LANE MUSIC (ASCAP), 3310 Mercury, Grapevine TX 76051. (817)481-4206. Owner: Hank Riddle. Music publisher. Estab. 1988. Publishes 20 songs/year; publishes 1-2 new songwriters/year. Hires staff songwriters. Pays standard royalty (sometimes more).
How to Contact: Submit demo tape by mail. Unsolicited submissions are OK. Prefers cassette with 3 songs and lyric sheet. SASE. Reports in 2 weeks.
Music: Mostly **country**, **pop** and **rock**; also **gospel**, **blues** and **jazz**. Published *Crazy Over You* (by Hank Riddle), recorded by Smith Sisters on Flying Fish Records (folk); *Until I Met You* (by Hank Riddle), recorded by Judy Rodman on MTM Records (country); and "Mid-nite Fever" (by Hank Riddle), recorded by Steve Young on RCA Records (country).

*SNOWCLIFF PUBLISHING (BMI), P.O. Box 82, De Ridder LA 70634. (318)462-3514. President: Cliff Shelder. Vice President: Gene Snow. Music publisher, record company (SME Records), record producer, music production company (SME Music). Estab. 1993. Publishes 10-15 songs/year; publishes 3-5 new songwriters/year. Pays standard royalty.
Affiliate(s): Snowcap Publishing (BMI).
How to Contact: Write or call first and obtain permission to submit a demo. Prefers cassette or DAT with no more than 3 songs and lyric sheet. Does not return material. Reports in 3-5 weeks.
Music: Contemporary Christian, country gospel and **country**; also **pop**, **jazz** and **blues**. Published "Granny" (by Cliff Shelder), recorded by Rebecca Yerg (contemporary Christian); "Put Your Lovin' Where Your Mouth Is" (by Cliff Shelder/Kellie Penney), recorded by Kellie Penney (country), both on SME Records; and *Glory Road* (by Jim Hall), recorded by Gene Snow on Smart Records (country gospel).
Tips: "We prefer songs with a positive message—not beer drinkin' music. Submit good quality demos in a neat package. Have your music performed in public and gauge the audiences response. If people keep asking to hear a particular song, we'd like to hear it too."

SOLID ENTERTAINMENT, (formerly AVC Music), Dept. SM, 11300 Magnolia Blvd., #1000, N. Hollywood CA 91601. (818)763-3535. President: James Warsinske. Music publisher. Estab. 1988. Publishes 30-60 songs/year; publishes 10-20 new songwriters/year. Pays standard royalty.
Affiliate(s): Harmonious Music (BMI).
How to Contact: Submit demo tape by mail. Unsolicited submissions are OK. Prefers cassette or VHS videocassette with 2-5 songs and lyric sheet. "Clearly labelled tapes with phone numbers." SASE. Reports in 1 month.
Music: Mostly **R&B/soul**, **pop** and **rock**; also **A/C**. Published "Let It Be Right," written and recorded by Duncan Faure on AVC Records (pop/rock); "Melissa Mainframe" (by Hohl/Rocca), recorded by Rocca on Life Records (pop/rap); and "In Service" (by Michael Williams), recorded by Madrok on AVC Records (rap).
Tips: "Be yourself, let your talents shine regardless of radio trends."

SONG FARM MUSIC (BMI), P.O. Box 24561, Nashville TN 37202. (615)742-1557. President: Tom Pallardy. Music publisher and record producer (T.P. Productions). Member NSAI. Estab. 1980. Publishes 2-5 songs/year; publishes 1-2 new songwriters/year. Pays standard royalty.
How to Contact: Write or call first and obtain permission to submit. Requires cassette with maximum 2 songs and lyric or lead sheet. SASE required with enough postage for return of all materials. Reports in 2-6 weeks.
Music: Mostly **country**, **R&B** and **pop**; also **crossover** and **top 40**. Published "Mississippi River Rat" (by J. Hall, R. Hall, E. Dickey), recorded by Tom Powers on Fountain Records (Cajun country); "Today's Just Not the Day" (by J. Bell, E. Bobbitt), recorded by Liz Draper (country); and "In Mama's Time" (by T. Crone), recorded by Pat Tucker on Radioactive Records (country/pop).
Tips: "Material should be submitted neatly and professionally with as good quality demo as possible. Songs need not be elaborately produced (voice and guitar/piano are fine) but they should be clear. Songs must be well constructed, lyrically tight, good strong hook, interesting melody, easily remembered; i.e., commercial!"

*SONY/ATV MUSIC PUBLISHING (ASCAP, BMI), 8 Music Square W., Nashville TN 37203. (615)726-8300. Fax: (615)244-6387. Director, Creative Services: Mr. Dale Dodsons. Music publisher. Estab. 1955. Publishes over 500 songs/year; publishes 0-20 new songwriters/year. Hires staff writers. "All contracts are negotiated individually."
Affiliate(s): Cross Keys (ASCAP), Tree (BMI).
  • Sony/ATV has been voted *Billboard*'s Country Music Publisher of the Year for 23 consecutive years.
How to Contact: Submit demo tape by mail. Unsolicited submissions are OK. Prefers cassette with 5 songs and lyric sheet. "Hits only, please." Does not return material. Reports in 2 weeks.
Music: Mostly **country** and **western**. Published "Let That Pony Run" (by Gretchen Peters), recorded by Pam Tillis on Arista Records (country); "Ain't Going Down 'till the Sun Comes Up" (by Kim Williams), recorded by Garth Brooks on Capitol Records (country); and "Neon Moon" (by Don Cook), recorded by Brooks & Dunn on Arista Records (country).
Tips: "Submit a good demo of a great song."

SOUND CELLAR MUSIC, 116 N. Peoria, Dixon IL 61021. (815)288-2900. Music publisher, record company, record producer, recording studio. Estab. 1987. Publishes 15-25 songs/year. Publishes 5 or 6 new songwriters/year. Pays standard royalty. "No charge obviously for publishing, but if we record the artist there is a small reduced fee for rental of our studio."
  • Sound Cellar Music's record label, Cellar Records, is listed in the Record Companies section.

How to Contact: Submit demo tape by mail. Unsolicited submissions are OK. Prefers cassette with 3 or 4 songs and lyric sheet. Does not return material. "We contact by phone only if we want to work with the artist."
Music: Mostly **metal**, **country** and **rock**; also **pop**, **rap** and **blues**. Published *Collins*, written and recorded by Snap Judgment (alternative); *Soul Searchin'*, written and recorded by Justice 4 (rock); and "Spill A Tear," written and recorded by Impetus (metal), all on Cellar Records.
Tips: "Be realistic about making it in the music business. It takes time and self-investment just like any business does. Forget about so-called overnight success."

SOUNdBYTE CORPORATION, Box 70219, Richmond VA 23255. (804)262-9940. Fax: (804)262-9387. Contact: Patrick D. Kelley. Music publisher. Pays standard royalty.
How to Contact: Submit demo tape by mail. Unsolicited submissions are OK. Prefers cassette with 2 songs and lyric sheet. "Please limit demo to 2 songs at a time. Be sure to include lyric sheet with a letter stating what you are seeking." SASE. Reports in 1 month.
Music: Mostly **country**, **gospel** and **children's**; also **folk**, **rock** and **pop**.

SOUNDS OF AICRAM (BMI), 375 Military Rd., Kalama WA 98265-0460. (360)673-2487. President: Ron Dennis Wheeler. Music publisher. Estab. 1964. Publishes 100 songs/year; 20-25 new songwriters/year. "Sometimes hires staff writers for special projects." Pays standard royalty.
Affiliate(s): Do It Now Publishing (ASCAP), RR&R Music (BMI) and McGibony Publishing (BMI).
• See the listing for RR&R Records in the Record Companies section, and RR&R Productions in the Record Producers section.
How to Contact: "Send a professionally recorded demo tape—if not, response time may be delayed. Unsolicited submissions are OK. Send music tracks with and without lead vocals. Lyric sheet and chords. Also send music score if possible. Prefers 15 ips and a cassette copy and DAT. Clarity is most important. SASE is a must if you want submission returned. Responds only if interested."
Music: **Gospel**, **rock** and **pop**; also **country** and **R&B**. "No New Age." Published "I Need You" (by Richard McGibony), co-published by EMI; "Reason," written and recorded by Richard McGibony; and "Two Shades of Blue" (by R. McGibony/R.D. Wheeler), recorded by Bill Scarbrough on Legends Records.

*SOUNDS-VISION MUSIC, P.O. Box 3691, La Mesa CA 91944-3691. Phone/fax: (619)460-1146. Owner: Rodion Hollman. Music publisher, record company, record producer and distributor. Estab. 1986. Publishes 30 songs/year. Publishes 3-4 new songwriters/year. "Royalty amount varies per contract."
Affiliate(s): Xpresh'N Series Music (BMI).
• See their listing in the Record Companies section.
How to Contact: Submit demo tape by mail. Unsolicited submissions are OK. Prefers cassette with 1-3 songs. Does not return material. Reports in 6 weeks.
Music: Mostly **flamenco**, **gypsy music** and **international**; also **classical guitar**. Published *Tarantas*, written and recorded by Daniel de Malaga (flamenco); *Granainas*, written and recorded by Alberto de Malaga (flamenco); and *Nos Volvemos a Querer*, written and recorded by Remedios Flores (flamenco), all on Sounds-Vision Records.
Tips: "Please do not send sheet music. Only reviews/quotes/etc. from major periodicals. We will test market pre-produced CDs for a minimal fee."

SOUTHERN MOST PUBLISHING COMPANY (BMI), P.O. Box 1461446, Laurie MO 65038. (314)374-1111. President/Owner: Dann E. Haworth. Music publisher and record producer (Haworth Productions). Estab. 1985. Publishes 10 songs/year; 3 new songwriters/year. Hires staff songwriters. Pays standard royalty.
Affiliates: Boca Chi Key Publishing (ASCAP).
• See the listing for Haworth Productions in the Record Producers section.
How to Contact: Write first and obtain permission to submit. Prefers cassette with 3 songs and lyric sheet. SASE. Reports in 6-8 weeks.
Music: Mostly **rock**, **R&B** and **country**; also **gospel** and **New Age**.
Tips: "Keep it simple and from the heart."

THE SPACEK CO., P.O. Box 741506, Dallas TX 75374. (903)882-1375. President: Ed Spacek. Music publisher. Estab. 1978. Pays standard royalty.
Affiliate(s): Woodcreek (ASCAP), Eagles Nest (BMI).
How to Contact: Submit demo tape by mail. Unsolicited submissions are OK. Prefers cassette. Does not return material. Reports in 1 month.
Music: All types.

SPHEMUSATIONS, 12 Northfield Rd., Onehouse, Stowmarket Suffolk 1P14 3HF **England**. Phone: 0449-613388. General Manager: James Butt. Music publisher. Estab. 1963. Publishes 200 songs/year; publishes 6 new songwriters/year. Pays 10% royalty.
How to Contact: Submit demo tape by mail. Unsolicited submissions are OK. Prefers cassette (or VHS or Beta videocassette). SAE and IRC. Reports in 3 months.
Music: Serious modern music. Published *The Romantic Cello* (by Brahms, Fauré, Casals, St. Saens), recorded by Gillian Benjamin; *Interinfinitus* (by James Butt), recorded by South Suffolk Symphonia; and *Spring Sonata* (by Beethoven), recorded by James Maddocks/James Butt, all on Sphemusations Records.
Tips: "Present yourself with a good sense of style."

SPRADLIN/GLEICH PUBLISHING (BMI), 4234 N. 45th St., Phoenix AZ 85018-4307. Manager: Lee Gleich. Music publisher. Estab. 1988. Publishes 4-10 songs/year; 2-4 new songwriters. Pays standard royalty.
Affiliate(s): Paul Lee Publishing (ASCAP).
How to Contact: Write first to obtain permission to submit. Prefers cassette with 3 songs and lyric or lead sheet. "It must be very good material, as I only have time for promoting songwriters who really care." SASE. Reports in 1 month.
Music: Mostly **country** geared to the US and European country markets. Published "I Gotta Learn to Dance" and "Love's Gone Crazy," both written and recorded by Bob Cesaro on Wild Sky Records (rock); and *Go Slow and Wait* (by Paul Spradlin), recorded by the Goose Creek Symphony on Goose Records (country).
Tips: "Send me a request letter, then send me your best song. We are now publishing mostly all country and rockabilly!"

SPRING ROSE MUSIC (BMI) (formerly Songfinder Music), 4 Reina Lane, Valley Cottage NY 10989. (914)268-7711. Owner: Frank Longo. Music publisher. Estab. 1987. Publishes 20 songs/year; publishes 5-10 new songwriters/year. Pays standard royalty.
Affiliate(s): Songfinder Music (ASCAP).
How to Contact: Submit demo tape by mail. Unsolicited submissions are OK. Prefers cassette with 2 songs and lyric sheets. SASE. "No SASE—no returns." Reports in 4 weeks.
Music: Mostly **country**, **pop**, **MOR** and **soft rock**; also **top 40/pop** and **uptempo country**. Published *Lovin*, written and recorded by Rich Micallef on Artistic Records (MOR); *Hurty Flirty Love*, written and recorded by Jerry Piper on Missile Records (country); and "Slow Night in Memphis" (by J. D'Allesandro), recorded by Elvis Spencer on Gold Wax Records (R&B).
Tips: "Listen to what's being played on the radio. Be professional. Good demos get good results. Up tempo positive lyrics are always wanted. Success needs no apology—failure provides no alibi. Egos are a dime a dozen—good songwriters have open ears and closed lips and pencils with big erasers to rewrite, rewrite, rewrite."

STABLE MUSIC CO. (BMI), 6503 Wolf Creek Pass, Austin TX 78749. (512)288-3370. Fax: (512)288-1926. Owner: Rex T. Sherry. Music publisher, record company (Thoroughbred Records) and record producer. Estab. 1967. Publishes 5-10 songs/year. Pays standard royalty.
How to Contact: Write first and obtain permission to submit. Prefers cassette with 2-4 songs and lyric sheet. SASE. Reports in 3 weeks.
Music: Mostly **country**; also **bluegrass**.
Tips: "Write material with a particular artist in mind."

STARBOUND PUBLISHING CO. (BMI), Dept. SM, 207 Winding Rd., Friendswood TX 77546. (713)482-2346. President: Buz Hart. Music publisher, record company (Juke Box Records, Quasar Records and Eden Records) and record producer (Lonnie Wright and Buz Hart). Estab. 1970. Publishes 35-100 songs/year; publishes 5-10 new songwriters/year. Pays standard royalty.
How to Contact: Write first and obtain permission to submit. Prefers cassette with 3 songs and lyric sheet. SASE. Reports in 2 months.
Music: Mostly **country**, **R&B** and **gospel**. Published "Butterfly" (by Pamela Parkins/Buz Hart), recorded by Frankie Laine on Score Records; "Let it Slide" (by James Watson/Buz Hart), recorded by Stan Steel on Gallery II Records; and "Country Boy's Dream" (by Gene Thomas/Buz Hart), recorded by Charlie Louvin, Waylon Jennings, and George Jones on Playback Records.

STEEL RAIN PUBLISHING (BMI), 437 Gilbert Ridge, Alexandria KY 41001. (606)635-1160. President/Manager: Sharon Karr. Estab. 1993. Publishes 10 songs/year; publishes 3 new songwriters/year. Pays standard writer's share.
How to Contact: Submit demo tape by mail. Unsolicited submissions are OK. Prefers cassette or VHS videocassette with 3 songs and lyric sheet. "Please print clearly, if not typed." Does not return material. Reports in 4-8 weeks.

Music: Mostly **country**, **country rock** and **country gospel**. Published *Steel Rain*, by Bryan Karr; *Run-Away Stage* and *Cross Roads* (by Bryan Karr/Sharon Karr), all recorded by Bryan Karr/Steel Rain on Sagegrass Records (country).

JEB STUART MUSIC CO. (BMI), Box 6032, Station B, Miami FL 33123. (305)547-1424. President: Jeb Stuart. Music publisher, record producer and management firm. Estab. 1975. Publishes 4-6 songs/year. Pays standard royalty.
• See the listing for Esquire International in the Record Producers section.
How to Contact: Submit demo tape by mail. Unsolicited submissions are OK. Prefers cassette or disc with 2-4 songs and lead sheet. SASE. Reports in 1 month.
Music: Mostly **gospel**, **jazz/rock**, **pop**, **R&B** and **rap**; also **blues**, **church/religious**, **country**, **disco** and **soul**. Published "Love in the Rough," "Guns, Guns (No More Guns)" and "Come On Cafidia," all written and recorded by Jeb Stuart on Esquire Int'l Records.

STYLECRAFT MUSIC CO. (BMI), P.O. Box 802, 953 Highway 51, Madison MS 39110. (601)856-7468. Professional Manager: Style Wooten. Music publisher, record company (Style Records, Styleway Records and Good News Records), record producer and booking agency. Estab. 1964. Publishes 20-65 songs/year; publishes 20 new songwriters/year. Pays standard royalty.
How to Contact: Submit demo tape by mail. Unsolicited submissions OK. Prefers cassette with 2-4 songs and "typewritten lyric sheet." SASE. Reports in 6-8 weeks.
Music: **Country** and **black gospel**. Published *Thankful*, *Joy* and *Friend Jesus* (by Robert Harris), all recorded by The Traveling Kings on Golden Rule Records.

SUCCES, Pynderslaan, Dendermonde 9200 **Belgium**. (52)21 89 87. Fax: (52)22 52 60. Director: Deschuyteneer Hendrik. Music publisher, record company and record producer. Estab. 1978. Publishes 400 songs/year. Hires staff songwriters. Pays standard royalty.
How to Contact: Submit demo tape by mail. Unsolicited submissions are OK. Prefers cassette (or VHS videocassette) with 3 songs. SAE and IRC. Reports in 2 months.
Music: Mostly **pop**, **dance** and **variety**; also **instrumental** and **rock**. Published "La Rasparam" (by R. Mondes), recorded by Am Biance on Dino Records; *Suddenly There's You* (by Mike Egan), recorded by Nicole Hugo on NHS Records; and "Niets of Niemand" (by H. Spider), recorded by Rudy Silvester on Scorpion Records.

SUN STAR SONGS, Box 1387, Pigeon Forge TN 37868. (423)429-4121. Fax: (423)429-7090. President: Tony Glenn Rast. Music publisher. Estab. 1965, reactivated 1992. Pays standard royalty.
How to Contact: Submit demo tape by mail. Unsolicited submissions OK. Prefers cassette with 3 songs and lyric sheets. SASE. Reports in 2 weeks.
Music: Mostly **country**, **Christian country-gospel** and **bluegrass**; also **pop-rock**. Published *Let's Go Racing* (by Rast/Ruby/Kabban), recorded by Nevada on SunStar Records (country); *If You Ain't Got Jesus* (by Jim S. Ales), recorded by Tommy Cash on Rejoice Records (gospel); and *You are the Christ* (by Tony Glenn Rast/Betty Ross), recording by Holly Robinson on Heartlight Records (gospel).
Tips: "Submit quality demos. Also interested in good lyrics for co-writing."

*SUNAPEE MUSIC GROUP, P.O. Box 270247, Nashville TN 37227-0247. (615)259-7588. Fax: (615)259-0103. Director of Production/Promotion: John Edman. Music publisher and record company. Publishes 50 songs/year; publishes 20 new songwriters/year. Pays standard royalty.
• Sunapee Music's record label, Silver Wing Records, is listed in the Record Companies section.
How to Contact: Write or call first and obtain permission to submit. Prefers cassette with 3-4 songs and lyric sheet. "We have a submission sheet that we send on request." Does not return material. Reports in 2-4 weeks.
Music: Mostly **contemporary country**, **traditional country** and **gospel**; also **contemporary Christian**, **R&B**, **blues** and **alternative rock**. Published *Rockin' Up The Country*, written and recorded by Johnny Southern; *If These Walls Could Talk*, written and recorded by Gene Burton; and *Gonna Build a Bar in the Back of My Car*, written and recorded by Keith Dominick, all on Silver Wing Records (country).

SUNFROST MUSIC, P.O. Box 231, Cedarhurst NY 11516-0231. (516)791-4795. Publisher: Steve Goldmintz. Estab. 1985. Publishes 36 songs/year. Publishes 1-2 new songwriters/year (usually by collaboration). Pays standard royalty.
Affiliate(s): Anglo American Music, Manchester, England.
How to Contact: Write first and obtain permission to submit. Prefers cassette. SASE. "Please send envelope, not postcard, with correct postage." Reports in 6 weeks.
Music: Mostly **pop**, **rock** and **folk**; also **country**. Published "Love is There" written and recorded by Steve Goldmintz on Sunfrost Records (pop).

Tips: "After the song is done, the work begins and your local contacts may be just as important as the unknown publisher that you are trying to reach. Build your own network of writers. Let's put the 'R' back into 'A&R.' "

SUNSONGS MUSIC/HOLLYWOOD EAST ENTERTAINMENT (BMI, ASCAP, SESAC), 52 N. Evarts Ave., Elmsford NY 10523. (914)592-2563. Professional Manager: Michael Berman. Music publisher, record producer and talent agency. Estab. 1981. Publishes 20 songs/year; publishes 10 new songwriters/year. Pays standard royalty; co-publishing deals available for established writers.
Affiliate(s): Media Concepts Music and Dark Sun Music (SESAC).
How to Contact: Submit demo tape by mail. Unsolicited submissions OK. Prefers cassette with 3-4 songs and lyric sheet. SASE. Reports in 2 months.
Music: Dance-oriented, techno-pop and **R&B**; also **rock (all styles)** and **top 40/pop**. Published "Total Satisfaction" (by J. Henderson/E. Dozier), recorded by EH DEE on Hendoz Records; "9 Christmas Cards" (arrangements by John Henderson), recorded by the Grand Rapmasters on BMG Records (R&B).
Tips: "Submit material with strong hook and know the market being targeted by your song."

SUPREME ENTERPRISES INT'L CORP., 12304 Santa Monica Blvd., 3rd Fl., Los Angeles CA 90025. (818)707-3481. Fax: (818)707-3482. G.M. Copyrights: Lisa Lew. Music publisher, record company and record producer. Estab. 1979. Publishes 20-30 songs/year; publishes 2-6 new songwriters/year. Pays standard royalty.
Affiliate(s): Fuerte Suerte Music (BMI).
How to Contact: Submit demo tape by mail. Unsolicited submissions are OK. Prefers cassette. Does not return material. "Please copyright material before submitting." Reports in 2-3 weeks if interested.
Music: Mostly **Latin pop, reggae in Cumbias Spanish and English** and **ballads in Spanish.** Published "Paso La Vida Pensando," recorded by Jose Feliciano on Motown Records; "Cucu Bam Bam" (by David Choy), recorded by Kathy on Polydor Records (reggae/pop); and "El Marciano," recorded by Coco Man on M.P. Records.
Tips: "A good melody is a hit in any language."

*SURESPIN SONGS (BMI), 1217 16th Ave. S., Nashville TN 37212. (615)327-8129. Fax: (615)327-0928. Music publisher. Estab. 1983. Publishes 25 songs/year; publishes 2 new songwriters/year.
Affiliate(s): Preston Sullivan Music (ASCAP).
How to Contact: Call first and obtain permission to submit. Prefers cassette with 3 songs. Does not return material. Reports in 2 months.
Music: Mostly **rock** and **country**.

SWEET GLENN MUSIC (BMI), P.O. Box 1067, Santa Monica CA 90406. (310)452-0116. Fax: (310)452-2585. Vice President Talent: Mr. Friedwin. Music publisher and management company. Estab. 1980. Publishes 3-5 songs/year; publishes 1 new songwriter/year. Royalty rate varies.
Affiliate(s): Sweet Karol Music (ASCAP).
How to Contact: Write first and obtain permission to submit. "You must write before submitting." Reports in 2 months.
Music: Mostly **retro R&B** and **progressive country**. Published "Rhythm of Romance" (by Scott), recorded by Randy Crawford.
Tips: "Must be part of a performing act or established producer/arranger-writer only!"

SWEET JUNE MUSIC (BMI), P.O. Box 2325, Rockport TX 78381. (512)729-4249. Fax: (512)729-5338. Owner: Tom Thrasher. Music publisher, record company (TBS Records) and record producer. Estab. 1963. Publishes 4 songs/year; publishes 1-3 new songwriters/year. Pays standard royalty.
How to Contact: Write first and obtain permission to submit. Prefers cassette or DAT with 3 songs and lyric and/or lead sheet. "Copyright all material *before* submitting!" Does not return material. Reports in 6 weeks.
Music: Mostly **Christian country, Southern gospel** and **traditional hymns**; also **bluegrass, folk** and **country**. Published "God Is Not Through With Me," written and recorded by Tom Thrasher (Christian country); "God Has Promised" (by Thomas R. Thrasher), recorded by Donna Bryant (Southern gospel); and *The Bible*, written and recorded by Kerry Patton (Christian country), all on TBS Records.
Tips: "Write and rewrite. Don't waste words."

*T.C. PRODUCTIONS/ETUDE PUBLISHING CO. (BMI), 121 Meadowbrook Dr., Somerville NJ 08876. (908)359-5110. Fax: (908)359-1962. President: Tony Camillo. Music publisher and record producer. Estab. 1992. Publishes 25-50 songs/year; publishes 3-6 new songwriters/year. Pays standard royalty.

Affiliate(s): We Iz It Music Publishing (ASCAP), Etude/Barcam (BMI).
How to Contact: Call first and obtain permission to submit a demo. Prefers cassette with 3-4 songs and lyric sheet. SASE. Reports in 2 weeks.
Music: Mostly **R&B** and **dance**; also **country** and **outstanding pop ballads**. Published "One of a Kind" (by Sandy Farina/Lisa Ratner), recorded by Vanessa Williams; "Waiting for Last Goodbye" and "I Feel a Song" (by Tony Camillo/Mary Sawyer), recorded by Gladys Knight, all on P.A.R. Records (R&B).

*TABITHA MUSIC, LTD., 2 Southernhay West, Exeter, Devon EX1 1J9, **United Kingdom**. Phone: 01392-499889. Fax: 01392-498068. Managing Director: Graham Sclater. Music publisher, record company (Tabitha and Willow Records) and record producer. MCPS, PRS. Member MPA. Estab. 1975. Publishes 25 songs/year; publishes 6 new songwriters/year. Pays standard royalty.
Affiliate(s): Domino Music and Dice Music.
How to Contact: Submit demo tape by mail. Unsolicited submissions are OK. Prefers cassette with 1-4 songs and lyric sheet. SAE and IRC. Reports in 1 month.
Music: Mostly **MOR** and **pop**; also **country**, **dance-oriented**, **Spanish**, **rock**, **soul** and **top 40**. Published "Aliens" (by Mark Fojo), recorded by Sovereign; "Not A Chance," written and recorded by Simon Galt; and "Teenage Love," written and recorded by A. Ford, all on Tabitha Records.

DALE TEDESCO MUSIC CO. (BMI, ASCAP), 16020 Lahey St., Granada Hills CA 91344. (818)360-7329. Fax: (818)886-1338. President: Dale T. Tedesco. General Manager: Betty Lou Tedesco. Music publisher. Estab. 1981. Publishes 20-40 songs/year; publishes 20-30 new songwriters/year. Pays standard royalty.
Affiliate(s): Tedesco Tunes (ASCAP).
How to Contact: Submit a demo tape—unsolicited submissions are OK. Prefers cassette with 1 song and lyric sheet. SASE or postcard for critique. "Dale Tedesco Music hand-critiques all material submitted. Only reviews 1 song. Free evaluation." Reports in 3-4 weeks.
Music: Mostly **pop**, **R&B** and **A/C**; also **dance-oriented**, **instrumentals** (for TV and film), **jazz**, **MOR**, **rock**, **soul** and **ethnic instrumentals**. Published *One Child* (by David Brisbin), recorded by Ernestine Anderson on Quest Records (jazz).

TENTEX MUSIC PUBLISHING (BMI), 6003 Brown Rock Trail, Austin TX 78749. (512)288-0793. Contact: George Watson. Music publisher. Estab. 1989. Publishes 3 songs/year; publishes 2 new songwriters/year. Pays standard royalty.
Affiliate(s): Los-Tex Music (ASCAP).
How to Contact: Write first and obtain permission to submit. Prefers cassette with 2 songs and typed lyric sheet. Does not return material. Reports in 6 weeks - 2 months.
Music: Mostly **country**, **R&B** and **pop**. Published "Love Ain't the Lottery" (by Tommy Byrd & Linda Hardy); "I Want What He's Having" (by Norm Sales & Darcy Green); and "Chutes and Ladders" (by Holly Watson).
Tips: "Write strong lyrics with a memorable melody and dynamite chorus. Submit a well-produced, high quality demo—no work tapes, please."

*THIRD WAVE PRODUCTIONS LIMITED, P.O. Box 563, Gander Newfoundland A1V 2E1 **Canada**. Phone: (709)256-8009. Fax: (709)256-7411. President: Arch. Bonnell. Music publisher, record company (Third Wave/Street Legal), distribution and marketing company. Estab. 1986. Publishes 20 songs/year; publishes 2 new songwriters/year.
• See their listing in the Record Companies section.
How to Contact: Submit demo tape by mail. Unsolicited submissions are OK. Prefers cassette or DAT with lyric sheet. SASE. Reports in 2 months.
Music: Mostly **traditional Newfoundland**, **Celtic/Irish**, **folk**; also **bluegrass**, **country** and **pop/rock**. Published *Salt Beef Junkie* and *He's a Part of Me* (by Buddy Wosisname), recorded by The Other Fellers (traditional); and *Nobody Never Told Me*, written and recorded by The Psychobilly Cadillacs (country), all on Third Wave Productions.

THIS HERE MUSIC (ASCAP), P.O. Box 277, Arnolds Park IA 51331. (712)338-2663. Fax: (712)338-2614. E-mail: thisheremu@aol.com. President: Rikk Colligan. Music publisher, record company, record producer and songcrafting workshop. Estab. 1991. Publishes 5 songs/year; publishes 2 new songwriters/year. Pays standard royalty.
How to Contact: Write, call or e-mail first and obtain permission to submit. Prefers cassette, list of goals for your music and 3 songs. "Simply produced cassette is fine. Send SASE and we'll critique your work." Does not return material. Reports in 6 months.
Music: Mostly **folk influenced**, **pop** and **rock**; also **Lutheran worship music**, **Bible Camp sing alongs** and **children's songs**. Published "Where You Are" (by R. Colligan), recorded by Sojourn on Sojourn Records (CCM); "Gravity," written and recorded by R. Colligan on This Here Music Records

(alternative); and "There's A Promise" (by R. Colligan), recorded by Hans Peterson on Dakota Road Records (worship).
Tips: "Prepare yourself for a complete lack of hype if you contact us. We're grass roots and would be happy to talk with you about your dreams and goals for your music. We can introduce you to a Midwest network of good people to help you make a living with your music."

TIKI ENTERPRISES, INC. (BMI, ASCAP), 195 S. 26th St., San Jose CA 95116. (408)286-9840. President: Gradie O'Neal. Music publisher, record company (Rowena Records) and record producer (Jeannine O'Neal and Gradie O'Neal). Estab. 1967. Publishes 40 songs/year; publishes 12 new song-writers/year. Pays standard royalty.
Affiliate(s): Tooter Scooter Music (BMI), Janell Music (BMI) and O'Neal & Friend (ASCAP).
● See the listing for Rowena Records in the Record Companies section.
How to Contact: Submit a demo tape by mail. Unsolicited submissions are OK. Prefers cassette with 3 songs and lyric or lead sheets. SASE. Reports in 3 weeks.
Music: Mostly **country, Mexican, rock/pop gospel, R&B** and **New Age**. Published "Yamor Indio," by Roy De Hoyos (Mexican Tex-Mex); "Palomita Triste," by Jaque Lynn (Mexican); and "I Know That I Know," by Jeannine O'Neal (contemporary Christian).

TOOTH AND NAIL MUSIC, P.O. Box 140136, Nashville TN 37214. Manager: Jenny Travis. Music publisher and record producer. Estab. 1993. Publishes 30 songs/year; publishes 3 new songwrit-ers/year. Pays standard royalty.
Affiliate(s): 1st Page Music (BMI).
How to Contact: Submit demo tape by mail. Unsolicited submissions are OK. Prefers cassette (or VHS videocassette) with 1-10 songs and lyric sheet. "Artists send a picture with tape—even Polaroid." SASE. Reports in 3 weeks.
Music: Mostly **pop, rock** and **R&B**. Published *Waiting For You* (by Daryo and Anderson Page) and *This Love* (by Stephany Delram and Zig), both recorded by Dream Street on Tooth & Nail Records.

TOPS AND BOTTOMS MUSIC (BMI), P.O. Box 1341, New York NY 10113. (212)366-6636. Fax: (212)366-4646. Director: Richard Dworkin. Music publisher. Estab. 1988. Publishes 5 songs/year; publishes 1 new songwriter/year. Pays standard royalty.
How to Contact: Submit demo tape by mail. Unsolicited submissions are OK. Prefers cassette (or VHS videocassette if available) with 3-5 songs and lyric sheet. Does not return material. Reports in 4 months.
Music: Music relating to gay/lesbian life. Published "Love Don't Need A Reason"(by Peter Allen/Michael Callen/Marsha Malamet), recorded by Peter Allen on MCA Records (ballad); *Living In War-time* and *Crazy World*, both written and recorded by Michael Callen on Significant Other Records (rock/ballad).

TRANSAMERIKA MUSIKVERLAG KG, (formerly CSB Kaminsky GMBH), Wilhelmstrasse 10, 23611 Bad Schwartan, **Germany**. Phone: (0451)21530. General Manager: Pia Kaminsky. GEMA, PRS, KODA, NCB, APRA. Music publisher and administrator. Estab. 1978. Publishes 2-4 songs/year; 1 new songwriter/year. Pays 50% if releasing a record; 85% if only administrating.
Affiliate(s): Loosong Copyright Service Ltd. (London, United Kingdom) and Leosong Music Austra-lia Pty. Ltd., Sydney.
How to Contact: Submit demo tape by mail. Unsolicited submissions are OK. Prefers cassette or VHS videocassette. Does not return material. Reports in 1-2 months.
Music: Mostly **pop**; also **rock, country, film music** and **reggae**. Published *Sandcastle* (by Dominic Suhle); *The City (Where You Live)* (by Dieter Hoffmann); and *Why Glorify* (by Dirk Latus), all recorded by Gary's Best Friend on Rockwerk Records.

TREASURE TROVE MUSIC (BMI), P.O. Box 48864, Los Angeles CA 90048. (213)739-4824. Creative Manager: Larry Rosenblum. Music publisher, record company (L.S. Disc) and record pro-ducer. Estab. 1987. Publishes 3-15 songs/year; publishes 1-5 new songwriters/year. Pays standard royalty.
How to Contact: Submit demo tape by mail. Unsolicited submissions are OK. Prefers cassette (or VHS videocassette or CD) with 1-10 songs and lyric sheet. SASE. Reports in 1 month.
Music: Mostly **rock, progressive rock** and **folk rock**; also **unique crossover, punk** and **rap**. Published "Nobody for President" (by Fenson and Peri Traynor); "Your Love is Like a Pizza" and "Fair Trade" (by Fenson), all recorded by the Bob Dole Band on L.S. Disc.
Tips: "Good songs always stand out no matter what the current trends might be. Don't ever give up!"

TRUSTY PUBLICATIONS (BMI), 8771 Rose Creek Rd., Nebo KY 42441. (502)249-3194. Presi-dent: Elsie Childers. Music publisher, record company (Trusty Records) and record producer. Member

CMA. Estab. 1960. Publishes 2-3 songs/year; publishes 2 new songwriters/year. Pays standard royalty.
 • Trusty's affiliated record label, Trusty Records, is listed in the Record Companies section.
How to Contact: Write or call first and obtain permission to submit. (Send SASE for any reply please.) Prefers cassette (or VHS videocassette) with 2-4 songs and lead sheet. Does not return material. Reports in 6 weeks.
Music: Country, R&B, rock, contemporary Christian, Southern gospel, jazz, line and Christian country and **dance.** Published *Ordinary Man* (by Barry Howard), *She's Gotta Have The Music* (by Barry Howard/Don Cottrell) and *Half The Man* (by Bobby Shane), all recorded by Barry Howard on Trusty Records.

*TWIN SPIN PUBLISHING (BMI), P.O. Box 2114, Valparaiso IN 46384. (219)477-2083. Fax: (219)477-4075. President: Tony Nicoletto. Music publisher, record company (KNG Records). Estab. 1990. Publishes 50 songs/year; publishes 12 new songwriters/year. Pays standard royalty.
 • Twin Spin's management company, Nic of Tyme Productions, can be found in the Managers and Booking Agents section.
How to Contact: Submit demo tape by mail. Unsolicited submissions are OK. Prefers cassette with 4-6 songs. "Send all important information: bio, song history, etc." Does not return material. Reports in 3-4 weeks.
Music: Mostly **rock, pop** and **alternative**; also **gospel** and **country**. Published "It's the Mick," written and recorded by Ray Maas (country); "Just Askin' " (by Jason Tarka), recorded by Alison's Mailbox (alternative); and "M-16" (by Alex Smith), recorded by Joker's Death & Taxes (rock), all on KNG Records.

TWIN TOWERS PUBLISHING CO., Dept. SM, 8833 Sunset Blvd., Penthouse West, Los Angeles CA 90069. (310)659-9644. President: Michael Dixon. Music publisher and booking agency (Harmony Artists, Inc.). Publishes 24 songs/year. Pays standard royalty.
How to Contact: Call first to get permission to submit a tape. Prefers cassette with 3 songs and lyric sheet. SASE. Will respond only if interested.
Music: Mostly **pop, rock** and **R&B**. Published "Magic," from *Ghostbusters* soundtrack on Arista Records; and "Kiss Me Deadly" (by Lita Ford) on RCA Records.

UBM (BMI, GEMA), Hohenstaufenring 43-45, 50674 Köln **Germany**. Phone: 240-2234. President: Uwe Buschkotter. Music publisher, record company and record producer. Estab. 1968. Publishes 100 songs/year; publishes 10 new songwriters/year. Pays standard royalty.
How to Contact: Submit demo tape by mail. Unsolicited submissions are OK. Prefers cassette (or VHS videocassette) and lead sheets. SAE and IRC. Reports in 1 week.
Music: Mostly **jazz, pop, MOR, funk** and **easy listening**; also **classical**. Published *Peckin' Order, Midnight Rendezvous* and *Louisiana Shuffle* (by Les Hooper), all recorded by various artists on UBM Records (fusion).

ULTIMATE PEAK MUSIC (BMI), P.O. Box 707, Nashville TN 37076. Manager: Danny Crader. Music publisher. Estab. 1992. Publishes 35 songs/year; publishes 4 new songwriters/year. Hires staff writers. Pays standard royalty.
How to Contact: Submit demo tape by mail. Unsolicited submissions are OK. Prefers cassette with 1-6 songs and lyric sheet. SASE. Reports in 6-8 weeks.
Music: Mostly **country** and **MTV pop/rock**. Published *Test of Time* and *Mathematics* (by Anderson Page/Billy Herzig); and *Colorful Romance* (by Daryl Girard), all recorded by Dream Street on Tooth And Nail Records (pop).
Tips: "Listen to the radio and compare your songs to the hits—not for recording quality, but for substance and content and structure—and be objective and realistic and honest with yourself."

UNIMUSICA INC. (ASCAP), 3191 Coral Way, Suite 110, Miami FL 33145. (305)442-7273. Fax: (305)442-1790. Manager: Maria Flores. Music publisher. Estab. 1981. Publishes 5,000 songs/year; publishes 500 new songwriters/year. Pays standard royalty.
Affiliate(s): Musica Unica Publishing (BMI).
How to Contact: Submit demo tape by mail. Unsolicited submissions are OK. Prefers cassette. Does not return material. Reports in 3 months.

 A BULLET introduces comments by the editor of *Songwriter's Market* indicating special information about the listing.

Music: Mostly **salsa**, **baladas** and **merengues**. Published *Situ te Vas* (by Roberto Morales/Enrique Iglesias), recorded by Enrique Iglesias on Fonovisa Records; *Bailando* (by Jose 'Chein' Garcia), recorded by Frankie Ruiz; *Mujer Prohibida* (by Carlos de La Cima), recorded by Hector Tricoche, both on Rodven Records.
Tips: "Supply record companies with the best possible demo."

VAAM MUSIC GROUP (ASCAP, BMI), P.O. Box 29688, Hollywood CA 90029-0688. (213)664-7765. President: Pete Martin. Music publisher and record producer. Estab. 1967. Publishes 9-24 new songs/year. Pays standard royalty.
Affiliate(s): Pete Martin Music.
● See the listing for Pete Martin/Vaam Productions in the Record Producers section.
How to Contact: Prefers cassette with 2 songs maximum and lyric sheet. SASE. Reports in 1 month. "Small packages only."
Music: **Top 40/pop**, **country** and **R&B**. "Submitted material must have potential of reaching top 5 on charts." Published "The Greener Years," recorded by Frank Loren on Blue Gem Records (country/MOR); "Bar Stool Rider" (by Peggy Hackworth); and "I Love a Cowboy," written and performed by Sherry Weston in the feature film "Far Out Man," with Tommy Chong (of Cheech & Chong comedy team) and also co-starring Martin Mull.
Tips: "Study the top 10 charts in the style you write. Stay current and up-to-date with today's market."

VALET PUBLISHING CO. (BMI), 2442 N.W. Market St., Suite 273, Seattle WA 98107. Administrative offices: 5503 Roosevelt Way NE, Seattle WA 98105. (206)524-1020. Fax: (206)524-1102. Publishing Director: Buck Ormsby. Music publisher and record company (Etiquette/Suspicious Records). Estab. 1961. Publishes 5-10 songs/year. Hires staff songwriters. Pays standard royalty.
● See the listing for John "Buck" Ormsby in the Record Producers section.
How to Contact: Call first and obtain permission to submit a demo tape. Prefers cassette with 3-4 songs and lyric sheets. SASE. Reports in 6-8 weeks.
Music: Mostly **R&B**, **rock** and **pop**; also **dance** and **country**.
Tips: "Production of tape must be top quality and lyric sheets professional."

VELOCITY PRODUCTIONS, Box 518, Leander TX 78646-0518. Contact: Review Coordinator. Music publisher and record producer. Estab. 1986. Publishes 10-20 songs/year; publishes 2-3 new songwriters/year. Pays standard royalty.
Affiliate(s): Velocity Publishing (BMI).
How to Contact: Write and obtain permission to submit. Prefers cassette (or VHS videocassette) with 1-4 songs and lyric sheet. SASE. Reports in 4-6 weeks.
Music: Mostly **children's**. Published "Will It Be My Turn to Love" (by J. Brehm-Stern), recorded by Heather Arn (MOR); *Tales From the Forest* and "Garden Bug Blues" (by J. Brehm-Stern), both recorded by Velocity Players, all on Velocity Records.
Tips: "Remember to improve your business skills as well as your creative skills."

VOKES MUSIC PUBLISHING (BMI), Box 12, New Kensington PA 15068-0012. (412)335-2775. President: Howard Vokes. Music publisher, record company, booking agency and promotion company.
● Vokes Music's record label, Vokes Music Record Co., is listed in the Record Companies section and their booking agency, Vokes Booking Agency, is listed in the Managers and Booking Agents section.
How to Contact: Submit cassette (3 songs only), lyric or lead sheet. SASE. Reports within a week.
Music: **Traditional country-bluegrass** and **gospel**. Published "A Million Tears" (by Duke & Null), recorded by Johnny Eagle Feather on Vokes Records; "I Won't Be Your Honky Tonk Queen" (by Vokes-Wallace), recorded by Bunnie Mills on Pot-Of-Gold Records; and "Break The News" (by Vokes-Webb), recorded by Bill Beere on Oakhill Records.
Tips: "We're always looking for country songs that tell a story, and only interested in hard-traditional-bluegrass, country and country gospel songs. Please no 'copy-cat songwriters.' "

WARNER/CHAPPELL MUSIC CANADA LTD. (SOCAN), 85 Scarsdale Rd. #101, Don Mills Ontario M3B 2R2 **Canada**. (416)445-3131. Fax: (416)445-2473. Creative Manager: Anne-Marie Smith. Music publisher.
How to Contact: Write first and obtain permission to submit a demo. Prefers cassette, bio, photo with 3 songs and lyric sheet. SAE and IRC. Reports in 2 months.
Music: Mostly **rock/pop** and **country**.

WARNER/CHAPPELL MUSIC, INC., 10585 Santa Monica Blvd., Third Floor, Los Angeles CA 90025-4950. (310)441-8600. This publisher prefers not to share information.

WATCHESGRO MUSIC (BMI), 9208 Spruce Mountain Way, Las Vegas NV 89134-6024. (702)363-8506. President: Eddie Carr. Music publisher. Estab. 1987. Publishes 100 songs/year; publishes 5 new songwriters/year. Pays standard royalty.
Affiliate(s): Watch Us Climb Music (ASCAP).
 • Watchesgro Music's record label, Interstate 40 Records, is listed in the Record Companies section.
How to Contact: Write first and obtain permission to submit. Prefers cassette. SASE. Reports in 1 week.
Music: Published "7th & Sundance" (by Aileen/Dempsey), recorded by Rita Aileen (country); "Eatin' My Words" (by M. Jones), recorded by Michael Jones; and "Precious Memories" (by D. Horn), recorded by Cindy Jane, all on Interstate 40 Records (country).

*WATONKA RECORDS CO. (ASCAP), 19523 Lockridge Dr., Spring TX 77373. President: Earl The Pearl Roberts. Music publisher, record company and record producer. Estab. 1974. Publishes 1-10 songs/year. Pays standard royalty.
How to Contact: Write first and obtain permission to submit. Unsolicited submissions are OK. Prefers cassette or VHS videocassette with 4 songs maximum and lyric/lead sheet. SASE. Reports in 2 weeks.
Music: Country, rock and **Tex Mex** only. Published "Destiny's Wings" (by Roberts/Wright), recorded by Ghost Who Walks; "Shootin' the Bull" (by Roberts/Callaway), recorded by Redman; and "Boots" (by ETP/Big John), recorded by Randy C., all on Watonka Records (country).
Tips: "If you believe in your completed songs, that's all that counts. Rock on with it. All the doors may be closed—keep knocking. Watonka is a small independent (Indy) publisher—very selective."

*WEAVER WORDS OF MUSIC (BMI), P.O. Box 803, Tazewell VA 24651. (703)988-6267. President: H. R. Cook. Music publisher and record company (Fireball Records). Estab. 1978. Publishes 12 songs/year; varying number of new songwriters/year. Pays standard royalty.
Affiliate(s): Weaver of Melodies Music (ASCAP).
How to Contact: Submit demo tape by mail. Unsolicited submissions are OK. Prefers cassette with 3 songs and lyric or lead sheets. SASE. Reports in 1 month.
Music: Mostly **country**. Published "Winds of Change," written and recorded by Cecil Surrett; "Texas Saturday Night" and "Old Flame Burning," written and recorded by H.R. Cook, all on Fireball Records (country).

BERTHOLD WENGERT (MUSIKVERLAG), Waldstrasse 27, D-76327, Pfinztal-Soellingen, Germany. Contact: Berthold Wengert. Music publisher. Pays standard GEMA royalty.
How to Contact: Prefers cassette and complete score for piano. SAE and IRC. Reports in 4 weeks. "No cassette returns!"
Music: Mostly **light music** and **pop**.

WEST & EAST MUSIC, Marianneng 25/2-5, A-1090 Vienna **Austria** (011)43-1-8941920. Fax: (011)43-1-4061792. MD: Harry Huber. Music publisher, record company and record producer. Estab. 1989. Publishes 100-130 songs/year. Pays standard royalty.
Affiliates: Jam! (the dance label).
How to Contact: Submit demo tape by mail. Unsolicited submissions are OK. Prefers cassette. SAE and IRC. Reports in 3-4 weeks.
Music: Mostly **dance** and **pop**. Published *Yowí Yowí*, recorded by Black Spaghetti; "Is It Love," recorded by The Real Stuff; and "Across the Universe" (by Huber), recorded by DJ Sonic, all on JAM! Records.

WESTUNES MUSIC PUBLISHING CO. (ASCAP), 1115 Inman Ave., Suite 330, Edison NJ 08820-1132. (908)548-6700. Fax: (908)548-6748. President/A&R Director: Victor Kaply. Professional Manager: Elena Petillo. Music publisher and management firm (Westwood Entertainment Group). Publishes 15 songs/year; publishes 2 new songwriters/year. Pays standard royalty.
 • Westunes Music's management firm, Westwood Entertainment, is listed in the Managers and Booking Agents section.
How to Contact: Write first and obtain permission to submit. Prefers cassette with 3 songs and lyric sheet. SASE. Reports in 6 weeks.
Music: Mostly **rock**; also **pop**. Published *Fearless*, written and recorded by Kevin McCabe; "I Can't Live My Life," written and recorded by Ground Zero, both on Westwood Records; and *Down & Dirty* (by Jim Forest), recorded by Kidd Skruff on Luiggi Records (Spain).
Tips: Submit a "neat promotional package with bio and lyrics."

WHEELERBOY ENTERTAINMENT (ASCAP), 901 Sixth St. SW, #103A, Washington DC 20024. (202)488-3266. Executive Director: George Wheeler, Jr. Music publisher and record producer. Estab. 1994. Publishes 12 songs/year. Pays standard royalty.

How to Contact: Submit demo tape by mail. Unsolicited submissions are OK. Prefers cassette (or VHS videocassette) with 3 songs and lyric sheet. SASE. Reports in 1 month.
Music: Mostly **Top 40 R&B**, **hip hop**, **club**, **dance** and **ballads**; also **fusion jazz funk** and **contemporary jazz funk**. Published "Lucky" and "Baby I'm Yours," both written by George Wheeler and recorded by Barbara Price on Wheelerboy Records.

WHITE CAT MUSIC, Suite 114, 10603 N. Hayden Rd., Scottsdale AZ 85260. (602)951-3115. Fax: (602)951-3074. Professional Manager: Frank Fara. Producer: Patty Parker. Music publisher. Member CMA, CCMA, BCCMA and BBB. Estab. 1978. Publishes 30 songs/year; publishes 20 new songwriters/year. "50% of our published songs are from non-charted and developing writers." Pays standard royalty.
Affiliate(s): Rocky Bell Music (BMI), How The West Was Sung Music (BMI), and Crystal Canyon Music (ASCAP).
How to Contact: Submit demo tape by mail. Unsolicited submissions are OK. Prefers cassettes only with 2 songs and lyric or lead sheet. SASE. Reports in 2 weeks.
Music: All styles of **country**—traditional to crossover. Published "Stop, Look & Listen" (by Roy G. Ownbey), recorded by Pam Ferens; "Another Love Song" (by Joseph Hurka/Jeff Larson), recorded by Jill Trace; and *Dale Evans Tribute: She Rode A Horse Called Buttermilk* (by Frank Fara/Patty Parker), recorded by Patty Parker, all on Comstock Records.
Tips: "Stack the odds in your favor by sending fewer songs—two to four at most, medium to up-tempo songs are always in demand. Long instrumental intros and breaks detract, go for a clear out-front vocal presentation."

WHITEWING MUSIC (BMI), 413 N. Parkerson Ave., Crowley LA 70526. (318)788-0773. Fax: (318)788-0776. Owner: J.D. Miller. Music publisher and record company (Master-Trak, Showtime, Par T, MTE, Blues Unlimited, Kajun, Cajun Classics). Estab. 1946. Publishes 12-15 songs/year. Publishes 6 new songwriters/year. Pays standard royalty.
Affiliate(s): Jamil Music (BMI).
● Whitewing Music's record label, Master-Trak Enterprises, is listed in the Record Companies section and Jay Miller is listed in the Record Producers section.
How to Contact: Submit demo tape by mail. Unsolicited submissions are OK. Prefers cassette (or videocassette) with 6 songs and lyric or lead sheets. Reports in 5-6 weeks.
Music: Mostly **country**, **rock** and **MOR**; also **cajun**. Published *Avec Amis* (by Lee Benoit); and *Old Fashion Love* (by Kenne Wayne).

*DEAN WHITNEY MUSIC ENTERPRISES (ASCAP, BMI), P.O. Box 632981, San Diego CA 92163-2981. (619)297-2310. Fax: (619)297-7246. E-mail: brnchild@aol.com or brnchild@ix.netcom.com. A&R Director: Rex Sampaga. Music publisher, record company (BrainChild Records) and record producer. Estab. 1979. Publishes 150 song/year. Publishes 1-2 new songwriters/year. Pays standard royalty.
Affiliate(s): DeWhit Music, Lil Bo-Dean Music, Seaneen Music (ASCAP), Brother Bear Music (BMI).
How to Contact: Call first and obtain permission to submit a demo. Prefers cassette with 10 songs. SASE. Reports in 1 month.
Music: Contemporary instrumental only. Published *Online*, written and recorded by J. Michael Verta; *Love's Gift* (by Tony Guerrero), recorded by Greg Vail; and *No Getting Over You* (by Daniel Ho), recorded by Kilauea, all on BrainChild Records (NAC).

WILCOM PUBLISHING (ASCAP), Box 4456, West Hills CA 91308. (818)348-0940. Owner: William Clark. Music publisher. Estab. 1989. Publishes 10-15 songs/year; publishes 1-2 new songwriters/year. Pays standard royalty.
How to Contact: Write first and obtain permission to submit a tape. Prefers cassette with 1-2 songs and lyric sheet. SASE. Reports in 3 weeks.
Music: Mostly **R&B**, **pop** and **rock**; also **country**. Published "Girl Can't Help It" (by W. Clark/D. Walsh/P. Oland), recorded by Stage 1 on Rockit Records (top 40).

SHANE WILDER MUSIC (BMI), P.O. Box 3503, Hollywood CA 90078. (805)251-7526. President: Shane Wilder. Music publisher, record producer (Shane Wilder Productions) and management firm (Shane Wilder Artist Management). Estab. 1960. Publishes 25-50 songs/year; publishes 15-20 new songwriters/year. Pays standard royalty.
● Shane Wilder's management firm, Shane Wilder Artists Management, is listed in the Managers and Booking Agents section.
How to Contact: Submit demo tape by mail. Unsolicited submissions are OK. Prefers cassette (or VHS videocassette) with 3 songs and lyric sheet. "Include SASE if you wish tape returned. Photo and resume should be sent if you're looking for a producer." Reports in 2 weeks.

Music: Mostly **traditional country**. Published "Goodbye Stew" (by Kimber Cunningham), recorded by Debbie Davis on Richway Records; "Cold & Lonesome Life" and "Under A Dark Desert Sky" (by Al and Alton Corey), recorded by Travis T. Wilson on TTW Records.
Tips: "See what is comin' out of Nashville and submit the same type strong country material. We only publish highly commercial songs. Constantly looking for songs that have a good story line. We publish country only and are a BMI company. Do not send ASCAP material."

WINSTON & HOFFMAN HOUSE MUSIC PUBLISHERS (ASCAP/BMI), 1680 N. Vine St., #318, Hollywood CA 90028. E-mail: sixties1@aol.com. President: Lynne Robin Green. Music publisher. Estab. 1958. Publishes 25 songs/year. Pays standard royalty.
Affiliates: Lansdowne Music Publishers (ASCAP), Bloor Music (BMI), Clemitco Publishing (BMI), Ben Ross Music (ASCAP), Triple Scale Music (BMI) and Vassars Music (ASCAP).
How to Contact: Submit demo tape by mail. Unsolicited submissions are OK. "Do not query first." Prefers cassette with 3 songs maximum and lyric sheet. "*Must* SASE, or *no* reply! No calls." Reports in 1 month.
Music: Mostly **R&B dance, ballads, hip hop, vocal jazz, alternative rock** and **R&B**; also **country** and **pop ballads**. Published *Thy Word*, written and recorded by Leon Patillo on Randolph Records (gospel); "Old Home Place" (by Webb/Jayne), recorded by Travis Tritt on Warner Bros. Records (country); and *There Is A Time* (by Dillard/Jayne), recorded by Panorama Ramblers on Word Records.
Tips: "Be selective in what you send. Be realistic about which artist it suits! Be patient in allowing time to place songs. Be open to writing for films—be interesting lyrically and striking melodically."

WITHOUT PAPERS MUSIC PUBLISHING INC., 2366 Woodhill Rd., Cleveland OH 44106. (216)791-2100, ext. 204. Fax: (216)791-7117. President: Michele Norton. Music publisher. Estab. 1992. Publishes 4 songs/year; publishes 2 new songwriters/year. Hires staff songwriters. Pays standard royalty.
How to Contact: Write or call first and obtain permission to submit. Prefers cassette with lyric sheet. SASE. Reports in 1 month.
Music: Mostly **rock, R&B** and **country** (with R&B or rock base); also **children's, classical, different** and **commercial**. Published "Brown's Blues" (by Stutz Bearcat), recorded by Butch Armstrong on Doubleneck Records (blues).
Tips: "Be patient and be willing to work with us and the song."

*WIZE WORLD OF MUZIC (BMI), P.O. Box 607321, Orlando FL 32860-7321. (407)291-6163. Publisher: Christopher R. Davis. Music publisher. Estab. 1994. Publishes 10-20 songs/year; publishes 2 new songwriters/year. Hires staff songwriters. Pays standard royalty.
How to Contact: Submit demo tape by mail. Unsolicited submissions are OK. Prefers cassette with 3 songs and lyric sheet, and bio. SASE. Reports in 3-4 weeks.
Music: Mostly **R&B, reggae (dance halls)** and **hip hop**; also **jazz, gospel** and **funk**. Published "Strapped," written and recorded by C.D. Wize (reggae); "Memory Lane" and "That's Love" (by Christopher Davis/Sharon Williams), recorded by Sharon Williams on (R&B), all on X-Slave Records.
Tips: "Be original and diligent. Keep it 'on the real.' Write about something that people can relate to. Submit a clean demo!"

WOODRICH PUBLISHING CO. (BMI), P.O. Box 38, Lexington AL 35648. (205)247-3983. President: Woody Richardson. Music publisher, record company (Woodrich Records) and record producer. Estab. 1959. Publishes 25 songs/year; publishes 12 new songwriters/year. Pays standard royalty.
● See the listing for Woodrich Records in the Record Companies section.
Affiliate(s): Mernee Music (ASCAP), Melstep Music (BMI) and Tennesse Valley Music (SESAC).
How to Contact: Submit demo tape by mail. Unsolicited submissions are OK. Prefers cassette with 2-4 songs. Prefers studio produced demos. SASE. Reports in 2 weeks.
Music: Mostly **country** and **gospel**; also **bluegrass, blues, choral, church/religious, easy listening, folk, jazz, MOR, progressive, rock, soul** and **top 40/pop**. Published *Somewhere Above Tennessee*, written and recorded by Jerry Piper on Missle Records; *Christmas of White* (by Barbara Jean Smith), recorded by Dianna L. Carter on BJ's Records; and *Chitlins and Mountain Oysters* (by Woody Richardson), recorded by Marty Whiddon on Woodrich Records.
Tips: "Use a studio demo if possible. If not, be sure the lyrics are extremely clear. Be sure to include a SASE with *sufficient* return postage."

 THE ASTERISK before a listing indicates that the listing is new in this edition. New markets are often the most receptive to unsolicited submissions.

WORLD FAMOUS MUSIC CO. (ASCAP), 1364 Sherwood Rd., Highland Park IL 60035. (847)831-3123. President: Chip Altholz. Music publisher, record producer. Estab. 1986. Publishes 25 songs/year; 3-4 new songwriters/year. Pays standard royalty.
How to Contact: Submit a demo tape by mail. Unsolicited submissions are OK. Prefers cassette with 3 songs and lyric sheet. SASE. Reports in 1 month.
Music: Mostly **pop**, **R&B** and **rock**. Published "Harmony," (by Altholz/Faldner), recorded by Barry Faldner on Amenter Records (ballad); and "Running" and "Serious," both written and recorded by Nick Bak on Pink Street Records.
Tips: "Have a great melody, a lyric that is visual and tells a story and a commercial arrangement."

WORSHIP MUSIC, 96 Fifth Avenue, Suite #11H, New York NY 10011. (212)366-4874. Fax: (212)604-0238. Co-president: Paul Burton. Music publisher and management company. Estab. 1995. Pays standard royalty.
Affiliate(s): Ceremony Music (ASCAP), Culto Music (BMI) and Windswept Pacific Entertainment Co.
How to Contact: Submit demo tape by mail. Unsolicited submissions are OK. Prefers cassette or DAT with 2-3 songs and lyric sheet. SASE. Reports in 4-6 weeks.
Music: Mostly **pop (top 40)**, **R&B**, **dance**, **rock**, and **country**. Published *Stimulate My Mind* (by Devalle S. Hayes), recorded by Sherry Johnson on Loose Cannon/Mercury Records (R&B); and *No Lover No Friend* (by Devalle S. Hayes), recorded by Groove.

YORGO MUSIC (BMI), 615 Valley Rd., Upper Montclair NJ 07043. (201)746-2359. President: George Louvis. Music publisher. Estab. 1987. Publishes 5-10 songs/year; publishes 3-5 new songwriters/year. Pays standard royalty.
How to Contact: Submit demo tape by mail. Unsolicited submissions are OK. Prefers cassette with 1-3 songs and lyric or lead sheets. "Specify if you are a writer/artist or just a writer." Does not return material. Reports in 2-3 months.
Music: Only **gospel** and **contemporary Christian**.

YOUR BEST SONGS PUBLISHING, 1210 Auburn Way N., Suite P171, Auburn WA 98002. General Manager: Craig Markovich. Music publisher. Estab. 1988. Publishes 3-7 songs/year; publishes 1-4 new songwriters/year. Query for royalty terms.
How to Contact: Submit demo tape by mail. Unsolicited submissions are OK. Prefers cassette with 1-3 songs and lyric sheet. "Submit your 1-3 best songs per type of music. Use separate cassettes per music type and indicate music type on each cassette." SASE. Reports in 1-2 months.
Music: Mostly **country**, **rock/blues** and **pop/rock**; also **progressive**, **A/C** and some **heavy metal**. Published "Hidden Gun" and "Farewell (My Love)," recorded by Brain Box on Cybervoc, Inc.
Tips: "We just require good lyrics, good melodies and good rhythm in a song."

ZAUBER MUSIC PUBLISHING (ASCAP), P.O. Box 5087, V.M.8.O., Vancouver, British Columbia V6B 4A9 **Canada**. (604)528-9194. Professional Manager: Martin E. Hamann. Music publisher and record producer. Estab. 1981. Publishes 3-5 songs/year; publishes 1-2 new songwriters/year. Hires staff writers. Pays standard royalty.
Affiliate(s): Merlin Productions and Zauberer Music (SOCAN).
 • See the listings for Merlin Productions in the Record Companies and Record Producers sections, and Merlin Management in the Managers and Booking Agents section.
How to Contact: Submit demo tape by mail. Unsolicited submissions are OK. Prefers cassette with lyric or lead sheet. SAE or IRC. Reports in 3 weeks.
Music: Mostly **dance**, **pop/R&B** and **rock**; also **techno** and **Euro-pop**. Published "Harmony Rave," written and recorded by Mode to Joy; and "Love Is Everything" (by Wolfgang/Wolfgang), recorded by Beverly Sills, all on Merlin Records (rock).
Tips: "Send 3 songs only, the most commercial first. Hire the best singer available. Uptempo songs work best. Have a strong lyric/melodic chorus."

*ZOMBA MUSIC PUBLISHING (ASCAP, BMI), 137-139 W. 25th St., New York NY 10001. (212)620-8744. Fax: (212)242-7462. Director: Tse Williams. Music publisher. Publishes 5,000 songs/year; publishes 25 new songwriters/year.
Affiliate(s): Zomba Enterprises, Inc. (ASCAP); Zomba Songs, Inc. (BMI).
How to Contact: Call first and obtain permission to submit a demo. Prefers cassette or DAT with 4 songs and lyric sheet. SASE.
Music: Mostly **R&B**, **pop** and **rap**; also **rock** and **alternative**. Published "You Are Not Alone" (by R. Kelly), recorded by Michael Jackson on Epic Records (pop); *Any Man Of Mine* (by Mutt Lange), recorded by Shania Twain on Mercury Records (country/pop); and "Can I Touch You There" (by Mutt Lange), recorded by Michael Bolton on Sony Records (pop).

Category Index

The Category Index is a good place to begin searching for a market for your songs. Below is an alphabetical list of 19 general music categories. If you write country songs and are looking for a publisher to pitch them, check the Country section in this index. Once you locate the entries for those publishers, read the music subheading *carefully* to determine which companies are most interested in the type of country music you write. Some of the markets in this section do not appear in the Category Index because they have not indicated a specific preference. Most of these said they are interested in "all types" of music. Listings that were very specific, or whose description of the music they're interested in doesn't quite fit into these categories, also do not appear here.

Adult Contemporary

Alexis; Alleged Iguana Music; Allegheny Music Works; Amiron Music; Antelope Publishing Inc.; Arylis Corporation; Audio Images Two Thousand Music Publishing; Axbar Productions; Bal & Bal Music Publishing Co.; Barren Wood Publishing; *Bay Ridge Publishing Co.; Betty Jane/Josie Jane Music Publishers; Blue Hill Music/Tutch Music; BOAM; Bradley Music, Allan; Buried Treasure Music; California Country Music; Camex Music; Christel Music Limited; *Country Rainbow Music; Country Star Music; Dean Enterprises Music Group; Denny Music Group; Duane Music, Inc.; *Fingerprint Songs; Gary Music, Alan; Green One Music; G-String Publishing; Hammel Associates, Inc., R.L.; Havasong Music; Hickory Valley Music; High-Minded Moma Publishing & Productions; Hitsburgh Music Co.; *Immortal Beloved Music Publishing; Inside Records/OK Songs; ISBA Music Publishing Inc.; Jaclyn Music; Ja/Nein Musikverlag GmbH; Joseph Music Inc., Patrick; Jump Music; *Just a Note; JW One Music Publishing Co.; Kansa Records Corporation; Kaupps & Robert Publishing Co.; Kingsport Creek Music Publishing; Kommunication Koncepts; Kozkeeozko Music; *Largo Music Publishing; Lineage Publishing Co.; Mento Music Group; Merry Marilyn Music Publishing; Montina Music; Music in the Right Keys Publishing Company; Nebo Ridge Publishing Company; New Rap Jam Publishing, A; Okisher Music; Omni 2000, Inc.; Operation Perfection; Otto Publishing Co.; Panchatantra Music Enterprises; Parravano Music; Pegasus Music; Pine Island Music; Prescription Company; R. J. Music; Riverhawk Music; *RNR Publishing; *Rob-Lee Music; Rockford Music Co.; Rondor Music International; Roots Music; Ryan Music, Joshua; S.M.C.L. Productions, Inc.; Segal's Publications; Sha-La Music, Inc.; Siegel Music Companies; Silicon Music Publishing Co.; Spring Rose Music; *Tabitha Music, Ltd.; Tedesco Music Co., Dale; UBM; Whitewing Music; Woodrich Publishing Co.; Your Best Songs Publishing

Alternative

Abalone Publishing; *Aladdin Music Group; *Al-Ky Music; AUM Circle Publishing; Baby Raquel Music; *Bay Ridge Publishing Co.; Big Snow Music; Camex Music; *Chicago Kid Productions; Clear Pond Music; Cottage Blue Music; Fat City Publishing; Flea Circus Music; *Funzalo Music; Genetic Music Publishing; Havasong Music; Interscope Music Publishing; JK Jam Music; Josena Music; Keno Publishing; Krude Toonz Music; Kwaz Song Music; *Largo Music Publishing; *Last Brain Cell; *Pas

---

 THE ASTERISK before a listing indicates that the listing is new in this edition. New markets are often the most receptive to unsolicited submissions.

Mal Publishing; Pen Cob Publishing Inc.; Planet Dallas Recording Studios; Prejippie Music Group; Primal Visions Music; *Rachel Marie Music Ltd.; Rana International & Affiliates Inc.; *Sunapee Music Group; Treasure Trove Music; *Twin Spin Publishing; Winston & Hoffman House Music Publishers; *Zomba Music Publishing

Blues

*Aladdin Music Group; Alexis; *Al-Ky Music; Bagatelle Music Publishing Co.; *Bahoomba Music; Bal & Bal Music Publishing Co.; *Bay Ridge Publishing Co.; Bearsongs; Blue Hill Music/Tutch Music; Christopher Publishing, Sonny; Davis & Davis Music; ESI Music Group; Fat City Publishing; Frozen Inca Music; Humanform Publishing Company; Ja/Nein Musikverlag GmbH; Kilowatt Music; *Last Brain Cell; Macman Music, Inc.; Martin's Music Publishing, Rod; Montina Music; Motex Music; Music in the Right Keys Publishing Company; Nervous Publishing; Okisher Music; Panchatantra Music Enterprises; Pollard Sound World; Prescription Company; *Promo; Prospector Three D Publishing; R. J. Music; *Rachel Marie Music Ltd.; *RNR Publishing; *Sea Dream Music; Silicon Music Publishing Co.; Sizemore Music; Slanted Circle Music; *Smokey Lane Music; *Snowcliff Publishing; *Sunapee Music Group; Woodrich Publishing Co.

Children's

Berandol Music Ltd.; Branch Group Music; *Colton Shows, Glenn; Davis & Davis Music; Flying Red Horse Publishing; *Kidsource Publishing; Lonny Tunes Music; Mighty Twinns Music; NSP Music Publishing Inc.; Omni 2000, Inc.; Paluch Company, J. S./World Library Publications, Inc.; Parravano Music; PPI/Peter Pan Industries; Prescription Company; Rhythms Productions; Segal's Publications; Silverhill Music; Soundbyte Corporation; This Here Music; Velocity Productions; Without Papers Music Publishing Inc.

Classical

Bad Habits Music Publishing; Clevère Musikverlag, R.D.; Ho-hum Music; *Immortal Beloved Music Publishing; Jae Music, Jana; *Musikverlag K. Urbanek; PPI/Peter Pan Industries; Rising Star Records and Publishers; Roots Music; UBM; Without Papers Music Publishing Inc.

Country

Abalone Publishing; Accent Publishing Co.; Aim High Music Company; *Aladdin Music Group; Alexis; *Al-Ky Music; Alleged Iguana Music; Allegheny Music Works; AlliSongs Inc.; Aquarius Publishing; Audio Images Two Thousand Music Publishing; Axbar Productions; Bagatelle Music Publishing Co.; Bal & Bal Music Publishing Co.; Barkin' Foe the Master's Bone; Barren Wood Publishing; *Bay Ridge Publishing Co.; *Beaverwood Audio-Video; Beecher Publishing, Earl; Best Buddies, Inc.; Betty Jane/ Josie Jane Music Publishers; Big Fish Music Publishing Group; Black Stallion Country Publishing; Blue Hill Music/Tutch Music; Blue Spur Entertainment, Inc./Git A Rope Publishing; BOAM; Bonnfire Publishing; Bradley Music, Allan; Brewster Songs, Kitty; Buried Treasure Music; Cactus Music and Winnebago Publishing; California Country Music; Calinoh Music Group; Cash Productions, Inc.; Castle Music Group; Cheavoria Music Co.; Cherie Music; Chestnut Mound Music Group; Christopher Publishing, Sonny; Cimirron Music; Cisum; Clear Pond Music; Clevère Musikverlag, R.D.; Coffee and Cream Publishing Company; Colstal Music; *Colton Shows, Glenn; *Copperfield Music Group; Cornelius Companies, The; Cottage Blue Music; Country Breeze Music; *Country Rainbow Music; Country Showcase America; Country Star Music; Cowboy Junction Flea Market and Publishing Co.; Craig Music, Loman; Cupit Music; D.S.M. Producers Inc.; Darbonne Publishing Co.; Davis & Davis Music; De Miles Music Company, The Edward; Dean Enterprises Music Group; Delev Music Company; Dell Music, Frank; Delpha's Music Publishers; Denny Music Group; Doc Publishing; Doss Music, Buster; *Dream Seekers Publishing; Duane Music, Inc.; Earitating Music Publishing;

*Earthscream Music Publishing Co.; Emandell Tunes; EMF Productions; *Enid, Oklahoma Music Publishing; ESI Music Group; Faiella Publishing, Doug; Famous Music Publishing Companies; Farr-Away Music; Fat City Publishing; *Fingerprint Songs; First Time Music (Publishing) U.K. Ltd.; *Flaming Star West Music; Flash International; Flea Circus Music; Focal Point Music Publishers; Fox Farm Recording; Frick Music Publishing Co.; Furrow Music; Gary Music, Alan; Giftness Enterprise; GlobeArt Inc.; Gold Music Publishing, Jay; Goodland Music Group Inc., The; Gowell Music, Richard E.; Green Meadows Publishing; Green One Music; G-String Publishing; Gypsy Heart Music; Halo International; Hammel Associates, Inc., R.L.; Havasong Music; Hawksbill Music; Henly Music Associates; Hickory Lane Publishing and Recording; Hickory Valley Music; *High Pockets Publishing Inc.; High-Minded Moma Publishing & Productions; Hitsburgh Music Co.; Ho-hum Music; Holton Music; Honk Music & Records — Musikverlag H. Gebetsroither; Humanform Publishing Company; *Immortal Beloved Music Publishing; Inside Records/OK Songs; Iron Skillet Music; *Jacksongs Music Publishing, d.t.; Jaclyn Music; Jae Music, Jana; Jaelius Enterprises; Jammy Music Publishers Ltd.; Jerjoy Music; *JoDa Music; Johnson Music, Little Richie; Jolson Black & White Music, Al; Jon Music; Joseph Music Inc., Patrick; *Just a Note; JW One Music Publishing Co.; Kansa Records Corporation; Kaupps & Robert Publishing Co.; Kaylee Music Group, Karen; Kel-Cres Publishing; *Kelly Entertainment, Robert; Kingsport Creek Music Publishing; *Kirchstein Publishing Co.; Kozkeeozko Music; Krude Toonz Music; Lari-Jon Publishing; *Last Brain Cell; Laurmack Music; Lilly Music Publishing; Lindsay Publishing, Doris; Lineage Publishing Co.; Lion Hill Music Publishing Co.; Lonny Tunes Music; Lovey Music, Inc.; Luick & Associates Music Publisher, Harold; M & T Waldoch Publishing, Inc.; McCartney Music; McCoy Music, Jim; McGibony Publishing; Mack Music, Danny; *Magic Message Music; Makers Mark Gold; Manny Music, Inc.; Mathes Company, The; Mento Music Group; Merry Marilyn Music Publishing; *Miller Music, Jody; Montina Music; Moon June Music; Motex Music; Music in the Right Keys Publishing Company; Nashville Sound Music Publishing Co.; National Talent; Nautical Music Co.; Nebo Ridge Publishing Company; Nervous Publishing; New Rap Jam Publishing, A; Newcreature Music; Non-Stop Music Publishing; Oh My Gosh Music; Okisher Music; Old Slowpoke Music; Omni 2000, Inc.; One Hot Note Music Inc.; *Ontrax Companies; Orchid Publishing; Otto Publishing Co.; Oyster Bay Music; Panchatantra Music Enterprises; Paradise Publications; Parravano Music; Pecos Valley Music; Pegasus Music; Pen Cob Publishing Inc.; Pine Island Music; Platinum Boulevard Publishing; *Platinum Gold Music; Pollard Sound World; Portage Music; Prescription Company; Pritchett Publications; Prospector Three D Publishing; Purple Haze Music; R. J. Music; Rana International & Affiliates Inc.; Ridge Music Corp.; Riverhawk Music; Rocker Music/Happy Man Music; Rockford Music Co.; Roots Music; Rose Hill Group; Rustron Music Publishers; Sabteca Music Co.; Saddlestone Publishing; Samuel Three Productions; Scott Music Group, Tim; *Second City Publishing; Segal's Publications; Sellwood Publishing; Siegel Music Companies; Silicon Music Publishing Co.; Silver Thunder Music Group; Silverhill Music; Simply Grand Music, Inc.; Siskatune Music Publishing Co.; Sizemore Music; *Smokey Lane Music; *Snowcliff Publishing; Song Farm Music; *Sony/ATV Music Publishing; Sound Cellar Music; Soundbyte Corporation; Sounds of Aicram; Southern Most Publishing Company; Spradlin/Gleich Publishing; Stable Music Co.; Spring Rose Music; Starbound Publishing Co.; Steel Rain Publishing; Stuart Music Co., Jeb; Stylecraft Music Co.; Sun Star Songs; *Sunapee Music Group; Sunfrost Music; *Surespin Songs; Sweet Glenn Music; Sweet June Music; *T.C. Productions/Etude Publishing Co.; *Tabitha Music, Ltd.; Tentex Music Publishing; *Third Wave Productions Limited; Tiki Enterprises, Inc.; Transamerika Musikverlag KG; Trusty Publications; *Twin Spin Publishing; Ultimate Peak Music; Vaam Music Group; Valet Publishing Co.; Vokes Music Publishing; Warner/Chappell Music Canada Ltd.; *Watonka Records Co.; *Weaver Words of Music; White Cat Music; Whitewing Music; Wilcom Publishing; Wilder Music, Shane; Winston & Hoffman House Music Publishers; Without Papers Music Publishing Inc.; Woodrich Publishing Co.; Worship Music; Your Best Songs Publishing

Dance

Abalone Publishing; Alexis; Aljoni Music Co.; *Al-Ky Music; Audio Music Publishers; Baby Raquel Music; Bad Habits Music Publishing; *Bartow Music; Brewster Songs, Kitty; Brothers Organisation, The; Clevère Musikverlag, R.D.; Coffee and Cream Publishing Company; D.S.M. Producers Inc.; Dagene Music; De Miles Music Company, The Edward; Delev Music Company; *Dream Seekers Publishing; Drive Music, Inc.; Duane Music, Inc.; *Fresh Entertainment; Gary Music, Alan; Genetic Music Publishing; G-String Publishing; Hit & Run Music Publishing Inc.; Honk Music & Records — Musikverlag H. Gebetsroither; Inside Records/OK Songs; *International Music Network Limited; ISBA Music Publishing Inc.; *JK Jam Music; Joey Boy Publishing Co.; Jump Music; *Kelly Entertainment, Robert; Kommunication Koncepts; Kozkeeozko Music; Lilly Music Publishing; M & T Waldoch Publishing, Inc.; Makers Mark Gold; Montina Music; *Musikverlag Rossori; Omni 2000, Inc.; One Hot Note Music Inc.; Phaja Music; *Power Voltage Music; Prejippie Music Group; Prescription Company; *Pretty Shayna Music; *Rob-Lee Music; Rockford Music Co.; Rose Hill Group; Ryan Music, Joshua; S.M.C.L. Productions, Inc.; Sha-La Music, Inc.; Siegel Music Companies; Siskatune Music Publishing Co.; Stuart Music Co., Jeb; Succes; Sunsongs Music/ Hollywood East Entertainment; *T.C. Productions/Etude Publishing Co.; *Tabitha Music, Ltd.; Tedesco Music Co., Dale; Trusty Publications; Valet Publishing Co.; West & East Music; Wheelerboy Entertainment; Winston & Hoffman House Music Publishers; Worship Music; Zauber Music Publishing

Folk

Alexis; Aquarius Publishing; BOAM; Cimirron Music; Clevère Musikverlag, R.D.; *Colton Shows, Glenn; Don Del Music; Earitating Music Publishing; First Time Music (Publishing) U.K. Ltd.; Green Meadows Publishing; Halo International; Heupferd Musikverlag GmbH; *Immortal Beloved Music Publishing; *Kirchstein Publishing Co.; Martin's Music Publishing, Rod; Montina Music; Motex Music; Omni 2000, Inc.; Panchatantra Music Enterprises; Parravano Music; Prescription Company; Rockford Music Co.; Roots Music; Rustron Music Publishers; Soundbyte Corporation; Sunfrost Music; Sweet June Music; *Third Wave Productions Limited; This Here Music; Woodrich Publishing Co.

Jazz

Alexander Sr. Music; Alexis; Aljoni Music Co.; Antelope Publishing Inc.; Arylis Corporation; Bad Habits Music Publishing; Bal & Bal Music Publishing Co.; *Bay Ridge Publishing Co.; Bearsongs; Brewster Songs, Kitty; Coast Line Events, Inc.; *Cunningham Music; D.S.M. Producers Inc.; Elect Music Publishing Company; Fat City Publishing; *Fingerprint Songs; Flash International; Genetic Music Publishing; Giftness Enterprise; GlobeArt Inc.; Happy Hour Music; Heupferd Musikverlag GmbH; Ho-hum Music; Honk Music & Records — Musikverlag H. Gebetsroither; Joey Boy Publishing Co.; *Kelly Entertainment, Robert; Laurmack Music; Lonny Tunes Music; Montina Music; Newcreature Music; Non-Stop Music Publishing; NSP Music Publishing Inc.; Okisher Music; Old Slowpoke Music; Omni 2000, Inc.; One Hot Note Music Inc.; Philippopolis Music; Platinum Boulevard Publishing; Prescription Company; Ridge Music Corp.; Rockford Music Co.; Slanted Circle Music; *Smokey Lane Music; *Snowcliff Publishing; Stuart Music Co., Jeb; Tedesco Music Co., Dale; Trusty Publications; UBM; Wheelerboy Entertainment; Winston & Hoffman House Music Publishers; *Wize World of Muzic; Woodrich Publishing Co.

Latin

Alexis; Happy Hour Music; Honk Music & Records — Musikverlag H. Gebetsroither; Inside Records/OK Songs; Johnson Music, Little Richie; Josena Music; *Latin American Music Co., Inc.; Manny Music, Inc.; Motex Music; Padrino Music Publishing; Ryan Music, Joshua; *Sounds-Vision Music; Supreme Enterprises Int'l Corp.; *Tabitha Music, Ltd.; Unimusica Inc.

Metal

*Bay Ridge Publishing Co.; Ho-hum Music; Keno Publishing; Kommunication Koncepts; M & T Waldoch Publishing, Inc.; *Pas Mal Publishing; Silverhill Music; Sound Cellar Music; Your Best Songs Publishing

New Age

Bad Habits Music Publishing; Dingo Music; Heupferd Musikverlag GmbH; High-Minded Moma Publishing & Productions; Ho-hum Music; Honk Music & Records — Musikverlag H. Gebetsroither; McCartney Music; Myko Music; Non-Stop Music Publishing; Platinum Boulevard Publishing; Primal Visions Music; Quark, Inc.; Rana International & Affiliates Inc.; Rising Star Records and Publishers; Rustron Music Publishers; Southern Most Publishing Company; Tiki Enterprises, Inc.

Novelty

Big Fish Music Publishing Group; Branch Group Music; Cisum; Colstal Music; Davis & Davis Music; Dean Enterprises Music Group; Doré Records; Furrow Music; Green One Music; *Immortal Beloved Music Publishing; Joey Boy Publishing Co.; JW One Music Publishing Co.; Lonny Tunes Music; Martin's Music Publishing, Rod; Moon June Music; Parravano Music; Riverhawk Music

Pop

Abalone Publishing; Accent Publishing Co.; Alexis; *Al-Ky Music; Alleged Iguana Music; Allegheny Music Works; Amiron Music; Aquarius Publishing; Audio Music Publishers; AUM Circle Publishing; Bad Habits Music Publishing; Bal & Bal Music Publishing Co.; Barkin' Foe the Master's Bone; Bartow Music; *Bay Ridge Publishing Co.; Beecher Publishing, Earl; Berandol Music Ltd.; Bernard Enterprises, Inc., Hal; Best Buddies, Inc.; Betty Jane/Josie Jane Music Publishers; Big Fish Music Publishing Group; Blue Hill Music/Tutch Music; Bourne Co. Music Publishers; Bradley Music, Allan; Brewster Songs, Kitty; Bronx Flash Music, Inc.; Brothers Organisation, The; Buried Treasure Music; California Country Music; Calinoh Music Group; Camex Music; Cash Productions, Inc.; Castle Music Group; Centium Entertainment, Inc.; Cheavoria Music Co.; *Chicago Kid Productions; Christel Music Limited; Cisum; Clear Pond Music; Clevère Musikverlag, R.D.; Coffee and Cream Publishing Company; *Copperfield Music Group; Cornelius Companies, The; Corporate Music; Cottage Blue Music; Craig Music, Loman; *Cunningham Music; D.S.M. Producers Inc.; Dagene Music; De Miles Music Company, The Edward; Dean Enterprises Music Group; Delev Music Company; Dell Music, Frank; Delpha's Music Publishers; Demi Monde Records & Publishing Ltd.; Dingo Music; *Dream Seekers Publishing; Drive Music, Inc.; Duane Music, Inc.; *Earthscream Music Publishing Co.; EMF Productions; ESI Music Group; Ever-Open-Eye Music; *Fingerprint Songs; First Time Music (Publishing) U.K. Ltd.; Focal Point Music Publishers; *Fresh Entertainment; Frick Music Publishing Co.; Frontline Music Group; *Funzalo Music; Gary Music, Alan; Genetic Music Publishing; *GFI West Music Publishing; Giftness Enterprise; GlobeArt Inc.; Gold Music Publishing, Jay; Gowell Music, Richard E.; Hammel Associates, Inc., R.L.; Havasong Music; Hawksbill Music; Henly Music Associates; High-Minded Moma Publishing & Productions; Hit & Run Music Publishing Inc.; Hit-Fabrik Musikverlag; Ho-hum Music; Inside Records/OK Songs; Interscope Music Publishing; ISBA Music Publishing Inc.; Jae Music, Jana; Jaelius Enterprises; Jammy Music Publishers Ltd.; Ja/Nein Musikverlag GmbH; Jasper Stone Music/JSM Songs; *JK Jam Music; Jolson Black & White Music, Al; Josena Music; Joseph Music Inc., Patrick; Jump Music; *Just a Note; JW One Music Publishing Co.; Kaupps & Robert Publishing Co.; *Kelly Entertainment, Robert; Keno Publishing; Kommunication Koncepts; Kozkeeozko Music; Laurmack Music; Lindsay Publishing, Doris; Lineage Publishing Co.; Lin's Lines; M & T Waldoch Publishing, Inc.; McCartney Music; Makers Mark Gold; Martin's Music Publishing, Rod; MCA Music Publishing; Mento Music Group; Mighty Twinns Music; Montina Music; *Motor Music Co.; Music Room Publishing Group, The; *Musikverlag Rossori; Myko

Music; Mymit Music Productions, Chuck; Namax Music Publishing; Nebo Ridge Publishing Company; New Rap Jam Publishing, A; Newcreature Music; Non-Stop Music Publishing; Omni 2000, Inc.; One Hot Note Music Inc.; *Ontrax Companies; Operation Perfection; Orchid Publishing; Oyster Bay Music; PeerMusic; Pegasus Music; Phaja Music; Pine Island Music; *Platinum Gold Music; Prescription Company; *Pretty Shayna Music; Primal Visions Music; Prospector Three D Publishing; Rana International & Affiliates Inc.; Raving Cleric Music Publishing/Euro Export Entertainment; Ren Maur Music Corp.; Rent-A-Song; Ridge Music Corp.; *Rob-Lee Music; Rocker Music/Happy Man Music; Rockford Music Co.; Roots Music; Rose Hill Group; Rustron Music Publishers; Ryan Music, Joshua; S.M.C.L. Productions, Inc.; Sabteca Music Co.; Saddlestone Publishing; *Sci-Fi Music; Scott Music Group, Tim; Segal's Publications; Sha-La Music, Inc.; Shaolin Music; Shu'Baby Montez Music; Siegel Music Companies; Silver Blue Music/Oceans Blue Music; Silver Thunder Music Group; Simply Grand Music, Inc.; Sizemore Music; *Smokey Lane Music; *Snowcliff Publishing; Solid Entertainment; Song Farm Music; Sound Cellar Music; Soundbyte Corporation; Sounds of Aicram; Spring Rose Music; Stuart Music Co., Jeb; Succes; Sun Star Songs; Sunfrost Music; Sunsongs Music/Hollywood East Entertainment; *Tabitha Music, Ltd.; Tedesco Music Co., Dale; Tentex Music Publishing; *Third Wave Productions Limited; This Here Music; Tiki Enterprises, Inc.; Tooth and Nail Music; Transamerika Musikverlag KG; *Twin Spin Publishing; Twin Towers Publishing Co.; UBM; Ultimate Peak Music; Vaam Music Group; Valet Publishing Co.; Warner/Chappell Music Canada Ltd.; Wengert, Berthold (Musikverlag); West & East Music; Westunes Music Publishing Co.; Wheelerboy Entertainment; Wilcom Publishing; Winston & Hoffman House Music Publishers; Woodrich Publishing Co.; World Famous Music Co.; Worship Music; Your Best Songs Publishing; Zauber Music Publishing; *Zomba Music Publishing

R&B

Accent Publishing Co.; Alexander Sr. Music; Alexis; Aljoni Music Co.; Allegheny Music Works; Amiron Music; Audio Music Publishers; Bad Habits Music Publishing; Bal & Bal Music Publishing Co.; Barkin' Foe the Master's Bone; *Bartow Music; *Bay Ridge Publishing Co.; Bernard Enterprises, Inc., Hal; Best Buddies, Inc.; Betty Jane/Josie Jane Music Publishers; BOAM; Bourne Co. Music Publishers; Bradley Music, Allan; Brewster Songs, Kitty; Bronx Flash Music, Inc.; Brothers Organisation, The; California Country Music; Camex Music; Cash Productions, Inc.; Castle Music Group; Centium Entertainment, Inc.; Cheavoria Music Co.; *Chicago Kid Productions; Cisum; Clevère Musikverlag, R.D.; *Coast Line Events, Inc.; Coffee and Cream Publishing Company; Corporate Music; Cottage Blue Music; Country Star Music; *Cunningham Music; D.S.M. Producers Inc.; Dagene Music; Davis & Davis Music; De Miles Music Company, The Edward; Dean Enterprises Music Group; Delev Music Company; Demi Monde Records & Publishing Ltd.; Dingo Music; *Dream Seekers Publishing; Drive Music, Inc.; Duane Music, Inc.; Elect Music Publishing Company; EMF Productions; Ever-Open-Eye Music; Famous Music Publishing Companies; *Fingerprint Songs; First Time Music (Publishing) U.K. Ltd.; Flash International; *Fresh Entertainment; Frontline Music Group; Frozen Inca Music; Furrow Music; Gary Music, Alan; Genetic Music Publishing; *GFI West Music Publishing; Giftness Enterprise; GlobeArt Inc.; Gowell Music, Richard E.; Green Meadows Publishing; Hammel Associates, Inc., R.L.; Hawksbill Music; Hit & Run Music Publishing Inc.; Honk Music & Records — Musikverlag H. Gebetsroither; *International Music Network Limited; Interplanetary Music; Interscope Music Publishing; ISBA Music Publishing Inc.; Jaelius Enterprises; Jasper Stone Music/JSM Songs; *JK Jam Music; Joey Boy Publishing Co.; *Just a Note; JW One Music Publishing Co.; Kansa Records Corporation; Kaupps & Robert Publishing Co.; Keno Publishing; Kingsport Creek Music Publishing; *Kirchstein Publishing Co.; Kommunication Koncepts; Kozkeeozko Music; *Last Brain Cell; Laurmack Music; Lin's Lines; M & T Waldoch Publishing, Inc.; McGibony Publishing; Macman Music, Inc.; Majestic Control; Makers Mark Gold; Mighty Twinns Music; Montina Music; *Motor Music Co.; Music in the Right Keys Publishing Company; Music Room Publishing Group, The; Mymit Music Productions, Chuck; Namax Music Publishing; Nervous Publishing; New Rap Jam Publishing, A; Newcreature Music; Non-Stop Music

Publishing; NSP Music Publishing Inc.; Okisher Music; Old Slowpoke Music; Omni 2000, Inc.; Operation Perfection; Oyster Bay Music; PeerMusic; Phaja Music; Platinum Boulevard Publishing; *Platinum Gold Music; Prescription Company; *Pretty Shayna Music; Purple Haze Music; Rana International & Affiliates Inc.; Raving Cleric Music Publishing/Euro Export Entertainment; Ren Maur Music Corp.; Rent-A-Song; *RNR Publishing; *Rob-Lee Music; Rondor Music International; Rustron Music Publishers; Ryan Music, Joshua; Sabteca Music Co.; Saddlestone Publishing; Scott Music Group, Tim; Second City Publishing; Segal's Publications; Sha-La Music, Inc.; Shu'Baby Montez Music; Siegel Music Companies; Silver Blue Music/Oceans Blue Music; Silver Thunder Music Group; Simply Grand Music, Inc.; Siskatune Music Publishing Co.; Sizemore Music; Solid Entertainment; Song Farm Music; Sound Cellar Music; Sounds of Aicram; Southern Most Publishing Company; Starbound Publishing Co.; Stuart Music Co., Jeb; *Sunapee Music Group; Sunsongs Music/Hollywood East Entertainment; Sweet Glenn Music; *T.C. Productions/Etude Publishing Co.; *Tabitha Music, Ltd.; Tedesco Music Co., Dale; Tentex Music Publishing; Tiki Enterprises, Inc.; Tooth and Nail Music; Trusty Publications; Twin Towers Publishing Co.; Vaam Music Group; Valet Publishing Co.; Wheelerboy Entertainment; Wilcom Publishing; Winston & Hoffman House Music Publishers; Without Papers Music Publishing Inc.; *Wize World of Muzic; Woodrich Publishing Co.; World Famous Music Co.; Worship Music; Your Best Songs Publishing; Zauber Music Publishing; *Zomba Music Publishing

Rap

Aljoni Music Co.; Audio Music Publishers; Barkin' Foe the Master's Bone; *Bay Ridge Publishing Co.; Dagene Music; Elect Music Publishing Company; Flash International; *Fresh Entertainment; Frozen Inca Music; Interscope Music Publishing; ISBA Music Publishing Inc.; Jasper Stone Music/JSM Songs; Joey Boy Publishing Co.; *Kelly Entertainment, Robert; Keno Publishing; Laurmack Music; Lin's Lines; Majestic Control; New Rap Jam Publishing, A; One Hot Note Music Inc.; Operation Perfection; Oyster Bay Music; *Platinum Gold Music; Shu'Baby Montez Music; Silver Blue Music/ Oceans Blue Music; Sound Cellar Music; Stuart Music Co., Jeb; Treasure Trove Music; Winston & Hoffman House Music Publishers; *Wize World of Muzic; *Zomba Music Publishing

Religious

Accent Publishing Co.; Aim High Music Company; *Aladdin Music Group; Alexander Sr. Music; Alexis; Allegheny Music Works; Audio Images Two Thousand Music Publishing; Bagatelle Music Publishing Co.; Bal & Bal Music Publishing Co.; Barkin' Foe the Master's Bone; Barren Wood Publishing; *Bay Ridge Publishing Co.; *Beaverwood Audio-Video; Beecher Publishing, Earl; Best Buddies, Inc.; Betty Jane/Josie Jane Music Publishers; Big Fish Music Publishing Group; Blue Spur Entertainment, Inc./Git A Rope Publishing; BOAM; Bradley Music, Allan; Cactus Music and Winnebago Publishing; California Country Music; Calinoh Music Group; Cash Productions, Inc.; Castle Music Group; Chestnut Mound Music Group; Cisum; *Coast Line Events, Inc.; Coffee and Cream Publishing Company; *Copperfield Music Group; Cornelius Companies, The; Cottage Blue Music; Country Breeze Music; Country Star Music; Cowboy Junction Flea Market and Publishing Co.; Craig Music, Loman; *Cunningham Music; Cupit Music; Darbonne Publishing Co.; Davis & Davis Music; Dell Music, Frank; Delpha's Music Publishers; Dingo Music; *Dream Seekers Publishing; Earitating Music Publishing; Emandell Tunes; EMF Productions; *Enid, Oklahoma Music Publishing; Ever-Open-Eye Music; Faiella Publishing, Doug; First Time Music (Publishing) U.K. Ltd.; *Flaming Star West Music; *Flammer Music, Harold; Flash International; Focal Point Music Publishers; Foster Music Company, Mark; Fox Farm Recording; Frick Music Publishing Co.; Frontline Music Group; Giftness Enterprise; GlobeArt Inc.; Green Meadows Publishing; Hammel Associates, Inc., R.L.; *Harbor Gospel Music Production; Heartbeat Music; Henly Music Associates; Hinds Feet Music; Hitsburgh Music Co.; Holton Music; Holy Spirit Music; Hutchins Music, Gregg; *Jacksongs Music Publishing, d.t.; Jaclyn Music; Jaelius Enterprises; Jerjoy Music; *JoDa Music;

Josena Music; *Just a Note; JW One Music Publishing Co.; Kansa Records Corporation; Kaupps & Robert Publishing Co.; Kaylee Music Group, Karen; Kingsport Creek Music Publishing; Kommunication Koncepts; Lari-Jon Publishing; *Last Brain Cell; Laurmack Music; LCS Music Group, Inc.; Lindsay Publishing, Doris; Lin's Lines; Lion Hill Music Publishing Co.; McCoy Music, Jim; McGibony Publishing; Mack Music, Danny; Makers Mark Gold; Manny Music, Inc.; Mathes Company, The; Mighty Twinns Music; *Miller Music, Jody; Montina Music; Motex Music; Music in the Right Keys Publishing Company; Namax Music Publishing; National Talent; Nebo Ridge Publishing Company; New Rap Jam Publishing, A; Newcreature Music; NSP Music Publishing Inc.; Oh My Gosh Music; Omni 2000, Inc.; Orchid Publishing; Otto Publishing Co.; Paluch Company, J. S./World Library Publications, Inc.; Panchatantra Music Enterprises; Parravano Music; Pollard Sound World; Pritchett Publications; Prospector Three D Publishing; *Rachel Marie Music Ltd.; Radiant Music; *RNR Publishing; Rocker Music/Happy Man Music; Roots Music; Saddlestone Publishing; Samuel Three Productions; Scott Music Group, Tim; Scrutchings Music; *Sea Dream Music; *Smokey Lane Music; *Snowcliff Publishing; Soundbyte Corporation; Sounds of Aicram; Southern Most Publishing Company; Starbound Publishing Co.; Steel Rain Publishing; Stuart Music Co., Jeb; Stylecraft Music Co.; Sun Star Songs; *Sunapee Music Group; Sweet June Music; This Here Music; Tiki Enterprises, Inc.; Trusty Publications; Twin Spin Publishing; Vokes Music Publishing; *Wize World of Muzic; Woodrich Publishing Co.; Yorgo Music

Rock

Abalone Publishing; Accent Publishing Co.; *Aladdin Music Group; *Al-Ky Music; All Rock Music; Alleged Iguana Music; Amiron Music; Aquarius Publishing; Audio Music Publishers; AUM Circle Publishing; Axbar Productions; Baby Raquel Music; Bad Habits Music Publishing; Bal & Bal Music Publishing Co.; *Bay Ridge Publishing Co.; *Baylor-Eselby Music; Beecher Publishing, Earl; Bernard Enterprises, Inc., Hal; Best Buddies, Inc.; Big Snow Music; BOAM; Brewster Songs, Kitty; Bronx Flash Music, Inc.; Brothers Organisation, The; Buried Treasure Music; California Country Music; Camex Music; Cash Productions, Inc.; Centium Entertainment, Inc.; Cherie Music; Christel Music Limited; Christopher Publishing, Sonny; Cisum; Clear Pond Music; Clevère Musikverlag, R.D.; *Colton Shows, Glenn; Corporate Music; Cottage Blue Music; Country Breeze Music; Country Star Music; *Cunningham Music; Cupit Music; D.S.M. Producers Inc.; Davis & Davis Music; De Miles Music Company, The Edward; Dean Enterprises Music Group; Demi Monde Records & Publishing Ltd.; Dingo Music; Doss Music, Buster; *Dream Seekers Publishing; Drive Music, Inc.; Duane Music, Inc.; Earitating Music Publishing; *Earthscream Music Publishing Co.; Editions Scipion; Elect Music Publishing Company; EMF Productions; ESI Music Group; Faiella Publishing, Doug; Famous Music Publishing Companies; Fat City Publishing; First Time Music (Publishing) U.K. Ltd.; *Flaming Star West Music; Flea Circus Music; Frick Music Publishing Co.; Frontline Music Group; Frozen Inca Music; *Funzalo Music; Gary Music, Alan; *GFI West Music Publishing; Giftness Enterprise; Gold Music Publishing, Jay; Green Meadows Publishing; Green One Music; G-String Publishing; Hammel Associates, Inc., R.L.; Havasong Music; Hawksbill Music; Heupferd Musikverlag GmbH; Hickory Lane Publishing and Recording; *High Pockets Publishing Inc.; High-Minded Moma Publishing & Productions; Hit & Run Music Publishing Inc.; Ho-hum Music; Honk Music & Records — Musikverlag H. Gebetsroither; *Immortal Beloved Music Publishing; Interscope Music Publishing; ISBA Music Publishing Inc.; *Jacksongs Music Publishing, d.t.; Jammy Music Publishers Ltd.; Ja/Nein Musikverlag GmbH; Jasper Stone Music/JSM Songs; *JK Jam Music; *JoDa Music; Jolson Black & White Music, Al; JW One Music Publishing Co.; Kaupps & Robert Publishing Co.; Kel-Cres Publishing; *Kelly Entertainment, Robert; Keno Publishing; Kilowatt Music; *Kirchstein Publishing Co.; Kommunication Koncepts; *Largo Music Publishing; Lari-Jon Publishing; *Last Brain Cell; Lilly Music Publishing; Lin's Lines; Lonny Tunes Music; M & T Waldoch Publishing, Inc.; McCoy Music, Jim; Macman Music, Inc.; *Magic Message Music; Martin's Music Publishing, Rod; Montina Music; Motex Music; Music Room Publishing Group, The; *Musikverlag Rossori; Myko Music; Mymit Music Productions, Chuck; Nebo Ridge Publishing Company; Nervous Publishing; New Rap Jam Publishing, A; Newcreature Music; Old Slowpoke Music; Omni 2000, Inc.; One Hot Note Music Inc.; *Ontrax Companies; Operation Perfection; PeerMusic; Pen Cob Publishing Inc.; Planet Dallas Recording Studios; Platinum Boulevard Publishing; Platinum Gold Music; Pollard Sound World; Portage Music; *Power Voltage Music; Prejippie Music Group; Prescription Company; *Pretty Shayna Music; Primal Visions Music; Pritchett Publications; *Promo; Prospector Three D Publishing; Purple Haze Music; R. J. Music; *Rachel Marie Music Ltd.; Rana International & Affiliates Inc.; Raving Cleric Music Publishing/Euro Export Entertainment; Ren Maur Music Corp.; Rent-A-Song; Ridge Music Corp.; *RNR Publishing; Rob-Lee Music; Rocker Music/Happy Man Music; Rockford Music Co.; Rondor Music International; Roots Music; Rose Hill Group; Ryan Music, Joshua; Saddlestone Publishing; *Sci-Fi Music; Scott Music Group, Tim; *Sea Dream Music; *Second City Publishing; Segal's Publications; Sha-La Music, Inc.; Shaolin Music; Siegel Music Companies; Silicon Music Publishing Co.; Simply Grand Music, Inc.; *Smokey Lane Music; Solid Entertainment; Sound Cellar Music; Soundbyte Corporation; Sounds of Aicram; Southern Most Publishing Company; Spring Rose Music; Steel Rain Publishing; Stuart Music Co., Jeb; Succes; Sun Star Songs; Sunfrost Music; Sunsongs Music/Hollywood East Entertainment; *Surespin Songs; *Tabitha Music, Ltd.; Tedesco Music Co., Dale; *Third Wave Productions Limited; This Here Music; Tiki Enterprises, Inc.; Tooth and Nail Music; Transamerika Musikverlag KG; Treasure Trove Music; Trusty Publications; *Twin Spin Publishing; Twin Towers Publishing Co.; Ultimate Peak Music; Valet Publishing Co.; Warner/Chappell Music Canada Ltd.; *Watonka Records Co.; Westunes Music Publishing Co.; Whitewing Music; Wilcom Publishing; Without Papers Music Publishing Inc.; Woodrich Publishing Co.; World Famous Music Co.; Worship Music; Your Best Songs Publishing; Zauber Music Publishing; *Zomba Music Publishing

World Music

Elect Music Publishing Company; Heupferd Musikverlag GmbH; Honk Music & Records — Musikverlag H. Gebetsroither; Inside Records/OK Songs; Keno Publishing; *Kirchstein Publishing Co.; *Latin American Music Co., Inc.; Lin's Lines; Manny Music, Inc.; PPI/Peter Pan Industries; Primal Visions Music; *Sounds-Vision Music; Supreme Enterprises Int'l Corp.; Tedesco Music Co., Dale; Transamerika Musikverlag KG; Whitewing Music; *Wize World of Muzic

---

✳ THE ASTERISK before a listing indicates that the listing is new in this edition. New markets are often the most receptive to unsolicited submissions.

Music Print Publishers

The music print publisher's function is much more specific than that of the music publisher. Music publishers try to exploit a song in many different ways: on records, videos, movies and radio/TV commercials, to name a few. But, as the name implies, music print publishers deal in only one publishing medium: print.

Although the role of the music print publisher has virtually stayed the same over the years, demand for sheet music has declined substantially. Today there are only a few major sheet music publishers in operation, along with many smaller ones.

Most songs fall into one of two general categories: popular or educational music. Popular songs are pop, rock, adult contemporary, country and other hits heard on the radio. They are printed as sheet music (for single songs) and folios (collections of songs). Educational material includes pieces for chorus, band, orchestra, instrumental solos and instructional books. In addition to publishing original compositions, print publishers will sometimes print arrangements of popular songs.

Most major publishers of pop music won't print sheet music for a song until a popular recording of the song has become a hit single, or at least is on the Billboard Hot 100 chart. Some of the companies listed here indicate the lowest chart position of a song they've published, to give you a better idea of the market.

Chart action is obviously not a factor for original educational material. What print publishers look for is quality work that fits into their publishing program and is appropriate for the people who use their music, such as school and church choirs, school bands or orchestras.

When dealing with music print publishers, it is generally unacceptable to send out simultaneous submissions; that is, sending identical material to different publishers at the same time. Since most of the submissions they receive involve written music, whether single lead sheets or entire orchestrations, the time they invest in evaluating each submission is considerable—much greater than the few minutes it takes to listen to a tape. It would be discourteous and unprofessional to ask a music print publisher to invest a lot of time in evaluating your work and then possibly pull the deal out from under him before he has given you an answer.

Writers' royalties range from 10-15% of the retail selling price of music in print. For educational material that would be a percentage of the price of the whole set (score and parts). For a book of songs (called a folio), the 10-15% royalty would be pro-rated by the number of songs by that writer in the book. Royalties for sheet music are paid on a flat rate per sheet, which is usually about one-fifth of the retail price. If a music publisher licenses print publishing to a music print publisher, print royalties are usually split evenly between the music publisher and songwriter, but it may vary. You should read any publishing contract carefully to see how print deals fit in, and consult an entertainment attorney if you have any questions.

ABINGDON PRESS (ASCAP, BMI), Dept. SM, 201 Eighth Ave. S., Nashville TN 37203. (615)749-6158. Senior Music Editor: Gary Alan Smith. Music print publisher. Publishes approximately 500 songs/year; publishes as many new songwriters as possible.
How to Contact: Submit manuscripts and a demo tape by mail. Unsolicited submissions are OK. "Unsolicited material must be addressed with Gary Alan Smith's name on the first line." Prefers no more than 4 songs per submission. "Please be sure name and address are on tapes and/or manuscripts." SASE. Reports in 6-8 weeks.

Music: Mostly **sacred choral** and **instrumental**.
Tips: "Focus material on small to mid-size, volunteer church choirs and musicians. Be flexible in your writing and be patient."

ALRY PUBLICATIONS, ETC., INC. (ASCAP), P.O. Box 36542, Charlotte NC 28236. (704)334-3413. Fax: (704)334-1143. President: Amy Rice Blumenthal. Music print publisher and music publisher. Estab. 1980. Publishes 20 pieces/year; mostly individual songs or educational material. Publishes 3-5 new songwriters/year. Pays 10% print royalty.
How to Contact: Submit demo tape by mail. Unsolicited submissions are OK. Prefers cassette and complete score or part(s). "Brief bio and any performance notes should be included." SASE. Reports 1-3 months.
Music: Mostly **classical**, **educational** and **chamber music**; also **original**, **popular** and **jazz**. Published "Serenade" (by David Uber)(chamber trio); "Flowers" (by Elizabeth Raum) (flute or oboe); and "Sacred Medley" (by Tommy Goff) (flute choir).
Tips: "Be aware of the market for sheet music/educational and classical."

MEL BAY PUBLICATIONS, INC. (BMI), P.O. Box 66, Pacific MO 63069-0066. E-mail: email@ melbay.com. Website: http://www.melbay.com. Vice President: William A. Bay. Music print publisher. Estab. 1947. Publishes 200 pieces/year (books, videos, CDs); mostly folios or educational material. Pays standard royalty.
How to Contact: Submit demo tape by mail. Unsolicited submissions are OK. Prefers cassette with book synopsis, outline, sample chapters. Does not return material. Reports in 4-6 weeks.
Music: Mostly **guitar**, **fretted instruments** and **keyboard**; also **percussion** and **instrumental**. Published *Emerald*, *Sardius* and *Topaz*, all written and recorded by Carlos Barbosa-Lima on Concord Jazz (Brazilian jazz).
Tips: "We are interested in books or anthologies, not isolated pieces."

BOSTON MUSIC CO. (ASCAP), 172 Tremont St., Boston MA 02111. (617)426-5100. Website: http://www.bostonian.com/music/bmc. Contact: Editorial Department. Music print publisher. Prints 100 pieces/year, both individual pieces and music books. Pays 10% royalty.
How to Contact: Write or call first and obtain permission to submit. SASE. Reports in 6-7 months.
Music: Choral pieces, educational material, instrumental solo pieces and **"piano instructional materials that piano teachers would be interested in."** Published "Jubilation!" (by Frederick Koch) (piano duet); "Hosanna In The Highest" (by Barbara Owen) (SAB choral); "Organic Rhapsody" (by Wynn-Anne Rossi) (violin/piano).
Tips: "Please submit only music suitable to our catalog—no vocal music, no pop or rock."

BOURNE COMPANY, 5 W. 37th St., New York NY 10018. (212)391-4300. Contact: Professional Manager. Music print publisher. Estab. 1917. Publishes educational material and popular music.
Affiliate(s): ABC Music, Ben Bloom, Better Half, Bogat, Burke & Van Heusen, Goldmine, Harborn, Lady Mac, Murbo Music.
• See their listing in the Music Publishers section.
How to Contact: Write first and obtain permission to submit. SASE. Reports in 3-6 months.
Music: Band pieces, choral pieces and **handbell pieces.** Published "You Can Count on Me" (by S. Cahn/N. Monath) (2 part choral); "Unforgettable" (by Gordon), recorded by Natalie Cole on Elektra Records (vocal duet); and "The Songs of Charlie Chaplin."

ECS PUBLISHING, Dept. SM, 138 Ipswich St., Boston MA 02215. (617)236-1935. President: Robert Schuneman. Music print publisher. Prints 200 pieces/year, mostly individual pieces and music books. Pays 10% royalty on sales and 50% on performance/license.
Affiliates: Galaxy Music Corporation (ASCAP), E.C. Schirmer Music Co. Inc. (ASCAP), Ione Press, Inc. (BMI), Highgate Press (BMI).
How to Contact: Query with complete score and tape of piece. Prefers cassette. "Submit a clean, readable score." SASE. Reports in 6-8 months.
Music: Choral pieces, orchestral pieces, instrumental solo pieces, instrumental ensemble pieces, methods books, books on music and **keyboard pieces**.

CARL FISCHER, INC. (ASCAP), 62 Cooper Square, New York NY 10003. (212)777-0900. Fax: (212)477-4129. Vice President, Publishing: Mr. Lauren Keiser. Music print publisher, music publisher. Estab. 1872. Publishes over 100 pieces/year; mostly individual songs, folios or educational material. Publishes 3-4 new composers/year. Lowest chart position held by a song published in sheet form is 40. Pays standard royalty.
Affiliates: Pembroke (BMI).
How to Contact: Write first and obtain permission to submit a demo. Prefers cassette with lead sheet and/or scores. SASE. Reports in 4 months.

Music: Mostly **sacred choral** and **band**. Published "Symphony #2" (by Howard Hanson), recorded by Seattle Symphony; "Waltzing Matilda" (traditional); and "Concerto for Left Hand" (by Lukas Foss).

MARK FOSTER MUSIC COMPANY, Box 4012, Champaign IL 61824-4012. (217)398-2760. Fax: (217)398-2791. President: Jane C. Menkhaus. Music print publisher, music publisher and retail music division. Estab. 1962. Publishes 20-30 pieces/year; mostly choral music and books. Publishes 3-4 new songwriters/year. Pays 5-10% over first 3,000 copies sold.
Affiliate(s): Fostco (ASCAP) and Marko (BMI).
• See their listing in the Music Publishers section.
How to Contact: Submit demo tape by mail. Unsolicited submissions are OK. Prefers cassette with 1 song and choral manuscript. If new composer/arranger, submit bio. SASE.
Music: Mostly **sacred SATB**, **secular SATB** and **sacred** and **secular treble** and **male choir music**; also **conducting books** and **Kodaly materials**. Published "Before Your Throne" (by Bradley Elling-boe); "City on the Hill" (by Marvin V. Curtis); and "Jubilant Song" (by René Clausen).
Tips: "Must be well-constructed piece to begin with, manuscript should be in decent format, preferably with keyboard reduction."

*GENEVOX MUSIC GROUP (ASCAP, BMI, SESAC), 127 Ninth Ave. N., Nashville TN 37234. (615)251-3770. Music print publisher. Estab. 1986. Director: Mark Blankenship. Prints 75-100 songs/year; publishes 10 new songwriters/year. Pays 10% royalty.
How to Contact: Submit demo tape and choral arrangement, lead sheet or complete score. Unsolicited submissions are OK. Prefers cassette with 1-5 songs. SASE. Reports in 2 weeks acknowledging receipt, 3 months response.
Music: Choral, **orchestral**, **instrumental solo** and **instrumental ensemble pieces**. "We publish all forms of choral sacred music for all ages, and instrumental for handbell, organ, piano and orchestra." Published "Go, Go Jonah," by Kathie Hill (children's choral musical); "Bless the Lord," arranged by Dave Williamson (praise/worship); and "God So Loved the World," arranged by Camp Kirkland and Tom Fettke (musical).
Tips: "Most of what we publish is designed for use by church choirs and instrumentalists. Middle-of-the-road, traditional anthems, hymn arrangements, praise and worship, contemporary and inspirational songs in an SATB/keyboard choral format stand the best chance for serious consideration."

HINSHAW MUSIC, INC. (ASCAP), Box 470, Chapel Hill NC 27514-0470. (919)933-1691. Editor: Don Hinshaw. Music print publisher. Estab. 1975. Prints 100 pieces/year, both individual pieces and music books. Publishes educational material. Pays 10% royalty.
Affiliate(s): Hindon Publications (BMI) and Chapel Hill Music (SESAC).
How to Contact: Write first and obtain permission to submit. After receiving permission, "Send the complete score. Lyric sheets and/or tapes alone are not acceptable. We do not review lyrics alone. Cassette tapes may be sent in addition to the written ms. Send clear, legible photocopies, *not* the original. Submit only 2 or 3 mss at a time that are representative of your work. An arrangement of a copyrighted work will not be considered unless copy of written permission from copyright owner(s) is attached. Once a ms has been submitted, do not telephone or write for a 'progress report.' Be patient." SASE. Reports in 1-4 months.
Music: Choral pieces and **organ**. Published "Music to Hear" (by G. Shearing); and *Magnificat* (by J. Rutter), recorded by Collegium.
Tips: "Submit your ms to only one publisher at a time. It requires considerable time and expense for us to thoroughly review a work, so we want the assurance that if accepted, the ms is available for publication. We are unable to 'critique' rejected works. A pamphlet, 'Submitting Music for Publication,' is available with SASE."

JUMP MUSIC, Langemunt 71, 9420 Aaigem, **Belgium**. Phone: (053)62-73-77. Estab. 1976. General Manager: Eddy Van Mouffaert. Music print publisher. Publishes educational material and popular music. Prints 150 songs/year, mostly individual songs. Pays 5% royalty.
• See their listing in the Music Publishers section.
How to Contact: Submit demo tape by mail. Unsolicited submissions are OK. Prefers cassette and lead sheet or complete score. Does not return material. Reports in 2 weeks.

MARKET CONDITIONS are constantly changing! If you're still using this book and it is 1998 or later, buy the newest edition of *Songwriter's Market* at your favorite bookstore or order directly from Writer's Digest Books.

Music: Pop, ballads, band pieces and **instrumentals**. Published *Tot Ziens* (by Eddy Govert), recorded by Eigentijdse Jevgd on Youth Sound Records (Flemish); "Go Go Go" (by Henry Spider), recorded by Rudy Silvester on Scorpion Records (Flemish); and *Onze Vader* (by Paul Severs), recorded by P.P. Michiels on Youth Sound Records (Flemish).

KALLISTI MUSIC PRESS, 810 S. Saint Bernard St., Philadelphia PA 19143-3309. (215)724-6511. E-mail: kallisti@pacs.pha.pa.us. Publisher: Andrew Stiller. Music print publisher. Estab. 1991. Publishes 12 pieces/year; mostly individual songs or folios. Publishes 1-2 new songwriters/year. Pays 30-50% royalty.
How to Contact: Write or call first and obtain permission to submit. Prefers cassette with résumé or bio, and complete list of works. "Cassette should include works covering the composer's full chronological and stylistic range. Résumé should indicate date of birth. Works list should indicate forces, duration, and date of each item. Do not send scores." SASE. Reports in 2 weeks.
Music: Mostly **"serious" music, new and old**; also **traditional/folk anthologies** and **jazz transcriptions**. Published *The Kairn of Koridwen* (by Charles Tomlinson Griffes) on Koch International Records (ballet); *Metaphors* (by Lejaren Hiller) on New World Records (guitar quartet); and *The Water is Wide, Daisy Bell* (by Andrew Stiller) on MMC Records (piano).
Tips: "Bear in mind that we want to publish music that will still be performed 200 years from now. All mss accepted for publication must be submitted in Finale or other music-notation software format of comparable sophistication."

THE LORENZ CORPORATION (ASCAP, BMI, SESAC), Box 802, Dayton OH 45401-0802. (513)228-6118. Contact: Editorial Department. Music print publisher. Estab. 1890. Publishes 500 titles/year; 10 new composers/year. Hires staff writers. Pays standard royalty.
How to Contact: Submit manuscript (completely arranged, not songs or lead sheets); tape not necessary. "No demos—only full arrangement." SASE. Reports in 4-6 weeks.
Music: Interested in **religious/Christian choral**, **high school, junior high, elementary choral** and **organ/piano music**; also **sacred** and **educational band music** and **handbell music**.
Tips: "Send in a legible copy. We do not produce vocal solo collections or sheet music. We encourage new composers/arrangers but do not use lead sheets or vocal solos, only fully arranged pieces for chorus, keyboard or handbell."

HAROLD LUICK & ASSOCIATES (BMI), Box B, Carlisle IA 50047. (515)989-3748. President: Harold Luick. Music print publisher. Prints 4-5 songs/year, mostly individual songs. Lowest chart position held by a song published in sheet form is 98. Pays 4% royalty.
 • See their listings in the Music Publishers and Record Producers sections.
How to Contact: Write and obtain permission to submit or submit through publisher or attorney. Prefers cassette or reel-to-reel and lyric sheet. SASE. Reports in 3 weeks.
Music: Mostly **traditional country**; also **novelty songs**. Published "Mrs. Used To Be," written and recorded by Joe Harris on River City Records (country).
Tips: "Send us song material that is conducive to type of market today. Good commercial songs."

*MUSIC BOX DANCER PUBLICATIONS LTD., 2600 John St. #220, Markham Ontario L3R 3W3 **Canada**. (905)475-1848. (905)474-9870. President: John Loweth. Music print publisher and music publisher. Estab. 1979. Publishes 20-30 pieces/year; mostly individual songs, folios and educational material. Publishes 2 new songwriters/year. Pays standard royalty.
 • See the listing for Berandol Music in the Music Publishers section and Berandol Records in the Record Companies section.
How to Contact: Submit demo tape by mail. Unsolicited submissions are OK. Prefers cassette. Does not return material. Reports in 2-3 months.
Music: Mostly **instrumental, piano** and **other instrumentation**. Published *Shadows of the Dancer*, written and recorded by Frank Mills (piano); *Fields*, written and recorded by Brian Langill (pop instrumental), both on MBD Records; and *Flute Quartet No. 1*, written and recorded by Daniel Theaker (instrumental) on DTee Records.
Tips: "You must have a professional demo, and indicate your achievements to date."

PLYMOUTH MUSIC CO., INC., 170 NE 33rd St., Ft. Lauderdale FL 33334. (305)563-1844. General Manager: Bernard Fisher. Music print publisher. Estab. 1953. Prints 50 pieces/year: individual pieces, individual songs, music books and folios. Pays 10% of retail selling price.
Affiliate(s): Aberdeen Music (ASCAP), Galleria Press (ASCAP), Walton Music (ASCAP) and Music for Percussion (BMI).
How to Contact: Submit demo tape by mail. Unsolicited submissions are OK. Prefers cassette and lead sheet or complete score. SASE. Reports in 2 weeks.

Music: Choral pieces and percussion music.
Tips: "Send choral music for church and school with cassette tape if available. Manuscripts should be legible."

THEODORE PRESSER CO. (ASCAP, BMI, SESAC), Dept. SM, One Presser Place, Bryn Mawr PA 19010. (215)525-3636. Fax: (215)527-7841. E-mail: presser@presser.com. Contact: Editorial Committee. Music print publisher. Member MPA. Publishes 90 works/year. Pays varying royalty.
Affiliate(s): Merion Music (BMI), Elkan-Vogel, Inc. (ASCAP), and Mercury Music Corp. (SESAC).
How to Contact: Submit demo tape by mail. Unsolicited submissions are OK. Prefers cassette with 1-2 works and score. "Include return label and postage." Reports in 1 month.
Music: Serious, educational and **choral music**. "We primarily publish serious music of emerging and established composers, and vocal/choral music which is likely to be accepted in the church and educational markets, as well as gospel chorals of high musical quality. We are *not* a publisher of song sheets or pop songs."
Tips: "Do not submit more than three works, unless requested. Do not send anything other than choral, educational or serious concert music. We do not do 'pop' music."

R.T.F.M., % Stewart House, Hillbottom Rd., Highwycombe, Buckinghamshire HP124HJ **United Kingdom**. Phone: (01630)647374. Fax: (01630)647612. A&R: Ron Lee. Music print publisher, music publisher. Publishes educational material and popular music. Prints 40 songs/year, mostly individual songs. Lowest chart position held by a song published in sheet form is 140. Royalty negotiable.
  • See the listings for LeMatt Music in the Record Companies section and R.T.L. Music in the Music Publishers section.
Affiliate(s): Lee Music, Pogo Records and R.T.L. Music.
How to Contact: Submit demo tape by mail. Unsolicited submissions are OK. Prefers cassette, DAT or video and lyric and lead sheets or complete score. Include photo and bio. SAE and IRC. Reports in 6 weeks.
Music: All types: band, orchestral, instrumental solo and **instrumental ensemble** pieces; also **radio, TV** and **film music** (specializes in jingles/background music). Published *Gotta Do It All Again*, written and recorded by Alvin Stardust on C.M.C. Records; *Wine, Women and Song*, written and recorded by Ricky Valance on Tring Records; and *I Hate School*, written and recorded by Suburban Studs on Anagram Records.

*SEA DREAM MUSIC, 236 Sebert Rd., London E7 0NP **England**. (0181)534-8500. Senior Partner: Simon Law. Music print publisher. Publishes educational material and popular music. Estab. 1976. Prints 20 songs/year, mostly individual songs. Has printed sheet music for uncharted songs. Pays 10% royalty per sheet sold.
Affiliate(s): Chain of Love Music, Crimson Flame, Ernvik Musik (Sweden), Really Free Music, Scarf Music Publishing.
  • See their listing in the Music Publishers section, as well as listings for Plankton Records in the Record Companies section and Sandcastle Productions in the Managers and Booking Agents section.
How to Contact: Write first and obtain permission to submit. Prefers cassette and lyric sheet. SAE and IRC. Reports in 3 months.
Music: Band and **choral pieces**. Published *Come And Talk About Jesus* (by Derek Llewellyn), recorded by Fresh Claim on Plankton Records (children's); *We Are One* (by Ben Okafor), recorded by Ben Okafor/Garth Hewitt on Word Records (reggae); and *Jesus Is The Living Way* (by Gill Hutchinson), recorded by Su Band on ICC Records (children's).
Tips: "We publish specifically Christian songs."

SHELLEY MUSIC, 1731 Red Bud Rd., Bolingbrook IL 60440. President: Guy Shelley. Music print publisher. Estab. 1992. Publishes 20-50 songs/year; publishes 4 new songwriters/year. Pays 10% standard sheet music royalty.
Affiliate(s): Guy Smilo Music (BMI).
How to Contact: Write first and obtain permission to submit. Prefers cassette with 1-3 songs and lyric sheet. SASE. Reports in 6 months. "No phone calls."
Music: Mostly **classical (educational)**. Published "The Ice Bear," "Jupiter" and "Prolog," all piano pieces written by Donna Shelley.
Tips: "Have a finished score and a clean demo. Only submit your best material."

WILLIAM GRANT STILL MUSIC (ASCAP), 4 S. San Francisco St., Suite 422, Flagstaff AZ 86001-5737. (520)526-9355. Estab. 1983. Manager: Judith Anne Still. Music print publisher. Publishes educational material and classical and popular music. Prints 2-3 arrangements/year; 2-3 new arrangers/year. Pays 10% royalty for arrangements sold. "We publish arrangements of works by William Grant

Still. This year we are especially interested in developing a catalog of clarinet arrangements, though other sorts of arrangements may be considered."

How to Contact: Write or call first and obtain permission to submit. Does not return material. Reports in 2 weeks.

Music: Mostly **instrumental solo pieces**. Published "Bayou Home" and "Memphis Man" (by Anthony Griggs); "Excerpt from *Troubled Island*" (by Bob McMahan); and "In Memoriam for William Grant Still" (by Christian Dupriez).

Tips: "Be intimately familiar with the work of Will Grant Still."

TPM/STUDIO, P.O. Box 3362, Greensboro NC 27401. (910)370-4441. E-mail: twpoteat@hamlet.un cg.edu. Owner: Terry Poteat. Music print publisher, vanity publisher. Estab. 1993. Publishes 15-20 pieces/year; mostly individual pieces. Royalty varies depending on composer and material but not less than 10%.

Affiliate(s): TPM/Studio Productions (ASCAP); Tom/Quincy Music (BMI).

How to Contact: Send as complete a submission as possible, including a short biography, publishing experiences (if any), and a list of compositions to date. Pieces already performed are of interest to us at this time. A recording is most beneficial."

Music: Mostly **modern jazz**, **chamber pieces** and/or **solos**, **sacred** and **secular choral**. Published "Black Rain" (by Kym Holliday), recorded by Ranid Woods on Jet Records (top 40); "Angels" (by Stephen Suber); and "Brighter Day," written by Terry Poteat.

Tips: "Send as complete a submission as possible, including a short biography, publishing experiences (if any), and a list of compositions to date. Pieces already performed are of interest to us at this time. A recording is most beneficial."

TRANSCONTINENTAL MUSIC PUBLICATIONS (ASCAP), Dept. SM, 838 Fifth Ave., New York NY 10021. (212)650-4101. Fax: (212)650-4109. Website: http://www.shamash.org/reform/uahc/transmp/. Senior Editor: Dr. Judith B. Tischler. Music print publisher. Estab. 1941. Pays 10% royalty. "We publish serious solo and choral Jewish music. The standard royalty is 10% except for rentals—there is no cost to the songwriter. Distributes audio cassettes and CDs if 50% or more of the content is published by Transcontinental. Currently producing CDs of children's songs and synagogue choral Jewish music."

Affiliate(s): New Jewish Music Press (BMI).

How to Contact: Query first. Prefers cassette. "We usually do not accept lead sheets. Most all of our music is accompanied. Full and complete arrangements should accompany the melody." SASE. Reports in 1 month.

Music: Only **Jewish vocal** and **Jewish choral**. Published "Numi Numi" by Stern (classical); "Biti" (by Isaacson) (Bat Mitzvah Solo) and "Shalom Aleichem" (by Kalmanoff), recorded by Milnes on Ross Records (choral).

TRILLENIUM MUSIC CO. (ASCAP), P.O. Box 88, Tunbridge VT 05077. (802)889-3354. President: Don Stewart. Music print publisher. Estab. 1986. Publishes 10-15 pieces/year; mostly educational material or serious music. Publishes 1 new songwriter/year. Pays purchase amount.

How to Contact: Write first and obtain permission to submit a demo. Prefers cassette with lead sheet and complete materials, if possible. SASE. Reports in 3 months.

Music: Mostly **serious, jazz-derived**. Published "Seven Little Etudes," "A Book of Sliding Things" and "Gesualdo Stanzas" (by Don Stewart).

VIVACE PRESS, NW 310 Wawawai Rd., Pullman WA 99163. (509)334-4660. Fax: (509)334-3551. Contact: Jonathan Yordy. Music print publisher. Estab. 1990. Publishes 40 pieces of music/year; publishes several new composers/year. Pays 10% royalty for sheet music sales.

How to Contact: Submit demo tape and sheet music. Unsolicited submissions OK. Prefers cassette. SASE. Reports in 1-2 weeks.

Music: Chamber music, with an emphasis on **historical classical** and **contemporary classical keyboard**. Published "Prelude For Organ," by Fanny Mendelssohn (organ); "Toccata For Harpsichord," by Emma Lou Diemer (harpsichord); and "Electric Church and The Walls of Jerusalem," by Robert Starer (piano).

Tips: "High-quality submissions in all categories considered."

FRANK E. WARREN MUSIC SERVICE (ASCAP), P.O. Box 650006, W. Newton MA 02165. (617)332-5394. Owner/operator: Frank E. Warren. Music print publisher. Estab. 1994. Publishes 25-50 pieces/year; mostly educational material. Publishes 5-25 new songwriters/year. Pays 12.5% of sales.

Affiliate(s): Earnestly Music (BMI).

How to Contact: Write or call first and obtain permission to submit a demo (and scores). Prefers clear manuscript or score, cassette optional (desirable). "Present everything (music, cassette, other supporting materials) in an orderly fashion that is explained well in a cover letter." SASE. Reports in 6-8 weeks.

Music: Mostly **chamber music, choral music** and **transcriptions/arrangements**; also **educational materials, string orchestra.** Published *Quintet No. 2 for Brass* (by Kenneth Amis), recorded by Empire Brass on Hard Press Records; *Divertimento for Reed Trio* (by David L. Post); and *Piano Trio No. 1* (1993) (by Frederick Koch), recorded by Elysian Trio on Truemedia Records.

Tips: "Provide camera-ready scores that meet industry standards in regard to notation and score layout. Be patient, and at the same time prepared to respond to publisher deadline dates in a timely manner. Don't be afraid to ask questions. Frank E. Warren Music Service is a composer-friendly organization, with flexible terms in helping to meet the needs of composers. Our primary concern is the distribution of music and the development of the composer's career. The compositions in our catalogue are from emerging, advanced, and professional composers. We welcome submissions from writers, and inquiries from dealers and libraries."

THE WILLIS MUSIC COMPANY, 7380 Industrial Rd., Florence KY 41022-0548. (606)283-2050. Estab. 1899. Editor: David B. Engle. Music print publisher. Publishes educational material. Prints 100 publications/year; "no charted songs in our catalog." Pays 5-10% of retail price or outright purchase.

Affiliate: Harry Fox Agency.

How to Contact: Prefers fully notated score. SASE. Reports in 3 months.

Music: Mostly **early level piano teaching material**; also **instrumental solo pieces, method books** and "supplementary materials—educational material only."

Record Companies

The role of the record company is to record and release records, cassettes and CDs—the mechanical products of the music industry. They sign artists to recording contracts, decide what songs those artists will record, and determine which songs to release. They are also responsible for providing recording facilities, securing producers and musicians, and overseeing the manufacture, distribution and promotion of new releases.

MAJOR LABELS AND INDEPENDENT LABELS

Major labels and independent labels—what's the difference between the two? Major labels are defined as those record companies distributed by one of the "Big 6" distribution companies: BMG, CEMA, Polygram, Sony Music, UNI and WEA. Distribution companies are wholesalers that sell records to retail outlets. Independent labels go through smaller distribution companies to distribute their product. They usually don't have the ability to distribute records in massive quantities as the major distributors do. However, that doesn't mean independent labels aren't able to have hit records just like their major counterparts. Walt Disney Records is an independent label that has had phenomenal success with soundtracks such as *Pocahontas* and *The Lion King*. Other examples include Tommy Boy Records, which sold over a million records with Coolio's *Gangsta's Paradise*; California indie Epitaph Records, which had huge success with Offspring's *Smash*, selling more than five million copies of that record, which remains on the chart more than two years after its release; and folk label Rounder Records, which helped bring Alison Krauss to the public eye by selling over 2 million copies of her release *Now That I've Found You: A Collection*.

Most, but not all, of the companies listed in this section are independent labels. They are usually the most receptive to receiving material from new artists. Major labels spend more money than most other segments of the music industry; the music publisher, for instance, pays only for items such as salaries and the costs of making demos. Record companies, at great financial risk, pay for many more services, including production, manufacturing and promotion. Therefore, major labels must be very selective when signing new talent. Also, the continuing fear of copyright infringement suits has closed avenues to getting new material heard by the majors. Most don't listen to unsolicited submissions, period. Only songs recommended by attorneys, managers and producers who record company employees trust and respect are being heard by A&R people at major labels. But that doesn't mean all major labels are closed to new artists. Several major labels are listed in this year's *Songwriter's Market*, including Atlantic Records, Arista Records, Elektra Entertainment, Jive Records, MCA Records and Zoo Entertainment. Following submission policies carefully and presenting a professional package could get you an attentive audience at a major label.

But the competition is fierce at the majors, so independent labels should not be overlooked. Since they're located all over the country, indie labels are easier to contact and can be important in building a local base of support for your music (consult the Geographic Index at the back of the book to find out which companies are located near you). Independent labels usually concentrate more on a specific type of music, which will help you target those companies your submission should be sent to. And since the staff at an indie label is smaller, there are fewer channels to go through to get your music heard by the decision makers in the company.

If you're interested in getting a major label deal, it makes sense to look to independent record labels to get your start. Independent labels are seen by many as a stepping stone to a major recording contract. Very few artists are signed to a major label at the start of their careers; usually, they've had a few independent releases that helped build their reputation in the industry. Major labels watch independent labels closely to locate up-and-coming bands and new trends. In the current economic atmosphere at major labels—with extremely high overhead costs for developing new bands and the fact that only 10% of acts on major labels actually make any profit—they're not willing to risk everything on an unknown act. Most major labels won't even consider signing a new act that hasn't had some indie success.

But independents aren't just farming grounds for future major label acts; many bands have long term relationships with indies, and prefer it that way. While they may not be able to provide the extensive distribution and promotion that a major label can (though there are exceptions), indie labels can help an artist become a regional success, and may even help the performer to see a profit as well. With the lower overhead and smaller production costs that an independent label operates on, it's much easier to be a "success" on an indie label than on a major.

Independent record labels can run on a small staff, with only a handful of people running the day-to-day business. Major record labels are more likely to be divided into the following departments: A&R, sales, marketing, promotion, product management, artist development, production, finance, business/legal and international.

The A&R department is staffed with A&R reps who search out new talent. They go out and see new bands, listen to demo tapes, and decide which artists to sign. They also look for new material for already signed acts, match producers with artists and oversee recording projects. Once an artist is signed by an A&R rep and a record is recorded, the rest of the departments at the company come into play.

The sales department is responsible for getting a record into stores. They make sure record stores and other outlets receive enough copies of a record to meet consumer demand. The marketing department is in charge of publicity, advertising in magazines and other media, promotional videos, album cover artwork, in-store displays, and any other means of getting the name and image of an artist to the public. The promotion department's main objective is to get songs from a new album played on the radio. They work with radio programmers to make sure a product gets airplay. The product management department is the ringmaster of the sales, marketing and promotion departments, assuring that they're all going in the same direction when promoting a new release. The artist development department is responsible for taking care of things while an artist is on tour, such as setting up promotional opportunities in cities where an act is performing. The production department works with the actual manufacture and printing of the record, making sure it gets shipped to distributors in a timely manner. People in the finance department compute and distribute royalties, as well as keep track of expenses and income at the company. The business/legal department takes care of contracts, not only between the record company and artists but with foreign distributors, record clubs, etc. And finally, the international department is responsible for working with international companies for the release of records in other countries.

LOCATING A RECORD LABEL

With the abundance of record labels out there, how do you go about finding one that's right for the music you create? First, it helps to know exactly what kind of music a record label releases. Become familiar with the records that a company has released, and see if they fit in with what you're doing. Each listing in this section details the type of music a particular record company is interested in releasing. You will want to refer to the Category Index, located at the end of this section, to help you find those companies most receptive to the type of music you write.

Recommendations by key music industry people are an important part of making contacts with record companies. Songwriters must remember that talent alone does not guarantee success in the music business. You must be recognized through contacts, and the only way to make contacts is through networking. Networking is the process of building an interconnecting web of acquaintances within the music business. The more industry people you meet, the larger your contact base becomes, and the better are your chances of meeting someone with the clout to get your demo into the hands of the right people. If you want to get your music heard by key A&R representatives, networking is imperative.

Networking opportunities can be found anywhere industry people gather. A good place to meet key industry people is at regional and national music conferences and workshops. There are many held all over the country for all types of music (see the Workshops and Conferences section for more information). You should try to attend at least one or two of these events each year; it's a great way to increase the number and quality of your music industry contacts.

Another good way to attract A&R people is to make a name for yourself as an artist. By starting your career on a local level and building it from there, you can start to cultivate a following and prove to labels that you can be a success (see the Performing Songwriter Roundtable on page 23 for information on three singer/songwriters who are successful on their own). A&R people figure if an act can be successful locally, there's a good chance they could be successful nationally. Start getting booked at local clubs, and start a mailing list of fans and local media. Once you gain some success on a local level, branch out. All this attention you're slowly gathering, this "buzz" you're generating, will not only get to your fans but to influential people in the music industry as well.

RECORD COMPANY CONTRACTS

Once you've found a record company that is interested in your work, either major or independent, the next step is signing a contract. Independent label contracts are usually not as long and complicated as major label ones, but they are still binding, legal contracts. Make sure the terms are in the best interest of both you and the label. Avoid anything in your contract that you feel is too restrictive. It's important to have your contract reviewed by a competent entertainment lawyer. A basic recording contract can run from 40-100 pages, and you need a lawyer to help you understand it. A lawyer will also be essential in helping you negotiate a deal that is in your best interest.

Recording contracts cover many areas, and just a few of the things you will be asked to consider will be: What royalty rate is the record label willing to pay you? What kind of advance are they offering? How many records will the company commit to? Will they offer tour support? Will they provide a budget for video? What sort of a recording budget are they offering? Are they asking you to give up any publishing rights? Are they offering you a publishing advance? These are only a few of the complex issues raised by a recording contract, so it's vital to have an entertainment lawyer on your side when discussing a recording contract, whether with a major label or an independent.

SUBMITTING TO RECORD COMPANIES

When submitting to a record company, major or independent, a professional attitude is imperative. Just because independent companies are small doesn't mean you should forget professionalism. When submitting material to a record company, be specific about what you are submitting and what your goals are. If you are strictly a songwriter and the label carries a band you believe would properly present your song, state that in your cover letter. If you are an artist looking for a contract, make sure you showcase your strong points as a performer. Whatever your goals are, follow submission guidelines closely, be as neat as possible and include a top-notch demo. If you need more information concerning a company's requirements, write or call for more details. (For more information on submitting your material, see Getting Started on page 5.)

A & M RECORDS, 1416 N. LaBrea Ave., Hollywood CA 90028-7596. (213)469-2411. This record company prefers not to share information.

A & R RECORDS, 900 19th Ave. S., Suite 207, Nashville TN 37212. (615)329-9127. Owner/President: R. Steele/David Steele. Labels include South Side of Heaven Records, Aarrow Records. Record company, record producer, music publisher and talent development/booking. Estab. 1986. Releases 10 CDs/year. Royalty varies, depending on individual agreement. Pays statutory rate to publisher per song on record.
How to Contact: Submit demo tape by mail. Unsolicited submissions are OK. But must be coded: "Songwriter's Market." Prefers cassette with 2 songs and lyric sheet. "We are currently working with writer/artists only. We are not currently soliciting songs from outside writers who are not singers." SASE. Reports in 1-2 months.
Music: Mostly **country**, **gospel** and **alternative/folk/bluegrass**; also **Cajun**, **instrumental (fiddle)** and **children's**. Released *Family Ties* (by Steele/Knights), recorded by David Steele on A&R Records; *Shooting Star* (by Reynolds/Steele), recorded by Bethany Reynolds on Aarrow Records; and *Up For an Oscar* (by David Steele), recorded by Ruthie Steele on A&R Records. Other artists include Tricia Torline, Lollie Ellis, Nashville Kelly, Kelli Steele, Randy Cox, Carl L'Amour, Mark Thomsen and Houston Carter.
Tips: "Only dedicated, business-minded artists can be considered. Identifiable, unique voice is a must."

*ALADDIN RECORDINGS, P.O. Box 121626, Nashville TN 37212. (615)726-3556. Contact: A&R Department. Record company. Estab. 1996. Releases 6 singles, 3 LPs and 3 CDs/year. Pays negotiable royalty to artists on contract; statutory rate to publisher per song on record.
How to Contact: Submit demo tape by mail. Unsolicited submissions are OK. Prefers cassette with 3 songs and lyric sheet. "Send all pertinent information." SASE. Reports in 1 month.
Music: Mostly **country**, **rock** and **alternative**; also **blues**, **gospel** and **contemporary/R&B**. Released *What Do Ya Say*, written and recorded by Jay S. Kay (alternative); *Country Girl*, written and recorded by Scott Dawson (country); and "The Greatest Mistake of My Life" (by David Smith), recorded by Mary Aldrich (contemporary).
Tips: "We are looking for songs and artists with a different approach. We need more artists and songs to possibly place with major record companies and also for possible placement in movies, soundtracks, commercials and television programs."

ALBATROSS RECORDS, 2405 Wentworth St., Houston TX 77004. (713)521-2616. Marketing/Sales: Craig Baham. Labels include R&D Productions and FW Records. Record company. Estab. 1990. Releases 20 singles, 10 LPs and 10 CDs/year. Pays negotiable royalty to artists on contract; statutory rate to publisher per song on record.
How to Contact: Submit demo tape by mail. Unsolicited submissions are OK. Prefers cassette with lyric and lead sheets. Does not return material. Reports in 2-3 weeks.
Music: Mostly **R&B**, **rap** and **Latino/TexMex**; also **jazz**, **country** and **blues**. Released *What's Really Going On*, written and recorded by 4-Deep (rap); *What's It All About*, written and recorded by Aduo (rap); and *Imma Holla Atcha*, written and recorded by McKeldocheous, all on Albatross Records.

ALISO CREEK PRODUCTIONS INCORPORATED, Box 8174, Van Nuys CA 91409. (818)787-3203. President: William Williams. Labels include Aliso Creek Records. Record company. Estab. 1987. Releases 4 CDs/year. Pays negotiable royalty to artists on contract; pays statutory rate to publisher per song on record.

THE ASTERISK before a listing indicates that the listing is new in this edition. New markets are often the most receptive to unsolicited submissions.

INSIDER REPORT

R&B and rap becoming more artist-driven

"I've noticed more and more that A&R people are trying to find artists who write their own music, so that means writers may have a tougher time getting their songs placed," says David McPherson, director of A&R for Jive Records. Jive's roster includes many successful R&B and rap acts, including R. Kelly, A Tribe Called Quest, and Aaliyah. "Right now about half my acts are artists who write their own stuff. Many are artist/producers."

This is almost always the case with rap artists, he says. On the other hand, R&B artists, like pop artists, do cut songs from outside writers, but the field is slowly becoming more artist-driven. "R&B is very producer-driven," McPherson says, "and as a result so much of what's out there is starting to

David McPherson

sound alike. You can identify material from the different studios—they use the same top five producers and writers every time. So now, A&R people are looking for artists who can bring their own definitive sound to the table. I expect R&B will become more like rock, where each artist is known for their own unique sound."

Trends in the rap industry are somewhat different. The challenge facing rap today, says McPherson, is one of exposure. More and more black and urban radio stations are refusing to play material that contains violent, sexually explicit lyrics. "We live in tough times, with a lot of murder and crime," he says. "Radio stations are responding to that by cutting out anything they feel might incite violence." This has been a long-standing problem with rap, of course, because the point of much rap music is to reflect an increasingly violent world. Rap has staying power, says McPherson, but artists, producers and record companies will have to find alternative ways to promote records to rap audiences.

Another trend which may affect rap in subtle ways and R&B more directly is the return of pop music. "The state of the world is such that people want to hear music that makes them feel good. They still want to learn the truth, but they want lyrics that are more meaningful and music that is more musical. They want prettier melodies, more heartfelt lyrics."

That's why acts such as Seal, D'Angelo and Dionne Farris are doing so well, he says. They've almost created a new hybrid genre, one that could be called rap and R&B alternative. "Real songs are coming back."

Writers interested in learning more about this new trend in R&B should look to country music, says McPherson. "Nashville songwriters write songs that have a lot of crossover potential. They understand that songs should tell stories. They seem to have more of an understanding of what songs really are than just about anybody.

"What I look for in a song is a great melody and what I like to call the 'common touch.' The lyrics have to be about something the majority of people can relate to, a story people can understand. Even the melody should have that common touch; people should be able to hum it or sing along with the song."

McPherson finds songs through a variety of channels. He's in constant touch with producers, music publishers, artists and songwriters. While Jive Records' official policy is "no unsolicited submissions," he says he is always open to them. "I will listen to unsolicited tapes and demos. You never know what you'll get in the mail." Yet much of what he receives he cannot use because the songwriter or artist sending the material has sent the wrong type of song. "Sometimes the songs are so far off. They must send material that fits the genre or the artists I work with."

Songwriters need to do some research before they begin sending out demo tapes, he says. Call or write first and find out what an A&R representative is looking for and what artists he or she works with. Then ask if you can send a tape before sending one in.

Writers must also learn to be patient. "One misconception new writers seem to have is that A&R people make snap decisions. We wait for the right songs and we spend a lot of time thinking about the songs we find. There's a lot of thought and care put into the process."

Another mistake newer writers make is not putting their names, phone numbers and addresses directly on the tape, as well as on the case. It sounds like a simple thing, but McPherson says he once had two songs sent to him he wanted to work with but couldn't because there was no identifying material on the tape. He gets about 1,000 tapes or demos a week and cases can get mixed up.

Writers need to do their homework on the business side of things too, he says. "Read books like *Songwriter's Market* and other books on the songwriting business. Learn about rights and getting your material copyrighted. Attend seminars and conferences to learn the ins and outs of the business."

Now is an excellent time for the savvy songwriter. With movie scores, CD-ROM games and other licensing deals, songwriters have more venues available to get their work heard than ever before, says McPherson. It's important to stay on top of issues concerning the rights of songwriters. ASCAP and BMI have been exploring these areas and offer a lot of good advice helpful to songwriters.

Networking is the key, McPherson says. There are many conferences sponsored by the various trade magazines in the industry to help songwriters keep abreast of trends. Rap and R&B writers should subscribe to at least one of these trade publications. In addition to *Billboard*, leading magazines in the field include *Black Radio Exclusive, Jack the Rapper, The Gavin Report* and *Urban Network*.

Lastly, says McPherson, "Do everything you can to learn the business and perfect your craft. Listen to what's out there. Listen to the radio. Know your competition. There's a lot to learn."

—Robin Gee

How to Contact: Do not call. Write first and obtain permission to submit. Prefers cassette with 3 songs and lyric sheet. SASE. Reports in 3-4 weeks.
Music: Mostly **acoustic** and **children's music**; also **Latin rock**. Released *Perdido El Silencio*, written and recorded by Valerio on Aliso Creek Records.
Tips: "We are looking for career singer/songwriters with well-developed material and performance skills and the desire to tour."

*ALL STAR PROMOTIONS, P.O. Box 1130, Tallevast FL 34270. (813)351-3253. Vice President/ A&R: Bob Francis. Labels include Castle Records, TCB Records, Rock Island Records, Jade Records, Phoenix Records, Heavy Weather Records. Record company, record producer and music publisher. Estab. 1967. Releases 18 singles, 6 12" singles, 6 LPs and 6 CDs/year. Pays 6-10% royalty to artists on contract; statutory rate to publisher per song on record.
  • See the listing for Rob-Lee Music in the Music Pubishers section.
How to Contact: Submit demo tape by mail. Unsolicited submissions are OK. "Tapes are not returned." Prefers cassette (or VHS videocassette if available) with 6 songs. Does not return material. Reports in 1 month.
Music: Mostly **rock**, **dance** and **R&B/funk**; also **AOR** and **MOR**. Released "Doolin' Dalton," written and recorded by Ed Reid on Ocean Records (folk); *Nasty As They Wanna Be* (by D. Lawrence), recorded by Nasty Boys on Castle Records (rock); and "Ultimate Male" (by P. Lucic), recorded by Noelle on Jade Records (dance). Other artists include Phoenix, Heavy Weather, Grumpy, Murray Woods, Derrick Dukes, The Big Cheese, Bambi, Hot Shot and TCB Band.
Tips: "Submit quality demo (not merely acoustic guitar and vocal) on quality cassette in order to give us a chance to hear the potential of the tune or the artist. Poor quality tapes get minimum consideration."

ALLEGHENY MUSIC WORKS, 306 Cypress Ave,. Johnstown PA 15902. (814)535-3373. Managing Director: Al Rita. Labels include Allegheny Records. Record company, music publisher (Allegheny Music Works Publishing/ASCAP and Tuned on Music/BMI). Estab. 1991. Pays 10-12% royalty to artists on contract; statutory rate to publisher per song on record.
  • See their listing in the Music Publishers section.
How to Contact: Submit demo tape by mail. Unsolicited submissions are OK. Prefers cassette with 3 songs and lyric sheet or lead sheet. SASE. Reports in 2-4 weeks.
Music: Mostly **country (all styles)**; also **pop**, **A/C**, **R&B** and **inspirational**. Released "Drive" (by Karen McDermott), recorded by Gerry Moffett; "My Best Friend" (by Linda Fox Vartanian/Andrew Amoroso), recorded by Rich Mead; and "Sleeping With the Dog" (by Jubal Stevens), recorded by Mark McLelland and Wanda Copier, all on Allegheny Records.
Tips: "Send us material that stands out lyrically and melodically."

*ALPHA RECORDING CO., 4056 Shady Valley Dr., Arlington TX 76013. Phone/fax: (817)274-5530. Owner: Samuel Egnot. Record company, music publisher (Samuel Three Productions). Estab. 1992. Releases 6 singles, 6 LPs and 2 CDs/year. Pays negotiable royalty to artists on contract.
  • See the listing for Samuel Three Productions in the Music Publishers section.
How to Contact: Submit demo tape by mail. Unsolicited submissions are OK. SASE. Reports in 2 months.
Music: Mostly **country** and **gospel**. No rap or heavy metal. Released "You Didn't Tell Me" (by S. Egnot), recorded by Sam Younger; "I've Fallen Agein," written and recorded by Sami McLemorec; and "Lady From Muleshoe" (by Ted Disko), recorded by Sam Younger, all on Alpha Recording Co.

ALPHABEAT, Box 12 01, D-97862 Wertheim/Main, **Germany**. Phone: (09342)841 55. Owner: Stephan Dehn. A&R Manager: Andreas Paul. Creative Services: Heiko Köferl. Record company and record producer. Releases vary "depending on material available." Also works through "license contract with foreign labels." Payment to artists on contract "depends on product."
How to Contact: Submit demo tape by mail. Unsolicited submissions are OK. Prefers cassette (or PAL videocassette) with maximum of 3 songs and lyric sheet. "When sending us your demo tapes, please advise us of your ideas and conditions." SAE and IRC. Reports in 2 weeks.
Music: Mostly **dance/disco/pop**, **synth/pop** and **electronic**; also **R&B**, **hip hop/rap** and **ballads**. Artists include Red Sky, Fabian Harloff, Silent Degree, Mode Control, Mike M.C. & Master J., Skyline, Lost in the Dessert and Oriental Bazar.
Tips: "We are a distributor of foreign labels. If foreign labels have interest in distribution of their productions in Germany (also Switzerland and Austria) they can contact us. We distribute all styles of music of foreign labels. Please contact our 'Distribution Service' department."

ALYSSA RECORDS, Box 587, Farmingville NY 11738. President: Andy Marvel. Labels include Ricochet Records. Record company, music publisher (Andy Marvel Music/ASCAP, Bing Bing Bing Music/ASCAP and Andysongs/BMI) and record producer (Marvel Productions). Estab. 1981. Releases

12-15 singles, 1 12" single and 4 LPs/year. Pays standard royalty to artists on contract; statutory rate to publisher per song on record.
How to Contact: Write first and obtain permission to submit. Prefers cassette or CD with 3 songs and lyric sheet. Return only with SASE. "Do not call." Reports in 2 months.
Music: Mostly **pop**, **R&B** and **Top 40**; also **country**.

AMERICAN MUSIC NETWORK, INC., P.O. Box 7018, Warner Robins GA 31095. (912)953-2800. President: Robert R. Kovach. Labels include Scaramouche Recordings. Record company, record producer and music marketing corp. Estab. 1986. Releases 25 singles, 12 LPs and 12 CDs/year. Pays varying royalty to artists on contract; statutory rate to publisher per song on record.
How to Contact: Submit demo tape by mail. Unsolicited submissions are OK. Prefers cassette with 4 songs and lyric sheet. "We need name, address and telephone number." SASE. Reports in 4 months.
Music: Mostly **country**, **A/C** and **bluegrass**; also **rock**, **gospel** and **other forms**. Released "Easy On Your Feet," written and recorded by Theresa Justus (A/C); "Real Country Livin'," written and recorded by Little Rudy (country); and "What Happens To Love," written and recorded by Wayne Little (country), all on Scaramouche Recordings. Other artists include Napoleon Starke, Ron Sullivan and Dusty Shelton.
Tips: "We are looking for a whole new stable of artists."

AMERICATONE RECORDS INTERNATIONAL USA, 1817 Loch Lomond Way, Las Vegas NV 89102-4437. (702)384-0030. Fax: (702)382-1926. Estab. 1975. Record company, producer and music publisher. Releases 8 CDs and cassettes/year. Pays standard royalty.
Affiliate(s): The Rambolt Music International (ASCAP), Christy Records International.
How to Contact: Submit demo tape by mail. Prefers cassette or CD. SASE. Reports in 1 month.
Music: Mostly **country**, **jazz**, **rock**, **Spanish** and **classic ballads**. Released *Caribbean Jazz*, written and recorded by Anthony Diazz; *Coming Home*, written and recorded by Jim "Bo" Evans; and *Big Band Jazz*, recorded by Ladd McIntosh, all on Americatone International Records.

*AMIRON MUSIC/AZTEC PRODUCTIONS, 20531 Plummer St., Chatsworth CA 91311. (818)998-0443. General Manager: A. Sullivan. Labels include Dorn Records and Aztec Records. Record company, booking agency and music publisher (Amiron Music). Releases 2 singles/year. Pays 10% maximum royalty to artists on contract; standard royalty to songwriters on contract. Pays statutory rate to publishers.
  • Amiron Music's management firm, AKO Productions, is listed in the Managers and Booking Agents section.
How to Contact: Prefers cassette and lead sheet. SASE. Reports in 3 weeks.
Music: **Dance**, **easy listening**, **folk**, **jazz**, **MOR**, **rock** ("no heavy metal") and **top 40/pop**. Released "Look In Your Eyes," recorded by Newstreet; and "Midnight Flight," recorded by Papillon.
Tips: "Be sure the material has a hook; it should make people want to make love or fight. Write something that will give a talented new artist that edge on current competition."

*ANTIPHON INTERNATIONAL, P.O. Box 1351, Island Heights NJ 08753. (908)270-4970. President: J.D. Kucharik. Labels include Antiphon Records, Gospel Underground. Record company, music publisher (Rachel Marie Music Ltd./ASCAP). Estab. 1991. Releases 2 singles, 2 LPs and 3 CDs/year. Pays negotiable royalty to artists on contract; statutory rate to publisher per song on record.
  • Antiphon's publishing company, Rachel Marie Music, is listed in the Music Publishers section.
How to Contact: Write first and obtain permission to submit. Prefers cassette with 3 songs and lyric sheet. "Send SASE for response." Does not return material. Reports in 3-5 weeks.
Music: Mostly **gospel/rock**, **alternative/rock** and **Christian**; also **blues** and **gospel/blues**. Released *James David* (by J.D. Kucharik), recorded by James David (gospel/rock); *Dean Mathias*, written and recorded by Dean Jay Mathias (Christian/pop); and *Dream Child* (by J.D. Kucharik), recorded by Dream Child (rock), all on Antiphon Records. Other artists include Destination Goat.
Tips: "Music has to come from the heart. Writing, and the recording (even rough demos), should reflect the mood and the feeling for which it was intended. Draw the listener in! We look for lyrics that are positive in nature. A message of social or spiritual change is encouraged; we respect artists with vision and a professional and new approach to styles and sound."

*ARIAL RECORDS, Box 881, Black Diamond, Alberta T0L 0H0 **Canada**. Manager: Tim Auvigne. Record company, management firm, booking agent and music publisher (Ster N' Ster Publishing). Estab. 1989.
How to Contact: Submit demo tape by mail. Unsolicited submissions are OK. Prefers cassette or VHS videocassette with 3 songs and lyric sheet. SASE. Reports in 1 month.
Music: Mostly **country**; also **pop**. Current acts include Brent McAthey (country singer/songwriter).
Tips: "Have your songs copywritten first; then let as many people hear them as will listen!"

*ARIANA RECORDS, 1336 S. Avenida Polar #C208, Tucson AZ 85710. (520)790-7324. President: James M. Gasper. Labels include Egg White Records. Record company, music publisher, record producer. Estab. 1980. Releases 2 singles, 4 LPs and 4 CDs/year. Pays negotiable royalty to artists on contract; negotiable rate to publisher per song on record.
How to Contact: Submit demo tape by mail. Unsolicited submissions are OK. Prefers cassette or ½″ VHS videocassette. SASE. Reports in 1-2 months.
Music: Mostly **New Age/atmospheric**, **rock**, **folk rock** and **funk jazz**; also **completed projects**. Released *Never Be Rich*, written and recorded by Tom Privett (rock); *Dancing Animals*, written and recorded by Scuba Tails (New Age), both on Ariana Records; and *Get On It*, written and recorded by Undercover Band on Egg White Records (funk pop). Other artists include The Fellowship, Jtiom, The Three F's and The Mystics.
Tips: "A great song should be able to stand alone one voice, one instrument or one full band."

ARION RECORDS, P.O. Box 16046, Chattanooga TN 37416-0046. President/Owner: Steve Babb. Record company, music publisher (Sound Resources/BMI) and recording studio. E-mail: audio111@aol.com. Website: www.pacificrim.net/~lspeed/glassh/ghpage1.html. Estab. 1992. Releases 3-5 CDs/year. Pays 10% royalty to artists on contract; statutory rate to publishers per song on record.
How to Contact: Submit demo tape by mail. Unsolicited submissions are OK. Prefers DAT, CD or cassette (metal if possible). Does not return material. Reports in 2 months "if interested."
Music: Mostly **progressive rock** and **art rock**. Released *Journey of the Dunadan* and *Perelandra*, written and recorded by Glass Hammer; and *Love Changes*, recorded by Tracy Cloud, all on Arion Records. Other artists include Stephen DeArque, Privy Member, Fred Schendel and They're Made Out of Meat.
Tips: "We define progressive rock as being reminiscent of ELP, Yes, Genesis, etc. If your music fits that definition, we are interested. If your music somehow redefines progressive rock, we would be interested in that as well."

*ARISTA RECORDS, 6 W. 57th St., New York NY 10019. Fax: (212)977-9843. Contact: A&R. Record company.
• Arista Records currently commands 23% of the singles market share in the record industry.
How to Contact: Write first and obtain permission to submit. Prefers cassette or DAT. Does not return submissions. Reports in 4-6 weeks.
Music: Mostly **pop/urban hits**, **rock hits** and **mass appeal smashes**. Released *Waiting to Exhale* (soundtrack); *The Greatest Hits Collection*, recorded by Alan Jackson (country); and *The Bridge*, recorded by Ace of Base (pop), all on Arista Records. Other artists include Deborah Cox, Sarah McLachlan, Real McCoy, Kenny G.
Tips: "Submit songs that are well produced with in-depth lyrics and strong melodies. We often get songs with one line hooks and underdeveloped verses that sound good, but do not stand up to scrutiny. Only send the best of the best—uptempos are always needed!"

*ARKADIA ENTERTAINMENT CORP., 34 E. 23rd St., New York NY 10010. (212)674-5550. (212)979-0266. Contact: A&R Song Submissions. Labels include Arkadia Jazz, Arkadia Classical, Arkadia Now and Arkadia Allworld. Record company, music publisher (Arkadia Music), record producer (Arkadia Productions) and Arkadia Video. Estab. 1995. Releases 6 singles, 12 LPs and 22 CDs/year. Pays statutory rate to publisher per song on record.
How to Contact: Submit demo tape by mail. Unsolicited submissions are OK. Prefers cassette, DAT or VHS videocassette with 3-4 songs and lyric and lead sheets. SASE. Reports ASAP.
Music: Mostly **jazz, pop/R&B** and **rock**; also **world**. Released *Velvet Moon*, recorded by Velvet Moon; *In the Spirit*, recorded by In the Spirit; and *Michel Gallois*, recorded by Michel Gallois, all on Arkadia Records.

ASSOCIATED ARTISTS MUSIC INTERNATIONAL, Maarschalklaan 47, 3417 SE Montfoort, **The Netherlands**. Phone/fax: 31-3484-72860. Release Manager: Joop Gerrits. Labels include Associated Artists, Disco-Dance Records and Italo. Record company, music publisher (Associated Artists International/BUMA-STEMRA, Hilversum Happy Music/BUMA-STEMRA, Intermedlodie/BUMA-STEMRA and Hollands Glorie Productions), record producer (Associated Artists Productions) and TV promotions. Estab. 1975. Releases 10 singles, 25 12″ singles, 6 LPs and 6 CDs/year. Pays 14% royalty to artists on contract; variable amount to publishers.

 THE ASTERISK before a listing indicates that the listing is new in this edition. New markets are often the most receptive to unsolicited submissions.

How to Contact: Submit demo tape by mail. Unsolicited submissions OK. Prefers compact cassette or 19 cm/sec reel-to-reel (or VHS videocassette) with any number of songs and lyric or lead sheets. Records also accepted. SAE and IRC. Reports in 6 weeks.
Music: Mostly **dance**, **pop**, **house**, **hip hop** and **rock**. Released "La Luna" (by P. Prins), recorded by The Ethics on Virgin Records (dance); *Freedom*, written and recorded by D.J. Bobo on ZYX Records (dance); and "Labia" (by P. Prins), recorded by Indica on M.M. Records (dance). Other artists include Clubhouse, Silvio Pozzoli, Eating Habits, D.S.K. and Mikko Mission.
Tips: "We invite producers and independent record labels to send us their material for their entry on the European market. Mark all parcels as 'no commercial value—for demonstration only.' We license productions to record companies in all countries of Europe and South Africa. Submit good demos or masters."

*ATLANTIC RECORDS, 75 Rockefeller Plaza, New York NY 10019. (212)275-2300. Fax: (212)275-2315. E-mail: jillian_schwartz@wmg.com or chargzvisa@aol.com. Assistant to Senior Vice President Craig Kallman: Jillian Schwartz. "Craig Kallman is also President of Big Beat Records and Tag Records." Record company. Pays negotiable royalty to artists on contract; negotiable rate to publisher per song on record.
• See the interview with Atlantic A&R rep Tom Carolan in the 1996 *Songwriter's Market*.
How to Contact: Submit demo tape by mail. Unsolicited submissions are OK. Prefers cassette and press info on songwriter/artist. "Send as much information as possible." Does not return material. "Send material for Changing Faces, Robin S. and Robyn Springer."

aUDIOFILE TAPES, 209-25 18th Ave., Bayside NY 11360. Sheriff, aT County: Carl Howard. Cassette-only label of alternative music. Estab. 1984. Produces about 25 cassettes/year. "Money is solely from sales. Some artists ask $1 per tape sold."
How to Contact: Write first to obtain permission to submit. Prefers cassette. "Relevant artist information is nice. Master copies accepted on hi-bias or metal analog tape, or DAT." SASE. Reports in 3-6 weeks.
Music: Mostly **psych/electronic rock**, **non-rock electronic music** and **progressive rock**; also **free jazz** and **world music**. Released *Prozak*, recorded by The Conspiracy (alternative rock); *Compiled Wounds*, recorded by Wound: experiment (collage electronic); and *Bobo*, recorded by If, Bwana (improvised/electronic), all on audiofile Tapes. Other artists include Thru Black Holes Band, Sphinx, Arnold Mathes, Piume e Sangue, Klimperei and Mana Erg.
Tips: "Please, no industrial music, no deliberately shocking images of racism and sexual brutality. And no New Age sleeping pills. Unfortunately, we are not in a position to help the careers of aspirant pop idols. Only true devotees *really* need apply. I mean it—money does not exist here. No artist has ever been under contract; this is real underground informal stuff."

AVALANCHE COMMUNICATIONS, (formerly Bonaire Management Inc.), 3018 Paulcrest Dr., Los Angeles CA 90046. (213)650-9095. E-mail: avalanche@bonaire.com. Website: http://www.bonaire.com. President: Clive Corcoran. Labels include Bonaire and Avalanche. Record company, music publisher, record producer. Estab. 1977. Releases 2 singles, 15 CDs/year. Pays statutory royalty to publisher per song on record.
How to Contact: Write first and obtain permission to submit. Prefers cassette (or VHS videocassette if available) with 3 songs and 3 lyric sheets. SASE.
Music: Mostly **rock** and **pop**. Released *Gasoline*, recorded by Noodle Horse (alternative); *Battle Lines*, recorded by John Wetton (progressive rock); and *Some of the Best of Gene Loves Jezebel*, recorded by Gene Loves Jezebel (rock), all on Avalanche Records.

AZRA INTERNATIONAL, Box 459, Maywood CA 90270. (213)560-4223. A&R: Jeff Simins. Labels include World Metal, Metal Storm, Azra, Iron Works, Not So Famous David's Records and Masque Records. Record company. Estab. 1978. Releases 10 singles, 5 LPs, 5 EPs and 5 CDs/year. "Artists usually carry their own publishing." Pays 10% royalty to artists on contract; statutory rate to publisher per song on record.
How to Contact: Submit demo tape by mail. Unsolicited submissions are OK. Prefers cassette (or VHS videocassette) with 3-5 songs and lyric sheet. Include bio and photo. SASE. Reports in 2 weeks.
Music: Mostly **rock**, **heavy metal** and **New Age**; also **novelty**. Released "The Road," written and recorded by Jason Ebs on Azra International (rock); *Cell 13* (by Sean Hutch), recorded by Torso (metal); and *Live* (by Chris Fogelson), recorded by Subjugator (metal), both on Iron Works Records. Other artists include Alan Ichyasu, Birdhouse, Skif Dank, Acid Face, Civic Idiots, Rotten Rod, Concerto, Pipedreams and Hyperchild.
Tips: "Make sure your songs are timeless; don't follow the current trends."

AZTLAN RECORDS, P.O. Box 5672, Buena Park CA 90622. (714)826-7151. Manager: Carmen Ortiz. Record company and record distributor. Estab. 1986. Releases 1 LP and 1 CD/year. Royalty paid to artist on contract varies.

How to Contact: Write first and obtain permission to submit. SASE.
Music: Mostly **alternative**, **industrial** and **experimental**; also **gothic**, **performance poetry** and **ethnic**. Released *Nirvana*, written and recorded by 12 artists (compilation); *Awaken*, written and recorded by 7 artists (compilation); and *Der Kirshenwasser*, written and recorded by Angel of the Odd (alternative), all on Aztlan Records. Other artists include Cecilia±, Dichroic Mirror, Pleasure Center and Spiderbaby.
Tips: "Die rather than compromise what you are doing. Music is your life."

BABY FAZE RECORDS & TAPES, 45 Pearl St., San Francisco CA 94103. (415)495-5312. Big Cheese: g. miller marlin. Labels include Dog Bite Records (singles-only label), Sound Waves (So Wave Back). Record company and record producer (g. miller marlin, David S. Willers). Estab. 1989. Releases 20 singles and 10 cassettes/year
How to Contact: Submit demo tape by mail. Unsolicited submissions are OK. Prefers cassette (or VHS videocassette). "We encourage submissions of all types and genres of music." Does not return material.
Music: Mostly **alternative**, **industrial** and **rock**; also **rap**, **pop** and **R&B funk**. Released *King Size Size Queen* (by g. miller marlin), recorded by Cat Howdy (industrial); *Sweet, Light, Crude* (by S. Fievet), recorded by LMNOP; and *Choice Cuts* (by Kenyata Sullivan), recorded by Pandora's Lunch Box (alternative), all on Baby Faze Records. Other artists include Eric Mars, Secret Team, Hangboxers, Threnody, Into Decline, Broken Toys and God's Favorite.
Tips: "Submit anything with a short release, intent letter or note, and if used in the future, we'll be in touch—so don't forget to include a contact name and address with all submissions (photos and band bios are also helpful.)"

babysue, P.O. Box 8989, Atlanta GA 30306. (404)875-8951. Website: http://babysue.com. President/Owner: Don W. Seven. Record company. Estab. 1983. Releases 2 singles, 5 LPs, 2 EPs and 7 CDs/year. Pays 15% royalty to artists on contract; varying royalty to publisher per song on record.
• babysue also has a listing in the Managers and Booking Agents section.
How to Contact: Submit demo tape by mail. Unsolicited submissions are OK. Prefers cassette with any number of songs. Does not return material. Reports in 2 months. "We only report back if we are interested in the artist or act."
Music: Mostly **rock**, **pop** and **gospel**; also **heavy metal**, **punk** and **classical**. Released *Camera-Sized Life*, written and recorded by LMNOP (rock); *Mush It Up*, written and recorded by The Mushcakes (folk); and *All Tied Down*, written and recorded by The Shoestrings, all on babysue records.
Tips: "Send us cash (just kidding). Actually, we're just into sincere, good stuff."

BACKSTREET RECORDS, P.O. Box 350, Terryville CT 06786. (860)584-0606. Fax: (860)584-8197. E-mail: bkstrecrds@aol.com. Website: http://www.he.net/~mystprod/flymain.html. A&R: Brian Krenicki. Record company. Estab. 1994. Releases 3 LPs, 1 EP and 3 CDs/year. Pays negotiable royalty to artists on contract; negotiable rate to publisher per song on record.
How to Contact: Write or call first and obtain permission to submit a demo. Prefers cassette with 4 songs. Does not return material. Reports in 2 months.
Music: Mostly **rock**, **hard rock** and **alternative**. Released *Under Covers*, recorded by Trixter (rock); *John Flywheel*, written and recorded by John Flywheel; and *Faces of Cain*, written and recorded by Grady Cain, all on Backstreet Records. Other artists include Meliah Rage and Axis-Y.

BAGATELLE RECORD COMPANY, P.O. Box 925929, Houston TX 77292. President: Byron Benton. Record company, record producer and music publisher (Floyd Tillman Music Co.). Releases 20 singles and 10 LPs/year. Pays negotiable royalty to artists on contract.
• See the listing for Bagatelle Music in the Music Publishers section.
How to Contact: Submit demo tape by mail. Prefers cassette and lyric sheet. SASE. Reports in 2 weeks.
Music: Mostly **country**; also **gospel**. Released "This is Real," by Floyd Tillman (country); "Lucille," by Sherri Jerrico (country); and "Everything You Touch," by Johnny Nelms (country). Other artists include Jerry Irby, Bobby Beason, Bobby Burton, Donna Hazard, Danny Brown, Sonny Hall, Ben Gabus, Jimmy Copeland and Johnny B. Goode.

BANDIT RECORDS, P.O. Box 111480, Nashville TN 37222. (615)331-1219. President: Loman Craig. Vice President: Tommy Hendrick. Labels include HIS Records (gospel). Record company and record producer (Loman Craig Productions). Estab. 1979. Releases 5 singles and 2 LPs/year. Pays statutory rate to publisher per song on record. "There is a charge for demo and custom sessions."
How to Contact: Submit demo tape by mail. Unsolicited submissions are OK. Prefers cassette with 2-3 songs and lyric sheet. SASE. Reports in 4-6 weeks.
Music: Mostly **country**, **ballads** and **gospel**. Released *One and the Same* (by Loman Craig/Tommy Hendrick) and *Cross My Heart* (by Chad Allen), both recorded by Loman Craig on Bandit Records;

and *Conviction* (by Justin Sullivan), recorded by Mt. Zion Singers on HIS Records.
Tips: "Send a clear sounding demo and readable lyric sheets. Since we are a small independent record label, we do have to charge for services rendered."

*BASSET HOUND PRODUCTIONS, 527 N. Azuza Ave. #280, Covina CA 91722. (818)453-1825. Producer/A&R Rep: Sean Hutch. Record company, music publisher (Basset Hound Publishing), record producer (Sean Hutch) and booking agency. Estab. 1995.
How to Contact: Submit demo tape by mail. Unsolicited submissions are OK. Prefers cassette or CD, bio, résumé and picture with lyric and lead sheets. SASE.
Music: Mostly **alternative rock, techno** and **industrial**; also **hard rock, gothic** and **dance.** Released *Torso*, written and recorded by Torso on Ironworks:Azra Records (industrial/techno).

*BCN/BEACON RECORDS, P.O. Box 3129, Peabody MA 01961. (508)762-8400. E-mail: bcnrecords@aol.com. Principal: Tony Ritchie. Labels include VISTA Records. Record company and music publisher. Releases 12-15 CDs/year. Pays standard royalty to artists on contract; statutory rate to publisher per song on record.
How to Contact: Submit demo tape by mail. Unsolicited submissions are OK. Does not return material. Reports in 2-3 weeks.
Music: Mostly **folk, Celtic** and **folk-rock**; also **country, New Age** and **blues.** Recorded *Were You At The Rock* (by various), recorded by Aine Minogue; *Shoes That Fit Like Sand*, written and recorded by Diane Taraz; and *Of Age* (by Fowler/Shulman), recorded by Aztec Two-Step, all on BLN/Beacon Records. Other artists include Gail Rundlett, Pendragon and MacIsaac & Ross.

BELMONT RECORDS, 484 Lexington St., Waltham MA 02154. (617)891-7800. President: John Penny. Labels include Waverly Records. Record company and record producer. Pays standard royalty to artists on contract; statutory rate to publisher per song on record.
How to Contact: Write first and obtain permission to submit. Prefers cassette with 3 songs and lyric sheet. SASE. Reports in 3 weeks.
Music: Mostly **country.** Released *One Step At a Time*, recorded by Cheri Ann on Belmont Records (C&W); and *Tudo Bens Sabe*, recorded by Familia Penha (gospel). Other artists include Stan Jr., Tim Barrett, Jackie Lee Williams, Robin Right, Mike Walker and Dwain Hathaway.

BERANDOL MUSIC, 2600 John St., Unit 220, Markham, Ontario L3R 3W3 **Canada**. (905)475-1848. A&R: Ralph Cruickshank. Record company, music publisher (Berandol Music/SOCAN). Estab. 1947. Pays 10% royalty to artists on contract; statutory rate to publisher per song on record.
● Berandol Music is also listed in the Music Publishers section.
How to Contact: Submit demo tape by mail. Unsolicited submissions are OK. Prefers cassette with 4 songs. Does not return material. Reports in 3 weeks.
Music: Mostly **instrumental, children's** and **CHR (top 40).**

BIG BEAR RECORDS, Box 944, Birmingham, B16 8UT, **United Kingdom**. Phone: 44-021-454-7020. Fax: 44-021-454-9996. A&R Director: Jim Simpson. Labels include Truckers Delight and Grandstand Records. Record company, record producer and music publisher (Bearsongs). Releases 6 LPs/year. Pays 8-10% royalty to artists on contract; 8¼% to publishers for each record sold. Royalties paid directly to songwriters and artists or through US publishing or recording affiliate.
● Big Bear's publishing affiliate, Bearsongs, is listed in the Music Publishers section, and Big Bear is listed in the Record Producers section.
How to Contact: Submit demo tape by mail. Unsolicited submissions are OK. Prefers 7½ or 15 ips reel-to-reel, DAT, or cassette (or videocassette) and lyric sheet. Does not return material. Reports in 3 weeks.
Music: **Blues** and **jazz.** Released *I've Finished with the Blues* and *Blues for Pleasure* (by Skirving/Nicholls), both recorded by King Pleasure and the Biscuit Boys (jazz); and *Side-Steppin'* (by Barnes), recorded by Alan Barnes/Bruce Adams Quintet (jazz), all on Big Bear Records. Other artists include Lady Sings the Blues, Bill Allred and Kenny Baker's Dozen.

BIG POP, P.O. Box 12870, Philadelphia PA 19108. (215)551-3191. Fax: (215)467-2048. Contact: A&R Dept. Record company. Estab. 1993. Releases 8 singles, 6 LPs/CDs and 2 EPs/year. Pays variable royalty to artists on contract; reduced statutory rate to publisher per song on record.
How to Contact: Write first and obtain permission to submit. Prefers cassette (or VHS videocassette if available) with 3-4 songs and lyric sheet. "We are looking for artist/songwriters. None of our current artists perform other writers' material. Please send a complete press kit with bios, photos and tearsheets with submission." SASE. Reports in 2-3 months.
Music: Mostly **modern rock** and **top 40.** Released *The Dust Has Come to Stay* (by M. Bund), recorded by Mexico 70; *Space Flyer*, written and recorded by Melting Hopefuls; and "Get Along," written and recorded by The Holy Cows, all on Big Pop Records. Other artists include All About Chad.

Tips: "We're interested in artists and songs. Your image and concept of where you fit in should be defined before we get involved. The quality of your songs—structure, hooks and lyrics—is very important to us. And generally, you shouldn't imitate others' styles. Be original!"

BIG ROCK PTY. LTD., P.O. Box, Dulwich Hill, NSW 2203 **Australia**. Phone (02)5692152. A&R Manager: Chris Turner. Labels include Big Rock Records, Sound Energy. Record company, music publisher (A.P.R.A.), record producer (Big Rock P/L). Estab. 1979. Releases 5 singles, 10 LPs and 10 CDs/year. Pays 5% royalty to artists on contract.
How to Contact: Submit demo tape by mail. Unsolicited submissions are OK. Prefers cassette with 6 songs and lyric sheet. SAE and IRC. Reports in 6 weeks.
Music: Mostly **rock**, **R&B** and **pop**.

BLACK & BLUE, 400D Putnam Pike, Suite 152, Smithfield RI 02917. (401)949-4887. New Talent Manager: Larry Evilelf. Record company. Releases 3-8 EPs, 5 CDs/cassettes year. Pays statutory rate to publisher per song on record.
How to Contact: Submit demo tape by mail. Unsolicited submissions are OK. Prefers cassette (or VHS videocassette) with 3 songs and lyric sheet or lead sheet. Does not return material. Reports in 1 month. Replies only if interested.
Music: Mostly **eclectic**, **alternative rock** and **hardcore**; also **speed metal**, **C&W** and **grind core**. Released *Hung Over and Stoned* (by Don McCloud), recorded by Bloody Mess (punk); *Money* (by Lena Luna), recorded by Cedar Street Sluts (punk); and *Baby Elvis* (by Don Hall/Dick Gingras/Tom D'Agostino), recorded by Algae Afterbirth (punk), all on Black & Blue Records. Other artists include 10-96, Dishwater and Blue Nouveaux.
Tips: "We are interested in working with performing songwriters more than just songwriters."

BLACK DIAMOND RECORDS INC., P.O. Box 8073, Pittsburg CA 94565. (510)568-7036. Fax: (510)636-0614. President: Jerry "J." Vice President: Maurice Belcher. Labels include Ricochet Records, "In The House" Records, Hittin' Hard Records, Flash Point Records, Stay Down Records and Jairus Records. Record company, music publisher and record producer (Bobelli Productions, In The House Productions). Estab. 1988. Pays 5½-16% royalty to artists on contract; statutory rate to publisher per song on record.
   • See the listing for Its Happening Present Entertainment in the Managers and Booking Agents section.
How to Contact: Write or call first and obtain permission to submit. Prefers cassette with 2-4 songs, photo and lyric sheet. Does not return material. Reports in 3 months.
Music: Mostly **R&B**, **hip hop**, **country/jazz** and **hip hop rap**; also **jazz**, **blues** and **rock**. Released "When U Come Over Tonight" (by M. Veasie/K. Mitchell), recorded by Flikk (R&B); "This Is How It Goes" (by M. Shiehadahd/M. Garton), recorded by Marty "G" (hip hop/rap); and "Nubian Queen" (by Nubian Cartel/B. Ford), recorded by Nubian Cartel, all on Black Diamond Records. Other artists include Deanna Dixon, Proper J, Jerry J, Lyndarne and Acyte 2.

BLACK DOG RECORDS, 701 Spanish Main #64, Cudjoe Key FL 33042-4333. (305)745-3164. Executive Director: Marian Joy Ring. A&R Contact: Rusty Gordon (Rustron Music Productions), 1156 Park Lane, West Palm Beach, FL 33417. (407)686-1354. Record company. Estab. 1989. Releases 2-6 singles and 3 LPs/year. Pays standard royalty to artists on contract; statutory rate to publisher per song on record.
How to Contact: Submit demo tape by mail. Unsolicited submissions are OK. Prefers cassette with 3-6 songs and lyric or lead sheet. Does not return material. Reports in 4-6 weeks.
Music: Mostly **pop**, **R&B** and **folk-rock**; also **New Age** and **cabaret**. Released *Yemanjah*, *Water Over the Dam* and *3 Teenage Mothers*, all written and recorded by Marian Joy Ring on Black Dog Records. Other artists include Woody Allen and Quint Lange.

BLUE GEM RECORDS, P.O. Box 29688, Hollywood CA 90029. (213)664-7765. Contact: Pete Martin. Record company and record producer (Pete Martin Productions). Estab. 1981. Pays 6-15% royalty to artists on contract; statutory rate to publisher per song on record.
   • See the listings for Pete Martin/Vaam Productions in the Record Producers section and Vaam Music Group in the Music Publishers section.

REMEMBER: Don't "shotgun" your demo tapes. Submit only to companies interested in the type of music you write. For more submission hints, refer to Getting Started on page 5.

How to Contact: Submit demo tape by mail. Unsolicited submissions are OK. Prefers cassette with 2 songs. SASE. Reports in 3 weeks.
Music: Mostly **country** and **R&B**; also **pop/top 40** and **rock**. Released "The Greener Years," written and recorded by Frank Loren (country); "It's a Matter of Loving You" (by Brian Smith), recorded by Brian Smith & The Renegades (country); and "Two Different Women" (by Frank Loren and Greg Connor), recorded by Frank Loren (country), all on Blue Gem Records. Other artists include Sherry Weston (country).
Tips: "Study the top 10 on charts in your style of writing and be current!"

BLUE WAVE, 3221 Perryville Rd., Baldwinsville NY 13027. (315)638-4286. President/Producer: Greg Spencer. Labels include Blue Wave/Horizon. Record company, music publisher (G.W. Spencer Music/ASCAP) and record producer (Blue Wave Productions). Estab. 1985. Releases 3 LPs and 3 CDs/year. Royalty to artists on contract varies; pays statutory rate to publisher per song on record.
How to Contact: Submit demo tape by mail. Unsolicited submissions are OK. Prefers cassette (or VHS or Beta videocassette—live performance only) and as many songs as you like. SASE. "We contact only if we are interested." Reports in 1 month.
Music: Mostly **blues/blues rock**, **roots rock** and **roots R&B/soul**; also **roots country/rockabilly** or **anything with "soul."** Released *Now I'm Good* (by Richard Newell), recorded by King Biscuit Boy; *Good Times Guaranteed* (by Don Walsh), recorded by Downchild Blues Band; *and Mama Lion* (by Nick Graunites), recorded by Kim Lembo, all on Blue Wave Records.

*BMX ENTERTAINMENT, P.O. Box 10857, Stamford CT 06904. (203)352-3569. Fax: (203)357-1676. President: Mauris Gryphon. Labels include Red Tape Records. Record company. Estab. 1984. Releases 7 singles, 7 12″ singles, 7 LPs, 7 EPs and 7 CDs/year. Pays 10-12% royalty to artists on contract.
How to Contact: Submit demo tape by mail. Unsolicited submissions are OK. Prefers cassette (or VHS videocassette if available) with 4 songs. "Send résumé, photo, management arrangements, if any." SASE. Reports in 2 weeks.
Music: Mostly **country**, **R&B** and **rock**; also **rap**, **pop**, **jazz** and **salsa**. Released "You & I," written and recorded by Edwin Rivera (ballad); "Hot As Fire," written and recorded by Damm Samm (rock); and "Tick Tica Tock," written and recorded by Tic Tock (reggae), all on BMX Entertainment. Other artists include K. Nice, Head Banger, Singles, Donald Murray and Tom Adams.

BNA RECORDS, (formerly BNA Entertainment), 1 Music Circle North, Nashville TN 37203. (615)313-4300. Fax: (615)313-4303. Contact: A&R Dept. Record company. Estab. 1990. Pays standard royalty to artists on contract; statutory rate to publisher per song on record.
How to Contact: Call first and obtain permission to submit. Prefers cassette or videocassette with 2 songs and lyric sheet. "We prefer that writers submit via a publisher." Refuses unsolicited submissions. Reply time "depends on the project."
Music: Mostly **country**. Artists include Jesse Hunter, John Anderson, Kenny Chesney, Lonestar and Lorrie Morgan.
Tips: "Put together a presentable package and showcase."

BODARC PRODUCTIONS, 4225 N. Hall St., Dallas TX 75219. (214)526-1062. Fax: (214)526-0223. Producer: Robert Weigel. Record company. Estab. 1980. Releases 5-6 LPs and 5-6 CDs/year. Pays negotiable royalty to artists on contract; statutory rate to publisher per song on record.
How to Contact: Submit demo tape by mail. Unsolicited submissions are OK. Prefers cassette. Does not return material. Reports in 3 months.
Music: Mostly **modern/disco**, **aerobics jazz** and **ballroom dancing**; also **children's songs** and **non lyric**. Released *Joy of Ballet*, recorded by Lynn Stanford; *Tap With a Talent* and *Critters and Countries*, both recorded by Steven Mitchell, all on Bodarc Productions.
Tips: "We need music for dance classes—ballet, tap, jazz, ballroom, without lyrics."

BOLD I RECORDS, 2124 Darby Dr., Massillon OH 44646. (216)833-2061. A&R Dept.: Nick Boldi. Labels include Rox Town Records. Record company, record producer and music publisher (Bolnik Music/BMI). Estab. 1986. Releases 2 CDs/year. Pays 6% royalty on net to artists on contract; statutory rate to publisher per song on record.
How to Contact: Submit demo tape by mail. Unsolicited submissions are OK. Prefers cassette with 4 songs and lyric sheet. Does not return material. Reports in 10 weeks.
Music: Mostly **new country**, **rockabilly** and **ballads**. "We are not interested in rap, jazz, blues or heavy metal." Released "Bucken Bull Inn" and "Needa Needa," recorded by Kody Stormn (country); and "Who Do You Want Me To Be" (by Joey Welz/Lou Mishiff), recorded by Joey Welz (rockabilly).

BOLIVIA RECORDS, 1219 Kerlin Ave., Brewton AL 36426. (205)867-2228. President: Roy Edwards. Labels include Known Artist Records. Record company, record producer and music publisher

(Cheavoria Music Co.). Estab. 1972. Releases 10 singles and 3 LPs/year. Pays 5% royalty to artists on contract; statutory rate to publishers for each record sold.

- Bolivia Records' publishing company, Cheavoria Music, is listed in the Music Publishers section and Known Artist Productions is listed in the Record Producers section.

How to Contact: Submit demo tape by mail. Unsolicited submissions are OK. Prefers cassette with 3 songs and lyric sheet. SASE for reply. All tapes will be kept on file. Reports in 1 month.

Music: Mostly **R&B**, **country** and **pop**; also **easy listening**, **MOR** and **soul**. Released "If You Only Knew" (by Horace Linsky), recorded by Roy Edwards; "Make Me Forget" (by Horace Linsky), recorded by Bobbie Roberson, both on Bolivia Records; and "We Make Our Reality," written and recorded by Brad Smiley on Known Artist Records. Other artists include Jim Portwood.

BOOGIE BAND RECORDS, 6245 Bristol Pkwy., Suite 206, Culver City CA 90230. Contact: Larry McGee. Labels include Classic Records and Mega Star Records. Record company, music publisher (Operation Perfection Publishing), record producer (Intrigue Productions) and management firm (LMP Management). Estab. 1976. Releases 6 singles, 3 12" singles, 1 LP, 4 EPs and 2 CDs/year. Pays 10% royalty to artists on contract; statutory rate to publishers per song on record.

- Boogie Band's publishing company, Operation Perfection, is listed in the Music Publishers section; their management firm, LMP Management, is in the Managers and Booking Agents section; and Intrigue Productions is listed in the Record Producers section.

How to Contact: Write first and obtain permission to submit. Prefers cassette with 1-4 songs and lyric sheet. SASE. Reports in 2 months. "Please only send professional quality material."

Music: **Urban contemporary**, **dance**, **rock**, **MOR/A/C**, **pop**, **rap** and **R&B**. Released *Starflower* (by Joe Cacamisse), recorded by Star Flower (A/C); *Too Tough* (by Terrence Jones), recorded by En-Tux (pop); and *Got It Goin' On* (by Alan Walker), recorded by Executives, all on Mega Star Records. Other artists include Wali Ali, A. Vis and Denise Parker.

Tips: "Make your song as commercial, crossover and as current as possible. Be sure to use current arrangements as well as song structure."

BOUQUET RECORDS, Bouquet-Orchid Enterprises, P.O. Box 1335, Norcross GA 30091. (770)798-7999. President: Bill Bohannon. Record company, music publisher (Orchid Publishing/BMI), record producer (Bouquet-Orchid Enterprises) and management firm. Releases 3-4 singles and 2 LPs/year. Pays 5-8% maximum royalty to artists on contract; pays statutory rate to publishers for each record sold.

- Bouquet Records' publishing company, Orchid Publishing, is listed in the Music Publishers section and Bouquet-Orchid Enterprises is in the Managers and Booking Agents section.

How to Contact: Submit demo tape by mail. Unsolicited submissions are OK. Prefers cassette with 3-5 songs and lyric sheet. SASE. Reports in 1 month.

Music: Mostly **religious** (contemporary or country-gospel, Amy Grant, etc.), **country** ("the type suitable for Clint Black, George Strait, Patty Loveless, etc.") and **Top 100** ("the type suitable for Billy Joel, Whitney Houston, R.E.M., etc."); also **rock** and **MOR**. Released *Blue As Your Eyes* (by Bill Bohannon), recorded by Adam Day (country); *Take Care of My World* (by Bob Freeman), recorded by Bandoleers (top 40); and *Making Plans* (by John Harris), recorded by Susan Spencer (country), all on Bouquet Records.

Tips: "Submit 3-5 songs on a cassette tape with lyric sheets. Include a short biography and perhaps a photo. Enclose SASE."

*BRAINCHILD RECORDS, P.O. Box 632981, San Diego CA 92163-2981. (619)297-2310. Fax: (619)297-7246. E-mail: brnchild@aol.com or brnchild@ix.netcom.com. A&R Director: Rex Sampaga. Record company, music publisher (Brother Bear Music/DeWhit Music) and record producer (Dean Whitney). Estab. 1984. Releases 4 LPs and 4 CDs/year. Pays negotiable royalty to artists on contract; statutory rate to publisher per song on record.

How to Contact: Call first and obtain permission to submit. Prefers cassette or DAT. SASE. Reports in 1 month.

Music: **Contemporary instrumental** only. Released *The Phoenix*, written and recorded by J Michael Verta; *E-Motion* (by various), recorded by Greg Vail; and *Diamond Collection* (by various), recorded by Kilauea, all on BrainChild Records (NAC).

*BREEDEN MUSIC GROUP, 50 Music Square West, Suite 303, Nashville TN 37203. (615)327-1515 or (615)327-2121. Fax: (615)327-9095. Director of A&R: Mitzi Mason. Labels include Ram and Portland Ltd. Record company, music publisher (Plaque Music/BMI; LePanto Music/ASCAP) and record producer (Gene Breeden/Dennis Payne). Estab. 1968. Releases 10 CDs and 10 cassettes/year. Pays statutory rate to publisher per song on record.

How to Contact: Submit demo tape by mail. Unsolicited submissions are OK. Prefers cassette or videocassette with 3-5 songs and lyric sheet. "Also include photo, bio and list of goals and ambitions." Does not return material. Reports in 6-8 weeks.

Music: Mostly **country**, **gospel** and **blues/R&B**; also **light rock**, **bluegrass** and **pop**. Released "Tucson," recorded by Johnny "U" (country); *I Want my Rib Back*, recorded by Steve Anthony (country); and *Speak To My Heart*, recorded by Brooke Shannon (gospel), all on Ram Records. Other artists include Tim White, Troy and Teddy Malone.
Tips: "Do the best job you can on your work—writing, arrangement and production. Demos are very important in placing material."

BRENTWOOD MUSIC, One Maryland Farms, Suite 200, Brentwood TN 37027. (615)373-3950. Fax: (615)373-8612. Attn: Publishing. Labels include Brentwood Records, Brentwood Kids Co., Brentwood Bluegrass, Brentwood Jazz, Smoky Mtn. Music, Spotted Dog, Ransom, Essential. Record company and music publisher. Estab. 1981. Releases 10-15 singles, 75-100 cassettes, 75-100 CDs/year. Pays various percent royalty to artists on contract; statutory rate to publisher per song on record.
How to Contact: Call first (extension 303) and obtain permission to submit. Prefers cassette with lyric or lead sheet. Does not return material. "Reports once per quarter."
Music: Mostly **contemporary Christian**, **children's** and **religious choral**; also **bluegrass** and **positive country**. Released "Runs in the Blood" (by Jeff Silvey/Jeff Jansen); "Trailerhitch" (by Brian Cumming/Alice Townsend), both recorded by Ken Holloway on Ransom Records (Christian country); and "Revolution" (by Daryl Youngblood), recorded by Imagine This on Essential Records (rock).

BRIARHILL RECORDS, 3484 Nicolette Dr., Crete IL 60417. (708)672-6457. A&R Director: Danny Mack. Record company, music publisher (Syntony Publishing/BMI), record producer (The Danny Mack Music Group). Estab. 1983. Releases 3-4 singles, 1 LP, 2 EPs and 1 CD/year. Pays negotiable royalty to artists on contract; statutory rate to publisher per song on record.
 • Briarhill's publishing company, Danny Mack Music, is listed in the Music Publishers section.
How to Contact: Submit demo tape by mail. Unsolicited submissions are OK. Prefers cassette with 3 songs and lyric sheet. SASE. Reports in 4-5 weeks.
Music: Mostly **country**, **novelty** and **polka**; also **southern gospel** and **Christmas**. Released "Country Love Song" (by Jim Garrison), recorded by Danny Mack; "Sunshine Stone," written and recorded by Keith Scott; and "Sad State of Affairs" (by Danny Mack), recorded by Rebecca Thompson, all on Briarhill Records.
Tips: "Be patient and don't expect others to invest financially to support your career goals. It's unrealistic."

BRIGHT GREEN RECORDS, P.O. Box 24, Bradley IL 60915. (815)932-7455. Fax: (815)932-0933. E-mail: deadmykel@aol.com. Contact: Mykel Boyd. Record company and record producer. Estab. 1989. Releases 8 singles, 6 LPs, 2 EPs and 6 CDs/year. Royalty varies; depends on agreement.
How to Contact: Submit demo tape by mail. Unsolicited submissions are OK. Prefers cassette, DAT or VHS videocassette with lyric sheet. Does not return material. Reports in 1 month.
Music: Mostly **experimental**, **electronic** and **jazz**; also **noise**. Released *Black Dahlia*, written and recorded by Black Dahlia (dark rock); *A Dream Within A Dream*, written and recorded by various artists (experimental); and *Fix Your Snack*, written and recorded by Foo (rock), all on Bright Green Records. Other artists include Angelhood, Trespassers W, Angry Red Planet and Cage.
Tips: "Don't be afraid to experiment, there is a real market for off the wall strange music, and we release it!"

BROKEN RECORDS INTERNATIONAL, 305 S. Westmore Ave., Lombard IL 60148. (708)916-6874. E-mail: 756630.0544@compuserve.com. International A&R: Roy Bocchieri. Record company. Estab. 1984. Payment negotiable.
How to Contact: Submit demo tape by mail. Unsolicited submissions are OK. Prefers cassette or CD (or VHS videocassette) with at least 2 songs and lyric sheet. Does not return material. Reports in 8 weeks.
Music: Mostly **rock**, **pop** and **dance**; also **acoustic** and **industrial**. Released *Electric*, written and recorded by LeRoy (pop); and *Hallowed Ground*, written and recorded by Day One (alternative), both on Broken Records.

BSW RECORDS, P.O. Box 2297, Universal City TX 78148. (210)659-2557. President: Frank Willson. Record company, music publisher (BSW Records/BMI) and record producer. Estab. 1987. Releases 12 singles, 4 LPs and 6 CDs/year. Pays standard royalty to artists on contract; statutory rate to publisher per song on record.
 • BSW's president, Frank Willson, is listed in the Record Producers section and their managment firm, Universal Music Marketing, is listed in the Managers and Booking Agents section.
How to Contact: Submit demo tape by mail. Unsolicited submissions are OK. Prefers cassette (or ¾" videocassette) with 3 songs and lyric sheet. SASE. Reports in 5 weeks.
Music: Mostly **country**, **rock** and **blues**. Released *Ice Mountain*, written and recorded by Maria Rose; *Ten Days In the Saddle*, written and recorded by Wes Wiginton; and *Let Me Be the One*, written and

recorded by Patty David, all on BSW Records. Other artists include Jess DeMaine, Andy Johnson, Tom Clark, C. Howard, Craig Robbins, Rusty Doherty, Stan Crawford and Mike Lord.

*C.E.G. RECORDS, INC., 102 E. Pikes Peak Ave., #600, Colorado Springs CO 80903. (719)632-0227. Fax: (719)634-2274. President: Robert A. Case. Record company and music publisher (New Pants Publishing/ASCAP, Old Pants Publishing/BMI). Estab. 1989. Releases 3-4 LPs and 3-4 CDs/year. Pays negotiable royalty to artists on contract.
How to Contact: Submit demo tape by mail. Unsolicited submissions are OK. Prefers cassette with 3-5 songs and lyric sheet. "Include a brief history of songwriter's career. Songs submitted must be copywritten or pending with copyright office." Does not return material. Reports in 3-4 months.
Music: Mostly **pop**, **rock** and **country**. Released *Sound of the Rain*, written and recorded by Silence; *Like No One Else* and *Woodland*, written and recorded by Lisa Bigwood, all on C.E.G. Records.
Tips: "Think of the music business as a job interview. You must be able to sell yourself and the music is your baby. You have to be strong and not deal with rejection as a personal thing. It is not a rejection of you, it's a rejection of the music. Most songwriters don't know how to communicate with labels. The best way is to start a friendship with people at the label."

CAFFEINE DISK, 21252 Beach Blvd., #210, Huntington Beach CA 92648. (714)375-4264. A&R Director: John Notsure. Record company. Estab. 1992. Releases 3 singles, 3 LPs, 4 EPs and 3 CDs/year. "Special arrangements are often made."
How to Contact: Submit demo tape by mail. Unsolicited submissions are OK. Prefers cassette with 3-4 songs, bio and press. Does not return material. Reports in 3-6 weeks. ("Be patient!")
Music: Punk. Released *Seized the Day*, recorded by Blind Justice; *Reunité*, recorded by SHIV; and *Crashland*, recorded by the Gravel Pit, all on Caffeine Disk Records. Other artists include Quest of the Moonbreed, Flowerland, Laurels, The Streams, The Philistines Jr. and Mighty Purple.
Tips: "Send punk only!"

CAMBRIA RECORDS & PUBLISHING, Box 374, Lomita CA 90717. (310)831-1322. Fax: (310)833-7442. Director of Recording Operations: Lance Bowling. Labels include Charade Records. Record company and music publisher. Estab. 1979. Pays 5-8% royalty to artists on contract; statutory rate to publisher for each record sold.
How to Contact: Write first to obtain permission to submit. Prefers cassette. SASE. Reports in 2 months.
Music: Mostly **classical**. Released *Songs of Elinor Remick Warren* on Cambria Records. Other artists include Marie Gibson (soprano), Mischa Leftkowitz (violin), Leigh Kaplan (piano), North Wind Quintet and Sierra Wind Quintet.

CANYON RECORDS AND INDIAN ARTS, 4143 N. 16th St., Phoenix AZ 85016. (602)266-4823. Owner: Bob Nuss. Labels include Indian House, Indian Sounds. Record company, distributor of American Indian recordings. Estab. 1984. Releases 50 cassettes and 20 CDs/year. Royalty varies with project.
 • Note that Canyon Records is a very specialized label, and only wants to receive submissions by Native American artists.
How to Contact: Write or call first and obtain permission to submit. Prefers cassette or VHS videocassette. SASE. Reports in 2 months.
Music: Music by American Indians—any style (must be enrolled tribal members). Released *Islands of Bows*, written and recorded by R. Carlos Nakai (Native flute); *Southern Scratch Vol. 3*, written and recorded by Ron Joaquim and Southern Scratch (polkas), both on Canyon Records; and *Tewa Indian Women's Choir of San Juan Pueblo* (traditional), on Indian House Records. Other artists include Black Lodge Singers, John Rainer, Tree Cody and Joanne Shenandoah.
Tips: "We deal only with American Indian performers. We do not accept material from others. Please include tribal affiliation. *No* New Age 'Indian style' material."

CAPITOL RECORDS, 1750 N. Vine St., Hollywood CA 90028-5274. (213)462-6252. This record company prefers not to share information.

CAPSTAN RECORD PRODUCTION, P.O. Box 211, East Prairie MO 63845. (314)649-2211. Contact: Joe Silver or Tommy Loomas. Labels include Octagon and Capstan Records. Record company, music publisher (Lineage Publishing Co.) and record producer (Silver-Loomas Productions). Pays 3-5% royalty to artists on contract.
 • Capstan's publishing affiliate, Lineage Publishing Co., can be found in the Music Publishers section and Staircase Promotion can be found in the Managers and Booking Agents section.
How to Contact: Write first to obtain permission to submit. Prefers cassette (or VHS videocassette) with 2-4 songs and lyric sheet. "Send photo and bio." SASE. Reports in 1 month.

Music: Country, easy listening, MOR, country rock and **top 40/pop.** Released "Country Boy" (by Alden Lambert); "Yesterday's Teardrops" and "Round & Round," written and recorded by The Burchetts. Other artists include Bobby Lee Morgan, Skidrow Joe, Vicarie Arcoleo and Fleming.

CARE FREE RECORDS GROUP, Box 2463, Carefree AZ 85377. (602) 230-4177. Vice President: Doya Fairbanks. Labels include Blue Mesa and Tempe. Record company, record producer, music publisher, distribution and promotion company. Estab. 1990. Releases 6 singles, 4 12″ singles, 12 LPs, 5 EPs and 12 CDs/year. Pays varying royalty to artists on contract and to publisher per song on record.
   • Care Free is also listed in the Record Producers section, and their publishing affiliate, Ho-Hum Music, is listed in the Music Publishers section.
How to Contact: Submit demo tape by mail. Unsolicited submissions are OK. Prefers cassette (or VHS videocassette if available) with 4-6 songs. SASE. Reports in 1 month.
Music: Mostly **country, jazz** and **classical**; also **rock, metal** and **New Age.** Released *Pablo,* written and recorded by Pablo on Blue Mesa Records (pop); *The Totem Pole* (by Doug), recorded by Totem Pole (pop); and *Harold's Coral,* written and recorded by Harold's Coral (country), both on Care Free Records. Other artists include Paul Conseio, Arisnal and Gypsy Wind.

CARLYLE RECORDS, INC., 1217 16th Ave. South, Nashville TN 37212. (615)327-8129. President: Laura Fraser. Record company. Estab. 1986. Releases 3 12″ singles, 6 LPs, 4 EPs and 6 CDs/year. Pays compulsory rate to publisher per song on record.
   • See the listing for Carlyle Productions in the Record Producers section and Carlyle Management in the Managers and Booking Agents section.
How to Contact: Submit demo tape by mail. Unsolicited submissions are OK. Prefers cassette (or VHS videocassette). Does not return unsolicited material. Reports in 1 month.
Music: Mostly **rock.** Released "Orange Room" (by Michael Ake), recorded by the Grinning Plowmen; *All Because of You,* written and recorded by Dorcha; and *Sun* (by John Elliot), recorded by Dessau, all on Carlyle Records.

*CAROLINE RECORDS, INC., 114 W. 26th St., 11th Floor, New York NY 10001. (212)886-7500. Website: http://www.caroline.com. Director A&R/Label Operations: Brian Long. Exclusive manufacturing and distribution of EG, Astralwerks (electronic) and Real World (world music), Vernon Yard (alternative rock), Instant Mayhem (alternative rock), Scamp (retrocool), Mercator (world) and Gyroscope (eclectic). Record company and independent record distributor (Caroline Records Inc.). Estab. 1979. Releases 10-12 12″ singles and 100 CDs/year. Pays varying royalty to artists on contract; statutory rate to publisher per song.
How to Contact: Submit demo tape by mail. Unsolicited submissions are OK. Prefers cassette with lead sheets and press clippings. SASE. Reports in 3 months.
Music: Mostly **alternative/indie rock.** Released *Three Sheets to the Wind,* written and recorded by Idaho on Caroline Records; *Ben Folds Five,* written and recorded by Ben Folds Five on Passenger/Caroline Records; and *Transmission,* written and recorded by Low on Vernon Yard/Caroline Records. Other artists include Acetone, Tanner, Sincola, Lidattusik, Capsize 7, Maids of Gravity, Adrian Belew and Chemical Brothers.
Tips: "We are open to artists of unique quality and enjoy developing artists from the ground up. We listen to all types of 'alternative' rock, metal, funk and rap but do not sign mainstream hard rock or dance. We send out rejection letters so do not call to find out what's happening with your demo."

CASARO RECORDS, 932 Nord Ave., Chico CA 95926. (916)345-3027. Contact: Hugh Santos. Record company and record producer (RSA Productions). Estab. 1988. Releases 5-8 LPs/year. Pays variable royalty to artists on contract; statutory rate to publisher per song on record.
How to Contact: Write first and obtain permission to submit. Prefers cassette with full project demo and lyric sheet. Does not return material. Reports in 3 months.
Music: **Jazz** and **country**; also **R&B** and **pop.** Released *Jesus My Master,* written and recorded by Curt Collins (gospel); *Forever High,* written and recorded by David Sheehy (folk/rock); and *Liberty Waltz,* written and recorded by Cindy Smith (folk/rock), all on Casaro Records. Other artists include Lesley McDaniel, Jeff Dixon, Lory Dobbs and Charlie Robinson.
Tips: "Produce your song well (in tune—good singer). It doesn't need to be highly produced—just clear vocals. Include lyric sheet."

*CASTLE VON BUHLER RECORDS, 16 Ashford St., Boston MA 02134. E-mail: cvb@drawbridge.com. Website: http://cvb.drawbridge.com. Labels include PussyKitty Records. Record company and management firm. Estab. 1993. Releases 2 singles, 1 LP and 5 CDs/year. Pays negotiable royalty to artists on contract.
How to Contact: Submit demo tape by mail. Unsolicited submissions are OK. "No calls please." Prefers cassette with 3-5 songs and band photo. Does not return material. "We only report back if interested."

Music: Mostly **alternative**, **techno** and **ethnic**; also **ambient**, **classical** and **gothic**. Released *Anon*, written and recorded by various artists (alternative); *The Cruelty of Children*, written and recorded by Sirensong (alternative); and *Soon*, written and recorded by various artists (alternative), all on Castle von Buhler Records. Other artists include Turkish Delight, The Moors, Women of Sodom, Adam von Buhler and Veronica Black Morpheus Nipple.

Tips: "Send a tape with a photo and a personal handwritten note and never call."

CAT'S VOICE PRODUCTIONS, P.O. Box 1361, Sanford ME 04073. (207)490-3676. Owner: Tom Reeves. Record company, music publisher (Rahsaan Publishing/ASCAP), record producer and recording studio. Estab. 1982. Releases 2 singles, 4 12″ singles and 4 CDs/year. Pays 15-20% royalty to artists on contract; statutory royalty to publishers per song on record.

How to Contact: Submit demo tape by mail. Unsolicited submissions are OK. Prefers cassette (or VHS videocassette) with 3 songs and lyric sheet. "Publishing requires laser copy sheet music." SASE. Reports in 2 weeks.

Music: **Rock**, **R&B** and **country**; also **New Age** and **alternative**. Released "Friends of Friends" and "Forever," both written and recorded by Paul Wilcox; and *Robert Hartwell*, written and recorded by Robert Harwell, all on Cat's Voice Records. Other artists include Buddy Sullivan, Andy Henry, David Hartwell, Loaded Soul, Billy DeNuzzio and Carl Armano.

CEDAR CREEK RECORDS™, 44 Music Square East, Suite 503, Nashville TN 37203. (615)252-6916. Fax: (615)327-4204. President: Larry Duncan. Record company, music publisher (Cedar Creek Music/BMI and Cedar Cove Music/ASCAP), record producer (Cedar Creek Productions). Estab. 1992. Releases 20 singles, 5 LPs and 5 CDs/year. Pays 10% royalty to artists on contract; statutory rate to publisher per song on record.

● You can find listings for Cedar Creek Productions in the Record Producers and Managers and Booking Agents sections.

How to Contact: Submit demo tape by mail. Unsolicited submissions are OK. Prefers cassette (or VHS videocassette). Does not return material. Reports in 2 months.

Music: Mostly **country**, **country/pop**, **country/R&B**, **Southern gospel** and **Christian contemporary**; also **pop**, **R&B**, **Christian country**, **contemporary jazz** and **light rock**. Released "When The Sun Goes Down Over Dixie" (by Brian McCardle/John Georgette); "What Would Jeff And Robert Say Today" (by Deke Little/Lynn Guyo); "Ride Rebels Ride" (by Deke Little/Tex Henley/Eldon Money), all recorded by Lynn Guyo on Interstate Records.

Tips: "Submit your best songs on a good fully produced demo or master using a great singer."

CELLAR RECORDS, 116 N. Peoria, Dixon IL 61021. (815)288-2900. E-mail: tjoos@aol.com. Owners: Todd Joos or Bob Brady. Record company, music publisher (Sound Cellar Music/BMI), record producer (Todd Joos), recording studio (Cellar Studios). Estab. 1987. Releases 4-6 singles, 12 cassettes, 6 EPs, 6-8 CDs/year. Pays 100% royalty to artists on contract; statutory rate to publisher per song on record. Charges in advance "if they use our studio to record."

● Cellar Records' publishing affiliate, Sound Cellar Music, can be found in the Music Publishers section.

How to Contact: Submit demo tape by mail. Prefers cassette (or VHS videocassette if available) with 3-4 songs and lyric sheet. Does not return material. "If we like it we will call you."

Music: Mostly **metal**, **country** and **rock**; also **pop**, **rap** and **blues**. Released *Soul Searchin'*, recorded by Justice 4 (alternative); *Snap Judgment*, recorded by Snap Judgment (hard rock); and "Spill A Tear," recorded by Impetus (death metal), all on Cellar Records. Other artists include Pandemonium Carnival, Mass, Atonement, Manic Oppression, Pierce and Light, Lefwitch, Blind Witness and Drastic Measures.

Tips: "Make sure that you understand that your band is business and you must be willing to self invest time, effort and money just like any other new business. We can help you but you must also be willing to help yourself."

CENTIUM ENTERTAINMENT, INC., 373 S. Robertson Blvd., Beverly Hills CA 90211. (310)854-4966. Fax: (310)854-3966. President: Arthur Braun. Labels include Centium Records. Record company and music publisher (Centium Entertainment, Inc.). Estab. 1994. Releases 6 singles, 2 LPs, 10 EPs and 6 CDs/year. Pays negotiable royalty to artists on contract; statutory rate to publisher per song on record.

● See the interview with President Arthur Braun in the Music Publishers section. Centium Entertainment released "I Live For Your Love," recorded by Natalie Cole, which won BMI's one million performance award in 1994. They also have a listing in the Music Publishers section.

How to Contact: Submit demo tape by mail. Unsolicited submissions are OK. Prefers cassette with lyric sheet. SASE. Reports in 4-6 weeks.

Music: Mostly **R&B**, **rock** and **dance**; also **country**. Released "I Live For Your Love" (by Werfel/Reswick/Rich), recorded by Natalie Cole on Manhattan Records; "Never Give Up on a Good Thing," written and recorded by Monie Love on London Records; and "I Don't Give My Love to Just Anybody," written and recorded by Laura Enea on Next Plateau Records.

CEREBRAL RECORDS, 1236 Laguna Dr., Carlsbad CA 92008. (619)434-2497. Publicist: Carol Leno. Record company, music publisher (Cerebral Records/BMI), record producer (Cerebral Records) and recording studio. Estab. 1991. Releases 1-3 LPs and 1-3 CDs/year. Pays negotiable royalty.
How to Contact: Write first and obtain permission to submit. Prefers cassette. SASE. Reports in 2 months.
Music: Mostly **progressive rock**. Released *Broken Hands*, *I Am Myself* and *On With the Show*, all written and recorded by State of Mind on Cerebral Records.
Tips: "Have fun. Write songs you like. Cover 'em with hooks and fill 'em with intelligence. Keep on growing as an artist."

CHA CHA RECORDS, P.O. Box 321, Port Washington WI 53074. (414)284-9777. President: Joseph C. De Lucia. Labels include Cap and Debby. Record company, record producer, and music publisher (Don Del Music/BMI). Estab. 1955. Pays negotiable royalty to artists on contract; negotiable rate to publishers per song on record.
  • Cha Cha's publishing affiliate, Don Del Music, is listed in the Music Publishers section.
How to Contact: Write first and obtain permission to submit. Prefers cassette with 4-6 songs and lyric sheet. SASE. Reports in 3 months.
Music: **Acoustic** and **folk**.

CHATTAHOOCHEE RECORDS, 15230 Weddington St., Van Nuys CA 91411. (818)788-6863. Contact: Chris Yardum. Record company and music publisher (Etnoc/Conte). Member NARAS. Releases 4 singles/year. Pays negotiable royalty to artists on contract.
How to Contact: Submit demo tape by mail. Unsolicited submissions are OK. Prefers cassette with 2-6 songs and lyric sheet. Does not return material. "We contact songwriters if we're interested."
Music: **Rock**.
Tips: "Send it in. If we're interested, we'll contact you in six to eight weeks."

CHERRY STREET RECORDS, P.O. Box 52681, Tulsa OK 74152. (918)742-8087. President: Rodney Young. Record company and music publisher. Estab. 1990. Releases 2 CD/year. Pays 5-15% royalty to artists on contract; statutory rate to publisher per song on record.
How to Contact: Write first and obtain permission to submit. Prefers cassette (or Beta or VHS videocassette) with 4 songs and lyric sheet. SASE. Reports in 6-8 weeks.
Music: **Rock, country** and **R&B**; also **jazz**. Released *Blue Dancer* (by Chris Blevins) and *Hardtimes* (by Brad Absher), both on CSR Records (country rock); also *She Can't Do Anything Wrong* (by Davis/ Richmond), recorded by Bob Seger on Capitol Records.
Tips: "We are a songwriter label—the song is more important to us than the artist. Send only your best four songs."

CHRISMARIE RECORDS, P.O. Box 934273, Margate FL 33442-8034. Fax: (954)427-1819. A&R Director: Peggy Cooney. Producer: Joseph W. Nudo. Record company. Estab. 1990. Releases 2 singles, 2 LPs and 1 CD/year. Pays 5-10% royalty to artists on contract; statutory rate to publisher per song on record.
  • See the listings for Rana International & Affiliates in the Music Publishers and Managers and Booking Agents sections.
How to Contact: Submit demo tape by mail. Unsolicited submissions are OK. Prefers VHS videocassette with 2-4 songs and lyric sheet. Does not return material. Reports in 12-16 weeks.
Music: Mostly **pop**, **rock** and **ballads**; also **country**, **R&B** and **new music**. Released *Dream On*, written and recorded by Niko (pop); "Anita," written and recorded by Adamos (rock ballad); and "Glass of Wine," written and recorded by Festa (pop), all on Chrismarie Records. Other artists include Red Rose, Adriana, Motion, Burgandy Row and Bitterr Tides.
Tips: "We are interested in original material only! The quality of your demo projects, your talent and the music should *never* overpower the lyrics. We strongly encourage submissions of VHS videocassettes. Need not be professionally done. Stay positive! All submissions must include name, phone number and SASE for response."

*CHRISTIAN MEDIA ENTERPRISES, 4041 W. Wheatland, Suite 156-372, Dallas TX 75237. Phone/fax: (214)283-2780. Owner: Craig R. Miles. Labels include Break Through Records, CME Records. Record company, music publisher (CME Publishing Co./ASCAP) and record producer (Craig R. Miles). Estab. 1988. Pays negotiable royalty to artists on contract; statutory rate to publisher per song on record.

How to Contact: Write first to arrange personal interview or submit demo tape by mail. Unsolicited submissions are OK. Prefers cassette, DAT or VHS videocassette with 3 songs and lyric and lead sheet. Does not return material. Reports in 2-3 months.
Music: Mostly **contemporary Christian, contemporary gospel** and **jazz gospel**. Released "I've Found Joy" (by Craig Miles), recorded by Onyx on CME Records (CCM). Other artists include Paul T. and Jason Watson.
Tips: "Be committed; be patient; be professional; be ready. Success is obtained when opportunity meets preparation."

CIMIRRON/RAINBIRD RECORDS, 607 Piney Point Rd., Yorktown VA 23692. (804)898-8155. President: Lana Puckett. Vice President: Kim Person. Record company. Releases at least 3 CDs and cassettes/year. Pays variable royalty to artists on contract; negotiable rate to publisher per song on record.
• See the listing for Cimirron Music in the Music Publishers section.
How to Contact: Write or call first and obtain permission to submit. Prefers cassette with 1-3 songs and lyric sheet. SASE. Reports in 3 months.
Music: Mostly **country-bluegrass, New Age** and **pop**. Released *Nutcracker Suite* and *Guitar Town*, written and recorded by Steve Bennett (guitar); and "Christmas Love" (by Lana Puckett and Kim Person), recorded by Lana & Kim, all on Cimirron/Rainbird Records.

CITA COMMUNICATIONS INC., Dept. SM, 530 Pittsburgh Rd., Butler PA 16001. (412)586-6552. E-mail: citatb@isrv.com. A&R/Producer: Mickii Taimuty. Labels include Phunn! Records and Tropē Records. Record company. Estab. 1989. Releases 3 singles, 2 EPs and 2 CDs/year. Pays artists 10% royalty on contract. Pays statutory rate to publisher per song on record.
How to Contact: Submit demo tape by mail. Unsolicited submissions are OK. Prefers cassette (or VHS, Beta or ¾" videocassette) with a maximum of 6 songs and lyric sheets. SASE. Reports in 6 weeks.
Music: Mostly **alternative, new country** and **rock gospel**; also **rock/dance**. Released "Hold Me Now" and "I Cross My Heart" (by Taimuty/Nelson), recorded by Melissa Anne on Phunn! Records; and "Fight the Fight," written and recorded by M.J. Nelson on Tropē Records. Other artists include Most High, Sister Golden Hair and Countdown.

CLEOPATRA RECORDS, 8726 S. Sepulveda Blvd., Suite D-82, Los Angeles CA 90045. (310)305-0172. Fax: (310)821-4702. Contact: A&R. Labels include Zoth Ommog, Hypnotic, Hard Records Europe and Cherry Red. Record company. Estab. 1991. Releases 5 singles, 10 LPs, 5 EPs and 100 CDs/year. Pays 10-14% royalty to artists on contract; negotiable rate to publisher per song on record.
How to Contact: Submit demo tape by mail. Unsolicited submissions are OK. Prefers cassette or VHS videocassette with 5 songs and lyric sheet. Does not return material. Reports in 1 month.
Music: Mostly **industrial, gothic** and **ambient**; also **trance, space rock** and **electronic**. Released *Thoth*, written and recorded by Nik Turner (electronic/space rock); *Lost Minds* (by Rozz Williams/Evao), recorded by Christian Death (gothic); and *Lucy is Red*, written and recorded by Nosferato (gothic), all on Cleopatra Records. Other artists include Controlled Bleeding, Helios Creed, Rosetta Stone and Psychic TV.
Tips: "Don't write your music thinking of a hit record for the mainstream."

COLUMBIA RECORDS, 550 Madison Ave., New York NY 10022. (212)833-8000. This record company prefers not to share information.

COM-FOUR, 7 Dunham Place, Brooklyn NY 11211. (718)599-2205. Label Manager: Albert Garzon. Record company. Estab. 1985. Releases 5-10 singles and 10 CDs/year. Pays various royalties to artists on contract.
How to Contact: Submit demo tape by mail. Unsolicited submissions are OK. Prefers cassette (or VHS videocassette if available), or finished CD with 5-7 songs. Does not return material. "We only respond if we like material."
Music: Mostly **rock** and **post-punk**; also **ethnic** and **jazz**. Released recordings from such groups as Psychic TV, King Tubby and The Upsetters.
Tips: "Be original and have some talent. Be willing and ready to work hard touring, promoting, etc."

COMMA RECORDS & TAPES, Postbox 2148, 63243 Neu-Isenburg, **Germany**. Phone: (6102)52696. Fax: (6102)52696. General Manager: Roland Bauer. Labels include Big Sound, Comma International and Max-Banana-Tunes. Record company. Estab. 1969. Releases 50-70 singles and 20 LPs/year. Pays 7-10% royalty to artists on contract.
• Comma Records' publishing company, R.D. Clevère Musikverlag, is listed in the Music Publishers section.

How to Contact: Prefers cassette and lyric sheet. Reports in 3 weeks. "Do not send advanced letter asking permission to submit, just send your material, SAE and minimum two IRCs."
Music: Mostly **pop**, **disco**, **rock**, **R&B** and **country**; also **musicals** and **classical**.

COMSTOCK RECORDS LTD., 10603 N. Hayden Rd., Suite 114, Scottsdale AZ 85260. (602)951-3115. Fax: (602)951-3074. Production Manager/Producer: Patty Parker. President: Frank Fara. Record company, music publisher (White Cat Music/ASCAP, Rocky Bell Music/BMI, How the West Was Sung Music/BMI), Nashville Record Production and International and U.S. Radio Promotions. Member CMA, BBB, CCMA, BCCMA, British CMA and AF of M. "Comstock Records, Ltd. has three primary divisions: Production, Promotion and Publishing. We distribute and promote both our own Nashville produced recordings and already completed country or pop/rock CDs or DATs ready for CD manufacturing. We offer CD design and mastering for products we promote." Releases 24-30 CD singles and 6-8 CDs/year. Pays 10% royalty to artists on contract; statutory rate to publishers for each record sold. "Artists pay distribution and promotion fee to press and release their masters."
  • Comstock Records' publishing company, White Cat Music, is listed in the Music Publishers section and Patty Parker can be found in the Record Producers section.
How to Contact: Submit demo tape by mail. Unsolicited submissions are OK. Prefers CD or cassette (or VHS videocassette) with 1-4 songs "plus word sheet. Enclose stamped return envelope if cassette is to be returned." Reports in 2 weeks.
Music: Released "No One Ever Died From A Broken Heart" (by Hayward Simpson), recorded by Danielle St. Pierre; "Darlin' Rita," written and recorded by Ty Tomes; and "Ride Me Home" (by George F. Spicka/Jane Lamar), recorded by Jane Lamar & Snidely's Daughter, all on Comstock Records. Other artists include Pam Ferens, Christopher Lee Clayton, Zo Carroll, Sharon Lee Bearers, No Where Dreamer, Distant Cousins and Marshall Kipp Project.
Tips: "Go global with your music and talent. The overseas radio market is fertile ground for North American country and pop/rock acts. Likewise U.S. Radio is open to the fresh new sounds that foreign artists bring to the airwaves. Good songs and good singers are universal."

CONTINENTAL RECORDS, 744 Joppa Farm Rd., Joppatowne MD 21085. (410)679-2262. CEO: Ernest W. Cash. Record company and music publisher (Ernie Cash Music/BMI). Estab. 1986. Pays 10% royalty to artists on contract; statutory rate to publisher per song on record.
  • See the listings for Cash Productions Inc. in the Music Publishers and Managers and Booking Agents sections.
How to Contact: Call first and obtain permission to submit. Prefers cassette (or VHS videocassette) with 3 songs and lyric sheet. SASE. Reports in 2 weeks.
Music: Mostly **country** and **gospel**. Artists include The Short Brothers.

COUNTRY BREEZE RECORDS, 1715 Marty, Kansas City KS 66103. (913)384-7336. President: Ed Morgan. Labels include Angel Star Records and Midnight Shadow Records. Record company, music publisher (Country Breeze Music/BMI and Walkin' Hat Music/ASCAP). Releases 15 7" singles and 20 cassettes and 15-20 CDs/year. Pays 25% royalty to artists on contract; statutory rate to publisher per song on record.
  • Country Breeze's publishing company, Country Breeze Music, is listed in the Music Publishers section.
How to Contact: Submit demo tape by mail. Unsolicited submissions are OK. Prefers studio-produced demo with 3 songs and lyric sheet. SASE. Reports in 2 weeks.
Music: All types **country**. Released "I Can't Believe I Said Goodbye" (by E. Morgan/E. Livermore), recorded by Tanya Poe on Country Breeze Records (country); "Higher This Time" (by Diane Kemp), recorded by Tommy Moon; and "The Hand That Holds Onto Mine," written and recorded by Keith Loyd, both on Angel Star Records (gospel). Other artists include Southern Comfort, Second Coming Singers, Hal Henderson and Tom Anderson.
Tips: "Do not submit material and call me three days later wanting to know if it's recorded yet. It takes time."

COUNTRY STAR INTERNATIONAL, 439 Wiley Ave., Franklin PA 16323. (814)432-4633. President: Norman Kelly. Labels include CSI, Country Star, Process and Mersey Records. Record company, music publisher (Country Star/ASCAP, Process and Kelly/BMI) and record producer (Country Star Productions). Member AFM and AFTRA. Estab. 1970. Releases 5-10 singles and 5-10 LPs/

REFER TO THE CATEGORY INDEX (at the end of this section) to find exactly which companies are interested in the type of music you write.

year. Pays 8% royalty to artists on contract; statutory rate to publisher per song on record.

● See the listings for Country Star Music in the Music Publishers section and Country Star Attractions in the Managers and Booking Agents section.

How to Contact: Submit demo tape by mail. Unsolicited submissions are OK. Prefers cassette with 2-4 songs and typed lyric or lead sheet. SASE. "No SASE no return." Reports in 1 week.

Music: Mostly **C&W** and **bluegrass**. Released "Teardrops Still Fall" (by N. Kelly/J. Barbaria), recorded by Larry Piefer (country); "Western Dawn" (by J. E. Meyers), recorded by Jeffrey Connors, both on Country Star Records; and "God Specializes," written and recorded by Sheryl Friend on Process Records. Other artists include Junie Lou and Bob Stamper.

*COUNTRY STYLE RECORDS, P.O. Box 732, Hominy OK 74035. (918)885-2337. Fax: (918)885-6498. President: Geri WyNell. Record company, music publisher (Country Style Country Music Inc.) and record producer (Ken Peade). Estab. 1995. Pays negotiable royalty to artists on contract; negotiable rate to publisher per song on record.

How to Contact: Submit demo tape by mail. Unsolicited submissions are OK. Prefers cassette or VHS videocassette. Does not return material. Reports in 1-4 weeks.

Music: Mostly **country**, **bluegrass** and **gospel**; also **easy listening**. Released *Country Style Forever*, written and recorded by Geri Wynell; "Every Step of the Way," written and recorded by John Kurtz; and "A Country Girl's Heart" (by G. WyNell/W. Griffith), recorded by Geri WyNell, all on Country Style Records. Other artists include Gail Hinton, Kathy Myers, Apache, Ronnie Barrett, Peggy Davis, Joy West, Richard Vines and Mary Lindley.

Tips: "Be yourself! Don't try to be something you're not. Just be willing to work hard. We all work hard for our aritsts and songwriters. Be serious about your music career! Always create your own image and style."

COWGIRL RECORDS, Box 6085, Burbank CA 91510. Contact: Vice President. Record company and music publisher (Kingsport Creek). Estab. 1980. Pays statutory rate to publishers for each record sold.

● See the listing for Kingsport Creek Music in the Record Producers section.

How to Contact: Submit demo tape by mail. Unsolicited submissions OK. Prefers cassette (or VHS videocassette) with any number of songs and lyric sheet or lead sheet. Does not return unsolicited material. "Include a photo and bio if possible."

Music: Mostly **country, R&B, MOR** and **gospel**. Released "Leading Me On," "Pick Up Your Feet" and "With Me Still," all written and recorded by Melvena Kaye on Cowgirl Records.

*CRITIQUE RECORDS, INC., 50 Cross St., Winchester MA 01890. (617)729-8137. Fax: (617)729-2320. Director of A&R: Ian-John. Labels include Popular Records, Inc. Record company and record producer (Ian-John). Releases 8 LPs and 24 CDs/year. Pays negotiable royalty to artists on contract; statutory rate to publisher per song on record.

● One of Critique's releases, "Total Eclipse of the Heart" by Nikki French, was one of *Billboard*'s top selling singles of 1995, selling over 600,000 copies.

How to Contact: Call first and obtain permission to submit a demo. Prefers cassette with 3 songs and lyric and/or lead sheet. SASE. Reports in 3 weeks.

Music: Mostly **dance-pop, R&B, hip-hop, rock** and **alternative**; also **country, house-techno** and **trance-HiNRG**. Released "Total Eclipse of the Heart," recorded by Nikki French; "Get Ready for This," recorded by 2 Unlimited; and "Stayin' Alive," recorded by N-trance, all on Critique Records (dance). Other artists include David Hasselhoff, X-Press, Digital Underground, Marty Haggard, McPotts and Ian-John.

*CTI RECORDS, 88 University Place, New York NY 10003. (212)645-9302. Fax: (212)727-0415. Vice President of Operations: John W. Taylor. National Marketing Director: Dave Anderson. Record company, music publisher (Char-Liz Music/BMI, Three Brothers Music/ASCAP) and record producer (Creed Taylor, John W. Taylor). Estab. 1965. Releases 2 singles, 6 CDs/year. Pays negotiable royalty to artists on contract.

How to Contact: Submit demo tape by mail. Unsolicited submissions are OK. "Please do not send elaborate packages. Only cover letter, actual demo and musician roster." Does not return material. Reports in 1-2 weeks.

Music: Mostly **new music, R&B, jazz** and **acid jazz**; also **jazz**. Released *Evolution*, written and recorded by Thus Spoke Z on Kudu Records (acid jazz); *Vineland Dreams*, written and recorded by Steve Laury (contemporary jazz); and *I'll Be Over You*, recorded by Larry Coryell/Peabo Bryson (contemporary R&B), both on CTI Records. Other artists include Ted Rosenthal, Freddie Hubbard and Donald Harrison.

Tips: "An artist should be familiar with radio formats and *Billboard* charts and know where music is heard, i.e., clubs, record stores, etc. if the music does not adhere to any particular radio format."

*DAGENE/CABLETOWN RECORDS, (formerly Dagene Records), P.O. Box 410851, San Francisco CA 94141. (415)822-1530. President: David Alston. Record company, music publisher (Dagene Music) and record producer (David-Classic Disc Productions). Estab. 1993. Pays standard royalty to artists on contract; statutory rate to publisher per song on record.
    • See the listing for Golden City International in the Managers and Booking Agents section.
How to Contact: Write or call first and obtain permission to submit. Prefers cassette (or VHS videocassette) with 2 songs and lyric sheet. SASE. Reports in 1 month.
Music: Mostly **R&B/rap**, **dance** and **pop**; also **gospel**. Released "Maxin" (by Marcus Justice/Bernard Henderson), recorded by 2 Dominatorz on Dagene Records; "Love Don't Love Nobody" (by David Alston), recorded by Rare Essence on Cabletown Records; and "Why Can't I Be Myself" (by David Alston), recorded by David Alston on E-lect-ric Recordings. Other artists include Chapter 1.

ALAN DALE PRODUCTIONS, 1630 Judith Lane, Indianapolis IN 46227. (317)786-1630. President: Alan D. Heshelman. Labels include ALTO Records. Record company. Estab. 1990.
How to Contact: Submit demo tape by mail. Unsolicited submissions are OK. Prefers cassette with 3 songs. SASE. Reports in 4-6 weeks.
Music: Mostly **adult contemporary**, **country**, **jazz**, **gospel** and **New Age**. Released "Little Boys Like Lookin' " (by Alan Dale), recorded by Taurus (country); "Fire, Ice 'n' Thunder (by Alan Dale), recorded by JAG (pop); and "Forever Loving You" (by Alan Dale), recorded by J.J. Lake (A/C), all on A.D.P. Records. Other artists include Still Water.
Tips: "Create a writing style with good paraphrasing and excellent vocals."

DANCER PUBLISHING CO., 166 Folkstone, Brampton, Ontario L6T 3M5 **Canada**. (905)791-1835. President: David Dancer. Labels include Cougar Records. Record company and music publisher. Estab. 1991. Releases 6 singles and 4 CDs/year. Pays 10% royalty to artists on contract; statutory rate to publisher per song on record.
How to Contact: Submit demo tape by mail. Unsolicited submissions are OK. Prefers cassette with 4 songs and lyric sheet. Does not return material. Reports in 1 month.
Music: Mostly **country**, **bluegrass** and **light rock**. Released "Old Habits Die Hard," (by Don Mittan) and "It's a Hello Goodbye World" (by Leonard H. Kohls), both on Cougar Records.

*DARGASON MUSIC, P.O. Box 189, Burbank CA 91503-0189. (818)846-4981. Fax: (818)846-2294. Administrative Assistant: Michael Kowalski. Record company and music publisher (Dolmen Music). Estab. 1984. Releases 2-3 LPs and 2-3 CDs/year. Pays negotiable royalty to artists on contract; statutory rate to publisher per song on record.
How to Contact: Submit demo tape by mail. Unsolicited submissions are OK. Prefers cassette or VHS videocassette. SASE. Reports in 6 weeks.
Music: Mostly **folk instrumental**, **contemporary vocal** and **contemporary instrumental**. Released *Celtic Treasures*, recorded by Joemy Wilson (instrumental/folk); *Treasures of the Celtic Harp*, recorded by Kim Robertson (instrumental folk); and *The Classical Banjo*, recorded by John Bullard (folk/classical), all on Dargason Records. Other artists include Kim Angelis and John Bullard.

DEADEYE RECORDS, P.O. Box 5022-347, Lake Forest CA 92630. (714)768-0644. E-mail: deadeye@deltanet.com. Website: www.deltanet.com/~user/deadeye. Manager: Karen Jenkins. Labels include Thunderzone Records. Record company. Estab. 1992. Releases 3 CDs/year. Pays varying royalty to artists on contract; statutory rate to publisher per song on record.
How to Contact: Write first and obtain permission to submit. Prefers cassette (or videocassette if available) with 3 songs and lyric sheet. Does not return material. Reports in 2 months.
Music: Mostly **country**, **rock** and **blues**; also **R&B**. Released *Ragin' Wind* (by Frank Jenkins), recorded by Diamondback on Deadeye Records (country).

*DECIBEL, 17125C W. Bluemound Rd., #122, Brookfield WI 53008. Phone/fax: (414)454-0775. E-mail: decibel@earth.execpc.com. Website: http://execpc.com/decibel.html. President: Tom Muschitz. Labels include feedback. Record company. Estab. 1994. Releases 8 CDs/year. Pays negotiable royalty to artists on contract; statutory rate to publisher per song on record.
How to Contact: Submit demo tape by mail. Unsolicited submissions are OK. Prefers cassette or DAT. "Any submissions welcome." SASE. Reports in 3 weeks.
Music: Mostly **industrial**, **electronic** and **experimental**; also **gothic**, **metal** and **punk**. Released *desolate*, recorded by Alien Faktor (experimental/industrial); *Gigapus*, recorded by Severed Heads (dance); and *Stillbirth*, recorded by Oneiroid Psychosis (gothic industrial), all on decibel Records. Other artists include No One, Impact Test, fuckface, Morpheus Sister and Sirvix.
Tips: "Feel free to send creative, sincere works. Derivative electronic compositions will not be responded to."

*DEEP SIX RECORDS, 8033 Sunset Blvd., #448, Los Angeles CA 90046. Phone/fax: (213)654-7674. E-mail: the deep6co@aol.com. Contact: Mark James. Record company, music publisher (Whatever Music/BMI) and record producer (King James, Ltd.). Estab. 1995. Releases 4 singles, 2-4 LPs and 2-4 CDs/year. Pays negotiable royalty to artists on contract; statutory rate to publisher per song on record.
How to Contact: Write first and obtain permission to submit. Prefers cassette with 3-4 songs and lyric sheet (if available). Does not return material. Reports in 6-8 weeks.
Music: Mostly **commercial/alternative**, **modern rock** and **roots**. Released *Used* (by B. Small), recorded by The Hangmen (rock); *Sin Factory*, written and recorded by Kim Salmon and Surrealists (rock); and *Maxfield Rabbit*, written and recorded by Maxfield Rabbit, all on Deep Six Records.
Tips: "We also license masters from other territories for U.S. release."

*DEF BEAT RECORDS, 38 Cassis Dr., Etobicoke M9V 4Z6 **Canada**. (416)746-6205. Fax: (416)586-0853. President: Dalbert Myrie. A&R: Junior Smith. Labels include Worrel Productions, Myrie Associates Labels and DBR Records. Record company, music publisher (De La Musique Publishing, M.A.L. Music Publishing), record producer (Dalbert Myrie, D. Fresh) and management company (DBR Management). Estab. 1986. Releases 12 singles, 4 LPs, 3 EPs and 10 CDs/year. Pays negotiable royalty to artists on contract; ¾ statutory rate to publisher per song on record.
How to Contact: Write or call first and obtain permission to submit. Prefers cassette or VHS videocassette. SASE. Reports in 6 weeks.
Music: Mostly **soul**, **R&B**, **hip-hop** and **dance**; also **reggae**, **Euro** and **house**. Released *2-Versatile*, written and recorded by 2-Versatile; *Smooth & Soft*, written and recorded by Gentlemen X; and *Respect My Boundary*, written and recorded by D.M.W., all on Def Beat Records. Other artists include Mercia Bunting, Afterlife, MiC'N Gz Crew, D. Fresh, D'S Girls, Black Chrome, JC and Raynaldo.
Tips: "Make sure your contact lists are updated on a regular basis. Make sure when you are submitting a tape (songs), it is the best representation of your work."

DEJADISC, INC., P.O. Box 788, San Marcos TX 78667-0788. (512)392-6610. Fax: (512)754-6886. Director of Product Development: Steve Wilkison. Record company. Estab. 1992. Releases 6 LPs and 6 CDs/year. Pays 10-12% royalty to artists on contract; statutory rate to publisher per song on record.
How to Contact: Submit demo tape by mail. Unsolicited submissions are OK. Prefers cassette or VHS videocassette with 5-10 songs and lyric sheet. "Keep it simple and be neat." Does not return material. Reports in 1-2 months.
Music: Mostly **folk**, **rock** and **country**. Released *Love & Trust*, written and recorded by Michael Fracasso (folk); *Brand New Ways*, written and recorded by Don McCalister (country); and *Trashman Shoes* (by Slattery/Kassens), recorded by Shoulders (rock), all on Dejadisc Records. Other artists include David Rodriguez, Elliott Murphy, Sarah Elizabeth Campbell, Lisa Mednick and Coffee Sergeants.
Tips: "Our focus is primarily devoted to folk, singer-songwriter, country and rock recordings. We look for strong, unique and original songwriters."

DEMI MONDE RECORDS AND PUBLISHING, LTD., Foel Studio, Llanfair Caereinion, Powys, Wales, **United Kingdom**. Phone/fax: (01938)810758. Managing Director: Dave Anderson. Record company and music publisher (Demi Monde Records & Publishing, Ltd.) and record producer (Dave Anderson). Estab. 1983. Releases 5 12" singles, 10 LPs and 6 CDs/year. Pays 10% royalty to artists on contract; statutory rate to publisher per song on record.
  ● See their listings in the Music Publishers and Record Producers sections.
How to Contact: Submit demo tape by mail. Unsolicited submissions are OK. Prefers cassette with 3-4 songs. SAE and IRC. Reports in 6 weeks.
Music: **Rock**, **R&B** and **pop**. Released *Hawkwind*, *Amon Duul II & Gong* and *Groundhogs* (by T.S. McPhee), all on Demi Monde Records.

DIGITALIA RECORDS, 480 Valley Rd., Suite B11, Montclair NJ 07043-1855. (201)746-9500. Vice President/A&R: Charles Farley. Record company and record producer. Estab. 1992. Releases 10 12" singles/year. Pays 10% royalty to artists on contract; statutory rate to publisher per song on record.
How to Contact: Submit demo tape by mail. Unsolicited submissions are OK. Prefers cassette (or VHS videocassette) with 2-3 songs and lyric sheet. Reports in 5 weeks.
Music: **Rap** and **dance**. Released "Joo Ought To Know, Mang," written and recorded by Hector from East 177; "Elephant Ears," written and recorded by Sneak (rap); and "Nod Ya Head," written and recorded by Dirt Money, all on Digitalia Records.

Tips: "Research what the components of a hit record are *before* you submit. Learn the difference between a good song and good record."

*DIRECT RECORDS, INC., P.O. Box 8205, Chicago IL 60680 or 600 Pickard West, Mt. Pleasant MI 48858. (800)770-6792. Contact: A&R Department. Labels include B.D.A. Independent music distributor. Estab. 1994. Releases 5-10 singles, 5-7 LPs and 5-7 CDs/year. Pays negotiable rate to artists on contract and to publisher per song on record.
How to Contact: Submit demo tape by mail. Unsolicited submissions are OK. Prefers cassette, CDs or albums. "Should be a complete promo package including release, photos, bios, etc." Does not return material. Reports in 4-6 weeks.
Music: All styles. Released *Another Roadside Attraction* (by Dan Davis), recorded by Pablo's Dog on Pablo's Dog Records (alternative); *Picture This*, written and recorded by Ray Dunn (folk rock); and *Just Beginning*, written and recorded by George Feith (country), both on B.D.A. Records.
Tips: "Always look for opportunities to sell and distribute your music. Exposure is the key to creating interest in your music."

DMT RECORDS, 11714-113th Ave., Edmonton Alberta T5G 0J8 **Canada**. (403)454-6848. Fax: (403)454-9291. E-mail: dmt@ccinet.ab.ca. A&R: Gerry Dere. President: Danny Makarus. Record company, music publisher (La Nash Publishing/Danny Makarus Music) and record producer (Gerry Derre). Estab. 1986. Releases 4 singles, 3-6 LPs, 1 EP and 3-6 CDs/year. Pays negotiable royalty to artists on contract; negotiated rate to publishers per song on record.
How to Contact: Submit demo tape by mail. Unsolicited submissions are OK. Prefers cassette with 4 songs and lyric sheet. Does not return material. Reports in 1 month (if interested).
Music: Mostly **country, pop-soft rock** and **MOR**. Released "Darlin When I'm Gone" (by D. Larabie), recorded by 5 Wheel Drive (country); "Gotta Get Back" (by K. Repkow), recorded by High Park (rock); and *North American Breed* (by B. Cree/D. Cree), recorded by Rising Cree (ethnic), all on DMT Records.
Tips: "Our mainstay is today's country music—we are interested in mainstream country music."

*DON'T RECORDS, P.O. Box 11513, Milwaukee WI 53211. (414)224-9023. Fax: (414)224-8021. E-mail: dont@execpc.com. VP of A&R: Joe Vent. Record company. Estab. 1991. Releases 6 LPs/year. Pays negotiable royalty to artists on contract; statutory rate to publisher per song on record.
How to Contact: Submit demo tape by mail. Unsolicited submissions are OK. Prefers cassette. "Send studio quality material." Does not return material. Reports in 2 months.
Music: Mostly **pop/rock** and **alternative**; also **polka**. Released *Upstroke for Downfolk*, written and recorded by Paul Cebar & The Milwaukeeans (pop); *Star of Desire* (by Scott & Brian Wooldridge), recorded by Wooldridge Brothers (pop); and *Gag Me with Spoon*, written and recorded by various (pop), all on Don't Records. Other artists include Pet Engine and Yell Leaders.
Tips: "Play a lot and be selling your own release when you send us material."

DRAG CITY, INC., P.O. Box 476867, Chicago IL 60647. (312)455-1015. President: Daniel Koretzky. Labels include Sea Note. Record company. Estab. 1989. Releases 10 singles, 10 LPs, 5 EPs and 10 CDs/year. Pays 50/50 profit split.
How to Contact: Submit demo tape by mail. Unsolicited submissions are OK. Prefers cassette. Does not return material. Does not report back on submissions "unless we're interested."
Music: Mostly **rock** and **country**. Released "Back to School," recorded by Royal Trux; *Julius Caesar*, recorded by Smog; and *Funny Farm*, recorded by King Kong, all on Drag City. Other artists include The Red Crayola, Palace Brothers, The Silver Jews, Mantis, Burnout, Gastr del Sol and Hot Toasters.

*DRIVE ENTERTAINMENT, 10351 Santa Monica Blvd., Los Angeles CA 90025. (310)553-3490. Fax: (310)553-3373. E-mail: drive@earthlink.net. President: Don Grierson. Labels include Drive Archive. Record company and music publisher (Drive Music, Donunda Music). Estab. 1992. Releases 50 LPs and 50 CDs/year. Pays negotiable royalty to artists on contract; statutory rate to publisher per song on record.
• See the listing for Drive Music in the Music Publishers section.
How to Contact: Submit demo tape by mail. Unsolicited submissions are OK. Prefers cassette and DAT with 3 songs and lyric sheet. SASE. Reports in 4 weeks.

● **A BULLET** introduces comments by the editor of *Songwriter's Market* indicating special information about the listing.

Music: Mostly **pop**, **rock** and **Triple A**; also **dance**. Released *Night Ranger*, written and recorded by Night Ranger on Drive Entertinment (rock); *House Of Love*, written and recorded by various on VRG Records (dance); and *Drop Till You Dance*, written and recorded by various on Big Fish Records (dance).

*EARTH FLIGHT PRODUCTIONS, P.O. Box 158, Poughquaq NY 12570. Fax: (914)724-3739. E-mail: earthflight@delphi.com. Head of A&R: Craig Peyton. Record company. Estab. 1990. Releases 2 LPs and 2 CDs/year. Pays negotiable royalty to artists on contract; statutory rate to publisher per song on record.
How to Contact: Submit demo tape by mail. Unsolicited submissions are OK. Prefers cassette. Does not return material. Reports in 2 months.
Music: Mostly **acid jazz**, **fusion jazz** and **contemporary jazz**; also **instrumental world**. Released *Latitude One*, recorded by Latitude (AA); *Tropical Escape* and *The Web*, both recorded by Craig Peyton (acid/jazz), all on Earth Flight Records.
Tips: "Please only submit material if you have an established track record and understand the indie market."

EARTHTONE/SONIC IMAGES, P.O. Box 691626, W. Hollywood CA 90069. (213)650-1000. Fax: (213)650-1016. E-mail: brad@sonicimages.com. Director of A&R: Brad Pressman. Record company. Estab. 1991. Releases 3 singles and 11 CDs/year. Pays negotiable royalty to artists on contract; statutory rate to publisher per song on record.
How to Contact: Submit demo tape by mail. Unsolicited submissions are OK. Prefers DAT or CD (for finished product deals) with 5 songs. Does not return material. Reports in 3 weeks.
Music: Mostly **ambient/world**. Artists include Christopher Franke, Shadowfax, Mercs, Mark Shreve and Solar System.
Tips: "Make it easy on us. Send me a DAT or CD and let me know if it is a finished album deal or if recording funds are necessary. Looking for Flamenco guitar music à la 'B-Tribe.' Finished masters are certainly welcome."

EASTERN FRONT RECORDS, INC., 7 Curve St., Medfield MA 02052. (508)359-8003. Fax: (508)359-8090. E-mail: eastfront1@aol.com. Vice President: Robert Swalley. Record company and music publisher (Eastern Front Publishing). Estab. 1991. Releases 4-6 LPs and 4-6 CDs/year. Pays negotiable royalty to artists on contract; statutory rate to publisher per song on record.
● Eastern Front Records, Inc. is distributed nationally by Distribution North America (DNA).
How to Contact: Call first and obtain permission to submit a demo. Prefers cassette or DAT with 3 songs and lyric sheet. "Lyrics matter. If we accept the submission, we expect the artist/management to provide press kit and photo. Artist should feel free to call us to follow up—we are e-mail friendly!" Does not return material. Reports in 1-2 months.
Music: Mostly **rock/pop**, **contemporary folk** and **acoustic singer/songwriters**. Released *Stranger to This Land*, written and recorded by Barbara Kessler; *Singing For the Landlord*, written and recorded by Greg Greenway; and *Little Town*, written and recorded by Kevin Connolly, all on Eastern Front Records. Others artists include Martin Sexton and Peter Mulvey.
Tips: "Be prepared to put in hard work including touring. Lyrics matter—not expecting full production demo but we expect a well recorded vocal and a well thought-out representation of the material. Distinctive vocals a major plus!"

*ELASTIC RECORDS, P.O. Box 17598, Anaheim CA 92817. (714)772-6547. Owner: Amin Ghashghai. Record company. Estab. 1990. Releases 3 singles and 2 CDs/year. Pays negotiable royalty to artists on contract.
How to Contact: Submit demo tape by mail. Unsolicited submissions are OK. Prefers cassette, DAT, VHS videocassette, LP or CD. Does not return material.
Music: Mostly **rock** and **punk**. Released *Here, There and Nowhere*, written and recorded by Milestone (punk); "School Lunch Victim," written and recorded by Enemy (punk); and "Don't Bother Knockin," written and recorded by Fu Manchu (rock), all on Elastic Records. Other artists include Virginia's Scrapings, Stranger Death 19, Loco, Hedgerod and Pale.

*ELEKTRA ENTERTAINMENT GROUP, 345 N. Maple Dr., Beverly Hills CA 90210. (310)288-3814. Fax: (310)274-9491. Director of A&R: Lara Hill. Record company.
How to Contact: Submit demo tape by mail. Unsolicited submisssions are OK. Prefers cassette or DAT with 3 songs. Does not return material. Reports in 3 months.
Music: Mostly **alternative/modern rock**. Released *Tigerlily*, recorded by Natalie Merchant; *New Beginning*, recorded by Tracy Chapman; and *Black Love*, recorded by Afghan Whigs, all on Elektra Entertainment.

EMA MUSIC INC., P.O. Box 91683, Washington DC 20090-1683. (202)319-1688. Fax: (202)575-1774. President: Jeremiah N. Murphy. Director of Promotions: Benjamin R. Stukes. Record company.

Estab. 1993. Releases 2 LPs and 2 CDs/year. Pays statutory rate to publisher per song on record.
How to Contact: Submit demo tape by mail. Prefers cassette with lyric or lead sheet. "Do not call." SASE. Reports in 3 months.
Music: Mostly **gospel** and **contemporary Christian**. Released *Just Jesus* (by M. Brown); *I Must* (by J. Murphy); and *Blessed Assurance* (by P. Crosby), all recorded by J. Murphy on EMA Records (gospel).

EMERALD CITY RECORDS, P.O. Box 26341, Dayton OH 45426. (513)837-4854. Fax: (513)837-2327. President: Jack Froschauer. Creative Director: Chris Tanner. Record company. Estab. 1992. Pays negotiable royalty to artists on contract; statutory rate to publisher per song on record.
• Emerald City's publishing company, Barren Wood Publishing, is listed in the Music Publishers section.
How to Contact: Submit demo tape by mail. Unsolicited submissions are OK. Prefers cassette or DAT with 1-4 songs and lyric or lead sheet. "If sending cassette, studio quality please." SASE. Reports in 4-6 weeks.
Music: Mostly **A/C**, **country** and **contemporary Christian**. Released "I've Got the Lord In Me" (by David Schafer), recorded by David Schafer with Stephen Seifert (gospel); "Come Out From the Storm" (by Kent Pritchard), recorded by Kent Pritchard & God's Will (rock); and "Goochee Goochee" (by Jack Froschauer), recorded by Cadillac Jack & the Reel-Time All-Stars, all on Emerald City Records.

*EMF PRODUCTIONS, 1000 E. Prien Lake Rd., Lake Charles LA 70601. Phone/fax: (318)474-0435. Owner: Ed Fruge. Record company and record producer. Estab. 1977. Releases 3 singles, 3 LPs and 3 CDs/year. Pays negotiable royalty to artists on contract; statutory rate to publisher per song on record.
• See their listing in the Music Publishers section.
How to Contact: Submit demo tape by mail. Unsolicited submissions are OK. Prefers cassette and lyric sheet. Does not return material. Reports in 6 weeks.
Music: Mostly **pop**, **R&B** and **country**.

EPIC RECORDS, 550 Madison Ave., New York NY 10022. (212)833-8000. This record company prefers not to share information.

ESB RECORDS, P.O. Box 6429, Huntington Beach CA 92615-6429. (714)962-5618. Executive Producers: Eva and Stan Bonn. Record company, music publisher (Bonnfire Publishing/ASCAP, Gather' Round/BMI) and record producer (ESB Records). Estab. 1987. Releases 1 single, 1 LP and 1 CD/year. Pays negotiable royalty to artists; pays statutory rate to publisher per song on record.
• ESB's publishing affiliate, Bonnfire Publishing, is listed in the Music Publishers section.
How to Contact: Submit demo tape by mail. Unsolicited submissions are OK. SASE. Reports in 1 month.
Music: Country, all formats. Released "Toe Tappin Country Man" (by Jack Schroeder), recorded by John P. Swissholm; "She's Just a Dreamer" (by Jim Weaver/Bobby Lee Caldwell) and "Sounds of the Universe" (by Stan Bonn/Eddie Sheppard), both recorded by Bobby Lee Caldwell, all on ESB Records (country).
Tips: "Be worldwide and commercial in lyrics. Be professional in all aspects of the music industry."

ETHEREAN MUSIC/VARIENA PUBLISHING, 9200 W. Cross Ave., #510, Littleton CO 80123. (303)973-8291. Fax: (303)973-8499. E-mail: etherean@aol.com. Contact: A&R Department. Labels include Elation Artists, Native Spirit, EM Pop. Record company and music publisher. Estab. 1979. Releases 4-10 CDs/year. Royalty negotiable.
How to Contact: Submit demo tape by mail. Unsolicited submissions are OK. Prefers cassette (or VHS videocassette if available) with all songs and lyric or lead sheet; include photo and tearsheets. "Must include on package, 'unsolicited materials enclosed'." SASE. Reports in 3 months.
Music: Mostly **New Age/ethnic**, **jazz/contemporary** and **instrumental/world**; also **pop**. Released *Night Fire* (by various), recorded by Bryan Savage on Elation Artists Records; *Sons of Somerlied*, written and recorded by Steve McDonald; and *In the Presence of Angels*, written and recorded by Dik Darrell, both on Etherean Records. Other artists include Denean, Kenny Passarelli and Laura Theodore.

 THE ASTERISK before a listing indicates that the listing is new in this edition. New markets are often the most receptive to unsolicited submissions.

FACTORY BEAT RECORDS, INC., 521 Fifth Ave., New York NY 10175. (212)757-3638. A&R Director: Rena L. Romano. Labels include R&R, Ren Rom and Can Scor Productions, Inc. Record company, record producer and music publisher (Ren Maur Music Corp.). Releases 4 12" singles and 2 LPs/year. Pays 10% royalty to artists on contract; statutory rate to publisher for each record sold.
• Factory Beat's publishing company, Ren Maur Music Corp., is listed in the Music Publishers section.
How to Contact: Submit demo tape by mail. Unsolicited submissions are OK. Prefers cassette with 4 songs and lead sheet. SASE. Reports in 1 month. "Do not phone—we will return material."
Music: Mostly **R&B**, **pop rock** and **country**; also **gospel**. Released *Mama's Baby, South of the Border* and *Make My Day* (by B. Nichols), all recorded by Lucia Rena on Factory Beat Records.

FAME AND FORTUNE ENTERPRISES, P.O. Box 121679, Nashville TN 37212. (615)244-4898. Producers: Jim Cartwright and Scott Turner. Labels include Fame and Fortune Records and National Foundation Records. Record company, music publisher (Pitchin' Hits Music/BMI) and record producer. Estab. 1976. Releases 6 singles, 6 LPs and 6 CDs/year. Pays statutory rate to publisher per song on record.
How to Contact: Submit demo tape by mail. Unsolicited submissions are OK. Prefers cassette (or VHS videocassette) with 4 songs and lyric sheet. SASE (with correct postage). Reports in 6-10 weeks.
Music: Mostly **country, MOR, med. rock, contemporary Christian, gospel** and **pop**. Released "Rise Above It," (by Steve Rose), recorded by Brittany Hale on GBS Records (country); "The Mule Jumped Over the Moon" (by Bobbe Sullivan), recorded by Bonnie Lou Bishop; and "Innocent Til Proven Lonely" (by Shayne Vaughn), recorded by A.J. Stone, both on Fame & Fortune Records. Other artists include Angel Connell, Chuck Lohmann, Arden Gatlin, Rudy Parris, Julie Carter and Marty James.
Tips: "We have expanded our company and now have Fame & Fortune Management (artist development and management). Potential artists *must have* financial backers in place. Contact Jim Cartwright."

FAT CITY ARTISTS, 1906 Chet Atkins Place, Suite 502, Nashville TN 37212. (615)320-7678. Fax: (615)321-5382. Vice President: Rusty Michael. Record company, music publisher (Fort Forever/BMI), record producer (Creative Communications Workshop) and booking agency (Fat City Artists). Estab. 1972. Releases 4-6 singles, 4-6 LPs, 4-6 EPs and 4-6 CDs/year. Pays 12-15% royalty to artist on contract for demo work; statutory rate to publisher per song on record.
• See their listing in the Managers and Booking Agents section, as well as the listing for Fat City Publishing in the Music Publishers section.
How to Contact: Submit demo tape by mail. Unsolicited submissions are OK. Prefers cassette (or VHS videocassette) with 4-6 songs and lyric sheet. SASE. Reports in 6 weeks.
Music: Mostly **rock, country** and **blues**; also **alternative, rockabilly** and **jazz**.
Tips: "Provide us with as much information as you can with regard to your material and act and we will provide you with an evaluation as soon as possible. Our advertising/promotion division specializes in developing effective artist promotional packages, including demos, videos, video press kits, photography and copy. We will evaluate your present promotional material at no cost."

FEARLESS RECORDS, P.O. Box 11111, Whittier CA 90603-0111. (310)946-9766. E-mail: mmroch @ix.netcom.com or mjmspike@aol.com. A&R Directors: Steve James or Michael Joseph. Record company, music publisher (Shelf Music/BMI) and record producer. Estab. 1990. Releases 5 LPs and 2 CDs/year. Pays 15% royalty to artists on contract; statutory rate to publisher per song on record.
How to Contact: Submit demo tape by mail. Unsolicited submissions are OK. Prefers cassette or CD with 4 songs and lyric sheet. Does not return material. Reports in 3 months.
Music: Mostly **country, pop** and **punk rock**.

FICTION SONGS, 1540 Broadway, 39th Floor, New York NY 10036. (212)930-4910. Fax: (212)930-4736. E-mail: jdloveless@aol.com. Director A&R: Jonathan Daniel. Record company and music publisher. Estab. 1977.
How to Contact: Submit demo tape by mail. Unsolicited submissions are OK. Prefers cassette. Does not return material.
Music: Mostly **alternative** and **rock**. Artists include The Cure, Primitive Radio Gods, NY Loose, God Machine and Weknowwhereyoulive.

*FINK-PINEWOOD RECORDS, P.O. Box 5241, Chesapeake VA 23324. (804)627-0957. Labels include Bay Port Records. Record company. Estab. 1954.
How to Contact: Submit demo tape by mail. Unsolicited submissions are OK. Prefers cassette with 2 songs. SASE. Reports in 3 weeks.
Music: Mostly **soul-blues** and **soul-gospel**.
Tips: "Try to work with a growing small label, one that is unknown with commercial broadcasting media!"

*FIREANT, 2009 Ashland Ave., Charlotte NC 28205. Phone/fax: (704)335-1400. E-mail: fireants@ao l.com. Website: http://kiwi.futuris.net/mabels/fireant.html. Owner: Lew Herman. Record company, music publisher (Fireant Music) and record producer (Lew Herman). Estab. 1990. Releases 3 CDs/year. Pays negotiable royalty to artists on contract; statutory royalty to publisher per song on record.
How to Contact: Submit demo tape by mail. Unsolicited submissions are OK. Prefers cassette, DAT or videocassette. Does not return material.
Music: "Anything except New Age and MOR. No disco, either." Mostly **progressive, traditional** and **musical hybrids**. Published *Pachuco Cadaver* (by Don Van Vliet), recorded by Eugene Chadbourne/Jimmy Carl Black (pop/jazz/folk/blues); *Dancing With Daddy G* (traditional/arranged by the Tigers), recorded by the Tigers (gospel); and *Ready to Roll* (traditional), recorded by Red Hots (traditional/country), all on Fireant. Other artists include Mr. Peters' Belizian Boom and Chime Band.

FIRST TIME RECORDS, Sovereign House, 12 Trewartha Rd., Praa Sands, Penzance, Cornwall TR20 9ST **England**. (01736)762826. Fax: (01736)763328. Managing Director A&R: Roderick G. Jones. Labels include Pure Gold Records, Rainy Day Records and Mohock Records. Registered members of Phonographic Performance Ltd. (PPL). Record company and music publisher (First Time Music Publishing U.K. Ltd./MCPS/PRS) and record producer (First Time Management & Production Co.). Estab. 1986. Royalty to artists on contract varies; pays statutory rate to publisher per song on record subject to deal.
  ● See the listings for First Time Music Publishing in the Music Publishers section and First Time Management in the Managers and Booking Agents section.
How to Contact: Prefers cassette with unlimited number of songs and lyric or lead sheets, but not necessary. SAE and IRC. Reports in 1-3 months.
Music: Mostly **country/folk, pop/soul/top 20** and **country with an Irish/Scottish crossover**; also **gospel/Christian** and **HI NRG/dance**. Released *Songwriters and Artistes Compilation Volume III*, on Rainy Day Records; "The Drums of Childhood Dreams," written and recorded by Pete Arnold on Mohock Records (folk); and *The Light and Shade of Eddie Blackstone*, written and recorded by Eddie Blackstone on T.W. Records (country).
Tips: "Writers should learn patience, tolerance and understanding of how the music industry works, and should present themselves and their product in a professional manner and always be polite. Listen to constructive criticism and learn from the advice of people who have a track record in the music business. Your first impression may be the only chance you get, so it is advisable to get it right from the start."

*FLIP RECORDS, 433 W. Broadway, New York NY 10012. (212)925-2527. Fax: (212)925-2507. President: S. Jordan Schur. Record company. Estab. 1994. Releases 6 singles, 4-6 LPs, 1-2 EPs and 4-6 CDs/year. Pays 6-12% royalty to artists on contract.
How to Contact: Submit demo tape by mail. Unsolicited submissions are OK. Prefers cassette. Does not return material. Reports in 2 weeks.
Music: Mostly **alternative**. Released *Big Hate* (by B. Stanger), recorded by Big Hate (alternative); and *La Vista Hotheads* (by G. Uhlenbrock), recorded by La Vista Hotheads (alternative), both on Flip Records.
Tips: "Have a hard, unique, fat sound."

FLYING HEART RECORDS, Dept. SM, 4026 NE 12th Ave., Portland OR 97212. (503)287-8045. Owner: Jan Celt. Record company. Estab. 1982. Releases 2 LPs and 1 EP/year. Pays variable royalty to artists on contract; negotiable rate to publisher per song on record.
  ● See the listing for Jan Celt in the Record Producers section.
How to Contact: Submit a demo tape by mail. Unsolicited submissions are OK. Prefers cassette with 1-10 songs and lyric sheets. Does not return material. "SASE required for *any* response." Reports in 3 months.
Music: Mostly **R&B, blues** and **jazz**; also **rock**. Released "Get Movin" and "Down Mexico Way" (by Chris Newman), recorded by Napalm Beach (rock); and "Which One Of You People" (by Jan Celt), recorded by The Esquires (R&B), all on Flying Heart Records. Other artists include Janice Scroggins, Tom McFarland, Obo Addy, Snow Bud and The Flower People.
Tips: "Express your true feelings with creative originality and show some imagination. Use high quality cassette for best sound."

FOUNTAIN RECORDS, P.O. Box 35005 AMC, Greensboro NC 27425. (910))882-9990. President: Doris W. Lindsay. Record company, music publisher (Better Times Publishing/BMI, Doris Lindsay Publishing/ASCAP) and record producer. Estab. 1979. Releases 3 singles and 1 LP/year. Pays 5% royalty to artists on contract; statutory rate to publisher per song on record.
  ● See the listing for Doris Lindsay Publishing in the Music Publishers section.
How to Contact: Submit demo tape by mail. Unsolicited submissions are OK. Prefers cassette with 2 songs and lyric sheets. SASE. Reports in 2 months.

Music: Mostly **country, pop** and **gospel**. Released *Two Lane Life* (by D. Lindsay), recorded by Mitch Snow; "Grandma Bought A Harley" (by S. Rosario), recorded by Glenn Mayo; *Service Station Cowboy* (by Hoss Ryder), recorded by David Johnson, all on Fountain Records.
Tips: "Have a professional demo and include phone and address on cassette."

FRESH ENTERTAINMENT, 1315 Simpson Rd. NW, Suite 5, Atlanta GA 30314. (404)642-2645. Vice President, Marketing/A&R: Willie Hunter. Record company and music publisher (Hserf Music/ ASCAP, Blair Vizzion Music/BMI). Releases 5 singles and 2 LPs/year. Pays 7-10% royalty to artists on contract; statutory rate to publisher per song on record.
  • See their listing in the Music Publishers section.
How to Contact: Submit demo tape by mail. Unsolicited submissions are OK. Prefers cassette (or VHS videocassette) with at least 3 songs and lyric sheet. SASE. Reports in 4-6 weeks.
Music: Mostly **R&B, rock** and **pop**; also **jazz, gospel** and **rap**. Released "Nasty Dancer," "Mega Mix" and "Donkey Kung" (by Taz/Kilo), all recorded by Kilo on Ichiban Records. Other artists include Chris Gantt, DJ Taz, Jimmy Calhoun, Charles Pettaway, Cirocco, McIntosh and Vivian Memefee.
Tips: "Be creative in packaging material."

FULLMOON ENTERTAINMENT/MOONSTONE RECORDS, 3030 Andrita St., Los Angeles CA 90065. (213)341-5959. Fax: (213)341-5960. Contact: A&R Dept. Record company and music publisher (Talex Music/BMI, Terror Tunes/ASCAP). Estab. 1991. Releases 8 CDs/year. Pays negotiable royalty to artists on contract.
How to Contact: Submit demo tape by mail. Unsolicited submissions are OK. Prefers cassette (or VHS-NTSC videocassette) with 3-5 songs and lyric sheet. SASE. Reports in 1 month.
Music: Mostly **hard rock, rock** and **alternative/dance**; also **pop** and **blues**. Released *Bad Channels* (by Blue Oyster Cult); "Pain" (by Rhino Bucket); and *Terrified*, written and recorded by Quiet Riot, all on Moonstone Records. Other artists include David Arkenstone and Pino Donnagio.
Tips: "Your songs must be competitive (in content and presentation) with the best writers out there. We are a film and record company and work with only the best—the best old pros and the best new comers."

GEFFEN/DGC RECORDS, 9130 Sunset Blvd., Los Angeles CA 90069-6197. (310)278-9010. This record company prefers not to share information.

GENERAL BROADCASTING SERVICE (GBS Records), 203 Gates Dr., Hendersonville TN 37075-4961. (615)826-2605. Fax: (615)826-2607. Owner/producer: Ernie Bivens. Labels include Nashville American, Chory International, Kingford Records. Record company, music publisher (GBS Music/SESAC, Bivens Music/BMI), record producer (Ernie Bivens) and promotions company. Pays standard royalty for artists on contract; statutory rate to publishers per song on record.
How to Contact: Submit demo tape by mail. Unsolicited submissions are OK. Prefers "any format" tape with 2-4 songs and lyric sheet. Does not return material. Reports in 2-4 weeks.
Music: Mostly **country (all types)**, **gospel** and **southern rock**. Released "Country's Cool," written and recorded by Carl Freberg; "Too Late For The Show" (by Ernie Bivens), recorded by David Chamberlain; and "Tell Me Tell Me True" (by Karen Donovan), recorded by G. Shuman/B. Kelly, all on GBS Records. Other artists include Brittany Hale, Dallas Morris, Janis Leigh, Melba Montgomery and Karen Donovan.

GENERIC RECORDS, INC., 433 Limestone Rd., Ridgefield CT 06877. (203)438-9811. President: Gary Lefkowith. Labels include Outback, GLYN. Record company, music publisher (Sotto Music/ BMI) and record producer. Estab. 1976. Releases 1-2 singles, 1-2 12″ singles, 1 LP and 1 CD/year. Pays 5% royalty to artists on contract; statutory rate to publisher per song on record.
How to Contact: Call for permission to submit a demo. Prefers cassette with 2-3 songs. SASE. Reports in 4 weeks.
Music: Mostly **alternative rock, rock** and **pop**; also **country** and **rap**. Released *Disconnected* and *Hi fi*, both recorded by Hi fi.
Tips: "Concentrate on making the music great. Everything else will fall into place if you're in the groove."

GLOBAL PACIFIC RECORDS/BLACKHORSE ENTERTAINMENT, 1275 E. MacArthur St., Sonoma CA 95476. (707)996-2748. Fax: (707)996-2658. A&R Director: Howard Sapper. Record

---

THE TYPES OF MUSIC each listing is interested in are printed in boldface.

company and music publisher (Global Pacific Publishing). Releases 10 singles, 12 LPs and 12 CDs/year.

How to Contact: Call first and obtain permission to submit. Prefers cassette with 3 songs. "Note style of music on envelope." Does not return material. Reports in 3 months.

Music: Mostly **New Age, pop, jazz, alternative rock** and "**pop/quiet storm**;" also **classical**. Artists include Bob Kindler, David Friesen, Georgia Kelly, Ben Tavera King, Paul Greaver, Morgan Fisher, Steve Kindler and Charles Michael Brotman.

Tips: "Write us a hit! Know your label and market you are targeting."

GOLD CITY RECORDS, INC., 10 Deepwell Farms Rd., S. Salem NY 10540. (914)533-5096. Fax: (914)533-5097. President: Chris Jasper. Vice President/General Counsel: Margie Jasper. Labels include Gold City Label. Record company. Estab. 1986. Releases 5-10 singles, 5-10 12″ singles, 3-5 LPs and 3-5 CDs/year. Pays statutory rate to publisher per song on record.

How to Contact: Submit demo tape by mail. Unsolicited submissions are OK. Prefers cassette with 3 songs and lyric sheets. SASE. Reports in 4-6 weeks.

Music: Mostly **R&B/gospel**. Released *Praise The Eternal* and *Deep Inside*, written and recorded by Chris Jasper; and *Outfront*, written and recorded by Outfront, all on Gold City Records.

GOLDEN TRIANGLE RECORDS, 1051 Saxonburg Blvd., Glenshaw PA 15116. Producer: Sunny James. Labels include Rockin Robin and Shell-B. Music publisher (Golden Triangle/BMI) and record producer (Sunny James). Estab. 1987. Releases 8 singles, 6 12″ singles, 10 LPs and 19 CDs/year. Pays 10% royalty to artists on contract; statutory rate to publishers per song on record.

● See the listing for Sunny James in the Record Producers section.

How to Contact: Submit demo tape by mail. Unsolicited submissions are OK. Prefers cassette, 15 IPS reel-to-reel (or ½″ VHS videocassette) with 3 songs and lyric or lead sheets. SASE. Reports in 1 month.

Music: Mostly **progressive R&B, rock** and **A/C**; also **jazz** and **country**. Released "Astor" (by S. Bittner), recorded by P. Bittner on Shell-B Records (rock); "Those No's" (by R. Cvetnick), recorded by J. Morello on Rockin Robin Records (R&B); and "Most of All" (by F. Johnson), recorded by The Marcels on Golden Triangle Records (A/C). Other artists include The original Mr. Bassman Fred Johnson of the Marcels (Blue Moon).

GRACELAND ENTERTAINMENT, (formerly Frontline Music Group), Box 28450, Santa Ana CA 92799-8450. Contact: Kenny Hicks. Labels include Frontline Records, MYX Records, Graceland Records, Alarma Records. Record company, music publisher (Broken Songs/ASCAP, Carlotta Music/BMI). Estab. 1985. Releases 30 CDs/year. Pays statutory rate to publisher per song on record.

● See the listing for Frontline Music Group in the Music Publishers section.

How to Contact: Submit demo tape by mail. Unsolicited submissions are OK. Prefers cassette (or VHS videocassette) with 3-4 songs and typed lyric sheet. Does not return material. "We only reply on those of interest—but if you've not heard from us within 1-2 months we're not interested."

Music: Mostly **gospel/contemporary/Christian, rock/pop** and **R&B**; also **worship** and **praise**. Released "Light of Love" (by Steve Harvey/Gary Brown), recorded by Angie and Debbie Winans on Frontline Records (R&B); *Get On Up* (by Blackwell/Massey/Dunn), recorded by Scott Blackwell on MYX Records (dance); and *Shine* (by Sprinkle/Sprinkle/Hunter/Barber), recorded by Poor Ol' Lou on Alarma Records (rock). Other artists include CMC's, Everyday Life, Gospel Gangstas.

Tips: "Put your best songs at the top of the tape. Submit a *brief* background/history. Listen to product on the label and try writing for a specific artist. Be professional; please don't hound the label with calls."

GRASS ROOTS RECORD & TAPE/LMI RECORDS, Box 532, Malibu CA 90265. (213)463-5998. President: Lee Magid. Record company, record producer, music publisher (Alexis/ASCAP, Marvelle/BMI, Lou-Lee/BMI) and management firm (Lee Magid Management Co.). Member AIMP, NARAS. Estab. 1967. Releases 4 LPs and 4 CDs/year. Pays 2-5% royalty to artists on contract; statutory rate to publishers per song on record.

● Grass Roots Record's publishing company, Alexis, is listed in the Music Publishers section, and President Lee Magid is listed in the Record Producers section.

How to Contact: Submit demo tape by mail. Unsolicited submissions are OK. Prefers cassette with 3 songs and lyric sheet. "Please, no 45s." Does not return material. Reports in 6-8 weeks.

Music: Mostly **pop/rock, R&B, country, gospel, jazz/rock** and **blues**; also **bluegrass, children's** and **Latin**. Released "Yours is a Mighty Hand" (by C. Rhone), recorded by Tramaine Hawkins on Sony Records (gospel); "He's Always There" (by J.M. Hides), recorded by Tata Vega on Quest Records (pop); and "It's Too Late," written and recorded by Zad. Other artists include John Michael Hides, Julie Miller.

GREEN BEAR RECORDS, Rockin' Chair Center Suite 103, 1033 W. State Highway 76, Branson MO 65616. (417)334-2383. Fax: (417)334-2306. President: George J. Skupien. Labels include Green One Records and Bear Tracks Records. Record company, music publisher (Green One Music/BMI), and record producer (George Skupien). Estab. 1992. Releases 3-4 singles, 1-10 LPs and 2-6 CDs/year. Pays 10% royalty to artists on contract; statutory rate to publisher per song on record.
• Green Bear's publishing company, Green One Music, is listed in the Music Publishers section.
How to Contact: Submit demo tape by mail. Unsolicited submissions are OK. Prefers cassette or DAT with 4-6 songs and lyric or lead sheet. Does not return material. Reports in 6-8 weeks.
Music: Mostly **polkas, waltzes** and **country**; also **Southern gospel, MOR** and **light rock**. Released "My Last Cowboy Song," written and recorded by George Skupien (country); "An American Tradition" (by George Skupien), recorded by The Stagemen (polka); and "Keep On Keepin' On," written and recorded by Matt Row'd (country), all on Green Bear Records. Other artists include D. Mack, B. Jackson, Ted Thomas, Rudy Negron and The Mystics.
Tips: "Submit a well-produced, studio quality demo of your material on cassette or DAT with a clean vocal up front. If possible, submit your demo with and without lead vocal for presentation to recording artists."

GREEN VALLEY RECORDS, P.O. Box 515, 314 S. Jasper St., Olney IL 62450. (618)395-1205 or (618)393-6426. President: Robert B. Britton. Record company and record producer. Estab. 1990. Releases 8-15 CDs/year. Pays 25% royalty to artists on contract; statutory rate to publisher per song on record.
How to Contact: Submit demo tape by mail. Unsolicited submissions are OK. Prefers cassette with 3-5 songs and lyric sheet. SASE. Reports in 3-4 weeks.
Music: Mostly **country, contemporary ballads** and **love songs** and **inspirational gospel**. Released *What Love Can Do*, written and recorded by Kathie Reece; and "Too Hot to Sleep," written and recorded by Stevie Raymon, both on Green Valley Records. Other artists include Nancy Steinman and Jamie Harper.

GUESTSTAR RECORDS, 17321 Ritchie Ave. NE, Sand Lake MI 49343-9475. President: Raymond G. Dietz, Sr. Record company, record producer and music publisher (Sandlake Music/BMI). Estab. 1967. Releases 8 singles, 2 LPs and 2 CDs/year. Royalty varies to artist on contract, "depending on number of selections on product; 2 ½¢/per record sold; statutory rate to publisher per song on record."
• See the listing for Guestar Entertainment Agency in the Managers and Booking Agents section.
How to Contact: Submit demo tape by mail. Unsolicited submissions are OK. Prefers cassette (or VHS videocassette) with lyric and lead sheet. "Send a SASE with submissions." Does not return material. Reports in 1 week.
Music: Mostly **country rock** and **country**; also **religious/country** and **mountain songs**. Released *Best of Mountain Man* (by Mike Gillette/Raymond Dietz); "Proud to be Your Boy" and "Back on the Job" (by Raymond Dietz), all recorded by Mountain Man on Gueststar Records (country). Other artists include Jamie "K" and Sweetgrass Band.
Tips: "Songwriters: send songs like you hear on the radio. Keep updating your music to keep up with the latest trends. Artists: send VHS video and press kit."

GUITAR RECORDINGS, 10 Midland Ave., Port Chester NY 10573. (914)935-5200. Fax: (914)937-0614. Contact: Label Director. Labels include Guitar Acoustic, Classic Cuts. Record company. Estab. 1989. Releases 4-6 cassettes and 4-6 CDs/year. Pays varying royalty to artists on contract.
How to Contact: Submit demo tape by mail. Unsolicited submissions are OK. Prefers cassette with 3 songs. Include bio, photo, press kit. Does not return material. Reports in 6 months.
Music: Mostly **rock, classic/blues** and **jazz/acoustic**; also **alternative**. Released *Any Road*, written and recorded by Randy Bachman; *Wood—Against The Grain* (by Mark Wood), recorded by Wood; and *Hairpick*, written and recorded by Blues Saraceno, all on Guitar Recordings (rock). Other artists include Brad Gillis.
Tips: "Submit your best (original) material, with no excuses! We send out rejection letters, so please do not call for an update on your demo."

HOW TO GET THE MOST out of *Songwriter's Market* (at the front of this book) contains comments and suggestions to help you understand and use the information in these listings.

HALLWAY INTERNATIONAL RECORDS/1ST COAST POSSE MIXES, 8017 International Village Dr., Jacksonville FL 32211. (904)765-8276. Record company, music publisher (Aljoni Music Co./BMI, Hallmarque Musical Works, Ltd./ASCAP), record producer (Hallways to Fame Productions) and video makers (Cosmic Eye). Estab. 1971. Releases 4-6 singles, 8 12″ singles and 6 LPs/year. Royalty negotiated per contract.

• Hallway International's publishing company, Aljoni Music, is listed in the Music Publishers section.

How to Contact: Submit demo tape by mail. Unsolicited submissions are OK. Prefers cassette (or VHS videocassette) with 2-4 songs and lyric or lead sheet. Does not return material. Reports in 6-8 weeks.

Music: Mostly **rap, R&B** and **jazz**; also **world** (others will be considered). Released "Upside Down Valentine" (by Ron "Cos" Hall), recorded by Da Hood Plus (rap) and "Runnin' 2 U" (by Maya D./Al Money), recorded by Maya D., both on 1st Coast Posse Records; and *All Hall* , written and recorded by Al Hall Jr. on Hallway International Records (world jazz). Other artists include Akshun Jaxon and GPH₂N.

Tips: "Rap, R&B-dance, jazz-world is what we do best—so, send your best and we'll do the rest!!"

HAMMERHEAD RECORDS, INC., 41 E. University Ave., Champaign IL 61820. (217)355-9052. Fax: (217)355-9057. E-mail: hammerhd@prairienet.org. Website: http://www.shout.net/~hammerhd/. A&R: Todd Thorstenson and Jeff Markland. Record company. Estab. 1993. Releases 4 CDs/year. Pays negotiable royalty to artists on contract; statutory rate to publisher per song on record.

How to Contact: Submit demo tape by mail. Unsolicited submissions are OK. Prefers cassette. "Include any press, bio, reviews, etc." Does not return material. Reports in 2 weeks.

Music: Mostly **rock—all forms**. Released *Chateau*, recorded by Free Range Chicken (psychosurf rock); "Better Off At Home" (by Jon Pheloung/Paul Colussi), recorded by The Bludgers (folk rock); and "Hack," written and recorded by Third Stone (hard rock), all on Hammerhead Records. Other artists include The Mess and Cain.

Tips: "We work very closely with all of our artists and greatly appreciate honesty and integrity."

HAPPY MAN RECORDS, Box 73, 4501 Spring Creek Dr., Bonita Springs FL 33923. (813)947-6978. Executive Producer: Dick O'Bitts. Labels include Condor, Con Air. Record company, music publisher (Rocker Music/BMI, Happy Man Music/ASCAP) and record producer (Rainbow Collection Ltd.). Estab. 1972. Releases 4-6 singles, 4-6 12″ singles, 4-6 LPs and 4 EPs/year. Pays negotiable royalty to artists on contract; statutory rate to publisher per song on record.

• Happy Man's publishing company, Rocker Music/Happy Man Music, can be found in the Music Publishers section.

How to Contact: Submit demo tape by mail. Unsolicited submissions are OK. Prefers cassette (or VHS videocassette) with 3-4 songs and lyric sheet. SASE. Reports in 4 weeks.

Music: All types. Released *Meet the Challengers* (by Dan Mitchell) and *Baby Here's The Key* (by Wallace/Skinner), both recorded by Challengers (country); *4 More For the Road*, written and recorded by Overdue (rock), all on Happy Man Records. Other artists include Ray Pack, Crosswinds, Carl Hallsman and Colt Gipson.

*HEATH & ASSOCIATES, E. Saint Catherine, #1058, Louisville KY 40204. (502)637-2877. General Partner: John V. Heath. Labels include Hillview Records and Estate Records. Record company, music publisher (Two John's Music/ASCAP) and record producer (MVT Productions and Just a Note/BMI). Estab. 1979. Releases 8-10 singles, 3 12″ singles, 4-5 LPs, 3 EPs and 3 CDs/year. Pays 10% royalty to artists on contract; statutory rate to publisher per song on record.

How to Contact: Submit demo tape by mail. Unsolicited submissions are OK. Prefers cassette, 7½ ips reel-to-reel or VHS videocassette with 3 songs and lead sheets. SASE. Reports in 2 weeks.

Music: Mostly **pop, country, R&B** and **MOR**; also **gospel**. Released "Dry Those Tears," written and recorded by Donald Dodd on Hillview Records (MOR); "Hot," written and recorded by The Word on Estate Records (gospel); and "Crazy Trucker," written and recorded by Michael Palko on Hillview Records (country). Other artists include Terry Burton, Moody and Louisville.

Tips: "Be professional in submissions."

HOT WINGS ENTERTAINMENT, 429 Richmond Ave., Buffalo NY 14222. (716)884-0248. Manager, A&R: Dale Anderson. Record company (Hot Wings Records), music publisher (Buffalo Wings Music/BMI). Estab. 1994. Releases 2 LPs and 2 CDs/year. Pays 10% to artists on contract; statutory rate to publisher per song on record.

How to Contact: Call first and obtain permission to submit. Prefers cassette with 3 or more songs. Does not return material. Reports in 3-4 months.

Music: Mostly **folk/acoustic, alternative rock** and **jazz**. (Preference to artists from Upstate New York.) Released *No Illusions*, a compilation of songs from 15 Buffalo women singer-songwriters; and *Life in the First Person* (by Alison Pipitone).

Tips: "Make honest, uncomplicated music with a strong personal point of view."

HOWDY RECORDS, 1810 S. Pea Ridge Rd., Temple TX 76502. (817)773-8001 or (817)939-8000. Fax: (817)773-1515, ext. 156. Owner: Andy Anderson. Labels include Border Serenade and Up Yonder. Record company, music publisher (Heart O' Country) and record producer (Lonnie Wright). Estab. 1960. Releases 18 singles, 6 EPs and 12 CDs/year. Pays 2.5% royalty to artists on contract; 2.5% rate to publisher per song on record.
How to Contact: Write or call first and obtain permission to submit a demo or to arrange personal interview. Prefers cassette with 10 songs and lyric sheet. Does not return material. Reports in 4-8 weeks.
Music: Mostly **country**, **religious** and **Tex-Mex**. Released *Loving You* (by A. Anderson), recorded by Juan Ortiz on Border Serenade Records (Tex-Mex); "Once Too Often" (by A. Anderson), recorded by Val-Eria on Howdy Records (country); and "So Soon" (by Valerie Perticle), recorded by James Andrews on Up Yonder Records (rock). Other artists include Billie Ray, Paul Aquilar and William Bennett.

*****HYPNOTIC RECORDINGS**, P.O. Box 7347, Fullerton CA 92634. (213)312-4343. A&R Rep: Armando Vega. Record company. Estab. 1995. Releases 2 singles, 4 LPs and 4 EPs and 4 CDs/year. Pays negotiable royalty to artists on contract; statutory rate to publisher per song on record.
How to Contact: Submit demo tape by mail. Unsolicited submissions are OK. Prefers cassette or VHS videotape with 3 songs. SASE. Reports in 1 month.
Music: Mostly **heavy metal**, **loud rock** and **hard rock**. Released *Wicked From the Womb* and "Erroresistable," both written and recorded by Hyperchild. Other artists include In Search Of and Rated R.

*****IMI RECORDS**, 541 N. Fairbanks Court, Chicago IL 60611. (312)245-9334. Fax: (312)245-9327. Contact: Head of A&R (specify style: rock, jazz, urban). Record company and music publisher (Vertical City Music Inc./BMI; 2 Beep Music Inc./ASCAP). Estab. 1993. Releases 8 singles, 5-7 LPs, 2-3 EPs and 4-8 CDs/year. Pays negotiable royalty to artists on contract; negotiable rate to publishers per song on record.
● IMI is an independent label with international distribution. However, some releases are also released through individual affiliations with Atlantic, Sony, MCA and other major labels, depending on the project.
How to Contact: Submit demo tape by mail. Unsolicited submissions are OK. Prefers cassette or DAT, ½″ VHS videocassette, pictures, bios and press (if any). "Be very specific on what you're looking for in a label. Artist/songwriter, band, producer looking for a deal with specific artist, label looking for promotion and/or distribution. Above all, please be professional!" Does not return material. Reports in 4 weeks.
Music: Mostly **alternative/modern rock**, **urban R&B** and **jazz (traditional and progressive)**; also **artists (individual and bands)**, **producers** and **small label affiliations**. Released "Mindblowing," written and recorded by David Josias on IMI/Lava/Atlantic R&B; "The Falling Wallendas" (by Scott Bennett/Allen Keller), recorded by The Falling Wallendas (rock/pop); and *Jazz Wagon* (by Jon Weber/various), recorded by Jon Weber (jazz), both on IMI Records. Other artists include Vallejo.
Tips: "Research a label's work, as not all labels are appropriate for all artists. Be open to creative criticism as it is a team-oriented endeavor with regards to artists' careers and directions. Remember, the intention is to sell records. Great records don't come easy, so prepare to be flexible and grow."

INFERNO RECORDS, P.O. Box 28743, Kansas City MO 64118. (816)454-7638. E-mail: murtham @maplewoods.cc.mo.us. A&R Director: Mark Murtha. Record company. Estab. 1989. Releases 6 LPs, 4 EPs and 4 CDs/year. Pays standard royalty to artists on contract; statutory rate to publisher per song on record.
How to Contact: Write first and obtain permission to submit. Prefers cassette with 4 songs. SASE. Reports in 1 month.
Music: Mostly **rock**, **alternative** and **country**. Released *Awake*, recorded by London Drive (rock); *We're Pretty Good—If You Turn Your Head*, recorded by Bad Hair Day (rock); and *Mass Spewage*, recorded by Phantasmagoria (alternative), all on Inferno Records. Other artists include Toymaker's Dream and CIZI.

MARKET CONDITIONS are constantly changing! If you're still using this book and it is 1998 or later, buy the newest edition of *Songwriter's Market* at your favorite bookstore or order directly from Writer's Digest Books.

Tips: "We're primarily looking for talented self-starters who have professional recordings ready for release. We release an annual compilation of unsigned artists."

INTERSOUND INC., P.O. Box 1724, Roswell GA 30077. (770)664-9262. Fax: (404)664-7316. A&R Rep (rock): Dick Bozzi; Gospel: James Bullard; Rap: J.W. Sewell and Ron Patterson. Labels include Branson and So-Lo Jam. Record company, music publisher and distributor. Estab. 1982. Releases 6-10 singles and 150 CDs/year. Pays negotiable royalty to artists on contract; negotiable rate to publisher per song on record.
How to Contact: Write or call first and obtain permission to submit. Prefers cassette with 3 songs. "We will contact the songwriter when we are interested in the material." Does not return material. Reports in 2 months.
Music: Mostly **rock, gospel** and **country**; also **rap, swing** and **classical**. Released *Back to the Innocence*, written and recorded by Jonathan Cain (rock); *Ronnie James and the Jez Hot Swing Club*, written and recorded by Ronnie James (swing); and *Hold On* (by Michael Scott), recorded by Michael Scott and the Outreach Choir (gospel), all on Intersound Inc. Other artists include Way 2 Real (rap), Jennifer Holliday (gospel), The Gatlin Brothers (country) and The Bellamy Brothers (country).
Tips: "Intersound is only interested in non-signed, non-published writers."

INTERSTATE 40 RECORDS, 9208 Spruce Mountain Way, Las Vegas NV 89134. (702)363-8506. President: Eddie Lee Carr. Labels include Tracker Records. Record company and music publisher (Watchesgro Music/BMI and Watch Us Climb/ASCAP). Estab. 1979. Releases 12 singles, 1 LP and 2 CDs/year. Pays 50% royalty to artists on contract; statutory rate to publisher per song on record.
• Interstate 40's publishing company, Watchesgro Music, can be found in the Music Publishers section.
How to Contact: Submit demo tape by mail. Unsolicited submissions are OK. Prefers cassette with 3 songs. SASE. Reports in 2 weeks.
Music: Mostly **country**. Movie and TV credits include "Blues Bros. II," "The Christopher Columbus Story" and "Cochise."

JABALA MUSIC, 155B Quincy Ct., Bloomingdale IL 60108. Phone/fax: (708)529-7127. General Manager: Carolyn Ford. Labels include Spanda Music, Great American Song Machine. Record company and music publisher. Estab. 1976. Releases 6 singles, 6 LPs and 6 CDs/year. Royalty varies; pays statutory rate to publisher per song on record.
How to Contact: Submit demo tape by mail. Unsolicited submissions are OK. Prefers cassette (or VHS videocassette) with 6 songs and lyric or lead sheet. Does not return material. Reports in 2 months.
Music: Mostly **rock, country, New Age** and **folk**; also **classical guitar** and **original music**. Released "Cross the Waters" and "We All Need," written and recorded by Sedona on CASM Records (country); and "Jungle Women," written and recorded by Chickie and Chicks on Spanda Records (New Age). Other artists include Sisters and Caere Ford.

JALYN RECORDING CO., 306 Millwood Dr., Nashville TN 37217. (615)366-9999. President: Jack Lynch. Labels include Nashville Bluegrass and Nashville Country Recording Company. Record company, music publisher (Jaclyn Music/BMI, JLMG Music/ASCAP), record producer, film company (Nashville Country Productions) and distributor (Nashville Music Sales). Estab. 1963. Releases 1-12 LPs/year. Pays statutory royalty to artists on contract; statutory rate to publisher per song on record.
• See the listings for Jaclyn Music in the Music Publishers section and Nashville Country Productions in the Record Producers section.
How to Contact: Submit demo tape by mail. Unsolicited submissions are OK. Prefers cassette with 1-4 songs and lyric sheet. SASE. Reports in 1 month.
Music: **Country, bluegrass, gospel** and **MOR**. Released *Time Will Tell* (by T.E. Morris), recorded by Odie Gal on NCP-19961 Records; *There'll Never Be Another* (by J.D. Lynch), recorded by Jack Lynch on NBC-19941 Records; and *I'm Wanted* (by Barbara Jackson), recorded by Don Hendrix on NCP-19964 Records.
Tips: "Send good performance on cassette, bio, picture and SASE."

JAMAKA RECORD CO., 3621 Heath Lane, Mesquite TX 75150. (214)279-5858. Contact: Jimmy Fields. Labels include Felco and Kick Records. Record company, record producer and music publisher (Cherie Music/BMI). Estab. 1955. Releases 2 singles/year. Pays .05% royalty to artists on contract; statutory rate to publisher for each record sold.
• Jamaka Record Co.'s publishing company, Cherie Music, is listed in the Music Publishers section.
How to Contact: Prefers cassette with lyric sheet. "A new singer should send a good tape with at least 4 strong songs, presumably recorded in a professional studio." Does not return material without return postage and proper mailing package.

Music: Country and **progressive country**. Released "Cajun Baby Blues" and "If You Call This Loving," recorded by Steve Pride.
Tips: "Songs should have strong lyrics with a good story, whether country or pop."

JAMOTÉ MUSIC GROUP, (formerly Madflow Recordings), P.O. Box 5167, E. Orange NJ 07019. (201)672-5052. Fax: (201)672-4969. Director A&R: Maurice Nusom. Record company. Estab. 1996. Pays 13% royalty to artists on contract; statutory rate to publisher per song on record.
How to Contact: Submit demo tape by mail. Unsolicited submissions are OK. Prefers cassette with 3 songs, bio, cover letter, 8×10 b&w photo (complete press kit). SASE. Reports in 1 month.
Music: Mostly **rap/hip hop**, **breakbeats**, **house** and **dance**.
Tips: "We are very picky about rap music submissions! We ask that the music submitted have strong beats and tight lyrics with meaning. (We listen for styles like Wu-tang, Boot Camp Clik, Onyx, Lost Boys.) We want something different!"

J&J MUSICAL ENTERPRISES LTD., P.O. Box 575, Kings Park NY 11754. Contact: Frances Cavezza. Labels include JAJ Records. Record company and record production. Estab. 1983. Releases 1-2 CDs/year. Pays variable royalty.
How to Contact: Write first and obtain permission to submit. Prefers cassette with 4 songs and lyric sheet. SASE. Reports in 1 month. "Typed letters preferred."
Music: Mostly **progressive** and **jazz**. Released *Shorts*, *Picnic* and *Tools*, all written and recorded by Jeneane Claps on JAJ Records (jazz).
Tips: "Letters should be neat, short and provide some kind of reply card."

JAV RECORDS, P.O. Box 3873, Dallas TX 75208. (214)424-6750. A&R Director: Johnny Valladarez. Record company and music publisher (Dark Soul Music/BMI). Estab. 1992. Releases 5 singles, 2 LPs, 1 EP and 1 CD/year. Pays negotiable royalty to artists on contract; statutory rate to publisher per song on record.
How to Contact: Submit demo tape by mail. Unsolicited submissions are OK. Prefers cassette with 3 songs and lyric sheet. "Make sure demo is recorded on good quality tape. Preferably chrome or metal. Any information relating to artist's past accomplishments is welcomed." Does not return material. Reports in 2 months.
Music: Mostly **alternative**, **hard rock** and **college rock**; also **punk rock**, **heavy metal** and **anything adventurous**. Released "Secret Lover," written and recorded by Johnny Diamond (alternative); "Tom's Lean Years," written and recorded by Moisture Missiles (alternative); and "Blackness," written and recorded by Arnold Layne (alternative); all on JAV Records.
Tips: "Be on the cutting edge while incorporating today's musical styles in your songwriting. Write something that is different yet will appeal to a mass audience."

*JIVE RECORDS, 137-139 W. 25th St., New York NY 10001. (212)620-8739. Fax: (212)337-0990. Director of A&R: David McPherson. Record company. Estab. 1982. Releases 23 singles and 23 CDs/year.
● For more information, see the interview with Jive's Director of A&R David McPherson in this section.
How to Contact: Write or call first and obtain permission to submit. Prefers cassette. Does not return material. Reports in 2 weeks.
Music: Mostly **R&B**, **pop** and **rap**. Released *R. Kelly*, recorded by R. Kelly; *Age Ain't Nothin' But A Number*, recorded by Aaliyah; and *Midnight Marauders*, recorded by A Tribe Called Quest, all on Jive Records.
Tips: "Make the best material possible."

JOEY BOY RECORDS INC., 3081 NW 24th St., Miami FL 33142. (305)635-5588. Contact: Aldo Hernandez. Labels include J.R. Records, American Faith Records. Record company. Estab. 1985. Releases 50 singles, 50 12″ singles, 15-20 LPs and 15-20 CDs/year. Pays 6% royalty to artists on contract; statutory rate to publisher per song on record.
● See the listing for Joey Boy Publishing in the Music Publishers section.
How to Contact: Submit demo tape by mail. Unsolicited submissions are OK. Prefers cassette with 3 songs and lyric sheet. SASE. Reports in 6-8 weeks.

 **A BULLET** introduces comments by the editor of *Songwriter's Market* indicating special information about the listing.

Music: Mostly **bass**, **rap** and **dance**; also **jazz** and **comedy**. Released *Bass Rave* (by Bass Master Ace), recorded by David Suggs; *Trunk-A-Funk* (by Bass Patrol), recorded by Brian Graham/Robert Lewis; and "Get It Boy" (by Fresh Celeste), recorded by Celeste Mills, all on Joey Boy Records. Other artists include The Dogs, M-4-Sers and DF Fury.
Tips: "Be respectful and polite to people at all times when calling a place of business, even if they are not telling you what you want to hear."

JUSTIN TIME RECORDS INC., 5455 Pare, Suite 101, Montreal Quebec H4P 1P7 **Canada**. (514)738-9533. A&R Directors: Jean-Pierre Leduc and Denis Barnabé. Labels include Just a Memory Records. Record company, music publisher (Justin Time Publishing and Janijam Music/SOCAN) and record producer (Jim West). Estab. 1982. Releases 12 LPs and 12 CDs/year. Pays statutory rate to publisher per song on record.
How to Contact: Submit demo tape by mail. Unsolicited submissions are OK. Prefers cassette (or VHS videocassette if available) with at least 5 songs and lyric sheet. Does not return unsolicited material. Reports in 3 months.
Music: Mostly **jazz**, **blues** and **gospel**; also **French pop**, **comedy** and **cajun**. Released *A Timeless Place* (by Jimmy Rowles/Johnny Mercer), recorded by Jeri Brown/Jimmy Rowles (jazz); *Jubilation VI*, written and recorded by Montreal Jubilation Gospel Choir (gospel); and "Heat Seeking Missile," written and recorded by Bryan Lee (blues), all on Justin Time Records.
Tips: "Offer a project that is unlike everything else. So many records are pleasant, but don't offer an angle that can help spread awareness about them."

*K-ARK RECORDS, 400 Montego Cove, Hermitage TN 37076. (615)391-3450. Contact: Office Staff. Record company, music publisher, record producer (Nolan Capps). Estab. 1955. Releases 12 singles, 12 LPs and 12 CDs/year. Pays negotiable royalty to artists on contract; statutory rate to publisher per song on record.
How to Contact: Submit demo tape by mail. Unsolicited submissions are OK. Prefers cassette with 10 songs and lyric sheet. Does not return material. Reports in 2 weeks.
Music: Mostly **country**; also **gospel**. Released "I Go Home" (by Odel Usher), recorded by David Houston; *Bryan Key*, written and recorded by Bryan Key; and "I Cry" (by Onie Wheeler), recorded by Warner Mack, all on K-ark Records.

KAUPP RECORDS, Box 5474, Stockton CA 95205. (209)948-8186. President: Nancy L. Merrihew. Record company, music publisher (Kaupps and Robert Publishing Co./BMI) and record producer (Merri-Webb Productions). Estab. 1990. Releases 1 single and 4 LPs/year. Pays standard royalty to artists on contract; statutory rate to publisher per song on record.
• Kaupp Records' publishing company, Kaupps and Robert Publishing, can be found in the Music Publishers section.
How to Contact: Write first and obtain permission to submit. Prefers cassette (or VHS videocassette if available) with 3 songs. SASE. Reports in 3 months
Music: Mostly **country**, **R&B** and **A/C rock**; also **pop**, **rock** and **gospel**. Released "Freedom Bound" and "Kiss A Lot of Frogs" (by N. Merrihew), recorded by Nanci Lynn; and "Mountain of Hurt" (by K. Birmingham/D.J. Birmingham), recorded by Birmingham Country, all on Kaupp Records.
Tips: "Know what you want, set a goal, focus in on your goals, be open to constructive criticism, polish tunes and keep polishing."

KEEPING IT SIMPLE AND SAFE, INC., (formerly Homebased Entertainment Co.), 622 State St. Room 36, Springfield MA 01109. (413)747-4604. E-mail: kiss@aol.com. President: Timothy Scott. Labels include Night Owl Records, Grand Jury Records, Second Time Around Records, Southend-Essex Records. Record company. Estab. 1993. Releases 3 singles, 2 LPs and 2 CDs/year. Pays 15-25% royalty to artists on contract; statutory rate to publisher per song on record.
• See the listing for Tim Scott Music Group in the Music Publishers section.
How to Contact: Submit demo tape by mail. Unsolicited submissions are OK. Prefers cassette, CD or VHS videocassette with 3-5 songs and lyric sheet. SASE. Reports in 2 months.
Music: Mostly **pop**, **R&B**, and **rap**; also **country**, **rock** and **gospel**. Released "What About Me," (by Tim Scott), recorded by Sweet Tooth on Southend Essex Records; "Forever Yours" (by Tim Scott), recorded by Loveworld; and "Everything I Do" (by Tim Scott), recorded by S.E.D., both on Night Owl Records.

KEPT IN THE DARK RECORDS, 332 Bleeker St., K-132, New York NY 10014. E-mail: sakin@rtd.com. President: Larry A. Sakin. Record company. Estab. 1988. Releases 2-3 singles and 3-4 CDs/year. Pays negotiable royalty to artists on contract.
How to Contact: Submit demo tape by mail. Unsolicited submissions are OK. Prefers cassette with 3-5 songs and lyric sheet. SASE. Reports in 2 weeks.

Music: Mostly **rock**, **R&B** and **country**; also **jazz**. Released *Fugufish*, written and recorded by Way Past Cool (jazz/funk); *You're Not the Boss of Me*, written and recorded by The Eyepennies (rock); and *Grimble Wedge*, written and recorded by Grimble Wedge (rock), all on Kept In The Dark Records. Other artists include Recliner, Tony Faye, Passionflies and Molly Who.
Tips: "Think of your art as product and market it as such. Don't be in a hurry. Think of us like an employer rather than a business partner. We want to market anything that we feel will set an audience on its ear."

KINGSTON RECORDS, 15 Exeter Rd., Kingston NH 03848. (603)642-8493. Coordinator: Harry Mann. Record company and music publisher (Strawberry Soda Publishing/ASCAP). Estab. 1988. Releases 3-4 singles, 2-3 12″ singles, 3 LPs and 2 CDs/year. Pays 3-5% royalty to artists on contract; statutory rate to publisher per song.
• See their listing in the Record Producers section.
How to Contact: Write first and obtain permission to submit. Prefers cassette, 15 ips reel-to-reel or videocassette with 3 songs and lyric sheet. Does not return material. Reports in 6-8 weeks.
Music: Mostly **rock**, **country** and **pop**; "no heavy metal." Released *Two Lane Highway*, written and recorded by Doug Mitchell Band on Kingston Records (folk/rock).
Tips: "Working only with N.E. and local talent."

KOTTAGE RECORDS, Box 121626, Nashville TN 37212. (615)726-3556. President: Neal James. Record company, music publisher (Cottage Blue Music/BMI) and record producer (Neal James). Estab. 1979. Releases 4 singles, 2 LPs and 3 CDs/year. Pays standard royalty to artists on contract; statutory rate to publisher per song on record.
• Kottage Records' publishing company, Cottage Blue Music, is listed in the Music Publishers section, and President Neal James is listed in the Record Producers section.
How to Contact: Submit demo tape by mail. Unsolicited submissions are OK. Prefers cassette with 2 songs and lyric sheet. SASE. Reports in 1 month.
Music: Mostly **country**, **rock/pop** and **gospel**; also **R&B** and **alternative**. Released "What Do Ya Say," written and recorded by Jay S. Kay (alternative); *I Close My Eyes*, written and recorded by Judie Bell (contemporary); and "Generic People" (by Darrell Hughes), recorded by Allusion (rock), all on Kottage Records. Other artists include P.J. Hawk.

KSM RECORDS, 2305 Vista Court, Coquitlam British Columbia V3J 6W2 **Canada**. (604)202-3644. Fax: (604)469-9359. A&R Rep: David London. Record company, music publisher (Kwaz Song Music) and record producer (David London). Estab. 1991. Releases 2-5 singles and 2-5 CDs/year. Pays negotiable rate to artists on contract; statutory rate to publisher per song on record.
• KSM Records' publishing company, Kwaz Song Music, is listed in the Music Publishers section.
How to Contact: Submit demo tape by mail. Unsolicited submissions are OK. Prefers cassette or VHS videocassette and press material. Does not return material. Reports in 1 month.
Music: Mostly **industrial**, **Gothic**, **techno**, **heavy/extreme**, **electronic** and **experimental**. Released *Assume The Position* (by Bryan Kortness), recorded by Jagd Wild; *Debut* (by Chris Engel), recorded by Dripping Rictus; and *Oracle Pool*, written and recorded by various artists, all on KSM Records. Other artists include Daed21, Idiot Stare, Fourthman, Reanimated Soul, Bytet, Colour Clique, Structure and Pee.

L.A. RECORDS, P.O. Box 1096, Hudson, Quebec J0P 1H0 **Canada**. (613)780-1163. Fax: (514)458-2819. A&R: Mike Lengies. Labels include Idle Music. Record company, music publisher (G-String Publishing) and record producer (M. Lengies). Estab. 1991. Releases 20-40 singles and 5-8 CDs/year. Pays negotiable royalty to artists on contract; statutory rate to publishers per song on record.
• L.A. Records' publishing company, G-String Publishing, is listed in the Music Publishers section and their management firm, M.B.H. Music Management, is listed in the Managers and Booking Agents section.
How to Contact: Submit demo tape by mail. Unsolicited submissions are OK. Prefers cassette or DAT with 3 songs and lyric sheet. SASE. Reports in 2 months.
Music: Mostly **commercial rock**, **alternative** and **A/C**; also **country** and **dance**. Released *Stoned Again* (by various), recorded by Pete Zaman; *Li'l Crack In My Mirror* (by various), recorded by Jessica Ehrenworth; and *Lonely Days* (by various), recorded by Tommy Hayes, all on L.A. Records. Other artists include Sharon Costello, On The Edge, Andy Jameson, Electric Vomit.
Tips: "Know your craft; have great lyrics and good melody. Song must create a strong emotional reaction, and must be radio friendly and under four minutes."

L.A. RECORDS, 26068 Regency Club Ct., Suite 7, Warren MI 48089. Music Director: Jack Timmons. Labels include Stark Records, R.C. Records, Fearless. Record company, record producer and music publisher (Abalone Publishing). Estab. 1984. Releases 20-30 singles, 1-10 12″ singles, 20-30 LPs, 1-

5 EPs and 2-15 CDs/year. Pays 10% royalty to artists on contract; statutory rate to publisher per song on record.

- L.A. Records' publishing company, Abalone Publishing, is listed in the Music Publishers section.

How to Contact: Submit demo tape by mail. Unsolicited submissions are OK. Prefers cassette with 1-10 songs and lyric sheet. "It is very important to include a cover letter describing your objective goals." SASE. Reports in 1 month.

Music: Mostly **rock/hard rock**, **heavy metal** and **pop/rock**; also **country/gospel**, **MOR/ballads**, **R&B**, **jazz**, **New Age**, **dance** and **easy listening**. Released *Tripper* (by J. Scott), recorded by The Pistol Kids (rock); "Renegade" (by Kate Smahl), recorded by Licks (dance); and *Love's Tough* (by Sam Steel), recorded by The Stars (pop/rock), all on L.A. Records. Other artists include The Simmones, Kevin Stark, The Comets, Fearless.

Tips: "Don't be afraid to indulge, pursue and aim forward. Attitude and taking chances are crucial."

*L. P. S. RECORDS, INC., 2140 St. Clair St., Bellingham WA 98226-4016. (360)733-3807. President: Mrs. Renie Peterson. Record company, music publisher (Heartstone/BMI; Cherrystone/ASCAP; Fourth Corner/SESAC) and record producer (Renie Peterson). Estab. 1970. Releases 1 CD/year. Pays 80¢/CD (US); 40¢/CD (foreign); 60¢/CAS (US); 30¢/CAS (foreign) to artists on contract.

How to Contact: Submit demo tape by mail. Unsolicited submissions are OK. Prefers cassette ("studio demos only") with 3 songs and typed lyric sheet. "Do not include lengthy letters about the songs; we're only interested in unpublished songs. Looking for songs by established songwriters (country primarily). Only accredited BMI, ASCAP or SESAC songwriters should apply." SASE. Reports in 1 week.

Music: Mostly **country**; also **Southern gospel**. Released *Out On Her Own* (by various), recorded by Donna Vallance on LPS Records (country).

Tips: "Study what's airing on Top 40 country radio, learn your craft, send neat submissions. Teamwork is important; as is having the ability to get out on the road, meet people and sell records. Charisma and talent are prime as well as personal appearance."

LAMAR MUSIC GROUP, P.O. Box 412, New York NY 10462. Associate Director: Darlene Barkley. Labels include Lamar, MelVern, Wilson, Pulse Music and Co. Pub. Record company, music publisher, and workshop organization. Estab. 1984. Releases 10-12 12″ singles and 2-4 LPs/year. Pays standard royalty to artists on contract; statutory rate to publisher per song. "We charge only if we are hired to do 'work-for-hire' projects."

How to Contact: Write first and obtain permission to submit. Prefers cassette with 2 songs. Does not return material. Reports in 1 month.

Music: Mostly **R&B**, **rap** and **pop**. Released "I Am So Confused," written and recorded by Eemence on Lamar Records; "Heavenly," recorded by Vern Wilson on Motown Records; and "Feel Like a Woman" (by Wilson/Johnson), recorded by S. Taylor on MelVern Records (R&B/ballad). Other artists include Barry Manderson and Co/Vern.

Tips: "Must have managers or agents knowledgable in marketing with a promotional plan of action and the necessary funding to support the plan."

*LAMON RECORDS, P.O. Box 25371, Charlotte NC 28229. (704)882-8845. Fax: (704)545-1940. A&R: D. Moody. Labels include Pan Handle. Record company and music publisher (Laymond Publishing Inc.). Estab. 1962. Releases 10 singles, 10 LPs, 5 EPs and 5 CDs/year. Pays negotiable royalty to artists on contract; statutory rate to publisher per song on record.

How to Contact: Submit demo tape by mail. Unsolicited submissions are OK. Prefers cassette with 3 songs and lyric sheet. SASE. Reports in 2 months.

Music: Mostly **rock**, **country** and **gospel**; also **R&B** and **soul**.

LANDMARK COMMUNICATIONS GROUP, Box 1444, Hendersonville TN 37077. Producer: Bill Anderson, Jr. Labels include Jana and Landmark Records. Record company, record producer, music publisher (Newcreature Music/BMI and Mary Megan Music/ASCAP) and management firm (Landmark Entertainment). Releases 10 singles, 8 LPs and 8 CDs/year. Pays 5-7% royalty to artists on contract; statutory rate to publisher for each record sold.

How to Contact: Prefers 7½ ips reel-to-reel or cassette with 4-10 songs and lyric sheet. SASE. Reports in 1 month.

LISTINGS OF COMPANIES in countries other than the U.S. have the name of the country in boldface type.

Music: Country/crossover, gospel, jazz, R&B, rock and top 40/pop. Released *Joanne Cash Yates Live . . . w/Johnny Cash* on Jana Records (gospel); "You Were Made For Me," by Skeeter Davis and Teddy Nelson on Elli Records/Norway; and "The Tradition Continues" (by Vernon Oxford), recorded on Landmark Records (country).

LANDSLIDE RECORDS, 1800 Peachtree St., Suite 333, Atlanta GA 30309. (404)355-5580. President: Michael Rothschild. Record company, music publisher (Frozen Inca Music/BMI) and record producer. Estab. 1981. Releases 2 12″ singles, 6 LPs and 6 CDs/year. Pays negotiable royalty to artists on contract; negotiable rate to publisher per song on record.
  • See the listing for Landslide's publishing company, Frozen Inca Music, in the Music Publishers section.
How to Contact: Submit demo tape by mail. Unsolicited submissions are OK. Prefers cassette with 6-12 songs and lyric sheet. SASE. Reports in 1 month.
Music: Mostly R&B, blues and rap; also jazz. Released *Strange Voices* (by various), recorded by Bruce Hampton (rock/jazz); *Freak Doggin'* (by Gerald Jackson/various), recorded by various artists (hip hop); and *Navigator*, written and recorded by Paul McCandless (jazz), all on Landslide Records..

LANOR RECORDS, Box 233, 329 N. Main St., Church Point LA 70525. (318)684-2176. Contact: Lee Lavergne. Record company and music publisher (Jon Music/BMI). Releases 8-10 cassettes a year. Pays 3-5% royalty to artists on contract; statutory rate to writers for each record sold.
  • Lanor Records' publishing company, Jon Music, is listed in the Music Publishers section.
How to Contact: Prefers cassette with 2-6 songs. SASE. Reports in 2 weeks.
Music: Mostly country; also rock, soul, zydeco, cajun and blues. Released *Cajun Pickin'*, recorded by L.A. Band (cajun); *Rockin' with Roy*, recorded by Roy Currier; and *Zydeco All Night*, recorded by Joe Walker (zydeco), all on Lanor Records.
Tips: Submit "good material with potential in today's market. Use good quality cassettes—I don't listen to poor quality demos that I can't understand."

LARI-JON RECORDS, 325 W. Walnut, Rising City NE 68658. (402)542-2336. Owner: Larry Good. Record company, music publisher (Lari-Jon Publishing/BMI) and record producer (Lari-Jon Productions). Estab. 1967. Releases 15 singles and 5 LPs/year. Pays varying royalty.
  • Lari-Jon Publishing, Lari-Jon Productions and Lari-Jon Promotions are listed in the Music Publishers, Record Producers and Managers and Booking Agents sections, respectively.
How to Contact: Submit demo tape by mail. Unsolicited submissions are OK. Prefers cassette with 5 songs and lyric sheet. SASE. Reports in 2 months.
Music: Mostly country, gospel-Southern and '50s rock. Released "Glory Bound Train," written and recorded by Tom Campbell; *Country Blues,* written and recorded by Larry Good (country); and *Her Favorite Songs*, written and recorded by Johnny Nace (country), all on Lari-Jon Records. Other artists include Kent Thompson and Brenda Allen.

LARK RECORD PRODUCTIONS, INC., P.O. Box 35726, Tulsa OK 74153. (918)786-8896. E-mail: janajae@aol.com. Website: http://home.aol.com/janajae. Vice-President: Kathleen Pixley. Record company, music publisher (Jana Jae Music/BMI) and record producer (Lark Talent and Advertising). Estab. 1980. Payment to artists on contract negotiable; statutory rate to publisher per song on record.
  • See the listings for Jana Jae Music in the Music Publishers section, Lark Talent and Advertising in the Record Producers section and Jana Jae Enterprises in the Managers and Booking Agents section.
How to Contact: Submit demo tape by mail. Unsolicited submissions are OK. Prefers cassette or VHS videocassette with 3 songs and lead sheets. Does not return material.
Music: Mostly country, bluegrass and classical; also instrumentals. Released "Fiddlestix" (by Jana Jae); "Mayonnaise" (by Steve Upfold); and "Flyin' South" (by Cindy Walker), all recorded by Jana Jae on Lark Records (country). Other artists include Syndi, Hotwire and Matt Greif.

***LBI RECORDS**, P.O. Box 328, Jericho VT 05465. (802)899-3787. Fax: (802)899-3805. President: Bobby Hackney. Record company and record producer. Estab. 1986. Releases 12 singles, 2 LPs and 2 CDs/year. Pays negotiable royalty to artists on contract; statutory rate to publisher per song on record.
How to Contact: Submit demo tape by mail. Unsolicited submissions are OK. Prefers cassette with 3 songs and lyric sheet. SASE. Reports in 4-5 weeks.
Music: Mostly reggae, R&B and jazz; also poetry and hip hop/funk/rap. Released *The Hotter, The Better* and *Reggae Mood* (by B. Hackney), both recorded by Lambsbread (reggae); and "African Princess," written and recorded by Mikey Dread (reggae), all on LBI Records. Other artists include Kerry Taylor and Trini.

LBJ PRODUCTIONS, 8608 W. College St., French Lick IN 47432. (812)936-7318. E-mail: lbjprod @intersource.com. Website: http://intersource.com/~lbjprod. Director A&R: Janet S. Jones. Owner/

Producer: Larry Jones. Labels include Stone Country Records, SCR Gospel, SCR Rock. Record company, music publisher (Plain Country Publishing/ASCAP, Riff-Line Publishing/BMI), record producer (LBJ Productions) and producer of radio-spot ads and jingles. Estab. 1989. Releases 2-4 singles, 3-6 LPs, 2-3 EPs and 1-2 CDs/year. Pays 10-15% royalty to artists on contract; statutory rate to publisher per song on record.

How to Contact: Write first and obtain permission to submit. Prefers cassette (or VHS videocassette) with 4-6 songs and lyric sheet. SASE. Reports in 6-8 weeks.

Music: Mostly **country**, **gospel** and **rock**; also **R&B**, **MOR** and **pop**. Released "Angel" (by Bruce Taylor), recorded by Borrowed Time on SCR Rock Records; "Smooth Operator" (by Wagner/Troutman), recorded by Heart & Soul on Riff Line Records (R&B); and *This Bud Ain't For You* (by Easterday/Fred), recorded by Bobby Easterday on SCR Records. Other artists include Rita White, Gordon Ray, C.L. Jones and Terry Tiallon.

Tips: "Make a good first impression. Put the song on your demo tape that you think is strongest first. If you catch our ear we'll listen to more music. We are not looking for someone that does imitations, we need new and exciting people with styles that cry out for attention. But remember, make your submissions to the point and professional—we'll decide if you've got what we want."

LE MATT MUSIC LTD., % Stewart House, Hill Bottom Rd., Highwycombe, Buckinghamshire, HP12 4HJ **England**. Phone: (01630)647374. Fax: (01630)647612. Contact: Ron or Cathrine Lee. Labels include Swoop, Zarg Records, Genouille, Pogo and Check Records. Record company, record producer and music publisher (Le Matt Music, Ltd., Lee Music, Ltd., R.T.F.M. and Pogo Records, Ltd.). Member MPA, PPL, PRS, MCPS. Estab. 1972. Releases 30 12″ singles, 20 LPs and 20 CDs/year. Pays negotiable royalty to artists on contract; negotiable rate to publisher for each record sold. Royalties paid to US songwriters and artists through US publishing or recording affiliate.

• Le Matt Music's publishing company, R.T.L. Music, is listed in the Music Publishers section, and R.T.F.M. is listed in the Music Print Publishers section.

How to Contact: Submit demo tape by mail. Unsolicited submissions are OK. Prefers CD, cassette or DAT (or VHS 625 PAL standard videocassette) with 1-3 songs and lyric sheet. Include bio and still photos. SAE and IRC. Reports in 6 weeks.

Music: Mostly interested in **pop/top 40**; also interested in **bluegrass**, **blues**, **country**, **dance-oriented**, **easy listening**, **MOR**, **progressive**, **R&B**, **'50s rock**, **disco**, **new wave**, **rock** and **soul**. Released *Children of the Night*, *Witch Woman* and *Dance of Death*, all written by Ron Dickson and recorded by Nightmare on ZARG Records (shock rock). Other artists include Johnny Moon, Hush, Dead Fish and Daniel Boone.

*LIQUID MEAT RECORDS, P.O. Box 460692, Escondido CA 92046-0692. (619)753-8734. E-mail: liqmeat@ix.netcom.com. Director of A&R: Mollie Ehn. Labels include Slurr Records. Record company. Estab. 1992. Releases 7-8 singles, 2-4 LPs, 1-3 EPs and 2-4 CDs/year. Pays negotiable royalty to artists on contract; statutory rate to publisher per song on record.

How to Contact: Submit demo tape by mail. Unsolicited submissions are OK. Prefers cassette with 4 or more songs and lyric sheet. "We cannot respond to all submissions. If we are interested we will respond." Does not return material. Reports in 2 months.

Music: Mostly **punk**, **noise-rock** and **pop**; also **industrial**, **techno** and **rave**. Released *Fairplay*, written and recorded by Everready (punk); "Getting Along. . ." (by Dave Thirsty), recorded by Thirsty (punk); and "Know" (by Dave Quinn), recorded by Tiltwheel (punk), all on Liquid Meat Records. Other artists include Bob "Bondex" Johnston, Stink, Discount and Hemlock.

Tips: "Write songs that mean something—be original, and don't ever give up."

*LIVE OAK RECORDS, 735 El Paseo, Lakeland FL 33805. (941)686-4952. Fax: (941)686-8730. Label Director: Robert Renfro. Record company. Estab. 1993. Releases 1-10 singles, 1-6 LPs, 1-10 EPs and 1-6 CDs/year. Pays negotiable royalty to artists on contract; statutory rate to publisher per song on record.

How to Contact: Submit demo tape by mail. Unsolicited submissions are OK. Prefers cassette with 1-4 songs and lyric/lead sheet. "If you are an artist seeking a record deal, include a photo, bio and press kit." SASE. Reports in 8 weeks.

Music: Mostly **pop**, **dance** and **rock**; also **R&B**, **alternative** and **country**. Released "You Heard the Man" (by Renfro/Veenstra), recorded Xeonod (dance); "My Next Ex-Wife" (by Renfro/Veenstra), recorded by The Painters (country); and "Gimme Summa Whatcha Good For" (by Renfro/Veenstra), recorded by ESAS (dance), all on Live Oak Records.

Tips: "Remember, no one cares as much about your success as you do. So understand and be involved in every aspect of your career. Call me. My advice is free and I'm always willing to help struggling artists (I've been there)."

LOCONTO PRODUCTIONS/SUNRISE STUDIO, 10244 NW 47 St., Sunrise FL 33351. (305)741-7766. President: Frank X. Loconto. Labels include FXL Records. Record company, music

publisher (Otto Music Publishing/ASCAP) and recording studio. Estab. 1978. Releases 10 singles, 10 cassettes/albums and 5 CDs/year. Pays negotiable royalty to artists on contract; statutory rate to publisher per song on record.
- Loconto Productions is also listed in the Record Producers section, and their publishing affiliate, Otto Publishing, is listed in the Music Publishers section.

How to Contact: Submit demo tape by mail. Unsolicited submissions are OK. Prefers cassette with lyric sheet or lead sheet. SASE. Reports in 2-3 months.

Music: Released *Love Is In The Air* (by various), recorded by Michael Moog (disco); *Totally Me*, written and recorded by Bob Orange (pop/gospel); and *New Life In Christ* (by various), recorded by Scott Dewey (gospel), all on FXL Records. Other artists include Michael Moog, Roger Bryant, Bill Dillon and Bob Orange.

Tips: "Be sure to prepare a professional demo of your work and don't hesitate to seek 'professional' advice."

LONESOME WIND CORPORATION, 111 E. Canton St., Broken Arrow OK 74012-7140. (800)210-4416. President: Marty R. Garrett. Labels include Lonesome Wind Records. Record company, record producer, music publisher and entertainment consultant. Estab. 1988. Releases 3-4 EPs and 1 CD/year. Pays 7-10% royalty to artists on contract; statutory rate to publisher per song on record.

How to Contact: Write or call first and obtain permission to submit. Prefers cassette with 4-5 songs and lyric or lead sheet with chord progressions listed. Does not return material. Reports in 3 weeks.

Music: Straight-up, honky tonk, country or **scripturally-based gospel**. Released *Too Free Too Long* (by Cliff Voss), recorded by Mark Cypert on Stormy Heart Records; and *Carry Me Over*, written and recorded by The Cripple Jimmi Band on Kid Mega Records.

Tips: "We concentrate strictly on securing funding for artists who intend to record and release CD quality products to the public for sale. Artists will need to be prepared to educate themselves as to what is required. We do not require professional demos to submit, but make sure vocals are distinct, upfront and up-to-date. I personally listen and respond to each submission I receive, so call to see if we are currently reviewing for an upcoming project."

*LONNY TUNES, P.O. Box 460086, Garland TX 75046. (214)497-1616. President: Lonny Schonfeld. Record company, record producer and music publisher (Lonny Tunes/BMI). Estab. 1988. Releases 8-10 singles, 8-10 LPs and 2 CDs/year. Pays 20% (of wholesale) to artists on contract; statutory rate to publisher per song on record.
- See their listing in the Music Publishers section, as well as the listing for Lonny Schonfeld in the Managers and Booking Agents section.

How to Contact: Submit demo tape by mail. Unsolicited submissions are OK. Prefers cassette or VHS videocassette with 3-5 songs and lyric sheet. "Professional quality only." Does not return material. Reports in 6-8 weeks.

Music: Mostly **country, children's** and **rock**; also **jazz** and **comedy**. Released "Baby, With You" (by L. Schonfeld/R. Stout), recorded by Randy Stout (pop); *James Blonde 006.95* (by Marty Brill), recorded by various artists; and "One Word Question" (by L. Schonfeld), recorded by David Wilson, all on Lonny Tunes Records.

*LOTUS RECORDS, P.O. Box 669, Ansonia Station, New York NY 10023. (212)586-1056. Fax: (212)586-3342. E-mail: lotusrec@aol.com. Contact: A&R Department. Record company. Estab. 1994. Releases 6 CDs/year. Pays statutory rate to publishers per song on record.

How to Contact: Write or call first and obtain permission to submit. Prefers cassette and photos/bios. Does not return material. Reports in 4 weeks.

Music: Mostly **acid jazz, trip-hop** and **dance**.

LRJ, Box 3, Belen NM 87002. (505)864-7441. Manager: Tony Palmer. Labels include Little Richie and Chuckie. Record company. Estab. 1959. Releases 5 singles and 2 LPs/year.
- See the listings for Little Richie Johnson Music in the Music Publishers section, and Little Richie Johnson in the Record Producers and Managers and Booking Agents sections.

How to Contact: Submit demo tape by mail. Unsolicited submissions are OK. Prefers cassette. Does not return material. Reports in 1 month.

Music: Mostly **country**. Released "Sing Me a Love Song," written and recorded by Myrna Lorrie; "Auction of My Life," written and recorded by Joe King; and "Helpless," recorded by Alan Godge, all on LRJ Records.

LUCIFER RECORDS, INC., Box 263, Brigantine NJ 08203-0263. (609)266-2623. President: Ron Luciano. Labels include TVA Records. Record company, music publishers (Ciano Publishing and Legz Music), record producers (Pete Fragale and Tony Vallo) and management firm and booking agency (Ron Luciano Music Co. and TVA Productions). "Lucifer Records has offices in South Jersey; Palm Beach, Florida; Sherman Oaks, California; and Las Vegas, Nevada."

How to Contact: Call or write to arrange personal interview. Prefers cassette with 4-8 songs. SASE. Reports in 3 weeks.
Music: **Dance, easy listening, MOR, rock, soul** and **top 40/pop.** Released "I Who Have Nothing," by Spit-N-Image (rock); "Lucky," by Legz (rock); and "Love's a Crazy Game," by Voyage (disco/ballad). Other artists include Bobby Fisher, Jerry Denton, FM, Zeke's Choice and Al Caz.

*LYRA HOUSE, LTD., 4750 N. Central, Suite 7N, Phoenix AZ 85012. (602)234-1809. Fax: (602)230-1991. E-mail: naaf@aol.com. Managing Director: Marc Parella. Record company and arts foundation. Estab. 1989. Releases 5 CDs/year.
How to Contact: "Lyra House does not work with songwriters. We are a classical/concert music label. Accepts demos by invitation only."
Music: Mostly **classical, contemporary concert music** and **orchestral**; also **ecletic new music** and **serious film scores.** Released *A Feast of Beethoven* and *A Festival of Chopin*, both recorded by Dickran Atamial; and *Bolet in Memorium*; recorded by Jorge Bolet, all on Lyra House Records. Other artists include Donald Keats, Luis Gonzales and Marc Parella.
Tips: "We do not work with popular songwriters. Persons interested in recording with Lyra House must first submit a proposal to our parent organization, North American Artists Foundation, at the above address."

*M.E.G. RECORDS CO., 2069 Zumbehl Rd., #27, St. Charles MO 63303. (314)447-1652. Fax: (314)447-1652. President: Brian Gleason. Record company, music publisher (Cow Jumping Over the Moon Music/BMI) and record producer (Brian Gleason). Estab. 1995. Pays negotiable royalty to artists on contract; statutory rate to publisher per song.
How to Contact: Submit demo tape by mail. Unsolicited submissions are OK. Prefers cassette or VHS videocassette with 3-4 songs, pictures, bio, work history (résumé), day and nighttime phone numbers and lyric sheet. "Prefer writer and artist to be the same, but will accept material from either." SASE. Reports in 3-6 months.
Music: Mostly **country, country rock** and **Christian.** Released *This Old House*, written and recorded by Brian Winslow on M.E.G. Records (country).
Tips: "Submit original material only, clean vocal and guitar is adequate. Prefer singer/songwriter submissions."

MAGNUM MUSIC CORP. LTD., 8607 128th Ave., Edmonton, Alberta T5E 0G3 **Canada**. (403)476-8230. Fax: (403)472-2584. General Manager: Bill Maxim. Record company. Estab. 1982. Pays standard royalty.
Affiliate(s): High River Music Publishing (ASCAP), Ramblin' Man Music Publishing (BMI).
• See their listing in the Managers and Booking Agents section.
How to Contact: Write or call first and obtain permission to submit. Prefers cassette (or VHS videocassette) with 3 songs and lyric sheet. Does not return material. Reports in 2 months.
Music: Mostly **country, gospel** and **contemporary**; also **pop, ballads** and **rock**. Published *Pray for the Family* and *Emotional Girl*, both written and recorded by C. Greenly (country); and *Don't Worry 'Bout It*, written and recorded by T. Anderson (country), all on Magnum Records.

MAKESHIFT MUSIC, P.O. Box 557, Blacktown, NSW 2148 **Australia**. Phone: (612)626-8991. Manager: Peter Bales. Record company, music publisher (Aria and Apra). Estab. 1980. "Makeshift Music is an administration and production company specializing within the recording and publishing fields of the music industry. Product and material is now leased out to third party companies such as BMG, Sony, Mushroom, etc." Pays statutory rate to publisher per song on record.
How to Contact: Submit demo tape by mail. Unsolicited submissions are OK. Prefers cassette (or PAL/VHS videocassette if available) with 2-3 songs and lyric sheet. SAE and IRC. Reports in 2-3 months where possible.
Music: Mostly **rock/pop.** Artists include The Generator, Frank Seckold, Chimps and The Sessions.

MALACO RECORDS, 3023 W. Northside Dr., Jackson MS 39213. (601)982-4522. Executive Director: Jerry Mannery. Record company. Estab. 1986. Releases 20 projects/year. Pays 8% royalty to artists on contract; statutory rate to publisher per song.
How to Contact: Submit demo tape by mail. Unsolicited submissions are OK. Prefers cassette (or VHS videocassette). Does not return material.
Music: Mostly **traditional** and **contemporary gospel.** Artists include Mississippi Mass Choir, Ricky Dillard and the New Generation Chorale, Jackson Southernaires and Dorothy Norwood.

*THE MAN ON PAGE 602, 708 W. Euclid, Pittsburg KS 66762. (316)231-6443. Labels include Antique, Catfish, Cisum and Big Brutus. Record company, music publisher and record producer. Estab. 1975. Pays statutory royalty to publisher per song on record.
• See the listing for Cisum in the Music Publishers section.

How to Contact: Write or call first and obtain permission to submit. Prefers cassette with 2 songs and lyric sheet. Does not return material. Reports in 3 weeks.
Music: Mostly **country, gospel** and **R&B**; also **easy rock**. Released "Shade Tree Mechanic" (by Gene Strassey); "Tennessee River Blues" (by Jack Barlow); and "Lookin' At Our Hero" (by Mister X), all on Antique Records.

MANNY MUSIC, INC., 2035 Pleasanton Rd., San Antonio TX 78221-1306. (210)924-2224. Fax: (210)924-3338. E-mail: amen@icsi.net. Website: http://www.ordanet.com:1995/Manny/manny.html. Publishing Dept.: Pete Rodriguez. Labels include Manny Records, RP Records and Tapes, AMS Records (gospel line). Record company, record producer and music publisher (Manny Music/BMI, Rosman Music/ASCAP, Texas Latino/SESAC). Estab. 1963. Releases 20-35 singles and 10-15 CDs/year. Pays variable royalty to artists on contract; statutory rate to publisher per song on record.
• See the listing for Manny Music in the Music Publishers section.
How to Contact: Submit demo tape by mail. Unsolicited submissions are OK. Prefers cassette and lyric sheet. "Allow three or four weeks before calling to inquire about submission." SASE. Reports in 12-18 weeks.
Music: Mostly **Spanish**, **Tex-Mex** or **Tejano** and **Spanish gospel**; also **C&W**, **pop** and **rock**. Released *Siempra Contigo*, written and recorded by Culturas; and *Tu Eros Mia*, written and recorded by Oscar G, both on Manny/WEA Records. Other artists include La Tropa F, Sunny Ozuna, George Rivas, Johnny Bustamante, Raul Alberto, Esmeralda, Baby Phaze, Roel Martinez and Texas Latino.
Tips: "Have a good storyline, good hook, catchy melody. Not too cerebral—music is fun!"

JOHN MARKS RECORDS, 19 Wright Ave., Wakefield RI 02879. (401)782-6298. Fax: (401)792-8375. Owner: John Marks. Record company. Estab. 1991. Releases 4 CDs/year. Royalty varies.
How to Contact: Write first and obtain permission to submit. Prefers cassette (analog or DAT) or CD. "Primarily interested in master tapes suitable for licensing." SASE. Reports in 1 month.
Music: Mostly **classical** and **jazz**; also, **new music**. Released *Transylvanian Software*, written and recorded by Guy Klucevsek (alternative); *Blue Skies*, recorded by Harry Allen Quartet (jazz); and *Bach Cello Suites*, recorded by Nathaniel Rosen, all on John Marks Records.
Tips: "Have something meaningful and beautiful to say, and record it with wonderful sound quality."

MASTER-TRAK ENTERPRISES, Dept. SM, 413 N. Parkerson, Crowley LA 70526. (318)788-0773. General Manager and Chief Engineer: Mark Miller. Labels include Master-Trak, Showtime, Kajun, Blues Unlimited, Par T and MTE Records. Record company and recording studio. Releases 20 singles and 6-8 LPs/year. Pays 7% artist royalty.
• See the listing for Whitewing Music in the Music Publishers section and Jay Miller in the Record Producers section.
How to Contact: Submit demo tape by mail. Unsolicited submissions are OK. Prefers cassette and lead sheet. Does not return material.
Music: Mostly **country**, **rock**, **R&B**, **cajun**, **blues** and **zydeco**. Released "That's When I Miss You" (by J. Runyo), recorded by Sammy Kershaw; "Please Explain," written and recorded by Wade Richards, both on MTE Records; and "My Heart Is Hurting," written and recorded by Becky Richard on Kajun Records. Other artists include Al Ferrier, Fernest & The Thunders, River Road Band, Clement Bros., Lee Benoit and Kenné Wayne.
Tips: "The song is the key. If we judge it to be a good song, we record it and it sells, we are happy. If we misjudge the song and/or the artist and it does not sell, we must go back to the drawing board."

THE MATHES COMPANY, P.O. Box 22653, Nashville TN 37202. (615)252-6912. Owner: David Mathes. Labels include Rising Star (custom), Star Image (country), Heirborn (country gospel), Kingdom (Christian). Record company and record producer. Estab. 1962. Releases 12-15 LPs and 10 CDs/year. Pays 10-23% royalty to artists on contract; statutory rate to publisher per song on record.
• See their listing in the Music Publishers section, as well as a listing for David Mathes Productions in the Record Producers section.
How to Contact: Submit demo tape by mail. Unsolicited submissions are OK. "No certified mail accepted." Prefers cassette (or VHS videocassette) with 2-3 songs and lyric sheet. SASE. Reports in 1 month.
Music: Mostly **gospel** and **country**; also **spoken word**, **MOR** and **instrumental**. Released *My Love For You* (by David & Deanna Mathes), recorded by Warner Mack on Sapphire Records (country); and *My Ole Guitar*, written and recorded by Gene Taylor on Music of America Records. Other artists include The Ballards, Johnny Newman, DeAnna, Nashville Sidemen & Singers, and Harry House.
Tips: "Songs must be positive country or gospel, with strong messages, not out of date and not political or controversial. Artists must have unique vocal style, good stage presence, have past performances and long term commitment."

MAUI ARTS & MUSIC ASSOCIATION, Suite 208, P.O. Box 356, Paia, Maui HI 96779. (808)874-7573. E-mail: dream@maui.net. Website: http://www.maui.net/~dream. A&R Public Submissions: Jason Q. Publik. Labels include Survivor, Maui No Ka Oi, Revelation, Maui Country. Record company, record producer, music publisher and environmental association. Estab. 1974. Releases 1-12 singles, 1-12 LPs and 1-12 CDs/year. Pays 5-15% royalty to artists on contract; statutory royalty to publisher per song on record.
How to Contact: Submit demo tape by mail. Unsolicited submissions are OK. Prefers cassette or videocassette with 3 songs and lyric or lead sheet. SASE. Reports in 2-4 weeks.
Music: Mostly **pop**, **rock** and **blues**; also **country**, **jazz** and **instrumental**. Released "Unlock The Hope" (by Lono), recorded by Jason on Maui Country Records (pop).

THE MAVERICK GROUP, 1122 Colorado St., Suite 1702, Austin TX 78751. (512)472-7137. Fax: (512)476-1257. E-mail: charlytex@aol.com. Managing Director: Charly Mann. Record company. Estab. 1989. Releases 5 LPs and 6 CDs/year. Pays negotiable royalty to artists on contract; statutory rate to publisher per song on record.
How to Contact: Write or call first and obtain permission to submit a demo. Prefers cassette or ½" or ¾" videocassette with 3 songs and lyric sheet. Does not return material. Reports in 2 weeks.
Music: Mostly **adult alternative**, **progressive country** and **progressive rock**; also **acoustic singer/songwriter**. Released *Camel Rock*, written and recorded by Chuck Pyle (progressive country); *Nights at the Chez*, written and recorded by David Roth (acoustic); and *Tales From the Erogenous Zone* (by Dan HR), recorded by HR (progressive rock), all on Maverick Records. Other artists include Kurt Kempter and the Southern Lights.

MCA RECORDS, 1755 Broadway, 8th Floor, New York NY 10019. (212)841-8000. East Coast A&R Director: Hans Haedelt. Vice President: Michael Rosenblatt. Labels include Costellation, Cranberry, Curb, London, Zebra and Philly World. Record company and music publisher (MCA Music).
  • Two of MCA's artists, Vince Gill and the Mavericks, won Grammys in 1996.
How to Contact: Call first and obtain permission to submit. Prefers cassette (or VHS videocassette) and lyric or lead sheet. SASE. Clearly label demo with name, address and phone number.

MCI ENTERTAINMENT GROUP, P.O. Box 8442, Universal City CA 91608. (818)506-8533. Fax: (818)506-8534. Vice President A&R: Jaeson Effantic. Labels include Bouvier, Credence, PPL. Record company. Estab. 1979. Releases 10-30 singles, 12 12" singles, 6 LPs and 6 CDs/year. Pays 15% royalty to artists on contract; statutory rate to publisher per song on record.
  • See the listings for Pollybyrd Publications in the Music Publishers section and Sa'mall Management in the Managers and Booking Agents section.
How to Contact: Write or call first and obtain permission to submit. Prefers cassette or videocassette with 2 songs. SASE. Reports in 6 weeks.
Music: Released *We The People People* (by J. Jarrett), recorded by The Band AKA (pop); *What Up With This* (by Scotti), recorded by Lejenz (pop); and *Phyne as I Can Be* (by Maxx Diamond), recorded by I.B. Phyne (pop); all on Sony/PPL Records. Other artists include Phuntain, Buddy Wright, Riki Hendrix, Condottiere and D.M. Groove.
Tips: "Educate yourself—be positive, open minded, be commercial-oriented and remember that the world changes and so does the public's taste in music."

MCR, Rt. 1 Box 70G, Dale TX 78616. (512)398-7519. Owner: Don Jones. Labels include Misty, Texas Gold. Record company, record producer, music publisher and artist career development. Estab. 1968. Releases 5 singles and 10 CDs/year. Pays standard royalty to artists on contract; statutory rate to publisher per song on record.
  • MCR's publishing affiliate, Motex Music, is listed in the Music Publishers section.
How to Contact: Submit demo tape by mail. Unsolicited submissions are OK. Prefers cassette with 4 songs and lyric sheet. SASE. Reports in 6 weeks.
Music: Mostly **country**, **gospel** and **blues**. Released *Hotter Than The Flame*, written and recorded by Winston James and the Drugstore Cowboys (country); "Lord Have Mercy" (by Lamar Mixon), recorded by Sandy Samples (gospel); and "Here's To You," written and recorded by Bud Robbins, all on Misty Records. Other artists include Karin Kaye and Dana Smith.
Tips: "Send press kit if available. MCR is a Texas-based independent record label dedicated to becoming a vehicle for the development of country talent."

MEGAFORCE WORLDWIDE ENTERTAINMENT, 14 Tennent Rd., Morganville NJ 07751. (908)591-1117. Fax: (908)591-1116. Website: http://www.web.com/crazedworld. Director of Publicity/A&R: Maria Ferrero. Labels include Megaforce Records Inc. Record company. Estab. 1983. Releases 5 LPs, 2 EPs and 5 CDs/year. Pays various royalties to artists on contract; ¾ statutory rate to publisher per song on record.

How to Contact: Submit demo tape by mail. Unsolicited submissions are OK. Prefers cassette (or ¾″ videocassette if available) with 4 songs. SASE. Reports ASAP.
Music: Mostly **rock**. Released *I Am Dog*, written and recorded by by Love in Reverse on Reprise Records (eclectic/ambient); *Filth Pig*, written and recorded by Ministry on Warner Bros. Records (heavy); and *Bif Naked*, written and recorded by Bif Naked on Her Royal Majesty's Records (pop). "We also manage Ministry, Testament, and Goudsthumb."
Tips: "Don't compromise—do what you want to do creatively."

*MEGAROCK RECORDS, P.O. Box 19131, Stockholm 10432 **Sweden**. (+46)8 151520. Fax: (+46)8 151530. Creative Manager: Magnus Soderkrist. Labels include Stars on The Rise, Active and Rock Treasures. Record company. Estab. 1993. Releases 10 singles, 2-5 EPs and 15 CDs/year. Pays negotiable royalty to artists on contract; statutory rate to publisher per song on record.
How to Contact: Submit demo tape by mail. Unsolicited submissions are OK. Prefers cassette with 5-10 songs and lyric sheet. SAE and IRC. Reports in 5-7 weeks.
Music: Mostly **melodic rock/AOR**, **mainstream pop/rock** and **progressive rock/pop**; also **acoustic rock/pop**, **heavy rock** and **hi-tech pop/rock**. Released *Revolution*, written and recorded by Bad Habit (melodic rock/AOR); *Ten'r Out*, written and recorded by Aces High (commercial hard rock), both on Megarock Records; and *Leon's Gettin' Larger*, written and recorded by City of Faith on Stars on the Rise Records (roots '70s rock). Other artists include Backyard Babies, The Quill, Ungreatful, Misha Calvin and Walk the Wire.
Tips: "Make sure to send your material to the right person and make a professional impression. Don't worry about sending too many songs, as we are actually around for the love of listening to music."

MEGATONE RECORDS INC., 7095 Hollywood Blvd. #349, Los Angeles CA 90028. (213)850-5400. Fax: (213)850-5302. E-mail: megatone.records@sonicnet.com. A&R: Thomas White. Labels include Megatech, Megahouse and Airwave. Record company. Estab. 1981. Releases 24 singles, 6 LPs and 6 CDs/year. Pays 7-12% royalty to artists on contract; 75% of statutory rate to publisher per song on record.
How to Contact: Submit demo tape by mail. Unsolicited submissions are OK. Prefers cassette with 3 songs and lyric sheet. "Looking for strong songs with great lyrical hooks and memorable melodies." SASE. Reports in 2-3 months.
Music: Mostly **dance/house/disco**, **alternative/new rock** and **electronic music**; also **power pop**, **punk** and **groove oriented music**. Released "Only You," recorded by T. Mace on Megatone Records (dance); and "Dead End World," recorded by Warehouse on Quality Records (pop). Other artists include Judy Tenuta, Ernest Kohl, Linda Imperial and Shades of Grey.
Tips: "Write music from your heart. Passion and inspiration always stand out in material. Remember it will always take longer than you planned to hear back from industry people."

MERKIN RECORDS INC., 310 E. Biddle St., Baltimore MD 21202. (410)234-0048. President: Joe Goldsborough. Labels include Protocool Records. Record company. Estab. 1988. Releases 5-6 singles, 5-10 LPs, 3-5 EPs, and 5-10 CDs/year. Pays 9-16% royalty to artists on contract; statutory rate to publisher per song on record. "Nothing if we don't get part of publishing."
How to Contact: Submit demo tape by mail. Unsolicited submissions are OK. Prefers cassette with 3 songs. "If we don't like, you might not hear from us. If you can't say something nice don't say anything at all." Does not return material. Reports in 2 weeks.
Music: Mostly **eclectic alternative rock**. Released *Bastards Of Melody* (by Andy Bopp), recorded by Love Nut (rock); *Onespot Fringehead*, written and recorded by Onespot Fringehead (alternative hard rock); and *Carload of Scenic Effects*, written and recorded by Gerty (alternative rock), all on Merkin Records. Other artists include Meatjack, Broad and Black Friday.
Tips: "We are looking for tour-ready, driven bands who write their own songs. Standard pop and metal will do better elsewhere."

MERLIN PRODUCTIONS, P.O. Box 5087, Vancouver British Columbia V6B 4A9 **Canada**. Phone/fax: (604)528-9194. President: Wolfgang Hamann. Record company, production company. Estab. 1979. Releases 5 singles, 3 LPs, 1 EP and 3 CDs/year. Pays negotiable royalty to artists on contract; statutory rate to publisher per song on record.
• See the listings for Zauber Music Publishing in the Music Publishers section and Merlin Management in the Managers and Booking Agents section.
How to Contact: Submit demo tape by mail. Unsolicited submissions are OK. Prefers cassette with 3 songs and lyric sheet. SAE and IRC. Reports in 3 weeks.
Music: Mostly **rock/pop**, **R&B** and **dance**; also **modern rock**. Released *Sunshine* and *Harmony*, both written and recorded by Mode to Joy (rock); and *Tattoo Man*, written and recorded by Wolfgang/Wolfgang (dance), all on Merlin Productions. Other artists include Teknoamedeus.

*METAL BLADE RECORDS, 2345 Erringer Rd., Suite 108, Simi Valley CA 93065. (805)522-9111. Fax: (805)522-9380. E-mail: mtlbldrcds@aol.com. A&R: Matthew Bower. Record company. Estab. 1982. Releases 20 LPs, 2 EPs and 20 CDs/year. Pays negotiable royalty to artists on contract.
How to Contact: Submit demo tape by mail. Unsolicited submissions are OK. Prefers cassette with 3 songs. Does not return material. Reports in 1-3 months.
Music: Mostly **heavy metal, industrial** and **punk**; also **hardcore, gothic** and **noise**. Released *Rag Na Roc*, recorded by Gwar (metal/punk); *Solar Lovers*, recorded by Cellestia Season (gothic/metal); and *Haunted*, recorded by Six Feet Under (heavy metal), all on Metal Blade Records. Other artists include Grip Inc., Decoryah, Galactic Cowboys, Masquerade, Cannibal Corpse, Sacred Reich, King Diamond and Fates Warning.
Tips: "Be critical of yourself; know when you have good songs and when you have bad songs. Metal Blade is known throughout the underground for quality metal-oriented acts."

MIGHTY RECORDS, 150 West End, Suite 6-D, New York NY 10023. (212)873-5968. Manager: Danny Darrow. Labels include Mighty Sounds & Filmworks. Record company, music publisher, record producer (Danny Darrow). Estab. 1958. Releases 1-2 singles, 1-2 12″ singles and 1-2 LPs/year. Pays standard royalty to artists on contract; statutory rate to publisher per song on record.
  ● Manager Danny Darrow also has a listing in the Record Producers section and the Rockford Music Co. can be found in the Music Publishers section.
How to Contact: Submit demo tape by mail. Unsolicited submissions are OK. "No phone calls." Prefers cassette with 3 songs and lyric sheet. SASE. Reports in 1-2 weeks.
Music: Mostly **pop, country** and **dance**; also **jazz**. Released *Impulse* (by D. Darrow); *Corporate Lady* (by Michael Green); and *Falling In Love* (by Brian Dowen), all recorded by Danny Darrow on Mighty Records.
Tips: "Listen to the top 40 hits and write better songs."

MIRROR RECORDS, INC., 645 Titus Ave., Rochester NY 14617. (716)544-3500. Vice President: Armand Schaubroeck. Labels include House of Guitars Records. Record company and music publisher. Royalty paid to artists varies; negotiable royalty to songwriters on contract.
How to Contact: Prefers cassette or record (or videocassette). Include photo with submission. SASE. Reports in 3-4 months.
Music: **Folk, progressive, rock, alternative, rap, R&B** and **blues**. Released "Rip It Out," recorded by Dirty Looks; "Taar," recorded by Burning Orange; and "Let's Go Get Stoned," recorded by the Chesterfield Kings.

MISSILE RECORDS, Box 5537 Kreole Station, Moss Point MS 39563. (601)475-2098. Fax: (601)475-7484. "No collect calls." President/Owner: Joe F. Mitchell. Record company, music publisher (Bay Ridge Publishing/BMI) and record producer. Estab. 1974. Releases 28 singles and 10 LPs/year. "Missile Records has national and international distribution." Pays "8-15¢ per song to new artists, higher rate to established artists"; statutory rate to publisher for each record sold.
How to Contact: Write first and obtain permission to submit. Include #10 SASE. "All songs sent for review must include sufficient return postage." Prefers cassette with 3-6 songs and lyric sheet. SASE. Reports in 6-8 weeks.
Music: Mostly **country, alternative, gospel, rap, heavy metal, jazz, bluegrass** and **R&B**; also **soul, MOR, blues, rock** and **pop**. Released *My Kind of Country* and "When Love Builds a House," recorded by Jerry Piper; and "Has Anyone Seen My Baby?", written and recorded by Herbert Lacey (R&B), all on Missile Records.
Tips: "Have faith in your ability. Set a goal and work to achieve it."

*MJM RECORDS, P.O. Box 1731, La Mirada CA 90637. President: Mark Joseph. Labels include Renaissance Recordings. Record company. Estab. 1991. Releases 3 CDs/year. Pays negotiable royalty to artists on contract; statutory rate to publisher per song on record.
How to Contact: Submit demo tape by mail. Unsolicited submissions are OK. Does not return material.
Music: Mostly **pop, rock** and **R&B**; also **alternative**. Released *Tamplin* and *Witness Box*, both written and recorded by Ken Tamplin; and Enemy Lines (by George Ochoa), recorded by Recon, all on MJM Records (rock). Other artists include Saviour Machine.

MODAL MUSIC, INC.™, Niels Bjerres VEJ 37, DK-8270 Hojbjerg, **Denmark**. Phone/fax: 45/8672 5050. Contact: President. Record company and agent. Estab. 1988. Releases 1-2 LPs/year. Pays negotiable royalty to artists on contract; negotiable rate to publisher per song on record.
How to Contact: Submit demo tape by mail. Unsolicited submissions are OK. Prefers cassette with bio, PR, brochures, any info about artist and music. Does not return material. Reports in 1-2 months.
Music: Mostly **ethnic, folk** and **world**. Released *Meet Your Neighbor's Folk Music*, recorded by Jutta & the Hi-Dukes (ethnic folk); *Lebedich und Frailach*, recorded by Ensemble M'chaiya (Jewish folk);

and *New Times*, recorded by Balkan Rhythm Band (Balkan-world), all on Modal Music Records.
Tips: "We must hear what you've done, but recording quality (for demos *only*) is not as important as performance and writing quality. We don't expect too many writers, however, due to the ethnic focus of the label. Make sure your name, address, and phone number are on *every item* you submit."

MODERN BLUES RECORDINGS, Box 248, Pearl River NY 10965. (914)735-3944. Owner: Daniel Jacoubovitch. Record company. Estab. 1985. Releases 1-2 LPs and 1-2 CDs/year. Pays varying royalty.
How to Contact: Call first and obtain permission to submit. Does not return material. Reports in 6-8 weeks.
Music: Blues, R&B, **soul** and rock. Released "Poison Kisses," written and recorded by Jerry Portnoy; "Ida's Song," written and recorded by J. Vaughn; and "Frances," written and recorded by Johnson/Maloney, all on Modern Blues Recordings. Other artists include Clayton Love, Tommy Ridgley and Little Hatch.

MODERN VOICES ENTERTAINMENT, LTD., 22 Yerk Ave., Ronkonkoma NY 11779. (516)585-5380. E-mail: 103016,252@compuserve.com. Website: http://www.Arts-Online.com/ModernVoices.html. President: Chris Pati. Record company and record producer. Estab. 1991. Releases 7-10 CDs/year. Pays 7-10% royalty to artists on contract; statutory rate to publisher per song on record.
How to Contact: Call first to obtain permission to submit. Prefers cassette (or videocassette) with 2-3 songs and lyric sheet. Does not return material. Reports in 2-3 months.
Music: Mostly **blues**, **gospel** and **R&B**; also **pop/rock**, **rap** and **alternative**. Released *Blufire*, written and recorded by Chris Pati (alternative); *Wax Poetic*, written and recorded by Wax Poetic; and *Heavenbound*, written and recorded by The Original Loving Brothers (gospel), all on Modern Voices Records. Other artists include Deborah Ann, Tony Mascolo, Marilyn Pardo and Cesco.

*MOJO RECORDS, 1547 14th St., Santa Monica CA 90404. (310)260-3181. Fax: (310)260-3172. A&R: Patrick McDowell. Record company, music publisher (Jay Rifkin/WADAUDEF?) and record producer (Jay Rifkin). Estab. 1995. Pays negotiable royalty to artists on contract; statutory rate to publisher per song on record.
How to Contact: Write first and obtain permission to submit. Prefers cassette with 3 songs and lyric sheet. Does not return material. Reports in 1-2 months.
Music: Mostly **alternative rock, modern rock** and **A/C**. Artists include Goldfinger and Sam Ellis.

*MONS RECORDS, Taubenplatz 42, Trippstadt **Germany** 67705. (49)6306-993222. Fax: (49)6306-993223. President: Thilo Berg. Record company, music publisher and record producer. Estab. 1992. Releses 30 CDs/year. Pays negotiable royalty to artists on contract; statutory rate to publisher per song on record.
 • Mons Records was voted the most successful independent label on the Top 100 Gavin jazz charts for 1995.
How to Contact: Submit demo tape by mail. Unsolicited submissions are OK. Prefers cassette. Does not return material. Reports in 1 month.
Music: Mostly **jazz** and **pop**. Released *It's a Wonderful World*, written and recorded by Allan Harris; and *Wish Me Love*, written and recorded by Dee Daniels, both on Mons Records (jazz).

MONTICANA RECORDS, P.O. Box 702, Snowdon Station, Montreal, Quebec H3X 3X8 **Canada**. General Manager: David P. Leonard. Labels include Dynacom. Record company, record producer and music publisher (Montina Music/SOCAN). Estab. 1963. Pays negotiable royalty to artists on contract.
 • Monticana's publishing company, Montina Music, can be found in the Music Publishers section and Monticana Productions can be found in the Record Producers section.
How to Contact: Submit demo tape by mail. Unsolicited submissions are OK. Prefers phonograph record (or VHS videocassette) and lyric sheet. Does not return material.
Music: Mostly **top 40, blues, country, dance-oriented, easy listening, folk, gospel, jazz, MOR, progressive, R&B, rock** and **soul**.

MOR RECORDS, 17596 Corbel Court, San Diego CA 92128. (619)485-1550. President: Stuart L. Glassman. Record company and record producer. Estab. 1980. Releases 3 singles/year. Pays 4% royalty to artists on contract; negotiable rate to publisher per song on record.
Affiliate(s): MOR Jazztime.
How to Contact: Submit demo tape by mail. Unsolicited submissions are OK. Prefers cassette (or VHS videocassette). SASE. Reports in 2-3 weeks.
Music: Mostly **pop instrumental/vocal MOR**; also **novelty**. Released *Run to the Movies*, written and recorded by Legends; *The Hour of Love*, written and recorded by Dennis Russell; and *Sandy Taggart Sings*, written and recorded by Sandy Taggart, all on MOR Records. Other artists include Frank Sinatra Jr., Dave Racan, Dave Austin, Wally Flaherty and Mr. Piano.

Tips: "Send original work. Do not send 'copy' work. Write lyrics with a 'hook.' "

*MOUNTAIN RECORDS, P.O. Box 1253, Easton PA 18044. (610)253-5744. Fax: (800)500-1339. Website: http://webtunes.com/~inotes/brodian.html. President: Stewart Brodian. Record company. Estab. 1983. Releases 1 single, 1 LP and 1 CD/year. Pays negotiable royalty to artists on contract; statutory rate to publisher per song on record.
How to Contact: Submit demo tape by mail. Unsolicited submissions are OK. Prefers cassette with any number of songs. SASE. Reports in 3 weeks.
Music: Mostly **pop, rock** and **alternative**; also **folk, industrial** and **heavy metal**. Released *Troubled Troubadour*, written and recorded by G.G. Allin (alternative); "Dinosaur Rocker," written and recorded by Stewart Brodian (folk); and *A Mountain of Metal*, written and recorded by various artists, all on Mountain Records. Other artists include the Zeros.
Tips: "Use wholesome lyrics—you can get your point across without swearing."

MSM RECORDS, Box 101, Sutton MA 01590. Publisher/Owner: John Scott. Labels include Hālo Records and Bronco Records. Record company and music publisher (Mount Scott Music/BMI and Pick The Hits Music/ASCAP). Estab. 1979. Releases 3-4 singles/year. Pays negotiated royalty to artists on contract; statutory rate to publisher per song on record.
How to Contact: Write first and obtain permission to submit. Prefers cassette with 2 songs and lyric sheet. SASE. Reports in 6 weeks.
Music: Mostly **folk, traditional country, contemporary country**, and **theater/musical works**. Released *Simply Classic Guitar* (by various), recorded by Joel Rivard (instrumental); *Same Old School*, written and recorded by Cactus (country), both on MSM Records; and *Duchess of Malfi* (by Jon Scott), recorded by Cliniqué Chamber Orchestra on Halo Records (theater score soundtrack). Other artists include Far North (folk/bluegrass) and Just Add Water.
Tips: "Follow submission guidelines. Pro demos preferred. Lead sheets best, but will accept typed lyric sheets. Will discuss acceptance of theater works for review/possible collaboration. Write and include synopsis (two page maximum) if submitting theater works."

MULE KICK RECORDS, 5341 Silverlode Dr., Placerville CA 95667. (916)626-4536. Owner: Doug McGinnis, Sr. Record company and music publisher (Freewheeler Publishing/BMI). Estab. 1949. Pays 25% royalty to artists on contract; statutory rate to publisher.
How to Contact: Submit demo tape by mail. Unsolicited submissions are OK. Prefers cassette with 6-10 songs and lyric and lead sheet. SASE. Reports in 1 week.
Music: Mostly **C&W** and **c-rock**; also **pop**. Released *A Tribute to Billy Hughes*, recorded by Doug McGinnis; *Pretending*, written and recorded by Diana Blair; and *Tribute Two*, written and recorded by Joaquim Murphy, all on Mule Kick Records.

MUSIC SERVICES & MARKETING, P.O. Box 7171, Duluth MN 55807. (218)628-3003. President: Frank Dell. Record company, music publisher (Frank Dell Music/BMI) and record producer (MSM). Estab. 1970. Releases 2 singles, 1 LP and 1 CD/year. Pays 10% royalty to artists on contract; statutory rate to publisher per song on record.
   ● Music Services & Marketing's publishing company, Frank Dell Music, is listed in the Music Publishers section.
How to Contact: Submit demo tape by mail. Unsolicited submissions are OK. Write first to arrange personal interview. Prefers cassette with 2 songs. SASE. Reports in 3 months.
Music: Mostly **country** and **gospel**. Released "Memories," written and recorded by Frank Dell on Country Legends Records. Other artists include Betty Lee, John Voit and Terry Panyon.

*MUSIKUS PRODUCTIONS, INC., 715 North Ave., New Rochelle NY 10801. (914)633-2506. President: Hugh Berberich. Record company. Estab. 1992. Releases 4 cassettes and 12 CDs/year. Pays 15% royalty to artists on contract; negotiable rate to publisher per song on record.
   ● One of Musikus Productions' artists, Carolina Slim, appears in the Madonna video "Secret."
How to Contact: Submit demo tape by mail. Unsolicited submissions are OK. Prefers cassette or DAT. SASE. Reports in 3 weeks.
Music: Mostly **pop, rock** and **R&B**; also **classical, show (musical)** and **blues**. Released *Society Blues*, written and recorded by Carolina Slim (blues); *Flood* (by Andy Toomson), recorded by Flood (rock);

MARKET CONDITIONS are constantly changing! If you're still using this book and it is 1998 or later, buy the newest edition of *Songwriter's Market* at your favorite bookstore or order directly from Writer's Digest Books.

and *Max Barros* (by various), recorded by M. Barros (classical) all on Musikus Productions, Inc. Other artists include Christine McCabe, Andrew Burns, Michael Svelen and Brian Hunter.

NERVOUS RECORDS, 7-11 Minerva Rd., London NW10 6HJ, **England**. Phone: 44(181)963-0352. E-mail: 100316.3456@compuserve.com. Website: http://194.60.72.96/www.nervousrecords. Managing Director: R. Williams. Record company (Rage Records), record producer and music publisher (Nervous Publishing and Zorch Music). Member MCPS, PRS, PPL, ASCAP, NCB. Releases 10 CDs/year. Pays 8-10% royalty to artists on contract; statutory rate to publisher per song on records. Royalties paid directly to US songwriters and artists or through US publishing or recording affiliate.
   • Nervous Records' publishing company, Nervous Publishing, is listed in the Music Publishers section.
How to Contact: Submit demo tape by mail. Unsolicited submissions are OK. Prefers cassette with 4-15 songs and lyric sheet. SAE and IRC. Reports in 6 weeks.
Music: Psychobilly and **rockabilly**. "No heavy rock, AOR, stadium rock, disco, soul, pop—only wild rockabilly and psychobilly." Released *Mobile Corrosion*, written and recorded by Darrel Higham; *Is It Cool*, by various artists; and *Lost In The Desert* (by Rasmussen), recorded by Taggy Towes, all on Nervous Records. Other artists include Voodoo Swing, Colbert Hamilton and the Quakes, Nitros, 3 Blue Teardrops.
Tips: "More rockabilly—quick!"

NEW BEGINNING RECORD PRODUCTIONS, Box 4773, Fondren Station, Jackson MS 39216-0773. A&R Manager: S. Wooten. Record company. "We will work with composers, lyric writers and collaborators on unusual songs. Also new unusual talent is welcome." Pays 10-20% royalty to artists on contract; statutory rate to publisher for each record sold.
How to Contact: Submit demo tape by mail. Unsolicited submissions are OK. Prefers cassette with 2-4 songs. SASE. Reports in 1 month.
Music: Mostly **country**; also **bluegrass** and **black gospel**. Released "A City Called Glory" and "The Angels Will Be Singing," recorded by Archie Mitchell on Four Winds Records; and "Heaven Bound" (by Spiritual Travelers), recorded by L.D. Tennial on Golden Rule Records.

NEW EXPERIENCE RECORDS/GRAND SLAM RECORDS, Box 683, Lima OH 45802. Contact: James Milligan. Record company, music publisher (A New Rap Jam Publishing/ASCAP and Party House Publishing/BMI), management (Creative Star Management) and record producer (James Milligan). Estab. 1989. Releases 15-20 singles, 5 12" singles, 3 LPs, 2 EPs and 2-5 CDs/year. Pays 8% royalty; statutory rate to publisher per song on record.
   • See the listings for A New Rap Jam Publishing in the Music Publishers section and New Experience Records in the Record Producers section.
How to Contact: Write or call first and obtain permission to submit. Address material to A&R Dept. or Carl Milligan, Talent Coordinator. Prefers cassette (or VHS videocassette) with 3-5 songs and lyric sheet. SASE. Reports in 1 month.
Music: Mostly **R&B**, **pop** and **rock/rap**; also **country**, **contemporary gospel** and **soul/top 40**. Released "Understanding," written and recorded by James Milligan/Anthony Milligan on N.E.R. Records (ballad); "Release Me" (by 419 SQad Gladys Knight), recorded by Thomas Roach/John Ward on Pump It Up Records (rap); and "I'm So Proud," produced by Curtis Mayfield and reissued by The Impressions on N.E.R. Records. Other artists include Carl Milligan (gospel singer), Richard Bamberger, Brooks, Melvin Brooks of the World Famous Impressions, Barbara Joyce Lomas and Generation X.

NOCTURNAL RECORDS, P.O. Box 399, Royal Oak MI 48068. (810)542-NITE. Fax: (810)542-4342. President: Chris Varady. Record company and record producer. Estab. 1988.
How to Contact: Submit demo tape by mail. Unsolicited submissions are OK. Prefers cassette or CD. Does not return material.
Music: Mostly **alternative rock**, **punk** and **alternative folk**; also **progressive**. Released *Falling*, written and recorded by Cathouse (alternative); "Tennessee Hustler," written and recorded by Mule (punk); and *Lying Next to You*, written and recorded by Wig (punk), all on Nocturnal Records.

NORTH STAR MUSIC, 22 London St., E. Greenwich RI 02818. (401)886-8888. President: Richard Waterman. Record company. Estab. 1985. Releases 5-10 LPs/year. Pays 4-10% royalty to artists on contract; statutory rate to publisher per song on record.
How to Contact: Submit demo tape by mail. Unsolicited submissions are OK. Prefers cassette with 4-5 songs and lyric sheet. Does not return material. Reports in 2 months.
Music: Mostly **instrumental**, **traditional jazz**, **contemporary** and **classical**. Released *Broadway Openings* (by various), recorded by Rick Johnson (jazz); *Eveningtide*, written and recorded by Bruce Foulke (contemporary); and *Prelude in Pastel*, written and recorded by Ron Murray (contemporary), all on North Star Records. Other artists include Judith Lynn Stillman, Greg Joy, Gerry Beaudoin, Cheryl Wheeler, Nathaniel Rosen and Swingshift.

Tips: "Send a professional looking, well thought-out presentation of your best material."

*NOT LAME RECORDINGS, 962 S. Clarkson St., Denver CO 80209. Phone/fax: (303)744-2684. E-mail: notlame@aol.com. Contact: Bruce Brodeen. Record company and distributor of indie power pop bands and labels. Estab. 1994. Releases 1-2 EPs and 3-4 CDs/year. Pays negotiable royalty to artists on contract; negotiable rate to publisher per song on record.
How to Contact: Submit demo tape by mail. Unsolicited submissions are OK. Prefers cassette, VHS videocassette, CD or LP with 3 songs. Does not return material. Reports in 3-4 weeks.
Music: Mostly **power pop**, **pop/punk** and **music with hooks!** Released *Double Dose of Pop* (by Mike Mazarella), recorded by The Rooks; *Symphony* (by Tony Perkins), recorded by Martin Luther Lennon; and "4 Song EP" (by various), recorded by Pez Band, all on Not Lame Records. Other artists include The Rockafellers, Cherry Twister, The Shambles and The Finns.
Tips: "Not Lame proudly embraces artists who are not ashamed of Beatle-esque hooks and harmonies in their craft."

NUCLEUS RECORDS, Box 282, 885 Broadway, Bayonne NJ 07002. President: Robert Bowden. Record company and music publisher (Roots Music/BMI). Member AFM (US and Canada). Estab. 1979. Releases 2 singles and 1 LP/year. Pays 25% royalty to artists on contract; statutory rate to publisher per song on record.
  • Nucleus Records' publishing company, Roots Music, is listed in the Music Publishers section, and Robert Bowden is listed in the Record Producers section.
How to Contact: Write first and obtain permission to submit. Prefers cassette (or videocassette) with any number songs and lyric sheet. Prefers studio produced demos. SASE. Reports in 1 month.
Music: Mostly **country** and **pop**; also **church/religious**, **classical**, **folk**, **MOR**, **progressive**, **rock** (**soft**, **mellow**) and **top 40**. Released "Henrey C.," "Always" and "Selfish Heart" (by Bowden), recorded by Marco Sission, all on Nucleus Records.

OAR FIN RECORDS, (formerly Metro Records), 216 Third Ave. N., Minneapolis MN 55401. (612)338-3833. Special Projects Coordinator: James Walsh. Record company, record producer, artist management and development/talent agency. Estab. 1991. Releases 3-4 singles, 1-2 EPs and 5-10 CDs/year. Pays 5-20% royalty to artists on contract; statutory rate to publisher per song on record.
How to Contact: Write or call first and obtain permission to submit. Prefers cassette (or VHS videocassette if available) with 3-4 songs and lyric sheet or lead sheet. SASE. Reports in 2-3 weeks.
Music: Mostly **pop**, **rock** and **country**; also **jazz**. Released *20 Years Ago Today*, (by Walsh/Challman), recorded by Gypsy (rock); *Buffalo Alice* (by Wilson/Sickels/Adams), recorded by Buffalo Alice (country); and *Night Life*, recorded by Down Right Tight (R&B), all on Oar Fin Records.
Tips: "Be prepared to make a commitment to the label and your career. The level of your commitment will be mirrored by our company. As an artist, be prepared to back up your recorded product live."

*OBLIVION ENTERTAINMENT, 1660 E. Herndon #135, Fresno CA 93720. (209)432-7329. Fax: (209)432-0147. Public Relations: Marlo Shay Boutté. Record company. Estab. 1992. Pays negotiable royalty to artists on contract; negotiable rate to publisher per song on record.
  • One of Oblivion's artists, Pusher, had a song appear in the Sylvester Stallone/Antonio Banderas film *Assassins*.
How to Contact: Submit demo tape by mail. Unsolicited submissions are OK. Prefers cassette with 3 songs and lyric sheet. Include photo. SASE. Reports in 3 weeks.
Music: Mostly **alternative**, **rock** and **soul**; also **easy listening** and **pop**. Released *Blisskreig* (by Laura Arias), recorded by Candy Planet (alternative); *Problems* (by Tommy Joy), recorded by Pusher (alternative); and *She's My Dream* (by Celia Farbe), recorded by Vodka (alternative), all on Oblivion. Other artists include Braindead Soundmachine and Lance Carlos.
Tips: "Be self motivated and be willing to put in the work and effort, playing every gig booked, self-publicity. Be open minded."

OCP PUBLICATIONS, 5536 NE Hassald, Portland OR 97213. (503)281-1191. Fax: (503)282-3486. Administrative Assistant/Submissions: Kathy Orozco. Labels include Candleflame and NALR. Record company, music publisher and record producer. Estab. 1977. Releases 20 LPs and 10 CDs/year. Pays 10% royalty to artists on contract; negotiable rate to publisher per song on record.
  • See the interview with OCP artists Mark Friedman and Janet Vogt in the 1996 *Songwriter's Market*.
How to Contact: Submit demo tape by mail. Unsolicited submissions are OK. Requires lead sheets (with chords, melody line and text minimum) with *optional* demo tape. Prefers cassette with lead sheet. "Detailed submission information available upon request." SASE. Reports in 3 months.
Music: Mostly **liturgical**, **Christian/listening** and **children's Christian**; also **choral Christian anthems** and **youth Christian anthems**. Released *If We Dare to Hope*, written and recorded by Bobby Fisher; *If God Is For Us*, written and recorded by Grayson Warren Brown; and *God Shines On You*,

written and recorded by Mark Friedman and Janet Vogt, all on OCP. "There are over 80 artists signed by OCP."
Tips: "Know the Catholic liturgy and the music needs therein."

OGLIO RECORDS, 901-A North Pacific Coast Hwy. #200, Redondo Beach CA 90277. (310)798-2252. Fax: (310)798-3728. Record company. Estab. 1992. Releases 20 LPs and 20 CDs/year. Pays negotiable royalty to artist on contract.
How to Contact: Write first and obtain permission to submit a demo. All formats. Does not return material. Reports in 6 weeks.
Music: Mostly **alternative rock** and **adult rock**.

OLD SCHOOL RECORDS, 179 Prospect Ave., Wood Dale IL 60191-2727. E-mail: oldschrec@aol. com. Owner/President: Peter J. Gianakopoulos. Record company, music publisher (Old School Records/Goosongs, ASCAP). Estab. 1992. Releases 1-2 singles, 1-2 LPs, 1-2 EPs, and 1-2 CDs/year. Pays 10-16% to artists on contract; statutory rate to publisher per song on record.
How to Contact: Submit demo tape by mail. Unsolicited submissions are OK. Prefers cassette with 3-5 songs and lyric sheet. SASE. Reports in 1 month.
Music: Mostly **alternative rock**, **blues** and **pop**; also **funk**, **punk** and **tribute albums**. Released *Muse* (by Peter Gaines), recorded by The Now (rock); *Goo*, written and recorded by Goo (rock); and *Resurrection of the Warlock—A Tribute to Marc Bolan & T. Rex*, recorded by various artists, all on Old School Records. Other artists include The Crüxshadows and Cosa Nostra.
Tips: "Be true to your craft. No matter how different the feel of music—take it to the style you feel like writing. Most artists may find their best writing style is different from their listening tastes."

*OMNI 2000 INC., 413 Cooper St., Camden NJ 08102. (609)963-6400. Fax: (609)964-FAX-1. President/Executive Producer: Michael Nise. Record company, music publisher and record producer. Estab. 1995. Pays negotiable royalty to artists on contract; statutory rate to publisher per song on record.
How to Contact: Write first and obtain permission to submit. Prefers cassette. SASE.
Music: Mostly **R&B**, **gospel** and **pop**; also **children's**.

ORBIT RECORDS, P.O. Box 120675, Nashville TN 37212. (615)883-9161. Owner: Ray McGinnis. Record company and music publisher (Nautical Music Co.). Estab. 1965. Releases 6-10 singles, 6 12″ singles and 4 CDs/year. Pays 5.25% royalty to artists on contract; statutory rate to publisher per song on record.
  ● Orbit Records' publishing affiliate, Nautical Music Co., is listed in the Music Publishers section.
How to Contact: Submit demo tape by mail. Unsolicited submissions are OK. Prefers cassette with 4 songs and lead sheet. SASE. Reports in 4-6 weeks.
Music: Country (ballads), **country rock** and **R&B**. Released "Falling" (by Alan Warren), recorded by Bo Jest; "I'm Gonna Be Strong" (by Gene Pitney), recorded by Michael Storm; and "Southern Living" (by McGregory/Hughes), recorded by Sonny Martin, all on Orbit Records.
Tips: "We like artists with individual styles, not 'copy cats'; be original and unique."

ORDER RECORDS, 441 E. Belvedere Ave., Baltimore MD 21212. (410)435-0993. Fax: (410)435-3513. E-mail: orderprod@aol.com. General Partner: Joyce Klein. Record company, record producer (Order Productions) and music publisher (Orderlottsa Music/BMI). Estab. 1985. Releases 3 CDs/year. Pays standard royalty to artists on contract; statutory rate to publisher per song on record.
  ● See the listing for Orderlottsa Music in the Music Publishers section.
How to Contact: Submit demo tape by mail. Unsolicited submissions are OK. Prefers cassette with 3 songs. SASE. Reports in 1 month.
Music: Contemporary instrumental only. Released *Unconquered Lions* (by W. Raymond), recorded by Uprising (reggae); *Keepers of the Light* and *Of Ancient Wisdom*, written and recorded by Jeff Order on Order Records (New Age).
Tips: "Don't expect any record label to invest in your career if you haven't done so first! Always include a SASE with your submissions. Make your compositions and songs interesting with clean melodies, good arrangements and well executed."

HOW TO GET THE MOST out of *Songwriter's Market* (at the front of this book) contains comments and suggestions to help you understand and use the information in these listings.

*ORINDA RECORDS, P.O. Box 838, Orinda CA 94563. (510)833-7000. A&R Director: Harry Balk. Record company. Pays negotiable rate to publisher per song on record.
How to Contact: Submit demo tape by mail. Unsolicited submissions are OK. Prefers cassette and lead sheet. Does not return material. Reports in 3 months.
Music: Mostly **pop**, **rock** and **jazz**.

P. & N. RECORDS, 61 Euphrasia Dr., Toronto, Ontario M6B 3V8 **Canada**. (416)782-5768. Fax: (416)782-7170. Presidents: Panfilo Di Matteo and Nicola Di Matteo. Record company, record producer and music publisher (Lilly Music Publishing). Estab. 1993. Releases 10 singles, 20 12″ singles, 15 LPs, 20 EPs and 15 CDs/year. Pays 25-50% royalty to artists on contract; statutory rate to publisher per song on record.
  ● P. & N.'s publishing affiliate, Lilly Music Publishing, is listed in the Music Publishers section.
How to Contact: Submit demo tape by mail. Unsolicited submissions are OK. Prefers cassette or videocassette with 3 songs and lyric or lead sheet. "We only contact if we are interested in the material." Does not return material. Reports in 1 month if interested.
Music: Mostly **dance**, **ballads** and **rock**. Released *My Life* and *Tonight* (by Marco A. Gomes), recorded by Riga; and "Kinta," written and recorded by Janet Di Matteo, all on P. & N. Records.

PAINT CHIP RECORDS, P.O. Box 12401, Albany NY 12212. (518)765-4027. President: Dominick Campana. Record company. Estab. 1992. Releases 2 singles and 4 CDs/year. Pays negotiable royalty to artists on contract.
How to Contact: Submit demo tape by mail. Unsolicited submissions are OK. Prefers cassette with 4 songs. "No guitar solos, fluffy keyboards, crappy production or lyrics with the word 'baby' in them. Our dream roster might include The Clash, The Jam, The Replacements and Billy Bragg. Current faves include Radiohead and Oasis." Does not return material. Reports in 6 weeks.
Music: Mostly **"alternative" guitar rock** (bands). Released *Bump Into Fate* by various artists; *Big Block* (by Crist/Pauley/Hogan), recorded by Bloom (alternative rock); and *Lughead* (by Ferrandino/Weiss/Blaine/Bell), recorded by Lughead, all on Paint Chip Records. Other artists include Queer For Astro Boy.
Tips: "Be honest. Don't depend on your music to generate steady income right away. Pour your soul into every song."

PARAGOLD RECORDS & TAPES, P.O. Box 292101, Nashville TN 37229-2101. (615)865-1360. Director: Teresa Parks Bernard. Record company, music publisher (Rainbarrel Music Co./BMI) and record producer. Estab. 1972. Releases 3 singles and 3 LPs/year. Pays statutory rate to publisher per song on record.
How to Contact: Write first and obtain permission to submit. Prefers cassette (or VHS videocassette) with 2 songs and lyric or lead sheet. SASE (#10 envelope not acceptable). Reports in 2 months.
Music: **Country**. Released "Rose & Bittercreek" and "Bottle of Happiness," written and recorded by Johnny Bernard; and "Daddy's Last Letter" (by J. Bernard), recorded by JLyne, all on Paragold Records (country). Other artists include Sunset Cowboys.
Tips: "We are only accepting limited material of the highest quality."

*PATTY LEE RECORDS, 6034 Graciosa Dr., Hollywood CA 90068. (213)469-5431. Assistant to the President: Susan Neidhart. Record company and record producer. Estab. 1985. Releases 1-2 singles, 1-2 EPs and 2-3 CDs/year. Pays negotiable royalty to artists on contract.
How to Contact: Send query postcard only. Does not return material.
Music: Mostly **New Orleans rock**, **bebop jazz** and **cowboy poetry**; also **eclectic**, **folk** and **country**. Released *Alligator Ball, Be Your Own Parade* and *Must Be the Mardi Gras*, all written and recorded by Armand St. Martin on Patty Lee Records (New Orleans rock). Other artists include Too Tall Timm, James T. Daughtry, Jim Sharpe, Curt Warren and Kevin Atkinson.
Tips: "Our label is small, which gives us the ability to develop our artists at their own rate of artistry. We are interested in quality *only,* regardless of the genre of music or style. Keep in mind that Patty Lee Records is not Warner Bros.! So patience and a good query letter are great starts."

*J. PAUL RECORDS, 1387 Chambers Rd., Columbus OH 43212. Phone/fax: (614)487-1911. Owner: Jim Bruce. Record company, music publisher (James Paul Music), record producer (Jim Bruce) and artist management. Estab. 1994. Releases 1-3 singles, 1-3 LPs and 1-3 CDs/year. Pays negotiable royalty to artists on contract; statutory rate to publisher per song on record.
How to Contact: Submit demo tape by mail. Unsolicited submissions are OK. Prefers cassette, DAT or VHS videotape with 1-3 songs. SASE. Reports in 4-6 weeks.
Music: Mostly **country**, **gospel** and **top 40/pop**; also **country rock**. Released *That's The Way* (by various), recorded by Debbie Collins on J. Paul Records.
Tips: "Upbeat songs a must, ballads OK for songwriters. Artist must have professional package and band in place and working."

PBM RECORDS, P.O. Box 1312, Hendersonville TN 37077-1312. (615)865-1696 Fax: (615)865-6432. E-mail: mgpbmrecds@aol.com. Owner: Michele Gauvin. Labels include Nashville Rocks! Records. Record company. "PBM also independently produces 2 television shows from Nashville." Estab. 1990. Releases 1-3 CDs/year. Pays statutory rate to publisher per song on record.
How to Contact: Call or write first and obtain permission to submit a demo. Prefers cassette or VHS videocassette with lyric sheet, photo and bio. SASE. Reports in 3-6 months.
Music: Mostly **country** and **rock**. Released "Don't Touch Me" (by Hank Cochran); "Half A Mind" (by Roger Miller); and "You're Not the Only Heart In Town" (by Lonnie Wilson), all recorded by Michele Gauvin on PBM Records (country). Other artists include Jim Woodrum.
Tips: "Send your best material and be persistent."

*PC! MUSIC COMPANY, 711 Eighth Ave., San Diego CA 92101. (619)236-0187. Fax: (619)236-1768. E-mail: califmsc@aol.com. Contact: Corbin Dooley. Record company, music publisher (PC! Acid, PC! Buddah) and record producer (Corbin Dooley). Estab. 1995. Releases 5 singles, 5 LPs and 5 CDs/year. Pays negotiable royalty to artists on contract.
How to Contact: Submit demo tape by mail. Unsolicited submissions are OK. Prefers cassette, DAT or videocassette. "It's always good to follow up repeatedly—then we know you are serious about your work." Returns material if requested. Reports in 1 week.
Music: Mostly **alternative**, **rock** and **hiphop/jazz**; also **acid jazz**, **lounge** and **techno**. Released albums by Another Society (metal) and Jack Johnson (alternative).
Tips: "Send us any original, unique material and be persistent in your follow up."

*PEACHTOWN RECORD CO. INC., 3625 Seilene Dr., College Park GA 30349. (404)761-8262. CEO/President: Bill Freeman. Record company, music publisher (Tasma Publishing) and record producer (Bill Fleetwood). Estab. 1965. Releases 4 singles, 3 LPs and 2 CDs/year.
How to Contact: Write first to arrange personal interview, or submit demo tape by mail. Unsolicited submissions are OK. Prefers cassette. SASE. Reports in 2 weeks.
Music: Mostly **spiritual** and **gospel**. Released *Born Again* (by Bill Fleetwood), recorded by Born Again on Peachtown Record Co. (spiritual).

*PERIDOT RECORDS, P.O. Box 8846, Cranston RI 02920. (401)785-2677. Owner/President: Amy Parravano. Record company, music publisher (Parravano Music) and record producer (Peridot Productions). Estab. 1992. Releases 2 singles, 1 LP and 1 CD/year. Pays 10% royalty to artists on contract; statutory rate to publisher per song on record.
● See the listings for Parravano Music in the Music Publishers section and Peridot Productions in the Record Producers section.
How to Contact: Submit demo tape by mail. Unsolicited submissions are OK. Prefers cassette or DAT with 6-10 songs and lyric sheet. SASE. Reports in 6 months.
Music: Mostly **country**, **country/rock** and **country/blues**; also **ballads**, **MOR** and **rockabilly**. Released *All Night Long* (by Mike DiSano), recorded by Joe Kemp on BJD Records (country); *One Last Try* (by Mike DiSano), recorded by Joe Kemp (country); and "Doctor of Romance" (by Amy Parravano), recorded by Amy Beth, both on Peridot Records.
Tips: "Send your best with commercial appeal."

*PERSPECTIVE RECORDS, 1416 N. LaBrea, Hollywood CA 90028. (213)469-2411. Fax: (213)856-7152. Sr. Director of A&R: Jr. Regisford. Record company.
How to Contact: Submit demo tape by mail. Unsolicited submissions are OK. Prefers cassette or VHS videocassette with 4 songs and lyric sheet. Does not return material. Reports in 4-6 weeks.
Music: Mostly **R&B**, **rap** and **pop**; also **gospel** and **jazz**. Released *The Icon Is Love*, recorded by Barry White; "I Like What You're Doing to Me" (by M.C. Young/B. Hank/W.G. Young), recorded by Joya; and "Love Today" (by T. Taylor/C. Farrar), recorded by Vertical Hold, all on A&M/Perspective Records.

*PHISST RECORDS CORPORATION, 1630 NW First Ave., #14481, Gainesville FL 32604. (904)378-9887. Fax: (904)373-0991. E-mail: phisst@grove.ufl.edu. Website: http://grove.ufl.edu/~phisst. Executive Director: George Telegadis. Labels include Roofinol Records. Record company. Estab. 1993. Releases 12-14 singles and 12-14 CDs/year. Pays negotiable royalty to artists on contract; statutory rate to publisher per song on record.
How to Contact: Submit demo tape by mail. Unsolicited submissions are OK. Prefers DAT, VHS videocassette, CD (preferably). "Send photo, bio, and best 3 press clippings, tour history and current routing. Include manager and booking agent information." Does not return material. Reports in 2 weeks.
Music: Mostly **mainstream alternative** and **heavy alternative**; also **techno/jungle**, **trip hop** and **ambient**. Released *Crave*, written and recorded by Skirt (mainstream alternative); *Embers*, written and recorded by Love Canal (heavy alternative); and *Propaganda/Rock The Vote*, written and recorded

by various artists (mainstream alternative), all on Phisst Records. Other artists include Life Like Feel, Information Society and Big Train.

Tips: "Have competent management. Have and be consistently booked within a region (5+ states, 15-20 dates per month). Have a finished full-length recording. We love to do licensing deals."

PHOENIX RECORDS, INC., Dept. SM, Box 121076, Nashville TN 37212-1076. (615)244-5357. President: Reggie M. Churchwell. Labels include Nashville International Records and Monarch Records. Record company and music publisher. Estab. 1971. Releases 5-6 CDs/year. Pays standard royalty to artists on contract; statutory rate to publisher per song on record.

How to Contact: Write first and obtain permission to submit. "You must have permission before submitting any material." Prefers cassette with lyric sheets. SASE. Reports in 1 month.

Music: Mostly **country** and **pop**; also **gospel**.

Tips: "We are looking for songs with strong hooks and strong words. We are not simply looking for songs, we are looking for hits."

*PICKWICK/MECCA/INTERNATION RECORDS, P.O. Box 725, Daytona Beach FL 32115. (904)252-4849. President: Clarence Dunklin. Record company. Estab. 1980. Releases 20 singles, 30 LPs and 30 CDs/year. Pays 5-10% royalty to artists on contract; negotiable rate to publisher per song on record.

• See the listing for Pritchett Publications in the Music Publishers section.

How to Contact: Submit demo tape by mail. Unsolicited submissions are OK. Prefers cassette with 12 songs and lyric or lead sheet. Does not return material.

Music: Mostly **gospel**, **disco** and **rock/pop**; also **country**, **ballads** and **rap**. Released *Give It To Me Baby* (by Loris Doby), recorded by Gladys Nighte; *Baby I Love You*, written and recorded by Joe Simmon; and *I Love Sweetie* (by Doris Doby), recorded by Bobby Blane.

PINECASTLE/WEBCO RECORDS, 5108 S. Orange Ave., Orlando FL 32809. (407)856-0245. Fax: (407)858-0007. E-mail: pinecast@nebula.ispace.com. Website: http://www.imageplaza.com/fl/music/pinecast. President: Tom Riggs. Record company. Estab. 1991. Releases 10-15 CDs/year. Pays varying royalty to artists on contract; statutory rate to publisher on record.

How to Contact: Write first and obtain permission to submit. Prefers cassette. Does not return material. Reports in 2 months.

Music: Mostly **bluegrass** and **related acoustic**. Released *The Ernest Tubb Record Folio*, recorded by Osborne Brothers on Pinecastle Records; *Born to Sing*, recorded by Larry Stephenson on Webco Records; and *Making the Rounds*, recorded by Terry Eldridge and Andrea Zohn on Pinecastle Records. Other artists include The New Coon Creek Girls, Bill Emerson, Reno Brothers and Rarely Herd.

Tips: "We listen to traditional bluegrass as well as contemporary bluegrass and try to keep a balance between them. We send out rejection letters so please don't call inquiring of the status of your demo."

PIRATE RECORDS, 221 W. 57th St., 8th Floor, New York NY 10019. (212)489-1500. A&R Department: Half Pint. Record company and music publisher (Majestic Control/BMI). Estab. 1994.

How to Contact: Submit demo tape by mail. Unsolicited submissions are OK. Prefers cassette with 3 songs. SASE. Reports in 8 weeks.

Music: Mostly **rap** and **R&B**. Released "Spread It Around" and "Bridge 95," both recorded by Kamakaze on Pirate Records.

*PISSED OFF RECORDS, INC., 320 N. Oakhurst Dr., Penthouse #13, Beverly Hills CA 90210. President/Head of A&R: Brent Lee Kendell. Record company and business management/representation. Estab. 1990. Releases 12 singles, 6 LPs and 5 CDs/year. Pays negotiable royalty to artists on contract; statutory rate to publisher per song on record.

How to Contact: Submit demo tape by mail. Unsolicited submissions are OK. Prefers cassette or VHS videocassette with 3 songs. "Send three songs; no blank tape; repeat first side on reverse; song contact number on cassette." SASE. Reports in 1 month.

Music: Mostly **pissed off/angry**, **punk/heavy metal** and **rock**. Released *Say Uncle* (by Williams/Thomas), recorded by Say Uncle; *Dogs of Pleasure* (by Edwards/Taylor), recorded by Dogs of Pleasure; and *Slam House* (by Patricks/Smith), recorded by Slamhouse (punk), all on Pissed Off Records. Other artists include Bogus Toms, Buzzzcock, Rocktwins, Buzz. . . , C.A.P., Trendlaser and Nuclear Waste.

Tips: "Find a label that represents your small niché in the music industry. Get noticed—get on the CMJ by submissions—get a following. Don't send blank tape!"

*PLANKTON RECORDS, 236 Sebert Rd., Forest Gate, London E7 0NP **England**. (0181)534-8500. Senior Partner: Simon Law. Labels include Sea Dream, Embryo Arts (licensed, Belgium) and Gutta (licensed, Sweden). Record company and music publisher (Sea Dream Music, Chain of Love Music, Crimson Flame, Scarf Music Publishing and Really Free Music). Estab. 1977. Releases 2 CDs,

2 LPs and 1 EP/year. Pays 10% royalty to artists on contract; statutory royalty to publisher per song on record.
   • See the listings for Sea Dream Music in the Music Publishers and Music Print Publishers sections, and Sandcastle Productions in the Managers and Booking Agents section.
How to Contact: Write first and obtain permission to submit. Prefers cassette with 3 songs and lyric sheet. SAE and IRC. Reports in 3 months.
Music: Mostly **funk/rock**, **R&B** and **gospel**; also **blues**. Released *Broken Man* (by Simon Law), recorded by Fresh Claim; *Artsong Song* (by Marc Catley), recorded by Paley's Watch; and *Chattabox* (by Derek Llewellyn), recorded by News Hounds, all on Plankton Records. Other artists include Vatten, Asylum, Ben Okafor, Trevor Speaks, Out of Darkness, Ruth Turner and Geoff Mann.
Tips: "We specialize in bands with a Christian bias, regardless of their musical style."

*PLATEAU MUSIC, P.O. Box 947, White House TN 37188. (615)672-8934. Fax: (615)672-4898. Owner: Tony Mantore. Record company and record producer. Estab. 1990. Releases 4 singles and 2 CDs/year. Pays negotiable royalty to artists on contract; statutory rate to publisher per song on record.
How to Contact: Submit demo tape by mail. Unsolicited submissions are OK. Prefers cassette with 4 songs and lyric sheet. Does not return material. Reports in 2 weeks.
Music: Mostly **country, gospel** and **rock**.

PLATINUM BOULEVARD RECORDS, 525 E. Moana Lane, Reno NV 89502. (702)827-4424. President: Lawrence Davis. Record company. Estab. 1986. Releases 2 singles and 1 LP/year. Pays negotiable royalty to artists on contract; negotiable rate to publisher per song on record.
   • See their listing in the Music Publishers section.
How to Contact: Submit demo tape by mail. Unsolicited submissions are OK. Prefers cassette (or VHS videocassette) with songs and lyric or lead sheets. Does not return material. "We report back only if interested."
Music: Mostly **rock**, **pop** and **R&B**; also **country**, **jazz** and **New Age**. Released *Hear My Heart*, written and recorded by Carl Driggs on Platinum Boulevard Records (pop).
Tips: "When presenting material indicate which artists you have in mind to record it. If you desire to be the recording artist please indicate."

PLATINUM PLUS RECORDS INTERNATIONAL (formerly Stop Hunger Records International), 1300 Division St., Nashville TN 37203. (615)242-4722. (800)767-4984. Fax: (615)242-1177. E-mail: platinumr@aol.com. Producer: Robert Metzgar. Record company and music publisher (Aim High Music/ASCAP, Bobby and Billy Music/BMI). Estab. 1971. Releases 16-17 singles, 25 LPs and 25 CDs/year. Pays statutory rate to publisher per song on record.
   • See the listings for Aim High Music in the Music Publishers section, Capitol Ad, Management and Talent in the Record Producers section and Capitol Management in the Managers and Booking Agents section.
How to Contact: Submit demo tape by mail. Unsolicited submissions are OK. Prefers cassette or VHS videocassette with 5-10 songs and lyric sheet. Does not return material. Reports in 3-4 weeks.
Music: Mostly **country, traditional country** and **pop country**; also **gospel, southern gospel** and **contemporary Christian**. Released *There By Now* (by T. Tucker), recorded by J. Leclere; *Country Boogie Baby* (by T. Williams), recorded by Legal Limit, both on Capitol Records; and *So Hello, Handsome* (by A. Davis), recorded by L. Davis on Sony Records. Other artists include Tommy Cash/ Mark Allen Cash (CBS-Sony), Carl Butler (CBS-Sony), Tommy Overstreet (CBS-Sony), Mickey Jones (Capitol), Glen Campbell Band and others.

PLAYBACK RECORDS, Box 630755, Miami FL 33163. (305)935-4880. Fax: (305)933-4007. Producer: Jack Gale. Labels include Gallery II Records, Ridgewood Records. Record company, music publisher (Lovey Music/BMI and Cowabonga Music/ASCAP) and record producer. Estab. 1983. Releases 20 CDs/year. Pays negotiable royalty; statutory rate to publisher per song on record.
   • Playback's publishing company, Lovey Music, is listed in the Music Publishers section, and Jack Gale is listed in the Record Producers section.
How to Contact: Submit demo tape by mail. Unsolicited submissions are OK. Prefers cassette (VHS videocassette if available) with 2 songs and lyric sheet. Does not return material. Reports in 2 weeks if interested.
Music: Mostly **country**. Released *Are You Sincere* (by W. Walker), recorded by Melba Montgomery (country); *Just Beyond the Pain* (by A. Butler), recorded by Charlie Louvin and Crystal Gayle (country); and *My Love Belongs to You* (by R. Rogers), recorded by Del Reeves, all on Playback Records. Other artists include Tommy Cash, Jimmy C. Newman, Jeannie C. Riley, Sammi Smith, Johnny Paycheck and Cleve Francis.
Tips: "Send only your best. Be open to suggestion. Remember . . . this is a business, not an ego trip."

PLAYBONES RECORDS, Box 20 33 12, D-20223 Hamburg, Eppendorfer Weg 7, D-20259 Hamburg **Germany**. Phone: (040) 4300339. Fax: (040)439.65.87. Producer: Arno v. Vught. Labels include Rondo Records. Record company, music publisher (Mento Music Group) and record producer (Arteg Productions). Estab. 1975. Releases 30 CDs/year. Pays 8-16% royalty to artists on contract.
 • See the listing for Mento Music Group in the Music Publishers section.
How to Contact: Submit demo tape by mail. Unsolicited submissions are OK. Prefers cassette. Does not return material. Reports in 2 weeks.
Music: Mostly **instrumentals**, **country** and **jazz**; also **background music**, **rock** and **gospel**. Released *Jazz* (by E. Stanbert), recorded by E. Kammler; *Loose One* (by Brun/Kuhles), recorded by Daniel & Claudia on Playbones; and *Born Again*, written and recorded by Reifegerste on DA Music. Other artists include H.J. Knipphals, Gaby Knies, Jack Hals, H. Hausmann, Crabmeat and M. Frommhold.

PMG RECORDS, Box 312897, Penobscot Station, Detroit MI 48231. President: Bruce Henderson. Record company, music publisher (Prejippie Music Group/BMI) and record producer (PMG Productions). Estab. 1990. Releases 6-12 12″ singles, 2 LPs and 2 EPs/year. Pays variable royalty to artists on contract; statutory rate to publisher per song on record.
 • See the listings for Prejippie Music Group in the Music Publishers and Record Producers sections.
How to Contact: Submit demo tape by mail. Unsolicited submissions are OK. Prefers cassette (or VHS videocassette) with 3-4 songs and lyric sheet. Include photo if possible. No calls please. SASE. Reports in 3 months.
Music: Mostly **funk/rock**, **techno/house** and **dance**; also **alternative rock** and **experimental**. Released "You Enjoy The Girl" and "Lolita," written and recorded by Bourgeoise Paper Jam (funk/rock); and "Windsong," written and recorded by Tony Webb (jazz). Other artists include Jezebel.
Tips: "A strong hook and melody line are your best weapons! We also look for originality."

POP RECORD RESEARCH, 10 Glen Ave., Norwalk CT 06850. (203)847-3085. Director: Gary Theroux. Labels include Surf City, GTP and Rock's Greatest Hits. Record company, music publisher (Surf City Music/ASCAP), record producer and archive of entertainment-related research materials (files on hits and hitmakers since 1877). Estab. 1962. Pays statutory rate to publisher per song on record.
 • See their listing in the Organizations section.
How to Contact: Submit demo tape by mail. Unsolicited submissions are OK. Prefers cassette (or VHS videocassette). Does not return material.
Music: Mostly **pop**, **country** and **R&B**. Released "The Declaration" (by Theroux-Gilbert), recorded by An American on Bob Records; "Thoughts From a Summer Rain," written and recorded by Bob Gilbert on Bob Records; and "Tiger Paws," written and recorded by Bob Gilbert on BAL Records. Other artists include Gary and Joan, The Nightflight Singers and Ruth Zimmerman.
Tips: "Help us keep our biographical file on you and your career current by sending us updated bios/press kits, etc. They are most helpful to writers/researchers in search of accurate information on your success."

*POWERHOUSE RECORDS, P.O. Box 14290, Austin TX 78761-4290. (512)928-4971. Fax: (512)928-4918. Owner: Tom Principato. Record company. Estab. 1983. Releases 1-2 CDs/year. Pays negotiable royalty to artists on contract; statutory rate to publisher per song on record.
How to Contact: Submit demo tape by mail. Unsolicited submissions are OK. Prefers cassette with lyric sheet. Does not return material. "We don't guarantee we will report back on all submissions."
Music: Mostly **rock**, **blues** and **jazz**; also **instrumental guitar music**. Released *In The Clouds* and *Tip of The Iceberg*, both written and recorded by Tom Principato (blues/rock); and *Trouble*, recorded by Nighthawks, all on Powerhouse Records. Other artists include Bob Margolin, John Mooney and Big Joe Maher.

PPI/PETER PAN INDUSTRIES, 88 St. Francis St., Newark NJ 07105. (201)344-4214. Director A&R: Marianne Eggleston. Labels include Compose Records, Current Records, Parade Video, Iron Bound Publishing/Compose Memories. Record company, music publisher and record producer (Dunn Pearson, Jr.) Estab. 1928. Releases more than 200 cassettes and CDs and 75-80 videos/year. Pays royalty per contract. "All services are negotiable!"
 • See their listing in the Music Publishers section.
How to Contact: Write to obtain permission to submit. Prefers cassette (or VHS videocassette if available) with 10 songs (full cassette) and lyric sheet. SASE. Reports in 3 months.
Music: **Pop** and **R&B**; also **jazz** and **New Age**. Released "Color Tapestry," written and recorded by Dunn Pearson, Jr. on Compose Records; "A Different Light," by David Friedman; and "The Trollies," by Dennis Scott, Grammy Award winner.
Tips: "Make sure all submissions are presented typed and professional. All recording must be mastered."

PRAVDA RECORDS, 3823 N. Southport, Chicago IL 60613. (312)549-3776. E-mail: pravdausa@a ol.com. Director of A&R: Mark Luecke. Labels include Bughouse. Record company. Estab. 1985. Releases 3-6 singles, 1 EP and 5-6 CDs/year. Pays 10-15% royalty to artists on contract; statutory rate to publisher per song on record.
How to Contact: Call first and obtain permission to submit. Prefers cassette with 3-4 songs. SASE. "Will contact only if interested."
Music: Mostly **rock**. Released *Parlez-vous Français?* (by W. Wisely), recorded by Willie Wisely Trio (pop); *Hear No Evil* (by G. Mercer), recorded by Wake Ooloo (rock); and *Summer Crashing*, written and recorded by Susan Voelz (pop/rock), all on Pravda Records. Other artists include Tiny Tim, The New Duncan Imperials, Javelin Boot.
Tips: "Be nice! Tour behind your release, don't take yourself too seriously."

PRESENCE RECORDS, 67 Candace Lane, Chatham NJ 07928-1115. (201)701-0707. President: Paul Payton. Record company, music publisher (Paytoons/BMI), record producer (Presence Productions). Estab. 1985. Pays 1-2% royalty to artists on contract; statutory rate to publisher per song on record.
How to Contact: Submit demo tape by mail. Unsolicited submissions are OK. "No phone calls." Prefers cassette with 2-4 songs and lyric sheet. SASE. Reports in 1 month. "Tapes not returned without prepaid mailer."
Music: Mostly **doo-wop ('50s)**, **rock**, **new wave rock** and **New Age**. Released "Ding Dong Darling," "Bette Blue Moon" and "Davilee/Go On" (by Paul Payton/Peter Skolnik), recorded by Fabulous Dudes (doo-wop), all on Presence Records.

PRIVATE MUSIC, 8750 Wilshire Blvd., Los Angeles CA 90211-2713. (310)358-4500. Fax: (310)358-4501. VP of A&R: Michael Gallelli. Record company. Estab. 1985. Releases 10 CDs/year.
  ● One of Private Music's artists, Etta James, won a Grammy in 1995 for Best Jazz Vocal Performance for her album *Mystery Lady (Songs of Billie Holiday)*.
How to Contact: Write first and obtain permission to submit. Prefers cassette with 4 songs and lyric sheet. SASE. Reports in 1 month.
Music: "Artists/bands/groups that feature well-crafted songs with strong melodies and unique point-of-view lyrics presented in a modern and contemporary musical setting." Released albums by Susan Werner (acoustic-rock), AJ Croce (rock/R&B), and Etta James (jazz), all on Private Music. Other artists include Taj Mahal, Dan Zanes, Chris Thomas, Yanni, Jennifer Warnes and Fabulous Thunderbirds.
Tips: "If a live act, put me on mailing list informing of show itineraries. If singer/songwriter, associate with BMI or ASCAP."

*PROVOCATIVE ENTERTAINMENT GROUP INC. RECORDINGS, 140-11 Dekruif Place, Suite 11G, New York NY 10475. Fax: (718)452-7179. President: Philip Anthony. Labels include Paris Club Records, N.A.M.E. Records, Third Rail Records. Record company and management firm. Estab. 1990. Releases 3 singles, 3 LPs and 3 CDs/year. Pays negotiable royalty to artists on contract; negotiable rate to publisher per song on record.
How to Contact: Fax first to verify submitting material. Prefers cassette and 8×10 with bio with 3 songs. SASE. Reports in 6 weeks.
Music: Mostly **hip hop R&B**, **smooth R&B** and **rap**; also **house**, **rock** and **alternative**. Released "Drop Da Beat," written and recorded by Paris Ford on P.E.G. Inc., "Beside Me," written and recorded by Lady Dee on Third Rail Records; and *Plunky Oness of Funk* (by various), recorded by Plunky on N.A.M.E. Records. Other artists include Buttaman, K. Jasper, T-Ski Valley, K-P featuring Chanita Renee and The Jam Boys.

*QUARK RECORDS, P.O. Box 7320 FDR Station, New York NY 10150. Phone/fax: (212)838-6775. E-mail: quarkent@aol.com. President: Curtis Urbina. Labels include Outer Limits. Record company and music publisher (Quarkette Music/Freedurb Music). Estab. 1984. Releases 4 singles and 2 LPs/year. Pays negotiable royalty to artists on contract; ¾ statutory rate to publisher per song on record.
How to Contact: Write first and obtain permission to submit a demo. Prefers cassette or DAT with 2 songs. SASE. Reports in 4-6 weeks.
Music: Mostly **instrumental/New Age**, **dance/pop** and **storytelling**. Released *Forgotten Times*, written and recorded by Mark P. Adler on Quark Records (New Age).

REMEMBER: Don't "shotgun" your demo tapes. Submit only to companies interested in the type of music you write. For more submission hints, refer to Getting Started on page 5.

*QV III MUSIC, 6922 Hollywood Blvd., Suite 907, Hollywood CA 90028. (213)957-6900. Fax: (213)957-6903. Contact: Steve Pina. Labels include Moola Records. Record company, music publisher (QV III Music) and record producer (Colada Productions). Estab. 1992. Releases 15 singles, 10-15 LPs, 2-4 EPs and 10-15 CDs/year. Pays negotiable royalty to artists on contract.
How to Contact: Submit demo tape by mail. Unsolicited submissions are OK. Prefers cassette or VHS videocassette and lyric sheet. SASE. Reports in 2 months.
Music: Mostly **pop/R&B**, **dance/rap** and **Latin**; also **country** and **movie themes**. Released "Definition" (by O. Epps), recorded by D. WolfPack on Emotional Records (rap); *Str 8 Up Loco*, written and recorded by various artists on Moola Records (rap); and "Let Me Go" (by Troy Banhoad), recorded by Teddy on Marloy Records (R&B). Other artists include Willie Hutch and Jerri Jhetto.
Tips: "Make sure you have done your songwriting homework: self-critiques, re-writes and presentable demos. We also do licensing for film and television. Credits include *Melrose Place*, *Harry & The Hendersons* and *Deadly Force*."

R.E.F. RECORDS, 404 Bluegrass Ave., Madison TN 37115. (615)865-6380. Contact: Bob Frick. Record company, record producer and music publisher (Frick Music Publishing Co./BMI). Releases 10 LPs/year. Pays statutory rate to publisher per song on record.
• See the listings for Frick Music Publishing in the Music Publishers section, as well as Bob Scott Frick in the Record Producers section and Bob Scott Frick Enterprises in the Managers and Booking Agents section.
How to Contact: Submit demo tape by mail. Unsolicited submissions are OK. Prefers 7½ ips reel-to-reel or cassette with 2 songs and lyric sheet. SASE. Reports in 1 month.
Music: **Country**, **gospel**, **rock** and **top 40/pop**. Released *The Right Track* (by Camp/Frick), recorded by Bob Scott Frick on R.E.F. Records.

*RADICAL RECORDS, 77 Bleecker St., Suite C2-21, New York NY 10012. (212)475-1111. Fax: (212)475-5676. E-mail: radical@chelsea.ios.com. A&R: Eric Rosen. Record company. "We also do independent radio and retail promotion." Estab. 1986. Releases 5 singles, 1 LP and 2 CDs/year.
How to Contact: Submit demo tape by mail. Unsolicited submissions are OK. Prefers cassette or CD. Does not return material. Reports in 1 month.
Music: Mostly **modern rock**, **pop** and **ska**; also **industrial** and **rock**. Released *O No No O Zone*, recorded by J.C.U. (punk); *Oi! Skampilation, Vol. I*, recorded by various artists (ska/oi!); and "Jazzy Wit Da Joint," recorded by Stressed Out (rap), all on Radical Records.
Tips: "Create the best possible demos you can and show a past of excellent self-promotion."

RAGE-N-RECORDS, 212 N. 12th St., Suite #3, Philadelphia PA 19107. (215)977-7777. E-mail: rage@netaxs.com. Website: www.ikonman.com. President: Vincent Kershner. Labels include Ikon. Record company, music publisher (RNR Publishing/ASCAP) and record producer (David Ivory). Estab. 1986. Pays various royalty to artist; statutory rate to publisher per song on record.
• See the listing for Ivory Productions in the Record Producers section and RNR Publishing in the Music Publishers section.
How to Contact: Submit demo tape by mail. Unsolicited submissions are OK. Prefers cassette or DAT (or VHS videocassette) with 3-5 songs and lyric sheet. SASE. Reports in 4-6 weeks.
Music: Mostly **rock**, **pop** and **blues**; also **R&B**. Released *Reindeer Games*, written and recorded by Pat Godwin (Xmas satirical); *Focus*, written and recorded by Slideways; and *Insight, Outtasight*, written and recorded by Stevie LaRocca, all on Ikon Records. Other artists include The Peaks, Don Himlin, Do or Die and The Cutaways!

RAMMIT RECORDS, 414 Ontario St., Toronto ON M5A 2W1 **Canada**. (416)923-7611. Fax: (416)923-3352. A&R, New Projects: Trevor G. Shelton. Record company, music publisher (Rammit Noise) and record producer (Trevor G. Shelton). Estab. 1983. Releases 5-10 singles, 5-10 12″ singles, 5 LPs, 5 cassettes and 5 CDs/year. Pays statutory rate to publisher per song.
• See their listing in the Record Producers section.
How to Contact: Submit demo tape by mail. Unsolicited submissions are OK. Prefers cassette with 4 songs. SAE and IRC. Reports in 3-4 weeks.
Music: Mostly **R&B**, **hip hop** and **dance**; also **alternative rock**. Released *2 Versatile* (by D. Myrie/R. Clarke), recorded by 2 Versatile (hip hop); and *Line Up In Paris* (by Lipwork Pub.), recorded by Line Up in Paris (rock), both on Rammit/A&M Records. Other artists include Martha and the Muffins, Machinations, Mystery Romance and Andy McLean.
Tips: "Realize you may be turned down, but work hard. Don't be discouraged by thank you—but no thanks form letters. Keep writing and if A&R departments suggest ideas of improving your material—listen to them, if you think comments are valid, use them."

RANDOM RECORDS, 22 Milverton Blvd., Toronto, Ontario M4J 1T6 **Canada**. (416)778-6563. President: Peter Randall. Record company, music publisher (Random Image Music), record producer

(Peter Randall). Estab. 1986. Releases 3 singles, 3 LPs, 1 EP and 3 CDs/year. Pays 15% royalty to artists on contract; statutory rate to publisher per song on record.
How to Contact: Submit demo tape by mail. Unsolicited submissions are OK. Prefers cassette, DAT or NTSC videocassette with no more than 2 songs and lyric sheet. SAE and IRC. Reports in 1 month.
Music: Mostly **pop**, **rock** and **country**; also **folk**. Released *The Raindogs* (by Farrar/Randall), recorded by Raindogs (pop rock); and *Slapped in the Face by a Rainbow*, written and recorded by Peter Randall (folk rock), both on Random Records. Other artists include Quadras, Timeline, Shaun Firth.
Tips: "Songwriters would be much better off to rewrite and re-work one song until it's killer, than to try and submit 18 passable songs. We have no time or reason to rewrite them for you."

*RAREFACTION, P.O. Box 170023, San Francisco CA 94117. (415)346-1840. E-mail: rmac@rarefaction.com. Website: http://www.rarefaction.com. Sound Designer: Ron MacLeod. Producer of CD-ROM sound libraries. Estab. 1995. Releases 3 CDs/year. Pays negotiable royalty to artists on contract; statutory rate to publisher per song on record.
How to Contact: Write or call first and obtain permission to submit. SASE. Reports in 1 month.
Music: Sound samples. Released *A Poke in the Ear With a Sharp Stick Vol. I-III.*

RAVE RECORDS, INC., 13400 W. Seven Mile Rd., Detroit MI 48235. (810)540-RAVE. Fax: (810)338-0739. E-mail: rave_rec@ix.netcom.com. Production Dept.: Derrick. Record company and music publisher (Magic Brain Music/ASCAP). Estab. 1992. Releases 2-4 singles and 2 CDs/year. Pays various royalty to artists on contract; statutory rate to publisher per song on record.
How to Contact: Submit demo tape by mail. Unsolicited submissions are OK. Prefers cassette with lyric or lead sheet. "Be sure to include all press/promotional information currently used." Does not return material. Reports in 2-4 months.
Music: Mostly **alternative rock** and **dance**. Released "Got To Hold On" and "All Mixed Up" (by Art Forest), recorded by Nicole; and "No Time Like Tomorrow" (by S. Sholtes/M. Hoffmeyer), recorded by Bukimi3, all on Rave Records. Other artists include Cyber Cryst and Dorothy.
Tips: "We are interested in artists who are new to the market place, but please include at least 4 songs on your demo. Also, if we have information regarding your demo, we will call you. Please do not call us about your submission."

RBW, INC., P.O. Box 14187, Parkville MO 64152. (816)587-5358. President: Russ Wojtkiewicz. Labels include RBW Record Co. and Blue City Records. Record company and production/recording broker. Estab. 1990. Releases 3-5 CDs/year. Pays varying royalty to artists on contract; statutory rate to publisher per song on record.
How to Contact: Submit demo tape by mail. Unsolicited submissions are OK. Prefers cassette or CD and lyric or lead sheet. "If no video, send recent b&w photo." Does not return material. Reports in 6-12 weeks.
Music: Mostly **blues**, **classical** and **jazz/big band**.
Tips: "Looking for artists with strong regional following, with or without recording track record. RBW/Blue City is looking for unique talent and sound. Will listen to all music submitted. Rejection letters will be sent. Do not call."

REACT RECORDINGS, 9157 Sunset Blvd., Suite 210, W. Hollywood CA 90069. (310)550-0233. Fax: (310)550-0235. A&R Director: Sebastian Jones. Record company and music publisher (Startup Music/ASCAP). Estab. 1994. Releases 10 singles, 12 LPs and 12 CDs/year. Pays negotiable royalty to artists on contract; ¾ rate to publisher per song on record.
How to Contact: Submit demo tape by mail. Unsolicited submissions are OK. Prefers cassette with 3-5 songs and lyric sheet. Does not return material. Reports in 3-4 weeks.
Music: Mostly **hip hop jazz**, **blues**, **dance** and **R&B**. Released "Back 2 Tha' Funk," written and recorded by Rodney O & Joe Cooley (rap); "Da' Nayborhoodz," written and recorded by Da' Nayborhoodz (rap); and "No Brain Cells," written and recorded by Insane Poetry (rap), all on React Records.

RED DOT/PUZZLE RECORDS, 1121 Market, Galveston TX 77550. (409)762-4590. President: A.W. Marullo, Sr. Record company, record producer and music publisher (A.W. Marullo Music/BMI). Estab. 1952. "We also lease masters from artists." Releases 14 12″ singles/year. Pays 8-10% royalty to artists on contract; statutory rate to publisher for each record sold.
How to Contact: Prefers cassette with 4-7 songs and lyric sheet. "Cassettes will not be returned. Contact will be made by mail or phone." Reports in 2 months.
Music: Rock/top 40 dance songs. Released "Do You Feel Sexy" (by T. Pindrock), recorded by Flash Point (Top 40/rock); "You Put the Merry in My Christmas," (by E. Dunn), recorded by Mary Craig (rock/pop country); and "Love Machine" (by T. Pindrock), recorded by Susan Moninger, all on Puzzle/Red Dot Records. Other artists include Joe Diamond, Billy Wayde, Jerry Hurtado and Tricia Matula.

Tips: "All songs amd masters must have good *sound* and be studio produced."

RED SKY RECORDS, P.O. Box 7, Stonehouse, Glos. GL10 3PQ **United Kingdom**. Phone: 01453-826200. Producer: Johnny Coppin. Record company (PRS) and record producer (Red Sky Records). Estab. 1985. Releases 2 albums per year. Pays 8-10% to artists on contract; statutory rate to publisher per song on record.
• See the listing for Johnny Coppin/Red Sky Records in the Record Producers section.
How to Contact: Write first and obtain permission to submit. Does not return material. Reports in 6 months.
Music: Mostly **rock/singer-songwriters**, **modern folk** and **roots music**. Released *Dead Lively!*, written and recorded by Paul Burgess; *Force of the River* and *A Country Christmas*, written and recorded by Johnny Coppin, all on Red Sky Records. Other artists include David Goodland.

*REDEMPTION RECORDS, P.O. Box 3244, Omaha NE 68103-0244. (712)328-2771. Fax: (712)328-9732. A&R: Ryan D. Kuper. Labels include Fahrenheit, Full Flavor and Mayhem. Record company. Estab. 1990. Releases 6-10 singles, 2 LPs, 2 EPs and 6 CDs/year. Pays negotiable royalty to artists on contract; statutory rate to publisher per song on record.
How to Contact: Submit demo tape by mail. Unsolicited submissions are OK. Prefers cassette with 4 songs and lyric and/or lead sheet. "Include band's or artist's goals." Does not return material. Reports in 2-4 weeks.
Music: Mostly **progressive rock**, **power pop** and **post hardcore**; also **hip hop**, **hardcore** and **punk**. Released *The Healing*, recorded by Martin's Dam (rock); *Goodbye To Alice*, recorded by Easter (rock); and *Suck Fumes*, recorded by Rosegarden Funeral (hard rock), all on Redemption Records. Other artists include Let's Rodeo, September, Downer and Anton Barbeau.
Tips: "Be prepared to tour to support the release. Make sure the current line-up is secure."

RED-EYE RECORDS, Wern Fawr Farm, Pencoed, Mid-Glam CF35 6NB **United Kingdom**. Phone: (0656)86 00 41. Managing Director: M.R. Blanche. Record company, music publisher (Ever-Open-Eye Music/PRS). Estab. 1979. Releases 4 singles and 2-3 LPs/year.
• Red-Eye Records' publishing company, Ever-Open-Eye Music, is listed in the Music Publishers section.
How to Contact: Submit demo tape by mail. Unsolicited submissions are OK. Prefers cassette (or VHS videocassette) or 7½ or 15 ips reel-to-reel with 4 songs. SAE and IRC. Does not return material.
Music: Mostly **R&B**, **rock** and **gospel**; also **swing**. Released "River River" (by D. John), recorded by The Boys; "Billy" (by G. Williams), recorded by The Cadillacs; and "Cadillac Walk" (by Moon Martin), recorded by the Cadillacs, all on Red-Eye Records. Other artists include Cartoon and Tiger Bay.

*REITER RECORDS LTD., 308 Penn Estates, East Stroudsburg PA 18301. (717)424-9599. Fax: (717)424-0452. E-mail: wwwreit.com. Vice President of A&R: Greg Macmillan. Record company. Estab. 1990. Releases 5 singles, 5-10 LPs and 5-10 CDs/year. Pays negotiable royalty to artists on contract; statutory rate to publisher per song on record.
How to Contact: Submit demo tape by mail. Unsolicited submissions are OK. Does not return material.
Music: Mostly **pop**, **jazz** and **rock**. Released *Black Rose '95*, written and recorded by various artists on Reiter Records. Other artists include Jim Cherry and Danger Zone.

REJOICE RECORDS OF NASHVILLE, 116 Roberta Dr., Hendersonville TN 37075. (615)264-1373. Owner: Gregg Hutchins. Record company and music publisher. Estab. 1993. Releases 3 CDs/year. Pays statutory rate to publisher per song on record.
• See the listing for Gregg Hutchins Music in the Music Publishers section.
How to Contact: Write first and obtain permission to submit. Prefers cassette with up to 3 songs and lyric sheet. Does not return material. "We don't report back unless we're interested."
Music: Mostly **southern gospel**, **country gospel** and **Christian country**; also **bluegrass gospel**. Released *Adam's Side* (by Jesse Wilson), recorded by Billy Walker (gospel); *Jordan's Banks*, written and recorded by Donnie & Vicky Clark (gospel); and "The Last Time I Fall" (by Jim Watters), recorded by Charlie Louvin, all on Rejoice Records. Other artists include Tommy Cash.

REPRISE RECORDS, 3300 Warner Blvd., Burbank CA 91505. (818)846-9090. This record company prefers not to share information.

THE TYPES OF MUSIC each listing is interested in are printed in boldface.

REVEAL, 777 Barb Rd., Vankleek Hill Ontario K0B 1R0 **Canada**. E-mail: tgbarn@hawk.igs.net. Website: http://www.hawk.igs.net/~tgbarn. President, A&R: Peter Riden. Record company, music publisher (Riden Stars Music/BMI) and record producer. Estab. 1976. Pays 5% of net profit to artists on contract; statutory rate to publisher per song on record.
How to Contact: Submit demo tape by mail. Unsolicited submissions are OK. Prefers cassette (or VHS videocassette) with 2-5 songs and lyric sheet. Does not return material. Reports in 2-3 months.
Music: Mostly **rock**, **progressive** and **country/pop**. Released *Front Lines*, written and recorded by Lugene Chivelas on Music Web Records; *Take A Look Around*, written and recorded by Leo John Niebudek; and *Society News* (by S. Child), recorded by Elizabeth DeBolt. Other artists include Brian Lockwood, H.P.N., John Wild, Jim Kruger, Concept, David Ball and Faces of Emotion.
Tips: "On July 1-7 every year there is a week long event being held at the Grand Barn, a 220-ft. long complex with stage where some of the selected artists will be invited to come, attend and/or perform. A unique chance to be heard and meet other unrecognized, deserving ones."

REVELATION RECORDS, P.O. Box 5232, Huntington Beach CA 92615. (714)375-4264. E-mail: info@revelationrecords.com. Owner: Jordan Cooper. Labels include Crisis. Record company. Estab. 1987. Releases 2 singles, 2 12″ singles, 6 LPs, 4 EPs and 10 CDs/year. Royalty varies. Pays various amounts to publisher per song on record.
How to Contact: Submit demo tape by mail. Unsolicited submissions are OK. Send demos to the attention of Fred Knot. Prefers cassette or VHS videocassette with 3 songs and lyric sheet. "Send photos and bio/press sheet if you have one." Does not return material. Reports in 2 months.
Music: Mostly **rock**, **hardcore/punk** and **thrash**; also **country**, **rap** and **disco**. Released "Do You Know Who You Are?," recorded by Texas Is The Reason; *Sights* (by Mike Ferraro), recorded by Mike Judge & Old Smoke (country-folk-blues); and "Looking Back," written and recorded by Bold, all on Revelation Records. Other artists include Farside, Into Another, Sense Field, Iceburn, ORANGE 9mm, Function, Shades Apart, Civ, Gorilla Biscuits, Quicksand, Sick of it All, Youth of Today, State of the Nation and Enginekid.
Tips: "Don't be inhibited when sending songs, we listen to everything. Don't be discouraged, our taste is not anything more than opinion."

RICHWAY RECORDS INTERNATIONAL, P.O. Box 110983, Nashville TN 37222. (615)731-6640. Fax: (615)731-9147. President: Wayne G. Leinsz. Record company, record producer and music publisher. Estab. 1991. Releases 20 LPs and 4 CDs/year. Pays 25% royalty to artists on contract; statutory rate to publisher per song on record.
  • Richway Records' publishing company, Lion Hill Music, is listed in the Music Publishers section.
How to Contact: Submit demo tape by mail. Unsolicited submissions are OK. Prefers cassette (or VHS videocassette if available) with 3 songs and lyric sheet. SASE. Reports in 1 month.
Music: Mostly **country**, **bluegrass** and **gospel**. Released *Jerry James & Country Thunder*, recorded by Jerry James (country); *Bobby Atkins & Margie Lynn*, recorded by Bobby Atkins and Margie Lynn (country); and "Stone Country" (by R. Guffnet/R. Pugh), recorded by Warren Ham (country), all on Richway Records. Other artists include Gates Millay, Michael Hollomon, Larry Elliott, James Michael Walts, Jack Reeves and Walt Timmerman.

RISING STAR RECORDS AND PUBLISHERS INC., 52 Executive Park South, Suite 5203, Atlanta GA 30329. (404)636-2050. President: Barbara Taylor. Record company, record distributor and music publisher. Estab. 1987. Releases 5-6 CDs/year. Pays negotiated royalty to artists on contract; negotiated rate to publisher per song on record.
  • Rising Star's publishing company is listed in the Music Publishers section.
How to Contact: Submit demo tape by mail. Unsolicited submissions are OK. Prefers cassette with 3 songs and press kit. SASE. Reports in 6 weeks.
Music: Mostly **contemporary instrumental**, **New Age**, **Celtic** and **classical**. Released "HEART-KEYS: The AIDS Memorial Album," by various artists (New Age piano); "Crossing to Ireland" (by Nancy Bick-Clark and Sara Johnson); and "Lake Serenity" (by various artists), all on Rising Star Records.

ROCK DOG RECORDS, P.O. Box 3687, Hollywood CA 90028. (213)661-0259. E-mail: patt2@net com.com. A&R Director: Gerry North. East Coast Division: Rock Dog Records, P.O. Box 884, Syosset NY 11791-0899. A&R Director: Maria Cuccia. Record company, record producer. Estab. 1987. Releases 3 singles, 1-3 12″ singles, 3-5 LPs, 1-3 EPs and 3 CDs/year. Pays negotiable royalty to artists on contract; statutory royalty to publisher per song on record. In house distribution through Saturn Studios.
How to Contact: Write first and obtain permission to submit. Prefers CD (or VHS videocassette) with 3-5 songs and lyric sheet. SASE. Reports in 1 month.

Music: Mostly **contemporary instrumental**, **jazz** and **ambiage (ambient/New Age)**. Released *A Separate Reality* and *Variations on a Dream*, both written and recorded by Brainstorm (Ambiage); and "Internal Peace," written and recorded by Elijah (New Age), all on Rock Dog Records. Other artists include Stratos Dimantis, Michael Halaas, The Daughters of Mary, Mark Round and Chasm.

*ROCKADELIC RECORDS, P.O. Box 742801, Dallas TX 75374-2801. (214)826-9379. Fax: (214)826-4290. Owner/President: Mark Millstone. Labels include Animus Oculus, Mind And Eye and Fungus. Record company. Estab. 1987. Releases 12 LPs and 6 CDs/year. Pays negotiable rate to artists on contract; single payment per album or CD project.
How to Contact: Submit demo tape by mail. Unsolicited submissions are OK. Prefers cassette or DAT or videotape. "Narrative and band photos helpful." Does not return material. Reports in 2 weeks.
Music: Mostly **rock**, **blues**, **'60s hard rock** and **psychedelia**. Released *Boozers* (by Paul Pennington), recorded by Boozers (hard rock/punk); *Sugar Cube Blues Band* (by Budley Bays), recorded by Sugar Cube Blues Band ('60s punk/psychedelia); and *Burnin' Rain* (by Mike Pemberton), recorded by Burnin' Rain ('60s rock), all on Rockadelic Records.
Tips: "We specialize in releasing previously unreleased studio album projects by hard rock/psychedelic groups from the late '60s and early '70s. Have put out nearly 50 releases since 1987."

ROCOCO RECORDS, P.O. Box 693, Seal Beach CA 90740-0693. (310)594-6641. Fax: (310)594-0041. Director of A&R: Kookie Wrigley, Jr. Record company, music publisher (Mean Streets Music) and record producer (Rocco Spagnola). Estab. 1990. Releases 5 singles and CDs/year. Pays negotiable royalty to artists on contract; statutory royalty to publisher per song on record.
How to Contact: Submit demo tape by mail. Unsolicited submissions are OK. Prefers cassette. "No phone calls. If we have any interest in the material, we shall contact the songwriter." Does not return material. Reports in 4 weeks.
Music: Mostly **rock, country** and **folk**. Released *L.A. River* (by Stanley Wycoff/Rocco Spagnola) and *Vale of Tears* (by Stanley Wycoff), both recorded by Bierce in L.A.; and *Blabbermouth* (by Dot Kincaid), recorded by Chix Wit Stix, all on Rococo Records. Other artists include The Blockz, The Triceps, Uncomfortable Seats, The Prisnors and The Calories.
Tips: "The songwriter should ask himself or herself, 'what makes this song worthy of attention?' The song should offer something new. It should not rehash the tired themes that dominate popular music unless it offers a new perspective on these themes. We particularly appreciate a wry sense of humor and we also encourage 'serious' themes. A song should not be submitted to us unless the songwriter is willing to be judged by each song submitted."

ROLL ON RECORDS®, 112 Widmar Pl., Clayton CA 94517. (510)672-8201. Owner: Edgar J. Brincat. Record company. Estab. 1985. Releases 2-3 LPs/cassettes/year. Pays 10% royalty to artists on contract; statutory rate to publisher per song on record.
   • See the listing for California Country Music in the Music Publishers section.
How to Contact: Submit demo tape by mail. Unsolicited submissions are OK. Prefers cassette with 3 songs and lyric sheet. SASE. Reports in 4-6 weeks.
Music: Mostly **contemporary/country**, **MOR** and **R&B**; also **pop**, **light rock** and **modern gospel**. Released "Broken Record" (by Horace Linsley/Dianne Baumgartner), recorded by Edee Gordon on Roll On Records; *Maddy* and *For Realities Sake* (both by F.L. Pittman/Madonna Weeks), recorded by Ron Bands/L.J. Reynolds on Life Records/Bellmark Records.
Tips: "Have patience . . . write a great song, then let us do the rest."

ROSEBUD RECORDS, P.O. Box 26044, Fraser MI 48026. (810)831-1380. Record company and publisher (Rose Music/BMI). Estab. 1990. Releases 5 singles, 3 LPs, and 10 CDs/year. Pays statutory rate to publisher per song on record.
How to Contact: Submit demo tape by mail. Unsolicited submissions are OK. Prefers cassette with 3 songs and lyric sheet. Must be coded: Songwriter AD-25. "Please make sure that your recording is of good quality and that all songs are copyrighted. Any information relating to the artist's past accomplishments is appreciated." Does not return material. Reports in 3-4 weeks.
Music: Mostly **country, pop/country, rock, contemporary Christian** and also **R&B/jazz**. Released "Forever Friends by Family G (R&B); "Song of Joy" by T. Senecal (MOR); and "Without A Cause" by Xavier John (pop). Other artists include Charade, Bad Toyz and the Avenue.
Tips: "We are looking for career-minded singer/songwriters with good commercial material, well developed, outstanding performance skills and a desire to be successful!"

ROTTEN RECORDS, P.O. Box 2157, Montclair CA 91763. (909)624-2332. Fax: (909)624-2392. President: Ron Peterson. Promotions/Radio/Video: Richard Shytlemeyer. Record company. Estab. 1985. Releases 3 LPs, 3 EPs and 3 CDs/year.
How to Contact: Submit demo tape by mail. Unsolicited submissions are OK. Prefers cassette. SASE. Reports in 2 months.

Music: Mostly **rock**, **alternative** and **commercial**; also **punk** and **heavy metal**. Released *No Longer Human*, recorded by STG on Rotten Records (industrial).
Tips: "Don't call and keep bugging us to listen to your demo—very annoying!"

ROUND FLAT RECORDS, P.O. Box 1676, Amherst NY 14226. E-mail: roundflat@aol.com. President: Curt Ippolito. Record company and distributor. Estab. 1989. Releases 10 singles and 6 CDs/year. Pays varying royalty to artists on contract; varying rate to publisher per song on record.
How to Contact: Submit demo tape by mail. Unsolicited submissions are OK. Prefers cassette (or VHS videocassette if available) with 5 songs and lyric sheet. Does not return material. Reports in 3-5 weeks.
Music: Mostly **alternative**, **hardcore** and **ska**; also **industrial**. Released "S/T," written and recorded by Chilihead; "2 Past 7," written and recorded by 1073; and "The Truth," written and recorded by Ink Marker, all on Round Flat Records. Other artists include Against All Hope, Cropdogs and Powertrip.

*ROWENA RECORDS, 195 S. 26th St., San Jose CA 95116. (408)286-9840. Fax: (408)286-9845. Owner: Grady O'Neal. Record company. Estab. 1967. Releases 8-12 LPs and 8-12 CDs/year. Pays statutory royalty to artists on contract; pays statutory rate to publisher per song on record.
- Rowena Records' publishing affiliate, Tiki Enterprises, has a listing in the Music Publishers section.
How to Contact: Submit demo tape by mail. Unsolicited submissions are OK. Prefers cassette with 2 songs and lyric sheet. SASE. Reports in 3 weeks.
Music: Mostly **gospel**, **country**, **pop**, and all styles of **Mexican**. Released *So Far So Good* (by various), recorded by Jaque Lynn (country); *I Know That I Know*, written and reocrded by Jeannine O'Neal (gospel); and *Los Metallcos*, recorded by Los Metallcos, all on Rowena Records.

ROYALTY RECORDS, 176 Madison Ave. 4th Floor, New York NY 10016. (212)779-0101. Fax: (212)779-3255. A&R: Dave R.. Labels include Mysterious Man Recordings. Record company. Estab. 1994. Releases 5 singles and 5 CDs/year. Pays negotiable royalty to artists on contract; statutory rate to publisher per song on record.
How to Contact: Submit demo tape by mail. Unsolicited submissions are OK. Prefers cassette or videocassette. Does not return material. Reports in 2 months.
Music: Mostly **heavy/alternative**. Released *Lite & Sweet*, written and recorded by Po' Boy Swing (alternative); and *Self Titled*, written and recorded by Track One A.B. (alternative), both on Royalty Records.

RR&R RECORDS, 375 Military Rd., Kalama WA 98625. A&R : Ron Dennis Wheeler. Labels include Rapture Records, Ready Records and Y'Shua Records. Record company, music publisher (Sounds of Aicram/BMI, Do It Now Publishing/ASCAP), record producer (Ron Dennis Wheeler). Estab. 1966. Releases 5 singles, 5 12″ singles, 5 LPs, 5 EPs and 5 CDs/year. Pays standard royalty to artists on contract; statutory rate to publisher per song on record.
- See the listings for Sounds of Aicram in the Music Publishers section and RR&R Music Productions, Inc. in the Record Producers section.
How to Contact: Submit demo tape by mail. Unsolicited submissions are OK. Prefers cassette and DAT with and without lead vocals with lyric and lead sheet. SASE. Reports if interested.
Music: Mostly **gospel**, **rock**, **pop**, **country** and **R&B**. Released "There's Someone for Each of Us," "One Perfect Man" (by R. McGibony) and "He's Keeping Me Strong" (by Irene Gaskings), all recorded by Ron Dennis Wheeler on RR&R Records. Other artists include Patty Weaver, Mike Brookshire, Jez Davidson, Linda Marr, Dennis Wheeler, Bob Nite Off, Mike Bell, Pam Jorden and Tammie Bridge.
Tips: "Do not try to copy another artist or style of music. Better production masters (if possible) get more attention quicker. Please have vocals clear and out front of music."

RUFFCUT PRODUCTIONS, 6472 Seven Mile, South Lyon MI 48178. Phone/fax: (810)486-0505. Producer: J.D. Dudick. Record company, music publisher (Al-Ky Music/BMI). Estab. 1991. Releases 4 singles and 4 CDs/year. Pays 10-14% royalty to artists on contract; statutory rate to publisher per song on record.
- See the listing for Al-Ky Music in the Music Publishers section and J.D. Dudick in the Record Producers section.
How to Contact: Submit demo tape by mail. Unsolicited submissions are OK. Prefers cassette with 2 songs and lyric sheet. Does not return material. Reports in 2 months.
Music: Mostly **rock**, **pop** and **country**; also **alternative**. Released *Something For Everyone* (by Bil Tol), recorded by Cidyzoo on Vehicle Garage; *Minddust* (by Chris Pierce), recorded by "Q"; and *Am I Different* (by Laya Phelps), recorded by Laya, both on Ruffcut Records. Other artists include Hubcaps, Jim Dean and Moon Toonsie.

Tips: "Write songs that mean something, and if other people like it (sincerely) let's hear it. Records sell on musical expression, not marketing hype. Remember to keep the vocals above the music."

RUSTRON MUSIC PRODUCTIONS, 1156 Park Lane, West Palm Beach FL 33417-5957. (407)686-1354. E-mail: p0086476@pbfreenet.seflin.lib.fl.us. Executive Director: Rusty Gordon. A&R Director: Ron Caruso. Labels include Rustron Records and Whimsong Records. "Rustron administers 22 independent labels for publishing and marketing." Record company, record producer and music publisher (Whimsong/ASCAP and Rustron Music/BMI). Estab. 1970. Releases 5-10 CDs/year. Pays variable royalty to artists on contract. "Artists with history of product sales get higher % than those who are 1st product with no sales track record." Pays statutory rate to publisher.
- See the listings for Rustron Music in the Music Publishers section and Rustron Music Productions in the Record Producers and Managers and Booking Agents section.
How to Contact: Submit demo tape by mail. Unsolicited submissions are OK. Prefers cassette with 3 songs and lyric sheet. "If singer/songwriter has independent product (cassette or CD) produced and sold at gigs—send this product." SASE required for all correspondence, no exceptions. Reports in 2-4 months.
Music: Mostly **mainstream** and **women's music**, **A/C**, **electric acoustic**, **pop (cabaret, blues)** and **blues (R&B, country and folk)**; also **New Age fusions** (instrumentals), **modern folk fusions**, **environmental** and **socio-political**. Released "Fit New Jersey Into The Everglades," written and recorded by Boomslang Swampsinger; "Love Lasts Longer" (by Rusty Gordon), recorded by Dana Adams; and "Reasons To Run" (by Jayne Margo-Reby/Vic Paul Bersok/Debbie Tyson), recorded by Jayne Margo-Reby, all on Rustron Records. Other artists include Whig Party, Deb Criss, Lori Surrency, Flash Silvermoon, Kathi Gibson and Chris Limardo, Star Smiley and Elysian Sex Drive.
Tips: "Find your own unique style; write well crafted songs with unpredictable concepts, strong hooks and definitive melody. New Age composers: evolve your themes and add multi-cultural diversity with instruments. Don't be predictable. Don't over-produce your demos and don't drown vocals."

SABRE PRODUCTIONS, P.O. Box 10147, San Antonio TX 78210. (210)533-6910. Producer: E.J. Henke. Labels include Fanfare, Satin, Legacy. Record company, record producer. Estab. 1965. Releases 48 singles, 5 LPs and 4 CDs/year. Pays 10% royalty to artists on contract; statutory rate to publisher per song on record.
How to Contact: Submit demo tape by mail. Unsolicited submissions are OK. Prefers cassette with 4 songs and lyric sheet. SASE. Reports in 2 weeks.
Music: Mostly **country** (all styles), **gospel** and **rock/R&B**. Released *Take A Number* (by Staggs/Norton/Wharton), recorded by Robert Beckom on Sabre Records (country); *Borderline Crazy* (by Betty Kay Miller), recorded by Darnell Miller on Fanfare Records (country); and "Hypnotized," (by Ted Snyder), recorded by Ace Diamond on Legacy Records (rockabilly). Other artists include Joe Terry, Suzie Rowles, Howard Alexander and Sunglows.
Tips: "Submit only your best material. Be patient and don't irritate your publisher, record label, etc."

SABTECA RECORD CO., Box 10286, Oakland CA 94610. (510)465-2805. President: Duane Herring. Creative Manager: Sean Herring. Record company and music publisher (Sabteca Music Co./ASCAP, Toyiabe Music Co./BMI). Estab. 1980. Releases 3 singles and 1 12" single/year. Pays 10% royalty to artists on contract; statutory rate to publisher per song on record.
Affiliate(s): Andre Romare Records.
- Sabteca's publishing company, Sabteca Music Co., can be found in the Music Publishers section.
How to Contact: Write first and obtain permission to submit. Prefers cassette with lyric sheet. SASE. Reports in 2 months.
Music: Mostly **R&B**, **pop** and **country**. Released "Sacrifice," "One Hundred Pounds of Love" and "One Day Man" (by Duane Herring/Tom Roller), recorded by Johnny B on André Romare Records (country). Other artists include Walt Coleman, Lil Brown and Lois Shayne.
Tips: "Improve your writing skills. Keep up with music trends."

SADDLESTONE RECORDS, 264 "H" Street Box 8110-21, Blaine WA 98230. Canada address: 6260-130 St., Surrey British Columbia V3X 1R6 **Canada**. (604)572-4232. Fax: (604)572-4282. President: Candice James. Labels include Silver Bow Records. Record company, music publisher (Saddlestone/BMI) and record producer (Silver Bow Productions). Estab. 1988. Releases 50 singles, 30 LPs and 30 CDs/year. Pays 15% royalty to artists on contract; statutory rate to publishers per song on record.
- See the listing for Saddlestone Publishing in the Music Publishers section, Silver Bow Productions in the Record Producers section and Silver Bow Management in the Managers and Booking Agents section.
How to Contact: Submit demo tape by mail. Unsolicited submissions are OK. Prefers cassette with 3-5 songs and lyric sheet. SASE. Reports in 3 months.

Music: Mostly **country**, **pop** and **rock**; also **R&B**, **gospel** and **children's**. Released *She Worships the Heart* (M. Mikulen/S. Lester Smith), recorded Clancy Wright (country); *Lonely*, written and recorded by George Armishaw (crossover); and *The Wine Remembers* (by Bruce Robbins), recorded by Pappy Hamel (E/L), all on Saddlestone Records. Other artists include Gary MacFarlane, Sunny & Houserockers, Randy Friskie, Tracy Todd, Joe Lonsdale, Blackwater Jack, Robert Rigby, John McCabe, Stan Giles, Gerry King and Clancy Wright.
Tips: "Send original material, studio produced, with great hooks."

SAHARA RECORDS AND FILMWORKS ENTERTAINMENT, 4475 Allisonville Rd., 8th Floor, Indianapolis IN 46205. (317)546-2912. President: Edward De Miles. Record company, music publisher (EDM Music/BMI) and record producer. Estab. 1981. Releases 15-20 CD singles and 5-10 CDs/year. Pays 9½-11% royalty to artists on contract; statutory rate to publishers per song on record.
• See the listings for Edward De Miles Music Company in the Music Publishers section, and Edward De Miles in the Record Producers section.
How to Contact: Write first and obtain permission to submit. Prefers cassette with 3-5 songs and lyric sheet. Does not return material. Reports in 1 month.
Music: Mostly **R&B/dance**, **top 40 pop/rock** and **contemporary jazz**; also **TV-film themes**, **musical scores** and **jingles**. Released "Hooked on U," "Dance Wit Me" and "Moments," written and recorded by Steve Lynn (R&B), all on Sahara Records. Other artists include Lost in Wonder, Dvon Edwards and Multiple Choice.
Tips: "We're looking for strong mainstream material. Lyrics and melodies with good hooks that grab people's attention."

SALEXO MUSIC, P.O. Box 18093, Charlotte NC 28218-0093. (704)536-0600. President: Samuel OBie. Record company. Estab. 1992. Releases 3 LPs and 3 CDs/year. Pays 2.5% royalty to artists on contract; variable rate to publisher per song on record.
How to Contact: Submit demo tape by mail. Unsolicited submissions are OK. Prefers cassette with 3 songs and lyric sheet. SASE. Reports in 3 months.
Music: Mostly **contemporary gospel**, **jazz** and **R&B**. Released *Vision & Message* (by Samuel A. OBie) (inspirational); *Communion* (by Samuel OBie Singers) (inspirational); and *He's My All & All* (by Fellowship Community Choir) (traditional), all on Salexo Records.

*SATIN RECORDS, P.O. Box 632, Snohomish WA 98291-0632. (206)546-3038. Partner: John W. Iverson. Labels include Seafair-Bolo Records. Record company and music publisher (Bolmin Publishing/BMI). Estab. 1982. Releases 2 singles, 4 LPs, 1 EP and 4 CDs/year. Pays negotiable royalty to artists on contract; statutory rate to publisher per song on record.
How to Contact: Write first and obtain permission to submit. Prefers cassette, DAT or CD with lyric sheet. SASE. Reports in 2 months.
Music: Mostly **R&B**, **jazz** and **rock**. Released "Come Softly To Me" (by Gary Troxel/Barbara Ellis/Gretchey Christopher) and "I'll Be Whatever You Want Me To Be" (by Antowaine Richardson), both recorded by The Main Attraction on Satin Records (R&B); and *The Poet* (by Michael Loveless), recorded by UMT Two O'Clock Band on Bolo Records (jazz). Other artists include The Scamhound Hunters.

*SATURN RECORDS, One Dormont Square, Pittsburgh PA 15216. (412)343-5222. Fax: (412)341-8164. Operations Director: James Quinn. Record company. Estab. 1982. Releases 10 singles, 5 LPs, 10 EPs and 5 CDs/year. Pays negotiable royalty to artists on contract; negotiable rate to publisher per song on record.
How to Contact: Call first and obtain permission to submit. Prefers cassette with 3 songs. Does not return material. Reports in 2 months.
Music: Mostly **alternative**, **A/C** and **jazz**; also **country**, **R&B** and **progressive**. Released *Too Much Too Soon* (by various), recorded by Sputz (A/C); *One Song At A Time* (by various), recorded by Larry Lee Jones (country); and *Enter At Your Own Risk* (by various), recorded by Misfits in the Attic (rap), all on Saturn Records. Other artists include Colette Barron, Ovalordians, Da Smoove One B.U.D., and The Mercurials.
Tips: "Be professional. Make sure that demo, promotional, and bio material are of the utmost professional quality."

 THE ASTERISK before a listing indicates that the listing is new in this edition. New markets are often the most receptive to unsolicited submissions.

SCENE PRODUCTIONS, Box 1243, Beckley WV 25802. (304)252-4836. President/Producer: Richard L. Petry. A&R: Carol Lee. Labels include Rising Sun and Country Bridge Records. Record company, record producer and music publisher (Purple Haze Music/BMI). Member of AFM. Releases 1-2 singles and 1-2 LPs/year. Pays 4-5% minimum royalty to artists on contract; standard royalty to songwriters on contract; statutory rate to publisher for each record sold. Charges "initial costs, which are conditionally paid back to artist."
- Scene Productions' publishing company, Purple Haze Music, is listed in the Music Publishers section.

How to Contact: Submit demo tape by mail. Unsolicited submissions are OK. Prefers cassette with 2-5 songs and lyric sheet. Prefers studio produced demos. SASE. Reports in 4-8 weeks.

Music: Mostly **country**, **top 40**, **R&B/crossover** and **pop/rock**; also **MOR**, **light** and **commercial rock**. Released "My Old Friend," written and recorded by Chuck Paul (pop) on Rising Sun Records; and "Home Sweet W.V.," written and recorded by Dave Runion on Country Bridge Records.

Tips: "Prepare ahead of time with a very good demo tape presenting your talent. Don't spend a lot on a taping and video. You need some kind of initial financial backing to get your career started. Remember you're investing in yourself. You'll need around $10,000 to get the proper exposure you need. Major labels require around 10 times this to sign you. Deal with a company that is reputable and has music with the trade people, *Billboard*, *Cash Box*, *R&R* and *Gavin*."

SCOTTI BROS. RECORDS, 808 Wilshire Blvd., 3rd Floor, Santa Monica CA 90401. (310)656-1100. Fax: (310)656-7430. Alternative A&R: Michael Roth. Labels include Street Life Records, Backyard Records. Record company and music publisher (AllAm Songs/BMI and AACI Songs/ASCAP). Estab. 1978. Releases 25 singles, 25 LPs, 3 EPs and 25 CDs/year.

How to Contact: Submit demo tape by mail. Unsolicited submissions are OK. Prefers cassette, photo and major press. Does not return material.

Music: Mostly **urban** and **alternative**. Released *12 Gauge*, written and recorded by 12 Gauge on Street Life Records (urban); *You Got Lucky* (by Tom Petty), recorded by various artists on Backyard Records (alternative); and *Alapallooza* (by various), recorded by Weird Al on Scotti Bros. Records. Other artists include James Brown, Gerald Alston, Freddie Jackson, The Young Dubliners, Truck Stop Love, Sweet Sable, Tina Moore, Breakdown, The Nylons, Alfonzo, China, Gold Teet and Craig G.

SCRATCHED RECORDS, 1611 Arvada Dr., Richardson TX 75081. (214)680-1830. President: Gerard LeBlanc. Labels include Spectre. Record company. Estab. 1990. Releases 6 singles and 3 CDs/year. Pays 50% royalty to artists on contract; statutory rate to publisher per song on record. "We split all expenses 50/50."

How to Contact: Submit demo tape by mail. Unsolicited submissions are OK. Prefers cassette. "Will respond if interested." Does not return material. Reports in 2 weeks.

Music: Mostly **alternative**, **punk** and **hardcore**; also **girl bands**. Released *A Reason to Care*, written and recorded by Humungus (punk); *Phurly*, written and recorded by Third Leg (hard core); and *We're From Texas*, written and recorded by 21 different bands (alternative), all on Scratched Records.

*SHAKY RECORDS, Box 71, Stn "C", Winnipeg Manitoba R3M 3X3 **Canada**. (204)932-5212. President: Shaky. Record company and music publisher (Shaky Publishing Co./SOCAN). Estab. 1984. Releases 2 LPs, 2 EPs and 1 CD/year.

How to Contact: Submit demo tape by mail. Unsolicited submissions are OK. Prefers cassette (or VHS videocassette if available) with 4-5 songs and lyric sheet. Does not return material. Reports in 1 month.

Music: Mostly **hard rock**, **heavy metal** and **rock**. Released *Strictly Business*, *Three The Hard Way* and *Bad Boys of Rock* (by B. Johnston), recorded by Lawsuit on Shaky Records. Other artists include The Shake.

Tips: "Build up your song catalog, look to other genres of music to expand your ideas in your type of music. Demo quality is important but songs come first. Write lots, choose wisely."

*SHANG RECORDS, 404 Washington Ave., Suite 680, Miami Beach FL 33139. (305)531-7755. Fax: (305)672-8952. President: Luther McKenzie. Record company. Releases 30 singles, 6 LPs and 36 CDs/year.

How to Contact: Call first and obtain permission to submit a demo. Prefers cassette, photos and bio. Does not return material. Reports in 1 month.

Music: Mostly **reggae**, **rap** and **R&B**; also **hip hop**. Released "Pull Up To The Bumper," recorded by Patra on Shang/550 Records; "Let's Get It On," recorded by Shabba Ranks on Sony/Epic Records; and "Scent of Attraction," recorded by Patra/Aaron Hall on Shang/550 Records. Other artists include Mad Cobra (Shang/Capitol recording artist).

SHAOLIN FILM & RECORDS, Box 58547, Salt Lake City UT 84158. (801)595-1123. President: Richard O'Connor. A&R: Don DelaVega. Labels include Shaolin Communications. Record company,

music publisher (Shaolin Music/ASCAP) and record producer (T.S. Coyote). Estab. 1984. Releases 4 singles, 2 LP, 2 CDs and 2 EPs/year.
• See the listing for Shaolin Music in the Music Publishers section.
How to Contact: Submit demo tape by mail. Unsolicited submissions are OK. Prefers cassette with 3-4 songs and lyric sheet. Include bio and press kit. Does not return material. Reports in 6 weeks.
Music: Mostly **rock**, **hard rock** and **pop**; also **soundtracks**. Released *American Zen: Level 1* and *Tai Chi Magic*, both written and recorded by Coyote on Shaolin Film and Records.

SHEFFIELD LAB RECORDING, 1046 Washington St., Raleigh NC 27605. (919)829-1154. Fax: (919)829-0047. A&R: Eric Conn/Tom Volpe. Labels include Audio Phile. Record company. Estab. 1968. Releases 10-20 CDs/year. Pays negotiable royalty to artists on contract.
How to Contact: Write or call first and obtain permission to submit a demo. Prefers cassette, CD or DAT with 3-4 songs and lyric sheet. Does not return material. Reports in 8-10 weeks.
Music: Mostly **classical**, **jazz** and **pop**; also **world music**. Released *Matter of Time*, by Michael Allen Harrison; and *River of My Own*, by Mark Terry, both on Sheffield Lab Recordings.
Tips: "Sheffield Music has been started as a sister label and will be recording 1-2 projects a month—rock, jazz, country, classical. We are also looking for high quality *completed* masters."

*SHIMMY-DISC, JAF Box 1187, New York NY 10116. (201)767-4620. Fax: (201)767-3766. President: Kramer. Labels include Kokopop, Strangelove and Shimmy-Boots. Record company and record producer (Kramer). Estab. 1987. Releases 10 CDs/year. Pays negotiable royalty to artists on contract; 75% of statutory rate to publisher per song on record.
• Shimmy-Disc was voted Best New York Label by the New York Press, and their president, Kramer, was voted Producer of the Year by *Rolling Stone* magazine in 1992. Kramer has produced artists such as Ween, Daniel Johnston, Urge Overkill, King Missle and GWAR.
How to Contact: Submit demo tape by mail. Unsolicited submissions are OK. Prefers cassette. Does not return material. Reports in 1 month.
Music: Mostly **alternative, underground** and **weird**; also **spoken word, soundtracks** and **Canterbury scene/U.K.** Released *Tattoo of Blood* (by Kramer/Jillette), recorded by the Captain Howdy; *Hit Men*, written and recorded by Daevid Allen & Kramer, both on Shimmy-Disc (alternative); and *Orgy of the Dead*, written and recorded by Ed Wood, Jr. on Strangelove Records (soundtrack). Other artists include Tin Ear, Dogbowl, Daved Hild, Hugh Hopper and E-trance.
Tips: Shimmy-Disc releases "music that cannot or will not be released on 'alternative' labels. We are one of the last truly independent labels in the U.S., along with Drag City and Touch & Go."

*SHIRO RECORDS, 8228 Sunset Blvd., 1st Floor, Los Angeles CA 90046. (213)654-2353. Fax: (213)654-2868. E-mail: shirorecs@aol.com. Record company. Estab. 1990. Releases 6 singles, 5 LPs and 5 CDs/year. Pays negotiable royalty to artists on contract; statutory rate to publisher per song on record.
How to Contact: Submit demo tape by mail. Unsolicited submissions are OK. Prefers cassette or CD with 5 songs and lyric or lead sheet. "We will contact the artist if interested in project." Does not return material. Reports in 2 weeks.
Music: Mostly **New Age, funk/jazz** abd **pop**; also **R&B, rap** and **rock/blues**. Released *Back to Reality*, written and recorded by Jeune (funk); *Ecstasy in Avila*, written and recorded by Quinn (New Age); and *Definition Aggro* (by Doug Carrson), recorded by Ultrahead (metal), all on Shiro Records. Other artists include Al Berry, Civilization, and Tomi Kita.

SILENT RECORDS, 340 Bryant St., 3rd Floor East, San Francisco CA 94107. (415)957-1320. Fax: (415)957-0779. E-mail: silent@sirius.com. Website: http://www.silent.org. President: Kim Cascone. Record company and record producer (Kim Cascone). Estab. 1986. Releases 20 CDs/year. Accepts LPs and CDs for consideration and distribution. Pays 15% of wholesale as royalty to artists on contract; negotiable rate to publishers per song on record.
Affiliate(s): Furnace, Sulphur.
How to Contact: Write first and obtain permission to submit. Prefers cassette (or VHS videocassette) with press kit (press clips, bio, etc.). Does not return material. Reports in 6 months.
Music: Mostly **ambient**. Released *Anechoic* (by Kim Cascone), recorded by The Heavenly Music Corporation; *Sonic Acupuncture*, recorded by ATOI; and *Born of Earth and Torments* (by T. Hendricks/B. Matys/R. Robinson), recorded by 23 Degrees, all on Silent Records. Other artists include 303 Terrorists, Deeper Than Space, Michael Mantra.
Tips: "Give up all hope of being rich and famous and create music because you love it."

SILVER WAVE RECORDS, P.O. Box 7943, Boulder CO 80306. (303)443-5617. Fax: (303)443-0877. E-mail: silwave@aol.com. Website: www.bodhi.com/swave. General Manager: Greg Fisher. Labels include Silver Planet Productions. Record company. Estab. 1986. Releases 6-8 LPs, and 6-8 CDs/year. Pays varying royalty to artists on contract and to publisher per song on record.

How to Contact: Write first and obtain permission to submit. Prefers cassette. "Call us two weeks after submitting to make sure it has been received. We will call if interested." SASE. Reports in 1 month.

Music: Mostly **world**, **New Age**, and **contemporary instrumental**. Released *Soul Nature*, written and recorded by Peter Kater (children's); *The World Sings Goodnight, Vol. 2*, recorded by Various World Voices (New Age); and *Vanishing Borders*, recorded by Danny Heines, all on Silver Wave Records. Other artists include Tom and Susan Wasinger and Jim Harvey, Davol, Steve Haun Wind Machine, Curandero, Trio Globo and Joanne Shenandoah.

Tips: "Realize we are primarily an instrumental music label, though we are always interested in good music. Songwriters in the genres of world, New Age and contemporary instrumental are welcome to submit demos. Please include radio and press info, along with bio."

*SILVER WING RECORDS, P.O. Box 270247, Nashville TN 37227-0247. (615)259-7588. (615)259-0107. Director of Production/Promotion: John Edman. Labels include Steele Wheel Records. Record company, music publisher (Sunapee Music Group) and record producer (W. Chad Webb Productions). Estab. 1991. Releases 40 singles, 8-10 LPs and 6 CDs/year. Pays negotiable royalty to artists on contract; statutory rate to publisher per song on record.

● Silver Wing's publishing company, Sunapee Music Group, is listed in the Music Publishers section.

How to Contact: Write or call first and obtain permission to submit. Prefers cassette with 3-4 songs and lyric sheet. "We have a submissions sheet that we send on request." Does not return material. Reports in 2-4 months.

Music: Mostly **contemporary country**, **traditional country** and **gospel**; also **contemporary Christian, R&B, blues** and **alternative rock**. Released *LuLu Salutes Patsy* (by various), recorded by LuLu Roman; *Rockin' Up the Country* (by various), recorded by Johnny Southern; and *If These Walls Could Talk* (by various), recorded by Gene Burton, all on Silver Wing Records (country). Other artists include Bryan Edman, Dellinger, Jami Hall and Keigh Dominick.

SIRR RODD RECORD & PUBLISHING CO., 2453 77th Ave., Philadelphia PA 19150-1820. President: Rodney J. Keitt. Record company, music publisher, record producer and management and booking firm. Releases 5 singles, 5 12″ singles and 2 LPs/year. Pays 5-10% royalty to artists on contract; statutory rate to publisher for each record sold.

How to Contact: Prefers cassette (or videocassette) with 3-5 songs and lyric sheet. SASE. Reports in 1 month.

Music: **Top 40**, **pop**, **gospel**, **jazz**, **dance** and **rap**. Released "All I Want For Christmas," by The Ecstacies; "Guess Who I Saw Today," by Starlene; and "Happy Birthday Baby," by Rodney Jerome Keitt.

SKY-CHILD RECORDS, 221 Linwood Ave., Buffalo NY 14209. President: Alvin Dahn. General Manager and Director of A&R: Edward Parker. Labels include Lucy-V Records. Record company. Estab. 1976. Releases 6 singles, 3 LPs and 3 CDs/year. Pays 5% royalty to artists on contract; statutory rate to publisher per song on record.

How to Contact: Write first and obtain permission to submit. Prefers cassette (or VHS videocassette if available) with 3-6 songs and lyric or lead sheet. Does not return material. Reports in 4-6 weeks.

Music: Mostly **pop/rock**, **rock** and **country**; also **blues**, **ballads**, **gospel**, **inspirational** and **classical**. Released *Almighty God* (by Nevile Brand), recorded by New Creation (gospel) and *Free Feeling* (by George Mobly), recorded by Friction (country), both on Sky-Child Records; and *Deadline*, written and recorded by Mark White on Lucy-V Records (rock). Other artists include Al & Jim, Barry James Band, Don Butternut, Alvin Dahn, Al & Jim, Peggy Walker and Affair.

Tips: "Make sure your material is well developed and submitted in a professional manner with a full press kit (if possible)."

*SMITHSONIAN/FOLKWAYS RECORDINGS, 955 L'Enfant Plaza, Suite 2600, Smithsonian Institute, Washington DC 20560. (202)287-3251. Fax: (202)287-3699. E-mail: cfpcs.folkways@ic.si.edu. Curator/director: Anthony Seeger. Labels include Folkways, Cook and Paredon. Record company and music publisher. Estab. 1948. Releases 25 CDs/year. Pays negotiable royalty to artists on contract and to publisher per song on record.

How to Contact: Write first and obtain permission to submit or to arrange personal interview. Prefers cassette or DAT. Does not return material. Reports in 3 months.

Music: Mostly **traditional U.S. folk music**, **world music** and **children's music**. "We only are interested in music publishing associated with recordings we are releasing. Do not send demos of songwriting only."

Tips "If you are a touring artist and singer/songwriter, consider carefully the advantages of a non-museum label for your work. We specialize in ethnographic and field recordings of people around the world."

SONIC GROUP, LTD., 15 Gloria Lane, Fairfield NJ 07004. (201)575-7460. President: Mark S. Berry. Record company, music publisher (Baby Raquel Music/ASCAP) and record producer (Mark S. Berry). Estab. 1984. Releases 1-2 CDs/year. Pays 10-14% royalty to artists on contract; statutory rate to publisher per song on record.
  • Sonic Group's publishing company, Baby Raquel Music, can be found in the Music Publishers section.
How to Contact: Submit demo tape by mail. Unsolicited submissions are OK. Prefers cassette or VHS videocassette with 3 songs and lyric sheet. Does not return material. Reports in 2 months.
Music: Mostly **alternative rock** and **metal progressive**. Current acts include Voivod, Elvis Manson, Michelin Slave, I Mother Earth, Headstones Bootsauce and Face Plate.

SOUND ACHIEVEMENT GROUP, INC., P.O. Box 24625, Nashville TN 37202. (615)883-2600. President: Royce B. Gray. Labels include New Wind Records, Sugar Mountain Records, Palace Records, Candle Records, Heart Reign Records, Image Records. Record company. Estab. 1985. Releases 15 singles, 15 LPs and 4 CDs/year. Pays 10% royalty to artists on contract; statutory rate to publisher per song on record.
How to Contact: Submit demo tape by mail. Unsolicited submissions are OK. Prefers cassette (or VHS videocassette) with 3 songs and lyric sheet. Does not return material. Reports in 3 months.
Music: Mostly **southern gospel**, **country gospel** and **MOR/inspirational**; also **contemporary gospel** and **Christmas songs**. Released *Whatever It Takes* (by Sam Johnson), recorded by Darla McFadden and *Glorious Hymns of Praise*, recorded by Giorgio Longdo, both on Candle Records; and *Sam's Songs III*, written and recorded by Sam Johnson on Image Records. Other artists include New Spirit Singers, Revelations, Paradise, Heather Stemann and Impact Brass & Singers.
Tips: "Submit quality demos with lyric sheets on all works."

SOUNDS-VISION MUSIC, P.O. Box 3691, La Mesa CA 91944. Phone/Fax: (619)460-1146. Fax: (800)447-1132. Owner: R.L. Hollman. Labels include Gypsy Power Records. Record company, record producer, music publisher (Xpresh'n series music/BMI) and record distributor. Estab. 1985. Releases 3 LPs and 3 CDs/year. Pays 10% royalty to artists on contract; varying amount to publisher per song on record.
  • See their listing in the Music Publishers section.
How to Contact: Submit demo tape by mail. Unsolicited submissions are OK. Prefers cassette (or videocassette if available) with 1 song. SASE. Reports in 6 weeks.
Music: Mostly **flamenco**, **Latin jazz** and **classical**; also **middle eastern**. Released *Poder Gitano*, written and recorded by Rodrigo; *Bulerias Trio* (by Rodrigo), recorded by La Familia Flores; and *Cansada de Querer*, written and recorded by Fernandea Romero, all on Sounds-Vision Records. Other artists include Remedios Flores, Angelita Agujetas, Alberto de Malaga, Daniel de Malaga, Angelita, Luana Moreno, Carlos Montoya, Manitas de Plata.
Tips: "Be open to our opinions and suggestions."

SOURCE UNLIMITED RECORDS, 331 E. Ninth St., New York NY 10003. Contact: S.J. Mollica. Record company. Estab. 1982. Releases 4 CDs/year. Pays 20% royalty to artists on contract; statutory rate to publisher per song on record.
How to Contact: Write first to obtain permission to submit.
Music: Released "A Night in the Life," "Self-Respect" and "Music From the Street," all written and recorded by Santo (urban folk).
Tips: "Write about what you know! Be original."

SPIRITUAL WALK RECORDS, P.O. Box 1674, Temple Hills MD 20757. (301)894-5467. Marketing Director: Yolanda Weir. Labels include Obadiah Records and J-Nozz Records. Record company, concert promoter and marketing company. Estab. 1993. Releases 4-5 singles, 5 LPs and 5 CDs/year. Pays 5% royalty to artists on contract; statutory rate to publisher per song on record.
How to Contact: Submit demo tape by mail. Unsolicited submissions are OK. Prefers cassette (or VHS videocassette if available) with 3 songs and lyric sheet. SASE. Reports in 6-8 weeks.
Music: Strictly **gospel** (all styles). Released "Jesus Is the Light" and "Glorify" (by Sara West), both recorded by The West Singers (traditional) on Spiritual Walk Records.
Tips: "Put your best and strongest song first. This determines whether or not we listen to the other songs on the tape. Strong vocals are a big plus."

SPLUNGE COMMUNICATIONS, INC., P.O. Box 71227, Milwaukee WI 53211. Phone/fax: (414)332-9795. E-mail: clancyc@execpc.com. C.E.O: Clancy Carroll. Record company and music publisher (Splungeorama Music/BMI). Estab. 1993. Releases 10 singles and 2 CDs/year. Pays negotiable royalty on artists on contract; statutory rate to publisher per song on record.

How to Contact: Submit demo tape by mail. Unsolicited submissions are OK. Prefers cassette with 4 songs. "Keep packaging simple and straight forward." Does not return material. Reports in 2-3 months.
Music: Mostly **alternative rock**, **folk** and **experimental**. Released "Looking for my Underground Umbrella" (by Kevin Kinney), recorded by Drop (alternative rock); "Eleven the Hard Way" recorded by Wanda Chrome and the Leather Pharaohs; and "I Left My Heart In Budapest," written and recorded by Chris Twining (punk folk), all on Splunge Communications.

STARCREST PRODUCTIONS, INC., 1602 Dellwood Court., Grand Forks ND 58201. (701)772-0518. President: George J. Hastings. Labels include Meadowlark and Minn-Dak Records. Record company, management firm and booking agency. Estab. 1970. Releases 2-6 singles and 1-2 LPs/year. Payment negotiable to artists on contract; statutory rate to publisher for each record sold.
How to Contact: Submit demo tape by mail. Unsolicited submissions are OK. Prefers cassette with 1-6 songs and lead sheet. SASE. Reports in 3 months.
Music: **Country** and **top 40/pop**. Released "You and North Dakota Nights" (by Stewart & Hastings), recorded by Mary Joyce on Meadowlark Records (country).

STARDUST, 341 Billy Goat Hill Rd., Winchester TN 37398. (615)649-2577. Fax: (615)649-2732. President: Barbara Doss. Labels include Stardust, Wizard, Doss, Kimbolon, Flaming Star. Record company, music publisher (Buster Doss Music/BMI) and record producer (Colonel Buster Doss). Estab. 1959. Releases 50 singles and 25 CDs/year. Pays 8-10% royalty to artists on contract; statutory rate to publisher per song on record.
- Buster Doss's publishing company, Buster Doss Music, is listed in the Music Publishers section, and he is also listed in the Record Producers and Managers and Booking Agents sections.

How to Contact: Write first and obtain permission to submit. Prefers cassette with 2 songs and lyric sheet. SASE. Reports "on same day received."
Music: Mostly **country**; also **rock**. Released "Come On In," recorded by Duane Hall on Stardust Records and "Rescue Me," recorded by Tommy D on Doss Records. Other artists include Linda Wunder, Rooster Quantrell, Don Sky, James Bryan and Dwain Gamel.

STARGARD RECORDS, Box 138, Boston MA 02101. (617)696-7474. Artist Relations: Janice Tritto. Labels include Oak Groove Records. Record company, music publisher (Zatco Music/ASCAP and Stargard Publishing/BMI) and record producer. Estab. 1985. Releases 9 singles and 1 LP/year. Pays 6-7% royalty to artists on contract; statutory rate to publisher per song on record.
How to Contact: Submit demo tape by mail. Unsolicited submissions are OK. Prefers cassette and lyric sheet. SASE. Reports in 2 months. "Sending bio along with picture or glossies is appreciated but not necessary."
Music: Mostly **R&B** and **dance/hip hop**. Released "Anything to Turn U On" and "Nasty Love" (by Floyd Wilcox), both recorded by U-Nek Aproach (R&B/hip hop); and "Give Your Love 2 Me" (by Chris Palmer), recorded by Jilly B., all on Stargard Records. Other artists include APB and Nasty Love Band.

STARTRAK RECORDS, INC., 2200 Evergreen St., Baltimore MD 21216. (410)225-7600. Fax:(410)557-0883. Vice President, A&R: Jimmie McNeal. Labels include Moe Records, D&L Records and JLM Records. Record company. Estab. 1989. Releases 3-4 singles, 3-4 12" singles, 4 LPs, 3 EPs and 6 CDs/year. Pays varying royalty.
How to Contact: Write or call to arrange personal interview, or submit demo tape by mail. Unsolicited submissions are OK. Prefers cassette (or VHS videocassette if available). SASE. Reports in 2 weeks.
Music: Mostly **R&B**, **rap** and **jazz**; also **gospel**, **rock/pop** and **country**. Released *Love Goddess* and *Magic Lady*, both recorded by Lonnie L. Smith on Startrak Records (jazz); and *Club Jazz*, recorded by Pieces of a Dream on Startrak/Capitol Records (jazz). Other artists include Terry Burrus, Dee D. McNeal and Tony Guy.
Tips: "Be original—we always look for new and fresh material with a new twist."

*STRICTLY RHYTHM RECORDS, 920 Broadway, Suite 1403, New York NY 10010. (212)254-2400. Fax: (212)254-2629. Contact: A&R Department. Labels include Phat Wax Records and Groove On Records. Record company. Estab. 1989. Releases 200 singles, 10 LPs, 10 EPs and 10 CDs/year. Pays negotiable royalty to artists on contract; statutory rate to publisher per song on record.
- Strictly Rhythm Records was voted *Billboard* magazine's #1 Dance Music Label in 1995.

How to Contact: Submit demo tape by mail. Unsolicited submissions are OK. Prefers cassette or DAT. "We will only contact you if there is interest in your submission." Does not return material.
Music: Mostly **dance**, **house** and **rap**. Released "Set U Free" (by G. Acosta/N. Renee), recorded by Planet Soul; "I Like To Move It" (by E. Morillot/M. Quashic), recorded by Reel 2 Real; and "Stay

Together" (by B. Reid/L. Vega), recorded by Barbara Tucker, all on Strictly Rhythm Records (dance). Other artists include Alexia, Elan and Winter Darling.

STRUGGLEBABY RECORDING CO., 2612 Erie Ave., P.O. Box 8385, Cincinnati OH 45208. (513)871-1500. Fax: (513)871-1510. A&R/Professional Manager: Pepper Bonar. Record company. Estab. 1983. Releases 3-4 CDs/year. Pays negotiable royalty to artists on contract; statutory (per contract) rate to publisher per song on record.
  • See the listings for Strugglebaby's affiliated company, Hal Bernard Enterprises, in the Music Publishers and Record Producers sections, and for Umbrella Artists Management in the Managers and Booking Agents section.
How to Contact: Submit demo tape by mail. Unsolicited submissions are OK. Prefers cassette with 3 songs and lyric sheet. SASE. Reports in 3-4 weeks.
Music: Mostly **modern rock, rock** and **R&B**. Released *Awkwardsville*, written and recorded by psychodots (modern rock); *Argentina*, written and recorded by The Blue Birds (R&B); and *Brian Lovely & the Secret*, written and recorded by Brian Lovely & the Secret (rock), all on Strugglebaby Recording.
Tips: "Keep it simple, honest, with a personal touch. Show some evidence of market interest and attraction and value as well as the ability to tour."

*SUN WEST MEDIA/UNCLE BIFF'S RECORDS, 1801 Oakland Blvd, Suite 315, Walnut Creek CA 94596. (510)906-8118. Fax: (510)939-3306. E-mail: sunwest mg@aol.com. President/Producer: Christopher Embree. Record company, record producer (Christopher Embree), film and video production and film stock library. Estab. 1993. Releases 3 LPs and 3 CDs/year. Pays negotiable royalty to artists on contract; statutory rate to publisher per song on record.
How to Contact: Submit demo tape by mail. Unsolicited submissions are OK. Prefers cassette or self-released CD. Include photo and bio. SASE. Reports in 3 weeks.
Music: Mostly **hard rock, aggressive "alternative"** and **AOR**; also **AAA**. Released *Caveat Emptor* and *Czars* (by Mohr/Rowell/Fuller/Johnson), recorded by Czars on Uncle Biff's Records.
Tips: "We attend all major industry gatherings such as Gavin, Foundations, SXSW, and CMJ when possible. Be there or you'll never get ahead of the game."

SUNCOUNTRY RECORDS, 2709 W. Pine Lodge, Roswell NM 88201. (505)622-0244. President: Ray Willmon. Record company and music publisher (Pecos Valley Music). Estab. 1989. Releases 1-2 singles, 1 CD/year. Pays 2-10% royalty to artists on contract; statutory rate to publisher per song on record.
  • SunCountry's publishing company, Pecos Valley Music, can be found in the Music Publishers section.
How to Contact: Submit demo tape by mail. Unsolicited submissions are OK. "No phone calls please—we will accept or reject by mail." Prefers cassette, CD or VHS videocassette with 2 songs maximum and lyric sheet. SASE. Reports in 6-8 weeks.
Music: Mostly **C&W, soft rock** and **gospel (country)**. Released "We're In Love," written and recorded by Jimmy Maples; and "Gone" and "Sometime," written and recorded by Bill Gates, all on SunCountry Records. Other artists include Jessie Wayne and Will Anderson.

*SUNDOWN RECORDS, P.O. Box 241, Newbury Park CA 91320. (805)499-9912. E-mail: sundown@adnetsol.com. Owner: Gilbert Yslas. Labels include Blue Sky Music. Record company, music publisher, record producer and music distributor. Estab. 1984. Releases 6-8 CDs/year. Pays negotiable royalty to artists on contract; statutory rate to publisher per song on record.
How to Contact: Write first and obtain permission to submit a demo. Prefers cassette. SASE. Reports in 2-3 weeks.
Music: Mostly **A/C, alternative** and **instrumental**; also **classical** and **New Age**. Released *X-mas Album*, written and recorded by Keith Emerson on Sundown Records (A/C); and *Soliloquy*, written and recorded by Kathie Touin on Blue Sky Records/Classical.

*SUNSET RECORDS, 12028 SW 75th St., Miami FL 33183. (305)273-0575. President: Rudy Ibarra. Record company, music publisher (Ridi Music) and record producer (Rudy Ibarra). Estab. 1995. Releases 1 CD/year. Pays negotiable royalty to artists on contract; statutory rate to publisher per song on record.
How to Contact: Submit demo tape by mail. Unsolicited submissions are OK. Prefers cassette or DAT with 4 songs. "When submitting, please be specific about your goals. Include additional information if necessary." SASE. Reports in 2 weeks.
Music: Mostly **instrumental, Latin** and **pop**; also **children's, rock** and **disco**. Released *Pirata Del Amor*, written and recorded by Ray Guiu on Sunset Records (Latin).
Tips: "Success is in the details. Never stop polishing your skills for they will take you where you want to be."

THE SUNSHINE GROUP, 275 Selkirk Ave., Winnipeg Manitoba R2W 2L5 **Canada**. (204)586-8057. Fax: (204)582-8397. A&R: Ness Michaels. Labels include Jamco International, Baba's Records, Cherish Records, Sunshine Records. Record company, music publisher (Rig Publishing), record producer (Brandon Friesen/Danny Schur.). Estab. 1974. Releases 85 LPs and 20 CDs/year. Pay negotiable to artists on contract and to publishers per song on record.
How to Contact: Submit demo tape by mail. Unsolicited submissions are OK. Prefers cassette or VHS videocassette with 3 songs and lyric sheet. "Send bios and pictures along with any press information." Does not return material. Reports in 1-2 months.
Music: Mostly **country, MOR** and **ethnic**; also **aboriginal, fiddle** and **old tyme**. Released "Peyote" (by Marty-Porte), recorded by Rain Dance, and "I've Got the Blues" written and recorded by Billy-Joe Green, both on Sunshine Records; and "Reservation Dog," recorded by Peacemaker on Jamco Records. Other artists include Peace Maker, Whitefish Bay Singers, Eyabay, Wigwam, Mishi Donovan, Charlie Goertzen, Rick Burt, Billy Simard.
Tips: "Must have original materials, management and a burning desire to succeed. Professional appearance and stage presence a must. Have professional promo kits. Video is important."

*SURESHOT RECORDS, P.O. Box 9117, Truckee CA 96162. (916)587-0111. Owner: Alan Redstone. Record company, record producer and music publisher. Estab. 1979. Releases 1 single and 1 LP/year. Pays statutory royalty to publisher per song on record.
How to Contact: Call first and obtain permission to submit. SASE. Reports in 2 weeks.
Music: Mostly **country, A/C** and **rock**; also **ballads**. Released "Love & Life," "Emily" and "Family History," all written and recorded by Alan Redstone on Sureshot Records (country).

SURPRIZE RECORDS, INC., 7231 Mansfield Ave., Philadelphia PA 19138-1620. (215)276-8861. President: W. Lloyd Lucas. Director of A&R: Darryl L. Lucas. Labels include SRI. Record company and record producer. Estab. 1981. Releases 4-6 singles, 1-3 12″ singles and 2 LPs/year. Pays 8-10 royalty to artists on contract; statutory rate to publisher per song on record.
• See the listing for Delev Music Company in the Music Publishers section.
How to Contact: Submit demo tape by mail. Unsolicited submissions are OK. Prefers cassette or VHS videocassette with 3 songs and lyric or lead sheet. Does not return material. Reports in 4-6 weeks. "We will *not* accept certified mail!"
Music: Mostly **R&B ballads, R&B dance oriented** and **crossover country**. Released *Pleasure* (by Jerry Dean) and *Say It Again* (by R. Hamersma/G. Magallan), both recorded by Jerry Dean (R&B); and "Fat Girls" (by B. Heston/L. Walker/E. Webb/J. Hudson), recorded by Keewee, all on Surprize Records. Other artists include Lamar (R&B).
Tips: "Be dedicated and steadfast in your chosen field whether it be songwriting and/or performing. Be aware of the changing trends. Watch other great performers and try to be as good, if not better. 'Be the best that you can be.' And as Quincy Jones says, 'Leave your egos at the door' and take all criticisms as being positive, not negative. There is always something to learn."

TANDEM RECORDS, 842 Stanton Rd., Burlingame CA 94010. (415)692-2866. Fax: (415)692-8800. E-Mail: trcdist@trcdist.com. Website: http://www.trcdist.com. A&R Representative: Dave Christian. Record company, music publisher (Atherton Music/ASCAP, Atherton Road Music/BMI). Estab. 1985. Pays statutory rate to publisher per song on record.
Affiliate(s): Speed Records.
How to Contact: Submit demo tape by mail. Unsolicited submissions are OK. Prefers cassette and lyric sheet. Does not return material. Reports in 1 month.
Music: Mostly **rap, R&B** and **gospel**; also **modern** and **dance**. Released *Pilot Me* (by Steven Roberts/D. Christian), recorded by Rev. Fleetwood Irving on Tandem Records (gospel); *Faith* (by Dave Sears), recorded by 7 Red 7; and *In Love Again*, written and recorded by Aria on Speed Records (dance). Other artists include Funklab All Stars, Van Damme, Rated X and Tenda Tee, What The Hell, Tabb Doe and Aria.
Tips: "Don't submit until you are sure you are submitting your best work."

TARGET RECORDS, Box 163, West Redding CT 06896. President: Paul Hotchkiss. Labels include Kastle Records. Record company, music publisher (Blue Hill Music/Tutch Music) and record producer (Red Kastle Prod.). Estab. 1975. Releases 6 singles and 4 compilation CDs/year. Pays statutory rate to publisher per song on record.
• Target Records' publishing company, Blue Hill Music/Tutch Music, is listed in the Music Publishers section and Red Kastle Productions is listed in the Record Producers section.
How to Contact: Write first and obtain permission to submit. Prefers cassette with 2 songs and lyric sheet. SASE. Reports in 2 weeks.
Music: **Country** and **crossover**. Released "Rock & Roll Heart" (by P. Hotchkiss), recorded by M. Terry; "Don't Say A Word," written and recorded by Jett Edson, both on Roto-Noto Records. Other artists include Beverly's Hillbilly Band, Bigger Bros., Malone & Hutch and Rodeo.

Tips: "Write songs people want to hear over and over. Strong commercial material."

TEETER-TOT RECORDS, Rt 1, Box 1658-1, Couch MO 65690. (417)938-4259. President/A&R Directors: Chad Sigafus/Terri Sigafus. Record company, record producer and music publisher. Estab. 1988. Releases 4 LPs/year. Pays negotiable royalty to artists on contract; statutory rate to publisher per song on record.
How to Contact: Submit demo tape by mail. Unsolicited submissions are OK. Prefers cassette with 4 songs. Does not return material. Reports in 1 month.
Music: Mostly **children's**, **all styles** and **Christian/children's**. Released *Water Color Ponies*, *Orange Tea & Molasses* and *Little Lamb, Little Lamb*, all written and recorded by Chad and Terri Sigafus on Teeter-Tot Records. Other artists include "Mr. Steve."
Tips: "In children's music, you must be sincere. It's not an easy market. It requires just as much in terms of quality and effort as any other music category. Your heart must be in it."

*THICK RECORDS, 1013 W. Webster #7, Chicago IL 60614. (312)244-0044. Fax: (312)244-2202. E-mail: thlck@aol.com. Contact: Zachary Einstein. Labels include Affiliated with Symbiotic (Buzz, Delmore, Anti Gravity, Fine Corinthian, Espresso). Record company. Estab. 1994. Releases 7-10 singles and 3-5 CDs/year.
How to Contact: Submit demo tape by mail. Unsolicited submissions are OK. Prefers cassette, CD or 7". "Put address directly on tape or CD booklet." Does not return material. Reports ASAP.
Music: Mostly **pop**, **punk** and **garage**; also **hardcore**, **slowcore** and **noize**. Released *I'm A Big Girl Now*, written and recorded by Judge Nothing (pop-punk); *Calliope*, written and recorded by Calliope (slowcore); and *Pill*, written and recorded by Orange (heavy garage), all on Thick Records. Other artists include Back of Dave, Dick Justice, The Laurels, Geezer Lake, Speed Duster, Not Rebecca and Liquor Bike.
Tips: "Be ready to work your own record, tour, tour, work, tour. Don't expect to be huge rock stars. Pay your dues and be independent. Become developed and exposed."

*THIRD WAVE PRODUCTIONS LTD. P.O. Box 563, Gander Newfoundland A1V 2E1 **Canada**. (709)256-8009. Fax: (709)256-7411. Manager: Wayne Pittman. President: Arch Bonnell. Labels include Street Legal Records. Record company, music publisher, distributor and agent. Estab. 1986. Releases 2 singles, 2 LPs and 2 CDs/year. Pays negotiable royalty to artists on contract; statutory rate to publisher per song on record.
• See their listing in the Music Publishers section.
How to Contact: Submit demo tape by mail. Unsolicited submissions are OK. Prefers cassette, DAT, and lyric sheet. SASE. Reports in 2 months.
Music: Mostly **folk/traditional**, **bluegrass** and **country**; also **pop**, **Irish** and **Christmas**. Published *Salt Beef Junkie*, written and recorded by Buddy Wasisname and Other Fellers (folk/traditional); *Newfoundland Bluegrass*, written and recorded by Crooked Stovepipe (bluegrass); and *Nobody Never Told Me*, written and recorded by The Psychobilly Cadillacs (rockabilly/country), all on Third Wave Productions. Other artists include Lee Vaughn.
Tips: "We are not really looking for songs but are always open to take on new artists who are interested in recording/producing an album. We market and distribute as well as produce albums. Not much need for 'songs' per se, except maybe country and rock/pop."

*THUMP RECORDS, INC., 3101 Pomona Blvd., Pomona CA 91768. (909)595-2144. Fax: (909)598-7028. President A&R: Bill Walker. General Manager: Pebo Rodriguez. Labels include Neurotic Records, Inc. Record company and music publisher (Walk-Lo/ASCAP). Estab. 1990. Releases 10 singles, 36 LPs, 6 EPs and 36 CDs/year. Pays 10% (negotiable) royalty to artists on contract; ¾ statutory rate to publisher per song on record.
How to Contact: Submit demo tape by mail. Unsolicited submissions are OK. Prefers cassette and lyric sheet. SASE. Reports in 2-4 weeks.
Music: Mostly **house**, **rap** and **ballads**; also **dance** and **industrial**. Released *Baby O.G.* (by Lawrence Patino), recorded by Slow Pain on Thump Records (rap); *Main Line* (by Steve Seibold), recorded Hate Dept. on Neurotic Records (industrial punk); and *Nayba Hood Queen* (by Jennifer Velarde), recorded by J.V. on Thump Records (rap). Other artists include Rocky Padilla and Deuce Mob.
Tips: "Provide Thump with positive upbeat music that has universal appeal."

*TOP RECORDS, Gall. del Corso, 4 Milano 20122 **Italy**. Phone: (02)76021141. Fax: (0039)276021141. Manager/Director: Guido Palma. Labels include United Colors Productions, Dingo Music, Kiwi Record, Smoking Record and Tapes. Estab. 1979. Record company and music publisher (Dingo Music). Releases 20 12" singles, 30 LPs, 15 EPs and 40 CDs/year. Pays standard royalty to artists on contract; statutory rate to publisher per song on record.
How to Contact: Submit demo tape by mail. Unsolicited submissions are OK. Prefers cassette (or videocassette) with 5 songs and lyric sheet. SAE and IRC. Reports in 1 month.

Music: Mostly **pop** and **dance**; also **soundtracks**. Released *Una Vecchia Cantone Italiana* (by Marrocchi), recorded by Rosanna Fratello; *Stammi Vincino* (by L. Albertelli), recorded by Rosanna Fratello; and *Raga-Ragazzina* (by A. De Bernardi), recorded by Alex Nardi, all on TOP Records.

TOP TEN HITS RECORDS INC., 6832 Hanging Moss Rd., Orlando FL 32807. (407)672-0101. Fax: (407)672-5742. President: Hector L. Torres. Labels include T.R., New Generation, Rana and CEG. Record company, music publisher and independent record distributor. Estab. 1979. Releases 20 singles, 15 LPs and 15-20 CDs/year. Pays varying royalty to artists on contract; statutory royalty to publisher per song on record.
How to Contact: Submit demo tape by mail. Unsolicited submissions are OK. Prefers cassette with lead sheet. SASE. Reports in 1 month.
Music: Mostly **Spanish: tropical/pop**, **salsa**, and **merengue**; also **Latin-jazz** and **cumbia**. Released *15 to Aniversario* (by Ringo Martinez), recorded by Datrullal 15 (merengue); *Now is the Time* (by Martin Arroyo), recorded by MAQ (jazz); and *Grupomania* (by various), recorded by Grupomania (merengue), all on Top Ten Hits Records. Other artists include Zona Roja, Bronx Horns, Bobby Valenin, Gran Daneses, Alfa 8 and Magnificos.
Tips: "We are an independent Latin record company specializing mostly in tropical rhythms and Latin jazz."

TRAC RECORD CO., 170 N. Maple, Fresno CA 93702. (209)255-1717. Owner: Stan Anderson. Record company and music publisher (Sellwood Publishing/BMI). Estab. 1972. Releases 5 singles, 5 LPs and 2 CDs/year. Pays 13% royalty to artists on contract; statutory rate to publisher per song on record.
 • See their listing in the Record Producers section, as well as a listing for Sellwood Publishing in the Music Publishers section.
How to Contact: Submit demo tape by mail. Unsolicited submissions are OK. Prefers cassette (or VHS videocassette) with 2-4 songs and lyric sheet. SASE. Reports in 3 weeks.
Music: **Traditional country** and **country rock**. Released *Long Texas Highway* (by Jessica James/Debbie D) and *Grandpa's Old Piano* (by Ray Richmond), recorded by Jessica James; and *Kick Me When I'm Down*, written and recorded by Jimmy Walker, all on TRAC Records.

*TRAVELER ENTERPRISES, 505 Erin Blue Place, Edmond, OK 73034. Vice President: Paul Palmer. Labels include Traveler Records. Record company, music publisher (Cooter Bug Music/BMI) and record producer (Crosbee Promotions). Estab. 1976. Releases 2-4 singles, 2-4 12" singles and 2 LPs/year. Pays lease rate to artists on contract.
How to Contact: Write first and obtain permission to submit. Prefers cassette with 2 songs and lyric sheet. SASE. Reports in 2 months.
Music: Mostly **country**. Released *Praying*, recorded by Bonnie Rairdon; *Tribute to the American Cowboy*, recorded by Rusty Rogers; and *Fragile*, recorded by the Class Band, all on Traveler Records. Other artists include Gary Bean.
Tips: "Be very selective on material you submit."

TREASURE COAST RECORDS (a division of Judy Welden Enterprises), 692 SE Port St. Lucie Blvd., Port St. Lucie FL 34984. Labels include Heartfelt Records (Christian music only). President: Judy Welden. Record company, music publisher (Songrite Creations Productions/BMI, Sine Qua Non Music/ASCAP) and record producer. Estab. 1992. Releases 75-100 singles and 6-8 CDs/year. Pays 10-15% royalty to artists on contract; statutory rate to publisher per song on record.
How to Contact: Submit demo tape by mail. Unsolicited submissions are OK. "Send only your best unpublished songs (1 or 2 max), bio, press, number of songs written, releases, awards, etc." Prefers cassette with 1 or 2 songs and lyric sheet. SASE. Reports in 3 weeks.
Music: Mostly **contemporary country, pop (A/C)** and **gospel**; also **R&B**. Released "Tonight You're Mine" (by Lew Brodsky/Paul Brand/Lori Kline), recorded by Lori Kline; "I Can Almost Hear An Angel" (by Dennis Blunt), recorded by Loralee Christensen; and "Daylight In Dixie" (by Keith Curry), recorded by Keith Curry & Derringer Band, all on Treasure Coast Records. Other artists include Alesia Panajota, Glenn Mayo, Erika Lee, Salt Creek, Rick Taylor, Trey Moyer, Larry LaVey and Paige Blind.

TREND RECORDS, P.O. Box 201, Smyrna GA 30081. (770)432-2454. President: Tom Hodges. Labels include Trendsetter, Atlanta's Best, Trend Star, Trend Song, British Overseas Airways Music, Trendex, and Stepping Stone Records. Record company, music publisher (Mimic Music/BMI, Skipjack Music/BMI and British Overseas Airways Music/ASCAP), record producer and management firm. Estab. 1965. Releases 4 singles, 14 LPs and 10 CDs/year. Pays 15% royalty to artists on contract; standard royalty to songwriters on contract; statutory rate to publisher per song on records.
 • Trend Records' publishing company, BOAM, can be found in the Music Publishers section.

How to Contact: Submit demo tape by mail. Unsolicited submissions are OK. Prefers cassette (or VHS videocassette) with 8-10 songs, lyric and lead sheet. SASE. Reports in 3 weeks.
Music: Mostly **R&B**, **country** and **MOR**; also **gospel**, **light rock** and **jazz**. Released *Nashville Sessions*, recorded by Jim Single; *Sweet Jesus*, recorded by Keith Bradford; and *A Big Smokin' Gun*, recorded by Hilda Gonzalez, all on Trend Records. Other artists include The Caps, "Little" Jimmy Dempsey, Candy Chase, Joe Terry, Charlie & Nancy Cole and Marion Frizzell.

TRIPLE X RECORDS, P.O. Box 862529, Los Angeles CA 90086-2529. (213)221-2204. Fax: (213)221-2778. A&R: Bruce Duff. Record company. Estab. 1986. Releases 5 singles, 10 LPs, 4 EPs and 25 CDs/year. Royalties not disclosed.
How to Contact: Call first and obtain permission to submit. "No unsolicited tapes, please." Prefers cassette. "Photo and bio are helpful." Does not return material. Reports in 1-2 months.
Music: Mostly **rock**, **industrial/goth** and **rap**; also **blues**, **roots** and **noise**. Released *Idjit Savant* (by Graves/Phillips/Lee), recorded by The Dickies (rock); *The Anti-Naturalists* (by Pfahler/Somoa), recorded by the Voluptuous Horror of Karen Black (rock); and *Bliss*, written and recorded by Jeff Dahl (rock), all on Triple X Records. Other artists include Rozz Williams, Bo Diddley, Angry Samoans, Vandals, Die Haut, Lydia Lunch and Miracle Workers.
Tips: "Looking for self-contained units that generate their own material and are willing and able to tour."

TRUMPETER RECORDS INC., 5660 E. Virginia Beach Blvd., Norfolk VA 23502. (804)455-8454. Fax: (804)461-4669. A&R: Tres Swann and Mike Lee. Subsidiary labels include Peacetime Records. Record company. Estab. 1991. Releases 2 singles, 2 EPs and 10 CDs/year. Pays varying royalty to artists on contract; statutory rate to publisher per song on record.
● See the listing for Pen Cob Publishing in the Music Publishers section and Sirocco Productions in the Managers and Booking Agents section.
How to Contact: Write or call first and obtain permission to submit. Prefers cassette or VHS videocassette. SASE. Reports in 3-4 weeks.
Music: Mostly **alternative/progressive** and **rock**. Released *Flow*, recorded by Egypt (alternative/progressive); and *Color of the Day*, recorded by Mundahs, both on Trumpeter Records. Other artists include Big Stoner Creek, Sea of Souls and Ashes.

TRUSTY RECORDS, 8771 Rose Creek Rd., Nebo KY 42441. (502)249-3194. President: Elsie Childers. Record company and music publisher (Trusty Publications/BMI). Member CMAA, CMA. Estab. 1960. Releases 2 CDs/year. Pays various standard to artists on contract; statutory rate to publisher for each record sold.
● See the listing for Trusty Publications in the Music Publishers section.
How to Contact: Write or call first and obtain permission to submit. Prefers cassette with 2-4 songs and lead sheet. Does not return material. Reports in 6 weeks (if SASE enclosed).
Music: Country, **blues**, **contemporary Christian**, **country Christian**, **easy listening**, **gospel**, **MOR**, **soul** and **top 40/pop**. Released *Aggravatin'* and *Hearin' Things* (by Elsie Childers), recorded by Barry Russell on Trusty Records (country).

TVT RECORDS, 23 E. Fourth St., New York NY 10003. (212)979-6410. Fax: (212)979-6489. Director of A&R: Tom Sarig. Labels include Tee Vee Toons, Wax Trax! Records, 1001 Sundays, Blunt Recordings, Fuel Records. Record company and music publisher (TVT Music). Estab. 1986. Releases 25 singles, 20 12″ singles, 40 LPs, 5 EPs and 40 CDs/year. Pays varying royalty to artists on contract; statutory rate to publisher per song on record.
How to Contact: Submit demo tape by mail. Unsolicited submissions are OK. Prefers cassette (or VHS videocassette if available). Does not return material. Reports in 6 weeks.
Music: Mostly **alternative rock**, **rap** and **techno**; also **jazz/R&B**. Released *Pretty Hate Machine* (by Trent Reznor), recorded by Nine Inch Nails (industrial rock); *Ring* (by Mike Connell), recorded by The Connells (alternative rock); and *Spirits*, written and recorded by Gil Scott-Heron (jazz/soul/rap), all on TVT Records. Other artists include Catherine, Mic Geronimo, Kinsui, DNote, Cords, KMFDM, Psykosonik, Rise Robots Rise, Jester, Chris Connelly, AFX, Autechre, EBN, Spooky-Ruben, Fledgling and Birdbrain.
Tips: "We look for seminal, ground breaking, genre-defining artists of all types with compelling live presentation. Our quest is not for hit singles but for enduring important artists."

THE TYPES OF MUSIC each listing is interested in are printed in boldface.

*28 RECORDS, 19700 NW 86 Court, Miami FL 33015-6917. Phone/fax: (305)829-8142. E-mail: rec28@aol.com. Website: http://www.webcom.com/~cyborg/28RECORDS. President/CEO: Eric Diaz. Record company. Estab. 1994. Releases 2 LPs and 4 CDs/year. Pays negotiable royalty to artists on contract; statutory rate to publisher per song on record.

How to Contact: Submit demo tape by mail. Unsolicited submissions are OK. Prefers cassette, VHS videocassette or CD (if already released on own label for possible distribution or licensing deals). If possible send promo pack and photo. "Please put Attn: A&R on packages." Does not return material. Reports in 1 month.

Music: Mostly **hard rock/modern rock**, **metal** and **alternative**; also **punk** and **death metal**. Released *Julian Day*, recorded by Helltown's Infamous Vandal (modern/hard rock); and *Mantra*, recorded by Derek Cintron (modern rock), both on 28 Records.

Tips: "Be patient and ready for the long haul. We strongly believe in nurturing you the artist/songwriter. If you're willing to do what it takes and have what it takes, we will do whatever it takes to get you to the next level. We are looking for artists to develop. We are a very small label but we are giving the attention that is a must for a new band as well as developed and established acts. Give us a call."

TWIN SISTERS PRODUCTIONS, INC., 1340 Home Ave., Suite D, Akron OH 44310. (800)248-TWIN. President: Kim Thompson. Record company. Estab. 1986. Releases 4-6 LPs/year. Pays negotiable royalty to artists on contract; statutory rate to publisher per song on record.

How to Contact: Call first and obtain permission to submit. Prefers cassette (or VHS videocassette if available). SASE. Reports in 1 month.

Music: **Children's** only (video and audio). Released *Safe & Sound*, *Spanish* and *French* (by K. Thompson), recorded by various artists on Twin Sisters Productions.

Tips: "We are mainly interested in children's educational and entertaining audio. Artists wishing to become children's performers and songwriters skilled in children's audio are asked to call first before submitting. A demo will be required."

*UNITY ENTERTAINMENT CORPORATION, 207 Ashland Ave., Santa Monica CA 90405. (310)581-2700. Fax: (310)581-2727. E-mail: unitylab1@aol.com. Director of A&R: Chris Maggiore. Labels include Unity Label Group, Meltdown Records, Surfdog Records, Countdown Records and White Cat Records. Record company. Estab. 1992. Releases 20 LPs and 20 CDs/year. Pays negotiable royalty to artists on contract; 75% statutory rate to publisher per song on record.

How to Contact: Submit demo tape by mail. Unsolicited submissions are OK. Prefers cassette, DAT and lyric sheet. Does not return material. Reports in 2 weeks.

Music: Mostly **jazz/NAC**, **AAA** and **alternative**. Released *Stuff*, written and recorded by Box The Walls (AAA); *The Whole Affair*, written and recorded by Izit (acid jazz), both on Countdown Records; and *Swirl*, written and recorded by Sprung Monkey on Surfdog Records (alternative). Other artists include Keiko Matsui, Paul Taylor, Gary Hoey, The Almighty Ultrasound, Issa Toone, Lava Diva, Valerie Carter and Kazy Matsui.

UNIVERSAL-ATHENA RECORDS (UAR Records), Box 1264, Peoria IL 61654-1264. (309)673-5755. A&R Director: Jerry Hanlon. Record company and music publisher (Jerjoy Music/BMI). Estab. 1978. Releases 1-2 singles and 1 LP/year. Pays standard royalty to artists on contract; statutory rate to publisher for each record sold.

• UAR's publishing affiliate, Jerjoy Music, is listed in the Music Publishers section.

How to Contact: Submit demo tape by mail. Unsolicited submissions are OK. Prefers cassette with 4-8 songs and lyric sheet. SASE. Reports in 2 weeks.

Music: **Country**. Released *When Autumn Leaves*, written and recorded by Clint Miller; *Livin' On Dreams* (by Eddie Grew); and *Shadows on the Wall* (by Matt Dorman), both recorded by Jerry Hanlon, all on HAR Records (country).

Tips: "Be extremely critical and make realistic comparisons of the commercial and professional value of your work before submission."

*URGENT MUSIC, INC., 8103 Brodie Lane #3, Austin TX 78745. (512)282-4036. Fax: (512)282-7548. E-mail: urgent@io.com. A&R Publishing: Christopher Shannon. Labels include Urgent Records, Heart & Soul Music, More Than Music Productions. Record company and music publisher (234 Music Publishing). Estab. 1988. Releases 16 singles, 12 LPs and 12 CDs/year. Pays negotiable royalty to artists on contract; statutory rate to publisher per song on record.

How to Contact: Submit demo tape by mail. Unsolicited submissions are OK. Prefers cassette and lyric sheet. "Keep it simple." Does not return material. Reports in 2 months.

Music: Mostly **contemporary Christian**, **country** and **pop**. Released *Arizona Highway*, written and recorded by Phillip Sanditer; *Moon Circles*, written and recorded by Santa Fe; and *Between The Lines*, written and recorded by Joseph Mills, all on Urgent Music. Other artists include Rob Frazier, Tom and Sherry Green.

Tips: "Submit demo with guitar or keyboard and vocal. The song and raw talent is the name of the game. Don't clutter things up with production on submission."

VAI DISTRIBUTION, 158 Linwood Plaza, Suite 301, Fort Lee NJ 07024. (201)944-0099. Fax: (201)947-8850. Promotion Director: Don Fergusson. Record company and distributor. Estab. 1983. Pays negotiable royalty to artists on contract; other amount to publisher per song on record.
How to Contact: Write or call first and obtain permission to submit a demo. Prefers cassette, DAT or NTSC videocassette. Does not return material. Reports in 2-3 weeks.
Music: Mostly **opera (classical vocal)**, **classical (orchestral)** and **classical instrumental/piano**; also **jazz**. Released *Susannah* (by Carlisle Floyd), recorded by New Orleans Opera Orchestra and Chorus; *Caliph's Magician* (by Gabriel Von Wayditch), recorded by Orchestra and Chorus of Budapest National Opera, all on VAI Audio. Other artists include Jon Vickers, Evelyn Lear and Thomas Stewart.

*VALTEC PRODUCTIONS, P.O. Box 2642, Santa Maria CA 93457. (805)934-8400. Owner/Producers: J. Anderson and J. Valenta. Labels include Imperial Records. Record company and record producer (Joe Valenta). Estab. 1986. Releases 20 singles, 15 LPs and 10 CDs/year. Pays negotiable royalty to artists on contract; statutory rate to publisher per song on record.
How to Contact: Submit demo tape by mail. Unsolicited submissions are OK. Prefers DAT with 4 songs and lyric sheet. Does not return material. Reports in 1-2 months.
Music: Mostly **country**, **top 40** and **A/C**; also **rock**. Released *Just Me* (by Joe Valenta) and *Hold On* (by Joe Valenta/J. Anderson), both recorded by Joe Valenta (top 40); and *Time Out (For Love)* (by Joe Valenta), recorded by Marty K. (country), all on Valtec Records.

VICTORY RECORDS, P.O. Box 146546, Chicago IL 60614. (312)666-8662. Fax: (312)666-8665. Victory Europe: Gönninger Str. 3 72793 Pfullingen **Germany**. Contact: Tony Brummel. Record company and distributor. Estab. 1989. Releases 4 singles, 4 LPs, 2 EPs and 4 CDs/year. Royalty varies; pays statutory rate to publisher per song on record.
How to Contact: Submit demo tape by mail. Unsolicited submissions are OK. Prefers cassette with lyric sheet. "Send us as much information as possible." Does not return material. Reports in 3 weeks.
Music: Mostly **hardcore** and **indie rock/punk**; also **rockabilly**. Released *Destroy the Machines*, recorded by Earth Crisis; *One Truth*, recorded by Strife; and *Fear City*, recorded by Hi Fi and the Roadburners, all on Victory Records (hardcore). Other artists include Snapcase, Warzone, Cause for Alarm.
Tips: "If you're not familiar with our label or bands, odds are we won't like your band. However, if you think your band is extreme enough, you might send your recording anyway."

VOKES MUSIC RECORD CO., Box 12, New Kensington PA 15068. (412)335-2775. President: Howard Vokes. Labels include Vokes and Country Boy Records. Record company, booking agency and music publisher. Releases 8 singles and 5 LPs/year. Pays 2½-4½% song royalty to artists and songwriters on contract.
  ● Vokes Music's publishing company, Vokes Music Publishing, is listed in the Music Publishers section and their booking agency, Vokes Booking Agency, is listed in the Managers and Booking Agents section.
How to Contact: Submit cassette only and lead sheet. SASE. Reports in 2 weeks.
Music: **Country**, **bluegrass** and **gospel-old time**. Released "Cherokee Trail Of Tears" and "City Of Strangers," recorded by Johnny Eagle Feather; and "Portrait Of An Angel," recorded by Lenny Gee, all on Vokes Records.

WALL STREET MUSIC, 1189 E. 14 Mile Rd., Birmingham MI 48009. (810)646-2054. Fax: (810)646-1957. E-mail: wallstmus@aol.com. A&R Director: Joe Sanders. Record company and music publisher (Burgundy Bros.). Estab. 1985. Releases 6 singles, 4 12" singles, 4 LPs, 4 EPs and 8 CDs/year. Pays 8-14% royalty to artists on contract; statutory rate to publisher per song on record.
  ● See their listing in the Record Producers section.
How to Contact: Call first and obtain permission to submit. Prefers cassette (or VHS videocassette if available) with 2 songs and photo. "Label all items completely." Does not return material. Reports in 6 weeks.
Music: Mostly **rap**, **hip hop** and **house**; also **rave**, **trance** and **R&B**. Released "Taste the Flava" (by Mike Buckholtz), recorded by Soulism; "Ooh LaLa" (by Lester Marlin), and *Nasty Sexual Thangs* (by Darell Campbell), both recorded by Simply Black, all on Wall Street Music. Other artists include Drueada and ANG.
Tips: "Be professional and realistic. If we sign you, we'll be looking for someone with a cooperative, partnership attitude."

THE WANSTAR GROUP, P.O. Box 6283, Charleston SC 29405. (803)853-5294. President/Executive Producer: Samuel W. Colston III. Labels include Tye Records and Chela Records. Record company, music publisher (Out On A Limb Publishing/BMI) and record producer (S. Colston III). Estab. 1990. Releases 3 singles, 2 LPs and 2 CDs/year. Pays negotiable royalty to artists on contract; negotiable amount to publisher per song on record.

How to Contact: Submit demo tape by mail. Unsolicited submissions are OK. Prefers cassette or VHS videocassette with 3 songs and lyric sheet. Does not return material. Reports in 3-4 weeks.

Music: Mostly **dance/pop** and **R&B**; also **contemporary gospel**. Released "Red is the Color, My Love," (by Colston/Wentworth), recorded by Royal Red on Tye Records (R&B). Other artists include CZAR Justice of DA 3rd Generation.

Tips: "Make sure the song happens immediately within 10 to 15 seconds. Continue to refine the production of the songs."

WARNER BROS. RECORDS, 3300 Warner Blvd., Burbank CA 91505-4694. (818)846-9090. This record company prefers not to share information.

WATUSI PRODUCTIONS, 516 Storrs, Rockwall TX 75087. Phone/fax: (214)771-3797. Producer: Jimi Towry. Labels include World Beatnik Records. Record company and record producer (Jimi Towry). Estab. 1983. Releases 4 singles, 3 LPs, 4 EPs and 3 CDs/year. Pays negotiable royalty to artists on contract; statutory rate to publisher per song on record.

How to Contact: Submit demo tape by mail. Unsolicited submissions are OK. Prefers cassette, DAT or VHS videocassette with 3 songs and lyric sheet. SASE. Reports in 3 weeks.

Music: Mostly **world beat, reggae** and **ethnic**; also **jazz, hip hop/dance** and **pop**. Released *The Island* and *A Live Montage* (by J. Towry), recorded by Watusi; and "Feels Like the Nite" (by J. Towry/J. Clemons), recorded by Dr. Clock, all on World Beatnik Records. Other artists include Jimi Towry, Wisdom Ogbor (Nigeria), Joe Latch (Ghana), Dee Dee Cooper, Ras Lyrix (St. Croix), Ras Kumba (St. Kitts), Lee Mitchell, Gary Mon.

WEDGE RECORDS, Box 290186, Nashville TN 37229-0186. (615)754-2950. President: Ralph D. Johnson. Labels include Dome Records and Fleet Records. Record company, music publisher (Big Wedge Music/BMI and Pro-Rite Music/ASCAP), record producer (Ralph D. Johnson). Estab. 1960. Releases 10 singles, 2 LPs and 2 CDs/year. Pays 10% royalty to artists on contract; statutory rate to publisher per song on record.

How to Contact: Write or call first to obtain permission to submit a demo. Prefers cassette and lyric or lead sheet. SASE. Reports in 2 weeks.

Music: Mostly **country** and **country crossover**; also **rock, gospel, pop** and **R&B**. Released *The Boogie Place* (by Roy August), recorded by Keith Bryant; "Little Hearts Hurt Too" (by Cale Groves/Steve Green), recorded by Stacy Edwards; and "I'm Gonna Leave You" (by Roy August), recorded by Kristina Crowley, all on Wedge Records.

WENCE SENSE MUSIC/BILL WENCE PROMOTIONS, P.O. Box 110829, Nashville TN 37222. Contact: Kathy Wence. Labels include Six-One-Five Records and Skyway Records. Record company, music publisher (Wence Sense Music/ASCAP), record producer (Bill Wence). Estab. 1984. Releases 4-8 singles, 4 CDs/year. Pays statutory rate to publishers per song on record.

How to Contact: Submit demo tape by mail. Unsolicited submissions are OK. Prefers cassette with 1 song. SASE. Reports in 2 weeks.

Music: Prefers **country**. Released "Homeless Heart" (by Buddy Blackmon/Karen Pell), recorded by Lori Smith (country); *The Shadows* (by various), recorded by Shadows, both on 615 Records; and *Kristie Dukes* (by various), recorded Kristie Dukes on Skyway Records (country). Other artists include Trena and Lanada Cassidy.

Tips: "Send only one song until we request more of you and be patient."

WESTPARK MUSIC - RECORDS, PRODUCTION & PUBLISHING, P.O. Box 260227, Rathenauplatz 4, 50515 Cologne **Germany**. (49)221 247644. Fax: (49)221 231819. Contact: Ulli Hetscher. Labels distributed by BMG Ariola and Indigo. Estab. 1986. Releases 3-4 singles and 10-12 CDs/year. Pays 8-14% royalty to artists on contract.

How to Contact: Submit demo tape by mail. Unsolicited submissions are OK. Prefers cassette with 5-6 songs and lyric sheets. Does not return material. Reports in 2-3 months.

Music: Everything apart from mainstream-pop, jazz, classical, country and hard rock/metal. "The only other criterion is: we simply should love it." Released albums by Glora Feidman (BMG), Dario Domingues (Westpark) and Paul Millns (BMG).

Tips: "Mark cassette clearly. No high quality cassettes expected. We only send letters back!!"

WHITE CAR RECORDS, 10611 Cal Rd., Baton Rouge LA 70809. (504)755-1400. Owner: Nelson Blanchard. Labels include Techno Sound Records. Record company, music publisher (White Car Music/BMI, Char Blanche/ASCAP) and independent record producer. Estab. 1980. Releases 6 singles, 4 12″ singles, 6 LPs, 1 EP and 2 CDs/year. Pays 7½-20% royalty to artists on contract; statutory rate to publisher per song on record.
How to Contact: Submit demo tape by mail. Unsolicited submissions are OK. Prefers cassette with 4 songs. Does not return material. Reports in 2 weeks.
Music: Mostly **country**, **rock** and **pop**; also **R&B**. Released "Time, You're No Friend of Mine," written and recorded by Howard Austin; "Closer to Heaven," written and recorded by Joey Dupuy, both on Techno Sound Records; and "I Read Between the Lines (by Stan Willis), recorded by Nelson Blanchard on White Car Records. Other artists include John Steve, B.J. Morgan and Bayon Country Band.

*WHITEHOUSE RECORDS, P.O. Box 34363, Chicago IL 60634. (312)583-7499. Fax: (312)583-2526. E-mail: wthouse@housedog.com. Label Manager: Rob Gillis. Labels include Waterdog Records. Record company. Estab. 1994. Releases 1 EP and 6 CDs/year. Pays negotiable royalty to artists on contract; statutory rate to publisher per song on record.
How to Contact: Submit demo tape by mail. Unsolicited submissions are OK. Prefers cassette or CD. Include cover letter, brief bio, itinerary and picture. SASE. Reports in 1 month.
Music: Mostly **rock**, **pop** and **folk**. Released "Adam McCarthy," written and recorded by Ralph Covert on Waterdog Records (rock); *Woodshed* (by Jason Narducy), recorded by Jason & Alison (rock); and *Making Models*, written and recorded by Eric Lugosch (folk), both on Whitehouse Records. Other artists include Soulvitamins, Lava Sutra, MysteryDriver, Al Rose & The Transcendos, the Bad Examples, The Spelunkers and Joel Frankel.
Tips: "While we are primarily interested in artists who write their own material and perform live regularly, we are open to the artist with just a great song or two interested in having it included on a compilation."

WIDELY DISTRIBUTED RECORDS, 1412 W. Touhy, Chicago IL 60626. (312)465-2558. E-mail: widely@aol.com. President: Jack R. Frank. Record company. Estab. 1988. Releases 3 EPs and 6 CDs/year. Pays 15% royalty to artists on contract; negotiable amount to publisher per song on record.
How to Contact: Submit demo tape by mail. Unsolicited submissions are OK. Prefers cassette. Does not return material. Reports in 6 months.
Music: Mostly **pop** and **rock**; also **spoken word**. Released *Zoomar* (by Tom Szidon), recorded by Joy Poppers; *Incorporated*, written and recorded by Lydia Tomkiw; and *Kick Ball*, written and recorded by The Impatients, all on Widely Distributed Records. Other artists include Vinyl Devotion and Green.

WINCHESTER RECORDS, % McCoy, Route 2, Box 114, Berkeley Springs WV 25411. (304)258-9381. Labels include Master Records and Real McCoy Records. Record company, music publisher (Jim McCoy Music, Clear Music, New Edition Music/BMI), record producer and recording studio. Releases 20 singles and 10 LPs/year. Pays standard royalty to artists; statutory rate to publisher for each record sold.
  • See the listings for Jim McCoy Music in the Music Publishers section and Jim McCoy Productions in the Record Producers section.
How to Contact: Write first and obtain permission to submit. Prefers 7½ ips reel-to-reel or cassette with 5-10 songs and lead sheet. SASE. Reports in 1 month.
Music: Bluegrass, **church/religious**, **country**, **folk**, **gospel**, **progressive** and **rock**. Released *Touch Your Heart*, written and recorded by Jim McCoy; "Leavin'," written and recorded by Red Steed, both on Winchester Records; and "The Taking Kind" (by Tommy Hill), recorded by J.B. Miller on Hilton Records. Other artists include Carroll County Ramblers, Bud Arnel, Nitelifers, Jubilee Travelers and Middleburg Harmonizers.

WIZMAK PRODUCTIONS, P.O. Box 477, Wingdale NY 12594. (914)877-3943. E-mail: wizmak @aol.com. Manager: Geri White. Record company and recording studio. Estab. 1986. Releases 6-8 cassettes and CDs/year. Pays 12% royalty to artists on contract; statutory rate to publisher per song on record.

REFER TO THE CATEGORY INDEX (at the end of this section) to find exactly which companies are interested in the type of music you write.

How to Contact: Submit demo tape by mail. Unsolicited submissions are OK. Prefers cassette with 3 songs and lyric sheet. "Also include news article or review of a recent performance." SASE. Reports in 6-12 weeks.
Music: Mostly **dulcimer/folk, traditional (American & Irish)** and **gospel**; also **contemporary, acoustic** and **singer/songwriter**. Released *The Faery Hills*, written and recorded by Mark Nelson; *The Hourglass*, written and recorded by Mike Casey; and *A Wizmak Sampler*, written and recorded by various artists; all on Wizmak Records. Artists include The Woods Tea Co., Ken Perlman and The Plaid Family.
Tips: "Know your direction, establish yourself as a performer on a regional level."

*WOLFTRAX RECORDS, P.O. Box 40007, Houston TX 77240-0007. President: Paul Domsalla. Record company, music publisher (Puro Cielo Music) and record producer (Paul Domsalla, Puro Cielo Productions). Estab. 1993. Releases 1 CD/year. Pays negotiable royalty to artists on contract; statutory rate to publisher per song on record.
How to Contact: Submit demo tape by mail. Unsolicited submissions are OK. Prefers cassette with 5 songs and lyric sheet. SASE. Reports in 2 months.
Music: Mostly **blues, rock** and **country rock**. Released *Texas Thunder*, recorded by The Benny Valerio Band on Wolftrax Records (blues). Other artists include Chiggers (rock) and Aberose.
Tips: "Don't try to write like anyone else. Write from the heart."

WONDERLAND RECORDS, 374 Treadwell St., Hamden CT 06514. (203)248-2170. Fax: (203)248-1460. E-mail: wonderland@wlr.com. Website: http://www.connix.com/~wlr. Record company. Estab. 1993. Releases 1-3 singles, 3-8 cassettes, 1-3 EPs and 3-8 CDs/year. Pays negotiable royalty to artist on contract; variable rate to publisher per song on record.
How to Contact: Call first and obtain permission to submit. Prefers cassette, DAT, VHS videocassette or CD with 3 songs. "All of these formats are fine—we listen to *at least* 3 songs! Please include full contact info—name, address, phone, etc. Cover letters are fine—any press or similar artist promotion materials are helpful." Does not return material. Reports in 1-1½ months.
Music: Mostly **original alternative music, creative expressive music** and **rock/pop**; also **acoustic artists** and **solo performers**. Released *Spill*, written and recorded by Gravityhead (alternative); *The Bench EP*, written and recorded by Sylph (alternative); and *Firenza*, written and recorded by Flood No. 9 (alternative), all on Wonderland Records. Other artists include Mightly Purple and Big Hot Sun.
Tips: "Submissions must include full contact information. The enclosure of materials which may help paint a fuller picture of the artist is a good thing. Quality over quantity, and be ready to answer questions if we dig you."

WOODRICH RECORDS, Box 38, Lexington AL 35648. (205)247-3983. President: Woody Richardson. Record company, music publisher (Woodrich Publishing Co./BMI, Mernee Music/ASCAP and Tennessee Valley Music/SESAC) and record producer (Woody Richardson). Estab. 1959. Releases 12 singles and 12 LPs/year. Pays 50% royalty to artists on contract; statutory rate to publisher per song on record.
• Woodrich's publishing affiliate, Woodrich Publishing, is listed in the Music Publishers section.
How to Contact: Submit demo tape by mail. Unsolicited submissions are OK. Prefers cassette with 4 songs and lyric sheet. "Be sure to send a SASE (not a card) with sufficient return postage." Reports in 2 weeks. "We prefer a good studio demo."
Music: Mostly **country**; also **gospel, comedy, bluegrass, rock** and **jazz**. Released *Somewhere Above Tennessee*, written and recorded by Jerry Piper on Missile Records (country); *Christmas of White* (by Barbara J. Smith), recorded by Dianna Carter on BJS Records (Christmas); and *Chitlins & Mt. Oysters* (by W. Richardson/Whiddon), recorded by Marty Whiddon on Woodrich Records (comedy).
Tips: "Use a good studio with professional musicians. Don't send a huge package. A business envelope will do. It's better to send a cassette *not in a box*."

*WORLD DISC PRODUCTIONS, 5987 Brooks Lane, Friday Harbor WA 98250. (360)378-3979. Fax: (360)378-3977. Associate Producer: Daniel Summer. Labels include World Disc Music, Nature Recordings and Planet Me! (children's). Record company, music publisher (White Wolf, Paradise) and record producer (Richard Hooper, Daniel Summer). Estab. 1985. Releases 20-22 CDs/year. Pays negotiable royalty to artists on contract; negotiable rate to publisher per song on record.
How to Contact: Submit demo tape by mail. Prefers cassette or DAT. "Don't call us, we'll call you." Does not return material. Reports in 1 week.
Music: Mostly **world music**. Released *Thunderdrums*, written and recorded by Scott Fitzgerald; *Spirits of the Ancestors*, written and recorded by Gary Richard; and *Native Soul*, written and recorded by Tony Lasley, all on World Disc Music. Other artists include Peter Sterling, Chris Michelle, David Hubbard, Daniel Summer and Allan Phillips.
Tips: "Make great music and let it speak for itself."

*WORSHIP & PRAISE RECORDS INC., P.O. Box 593 Times Square Station, New York NY 10108. Phone/fax: (703)330-9604. Executive Producer/CEO: Minister Maharold L. Peoples, Jr.. Record company and music publisher (Worship & Praise Publishing). Estab. 1994. Releases 2 LPs and 2 CDs/year. Pays negotiable royalty to artists on contract; statutory rate to publisher per song on record.
How to Contact: Submit demo tape by mail. Unsolicited submissions are OK. Prefers cassette with 2 songs and lyric sheet. "Please submit bios, press releases or any other pertinent information on writer/artist." Does not return material. Reports in 3-4 weeks.
Music: Mostly **contemporary Christian, traditional Christian** and **black gospel**. Released *The Lord's Been Good to Me* (by J.P. Wilson/Min. Maharold Peoples), recorded by Elder Curtis Brown; *We're in This World* (by Min. Maharold Peoples), recorded by NY Convention Mass Choir; and *I Don't Want to Miss Heaven* (by Min. Maharold Peoples), recorded by The Worship & Praise Mass Choir, all on Worship & Praise Records (gospel).
Tips: "Your arrangements should be original, not rearrangements. Lyrics should be in line with the Bible."

XEMU RECORDS, 244 W. 54th St., #1010, New York NY 10019. (212)957-2985. Fax: (212)957-2986. E-mail: xemu@chelsea.ios.com. Website: http://chelsea.ios.com/~xemu. A&R: Dr. Claw. Record company. Estab. 1992. Releases 4 CDs/year. Pays negotiable royalty to artists on contract; statutory rate to publisher per song on record.
How to Contact: Submit demo tape by mail. Unsolicited submissions are OK. Prefers cassette with 3 songs. Does not return material. Reports in 4-6 weeks.
Music: Mostly **alternative**. Released *Vertigo*, recorded by Poets & Slaves; *Hold The Lettuce*, recorded by Death Sandwich; and *Ouagadougou*, recorded by Borhina Faso, all on Xemu Records (alternative rock). Other artists include Neanderthal Spongecake, Baby Alive, Smile Zone and Scary Chicken.

YELLOW JACKET RECORDS, 10303 Hickory Valley, Ft. Wayne IN 46835. President: Allan Straten. Record company. Estab. 1985. Releases 8-10 singles, 1 LP and 1 CD/year. Pays 7-10% royalty to artists on contract; statutory rate to publisher per song on record.
 • See the listing for Hickory Valley Music in the Music Publishers section.
How to Contact: Submit demo tape by mail. Unsolicited submissions are OK. Prefers cassette with 3-4 songs and typed lyric sheet. Does not return material. Reports in 3-4 weeks.
Music: **Country** and **MOR**. Released "She's My X and I Know Y" (by D. Crisman/S. Grogg/A. Straten), "Lisa Marie" (by S. Grogg/A. Straten) and "She's My Number One Fan" (by R. Hartman/S. Grogg/A. Straten), all recorded by Tom Woodard on Pharoah Records. Other artists include Roy Allan, Mike Vernaglia, Rick Hartman and Darin Crisman.
Tips: "Be professional. Be prepared to rewrite. When sending material use 6×9 envelope—no staples."

YOUNG COUNTRY RECORDS/PLAIN COUNTRY RECORDS, P.O. Box 5412, Buena Park CA 90620. (619)245-2920. Owner: Leo J. Eiffert, Jr. Labels include Eiffert Records and Napoleon Country Records. Record company, music publisher (Young Country Music Publishing Co./BMI, Eb-Tide Music/BMI), record producer (Leo J. Eiffert, Jr). Releases 10 singles and 5 LPs/year. Pays negotiable royalty to artists on contract; negotiable rate to publishers per song on record.
How to Contact: Submit demo tape by mail. Unsolicited submissions are OK. "Please make sure your song or songs are copyrighted." Prefers cassette with 2 songs and lyric sheet. Does not return material. Reports in 3-4 weeks.
Music: Mostly **country, easy rock** and **gospel music**. Released *Like A Fool*, written and recorded by Pam Bellows; *Something About Your Love* (by Leo J. Eiffert, Jr.), recorded by Chance Waite Young (country); and *Cajunland*, written and recorded by Leo J. Eiffert, Jr., all on Plain Country Records. Other artists include Brandi Holland, Homemade, Crawfish Band, Larry Settle.

YOUNG STAR PRODUCTIONS, INC., 5501 N. Broadway, Chicago IL 60640. (312)989-4140. President: Starling Young, Jr. Labels include Gold Karat Records. Record company, music publisher (Gold Karat Records/ASCAP) and record producer. Estab. 1991. Releases 7-8 singles, 7 LPs, 10 EPs and 9 CDs/year. Pays 6-10% royalty to artists on contract; statutory rate to publisher per song on record or ½ of statutory if we do not own publisher.
How to Contact: Submit demo tape by mail. Unsolicited submissions are OK. Prefers cassette (or VHS videocassette) with 4 songs and lyric or lead sheet. "Insert photo and bio." Does not return material. Reports in 4-6 weeks.
Music: Mostly **urban, dance, blues/jazz** and **gospel**; also **pop/rock, country** and **alternative**. Released "Whatcha Gonna Do" (by Michael Hearn), recorded by Linda Clifford; *Emerald City*, written and recorded by Abstract; and "Land of Lost and Found," written and recorded by Mr. Kofé, all on Gold Karat Records.
Tips: "Be established well enough to be accepted as a producer, artist or songwriter seriously. Be patient enough to know that success doesn't happen overnight. But be creative and assertive enough

to be ready when it happens. Writing and performing music well is a gift not to be taken lightly."

YOUNGHEART MUSIC, Box 6017, Cypress CA 90630. (714)995-7888. President: James Connelly. Record company. Estab. 1975. Releases 1-2 LPs/year. Pays statutory rate.
How to Contact: Submit demo tape by mail. Unsolicited submissions are OK. SASE. Reports in 4 weeks.
Music: Mostly **children**'s and **educational**. Released "Three Little Pig Blues" and "A Man Named King," written and recorded by Greg Scelsa and Steve Millang, both on Youngheart Records.
Tips: "We are looking for original, contemporary, motivating music for kids. Songs should be fun, educational, build self-esteem and/or multicultural awareness. New original arrangements of classic songs or nursery rhymes will be considered."

ZERO HOUR RECORDS, 1600 Broadway, New York NY 10019. (212)957-1277. Fax: (212)957-1447. President: Ray McKenzie. Record company and music publisher. Estab. 1990. Releases 12 singles, 6-12 LPs, 3 EPs and 6-12 CDs/year. Pays 11-13% royalty to artists on contract; statutory rate to publisher per song on record.
How to Contact: Write first and obtain permission to submit a demo. Prefers cassette. Does not return material. Reports in 1 month.
Music: Mostly **rock**, **hip hop** and **spoken word**; also **acid jazz**, **ambient** and **techno**. Released *Altimeter* (by Houghton/Topalian), recorded by Altimeter (rock); *Word Up*, written and recorded by Wildlife (rock); and *22 Brides* (by L. Johnson/C. Johnson), recorded by 22 Brides (rock), all on Zero Hour Records. Other artists include Cucumbers and Voice In Time.
Tips: "Send us music that is very unique and unusual."

ZEROBUDGET RECORDS, P.O. Box 2044, La Crosse WI 54602. (608)783-5818. President/Director A&R: Stephen Harm. Distributed in Europe by Ché Records. "We distribute some titles on the Boat Records and Angry Seed labels." Record company. Estab. 1982. Pays negotiable royalty to artists on contract; negotiable rate to publisher per song on record.
How to Contact: Submit demo tape by mail. Unsolicited submissions are OK. Prefers cassette (or VHS ½" videocassette if available) and lyric sheet. Does not return material. Reports in 3 months.
Music: Mostly **alternative** and **industrial**; also **rock** and **pop**. Released "Fly" (by Virock/Reinders); "Carnival" (by Virock/Reinders/Meusy); and "Losin' My Grip" (by Peterson), all recorded by Space Bike on Zerobudget Records. Other artists include Hick, Bombpop and Norm's Headache.
Tips: "Don't follow trends—set 'em. No cliché is ever OK."

*ZOO ENTERTAINMENT, 8750 Wilshire Blvd., Beverly Hills CA 90211. A&R: David Maricich. Record company. Estab. 1971. Releases 5-10 singles and 15-20 LPs/year.
How to Contact: Submit demo tape by mail. Unsolicited submissions are OK. "3 to 4 song cassette or independent CD is best." Does not return material. "All submissions will be listened to within one month. We will contact the artist only if we are interested."
Music: Mostly **alternative minded rock/pop** (i.e., not necessarily the current flavor of the month. . . . but that's OK too). Released *Replicants*, written and recorded by Replicants; *100% Fun*, written and recorded by Matthew Sweet; and *Subliminal Plastic Motives*, written and recorded by Self, all on Zoo Entertainment. Other artists include Tool.
Tips: "Make sure your songs have focus both structurally and stylistically."

✳ THE ASTERISK before a listing indicates that the listing is new in this edition. New markets are often the most receptive to unsolicited submissions.

Category Index

The Category Index is a good place to begin searching for a market for your songs. Below is an alphabetical list of 19 general music categories. If you write rock music and are looking for a record company to submit your songs to, check the Rock section in this index. There you will find a list of record companies interested in hearing rock songs. Once you locate the entries for those record companies, read the Music subheading *carefully* to determine which companies are most interested in the type of rock music you write. Some of the markets in this section do not appear in the Category Index because they have not indicated a specific preference. Most of these said they are interested in "all types" of music. Listings that were very specific, or whose description of the music they're interested in doesn't quite fit into these categories, also do not appear here.

Adult Contemporary

*All Star Promotions; Allegheny Music Works; American Music Network, Inc.; *Amiron Music/Aztec Productions; Bolivia Records; Boogie Band Records; Capstan Record Production; Cimirron/Rainbird Records; Comstock Records Ltd.; *Country Style Records; Cowgirl Records; Dale Productions, Alan; DMT Records; Emerald City Records; Fame and Forture Enterprises; Golden Triangle Records; Green Bear Records; *Heath & Associates; Jalyn Recording Co.; Kaupp Records; L.A. Records (MI); L.A. Records (Canada); LBJ Productions; Le Matt Music Ltd.; Lucifer Records, Inc.; Magnum Music Corp. Ltd.; Mathes Company, The; Missile Records; *Mojo Records; Monticana Records; Nucleus Records; *Oblivion Entertainment; *Peridot Records; Roll On Records®; Rustron Music Productions; *Saturn Records; Scene Productions; *Sundown Records; Sunshine Group, The; *Sureshot Records; Treasure Coast Records; Trend Records®; Trusty Records; *Unity Entertainment Corporation; *Valtec Productions; Yellow Jacket Records

Alternative

A & R Records; *Aladdin Recordings; *Antiphon International; Aztlan Records; Baby Faze Records & Tapes; babysue; Backstreet Records; *Basset Hound Productions; Big Pop; Black & Blue; Bright Green Records; Caffeine Disk; *Caroline Records, Inc.; *Castle von Buhler Records; Cat's Voice Productions; Chrismarie Records; CITA Communications Inc.; Cleopatra Records; Com-Four; *Critique Records, Inc.; *decibel; *Deep Six Records; *Don't Records; *Elektra Entertainment Group; Fat City Artists; Fiction Songs; *Flip Records; *Fullmoon Entertainment/Moonstone Records; Generic Records, Inc.; Global Pacific Records/Blackhorse Entertainment; Guitar Recordings; Hot Wings Entertainment; *IMI Records; Inferno Records; JAV Records; Kottage Records; KSM Records; L.A. Records (Canada); *Live Oak Records; Maverick Group, The; Megatone Records Inc.; Merkin Records Inc.; Merlin Productions; Mirror Records, Inc.; MJM Records; Modern Voices Entertainment, Ltd.; *Mojo Records; *Mountain Records; Nocturnal Records; *Oblivion Entertainment; Oglio Records; Old School Records; Paint Chip Records; *PC! Music Company; *Phisst Records Corporation; PMG Records; *Provocative Entertainment Group Inc. Recordings; *Radical Records; Rammit Records; Rave Records, Inc.; Revelation Records; Rotten Records; Round Flat Records; Royalty Records; Ruffcut Productions; *Saturn Records; Scratched Records; Scotti Bros. Records; *Shimmy-Disc; *Silver Wing Records; Sonic Group, Ltd.; Splunge Communications, Inc.; Strugglebaby Recording Co.; *Sun West Media/Uncle Biff's Records; *Sundown Records; Tandem Records; *Thick Records; Trumpeter Records Inc.; TVT Records; *28 Records; *Unity Entertainment Corporation; Victory Records; Wonderland Records; Xemu Records; Young Star Productions, Inc.; Zero Hour Records; *Zerobudget Records; *Zoo Entertainment

Blues

*Aladdin Recordings; Albatross Records; *Antiphon International; *BCN/Beacon Records; Big Bear Records; Black Diamond Records Inc.; Breeden Music Group; BSW Records; Deadeye Records; Guitar Recordings; Justin Time Records Inc.; Maui Arts & Music Association; MCR; Mirror Records, Inc.; *Musikus Productions, Inc.; *Peridot Records; *Plankton Records; Powerhouse Records; RBW, Inc.; React Recordings; *Rockadelic Records; Rustron Music Productions; *Shiro Records; *Silver Wing Records; Sky-Child Records; Triple X Records; *Wolftrax Records; Young Star Productions, Inc.

Children's

A & R Records; Aliso Creek Productions Incorporated; Berandol Music; Bodarc Productions; Brentwood Music; Grass Roots Record & Tape/LMI Records; *Lonny Tunes; *Omni 2000 Inc.; Saddlestone Records; *Smithsonian/Folkways Recordings; *Sunset Records; Teeter-Tot Records; Twin Sisters Productions, Inc.; Youngheart Music

Classical

babysue; Cambria Records & Publishing; Care Free Records Group; *Castle von Buhler Records; Comma Records & Tapes; Global Pacific Records/Blackhorse Entertainment; Intersound Inc.; Jabala Music; Lark Record Productions, Inc.; *Lyra House, Ltd.; Marks Records, John; *Musikus Productions, Inc.; North Star Music; Nucleus Records; RBW, Inc.; Rising Star Records And Publishers Inc.; Sheffield Lab Recording; Sky-Child Records; Sounds-Vision Music; *Sundown Records; VAI Distribution

Country

A & R Records; *Aladdin Recordings; Albatross Records; Allegheny Music Works; *Alpha Recording Co.; Alyssa Records; American Music Network, Inc.; *Americatone Records International USA; *Arial Records; Bagatelle Record Company; Bandit Records; *BCN/Beacon Records; Belmont Records; Black & Blue; Black Diamond Records Inc.; Blue Gem Records; *BMX Entertainment; BNA Records; Bold 1 Records; Bolivia Records; Bouquet Records; *Breeden Music Group; Brentwood Music; Briarhill Records; BSW Records; *C.E.G. Records, Inc.; Capstan Record Production; Care Free Records Group; Casaro Records; Cat's Voice Productions; Cedar Creek Records™; Cellar Records; Centium Entertainment, Inc.; Cherry Street Records; Chrismarie Records; Cimirron/Rainbird Records; CITA Communications Inc.; Comma Records & Tapes; Comstock Records Ltd.; Continental Records; Country Breeze Records; Country Star International; *Country Style Records; Cowgirl Records; *Critique Records, Inc.; Dale Productions, Alan; Deadeye Records; Dejadisc, Inc.; DMT Records; Drag City, Inc.; Emerald City Records; *EMF Productions; ESB Records; Factory Beat Records, Inc.; Fat City Artists; Fearless Records; First Time Records; Fountain Records; General Broadcasting Service; Generic Records, Inc.; Golden Triangle Records; Grass Roots Record & Tape/LMI Records; Green Bear Records; Green Valley Records; Gueststar Records; *Heath & Associates; Howdy Records; Inferno Records; Intersound Inc.; Interstate 40 Records; Jabala Music; Jalyn Recording Co.; Jamaka Record Co.; *K-Ark Records; Kaupp Records; Keeping It Simple And Safe, Inc.; Kept In The Dark Records; Kingston Records; Kottage Records; *L. P. S. Records, Inc.; L.A. Records (MI); L.A. Records (Canada); Lamon Records; Landmark Communications Group; Lanor Records; Lari-Jon Records; Lark Record Productions, Inc.; LBJ Productions; Le Matt Music Ltd.; *Live Oak Records; Lonesome Wind Corporation; *Lonny Tunes; LRJ; *M.E.G. Records Co.; Magnum Music Corp. Ltd.; *Man on Page 602, The; Manny Music, Inc.; Master-Trak Enterprises; Mathes Company, The; Maui Arts & Music Association; Maverick Group, The; MCR; Mighty Records; Missile Records; Monticana Records; MSM Records; Mule Kick Records; Music Services & Marketing; New Beginning Record Productions; New Experience Records/Grand Slam Records; Nucleus Records; Oar Fin Records; Orbit Records; Paragold Records & Tapes; Patty Lee Records; *Paul Records, J.; PBM Records; *Peridot Records; Phoenix Records,

Inc.; *Pickwick/Mecca/Internation Records; Pinecastle/WEBCO Records; Plateau Music; Platinum Boulevard Records; Platinum Plus Records International; Playback Records; Playbones Records; Pop Records Research; *QV III Music; R.E.F. Records; Random Records; Rejoice Records Of Nashville; Reveal; Revelation Records; Richway Records International; Rococo Records; Roll On Records®; Rosebud Records; *Rowena Records; RR&R Records; Ruffcut Productions; Rustron Music Productions; Sabre Productions; Sabteca Record Co.; Saddlestone Records; *Saturn Records; Scene Productions; *Silver Wing Records; Sky-Child Records; Starcrest Productions, Inc.; Stardust; Startrak Records, Inc.; SunCountry Records; Sunshine Group, The; *Sureshot Records; Surprize Records, Inc.; Target Records; *Third Wave Productions Ltd.; Trac Record Co.; *Traveler Enterprises; Treasure Coast Records; Trend Records®; Trusty Records; Universal-Athena Records; *Urgent Music, Inc.; *Valtec Productions; Vokes Music Record Co.; Wedge Records; Wence Sense Music/Bill Wence Promotions; White Car Records; Winchester Records; *Wolftrax Records; Woodrich Records; Yellow Jacket Records; Young Country Records/Plain Country Records; Young Star Productions, Inc.

Dance

*All Star Promotions; Alpha-Beat; *Amiron Music/Aztec Productions; Associated Artists Music International; *Basset Hound Productions; Bodarc Productions; Boogie Band Records; Broken Records; Centium Entertainment, Inc.; CITA Communications Inc.; Comma Records & Tapes; *Critique Records, Inc.; *Dagene/Cabletown Records; *Def Beat Records; Digitalia Records; *Drive Entertainment; First Time Records; Fullmoon Entertainment/Moonstone Records; Jamoté Music Group; Joey Boy Records Inc.; L.A. Records (MI); L.A. Records (Canada); Le Matt Music Ltd.; *Live Oak Records; *Lotus Records; Lucifer Records, Inc.; Megatone Records Inc.; Merlin Productions; Mighty Records; Modern Voices Entertainment, Ltd.; Monticana Records; P. & N. Records; *Pickwick/Mecca/Internation Records; PMG Records; *Provocative Entertainment Group Inc. Recordings; *Quark Records; *QV III Music; Rammit Records; Rave Records, Inc.; React Recordings; Red Dot/Puzzle Records; Revelation Records; Rosebud Records; Sirr Rodd Record & Publishing Co.; Stargard Records; *Strictly Rhythm Records; *Sunset Records; Tandem Records; *Thump Records, Inc.; *Top Records; Wall Street Music; Wanstar Group, The; Watusi Productions; Young Star Productions, Inc.

Folk

A & R Records; *Amiron Music/Aztec Productions; *Ariana Records; *BCN/Beacon Records; Black Dog Records; Cha Cha Records; *Dargason Music; Dejadisc, Inc.; Eastern Front Records, Inc.; First Time Records; Hot Wings Entertainment; Jabala Music; Mirror Records, Inc.; Modal Music, Inc.™; Monticana Records; *Mountain Records; MSM Records; Nocturnal Records; Nucleus Records; *Patty Lee Records; Random Records; Red Sky Records; Rococo Records; Rustron Music Productions; *Smithsonian/Folkways Recordings; *Third Wave Productions Ltd.; *Whitehouse Records; Winchester Records; Wizmak Productions

Jazz

Albatross Records; Americatone Records International USA; *Amiron Music/Aztec Productions; *Ariana Records; *Arkadia Entertainment Corp.; audiofile Tapes; Big Bear Records; Black Diamond Records Inc.; *BMX Entertainment; Bodarc Productions; Bright Green Records; Care Free Records Group; Casaro Records; Cedar Creek Records™; Cherry Street Records; Com-Four; *CTI Records; Dale Productions, Alan; *Earth Flight Productions; Etherean Music/Variena Publishing; Fat City Artists; Flying Heart Records; Fresh Entertainment; Global Pacific Records/Blackhorse Entertainment; Golden Triangle Records; Grass Roots Record & Tape/LMI Records; Guitar Recordings; Hallway International Records/1st Coast Posse Mixes; Hot Wings Entertainment; *IMI Records; J&J Musical Enterprises Ltd.; Joey Boy Records Inc.; Justin Time Records Inc.; Kept In The Dark Records; L.A. Records (MI); Landmark Communications

Group; Landslide Records; *LBI Records; *Lonny Tunes; *Lotus Records; Marks Records, John; Maui Arts & Music Association; Mighty Records; Missile Records; *Mons Records; Monticana Records; North Star Music; Oar Fin Records; *Orinda Records; *Patty Lee Records; *PC! Music Company; *Perspective Records; Platinum Boulevard Records; Playbones Records; *Powerhouse Records; PPI/Peter Pan Industries; RBW, Inc.; React Recordings; *Reiter Records Ltd.; Rising Star Records and Publishers Inc.; Rock Dog Records; Rosebud Records; Sahara Records and Filmworks Entertainment; Salexo Music; Satin Records; *Saturn Records; Sheffield Lab Recording; *Shiro Records; Sirr Rodd Record & Publishing Co.; Startrak Records, Inc.; Trend Records®; TVT Records; *Unity Entertainment Corporation; VAI Distribution; Watusi Productions; Woodrich Records; Young Star Productions, Inc.; Zero Hour Records

Latin

Albatross Records; Aliso Creek Productions Incorporated; Americatone Records International USA; *BMX Entertainment; Grass Roots Record & Tape/LMI Records; Howdy Records; Manny Music, Inc.; *QV III Music; Sounds-Vision Music; *Sunset Records; Top Ten Hits Records Inc.

Metal

Azra International; babysue; Black & Blue; Care Free Records Group; Cellar Records; *decibel; *Hypnotic Recordings; JAV Records; L.A. Records (MI); *Metal Blade Records; Missile Records; *Mountain Records; *Pissed Off Records, Inc.; Rotten Records; *Shaky Records; Sonic Group, Ltd.; *28 Records

New Age

*Ariana Records; Azra International; *BCN/Beacon Records; Black Dog Records; Care Free Records Group; Cat's Voice Productions; Dale Productions, Alan; Etherean Music/Variena Publishing; Global Pacific Records/Blackhorse Entertainment; Jabala Music; L.A. Records (MI); Platinum Boulevard Records; PPI/Peter Pan Industries; Presence Records; *Quark Records; Rising Star Records and Publishers Inc.; Rock Dog Records; Rustron Music Productions; *Shiro Records; Silver Wave Records; *Sundown Records

Novelty

Azra International; Briarhill Records; Justin Time Records Inc.; *Lonny Tunes; MOR Records

Pop

Allegheny Music Works; Alphabeat; Alyssa Records; *Amiron Music/Aztec Productions; *Arista Records; *Arkadia Entertainment Corp.; Associated Artists Music International; Avalanche Communications; Baby Faze Records & Tapes; babysue; Berandol Music; Big Pop; Big Rock Pty. Ltd.; Black Dog Records; Blue Gem Records; *BMX Entertainment; Bolivia Records; Boogie Band Records; *Breeden Music Group; Broken Records; *C.E.G. Records, Inc.; Capstan Record Production; Care Free Records Group; Casaro Records; Cedar Creek Records™; Cellar Records; Chrismarie Records; Cimirron/Rainbird Records; Comma Records & Tapes; Comstock Records Ltd.; *Critique Records, Inc.; *Dagene/Cabletown Records; Demi Monde Records and Publishing, Ltd.; DMT Records; *Don't Records; *Drive Entertainment; Eastern Front Records, Inc.; *EMF Productions; Etherean Music/Variena Publishing; Factory Beat Records, Inc.; Fame and Forture Enterprises; Fearless Records; First Time Records; Fountain Records; Fresh Entertainment; Fullmoon Entertainment/Moonstone Records; Generic Records, Inc.; Global Pacific Records/Blackhorse Entertainment; Graceland Entertainment; Grass Roots Record & Tape/LMI Records; *Heath & Associates; *Jive Records; Justin Time Records Inc.; Kaupp Records; Keeping It Simple And Safe, Inc.; Kingston Records; Kottage Records; L.A. Records (MI); Lamar Music Group; Landmark Communications Group; LBJ Productions; Le Matt Music Ltd.; *Live Oak Records; Lucifer Records, Inc.; Magnum Music Corp. Ltd.; Makeshift Music; Manny

Music, Inc.; Maui Arts & Music Association; *Megarock Records; Megatone Records Inc.; Merlin Productions; Mighty Records; Missile Records; *MJM Records; Modern Voices Entertainment, Ltd.; *Mons Records; Monticana Records; MOR Records; *Mountain Records; Mule Kick Records; *Musikus Productions, Inc.; New Experience Records/Grand Slam Records; *Not Lame Recordings; Nucleus Records; Oar Fin Records; *Oblivion Entertainment; Old School Records; Omni 2000 Inc.; *Orinda Records; *Paul Records, J.; *Perspective Records; Phoenix Records, Inc.; *Pickwick/Mecca/Internation Records; Platinum Boulevard Records; Pop Records Research; PPI/Peter Pan Industries; *Quark Records; *QV III Music; R.E.F. Records; Rage-N-Records; Random Records; Red Dot/Puzzle Records; *Redemption Records; *Reiter Records Ltd.; Reveal; Roll On Records®; *Rowena Records; RR&R Records; Ruffcut Productions; Rustron Music Productions; Sabteca Record Co.; Saddlestone Records; Sahara Records and Filmworks Entertainment; Scene Productions; Shaolin Film & Records; Sheffield Lab Recording; *Shiro Records; Sirr Rodd Record & Publishing Co.; Sky-Child Records; Starcrest Productions, Inc.; Startrak Records, Inc.; *Sunset Records; *Thick Records; *Third Wave Productions Ltd.; *Top Records; Trusty Records; *Urgent Music, Inc.; *Valtec Productions; Wanstar Group, The; Watusi Productions; Wedge Records; White Car Records; *Whitehouse Records; Widely Distributed Records; Wizmak Productions; Wonderland Records; Young Star Productions, Inc.; *Zerobudget Records

R&B

*Aladdin Recordings; Albatross Records; All Star Promotions; Allegheny Music Works; Alphabeat; Alyssa Records; *Arkadia Entertainment Corp.; Baby Faze Records & Tapes; Big Rock Pty. Ltd.; Black Diamond Records Inc.; Black Dog Records; Blue Gem Records; Blue Wave; *BMX Entertainment; Bolivia Records; Boogie Band Records; Casaro Records; Cat's Voice Productions; Cedar Creek Records™; Cellar Records; Centium Entertainment, Inc.; Cherry Street Records; Chrismarie Records; Comma Records & Tapes; Cowgirl Records; *Critique Records, Inc.; *CTI Records; *Dagene/Cabletown Records; Deadeye Records; *Def Beat Records; Demi Monde Records and Publishing, Ltd.; *EMF Productions; Factory Beat Records, Inc.; *Fink-Pinewood Records; First Time Records; Flying Heart Records; Fresh Entertainment; Fullmoon Entertainment/Moonstone Records; Gold City Records, Inc.; Golden Triangle Records; Graceland Entertainment; Grass Roots Record & Tape/LMI Records; Hallway International Records/1st Coast Posse Mixes; *Heath & Associates; *IMI Records; *Jive Records; Kaupp Records; Keeping It Simple And Safe, Inc.; Kept In The Dark Records; Kottage Records; L.A. Records (MI); Lamar Music Group; *Lamon Records; Landmark Communications Group; Landslide Records; Lanor Records; *LBI Records; LBJ Productions; Le Matt Music Ltd.; Live Oak Records; Lucifer Records, Inc.; *Man on Page 602, The; Master-Trak Enterprises; Merlin Productions; Mirror Records, Inc.; Missile Records; MJM Records; Modern Blues Recordings; Modern Voices Entertainment, Ltd.; Monticana Records; *Musikus Productions, Inc.; New Experience Records/Grand Slam Records; *Oblivion Entertainment; Old School Records; *Omni 2000 Inc.; Orbit Records; *Perspective Records; Pirate Records; *Plankton Records; Platinum Boulevard Records; Pop Records Research; PPI/Peter Pan Industries; *Provocative Entertainment Group Inc. Recordings; *QV III Music; Rage-N-Records; Rammit Records; React Recordings; Red-Eye Records; Roll On Records®; Rosebud Records; Rowena Records; RR&R Records; Sabre Productions; Sabteca Record Co.; Saddlestone Records; Sahara Records and Filmworks Entertainment; Salexo Music; *Satin Records; *Saturn Records; Scene Productions; *Shang Records; *Shiro Records; *Silver Wing Records; Stargard Records; Startrak Records, Inc.; Strugglebaby Recording Co.; Surprize Records, Inc.; Tandem Records; Treasure Coast Records; Trend Records®; Trusty Records; TVT Records; Wall Street Music; Wanstar Group, The; Wedge Records; White Car Records; Young Star Productions, Inc.

Rap

Albatross Records; Alphabeat; Associated Artists Music International; Baby Faze Records & Tapes; Black Diamond Records Inc.; *BMX Entertainment; Boogie Band

Records; Cellar Records; *Critique Records, Inc.; *Dagene/Cabletown Records; *Def Beat Records; Digitalia Records; Fresh Entertainment; Generic Records, Inc.; Hallway International Records/1st Coast Posse Mixes; Intersound Inc.; Jamoté Music Group; *Jive Records; Joey Boy Records Inc.; Keeping It Simple And Safe, Inc.; Lamar Music Group; Landslide Records; *LBI Records; *Lotus Records; Mirror Records, Inc.; Missile Records; Modern Voices Entertainment, Ltd.; New Experience Rec/Grand Slam Records; *Perspective Records; *Pickwick/Mecca/Internation Records; Pirate Records; *Provocative Entertainment Group Inc. Recordings; *QV III Music; *Radical Records; Rammit Records; React Recordings; *Redemption Records; Revelation Records; *Shang Records; *Shiro Records; Sirr Rodd Record & Publishing Co.; Stargard Records; Startrak Records, Inc.; *Strictly Rhythm Records; Tandem Records; *Thump Records, Inc.; Triple X Records; TVT Records; Wall Street Music; Zero Hour Records

Religious

A & R Records; *Aladdin Recordings; Allegheny Music Works; *Alpha Recording Co.; American Music Network, Inc.; *Antiphon International; babysue; Bagatelle Record Company; Bandit Records; Bouquet Records; *Breeden Music Group; Brentwood Music; Briarhill Records; Cedar Creek Records™; *Christian Media Enterprises; CITA Communications Inc.; Comstock Records Ltd.; Continental Records; *Country Style Records; Cowgirl Records; *Dagene/Cabletown Records; Dale Productions, Alan; EMA Music Inc.; Emerald City Records; Factory Beat Records, Inc.; Fame and Fortune Enterprises; *Fink-Pinewood Records; First Time Records; Fountain Records; Fresh Entertainment; General Broadcasting Service; Gold City Records, Inc.; Graceland Entertainment; Grass Roots Record & Tape/LMI Records; Green Bear Records; Green Valley Records; Gueststar Records; *Heath & Associates; Howdy Records; Intersound Inc.; Jalyn Recording Co.; Justin Time Records Inc.; *K-Ark Records; Kaupp Records; Keeping It Simple And Safe, Inc.; Kottage Records; L.A. Records (MI); *L. P. S. Records, Inc.; *Lamon Records; Landmark Communications Group; Lari-Jon Records; LBJ Productions; Lonesome Wind Corporation; *M.E.G. Records Co.; Magnum Music Corp. Ltd.; Malaco Records; *Man on Page 602, The; Manny Music, Inc.; Mathes Company, The; MCR; Missile Records; Modern Voices Entertainment, Ltd.; Monticana Records; Music Services & Marketing; New Beginning Record Productions; New Experience Records/Grand Slam Records; Nucleus Records; OCP Publications; *Omni 2000 Inc.; *Paul Records, J.; *Peachtown Record Co. Inc.; *Perspective Records; Phoenix Records, Inc.; *Pickwick/Mecca/Internation Records; *Plankton Records; *Plateau Music; Platinum Plus Records International; Playbones Records; R.E.F. Records; Red-Eye Records; Rejoice Records Of Nashville; Richway Records International; Roll On Records®; Rosebud Records; *Rowena Records; RR&R Records; Sabre Productions; Saddlestone Records; Salexo Music; *Silver Wing Records; Sirr Rodd Record & Publishing Co.; Sky-Child Records; Sound Achievement Group, Inc.; Spiritual Walk Records; Startrak Records, Inc.; SunCountry Records; Tandem Records; Teeter-Tot Records; Trend Records®; Trusty Records; Urgent Music, Inc.; Vokes Music Record Co.; Wanstar Group, The; Wedge Records; Winchester Records; Woodrich Records; *Worship & Praise Records Inc.; Young Country Records/Plain Country Records; Young Star Productions, Inc.; Treasure Coast Records

Rock

*Aladdin Recordings; Aliso Creek Productions Incorporated; *All Star Promotions; American Music Network, Inc.; Americatone Records International USA; *Amiron Music/Aztec Productions; *Antiphon International; *Ariana Records; Arion Records; *Arista Records; *Arkadia Entertainment Corp.; Associated Artists Music International; audiofile Tapes; Avalanche Communications; Azra International; Baby Faze Records & Tapes; babysue; Backstreet Records; *Basset Hound Productions; *BCN/Beacon Records; Big Rock Pty. Ltd.; Black Diamond Records Inc.; Black Dog Records; Blue Gem Records; Blue Wave; *BMX Entertainment; Boogie Band Records; Bouquet Records; *Breeden Music Group; Broken Records; BSW Records; *C.E.G. Records, Inc.; Capstan Record Production; Care Free Records Group; Carlyle Records, Inc.;

Cat's Voice Productions; Cedar Creek Records™; Cellar Records; Centium Entertainment, Inc.; Cerebral Records; Chattahoochee Records; Cherry Street Records; Chrismarie Records; CITA Communications Inc.; Com-Four; Comma Records & Tapes; *Critique Records, Inc.; Deadeye Records; Deep Six Records; Dejadisc, Inc.; Demi Monde Records and Publishing, Ltd.; *Don't Records; Drag City, Inc.; *Drive Entertainment; Eastern Front Records, Inc.; *Elastic Records; Factory Beat Records, Inc.; Fame and Forture Enterprises; Fat City Artists; Fearless Records; Fiction Songs; Flying Heart Records; Fresh Entertainment; Fullmoon Entertainment/Moonstone Records; General Broadcasting Service; Generic Records, Inc.; Golden Triangle Records; Grass Roots Record & Tape/LMI Records; Green Bear Records; Gueststar Records; Guitar Recordings; Hammerhead Records, Inc.; *Hypnotic Recordings; Inferno Records; Intersound Inc.; Jabala Music; JAV Records; Kaupp Records; Keeping It Simple And Safe, Inc.; Kept In The Dark Records; Kingston Records; KSM Records; L.A. Records (MI); L.A. Records (Canada); *Lamon Records; Landmark Communications Group; Lanor Records; Lari-Jon Records; LBJ Productions; Le Matt Music Ltd.; *Live Oak Records; *Lonny Tunes; Lucifer Records, Inc.; Magnum Music Corp. Ltd.; Makeshift Music; *Man on Page 602, The; Manny Music, Inc.; Master-Trak Enterprises; Maui Arts & Music Association; Maverick Group, The; Megaforce Worldwide Entertainment; *Megarock Records; Merlin Productions; Mirror Records, Inc.; Missile Records; *MJM Records; Modern Blues Recordings; Modern Voices Entertainment, Ltd.; Monticana Records; *Mountain Records; *Musikus Productions, Inc.; New Experience Records/ Grand Slam Records; Nucleus Records; Oar Fin Records; *Oblivion Entertainment; Old School Records; Orbit Records; *Orinda Records; P. & N. Records; *Patty Lee Records; *Paul Records, J.; PBM Records; *PC! Music Company; *Peridot Records; *Pickwick/Mecca/Internation Records; *Pissed Off Records, Inc.; *Plankton Records; *Plateau Music; Platinum Boulevard Records; Playbones Records; PMG Records; *Powerhouse Records; Pravda Records; Presence Records; *Provocative Entertainment Group Inc. Recordings; R.E.F. Records; *Radical Records; Rage-N-Records; Random Records; Red Dot/Puzzle Records; Red Sky Records; *Redemption Records; Red-Eye Records; *Reiter Records Ltd.; Reveal; Revelation Records; *Rockadelic Records; Rococo Records; Roll On Records®; Rosebud Records; Rotten Records; RR&R Records; Ruffcut Productions; Sabre Productions; Saddlestone Records; *Satin Records; Scene Productions; *Shaky Records; Shaolin Film & Records; *Shiro Records; Sky-Child Records; Splunge Communications, Inc.; Stardust; Startrak Records, Inc.; Strugglebaby Recording Co.; *Sun West Media/Uncle Biff's Records; SunCountry Records; *Sunset Records; *Sureshot Records; Trac Record Co.; Trend Records®; Triple X Records; Trumpeter Records Inc.; *28 Records; *Valtec Productions; Victory Records; Wedge Records; White Car Records; Whitehouse Records; Widely Distributed Records; Winchester Records; *Wolftrax Records; Woodrich Records; Young Country Records/Plain Country Records; Young Star Productions, Inc.; Zero Hour Records; *Zerobudget Records

World Music

*Arkadia Entertainment Corp.; audiofile Tapes; Com-Four; *Def Beat Records; *Earth Flight Productions; Earthtone/Sonic Images; Etherean Music/Variena Publishing; Global Pacific Records/Blackhorse Entertainment; Hallway International Records/1st Coast Posse Mixes; LBI Records; *Modal Music, Inc.™; Rising Star Records and Publishers Inc.; *Shang Records; Sheffield Lab Recording; Silver Wave Records; *Smithsonian/Folkways Recordings; Sounds-Vision Music; Sunshine Group, The; Watusi Productions; *World Disc Productions

✱ THE ASTERISK before a listing indicates that the listing is new in this edition. New markets are often the most receptive to unsolicited submissions.

Record Producers

The independent producer can best be described as a creative coordinator. He's usually the one with the most creative control over a recording project and is ultimately responsible for the finished product. Although some larger record companies have their own in-house producers who work exclusively with artists signed to a particular label, it's common for a record company today to contract out-of-house, independent producers for recording projects.

Producers play a large role in deciding what songs will be recorded for a particular project, and are always on the lookout for new songs for their clients. They can be valuable contacts for songwriters because they work so closely with the artists whose records they produce. They usually have a lot more freedom than others in executive positions, and are known for having a good ear for hit song potential. Many producers are songwriters, musicians and artists themselves. Since they have a big influence on a particular project, a good song in the hands of the right producer at the right time stands a good chance of being cut. And even if a producer is not working on a specific project, he is well-acquainted with record company executives and artists, and can often get material through doors not open to you.

Even so, it can be difficult to get your tapes to the right producer at the right time. Many producers write their own songs and even if they don't write, they may be involved in their own publishing companies so they have instant access to all the songs in their catalogs. It's important to understand the intricacies of the producer/publisher situation. If you pitch your song directly to a producer first, before another publishing company publishes the song, the producer may ask you for the publishing rights (or a percentage thereof) to your song. You must decide whether the producer is really an active publisher who will try to get the song recorded again and again, or whether he merely wants the publishing because it means extra income for him from the current recording project. You may be able to work out a co-publishing deal, where you and the producer split the publishing of the song. That means he will still receive his percentage of the publishing income, even if you secure a cover recording of the song by other artists in the future. Even though you would be giving up a little bit initially, you may benefit in the future.

The listings that follow outline which aspects of the music industry each producer is involved in, what type of music he is looking for, and what records and artists he's recently produced. Study the listings carefully, noting the artists each producer works with, and consider if any of your songs might fit a particular artist's or producer's style.

Consult the Category Index at the end of this section to find producers who work with the type of music you write, and the Geographic Index at the back of the book to locate producers in your area.

INSIDER REPORT

Rundgren strives for timelessness in his songs

"I just like dropping rocks in my own well and seeing how long they take to hit the bottom while hearing what kinds of sounds they make along the way," says perpetually curious Todd Rundgren. He's a highly regarded producer, computer and video wizard, multi-talented musician, lyricist and singer, and one of pop's most innovative songwriters. All this and his rocks aren't close to hitting bottom.

Todd Rundgren

In Rundgren's realm songwriting is not so much an act of creation as it is a process of clarifying and confronting unclear ideas. "I have thoughts that don't make sense to me until I try to articulate and present them in a musical context," he says, contending this process forces his ideas to withstand deconstruction and thus either prove themselves or collapse. "As long as the idea is inside my head I can build as many excuses to support it as possible. But I bring it out into the cold light of day and suddenly the unsupportable clauses and self-referential nature of the idea become very visible. So for me writing songs is this high ritual of trying to understand things I don't feel I've adequately thought out, like assumptions I've made that are full of flaws and other kinds of psychological weaknesses."

Yet Rundgren rarely sits down to write a song with the intent of working through some cloudy idea. Instead it's as if the song offers him an invitation and he chooses to accept or decline. "What happens is I somehow get into this musical frame of mind—which is not something I can turn on or off—that's been building up over days and weeks. Once I start to ponder all the problems of realizing this idea in musical terms, I make myself sensitized to possible input—bits of disconnected inspiration—and try to put it all in some sort of form. But I don't look at songs as being ongoing projects. I look at songs as being events, and I build up to the event. If the event doesn't deliver, I usually never go back to it."

A key factor in discerning whether he should stay and mingle at the "event" or vacate it is a song's potential longevity. "I always think when I'm writing a song: What's this going to sound like to me in the distant future? Am I doing something that will pin me like a butterfly to this context, or have I created something that has an essentially organic nature where you can add water to it and it comes back to life later? Will it have importance, or in ten years will it seem charitably quaint and even just plain muddle-headed? Timelessness is what I'm striving for. I've often gone back and listened to my earlier material and

INSIDER REPORT, *continued*

some of it is very touching and personal but it's about stuff that doesn't happen to me anymore. So it's hard for me to identify because I'm not that same person. People ask me to sing 'Hello It's Me' and I can't because it has no relevance now. Frank Sinatra can always sing 'My Way' because he still believes it, but I can't sing the first song I ever wrote with anything like the same intent."

So does Rundgren think songs written for a particular time and place should just be shelved? Not at all. That's why he's convinced music should have an organic nature, an indefinite capacity to keep regrowing. For such growth to take place, though, a song might have to get passed like a torch from person to person. "By plugging in their own experience instead of mine, other people revivify a song that might seem dead to me. That's when the song becomes organic, and takes on a life of its own. It's not mine anymore."

Losing that selfish sense of "owning" a song is one of Rundgren's goals. He's taking steps to achieve it, too, particularly with his last two interactive CDs, *No World Order* (Rhino/Forward) and *The Individualist* (ION/BMG), which allow the listener to take thousands of pieces of information and recreate their own songs from Rundgren's database of melodies and lyrics. "I have no feeling of ownership with my songs," he says. "I'm lucky to be the first to experience it and then pass it on to others. For me songs are personal artifacts like fingernails. They grow off me. I can't claim to have total control over the process. I can't grow hair where there isn't any, and I can't stop my hair from growing either."

Having listeners identify with what you're trying to convey is one of the most satisfying rewards for an artist. And Rundgren is unfailing in this area; his core admirers simply call him "Todd," as if he's a personal friend. The reason for this sense of intimacy has a lot to do with Rundgren's conception of art. "I believe art is a public act of self-examination. The only difference between the average person wondering something about themselves and the artist wondering something is the artist does it out loud, and everyone watches. Fortunately the audience usually benefits because they recognize that process in themselves, and they may actually get some real pointers from the artist."

After almost 30 years of music-making, Rundgren continues to examine himself scrupulously. He now owns his own publishing, and has thus extricated himself from constraints that bind many artists. But becoming complacent is the last thing on his mind. "What I worry about now is how much I'm doing just out of habit. We've got to question what we've inherited, everything from the length and structure of songs to commercial influences. I want to stop thinking in so-called album concepts and just concentrate on the piece of material at hand, and worry about contextualizing it later. My feeling is that my music will only continue to be valuable if I can continue to purify it in that sense."

The ultimate purification for Rundgren rests in what he calls thoughtless creation. "Ultimately that's what I'd like to do. I'd like to not go around saying, 'Yeah. I'm a songwriter.' I'd like to be able to reach a point where songs are really a part of me. I want to dream songs, transcribe them and pass them along."

—*Don Prues*

"A" MAJOR SOUND CORPORATION, 80 Corley Ave., Toronto, Ontario M4E 1V2 **Canada**. Phone/fax: (416)964-4878. Producer: Paul C. Milner. Record producer and music publisher. Estab. 1989. Produces 12 LPs, 2 EPs and 12 CDs/year. Fee derived from sales royalty when song or artist is recorded, or outright fee from recording artist or record company.
How to Contact: Submit demo tape by mail. Unsolicited submissions are OK. Prefers cassette, DAT or VHS videocassette with 5 songs and lyric sheet (lead sheet if available). Reports in 2-6 months.
Music: Mostly **rock, A/C, alternative, pop** and **metal**; also **Christian** and **R&B**. Produced *Strange Hearts*, written and recorded by Gloria Blizzard on Amatish Records (acid jazz); *Cantos From A Small Room* (by Dario Decicio), recorded by I Am (rock); and "Thirst" (by Mark Zinkew), recorded by Zinq (alternative/dance). Other artists include Hokus Pick Manouver (Word/MCA) and Tribal Stomp.
Tips: "Strong pre-production is the key to developing a strong product."

ACR PRODUCTIONS, P.O. Box 5236, Lubbock TX 79408-5236. (806)792-3804. Owner: Dwaine Thomas. Record producer, music publisher (Joranda Music/BMI) and record company (ACR Records). Estab. 1986. Produces 120 singles, 8-15 12″ singles, 25 LPs, 25 EPs and 25 CDs/year. Fee derived from sales royalty when song or artist is recorded. "We charge for in-house recording only. Remainder is derived from royalties."
How to Contact: Submit demo tape by mail. Unsolicited submissions are OK. Prefers cassette (or VHS videocassette if available) with 5 songs and lyric sheet. Does not return material. Reports in 6 weeks if interested.
Music: Mostly **country swing, pop** and **rock**; also **R&B** and **gospel**. Produced *Corn Fusion*, written and recorded by Doug Deforest; "Shattered Dreams" and "One Way Ticket" (by Dwaine Thomas), recorded by Cheyenne, all on ACR Records.
Tips: "Be professional. No living room tapes!"

AIRWAVE PRODUCTION GROUP INC., 1916 28th Ave. S., Birmingham AL 35209. (205)870-3239. Producer: Marc Phillips. Record producer, music publisher and artist development company. Estab. 1985. Produces 5 singles, 2 12″ singles, 4 LPs, 5 EPs and 3 CDs/year. Fee derived from sales royalty when song or artist is recorded.
How to Contact: Submit demo tape by mail. Unsolicited submissions are OK. Prefers cassette with 3 songs and lyric sheet. SASE. Reports in 6-10 weeks.
Music: Mostly **rock, R&B** and **pop**; also **jazz, country** and **contemporary Christian**. Produced "Another Wheel" and "Take A Step," written and recorded by Kelly Garrett on Sony Records (country); and *House of Love* (by A.J. Vallejo), recorded by Vallejo (rock). Other artists include Parousia, 4 AM and Elvis' Grave.

AKO PRODUCTIONS, Dept. SM, 20531 Plummer, Chatsworth CA 91311. (818)998-0443. President: A. Sullivan. Record producer and music publisher (Amiron). Produces 2-6 singles and 2-3 LPs/year. Fee derived from sales royalty when song or artist is recorded.
  ● AKO Productions' publishing company, Amiron Music, is listed in the Music Publishers section.
How to Contact: Write first and obtain permission to submit. Prefers cassette (or Beta or VHS videocassette) and lyric sheet. SASE. Reports in 1 month.
Music: Pop/rock and **modern country**. Produced *Ladies in Charge*, written and recorded by C. Ratliff on AKO Records.

*ALADDIN PRODUCTIONS, P.O. Box 121626, Nashville TN 37212. (615)726-3556. Executive Director: Neal James. Record producer. Estab. 1996. Produces 6 singles, 3 LPs, 3 CDs/year. Fee derived from sales royalty when song or artist is recorded or outright fee from recording artist or record company.
How to Contact: Submit demo tape by mail. Unsolicited submissions are OK. Prefers cassette with 2 songs and lyric sheet. "Send any pertinent information for review." SASE. Reports in 1 month.
Music: Mostly **country, alternative** and **rock**; also **gospel, blues** and **contemporary**. Produced "It's Up To You" (by Jerry Fuller), recorded by Deuces Wild (country); *What Do Ya Say*, written and recorded by Jay S. Kay (rock); and *Who Knows* (by Jim Hughes/Will Graveman), recorded by John Madrid on Crosswind Records (contemporary).
Tips: "Quality is the only thing selling. Screen your material very carefully and only submit your best. We are looking for songs and artists with something different. We need artists and songs to

possibly place not only with major record companies, but also for possible placement in movies, soundtracks, commercials and television programs."

STUART J. ALLYN, Skylight Run, Irvington NY 10533. (212)486-0856. Associate: Jack Walker. Record producer. Estab. 1972. Produces 6 singles and 3-6 CDs/year. Fee derived from sales royalty and outright fee from recording artist and record company.
How to Contact: Write first and obtain permission to submit. Prefers DAT, CD, cassette or 15 ips reel-to-reel (or VHS videocassette) with 3 songs and lyric or lead sheet. Does not return material. Reports in 12 months.
Music: Mostly **pop, rock, jazz** and **theatrical**; also **R&B** and **country**. Produced Dizzy Gillespie's "Winter in Lisbon" on Milan Records; *Mel Lewis & Jazz Orchestra* on Atlantic Records (jazz); and *Me & Him*, on Columbia Records (film score). Other artists include Billy Joel, Aerosmith, Carole Demas, Harry Stone, Bob Stewart, The Dixie Peppers, Nora York, Buddy Barnes and various video and film scores.

ANGEL FILMS COMPANY, 967 Hwy. 40, New Franklin MO 65247-9778. (573)698-3900. Vice President Production: Matthew Eastman. Record producer and record company (Angel One). Estab. 1980. Produces 5 LPs, 5 EPs and 5 CDs/year. Fee derived from sales royalty when song or artist is recorded.
  • See their listing in the Advertising, AV and Commercial Music Firms section.
How to Contact: Submit demo tape by mail. Unsolicited submissions are OK. Prefers cassette (or VHS videocassette if available) with 3 songs. "Send only original material, not previously recorded, and include a bio sheet on artist." SASE. Reports in 1-2 months.
Music: Mostly **pop, rock** and **rockabilly**; also **jazz** and **R&B**. Produced *Haulki*, written and recorded by Bill Hoehne; *Fairy Bride*, written and recorded by Shariee (children's); and *G-String*, written and recorded by G-String, all on Angel One Records. Other artists include Julian James, Kello So, Cat Arkin, Stephanie Li Gee and Patrick Donovon.
Tips: "Don't be scared of rejection. It's the only way you learn."

APOPHIS MUSIC, 7135 Hollywood, Los Angeles CA 90046. (213)851-8552. Fax: (213)850-1467. Record Producer: Jimmy Stewart. Manager: Terri Tilton. Record producer. Estab. 1968. Produces 3 LPs and 3 CDs/year. Fee derived from sales royalty when song or artist is recorded or outright fee from recording artist.
How to Contact: Write or call first and obtain permission to submit a demo. Prefers cassette with 3 songs and lyric or lead sheet. SASE. Reports in 1-2 months.
Music: Mostly **jazz, alternative** and **rock**; also **R&B** and **classical**. Produced *The Touch*, written and recorded by Jimmy Stewart on BlackHawk Records (jazz); *Evolution of Jazz Guitar*, written and recorded by Jimmy Stewart on CPP/Belwin Records (jazz); and "Songs of My Friends," recorded by Toni Lee Scott on Love and Jazz Records (jazz). Other artists include Gary Crosby.

AROUND SOUNDS PUBLISHING (ASCAP), 4572 150th Ave. NE, Redmond WA 98052. (206)881-9322. Fax: (206)881-3645. Contact: Lary 'Larz' Nefzger. Record producer and music publisher. Estab. 1981. Produces 8 LPs and 8 CDs/year. Fee depends on negotiated agreement.
How to Contact: Write or call first and obtain permission to submit.

AURORA PRODUCTIONS, 7415 Herrington NE, Belmont MI 49306. Producer: Jack Conners. Record producer, engineer/technician and record company (Big Rock Records and Ocean Records). Estab. 1984. Produces 1 CD/year. Fee derived from outright fee from recording artist.
How to Contact: Write first and obtain permission to submit. Prefers cassette with 1 or 2 songs. SASE. Reports in 6 weeks.
Music: Mostly **classical, folk** and **jazz**; also **pop/rock** and **New Age**. Produced "Acousma," written and recorded by S.R. Turner on North Cedar Records; "Peace on Earth" (by John and Danny Murphy), recorded by Murphy Brothers on Ocean Records; and *The Burdons*, written and recorded by The Burdons on Big Rock Records.

AUSTIN RECORDING STUDIO, 4606 Clawson, Austin TX 78745. (512)444-5489. President: Wink Tyler. Record producer, music publisher. Estab. 1971. Produces 2 CDs/year. Fee derived from outright fee from recording artist or record company.

 THE ASTERISK before a listing indicates that the listing is new in this edition. New markets are often the most receptive to unsolicited submissions.

How to Contact: Call first and obtain permission to submit. Prefers cassette with 4 songs and lyric sheet. SASE. Reports in 4 weeks.
Music: Mostly **country**. Produced *Shane Delome*, written and recorded by Shane; *Wes Wiginton*, written and recorded by Wes Wiginton; and *Bone Glove* (by Steve Karma), recorded by Bone Glove, all on BSW Records. Other artists include Erwin Williams, Mark Monaco and Forced Direction.

BAL RECORDS, Box 369, LaCanada CA 91012-0369. (818)548-1116. President: Adrian Bal. Record producer and music publisher (Bal & Bal Music). Estab. 1965. Produces 1-3 CDs/year. Fee derived from sales royalty when song or artist is recorded.
   • Bal Records' publishing company, Bal & Bal Music, is listed in the Music Publishers section.
How to Contact: Submit demo tape by mail. Unsolicited submissions are OK. Prefers cassette with 3 songs and lyric sheet. SASE. Reports in 3 weeks-5 months.
Music: Mostly **MOR**, **country**, **jazz**, **R&B**, **rock** and **top 40/pop**; also **blues**, **church/religious**, **easy listening** and **soul**. Produced "Fragile" (by James Jackson), recorded by Kathy Simmons (rock); and "You're A Part of Me," written and recorded by Paul Richards (A/C), all on BAL Records.
Tips: "Write and compose what you believe to be commercial."

BASEMENT BOYS, INC., 510 Jasper St., Baltimore MD 21201. (410)383-8437. Fax: (410)383-7538. Vice President: Teddy Douglas. Record producer and music publisher (Basement Boys Music). Estab. 1986. Produces 20 singles, 10 12" singles, 3 LPs, 2 EPs and 3 CDs/year. Fee derived from sales royalty when song or artist is recorded.
How to Contact: Submit demo tape by mail. Unsolicited submissions are OK. Prefers cassette (or VHS videocassette if available) with 4 songs and lyric sheet (if possible). Does not return material. Reports in 3 weeks.
Music: Mostly **dance**, **R&B** and **underground music**. Produced "100% Pure Love" (by J. Steinhour/ T. Douglas/C. Waters) and "What I Need" (by C. Waters/R. Payton), both recorded by Crystal Waters on Mercury Records (dance/R&B). Other artists include RuPaul and Victoria Wilson James.
Tips: "Be innovative and write meaningful, catchy, strong songs and hooks."

HAL BERNARD ENTERPRISES, INC., P.O. Box 8385, Cincinnati OH 45208. (513)871-1500. Fax: (513)871-1510. President: Stan Hertzman. Record producer, record company (Strugglebaby Recording Co.) and music publisher (Sunnyslope Music Inc. and Bumpershoot Music Inc.). Produces 5 singles and 3-4 LPs/year. Fee derived from sales royalty.
   • See Hal Bernard's listing in the Music Publishers section, as well as listings for Strugglebaby Recording Co. in the Record Companies section and Umbrella Artists Management in the Managers and Booking Agents section.
How to Contact: Prefers cassette with 1-3 songs and lyric sheet. SASE. Reports in 1 month.
Music: Produced *Inner Revolution*, by Adrian Belew on Atlantic Records; *Awkwardsville*, recorded by psychodots on Strugglebaby Records; and *Thank You for the Dance*, recorded by Danny Morgan on Seagull Records.

BIG BEAR, Box 944, Birmingham, B16 8UT, **United Kingdom**. Phone: 44-21-454-7020. Managing Director: Jim Simpson. Record producer, music publisher (Bearsongs) and record company (Big Bear Records). Produces 10 LPs/year. Fee derived from sales royalty.
   • See the listings for Bearsongs in the Music Publishers section and Big Bear Records in the Record Companies section.
How to Contact: Write first about your interest, then submit demo tape and lyric sheet. Does not return material. Reports in 2 weeks.
Music: **Blues** and **jazz**.

BIG SKY AUDIO PRODUCTIONS, 1035 E. Woodland Ave. #2, Springfield PA 19064. (610)328-4709. Fax: (610)328-7728. Producer: Drew Raison. Record producer. Estab. 1990. Produces 5-7 EPs and 10-12 CDs/year. Fee negotiable.
How to Contact: Submit demo tape by mail. Unsolicited submissions are OK. Prefers cassette or VHS videocassette with 3 songs and lyric sheet. "Don't send it to us if it isn't copyrighted!" Does not return material. Reports in 4-6 weeks.
Music: **Rock**, **R&B** and **New Age**; also **anything with strong vocals**. Produced *Speak On It* (by Syracuse/Gilham), recorded by Blue Noise; *Get It Right*, written and recorded by Johnny DeFrancesco, both on VAM Records; and *I Have Forgotten*, written and recorded by David E. Williamson on Ospedale Records. Other artists include Trash Planet, John Swiegart, Theodozia, Daniel Pry, Robert Hazzard, Joey DeFrancesco and Dreamlovers.
Tips: "Be prepared. Have more tunes ready and packed to go. We want to see what you can do!"

BLAZE PRODUCTIONS, 103 Pleasant Ave., Upper Saddle River NJ 07458. (201)825-1060. Record producer, music publisher (Botown Music) multimedia company and management firm. Estab.

1978. Fee derived from sales royalty or outright fee from recording artist or record company.
   • See their listing in the Managers and Booking Agents section.
How to Contact: Submit demo tape by mail. Unsolicited submissions are OK. Prefers cassette (or VHS videocassette) with 1 or more songs and lyric sheet. Does not return material. Reports in 3 weeks.
Music: **Pop**, **rock** and **dance**. Produced *Anything Can Happen*, by Voices on Botown Records; and "Up On Blocks," recorded by Gearhead on Wild Boar Records.

PETER L. BONTA, 2200 Airport Ave., Fredericksburg VA 22401. (703)373-6511. Record producer. Estab. 1980. Produces 8-12 singles, 5-8 LPs and 4-6 CDs/year. Fee derived from sales royalty or outright fee from recording artist or record company.
How to Contact: Write or call first and obtain permission to submit. Prefers cassette with 3-4 songs and lyric sheet. SASE. Reports in 3-6 weeks.
Music: Mostly **roots rock**, **country rock** and **blues**; also **country** and **bluegrass**. Produced *Every Reason/Every Season*, written and recorded by Carolyn Jane on CU Records (country folk); *In The Clouds*, written and recorded by Tom Principato on Powerhouse Records (blues); and *Have Love, Will Travel* (by various artists), recorded by Bill Kirchen on Blacktop Records (roots rock). Other artists include Furlongs, Chip Monk and Tripping on Rats.

ROBERT BOWDEN, Box 282, 885 Broadway, Bayonne NJ 07002. President: Robert Bowden. Record producer, music publisher (Roots Music/BMI) and record company (Nucleus Records). Estab. 1979. Produces 3 singles and 1 LP/year. Fees derived from sales royalty when song or artist is recorded.
   • Robert Bowden's publishing company, Roots Music, is listed in the Music Publishers section, and his record label, Nucleus Records, is listed in the Record Companies section.
How to Contact: Write first and obtain permission to submit. Prefers cassette (or VHS videocassette if available) with 3 songs and lyric sheet. SASE. Reports in 1 month.
Music: Mostly **country**; also **pop**. Produced "Henrey C," "Always" and "Selfish Heart" (by Bowden), all recorded by Marco Sisison on Nucleus Records.

BRIDGES PRODUCTIONS, 340 Fillmore, San Francisco CA 94117. (415)552-4047. Producer: Jamie Bridges. Record producer. Estab. 1984. Produces 1-10 singles and 2-8 CDs/year. Fee derived from sales royalty when song or artist is recorded or outright fee from recording artist or record company.
How to Contact: Write first and obtain permission to submit. Prefers cassette or DAT with 1-10 songs and lyric sheet. Does not return material. Reports in 6 weeks.
Music: Mostly **alternative** and **rock**.

CAPITOL AD, MANAGEMENT & TALENT GROUP, 1300 Division St., Suite 200, Nashville TN 37203. (615)242-4722, (615)244-2440, (800)767-4984. Fax: (615)242-1177. E-mail: www.platinu mr@aol.com. Senior Producer: Robert Metzgar. Record producer, record company (Aim High Records, Hot News Records, Platinum Plus Records, SHR Records) and music publisher (Aim High Music Co./ASCAP, Bobby & Billy Music Co./BMI). Estab. 1971. Produces 35 singles, 12-15 12″ singles, 20 LPs, 15 EPs and 35 CDs/year. Fee derived from sales royalty when song or artist is recorded or outright fee from recording artist or record company.
   • Capitol's publishing company, Aim High Music, is listed in the Music Publishers section; Capitol Management and Talent is listed in the Managers and Booking Agents section; and their record company, Platinum Plus, is listed in the Record Companies section.
How to Contact: Submit demo tape by mail. Unsolicited submissions are OK. Prefers cassette (or videocassette) with 3-5 songs and lyric sheet. "We are interested in hearing only from *serious* artist/songwriters." Does not return material. Reports in 3-4 weeks.
Music: Mostly **country**, **gospel**, **pop** and **R&B**; also **jazz**, **contemporary Christian**, **rock** and **pop-rock**. Produced *Sounds of Music*, written and recorded by B. Enriquez on Sony Records (Latin); *Keep On Dancin'* (by H. Smiley), recorded by Satin (dance); and *Livin For The Dream* (M. Johnson), recorded by John Michael Montgomery (country), both on CBS Records. Other artists include Carl Butler (CBS/Sony), Tommy Cash (Columbia), Mickey Jones (Capitol), Tommy Overstreet (MCA Records), Warner Mack (MCA Records) and others.
Tips: "Getting Capitol Management on your team is the best thing you could ever do!"

CARE FREE RECORDS GROUP, P.O. Box 2463, Carefree AZ 85377. (602)230-4177. Vice President: Doya Fairbanks. Record producer, record company, music publisher (Ho-Hum Music), distributor and promotions company. Estab. 1990. Produces 6 singles, 4 12″ singles, 12 LPs, 5 EPs and 12 CDs/year. Fee derived from outright fee from record company.
   • See Care Free's listing in the Record Companies section, as well as a listing for their publishing company, Ho-Hum Music, in the Music Publishers section.
How to Contact: Submit demo tape by mail. Unsolicited submissions are OK. Prefers cassette (or VHS videocassette) with 4-6 songs. SASE. Reports in 1 month.

Music: Mostly **country**, **jazz** and **classical**; also **rock/pop**, **metal** and **New Age**. Produced *Modern Art/Primitive Music*, written and recorded by Pablo on Blue Mesa Records (pop); *The Totem Pole*, written and recorded by Totem Pole (pop); and *Harold's Coral*, written and recorded by Harold's Coral (country), both on Care Free Records. Other artists include Paul Conceio, Arsinal and Gypsy Wind.

CARLOCK PRODUCTIONS, 85 Sixth Ave., Apt. B, Brooklyn NY 11217. Producer: Dave Carlock. Record producer. Estab. 1990. Produces 6 LPs and 5 EPs/year. Fee derived from sales royalty when song or artist is recorded or outright fee from recording artist or record company.
How to Contact: Write first and obtain permission to submit. Prefers cassette (or VHS videocassette if available) with 3-5 songs and lyric sheet. Does not return material. Reports in 2 weeks.
Music: Mostly **pop/rock**, **A/C** and **rock (alternative)**; also **contemporary Christian** and **gospel**. Produced *Long Way Down*, recorded by Greg Shafritz (pop/rock); *Daisy's Red Gravy Train*, recorded by Daisy's Red Gravy Train (pop/rock); and *There's A Space* (by Christopher Beerman).
Tips: "If contacting me from outside of NY metro area (NY, NJ, CT), be prepared to travel to New York for my services. In this instance, please be serious if you submit!"

*CARLYLE PRODUCTIONS, 1217 16th Ave. South, Nashville TN 37212. (615)327-8129. President: Laura Fraser. Record producer, record company (Carlyle Records) and production company. Estab. 1986. Produces 6 singles and 6 LPs/CDs per year. Fee derived from sales royalty when song or artist is recorded.
● See the listings for Carlyle Records in the Record Companies section and Carlyle Management in the Managers and Booking Agents section.
How to Contact: Call first and obtain permission to submit. Prefers cassette with 3 songs and lyric sheet. Does not return material. Reports in 2 months.
Music: Mostly **rock**, **pop** and **country**. Produced *Exercise In Tension*, written and recorded by Dessau (dance); "Too Late," written and recorded by Vegas Cocks (rock); and *Songs From Beneath the Lake*, written and recorded by The Shakers (rock).

*DON CASALE MUSIC, INC., 377 Plainfield St., Westbury NY 11590. (516)333-7898. President: Don Casale. Record producer, music publisher (Elasac Music/ASCAP; Don Casale Music/BMI) and artist management. Estab. 1979. Fee derived from sales royalty when song or artist is recorded.
● See Don Casale's other listing in the Managers and Booking Agents section.
How to Contact: "Please write to me (with SASE) before you submit, explaining your goals. Include your bio and a recent photo." Reports in 1 month.
Music: "All styles in tune with the current market." Produced *All Fired Up*, written and recorded by Joanne Redding on ICR Records (country). Other artists include Susy Mathis, B Sweet, Bullet Proof Boyz and Penny Towers.
Tips: "I'm looking for unique artists and songs."

CEDAR CREEK PRODUCTIONS, 44 Music Square E., Suite 503, Nashville TN 37203. (615)252-6916. Fax: (615)327-4204. President: Larry Duncan. Record producer, record company (Cedar Creek Records™), music publisher (Cedar Creek Music/BMI and Cedar Cove Music/ASCAP) and artist management. Estab. 1981. Produces 20 singles, 5 LPs and 5 CDs/year. Fee derived from outright fee from recording artist.
● See their listing in the Managers and Booking Agents section; Cedar Creek Records is listed in the Record Companies section.
How to Contact: Submit demo tape by mail. Unsolicited submissions are OK. Prefers cassette (or VHS videocassette) with 4-6 songs and lyric sheet (typed). "Put return address and name on envelope. Put telephone number in packet." Does not return material. Reports in 2 months.
Music: Mostly **country**, **country/pop** and **country/R&B**; also **pop**, **R&B**; **southern/gospel/Christian contemporary**, **Christian country**, **contemporary jazz** and **light rock**. Produced "Ride Rebels Ride" (by Deke Little/Tex Henley/Eldon Money); "When The Sun Goes Down Over Dixie" (by Brian McCardle/John Georgell); and "What Would Jeff and Robert Say Today" (by Deke Little/Lynn Guyo), all recorded by Lynn Guyo on Interstate Records (country).
Tips: "Submit your best songs on a good fully produced demo or master."

JAN CELT, 4026 NE 12th Ave., Portland OR 97212. (503)287-8045. Owner: Jan Celt. Record producer, music publisher (Wiosna Nasza Music/BMI) and record company (Flying Heart Records). Estab. 1982. Produces 3-5 CDs/year.
● See the listing for Flying Heart Records in the Record Companies section.
How to Contact: Submit demo tape by mail. Unsolicited submissions are OK. Prefers high-quality cassette with 1-10 songs and lyric sheet. SASE. Reports in 4 months. "If calling, please check time zone."
Music: Mostly **R&B**, **rock** and **blues**; also **jazz**. Produced "Vexatious Progressions," written and recorded by Eddie Harris (jazz); "Bong Hit" (by Chris Newman), recorded by Snow Bud & the Flower

People (rock); and "She Moved Away" (by Chris Newman), recorded by Napalm Beach, all on Flying Heart Records. Other artists include The Esquires and Janice Scroggins.
Tips: "Be sure your lyrics are heartfelt; they are what makes a song your own. Abandon rigid stylistic concepts and go for total honesty of expression."

CHUCKER MUSIC, INC., 345 E. 80th St., 15H, New York NY 10021. (212)744-2312. President: Chuck Dembrak. Record producer and music publisher (Cool One Music/ASCAP). Estab. 1978. Produces 3-6 12″ singles and 1-2 LPs/year. Fees derived from sales royalty when song or artist is recorded.
How to Contact: Submit demo tape by mail. Unsolicited submissions are OK. Prefers cassette (or VHS videocassette if available) with 3-4 songs and lyric sheet. Does not return material. Reports in 4 weeks.
Music: Mostly **R&B, pop** and **rock**. Produced *Sunday Serenade* (by J. Roach), recorded by Double Digit on Chucker Records (jazz); *High on Blues* (by C. Collins), recorded by Finest Tasby on Shanachie Records (blues); and *Necessity* (by C. Frycki), recorded by Killing Words on Midnite Fantasy Records (rock). Other artists include Geri Mingori and Leslie Fradkin.

COACHOUSE MUSIC, P.O. Box 1308, Barrington IL 60011. (312)822-0305. Fax: (312)464-0762. President: Michael Freeman. Record producer. Estab. 1984. Produces 4 LPs and 4 CDs/year. Fees vary with project.
How to Contact: Write first and obtain permission to submit. Prefers cassette, DAT or CD with 3-5 songs and lyric sheet. SASE. Reports in 1 month.
Music: Mostly **pop**, **rock** and **blues**; also **alternative rock** and **progressive country**. Produced *Eat At Godot's*, written and recorded by Ralph Covert on Waterdog Records (pop/folk); *Dance All Night*, written and recorded by Chubby Carrier (zydeco); and *Sideways In Paradise* (by various), recorded by Jim Thackeray and John Mooney (folk/blues), both on Blind Pig Records. Other artists include Maybe/Definitely, Eleventh Dream Day, Magic Slim, Amarillo Kings, The Tantrums, The Pranks, Allison Johnson and Mick Freon.
Tips: "Be honest, be committed, strive for excellence."

COFFEE AND CREAM PRODUCTIONS, 1138 E. Price St., Philadelphia PA 19138. Producer: Bolden Abrams, Jr.. Record producer, music publisher (Coffee and Cream Publishing Company/ASCAP) and record company (Coffee and Cream Records). Produces 12 singles, 12 12″ singles and 6 LPs/year. Fee derived from sales royalty or outright fee from recording artist or record company.
How to Contact: Submit demo tape by mail. Unsolicited submissions are OK. Prefers cassette with 1-4 songs and lyric sheet. Does not return material. Reports in 2 weeks.
Music: Mostly **R&B, pop** and **country**; also **gospel** and **dance**. Produced "I Had A Talk With My Man" (by Leonard Caston/Billy Davis) and "Sly Like A Fox" (by Regine Urbach), both recorded by Joy Harvey; and "Drifting Away" (by Maurice Mertoli/Phil Nelson), recorded by Heather Murphy, all on Coffee and Cream Records.

COLLECTOR RECORDS, Box 2296, Rotterdam Holland 3000 CG **The Netherlands**. Phone: 186-604266. Fax: 186-604366. Research: Cees Klop. Record producer and music publisher (All Rock Music). Produces 2 singles and 30 CDs/year. Fee derived from outright fee from recording artist.
• See the listing for All Rock Music in the Music Publishers section.
How to Contact: Submit demo tape by mail. Unsolicited submissions are OK. Prefers cassette. SAE and IRC. Reports in 1-2 months.
Music: Mostly **'50s rock**, **rockabilly** and **country rock**; also **piano boogie woogie**. Produced *Boogie Woogie Bill*, written and recorded by Teddy Redell on Collector Records (rock); *Grand Hotel* (by Laurentis), recorded by Rockin' Vincent (rock); and *Coco Boogie*, written and recorded by Andre Valkering, both on Down South Records.

COMPLEX STUDIOS, 23937 Oakmont Place, West Hills CA 91304. (818)346-1432. Producer: David DeVore. Record producer. Estab. 1974. Fee derived from sales royalty when song or artist is recorded, or outright fee from record company.
How to Contact: Submit demo tape by mail. Unsolicited submissions are OK. Prefers cassette and lyric sheet. SASE. Reports in 3 weeks.
Music: Mostly **pop/rock**, **dance** and **ballads**; also **reggae** and **country**. Produced records by REO Speedwagon, Foreigner, Santana, Russ Ballard and Spirit.

JOHNNY COPPIN/RED SKY RECORDS, P.O. Box 7, Stonehouse, Glos. GL10 3PQ **UK**. Phone: 01453-826200. Record producer, music publisher (PRS) and record company (Red Sky Records). Estab. 1985. Produces 2 albums/year. Fee derived from sales royalty when song or artist is recorded.
• Red Sky Records is also listed in the Record Companies section.
How to Contact: Write first and obtain permission to submit. Does not return material. Reports in 6 months.

Music: Mostly **rock**, **modern folk** and **roots music**. Produced "A Country Christmas" and "Force of the River," written and recorded by Johnny Coppin; and "Dead Lively!," written and recorded by Paul Burgess, all on Red Sky Records. Other artists include David Goodland.

DANO CORWIN, 5839 Silvercreek Rd., Azle TX 76020. (817)530-7942. Record producer, music video and sound production company. Estab. 1986. Produces 6 singles, 3 12″ singles, 5 EPs and 2 CDs/year. Fee derived from sales royalty when song or artist is recorded, or outright fee from recording artist or record company.
How to Contact: Submit demo tape by mail. Unsolicited submissions are OK. Prefers cassette (or VHS videocassette if available) with 3 songs and lyric sheet. "Keep songs under 5 minutes. Only copyrighted material will be reviewed. Please do not send material without copyright notices." Does not return material. Reports in 6-8 weeks.
Music: Mostly **rock**; also **pop** and **dance**. Produced *Dimensions*, written and recorded by Silent Shame on MLM Records (rock); "Hello" (by W.J. Ross), recorded by RTIC; and "Early Dawn" (by T. Darren), recorded by Zeph, both on WW Records (rock). Other artists include Complete, Sir Gray Wolf and Drune.
Tips: "Write as many songs as possible. Out of a large quantity, a few quality songs may emerge."

COUNTRY STAR PRODUCTIONS, Box 569, Franklin PA 16323. (814)432-4633. President: Norman Kelly. Record producer, music publisher (Country Star Music/ASCAP, Kelly Music/BMI and Process Music/BMI) and record company (Country Star, Process, Mersey and CSI Records). Estab. 1970. Produces 5-8 singles and 5-8 LPs/year. Fee derived from sales royalty when song or artist is recorded.
How to Contact: Submit demo tape by mail. Unsolicited submissions are OK. Prefers cassette with 2-4 songs and typed lyric or lead sheet. SASE. Reports in 1 week.
Music: Mostly **country** (80%); also **rock** (5%), **MOR** (5%), **gospel** (5%) and **R&B** (5%). Produced "The Holiday Waltz" (by Wrightman/Stelzer), recorded by Debbie Soe; "Love Tree" (by Kelly/Brown), recorded by David Lee Wayne; and "It's Enough to Make a Woman Lose Her Mind" (by Bill Anderson), recorded by Junie Lou, all on Country Star Records. Other artists include Gary King.

*RANDALL COUSINS PRODUCTIONS, 148 Erin Ave., Hamilton, Ontario L8K 4W3 **Canada**. (905)796-8236. Contact: Randall Cousins. Record producer, record company (Roto Noto Music), music publisher (Alleged Iguana Music). Estab. 1984. Produces 25 singles, 3 LPs, 3 CDs/year.
 • Randall Cousins' publishing company, Alleged Iguana Music, is listed in the Music Publishers section.
How to Contact: Write first and obtain permission to submit a demo. Prefers cassette or DAT with 2 songs and lyric sheet. SASE. Reports in 1 month.
Music: Mostly **new country**, **country** and **pop/AC**; also **rock** and **R&B**. Produced "Still Lovin' You" (by R. Cousins/H. Kennedy), recorded by the Wrecking Crew (R&B); "See Me Thru," written and recorded by Shade Stone (rock); and "Gotta Get My Love" (by M. Lapointe/L. Logan), recorded by Lisa Logan (country), all on Roto Noto Records. Other artists include Annette Lightheart, Harold MacIntyre, Mark Severn, Lynne and the Rebels, Lone Star Oasis, Belloni Poni, Manon, Marvin Tweeter and The Long-Gone Band.

CREATIVE MUSIC SERVICES, 838 Fountain St., Woodbridge CT 06525. Owner: Craig Calistro. Record producer (Ace Record Company). Estab. 1989. Produces 50 singles, 20 12″ singles, 15 LPs and 15 CDs/year. Fee derived from sales royalty when song or artist is recorded or outright fee from recording artist or record company.
How to Contact: Submit demo tape by mail. Unsolicited submissions are OK. Prefers cassette (or VHS videocassette if available) and 1-3 songs and lyric and lead sheets. "Send photo if available." Does not return material. Reports in 3 weeks.
Music: Mostly **pop/top 40** and **dance**; also **jazz**. Produced "Tell Me" (by Craig Calistro), recorded by J. Lord; *Drummer Boy*, written and recorded by Ken Aldrich (jazz); and *Quiet Nights* (by Craig Calistro), recorded by Debbyess (MOR), all on Ace Records. Other artists include Mike Grella.

JERRY CUPIT PRODUCTIONS, Box 121904, Nashville TN 37212. (615)731-0100. Producer: Jerry Cupit. Record producer and music publisher. Estab. 1984. Fee derived from sales royalty or outright fee from artist.
 • See the listing for Cupit Music in the Music Publishers section.
How to Contact: Write first and obtain permission to submit. Send demo, bio, photo and SASE. Does not return material. Reports in 2-3 months.
Music: Mostly **country**, **Southern rock** and **gospel**; also **R&B**. Produced "Jukebox Junkie" (by Ken Mellons/Jerry Cupit/Janice Honeycutt) and *Where Forever Begins*, both recorded by Ken Mellons on

Epic Records; and *A Memory Never Dies* (by L. Thomas Miller/T. Lea Reynolds/J. Sonnier), recorded by Jo-El Sonnier on Rounder Records.

D.S.M. PRODUCERS, INC., 161 W. 54th St., New York NY 10019. (212)245-0006. Director of A&R: Nicole Weitz. Contact: Associate Producer. Record producer, music publisher and music library. Estab. 1979. Fee derived from sales royalty when song or artist is recorded.
 • See D.S.M.'s listings in the Music Publishing and Advertising, AV and Commercial Music Firms sections.
How to Contact: Write first and obtain permission to submit. Prefers cassette (or VHS videocassette) with 2 songs and lyric or lead sheet. SASE. Reports in 1-3 months. "Must include an SASE for submission."
Music: All styles. Produced *DSM Tunes Vol. 2*, *Dance America Vol. 2* and *Rock America Vol. 2*, written and recorded by various artists on AACL Records.
Tips: "It's getting more difficult for an artist who cannot present a master demo to a label. You're going to need financing for your demos/masters, but it's worth having a professional studio produce your first demos as they do it for a living. They can help you become an established artist/songwriter. Invest in yourself, and when you have the right product, you will be heard and you're on your way to success. Be sure to title and label your submissions."

D.S.O., INC., (formerly Davis Soto Orban Productions), 601 Van Ness, #E3425, San Francisco CA 94102. (415)775-9785. Fax: (415)775-3082. CEO: Glenn Davis. Record producer. Estab. 1984. Produces 3 LPs and 1 CD/year.
How to Contact: Submit demo tape by mail. Unsolicited submissions are OK. Prefers cassette (or CD or MS-DOS disc) with 4 songs and lyric sheet. Send full demo kit (bio, tape, tearsheets, pics, etc.) if possible. SASE. Reports in 4-6 weeks.
Music: Mostly **world beat**, **infusion** and **modern**; also **rock**, **classical/poetry** and **pop**. Produced *Where Heaven Begins* (by Orban/Davis), *Transparent Empire* (by Orban) and *Summertime* (by Gershwin), all recorded by DSO on On The Wing Records.

S. KWAKU DADDY, Box 424794, San Francisco CA 94142-4794. (707)769-9479. President: S. Kwaku Daddy. Record producer and record company (African Heritage Records Co.). Produces 6 LPs/year. Fee derived from sales royalty when song or artist is recorded.
How to Contact: Write or call first and obtain permission to submit. Prefers cassette. SASE. Reports in 2 weeks.
Music: Mostly **African pop**, **R&B** and **gospel**. Produced *Times of Change*, *Life's Rhythms* and *The Circle*, all written and recorded by S. Kwaku Daddy on African Heritage Records.
Tips: "Place emphasis on rhythm."

DANNY DARROW, 150 West End Ave., Suite 6-D, New York NY 10023. (212)873-5968. Manager: Danny Darrow. Record producer, music publisher, record company (Mighty Records) and Colley Phonographics—Europe. Estab. 1958. Produces 1-2 singles, 1-2 12" singles and 1-2 LPs/year. Fee derived from sales royalty when song or artist is recorded.
 • Danny Darrow's record company, Mighty Records, is listed in the Record Companies section, and the Rockford Music Co. is listed in the Music Publishers section.
How to Contact: Submit demo tape by mail. Unsolicited submissions are OK. "No phone calls." Prefers cassette with 3 songs and lyric sheet. SASE. Reports in 1-2 weeks.
Music: Mostly **pop**, **country** and **dance**; also **jazz**. Produced *Impulse* (by Danny Darrow); and *Falling In Love* (by Brian Rowen), both recorded by Danny Darrow on Mighty Records.

DATURA PRODUCTIONS, 4320 Sara St., #9, Burbank CA 91505. (818)558-1329. Fax: (818)558-7538. Owner: William Hanifan. Record producer. Estab. 1990. Fee derived from outright fee from record company.
How to Contact: Submit demo tape by mail. Unsolicited submissions are OK. Prefers cassette, CD or VHS videocassette with lyric and lead sheet. Does not return material. Reports in 4-6 weeks.
Music: Mostly **R&B**, **rock** and **alternative**; also **metal**, **country** and **pop**.

EDWARD DE MILES, 4475 Allisonville Rd., 8th Floor, Indianapolis IN 46205. (317)546-2912. President: Edward De Miles. Record producer, music publisher (Edward De Miles Music Co./BMI)

REFER TO THE CATEGORY INDEX (at the end of this section) to find exactly which companies are interested in the type of music you write.

and record company (Sahara Records). Estab. 1981. Produces 15-20 singles, 15-20 12″ singles, 5-10 LPs and 5-10 CDs/year. Fee derived from sales royalty when song or artist is recorded.

• See the listings for the Edward De Miles Music Co. in the Music Publishers section, as well as Sahara Records and Filmworks Entertainment in the Record Companies section.

How to Contact: Write first and obtain permission to submit. Prefers cassette (or VHS or Beta ½″ videocassette if available) with 1-3 songs and lyric sheet. SASE. "We do not return material." Reports in 1 month.

Music: Mostly **R&B/dance**, **top 40 pop/rock** and **contemporary jazz**; also **country**, **TV and film themes—songs and jingles**. Produced "Hooked on U," "Dance Wit Me" and "Moments," (by S. Page), recorded by Steve Lynn (R&B), all on Sahara Records. Other artists include D'von Edwards and Multiple Choice.

Tips: "Copyright all material before submitting. Equipment and showmanship a must."

DEEP SPACE RECORDS, 7560 Meadowlark Dr., Sebastopol CA 95472. (707)824-8145. Owner/Producer: Kenn Fink. Record producer. Estab. 1985. Produces 3 singles and 1 LP/year. Fee derived from sales royalty when song or artist is recorded or outright fee from recording artist or record company.

How to Contact: Write first and obtain permission to submit. Prefers cassette with 3-5 songs and lyric sheet. SASE. Reports in 5 weeks.

Music: Mostly **hard rock**, **electronic** (not necessarily New Age) and **blends of the two**. Produced *Lifesigns* and *Locked In The Basement* (by Kenn Fink), recorded by The Outcast on Deep Space Records (electronic/rock).

AL DELORY AND MUSIC MAKERS, 3000 Hillsboro Rd., #11, Nashville TN 37215. (615)292-2140. President: Al DeLory. Record producer and career consultant (DeLory Music/ASCAP). Estab. 1987. Fee derived from outright fee from recording artist, record company, career consultant fees.

How to Contact: Write or call first and obtain permission to arrange personal interview. Prefers cassette (or VHS videocassette). Does not return material.

Music: Mostly **pop**, **country** and **Latin**. Produced "Gentle On My Mind," "By the Time I Get to Phoenix" and "Wichita Lineman," all recorded by Glen Campbell.

DEMI MONDE RECORDS & PUBLISHING LTD., Foel Studio, Llanfair Caereinion, Powys, SY21 0DS **Wales**. Phone/fax: 01938-810758. Managing Director: Dave Anderson. Record producer, music publisher (PRS & MCPS) and record company (Demi Monde Records). Estab. 1982. Produces 5 singles, 15 12″ singles, 15 LPs and 10 CDs/year. Fee derived from sales royalty.

• See their listings in the Music Publishers and Record Companies sections.

How to Contact: Submit demo tape by mail. Unsolicited submissions are OK. Prefers cassette with 3 or 4 songs and lyric sheet. SAE and IRC. Reports in 6 weeks.

Music: Mostly **rock**, **pop** and **blues**. Produced *Average Man*, recorded by Mother Gong (rock); *Frozen Ones*, recorded by Tangle Edge (rock); and *Blue Boar Blues* (by T.S. McPhee), recorded by Groundhogs (rock), all on Demi Monde Records. Other artists include Gong and Hawkwind.

JOEL DIAMOND ENTERTAINMENT, Dept. SM, 5370 Vanalden Ave., Tarzana CA 91356. (818)345-2558. Executive Vice President: Scott Gootman. Contact: Joel Diamond. Record producer, music publisher and manager. Fee derived from sales royalty when song is recorded or outright fee from recording artist or record company.

How to Contact: Submit demo tape by mail. Unsolicited submissions are OK. Prefers cassette with 1-3 songs and lyric sheet. Does not return material. Reports in 1 month.

Music: **Dance**, **easy listening**, **country**, **R&B**, **rock**, **soul** and **top 40/pop**. Produced "One Night In Bangkok," by Robey; "Love is the Reason" (by Cline/Wilson), recorded by E. Humperdinck and G. Gaynor on Critique Records (A/C); and "After the Loving," recorded by E. Humperdinck.

COL. BUSTER DOSS PRESENTS, 341 Billy Goat Hill Rd., Winchester TN 37398. Producer: Col. Buster Doss. Fax: (615)649-2732. Record producer, record company (Stardust, Wizard) and music publisher (Buster Doss Music/BMI). Estab. 1959. Produces 100 singles, 10 12″ singles, 20 LPs and 10 CDs/year. Fee derived from sales royalty when song or artist is recorded.

• Buster Doss's publishing company, Buster Doss Music, is listed in the Music Publishers section, his management firm, Col. Buster Doss Presents, is in the Managers and Booking Agents section, and his record label, Stardust, is listed under Record Companies.

How to Contact: Write first and obtain permission to submit. Prefers cassette with 2 songs and lyric sheet. SASE. Reports in 1 day if interested.

Music: **Pop**, **country** and **gospel**. Produced *The Man I Love* (by Buster Doss), recorded by Jerri Arnold; "Let's Go Dancing" (by Buster Doss), recorded by Mike "Doc" Holliday; and "You Can't Take Texas Out of Me" (by Barbara Doss), recorded by "Bronco" Buck Cody, all on Stardust Records.

Other artists include R.B. Stone, Cliff Archer, Linda Wunder, Honey James, Don Sky, Shelly Streeter, Rooster Quantrell and Dwain Gamel.

*DOUBLE K ENTERTAINMENT, P.O. Box 1441, Franklin TN 37065. (615)368-7545. Producer: Eddie Kilroy. Record producer, music publisher (Rancho Vaquero Music/BMI). Estab. 1985. Produces 3-5 CDs/year.
How to Contact: Prefers cassette with 1 song and lyric sheet. SASE. Reports in 1-2 months.
Music: Mostly **country**, **Christian country** and **'50s rockabilly**. Artists include Zaca Creek and Mickey Gilley.
Tips: "Be professional and current and use good common sense when sending material. Make sure it has a 'market.' "

DOUBLETIME PRODUCTIONS, P.O. Box 710925, San Diego CA 92072. (619)448-1717. Producer: Jeff Forrest. Record producer, engineer. Estab. 1980. Produces 15 singles, 20 12″ singles, 12 LPs, 18 EPs and 20 CDs/year. Fee derived from outright fee from recording artist.
How to Contact: Call first and obtain permission to submit. Prefers cassette with 3 songs and lyric sheet. SASE. Reports in 3 weeks.
Music: Mostly **alternative**, **punk** and **rock**. Produced *Home Improvements*, written and recorded by Fluf on Cargo/Head Hunter Records (alternative); "Boil That Dust Speck," written and recorded by Mike Keneally on Guitar Recordings (alternative); and *Shrunken Head*, written and recorded by Dead Bolt on Cargo/Head Hunter Records (alternative). Other artists include aMiniature (Restless), Further (BMG) and 3 Mile Pilot (Cargo).
Tips: "Know what direction you are going in and be able to take constructive criticism."

DUANE MUSIC, INC., 382 Clarence Ave., Sunnyvale CA 94086. (408)739-6133. President: Garrie Thompson. Record producer and music publisher. Fee derived from sales royalty.
• See their listing in the Music Publishers section.
How to Contact: Prefers cassette with 1-2 songs. SASE. Reports in 1 month.
Music: **Blues**, **country**, **rock**, **soul** and **top 40/pop**. Produced "Wichita," on Hush Records (country); and "Syndicate of Sound," on Buddah Records (rock).

J.D. DUDICK, 6472 Seven Mile, South Lyon MI 48178. Phone/fax: (810)486-0505. Producer: J.D. Dudick. Record producer. Estab. 1990. Produces 10 singles and 3 CDs/year. Fee derived from sales royalty when song or artist is recorded or outright fee from recording artist or record company.
• J.D. Dudick's publishing company, Al-Ky Music, is listed in the Music Publishers section, and his record label, Ruffcut Productions, is in the Record Companies section.
How to Contact: Submit demo tape by mail. Unsolicited submissions are OK. Prefers cassette (or VHS videocassette) with 3 songs and lyric sheet. Does not return material. Reports in 2 months.
Music: Mostly **modern rock**, **country rock** and **alternative**; also **funk/pop** and **country**. Produced *Something For Everyone* (by Bil Tol), recorded by Cidyzoo on Vehicle Garage Records (rock); *Mind Dust* (by Chris Pierce), recorded by "Q" (modern rock); and *Am I Different Enuf* (by Laya Phelps), recorded by Laya, both on Ruffcut Records.

E.S.R. PRODUCTIONS, 40, Camperdown Terrace, Exmouth Devon EX8 1EQ **UK**. (01395)223577. Contact: John Greenslade. Record producer and record company (E.S.R.). Estab. 1965. Produces 4 singles and 10 LPs/year. Fee derived from sales royalty when song or artist is recorded.
• See the listing for E.S.R. Records in the Record Companies section.
How to Contact: Submit demo tape by mail. Unsolicited submissions are OK. Prefers cassette with 4 songs and lyric sheet. SAE and IRC. Reports in 3 weeks.
Music: Mostly **country**, **pop** and **R&B**. Produced "You Take My Love" and *Love Songs* (by J. Greenslade), recorded by Geri Ellen; and "Hey Lady" (by J. Greenslade), recorded by Johnny Solo, all on E.S.R. Records. Other artists include Caz Barron and Johnny Ramone.

EARMARK AUDIO, P.O. Box 196, Vashon WA 98070. (206)463-1980. Owner: Jerry Hill. Record producer. Estab. 1991. Produces 3 cassettes and 3 CDs/year. Fee derived from outright fee from recording artist.
How to Contact: Submit demo tape by mail. Unsolicited submissions are OK. Prefers cassette (or VHS videocassette) with 1 song and lead sheet. Does not return material.
Music: Mostly **rock**, **polka**, **contemporary** and **country**. Produced *Across the Plains Polka* (by Vern Meisner), recorded by Lyle and Lynn Schaefer (polka); *Troubled Hero*, written and recorded by Peter Morrow (modern) on Vestige Records; and *True Vine* (by True Vine), recorded by Jay Munger (Christian rock). Other artists include Randy Greco, Julie Hanson, Sylvia Storaasli and Smelter/Neves.

LEO J. EIFFERT, JR., Box 5412, Buena Park CA 90620. (619)245-2920. Owner: Leo J. Eiffert, Jr. Record producer, music publisher (Eb-Tide Music/BMI, Young Country Music/BMI) and record company (Plain Country). Estab. 1967. Produces 15-20 singles and 5 LPs/year. Fee derived from sales royalty when song or artist is recorded.

• Leo J. Eiffert, Jr.'s management firm, Crawfish Productions, is listed in the Managers and Booking Agents section.

How to Contact: Submit demo tape by mail. Unsolicited submissions are OK. Prefers cassette with 2-3 songs, lyric and lead sheet. SASE. Reports in 3-4 weeks.

Music: Mostly **country** and **gospel**. Produced "Daddy I Know," written and recorded by Pam Bellows on Plain Country Records; "Little Miss," written and recorded by Johnny Horton; and "My Friend," written and recorded by Leo J. Eiffert Jr., both on Young Country Records. Other artists include Homemade, Crawfish Band, Brandi Holland and David Busson.

Tips: "Just keep it real country."

EIGHT BALL MIDI & VOCAL RECORDING, 1250 NE 33rd Court, Pompano Beach FL 33064. (305)785-5248. Studio/Production Manager: Peter Brown. Record producer, record company (8 Ball) and engineer and demo facility. Estab. 1990. Produced 10-20 singles/year. Fee derived from outright fee from recording artist or record company.

How to Contact: Write or call first to arrange personal interview. Prefers cassette or DAT with 3-5 songs and lyric sheet. "We're not that big a deal here. We're a small business and welcome phone calls from prospective clients. Let's talk before you submit material." Does not return material. Reports in 3-4 weeks.

Music: Mostly **R&B jazz crossover**, **global big band** and **ethnic/Latino/Middle Eastern**; also **pop/ rock/fusion contemporary ballads**, **elemental/New Age** and **world music**. Produced *For Driving Only*, "Another Sunny Day" and "Drive By" (by Peter Brown), all recorded by Donna Peterson on 8 Ball Records. Other artists include Alec Kassaam and Rob Banks.

ESQUIRE INTERNATIONAL, Box 6032, Station B, Miami FL 33101-6032. (305)547-1424. President: Jeb Stuart. Record producer, music publisher and management firm. Produces 6 singles and 2 LPs/year. Fee derived from sales royalty or independent leasing of masters and placing songs.

• Esquire International's publishing company, Jeb Stuart Music, has a listing in the Music Publishers section.

How to Contact: Submit demo tape by mail. Unsolicited submissions are OK. Prefers cassette or disc with 2-4 songs and lead sheet. SASE. Reports in 1 month.

Music: **Blues**, **church/religious**, **country**, **dance**, **gospel**, **jazz**, **rock**, **soul** and **top 40/pop**. Produced "Go to Sleep, Little Baby" (by Jeb Stuart), recorded by Cafidia and Jeb Stuart; "Guns Guns (No More Guns)" and "No One Should Be Alone on Christmas," both written and recorded by Jeb Stuart, all on Esquire Int'l Records. Other artists include Moments Notice and Night Live.

Tips: "When sending out material make sure it is well organized, put together as neatly as possible and is of good sound quality."

THE ETERNAL SONG AGENCY, 6326 E. Livingston Ave., Suite 153, Reynoldsburg OH 43068. (614)868-9162. Executive Producer: Leopold Xavier Crawford. Record producer, record company and music publisher (Fragrance Records, Song of Solomon Records, Emerald Records, Lilly Records Ancient of Days Music, Anastacia Music). Estab. 1986. Produces 7-15 singles and 5 CDs/year. Fee derived from sales royalty when song or artist is recorded or outright fee from recording artist or record company.

How to Contact: Write first and obtain permission to submit. Prefers cassette (or videocassette) with 3 songs and lyric or lead sheet. "Send complete biography, pictures, tape. Type all printed material. Professionalism of presentation will get you an ear with us." SASE. Reports in 4-6 weeks.

Music: Mostly **pop music/top 40**, **country** and **instrumental**; also **contemporary Christian**, **Christian inspirational** and **southern gospel music**. Produced "Jesus" (by Leopold Crawford), recorded by Debbie Butsko; *Through Edens Eyes*, written and recorded by Leopold Crawford, both on Fragrance Records; and *Wings of the Wind*, written and recorded by Streets of Gold on Cathedral Sound Records. Other artists include Bloodbought, Provision and Tony and Gail Calloway.

Tips: "Develop people skills, be professional, be flexible, work hard, never stop learning."

EVOLVING PRODUCTIONS, 8850 Serrano Way, Kelseyville CA 95451. (707)277-7211. Owner/ President: Christopher Grinstead. Record producer and music publisher. Estab. 1987. Produces 2-4 singles, 3-6 cassettes and 2-3 CDs/year.

How to Contact: Submit demo tape by mail. Unsolicited submissions are OK. Prefers cassette or VHS videocassette with 2-6 songs and lyric sheet. "Supply SASE for return of material. Make sure phone number and address are on all cassettes and videos." SASE. Reports in 1-2 months.

Music: Mostly **A/C**, **MOR** and **country**; also **folk**, **pop/jazz** and **light rock**. Produced *Formations* and *So Much More*, written and recorded by Christopher Grinstead. Other artists include Ibhara Brothers, Brakes, Roxie and Bill Schmidt.

Tips: "I prefer to work with serious and professional songwriters and musicians. Make your packages and presentations appear professional. An amateur-looking package can hinder your initial presentation."

DOUG FAIELLA PRODUCTIONS, 19153 Paver Barnes Rd., Marysville OH 43040-8838. (513)644-8295. President: Doug Faiella. Record producer, music publisher (Doug Faiella Publishing/ BMI), record company (Studio 7 Records) and recording studio. Estab. 1984. Produces 10 singles and 5 LPs/year. Fee derived from outright fee from recording artist. "Charges a flat rate per song."
 • Doug Faiella Publishing is listed in the Music Publishers section.
How to Contact: Write first and obtain permission to submit. Include SASE. Prefers cassette with 3 songs and lyric sheets. Reports in 4 weeks.
Music: Mostly **country**, **gospel** and **rock**. Produced *Arize* (by Jeff Smith/Chris Smith/Mike Brookover), recorded by Arize on Arize Records (gospel rock); *Yesterday Country*, recorded by Dago Red on Studio 7 Records (country); and *VanScyocs*, recorded by Jim and Helen VanSyoc on VanSyoc Records (gospel).

DANNY FEDERICI'S SHARK RIVER MUSIC, 421 N. Rodeo Dr., Suite 15-5, Beverly Hills CA 90210. Phone/fax: (714)821-1810. Vice President: Bob Reed. Record producer, music publisher and new artist development and management. Estab. 1994. Fee derived by "case by case arrangement."
 • Danny Federici also has a listing in the Managers and Booking Agents section.
How to Contact: Write or call first and obtain permission to submit or to arrange personal interview. Prefers cassette, DAT or VHS videocassette with 3 songs, lyric sheet and performer(s) bio. "Include address and phone of contact person and SASE. Please copyright material." Does not return material. Reports in 3-4 weeks.
Music: Mostly **rock**, **country** and **R&B/soul**; also **alternative** and **New Age**.
Tips: "You must have a strong desire to succeed in this business and be willing to use the constructive criticism of others to achieve that success. As founding member of the E Street Band, Danny Federici's years of recording and touring with Bruce Springsteen, as well as Dave Edmunds and others, have given him experience, expertise and insight into all facets of the music business."

VITO FERA PRODUCTIONS, 345 Sprucewood Rd., Lake Mary FL 32746-5917. (407)321-3702. Fax: (407)321-2361. President, A&R: Vito Fera. Office Manager: Rhonda Fera. Record producer, music publisher (NSP Publishing/ASCAP, Fera Music Publishing/BMI). Estab. 1980. Produces 5 singles, 1 LP and 4 EPs/year. Fee derived from sales royalty when song or artist is recorded.
 • Vito Fera's publishing company, NSP Publishing, can be found in the Music Publishers section.
How to Contact: Submit demo tape by mail. Unsolicited submissions are OK. Prefers cassette or VHS videocassette with 3 songs maximum and lyric sheet. "Package song material carefully. To avoid damage to your tape, stamp or write *Please Hand Cancel* on the package. Always label (name, address and phone) both cassette and lyric sheets. Bio and photo helpful." SASE. Reports in 4-8 weeks.
Music: Mostly **jazz**, **R&B** and **rock/light**; also **children's**, **Christian** and **soundtracks**. Produced "The Magic is Hot" (by Vito Fera), recorded by The Neighbors (rock); "Two Can Play Your Game" (by M.L. Wolfgang/V. Fera), recorded by Judy Soto (country); and "Summer Dream" (by Jim Ivins) recorded by Zaughn Ivins (ballad), all on Spin Records. Other artists include Steve Clarke, Kari Regragui, Keith Hilley and Jerry Dean.
Tips: "Have songs that tell stories with simple hook lines and memorable melodies."

FINAL MIX MUSIC, (formerly Another Level Music Productions), 2219 W. Olive Ave., Suite 102, Burbank CA 91506. (818)840-9000. Contact: Rob Chiarelli. Record producer, record company (Metro Beat Records) and music publisher (Roachi World Music). Estab. 1989. Releases 12 singles, 3-5 LPs and 3-5 CDs/year. Fee derived from sales royalty when song or artist is recorded or outright fee from record company.
How to Contact: Call first and obtain permission to submit. Prefers cassette with 3 songs. "No lyric sheets, no pictures or bios. Just the cassette and SASE for return. Have titles, artist and contact info printed on cassette." SASE. Reports in 4-6 weeks.
Music: Most **dance**, **R&B** and **rap**. Produced *Mind Body and Song*, recorded by Jade on Giant Records; "You Know How We Do It," recorded by Ice Cube on Priority Records; and *Pronounced Jah-nay*, recorded by Zhane on Motown Records. Other artists include Queen Latifah, En Vogue, Naughty By Nature, Too Short, Boyz II Men, Dana Dane and Spice 1.

FLAIR PRODUCTIONS, 852 Glasgow Dr., Forest Park OH 45240. (513)851-5557. Director of Production: Craig R. Stevens. Director of Engineering: Thorold E. Todd. Record producer, recording studio and production company. Estab. 1985. Produces 10 LPs and 5 CDs/year. Fee derived from outright fee from recording artist.

How to Contact: Submit demo tape by mail. Unsolicited submissions are OK. Prefers cassette with no more than 10 songs and lyric sheet. "All material reviewed but not returned without SASE." Reports in 6 weeks.
Music: Mostly **country, gospel** and **R&B**; also **folk, blues** and **jazz**. Produced *Risin' Child*, written and recorded by Craig Stevens on Platinum Plus Records (gospel); *Just Another Demo*, written and recorded by Jeff Sample (Christian); and *Heart String Music* (by Tedd Swormstedt), recorded by James Breedwell (country). Other artists include Cynthia Richardson and David Tracy.
Tips: "Be willing to write, re-write and work hard. Don't be afraid of your own material."

BOB SCOTT FRICK, 404 Bluegrass Ave., Madison TN 37115. (615)865-6380. Contact: Bob Scott Frick. Record producer and music publisher (Frick Music Publishing). Estab. 1958. Produces 12 singles, 30 12″ singles and 30 LPs.
 ● Frick Music Publishing can be found in the Music Publishers section, Bob Scott Frick Enterprises is in the Managers and Booking Agents section and R.E.F. Records can be found in the Record Companies section.
How to Contact: Submit demo tape by mail. Unsolicited submissions are OK. Write first and obtain permission to submit.
Music: Produced "I Found Jesus in Nashville," recorded by Bob Scott Frick; "Love Divine," recorded by Backwoods; and "A Tribute," recorded by Visionheirs on R.E.F. (gospel). Other artists include Larry Ahlborn, Bob Myers Family, David Barton, The Mattingleys, Partners In Praise and Jim Pommert.

JACK GALE, Box 630755, Miami FL 33163. (305)935-4880. Fax: (305)933-4007. Contact: Jack Gale. Record producer, music publisher (Cowabonga Music/ASCAP, Lovey Music) and record company (Playback Records). Estab. 1983. Produces 48 singles and 20 CDs/year. Fee derived from sales royalty when song or artist is recorded.
 ● Jack Gale's publishing company, Lovey Music, can be found in the Music Publishers section, and his record label, Playback, is listed in the Record Companies section.
How to Contact: Submit demo tape by mail. Unsolicited submissions are OK. Prefers cassette (or VHS videocassette if available) with 2 songs maximum and lyric sheet. Does not return material. Reports in 2 weeks if interested.
Music: Mostly **contemporary country** and **country crossover**. Produced "Take This Job and Shove It" (by David Allen Coe), recorded by Johnny Paycheck (country); *Makin' Music* (by J. Barnes), recorded by Willie Nelson/Charlie Louvin/Waylon Jennings (country); and "Guess Things Happen That Way" (by Jack Clements), recorded by Johnny Cash/Tommy Cash (country), all on Playback Records. Other artists include Jeannine C. Riley, Melba Montgomery, Cleve Francis, Ernie Ashworth, Riley Coyle, David Frizzell, Margo Smith, Sammi Smith and Del Reeves.
Tips: "Send clean demo."

THE GLAND PUPPIES, INC., P.O. Box 376, Yorba Linda CA 92686 E-mail: klopp@neurosun.medsch.ucla.edu. President: Rikki Rockett. Record producer. Estab. 1989. Produces 7-10 singles and 2 LPs/year. Fee derived from sales royalty when song or artist is recorded.
How to Contact: Submit demo tape by mail. Unsolicited submissions are OK. Prefers cassette with 4-8 songs and lyric sheet. SASE. Reports in 2-3 months.
Music: Mostly **New Age, pop/dance** and **folk** songs; also **comedy, gypsy/dance** and **thrash metal**. Produced *Me, Myself and It*, written and recorded by Hemorrhoy Rogers (techno); *Listen to the Toilet* (by Fardel), recorded by Bill Harris (country); and *Deus X Cheesee* (by the Shitmonks), recorded by Joe et.al. (rap), all on Retarded Records. Other artists include Plepesisio-H, Spray Monkey, Cowbotto, Jim-Jim the Bob, the Dog Catchers and Burning Mr. Lane.

GLOBAL ASSAULT MANAGEMENT AND CONSULTING, 639 Garden Walk Blvd., #1632, College Park GA 30349. (707)994-1770. Producer/Engineer: David Norman. Record producer. Estab. 1986. Produces 6 singles, 5 LPs, 5 EPs and 4 CDs/year. Fee derived from outright fee from recording artist or record company.
How to Contact: Write first and obtain permission to submit. Prefers cassette with 5 songs. "Please send photo." SASE. Reports in 2 weeks.
Music: Mostly **funk** and **R&B**; also **techno**. Produced AC Black on Motown Records. Engineer for Peabo Bryson, Arrested Development, The Neville Bros. and Aaron Neville. Provides industry consultation for independent artists, management firms, record labels, and recording studios.

GOODKNIGHT PRODUCTIONS, 2854 Fountainhead Blvd., Melbourne FL 32935. Partners: Greg Vadimsky, Flip Dahlenburg. Record producer. Estab. 1992. Produces 4 acts per year. Produces demos and finished masters for artists and labels. Fee derived from outright fee from recording artist.

How to Contact: Submit demo tape by mail. Unsolicited submissions are OK. Prefers cassette with 3 songs and lyric sheet. Please fully detail budget, goals of project, deadlines, etc. SASE. Reports in 2 weeks.
Music: Mostly **pop** and **film music**. Produced soundtrack music for the films "In No Sense Lost," on Mendonca Records; "Mid-Life Crisis," on Wildcat Records; and "Motive" on Genie Records, all written and recorded by Greg Vadimsky. Other artist include Garrett Louis, Spectre and Greg Roberts.
Tips: "We are always looking for artists who have potential but need an experienced, patient ear in order to achieve the best possible recording. Please follow our submission instructions as closely as you can."

GUESS WHO?? PRODUCTIONS, 140-23 Einstein Loop North, Bronx NY 10475-4903. (718)671-1846. Director: David Pellot. Record producer. Estab. 1988. Produces 10-15 singles/year. Fee derived from sales royalty or outright fee from recording artist or record company. "May charge in advance for services, depending on deal made with artist or songwriter."
How to Contact: Submit demo tape by mail. Unsolicited submissions are OK. Include biography, résumé and picture if available. Prefers cassette and lyric sheet. Does not return material. Reports in 4-6 weeks.
Music: Mostly **house**, **rap** and **hip hop**; also **ballads**, **top 40/dance** and **R&B**.
Tips: "Please send only the type of music requested and submit a neat, professional package with a good quality demo."

HAILING FREQUENCY MUSIC PRODUCTIONS, 7438 Shoshone Ave., Van Nuys CA 91406. (818)881-9888. Fax: (818)881-0555. President: Lawrence Weisberg. Record producer, record company (Blowin' Smoke Records) and music publisher (Hailing Frequency Publishing). Estab. 1992. Produces 3 LPs and 3 CDs/year. Fee derived from sales royalty when song or artist is recorded or outright fee from artist.
   • See the listing for Blowin' Smoke Productions in the Managers and Booking Agents section.
How to Contact: Write or call first and obtain permission to submit a demo. Prefers cassette or VHS ½" videocassette. "Write or print legibly with complete contact instructions." SASE. Reports in 3-4 weeks.
Music: Mostly **contemporary R&B**, **blues** and **blues-rock**; also **songs for film**, **jingles for commercials** and **gospel (contemporary)**. Produced *Get the Urge!* (by Mark Will/Larry Knight), recorded by The Urge (alternative); *Bayou Blues* (by various), recorded by Carolyn Basley (blues/R&B); and *Too Hot!* (by Larry Knight/Aina Olsen), recorded by Larry Knight (R&B), all on Blowin' Smoke Records. Other artists include Raelene Romano and the Fabulous Smokettes.
Tips: "Always continue to be productive. If you submit material and it doesn't get placed or produced continue to write and put your songs down on tape!"

*HARLOW SOUND, 31 Harlow Crescent, Rexdale, Ontario M9V 2Y6 **Canada**. (416)241-0165. Owner/Engineer: Gregory English. Record producer, recording studio. Estab. 1984. Produces 15-25 CDs/year. Fees derived from outright fee from recording artist.
How to Contact: Write or call first to arrange personal interview. Prefers cassette or DAT with 3-5 songs. SAE and IRC. Reports in 1-3 weeks.
Music: Produced *Sing or Die*, written and recorded by Courage of Lassie; *Beyond 7*, written and recorded by Gordon Deppe; and *Random Order*, written and recorded by Random Order. Other artists include Viciousphere, Andy Curren.
Tips: "Be prepared for changes. Example: have three or four different choruses for any given song and be willing to try different things in the studio."

HAWORTH PRODUCTIONS, Box 1446, Laurie MO 65038. (314)374-1111. President/Producer: Dann E. Haworth. Record producer and music publisher (Southern Most Publishing/BMI). Estab. 1985. Produces 5 singles, 3 12" singles, 10 LPs, 5 EPs and 10 CDs/year. Fee derived from sales royalty when song or artist is recorded.
   • Haworth Productions' publishing company, Southern Most Publishing, is listed in the Music Publishers section.
How to Contact: Write first and obtain permission to submit. Prefers cassette or 7½ ips reel-to-reel with 3 songs and lyric or lead sheets. SASE. Reports in 6-8 weeks.
Music: Mostly **rock**, **country** and **gospel**; also **jazz**, **R&B** and **New Age**. Produced *Christmas Joy* (by Esther Kreak) on Serene Sounds Records. Other artists include The Hollowmen, Jordan Border, Jim Wilson, Tracy Creech and Tony Glise.
Tips: "Keep it simple and from the heart."

HEART CONSORT MUSIC, 410 First St. W., Mt. Vernon IA 52314. (319)895-8557. Manager: Catherine Lawson. Record producer, record company, music publisher. "We are a single in-house operation." Estab. 1980. Produces 2-3 CDs/year. Fee derived from sales royalty when song or artist is recorded.

How to Contact: Submit demo tape by mail. Unsolicited submissions are OK. Prefers cassette (or VHS videocassette if available) with 3 songs and 3 lyric sheets. SASE. Reports in 3 months.

Music: Mostly **jazz**, **New Age** and **contemporary**. Produced *Elena*, *Pachyderm* and *Underground*, all written and recorded by James Kennedy on Heart Consort Music (jazz).

Tips: "Be original, don't copy someone else's style. We are interested in jazz/New Age artists with quality demos and original ideas. We aim for an international market."

HICKORY LANE PUBLISHING AND RECORDING, P.O. Box 2275, Vancouver, British Columbia V6B 3W5 **Canada**. (604)987-3756. Fax: (604)987-0616. President: Chris Michaels. A&R Manager: David Rogers. Record producer, record company and music publisher. Estab. 1988. Produces 3 LPs/year. Fee derived from sales royalty when song or artist is recorded.

• See Hickory Lane's listing in the Music Publishers section.

How to Contact: Submit demo tape by mail. Unsolicited submissions are OK. Prefers cassette (or VHS videocassette if available) with 1-5 songs and lyric or lead sheet if available. SAE and IRC. Reports in 4-6 weeks.

Music: Country. Produced "Until Now" (by Steve Mitchell), recorded by Chris Michaels on Hickory Lane Records. Other artists include Steven James, Rick Kinderly and Rodney Austin.

Tips: "Send only original material, send your best. Keep vocals up front and make a professional presentation. Be patient."

HOAX PRODUCTIONS, 4220 Colfax, Suite 112, Studio City CA 91604. (818)506-8608. Fax: (818)769-4987. Producer/owner: Ross Hogarth. Record producer and recording engineer. Estab. 1987. Produces 5 singles and 10 LPs/year. Fee derived from sales royalty when song or artist is recorded, or outright fee from recording artist or record company.

How to Contact: Submit demo tape by mail. Unsolicited submissions are OK. Prefers cassette with 4-6 songs and lyric sheet. "I accept any type of material. A videotape is good for image if a cassette is also included." SASE. Reports in 2-4 weeks.

Music: Mostly **alternative**, **pop/rock** and **country**; also **world music**, **folk** and **eclectic**. Produced *Famous Last Words*, written and recorded by Al Stewart on Mesa/Blue Moon Records; *Renegade Gentleman*, written and recorded by Larry Carlton on GRP Records; and *Zydeco Party Band*, written and recorded by Zydeco Party Band on Varese/Sarabande Records. Other artists include Native Tongue, The Dakotahs and Outcast.

Tips: "Be honest, trust your instinct, do not try to be what you are not. Do not judge or compare yourself before you have had a chance to play the game. Expectations only breed disappointment."

HORRIGAN PRODUCTIONS, 26591 Briarwood Lane, San Juan Capistrano CA 92675. (714)347-8316. President/Owner: Tim Horrigan. Record producer and music publisher (Buck Young Music/BMI). Estab. 1982. Produces 5-10 singles, 3-5 LPs, 3-5 EPs and 3-5 CDs/year. Fee derived from outright fee from recording artist. "We do some work on spec but the majority of the time we work on a work-for-hire basis."

How to Contact: Submit demo tape by mail. Unsolicited submissions are OK. Prefers cassette (or VHS videocassette if available) with 1-3 songs and lyric sheets. SASE. "Please do not call first; just let your music do the talking. Will reply in 3 weeks if interested."

Music: Mostly **pop**, **rock** and **country**. Produced "The Silly Willy Workout," recorded by Brenda Colgate (children's); "Let it Shine," recorded by Jim Rule (children's); and "Gone, So Gone," recorded by Patti Shannon (country). Other artists include Mama Says (country), Nigel Kingsley (gospel), Juliet Lane (1994 "Star Search" winner) and Johnny Legend (rockabilly).

Tips: "Write from the heart with eyes on the charts."

HOUSE OF RHYTHM, 12403 Ventura Court, Suite G, Studio City CA 91604. (818)980-8887. Fax: (818)980-9111. President: Stuart Wiener. Producer: Mike Jett. Record producer and production company. Estab. 1991. Produces 3-5 singles, 3-5 12″ singles, 2 LPs, 2 EPs and 2 CDs/year. Fee derived from sales royalty when song or artist is recorded.

HOW TO GET THE MOST out of *Songwriter's Market* (at the front of this book) contains comments and suggestions to help you understand and use the information in these listings.

How to Contact: Submit demo tape by mail. Unsolicited submissions are OK. Prefers cassette with 3 songs and lyric sheet. "Do not call to follow up; if we like it we will call you." SASE. Reports in 1 month.

Music: Mostly **dance, pop, R&B** and **rock**; also **new artists** and **new producers**. Produced "The Truth" (by Mike Nally), recorded by SYSTM X on Innerkore Records (dance); "Nasty Groove" and "Lift Em" (by Mike Jett), both recorded by Cold Automatic Eyes on Crap Records (dance). Other artists include Natasha, Richard Grieco and L'Simone.

I.V.M. COMMUNICATIONS, Box 405, Rodney Ontario N0L 2C0 **Canada**. (519)785-2180. Manager: Martin Dibbs. Record producer and music publisher (Inverted Vision Music/SOCAN). Estab. 1978. Produces 4 LPs and 4 CDs/year. Fee derived from outright fee from recording artist or record company.
How to Contact: Submit demo tape by mail. Unsolicited submissions are OK. Prefers DAT or VHS videocassette with 3 songs and lyric sheet. Does not return submissions. Reports in 6 weeks.
Music: Mostly **pop/rock**, **funk/rap** and **reggae**; also **world/New Age**, **folk** and **alternative**. Produced *Memory Theatre*, written and recorded by Memory Theatre (rock); *Colourless*, written and recorded by Xpertise (funk); and *Sid Mild*, written and recorded by Sid Mild (alternative), all on IVM Records. Other artists include Denise Pelly, Chevy Blue, Charlie Clements, Arizona Geoff, Cross Currents.
Tips: "Be serious, reliable, willing to work hard. Talent would be nice too! Sense of humour also highly recommended."

INTRIGUE PRODUCTION, 6245 Bristol Pkwy., Suite 206, Culver CA 90230. (213)417-3084, ext. 206. Producer: Larry McGee. Record producer and record company (Intrigue Productions). Estab. 1986. Produces 6 singles, 3 12″ singles, 1 LP, 4 EPs and 2 CDs/year. Fee derived from sales royalty when song or artist is recorded.
  • See the listings for Operation Perfection in the Music Publishers section, Boogie Band Records in the Record Companies section and LMP Management Firm in the Managers and Booking Agents section.
How to Contact: Write first and obtain permission to submit. Prefers cassette or reel-to-reel (or VHS videocassette if available) with 1-4 songs and lyric sheets. "Please put your strongest performance upfront. Select material based on other person's opinions." SASE. Reports in 2 months.
Music: Mostly **R&B**, **pop**, **rap** and **rock**; also **dance** and **A/C**. Produced "Starflower" (by Joe Cacamisse), recorded by Starflower (A/C); "Too Tough" (by Terrence Jones), recorded by En-Tux (pop); and "Got It Going On" (by Alan Walker), recorded by Executives (R&B), all on Cross-Over Records. Other artists include Wali Ali, A. Vis and Denise Parker.
Tips: "Keep up with the latest song structures and the latest technology."

IVORY PRODUCTIONS, INC., 212 N. 12th St., Suite #3, Philadelphia PA 19107. (215)977-9777. Fax: (215)569-4939. Contact: Vincent Kershner, David Ivory. Record producer. Estab. 1986. Produces 10 CDs/year. Fee derived from "varying proportions of outright fee and royalties."
  • See the listing for Rage-N-Records in the Record Companies section.
How to Contact: Submit demo tape by mail. Unsolicited submissions are OK. Prefers cassette with 3 songs. SASE. Reports in 6-8 weeks.
Music: Mostly **rock** and **pop**. Produced *Excess In Moderation*, written and recorded by Pat Godwin on Blood Records (rock); and *Tony White*, written and recorded by Tony White on D.A. Music (jazz); and "Do You Want More?," written and recorded by The Roots on Geffen Records. Other artists include Steve LaRocca & Billy Freeze, Jimmy Bruno, The Spelvins, Crossbone Pie, Don Himlin, Iota, Do Or Die, Slide, The Peaks, O.M.S.F. and Black Harvest.
Tips: "For examples of our production work via the Internet reach us at rage@netaxs.com."

*JAG STUDIO, LTD., 3801-C Western Blvd., Raleigh NC 27606. (919)821-2059. Record producer, music publisher (Electric Juice Tunes/BMI), record company (JAG Records) and recording studio. Estab. 1981. Produces 12 singles and 8 CDs/year. Fee derived from outright fee from recording artist or record company.
How to Contact: Write first and obtain permission to submit. Does not return material. Reports in 1-2 months.
Music: Mostly **pop/dance**, **rap** and **rock**; also **country** and **gospel**. Produced *Lord of the Underworld* (by Black Sabbath), recorded by COC (rock); *Plymouth Rock*, written and recorded by Modern Pilgrims on Pilgrim Records (rock); and *Seekers & Finders*, written and recorded by Jamie Pahl on Mission Entertainment (rock). Other artists include Cry of Love, Johnny Quest, Bad Checks, John Custer, Ellen Harlow, Stacy Jackson, Doug Jervey, Larry Hutcherson, Automatic Slim and Six String Drag.
Tips: "Be prepared. Learn something about the *business* end of music first."

NEAL JAMES PRODUCTIONS, P.O. Box 121626, Nashville TN 37212. (615)726-3556. President: Neal James. Record producer, music publisher (Cottage Blue Music/BMI, Neal James Music/

BMI) and record company (Kottage Records). Estab. 1971. Produces 16 singles and 4 CDs and LPs/year. Fee derived from sales royalty when song or artist is recorded or outright fee from recording artist or record company.

• Neal James' publishing company, Cottage Blue Music, is listed in the Music Publishers section, his record label, Kottage Records, is listed in the Record Companies section and his management firm, James Gang Management, is listed in the Managers and Booking Agents section.

How to Contact: Submit demo tape by mail. Unsolicited submissions are OK. Prefers cassette (or VHS videocassette if available) with 2 songs and lyric sheet. SASE. Reports in 1 month.

Music: Mostly **country, pop/rock** and **R&B**; also **gospel, alternative** and **blues**. Produced *What Do Ya Say*, written and recorded by Jay S. Kay on Alternative Records; "Love Don't Lie" (by James/Lee), recorded by Deuces Wild on NJO Records; and "Country Girl," written and recorded by Scott Dawson on Crosswind Records. Other artists include Allen Hayes, Alan Height, Taylor Reed Band, Allusion Band, Artica and Bill Fraser.

SUNNY JAMES, 1051 Saxonburg Blvd., Glenshaw PA 15116. (412)487-6565. Producer: Sunny James. Record producer, music publisher, record company (Golden Triangle). Estab. 1987. Produces 2 singles, 8 12″ singles and 9 CDs/year. Fee derived from sales royalty when song or artist is recorded.

• See the listing for Golden Triangle Records in the Record Companies section.

How to Contact: Submit demo tape by mail—unsolicited submissions are OK. Prefers cassette, 15 ips reel-to-reel (or ½″ VHS videocassette if available) with 3 songs and lyric or lead sheet. Does not return material. Reports in 2 weeks.

Music: Mostly **R&B, country** or **rock**; also **A/C** and **jazz**. Produced "Miss Nellie" (by S. James), recorded by Marcia Astorialo on Golden Triangle Records; "Slippery Rocks," written and recorded by Robin Gretnick on Rockin' Robin Records; and "Here We Go Again" (by James/Harp), recorded by The Marcels on Golden Triangle Records. Other artists include Bobby Wayne (Atlantic Records), Steve Grice (The Boxtops), The Original Marcels, Bingo Mundy, Cornelius Harp, Fred Johnson, Richard Knauss, Brian (Badfinger) McClain and City Heat.

ALEXANDER JANOULIS PRODUCTIONS, 1957 Kilburn Dr., Atlanta GA 30324. (404)662-6661. CEO: Alex Janoulis. Record producer. Produces 6 singles and 2 CDs/year. Fee derived from sales royalty or outright fee from recording artist or record company.

How to Contact: Write first and obtain permission to submit. "Letters should be short, requesting submission permission." Prefers cassette with 1-3 songs. "Tapes will not be returned without SASE." Reports in 2 months.

Music: Mostly **top 40, rock** and **pop**; also **black** and **disco**. Produced *Hurricane Blues* (by R. Wilson/A. Janoulis), recorded by Roger Hurricane Wilson; *Blues in Dixieland* and *Poor Man Shuffle* (by R. Page), recorded by Bob Page Project, all on Hottrax Records. Other artists include Night Shadows, Starfoxx, Sheffield-Webb, Splatter and Big Al Jano.

*JANUS MANAGEMENT, 54A Brookmount Rd., Toronto Ontario M4L 3N2 **Canada**. Phone/fax: (416)698-6581. Producer/Engineer: Nick Blagona. Record producer. Estab. 1991. Produces 8 cassettes, 2 EPs, 6 CDs/year. Fee derived from outright fee from recording artist or record company, or reduced fee in form of advance from record company and small sales royalties.

How to Contact: Submit demo tape by mail. Unsolicited submissions are OK. Prefers cassette, DAT, VHS videocassette, promotional materials and lyric/lead sheet (if applicable). "Please include all applicable lyrics (typed)." SASE. Reports in 2-4 weeks.

Music: Mostly **rock, jazz** and **folk**; also **classical** and **filmscoring**. Produced *Naked Research* (by T. Warren), recorded by Naked Research on A&M Records (pop); *Singing Naked*, written and recorded by G. Koller/J. Michels (jazz); and *Mitchell's Corners*, written and recorded by Mitchell's Corners (folk rock). Other artists include Deep Purple, Kim Mitchell, April Wine.

Tips: "Don't close any musical doors. Never stop growing as a songwriter and performer. Only in this way will you achieve artistry."

*JAY BIRD PRODUCTIONS, 5 Highpoint Dr., RR #3, Stouffville, Ontario L4A 7X4 **Canada**. (905)640-4104. President: William Wallace. Record producer and music publisher (Smokey Bird Publishing). Estab. 1981. Produces 4 singles/year. Fee derived from sales royalty when song or artist is recorded or outright fee from recording artist.

How to Contact: Write first and obtain permission to submit. Prefers cassette or VHS videocassette with 3 songs and lyric sheet. Does not return material. Reports in 3 weeks.

Music: Mostly **country**; also **pop/rock**. Produced "Little Lies" (by W. Wallace), "Dreamin'" (by Steve Earle) and "Fine Line" (by W.W.H.G.), all recorded by Lawnie Wallace on MCA Records (country).

*JAY JAY PUBLISHING & RECORD CO., 35 NE 62nd St., Miami FL 33138. (305)758-0000. Owner: Walter Jagiello. Record producer, music publisher (BMI) and record company (Jay Jay Record, Tape and Video Co.). Estab. 1951. Produces 12 singles, 12 LPs and 12 CDs/year. Fee derived from sales royalty when song or artist is recorded.
How to Contact: Submit demo tape by mail. Unsolicited submissions are OK. Prefers cassette (or VHS videocassette if available) with 6 songs and lyric and lead sheet. "Quality cassette or reel-to-reel, sheet music and lyrics." SASE. Reports in 2 months.
Music: Mostly **ballads**, **love songs**, **country music** and **comedy**; also **polkas** and **waltzes**. Produced *National Hits* and *Fantastic* (by W.E. Jagiello), recorded by Li'L Wally; and *Back to the Beat* (by W.E. Jagiello), recorded by Ed Liszewski, all on Jay Jay Records. Other artists include Mil-Eu Duo, Eddie Kuta and Orchestra.

JAZMIN PRODUCTIONS, P.O. Box 92913, Long Beach CA 90809. (310)509-4470. Owner/Producer: Gregory D. Dendy. Record producer Estab. 1991. Produces 2-4 LPs/year. Fee derived from sales royalty when song or artist is recorded or outright fee from recording artist or record company.
How to Contact: Submit demo tape by mail. Unsolicited submissions are OK. Prefers cassette with lyric sheet. SASE. Reports in 2 months.
Music: Mostly **gospel**. Produced *Back to the Old School* (by various artists), recorded by Pentecostal Community Choir; and *Untitled* (by various artists), recorded by Gospel Music Workshop of America Youth Mass Choir. Other artists include Enlightment, Broderick Rice.
Tips: "A song is nothing but a bunch of words if no one ever hears it. Don't be afraid of selling your song!"

JAZZAND, 12 Micieli Place, Brooklyn NY 11218. (718)972-1220. President: Rick Stone. Record producer, music publisher and record company. Estab. 1984. Produces 1 LP/year. Fee derived from outright fee from recording artist or record company.
How to Contact: Write or call first and obtain permission to submit. Prefers cassette. Does not return material. Reports in 2 weeks.
Music: Mostly **jazz (straight ahead)**, **bebop** and **hard bop**. Produced *Blues for Nobody*, *Lullaby For Alex* and *Far East*, written and recorded by Rick Stone on Jazzand Records (jazz).
Tips: "We are only interested in acoustic, straight ahead jazz. Please do not send unsolicited demos. Call or write first!"

JERICHO SOUND LAB, Box 407, Jericho VT 05465. (802)899-3787. Owner: Bobby Hackney. Record producer, music publisher (Elect Music/BMI) and record company (LBI Records). Estab. 1988. Produces 5 singles, 2 12″ singles and 3 LPs/year. Fee derived from outright fee from recording artist or record company, or sales royalty when song or artist is recorded.
   • See the listing for Elect Music in the Music Publishers section.
How to Contact: Submit demo tape by mail. Unsolicited submissions are OK. Prefers cassette or VHS videocassette with 3-4 songs and lyric sheet. SASE. Reports in 4-6 weeks.
Music: Mostly **reggae**, **R&B** and **pop**; also **rock** and **jazz-poetry**. Produced "Natural Woman" (by B. Hackney), recorded by Lambsbread (reggae); "African Princess," written and recorded by Mikey Dread; and "Rockin in the Dance Hall" (by Trini/B. Hackney), recorded by Trini (dancehall), all on LBI Records.
Tips: "Make it plain and simple. Send only your best. Most producers know within 10 to 15 seconds if a song catches their attention."

*JGM RECORDING STUDIO, 4121 N. Laramie, Chicago IL 60641. Producer: Lito Manlucu. Record producer. Estab. 1991. Produces 1 single, 1 LP and 1 CD/year. Fee derived from sales royalty.
How to Contact: Submit demo tape by mail. Unsolicited submissions OK. Prefers cassette with 3 songs and lyric sheet. SASE. Reports in 1 month.
Music: Mostly **pop**, **R&B** and **rock**; also **foreign music** and **dance**. Produced "Blue Jean" (by Lito Manlucu), recorded by Jane Park on Independent Records (dance/pop).

JK JAM PRODUCTIONS, Saratoga Mall, Saratoga NY 12866. (518)584-9020. Director of A&R: Jamie Keats. Record producer and music publisher (JK Jam Music). Estab. 1990. Fee derived from sales royalty when song or artist is recorded, or outright fee from recording artist.

MARKET CONDITIONS are constantly changing! If you're still using this book and it is 1998 or later, buy the newest edition of *Songwriter's Market* at your favorite bookstore or order directly from Writer's Digest Books.

• See the listing for JK Jam Music in the Music Publishers section.
How to Contact: Call first and obtain permission to submit. Prefers cassette with 4 songs. "Mastered quality recordings only." Does not return material. Reports in 1-2 months.
Music: Mostly **alternative**, **R&B/dance** and **rock**; also **pop/country**. Produced *Paul Traudt*, written and recorded by Paul Traudt (alternative); *Doug Lawler*, written and recorded by Doug Lawler (pop/country); and *Tommy Higgins*, written and recorded by Tommy Higgins (rock), all on JK Jam Productions.
Tips: "Maintain originality. Don't be conditioned by proven formulas. Master your timing and performance. Let us tailor your sound for today's market."

LITTLE RICHIE JOHNSON, P.O Box 3, Belen NM 87002. (505)864-7441. Contact: Tony Palmer. Record producer, music publisher and record company (LRJ). Estab. 1959. Produces 6 singles, 3 12″ singles, 6 CDs and 6 LPs/year. Fee derived from sales royalty when song or artist is recorded.
• Little Richie Johnson's publishing company, Little Richie Johnson Music, is listed in the Music Publishers section; his management firm, Little Richie Johnson Agency, is listed in the Managers and Booking Agents section; and his record label, LRJ, is listed in the Record Companies section.
How to Contact: Write first and obtain permission to submit. Prefers cassette with 4 songs. SASE. Reports in 6 weeks.
Music: Mostly **country**. Produced *Moonlight, Roses and the Wine* (by Jerry Jaramillo), recorded Gabe Neito; *Ship of Fools*, recorded by Reta Lee; and *Honky Tonk Cinderella*, written and recorded by Jerry Jaramillo, all on LRJ Records. Other artists include Alan Godage.

RALPH D. JOHNSON, Dept. SM, 114 Catalpa Dr., Mt. Juliet TN 37122. (615)754-2950. President: Ralph D. Johnson. Record producer, music publisher (Big Wedge Music) and record company. Estab. 1960. Produces 10 singles/year. Fee derived from sales royalty.
How to Contact: Submit demo tape by mail. Unsolicited submissions are OK. Prefers cassette with maximum of 4 songs. SASE. Reports in 2 weeks.
Music: Mostly **country** and **novelty**. Produced "Boogie Man" (by Roy August/Willie Beery), recorded by Stacy Edwards; "Two Steppin Into My Heart" (by Roy August/Willie Beery), recorded by Keith Bryant; and "We Are Gonna Raise the Ole Barn Tonight" (by Roy August), recorded by Karey Osborne, all on Wedge Records. Other artists include Cindy Jackson, Calmus Sisters and Kathy Johnson.
Tips: "Have a good demo and typed lyric sheets."

JUNE PRODUCTIONS LTD., "Toftrees," Church Rd., Woldingham, Surrey CR3 7JH **England**. Managing Director: David Mackay. Record producer, music producer (Sabre Music) and record company (Tamarin, PRT Records). Estab. 1970. Produces 6 singles, 3 LPs and 3 CDs/year. Fee derived from sales royalty.
How to Contact: Submit demo tape by mail. Unsolicited submissions are OK. Prefers cassette with 1-2 songs and lyric sheet. SAE and IRC. Reports in 6 weeks.
Music: **MOR**, **rock** and **top 40/pop**. Produced *Sarah Jory* (by various), recorded by Sarah Jory on Ritz Records (country rock); *The Western Movies CD* (by various), cast recording on K-Tel Records (country rock); and *Access All Areas* (by the Kruger Bros./John Parr), recorded by the Kruger Bros. on Blue Martin Records (rock). Other artists include Jon English, Jeff Turner and John Parr.

KAREN KANE PRODUCER/ENGINEER, 17 Bodwin Ave., Toronto, Ontario M6P 1S4 **Canada**. (416)760-7896. Fax: (416)766-0453. Contact: Karen Kane. Record producer and recording engineer. Estab. 1978. Produces 5-10 singles and 5-10 CDs/year. Fee derived from outright fee from recording artist or record company and sales royalty.
How to Contact: Write first and obtain permission to submit. Unsolicited submissions are *not* OK. Does not return material. Reports in 2 weeks.
Music: Mostly **pop**, **alternative**, **R&B/reggae** and **acoustic**. Produced *Shape Shifters*, written and recorded by Ubaka Hill on Ladyslipper Records (African percussion); *Notes After the Rainstorm*, written and recorded by Vivianne LaRiviere; and *Different from the Rest*, written and recorded by Linda Worster (pop/acoustic). Other artists include Ken Dunn, April K. and Kiya Heartwood.
Tips: "Get proper funding to do your projects right."

MATTHEW KATZ PRODUCTIONS, 29903 Harvester Rd., Malibu CA 90265. (310)457-4844. President: Matthew Katz. Record producer, music publisher (After You Publishing/BMI) and record company (San Francisco Sound, Malibu Records). Produces 6 singles, 6 12″ singles and 2 CDs/year. Fee derived from sales royalty when song or artist is recorded, or outright fee from record company.
How to Contact: Submit demo tape by mail. Unsolicited submissions are OK. Prefers cassette (or 8mm videocassette) and lead sheet. Does not return material.

Music: Mostly **rock** and **country**. Produced Jefferson Airplane, Moby Grape, It's A Beautiful Day, Indian Puddin' & Pipe, Fraternity of Man and Tim Hardin.
Tips: "We're interested in original New Age material for Malibu Records and message songs. Not interested in 'Why is she making it with some other guy, not me?' "

GENE KENNEDY ENTERPRISES, INC., 3950 N. Mt. Juliet Rd., Mt. Juliet TN 37122. (615)754-0417. President: Gene Kennedy. Vice President: Karen Jeglum Kennedy. Record producer, independent distribution and promotion firm and music publisher (Chip 'N' Dale Music Publishers, Inc./ASCAP, Door Knob Music Publishing, Inc./BMI and Lodestar Music/SESAC). Estab. 1975. Produces 5-10 CDs/year. Fee derived from outright fee from recording artist or record company.
How to Contact: Submit demo tape by mail. Unsolicited submissions are OK. Prefers cassette with up to 3 songs and lyric sheet. "Do not send in a way that has to be signed for." SASE (appropriate size for tapes). Reports in 2 weeks.
Music: **Country** and **gospel**. Produced *Shot In the Arm* (by Ron Kimball/Don Collins) and *Helping Hands* (by Jimmy Elledge), recorded by Christian Dawn; and *Something's Wrong* (by Buddy Godair/Ed Dickey), recorded by Olan Miller, all on Door Knob Records. Other artists include Floyd Mitchell.

*KINGSPORT CREEK MUSIC, Box 6085, Burbank CA 91510. Contact: Vice President. Record producer and music publisher.
• Kingsport Creek Music's record label, Cowgirl Records, is listed in the Record Companies section.
How to Contact: Submit demo tape by mail. Unsolicited submissions are OK. Prefers cassette (or VHS videocassette). Does not return material. "Include photo and bio if possible."
Music: Mostly **country, MOR, R&B, pop** and **gospel**. Produced "Leading Me On," "Pick Up Your Feet" and "With Me Still," all written and recorded by Melvena Kaye on Cowgirl Records.

KINGSTON RECORDS AND TALENT, 15 Exeter Rd., Kingston NH 03848. (603)642-8493. Coordinator: Harry Mann. Record producer, music publisher (Strawberry Soda Publishing/ASCAP) and record company (Kingston Records). Estab. 1988. Produces 3-4 singles, 2-3 12″ singles, 2-3 LPs and 1-2 CDs/year. Fee derived from sales royalty. Deals primarily with NE and local artists.
• See their listing in the Record Companies section.
How to Contact: Write first and obtain permission to submit. Prefers cassette with 1-2 songs and lyric sheet. Does not return material. Reports in 6-8 weeks.
Music: Mostly **rock, country** and **pop**; "no heavy metal." Produced *5¢ Strawberry Soda* and "Message To You," written and recorded by Doug Mitchell; and *Songs Piped from the Moon*, written and recorded by S. Pappas, all on Kingston Records. Other artists include Bob Moore, Candy Striper Death Orgy, Pocket Band, Jeff Walker, J. Evans, NTM and Miss Bliss.

KMA, 1650 Broadway, Suite 900, New York NY 10019-6833. (212)265-1570. A&R Director: Morris Levy. Record producer and music publisher (Block Party Music/ASCAP). Estab. 1987. Produces 2 12″ singles, 3 LPs and 3 CDs/year. Fee derived from sales royalty or outright fee from recording artist or record company.
How to Contact: Submit demo tape by mail. Prefers cassette. SASE. Reports in 3 months.
Music: Mostly **R&B, dance** and **rap**; also **movie** and **ethnic**. Produced "I Found It," recorded by Daphne on Maxi Records; "Through the Day," recorded by Millenium on 143/Atlantic Records; and "I Want You for Me," recorded by Raw Stilo on dv8/A&M Records.
Tips: *"Original* lyrics a huge plus."

KNOWN ARTIST PRODUCTIONS, 1219 Kerlin Ave., Brewton AL 36426. (334)867-2228. President: Roy Edwards. Record producer, music publisher (Cheavoria Music Co./BMI, Baitstring Music/ASCAP) and record company (Bolivia Records, Known Artist Records). Estab. 1972. Produces 10 singles and 3 LPs/year. Fee derived from sales royalty when song or artist is recorded.
• Known Artist's publishing company, Cheavoria Music, is listed in the Music Publishers section, and their record label, Bolivia Records, is in the Record Companies section.
How to Contact: "Write first about your interest." Prefers cassette with 3 songs and lyric sheet. Reports in 1 month. "All tapes will be kept on file."
Music: Mostly **R&B, pop** and **country**; also **easy listening, MOR** and **soul**. Produced "Got To Let You Know," "You Are My Sunshine" and "You Make My Life So Wonderful," all written and recorded by Roy Edwards on Bolivia Records (R&B). Other artists include Jim Portwood, Bobbie Roberson and Brad Smiley.
Tips: "Write a good song that tells a good story."

KOOL BREEZE PRODUCTIONS, N. 81 Lane, P.O. Box 120, Loxahatchee FL 33470. (407)795-4232. Executive Director: Kevin Reeves. Marketing Manager: Debbie Reeves. Record producer, music

publisher. Estab. 1991. Produces 10 singles and 6 LPs/year. Fee derived from sales royalty when song or artist is recorded or outright fee from record company.
How to Contact: Submit demo tape by mail. Unsolicited submissions are OK. Prefers cassette and lyric sheet (typed and full size). "Commercially viable to industry standards. Strong hooks, definitive melody, uplifting lyrical concepts, SASE required for all correspondence, don't be predictable." SASE. Reports in 2 months.
Music: Mostly **pop contemporary (dance)**, **rock (pop, blues, folk, soft, jazz)**, **A/C** and **electric acoustic**; also **country (pop, blues)**, **blues (R&B, urban)** and **gospel**. Produced *Fatal Vision* (by Andy Atkins), recorded by Fatal Vision; *Dynamic Derrick and Boogie Brigade* (by Kevin Reeves), recorded by Dynamic Derrick and the Boogie Brigade, both on Kool Breeze Records; and *Jayne Reby*, written and recorded by Jayne Reby on Rustron Records.
Tips: "Always send SASE with proper postage if you want a reply."

ROBERT R. KOVACH, Box 7018, Warner Robins GA 31095-7018. (912)953-2800. Producer: Robert R. Kovach. Record producer. Estab. 1976. Produces 6 singles, 2 cassettes and 1 CD/year. Fee derived from sales royalty when song or artist is recorded.
How to Contact: Submit demo tape by mail. Unsolicited submissions are OK. Prefers cassette with 4 songs and lyric sheet. SASE. Reports in 4 months.
Music: Mostly **country** and **pop**; also **easy listening**, **R&B**, **rock** and **gospel**.

L.A. ENTERTAINMENT, 6367 Selma Ave., Hollywood CA 90028. (213)467-1411. Fax: (213)462-8562. Vice President/A&R: Glen D. Duncan. Record Producer (L.A. Entertainment), record company (Warrior Records) and music publisher (Songbroker Publishing/ASCAP). Estab. 1988. Fee derived from sales royalty when song or artist is recorded.
How to Contact: Submit demo tape by mail. Unsolicited submissions are OK. Prefers cassette (or videocassette if available) with 3 songs, lyric and lead sheet if available. "All written submitted materials (i.e. lyric sheets, letter, etc.) should be typed." SASE. Reports in 4-6 weeks.
Music: Mostly **alternative** and **R&B**.
Tips: "A hit song is a hit song, whether it is recorded in a professional environment or at your home. Concentrate first on the writing of your material and then record it to the best of your ability. A professional sounding recording may help the presentation of a song, but it will not make or break a true hit."

LANDMARK COMMUNICATIONS GROUP, P.O. Box 1444, Hendersonville TN 37077. Producer: Bill Anderson Jr. Record producer, music publisher (Newcreature Music/BMI) and TV/radio syndication. Produces 12 singles and 12 LPs/year. Fee derived from sales royalty.
● Landmark's publishing affiliate, Newcreature Music, is listed in the Music Publishers section.
How to Contact: Write first and obtain permission to submit. Prefers 7½ ips reel-to-reel or cassette (or videocassette) with 4-10 songs and lyric sheet. SASE. Reports in 1 month.
Music: Mostly **country crossover**; also **blues**, **country**, **gospel**, **jazz**, **rock** and **top 40/pop**. Produced "Good Love," written and recorded by Gail Score (R&B); "A Hero Never Dies," written and recorded by Joanne Cash Yates on Jana Records (gospel); and "Nothin' Else Feels Quite Like It" (by B. Nash/K. Nash/B. Anderson), recorded on TV Theme Records (country). Other artists include Skeeter Davis and Vernon Oxford.

LARI-JON PRODUCTIONS, 325 W. Walnut, Rising City NE 68658. (402)542-2336. Owner: Larry Good. Record producer, music publisher (Lari-Jon Publishing/BMI) and record company (Lari-Jon Records). Estab. 1967. Produces 10 singles and 5 LPs/year. Fee derived from sales royalty when song or artist is recorded.
● See the listings for Lari-Jon Publishing in the Music Publishers section, Lari-Jon Records in the Record Companies section and Lari-Jon Promotions in the Managers and Booking Agents section.
How to Contact: Submit demo tape by mail. Unsolicited submissions are OK. "Must be a professional demo." SASE. Reports in 2 months.
Music: **Country**, **gospel-Southern** and **'50s rock**. Produced "As Long As You Need Me" (by Larry Good), recorded by Tom Campbell; *Her Favorite Song*, written and recorded by Johnny Nace; and *Nebraskaland*, written and recorded by Larry Good, all on Lari-Jon Records. Other artists include Kent Thompson.
Tips: "Be professional in all aspects of the music business."

THE TYPES OF MUSIC each listing is interested in are printed in boldface.

LARK TALENT & ADVERTISING, Box 35726, Tulsa OK 74153. (918)786-8896. E-mail: janajae @aol.com. Owner: Jana Jae. Record producer, music publisher (Jana Jae Music/BMI) and record company (Lark Record Productions, Inc.). Estab. 1980. Fee derived from sales royalty when song or artist is recorded.
  • Jana Jae's publishing company, Jana Jae Music, can be found in the Music Publishers section, and her record label, Lark Records, can be found in the Record Companies section.
How to Contact: Submit demo tape by mail. Unsolicited submissions are OK. Prefers cassette or VHS videocassette with 3 songs and lead sheet. Does not return material.
Music: Mostly **country**, **bluegrass** and **classical**; also **instrumentals**. Produced "Fiddlestix" (by Jana Jae); "Mayonnaise" (by Steve Upfold); and "Flyin' South" (by Cindy Walker), all recorded by Jana Jae on Lark Records. Other artists include Sydni, Hotwire and Matt Greif.

JOHN LEAVELL, 2045 Anderson Snow, Spring Hill FL 34609. (904)799-6102. Producer: John Leavell. Record producer and recording studio. Estab. 1980. Produces 10-12 singles/year. Fee derived from outright fee from recording artist and record company.
How to Contact: Submit demo tape. Unsolicited submissions are OK. Prefers cassette (or VHS videocassette if available) with 4-5 songs and lyric sheet. SASE. Reports in 1 month.
Music: Mostly **Christian rock**, **Christian contemporary** and **gospel**; also **rock** and **country**. Produced "Sons of Thunder" (by Tom Butler), recorded by Sons of Thunder; *Mr. Hyde*, recorded by Mr. Hyde; and *Morning Star*, recorded by Morning Star, all on Leavell Records. Other artists include Greg Eadler, Jim Butler, Tom Martin, Final Stand and One Eyed Jack.
Tips: "Make the best first impression you can! Always keep writing new material."

LEEWAY ENTERTAINMENT GROUP, 100 Wilshire Blvd., 20th Floor, Santa Monica CA 90401. (310)260-6900. Fax: (310)260-6901. Branch: Leeway London, 177 High Street, Harelsden, London NW10 4TE **England**. Producer: Daniel Leeway. Record producer, music publisher, recording studios (The Leeway Studios, 32 Track Digital). Estab. 1991. Fee derived from sales royalty when song or artist is recorded, or outright fee from recording artist, unless other arrangements have been made.
How to Contact: Write or call first to arrange personal interview, or submit demo tape/CD by mail. Unsolicited submissions are OK. Prefers cassette, DAT or CD with 2 songs and lyric sheet. SASE. Reports in 1 month minimum.
Music: Mostly **dance**, **pop** and **New Age**.
Tips: "Send all submissions as though you were submitting a business proposal to an investor. We are not going to invest in you or your material if you are not willing to invest in yourself. Be well prepared, patient, and confident about your talents. We will contact you if we are interested. No phone calls please."

LINEAR CYCLE PRODUCTIONS, Box 2608, Sepulveda CA 91393-2608. Producer: R. Borowy. Record producer. Estab. 1980. Produces 15-25 singles, 6-10 12″ singles, 15-20 LPs and 10 CDs/year. Fee derived from sales royalty when song or artist is recorded.
How to Contact: Submit demo tape. Unsolicited submissions are OK. Prefers cassette or 7⅜ ips reel-to-reel (or ½″ VHS or ¾″ videocassette if available). SASE. Reports in 6 weeks to 6 months.
Music: Mostly **rock/pop**, **R&B/blues** and **country**; also **gospel** and **comedy**. Produced "Mess 'O Film" (by B. Beat), recorded by Olif Splash on Old-Art Records (alternative); "My Woodpooker And Mee" (by M. Pandancski), recorded by Ggrfaf on No Sound Records (alternative); and "She's Cryin' For My Beer" (by Dumb), recorded by Bill mcBill IV on Kuntry Records (country).
Tips: "If you can provide a demo reel on CD or high quality cassette, the more likely we'll audition it. No cheap tapes, or records!"

MICK LLOYD PRODUCTIONS, 1018 17th Ave. S., Nashville TN 37212. (615)329-9093. Fax: (615)329-9094. Administrative Assistant: Vicki Don. Record producer and music publisher. Estab. 1982. Produces 20 singles and 7 LPs/year. Fee derived from sales royalty when song or artist is recorded or outright fee from record company.
How to Contact: Submit demo tape by mail. Unsolicited submissions are OK. Prefers cassette with 2 songs and lyric sheets. Does not return material. Reports in 2 months.
Music: Mostly **country**, **rock** and **dance**. Produced *Memories & Me* (by various), recorded by Paul Hale on K-Tel Records; *Do You Wanna Dance* (by various), recorded by Bubba James Hudson on Quality Records; and *Signature* (by various), recorded by David Grey on BFE/BMG Records (country). Other artists include Slim Whitman, Johnny Lee, John MacNally, Shannon Kennedy.

LOCONTO PRODUCTIONS, Box 16540, Plantation FL 33318. (305)741-7766. President: Frank X. Loconto. Record producer and music publisher. Estab. 1978. Produces 10 cassettes/albums and 10 CDs/year. Fee derived from sales royalty or outright fee from songwriter/artist and/or record company.
  • Loconto Productions is also listed in the Record Companies section, and its publishing company, Otto Publishing Co., is listed in the Music Publishers section.

How to Contact: Submit demo tape by mail. Unsolicited submissions are OK. Prefers cassette. SASE. Reports in 2-3 months.
Music: Produced *Love Is In The Air* (by various), recorded by Michael Moog (dicso); *Let's Make Up*, written and recorded by Joseph Ford (gospel); and *Spacey's Wonderlings* (by Frank X. Loconto), recorded by Cherise Wyneken (children's), all on FXL Records. Other artists include J.T. Michaels, Bill Dillon, James Billie (folk music) and the Lane Brothers.

LONDON BRIJJ PRODUCTIONS, 817 E. Locust Ave., Philadelphia PA 19138. (215)438-9882. Producer/engineer: Jae London. Record producer, music publisher (Amaj Int'l Music/BMI) and production company. Estab. 1984. Produces 7 singles, 3 12" singles, 3 LPs and 2 CDs/year. Fee derived from sales royalty when song or artist is recorded or outright fee from record company.
How to Contact: Submit demo tape by mail. Unsolicited submissions are OK. Prefers cassette (or VHS videocassette if available) with 3 songs and lyric sheet. SASE. Reports in 1-2 months.
Music: Mostly **R&B**, **hip hop** and **ballads**; also **reggae** and **club/house**. Produced "Do Ya Luv" (by Jae London), recorded by April Luv (R&B); "Here's to You," written and recorded by Kenny Brown (ballad); and *Take It Slow* (by J. London/K. Brown), recorded by various, all on AMAJ Records. Other artists include Nicci, Keith Luggins, Zachary Scott and Bruce Turner.
Tips: "Stay sharply focused to what you do best and *network*. Never give up. Do your homework and learn the business."

HAROLD LUICK & ASSOCIATES, Box B, Carlisle IA 50047. (515)989-3748. Record producer, music industry consultant and music publisher. Produces 20 singles and 6 LPs/year. Fee derived from sales royalty, outright fee from artist/songwriter or record company, and from consulting fees for information or services.
 • See their listing in the Music Publishers and Music Print Publishers sections.
How to Contact: Call or write first. Prefers cassette with 3-5 songs and lyric sheet. SASE. Reports in 3 weeks.
Music: Traditional country, gospel, contemporary country and **MOR**. Produced *Everhart*, written and recorded by Bob Everhart; and *Ballads of Deadwood S.D.*, written and recorded by Don McLaughhlin. "Over a 12-year period, Harold Luick has produced and recorded 412 singles and 478 albums, 7 of which charted and some of which have enjoyed independent sales in excess of 30,000 units."
Tips: "We are interested in helping the new artist/songwriter make it 'the independent way.' Songwriters can increase their chances by understanding that recording and songwriting is a business. 80% of the people who travel to large recording/publishing areas of our nation arrive there totally unprepared as to what the industry wants or needs from them. Do yourself a favor. Prepare, investigate and only listen to people who are qualified to give you advice. Do not implement anything until you understand the rules and pitfalls. Being successful in the music world is not based on 'luck' alone. It is based on being prepared, educated and knowledgeable when luck does come along. So if you have been unlucky in the past, maybe you have just been unprepared!"

JIM McCOY PRODUCTIONS, Rt. 2, Box 114, Berkeley Springs WV 25411. President: Jim McCoy. Record producer and music publisher (Jim McCoy Music/BMI). Estab. 1964. Produces 12-15 singles and 6 LPs/year. Fee derived from sales royalty.
 • Jim McCoy's publishing company, Jim McCoy Music, can be found in the Music Publishers section, and his record label, Winchester Records, can be found in the Record Companies section.
How to Contact: Submit demo tape by mail. Unsolicited submissions are OK. Prefers cassette or 7½ or 15 ips reel-to-reel (or Beta or VHS videocassette if available) with 6 songs and lyric or lead sheets. Does not return material. Reports in 1 month.
Music: Mostly **country**, **rock** and **gospel**; also **country/rock** and **bluegrass**. Produced "Dyin' Rain" and "I'm Gettin Nowhere," both written and recorded by J.B. Miller on Hilton Records (country). Other artists include Mel McQuain, Red Steed, R. Lee Gray, John Aikens and Jim McCoy.

DINO MADDALONE PRODUCTIONS, 2367 208th St., #7, Torrance CA 90501. (310)782-0915. President: Dino Maddalone. Record producer. Estab. 1987. Produces 7 singles, 4 LPs, 2 EPs and 6 CDs/year. Fee derived from sales royalty when song or artist is recorded, or outright fee from recording artist or record company.
How to Contact: Write or call to obtain permission to submit. Prefers cassette or DAT with 3 songs and lyric sheet. SASE. "Send photo and any press." Reports in 1 month.
Music: Mostly **rock**, **R&B** and **alternative**; also **pop** and **ballads**. Produced "South Paw," written and recorded by Precious Death on Metro One/Sony Records (rock); "Lost For Words" (by Lizzy Grey), recorded by Spiders and Snakes on RKO/Sony (retro rock); and "Let it Go Let it Die," written and recorded by Barren Cross on Rugged Records (ballad).
Tips: "Believe in every note you write."

LEE MAGID PRODUCTIONS, Box 532, Malibu CA 90265. (213)463-5998. President: Lee Magid. Record producer and music publisher (Alexis Music, Inc./ASCAP, Marvelle Music Co./BMI, Gabal Music Co./SESAC), record company (Grass Roots Records and LMI Records) and management firm (Lee Magid Management). Estab. 1950. Produces 4 singles, 4 12″ singles, 8 LPs and 8 CDs/year. Fee derived from sales royalty.
- See the listings for Alexis Music in the Music Publishers section, and Grass Roots Record & Tape/LMI Records in the Record Companies section.

How to Contact: Submit demo tape by mail. Unsolicited submissions are OK. "Send cassette giving address and phone number; include SASE." Prefers cassette (or VHS videocassette) with 3-6 songs and lyric sheet. "Please only one cassette, and photos if you are an artist/writer." Does not return material. Reports in 8-10 weeks.

Music: Mostly **R&B**, **rock**, **jazz** and **gospel**; also **pop**, **bluegrass**, **church/religious**, **easy listening**, **folk**, **blues**, **MOR**, **progressive**, **soul**, **instrumental** and **Top 40**. Produced *Who Is He?* (by Calvin Rhone), recorded by Tramaine Hawkins on Sparrow Records; *Let's Pretend*, recorded by Zad on LMI Records; and "Jesus Is Just Alright" (by A. Reynolds), recorded by DC Talk on Forefront Records. Other artists include Pet Campbell, John M. Hides and Perry "The Prince" Walker.

Tips: "Stick with your belief and a good melody and lyric."

MAKERS MARK MUSIC PRODUCTIONS (ASCAP), 3033 W. Redner St., Philadelphia PA 19121. (215)236-4817. Producer: Paul E. Hopkins. Record producer. Estab. 1991. Produces 15 singles, 5 12″ singles and 4 LPs/year. Fee derived from outright fee from recording artist or record company.
- See the listing for Makers Mark Gold in the Music Publishers section.

How to Contact: Submit demo tape by mail. Unsolicited submissions are OK. Prefers cassette with 2-4 songs and lyric sheet. "Explain concept of your music and/or style, and your future direction as an artist or songwriter." Does not return material. Reports in 4-6 weeks (if interested).

Music: Mostly **R&B**, **dance/hip house**, **country** and **rap**. Produced "When Will My Heart Beat Again," "Last Kiss" and "Top of the World" (by Cheryl Forman/Paul Hopkins), all recorded by Rachel Scarborough. Other artists include Larry Larr, Paul Hopkins, Elaine Monk (R&B) and Andy Romano (R&B/pop).

PETE MARTIN/VAAM MUSIC PRODUCTIONS, Box 29688, Hollywood CA 90029-0688. (213)664-7765. President: Pete Martin. Record producer, music publisher (Vaam Music/BMI, Pete Martin Music/ASCAP) and record company (Blue Gem Records). Estab. 1982. Produces 12 singles and 5 LPs/year. Fee derived from sales royalty when song or artist is recorded.
- See the listings for Vaam Music Group in the Music Publishers section and Blue Gem Records in the Record Companies section.

How to Contact: Prefers cassette with 2 songs and lyric sheet. Send small packages only. SASE. Reports in 1 month.

Music: Mostly **top 40/pop**, **country** and **R&B**. Produced Sherry Weston, Frank Loren, Brian Smith & The Renegades, Victoria Limon, Brandy Rose, Estrella Tamaz and Cory Canyon.

Tips: "Study the market in the style that you write. Songs must be capable of reaching Top 5 on charts."

MASTERPIECE PRODUCTIONS & STUDIOS, P.O. Box 780283, Wichita KS 67278-0283. (316)683-8333. Owner/Producer: Tim M. Raymond. Record producer, studio owner, music publisher (ArtUnique Music/ASCAP). Estab. 1980. Produces 200 singles, 10 12″ singles, 25 LPs, 5 EPs and 20 CDs/year. Fee derived from sales royalty when song or artist is recorded or outright fee from recording artist or record company.

How to Contact: Submit demo tape by mail. Unsolicited submissions are OK. Prefers DAT (will accept VHS videocassette or cassette, also) with 4-6 songs and lyric sheet. "Please send a complete promo pack (photos, tapes and bio)." Does not return material. Reports in 2 months.

Music: Mostly **gospel (Christian)**, **pop (Top 40)**, **rock**, **New Age** and **country**; also **R&B**, **vocal jazz** and **rap**. Produced *Cat Paws* (by Lee Campbell-Towell), recorded by Cat Paws in Motion on Hal Leonard Records; *Comin' On Strong (Live In Concert)*, recorded by Carman on Myrrh Records; and *Jesus, Authentic & Amazing*, by various artists. Other artists include Tim Enloe, Earnest Alexander and Tyler Green.

Tips: "Emphasize your uniqueness! It's what makes the difference. We are always looking for a unique talent, whether it be an artist or songwriter."

● **A BULLET** introduces comments by the editor of *Songwriter's Market* indicating special information about the listing.

DAVID MATHES PRODUCTIONS, P.O. Box 22653, Nashville TN 37202. (615)252-6912. President: David W. Mathes. AF-FM licensed. Record producer. Estab. 1962. Produces 6-10 singles, 4-16 12" singles and 4-6 LPs/year. Fee derived from outright fee from recording artist.
• See the listings for the Mathes Company in the Music Publishers and Record Companies sections.
How to Contact: Submit demo tape by mail. Unsolicited submissions are OK. "No certified mail accepted." Prefers 7½ or 15 ips reel-to-reel or cassette (or videocassette) with 2-4 songs and lyric sheet. "Enclose correctly stamped envelope for demo return." Reports in 1 month.
Music: Mostly **country** and **gospel**; also **bluegrass**, **R&B** and **Top 40/pop**. Produced "Undefinable Love" (by Dorothy Hampton), recorded by Johnny Newman on Star Image Records (country); "Beulah Land" (by Squire Parsons), recorded by Harry House on Heirborn Records (gospel); and "Rag Doll For Christmas" (by Merle Baasch), recorded by DeAnna on Star Image Records (Christmas).
Tips: "Don't be anxious to record with a producer who charges a lot less but offers studio time to record an album in 10-20 hours. It pays to work with producers who have experience and integrity."

SCOTT MATHEWS, D/B/A HIT OR MYTH PRODUCTIONS, 36C Lisbon St., San Rafael CA 94901. Fax: (415)389-9682. President: Scott Mathews. Record producer and music publisher (Hang On to Your Publishing/BMI). Estab. 1975. Produces 6 CDs/year. Fee derived from recording artist or record company (with royalty points).
• Scott Mathews was runner up for producer of the year for a rock instrumental at the 1995 Grammy Awards.
How to Contact: Submit demo tape by mail. Unsolicited submissions are OK. Prefers cassette. SASE. Reports in 1-3 months. "Please, no phone calls."
Music: Mostly **rock/pop**, **country** and **R&B**. Produced *Plugged* (by Richard Greene/Scott Mathews), recorded by The Bobs on Rounder Records (a cappella); *Unknown Territories*, written and recorded by Dick Dale on Hightone Records (rock); and *Putt Levels*, written and recorded by John Wesley Harding on Sire Records (folk). Has produced Roy Orbison, Rosanne Cash, John Hiatt and many more. Has recorded with everyone from Barbra Streisand to Sammy Hagar, including The Beach Boys, Keith Richards, John Lee Hooker, Van Morrison, Huey Lewis, Bonnie Raitt and Eric Clapton to name but a few with over 12 million units sold to date.
Tips: "I am looking for singer/songwriters with emphasis on songs and great voices of any style. I am no longer placing songs or publishing outside material. If you feel strongly that your act is ready to make records, send a tape now! A&R people no longer sign acts with 'potential.' You've got to knock them out with your first shot. I try to make time in my schedule to take on acts that have not yet been signed to a label, produce a finished record that gets them a deal with the right label and add some more platinum to my office walls."

*MERLIN PRODUCTIONS, P.O. Box 5087 VMPO, Vancouver, British Columbia V6B 4A9 **Canada**. Phone/fax: (604)525-9194. President: Wolfgang Hamann. Record producer. Estab. 1979. Produces 5 singles, 3 LPs, 1 EP and 3 CDs/year. Fee derived from sales royalty when song or artist is recorded.
• See their listing in the Record Companies section, as well as Merlin Management in the Managers and Booking Agents section.
How to Contact: Submit demo tape by mail. Unsolicited submissions are OK. Prefers cassette with 3 songs and lyric and/or lead sheet. "Best songs first. Target your songs, i.e., Whitney Houston." SAE and IRC. Reports in 3 weeks.
Music: Mostly **modern rock**, **dance** and **R&B**; also **pop**. Produced *Sunshine*, written and recorded by Mode to Joy (rock); "F.R.E." (by A. Brown), recorded by Wolfgang/Wolfgang (dance); and "Love Is Everything" (by Wolfgang/Wolfgang), recorded by Beverly Sills, all on Merlin Records.

JAY MILLER PRODUCTIONS, 413 N. Parkerson Ave., Crowley LA 70526. (318)783-1601 or 788-0773. Contact: Jay Miller. Record producer and music publisher. Produces 50 singles and 15 LPs/year. Fee derived from sales royalty when song or artist is recorded.
• Jay Miller's publishing company, Whitewing Music, can be found in the Music Publishers section, and his record company, Master-Trak Enterprises, is listed in the Record Companies section.
How to Contact: Write or call first to arrange personal interview. Prefers cassette for audition.
Music: Mostly **country**; also **blues**, **Cajun**, **disco**, **folk**, **gospel**, **MOR**, **rock**, **Top 40/pop** and **comedy**. Produced *Zydecajun*, by Wayne Toups on Mercury Records; *Business Is Pleasure* (by Sammy Kershaw); and *Avec Amis* (by Lee Benoit). Other artists include Camey Doucet, Freddie Pate and Kenne' Wayne.

MR. WONDERFUL PRODUCTIONS, INC., 1730 Kennedy Rd., Louisville KY 40216. (502)774-1066. President: Ronald C. Lewis. Record producer, music publisher (Ron "Mister Wonderful" Music/BMI and 1730 Music/ASCAP) and record company (Wonderful Records and Ham Sem

Records). Estab. 1984. Produces 2 singles and 3 12″ singles/year. Fee is derived from sales royalty when song or artist is recorded.

How to Contact: Submit demo tape by mail. Unsolicited submissions are OK. Prefers cassette with 4 songs and lyric sheet. SASE. Reports in 2 weeks.

Music: Mostly **R&B**, **black gospel** and **rap**. Produced "Am I Good" (by Ron Lewis) and "Just Another In My Past" (by Pam Layne), both recorded by Amanda Orch (R&B); and *Tell Them*, recorded by Sylvester Gough, all on Wonderful Records.

A.V. MITTELSTEDT, 9717 Jensen Dr., Houston TX 77093. (713)695-3648. Producer: A.V. Mittelstedt. Record producer and music publisher (Sound Masters). Produces 100 singles, 10 LPs and 20 CDs/year. Fee derived from sales royalty and outright fee from recording artist.

How to Contact: Prefers cassette. SASE. Reports in 3 weeks.

Music: Mostly **country**, **gospel** and **crossover**; also **MOR** and **rock**. Produced "Too Cold at Home" (by Bobby Harding), recorded by Mark Chestnutt on Cherry Records (country); "Two Will Be One," written and recorded by Kenny Dale on Axbar Records (country); and "Shake Your Hiney" (by Gradual Taylor), recorded by Roy Head on Cherry Records (crossover country). Other artists include Randy Cornor, Bill Nash, Ron Shaw, Borderline, George Dearborne and Good, Bad and Ugly.

MODERN TRIBE RECORDS, (formerly Creative Life Entertainment, Inc.), 196 Tuxedo Ave., Highland Park MI 48203. (313)537-0590. Producer: Juan Shannon. Record producer, record company and music publisher. Estab. 1990. Produces 12 singles, 12 12″ singles, 2 LPs, 2 EPs and 2 CDs/year. "Fee varies depending on negotiation."

How to Contact: Submit demo tape by mail. Unsolicited submissions are OK. Prefers cassette (or VHS videocassette) with 3-4 songs, lyric sheet and photo for groups/artist wanting to be signed. "Name, address and phone number on tape and cassette box." SASE. Reports in 1-2 months.

Music: **Pop**, **R&B**, **hip hop (rap)**, **alternative** and **gospel & country**. Produced "Get That Booty Up" (by J. Shannon/A. Brown), recorded by Raw (bass); "Take Me Back" (by K. Bradley/T. Morrow), recorded by Joshua (R&B); and *Love Songs*, written and recorded by Juan Shannon (jazz), all on Modern Tribe Records. Other artists include 666 and Jack Housen.

Tips: "If you are not ready to drop everything you're doing and concentrate on your career don't send your tape. If Warner Bros. won't pick it up, neither will I."

GARY MOFFET, P.O. Box 941 N.D.G., Montreal, Quebec H4A 3S3 **Canada**. (514)487-8953. Contact: Gary Moffet. Record producer. Estab. 1985. Produces 3 LPs, 4 EPs and 3 CDs/year. Fee derived from sales royalty when song or artist is recorded.

● Gary Moffet's publishing company, Sci-Fi Music, is listed in the Music Publishers section.

How to Contact: Submit demo tape by mail. Unsolicited submissions are OK. Prefers cassette with 6 songs and lyric sheet. SAE and IRC. Reports in 6 weeks.

Music: Mostly **rock, pop** and **acoustic**. Produced *Back to Reality* (by T. Mitchell), recorded by Mindstorm on Aquarius Records (heavy rock); *See Spot Run* (by C. Broadbeck), recorded by See Spot Run on Primer Records (rock); and *The Storm*, written and recorded by Ray Lyell on Spy Records (rock). Other artists include Adam's Apples, Simon Says and The Perfect Sex.

MONA LISA RECORDS/BRISTOL STUDIOS, 169 Massachusetts Ave., Boston MA 02115. (617)247-8689. Executive Director: Ric Poulin. Record producer. Estab. 1987. Produces 50 singles and 10 CDs/year.

How to Contact: Call first to arrange personal interview. Prefers cassette and lyric sheet. Does not return material. Reports in 2 months.

Music: Mostly **dance**, **R&B** and **pop**; also **jazz** and **rock**. Produced *Future Classics* (by Ric Poulin/Sean Cooper), recorded by various artists on Mona Lisa Records (dance); "Call the Doctor" (by Poulin/Yeldham/Poulin), recorded by Bijou on Critique/Atlantic Records (dance); and "Dance to the Rhythm of the Beat" (by Ric Poulin), recorded by Jennifer Rivers on Associated Artists Int'l (dance). Other artists include Never Never, Sherry Christian, Zina, Damien, Aaron Brown, Amy Silverman and Leah Langfeld.

Tips: "Develop the frame of mind that whatever you do, you are doing it as a professional."

MONTICANA PRODUCTIONS, P.O. Box 702, Snowdon Station, Montreal, Quebec H3X 3X8 **Canada**. Executive Producer: David Leonard. Record producer. Estab. 1963. Fee negotiable.

● See the listings for Montina Music in the Music Publishers section and Monticana Records in the Record Companies section.

How to Contact: Submit demo tape by mail. Unsolicited submissions are OK. Prefers cassette, phonograph record (or VHS videocassette) with maximum 10 songs and lyric sheet. "Demos should be as tightly produced as a master." Does not return material.

Music: Mostly **top 40**; also **bluegrass**, **blues**, **country**, **dance-oriented**, **easy listening**, **folk**, **gospel**, **jazz**, **MOR**, **progressive**, **R&B**, **rock** and **soul**.

GARY JOHN MRAZ, 1324 Cambridge Dr., Glendale CA 91205. Producer: Gary Mraz. Record producer. Estab. 1984. Produces 6-12 12″ singles and 2-6 LPs/year. Fee derived from sales royalty or outright fee from record company.
How to Contact: Submit demo tape by mail. Unsolicited submissions are OK. Prefers cassette (or VHS videocassette if available) with 3 songs and lyric sheet. Does not return material. Reports in 1-2 months.
Music: Mostly **dance**, **pop** and **R&B**. Produced "Studio Voodoo," recorded by Mraz Price on Radio Magic Records. Other artists include Bush Baby.
Tips: "Get your finished product to the untapped college radio market."

MUSICLAND PRODUCTIONS, 911 NE 17th Ave., Ocala FL 34470. (352)622-5529. Owner: Bobby Land. Record producer. Estab. 1986. Produces 2 singles and 2 CDs/year. Fee derived from financial backers.
How to Contact: Write first and obtain permission to submit. Prefers cassette with 4 songs and lyric sheet. "Professional demos only." Does not return material. Reports in 1-2 weeks.
Music: Mostly **country** and **gospel**. Produced "Cowboy Lady," written and recorded by Curt Powers on MPR Records; and *Right Back Where We Ended*, recorded by Charles Allen on Pleasentville Records. Other artists include David Mathis.

MUSICOM MUSIC PRODUCTIONS, 20 Admiral Rd., St. Catharines Ontario LZP 1G6 **Canada**. (905)682-5161. Owners: Kevin Hotte and Andy Smith. Record producer, record company, music publisher (Creative Images Media Prod.) music publisher (The Sound Kitchen) and MIDI recording facility. Estab. 1992. Produces 1 cassette and 1 CD/year. Fee derived from sales royalty when song or artist is recorded, outright fee from record company or artist, or co-op production.
How to Contact: Submit demo tape by mail. Unsolicited submissions are OK. Prefers cassette or VHS videocassette with 4-6 songs and lyric or lead sheet. Does not return material. Reports in 1-2 months.
Music: Mostly **rock**, **New Age** and **progressive-alternative**; also **R&B**, **pop** and **jazz**. Produced *Windows* (by Kevin Hotte/Andy Smith), recorded by Musicom on Creative Images Records (power New Age).
Tips: "Be honest, be professional, be specific. Dare to be different. Don't expect to be able to quit your day job. We offer limited exposure to a target audience in Canada (mainly Ontario). You might not make a fortune but you will get some exposure. We are new, independent, open minded and above all we are just like you. If you're contacting us as a result of seeing our listing in *Songwriter's Market*, we would like to know."

MUST ROCK PRODUCTIONZ WORLDWIDE, 97-11 Horace Harding Expwy., Suite 2H, Corona NY 11368-4704. (718)595-1638. President: Ivan "DJ/DOC" Rodriguez. Record producer, recording engineer. Estab. 1980. Produces 5 singles, engineers 2 LPs, 3 EPs and 2 CDs/year. Fee derived from sales royalty when song or artist is recorded. "We do not shop deals."
How to Contact: Call first and obtain permission to submit. Prefers cassette (or VHS videocassette) and lyric sheet. Does not return material. Reports in 2-3 weeks.
Music: Mostly **hip-hop**, **R&B** and **pop**; also **soul**, **ballads** and **soundtracks**. Produced "Poor Georgie" (by MC Lyte/DJ DOC), recorded by MC Lyte on Atlantic Records (rap). Other artists include Caron Wheeler, The Hit Squad, The Awesome II, Black Steel Music, Underated Productions, EPMD, Redman, Dr. Dre & Ed-Lover, Das-EFX, Biz Markie, BDP, Eric B & Rakim, The Fugees, The Bushwackass, Shai and Pudgee.
Tips: "Services provided include production (pre/post/co), tracking, mixing, remixing, live show tapes, jingles, etc. Additional info available upon request."

NASHVILLE COUNTRY PRODUCTIONS, 306 Millwood Dr., Nashville TN 37217. (615)366-9999. President/Producer: Colonel Jack Lynch. Record producer, music publisher (Jaclyn Music/BMI), record companies (Jalyn and Nashville Country Productions) and distributor (Nashville Music Sales). Estab. 1987. Produces 1-12 LPs/year. Fee derived from sales royalty or outright fee from recording artist or record company. "We do both contract and custom recording."
  ● Jack Lynch's publishing company, Jaclyn Music, can be found in the Music Publishers section, and his record label, Jalyn Recording Co., is in the Record Companies section.
How to Contact: Submit demo tape by mail. Unsolicited submissions are OK. Prefers cassette with 1-2 songs and lyric or lead sheet. SASE. Reports in 1 month.
Music: Mostly **country**, **bluegrass**, **MOR** and **gospel**; also **comedy**. Produced *There'll Never Be Another*, written and recorded by Jack Lynch on NBC-19962 Records; *Time Will Tell* (by T.E. Morris), recorded by Odie Gal on NCP-19961 Records; and *Love Takes Time* (by Franklin Kincaid), recorded by Don Hendrix on NCP-19964 Records.
Tips: "Prepare a good quality cassette demo, send to us along with a neat lyric sheet for each song and a bio, picture and SASE."

NEBO RECORD COMPANY, Box 194 or 457, New Hope AL 35760. Manager: Jim Lewis. Record producer, music publisher (Nebo Ridge Publishing/ASCAP) and record company. Estab. 1985. Fee derived from sales royalty when song or artist is recorded.
How to Contact: Submit demo tape by mail. Unsolicited submissions are OK. Prefers cassette with 1 song and lyric sheet. "It is OK to send a videocassette, but not a must. Songwriters must send a SASE. Send a neat professional package. Send only 1 song." Does not return material. Reports "as soon as possible."
Music: Mostly **modern country, traditional country** and **gospel**; also **rock, R&B** and **pop**. Produced *I Can't Take It* (by Larry Clark), recorded by Brenda Watson (country); *Your Love Hurts Me* (by Ann Black), recorded by Jan Hillis (country); and "Hold Me Tight" (by Laura Davis), recorded by Jill Mack (gospel), all on Nebo Records. Other artists include Ricky Terry, Joe White, Sandy Brown, Mary Powers, Gail Prince, Cindy Hold, Brandy Down and Terry Rose.
Tips: "We need several female singers for our Nebo Record label. Female singers should send a personal bio, some full-length photos, and a demo cassette tape of their songs for a review. Also, SASE should be included."

BILL NELSON, 45 Perham St., W. Roxbury MA 02132. Contact: Bill Nelson. Record producer and music publisher (Henly Music/ASCAP). Estab. 1987. Produces 6 singles and 6 LPs/year. Fee derived from outright fee from recording artist.
• See the listing for Henly Music Associates in the Music Publishers section.
How to Contact: Submit demo tape by mail. Unsolicited submissions are OK. Prefers cassette with 3-4 songs and lyric sheet. Does not return material. Reports in 3-4 weeks.
Music: Mostly **country, pop** and **gospel**. Produced "Do You Believe in Miracles" (by B. Nelson), recorded by Part-Time Singers; "Big Bad Bruce" (by J. Dean); and "Don't Hurry With Love" (by B. Bergeron), both recorded by B.N.O., all on Woodpecker Records.

NEMESIS MEDIA LABS, 487 Pittsfield, Columbus OH 43085. (614)841-9980. Producer: Loren Moss. Record producer and full broadcast production facility. Estab. 1988. Produces 6 singles, 2 LPs and 2 EPs/year. Fee derived from sales royalty when song or artist is recorded or outright fee from recording artist or record company.
How to Contact: Submit demo tape by mail. Unsolicited submissions are OK. Prefers DAT or cassette (or ¾″ videocassette) with 4 songs and lyric sheet. "Include pictures and biographical information." SASE. Reports in 6 weeks.
Music: Mostly **corporate/post scoring, reggae** and **hip hop/rap**; also **world beat, dance/house** and **R&B/top 40**. Produced "Chill" (by Tamara Straughter), recorded by Teddy B on Tamareco Records (rap); *Learning to Walk*, written and recorded by Poets of Heresy on Private Records (alternative); and "Do You Miss Me," written and recorded by Misti Tuffs on Artists Label (jazz).

NEU ELECTRO PRODUCTIONS, P.O. Box 1582, Bridgeview IL 60455. (708)257-6289. Owner: Bob Neumann. Record producer, record company. Estab. 1984. Produces 16 singles, 16 12″ singles, 20 LPs and 4 CDs/year. Fee derived from outright fee from recording artist or record company.
How to Contact: Submit demo tape by mail. Unsolicited submissions are OK. Prefers cassette (or VHS videocassette if available) with 3 songs and lyric sheet or lead sheet. "Accurate contact phone numbers and addresses, promo packages and photos." SASE. Reports in 2 weeks.
Music: Mostly **dance, house, techno, rap** and **rock**; also **experimental, New Age** and **top 40**. Produced "Juicy," written and recorded by Juicy Black on Dark Planet International Records (house); "Make Me Smile," written and recorded by Roz Baker (house); and *Reactovate-6* (by Bob Neumann), recorded by Beatbox-D on N.E.P. Records (dance).
Tips: "Quality of production will influence profitability."

NEW EXPERIENCE RECORDS, Box 683, Lima OH 45802. Music Publisher: James L. Milligan Jr. Record producer, music publisher (A New Rap Jam Publishing), management (Creative Star Management) and record company (New Experience Records, Grand-Slam Records, Pump It Up Records). Estab. 1989. Produces 15-20 12″ singles, 2 LPs, 3 EPs and 2-5 CDs/year. Fee derived from sales royalty when song or artist is recorded or outright fee from record company, "depending on services required."
• See the listings for A New Rap Jam Publishing in the Music Publishers section and New

MARKET CONDITIONS are constantly changing! If you're still using this book and it is 1998 or later, buy the newest edition of *Songwriter's Market* at your favorite bookstore or order directly from Writer's Digest Books.

Experience/Grand Slam Records in the Record Companies section.
How to Contact: Write or call first and obtain permission to submit. Address material to
A&R Dept. or Talent Coordinator (Carl Milligan). Prefers cassette with a minimum of 3 songs and
lyric or lead sheet (if available). "If tapes are to be returned, proper postage should be enclosed and
all tapes and letters should have SASE for faster reply." Reports in 1 month.
Music: Mostly **pop**, **R&B** and **rap**; also **gospel**, **contemporary gospel** and **rock**. Produced *Sandy
Beach Cove*, written and recorded by Richard Bamberger Brooks (pop); "You Promise Me Love" (by
The Impressions), recorded by Brooks, Melvin (ballad); and "People Get Ready," written and recorded
by World Famous Impressions (dance), all on N.E.R. Records. Other artists include Mr. Ice and
Generation X.
Tips: "This is a very hard business to break into. Therefore first impressions are very important.
Spend the extra if it will better your submission. Use a good studio. Always include proper postage
and contact information. Labels want finished masters. If there is interest, we will contact you."

NEW HORIZON RECORDS, 3398 Nahatan Way, Las Vegas NV 89109. (702)732-2576. President:
Mike Corda. Record producer. Fee derived from sales royalty when song or artist is recorded.
How to Contact: Submit demo tape by mail. Unsolicited submissions are OK. Prefers cassette with
1-3 songs and lyric sheet. SASE. Reports in 3 weeks.
Music: Blues, easy listening, jazz and **MOR**. Produced "Lover of the Simple Things," "Offa the
Sauce" (by Corda & Wilson) and "Go Ahead and Laugh," all recorded by Mickey Rooney on Prestige
Records (London). Artists include Bob Anderson, Jan Rooney, Joe Williams, Robert Goulet and Bill
Haley and the Comets.
Tips: "Send good musical structures, melodic lines, and powerful lyrics or quality singing if you're
a singer."

NIGHTWORK RECORDS, 355 W. Potter Dr., Anchorage AK 99518. (907)562-3754. Contact:
Kurt Riemann. Record producer and music licensor (electronic). Produces 2 singles, 8 LPs and 2 CDs/
year. Fees derived from sales royalty.
How to Contact: Submit demo tape by mail. Unsolicited submissions are OK. Prefers cassette or
15 ips reel-to-reel with 2-3 songs "produced as fully as possible. Send jingles and songs on separate
reels." Does not return material. Reports in 1-2 months.
Music: Mostly **electronic**, **electronic jingles** and **Alaska-type music**. Produced *Alaska*, written and
recorded by Kurt Riemann; *Aracus*, written and recorded by Jennifer Stone, both on Nightworks
Records (New Age); and *Into the Night*, written and recorded by Jeanene Walker on Windsong Records
(country).

***OMARI PRODUCTIONS**, 420 Lincoln Rd., Miami Beach FL 33139. (305)535-1123. Fax:
(305)535-1124. President: Bernard Adell. Record producer. Fee derived from sales royalty when song
or artist is recorded.
How to Contact: Submit demo tape by mail. Unsolicited submissions are OK. Prefers cassette or
VHS videocassette with 3 songs and lyric sheet. Does not return material. Reports in 2 weeks.
Music: Mostly **R&B**, **hip hop** and **rock**; also **gospel** and **country**. Recently produced *Mangu*, written
and recorded by Mangu (rap, Island Records); *Mother Superior*, written and recorded by Mother
Superior (rap, Island Records); and *City Limits*, written and recorded by Mike City (R&B/hip hop,
Intersound So-lo Jam Records).
Tips: "Always be original. It's originality that sells."

OMNI 2000 INC., 413 Cooper St., Camden NJ 08102. (609)963-6400. Contact: Director A&R.
Record producer, music publisher and record company. Estab. 1995. Produces 1-5 singles and 1-5 LPs/
year. Fee derived from sales royalty when song or artist is recorded.
● See Omni 2000's listing in the Music Publishers section.
How to Contact: Write first and obtain permission to submit. Prefers cassette with 3 songs and lyric
sheet. SASE. Reports in 1-2 months.

JOHN "BUCK" ORMSBY/ETIQUETTE PRODUCTIONS, 2442 NW Market, Suite 273, Seattle WA 98107. (206)524-1020. Fax: (206)524-1102. Publishing Director: John Ormsby. Record producer and music publisher (Valet Publishing). Estab. 1980. Produces 1-2 singles, 3-5 LPs and 3-5 CDs/
year. Fee varies.
● See the listing for Valet Publishing in the Music Publishers section.
How to Contact: Submit demo tape by mail—"always looking for new material but please call
first." Prefers cassette (or VHS videocassette if available) with lyric or lead sheet. SASE. Reports in
6-8 weeks.
Music: R&B, rock, pop and country.
Tips: "Tape production must be top quality; lead or lyric sheet professional."

PANIO BROTHERS LABEL, Box 99, Montmartre, Saskatchewan S0G 3M0 **Canada**. Executive Director: John Panio, Jr. Record producer. Estab. 1977. Produces 1 single and 1 LP/year. Fee derived from sales royalty or outright fee from artist/songwriter or record company.
How to Contact: Submit demo tape by mail. Unsolicited submissions are OK. Prefers cassette with any number of songs and lyric sheet. SAE and IRC. Reports in 1 month.
Music: Country, dance, easy listening and **Ukrainian**. Produced *Ukranian Country*, written and recorded by Vlad Panio on PB Records.

PATTY PARKER, 10603 N. Hayden Rd., Suite 114, Scottsdale AZ 85260. (602)951-3115. Fax: (602)951-3074. Producer: Patty Parker. Record producer, record company (Comstock). Estab. 1978. Produces 18 CD singles and 4-5 CDs/year. Fee derived from outright fee from recording artist or recording company.
• See the listing for Comstock Records in the Record Companies section and White Cat Music in the Music Publishers section.
How to Contact: Submit demo tape by mail. Unsolicited submissions are OK. Prefers CD or cassette (or VHS videocassette if available) with 2-4 songs and lyric sheet. Voice up front on demos. SASE. Reports in 2 weeks.
Music: Mostly **country—traditional** to **crossover, western** and some **pop/rock**. Produced "Show Me What You Know About Love" (by Paul Gibson), recorded by Danielle St. Pierre; *Opposites Attract* (by Dave Favell/Pam Ferens), recorded by Pam Ferens; and *A Hot Dog & A Daiquiri*, written and recorded by Bill Crews, all on Comstock Records. Other artists include Sharon Lee Beavers, Colin Clark, Brigitte Burke, Phil West, Jill Trace and Pamela Nelson.
Tips: "With todays international scope of music I need good medium to up-tempo songs for European country singers whom I produce in Nashville. The U.S. artists I produce are also in need of good uptempo songs to catch the ears of radio programmers worldwide."

PEGASUS RECORDING, P.O. Box 578903, Chicago IL 60657. (312)880-5000. Senior staff producer: Gary Khan. Record producer. Estab. 1988. Produces 12 singles, 2 LPs, 3 EPs and 3 CDs/year. Fee determined by project.
How to Contact: Submit demo tape by mail. Unsolicited submissions are OK. Prefers cassette or VHS videocassette with 1-3 songs and lyric sheet. SASE. Reports in 3 weeks.
Music: Mostly **rock, alternative, soul, R&B** and **A/C**; also **country, blues, world beat, gospel, classical** and **jazz**. Produced *Vesna* (by Sieradzki/Khan) and *Bow Echo* (by Chris Hordorwick), both on Pegasus Records. Other artists include Kevin Augusta, Robbie Rhodes, Magellan, U.B.C., Frank Lucas, Bernard McBean, Lenox Mayes, Sugar Blue, Buddy Miles and Dave Mason.
Tips: "Submit songs from the heart, not last month's charts! At this stage, *simple* production please. Keyboard patches and reverbs don't sell artists or writers."

*PERENNIAL PRODUCTIONS, Box 109, 73 Hill Rd., Redding CT 06875. (203)938-9392. Owner: Sean McNamara. Record producer. Estab. 1992. Fee derived from outright fee from recording artist or record company.
How to Contact: Submit demo tape by mail. Unsolicited submissions are OK. Prefers cassette (or VHS videocassette) with 4-8 songs and lyric or lead sheet. "Include a promo pack." Does not return material. Reports in 1 month.
Music: Mostly **alternative rock, contemporary jazz** and **folk**. Produced *Feel the Heat*, written and recorded by Flashpoint on Flight Path Records (fusion jazz); *Gary Wofsey Introduces the Contemporary Philharmonic Orchestra*, written and recorded by Gary Wofsey; and "Dischord," written and recorded by John Nutscher on Caffeine Disk Records (alternative).
Tips: "Send a bio about yourself and explain your intentions for the music submitted."

PERIDOT PRODUCTIONS, 17 Woodbine St., Cranston RI 02910. (401)785-2677. President: Amy Parravano. Record producer, record company and music publisher. Estab. 1992. Produces 2 singles, 2 12" singles and 1 LP/year. Fee derived from outright fee from recording artist.
• See the listing for Parravano Music in the Music Publishers section and Peridot Records in the Record Companies section.
How to Contact: Submit demo tape by mail. Unsolicited submissions are OK. Prefers cassette with 3-4 songs and lyric sheet. SASE. Reports in 6 months.
Music: Mostly **country, gospel** and **folk**; also **MOR, children's, country blues, blues** and **novelty**. Produced "After All This Time" (by Mike DiSano), recorded by Joe Kempf on B.J.D. Wishing Away Records; "America" and "North Hampton Line" (by Amy Parravano), recorded by Amy Beth on Peridot Records.
Tips: "Lyrics with good messages are still getting listeners' attention."

PERSON TO PERSON PRODUCTIONS, 342 Norfolk Rd., Litchfield CT 06759-0546. (203)567-0546. Fax: (203)491-9083. President: Chris Brown. Record producer. Estab. 1979. Produces 4-5 LPs/

year. Fee derived from outright fee from recording artist or record company.
How to Contact: Write first and obtain permission to submit. Prefers cassette with 3 songs and lyric sheet. Does not return material. Reports in 1 month.
Music: Mostly **jazz, folk** and **ethnic**; also **pop** and **rock**. Artists include Paul Winter Consort and Bill Lauf Jr.

PHILLY BREAKDOWN, 216 W. Hortter St., Philadelphia PA 19119. (215)848-6725. President: Matthew Childs. Record producer, music publisher (Philly Breakdown/BMI) and record company (Philly Breakdown). Estab. 1974. Produces 3 singles and 2 LPs/year. Fee derived from sales royalty when song or artist is recorded.
How to Contact: Submit demo tape by mail. Unsolicited submissions are OK. Prefers cassette with 4 songs and lead sheet. Does not return material. Reports in 6-10 weeks.
Music: Mostly **R&B, hip hop** and **pop**; also **jazz, gospel** and **ballads**. Produced *The Magic of Clyde Terrell* (by various), recorded by Clyde Terrell (jazz); *This is Jazz* (by Clarence Patterson), recorded by Nina Bundy (jazz); and "To Those In Love" (by Jim Tompson), recorded by Gloria Clark (pop), all on Philly Breakdown Records. Other artists include Leroy Christy, Charlie Nesbitt, Kenny Gates, Jerry Walker and Emmit King.

JIM PIERCE, 101 Hurt Rd., Hendersonville TN 37075. (615)824-5900. Fax: (615)824-8800. President: Jim Pierce. Record producer, music publisher (Strawboss Music/BMI, Pier-Jac Music/ASCAP) and record company (Round Robin Records). Estab. 1974. Produces 50 singles, 5-6 EPs and 2-3 CDs/year. Fee derived from sales royalty or outright fee from recording artist. "Some artists pay me in advance for my services." Has had over 200 chart records to date.
How to Contact: Write first and obtain permission to submit or to arrange personal interview. Prefers cassette with any number of songs and lyric sheet. Does not return material. Reports in 2-3 months.
Music: Mostly **country, contemporary, country/pop** and **traditional country**. Produced "Don't Call Us, We'll Call You," written and recorded by Harlen Helgeson; "You Can't Keep a Good Love Down" (by Jerry Fuller), recorded by Lenny Valenson; and "If I Live To Be A Hundred" (by Mae Borden Axton), recorded by Arne Benoni, all on Round Robin Records (country). Other artists include Jimmy C. Newman, Margo Smith, Bobby Helms, Sammi Smith, Tim Gillis, Roy Drusky, Charlie Lowin, Melba Montgomery and Harlan Craig.
Tips: "Don't let a 'no' stop you from trying."

PINE ISLAND MUSIC, 9430 Live Oak Place, #308, Ft. Lauderdale FL 33324. (April-October: 4250 Marine Dr., #2335, Chicago IL 60613). (305)472-7757. President: Jack P. Bluestein. Record producer and music publisher. Estab. 1973. Produces 5-10 singles/year. Fee derived from sales royalty.
How to Contact: Artist: query, submit demo tape. Songwriter: submit demo tape and lead sheet. Prefers cassette or 7½ ips reel-to-reel with 1-4 songs. SASE. Reports in 1-2 months.
Music: Mostly **blues, country, easy listening, folk, gospel, jazz, MOR, rock, soul** and **top 40/pop**. Produced "Drivin' Nails," written and recorded by Gary Oakes; and *An Old Old Man* (by Beth Thliveris), recorded by Bernice Boyce, both on Quadrant Records. Other artists include Jeffrey Cash and Praise (gospel) and Paula Ma Yu-Fen.
Tips: "Write good saleable material and have an understandable demo made."

PLANET DALLAS, P.O. Box 191447, Dallas TX 75219. (214)521-2216. Fax: (214)528-1299. President: Rick Rooney. Record producer and music publisher (Stoli Music/ASCAP and Planet Mothership/BMI). Estab. 1984. Produces 8-12 LPs, 5-12 EPs and 8-12 CDs/year. Fee derived from sales royalty when song or artist is recorded.
  ● Planet Dallas also has a listing in the Music Publishers section.
How to Contact: Call first and obtain permission to submit a demo. Prefers cassette or DAT. SASE. Reports in 2-4 weeks.
Music: Mostly **pop/rock, R&B** and **country**; also **soul** and **instrumental**. Produced albums by Gone By Dawn on Burn Records (rock) and Tripping Daisy on Island Records (rock). Other artists include Fu Schnickens and MC 900 Ft. Jesus.
Tips: "There is no luck in this business, only the result of hard work, inspiration and determination."

POKU PRODUCTIONS, 176-B Woodridge Crescent, Nepran, Ontario K2B 759 **Canada**. (613)820-5715. President: Jon E. Shakka. Record producer. Estab. 1988. Produces 1 single and 1 12" single/year. Fee derived from sales royalty when song or artist is recorded.
How to Contact: Write or call first and obtain permission to submit. Prefers cassette (or VHS videocassette if available) with 4 songs and lyric sheet. SAE and IRC. Reports in 3 months.
Music: Mostly **funk, rap** and **house music**; also **pop, ballads** and **funk-rock**. Produced "Good Man/Woman," "The Book" and "Money" (by Poku), recorded by Jon E. Shakka on Poku Records.

PREJIPPIE MUSIC GROUP, Box 312897, Penobscot Station, Detroit MI 48231. President: Bruce Henderson. Record producer, music publisher (Prejippie Music Group/BMI) and record company (PMG Records). Estab. 1990. Produces 6-12 12″ singles, 2 LPs and 2 EPs/year. Fee derived from outright fee from record company.
• See their listing in the Music Publishers section, as well as PMG Records in the Record Companies section.
How to Contact: Submit demo tape by mail. Unsolicited submissions are OK. No phone calls please. Prefers cassette with 3-4 songs and lyric sheet. SASE. Reports in 3 months.
Music: Mostly **funk/rock** and **techno/house**; also **alternative rock** and **experimental music** (for possible jingle/scoring projects). Produced "You Enjoy the Girl" and "Lolita," written and recorded by Bourgeoisie Paper Jam; and "Windsong," written and recorded by Tony Webb, all on PMG Records.
Tips: "We're looking for songwriters who have a good sense of arrangement, a fresh approach to a certain sound and a great melody/hook for each song."

THE PRESCRIPTION CO., % D.F. Gasman, 5 Slocum Ave., Port Washington NY 10050. (516)767-1929. President: David F. Gasman. Vice President A&R: Kirk Nordstrom. Branch: 525 Ashbury St., San Francisco CA 94117. (415)553-8540. VP Sales: Bruce Brennan. Record producer and music publisher (Prescription Co./BMI). Fee derived from sales royalty when artist or song is recorded or outright fee from record company.
• See their listing in the Music Publishers section.
How to Contact: Write or call first about your interest then submit demo. Prefers cassette with any number of songs and lyric sheet. Does not return material. Reports in 1 month.
Music: Mostly **bluegrass**, **blues**, **children's**, **country**, **dance**, **easy listening**, **jazz**, **MOR**, **progressive**, **R&B**, **rock**, **soul** and **top 40/pop**. Produced "You Came In," "Rock 'n' Roll Blues" and *Just What the Doctor Ordered*, all recorded by Medicine Mike.
Tips: "We want quality—fads mean nothing to us. Familiarity with the artist's material helps too."

PRIVATE ISLAND TRAX, (formerly Mīmác Productions), 6520 Sunset Blvd., Hollywood CA 90028. (213)856-8729. Artist Services: Robyn Whitney. Record producer and studio-TRAX recording. Estab. 1979. Fee derived from outright fee from record company. "If not a spec deal, we are for hire for production services."
How to Contact: Submit demo tape by mail. Unsolicited submissions are OK. Prefers cassette (or VHS videocassette if available) with 4 songs and lyric sheet. "Not interested in rap, pop/dance or country. We specialize in hard rock, heavy metal, unique R&B and some mature pop." Does not return material. Reports in 3 months.
Music: Mostly **hard rock**, **heavy metal** and **funk/rock**; also **unique R&B**, **mature pop** and **mature Latin pop**. Produced *Total Eclipse*, written and recorded by Total Eclipse on A&M Records (rock); *Juicy Talk*, written and recorded by Jerry Riopelle on Warner Bros. Records (country rock); and *Music Speaks Louder than Words* (by G. Abbot/A. Barykin), recorded by Emmanuel on Sony Records (Latin pop).
Tips: "Have your act totally developed: exact genre of music, detailed image, perfected songs. We don't want to teach you your craft."

RAINBOW RECORDING, 113 Shamrock Dr., Mankato MN 56001. Phone/fax: (507)625-4027. Contact: Michael Totman. Record producer and recording studio. Estab. 1986. Produces 4 singles, 4 LPs and 1 EP/year. Fee derived from outright fee from recording artist or record company.
How to Contact: Submit demo tape by mail. Unsolicited submissions are OK. Prefers cassette, DAT or VHS videocassette with 4 songs and lyric sheet or lead sheet. Does not return material. Reports in 4-6 weeks.
Music: Mostly **rock**, **country** and **top 40**; also **old time**, **punk-alternative** and **R&B**. Produced *Hosanna Praise Group Songs*, recorded by Hosanna Praise Group (contemporary Christian); *Structure Lake Two*, recorded by Structure/Jody Miller (rock); and *Untitled*, recorded by Morning Star/John Weber (rock opera).

RAMMIT RECORDS, 414 Ontario St., Toronto Ontario M5A 2W1 **Canada**. (416)923-7611. President: Trevor G. Shelton. Record producer, record company and music publisher. Estab. 1988. Produces 3-4 singles, 4 LPs and 4 CDs/year. Fee derived from sales royalty when song or artist is recorded or outright fee from record company.

REFER TO THE CATEGORY INDEX (at the end of this section) to find exactly which companies are interested in the type of music you write.

• See their listing in the Record Companies section.
How to Contact: Submit demo tape by mail. Unsolicited submissions are OK. Prefers cassette or VHS videocassette with 4-5 songs. "Include letter outlining what it is you are looking for." SASE. Reports in 3 weeks.
Music: Mostly **urban dance** and **alternative rock**. Produced *2 Versatile* (by D. Myrie/R. Clark), recorded by 2 Versatile (hip hop/R&B); *Line Up In Paris*, recorded by Line Up in Paris, both on A&M Records; and *Korea*, (by Lipworns/Mull), recorded by Korea on MCA Records (hard/rock). Other artists include Cleo-Patra, Liberty, Silver and Marvin Gaye.

REALWORLD ENTERTAINMENT CORP., 23330 Commerce Park Rd., Cleveland OH 44122. (216)292-6566. Fax: (216)292-1765. Producers/music publishers: Howard Perl, Lee Mars. Record producer and music publisher. Estab. 1994. Produces 3 acts/year. Fee derived from sales royalty when song or artist is recorded.
How to Contact: Submit demo tape by mail. Unsolicited submissions are OK. Prefers DAT or cassette (or videocassette if available) with 1-4 songs. "Label every part of submission with phone number and name." SASE. Reports in 6 weeks.
Music: Mostly **R&B/urban, rap** and **pop**; also **alternative**. Produced "Hey Man Nice Shot" remixes for Filter (Warner/Reprise); "Make You Say Daddy" remixes for Twice! (Silas/MCA); and *A Low Down Dirty Shame* soundtrack (songs by Silk & Zhane). Other artists include Carey Kelly.
Tips: "Must keep an open mind and be willing to try new ideas."

RED KASTLE PRODUCTIONS, Box 163, West Redding CT 06896. President: Paul Hotchkiss. Record producer and music publisher. Produces 10 singles, 2 EPs, 2 LPs and 2 CDs/year. Fee derived from sales royalty.
• Red Kastle's publishing company, Blue Hill Music, is listed in the Music Publishers section, and their record label, Target Records, is in the Record Companies section.
How to Contact: Prefers cassette with 2 songs and lyric sheet. Include bio. SASE. Reports in 3 weeks.
Music: Mostly **country** and **country/pop**. Produced "Honky Tonk Darlin'" and "Thinking About You," (by P. Hotchkiss), recorded by Susan Rose Manning on Target Records (country); and "Destination You," written and recorded by Michael Terry on Roto Noto Records (country). Other artists include Big John Hartman, Beverly's Hill-Billy Band, Susan Rose, Jett and Road Dawgs.

REEL ADVENTURES, 9 Peggy Lane, Salem NH 03079. (603)898-7097. Chief Engineer/Producer: Rick Asmega. Record producer. Estab. 1972. Produces 45 singles, 1 12″ single, 20 LPs, 2 EPs and 6 CDs/year. Fee derived from sales royalty when song or artist is recorded, or outright fee from recording artist or record company.
How to Contact: Submit demo tape by mail. Unsolicited submissions are OK. Prefers cassette (or VHS/8mm videocassette) and lyric sheet. Include photos and résumé. SASE. Reports in 2-3 weeks.
Music: Mostly **pop, funk** and **country**; also **blues, reggae** and **rock**. Produced *Cry Sin* (by Peter Sin), recorded by Cry Sin (pop); *Reunion* (by Anne Saltmarsh), recorded by New Hampshire Notibles (easy listening), both on Indi Records; and *Lazy Smoke*, written and recorded by John Pollano on Onyx Records (easy rock). Other artists include Larry Sterling, Broken Men, Melvin Crockett, Fred Vigeant, Monster Mash, Carl Armand, Cool Blue Sky, Ransome, Backtrax, Push, Too Cool for Humans and Burn Alley.

RICHMOND ST. RECORDINGS, INC., 168 Railroad St., Huntington Station, NY 11746. (516)423-3246. President: Bill Falvey. Record producer. Estab. 1987. Produces 100 singles, 3-5 12″ singles, 20 LPs, 50 EPs and 3-5 CDs/year. Fee derived from outright fee from recording artist or record company and investors.
How to Contact: Write or call first to arrange personal interview. Prefers cassette (or 1/2″ VHS videocassette if available). SASE. Reports in 1-2 weeks.
Music: All types. Produced *Head Cleaners*, written and recorded by Marc Berge on Nickel Records (rock); *Laughing Boy* (by Carey Palmer/Kursh Kale), recorded by Rewind on LB Records (rock); and *Coronation* (by Matt Rothstein), recorded by Kig Box on R&R Records (rap). Other artists include Pure Dog, Smok'n Mirrors, Colt Daniel, Lenny Cocco & Chimes, Eileen Alexander, Gravity, Revisions and Jim Kohler.

ROCKSTAR PRODUCTIONS, P.O. Box 131, Southeastern PA 19399. Executive Vice President: Jeffrey Sacks. Director of Marketing: Roni Sacks. Record producer. Estab. 1988. Produces 5 singles/year. Fee derived from sales royalty when song or artist is recorded.
How to Contact: Submit demo tape by mail. Unsolicited submissions are OK. Prefers cassette with 2 songs and lyric sheet. Does not return material. Reports in 2 months.
Music: Mostly **rock** and **pop**. Produced "Clip & Save," "Sad Way" and "The Bell" (by S. Sax), all recorded by Wanderlust on RKS Records (rock). Other artists include Nancy Falkow.

Tips: "Musical tastes should include The Beatles, The Kinks, Queen, The Cars. Be original with classic rock roots."

MIKE ROSENMAN, 45-14 215 Place, Bayside NY 11361. (718)229-4864. Producer: Mike Rosenman. Record producer and arranger. Estab. 1984. Produces 2-4 singles/year. Fee derived from sales royalty or outright fee from recording artist.
How to Contact: Call first and obtain permission to submit. Prefers cassette (or VHS videocassette if available), with 2-4 songs and lyric sheet. Include address and phone number. Put phone number on cassette. Will not return any tapes without SASE. Reports in 2-3 months.
Music: Mostly **pop**, **R&B**, **dance** and **rock**. Produced "Don't Bite the Hand That Feeds You" (by Ellen Parker), recorded by Dope Enough For Ya on Homebase Records (rap/R&B); "My Love Is Deep" (by M. Rosenman/E. Parker), recorded by Sara Parker on Vestry Records (dance); and *Jamie Morad*, written and recorded by Jamie Morad on Pejwak Records (rap).
Tips: "Write a song that says something original and makes sense. Production quality is less important than content quality."

RR & R MUSIC PRODUCTIONS INC., 375 Military Rd., Kalama WA 98625. Owner/President: Ron Dennis Wheeler. Record producer, music publisher (Sounds of Aicram/BMI and Do It Now Publishing/ASCAP) and record company (RR&R, Rapture, Ready Records and Yshua Records). Estab. 1964. Produces 10-20 compilation CDs and 10-20 CDs/year.
• See the listings for Sounds of Aicram in the Music Publishers section and RR&R Records in the Record Companies section.
How to Contact: Submit demo tape by mail. Unsolicited submissions are OK. Prefers cassette (Type II) or DAT with lyric chords and lead sheet. "Demo should have lead vocal and music and also a recording of music tracks without vocals." SASE. Reports only if interested.
Music: All types except rap or New Age and satanic. Produced "Don't Take The Kids and Move Away" (by Vern Decato), recorded by Billy James on RR&R; "8×10 Framed In Gold" (by Richard McGibony), recorded by Joey Welz on Caprice Records; and "I Need You" (by R. McGibony), recorded by Billy James on Capitol/EMI Records.

RUSTRON MUSIC PRODUCTIONS, 1156 Park Lane, West Palm Beach FL 33417-5957. (407)686-1354. A&R Directors: Rusty Gordon, Ron Caruso and Kevin Reeves. Record producer, manager and music publisher (Rustron Music Publishers/BMI, Whimsong Publishing/ASCAP). Estab. 1970. Produces 6-10 LP/cassettes and 6 CDs/year. Fee derived from sales royalty or outright fee from record company distributorship. "This branch office reviews all material submitted for the home office in Ridgefield, CT."
• See their listings in the Record Companies and Managers and Booking Agents sections, as well as Rustron Music Publishers in the Music Publishers section.
How to Contact: Submit demo tape by mail. Unsolicited submissions are OK. Prefers cassette with 1-3 songs and lyric or lead sheet. "Songs should be 3½ minutes long or less and must be commercially viable for today's market. Exception: New Age fusion compositions 3-10 minutes each, ½ hour maximum. Singer/songwriters and collaborators are preferred." SASE required for all correspondence. Reports in 2-4 months.
Music: Mostly **progressive country**, **pop** (ballads, blues, theatrical, cabaret), **folk/rock**, and **A/C electric acoustic**; also **R&B**, **New Age folk fusion** and **New Age instrumentals**. Produced "Give A Damn" (by J. Margo-Reby/Debbie Tyson), recorded by Jayne Margo-Reby; "Are You The One," written and recorded by Star Smiley; and "You Know I Love You" (by Rusty Gordon/Eric Shafer), recorded by Dana Adams, all on Rustron Records. Other artists include Ellen Hines, Deb Criss, Robin Plitt, Lori Surrency, Gary Jess, Boomslang, Swampsinger and Terry Andrews.
Tips: "Write from the heart. Don't be redundant. Develop lyrical themes, be unpredictable. Compose definitve melodies. Develop your own unique sound, don't sound like anyone else."

SANDBOX PRODUCTIONS, 11684 Ventura Blvd., Suite 134, Studio City CA 91604. (818)386-9135. Fax: (818)386-2862. Producer/Engineer: Mark Wolfson. Record producer, engineer/music supervisor. Estab. 1972. Produces 2 12″ singles, 2 CDs and 4 film projects a year. Fee derived from sales royalty when song or artist is recorded or outright fee from record company.
• See the listing for The Sandbox in the Advertising, AV and Commercial Music Firms sections.
How to Contact: Submit demo tape by mail. Unsolicited submissions are OK. "No calls please." SASE. Reports in 6 weeks.
Music: Produced "Let's Make Love," for the film *Cool World*, recorded by Kim Basinger and Frank Sinatra Jr. on MCA Records; "Marie Down the Street," recorded by Stone Temple Pilots on Savage Records; and "Don't Want to Fall in Love," recorded by Jane Child on Warner Bros. Records.

RAY SANDERS COMPANY, Box 384252, Waikoloa HI 96738. (808)883-9383. Owner: Ray Sanders. Record producer and music publisher (Pacific Coast Music/BMI). Estab. 1954. Produces 24 singles

and 4-5 CDs/year. Fee derived from outright fee from recording artist or record company.
How to Contact: Submit lyrics only—must be typed! Unsolicited submissions are OK. No cassettes. SASE. Reports in 1 week.
Music: Country; also **country gospel**. Produced "I Love Country Music" (by Hal Johnson) on BJD Records (country); *After Loving You* (by Glady Mayes) and "Resting Place" (by Mary Norris) (country gospel), both on Silverdash Records, all recorded by Ray Sanders. Other artists include Denny Hamingson, Ed Riley and Straight Shot, Raising Cane, Dennis O'Niel, Lee Davis.
Tips: "You are always better off to work with a co-writer, publisher/record company with a *track record* of success. We have an open door policy to any good writer."

SAS CORPORATION/SPECIAL AUDIO SERVICES, 503 Broadway, Suite 520, New York NY 10012. (212)226-6271. Fax: (212)226-6357. Owner: Paul Special. Record producer. Estab. 1988. Produces 3 singles, 1 12″ single, 5 LPs, 1 EP and 5 CDs/year. Fee derived from sales royalty when song or artist is recorded or outright fee from recording artist or record company.
How to Contact: Submit demo tape by mail. Unsolicited submissions are OK. Prefers cassette with 1-10 songs and lyric sheet. SASE. Reports in 6-8 weeks.
Music: Hard rock, funk, rock, metal, alternative and **industrial**. Produced "Color Of Darkness," written and recorded by Maria Excommunikata on Megaforce Records (alternative); "Love U/Duke," written and recorded by Heads Up! on Emergo Records (funk rock); and "Hope/Emelda" (by Van Orden/Hoffman), recorded by The Ordinaires on Bar None Records (alternative). Other artists include Central Europe, Band Of Weeds, Peter Moffit and Kablama Chunk.
Tips: "Don't be afraid to bring up new and unusual ideas."

SEGAL'S PRODUCTIONS, 16 Grace Rd., Newton MA 02159. (617)969-6196. Contact: Charles Segal. Record producer, music publisher (Segal's Publications/BMI, Samro South Africa) and record company (Spin Records). Produces 6 singles and 6 LPs/year. Fee derived from sales royalty when song or artist is recorded.
    • See the listing for Segal's Publications in the Music Publishers section.
How to Contact: Submit demo tape by mail. Unsolicited submissions are OK. Prefers cassette (or videocassette) with 3 songs and lyric sheet or lead sheet of melody, words, chords. "Please record keyboard/voice or guitar/voice if you can't get a group." Does not return material. Reports in 3 months (only if interested).
Music: Mostly **rock, pop** and **country**; also **R&B** and **comedy**. Produced "What is This Love" (by Paul/Motou), recorded by Julia Manin (rock); "Lovely Is This Memory" (by Segal/Paul), recorded by Nick Chosn on AU.S. (ballad); and *There'll Come A Time* (by Charles Segal), recorded by Rosemary Wills on Spin Records (ballad). Other artists include Art Heatley, Dan Hill and Melanie.
Tips: "Make a good and clear production of cassette even if it is only piano rhythm and voice. Also do a lead sheet of music—words—chords."

SHARPE SOUND PRODUCTIONS, Box 140536, Nashville TN 37214. (615)449-7781. Producer/Engineer: Ed Sharpe. Record producer. Estab. 1990. Fee derived from sales royalty or outright fee from recording artist or record company.
How to Contact: Submit demo tape by mail. Unsolicited submissions are OK. Prefers cassette (or VHS videocassette if available) with 4 songs and lyric sheet. SASE. Reports in 1 month.
Music: All types. Produced *Johnny B!*, written and recorded by John Bellar on Belotes Ferry Records (country/jazz); "Heavy" (by Dan Gunn), recorded by Velocipede on REX Records (rock/Christian); and *Cherokee Legends*, written and recorded by Ed Sharpe on Cherokee Publications (spoken word).
Tips: "Exhibit a personal and unique angle to your music."

SHU'BABY MONTEZ MUSIC, P.O. Box 28816, Philadelphia PA 19151. (215)473-5527. General Manager: Leroy Schuler. Record producer. Estab. 1990. Produces 6 singles, 25 12″ singles and 3 LPs/year. Fee derived from sales royalty when song or artist is recorded.
How to Contact: Call first and obtain permission to submit. Prefers cassette with 4 songs and lyric sheet. SASE. Reports in 5 weeks.
Music: Mostly **R&B, hip-hop** and **funk**. Produced *Free Style* (by Shu'Baby/K. Chaney/V. Butler), recorded by Shu'Baby; "Your Love Is So Sweet" and "Express Yourself" (by James Lewis/Shu'-Baby), recorded by James Lewis, all on Urban Logic Records.

SILVER BOW PRODUCTIONS, 6260 130 St., Surrey, British Columbia V3X 1R6 **Canada**. (604)572-4232. Fax: (604)572-4252. A&R: Candice James. Record producer. Estab. 1986. Produces 16 singles, 4 LPs and 6 CDs/year. Fee derived from outright fee from recording artist.
How to Contact: Call first and obtain permission to submit. Prefers cassette with 2 songs and lyric sheet. Does not return material. Reports in 6 weeks.
Music: Mostly **country, pop**, and **rock**; also **gospel, blues** and **jazz**. Produced *Fragile-Handle With Care*, written and recorded by Razzy Bailey on SOA Records (country); *Sugar* (erotic mix) (by Martin

Richmond), recorded by Martini (rock); and *Somewhere Downtown* (by Marsh Gardner), recorded by Clancy Wright on Saddlestone Records (country). Other artists include Rex Howard, Gerry King, Joe Lonsdale, Barb Farrell, Dorrie Alexander, Peter James, Matt Audette and Cordel James.

*SILVER THUNDER MUSIC GROUP, P.O. Box 41335, Nashville TN 37204. Phone/fax: (615)391-5035. President: Rusty Budde. Record producer, record company (Silver Thunder Records), music publisher (Silver Thunder Publishing), management firm. Estab. 1982. Produces 20 singles, 5-7 LPs and 5-7 CDs/year. Fee derived from sales royalty when song or artist is recorded or outright fee from recording artist or record company.
How to Contact: Write first and obtain permission to submit a demo or arrange personal interview. Prefers cassette. "Artists should submit 8 × 10 photo along with demo tape." Does not return material. Reports in 6-16 weeks.
Music: Mostly **country, rock** and **R&B**; also **gospel** and **pop**. Produced *What's Not To Love* (by D.J. Music), recorded by Heather Hartsfield (country); and *Radio Active* (by G. McCorkel), recorded by J.D. Treece (country), both on STR Records. Other artists include Rod Woodson, Jeff Samules, Jodi Collins and Bryan West.

*SIMON SEZ PRODUCTIONS, 5320 Riverton #3, North Hollywood CA 90160-3399. Phone/fax: (818)506-8682. President: Mitch Farber. Record producer. Estab. 1990. Produces 10 singles, 12 LPs, 4 EPs and 14 CDs/year. Fee derived from sales royalty when song or artist is recorded.
How to Contact: Submit demo tape by mail. Unsolicited submissions are OK. Prefers DAT. Does not return material. Reports in 3 weeks.
Music: Mostly **rock, country** and **jazz**; also **jingles**. Produced "Gone" (by Ellen Knorr), recorded by Black on BK Records (rock); and "Raindance," written and recorded by Joy Basu on Shrapnel Records (rock). Other artists include X's for Eyes.

*MIKE SISKIND PRODUCTIONS, 285 Chestnut St., West Hempstead NY 11552. (516)489-0738. Fax: (516)565-9425. E-mail: platear1@aol.com. Producer: Mike Siskind. Record producer. Estab. 1993. Produces 1-2 singles, 1-2 LPs and 1-2 CDs/year. Fee derived from sales royalty when song or artist is recorded or outright fee from recording artist or record company.
How to Contact: Submit demo tape by mail. Unsolicited submissions are OK. Prefers cassette with 3 songs and lyric sheet. "Serious acts only." SASE. Reports in 2-3 months.
Music: Mostly **rock, folk** and **country** (work best with women singers); also **pop** and **A/C**. Produced *Oconoluftee Lullaby* and *No Mercy*, written and recorded by Georgi Smith on Red Hand Records (rock); and *New York City Night*, written and recorded by Michael Ellis on Storehouse Records (rock).
Tips: "Be a pro, be prepared and be willing to take constructive criticism. My goal is the same as yours, to get the best possible product. Any suggestion is not a personal attack, but an attempt to bring out the best in everyone."

SLAVESONG CORPORATION, INC., P.O. Box 41233, Dallas TX 75241-0233. (214)225-1903. Chief Executive Officer: Keith Hill. Record producer and music publisher. Estab. 1991. Produces 2 singles, 2 12″ singles, 1 LP, 1 EP and 1 CD/year. Fee derived from sales royalty when song or artist is recorded or outright fee from recording artist.
How to Contact: Submit demo tape by mail. Unsolicited submissions are OK. Prefers cassette (or VHS videocassette) with 3-5 songs and lyric sheet. Send photo. SASE. Reports in 1 month.
Music: Mostly **R&B/dance, reggae** and **jazz**; also **world beat**. Produced "Oil Spill" and "Hi In My Hello" (by S.W./G.C.), recorded by George Clinton on Warner Bros. Records (R&B); and "Why?" (by S.W./K.H./2 Pos.), recorded by Two Positive M.C. on Slavesong Records (rap). Other artists include X-Slave and Gold Tee.

SMASH THE RADIO PRODUCTIONS, 13659 Victory #456, Van Nuys CA 91401. (818)365-4425. Fax: (818)904-0512. Producers: Steven T. Easter and Chris Wade-Daumerst. Record producer, record company (Smash the Radio/Mushi-Mushi) and music publisher (Easter Eyes Music/BMI). Estab. 1987. Produces 2 singles, 2 EPs and 2 CDs/year. Fee derived from sales royalty when song or artist is recorded or outright fee from recording artist or record company.
How to Contact: Submit demo tape by mail. Unsolicited submissions are OK. Prefers cassette or DAT (or VHS videocassette) with 4 songs and lyric sheet. SASE. Reports in 3 weeks.
Music: Mostly **Techno/house, pop** and **reggae**; also **alternative, R&B** and **rap**. Produced "Skating on Thin Ice" (by Steve Easter/Buff Bullen), recorded by Wailing Wall (alternative); "Hold Me/Sex Bass" (by Steve EAster/Chris Wade), recorded by House Arrest (house), both on Smash the Radio Records; and "Turning Nuttin 2 Something" (by Chris Wade/Steve Easter), recorded by E'Clipz on Mushi-Mushi Records (rap). Other artists include Dooley Boys, Jah-Moon, Sweet Cheeks, Harry Willis, Neil Kramer.
Tips: "Present a professional demo pack and pay attention to detail."

S'N'M RECORDING/HIT RECORDS NETWORK, 403 Halkirk, Santa Barbara CA 93110. (805)964-3035. Producers: Cory Orosco and Ernie Orosco. Record producer, record company (Night City Records, Warrior Records, Tell International Records), music publisher. Estab. 1984. Produces 4 singles, 2 12″ singles, 4 LPs, 2 EPs and 2-4 CDs/year.
How to Contact: Submit demo tape by mail. Unsolicited submissions are OK. Prefers VHS videocassette if available with 4 songs and lyric sheet. Does not return material. Reports in 2 months.
Music: Mostly **pop-rock, country** and **top 40**; also **top 40 funk, top 40 rock** and **top 40 country**. Produced *Club Songs* (by Ed Drayton), recorded by Free Cats; *Heartaches & Old Songs*, written and recorded by Mickey Guinn; and *Jargon* (by Tim Gates/Jargon), recorded by Jargon, all on Hit Records. Other artists include New Vision, Jade, Ernie and the Emperors, Hollywood Heros, Cornelius Bumpus (Doobie Brothers), Tim Bogert (Vanilla Fudge, Jeff Beck), Floyd Sneed (3 Dog Night), Wayne Lewis.
Tips: "Keep searching for the infectious chorus hook and don't give up."

SOUND CELL, 601 Meridian St., Huntsville AL 35801. (205)539-1868. Fax: (205)533-1622. Contact: Doug Smith. Record producer, record company and music publisher. Estab. 1981.
How to Contact: Write first and obtain permission to submit a demo. Prefers cassette. Does not return material. Reports in 1 month.
Music: Mostly **country, folk** and **bluegrass**; also **R&B** and **pop**. Produced Brian McKnight, Pierce Pettis, Claire Lynch, Take 6 and Vova Nova.

SOUND CONTROL PRODUCTIONS, 2813 Azalea Place, Nashville TN 37204. (615)269-5638. Producer: Mark. Record producer and record company (Mosrite Records). Estab. 1982. Produces 30 singles, 8 LPs and 2 CDs/year. Fee derived from sales royalty or outright fee from recording artist or record company—"sometimes all or a combination of these." Charges 50% in advance for services.
How to Contact: Submit demo tape by mail. Unsolicited submissions are OK. Prefers cassette with 3 songs and lyric sheet. "Don't submit anything in which you need to explain what the song or you are trying to say—let the performance do that." Does not return material. Reports in 8 weeks.
Music: Mostly **country, gospel** and **bluegrass**; also **Christmas**. Produced *Paddy Kelly* (by various), recorded by Paddy Kelly (country); *The Thorntons* (by various), recorded by Thorntons on Bridge Records (gospel); and *The Lewis Family* (by various), recorded by The Lewistown on Benson Records (gospel bluegrass).

SOUND SERVICES, 39867 Fremont Blvd., Apt. 505, Fremont CA 94538. (510)657-3079. Owner: Curtis Autin. Record producer. Estab. 1986. Produces 1 single and 2 LPs/year. Fee derived from outright fee from recording artist.
How to Contact: Submit demo tape by mail. Unsolicited submissions are OK. Prefers cassette (or VHS videocassette) with 1 song and lyric or lead sheet. SASE. Reports in 1 week.
Music: Mostly **rock, R&B** and **pop**; also **jazz**. Produced "People" (by Cardell Porter); "Lone Wolf" and *Night Ryder*, both by Dave Hamlett, all on Sound Services Records.
Tips: "I'm looking for artists and artists/songwriters."

SOUND SOUND/SAVAGE FRUITARIAN, P.O. Box 22999, Seattle WA 98122-0999. (206)322-6866. Fax: (206)720-0075. Owner: Tom Fallat. Record producer and recording studio. Estab. 1991. Produces 8 LPs and 5 CDs/year. Fee derived from outright fee from recording artist or record company.
How to Contact: Write or call first and obtain permission to submit a demo. Prefers cassette with 1 song and lyric or lead sheet. SASE. Reports in 2 months.
Music: Mostly **pop/rock/alternative, jazz** and **New Age**; also **anything unusual**. Produced *Victim of the Gat* (by Zone & Mac Tenshun), recorded by Lethal Crew (rap); *Led Jaxson* (by Doug Caulkins/Mark Malloy), recorded by Led Jaxson (blues); and *The Ocean Shows the Sky*, written and recorded by Joe Panzetta (folk/pop). Other artists include Robin Wes, Mecca Normal and Mojo Skill.
Tips: "Be unique, authentic and creative. We're more interested in honest expression than quick money making music."

SOUNDBOARD STUDIOS, 2600 Kennedy Blvd., Jersey City NJ 07306. (201)451-6140. Producer: Paul Harlyn. Record producer. Estab. 1984. Produces 5 singles, 2 EPs and 4 CDs/year. Fee derived from outright fee from record company.

REMEMBER: Don't "shotgun" your demo tapes. Submit only to companies interested in the type of music you write. For more submission hints, refer to Getting Started on page 5.

How to Contact: Submit demo tape by mail. Unsolicited submissions are OK. Prefers cassette with 3 songs. SASE. Reports in 1 month.

Music: Mostly **trance dance**, **pop dance** and **alternative rock/dance**; also **alternative rock**. Produced *Poppyseed (Blue Daze)* (by Paul Harlyn/Scott Slachter), recorded by Poppyseed on CNS Records; "Guantantamera" (by Jose Marti/H. Angulo/P. Seager), recorded by J.M. Dorathan on Polygram Records; and *Indian Spirets* (by Paul Harlyn), recorded by Harlyn on Radikal/BMG Records. Other artists include Great Barrier.

Tips: "Be your true self! Do your one thing better than anyone else."

SOUNDSTAGE SOUTH, 462 Safari Dr., Memphis TN 38111. (901)363-3345. President: Fred B. Montgomery. Record producer and artist development. Estab. 1990. Fee derived from sales royalty when song or artist is recorded. "SoundStage intends to provide a Rehearsal/Production Facility to area contemporary musicians and songwriters on a daily and monthly rental basis—to include a demo recording studio, private rehearsal studios and showcase room."

How to Contact: Submit demo tape by mail. Unsolicited submissions are OK. Prefers cassette (or VHS videocassette if available) with 3 songs and lyric sheet. Does not return material. Reports in 2-8 weeks.

Music: Mostly **rock**, **blues rock** and **contemporary country**; also **country/rock**.

Tips: "I have represented selected songwriters/artists in the Memphis/Mid-South area in development, pre-production, demo production and general support in shopping original material to publishers and labels."

SPHERE PRODUCTIONS, Box 991, Far Hills NJ 07931-0991. (908)781-1650. Fax: (908)781-1693. President: Tony Zarrella. Talent Manager: Louisa Pazienza. Record producer, artist development, management and placement of artists with major/independent labels. Produces 5-6 singles and 3 CDs/year. Estab. 1988.

How to Contact: Submit demo tape by mail. Unsolicited submissions are OK. Prefers cassette or CD (or VHS videocassette) with 3-5 songs and lyric sheets. "Must include: photos, press, résumé, goals and specifics of project submitted, etc." SASE. Reports in 10-12 weeks.

Music: Specializes in **pop/rock (mainstream)**, **progressive/rock**, **New Age** and **crossover country/pop**; also **film soundtracks**. Produced *Take This Heart*, *It's Our Love* and *You and I (Are Dreamers)* (by T. Zarrella), recorded by 4 of Hearts (pop/rock) on Sphere Records. Also represents Oona Falcon, Sky-King, Traveller, Forever More and Elexus Quinn & Ziggy True (the "Nothing is Meaningless Project").

Tips: "Be able to take direction and have trust and faith in yourself, your producer and manager. Currently seeking artists/groups incorporating various styles into a focused mainstream product."

STUART AUDIO SERVICES, 11 Ridgeway Ave., Gorham ME 04038. (207)839-3569. Producer/Owner: John A. Stuart. Record producer and music publisher. Estab. 1979. Produces 1-2 singles, 3 LPs and 3 CDs/year. Fee derived from sales royalty when song or artist is recorded, outright fee from recording artist or record company, or demo and consulting fees.

How to Contact: Write or call first and obtain permission to submit or to arrange a personal interview. Prefers cassette with 4 songs and lyric sheet. SASE. Reports in 3-4 weeks.

Music: Mostly **alternative folk-rock**, **rock** and **country**; also **contemporary Christian**, **children's** and **unusual**. Produced *Hungry Eyes*, written and recorded by Noel Paul Stookey on Gold Castle Records (new folk); *Winter to Summer*, written and recorded by John A. Stuart on C.T.W. Records (soundtrack); and *Signs of Home* (by Romanow/Rowe), recorded by Schoonner Fare on OuterGreen Records (folk). Other artists include Bates Motel, Chris Heard, Al Mossberg, Bodyworks, Jim Newton, Rick Charette and music for *Sesame Street* (soundtrack work).

STUDIO RECORDING, 425 Coloma, Sausalito CA 94965. (415)332-6289. Fax: (415)332-0249. Manager/Co-owner: Joel Jaffe. Record producer and engineer. Estab. 1983. Produces 6-8 LPs and 6-8 CDs/year. Fee derived from sales royalty when song or artist is recorded or outright fee from record company.

How to Contact: Call first and obtain permission to submit demo. Prefers cassette with 3-4 songs and lyric sheet. Does not return material. Reports in 1-2 months. "No response means not accepting material."

Music: Mostly **rock**, **alternative** and **pop**; also **country** and **R&B**. Engineered and co-produced *Sneetches*, written and recorded by Sneetches on SpinART/Sony Records (rock); *Stylistics* (by D. Glass), recorded by Stylistics on Bellmark Records (R&B); and *Beggars*, recorded by Beggars on Island Records (alternative). Other artists include Michael Been, Lenny Williams and Huey Lewis & The News.

Tips: "Be commercial! Direction of music to a format is essential."

PRESTON SULLIVAN ENTERPRISES, Dept. SM, 1217 16th Ave. S., Nashville TN 37212. (615)327-8129. President: Preston Sullivan. Record producer. Produces 10 singles and 4 LPs/year.
How to Contact: Submit demo tape by mail. Unsolicited submissions are OK. Prefers cassette (or videocassette) and lyric sheet. Does not return unsolicited material. Reports in 3 weeks.
Music: Mostly **hard rock, alternative rock, pop** and **R&B**. Produced "The Grinning Plowman" (by Michael Ake), recorded by The Grinning Plowmen (pop/rock); "Dessau" (by John Elliott), recorded by Dessau (dance); and "Dorcha," recorded by Dorcha (rock), all on Carlyle Records.

SYNDICATE SOUND, INC., 475 Fifth St., Struthers OH 44471. (216)755-1331. President: Jeff Wormley. Record producer, audio and video production company and record and song promotion company. Estab. 1981. Produces 6-10 singles and 15-20 CDs/year. Fee derived from sales royalty when song or artist is recorded or outright fee from recording artist or record company.
How to Contact: Submit demo tape by mail. Unsolicited submissions are OK. "Please send a promo package or biography (with pictures) of artist, stating past and present concerts and records." SASE. Reports in 4-6 weeks.
Music: Mostly **rock, pop** and **Christian rock**; also **country, R&B** and **alternative**. Produced "If At First You Don't Succeed" (by Dane Harris/Trish Reed), recorded by Trish Reed on RIPG Records; "Kitty Karry All" (by Dave Lisko), recorded by the Smarties; and "Oh-10," written and recorded by Ray Royal on Naughty Boyz Records. Other artists include Medicine Train, Freudian Slip, The Evergreens, Psycho Cafe, Gilroy's Kite, Jason Hairston and Madness.

*WILLIAM SZAWLOWSKI PRODUCTIONS & VENTURA MUSIC PUBLISHING, 7195 Mauriac, Brossard Quebec J4Y 1T8 **Canada**. Phone/fax: (514)678-3629. E-Mail: ventura@vir.com. President: Bill Szawlowski. Record producer. Estab. 1974. Produces 3 singles, 2 LPs and 3 CDs/year. Fee derived from sales royalty when song or artist is recorded.
How to Contact: Submit demo tape by mail. Unsolicited submissions are OK. Prefers 4 songs and lyric/lead sheet. "Cassette clearly marked: title, date of composition. Include picture and bio, letter of intention." SASE. Reports in 6 weeks.
Music: Mostly **rock, MOR** and **country**; also **dance, heavy rock** and **pop**. Produced *If I Were* (by Habre & Eon), recorded by Anxiety on Musicor Records (rock); *Gypsy Road* (by Anthony/Vanderbol), recorded by Garry Anthony on 2M Records (rock); and *Denise Murray* (by Murray & Lang), recorded by Denise Murray (country). Other artists include Sun City Rockers and Soul Stripper.

TALENT RECOGNITION SERVICES, P.O. Box 27745, Tempe AZ 85285-7745. Fax: (602)431-9225. General Manager: Donny Walker. Record producer and radio promoter. Estab. 1983. Produces 5-10 singles and 6-10 CDs/year. Fee derived from sales royalty when song or artist is recorded, outright fee from recording artist or record company, or investors.
How to Contact: Write first and obtain permission to submit or to arrange personal interview. Prefers cassette or VHS videocassette with 3-5 songs. Does not return material. Reports in 4-6 weeks.
Music: Mostly **rock, alternative** and **loud country**. Produced *Honey's Bone Yard*, written and recorded by Honey's Bone Yard on MSG Records; *Her Vanished Grace*, Her Vanished Grace on HVG Records; and *Unsigned & Deadly*, written and recorded by various artists on MSG Records.

TEXAS FANTASY MUSIC, 2932 Dyer St., Dallas TX 75205. (214)691-5318. Fax: (214)692-1392. Creative Director: Barbara McMillen. Record producer and music publisher (Showcat Music). Estab. 1982. Produces 35 singles/year. Fee derived from synchronization fees.
How to Contact: Submit demo tape by mail. Unsolicited submissions are OK. Prefers cassette with 2 songs and lyric sheet (if applicable). Does not return material. Reports in 6 weeks.
Music: Mostly **instrumental for film** and **all styles**. Produced *Theme for Billy Bob Country Countdown* (by Barbara McMillen/Don Ashley) syndicated TV show; *Theme for Impact* (by Don Ashley) syndicated TV; and *When I Was A Dinosaur Musical* (by Beverly Houston/Barbara McMillen/Richard Theisen), recorded by various artists on Remarkable Records (children's).

*TEXAS MUSIC MASTERS/WRIGHT PRODUCTIONS, 11231 Hwy. 64 E., Tyler TX 75707. Record producer. 30 years in business. Fee derived from outright fee from record company.
• See their listing in the Managers and Booking Agents section.
How to Contact: Submit demo tape by mail. Unsolicited submissions are OK. Prefers cassette with 3 songs and lyric sheet. SASE. Reports in 1 month.

 THE ASTERISK before a listing indicates that the listing is new in this edition. New markets are often the most receptive to unsolicited submissions.

Music: Mostly **country, gospel** and **blues**. Produced "The Road" (by Gene LeDoux), recorded by David Darst on Starquest Records; "Neon Glow," written and recorded by Jim Needham on Jukebox Records; and *Blue Jean* (by Alan Greene), recorded by Glen English on Starquest Records.

TMC PRODUCTIONS, P.O. Box 12353, San Antonio TX 78212. (210)829-1909. Producer: Joe Scates. Record producer, music publisher (Axbar Productions/BMI, Scates & Blanton/BMI and Axe Handle Music/ASCAP), record company (Axbar, Trophy, Jato, Prince and Charro Records) and record distribution and promotion. Produces 8-10 singles, 3-4 LPs and 4-6 CDs/year. Fee derived from sales royalty.
• TMC Productions' publishing company, Axbar, can be found in the Music Publishers section.
How to Contact: Write or call first and obtain permission to submit. Prefers cassette with 1-5 songs and lyric sheet. Does not return material. Reports "as soon as possible, but don't rush us."
Music: Mostly **traditional country**; also **blues, comedy** and **rock (soft)**. Produced "Chicken Dance" (traditional), recorded by George Chambers and "Hobo Heart," written and recorded by Juni Moon, both on Axbar Records. Other artists include Rick Will, Wayne Carter, Kathi Timm, Leon Taylor and Kenny Dale.

TOMSICK BROTHERS PRODUCTIONS, 21271 Chardon Rd., Dept. SM, Euclid OH 44117. (216)481-8380. President: Ken Tomsick. Record producer. Estab. 1982. Produces 2-5 LPs/year. Also produces original music for TV, radio, video and ad jingles. Fee derived from outright fee from recording artist.
How to Contact: Submit demo tape by mail. Unsolicited submissions are OK. Prefers cassette. Does not return material. Reports in 3 months.
Music: Mostly **ethnic, polka, jazz** and **alternative**. Produced *Soundbones* (by Tomsick Brothers), recorded by Tomsix; *Medium Head Boy*, written and recorded by Medium Head Boy, both on Behemoth Records; and *Slovenian Carousel*, written and recorded by Nancy Hlad.

TRAC RECORD CO., 170 N. Maple, Fresno CA 93702. (209)255-1717. Owner: Stan Anderson. Record producer, music publisher (Sellwood Publishing/BMI) and record company (TRAC Records). Estab. 1972. Produces 5 12" singles, 5 LPs and 5 CDs/year. Fee derived from outright fee from recording artist or outside investor.
• TRAC Records is also listed in the Record Companies section, and their publishing company, Sellwood Publishing, is listed in the Music Publishers section.
How to Contact: Submit demo tape by mail. Unsolicited submissions are OK. Prefers cassette with 3 songs and lyric sheet. "Studio quality." SASE. Reports in 3 weeks.
Music: Mostly **traditional country** and **country**. Produced *Long Texas Highway* (by Jessica James/Debbie D.), recorded by Jessica James; *Grandpa's Old Piano* (by Ray Richmond), recorded by Jessica James; and *Kick Me When I'm Down*, written and recorded by Jimmy Walker; all on TRAC Records (country). Other artists include Craig Jensen, The Country Connection.

THE TRINITY STUDIO, P.O. Box 1417, Corpus Christi TX 78403. (512)880-9268. Owner: Jim Wilken. Record producer and recording studio. Estab. 1988. Fee is negotiable.
How to Contact: Submit demo tape by mail. Unsolicited submissions are OK. Prefers cassette (or VHS videocassette if available). Does not return material. Reports in 1 month.
Music: Mostly **Christian-country**. Produced *Miracle Man* (by Merrill Lane), recorded by Leah (country); *The Train Song*, written and recorded by Merrill Lane, both on TC Records (country); and *Mark Ten Going Down*, written and recorded by Lofton Kline (country). Other artists include Kerry Patton, Lucy McGuffin, Jimmy Louis and Charlotte McGee.
Tips: "You must maintain a positive attitude about your career. Have faith in your work and don't get discouraged—keep at it."

TRIPLANE PRODUCTION, 120 Cloud Crest Dr., Henderson NV 89015. (702)564-3794. Producer: Vales Crossley. Record producer and music publisher. Estab. 1978. Produces 6 singles, 2 12" singles, 3 LPs, 3 EPs and 2 CDs/year. Fee derived from sales royalty when song or artist is recorded.
How to Contact: Write or call first and obtain permission to submit. Prefers cassette (or videocassette if available) with 3-6 songs and lyric sheet. Does not return unsolicited material. Reports in 4-6 weeks.
Music: Mostly **top 40, R&B, soul** and **rap**; also **New Age** and **rock**. Produced "Lapp Dog" (by S. Spann), recorded by Sweet Luie on Cryptic Records; "Hittin' Fo" (by R. Nullems), recorded by Baby Jon on Thump Records; and "Same Heart" (by V. Crossley/C. Burton), recorded by Twin Force on Dynasty Records. Other artists include Platters, Chrissie Zastrow and The Henleys.

Tips: "Be as ready to take care of business as you are to record."

12 METER PRODUCTIONS, 7808 Green Lake Rd., Fayetteville NY 13066. (315)637-6656. Producers: Matt Tucker and Chris Horvath. Record producer. Estab. 1988. Produces 1-5 singles, 1-5 12″ singles 1-2 LPs and 1-2 CDs/year. Fee derived from sales royalty or outright fee from recording artist or record company.
How to Contact: Submit demo tape by mail. Unsolicited submissions are OK. Prefers cassette (or VHS videocassette if available) with 1-5 songs and lyric sheet. "Send photo, press kit or bio if available. No calls." Does not return material. Reports in 2-3 months.
Music: Mostly **top 40/pop**, **dance** and **rock**; also **rap** and **R&B**. Produced "Incident at Big Sky" (by Tucker), recorded by DMOC (ambient); and *Please* (by D. Murray/J. Murray), recorded by Love Is Blue (techno), both on Murmur Records. Other artists include Jodi and Disgruntled Postal Workers.
Tips: "Send what you feel is your best work. Don't restrict yourself to one type of music. We listen to everything. Please tell us what we can do to help you. We are record producers, we can't get you a record contract, so don't ask."

TWIST TUNES, 807 Canyon Creek, Austin TX 78746. Phone/fax: (512)328-1836. Producer/Owner: Michael Donegani. Record producer. Estab. 1977. Produces 3 singles, 4 LPs, 1 EP and 2 CDs/year. Fee derived from outright fee from recording artist.
How to Contact: Call first and obtain permission to submit a demo. Prefers cassette with 3 songs and lyric sheet. SASE. Reports in 2 weeks.
Music: Mostly **personal**, **different** and **clear**; also **rock**, **pop** and **country**. Produced *Sprit Child*, written and recorded by Sprit Child (Christian); *Rita*, written and recorded by 47 Indians (rockabilly); and *Best Of*, written and recorded by Double O' Soul (jazz), all on Private Records. Other artists include John Lynsley, 2:AM, Chris Otcasek, Hassel & Twist, Lendahand, Mean Streets and Danny Click.

*UP FRONT MANAGEMENT, 1906 Seward Dr., Pittsburg CA 94565. Phone/fax: (510)427-7210. CEO/President: Charles Coke. Record producer, record company (Man Network/Heavyweight Productions) and music publisher (Brother Frog Music). Estab. 1980. Produces 10 singles, 10 LPs, 4 EPs and 10 CDs/year. Fee derived from upfront fee and percentage.
   • See their listing in the Managers and Booking Agents section.
How to Contact: Submit demo tape by mail. Unsolicited submissions are OK. Prefers cassette or CD with lyric sheet. Does not return material. Reports in 2 weeks.
Music: Mostly **rock**, **country** and **R&B**; also **jazz**, **alternative** and **blues**. Produced *Vorrice*, written and recorded by Vorrice (R&B); and *Crush*, written and recorded by Crush (rock). Other artists include Derrick Houghes (Motown), Tiggi Clay (Motown), Fizzy Quick (Motown) and Workforce (Scotti Bros.).
Tips: "Never write over the heads of the people you're trying to reach."

VECTOR SOUND, P.O. Box 66417, Chicago IL 60666. Owner/manager: Lucien Vector. Record producer. Estab. 1989. Produced 10-20 singles and 2-3 CDs/year. Fee derived from sales royalty when song or artist is recorded or outright fee from recording artist or record company.
How to Contact: Submit demo tape by mail. Unsolicited submissions are OK. Prefers cassette or VHS videocassette with lyric sheet. Does not return material. Reports in 2-4 weeks.
Music: Mostly **alternative rock** and **pop**; also **soundtracks**. Produced "Liberum Ghetto" (by Johny K/Doc Vec), recorded by Johny K on No Slop Pop Records (pop/rock); "Be My Friend" and "Promise," written and recorded by Koko Kitu on Kivi Music (pop/rock). Current artists include Nancy Davis, Stan Borys and Lukla.

CHARLES VICKERS MUSIC ASSOCIATION, Box 725, Daytona Beach FL 32015-0725. (904)252-4849. President/Producer: Dr. Charles H. Vickers D.M. Record producer, music publisher (Pritchett Publication/BMI, Alison Music/ASCAP) and record company (King of Kings Records, L.A. International Records and Bell Records International). Produces 3 singles and 6 LPs/year. Fee derived from sales royalty.
How to Contact: Write first and obtain permission to submit. Prefers 7½ ips reel-to-reel or cassette with 1-6 songs. SASE. Reports in 1 week.

HOW TO GET THE MOST out of *Songwriter's Market* (at the front of this book) contains comments and suggestions to help you understand and use the information in these listings.

Music: Mostly **church/religious**, **gospel** and **hymns**; also **bluegrass**, **blues**, **classical**, **country**, **easy listening**, **jazz**, **MOR**, **progressive**, **reggae (pop)**, **R&B**, **rock**, **soul** and **top 40/pop**. Produced *Have You Heard of That Holy City*, *Every Feeling I Have Comes From God*, and *Christ Is Mine*, all written and recorded by Charles Vickers on King of King Records. Other artists include James Franklin, Gladys Nighton and Charles Gardy.

WILLIAM F. WAGNER, Dept. SM, 14343 Addison St., Suite 221, Sherman Oaks CA 91423. (818)905-1033. Contact: Bill Wagner. Record producer. Estab. 1957. Produces 4-6 singles, 2-4 LPs and 2-4 CDs/year. Fee derived from sales royalty or outright fee from recording artist.
How to Contact: Submit demo tape by mail. Unsolicited submissions are OK. Prefers cassette with 1-5 songs and lead sheets. "Material should be copyrighted." SASE. Reports in 1 month.
Music: Mostly **top 40**, **pop**, **country** and **jazz**; also **blues**, **choral**, **gospel**, **easy listening**, **MOR**, **progressive**, **rock** and **soul**. Produced *The Island* (by Allen and Marilyn Bergman), recorded by Sandy Graham; *Strike Up The Band* (by Gershwin), recorded by Page Cavanaugh; and *All The Things You Are* (by Kern/Hammerstein), recorded by Rick Whitehead, all on Starline Records (jazz). Other artists include the U.S. Air Force Orchestra.
Tips: "Keep writing. Quit worrying about publishing (Irving Berlin had 1,200 copyrights before he started his own publishing company)."

WALL STREET PRODUCTIONS, 1189 E. 14 Mile, Birmingham MI 48009. (810)646-2054. Fax: (810)646-1957. Executive Producers: Tim Rochon and Joe Sanders. Record producer, record company, music publisher. Estab. 1985. Produces 6 singles, 4 12″ singles, 3 LPs and 6 CDs/year. Fee derived from sales royalty when song or artist is recorded.
  • See their listing in the Record Companies section.
How to Contact: Call first and obtain permission to submit. Prefers cassette (or videocassette if available) with 2 songs and lyric sheet. "Label all materials completely." Does not return material. Reports in 6 weeks.
Music: Mostly **rap**, **hip hop** and **dance**; also **R&B** and **jazz**. Produced "Taste the Flava" (by Mike Buckholtz), recorded by Soulism; "Ooh La La" (by Lester Marlin) and *Nasty Sexual Thangs* (by Darrell Campbell), both recorded by Simply Black, all on WSM Records. Other artists include Drueada and ANG.
Tips: "Be original and don't use samples."

*WALTON RECORD PRODUCTIONS, P.O. Box 218146, Nashville TN 37221-8146. (615)646-0506. Executive Producer: Jimmy Walton. Project Director: S. Hardesty. Record producer, record company and music publisher (JW One Music Publishing/BMI, Jimmy Walton Music Publishing/ASCAP). Estab. 1963. Produces 6-20 CDs/year. Fee derived from sales royalty when song or artist is recorded or outright fee from recording artist.
  • See the listing for JW One Music Publishing in the Music Publishers section.
How to Contact: Submit demo tape by mail. Unsolicited submissions are OK. Prefers cassette with 1-4 songs and lyric sheet. "Lyric sheets must be clearly printed. Submit proof of copyright ownership. Artist and performing groups send bio and photo." SASE. Reports in 1-8 weeks.
Music: Mostly **country ballads**, **new country/uptempo**, **pop/MOR** and **comedy**; also **R&B**, **lite rock** and **modern gospel**. Produced *How Many Heartaches* (by Herman House), recorded by Cheryl Di Blasi; *Down In Louisiana* (by Jimmy Walton/Ken Michaels), recorded by Wade McCurdy; and *Line Dancer* (by Bobby Ray Martin), recorded by Bobby Ray, all on Walton Records. Other artists include Suzy Q, Bob Bates and Phil Capuano.
Tips: "The industry operates on a drastically different level today. They are looking for finished product that has been produced professionally. Be patient and the time and effort will pay off. The good songs sell because of the proper steps taken at the appropriate time."

THE WEISMAN PRODUCTION GROUP, 449 N. Vista St., Los Angeles CA 90036. (213)653-0693. Contact: Ben Weisman. Record producer and music publisher (Audio Music Publishers). Estab. 1965. Produces 10 singles/year. Fee derived from sales royalty when song or artist is recorded.
  • The Weisman Production Group's publishing company, Audio Music Publishers, is listed in the Music Publishers section.
How to Contact: Submit demo tape by mail. Unsolicited submissions are OK. Prefers cassette with 3-10 songs and lyric sheet. SASE. "Mention *Songwriter's Market*. Please make return envelope the same size as the envelopes you send material in, otherwise we cannot send everything back. Just send tape." Reports in 4-8 weeks.
Music: Mostly **R&B**, **soul**, **dance**, **rap** and **top 40/pop**; also **all types of rock**.
Tips: "Work on hooks and chorus, not just verses. Too many songs are only verses."

WESTWIRES DIGITAL USA, 1042 Club Ave., Allentown PA 18103. (610) 435-1924. Contacts: Wayne Becker and Larry Dix. Record producer and production company. Fee derived from sales royalty or outright fee from record company.

How to Contact: Submit demo tape by mail. Unsolicited submissions are OK. Prefers cassette (or VHS videocassette if available) with 3 songs and lyric sheet. SASE. Reports in 1 month.
Music: R&B, **dance**, **alternative**, **folk** and **improvisation**. Produced *Flying Discs of Luv*, recorded by Trap Door on Interstellar Discs. Other artists include Danielle Lubene.
Tips: "We're interested in artists who have performance value. Especially interested in singer/song-writers."

TOM WILLETT, TOMMARK RECORDS, 7560 Woodman Place, #G3, Van Nuys CA 91405. (818)994-4862. Owners: Tom Willett and Mark Thornton. Record producer, music publisher (Schmerdley Music/BMI) and record company (Tomark Records). Estab. 1988. Produces 1 single and 1 CD/year.
How to Contact: Submit demo tape by mail. Unsolicited submissions are OK. Prefers cassette (or VHS videocassette if available) with any number of songs and lyric sheets. SASE. Reports in 4 weeks.
Music: Mostly **country** and **novelty**; also **folk**.

*WILLOW SHADE RECORDS, 40 Brookside Rd., Westford MA 01886-1801. Business Manager: Susan Webber. Record producer, record company. Estab. 1986. Produces 3-4 CDs/year. Fee derived from sales royalty when song or artist is recorded.
How to Contact: Submit demo tape by mail. Unsolicited submissions are OK. Prefers cassette with 2-4 songs and lead sheet, score. Does not return material. Reports in 2 months.
Music: Mostly **instrumental**, **acoustic** and **classical**; also **New Age**, **jazz** and **electronic**. Produced *New Interpretations*, recorded by Kevin Gallagher (classical); *Cumberland Consort*, written and recorded by Sharon Law, David Kelsey and Stephen Webber (instrumental); and *Angel Christmas*, written and recorded by various artists (classical/jazz), all on Willow Shade Records. Other artists include Brenda Stuart, Martha Kelsey, Shane Adams and Doug Woodson.
Tips: "High quality original or classical instrumental music is what we are looking for. Submit on high quality high-bias tape."

FRANK WILLSON, Box 2297, Universal City TX 78148. (210)659-2557. Producer: Frank Willson. Record producer and record company (BSW Records). Estab. 1987. Produces 4 singles, 12-15 12″ singles, 10-12 LPs, 3 EPs and 5 CDs/year. Fee derived from sales royalty when song or artist is recorded.
• Frank Willson's record company, BSW Records, can be found in the Record Companies section and his management firm, Universal Music Marketing, is in the Managers and Booking Agents section.
How to Contact: Submit demo tape by mail. Unsolicited submissions are OK. Prefers cassette with 3-4 songs and lyric sheets. SASE. Reports in 4-5 weeks.
Music: Mostly **country**. Produced *Ice Mountain*, written and recorded by Maria Rose; *Ten Days In The Saddle*, written and recorded by Wes Wiginton; and *Let Me Be The One*, written and recorded by Patty David, all on BSW Records. Other artists include Craig Robbins.

WIZARDS & CECIL B, 1111 Second St., San Rafael CA 94901. (415)453-0335. Producers: James Fischer and Pete Slauson. Record producer and music publisher. Estab. 1978. Produces 10 singles, 10 12″ singles, 15 LPs and 15 CDs/year. Fee derived from sales royalty when song or artist is recorded, outright fee from recording artist or record company and/or 24-track studio income.
How to Contact: Submit demo tape by mail. Unsolicited submissions are OK. Prefers cassette with several songs. Does not return material. Reports in 1-2 months.
Music: All kinds. Produced "New Riders of Purple Sage," recorded by W&CB on MU Records; "Nick Gravenities," recorded by In Mix on MU Records; and "Reggae on the River" for Warner Brothers Records. Other artists include Caribbean All Stars with Carlos Santana and Shana Morrison, and Caledonia.

WLM MUSIC/RECORDING, 2808 Cammie St., Durham NC 27705-2020. (919)471-3086. Owner: Watts Lee Mangum. Record producer, recording studio (small). Estab. 1980. Produces 6-8 singles/year. Fee derived from outright fee from recording artist. "In some cases—an advance payment requested for demo production."
How to Contact: Submit demo tape by mail. Unsolicited submissions are OK. Prefers cassette with 2-4 songs and lyric or lead sheet (if possible). SASE. Reports in 4-6 months.
Music: Mostly **country**, **country/rock** and **blues/rock**; also **pop**, **rock** and **R&B**. Produced "High Time" and "Heart of Stone," written and recorded by Clayton Wrenn; and "Crown Royal Nights," written and recorded by Alan Dunn, all on WLM Records. Other artists include Barry Hayes, Pamela Rhea, Ron Davis, John Davis, Clint Clayton, Maria Barbour and Melanie Barbour.
Tips: "Submit good demo tapes with artist's ideas, words, and music charted if possible. Be specific and realistic in your goals, but don't waiver in your desire to achieve them!"

*STEVE WYTAS PRODUCTIONS, Dept. SM, 11 Custer St., West Hartford CT 06110. (860)953-2834. Contact: Steven J. Wytas. Record producer. Estab. 1984. Produces 4-8 singles, 3 LPs, 3 EPs and 4 CDs/year. Fee derived from outright fee from recording artist.

How to Contact: Submit demo tape by mail. Unsolicited submissions are OK. Prefers cassette (or VHS ¾" videocassette) with several songs and lyric or lead sheet. "Include live material if possible." Does not return material. Reports in 2 months.

Music: Mostly **rock, pop, top 40** and **country/acoustic**. Produced *Better Lonely Days*, recorded by Hannah Cranna on Big Deal Records (rock); *Land of Steady Habits*, recorded by Big Train on Bolt Records (rock); and *Movable Beast*, recorded by All The Voices on Turnip Records (rock). Other artists include King Hop!, Under the Rose, The Shells, The Gravel Pit and G'nu Fuz.

Category Index

The Category Index is a good place to begin searching for a market for your songs. Below is an alphabetical list of 19 general music categories. If you write dance music and are looking for a record producer to submit your songs to, check the Dance section in this index. There you will find a list of record producers who work with dance music. Once you locate the entries for those producers, read the music subheading *carefully* to determine which companies are most interested in the type of dance music you write. Some of the markets in this section do not appear in the Category Index because they have not indicated a specific preference. Most of these said they are interested in "all types" of music. Listings that were very specific, or whose description of the music they're interested in doesn't quite fit into these categories, also do not appear here.

Adult Contemporary

"A" Major Sound Corporation; Bal Records; Carlock Productions; Country Star Productions; *Cousins Productions, Randall; Diamond Entertainment, Joel; Evolving Productions; Hickory Lane Publishing and Recording; Intrigue Production; James, Sunny; June Productions Ltd.; *Kingsport Creek Music; Known Artist Productions; Kool Breeze Productions; Kovach, Robert R.; Luick & Associates, Harold; Magid Productions, Lee; Miller Productions, Jay; Mittelstedt, A.V.; Monticana Productions; Nashville Country Productions; New Horizon Records; Panio Brothers Label; Pegasus Recording; Peridot Productions; Pine Island Music; Planet Dallas; Prescription Co., The; Rustron Music Productions; *Siskind Productions, Mike; *Szawlowski Productions & Ventura Music Publishing, William; Vickers Music Association, Charles; Wagner, William F.; *Walton Record Productions

Alternative

"A" Major Sound Corporation; *Aladdin Productions; Apophis Music; Bridges Productions; Carlock Productions; Coachouse Music; D.S.O., Inc.; Datura Productions; Doubletime Productions; Dudick, J.D.; Federici's Shark River Music, Danny; Hoax Productions; I.V.M. Communications; James Productions, Neal; JK Jam Productions; Kane Producer/Engineer, Karen; L.A. Entertainment; Maddalone Production, Dino; *Merlin Productions; *Modern Tribe Records; Musicom Music Productions; Pegasus Recording; *Perennial Productions; Prejippie Music Group; Rainbow Recording; Rammit Records; Realworld Entertainment Corp.; SAS Corporation/Special Audio Ser-

THE ASTERISK before a listing indicates that the listing is new in this edition. New markets are often the most receptive to unsolicited submissions.

vices; Smash the Radio Productions; Sound Sound/Savage Fruitarian; Soundboard Studios; Stuart Audio Services; Studio Recording; Sullivan Enterprises, Preston; Syndicate Sound, Inc.; Talent Recognition Services; Tomsick Brothers Productions; *Up Front Management; Vector Sound; Westwires Digital USA

Blues

*Aladdin Productions; Bal Records; Big Bear; Bonta, Peter L.; Coachouse Music; Demi Monde Records & Publishing Ltd.; Duane Music, Inc.; Esquire International; Flair Productions; Hailing Frequency Music Productions; James Productions, Neal; Kool Breeze Productions; Landmark Communications Group; Linear Cycle Productions; Magid Productions, Lee; Miller Productions, Jay; Monticana Productions; New Horizon Records; Pegasus Recording; Peridot Productions; Pine Island Music; Prescription Co., The; Reel Adventures; Silver Bow Productions; *Texas Music Masters/Wright Productions; TMC Productions; Triplane Production; *Up Front Management; Vickers Music Association, Charles; WLM Music/Recording

Children's

Fera Productions, Vito; Hickory Lane Publishing and Recording; Peridot Productions; Prescription Co., The; Stuart Audio Services

Classical

Apophis Music; Aurora Productions; Care Free Records Group; D.S.O., Inc.; *Janus Management; Lark Talent & Advertising; Pegasus Recording; Vickers Music Association, Charles; *Willow Shade Records

Country

ACR Productions; Airwave Production Group Inc.; AKO Productions; *Aladdin Productions; Allyn, Stuart J.; Bal Records; Bonta, Peter L.; Bowden, Robert; Capitol Ad, Management & Talent Group; Care Free Records Group; *Carlyle Productions; Cedar Creek Productions; Coachouse Music; Coffee and Cream Productions; Complex Studios; Country Star Productions; *Cousins Proudctions, Randall; Cupit Productions, Jerry; Darrow, Danny; Datura Productions; De Miles, Edward; DeLory and Music Makers, Al; Diamond Entertainment, Joel; Doss Presents, Col. Buster; *Double K Entertainment; Duane Music, Inc.; Dudick, J.D.; E.S.R. Productions; Earmark Audio; Eiffert, Jr., Leo J.; Esquire International; Eternal Song Agency, The; Evolving Productions; Faiella Productions, Doug; Federici's Shark River Music, Danny; Flair Productions; Gale, Jack; Haworth Productions; Hickory Lane Publishing and Recording; Hoax Productions; Horrigan Productions; *Jag Studio, Ltd.; James Productions, Neal; James, Sunny; *Jay Bird Productions; *Jay Jay Publishing and Record Co.; JK Jam Productions; Johnson, Little Richie; Johnson, Ralph D.; Kennedy Enterprises, Inc., Gene; *Kingsport Creek Music; Kingston Records and Talent; Known Artist Productions; Kool Breeze Productions; Kovach, Robert R.; Landmark Communications Group; Lari-Jon Productions; Lark Talent & Advertising; Leavell, John; Linear Cycle Productions; Lloyd Productions, Mick; Luick & Associates, Harold; McCoy Productions, Jim; Magid Productions, Lee; Makers Mark Music Productions; Martin, Pete/Vaam Music Productions; Masterpiece Productions & Studios; Mathes Productions, David; Mathews, d/b/a Hit Or Myth Productions, Scott; Miller Productions, Jay; Mittelstedt, A.V.; *Modern Tribe Records; Monticana Productions; Musicland Productions; Nashville Country Productions; Nebo Record Company; Nelson, Bill; *Omari Productions; Ormsby, John "Buck"/Etiquette Productions; Panio Brothers Label; Parker, Patty; Pegasus Recording; Peridot Productions; Pierce, Jim; Pine Island Music; Planet Dallas; Prescription Co., The; Rainbow Recording; Red Kastle Productions; Reel Adventures; Rustron Music Productions; Sanders Company, Ray; Segal's Productions; Silver Bow Productions; *Silver Thunder Music Group; Simon Sez Productions; *Siskind Productions, Mike; S'N'M Recording/Hit Records Network; Sound Cell; Sound Control Productions; Soundstage South; Sphere Productions; Stuart Audio Services; Studio Recording; Syndicate Sound, Inc.; *Szawlowski Productions & Ventura Music Publishing, William; Talent Recognition Services; *Texas Music Masters/Wright Productions; TMC Productions; Trac Record Co.; Trinity Studio, The; Twist Tunes; *Up Front Management; Vickers Music Association, Charles; Wagner, William F.; *Walton Record Productions; Willett, Tommark Records, Tom; Willson, Frank; WLM Music/Recording; Wytas Productions, Steve

Dance

Basement Boys, Inc.; Blaze Productions; Coffee and Cream Productions; Complex Studios; Corwin, Dano; Creative Music Services; Darrow, Danny; De Miles, Edward; Diamond Entertainment, Joel; Esquire International; Final Mix Music; Gland Puppies, Inc., The; Guess Who?? Productions; House of Rhythm; Intrigue Production; *Jag Studio, Ltd.; Janoulis Productions, Alexander; JGM Recording Studio; JK Jam Productions; KMA; Leeway Entertainment Group; Lloyd Productions, Mick; London Brijj Productions; Makers Mark Music Productions; *Merlin Productions; Miller Productions, Jay; Mona Lisa Records/Bristol Studios; Monticana Productions; Mraz, Gary John; Nemesis Media Labs; Neu Electro Productions; Panio Brothers Label; Poku Productions; Prejippie Music Group; Prescription Co., The; Rammit Records; Realworld Entertainment Corp.; Rosenman, Mike; Slavesong Corporation, Inc.; Smash The Radio Producions; Soundboard Studios; *Szawlowski Productions & Ventura Music Publishing, William; 12 Meter Productions; Wall Street Productions; Weisman Production Group, The; Westwires Digital USA

Folk

Aurora Productions; Coppin, Johnny/Red Sky Records; Evolving Productions; Flair Productions; Gland Puppies, Inc., The; Hoax Productions; I.V.M. Communications; *Janus Management; Magid Productions, Lee; Miller Productions, Jay; Moffet, Gary; Monticana Productions; *Perennial Productions; Peridot Productions; Person to Person Productions; Pine Island Music; Rustron Music Productions; *Siskind Productions, Mike; Sound Cell; Stuart Audio Services; Westwires Digital USA; Willett, Tommark Records, Tom

Jazz

Airwave Production Group Inc.; Allyn, Stuart J.; Angel Films Company; Apophis Music; Aurora Productions; Bal Records; Big Bear; Capitol Ad, Management & Talent Group; Care Free Records Group; Cedar Creek Productions; Celt, Jan; Creative Music Services; Darrow, Danny; De Miles, Edward; Esquire International; Evolving Productions; Fera Productions, Vito; Flair Productions; Haworth Productions; Heart Consort Music; James, Sunny; *Janus Management; Jazzand; Landmark Communications Group; Magid Productions, Lee; Masterpiece Productions & Studios; Mona Lisa Records/Bristol Studios; Monticana Productions; Musicom Music Productions; New Horizon Records; Pegasus Recording; *Perennial Productions; Person to Person Productions; Philly Breakdown; Pine Island Music; Prescription Co., The; Silver Bow Productions; Simon Sez Productions; Slavesong Corporation, Inc.; Sound Services; Sound Sound/Savage Fruitarian; Tomsick Brothers Productions; *Up Front Management; Vickers Music Association, Charles; Wagner, William F.; Wall Street Productions; *Willow Shade Records

Latin

DeLory And Music Makers, Al; Eight Ball MIDI & Vocal Recording; Private Island Trax

Metal

Care Free Records Group; Datura Productions; Gland Puppies, Inc., The; Private Island Trax; SAS Corporation/Special Audio Services

New Age

Aurora Productions; Big Sky Audio Productions; Care Free Records Group; Collector Records; Eight Ball MIDI & Vocal Recording; Federici's Shark River Music, Danny; Gland Puppies, Inc., The; Haworth Productions; Heart Consort Music; I.V.M. Communications; Leeway Entertainment Group; Masterpiece Productions & Studios; Musicom Music Productions; Neu Electro Productions; Rustron Music Productions; Sound Sound/Savage Fruitarian; Sphere Productions; Triplane Production; *Willow Shade Records

Novelty

Gland Puppies, Inc., The; *Jay Jay Publishing And Record Co.; Johnson, Ralph D.; Linear Cycle Productions; Miller Productions, Jay; Nashville Country Productions; Peridot Productions; Segal's Productions; TMC Productions; Willett, Tommark Records, Tom

Pop

ACR Productions; Airwave Production Group Inc.; AKO Productions; Allyn, Stuart J.; Angel Films Company; Aurora Productions; Bal Records; Blaze Productions; Bowden, Robert; Capitol Ad, Management & Talent Group; Care Free Records Group; Carlock Productions; *Carlyle Productions; Cedar Creek Productions; Chucker Music, Inc.; Coachouse Music; Coffee and Cream Productions; Complex Studios; Corwin, Dano; *Cousins Productions, Randall; Creative Music Services; D.S.O., Inc.; Darrow, Danny; Datura Productions; De Miles, Edward; DeLory And Music Makers, Al; Demi Monde Records & Publishing Ltd.; Diamond Entertainment, Joel; Doss Presents, Col. Buster; Duane Music, Inc.; Dudick, J.D.; E.S.R. Productions; Eight Ball MIDI & Vocal Recording; Esquire International; Eternal Song Agency, The; Evolving Productions; Gland Puppies, Inc., The; GoodKnight Productions; Guess Who?? Productions; Hoax Productions; Horrigan Productions; House of Rhythm; I.V.M. Communications; Intrigue Production; Ivory Productions, Inc.; *Jag Studio, Ltd.; James Productions, Neal; Janoulis Productions, Alexander; *Jay Bird Productions; Jericho Sound Lab; JGM Recording Studio; JK Jam Productions; June Productions Ltd.; Kane Producer/Engineer, Karen; Katz Productions, Matthew; *Kingsport Creek Music; Kingston Records and Talent; Known Artist Productions; Kool Breeze Productions; Kovach, Robert R.; Landmark Communications Group; Leeway Entertainment Group; Linear Cycle Productions; Maddalone Production, Dino; Magid Productions, Lee; Martin, Pete/Vaam Music Productions; Masterpiece Productions & Studios; Mathes Productions, David; Mathews, d/b/a Hit Or Myth Productions, Scott; *Merlin Productions; Miller Productions, Jay; *Modern Tribe Records; Moffet, Gary; Mona Lisa Records/Bristol Studios; Monticana Productions; Mraz, Gary John; Musicom Music Productions; Must Rock Productionz Worldwide; Nebo Record Company; Nelson, Bill; Nemesis Media Labs; Neu Electro Productions; New Experience Records; Ormsby, John "Buck"/Etiquette Productions; Parker, Patty; Person to Person Productions; Philly Breakdown; Pine Island Music; Planet Dallas; Poku Productions; Prescription Co., The; Private Island Trax; Rainbow Recording; Realworld Entertainment Corp.; Red Kastle Productions; Reel Adventures; Rockstar Productions; Rosenman, Mike; Rustron Music Productions; Segal's Productions; Silver Bow Productions; *Silver Thunder Music Group; *Siskind Productions, Mike; Smash the Radio Productions; S'N'M Recording/Hit Records Network; Sound Cell; Sound Services; Sound Sound/Savage Fruitarian; Sphere Productions; Studio Recording; Sullivan Enterprises, Preston; Syndicate Sound, Inc.; *Szawlowski Productions & Ventura Music Publishing, William; Triplane Production; 12 Meter Productions; Twist Tunes; Vector Sound; Vickers Music Association, Charles; Wagner, William F.; *Walton Record Productions; Weisman Production Group, The; WLM Music/Recording; Wytas Productions, Steve

R&B

"A" Major Sound Corporation; ACR Productions; Airwave Production Group Inc.; Allyn, Stuart J.; Angel Films Company; Apophis Music; Bal Records; Basement Boys,

282 Songwriter's Market '97

Inc.; Big Sky Audio Productions; Capitol Ad, Management & Talent Group; Cedar
Creek Productions; Celt, Jan; Chucker Music, Inc.; Coffee and Cream Productions;
Country Star Productions; *Cousins Proudctions, Randall; Cupit Productions, Jerry;
Daddy, S. Kwaku; Datura Productions; De Miles, Edward; Diamond Entertainment,
Joel; Duane Music, Inc.; E.S.R. Productions; Eight Ball MIDI & Vocal Recording;
Esquire International; Federici's Shark River Music, Danny; Fera Productions, Vito;
Final Mix Music; Flair Productions; Global Assault Management and Consulting;
Guess Who?? Productions; Hailing Frequency Music Productions; Haworth Produc-
tions; House of Rhythm; Intrigue Production; James Productions, Neal; James, Sunny;
Janoulis Productions, Alexander; Jericho Sound Lab; JGM Recording Studio; JK Jam
Productions; Kane Producer/Engineer, Karen; *Kingsport Creek Music; KMA; Known
Artist Productions; Kovach, Robert R.; L.A. Entertainment; Linear Cycle Productions;
London Brijj; Maddalone Production, Dino; Magid Productions, Lee; Makers Mark
Music Productions; Martin, Pete/Vaam Music Productions; Masterpiece Productions &
Studios; Mathes Productions, David; Mathews, d/b/a Hit Or Myth Productions, Scott;
*Merlin Productions; Mr. Wonderful Productions, Inc.; *Modern Tribe Records; Mona
Lisa Records/Bristol Studios; Monticana Productions; Mraz, Gary John; Musicom Mu-
sic Productions; Must Rock Productionz Worldwide; Nebo Record Company; Nemesis
Media Labs; New Experience Records; *Omari Productions; Ormsby, John "Buck"/
Etiquette Productions; Pegasus Recording; Philly Breakdown; Pine Island Music;
Planet Dallas; Prescription Co., The; Private Island Trax; Rainbow Recording; Rammit
Records; Realworld Entertainment Corp.; Rosenman, Mike; Rustron Music Produc-
tions; Segal's Productions; Shu'Baby Montez Music; *Silver Thunder Music Group;
Slavesong Corporation, Inc.; Smash the Radio Productions; Sound Cell; Sound Ser-
vices; Studio Recording; Sullivan Enterprises, Preston; Syndicate Sound, Inc.; Triplane
Production; 12 Meter Productions; *Up Front Management; Vickers Music Association,
Charles; Wagner, William F.; Wall Street Productions; *Walton Record Productions;
Weisman Production Group, The; Westwires Digital USA; WLM Music/Recording

Rap

Final Mix Music; Guess Who?? Productions; I.V.M. Communications; Intrigue Produc-
tion; *Jag Studio, Ltd.; KMA; London Brijj; Makers Mark Music Productions; Master-
piece Productions & Studios; Mr. Wonderful Productions, Inc.; *Modern Tribe Records;
Must Rock Productionz Worldwide; Nemesis Media Labs; Neu Electro Productions;
New Experience Records; *Omari Productions; Philly Breakdown; Poku Productions;
Realworld Entertainment Corp.; Shu'Baby Montez Music; Smash the Radio Produc-
tions; Triplane Production; 12 Meter Productions; Wall Street Productions; Weisman
Production Group, The

Religious

"A" Major Sound Corporation; ACR Productions; Airwave Production Group Inc.;
*Aladdin Productions; Bal Records; Capitol Ad, Management & Talent Group; Carlock
Productions; Cedar Creek Productions; Coffee and Cream Productions; Country Star
Productions; Cupit Productions, Jerry; Daddy, S. Kwaku; Doss Presents, Col. Buster;
*Double K Entertainment; Eiffert, Jr., Leo J.; Esquire International; Eternal Song
Agency, The; Faiella Productions, Doug; Fera Productions, Vito; Flair Productions;
Hailing Frequency Music Productions; Haworth Productions; Hickory Lane Publishing
and Recording; *Jag Studio, Ltd.; James Productions, Neal; Jazmin Productions; Ken-
nedy Enterprises, Inc., Gene; *Kingsport Creek Music; Kool Breeze Productions; Ko-
vach, Robert R.; Landmark Communications Group; Lari-Jon Productions; Leavell,
John; Linear Cycle Productions; Luick & Associates, Harold; McCoy Productions,
Jim; Magid Productions, Lee; Masterpiece Productions & Studios; Mathes Productions,
David; Miller Productions, Jay; Mr. Wonderful Productions, Inc.; Mittelstedt, A.V.;
*Modern Tribe Records; Monticana Productions; Musicland Productions; Nashville
Country Productions; Nebo Record Company; Nelson, Bill; New Experience Records;
*Omari Productions; Pegasus Recording; Peridot Productions; Philly Breakdown; Pine
Island Music; Sanders Company, Ray; Silver Bow Productions; *Silver Thunder Music

Group; Sound Control Productions; Stuart Audio Services; Syndicate Sound, Inc.; *Texas Music Masters/Wright Productions; Trinity Studio, The; Vickers Music Association, Charles; Wagner, William F.; *Walton Record Productions

Rock

"A" Major Sound Corporation; ACR Productions; Airwave Production Group Inc.; AKO Productions; *Aladdin Productions; Allyn, Stuart J.; Angel Films Company; Apophis Music; Aurora Productions; Bal Records; Big Sky Audio Productions; Blaze Productions; Bonta, Peter L.; Bridges Productions; Capitol Ad, Management & Talent Group; Care Free Records Group; Carlock Productions; *Carlyle Productions; Cedar Creek Productions; Celt, Jan; Chucker Music, Inc.; Coachouse Music; Collector Records; Complex Studios; Coppin, Johnny/Red Sky Records; Corwin, Dano; Country Star Productions; *Cousins Productions, Randall; Cupit Productions, Jerry; D.S.O., Inc.; Datura Productions; Deep Space Records; Demi Monde Records & Publishing Ltd.; Diamond Entertainment, Joel; *Double K Entertainment; Doubletime Productions; Duane Music, Inc.; Dudick, J.D.; Earmark Audio; Eight Ball MIDI & Vocal Recording; Esquire International; Evolving Productions; Faiella Productions, Doug; Federici's Shark River Music, Danny; Fera Productions, Vito; Hailing Frequency Music Productions; Haworth Productions; Hickory Lane Publishing and Recording; Hoax Productions; Horrigan Productions; House of Rhythm; I.V.M. Communications; Intrigue Production; Ivory Productions, Inc.; *Jag Studio, Ltd.; James Productions, Neal; James, Sunny; Janoulis Productions, Alexander; *Janus Management; *Jay Bird Productions; Jericho Sound Lab; JGM Recording Studio; JK Jam Productions; June Productions Ltd.; Katz Productions, Matthew; Kingston Records and Talent; Kool Breeze Productions; Kovach, Robert R.; Landmark Communications Group; Lari-Jon Productions; Leavell, John; Linear Cycle Productions; Lloyd Productions, Mick; McCoy Productions, Jim; Maddalone Production, Dino; Magid Productions, Lee; Masterpiece Productions & Studios; Mathews, d/b/a Hit Or Myth Productions, Scott; Miller Productions, Jay; Mittelstedt, A.V.; Moffet, Gary; Mona Lisa Records/Bristol Studios; Monticana Productions; Musicom Music Productions; Nebo Record Company; Neu Electro Productions; New Experience Records; *Omari Productions; Ormsby, John "Buck"/Etiquette Productions; Parker, Patty; Pegasus Recording; Person to Person Productions; Pine Island Music; Planet Dallas; Poku Productions; Prejippie Music Group; Prescription Co., The; Private Island Trax; Rainbow Recording; Reel Adventures; Rockstar Productions; Rosenman, Mike; SAS Corporation/Special Audio Services; Segal's Productions; Silver Bow Productions; *Silver Thunder Music Group; Simon Sez Productions; *Siskind Productions, Mike; S'N'M Recording/Hit Records Network; Sound Services; Sound Sound/Savage Fruitarian; Soundstage South; Sphere Productions; Stuart Audio Services; Studio Recording; Sullivan Enterprises, Preston; Syndicate Sound, Inc.; *Szawlowski Productions & Ventura Music Publishing, William; Talent Recognition Services; TMC Productions; Triplane Production; 12 Meter Productions; Twist Tunes; *Up Front Management; Vickers Music Association, Charles; Wagner, William F.; *Walton Record Productions; Weisman Production Group, The; WLM Music/Recording; Wytas Productions, Steve

World Music

Complex Studios; D.S.O., Inc.; Daddy, S. Kwaku; Eight Ball MIDI & Vocal Recording; Hoax Productions; I.V.M. Communications; Jericho Sound Lab; JGM Recording Studio; Kane Producer/Engineer, Karen; KMA; London Brijj; Nemesis Media Labs; Pegasus Recording; Person to Person Productions; Reel Adventures; Slavesong Corporation, Inc.; Smash the Radio Productions; Tomsick Brothers Productions; Vickers Music Association, Charles

---

✱ **THE ASTERISK** before a listing indicates that the listing is new in this edition. New markets are often the most receptive to unsolicited submissions.

Managers and Booking Agents

Of all the music industry players surrounding successful artists, managers are usually the people closest to the artists themselves. The artist manager can be a valuable contact, both for the songwriter trying to get songs to a particular artist and for the songwriter/performer. Getting songs to an artist's manager is yet another way of attempting to get your songs recorded, since the manager may play a large part in deciding what material his client uses. For the performer seeking management, a successful manager should be thought of as the foundation for a successful career. Therefore, it pays to be extremely careful when seeking management to represent you.

Choosing a manager can be one of the most important decisions you can make as a songwriter or performer. The relationship between a manager and his client relies on mutual trust. A manager works as the liaison between you and the rest of the music industry, and he must know exactly what you want out of your career in order to help you achieve your goals. His handling of publicity, promotion and finances, as well as the contacts he has within the industry, can make or break your career. You should never be afraid to ask questions about any aspect of the relationship between you and a prospective manager. Always remember that a manager works *for the artist*. A good manager is able to communicate his opinions to you without reservation, and should be willing to explain any confusing terminology or discuss plans with you before taking action. A manager needs to be able to communicate successfully with all segments of the music industry in order to get his client the best deals possible. He needs to be able to work with booking agents, publishers, lawyers and record companies. Keep in mind that you are both working together toward a common goal: success for you and your songs. Talent, originality, professionalism and a drive to succeed are qualities that will attract a manager to an artist—and a songwriter.

The function of the booking agent is to find performance venues for their clients. They usually represent many more acts than a manager does, and have less contact with their acts. A booking agent charges a commission for his services, as does a manager. Managers usually ask for a 15-50% commission on an act's earnings; booking agents usually charge around 10%.

Before submitting to a manager or booking agent, be sure you know exactly what you need. If you're looking for someone to help you with performance opportunities, the booking agency is the one to contact. They can help you book shows either in your local area or throughout the country. If you're looking for someone to help guide your career, you need to contact a management firm. Some management firms may also handle booking; however, it may be in your best interest to look for a separate booking agency. A manager should be your manager—not your agent, publisher, lawyer or accountant. It pays to have a team of people working to get your songs heard, adding to the network of professionals guiding your career and making valuable contacts in the industry.

The firms listed in this section have provided information about the types of music they work with and the types of acts they represent. You'll want to refer to the Category Index at the end of this section to find out which companies deal with the type of music you write, and the Geographic Index at the back of the book to help you locate companies near where you live. Each listing also contains submission requirements and information about what items to include in a press kit, and will also specify whether the company is a management firm or a booking agency. Remember that your submission represents you as an artist, and should be as organized and professional as possible.

ABBA-TUDE ENTERTAINMENT, 1875 Century Park East, 7th Floor, Los Angeles CA 90067. (310)788-2666. Fax: (818)735-0543. Attorney At Law: Mark "Abba" Abbattista. Management firm, music publisher (Abba-Cadaver), attorney. Estab. 1991. Represents individual artists, groups, songwriters, producers, artists from anywhere; currently handles 4 acts. Reviews material for acts.
How to Contact: Submit demo tape by mail. Unsolicited submissions are OK. Prefers cassette or CD with 3-4 songs and lead sheet. If seeking management, press kit should include bio, CD, tape, photo. "Be sure to put name and phone number on inside of tape." SASE. Reports in 2-4 weeks.
Music: Mostly **quality**; also **established acts**. Works primarily with bands, solo artists, singers, guitarists. Current acts include Souls at Zero (metal band), Skeletones (ska).

*ADB MANAGEMENT GROUP, 31 Queen St., Williamstown Victoria 3016 **Australia**. (613)9-397-2018. Fax: (613)9-427-9718. Manager/Promoter: Alan D. Buckland. Management firm and promoter. Estab. 1986. Represents individual artists, groups and songwriters from anywhere; currently handles 3 acts. Receives 20% commission. Reviews material for acts.
How to Contact: Submit demo tape by mail. Unsolicited submissions are OK. Prefers cassette or PAL videocassette with 3 songs and lyric and lead sheets. If seeking management, press kit should include any press, bio, photos, tapes or video; anything you think may help. Does not return material. Reports in 2 months; "if it's a hit song, 5 minutes."
Music: **All styles.** Works primarily with bands and singer/songwriters. Current acts include Joe Rais (Warner Bros.), Lounge Hounds (Solid Music/Mushroom Music) and Steve Zammit (songwriter/singer, pop/rock).
Tips: "Even Paul McCartney writes bad songs. Never lose your faith, keep writing."

ADELAIDE ROCK EXCHANGE, 186 Glen Osmond Rd., Fullarton SA **Australia** 5063. Phone: (08)338-1844. E-mail: kram@adam.com.au. Director: Mark Draper. Management firm and booking agency. Estab. 1982. Represents national and international artists and groups. Currently handles 30 acts. Receives 10-15% commission. Reviews material for acts.
How to Contact: Submit demo tape by mail. Unsolicited submissions are OK. Prefers cassette (or VHS videocassette if available). SAE and IRC. Reports in 2 months.
Music: Mostly **rock**, **pop** and **R&B**; also **duos**, **solos** and **sight artists**. Primarily works with recording bands, dance and concept bands. Current acts include Zep Boys (Led Zeppelin concept band), High Voltage (AC/DC concept band), Chunky Custard ('70s glam rock show band) and Ian Polites (pianist/vocalist).
Tips: "Please have all demo tapes, bios and photos with a track list and, most importantly, contact numbers and addresses."

THE AFRICAN DIASPORA PROJECT, P.O. Box 470642, San Francisco CA 94147-0642. (415)398-8336. Fax: (415)567-0195. Executive Director: Pietro Giacomo Poggi. Management firm, booking agency. Represents individual artists and/or groups and songwriters from anywhere; currently handles 7 acts. Receives 10-20% commission. Reviews material for acts.
How to Contact: Call first and obtain permission to submit. Prefers cassette or VHS videocassette and lyric sheet. Does not return material. If seeking management, press kit should include cover letter, bio, photo, lyrics, press clips, CD or tape demo. Does not return material. Reports in 2-3 weeks.
Music: Only interested in **music from the African Diaspora**, especially **African**, **Caribbean** and **Latin**. Current acts include Sol Y Luna (Calenko), Jungular Grooves (International Soul), Cool Breeze (Musique Tropique).
Tips: "Be innovative, speak with an original voice, be authentic, be dedicated and willing to go all out, and above all, be realistic and willing to learn."

AFTERSCHOOL PUBLISHING COMPANY, P.O. Box 14157, Detroit MI 48214. (313)894-8855. President: Herman Kelly. Management firm, booking agency, record company (Afterschool Co.) and music publisher (Afterschool Pub. Co.). Estab. 1978. Represents individual artists, songwriters, producers, arrangers and musicians. Currently handles 20 acts. Reviews material for acts.

THE ASTERISK before a listing indicates that the listing is new in this edition. New markets are often the most receptive to unsolicited submissions.

INSIDER REPORT

Artists need to find new ways to promote themselves

How much and what type of things your manager does for you depend on your level of experience in the music field, says Debbie Schwartz, co-owner (with partner Dennis Colligan) of DSM Management. "With what we call a baby band, we may act as a booking agent and offer recording advice," says Schwartz.

"If the act is just starting out," echoes Colligan, "we do everything. We even become a paralegal and accounting firm." Ideally, however, he prefers bands do their share of promoting themselves and take charge of their own careers.

"A lot of new performers seem to think that once they have a manager all the work is done— that having management is some sort of magic bul-

Dennis Colligan/Debbie Schwartz

let that will lead to success," he says. "There's a lot of work on both ends, and artists have to be prepared to pick up their piece of the whole process.

"Don't count on all your problems being solved when you sign with a manager," he says. "A lot of new people come to us with high expectations about what we can do, but it's best to invest those expectations in yourself and your ability. Even when you get a recording contract, it's still just the beginning."

No matter what their level of experience, artists should look for managers who have a real interest in them. A lot of energy is involved in promoting a band or artist, says Schwartz, and a manager must believe in the acts she works with. "You should look for someone you really feel comfortable with. After all, building a career does not happen overnight. It's a long-term process."

Both Schwartz and Colligan had a lot of experience in the music business before they started their partnership three years ago. Schwartz has been a manager for 20 years and Colligan is a songwriter and performer. They've worked with new bands such as Wanderlust, who are signed to RCA Records, and with veteran songwriter/performers such as David Sancious, who has been recording for several years and whose work can be heard on recordings by Sting, Bruce Springsteen and Peter Gabriel.

Sancious came to DSM with his own following and several established contacts in the field. Newer artists should try everything they can to build a following on their own, even before they seek management, Schwartz says. "Record your own CD, develop a mailing list and pass out flyers," she says. "Play out whenever and wherever possible."

INSIDER REPORT, *Colligan/Schwartz*

Schwartz and Colligan note that in rock music, the trend is toward working with performers who are also writers. With the exception of Nashville, it's getting harder for writers who are not performers to find people to cover their songs. But there are ways. "The best way is to try to hook up with a performer directly," says Schwartz. "Go see new music and find out if you can co-write with a band member. A lot of writers become writer-producers."

Schwartz and Colligan advise writers to be very careful when signing contracts with a manager. "Don't sign a contract that puts a third party in control of your royalties," says Colligan. "Watch out for managers who ask for a share in your royalties or those who ask for money up front. A manager should get about 20 percent of your earnings. They should not be getting a piece of your publishing pie as well."

Artists should continue to promote themselves even after they have a manager. Lately, Colligan notes, more performers and songwriters are developing their own World Wide Web pages—doing anything to get their names out there. The bottom line, he says, is to be on the lookout for new ways to promote your work.

—Robin Gee

How to Contact: Submit demo tape by mail. Unsolicited submissions are OK. Prefers cassette with 3 songs and lyric or lead sheet. If seeking management, include résumé, photo with demo tape and bio in press kit. SASE. Reports in 2 weeks.
Music: Mostly **pop**, **jazz**, **rap**, **country** and **folk**. Works primarily with small bands and solo artists. Current acts include Black Prince.

AIR TIGHT MANAGEMENT, P.O. Box 113, Winchester Center CT 06094. (203)738-9139. Fax: (203)738-9135. President: Jack Forchette. Management firm. Estab. 1969. Represents individual artists, groups or songwriters from anywhere; currently handles 6 acts. Receives 20% commission. Reviews material for acts.
How to Contact: Submit demo tape by mail. Unsolicited submissions are OK. Prefers cassette (or VHS videocassette). If seeking management, press kit should include photos, bio and recorded material. "Follow up with a fax, not a phone call." Does not return material.
Music: Mostly **rock**, **country** and **jazz**. Current acts include Bill Champlin (singer/songwriter/musician), Carmen Grillo (singer/songwriter/musician) and Kal David (blues recording artist).

AKO PRODUCTIONS, 20531 Plummer, Chatsworth CA 91311. (818)998-0443. President: A.E. Sullivan. Management firm, booking agency, music publisher and record company (AKO Records, Dorn Records, Aztec Records). Estab. 1980. Represents local and international artists, groups and songwriters; currently handles 5 acts. Receives 5-25% commission. Reviews material for acts.
 • AKO's record label, Amiron Music/Aztec Productions, is listed in the Record Companies section.
How to Contact: Write or call first and obtain permission to submit. Prefers cassette with maximum of 5 songs and lyric sheet. If seeking management, include cassette, videotape if available, picture and history in press kit. SASE. Reports in 2-8 weeks.
Music: Mostly **pop**, **rock** and **top 40**. Works primarily with vocalists, dance bands and original groups. No heavy metal. Current acts include Big Bang (pop), Everyday People (pop) and CoCo Ratcliff (R&B).

MARK ALAN AGENCY, P.O. Box 21323, St. Paul MN 55121. President: Mark Alan. Management firm and booking agency. Represents individual artists and groups; currently handles 9 acts. Receives 15-20% commission. Reviews material for acts.
 • Mark Alan's publishing company, Big Snow Music, is listed in the Music Publishers section.
How to Contact: Write first and obtain permission to submit. If seeking management, press kit should include demo tape, photos, biography and reviews. Prefers cassette (or VHS videocassette if

available) with 3 songs. Does not return material. Reports in 1-3 months.

Music: **Rock**, **alternative**, **pop** and **black contemporary**. Works primarily with groups and solo artists. Current acts include Airkraft (rock band), Zwarté (rock band), Crash Alley (rock band), Mr. Happy (alternative), Toy Box (rock), Lost Horizon (rock), Jon Doe (rock), 7 Day Weekend (rock).

Tips: "We work with bands that tour nationally and regionally and record their original songs and release them on major or independent labels. We book clubs, colleges and concerts."

*ALERT MUSIC INC., 41 Britain St., Suite 305, Toronto Ontario M5A 1R7 **Canada**. (416)364-4200. Fax: (416)364-8632. E-mail: alert@inforamp.net. President: W. Tom Berry. Management firm, music publisher (Trelatunes) and record company. Represents local and regional individual artists, groups and songwriters; currently handles 4 acts. Reviews material for acts.

How to Contact: Write first and obtain permission to submit a demo. Prefers cassette or CD. If seeking management, press kit should include photo, bio, fact sheet, cassette or CD. Does not return material.

Music: Mostly **rock** and **pop**. Works primarily with bands and singer/songwriters. Current acts include Holly Cole (pop vocalist), Kim Mitchell (rock singer/songwriter) and The Breits (rock group).

ALEXAS MUSIC PRODUCTIONS, 1935 S. Main St., Suite 433, Salt Lake City UT 84115. (801)467-2104. President: Patrick Melfi. Management firm, booking agency and record company (Alexas Records/ASCAP). Estab. 1976. Represents local, regional or international individual artists, groups and songwriters; currently handles 14 acts. Receives 15% commission. Reviews material for acts.

How to Contact: Write or call first and obtain permission to submit. Submit VHS videocassette only with 1-3 songs and lyric sheets. If seeking management, include bio, video, demo and press kit. SASE. Reports in 10 weeks.

Music: Mostly **country** and **pop**; also **New Age** and **gospel**. Represents well-established bands and vocalists. Current acts include A.J. Masters (singer/songwriter), Randy Meisner (Eagles, Poco), Juice Newton and Fats Johnson.

Tips: "Be strong, be straight and be persistent/no drugs."

*ALL ACCESS ENTERTAINMENT MANAGEMENT GROUP, INC., 425 Madison Ave., #802, New York NY 10017. (212)980-3101. Fax: (212)980-3510. E-mail: mad425@aol.com. Manager: Amy McFarland. Management firm. Estab. 1994. Represents local and regional (Northeast) individual artists and groups; currently handles 4 acts. Receives 20% commission. Reviews material for acts.

How to Contact: Submit demo tape by mail. Unsolicited submissions are OK. Prefers cassette with current press (if any) and photo. SASE. Reports in 6-8 weeks.

Music: Mostly **alternative/pop** and **rock**; also **country**. Works primarily with singer/songwriters and bands. Current acts include Carly Simon (Arista Records), Daryl Hall & John Oates (Arista Records, pop), Screaming Headless Torsos (Discovery/WB, funk/alternative), Thin Lizard Dawn (RCA Records, alternative/pop) and Stacy Wilde (Tom Petty-esque).

Tips: "To use a baseball analogy . . . we are looking for rookies of the year."

ALL MUSICMATTERS, P.O. Box 6156, San Antonio TX 78209. (210)651-5858. President: Jean Estes. Management firm and booking agency. Represents artists from anywhere.

How to Contact: Write first and obtain permission to submit. Prefers cassette. Does not return material. Reports in 1 month.

Music: Mostly **jazz**. Current acts include True Diversity (jazz group).

ALL STAR MANAGEMENT, 1229 S. Prospect St., Marion OH 43302-7267. (614)382-5939. President: John Simpson. Management firm, booking agency. Estab. 1990. Represents individual artists, groups and songwriters artists from anywhere; currently handles 9 acts. Receives 15-20% commission. Reviews material for acts.

How to Contact: Submit demo tape by mail. Unsolicited submissions are OK. Prefers cassette or videocassette with 3 songs and lyric or lead sheet. If seeking management, press kit should include audio with 3 songs, bio, 8×10 photo or any information or articles written on yourself or group, video if you have one. SASE. Reports in 2 months.

Music: Mostly **country**, **country rock** and **Christian country**; also **gospel** and **rock**. Works primarily with bands and singers/songwriters. Current acts include Leon Seiter (country singer/songwriter), Debbie Robinson (country) and Christopher Troy (country).

Tips: "Don't give up; write what you like. The industry will look at close-to-the-heart songs."

*ALL STAR PROMOTIONS, P.O. Box 1130, Tallevast FL 34270. (941)351-3253. Fax: (941)355-8114. VP of A&R: Bob Francis. Management firm, booking agency, music publisher (Rob-Lee Music, TCB Music, Pyramid Music), record company (Castle Records, Trade Records, TCB Records) and record producer (Rob Russen). Estab. 1966. Represents individual artists, groups and songwriters from

anywhere; currently handles 9 acts. Receives 15% commission. Reviews material for acts.
How to Contact: Submit demo tape by mail. Unsolicited submissions are OK. Prefers cassette or VHS videocassette with 6-10 songs. If seeking management, press kit should include bio, photo and references. Does not return material. Reports in 4 weeks.
Music: Mostly **rock**, **R&B** and **blues**. Works primarily with self-contained bands and singer/songwriters. Current acts include Murray Woods and Tangled Blue (self-contained blues/rock band), David "Googie" Lawrence (R&B vocalist, singer/songwriter) and Suzette Dorsey (vocalist).
Tips: "Submit master quality demos. Raw, unedited, uncut 'home' demos don't get any consideration at all."

ALL STAR TALENT AGENCY, Box 82, Greenbrier TN 37073. (615)643-4208. Agent: Joyce Kirby. Booking agency. Estab. 1966. Represents professional individuals, groups and songwriters; currently handles 6 acts. Receives 10% commission. Reviews material for acts.
How to Contact: Submit demo tape by mail. Unsolicited submissions are OK. Prefers cassette with 4 songs (can be cover songs) and lead sheet (VHS videocassette if available). If seeking management, press kit should include bios and photos. SASE. Reports in 6 weeks.
Music: Mostly **country**; also **bluegrass**, **gospel**, **MOR**, **rock (country)** and **top 40/pop**. Works primarily with dance, show and bar bands, vocalists, club acts and concerts. Current acts include Alex Houston (MOR), Jesse Chavez (country/gospel) and Jack Greene (country).

MICHAEL ALLEN ENTERTAINMENT DEVELOPMENT, P.O. Box 111510, Nashville TN 37222. (615)754-0059. Contact: Michael Allen. Management firm and public relations. Represents individual artists, groups and songwriters; currently handles 3 acts. Receives 15-25% commission. Reviews material for acts.
How to Contact: Submit demo tape by mail. Unsolicited submissions are OK. Prefers cassette (or VHS videocassette) with 3 songs and lyric or lead sheets. If seeking management, press kit should include photo, bio, press clippings, letter and tape. SASE. Reports in 3 months.
Music: Mostly **country**, **pop** and **R&B**; also **rock** and **gospel**. Works primarily with vocalists and bands. Currently doing public relations for Shotgun Red, Ricky Lynn Gregg and Easy Street.

AMAZING MAZE PRODUCTIONS, P.O. Box 282, Cranbury NJ 08512. (609)426-1277. Fax: (609)426-1217. Contact: Michael J. Mazur II. Management firm. Estab. 1987. Represents groups from anywhere. Commission varies. Reviews material for acts.
How to Contact: Submit demo tape by mail. Unsolicited submissions are OK. Prefers cassette (or VHS videocassette) with 2 songs. If seeking management, press kit should include CD/cassette, photo, bio and video. Does not return material.

AMERICAN ARTIST, INC., 17 Orchard Ave., Somerdale NJ 08083. (609)566-1232. Fax: (609)435-7453. President: Anthony J. Messina. Management firm and booking agent. Represents individual artists and groups from anywhere; currently handles 30 acts. Receives 15% commission. Reviews material for acts.
How to Contact: Submit demo tape by mail. Unsolicited submissions are OK. Prefers cassette or videocassette with 3 songs. Does not return material. Reports in 1 month.
Music: Mostly **R&B**, **rap** and **Top 40**. Current acts include Harold Melvin and the Bluenotes (R&B), Ben E. King (R&B) and Jimmy Harnen (Top 40).

AMERICAN FAMILY TALENT, P.O. Box 87, Skidmore MO 64487. (816)928-3631. Personal Manager: Jonnie Kay. Management firm (Festival Family Ent. Ltd.), music publisher (Max Stout Publishing/BMI) and record company (Max Stout Records). Estab. 1973. Currently handles 7 acts. Receives 15% commission. Reviews material for acts.
How to Contact: Submit demo tape by mail. Unsolicited submissions are OK. Prefers cassette (or videocassette of performance) with 2 songs with lyric and lead sheets. If seeking management, press kit should include bio, 8×10 photo, audio tape and videotape. Does not return material. Reports in 2 months.
Music: Mostly **ballads**, **pop** and **country**; also **patriotic**. Works primarily with variety showbands and dance bands. Current acts include Britt Small and Festival (brass band/variety), Matt and Robyn Rolf (country show band) and Texas the Band (variety showband).
Tips: "Be patient, we receive large amounts."

AMOK INC., 202-243 Main St. E., Milton Ontario L9T 1P1 **Canada**. (905)876-3550. Fax: (905)876-3552. E-mail: amok@inforamp.net. Website: http://www.netbistro.com/amok2/index.html. Contact: Lorenz Eppinger. Management firm and booking agent. Estab. 1985. Represents groups from anywhere. Currently handles 14 acts. Receives 15-20% commission.
How to Contact: Submit demo tape by mail. Unsolicited submissions are OK. Prefers cassette, VHS videocassette or CD if available, with lyric sheet. If seeking management, press kit should include bio,

past performances, photo, cassette, CD or video. "Due to the large amount of submissions we receive we can only respond to successful applicants." Does not return material.

Music: Mostly **world beat**, **new roots** and **folk**. Works primarily with bands in the world music and new roots field; no mainstream rock/pop. Current acts include Courage of Lassie (new roots, Beggars Banquet/PolyGram), Ashkaru (world beat, Triloka/Worldly Music) and Tarig Abubakar & The Afro Nubians (pan African, Stern's Africa).

*ANDERSON ASSOCIATES COMMUNICATIONS GROUP, 128 Bennett Ave., Yonkers NY 10701. (914)376-8724. Fax: (914)376-2870. CEO: Richard Papaleo. Management firm. Estab. 1992. Represents individual artists and groups from anywhere; currently handles 5 acts. Receives 15-20% commission. Reviews material for acts.

How to Contact: Submit demo tape by mail. Unsolicited submissions are OK. Prefers cassette, bio and/or picture with 3 songs and lead sheet. If seeking management, press kit should include cassette with 3 songs (video OK), bio and picture. SASE. Reports in 2-3 weeks.

Music: Mostly **R&B**, **pop/dance** and **pop/rock**; also **A/C**, **pop/mainstream** and **mainstream rock**. Current acts include Jackie Cohen (dance/R&B), Les Barron (R&B) and Cuba Gooding (pop/R&B).

Tips: "We work hard for all of our clients and will not recommend any deal to our client unless it is the right deal. We are in for the long term and not short term. We are not into the quick cash!"

*AQUILA ENTERTAINMENT, 215 Girard SE, Albuquerque NM 87106. (505)256-1488. Fax: (505)254-0879. Music Producer/Publisher: Rick Mata. Management firm, music publisher (Rick Mata) and record producer (Rick Mata). Estab. 1990. Represents individual artists, groups and songwriters from anywhere; currently handles 7 acts. Reviews material for acts.

How to Contact: Submit demo tape by mail. Unsolicited submissions are OK. Prefers cassette with 2 songs and lyric sheet. If seeking management, press kit should include tape with 3 songs, bio and photos. "Best (uptempo) song first!" SASE. Reports in 6 weeks.

Music: Mostly **alternative**, **New Age** and **progressive rock**; also **contemporary**, **Latin** and **classical guitar compositions**. Works primarily with bands, songwriters/musicians and composers. Current acts include Agony (band), Diablo (band) and Rick Nyte (singer/songwriter/composer).

Tips: "Write about topics people can relate to, and be as unique and original as possible. The industry is full of songs that sound alike. It is important to stand out."

ARDENNE INT'L INC., 1800 Argyle St., Suite 444, Halifax, N.S. B3J 3N8 **Canada**. (902)492-8000. Fax: (902)423-2143. E-mail: ardenne@fox.nstn.ca. Website: http://emporium.turnpike.net/A/AAllen/ardenne.events.html. President: Michael Ardenne. Management firm, record company (Ardenne Int'l Music). Estab. 1988. Represents local, individual artists and songwriters from anywhere; currently handles 3 acts. Receives 20% commission. Reviews material for acts.

How to Contact: Call first and obtain permission to submit. Prefers cassette with lyric sheet. "Put name, address, phone number and song list on the tape. Send maximum 3 songs." If seeking management, include b&w photo, bio, chart placings. Does not return material. Reports in 2-6 weeks.

Music: Mostly **country**, **pop** and **soft rock**. Works primarily with vocalists/songwriters. Current acts include LezLee (country), Annick Gagnon (pop/soft rock) and Trina (country).

Tips: "Be ruthless in your pursuit of the lyric and make sure the song travels from beginning to end. It has to go places!"

ARIMTE ENTERTAINMENT LTD. (formerly Arimte Management), 9675-125th St., Surrey British Columbia V3V 4X9 **Canada**. (604)589-1063. Fax: (604)589-4330. President: Rodney Turner. Vice President: Sharon Amrolia. Management firm and booking agency. Estab. 1991. Represents individual artists and groups from anywhere; currently handles 4 acts. Receives 20% commission. Reviews material for acts.

How to Contact: Submit demo tape by mail. Unsolicited submissions are OK. Prefers cassette with 3 songs and lyric sheet. If seeking management, press kit should include bio, photo, cassette and any other possible information. Does not return material. Reports in 2 weeks.

Music: Mostly **R&B**, **pop** and **funk/hip hop**; also **rock**, **alternative** and **jazz**. Currently represents Bassic Instincts (hip hop), Cuva (R&B) and Danielle (R&B).

Tips: "Write great songs for yourself if not the industry, but if you are working with an artist write great songs for the artist with whom you're working."

ARKLIGHT MANAGEMENT CO., P.O. Box 261, Mt. Vernon VA 22121. (703)780-4726. Manager: Vic Arkilic. Management firm. Estab. 1986. Represents local individual artists and groups; currently handles 1 act. Receives 15% commission. Reviews material for acts.

How to Contact: Submit demo tape by mail. Unsolicited submissions are OK. Prefers cassette (or VHS videocassette) with 4 songs and lyric sheet. If seeking management, include photo, bio, tape, video and lyric sheets. SASE. Reports in 3 months.

Music: Mostly **rock**, **pop** and **folk**. "We work with self-contained groups who are also songwriters."
Tips: "Please submit finished demos only!"

*ARRIVED ALIVE MANAGEMENT INC., 4 Accord Station, Hingham MA 02018. (617)695-3223. Fax: (617)695-3503. E-mail: aam@world.std.com. President: Jack Merry. Management firm. Estab. 1992. Represents individual artists, groups and songwriters from anywhere; currently handles 3 acts. Receives 15-20% commission. Reviews material for acts.
How to Contact: Submit demo tape by mail. Unsolicited submissions are OK. Prefers cassette or videocassette with 3-5 songs and lyric sheet. If seeking management, press kit should include picture, recent press, 12 month history on touring. Does not return material. Reports in 1-2 months.
Music: Mostly **rock**, **alternative** and **dance**; also **blues**, **country** and **jazz**. Current acts include Seventh Son (hard rock), Zen Lunatic (alternative rock) and Laurie Gettman (AOR).

ARSLANIAN & ASSOCIATES, INC., 6671 Sunset Blvd., #1502, Hollywood CA 90028. (213)465-0533. Management firm. Represents local individual artists and groups; currently handles 4 acts. Receives 20% commission. Reviews material for acts.
How to Contact: Call first and obtain permission to submit. Prefers cassette with 3 songs. If seeking management, press kit should include photo and bio. Does not return material. Reports in 1 month.
Music: Mostly **alternative** and **rock**. Works primarily with singer/songwriters in bands. Current acts include Farm Animals (roots rock led by singer/songwriter Jerold Aram), Fabian and Tommy Sands.

ARTIST REPRESENTATION AND MANAGEMENT, 1257 Arcade St., St. Paul MN 55106. (612)483-8754. Fax: (612)776-6338. Office Manager: Roger Anderson. Management firm, booking agency. Estab. 1983. Represents artists from anywhere; currently handles 15 acts. Receives 15% commission. Reviews material for acts.
How to Contact: Submit demo tape by mail. Unsolicited submissions are OK. Prefers cassette (or videocassette) with 3 songs and lyric sheet. If seeking management, press kit should include demo tape or videotape, preface, bio, etc. "Priority is placed on original artists with product who are willing to tour." Does not return material. Reports in 2 weeks.
Music: Mostly **rock**, **heavy metal** and **R&B**; also **southern rock** and **pop**. Works primarily with bands. Current acts include Crow (R&B, rock), Austin Healy (southern rock), Strawberry Jam & Hifi Horns (R&B), Nick St Nicholas & the Lone Wolf (rock), Fergie Frederikson (former lead vocalist for Toto) and Knight Crawler (contemporary hard rock).

ARTISTS ONLY, INC., 152-18 Union Turnpike, Flushing NY 11367. (718)380-4001. Fax: (718)591-4590. President: Bob Currie. Management firm, music publisher (ASCAP/Sun Face Music, BMI/Shaman Drum), record producer. Estab. 1986. Represents individual artists and/or groups, songwriters, producers and engineers from anywhere; currently handles 6 acts. Receives 20% commission. Reviews material for acts.
How to Contact: Submit demo tape by mail. Unsolicited submissions are OK. Prefers cassette or VHS videocassette with 2 songs and lyric sheet. If seeking management, press kit should include 3 song demo, photo and contact information including phone numbers. "If you want material returned, include stamped, self-addressed envelope." Reports in 2-3 weeks.
Music: Mostly **urban contemporary**, **dance** and **rap/rock**; also **popular (ballads)**, **Spanish** and **rock**. Works primarily with singer/songwriters and self-contained bands. Current acts include Tony Terry (singer/songwriter), Sweet Sensation (group) and Betty Dee (Latin).
Tips: "We only want your best, and be specific with style. Quality, not quantity."

ATCH RECORDS AND PRODUCTIONS, Suite 380, Fondren, Houston TX 77096-4502. (713)981-6540. Chairman/CEO: Charles Atchison. Management firm, record company. Estab. 1989. Represents local, regional and international individual artists, groups and songwriters; currently handles 3 acts. Receives 20% commission. Reviews material for acts.
How to Contact: Submit demo tape by mail. Unsolicited submissions are OK. Prefers cassette with 2 songs and lyric sheet. If seeking management, include bio, photo, demo and lyrics. Does not return material. Reports in 3 weeks.
Music: Mostly **R&B**, **country** and **gospel**; also **pop**, **rap** and **rock**. Works primarily with vocalists and groups. Current acts include B.O.U. (rap), Blakkk Media (rap) and Premier.
Tips: "Send a good detailed demo with good lyrics. Looking for wonderful love stories, also songs for children."

ATI MUSIC, 75 Parkway Ave., Markham, Ontario L3P 2H1 **Canada**. (905)294-5538. President: Scoot Irwin. Management firm, music publisher and record company. Estab. 1983. Represents individual artists, groups from anywhere. Currently handles 8 acts. Receives 15% commission. Reviews material for acts.

How to Contact: Submit demo tape by mail. Unsolicited submissions are OK. Prefers cassette (or VHS videocassette) with 2-3 songs and lyric sheet. If seeking management, press kit should include photo (2 different), bio and background. "Don't load with press clippings." Does not return material. Reports in 2-3 weeks.
Music: Mostly **country** and **gospel**. Current acts include Dick Damron (country/country gospel), Allana Myrol (contemporary country) and Billy Charne.
Tips: "Material should be compatible with today's market."

ATLANTIC ENTERTAINMENT GROUP, 1125 Atlantic Ave., #700, Atlantic City NJ 08401-4806. (609)823-6400. Fax: (609)345-8683. Director of Artist Services: Scott Sherman. Management firm, booking agency. Represents individual artists and groups from anywhere; currently handles over 60 acts. Receives 10-20% commission. Reviews material for acts.
How to Contact: Submit demo tape by mail. Unsolicited submissions are OK. Prefers cassette, CD or VHS videocassette with 3 songs and lyric or lead sheet. If seeking management, press kit should include bio and reviews. SASE. Reports in 2-4 weeks.
Music: Mostly **dance**, **R&B** and **contemporary**; also **house**, **rock** and **specialty**. Current acts include Jennifer Holliday (singer), Candace Jourdan (singer/writer), Candy J (singer/songwriter), C&C Music Factory, Deborah Cooper and Ernest Kohl.

babysue, P.O. Box 8989, Atlanta GA 30306. (404)875-8951. Website: http://babysue.com. President: Don W. Seven. Management firm, booking agency, record company (baby sue). "We also publish a magazine which reviews music." Estab. 1983. Represents local, regional or international individual artists, groups and songwriters; currently handles 4 acts. Receives 15% commission. Reviews material for acts.
• babysue's record label is listed in the Record Companies section.
How to Contact: Submit demo tape by mail. Unsolicited submissions are OK. Prefers cassette (or VHS videocassette if available) with 4 songs and lyric sheets. Does not return material. Reports in 2 months.
Music: Mostly **rock**, **pop** and **alternative**; also **country** and **religious**. Works primarily with multi-talented artists (those who play more than 1 instrument). Current acts include LMNOP (rock), Mush-cakes (folk) and the Mommy (heavy metal).

BANDSTAND (INTERNATIONAL) ENTERTAINMENT AGENCY, P.O. Box 1010, Simcoe, Ontario N3Y 5B3 **Canada**. (519)426-0000. Fax: (519)426-3799. Florida Address: Unit 392, 1475 Flamingo Drive, Englewood FL 34224. President: Wayne Elliot. Management firm, booking agency. Estab. 1965. Represents individual artists and groups from anywhere. Currently handles 3 acts. Receives 10-15% commission. Reviews material for acts.
How to Contact: Submit demo tape by mail. Unsolicited submissions are OK. If seeking management, press kit should include promo, video and demo. Does not return material. Reports in 1 month.
Music: Mostly **rock** and **country**; also **novelty acts**. Works primarily with vocalists and bands. Current acts include Kirby Ellis, Peggy Pratt and Bill Cayley.
Tips: "A good promo kit is a must! To be a winner, you must look like a winner!"

*BARNARD MANAGEMENT SERVICES (BMS), 1443 Sixth St., Santa Monica CA 90401. (310)587-0771. Agent: Russell Barnard. Management firm. Estab. 1979. Represents artists, groups and songwriters; currently handles 3 acts. Receives 10-20% commission. Reviews material for acts.
How to Contact: Write first and obtain permission to submit. Prefers cassette with 3-10 songs and lead sheet. Artists may submit VHS videocassette (15-30 minutes) by permission only. Does not return material. Reports in 2 months.
Music: Mostly **country crossover**; also **blues**, **country**, **R&B**, **rock** and **soul**. Works primarily with country crossover singers/songwriters and show bands. Current acts include Helen Hudson (singer/songwriter), Mark Shipper (songwriter/author) and Mel Trotter (singer/songwriter).
Tips: "Semi-produced demos are of little value. Either save the time and money by submitting material 'in the raw,' or do a finished production version."

*BASSLINE ENTERTAINMENT, INC., P.O. Box 2394, New York NY 10185. (212)769-6956. Fax: (212)874-9690. Executive Director: Sharon Williams. Management firm, artist development. Estab. 1993. Represents local and regional individual artists, groups and songwriters; currently handles 4 acts. Receives 20% commission. Reviews material for acts.
How to Contact: Submit demo tape by mail. Unsolicited submissions are OK. Prefers cassette or DAT or VHS videocassette. If seeking management, press kit should include bio (include physical description), demo picture and accurate contact telephone number. SASE. Reports in 2-3 weeks.
Music: Mostly **pop**, **R&B**, **club/dance** and **hip hop/rap**; also **Latin** and **rock**. Works primarily with singer/songwriters, rappers and bands. Current acts include E.C. Trybe (Latin/dance singing group) and The Revelations (rap group).

DICK BAXTER MANAGEMENT, P.O. Box 1385, Canyon Country CA 91386. (805)268-1659. Owner: Dick Baxter. Management firm and music publisher. Estab. 1963. Represents individual artists and groups from anywhere. Currently handles 3-5 acts. Receives 15-20% commission. Reviews material for acts.
How to Contact: Write first and obtain permission to submit. Prefers cassette (or VHS videocassette if available) with 3 or more songs and lyric sheet. If seeking management, press kit should include photos, bio, press clips, audio and video if available. Does not return material. Reports in 2 weeks.
Music: Mostly **country**, **gospel** and **pop**. Current acts include Dean Dobbins (country singer/songwriter), Ted & Ruth Reinhart (cowboy/western) and Steve Viall (country/pop).

BEACON KENDALL ENTERTAINMENT, 24 Thorndike St., Cambridge MA 02124. Contact: Warren Scott. Management firm and booking agency. Estab. 1988. Represents individual artists, groups, songwriters from anywhere; currently handles 12 acts. Receives 15-25% commission. Reviews material for acts.
How to Contact: Submit demo tape by mail. Unsolicited submissions are OK. Prefers cassette, CD or VHS videocassette with 6 songs and lyric sheet. If seeking management, press kit should include tape, picture, bio, video, press, etc. Does not return material. Reports in 6-8 weeks.
Music: Mostly **rock**, **alternative** and **R&B**. Works primarily with bands. Current acts include Heavy Metal Horns (R&B, jazz), Monster Mike Welch and Tree (hardcore).

*BIG BEAT PRODUCTIONS, INC., 1515 University Dr., Coral Springs FL 33071. (954)755-7759. Fax: (954)755-8733. President: Richard Lloyd. Management firm, booking agency. Estab. 1986. Represents individual artists, groups, songwriters from anywhere; currently handles 250 acts. Receives 15-20% commission. Reviews material for acts.
How to Contact: Submit demo tape by mail. Unsolicited submissions are OK. Prefers cassette or VHS videocassette with 5 songs and lyric and lead sheets. If seeking management, press kit should include video, audio, bio and 8×10 photo. Does not return material. Reports in 4-6 weeks.
Music: Mostly **pop/rock**, **country/variety** and **jazz/contemporary**; also **all types**. Current acts include Jonny Loew (singer/songwriter), Tina Robin (singer) and Carlos Manuel Santana (singer).

*BIG BOY RECORDS & ARTIST MANAGEMENT, P.O. Box 53297, Chicago IL 60653. (312)684-0021. President: Bill Collins. Management firm, booking agent and record company. Represents individual artists and groups from anywhere; currently handles 2 acts. Reviews material for acts.
How to Contact: Submit demo tape by mail. Unsolicited submissions are OK. Prefers cassette. Does not return material. Reports in 3 weeks.
Music: Mostly **blues**, **R&B** and **soul**. Current acts include Little Johnny Taylor (blues/soul) and Kid Dynamite (soul).

*BIG HAND, 67-2001 Bonnymede Dr., Mississauga Ontario L5J 4H8 **Canada**. (905) 855-3277. Fax: (905)855-2882. E-mail: puddin@interlog.com. President: Rick Gratton. Management firm, booking agency and music publisher (Maureen B. Close Publishing). Estab. 1993. Represents local and Southern Ontario individual artists, groups and songwriters; currently handles 2 acts. Receives 15% commission. Reviews material for acts.
How to Contact: Submit demo tape by mail. Unsolicited submissions are OK. Prefers cassette or VHS videocassette with lyric and/or lead sheet. If seeking management, press kit should include bio, tape, video, press clippings and photo. SAE and IRC. Reports in 2 months.
Music: Mostly **R&B/soul**, **blues** and **funk**; also **jazz**, **rock/pop** and **fusion**. Works primarily with drummers, bands, songwriters and instrumentalists. Current acts include The Maureen Brown Band (blues/R&B/jazz) and Big Hand (funk/R&B/blues big band).

BIG J PRODUCTIONS, 2516 S. Sugar Ridge, Laplace LA 70068. (504)652-2645. Agent: Frankie Jay. Booking agency. Estab. 1968. Represents individual artists, groups and songwriters; currently handles over 50 acts. Receives 15-25% commission. Reviews material for acts.
How to Contact: Write or call first and obtain permission to submit. Prefers cassette (or VHS videocassette if available) with 3-6 songs and lyric or lead sheet. "It would be best for an artist to lip-sync to a prerecorded track. The object is for someone to see how an artist would perform more than simply assessing song content." Does not return material. Reports in 2 weeks.
Music: Mostly **rock**, **pop** and **R&B**. Works primarily with groups with self-contained songwriters. Current acts include Zebra (original rock group), Crowbar (heavy metal) and Kyper (original dance).
Tips: "Have determination. Be ready to make a serious commitment to your craft because becoming successful in the music industry is generally not an 'overnight' process."

*J. BIRD ENTERTAINMENT AGENCY, 4905 S. Atlantic, Daytona Beach FL 32127. (904)767-1919. Fax: (904)767-1019. President: John Bird II. Management firm, booking agency, record company. Estab. 1963. Represents individual artists, groups and songwriters from anywhere; currently

handles 55 acts. Receives 15-20% commission. Reviews material for acts.
How to Contact: Submit demo tape by mail. Unsolicited submissions are OK. Prefers cassette or VHS videocassette and photo with 3 songs and lyric sheet. Does not return material. Reports in 2 weeks.
Music: Mostly **rock**, **top 40** and **country**. Current acts include Kansas, Little River Band and ELO.

BISCUIT PRODUCTIONS INC., H-117, 3315 E. Russell Rd., Las Vegas NV 89120. (702)451-1796. President: Steve Walker. Management firm. Estab. 1989. Represents individual artists and groups from anywhere; currently handles 3 acts. Receives 20% commission. Reviews material for acts.
How to Contact: Submit demo tape by mail. Prefers cassette or VHS videocassette. Does not return material. Reports in 2 months.
Music: Mostly **rap**, **R&B** and **dance**; also **pop** and **alternative**. Current acts include Mr. Freeze, Biscuit and Brand X.
Tips: "Believe in yourself and your work. If we can believe in you as well, it may work."

BLACK STALLION COUNTRY PRODUCTIONS, INC., P.O. Box 368, Tujunga CA 91043. (818)352-8142. President: Kenn E. Kingsbury, Jr.. Management firm, production company and music publisher (Black Stallion Country Publishing/BMI). Estab. 1979. Represents individual artists from anywhere; currently handles 5 acts. Receives 15-25% commission. Reviews material for acts.
  • Black Stallion's publishing company, Black Stallion Country Publishing, can be found in the Music Publishers section.
How to Contact: Submit demo tape by mail. Unsolicited submissions are OK. Prefers cassette with 3 songs and lyric sheet. SASE. Reports in 2 months.
Music: Mostly **country**, **R&B** and **A/C**. Works primarily with country acts, variety acts and film/TV pictures/actresses. Current acts include Lane Brody (singer country), Thom Bresh (musician) and Gene Bear (TV host).
Tips: "Be professional in presentation. Make sure what you present is what we are looking for (i.e., don't send rock when we are looking for country)."

*BLACKGROUND, 9000 Sunset Blvd., Hollywood CA 90069. (310)247-0344. Fax: (310)247-0347. A&R: Al Carter. Management firm and record company. Estab. 1993. Represents individual artists, groups, songwriters and producers from anywhere; currently handles 4 acts. Reviews material for acts.
How to Contact: Call first and obtain permission to submit. Prefers cassette or DAT with 3 or 4 songs. If seeking management, press kit should include picture, bio, 3 or 4 songs, name and contact number on cassette or DAT. Does not return material. Reports in 2-3 weeks.
Music: Mostly **R&B**, **hip hop** and **gospel**. Works primarily with songwriters/producers, musicians. Current acts include R. Kelly (R&B singer, producer and songwriter), Aaliyah (R&B singer) and The Winans (gospel singers, producers and songwriters).
Tips: "Submit complete songs with original music. Emphasis should be on strong hooks with commercial R&B appeal."

BLANK & BLANK, 1530 Chestnut St., Suite 308, Philadelphia PA 19102. (215)568-4310. Treasurer, Manager: E. Robert Blank. Management firm. Represents individual artists and groups. Reviews material for acts.
How to Contact: Submit demo tape by mail. Unsolicited submissions are OK. Prefers videocassette. Does not return material.

BLAZE PRODUCTIONS, 103 Pleasant Ave., Upper Saddle River NJ 07458. (201)825-1060. Fax: (201)825-4949. E-mail: blazepro@ix.netcom.com. Office Manager: Toni Lynn. Management firm, music publisher (Botown Music), production company, record company (Wild Boar Records). Represents local, individual artists, groups and songwriters from anywhere; currently handles 6 acts. Receives 15-20% commission. Reviews material for acts.
  • See their listing in the Record Producers section.
How to Contact: Submit demo tape by mail. Unsolicited submissions are OK. Prefers cassette or VHS videocassette with 3-5 songs and lyric sheet. If seeking management, press kit should include tape, lyrics, picture, bio and "something that gets across the band's vibe." Does not return material. Reports in 1 month.
Music: Mostly **modern rock** and **all music**; also **tribute acts**. "If you're the *best* we want to represent you. The best band, kazoo orchestra, tribute act, etc. Any type of music or act." Works primarily with bands and solo artists. Current acts include Dog Voices (regional touring act), Danny V's 52nd St. (tribute to Billy Joel), Hot Legs (tribute to Rod Stewart) and Waxface (Wild Boar Records/modern rock).
Tips: "Be persistent, yet polite, and be as creative as possible with your materials. A press kit should contain the band's vibe, not just a bio."

*BLOWIN' SMOKE PRODUCTIONS, 7438 Shoshone Ave., Van Nuys CA 91406-2340. (818)881-9888. Fax: (818)881-0555. President: Larry Knight. Management firm and record producer. Estab. 1990. Represents local and West Coast individual artists and groups. Currently handles 5 acts. Receives 10-15% commission. Reviews material for acts.
- See the listing for Hailing Frequency Music in the Record Producers section.
How to Contact: Write or call first and obtain permission to submit. Prefers cassette. If seeking management, press kit should include résumé, photo, bios, contact telephone numbers and any info on legal commitments already in place. SASE. Reports in 3-4 weeks.
Music: Mostly **R&B**, **blues** and **blues-rock**. Works primarily with single and group vocalists and a few R&B/blues bands. Current acts include Carolyn Basley (formerly with Ike & Tina Turner), The Smokettes (female vocal trio) and The Blowin' Smoke Rhythm & Blues Band.

THE BLUE CAT AGENCY/EL GATO AZUL AGENCY, P.O. Box 341, Gridley CA 95948. Phone/fax: (916)846-0108. E-mail: klkindig@ecst.csuchico.edu. Owner/agent: Karen Kindig. Management firm and booking agency. Estab. 1989. Represents individual artists and/or groups from anywhere; currently handles 4 acts. Receives 10-15% commission. Reviews material for acts.
How to Contact: Write or call first and obtain permission to submit. Prefers cassette. If seeking management, press kit should include demo tape, bio and press clippings (photo optional). SASE. Reports in 6 weeks.
Music: Mostly **Latin jazz**, **rock/pop "en español"** and any other style "en español." Works primarily with singer/songwriters, instrumentalists and bands. Current acts include Ylonda Nickell (alto saxophonist), Mark Little (pianist), Alejandro Santos (flutist/composer) and Richard Marañon (singer/songwriter/guitarist).
Tips: "Never lose sight of your musical goals and persevere until you reach them."

*BLUE SKY ARTIST MANAGEMENT, 761 N. Washington, Minneapolis MN 55401. (612)332-3909. Fax: (612)288-0918. Artist Managers: Miki Mulvehill and James Klein. Management firm. Estab. 1994. Represents individual artists, groups and songwriters from anywhere; currently handles 7 acts. Receives 10-15% commission. Reviews material for acts.
How to Contact: Submit demo tape by mail. Unsolicited submissions are OK. Prefers cassette with 4 songs and lyric sheet. If seeking management, press kit should include photo and music. SASE. Reports in 1 month.
Music: Mostly **roots/rock**, **blues** and **country**. Works primarily with Americana roots/rock artists. Current acts include Luther Allison, Jonny Lang, Molly and the Makers, Jim Thackery and the Drivers, GB Leighton, Blackie Ford and the Revelators and Syl Johnson.

GEOFFREY BLUMENAUER ARTISTS, 11846 Balboa Blvd., #204, Granada Hills CA 91344. (818)893-1896. Fax: (818)893-2796. President: Geoffrey Blumenauer. Vice President: Randy St. George. Management firm, booking agency. Estab. 1989. Represents national individual artists and groups and songwriters; currently handles 15 acts. Receives 15-20% commission. Reviews material for acts.
How to Contact: Submit demo tape by mail. Unsolicited submissions are OK. Prefers cassette with 3 songs and lyric or lead sheet. If seeking management, press kit should include picture, bio, history. SASE. "We contact if interested only."
Music: Mostly **rock/blues**, **country** and **jazz**; also **folk**, **bluegrass** and **pop**. Current acts include Robby Krieger (Doors), Nicolette Larson, Jim Messina, Maria Muldaur (pop/blues/R&B) and Randy Meisner (Eagles).
Tips: "Submit three of your best songs and follow up with additional materials."

*BOHEMIA ENTERTAINMENT GROUP, 8159 Santa Monica, #202, Los Angeles CA 90046. (213)848-7966. Fax: (213)848-9069. Management firm. Estab. 1992. Represents individual artists and groups from anywhere; currently handles 3 acts. Receives 15% commission. Reviews material for acts.
How to Contact: Submit demo tape by mail. Unsolicited submissions are OK. Prefers cassette. If seeking management, press kit should include a tape (cassette) with a little blurb written about the band. "If we want to pursue the act we will; otherwise we will send a note. If you do want a critique, send a note and we will do it free of charge." Does not return material. Reports in 3 weeks.
Music: Mostly **alternative** and **adult alternative**. Works primarily with punk and alternative bands.

BOJO PRODUCTIONS INC., 3935 Cliftondale Place, College Park GA 30349. (404)969-1913. Management firm and record company (Bojo Records). Estab. 1982. Represents local, regional or international individual artists, groups and songwriters; currently handles 3 acts. Receives 20% commission. Reviews material for acts.

How to Contact: Submit demo tape by mail. Unsolicited submissions are OK. Prefers cassette (or videocassette if available) with 3 songs and lyric or lead sheets. If seeking management, press kit should include resume, tape or video. SASE. Reports in 3 weeks.
Music: Mostly **R&B**, **gospel** and **country**; also **MOR**. Works primarily with vocalists and dance bands. Current acts include Rita Graham (jazz), George Smith (jazz singer) and Tommy Gill (piano).
Tips: "Send clean recording tape with lead sheets."

BOUQUET-ORCHID ENTERPRISES, P.O. Box 1335, Norcross GA 30091. (770)798-7999. President: Bill Bohannon. Management firm, booking agency, music publisher (Orchid Publishing/BMI) and record company (Bouquet Records). Represents individuals and groups; currently handles 4 acts. Receives 10-15% commission. Reviews material for acts.
  • See the listings for Orchid Publishing in the Music Publishers section and Bouquet Records in the Record Companies section.
How to Contact: Submit demo tape by mail. Unsolicited submissions are OK. Prefers cassette (or videocassette if available) with 3-5 songs, song list and lyric sheet. Include brief résumé. If seeking management, press kit should include current photograph, 2-3 media clippings, description of act, and background information on act. SASE. Reports in 1 month.
Music: Mostly **country**, **rock** and **top 40/pop**; also **gospel** and **R&B**. Works primarily with vocalists and groups. Current acts include Susan Spencer, Jamey Wells, Adam Day and the Bandoleers.

BRASSWIND ARTIST MANAGEMENT, P.O. Box 9895, College Station TX 77842. (409)693-5514. E-mail: dcooper@cy-net.net. Website: http://www.Brasswind.com. Personal manager: David O. Cooper. Management firm and music publisher (Brasswind Music Publishing). Estab. 1983. Represents individual artists. Currently handles 1 act. Reviews material for acts.
How to Contact: Call first and obtain permission to submit a demo. Prefers cassette with 3-4 songs and lyric sheet. SASE. Reports in 2-4 weeks.
Music: Country, **children's** and **contemporary Christian**. Currently represents Jack Houston (country and children's singer/songwriter, TV host).
Tips: "We are currently in need of adult country songs that touch on children's themes and strong country and Christian songs for radio and music video airplay."

BROTHERS MANAGEMENT ASSOCIATES, 141 Dunbar Ave., Fords NJ 08863. (201)738-0880. President: Allen A. Faucera. Management firm and booking agency. Estab. 1972. Represents artists, groups and songwriters; currently handles 25 acts. Receives 15-20% commission. Reviews material for acts.
How to Contact: Write first and obtain permission to submit. Prefers cassette (or VHS videocassette if available) with 3-6 songs and lyric sheets. Include photographs and resume. If seeking management, include photo, bio, tape and return envelope in press kit. SASE. Reports in 2 months.
Music: Mostly **pop**, **rock**, **MOR** and **R&B**. Works primarily with vocalists and established groups. Current acts include Waterfront (R&B), Glen Burtnik (pop rock) and Alisha (pop/dance).
Tips: "Submit very commercial material—make demo of high quality."

BULLSEYE ENTERTAINMENT, P.O. Box 7297, Cut-N-Shoot TX 77303-0297. E-mail: lbowley@aol.com. Contact: Lee Bowley, Jr. Management firm and music publisher (K-Bowley Publishing/ASCAP, Bowley's Red Snapper Publishing/BMI). Estab. 1991. Represents individual artists and songwriters from anywhere.
How to Contact: Submit demo tape by mail. Unsolicited submissions are OK. Prefers cassette (or VHS videocassette) with 3 songs and lyric sheet. If seeking management, press kit should include bio, photo and tape. Does not return material. Reports in 3 months.
Music: Mostly **country** and **Christian**. Works primarily with vocalists, singer/songwriters and bands. Reviews material for Doug Supernaw (singer/songwriter).
Tips: "We are moving heavily into Christian music with the exception of reviewing material for Doug Supernaw. You have ten seconds to interest your listener. If the song doesn't catch me in ten seconds, it won't anyone else either."

DOTT BURNS TALENT AGENCY, 478 Severn, Tampa FL 33606. (813)251-5882. Owner: Dott Burns. Estab. 1970. Represents individual artists, groups, actors, celebrities from coast to coast; cur-

---

MARKET CONDITIONS are constantly changing! If you're still using this book and it is 1998 or later, buy the newest edition of *Songwriter's Market* at your favorite bookstore or order directly from Writer's Digest Books.

rently handles 2 acts. Receives 10% commission. Reviews material for acts.
How to Contact: Submit demo tape by mail. Unsolicited submissions are OK. "Experienced performers only." Prefers cassette with 1-3 songs. SASE. Reports in 1-2 weeks.
Music: Mostly **country**, **jazz** and **pop**. Current acts include Platters, Peter Palmer and Aniko Ferrell (duo), John Tippanelli (entertainer and impressionist) and the Shirelles.

C & M PRODUCTIONS MANAGEMENT GROUP, 5114 Albert Dr., Brentwood TN 37027. (615)371-5098. Fax: (615)371-5317. Manager: Ronald W. Cotton. Management firm, booking agency and music publisher. Represents international individual artists; currently handles 5 acts. Receives 15% commission. Reviews material for acts.
How to Contact: Submit demo tape by mail. Unsolicited submissions are OK. Prefers cassette (or VHS videocassette if available) with 3 songs and lead sheets. If seeking management, include picture, tape and bio in press kit. Does not return material. Reports in 2 weeks.
Music: Mostly **country**, **gospel** and **pop**. Current acts include Jeff Scott, Ronna Reeves (country), Joel Nava (country), Davis Daniel (country) and Danni Leigh (country).

CAPITOL MANAGEMENT & TALENT, 1300 Division St., Suite 200, Nashville TN 37203. (800)767-4984; (615)244-2440; (615)244-3377. Fax: (615)242-1177. Producer: Robert Metzgar. Management firm, booking agency, music publisher (Aim High Music Co., Bobby & Billy Music) and record company (Stop Hunger Records International, Aim High Records, Hot News Records, Platinum Plus Records, SHR Records). Estab. 1971. Represents local, regional or international individual artists, groups and songwriters; currently handles 24 acts. Receives 15% commission. Reviews material for acts.
- Capitol Management's publishing company, Aim High Music, is listed in the Music Publishers section, Capitol Management is listed in the Record Producers section, and their record label, Stop Hunger Records, is listed in the Record Companies section.
How to Contact: Submit demo tape by mail. Unsolicited submissions are OK. Prefers cassette (or videocassette of live performance, if available). If seeking management, include photo, bio, resume and demo tape. Does not return material. Reports in 2 weeks.
Music: Mostly **traditional country**, **contemporary country** and **southern gospel**; also **pop rock**, **rockabilly** and **R&B**. Works primarily with major label acts and new acts shopping for major labels. Current acts include Tommy Cash (CBS Records), Tommy Overstreet (CBS Records), Mark Allen Cash, Mickey Jones, The Glen Campbell Band (Warner Bros.) and Billy Walker (MCA Records).
Tips: "Call us on our toll-free line for advice before you sign with anyone else."

*CARLYLE MANAGEMENT, 1217 16th Ave. South, Nashville TN 37212. (615)327-8129. Fax: (615)321-0928. President: Laura Fraser. Management firm. Estab. 1990. Represents individual artists and groups from anywhere. Currently handles 4 acts.
- See the listings for Carlyle Records in the Record Companies section and Carlyle Productions in the Record Producers section.
How to Contact: Call first and obtain permission to submit. Prefers cassette with 3 songs. If seeking management, press kit should include tape, photo, bio and press. Does not return material. Reports in 2 months.
Music: Mostly **rock** and **country**. Current acts include Aven Kepler (folk), The Vegas Cocks (rock) and The Grinning Plowmen (rock).

*DON CASALE MUSIC, INC., 377 Plainfield St., Westbury NY 11590. (516)333-7898. President: Don Casale. Management firm, music publisher (Elasac Music/ASCAP; Don Casale Music/BMI) and record producer. Estab. 1979. Currently handles 6 acts. Receives 20-25% commission.
- See Don Casale's other listing in the Record Producers section.
How to Contact: "Please write to me (with SASE) before you submit, explaining your goals. Include your bio and a recent photo." Reports in 1 month.
Music: "All styles in tune with the current market." Current acts include Susy Mathis (pop singer), Chris Stone (rock singer) and B Sweet (pop singer).
Tips: "I'm looking for unique artists and songs."

*CASH PRODUCTIONS, INC., 744 Joppa Farm Rd., Joppa Towne MD 21085. Phone/fax: (410)679-2262. President: Ernest W. Cash. Management firm, music publisher (Ernie Cash Music/BMI), record company (Continental Records). Estab. 1988. Represents local, regional or international individual artists, groups and songwriters. Currently represents 1 act. Receives 20% commission. Reviews material for acts.
- See their listing in the Music Publishers section, as well as a listing for Continental Records in the Record Companies section.
How to Contact: Write or call first to obtain permission to submit. Prefers cassette (or VHS videocassette if available) with 3 songs and lyric and lead sheet. SASE. Reports in 2 weeks.

Music: Mostly **country**, **pop** and **gospel**; also **contemporary**, **light rock** and **blues**. Works primarily with individual country artists and groups. Current acts include The Short Brothers.
Tips: "Above all be honest with me and I will work with you. Please give me time to review your material and give it a justifiable chance with our music group."

CAVALRY PRODUCTIONS, P.O. Box 70, Brackettville TX 78832. (210)563-2759. Contact: Rocco Fortunato. Management firm and record company. Estab. 1979. Represents regional (Southwest) individual artists and groups; currently handles 2 acts. Receives 10-30% comission. Reviews material for acts.
How to Contact: Submit demo tape by mail. Unsolicited submissions are OK. Prefers cassette with 3 songs and lyric sheet. "We only return material we find unuseable for our artist library." If seeking management, press kit should include picture, tape (cassette), goals, experience. Reports in 1-2 months.
Music: Mostly **country** and **Hispanic**; also **gospel** and **novelty**. Works primarily with single vocalists and various vocal groups with "2 to 4 voices." Current acts include Darryl Earwood (country) and Jose Lujan (Tejano).
Tips: "Material 'in the raw' is OK if you are willing to work with us to develop it. Make songs available to our artists for review from our library of possibilities. Songs not used immediately may be useable in the future. We will promote artist/writer collaborations where styles warrant. We are looking for artist/writer chemistry. Co-operation in working or developing submitted material is a big plus."

CEDAR CREEK PRODUCTIONS AND MANAGEMENT/CEDAR COVE MUSIC (AS-CAP), 44 Music Square E., Suite 503, Nashville TN 37203. (615)252-6916. Fax: (615)327-4204. President: Larry Duncan. Management firm, music publisher (Cedar Creek Music/BMI), record company (Cedar Creek Records) and record producer. Estab. 1992. Represents individual artists, groups and songwriters from anywhere; currently represents 1 act. Receives 20% of gross. Reviews material for acts.
  • See their listing in the Record Producers section; Cedar Creek Records can be found in the Record Companies section.
How to Contact: Submit demo tape by mail. Unsolicited submissions are OK. Prefers cassette (or VHS videocassette) with 4-6 songs and lyric sheet. If seeking management, press kit should include 8×12 color or b&w picture, bio, 4-6 songs on cassette tape and VHS video if available. Does not return material. Reports in 2 months.
Music: Mostly **country**, **country/pop** and **country/R&B**; also **pop**, **southern gospel/Christian contemporary**, **R&B**, **Christian country**, **contemporary jazz** and **light rock**. Works primarily with vocalists, singer/songwriters and groups. Current acts include Lynn Guyo.
Tips: "Submit your best songs and a good full demo with vocal upfront with five instruments on tracks backing the singer."

*CHABU PRODUCTIONS, 9735 Hidden Falls, San Antonio TX 78250. (210)509-0093. Fax: (210)509-0091. Owner: Pilar Chapa. Management firm. Estab. 1994. Represents Southwest regional groups; currently handles 2 acts. Receives 15% commission. Reviews material for acts.
How to Contact: Submit demo tape by mail. Unsolicited submissions are OK. Prefers cassette with lyric sheet. If seeking management, press kit should include video and/or current photo, cassette and biography. Does not return material. Reports in 2 weeks.
Music: Mostly **Tejano**, **top 40** and **rock**. Works primarily with Tejano groups who crossover into top 40. Current acts include Dee Y Grupo Vigo (Tejano band) and Mi Orgullo (Tejano band).
Tips: "Always copyright your songs and keep track of who you send your songs to. Also be careful which publishing company you use."

CIRCUIT RIDER TALENT & MANAGEMENT CO., 123 Walton Ferry Rd., Hendersonville TN 37075. (615)824-1947. Fax: (615)264-0462. President: Linda S. Dotson. U.K. office: 8 The Lindens, Mascot Rd., Watford Herts WD1 3RE **UK**. 011-44-1923-819415. Management firm, booking agency and music publisher (Channel Music, Cordial Music). Represents individual artists, songwriters and actors. Currently handles 9 acts (for management) but works with a large number of recording artists, songwriters, actors, producers. (Includes multi Grammy-winning producer/writer Skip Scarborough). Receives 10-15% commission. Reviews material for acts.
How to Contact: Write or call first and obtain permission to submit. Prefers cassette (or videocassette) with 3 songs and lyric sheet. If seeking management, press kit should include bio, photo and tape with 3 songs. Videocassettes required of artist's submissions. SASE. Reports in 6-8 weeks.
Music: Mostly **pop**, **country** and **gospel**; also **R&B** and **comedy**. Works primarily with vocalists, special concerts, movies and TV. Current acts include Sian Michael Townley (pop), Cam-Keyz (R&B), Willie John Ellison (blues), Frank White (blues), Alton McClain (gospel), Brad Martin (country), Hammond Brothers (country) and Doug Swander (country).

Tips: "Artists, have your act together. Have a full press kit, videos and be professional. Attitudes are a big factor in my agreeing to work with you (no egotists). This is a business and your career we will be building."

CLASS ACT PRODUCTIONS/MANAGEMENT, P.O. Box 55252, Sherman Oaks CA 91413. (818)980-1039. President: Peter Kimmel. Management firm, music publisher, production company. Estab. 1985. Represents local, national or international artists, groups, songwriters, actors and screenwriters. Currently handles 2 acts. Receives 20% commission. Reviews material for acts.
How to Contact: Submit demo tape by mail. Unsolicited submissions are OK. Include cover letter, pictures, bio, lyric sheets (essential), and cassette tape or CD in press kit. SASE. Reports in 1 month.
Music: Mostly **rock, pop** and **alternative**; also **R&B** and **new country (western beat).**

CLASSIC ROCK ENTERTAINMENT AGENCY, 12700 Park Central Dr. #1404, Dallas TX 75251. (214)239-2503. Fax: (214)788-5013. E-mail: tpars@aol.com. Owner: Traci L. Parsons. Booking agent. Estab. 1992. Represents individual artists and groups from anywhere. Currently handles 80 acts. Receives 10-20% commission. Reviews material for acts.
How to Contact: Call first and obtain permission to submit a demo. Prefers cassette with 4 songs and lyric or lead sheet. If seeking management, press kit should include picture, biography of members, demo cassette, experience with music (references). "Please allow management company to have 6-8 weeks to review original material and consult with publishers." Does not return material. Reports in 2-6 weeks.
Music: **Classic rock/dance**, **jazz/blues** and **funk/alternative**; also **folk**, **country/bluegrass** and **rap/contemporary R&B**. Works primarily with bands, solos, duets and trios. Current acts include Random Axis (band), In the House (original) and Emerald City (cover music band/dance).

CLOCKWORK ENTERTAINMENT MANAGEMENT AGENCY, 227 Concord St., Haverhill MA 01830. (508)373-5677. President: Bill Macek. Management firm. Represents groups and songwriters throughout New England. Receives 15% commission.
How to Contact: Query or submit demo tape. Prefers cassette or CD with 3-12 songs. "Also submit promotion and cover letter with interesting facts about yourself." Does not return material unless accompanied by SASE. Reports in 1 month.
Music: **Rock (all types)** and **top 40/pop**. Works primarily with bar bands and original acts.

*****CLOUSHER PRODUCTIONS**, P.O. Box 1191, Mechanicsburg PA 17055. (717)766-7644. Fax: (717)766-1490. Owner: Fred Clousher. Booking agency and production company. Estab. 1972. Represents groups from anywhere; currently handles over 100 acts.
How to Contact: Submit demo tape by mail. Unsolicited submissions are OK. Prefers VHS videocassette. If seeking bookings, press kit should include glossies, video demo tape and bio. Does not return material. "Performer should check back with us!"
Music: Mostly **country, old rock** and **ethnic** (German, Italian, etc.); also **dance bands** (regional) and **classical quartets**. "We work mostly with country, old time R&R, regional variety dance bands, tribute acts, and all types of variety acts." Current acts include Robin Right (country vocalist), Johnny Kai Hawaiian Style and Tribute To The Beatles.
Tips: "The songwriters we work with are entertainers themselves, which is the aspect we deal with. They usually have bands or do some sort of show, either with tracks or live music. We engage them for stage shows, dances, strolling, etc. We do not publish music or submit performers to recording companies for contracts. We strictly set up live performances for them!"

*****THE NEIL CLUGSTON ORGANIZATION PTY. LTD.**, P.O. Box 387 Glebe, Sydney, N.S.W. 2037 **Australia**. (02)5523277. Fax: (02)5523713. E-mail: nco@geko.net.au. Managing Director: Neil Clugston. Management firm. Estab. 1989. Represents individual artists, groups and actors from anywhere; currently handles 6 acts. Reviews material for acts.
How to Contact: Submit demo tape by mail. Unsolicited submissions are OK. Prefers cassette (or PAL VHS videocassette) with 2 songs and lyric sheet. If seeking management, press kit should include bio, photo, cassette. Does not return material. Reports in 1 month.
Music: Mostly **rock, pop** and **dance**; also **A/C**. Current acts include Alyssa Jane Cook (singer/actor), Nick Howard (R&B/pop singer) and Shelli Greene (R&B/pop).

HOW TO GET THE MOST out of *Songwriter's Market* (at the front of this book) contains comments and suggestions to help you understand and use the information in these listings.

Tips: "Only send hits."

*CODY ENTERTAINMENT GROUP, P.O. Box 456, Winchester VA 22604. Phone/fax: (540)722-4625. President: Phil Smallwood. Management firm and booking agency. Estab. 1975. Represents individual artists and groups from anywhere; currently handles 32 acts. Receives 10-20% commission.
How to Contact: Submit demo tape by mail. Unsolicited submissions are OK. Prefers cassette, DAT or videocassette with 3 songs and lead sheet. Does not return material. Reports in 2 weeks.
Music: Mostly **show acts** and **writers of love songs**. Current acts include Tyler (country recording act), Phil Zuckerman (writer) and Arlo Haines (writer/performer).

RAYMOND COFFER MANAGEMENT, Suite 1, Hadleigh House, 96 High St., Bushey Herts WD2 3DE **UK**. (081)420-4430. Fax: (081)950-7617. Contact: Raymond Coffer. Management firm. Estab. 1984. Represents local, regional and international individual artists and groups; currently handles 6 acts.
How to Contact: Submit demo tape by mail. Unsolicited submissions are OK. Prefers cassette (or PAL or VHS smvideocassette if available) with 3 songs and lyric sheet. If seeking management, press kit should include 3 songs and publicity photos. Does not return unsolicited material. Reports in 2 months.
Music: Mostly **rock** and **pop**. Works primarily with bands. Current acts include Cocteau Twins, Swell, The Sundays, Electrafixion, Cecil and Agnes.
Tips: "You must be a performer or member of a performing band."

COLWELL ARTS MANAGEMENT, RR#1, New Hamburg, Ontario N0B 2G0 **Canada**. (519)662-3499. Fax: (519)662-2777. Director: Jane Colwell. Management firm, booking agency. Estab. 1985. Represents individual artists, groups from anywhere. Currently handles 15 acts. Receives 10-20% commission. Reviews material for acts.
How to Contact: Submit demo tape by mail. Unsolicited submissions are OK. Prefers cassette (or VHS videocassette) with 4 contrasting songs. If seeking management, press kit should include tape, photo, resume, reviews, 2 letters of recommendation. SASE. Reports in 3 weeks.
Music: Mostly **classical**. Works primarily with singers. Current acts include Henriette Schellenberg (soprano) and Laughton & Humphreys (trumpet/soprano).
Tips: "Be prepared. Be honest. Have something special to offer."

COMMUNITY MUSIC CENTER OF HOUSTON, 5613 Almeda, Houston TX 77004. (712)523-9710. Managing Director: Ron Scales. Management firm and booking agency. Estab. 1979. Represents international individual artists and groups; currently handles 8 acts. Receives 10-20% commission. Reviews material for acts.
How to Contact: Submit demo tape by mail. Unsolicited submissions are OK. Prefers cassette (VHS videocassette if available) with 4 songs and lyric or lead sheet. Does not return material. Reports in 2-6 months.
Music: **Jazz**, **R&B** and **blues**; also **gospel** and **folk**. Works primarily with solo vocalists, vocal groups and jazz bands. Current acts include Rhapsody (jazz vocal ensemble), Scott Joplin Chamber Orchestra (classical music by African-American composers) and Jazz Revisited (Dixieland trio).

CONCEPT 2000 INC., 2447 W. Mound St., Columbus OH 43204. President: Brian Wallace. Management firm and booking agency (Concept 2000 Music/ASCAP). Estab. 1981. Represents international individual artists, groups and songwriters; currently handles 7 acts. Receives 10-20% commission. Reviews material for acts.
How to Contact: Submit demo tape by mail. Unsolicited submissions are OK. Prefers cassette with 4 songs. If seeking management, include photo and bio. Does not return material. Reports in 2 weeks.
Music: Mostly **country**, **gospel** and **pop**; also **jazz**, **R&B** and **soul**. Current acts include Bryan Hitch (gospel), The Breeze (country), The Andrew Jackson Piano Forte, Shades of Grey (R&B/soul), Ras Matunji and Earth Force (reggae), Marilyn Cordial (pop) and Gene Walker (jazz).
Tips: "Send quality songs with lyric sheets. Production quality is not necessary."

CONSCIENCE MUSIC, P.O. Box 740, Oak Park IL 60303. Phone/fax: (312)889-1177. Owner/Manager: Karen M. Smith. Management firm, record company (TOW Records) and Glow in the Dark Rehearsals. Estab. 1985. Represents individual artists, groups and songwriters from anywhere. Currently handles 4 acts. Receives 15% commission. Reviews material for acts.
How to Contact: Submit demo tape by mail. Unsolicited submissions are OK. Prefers cassette or current release with 2-3 songs and lyric sheet. If seeking management, press kit should include current reviews, bio or letter with band or artist objectives. "Cannot overemphasize the importance of having objectives you are ready to discuss with us." SASE. Reports in 2 months.
Music: Mostly **rock** and **pop**; also **visual artists**, **writers** and **models**. Works primarily with alternative "indie" bands in the States and Great Britain. Currently represents Wait For Light (guitar rock band),

Keith Kessinger (commercial rock songwriter) and PO! (U.K. pop band).
Tips: "Always do your best, write songs for your own enjoyment firstly and focus on your goals and ambitions. Be gracious and hard working."

*COOKMAN INTERNATIONAL, 5625 Willowcrest Ave., North Hollywood CA 91601. Fax: (818)763-1398. Management firm and music publisher (El Leon Music). Estab. 1989. Represents individual artists, groups and songwriters from anywhere; currently handles 4 acts. Receives 15% commission. Reviews material for acts.
How to Contact: Submit demo tape by mail. Unsolicited submissions are OK. Prefers cassette with 3 songs and lyric sheet. Include a bio and photo." SASE. Reports in 2 weeks.
Music: Mostly **Latin music**. Works primarily with bands and singer/songwriters. Current acts include Fabulosos Cadillacs (platinum-selling Latin rock band) and Todos Tos Muertos (Latin alternative act).

COOL RECORDS, (formerly Neville L. Johnson and Associates), 11726 San Vicente Blvd., Suite 418, Los Angeles CA 90049. (310)826-2410. Fax: (310)846-5450. General Manager: Tracey O'Brien. Entertainment law firm. Estab. 1978. Represents individual artists and/or groups from anywhere; currently handles 2 acts. Receives 10% commission.
How to Contact: Call first and obtain permission to submit. Prefers cassette or CD. If seeking management, press kit should include picture, bio, press clippings. SASE. Reports in 2 weeks.
Music: Mostly **alternative rock, singer/songwriter** and **alternative country**; open to suggestion. Currently represents (as an attorney) Patrick Moraz (keyboard), Bug Music, Academy of Country Music.
Tips: "We are part of a team and it's a lot of hard work. Be diplomatic at all times."

CORVALAN-CONDLIFFE MANAGEMENT, 563 Westminster Ave., Venice CA 90291. (310)399-8625. Manager: Brian Condliffe. Management firm. Estab. 1982. Represents local and international individual artists, groups and songwriters; currently handles 3 acts. Receives 15% commission. Reviews material for acts.
How to Contact: Call first and obtain permission to submit. Prefers cassette with 4-6 songs. If seeking management, include bio, professional photo and demo. SASE. Reports in 2 months.
Music: Mostly **R&B, pop** and **rock**; also **Latin**. Works primarily with alternative rock and pop/rock/world beat club bands. Current acts include Ramiro Medina, Eleanor Academia and Adam Rudolph.
Tips: "Be professional in all aspects of your kit and presentation. Check your grammar and spelling in your correspondence/written material. Know your music and your targeted market (rock, R&B, etc.)."

COUNTDOWN ENTERTAINMENT, 109 Earle Ave., Lynbrook NY 11563. (516)599-4157. President: James Citkovic. Management firm, consultants. Estab. 1983. Represents local, regional and international individual artists, groups, songwriters and producers; currently handles 2 acts. Receives 20-30% commission.
How to Contact: Submit demo tape by mail. Unsolicited submissions are OK. "Please, no phone calls." Prefers cassette or VHS (SP speed videocassette) if available with lyric sheet. If seeking management, include cassette tape of best songs, 8×10 pictures, VHS video, lyrics, press and radio playlists in press kit. Does not return material. Reports in 1 month.
Music: Mostly **pop/rock, modern music** and **alternative/dance**; also **R&B, pop/dance, industrial/techno** and **hard rock**. Deals with all styles of artists/songwriters/producers. Current acts include World Bang (alternative/metal/industrial rock), The Choclate Hippies (pop/funk/R&B/alternative/rock), and Ken Kushner and Drew Miles (producers).
Tips: "Send hit songs, only hit songs, nothing but hit songs."

COUNTRY STAR ATTRACTIONS, 439 Wiley Ave., Franklin PA 16323. (814)432-4633. Contact: Norman Kelly. Management firm, booking agency, music publisher (Country Star Music/ASCAP) and record company (Country Star, Process, Mersey and CSI Records). Estab. 1970. Represents artists and musical groups; currently handles 6-10 acts. Receives 10-15% commission. Reviews material for acts.
● See the listings for Country Star Music in the Music Publishers section, Country Star International in the Record Companies section and Country Star Productions in the Record Producers section.
How to Contact: Write first to arrange personal interview. Prefers cassette with 2-4 songs and typed lyric or lead sheet; include photo. SASE. Reports in 2 weeks.
Music: Mostly **country** (85%); **rock** (5%), **gospel** (5%) and **R&B** (5%). Works primarily with vocalists. Current acts include Junie Lou and Bobbie Sue (country singers).

COUNTRYWIDE PRODUCERS, 2466 Wildon Dr., York PA 17403. (717)741-2658. President: Bob Englar. Booking agency. Represents individuals and groups; currently handles 8 acts. Receives 10-15% commission. Reviews material for acts.

How to Contact: Query or submit demo with videocassette of performance, if available. Include photo. SASE. Reports in 1 week.
Music: Bluegrass, blues, classical, **country** and **disco**; also **folk**, **gospel**, **jazz**, **polka**, **rock (light)**, **soul** and **top 40/pop**. Works primarily with show bands. Current acts include Carroll County Ramblers (bluegrass), Ken Lightner (country), Rhythm Kings (country), Junction (variety), the Bruce Van Dyke Show (variety) and Big Wheeley & the White Walls (country rock).

COURTRIGHT MANAGEMENT INC., 201 E. 87th St., New York NY 10128. (212)410-9055. Contacts: Hernando or Doreen Courtright. Management firm. Estab. 1984. Represents local, regional and international individual artists, groups, songwriters and producers. Currently handles 3 acts. Receives 20% commission. Reviews material for acts.
How to Contact: Call first and obtain permission to submit. Prefers cassette (or VHS videocassette if available) with 3 or 4 songs and lyric sheet. If seeking management, include photos, bio, video, tape and press in press kit. Does not return material. Reports in 1 month.
Music: Mostly **rock**, **alternative** and **metal**; also **pop** and **blues**. Current acts include Deena Miller (alternative) and various producers, such as Neil Kernon, Mark Dodson, Eddie Kramer and many others.

CRANIUM MANAGEMENT, P.O. Box 240, Annadale NSW 2038 **Australia**. E-mail: cranium@ent ernet.com.au. Manager: Peter "Skip" Beaumont-Edmonds. Management firm. Estab. 1992. Represents individual artists, groups and songwriters from anywhere. Currently handles 5 acts. Receives 17-20% commission. Reviews material for acts.
How to Contact: Write or call first and obtain permission to submit a demo. Prefers cassette. "The minimum—don't waste money on being elaborate. Talent will show through. Be sensible—if it doesn't suit us don't send it." If seeking management, include demo tape, press release/bio and cover letter in press kit. Does not return material. Reports in 1 month.
Music: Mostly **alternative** and **pop**; also **country**. Works primarily with pop/rock, alternative bands; singer/songwriters. Current acts include Mental As Anything, Dog Trumpet, Louis Tillett and David Mason-Cox.

CRASH PRODUCTIONS, P.O. Box 40, Bangor ME 04402-0040. (207)794-6686. Manager: Jim Moreau. Booking agency. Estab. 1967. Represents individuals and groups; currently handles 9 acts. Receives 10-25% commission.
How to Contact: Submit demo tape by mail. Unsolicited submissions are OK. Prefers cassette (or VHS videocassette if available) with 4-8 songs. "To all artists who submit a video: We will keep it on file for presentation to prospective buyers of talent in our area—no longer than 15 minutes please. The quality should be the kind you would want to show a prospective buyer of your act." Include résumé and photos. "We prefer to hear groups at an actual performance." If seeking management, include 8×10 b&w photos, résumé, cassette, press clips and a videocassette in press kit. Does not return material. Reports in 3 weeks.
Music: Mostly **'50s-'60s**, **country rock** and **top 40**; also **rock** and **Polish**. Works primarily with groups who perform at night clubs (with an average of 150-200 patrons) and outdoor events (festivals and fairs). Current acts include Coyote (country rock), Ridge Kickers and Allison Ames & the Flames.
Tips: "My main business is booking acts to entertainment buyers. To sell them I must have material that tells potential buyers you are great and they need you. A photocopied press kit does not do it."

CRAWFISH PRODUCTIONS, Box 5412, Buena Park CA 90620. (619)245-2920. Producer: Leo J. Eiffert, Jr. Management firm, music publisher (Young Country/BMI) and record company (Plain Country Records). Estab. 1968. Represents local and international individual artists and songwriters; currently handles 4 acts. Commission received is open. Reviews material for acts.
• See the listing for Leo J. Eiffert, Jr. in the Record Producers section.
How to Contact: Submit a demo tape by mail. Unsolicited submissions are OK. Prefers cassette with 2-3 songs and lyric sheet. SASE. Reports in 3 weeks.
Music: Mostly **country** and **gospel**. Works primarily with vocalists. Current acts include Brandi Holland, Teeci Clarke, Joe Eiffert (country/gospel), Crawfish Band (country) and Homemade.

*CREATIVE MANAGEMENT GROUP, 701 N. Hollywood Way, Suite 108, Burbank CA 91505. Phone/fax: (818)566-8461. Contact: Michael Phelan. Management firm. Estab. 1995. Represents individual artists and groups from anywhere; currently handles 2 acts. Reviews material for acts.
How to Contact: Prefers cassette and bio with 3 songs. If seeking management, press kit should include bio, photo and press. Does not return material. "Will only report back if interested."
Music: Mostly **rock** and **alternative**. Current acts include Michael Lee Firkins and The Black Symphony.

CREATIVE STAR MANAGEMENT, 615 E. Second St., Lima OH 45804. Department of Creative Services: James Milligan. Address country material to: Robin Lynnell, P.O. Box 5678, Lima OH 45802.

Management firm, booking agency, music publisher (Party House Publishing/BMI), record company (New Experience Records/Grand Slam Records/J.K. Records). Estab. 1989. Represents individual artists, groups, songwriters from anywhere. Currently handles 18 acts. Receives 15-20% commission. Reviews material for acts.
- Creative Star Management's publishing company, A New Rap Jam Publishing, is listed in the Music Publishers section, and their record label, New Experience Records/Grand Slam Records, is listed in the Record Companies section.

How to Contact: Write first and obtain permission to submit. Prefers cassette (or VHS videocassette) with 3-5 songs and lyric sheet. If seeking management, press kit should include press clippings, bios, résumé, 8×10 glossy photo, any information that will support material and artist. SASE. Reports in 1 month.

Music: Mostly **R&B, pop** and **country**; also **rap, contemporary gospel** and **soul/funk**. Current acts include T.M.C. (R&B/group), Richard Bamberger, James Junior, The Impressions, Lance H. Hass (pop), Vanesta Compton (soul) and Barbara Lomaz.

Tips: "Be very professional, know the business and your market. This is a very tough business sometimes to break into. Be prepared to offer your best."

CRISS-CROSS INDUSTRIES, 24016 Strathern St., West Hills CA 91304. (818)710-6600. Fax: (818)719-0222. President: Doc Remer. Management firm and music publisher (Menachan's Music/ASCAP, Eyenoma Music/BMI). Estab. 1984. Represents individual artists, groups and songwriters from anywhere; currently handles 1 act. Reviews material for acts.

How to Contact: Write first and obtain permission to submit. Prefers cassette (or VHS videocassette if available) with 3 songs and lyric sheet. If seeking management, press kit should include photo, bio and credits. SASE. Reports in 3-4 weeks.

Music: Mostly **R&B** and **pop**. Works primarily with vocalists and self contained bands. Current acts include Chill Factor (band).

Tips: "You must currently be a working act. Make the words to the songs so they can be understood. The music should not be as loud as the vocals."

*CROSSFIRE ENTERTAINMENT, 1026A Third Ave., New York NY 10021. (212)832-5869. Fax: (212)832-6926. President: Will Botwin. Management firm and music publisher. Works with artists from anywhere; currently handles 11 acts. Reviews material for acts.

How to Contact: "We accept referrals through performing rights organizations only."

Music: Mostly **country, alternative** and **rock**. Current acts include Jimmie Dale Gilmore (alternative), Daniel Tashien (alternative) and Lisa Germano (alternative).

*CROSSOVER ENTERTAINMENT, P.O. Box 1912, Peter Stuyvesant Station, New York NY 10010. (212)889-1936. Fax: (212)889-5346. E-mail: spainin65@aol.com. Contact: Adrienne Lenhoff. Management firm. Estab. 1989. Represents individual artists and songwriters from anywhere. Receives 20% commission.

How to Contact: Submit demo tape by mail. Unsolicited submissions are OK. Prefers cassette, videocassette, CD or vinyl. If seeking management, press kit should include tape, relevant press and/or bio. SASE. Reports in 4-8 weeks.

Music: Mostly **alternative rock**. Works primarily with bands and singer/songwriters. Current acts include Idle (Big Deal Records), Cords (Dutch alternative band) and Emperor Norton Records.

*CROWE ENTERTAINMENT INC., 1030 17th Ave. S., Nashville TN 37212-2202. (615)327-0411. Fax: (615)329-4289. President: Jerry Crowe. Management firm, music publisher (Midnight Crow/ASCAP, Cro Jo/BMI). Estab. 1986. Represents individual artists and/or groups and songwriters from anywhere; currently handles 6 acts. Receives 20% commission. Reviews material for acts.

How to Contact: Submit demo tape by mail. Unsolicited submissions are OK. Prefers DAT, CD or cassette with no more than 3 songs and lyric sheet. If seeking management, press kit should include bio, picture, tape. SASE. Reports in 2-3 weeks.

Music: Mostly **country**. Current acts include Darryl and Don Ellis (Sony/Epic recording artists), Six-Gun (country band), Jackie Lynn (country), Karen Donovan (country) and John Primm (Christian country).

CYCLE OF FIFTHS MANAGEMENT, INC., 331 Dante Ct., Suite H, Holbrook NY 11741-3800. (516)467-1837. Fax: (516)467-1645. E-mail: fifths@aol.com. Vice President/Business Affairs: James Reilly. Management firm. Represents individual artists and/or groups from anywhere; currently handles 3 acts. Receives 20% commission. Reviews material for acts.

How to Contact: Send demo tape by mail. Unsolicited submissions are OK. Prefers cassette. Does not return material. Reports in writing, in 6-8 weeks.

Music: Mostly **rock** and **alternative**. Works primarily with established groups. Current acts include Eric Brunman (singer/songwriter), Solitude (Intercord Records) and Dominic Esposito (singer/songwriter).

D & M ENTERTAINMENT AGENCY, P.O. Box 19242, Johnston RI 02919. (401)944-6823. President and Manager: Ray DiMillio. Management firm and booking agency. Estab. 1968. Represents local groups; currently handles 33 acts. Receives 15% commission. Reviews material for acts.
How to Contact: Submit demo tape by mail. Unsolicited submissions are OK. Prefers cassette (or VHS videocassette) with 3 songs and lyric or lead sheet. SASE. Reports in 2 weeks.
Music: Mostly **R&B** and **pop**; also **rock**. Current acts include New Soul Nation, Sunshyne and Trilogy.

D&D TALENT ASSOCIATES, P.O. Box 254, Burkeville VA 23922. (804)767-4223. Owner: J.W. Dooley, Jr. Booking agency. Estab. 1976. Currently handles 2 acts. Receives 15% commission. "Reviews songs for individuals in the jazz and '40s-'50s field only."
How to Contact: Write first and obtain permission to submit. Prefers cassette (or videocassette) with 1-6 songs and lead sheet. SASE. Reports in 2-3 weeks.
Music: Mostly **jazz** and **'40s-'50s music**. Works primarily with vocalists and comics. Current acts include Johnny Pursley (humorist) and David Allyn (vocalist).
Tips: "Just send demos of Tin Pan Alley (great American popular song) type of music. No rock, no country."

DAS COMMUNICATIONS, LTD., 83 Riverside Dr., New York NY 10024. (212)877-0400. Management firm. Estab. 1975. Represents individual artists, groups and producers from anywhere; currently handles 14 acts. Receives 20% commission. Reviews material for acts.
How to Contact: Call first to obtain permission to submit. Reports in 1 month. Prefers demo with 3 songs, lyric sheet and photo. Does not return material.
Music: Mostly **rock**, **pop**, **R&B** and **alternative**. Current acts include Spin Doctors (rock), The Hatters (rock), Mantussa (metal), Milo Z (funk-rock), Jimmy Cliff (reggae), Jim Steinman (producer/songwriter), Diana King (R&B/reggae), Brownstone (R&B), Fugees (hip hop), Joan Osborne (rock) and Keith Thomas (producer/songwriter).

*DCA PRODUCTIONS, 437 W. 44th St., New York NY 10036. (212)245-2063. Fax: (212)245-2367. E-mail: dcaplus@panix.com. Contact: Kate Magill. Booking agency. Estab. 1975. Represents individual artists, groups and songwriters from anywhere; currently handles 22 acts. Reviews material for acts.
How to Contact: Submit demo tape by mail. Unsolicited submissions are OK. Prefers cassette or VHS videocassette with 2 songs. "All materials are reviewed and kept on file for future consideration. No material is returned. We do not report back, only if interested."
Music: Mostly **acoustic**, **rock** and **mainstream**; also **cabaret** and **theme**. Works primarily with acoustic singer/songwriters, top 40 or rock bands. Current acts include Roger Gillan (singer/songwriter), The Nudes (acoustic alternative music) and Val Vigoda Band (alternative rock).
Tips: "Please do not call for a review of material."

THE EDWARD DE MILES COMPANY, Vantage Point Towers, 4475 N. Allisonville Rd., 8th Floor, Indianapolis, IN 46205. (317)546-2912. President & CEO: Edward De Miles. Management firm, booking agency, entertainment/sports promoter and TV/radio broadcast producer. Estab. 1984. Represents film, television, radio and musical artists; currently handles 15 acts. Receives 10-20% commission. Reviews material for acts. Regional operations in Chicago, Dallas, Houston and Nashville through marketing representatives. Licensed A.F. of M. booking agent.
How to Contact: Write first and obtain permission to submit or to arrange personal interview. Prefers cassette with 3-5 songs, 8x10 b&w photo, bio and lyric sheet. "Copyright all material before submitting." If seeking management, include demo cassette with 3-5 songs, 8 × 10 b&w photo and lyric sheet in press kit. SASE. Reports in 1 month.
Music: Mostly **country**, **dance**, **R&B/soul**, **rock**, **top 40/pop** and **urban contemporary**; also looking for material for television, radio and film productions. Works primarily with dance bands and vocalists. Current acts include Lost in Wonder (progressive rock), Steve Lynn (R&B/dance), Multiple Choice (rap) and D'vou Edwards (jazz).
Tips: "Performers need to be well prepared with their presentations (equipment, showmanship a must)."

*DEBUTANTE MANAGEMENT, 3603 Corp. Kennedy St., Bayside NY 11361. Phone/fax: (718)357-4867. E-mail: debmgmt@aol.com. President: J. Miller. Management firm. Estab. 1989. Represents individual artists from anywhere; currently handles 3 acts. Receives 10-25% commission.

How to Contact: Submit demo tape by mail. Unsolicited submissions are OK. Prefers CD, cassette or VHS videocassette. "Make sure there's a contact phone number." Does not return material. Reports in 2 months.
Music: Mostly **rock, punk** and **alternative**; also **great songs** and **great music**. Works primarily with bands and solo performers. Current acts include Tommy Floyd (blues based, 3-chord rock).

*DEPTH OF FIELD MANAGEMENT, 1501 Broadway, Suite 1304, New York NY 10019. (212)302-9200. Fax: (212)382-1639. Contact: Peter McCallum. Management firm. Represents individual artists and groups from anywhere; currently handles 6 acts. Receives variable commission.
How to Contact: Submit demo tape by mail. Unsolicited submissions are OK. Prefers cassette with 3 or more songs. If seeking management, press kit should include bio and cassette. "Don't submit 'rough' mixes/recordings." Does not return material.
Music: Mostly **rock** and **alternative**. Current acts include Andreas Vollenweider (Swiss harpist), Michael Brecker (jazz saxophonist) and Randy Brecker (jazz trumpeter).

LIESA DILEO MANAGEMENT, P.O. Box 414731, Miami Beach FL 33141. President: Liesa DiLeo. Management firm, booking agency, music publisher. Estab. 1984. Represents individual artists, groups, songwriters, and actors from anywhere; currently handles 4 acts. Receives 20-30% commission. Reviews material for acts.
How to Contact: Submit demo tape by mail. Unsolicited submissions are OK. Prefers cassette with 2 songs and lyric sheet. If seeking management, press kit should include photo, bio, press clippings, video, cassette. SASE. Reports in 1 month.
Music: **Rock, pop, Latin, salsa** and **R&B**.

ANDREW DINWOODIE MANAGEMENT, P.O. Box 5052, Victoria Point QLD 4165 **Australia**. Phone: (07)32070502. Manager: Andrew Dinwoodie. Management firm, booking agency. Estab. 1983. Represents regional (Australian) individual artists, groups and songwriters; currently handles 3 acts. Receives 10-20% commission. Reviews material for acts.
How to Contact: Submit demo tape by mail. Unsolicited submissions are OK. Prefers cassette (VHS PAL if available) with lyric sheet. SAE and IRC. Reports in 6 weeks.
Music: Mostly **country, R&B** and **rock/pop**; also **bluegrass, swing** and **folk**. Current acts include Bullamakanka, Donna Heke and Bluey the Bastard.
Tips: "Be imaginative and stay your own individual; don't try to conform to the norm if you are different."

DIRECT MANAGEMENT, 645 Quail Ridge Rd., Aledo TX 76008-2835. Owner: Danny Wilkerson. Management firm and booking agency. Estab. 1986. Represents individual artists and/or groups from anywhere; currently handles 5 acts. Receives 10-20% commission. Reviews material for acts.
How to Contact: Submit demo tape by mail. Unsolicited submissions are OK. Prefers cassette (or VHS videocassette) with 3 songs. If seeking management, press kit should include bio, cassette or CD, photo, reviews. Does not return material. Reports in 1 month.
Music: Mostly **college rock, Christian** and **children's**. Current acts include Waltons (pop/rock), Generation Rumble (alternative) and The EPs (rock).

DME MANAGEMENT, 1020 Pico Blvd. Suite A, Santa Monica CA 90405. (310)396-5008. Fax: (310)390-1966. President: David Ehrlics. Management firm, record company (Laser Records) and music publisher (Dukare Music). Estab. 1992. Represents individual artists, groups, songwriters, producers and engineers from anywhere; currently handles 5 acts. Receives 15-20% commission. Reviews material for acts.
How to Contact: Submit demo tape by mail. Unsolicited submissions are OK. Prefers cassette. Does not return material. Reports in 1 month.
Music: Mostly **urban/rap, R&B** and **rock—made in England**. Current acts include Gravediggaz (rap, Gee Street/Island Records), Rob Bacon (urban/funk/soul, Loose Cannons/Polygram) and Afterworld (R&B/rap).

DMR AGENCY, Galleries of Syracuse, Suite 250, Syracuse NY 13202-2416. (315)475-2500. Contact: David M. Rezak. Booking agency. Represents individuals and groups; currently handles 30 acts. Receives 15% commission.

REFER TO THE CATEGORY INDEX (at the end of this section) to find exactly which companies are interested in the type of music you write.

How to Contact: Submit demo tape by mail. Unsolicited submissions are OK. Submit cassette (or videocassette) with 1-4 songs and press kit. Does not return material.
Music: Mostly **rock (all styles)**, **pop** and **blues**. Works primarily with cover bands. Current acts include Joe Whiting (R&B), Tryx (rock) and Windsong (pop).
Tips: "You might want to contact us if you have a cover act in our region. Many songwriters in our area have a cover group in order to make money."

*DR. SHAY'S, 174 N. Wellwood Ave., Lindenhurst NY 11757. (516)956-1000. Contact: Bobby Shay or Jay Cee Shay. Booking agency. Estab. 1993. Represents individual artists, groups, songwriters, comedians and magicians from anywhere; currently handles 24 acts. Receives 10% commission. Reviews material for acts.
How to Contact: Submit demo tape by mail. Unsolicited submissions are OK. Prefers cassette. Does not return material. "Call 4-6 weeks after sending."
Music: Mostly **rock**, **alternative** and **jazz**; also **dance**, **blues** and **comedy**. Current acts include Julian Dean (magician/comedian), Guy Fawkes (actor) and Tap Tap the Chisler (alternative rock).

*JAMES R. DORAN, P.C., 1949 E. Sunshine, #1-130, Springfield MO 65804. (417)882-9090. Fax: (417)882-2529. Owner: James R. Doran. Management firm, booking agency. Estab. 1975. Represents individual artists, groups and songwriters from anywhere; currently handles 5 acts. Receives variable commission. Reviews material for acts.
How to Contact: Submit demo tape by mail. Unsolicited submissions are OK. Prefers cassette. If seeking management, press kit should include bio. SASE. Reports in 2 weeks.
Music: Mostly **country**; also **rock**. Current acts include Ray Price (country artist).

COL. BUSTER DOSS PRESENTS, 341 Billy Goat Hill Rd., Winchester TN 37398. (615)649-2577. Fax: (615)649-2732. Producer: Col. Buster Doss. Management firm, booking agency, record company (Stardust Records) and music publisher (Buster Doss Music/BMI). Estab. 1959. Represents individual artists, groups, songwriters and shows; currently handles 14 acts. Receives 15% commission. Reviews material for acts.
  • Buster Doss's publishing company, Buster Doss Music, is listed in the Music Publishers section, and his record label, Stardust, is in the Record Companies section. Buster Doss is also listed under Record Producers.
How to Contact: Write first and obtain permission to submit. Prefers cassette with 2-4 songs and lyric sheet. If seeking management, press kit should include demo, photos, video if available and bio. SASE. Reports back on day received.
Music: **Country**, **gospel** and **progressive**. Works primarily with show and dance bands, single acts and package shows. Current acts include Mike "Doc" Holliday, "Rooster" Quantrell, Dee Dee Tompkins, Linda Wunder, The Border Raiders, "Bronco" Buck Cody and Jerri Arnold (country).

*DRASTIC MEASURES, INC., 4511 Balmoral Rd., Kennesaw GA 30144. (770)425-6543. President: Nancy Camp. Management firm. Estab. 1991. Represents local and regional (United States and Canada) groups; currently handles 2 acts. Receives 20% commission.
  • One of Drastic Measures' artists, Stuck Mojo, received awards for Best Metal/Hardcore Band and Best Rap/Hip Hop Band at the 1995 Atlanta Music Awards.
How to Contact: Submit demo tape by mail. Unsolicited submissions are OK. Prefers cassette or VHS videocassette with minimum of 3 songs and lyric sheet. If seeking management, press kit should include photo, bio, cassette (minimum 3 songs), video (if available), tearsheets, cover letter stating objective, tour history and current itinerary. Does not return material. Reports 4-6 weeks.
Music: Mostly **hard rock** and **heavy alternative rock**; also **pop metal** and **punk**. Works primarily with bands. Current acts include Stuck Mojo (Century Media Records, hard rock band) and Lush Life (alternative rock band).
Tips: "Don't attempt to write a hit, or what you think the industry wants to hear. Write what you feel, and write what you know about."

DSM MANAGEMENT, 794 Bear Hill Rd., Berwyn PA 19312. (610)647-3443. Fax: (610)408-8661. E-mail: dendeb@aol.com. Contact: Debbie Schwartz or Dennis Colligan. Management firm. Estab. 1980. Represents individual artists, groups and songwriters from anywhere; currently handles 3 acts. Receives 20% commission.
  • See the interview with DSM's Debbie Schwartz and Dennis Colligan in this section.
How to Contact: Submit demo tape by mail. Unsolicited submissions are OK. Prefers cassette with 4-6 songs and lyric sheet. If seeking management, press kit should include demo tape and picture with bio and/or press. Does not return material. Reports in 3 weeks "with artist making the follow-up call."
Music: Mostly **rock**, **alternative/folk** and **pop**. Primarily works with singer/songwriters and bands with main songwriter lead vocalist. Current acts include Wanderlust (RCA Records, pop/rock) and David Sancious (artist/producer).

Tips: "Submit demo tape by mail with follow-up 3-4 weeks after submission. Keep package simple."

DUCKWORTH/ATLANTICA, 198 Duckworth St., St. John's Newfoundland A1C 165 **Canada**. (709)753-9292. President: Fred Brokenshire. Management firm, record company (Duckworth/Atlantica) and distributor. Estab. 1990. Represents local and Atlantic Canadian individual artists and groups. Currently handles 42 acts. Reviews material for acts.
How to Contact: Submit demo tape by mail. Unsolicited submissions are OK. Prefers cassette and press/bio kit. "3 songs max per tape, properly labelled." Does not return material. Reports in 1-2 months.
Music: Mostly **Celtic traditional**, **Celtic rock** and **singer/writer ballads**. Works primarily with folk, folk-rock bands, singer-songwriters. Current acts include Irish Descendants (Celtic folk band), Damhnait Doyle (female singer/writer) and Sandbox (pop band).
Tips: "Know the artists we are working with; send us quality demos, and don't forget your name and number."

EAO MUSIC CORPORATION OF CANADA, P.O. Box 1240, Station "M," Calgary, Alberta T2P 2L2 **Canada**. (403)228-9388. Fax: (403) 229-3598. E-mail: eao.music@cia.com. President: Edmund A. Oliverio. Management firm and record company. Estab. 1985. Represents individual artists, groups and songwriters from western Canada (aboriginal artists). Currently handles 39 acts. Receives 15% commission. Reviews material for acts.
How to Contact: Submit demo tape by mail. Unsolicited submissions are OK. Prefers cassette with 3 songs and lyric and lead sheets. If seeking management, press kit should include b&w glossy photo, cassette tape, bio, media clippings and list of venues and festivals performed. SAE and IRC. Reports in 2 weeks.
Music: Mostly **country, folk** and **native (aboriginal)**; also **rock**. Works primarily with singer/songwriters. Current acts include Activate (modern reggae), Young Eagles (pow wow country rock), Feeding Like Butterflies (folk rock/Celtic) Dean McWhittee and Lesley Schaltz (folk singer/songwriter).
Tips: "Be upfront and honest. Establish your long term goals and short term goals. Have you joined your music associations (i.e., CMA, etc.)?"

EARTH TRACKS ARTISTS AGENCY, 4809 Ave. N., Suite 286, Brooklyn NY 11234. Managing Director-Artist Relations: David Krinsky. Management firm. Estab. 1990. Represents individual artists, groups and songwriters from anywhere; currently handles 2 acts. Receives 15% commission. Reviews material for acts.
How to Contact: Submit demo tape by mail. Unsolicited submissions are OK, accompanied by release form and SASE. "Do not call to submit tapes. Mail in for review. No calls will be returned, unsolicited or accepted, under any conditions." Prefers cassette with 3-6 songs and lyric sheet. If seeking management, include 1 group photo, all lyrics with songs, a cassette/CD of 3-6 original songs and the ages of the artists. Does not return material. Reports in 2-6 weeks. "We will contact artist if interested."
Music: Mostly **commercial rock** (all kinds), **pop/dance**, **alternative** and **post modern rock/folk rock**. No rap or metal. Works primarily with commercial, original, solo artists and groups, songwriters in the rock, pop, areas (no country, thrash or punk). Current acts include Bloody Jack (alternative) and Publius (alternative).
Tips: "Submit a package of completed songs along with lyrics, photo of artist/group, or songwriter credits if any. A video on VHS accepted if available. If no package available send a cassette of what you as an artist consider best represents your style. Strong meaningful songs are preferred, as well as light pop rock for top 40 release. Will submit quality songwriter's material to name artists. All materials must be accompanied by a release form and all songs must be copyrighted. Bands influenced by Pink Floyd especially sought. Also bands influenced by the Beatles and Dylan/Petty."

*EBI INC., 928 Broadway, Suite 405, New York NY 10010. (212)228-8300. Fax: (212)228-8495. E-mail: inpress@aol.com. Contact: Ellen Bello. Management firm. Estab. 1990. Represents individual artists, groups and songwriters. Receives 20% commission. Reviews material for acts.
How to Contact: Write or call first and obtain permission to submit. Prefers cassette or VHS videocassette with lyric sheet. Does not return material. Reports in 4-6 weeks.
Music: Mostly **Native American**, **alternative rock** and **mainstream**; also **country**. Works primarily with singer/songwriters and bands. Current acts include ULALI (Native American women, a cappella singers) and Joan Armatrading.

ELLIPSE PERSONAL MANAGMENT, % Boxholder 665, Manhattan Beach CA 90267. Phone/fax: (310)546-2224. Contact: Mr. L. Elsman. Management firm. Represents local individual artists, vocalists and vocalist/songwriters. Receives 15% commission and up (P.M. contract). Reviews material for acts.

How to Contact: Submit demo by mail. Prefers cassette with 3 songs. Does not return material. Reports in 5 weeks.
Music: Mostly **pop/rock**, **R&B/dance** and **AOR**. Current acts include Eric Tage Trio.
Tips: "Young vocalists and vocalist/songwriters who have fame and fortune as their goal may write, fax or call. Saturday calls between 10 a.m. and 2 p.m. Pacific time are OK (fax 24 hours)."

GINO EMPRY ENTERTAINMENT, 120 Carlton St., Suite 315, Toronto M5A 4K2 **Canada**. (410)928-1044. Fax: (416)928-1415. E-mail: gempry@idirect.com. President: Gino Empry. Management firm, booking agent, public relations. Estab. 1970. Represents individual artists, groups, songwriters and actors from anywhere; currently handles 12 acts. Receives 10-15% commission. Reviews material for acts.
How to Contact: Submit demo tape by mail. Unsolicited submissions are OK. Prefers cassette or VHS videocassette with lyric sheet. If seeking management, press kit should include résumé and newspaper reprints. Does not return material. Reports in 2 months.
Music: Mostly **pop**, **country** and **jazz/blues**; also **theatrical**. Works primarily with singer/songwriters, actors, dancers and soloists. Current acts include Roch Voisine (singer/composer), Andre Gagnon (composer), Patrick Norman (singer/composer) and Richard Samuels (singer/composer).

ENTERCOM, 579 Richmond St. W. Suite 401, Toronto, Quebec M5V 1Y6 **Canada**. (416)504-1620. Fax: (416)938-1310. Manager: James MacLean. Management firm. Estab. 1989. Represents groups from anywhere; currently handles 4 acts. Receives 20% commission. Reviews material for acts.
How to Contact: Submit demo tape by mail. Unsolicited submissions are OK. Prefers cassette. Does not return material. Reports in 6 weeks.
Music: Mostly **alternative**, **pop**, **rock** and **metal**. Works primarily with original cutting edge bands. Current acts include Doughboys (power punk pop, A&M Records), Voivod (cybermetal/punk, Hypnotic/A&M Records) and Lamprey (pop, BMG Records).
Tips: "Send to recommended people or companies. Random solicitation is useless. Research and educate yourself. If you come across as professional and down to earth you'll get a lot further. Forget what's popular at the moment. All music is current again or recycled, so write from the experience of your life, not anyone else's. Be true to yourself. Don't follow a trend, lead music into a new dimension. Create your own!"

THE ENTERTAINMENT GROUP, 9112 Fireside Dr., Indianapolis IN 46250. President: Bob McCutcheon. Management firm. Estab. 1987. Represents local, regional and international individual artists and groups; currently handles 3 acts. Receives 20% commission.
How to Contact: Write first and obtain permission to submit. Prefers cassette with 3 songs. If seeking management include photo and tape. SASE. Reports in 1 month.
Music: Mostly **hard rock** and **R&B**. Current acts include The Remainder (college radio), The Common (college radio) and Jon Huffman Project (alternative).
Tips: "Be patient and write what you really feel—the patience comes in while you wait for your writing to mature to the point that it can cause a stir in the industry to point in your direction."

ENTERTAINMENT INTERNATIONAL USA, P.O. Box 7189, Canton OH 44705-0189. (216)454-2095. A&R: Paulette Winderl. Management firm, booking agency, music publisher. Estab. 1969. Represents individual artists and/or groups, songwriters from anywhere; currently handles 10 acts. Receives 10% commission. Reviews material for acts.
How to Contact: Submit demo tape by mail. Unsolicited submissions are OK. Prefers cassette or VHS/Beta videocassette with 4 songs and lyric sheet. If seeking management, press kit should include bio, demo and photos. SASE. Reports in 1 month.
Music: All types. Current acts include Sirene (R&B), Mary White (country) and Unique (folk).
Tips: "Put your package together carefully in a professional manner."

ENTERTAINMENT RESOURCE MANAGEMENT (ERM), One Highway 20 West, P.O. Box 784, Fonthill, Ontario L0S 1E0 **Canada**. (905)892-5086. Fax: (905)892-5545. E-mail: herchmer@vaxxine.com. President: Vincent C. Herchmer. Management firm, booking agent and music publisher (ERM Publishing). Estab. 1991. Represents individual artists, groups and songwriters from anywhere; currently handles 4 acts. Receives 10-15% commission. Reviews material for acts.

● **A BULLET** introduces comments by the editor of *Songwriter's Market* indicating special information about the listing.

How to Contact: Submit demo tape by mail. Unsolicited submissions are OK. Prefers cassette (videocassette for management or booking only) with 3 songs and lyric and lead sheets. If seeking management, press kit should include demo tape (3 songs including 1 down tempo), manufactured CD or cassette if artist has recorded for distribution, professionally shot 8x10 photo, musical background and press clippings. "A 10-15 minute video is desired when artist lives outside our regional area." SAE and IRC. Reports in 1 month.
Music: Mostly **pop, country** and **rock**; also **alternative, Celtic** and **jazz**. "We tend to work mostly with pop singers/songwriters." Current acts include Brian Hawthorn (pop singer/songwriter), Still Life (original alternative band) and Wayne McNeil (country singer/songwriter).
Tips: "Good songwriting is based on life experience. Observe the lives of others as well as your own. Read as much as possible."

ENTERTAINMENT SERVICES INTERNATIONAL, 6400 Pleasant Park Dr., Chanhassen MN 55317. (612)470-9000. Fax: (612)474-4449. Owner: Randy Erwin. Booking agency. Estab. 1988. Represents groups from anywhere; currently handles 20 acts. Receives 10-20% commission. Reviews material for acts.
How to Contact: Submit demo tape by mail. Unsolicited submissions are OK. Prefers CD or VHS videocassette. If seeking management, press kit should include photos, biography, instrumentation, references, list of places performed, reviews, video, cassette or CD. SASE. Reports in 1-2 weeks.
Music: Mostly **rock, R&B, alternative rock** and **country**. Works primarily with bands.

ENTERTAINMENT WORKS, 2400 Poplar Dr., Baltimore MD 21207. (410)265-6519. President: Nancy Lewis. Management firm, booking agency and public relations/publicity firm. Estab. 1989. Represents regional and international groups; currently handles 3 acts. Receives 15-20% commission. Reviews material for acts.
How to Contact: Write or call first and obtain permission to submit. Prefers cassette with 3 songs "plus biography/publicity clips/photo." If seeking management, include group biography, individual biographies, 8×10 b&w glossy, all press clips/articles, PA requirements list and stage plot in press kit. Does not return material. Reports in 6 weeks.
Music: **Reggae.** Works primarily with vocalists/dance bands. Current acts include Winston Grennan Ska Rocks Band, the Original Jamaican All Stars and Jah Levi & the Higher Reasoning (all reggae).
Tips: "Start with a phone call to introduce yourself, followed by a well-recorded 3-song demo, band member biographies, photo and all publicity clips. This agency works only with reggae artists."

ETERNAL RECORDS/SQUIGMONSTER MANAGEMENT, 1598 E. Shore Dr., St. Paul MN 55106-1121. (612)771-0107. President/Owner: Robert (Squiggy) Yezek. Management firm, record company (PMS Records). Estab. 1983. Represents groups from anywhere; currently handles 20 acts. Reviews material for acts.
How to Contact: Submit demo tape by mail. Unsolicited submissions are OK. Prefers CD (if available) with songs (no limit) and lead sheet. If seeking management, press kit should include CD or tape, bio, promo package and any press. Does not return material. Reports in 1 month.
Music: Mostly **alternative rock, heavy metal** and **hard rock**; also **comedy** and **new pop**. Current acts include No Man's Land (alternative metal), Power Play and Zombie.
Tips: "You must be willing to work hard and be dedicated to your goal of success."

SCOTT EVANS PRODUCTIONS, 4747 Hollywood Blvd., #112, Hollywood FL 33021-6503. (305)963-4449. Artistic Director: Scott Evans. Management firm and booking agency. Estab. 1979. Represents local, regional or international individual artists, groups, songwriters, comedians, novelty acts, dancers and theaters; currently handles more than 50 acts. Receives 25% commission. Reviews material for acts.
How to Contact: Submit demo tape by mail. Unsolicited submissions are OK. Prefers cassette (or ½″ videocassette if available) with 3 songs. If seeking management, include picture, résumé, flyers, cassette or video tape. Does not return material.
Music: Mostly **pop, R&B** and **Broadway**. Deals with "all types of entertainers; no limitations." Current acts include Scott Evans and Company (variety song & dance), Dori Zinger (female vocalist), Jeff Geist, Perfect Parties and Joy Deco (dance act).
Tips: "Submit neat, well put together, organized press kit."

EVE'S CRADLE, 1717 Whitney Way, Austin TX 78741. (512)385-1465. Fax: (512)385-1425. Owner: Tammy Moore. Management firm. Estab. 1990. Represents individual artists, groups and songwriters from anywhere; currently handles 3 acts. Receives 15% commission. Reviews material for acts.
How to Contact: Call first and obtain permission to submit. Prefers cassette or VHS videocassette with 4 songs and lyric and lead sheet. If seeking management, press kit should include photo, song list, press, bio and tape. Does not return material. Reports in 1 month.

Music: Mostly **rock**, **alternative rock** and **country**; also **blues rock**. Current acts include Lead Shoe Ballet (rock band), The Contradicks (punk band) and David Young (songwriter).

*EXCLESISA BOOKING AGENCY, 122 Iris Ave., Jackson MS 39206. Phone/fax: (601)366-0220. Booking Managers/Owners: Roy and Esther Wooten. Booking agency. Estab. 1989. Represents groups from anywhere. Receives 10% commission. Reviews material for acts.
How to Contact: Submit demo tape by mail. Unsolicited submissions are OK. Prefers cassette or videocassette. If seeking management, press kit should include CD or cassette, videocassette, pictures and bio. Does not return material. Reports in 1-2 months.
Music: Gospel only. Current acts include The Jackson Southernaires, Slim & The Supreme Angels and The Mississippi Seminar Choir.
Tips: "Make sure your demo is clear with a good sound so the agent can make a good judgment."

*JAMES FAITH ENTERTAINMENT, P.O. Box 346, Port Jefferson NY 11777. (516)331-0808. Fax: (516)331-0994. President: James Faith. Management firm and booking agency. Estab. 1989. Represents individual artists, groups and songwriters from anywhere; currently handles 5 acts. Receives 10-15% commission. Reviews material for acts.
How to Contact: Call first and obtain permission to submit. Prefers cassette or VHS videocassette (if available) with 6 songs and lyric and/or lead sheet. If seeking management, press kit should include audio—cassette, CD, etc., explain how and who recorded it; print—bio, references, photos; video—if available; and personal letter—explain what you are looking for in management. List desires, expectations, personal beliefs and goals. Does not return material. Reports in 2 months.
Music: Mostly **jazz**, **rock**, **folk**, **blues** and **funk**; also **classical**, **world** and **big band**. Works primarily with soloists, bands and singer/songwriters. Current acts include Peter Duchin (big band and society music), Big Picnic (13 piece funk band) and Subject to Change (jazz trio).
Tips: "Have all info presented clearly and professionally."

FAME INTERNATIONAL, 939 Kimball St., Philadelphia PA 19147. (215)629-0709. Exec. V.P. Productions: Albert R. Bauman. Management firm and music publisher (Jazz Lady Publishing/ASCAP). Estab. 1986. Represents individual artists, groups, songwriters and specialty acts from anywhere; currently handles 16 acts. Receives 10-25% commission. Reviews material for acts.
How to Contact: Submit demo tape by mail. Unsolicited submissions are OK. Prefers cassette or VHS videocassette with 3 songs. If seeking management, press kit should include as much relevant material as possible—head shot, bio, reviews, list of previous year's engagements, contracted future dates and commitments. Does not return material. Reports in 2 weeks.
Music: Mostly **jazz** and **country**; also **specialty acts for casinos and cruises**. Works primarily with vocalists, singer/songwriters, big bands and comedy acts. Current acts include Nancy Kelly (jazz singer), Jim Craine, the Bob Crosby Orchestra and The Guy Lombardo Orchestra.
Tips: "On cover letter, be as specific as possible in describing your career goals and what has prevented you from attaining them thus far. Be honest."

*FAST LANE PRODUCTIONS, P.O. Box 3337, Virginia Beach VA 23454. (804)481-9662. Fax: (804)481-9227. E-mail: fastlan@exis.net. Agent: George Michailow. Booking agency and consultant for overseas artists seeking US licensing/distribution. Represents individual artists and groups from anywhere; currently handles 40 acts. Receives 15% commission. Reviews material for acts.
How to Contact: Submit demo tape by mail. Unsolicited submissions are OK. Prefers cassette, ½″ NTSC or CD (preferred). If seeking management, press kit should include bio, press, tour history—min. 1 year (including: date, venue and capacity, headliner or opener, fee and attendance info), tech rider (including: stage plan, mic assignment list), backline required and personnel list for all traveling (including each person's function, if not sure, list function as TBA). "Submit only relevant materials (listed above), no playbills, copies of ads or posters, etc." Does not return material. Reports in 2 weeks.
Music: Mostly **world beat**, **reggae** and **African pop**; also **Latin**, **New Age** and **ska**. Works primarily with music acts capable of touring. Current acts include Inner Circle (reggae), Lucky Dube (pop reggae/South African) and Culture (roots reggae/Jamaican).
Tips: "Have a record company willing to provide adequate promotional and tour support."

FASTBACK MANAGEMENT, 1321 Sixth Ave., San Francisco CA 94122. (415)564-7404. Fax: (415)564-2927. E-mail: spydogydog@aol.com. Contact: Cathy Cohn. Management firm. Estab. 1992. Represents individual artists and groups from anywhere; currently handles 2 acts. Reviews material for acts.
How to Contact: Submit demo tape by mail. Unsolicited submissions are OK. Prefers cassette or VHS videocassette. If seeking management, press kit should include artist history (bio), press and tape. SASE.
Music: All types. Current acts include Meat Beat Manifesto (industrial dance) and Stephen Yerkey (alternative folk/country singer-songwriter).

FAT CITY ARTISTS, 1906 Chet Atkins Place, Suite 502, Nashville TN 37212. (615)320-7678. Fax: (615)321-5382. President: Rusty Michael. Management firm, booking agency, lecture bureau and event management consultants. Estab. 1972. Represents international individual artists, groups, songwriters and authors; currently handles over 100 acts. Receives 20% commission. Reviews material for acts.
• See their listing in the Record Companies section, and the listing for Fat City Publishing in the Music Publishers section.
How to Contact: Submit demo tape and any other promotional material by mail. Unsolicited submissions are OK. Prefers cassette, CD or video with 4-6 songs. Does not return material. Reports in 2 weeks.
Music: Mostly **rock**, **top 40**, **country** and **blues**; also **rockabilly**, **alternative** and **jazz**. "To date our company has agreements with 140 artists that represent every genre of music." Current acts include Big Brother & The Holding Co., Duane Eddy (rock), The Belmont Playboys (rockabilly), Michael Dillon & Guns, Del Reeves (country), Wet Willie (blues), Nina Simone and Stanley Turrentine (jazz).
Tips: "Send all available information including audio, video, photo and print. Creative Communications Workshop, our advertising/promotion division, specializes in developing effective artist promotional packages, including demos, videos, photography and copy. We will evaluate your present promotional material at no cost."

FCC MANAGEMENT, P.O. Box 23329, Nashville TN 37202. Phone/fax: (615)742-6333. E-mail: frankccorp@aol.com. Vice President: Frank Callari. Management firm. Estab. 1990. Represents individual artists and/or groups and songwriters from anywhere; currently handles 4 acts. Receives 15-20% commission. Reviews material for acts.
How to Contact: Write first and obtain permission to submit. Prefers cassette or VHS videocassette with 3 songs and lyric or lead sheet. If seeking management, press kit should include tape, résumé, photo, bio and press. Does not return material. Reports in 2-4 weeks.
Music: Mostly **country**, **alternative rock** and **reggae**. Current acts include The Mavericks (country), Junior Brown (country), Dean Miller (country) and Jerry Radigan (country).

DANNY FEDERICI'S SHARK RIVER MUSIC, 421 N. Rodeo Dr., Suite 15-5, Beverly Hills CA 90210. Phone/fax: (714)821-1810. Vice President: Bob Reed. Management firm, music publisher, record producer and new artist development. Estab. 1994. Represents individual artists, groups and songwriters from anywhere; currently handles 6 acts. Receives 10-15% commission. Reviews material for acts.
• See their listing in the Record Producers section.
How to Contact: Write or call first to obtain permission to submit or to arrange personal interview. Prefers cassette, DAT or VHS videocassette with 3 songs, lyric sheet and performer(s) bio. If seeking management, press kit should include photo, performance and recording history. "Copyright material. Include contact person(s) name, address and phone number and SASE." Does not return material. Reports in 3-4 weeks.
Music: Mostly **rock, country** and **R&B/soul**; also **alternative** and **New Age**. Current acts include Sacred Hearts (blues/R&B band, House of Blues band), The Bunker Boys (film/TV scores) and Revenge (rock band).
Tips: "You must have a strong desire to succeed in this business and be willing to use the constructive criticism of others to achieve that success. As founding member of the E Street Band, Danny Federici's years of recording and touring with Bruce Springsteen, as well as Dave Edmunds and others, have given him experience, expertise and insight into all facets of the music business."

S.L. FELDMAN & ASSOCIATES, 1505 W. Second Ave., #200, Vancouver, British Columbia V6H 3Y4 **Canada**. (604)734-5945. Fax: (604)732-0922. Contact: Janet York. Management firm and booking agency. Estab. 1970. Represents individual artists and groups from anywhere; currently handles over 100 acts.
How to Contact: Submit demo tape by mail. Unsolicited submissions are OK. Prefers cassette and lyric sheet. If seeking management, include photo, bio, cassette, video (if available) in press kit. SAE and IRC. Reports in 6-8 weeks.
Music: Current acts include Bryan Adams, The Chieftains, Mae Moore, Odds, Sarah McLachlan and Spirit of the West.

FRED T. FENCHEL ENTERTAINMENT AGENCY, 2104 S. Jefferson Avenue, Mason City IA 50401. (515)423-4177. Fax: (515)423-8662. General Manager: Fred T. Fenchel. Booking agency. Estab. 1964. Represents local and international individual artists and groups; currently handles up to 10 acts. Receives 20% commission. Reviews material for acts.
How to Contact: Submit demo tape by mail (videocassette if available). Unsolicited submissions are OK. Does not return material. Reports in 3 weeks.

Music: Mostly **country**, **pop** and some **gospel**. Works primarily with dance bands and show groups; "artists we can use on club dates, fairs, etc." Current acts include The Memories, "Hot" Rod Chevy, The Sherwin Linton Show and Convertibles. "We deal primarily with established name acts with recording contracts, or those with a label and starting into popularity."

Tips: "Be honest. Don't submit unless your act is exceptional rather than just starting out, amateurish and with lyrics that are written under the pretense they are qualified writers."

*B.C. FIEDLER MANAGEMENT, 102-40 Alexander St., Toronto Ontario M4Y 1B5 **Canada**. (416)967-1421. Fax: (416)967-1991. Partners: B.C. Fiedler/Elisa Amsterdam. Management firm, music publisher (B.C. Fiedler Publishing) and record company (Sleeping Giant Music). Estab. 1964. Represents individual artists, groups and songwriters from anywhere; currently handles 6 acts. Receives 20-25% or consultant fees. Reviews material for acts.

How to Contact: Call first and obtain permission to submit. Prefers cassette or VHS videocassette with 3 songs and lyric sheet. If seeking management, press kit should include bio, list of concerts performed in past two years including name of venue, repertoire, reviews and photos. Does not return material. Reports in 2 months.

Music: Mostly **classical/crossover**, **voice** and **pop**; also **country**. Works primarily with classical/crossover ensembles, instrumental soloists, operatic voice and pop singer/songwriters. Current acts include Liona Boyd (classical guitar), Canadian Brass (brass quintet) and Pamela Morgan (singer/songwriter).

Tips: "Invest in demo production using best quality voice and instrumentalists. If you write songs, hire the talent to best represent your work. Submit tape and lyrics. Artists should follow up 6-8 weeks after submission."

FIRESTAR PROMOTIONS INC., P.O. Box 165, 1896 W. Broadway, Vancouver, B.C. V6J 1Y9 **Canada**. Phone/fax: (604)732-4012. President: Frances Wennes. Management firm and record producer. Estab. 1991. Works with individual artists and songwriters from anywhere; currently handles 3 acts. Receives 25% commission. Reviews material for acts.

How to Contact: Submit demo tape by mail. Unsolicited submissions are OK. Prefers cassette or VHS videocassette with letter and picture. If seeking management, press kit should include one page biography, references, picture, cassette, introduction letter, contact person, address and telephone number. Does not return material. Reports in 3 months.

Music: Mostly **New Age** and **instrumental**. Current acts include Firestar (angelic folk harpist), Blue Confusion (folk duo) and Jerry Wennes & the Happy Wanderers (European polka band).

Tips: "Have your personal finances in control. Do not ask for financial support."

FIRST TIME MANAGEMENT, Sovereign House, 12 Trewartha Rd., Praa Sands-Penzance, Cornwall TR20 9ST **England**. Phone: (01736)762826. Fax: (01736)763328. Managing Director: Roderick G. Jones. Management firm. Estab. 1986. Represents local, regional and international individual aritsts, groups and songwriters. Receives 20% commission. Reviews material for acts.

• See the listings for First Time Records in the Record Companies section and First Time Music in the Music Publishers section.

How to Contact: Submit demo tape by mail. Unsolicited submissions are OK. Prefers cassette or 15 ips reel-to-reel (or VHS videocassette) with 3 songs and lyric sheets. SAE and IRC. Reports in 4-8 weeks.

Music: Mostly **dance**, **top 40**, **rap**, **country**, **gospel** and **pop**; also **all styles**. Works primarily with songwriters, composers, vocalists, groups and choirs. Current acts include Pete Arnold (folk) and Willow.

Tips: "Become a member of the Guild of International Songwriters and Composers. Keep everything as professional as possible. Be patient and dedicated to your aims and objectives."

FIVE STAR ENTERTAINMENT, 10188 Winter View Dr., Naples FL 33942. (941)566-7701. Fax: (941)566-7702. Co-owners: Sid Kleiner and Trudy Kleiner. Booking agency. Estab. 1976. Represents local and regional individual artists and groups; currently handles 400 acts. Receives 15-30% commission. Reviews material for acts.

• See the listing for Sid Kleiner Music Enterprises in the Advertising, AV and Commercial Music Firms section.

How to Contact: Submit demo tape by mail. Unsolicited submissions are OK. Prefers cassette or VHS videocassette with 4 songs and lyric or lead sheet. If seeking management, press kit should include song list, demo, video equipment list and references. SASE. Reports in 4-6 weeks.

Music: Mostly **MOR**, **country** and **folk**. Current acts include Dave Kleiner (folk singer), Sid Kleiner (guitarist) and Magic Diamond (magic act).

*5 STAR MUSIC GROUP/MIKE WADDELL & ASSOCIATES, 4301 S. Carothers Rd., Franklin TN 37064. (615)790-7452. Fax: (615)790-9958. E-mail: fivestar01@aol.com. President: Mike Wad-

dell. Management firm, music publisher and record producer (James Hudson). Estab. 1977. Represents regional individual artists and songwriters; currently handles 2 acts. Receives variable commission. Reviews material for acts.
How to Contact: Submit demo tape by mail. Unsolicited submissions are OK. Prefers cassette, DAT or ½″ VHS videocassette with 3 songs and lyric sheet. If seeking management, press kit should include tape, bio, picture and press information. "Should we be interested in any material received, we will contact the writer or artist by telephone or mail. All material should be copyrighted prior to submission." Does not return material. Reports in 3 weeks.
Music: Mostly **country**, **rock** and **Christian**. Current acts include Nathan Whitt (alternative), Gerd Rube (Germany) and Johnathon Bloom (alternative).
Tips: "Research the song market and be confident that your songs will hold up. Do not waste the valuable time of publishers and labels with anything less than professional songs. In past years we have signed songs from submissions via the mail. One of those, Reece Wilson, was named BMI writer of the year in 1995."

FLASH ATTRACTIONS AGENCY, 38 Prospect St., Warrensburg NY 12885. (518)623-9313. Agent: Wally Chester. Management firm and booking agency. Estab. 1952. Represents artists and groups; currently handles 106 acts. Receives 15-20% commission. Reviews material for acts.
How to Contact: Submit demo tape by mail. Unsolicited submissions are OK. Prefers cassette for singers, VHS videocassette for acts, with 1-6 songs with lead and lyric sheets. If seeking management, press kit should include professionally-done videotape or cassette, 8×10 photo, resume, letters of recommendation, song list and history of the act. Songwriters should include professionally-done cassette, lead sheet, lyrics and music. SASE. Reports in 2 months.
Music: Mostly **country**, **calypso**, **Hawaiian** and **MOR**; also **blues**, **dance**, **easy listening**, **jazz**, **top 40**, **country rock** and **Latin**, plus **American Indian Shows**. Works primarily with vocalists, dance bands, lounge acts, floor show groups and ethnic shows. Current acts include Mirinda James (blues/rock), Lori Afo and "Island Call," The Country Belles (all girl variety band), The Ronnie Prophet Country Music Show, Hank Thompson and His Brazos Valley Boys (country music legend), Prince Pablo's Caribbean Extravaganza (steel drum band and floor show), and Bobby Dick and the Sundowners ('50s-'60s specialty act).
Tips: "Submit songs that have public appeal, good story line and simplicity."

FLINTER MUSIC (buba), (formerly aaLN International), PB15, Antwerp 17, B-2018, Antwerp **Belgium**. +(0)32480376. Fax: +(0)32483186. President: Luc Nuitten. Management firm, booking agency. Estab. 1991. Represents artists from anywhere; currently handles 6 acts. Receives 15% commission.
How to Contact: Submit demo CD by mail. Prefers CD or VHS videocassette (PAL) with 3 songs. If seeking management, press kit should include VHS video, CD, references, photos, bio, press book financial dossier. "Always looking for new talent—please present a complete neat and self-explanatory promo kit." Does not return material. Reports in 2 months.
Music: Mostly **jazz** and **world music**. Works primarily with concert tour bands, festival bands and European touring acts.

FOGGY DAY MUSIC, P.O. Box 99, Newtonville MA 02160. (617)969-0810. Fax: (617)969-6761. Owner: Paul Kahn. Management firm, booking agency and music publisher (Foggy Day Music). Represents individual artists, groups and songwriters from anywhere; currently handles 5 acts. Commission varies. Reviews material for acts.
How to Contact: Submit demo tape by mail. Unsolicited submissions are OK. Prefers cassette with lyric sheet. "No management submissions." Does not return material.
Music: **Folk**, **country** and **rock**; also **world music** and **blues**. Current acts include Luther Johnson (blues singer), Paul Bernard (folk singer/songwriter) and J.B. Hulto (blues singer).
Tips: "Simple recorded demo is OK, with lyrics."

FOLEY ENTERTAINMENT, P.O. Box 642, Carteret NJ 07008. (908)541-1862. Fax: (908)541-1862. President: Eugene Foley, J.D., Ph.D. Management firm. Estab. 1989. Represents individual artists and/or groups and songwriters from anywhere. Receives 20% commission. Reviews material for acts.

HOW TO GET THE MOST out of *Songwriter's Market* (at the front of this book) contains comments and suggestions to help you understand and use the information in these listings.

How to Contact: Submit demo tape by mail. Unsolicited submissions are OK. Copyright all material before you send it. Reports in 1 month if SASE is enclosed. Does not return material.
Music: Mostly **rock**, **alternative**, **pop**, **country** and **R&B**. Currently represents Razamanaz (hard rock), Danny Grae (country) and Joyride (dance/R&B).
Tips: "We are a national firm with clients from all across the United States. Our staff is comprised of friendly, experienced, and highly educated people who are eager to work hard for you and your career. Other services include: tape shopping, career and business advice, biography and press kit design, tour coordination and a full legal department. Please write or call for our free brochure."

*MITCHELL FOX MANAGEMENT INC., 212 Third Ave. N., Nashville TN 37201. (615)259-0777. Fax: (615)259-2956. E-mail: fox@laststraw.com. President: Mitchell Fox. Management firm. Estab. 1980. Represents individual artists, groups and songwriters from anywhere; currently handles 6 acts. Receives 10-15% commission. Reviews material for acts.
How to Contact: Submit demo tape by mail. Unsolicited submissions are OK. Prefers cassette with 4 songs and lyric sheet. If seeking management, press kit should include music, pictures and press clippings. Does not return material. Reports in 3-4 weeks.
Music: Mostly **country rock**, **1940-'50s country** and **world music**; also **jazz** and **rock**. Current acts include The Kentucky Head Hunters (country band), Mary Brown (country singer) and Gary Nicholson (AAA artist, country songwriter).

PETER FREEDMAN ENTERTAINMENT, 1790 Broadway, Suite 1316, New York NY 10019. (212)265-1776. Fax: (212)265-3678. E-mail: pfent@aol.com. President: Peter Freedman. Director: Steve Smith. Management firm. Estab. 1986. Represents individual artists, groups and songwriters from anywhere; currently handles 3 acts. Receives 15-20% commission. Reviews material for acts.
How to Contact: Write or call first and obtain permission to submit. Prefers cassette (or VHS videocassette) with 1-2 songs. If seeking management, press kit should include 3-4 song demo, short bio and picture. Does not return material. Reports in 3-4 weeks.
Music: Mostly **alternative/pop**, **dance** and **R&B/pop**. Works primarily with bands and solo artists. Current acts include Live (modern rock), Muse (modern rock) and The Ocean Blue (modern rock).
Tips: "Write, write and write some more."

BOB SCOTT FRICK ENTERPRISES, 404 Bluegrass Ave., Madison TN 37115. (615)865-6380. President: Bob Frick. Booking agency, music publisher (Frick Music Publishing Co./BMI and Sugarbaker Music Publishing/ASCAP) and record company (R.E.F. Recording Co). Represents individual artists and songwriters; currently handles 5 acts. Reviews material for acts.
  • Bob Scott Frick's publishing company, Frick Music Publishing, is listed in the Music Publishers section; his record label, R.E.F. Records, is in the Record Companies section; and he is listed in the Record Producers section.
How to Contact: Submit demo tape by mail, or write or call first to arrange personal interview. Prefers cassette with 3 songs and lyric sheet. SASE. Reports in 1 month.
Music: Mostly **gospel**, **country** and **R&B**. Works primarily with vocalists. Current acts include Larry Ahlborn (singer), Bob Myers (singer), Teresa Ford, Eddie Isaacs, Scott Frick, Jim and Ruby Mattingly, David Barton and Partners in Praise.

KEN FRITZ MANAGEMENT, 648 N. Robertson Blvd., Los Angeles CA 90069. (310)854-6488. Fax: (310)854-1015. E-mail: fritzed1@aol.com. Associate Manager: Pamela Byers. Management firm. Represents individual artists and groups from anywhere; currently handles 4 acts. Receives 15% commission. Reviews material for acts.
How to Contact: Write or call first and obtain permission to submit. Prefers cassette (or VHS videocassette) with 2-3 songs and lyric sheet. "Submissions should be short and to the point." SASE. Reports in 1-2 months.
Music: Mostly **alternative**, **rock** and **pop**; also **jazz** and **kids**. Current acts include George Benson (jazz guitar/vocalist) Peter, Paul & Mary (folk singer/songwriters), Michael Feinstein (American popular song/piano and vocalist) and Rebekah Del Rio (country singer/songwriter).

FUDPUCKER ENTERTAINMENT, P.O. Box 6593, Branson MO 65615. (417)336-4188. President: Wes Ranstad. Management firm, music publisher (Fudpucker Publishing) and record company (Vista Int'l). Estab. 1965. Represents individual artists from anywhere; currently handles 3 acts. Receives 15% commission. Reviews material for acts.
How to Contact: Submit demo tape by mail. Unsolicited submissions are OK. Prefers cassette or VHS videocassette with 4 songs and lyric sheet. If seeking management, send full press kit with all available information. SASE. Reports in 3-4 weeks.
Music: Mostly **country**, **comedy** and **novelty songs**. Works primarily with singers, comedians and bands. Current acts include Elmer Fudpucker (comedian, singer), James Walls (band) and Dexter (comedian, singer).

Tips: "Be professional on and off stage. A good image and reputation is 50% of success. The other 50% is talent and hard work."

FUTURE STAR ENTERTAINMENT, 315 S. Beverly Dr., Beverly Hills CA 90212. (310)553-0990. President: Paul Shenker. Management firm. Estab. 1982. Represents individual artists and groups from anywhere; currently handles 3 acts. Receives 20% commission. Reviews material for acts.
How to Contact: Write or call first and obtain permission to submit. Prefers cassette (or VHS videocassette) with 3-5 songs and lyric sheet. If seeking management, press kit should include photo, bio, tape or CD and press material. Does not return material. Reports in 6 weeks.
Music: Mostly **rock, pop** and **R&B**. Works primarily with rock bands. Current acts include Sway (alternative pop), Rachel Paschall (acoustic solo artist) and Tom Batoy (solo pop artist).

GALLUP ENTERTAINMENT, 93-40 Queens Blvd., Rego Park NY 11374. (718)897-6428. Fax: (718)997-7531. President: A. Gallup. Management firm. Estab. 1986. Represents individual artists and/or groups from anywhere; currently handles 5 acts. Receives 15% commission. Reviews material for acts.
How to Contact: Submit demo tape by mail. Unsolicited submissions are OK. Prefers cassette and lyric or lead sheet. If seeking management, press kit should include demo tape, bio, photo and clippings. Does not return material. Reports in 3-4 months.
Music: Mostly **rock** and **country**. Current acts include Tommy Sands (singer), Excellents (doo-wop) and Cathy Jean and the Roomates (doo-wop).

*GLAD PRODUCTIONS, P.O. Box 418, Purcellville VA 22132. (540)338-2017. Fax: (540)338-7319. E-mail: glad@mediasoft.net. Vice President: Don Nalle. Management firm, booking agency, music publisher (Champion of Love Music/ASCAP, Aux Send Music/BMI) and record producer (Ed Nalle). Estab. 1976. Represents individual artists, groups and songwriters from anywhere; currently handles 2 acts. Receives 20% commission. Reviews material for acts.
How to Contact: Submit demo tape by mail. Unsolicited submissions are OK. Prefers cassette with 3 songs and lyric sheet. If seeking management, press kit should include photo, bio, references and demo. Does not return material. "No response guaranteed." Reports in 6 weeks.
Music: Mostly **Christian** (any style). Current acts include Glad (vocal group) and Ron Larson (singer/songwriter/guitarist).
Tips: "Lyrical integrity is considered first, i.e., both the quality of the writing and the thematic direction."

*GLO GEM PRODUCTIONS, INC., 2640 Huckleberry, Port Huron MI 48060. (810)984-4471. Producer/Director: James David. Management firm and booking agency. Estab. 1976. Represents individual artists, groups and songwriters from anywhere; currently handles 15 acts. Receives 20% commission. Reviews material for acts.
How to Contact: Submit demo tape by mail. Unsolicited submissions are OK. Prefers cassette or ½" VHS videocassette. If seeking management, press kit should include bio, recent press, photo or video. Does not return material. Reports in 2 months.
Music: Mostly **pop, country** and **jazz**; also **MOR**. Works primarily with bands, singer/songwriters and variety acts. Current acts include Cliff Erickson (singer/songwriter), B.A.S.I.C. (Boys Always Singing in Class) (pop quartet) and Pixee Wales (variety performer).
Tips: "Any sentence you ever say is the first line to your song."

GMI ENTERTAINMENT INC., (formerly Gibson Management Inc.), 666 Fifth Ave., #302, New York NY 10103. (212)541-7400. Fax: (212)541-7547. Vice President: Karen Gibson Lampiasi. Management firm, music publisher (Hats Off Music/ASCAP, Hats On Music/BMI). Estab. 1987. Represents individual artists and songwriters from anywhere; currently handles 5 acts. Receives 20% commission. Reviews material for acts.
How to Contact: Write first and obtain permission to submit. Prefers cassette with 3 songs and lyric sheet. If seeking management, press kit should include photo, bio, cassette, press (if any) and lyrics. Does not return material. Reports in 3 months.
Music: Mostly **country, pop** and **R&B**. Works primarily with vocalists and singer/songwriters.
Tips: "Make sure the demos are clear and well-done. Spending a lot of money on production doesn't make the song any better. However, be sure the demos accurately reflect the feel and direction of the song. Use a professional singer if possible to avoid the listener being distracted by the vocal performance."

GOLDEN BULL PRODUCTIONS, P.O. Box 15142, Minneapolis MN 55415. (612)649-4631. Manager: Jesse Dearing. Management firm. Estab. 1984. Represents local and regional (Midwest) individual artists, groups and songwriters; currently handles 4 acts. Receives 12-20% commission. Reviews material for acts.

How to Contact: Submit demo tape by mail. Unsolicited submissions are OK. Prefers cassette (or VHS videocassette) with 4-5 songs and lyric or lead sheet. If seeking management, include demo tape, bio and 8×10 black and white photo in press kit. Does not return material. Reports in 8-12 weeks.
Music: Mostly **R&B**, **pop** and **rock**; also **gospel**, **jazz** and **blues**. Works primarily with vocalists, bands. Current acts include Lost and Found (R&B band), Keith Steward (songwriter) and A. Lock (singer).

*GOLDEN CITY INTERNATIONAL, Box 410851, San Francisco CA 94141. (415)822-1530. Fax: (415)695-1845. A&R Rep: Mr. Alston. Management firm. Estab. 1993. Represents regional (California area) individual artists and groups; currently handles 3 acts. Receives 15-20% commission. Reviews material for acts.
• See the listing for Dagene/Cabletown Records in the Record Companies section.
How to Contact: Write or call first and obtain permission to submit. Prefers cassette or VHS videocassette with 2-3 songs. If seeking management, press kit should include a complete bio and current photo along with cassette or CD of recent material. SASE. Reports in 1 month.
Music: Mostly **R&B/dance**, **rap** and **pop**; also **gospel** and **dance**. Current clients include Rare Essence (vocal group), Marcus Justice (writer/artist) and David Alston (producer).

GOLDEN GURU ENTERTAINMENT, 301 Bainbridge St., Philadelphia PA 19147. (215)574-2900. Fax: (215)440-7367. Owners: Eric J. Cohen, Esq. and Larry Goldfarb. Management firm, music publisher and record company. Estab. 1988. Represents individual artists, groups and songwriters from anywhere; currently handles 5 acts. Reviews material for acts.
How to Contact: Submit demo tape by mail. Unsolicited submissions are OK. Prefers cassette (or VHS videocassette) with 3-6 songs. If seeking management, press kit should include tape, press, photo, etc. SASE. Reports in 3-4 weeks.
Music: Mostly **rock**, **singer/songwriters**, **urban** and **pop**; "anything that is excellent!" Current acts include Jeffrey Gaines, Ben Arnold and Susan Werner (all 3 are major label recording artists).
Tips: "Be patient for a response. Our firm also renders legal and business affairs services. We also do bookings for the Tin Angel, the premier acoustic venue (200 capacity) in Philadelphia."

GRASS MANAGEMENT, 13546 Cheltenham Dr., Sherman Oaks CA 91423. (818)788-1777. Fax: (818)783-1542. President: Clancy Grass. Management firm. Estab. 1976. Represents individual artists, groups and songwriters from anywhere; currently handles 3 acts. Receives 15% commission. Reviews material for acts.
How to Contact: Submit demo tape by mail. Unsolicited submissions are OK. Prefers cassette or VHS videocassette with 1-6 songs and lyric sheet. If seeking management, press kit should include tape (audio and video if possible), photo and résumé. SASE. Reports in 2 weeks.
Music: Mostly **country**, **rock** and **R&B**; also **pop/rock** and **new world**. Works primarily with singer/songwriters, bands and writers. Current acts include Darryl Phinnessee (R&B/soul), MD Blessing (country rock) and Ripley Fairchild (pop/soul).
Tips: "Make submissions timely, cleanly with the adage 'less is more' in mind. Be honest and leave out all 'hype.' It's on the page or it isn't."

GREAT LAKES COUNTRY TALENT AGENCY, 167 Sherman, Rochester NY 14606. (716)647-1617. President: Donald Redanz. Management firm, booking agency, music publisher, record company and record producer. Estab. 1988. Represents individual artists and/or groups, songwriters from anywhere; currently handles 5 acts. Receives 15-20% commission. Reviews material for acts.
How to Contact: Submit demo tape by mail. Unsolicited submissions are OK. Prefers cassette with 4 songs. If seeking management, press kit should include picture, places played and tape. SASE. Reports in 1 month.
Music: Mostly **country**, **gospel**, and **top 40**; also **bluegrass**. Works primarily with vocalists, singer/songwriters and bands. Current acts include Donnie Lee Baker (country), Tony Starr (songwriter) and Jimmy C (top 40).
Tips: "Write heart-touching songs."

CHRIS GREELEY ENTERTAINMENT, P.O. Box 593, Bangor ME 04402-0593. (207)827-4382. General Manager: Christian D. Greeley. Management firm, shopping/contact service, consultation.

REMEMBER: Don't "shotgun" your demo tapes. Submit only to companies interested in the type of music you write. For more submission hints, refer to Getting Started on page 5.

Estab. 1986. Represents local, regional and international individual artists, groups and songwriters; currently handles 5 acts. Receives 10% commission. Reviews material for acts.
How to Contact: Submit demo tape by mail. Unsolicited submissions are OK. "Don't call!" Prefers cassette (or VHS videocassette if available) with 1-4 songs. SASE. Reports in 1 month.
Music: Mostly **rock, country** and **pop**. "I'm open to anything marketable." Wide range of musical styles. Current acts include Hey Mister (acoustic duo), Keith Tasker (solo guitarist) and Gabrielle Greeley (vocalist).
Tips: "Treat your music interests as a business venture. Don't be afraid to work hard and spend money to get where you want to go."

TIM GREENE ENTERTAINMENT, 6312 Hollywood Blvd., Suite 165, Hollywood CA 90028. (213)368-8100. President: Tim Greene. Management firm, record company (Greene Group Records) and record producer. Estab. 1983. Represents individual artists and groups from anywhere; currently handles 2 acts. Receives 10-15% commission. Reviews material for acts.
How to Contact: Submit demo tape by mail. Unsolicited submissions are OK. Prefers cassette or VHS videocassette. If seeking management, press kit should include bio, head shot, video and cassette tape. SASE. Reports in 3 weeks.
Music: Mostly **R&B, hip hop** and **rap**. Current acts include Rappin Granny (has appeared on Regis & Kathie Lee, CNN News, Today Show, Arsenio Hall) and Fat Daddy (rapper/producer).

GREIF-GARRIS MANAGEMENT, 2112 Casitas Way, Palm Springs CA 92264. (619)322-8655. Fax: (619)322-7793. Vice President: Sid Garris. Management firm. Estab. 1961. Represents individual artists and/or groups, songwriters from anywhere; currently handles 2 acts. Commission varies. Reviews material for acts.
How to Contact: Submit demo tape by mail. Unsolicited submissions are OK. Prefers cassette. SASE. Reports in 1 month.
Music: All types. Current acts include The New Christy Minstrels (folk) and Soulfolk (funky folk).

*GSI, INC., P.O. Box 56757, New Orleans LA 70156. (504)948-4848. Fax: (504)943-3381. C.E.O.: John Shoup. Management firm, music publisher, record company, record producer and television producer (network). Estab. 1990. Represents groups and songwriters from anywhere; currently handles 1 act. Reviews material for act.
How to Contact: Write first and obtain permission to submit a demo. Prefers cassette with 1 song and lyric and lead sheet. Does not return material.
Music: Mostly **jazz**. Current acts include Bobby Short, Manhattan Transfer, Bela Fleck, Charlie Byrd, Bill Monroe, Silver Sage and Dukes of Dixieland.

GUESTSTAR ENTERTAINMENT AGENCY, 17321 Ritchie Ave. NE, Sand Lake MI 49343-9475. (616)636-5068. President: Raymond G. Dietz, Sr. Management firm, booking agency, music publisher (Sandlake Music/BMI), record company (Gueststar Records, Inc.), record producer and record distributor (Gueststar Music Distributors). Represents individual artists, groups, songwriters and bands from anywhere; currently handles 3 acts. Receives 20% commission. Reviews material for acts.
• Gueststar Entertainment's record company, Gueststar Records, is listed in the Record Companies section.
How to Contact: Submit demo tape by mail. Unsolicited submissions are OK. Prefers cassette or VHS videocassette with unlimited songs, but send your best with lyric or lead sheet. If seeking management, press kit should include photo, demo tape, bio, music résumé and VHS videocassette (live on stage) if possible. Does not return material. Reports in 1 week.
Music: Mostly **contemporary country**, **hit country** and **traditional country**; also **contemporary Christian**, **MOR** and **mountain songs**. Current acts include Mountain Man (singer), Jamie "K" (singer) and Sweetgrass (band).
Tips: "Send songs like you hear on the radio—keep updating your music to keep up with the latest trends."

H.L.A. MUSIC, 313 N. 36th St., Belleville IL 62223. (618)236-1651. Fax: (618)277-9425. President: Randy Forker. Management firm. Estab. 1987. Represents groups from anywhere; currently handles 3 acts. Receives 15-20% commission. Reviews material for acts.
How to Contact: Submit demo tape by mail. Unsolicited submissions are OK. Prefers cassette or VHS videocassette with 2 songs and lyric sheet. If seeking management, press kit should include photo, bio, tape and contact number. Does not return material. Reports in 6 weeks.
Music: Mostly **rock**, **metal** and **rap/hip hop**. Works primarily with bands. Current acts include Bronx Zoo (rock/metal), Phatal Burth (rap/hip hop) and Busgy (rock).

HALE ENTERPRISES, Rt. 1, Box 49, Worthington IN 47471-9310. (812)875-3664. Contact: Rodger Hale. Management firm, booking agency and record company (Projection Unlimited). Estab. 1976. Represents artists, groups, songwriters and studio musicians; currently handles 15 acts. Receives 10-15% commission. Reviews material for acts.
How to Contact: Query by mail or call to arrange personal interview. Prefers cassette (or videocassette) with 2-10 songs and lyric sheet. If seeking management include current promo pack *or* photo, video-audio tape, clubs currently performing, short performance history and equipment list (if applicable). Does not return material. Reports in 2 weeks.
Music: Mostly **country** and **top 40**; also **MOR**, **progressive**, **rock** and **pop**. Works primarily with show bands, dance bands and bar bands. Current acts include Indiana (country show band), Seventh Heaven (top 40 show) and Cotton (show band).

BILL HALL ENTERTAINMENT & EVENTS, 138 Frog Hollow Rd., Churchville PA 18966-1031. (215)357-5189. Fax: (215)357-0320. Contact: William B. Hall III. Booking agency and production company. Represents individuals and groups; currently handles 20-25 acts. Receives 15% commission. Reviews material for acts.
How to Contact: Submit demo tape by mail. Unsolicited submissions are OK. Prefers cassette (or videocassette of performance) with 2-3 songs "and photos, promo material and record or tape. We need quality material, preferably before a 'live' audience." Does not return material. Reports in 2-4 months.
Music: Marching band, **circus** and **novelty**. Works primarily with "unusual or novelty attractions in musical line, preferably those that appeal to family groups." Current acts include Fralinger and Polish-American Philadelphia Championship Mummers String Bands (marching and concert group), Erwin Chandler Orchestra (show band), "Mr. Polynesian" Show Band and Hawaiian Revue (ethnic group), the "Phillies Whiz Kids Band" of Philadelphia Phillies Baseball team, Wm. (Boom-Boom) Browning Circus Band (circus band), Paul Cirilis Band, Philadelphia German Brass Band (concert band) and Vogelgesang Circus Calliope.
Tips: "Please send whatever helps me to most effectively market the attraction and/or artist. Provide me with something that gives you a clear edge over others in your field!"

*THE HARBOUR AGENCY PTY. LTD., P.O. Box KX300, Kings Cross 2011 NSW **Australia**. Booking Agency: Michael L. Harrison. Booking agency. Estab. 1979. Represents individual artists and groups from anywhere; currently handles 68 acts. Receives 10% commission. Reviews material for acts.
How to Contact: Submit demo tape by mail. Unsolicited submissions are OK. Prefers cassette. If seeking management, press kit should include bio, photo, video and demo. Does not return material. Reports in 3 months.
Music: Mostly **rock**, **pop** and **grunge**. Current acts include Midnight Oil, Crowded House, Divinyls and Frente.
Tip: "Write hits and always keep trying."

DUSTIN HARDMAN MANAGEMENT, P.O. Box 151077, Tampa FL 33684-1077. (813)932-3555. Fax: (813)876-5140. President: Dustin Hardman. Management firm. Estab. 1990. Represents groups from anywhere; currently handles 2 acts. Receives 20% commission. Reviews material for acts.
How to Contact: Submit demo tape by mail. Unsolicited submissions are OK. Prefers cassette with 3 songs and lyric sheet. If seeking management, press kit should include a photo, biography that is current but to the point, 2 or 3 song tape and contact info. "Make all submissions to the Attn. of Dustin Hardman." Does not return material. Reports in 3-4 weeks.
Music: Mostly **hard music**, **alternative** and **pop/dance rock**. "All artists are worked on a level to achieve international acceptance, so only serious artists need apply." Current acts include Empyria, Oppressor and Kamelot.
Tips: "My organization looks for serious and professional clients that want to achieve only the best in their genre. Represent yourself as you would want to be recognized."

HARDWAY MUSIC MANAGEMENT, P.O. Box 540, Dearborn Heights MI 48127. (313)278-6068. E-mail: kegegnn.com. Owner: Mark S. Shearer. Management firm. Estab. 1987. Represents individual artists and groups from anywhere; currently handles 3 acts. Receives 15-20% commission. Reviews material for acts.
How to Contact: Submit demo tape by mail. Unsolicited submissions are OK. Prefers cassette (or VHS videocassette) with 4 songs. If seeking management, include photo and video if possible in press kit. "We will contact you if interested." Does not return material. Reports in 2 weeks.
Music: Mostly **rock**, **alternative** and **dance**. Works primarily with bands. Current acts include Sex, Love and Money (Rockworld/Sony), Five Story Fall (Puppethead Records) and Love & War (rock).
Tips: "Have the best possible sounding demo tape you can, and always present your material in a professional manner."

M. HARRELL & ASSOCIATES, 5444 Carolina, Merrillville IN 46410. (219)887-8814. Owner: Mary Harrell. Management firm and booking agency. Estab. 1984. Represents individual artists, groups, songwriters, all talents—fashion, dancers, etc.; currently handles 40-60 acts. Receives 10-15% commission. Reviews material for acts.
How to Contact: Submit demo tape by mail. Unsolicited submissions are OK. Prefers cassette or videocassette with 2-3 songs. If seeking management, press kit should include résumé, bio, picture and videocassette (if available). "Keep it brief and current." SASE. Reports in 2-3 weeks.
Music: Mostly **country** and **R&B**. Current acts include Bill Shelton and 11th Ave. ('50s music), Mark Spencer and Faith (alternative), Sam Baker (gospel) and Julian Michaels (country/R&B).
Tips: "Try to study the commercial market and be honest in pursuing same; write what you feel."

HAWKEYE ATTRACTIONS, 102 Geiger St., Huntingburg IN 47542. (812)683-3657. President: David Mounts. Booking agency. Estab. 1982. Represents individual artists and groups. Currently handles 1 act. Receives 10% commission. Reviews material for acts.
How to Contact: Submit demo tape by mail. Unsolicited submissions are OK. Prefers cassette with 4 songs and lyric sheet. SASE. If seeking management, press kit should include bio, press clippings, 8×10 b&w glossy, cassette. Reports in 9 weeks.
Music: Mostly **country** and **western swing**. Works primarily with show bands, Grand Ole Opry style form of artist and music. Current acts include Bill Mounts and Midwest Cowboys (country/western swing).
Tips: "Don't copy anybody, just be yourself. If you have talent it will show through."

*HEADLINE MANAGEMENT, 125 E. 88th St., Suite 2A, New York NY 10028. Phone/fax: (212)410-6722. Vice President: Max Rosen. Management firm. Estab. 1991. Represents individual artists and groups from anywhere; currently handles 3 acts. Receives 20% commission. Reviews material for acts.
How to Contact: Submit demo tape by mail. Unsolicited submissions are OK. Prefers cassette or VHS videocassette with 3 songs. If seeking management, press kit should include 3 song demo, photo and strong press. Does not return material. Reports in 3 weeks.
Music: Mostly **modern rock** and **pop**. Works with alternative bands and pop singer/songwriters.
Tips: "Write good songs and do not send anything that is not your best work to anyone."

*HEADLINE TALENT INC., 1650 Broadway, New York NY 10019. (212)581-6900. Fax: (212)581-6906. Head of Music Department: Glen Knight. Booking agency. Estab. 1975. Represents individual artists and groups from anywhere; currently handles 10 acts. Receives 10-15% commission. Reviews material for acts.
How to Contact: Submit demo tape by mail. Unsolicited submissions are OK. Prefers cassette or videocassette with 6 songs. If seeking management, press kit should include picture, bio and reviews. Does not return material. Reports in 2-3 weeks.
Music: Mostly **rock**, **R&B**, **blues** and **country**; also "anything that sounds good." Current acts include JoAnne Johnson (piano player), The Persuasions (a cappella) and The Elephants (classic rock).

HIGH ENERGY MANAGEMENT, P.O. Box 30421, Philadelphia PA 19103. Owner: Mrs. D. Kendricks. Management firm. Estab. 1989. Represents individual artists and groups from anywhere; currently handles 4 acts. Receives 20% commission. Reviews material for acts.
How to Contact: Submit demo tape by mail. Unsolicited submissions are OK. Prefers cassette or videocassette with picture/bio. SASE. Reports in 2 weeks.
Music: Mostly **pop**, **R&B/contemporary**, **commercial rap** and **jazz**.

*STEVE HILL ENTERTAINMENT MANAGEMENT, P.O. Box 250013, Atlanta GA 30325. (404)352-9999. A&R Dept.: Steve Hill. Management firm and record company (New South Records). Estab. 1994. Represents individual artists, groups and songwriters from anywhere; currently handles 4 acts. Receives 10% commission. Reviews material for acts.
How to Contact: Write first and obtain permission to submit. Prefers cassette with 3 songs and lyric sheet. If seeking management, press kit should include 8×10 b&w photo, list of songs, equipment list, résumé of experience and performance, any press. "Please include stamped self addressed return envelope and current phone number." SASE. Reports in 3 months.
Music: Mostly **pop/CHR**, **R&B/dance** and **contemporary country**; also **A/C**, **alternative**, **gospel** and **metal**. Works primarily with singer/songwriters and groups. Current acts include Evan & Jaron (singer/songwriters), Cosmic Gypsies (rock act) and Phil Thomson (singer/songwriter).

*HIT CITY RECORDS, P.O. Box 64895, Baton Rouge LA 70896. (504)925-0288. Fax: (504)336-0076 (call first). President: Henry Turner. Management firm, booking agency, music publisher (Turner's World Publishing Co.), record company and record producer (Turner Productions). Estab. 1984. Represents individual artists, groups and songwriters from anywhere; currently handles 4 acts. Reviews material for acts.

How to Contact: Submit demo tape by mail. Unsolicited submissions are OK. Prefers cassette, DAT or videocassette with 3 songs and lyric sheet. If seeking management, press kit should include list of accomplishments, background and references. Does not return material. Reports in 2 weeks.

Music: Mostly **country, Southern gospel** and **blues**; also **reggae, folk** and **world music**. Current acts include Henry Turner Jr. & Flavor (reggae), Rappin' Red (rap/rock) and Eldon Ray & Cross Country (country).

Tips: "Be in reality. Realize that music is a business. Be patient and don't expect anyone to invest anything that you don't."

hm MANAGEMENT, 102 N. Washington Ave., Dunellen NJ 08812-1244. (908)968-4084. Fax: (908)756-9053. Contact: Helen Majeski. Management firm. Represents Northeast individual artists and groups; currently handles 4 acts. Reviews material for acts.

How to Contact: Submit demo tape by mail. Unsolicited submissions are OK. Prefers cassette. If seeking management, press kit should include bio, photo, press and tape. SASE. Reports in 2-3 weeks.

Music: Mostly **alternative**. Works primarily with bands and individual artists. Current acts include Mudd Helmut and Cadillac Dirt Band.

DOC HOLIDAY PRODUCTIONS, 10 Luanita Lane, Newport News VA 23606. (804)930-1814. President: Doc Holiday. Management firm, booking agent, music publisher (Doc Holiday Productions and Publishing/ASCAP, Doc Publishing/BMI and Dream Machine Publishing/SESAC), record producer and record company (Tug Boat International). Estab. 1985. Represents international individual artists, groups and songwriters; currently handles 46 acts. Receives 10-15% commission. Reviews material for acts.

• See the listing for Doc Publishing in the Music Publishers section.

How to Contact: Submit demo tape by mail. Unsolicited submissions are OK. Prefers cassette (or VHS videocassette if available) with 1 song and lyric sheet. If seeking management, include 8×10 photo, press clippings, bio, VHS, performance history, press experiments and demo tape in press kit. Does not return material. Reports in 2 weeks.

Music: Mostly **country, pop** and **R&B**; also **gospel** and **rap**. Works primarily with vocalist dance bands. Current acts include Wyndi Renee (country), Doc Holiday (rock), the Fortunes (top 40), the Johnson Family (gospel), Doug "The Ragin Cajun" Kenshaw (cajun), Big Al Downing (country) and Drew Kleeber (rock).

HOLOGRAM ENTERTAINMENT, (formerly Nason Enterprises, Inc.), 2219 Polk St. NE, Minneapolis MN 55418-3713. (612)781-8353. Fax: (612)781-8355. President: Christopher Nason. Management firm, record label, video production and music publisher. Estab. 1989. Represents individual artists, groups and songwriters from anywhere. Commission rate varies. Reviews material for acts.

How to Contact: Submit demo tape by mail. Unsolicited submissions are OK. Prefers cassette (or VHS videocassette) with 1-3 songs and lyric sheet. If seeking management, press kit should include photo, bio, lyric sheets, cassette and/or CD, clubs and regions performed. "Label everything." SASE. Reports in 2 months.

Music: Mostly **commercial radio, rock/heavy metal, alternative, crossover/pop, country** and **R&B**.

*HOOKER ENTERPRISES, 1325 El Hito Circle, Pacific Palisades CA 90272. (310)573-1309. Fax: (310)573-1313. E-mail: hook1325@aol.com. President: Jake Hooker. Management firm, music publisher, record company and record producer. Estab. 1976. Represents individual artists, groups and songwriters from anywhere; currently handles 3 acts. Receives 20% commission. Reviews material for acts.

How to Contact: Write first and obtain permission to submit. Prefers cassette or DAT. If seeking management, press kit should include bio, picture and cassette (or CD). Does not return material. Reports in 1 month.

Music: Mostly **rock** and **New Age**. Works primarily with solo artists (but groups OK). Current acts include Edgar Winter (rock artist), Larry Blank (composer) and Streak (rock group).

HORIZON MANAGEMENT INC., P.O. Box 8538, Endwell NY 13762. (607)785-9670. Contact: New Talent Department. Management firm, booking agency and concert promotion. Estab. 1967. Represents regional, national and international artists, groups and songwriters; currently handles 1,500 acts. Receives 20% commission. Reviews material for acts.

How to Contact: Write or call first and obtain permission to submit. Prefers cassette (or VHS videocassette if available) with 1-4 songs and 1 lyric or lead sheet. Send photo, bio, song list, equipment list, audio and/or video, press clippings, reviews, etc. Does not return material. Reports in 1 week.

Music: **All styles**, originals or covers. Current acts include the cast of Beatlemania (Broadway show), The Boxtops (oldies) and Blue Norther (jazz).

IMAGE PROMOTIONS INC., 1581 General Booth Blvd., Suite #107, Virginia Beach VA 23454. Phone/fax: (804)491-6632. E-mail: kimagepro@aol.com. President: Kim I. Plyler. Management firm and public relations. Estab. 1992. Represents individual artists, groups and songwriters from anywhere; currently handles 4 acts. Receives 15-20% commission. Reviews material for acts.
How to Contact: Submit demo tape by mail. Unsolicited submissions are OK. Prefers cassette or CD (or VHS videocassette) with 3 songs and lyric sheet. If seeking management, press kit should include video, audio cassette, photo (b&w 8×10), biography and any press items. SASE. Reports in 3½ weeks.
Music: Mostly **acoustic rock**, **folk** and **progressive**; also **country** and **R&B**. Works primarily with singer/songwriters. "We will accept material from progressive and country bands. We work a lot with the college market." Current acts include Tammy Gardner (folk singer/songwriter), The Mann Sisters (country duo/band) and Lewis McGehee (acoustic rock/songwriter).

IMANI ENTERTAINMENT INC., P.O. Box 150-139, Brooklyn NY 11215. (718)622-2132. Directors: Guy Anglade and Alfred Johnston. Management firm, music publisher (Imani Hits/BMI). Estab. 1991. Represents individual artists, groups, songwriters, producers and remixers from anywhere; currently handles 1 act. Receives 15-20% commission. Reviews material for acts.
How to Contact: Submit demo tape by mail. Unsolicited submissions are OK. Prefers cassette (or VHS videocassette) with 3 songs. If seeking management, press kit should include a bio, photograph and demo tape. SASE. Reports in 4-6 weeks.
Music: Mostly **R&B** and **hip-hop**. Works primarily with vocalists, singer/songwriters. Current acts include Infinite (unsigned artist).
Tips: "Be specific and to the point."

*IMMIGRANT MUSIC INC., 3575 Blvd. St. Laurent #409, Montreal Quebec H2X 2T7 **Canada**. Phone/fax: (514)849-5052. E-mail: deckmktg@generation.net. President: Dan Behrman. Management firm, booking agency and music publisher (Balenjo Music). Estab. 1979. Represents individual artists, groups and songwriters from anywhere; currently handles 6 acts. Receives 20% commission. Reviews material for acts.
How to Contact: Submit demo tape by mail. Unsolicited submissions are OK. Prefers cassette, VHS videocassette, CD or vinyl with 4 songs. If seeking management, press kit should include bio, press clippings, photo, references, recordings, technical and personal rider and requirements if known. Does not return material. Reports in 2 weeks.
Music: Mostly **world music**, **original ethnic** and **new acoustic music**; also **singer/songwriters**, **folk** and **ethnic/ambient**. Current acts include Boukman Eksperyans (Island Records, vodou-roots band), Simbi (Xenophile Records, vodou-roots band) and David Broza (Mesa-Blue Moon, singer/songwriter).
Tips: "Don't try to cater to the trend or to the industry. Express yourself and don't try to please or entertain. Guts, intelligence, sensitivity, good taste and originality can definitely mix well. Big egos and prima-donnas are not welcome; patience and a willingness to work hard and diligently are a must. We do not believe in overnight success, but rather in a big range, one step at a time career based on common sense and professionalism."

PAUL INSINNA MANAGEMENT, 222 Park Ave., White Plains NY 10604. Contact: Paul Insinna. Management firm. Estab. 1993. Represents individual artists, groups and songwriters from anywhere; currently handles 3 acts. Receives 10-20% commission. Reviews material for acts.
How to Contact: Write or call first and obtain permission to submit. Prefers cassette with lyric sheet. If seeking management, press kit should include photo, bio, demo and press clips. SASE. Reports in 6-9 weeks.
Music: **R&B**, **A/C** and **acoustic** (singer/songwriter); also **rap** and **dance**. Current acts include Edwin Lugo (R&B), G-Fellas (rap) and Craig Mack (rap artist).

INTERMOUNTAIN TALENT, P.O. Box 942, Rapid City SD 57709. (605)348-7777. Owner: Ron Kohn. Management firm, booking agency and music publisher (Big BL Music). Estab. 1978. Represents individual artists, groups and songwriters; currently handles 20 acts. Receives 15% commission. Reviews material for acts.
How to Contact: Submit demo tape by mail. Unsolicited submissions are OK. Prefers cassette with 3 songs and lyric sheet. Artist may submit videocassette. If seeking management, include tape, video and photo in press kit. SASE. Reports in 1 month.
Music: Mostly **rock**; also **country/rock**. Current acts include Double Trouble (band), Curtis Knox (solo), Road House (band) and Under the Mercy (duo).

*INTERNATIONAL ENTERTAINMENT BUREAU, 3612 N. Washington Blvd., Indianapolis IN 46205. (317)926-7566. Contact: David Leonards. Booking agency. Estab. 1972. Represents individual artists and groups from anywhere; currently handles 137 acts. Commission varies. Reviews material for acts.

How to Contact: Submit demo tape by mail. Unsolicited submissions are OK. Prefers VHS videocassette. If seeking management, press kit should include picture, testamonials, sample song list and press clippings. "Do not call us, please." Does not return material. Reports in 6 months.
Music: Mostly **rock**, **country** and **A/C**; also **jazz**, **nostalgia** and **ethnic**. Works primarily with bands, comedians and speakers. Current acts include Five Easy Pieces (A/C), Doug Lawson (country) and Oliver Syndrome (rock).

ITS HAPPENING PRESENT ENTERTAINMENT, P.O. Box 222, Pittsburg CA 94565. (510)980-0893. Fax: (510)636-0614. President: Bobellii Johnson. Management firm, booking agency and record company (Black Diamond Records, Flash Point Records, Triple Beam Records, Stay Down Records, Hitting Hard Records and D. City Records). Estab. 1989. Represents local, regional or international individual artists and songwriters; currently handles 12 acts. Receives 5-15% commission. Reviews material for acts.
 • See the listing for one of Its Happening Present's record companies, Black Diamond Records, in the Record Companies section.
How to Contact: Write first and obtain permission to submit. Prefers cassette with 2 songs and lyric sheet. If seeking management, press kit should include 8 × 10 photo, bio, video, 2-song demo, demo voice tape and lyric sheet. Does not return material. Reports in 2-6 months.
Music: Mostly **pop**, **R&B** and **jazz**; also **rap**, **country** and **classical**. Works primarily with vocalist songwriters, rap groups, bands and instrumentalists. Current acts include Deanna Dixon (R&B), Profile 'J' (rap), Format (R&B vocal group), Marty "G." (rapper) and Lyn Durné.
Tips: "Please, copyright all your material as soon as possible. Don't let anyone else hear it until that's done first. You have to be swift about hearing, slow about speaking and slow about giving. Be true to your art or craft."

J & V MANAGEMENT, 143 W. Elmwood, Caro MI 48723. (517)673-2889. Management: John Timko. Management firm, booking agency, music publisher. Represents local, regional or international individual artists, groups and songwriters; currently handles 3 acts. Receives 10% commission. Reviews material for acts.
How to Contact: Submit demo tape by mail. Unsolicited submissions are OK. Prefers cassette with 3 songs maximum and lyric sheet. If seeking management, include cassette tape, photo and short reference bio in press kit. SASE. Reports in 2 months.
Music: Mostly **country**. Works primarily with vocalists and dance bands. Current acts include John Patrick (country), Alexander Depue (fiddle) and Most Wanted (country).

*JACKSON ARTISTS CORP., (Publishing Central), Suite 200, 7251 Lowell Dr., Shawnee Mission KS 66204. (913)384-6688. CEO: Dave Jackson. Booking agency (Drake/Jackson Productions), music publisher (All Told Music/BMI, Zang/Jac Publishing/ASCAP and Very Cherry/ASCAP), record company and record producer. Represents artists, groups and songwriters; currently handles 12 acts. Receives 15-20% commission. Reviews material for acts.
How to Contact: Submit demo tape by mail. Unsolicited submissions are OK. Prefers cassette (or VHS videocassette of performance if available) with 2-4 songs and lead sheet. "List names of tunes on cassettes. May send up to 4 tapes. Although it's not necessary, we prefer lead sheets with the tapes—send 2 or 3 that you are proud of. Also note what 'name' artist you'd like to see do the song. We do most of our business by phone. We prefer good enough quality to judge a performance, however, we do not require that the video or cassettes be of professional nature." Will return material if requested with SASE. Reports in 3 months.
Music: Mostly **gospel**, **country** and **rock**; also **bluegrass**, **blues**, **easy listening**, **disco**, **MOR**, **progressive**, **soul** and **top 40/pop**. Works with acts that work grandstand shows for fairs as well as bar bands that want to record original material. Current acts include Dixie Cadillacs (country/rock), Britt Hammond (country), The Booher Family (bluegrass/pop/country), Paul & Paula, Bill Haley's Comets, Max Groove (jazz) and The Dutton Family (classical to pop).
Tips: "Be able to work on the road, either as a player or as a group. Invest your earnings from these efforts in demos of your originals that have been tried out on an audience. And keep submitting to the industry."

*JACOBS MANAGEMENT, 382-C Union, Campbell CA 95008. (408)559-1669. Fax: (408)559-6664. E-mail: midnitemgt@aol.com. Owner: Mitchell Jacobs. Management firm. Estab. 1988. Represents individual artists and groups from anywhere; currently handles 2 acts. Receives 15% commission. Reviews material for acts.
How to Contact: Write or call first and obtain permission to submit. Prefers cassette with 3 songs and lyric sheet. SASE. Reports in 1 month.
Music: Mostly **rock**, **R&B** and **roots**. Works primarily with singer/songwriters, bands. Current acts include Loved Ones and Katharine Chase.
Tips: "Send your three best songs. Write from the heart and be professional."

JAM ENTERTAINMENT & EVENTS, (formerly Jam—A Complete Entertainment Agency), 2900 Bristol St. E-201, Costa Mesa CA 92626. (714)556-9505. Agent: Dennis Morrison. Booking agency. Estab. 1974. Represents primarily local and West Coast individual artists, groups, songwriters, all forms of entertainment; currently handles 2,000 acts. Receives 10-15% commission. Reviews material for acts.
How to Contact: Submit demo tape by mail. Unsolicited submissions are OK. Prefers cassette or videocassette and 5-10 songs with lyric or lead sheet. If seeking management, press kit should include any and all bio information. Does not return material. Reports in 4-6 weeks.
Music: Mostly **classic rock**, **R&B** and **blues**; also **jazz**, **pop** and **country**. Works primarily with bands of all genres, singers and songwriters. Current acts include Coasters (soul), Ohio Players (soul) and R.B. Stone (country).

JAMES GANG MANAGEMENT, P.O. Box 121626, Nashville TN 37212. (615)726-3556. Contact: Neal James. Management firm, music publisher (Cottage Blue Music), record company (Kottage Records) and record producer. Estab. 1991. Represents individual artists and/or groups, songwriters from anywhere; currently handles 3 acts. Reviews material for acts.
  ● James Gang's publishing affiliate, Cottage Blue Music, is listed in the Music Publishers section, and their record label, Kottage Records, is listed in the Record Companies section; Neal James Productions is listed in the Record Producers section.
How to Contact: Submit demo tape by mail. Unsolicited submissions are OK. Prefers cassette and lyric sheet. If seeking management, press kit should include full bio, photo, cassette, references, list of clubs played. SASE. Reports in 1 month.
Music: Mostly **country**, **pop** and **gospel**; also **R&B**, **beach**, **blues** and **alternative rock**. Works primarily with vocalists, singer/songwriters, bands. Current acts include P.J. Hawk (country), Terry BarBay (contemporary), Judie Bell (contemporary/country), Scott Dawson (country) and Allusion Band (alternative rock).

ROGER JAMES MANAGEMENT, 10A Margaret Rd., Barnet, Herts EN4 9NP **England**. Phone: (0181)440-9788. Professional Manager: Laura Skuce. Management firm and music publisher (R.J. Music/PRS). Estab. 1977. Represents songwriters. Receives 50% commission (negotiable). Reviews material for acts.
  ● See the listing for R.J. Music in the Music Publishers section.
How to Contact: Submit demo tape by mail. Unsolicited submissions are OK. Prefers cassette with 3 songs and lyric sheet. Does not return material.
Music: Mostly **pop**, **country** and "any good song."

JANA JAE ENTERPRISES, P.O. Box 35726, Tulsa OK 74153. (918)786-8896. Vice President: Kathleen Pixley. Booking agency, music publisher (Jana Jae Publishing/BMI) and record company (Lark Record Productions, Inc.). Estab. 1979. Represents individual artists and songwriters; currently handles 12 acts. Receives 15% commission. Reviews material for acts.
  ● Jana Jae's publishing company, Jana Jae Publishing, is listed in the Music Publishers section, and its record label, Lark Records, is listed in the Record Companies section.
How to Contact: Submit demo tape by mail. Prefers cassette (or videocassette of performance if available). SASE.
Music: Mostly **country**, **classical** and **jazz instrumentals**; also **pop**. Works with vocalists, show and concert bands, solo instrumentalists. Represents Jana Jae (country singer/fiddle player), Matt Greif (classical guitarist), Sydni (solo singer) and Hotwire (country show band).

JAS MANAGEMENT, 2141 W. Governor's Circle, Suite H, Houston TX 77092. (713)683-0806. Manager: Tony Randle. Management firm, booking agency. Estab. 1988. Represents individual artists and/or groups and songwriters from anywhere; currently handles 20 acts. Receives 10-20% commission. Reviews material for acts.
How to Contact: Submit demo tape by mail. Unsolicited submissions are OK. Prefers cassette with 4 songs. If seeking management, press kit should include cassette, bio, pictures and press (if any). SASE. Reports in 2 months.
Music: Mostly **rap**, **R&B** and **gospel**. Works primarily with rapper/songwriters. Current acts include Scarface, Geto Boys and DMG.

LISTINGS OF COMPANIES in countries other than the U.S. have the name of the country in boldface type.

*JAZZ-ONE PRODUCTIONS INC., 575 Laramie Lane, Mahwah NJ 07430. (201)934-9759. Fax: (201)934-1679. President: Caprice Titone. Management firm and booking agency. Estab. 1991. Represents individual artists and groups from anywhere; currently handles 10 acts. Receives 10% commission. Reviews material for acts.

How to Contact: Call first and obtain permission to submit. Prefers cassette or VHS videocassette. If seeking management, press kit should include bio, press, reviews, pictures and videocassette. Does not return material. Reports in 3 weeks.

Music: Mostly **jazz** and **blues**. Works primarily with jazz acts. Current acts include Harry "Sweets" Edison, Lionel Hampton Orchestra, Inc. and Junior Mance.

*JERIFKA PRODUCTIONS, INC., 730 Oakmount Ave., #102, Las Vegas NV 89109-1442. (702)593-3602. Fax: (702)732-0847. E-mail: robvale@accessnv.com. A&R: Robert Vale. Management firm, booking agency, music publisher (Ritvale Music Corp./ASCAP; Robvale Music/BMI) and record company (The Robert Vale Record Company). Estab. 1969. Represents individual artists, groups and songwriters from anywhere; currently handles 8 acts. Receives 10% commission. Reviews material for acts.

How to Contact: Submit demo tape by mail. Unsolicited submissions are OK. Prefers cassette, DAT or VHS videocassette with 1 song, lyric and lead sheet. SASE. Reports in 2 weeks.

Music: Mostly **rock**, **alternative** and **New Age**. Current acts include Jerry Vale, James Moyer Blues Experience and Question Mark.

LITTLE RICHIE JOHNSON AGENCY, Box 3, Belen NM 87002. (505)864-7441. Fax: (505)864-7442. Manager: Tony Palmer. Management firm, music publisher (Little Richie Johnson Music) and record company (LRJ Records). Estab. 1958. Represents individual artists from anywhere; currently handles 4-6 acts. Reviews material for acts.

• Listings for Little Richie Johnson Music can be found in the Music Publishers section; Little Richie Johnson in the Record Producers section; and one for LRJ Records can be found in the Record Companies section.

How to Contact: Write first and obtain permission to submit. Prefers cassette. If seeking management, press kit should include tape, bio and any other important information. SASE. Reports in 6 weeks.

Music: Mostly **country**; also **Spanish**. Works primarily with vocalists and singers. Current acts include Alan Godage, Faron Young, Kim Frazee, Reta Lee and Gabe Neito.

*JOY ARTIST MANAGEMENT, INC., 4445-B Breton Rd., Suite 108, Kentwood MI 49548. (616)249-3931. Fax: (616)249-0736. Senior Partner: Malinda P. Sapp. Management firm, booking agency and music publisher (Butterbean Music). Estab. 1991. Represents individual artists, groups, songwriters and musicians from anywhere; currently handles 3 acts. Receives 15% commission. Reviews material for acts.

How to Contact: Submit demo tape by mail. Unsolicited submissions are OK. Prefers cassette and portfolio/discography/bio with lead sheet. If seeking management, press kit should include picture (8½ × 11 b&w preferable), discography, bio and demo. "Follow up with a phone call 30 days after submission." Does not return material. Reports in 1 month.

Music: Mostly **gospel** and **contemporary gospel**. Works primarily with choirs, groups and soloists. Current acts include Marvin L. Sapp (Word recording artist), Joy Crusade Chorale (recording gospel choir) and Integrity (gospel group).

Tips: "Submit a summary of your goals and desires. Follow up 30 days after submission of press pack. We are a full service management team specializing in marketing and mediation. Available for management or specific contracted services (tour support, booking, merchandise, etc.)."

C. JUNQUERA PRODUCTIONS, P.O. Box 393, Lomita CA 90717. (213)325-2881. Co-owner: C. Junquera. Management consulting firm and record company (NH Records). Estab. 1987. Represents local, regional and international individual artists and songwriters; currently handles 3 acts. Receives a flat fee for consulting, percentage for business management. Reviews material for acts.

How to Contact: Submit demo tape by mail. Unsolicited submissions are OK. Prefers cassette with 1-3 songs and lyric sheet. If seeking management, include 8 × 10 photo, bio, photocopies of news articles and sample of product. SASE. Reports in 1-2 months.

Music: Mostly **traditional country** and **country pop**; also **easy listening**. Works primarily with vocalists. Current recording acts include Nikki Hornsby (singer/songwriter), N. Kelel (songwriter) and Eric Oswald (songwriter).

Tips: "Be specific on goals you wish to obtain as artist or songwriter—submit a sample of your product and don't give up! Obtain outside financial support for production of your product—invest your talent, not your own money."

JUPITER PRODUCTIONS, 7751 Greenwood Dr., St. Paul MN 55112. (612)784-9654. C.E.O.: Lance King. Management firm, booking agency and record company (Nightmare). Estab. 1983. Represents individual artists, groups, songwriters from anywhere; currently handles 10 acts. Receives 10-15% commission. Reviews material for acts.
How to Contact: Write first and obtain permission to submit. Prefers cassette or VHS videocassette with 4 songs and lyric sheet. If seeking management, press kit should include 8 × 10 photo, poster (if available), song list, if self contained production or not and press clippings. "Send only important information." SASE. Reports in 4-6 weeks.
Music: Mostly **cutting edge rock**, **melodic metal** and **grunge**; also **rap metal** and **progressive rock**. Works primarily with vocalists, singer/songwriters and bands. Current acts include Gemini (metal), The King's Machine (melodic groove with attitude) and Boneyard (industrial grind, groove).

SHELDON KAGAN PRODUCTIONS, 95 McConnell, Dorval, Quebec H9S 5L9 **Canada**. (514)631-2160. Fax: (514)631-4430. President: Sheldon Kagan. Booking agency. Estab. 1965. Represents local individual artists and groups; currently handles 4 acts. Receives 10-20% commission. Reviews materials for acts.
How to Contact: Submit demo tape by mail. Unsolicited submissions are OK. Prefers cassette (or VHS videocassette) with 6 songs. SASE. Reports in 3 weeks.
Music: Mostly **top 40**. Works primarily with vocalists and bands.

*KALEIDOSCOPE MUSIC, 5337 W. Acoma Dr., Glendale AZ 85306. (602)547-2606. Owner: Tricia Kale. Management firm. Estab. 1991. Represents individual artists and groups from anywhere; currently handles 3 acts. Receives 15-20% commission.
How to Contact: Submit demo tape by mail. Unsolicited submissions are OK. Prefers cassette or DAT with 3 songs and lyric sheet. If seeking management, press kit should include bio, picture, press clippings and cassette or CD. SASE. Reports in 6 weeks.
Music: Mostly **rock**; also **country**. Works primarily with bands. Current acts include Marionette (rock band), David Gillespie (drummer) and Voodoo Scream (rock band).

*KAUFMAN HILL MANAGEMENT, 333 S. State St., Concourse Level, Chicago IL 60604. (312)427-3550. Contact: Don Kaufman or Shawn Hill. Estab. 1982. Represents individual artists, groups and songwriters; currently handles 3 acts. Receives 20% commission. Reviews material for acts.
How to Contact: Submit demo tape by mail. Unsolicited submissions are OK. Prefers cassette (or VHS videocassette if available) with 2-6 songs and photo. If seeking management, include photo, cassette, note as to why submitting. Does not return material. Reports back only if interested.
Music: **Rock**, **R&B**, **pop**, **dance** and **A/C**. Works primarily with singer/songwriters, bands, groups and vocalists. Current acts include Larry Heard/Mr. Fingers (dance, R&B, jazz, A/C), Appeal (R&B vocal group) and Jaffar (R&B, A/C).
Tips: "Submit by mail. If we can help you, we will be in touch."

*KENWAN'S PRODUCTIONS, 105 Mimosa Lane, Elizabeth City NC 27909. (800)822-3029. Fax: (919)338-1962. President: Kent O'Neal Felton. Management firm, booking agency, music publisher, record company, record producer and public relations. Estab. 1989. Represents individual artists, groups and songwriters from anywhere; currently handles 3 acts. Receives 15% commission. Reviews material for acts.
How to Contact: Submit demo tape by mail. Unsolicited submissions are OK. Prefers cassette, DAT or VHS videocassette with 4 songs and lyric and/or lead sheet. If seeking management, press kit should include cassette, bio and résumé. Does not return material. Reports in 1 month.
Music: Mostly **gospel**, **R&B** and **jazz**; also **contemporary gospel**. Works primarily with bands and individual artists. Current acts include Big Nick and the Mighty Gospel Wonders (gospel artist), Little Neal and the Disciples (gospel artist) and Atmosphere (R&B artist).

KKR ENTERTAINMENT GROUP, 1300 Clay St., 6th Floor, Oakland CA 94612. (510)464-8024. Fax: (510)763-9004. Administrator: Keith Washington. Management firm. Estab. 1989. Represents individual artists, groups and producers from anywhere. Reviews material for acts.
How to Contact: Call first and obtain permission to submit. Prefers cassette. If seeking management, press kit should include tape and photo (if available). "We do not accept unsolicited material." SASE. Reports in 2 weeks.
Music: Mostly **R&B**, **rap** and **rock**. Current acts include E-A-Ski & CMT (producer/artist), Spice One (Jive recording artist) and Christion (R&B group).
Tips: "Always learn who you are working with and stay involved in everything."

BOB KNIGHT AGENCY, 185 Clinton Ave., Staten Island NY 10301. (718)448-8420. President: Bob Knight. Management firm, booking agency, music publishing and royalty collection firm. Estab.

1971. Represents artists, groups and songwriters; currently handles 3 acts. Receives 10-20% commission. Reviews material for acts and for submission to record companies and producers.

How to Contact: Submit demo tape by mail. Unsolicited submissions are OK. Prefers cassette (or videocassette) with 5 songs and lead sheet "with bio and references." If seeking management, include bio, videocassette and audio cassette in press kit. SASE. Reports in 2 months.

Music: Mostly **top 40/pop**; also **easy listening**, **MOR**, **R&B**, **soul** and **rock** (**nostalgia '50s and '60s**). Works primarily with recording and name groups and artists—'50s, '60s and '70s acts, high energy dance, and show groups. Current acts include The Tymes (oldies), Delfonics (R&B nostalgia) and Big Smoothies (nostalgia).

*KRC RECORDS & PRODUCTIONS, HC 73, Box 5060, Harold KY 41635. (606)478-2169. President: Keith R. Carter. Management firm, booking agency, music publisher and record company. Estab. 1987. Represents local and regional individual artists; currently handles 1 act. Receives 15% commission. Reviews material for acts.

How to Contact: Submit demo tape by mail. Unsolicited submissions are OK. Prefers cassette or videocassette with 1-10 songs and lyric sheet. "Feel free to send any material." Does not return material.

Music: Mostly **country**; also **gospel** and **bluegrass**. Current acts include Kimberly Carter (singer).

*KRIETE, KINCAID & FAITH, 1574-61st St., Brooklyn NY 11219. (718)259-1402. Fax: (718)259-0634. E-mail: kkfmgmt@aol.com. Contact: Ken Kriete. Management firm. Estab. 1990. Represents individual artists and groups from anywhere; currently handles 7 acts. Receives variable commission.

How to Contact: Submit demo tape by mail. Unsolicited submissions are OK. Prefers cassette or VHS-NTSC videocassette with 3-4 songs. If seeking management, press kit should include CD or cassette, photo, bio, VHS if possible. Small amount of relevant press. Does not return material. Reports in 1 month.

Music: Mostly **hard alternative**. Works primarily with bands, singer/songwriters and producers. Current acts include Type O Negative, Life of Agony and The Misfits.

KUPER PERSONAL MANAGEMENT, (formerly Kuper-Lam Management), P.O. Box 66274, Houston TX 77266. (713)520-5791. Fax: (713)523-1048. E-mail: kuper_i@hccs.cc.tx.us. President: Ivan Kuper. Management firm, music publisher (Kuper-Lam Music/BMI). Estab. 1995. Represents individual artists, groups and songwriters from anywhere; currently handles 3 acts. Receives 20% commission. Reviews material for acts.

How to Contact: Submit demo tape by mail. Unsolicited submissions are OK. Prefers cassette. If seeking management, press kit should include photo, bio (one sheet) tearsheets (reviews, etc.) and cassette. Does not return material. Reports in 2 months.

Music: Mostly **singer/songwriters**, **urban contemporary** and **alternative college rock**. Works primarily with self-contained and self-produced artists. Current acts include Def Squad (rap), Champ X (activist) and Philip Rodriguez (songwriter).

Tips: "Create a market value for yourself, produce your own master tapes, create a cost-effective situation."

L.D.F. PRODUCTIONS, P.O. Box 406, Old Chelsea Station, New York NY 10011. (212)925-8925. President: Mr. Dowell. Management firm and booking agency. Estab. 1982. Represents artists and choirs in the New York area. Currently handles 1 act. Receives 20-25% commission. Reviews material for act.

How to Contact: Write first and obtain permission to submit. Prefers cassette (or videocassette of performance—well-lighted, maximum 10 minutes) with 2-8 songs and lyric sheet. Does not return material. Reports in 1 month. "Do not phone expecting a return call unless requested by L.D.F. Productions. Videos should be imaginatively presented with clear sound and bright colors."

Music: Mostly **gospel**, **pop**, **rock** and **jazz**. Works primarily with inspirational and contemporary pop artists. Current acts include L.D. Frazier (gospel artist/lecturer).

Tips: "Those interested in working with us must be original, enthusiastic, persistent and sincere."

LANDSLIDE MANAGEMENT, 928 Broadway, New York NY 10010. (212)505-7300. Principals: Ted Lehrman and Libby Bush. Management firm and music publisher (Kozkeeozko Music). Estab. 1978. Represents singers, singer/songwriters and actor/singers; currently handles 15 acts. Receives 15% commission. Reviews material for acts.

How to Contact: Write or call first to obtain permission to submit. "Potential hit singles only." SASE. "Include picture, résumé and (if available) ½" videocassette if you're submitting yourself as an act." Reports in 6 weeks.

Music: **Dance-oriented**, **MOR**, **rock** (**soft pop**), **soul**, **top 40/pop** and **country/pop**. Current acts include Deborah Dotson (soul/pop/jazz), Sara Carlson (pop/rock) and Patrick Boyd (pop).

LARI-JON PROMOTIONS, 325 W. Walnut, P.O. Box 216, Rising City NE 68658. (402)542-2336. Owner: Larry Good. Music publisher (Lari-Jon Publishing Co./BMI) and record company (Lari-Jon Records). "We also promote package shows." Represents individual artists, groups and songwriters; currently handles 5 acts. Receives 15% commission. Reviews material for acts.
   ● Lari-Jon Publishing is listed in the Music Publishers section; Lari-Jon Records is listed in the Record Companies section; and Lari-Jon Promotions is listed in the Managers and Booking Agents section.
How to Contact: Submit demo tape by mail. Unsolicited submissions are OK. Prefers cassette with 5 songs and lyric sheet. If seeking management, include 8×10 photos, cassette, videocassette and bio sheet in press kit. SASE. Reports in 2 months.
Music: Mostly **country, gospel** and **'50s rock**. Works primarily with dance and show bands. Represents Kent Thompson (singer), Nebraskaland 'Opry (family type country show) and Brenda Allen (singer/comedienne).
Tips: "Be professional in all aspects of the business."

LAZY BONES RECORDINGS/PRODUCTIONS, INC., 9594 First Ave. NE, Suite 230, Seattle WA 98115-2012. (206)820-6632. Fax: (310)457-7632. President: Scott Schorr. Management firm and record company (Lazy Bones Recordings). Estab. 1992. Represents individual artists and groups from anywhere; currently handles 3 acts. Receives 18-20% commission. Reviews material for acts.
How to Contact: Submit demo tape by mail. Unsolicited submissions are OK. Prefers cassette, VHS videocassette or CD with 4 songs (minimum). If seeking management, press kit should include demo tape, picture, contact number with address, video (if available) and any press. Does not return material. Reports in 1 month.
Music: Mostly **alternative rock, singer/songwriters** and **hip-hop**; also **any other music**—*except* country. Works primarily with bands or singer/songwriters. Current acts include Neros Rome (psychedelic alternative rock), Turntable Bay (hip-hop/dance hall) and Headland (pop rock).

LENTHALL & ASSOCIATES, (formerly Hulen Enterprises), Falcon Ave., Suite 2-2447, Ottawa, Ontario K1V 8C8 **Canada**. (613)738-2373. Fax: (613)523-7941. President, General Manager: Helen Lenthall. Management firm and record production. Represents individual artists, groups and songwriters from all territories. Reviews material for acts.
How to Contact: Submit demo tape by mail. Unsolicited submissions are OK. Prefers cassette (or VHS videocassette) with 3-8 songs maximum and lyric sheet or lead sheet. If seeking management, press kit should include bio, media package, photos, reviews, tracking if available. SAE and IRC. Reports ASAP.
Music: Mostly **soul, pop/rock** and **country**; also **hip hop, rap** and **gospel**. Primarily works with bands and vocalists.

LEVINSON ENTERTAINMENT VENTURES INTERNATIONAL, INC., 1440 Veteran Ave., Suite 650, Los Angeles CA 90024. (213)460-4545. E-mail: leviinc@aol.com. President: Bob Levinson. Management firm. Estab. 1978. Represents national individual artists, groups and songwriters; currently handles 3 acts. Receives 15-25% commission. Reviews material for acts.
How to Contact: Write first and obtain permission to submit. Prefers cassette (or VHS videocassette) with 6 songs and lead sheet. "Inquire first. Don't expect tape to be returned unless SASE included with submission and specific request is made." Reports in 2-4 weeks.
Music: Rock, MOR, R&B and country. Works primarily with rock bands and vocalists.
Tips: "Should be a working band, self-contained and, preferably, performing original material."

RICK LEVY MGT, 1881 S. Kirkman Rd., #715, Orlando FL 32811. (407)521-6135. Fax: (407)521-6153. President: Rick Levy. Office manager: Leiza Levy. Management firm, booking agency, music publisher (Flying Governor Music/BMI) and record company (Luxury Records). Estab. 1985. Represents local, regional or international individual artists and groups; currently handles 4 acts. Receives 15-20% commission. Reviews material for acts.
How to Contact: Submit demo tape by mail. Unsolicited submissions are OK. Prefers cassette (or VHS videocassette if available) with 3 songs and lyric sheet. If seeking management, include tape, VHS video, photo and press. SASE. Reports in 1 month.
Music: Mostly **R&B** (no rap), **pop, country** and **oldies**. Current acts include Jay & Techniques ('60s hit group), Rock Roots (variety-classic rock, rockabilly), Levy/Stocker (songwriters), and Robert "Boz" Boswell (country artist).
Tips: "In this business, seek out people better and more successful than you. Learn, pick their brains, be positive, take criticism and keep pluggin' no matter what."

*LITTLE BIG MAN BOOKING, 39A Gramercy Place N., New York NY 10010. (212)598-0003. Fax: (212)598-0249. President: Marty Diamond. Booking agency. Estab. 1994. Represents national acts with recording deals *only*; currently handles 35 acts. Receivew 10% commission. Reviews material for acts.

How to Contact: Submit demo tape by mail. Unsolicited submissions are OK. Prefers cassette or CD with 4 songs. "Don't be a pest!" Does not return material. Reports in 1 month.

Music: Mostly **alternative music**. Current acts include Sarah McLachlan, Michelle Shocked, Letters to Cleo, Chieftains, The Auteurs, Tricky and Whale.

Tips: "Develop a base in your hometown. Create a database of contacts."

*LIVE-WIRE MANAGEMENT, P.O. Box 653, Morgan Hill, CA 95038. (408)778-3526. Fax: (408)453-3836. President: Bruce Hollibaugh. Management firm. Estab. 1990. Represents individual artists and groups from anywhere; currently handles 2 acts. Receives 15-25% commission. Reviews material for acts.

How to Contact: Submit demo tape by mail. Unsolicited submissions are OK. Prefers DAT with 3-6 songs and lyric sheet. If seeking management, press kit should include what region you are currently performing in; how often you are doing live shows; any reviews; photos. Does not return material. Reports in 2-4 weeks.

Music: Mostly **pop**, **acoustic pop** and **New Age**; also **jazz**, **R&B** and **country**. Works primarily with bands and singer/songwriters. Current acts include Tommy Elskes (singer/songwriter) and The Bartron Tyler Group (acoustic jazz).

*LIVING EYE PRODUCTIONS LTD., P.O. Box 12956, Rochester NY 14612. (716)544-3500. Fax: (716)544-8860. Manager: Carl Labate. Management firm, music publisher (Pussy Galore Publishing/BMI) and record producer (Andy Babiuk and Greg Prevost). Estab. 1982. Represents individual artists, groups and songwriters from anywhere; currently handles 4 acts. Receives 20% commission. Reviews material for acts.

How to Contact: Submit demo tape by mail. Unsolicited submissions are OK. Prefers cassette and "what the artist feels necessary." Does not return material. Reports in 2 weeks.

Music: Mostly **'60s rock**, **'50s rock** and **blues**; also **folk rock** and **surf**. Works primarily with bands that can tour to promote record releases. Current acts include The Chesterfield Kings (rock), The Mean Red Spiders (rock) and The Flat Tops ('50s rock).

Tips: "We don't like trendy new stuff. Don't follow fads, create your own music by having good rock-n-roll influences."

LMP MANAGEMENT FIRM, 6245 Bristol Pkwy., Suite 206, Culver City CA 90230. Contact: Larry McGee. Management firm, music publisher (Operation Perfection, Inc.) and record company (Boogie Band Records Corp.). Represents individual artists, groups and songwriters; currently handles 10 acts. Receives 35% commission. Reviews material for acts.

• LMP's publishing company, Operation Perfection Inc., is listed in the Music Publishers section; Intrigue Production is in the Record Producers section; and their record label, Boogie Band Records, is listed in the Record Companies section.

How to Contact: Write first and obtain permission to submit. Prefers cassette (or videocassette of performance) with 1-4 songs and lead sheet. "Try to perform one or more of your songs on a local TV show. Then obtain a copy of your performance. Please only send professional quality material. Keep it simple and basic." If seeking management, include audio cassette, videocassette, photo and any additional promotional materials in press kit. SASE. Reports in 2 months.

Music: Mostly **pop-oriented R&B**; also **rock** and **MOR/adult contemporary**. Works primarily with professionally choreographed show bands. Current acts include Wali Ali, A. Vis and Denise Parker.

LONG ARM TALENT, 1657 Angelus Ave., Los Angeles CA 90026. (213)663-2553. Fax: (213)663-0851. E-mail: longarm@earthlink.net. Contact: Chris Lamson. Management firm. Estab. 1986. Represents individual artists and groups from anywhere. Currently handles 3 acts. Receives 20% commission.

How to Contact: Submit demo tape by mail. Unsolicited submissions are OK. Prefers cassette with 3 songs and lyric sheet. If seeking management, press kit should include photo, press and touring experience. Does not return material. Reports in 2 weeks.

Music: Mostly **alternative**, **rock** and **AAA (adult)**. Current acts include Stan Ridgway (alternative rock), Box The Walls (AAA) and Ultraviolet (alternative rock).

REMEMBER: Don't "shotgun" your demo tapes. Submit only to companies interested in the type of music you write. For more submission hints, refer to Getting Started on page 5.

*LONG DISTANCE ENTERTAINMENT, P.O. Box 223907, Hollywood FL 33022. (407)369-0755. Fax: (305)962-0015. President: Darlene Delano. Management firm, booking agency and public relations firm. Estab. 1988. Represents individual artists, groups and songwriters from anywhere; currently handles 6 acts. Management receives 15% commission; booking 10%; public relations fee structure. Reviews material for acts.
How to Contact: Call first and obtain permission to submit. Prefers cassette or VHS videocassette with 3 songs. If seeking management, press kit should include photo, bio and press copies. "Publicist submission should include the same material." Does not return material. Reports in 2 weeks.
Music: Mostly **rock**, **alternative** and **Latin**; also **country**, **industrial** and **pop**. Current acts include Carmine Appice (drummer/songwriter/singer), Alex Kane (guitarist/songwriter/singer) and Killing Butterflies with Bazookas (alternative).
Tips: "Be persistent, professional, and true to your art."

*LOWELL AGENCY, 4043 Brookside Court, Norton OH 44203. (216)825-7813. Contact: Leon Seiter. Booking agency. Estab. 1985. Represents regional (Midwest and Southeast) individual artists; currently handles 3 acts. Receives 10% commission. Reviews material for acts.
How to Contact: Submit demo tape by mail. Unsolicited submissions are OK. Prefers cassette with 4 songs and lyric sheet. If seeking management, include demo cassette tape and SASE in press kit. Does not return material. Reports in 2 months.
Music: Mostly **country**. Works primarily with country vocalists. Current acts include Leon Seiter (country singer/entertainer/songwriter), Ford Nix (bluegrass singer and 5 string banjo picker) and Tom Durnen (country singer, co-writer of "Heartbreak Hotel").

RICHARD LUTZ ENTERTAINMENT AGENCY, 5625 0 St., Lincoln NE 68510. (402)483-2241. General Manager: Cherie Worley. Management firm and booking agency. Estab. 1964. Represents individuals and groups; currently handles 100 acts. Receives 20% commission. Reviews material for acts.
How to Contact: Submit demo tape by mail. Unsolicited submissions are OK. Prefers cassette (or videocassette) with 5-10 songs "to show style and versatility" and lead sheet. "Send photo, résumé, tape, partial song list and include references. Add comedy, conversation, etc., to your videocassette. Do not play songs in full—short versions preferred." If seeking management, include audio cassette and photo in press kit. SASE. Reports in 2 weeks.
Music: Mostly **top 40** and **country**; also **dance-oriented** and **MOR**. Works primarily with bar and dance bands for lounge circuit. "Acts must be uniformed." Current acts include Sherwin Linton (country), Sweet 'N' Sassy (variety) and Endless Summer (nostalgia).

*M. &. G. ENTERTAINMENT CONSORTIUMS, INC., Executive Plaza East, 130 Spearman St., Lumberton NC 28358. (910)738-3793. Fax: (910)618-1760. Management firm (Technique Management), booking agency (Headline Booking Agency), music publisher (AZ Music), record company and record producer. Estab. 1972. Represents individual artists, groups, songwriters from anywhere; currently handles 35 acts. Receives 15% commission. Reviews material for acts.
How to Contact: Submit demo tape by mail. Unsolicited submissions are OK. Prefers cassette or DAT or VHS videocassette with lyric and/or lead sheet. If seeking management, press kit should include bio, prior commitments. "Cover letter mandatory." SASE. Reports in 2 weeks.
Music: Mostly **contemporary**, **rock** and **rap**; also **gospel**, **jazz** and **country**. Works primarily with singers, performing artists. Current acts include Psalmist (contemporary gospel), The Rickochet Mob featuring Big Cee, Scientific (rapper) and Allah's Annointed Gospel Singers.

M & M TALENT AGENCY INC., 146 Round Pond Lane, Rochester NY 14662. (716)723-3334. Contact: Carl Labate. Management firm and booking agency. Represents artists and groups; currently handles 1 act. Receives 20-25% commission.
How to Contact: Submit demo tape by mail. Unsolicited submissions are OK. Prefers cassette (or CD) with minimum 3 songs and lyric sheet. May send video if available; "a still photo would be good enough to see the type of performance; if you are a performer, it would be advantageous to show yourself or the group performing live. Theme videos are not helpful." If seeking management, include photos, bio, markets established, tape and/or videos. Does not return material. Reports in 3-4 weeks.
Music: **Blues**, **rock** and **R&B**. Works primarily with touring bands and recording artists. Current acts include The Chesterfield Kings (alternative rock, international touring band).
Tips: "My main interest is with groups or performers that are currently touring or ready to do so. And are at least 60% percent original. Strictly songwriters should apply elsewhere."

M.B.H. MUSIC MANAGEMENT, P.O. Box 1096, Hudson, Quebec J0P 1H0 **Canada**. (613)780-1163. Fax: (514)458-2819. Manager: Tanya Hart. Management firm. Estab. 1982. Works with local and regional individual artists and groups; currently handles 4 acts. Receives 20-30% commission. Reviews material for acts.

• M.B.H.'s publishing company, G-String Publishing, can be found in the Music Publishers section, and their record label, L.A. Records, is in the Record Companies section.
How to Contact: Submit demo tape by mail. Unsolicited submissions are OK. Prefers cassette or DAT with 3 songs and lyric sheet. If seeking management, press kit should include demo, 8 × 10 glossy, bio/résumé and song list. SASE. Reports in 2 months.
Music: Mostly **commercial rock**, **alternative** and **A/C**; also **country** and **dance**. Works primarily with singer/songwriters and solo artists. Current acts include Jessica Ehrenworth (dream pop singer), Tommy Hayes (vocal impersonator) and Pete Zaman (punk rock comedy).
Tips: "Know your craft. Great lyrics can save a bad melody. Songs must create an emotion on the first listen. Keep the songs under four minutes."

THE McDONNELL GROUP, 27 Pickwick Lane, Newtown Square PA 19073. (610)353-8554. Contact: Frank McDonnell. Management firm. Estab. 1985. Represents local, regional or international individual artists, groups and songwriters; currently handles 5 acts. Receives 20-25% commission. Reviews material for acts.
How to Contact: Write first and obtain permission to submit. Prefers cassette (or VHS videocassette if available) with 4 songs and lyric sheet. If seeking management, include press, tape or video, recent photos, bio. SASE. Reports in 1 month.
Music: Mostly **rock**, **pop** and **R&B**; also **country** and **jazz**.. Current acts include Johnny Bronco (rock group), Mike Forte (producer/songwriter) and Pat Martino (jazz guitarist).

*McGILLIS MUSIC PUBLISHING CO., 2895 Biscayne Blvd., #455, Miami FL 33137. (305)460-3547. President: Darrin McGillis. Management firm, music publisher and record company (McGillis Records). Estab. 1988. Represents individual artists and songwriters from anywhere; currently handles 5 acts. Receives 25% commission. Reviews material for acts.
How to Contact: Submit demo tape by mail. Unsolicited submissions are OK. Prefers cassette with 4 songs and lyric sheet. If seeking management, press kit should include head shot photo, full body photo and cassette with vocals. SASE. Reports in 2 weeks.
Music: Mostly **dance**, **pop** and **Spanish pop**; also **house music**, **Salsa** and **light rock**. Works primarily with bilingual dance and pop artists that appeal to a young audience. Current acts include Menudo (pop/Spanish/dance), Joel (pop/Spanish/dance) and Explosion (pop/Spanish/dance).

*MADSTORM PRODUCTION COMPANY, 66 Wrentham St., Dorchester, MA 02124. (617)825-6875. Director: Edgiton Farquharson. Management firm and record producer. Estab. 1992. Represents regional individual artists and songwriters; currently handles 5 acts. Receives 20% commission. Reviews material for acts.
How to Contact: Submit demo tape by mail. Unsolicited submissions are OK. Prefers cassette, DAT or videocassette. If seeking management, press kit should include bio, picture and music type. SASE. Reports in 3 weeks.
Music: Mostly **reggae**, **rap** and **urban contemporary**; also **rappers**, **reggae singers** and **DJ's**. Current acts include Fitzroy Francis (reggae singer), Karen Brown (singer) and Kenroy Scott (DJ/rapper).

MAGNUM MUSIC CORPORATION LTD., 8607-128 Avenue, Edmonton Alberta **Canada** T5E 0G3. (403)476-8230. Fax: (403)472-2584 Manager: Bill Maxim. Booking agency, music publisher (Ramblin' Man Music Publishing/PRO, High River Music Publishing/ASCAP) and record company (Magnum Records). Estab. 1984. Represents international individual artists, groups and songwriters; currently handles 4 acts. Receives 15% commission. Reviews material for acts.
• See their listing in the Record Companies section.
How to Contact: Write or call first and obtain permission to submit. Prefers cassette with 3-4 songs. If seeking management, include tape or CD, photo, press clippings and bio in press kit. SAE and IRC. Reports in 6-8 weeks.
Music: Mostly **country** and **gospel**. Works primarily with "artists or groups who are also songwriters." Current acts include Catheryne Greenly (country), Thea Anderson (country) and Gordon Cormier (country).
Tips: "Prefers finished demos."

MANAGEMENT PLUS, P.O. Box 680788, San Antonio TX 78268. (210)521-7948. Fax: (210)521-9061. Manager/Agent: Bill Angelini. Management firm and booking agency. Estab. 1980. Represents individual artists and groups from anywhere; currently handles 5 acts. Receives 10-20% commission. Reviews material for acts.
How to Contact: Submit demo tape by mail. Unsolicited submissions are OK. Prefers cassette, VHS videocassette and biography. If seeking management, press kit should include pictures, bios and discography. Does not return material. Reports in 1 week.
Music: Mostly **Latin American**, **Tejano** and **international**; also **Norteño** and **country**. Current acts include Los Padrez (Tejano), Anna Roman (Tejano) and Jorge Alejandro (Tejano)

THE MANAGEMENT TRUST LTD., 309B, 219 Dufferin St., Toronto, Ontario M6K 3J1 **Canada**. (416)532-7080. Fax: (416)532-8852. Contact: Jake Gold, Allan Gregg, Shelley Stertz. Management firm. Estab. 1986. Represents local, regional (Canada), individual artists and/or groups; currently handles 4 acts.
How to Contact: Call first and obtain permission to submit. If seeking management, press kit should include CD or tape, bio, photo and press. SAE and IRC. Reports in 4-6 weeks.
Music: All types. Current acts include The Tragically Hip (MCA Canada, Atlantic US), The Watchmen (MCA Canada), Ursula (MCA/Sumo) and David Gogo (EMI Music Canada).

MANAPRO ENTERTAINMENT, 82 Sherman St., Passaic NJ 07055. (201)777-6109. Fax: (201)458-0303. President: Tomasito Bobadilla. Management firm, record company, music publisher and record producer. Estab. 1988. Represents individual artists and/or groups from anywhere; currently handles 3 acts. Receives 20% commission. Reviews material for acts.
How to Contact: Submit demo tape by mail. Unsolicited submissions are OK. Prefers cassette (or VHS videocassette if available) with 3 songs and lyric sheet. If seeking management, press kit should include bio, 8 × 10 photo, 3-song demo and fact sheet. SASE. Reports in 3-6 months.
Music: Mostly **dance**, **pop** and **contemporary**; also **R&B** and **alternative**. Works primarily with vocalists and bands. Current acts include Giovanni Irepante (singer), Opty Gomez (songwriter) and Renew (R&B).

*MARK ONE-THE AGENCY, P.O. Box 62, Eastwood 5063 **South Australia**. (08)338-1844. Fax: (08)338-1793. E-mail: krqm@adam.com.au. Owner: Mark Draper. Management firm, booking agency and music publisher. Estab. 1981. Represents individual artists, groups, songwriters from anywhere; currently handles 20 acts. Receives 10-20% commission. Reviews material for acts.
How to Contact: Submit demo tape by mail. Unsolicited submissions are OK. Prefers cassette (or VHS videocassette) with 3 songs and lyric sheet. If seeking management, press kit should include photograph, 1 page bio and comprehensive contact list. SAE and IRC. Reports in 2 months.
Music: Mostly **rock**, **pop** and **dance**. Works primarily with bands. Current acts include Capacity Max (contemporary rock), Radio Ga Ga and Jungle Alley (rock band).
Tips: "Be honest, reliable and available."

MARSUPIAL LTD., Roundhill Cottage, The Ridge, Cold Ash, Newbury, Berks RG 16 9HZ **United Kingdom**. (0635)862200. Record Producer, Artist Manager: John Brand. Management firm, music publisher and record producer. Estab. 1990. Represents individual artists and/or groups, songwriters, producers and remixers from anywhere; currently handles 3 acts. Receives 20% commission. Reviews material for acts.
How to Contact: Submit demo tape by mail. Unsolicited submissions are OK. Prefers cassette or PAL videocassette with 4 songs and lyric sheet. If seeking management, press kit should include tape, photos, video (if possible) and any press. SAE and IRC. Reports in 6 weeks.
Music: All types. Current acts include Pooka (Rough Trade/Atlantic Records), Kyra (Virgin Records, blues/house) and Sally Anne Marsh (Love This Records/pop).

RICK MARTIN PRODUCTIONS, 125 Fieldpoint Road, Greenwich CT 06830. (203)661-1615. E-mail: easywayric@aol.com. President: Rick Martin. Personal manager and independent producer. Holds the Office of Secretary of the National Conference of Personal Managers. Represents actresses and vocalists; currently handles 2 acts. Receives 15-25% commission. "Occasionally, we are hired as consultants, production assistants or producers of recording projects."
How to Contact: Submit demo tape by mail. Unsolicited submissions are OK. "Enclose an SASE if you want tape back. Do not write for permission—will not reply, just send material. Photos are a must." Prefers cassette (or VHS videocassette) with 2-4 songs. "Don't worry about an expensive presentation to personal managers or producers; they'll make it professional if they get involved." SASE. Reports in 4 weeks.
Music: Top 40, **dance** and **easy listening**. No rock or folk music. Produces vocal groups and female vocalists. Current acts include Marisa Mercedes (vocalist/pianist/songwriter) and Rob and Steve (songwriters/vocalists).
Tips: "The tape does not have to be professionally produced—it's really not important what you've done—it's what you can do now that counts."

PHIL MAYO & COMPANY, P.O. Box 304, Bomoseen VT 05732. (802)468-5011. President: Phil Mayo. Management firm and record company (AMG Records). Estab. 1981. Represents international individual artists, groups and songwriters; currently handles 3 acts. Receives 20% commission.
How to Contact: Submit demo tape by mail. Unsolicited submissions are OK. Prefers cassette and/or CD with 3 songs and lyric or lead sheet. If seeking management, include bio, photo and lyric sheet in press kit. Does not return material. Reports in 1-2 months.

Music: Mostly **rock**, **pop** and **country**; also **blues** and **Christian pop**. Works primarily with dance bands, vocalists and rock acts. Current acts include The Drive (R&B), Athena and Blind Date.

MC PROMOTIONS & PUBLIC RELATIONS, 8504 Willis Ave., #6, Panorama City CA 91402. (818)892-1741. Management firm. Currently handles 3 acts. Receives 10% commission. Reviews material for acts.
How to Contact: Submit demo tape by mail. Unsolicited submissions are OK. Prefers cassette (or videocassette). Does not return material. Reports in 4-5 weeks.
Music: Mostly **country**. Works primarily with vocalists. Current acts include Sierra Highway, Deina Blair and John Campbell.

*MELODY'S MUSIC, 2429 Ninth Ave., Los Angeles CA 90018. (213)971-1970. Agent: Melody Rhyness. Management firm, music publisher (Melody's Music Publishing). Estab. 1990. Represents songwriters from anywhere; currently handles 2 acts. Receives 15% commission. Reviews material for acts.
How to Contact: Write first and obtain permission to submit submit a demo. Prefers cassette or VHS videocassette. SASE. Reports in 2 weeks.
Music: Mostly **R&B**, **gospel** and **jazz**. Works primarily with songwriters.

*MERLIN MANAGEMENT CORP., P.O. Box 5087 V.M.P.O., Vancouver, British Columbia V6B 4A9 **Canada**. Phone/fax: (604)525-9194. President: Wolfgang Hamman. Management firm. Estab. 1979. Represents individual artists, groups, songwriters and producers from anywhere; currently handles 3 acts. Receives 20-25% commission. Reviews material for acts.
• See the listings for Merlin Productions in the Record Companies and Record Producers sections.
How to Contact: Write or call first and obtain permission to submit demo. Prefers cassette with 3 songs and lyric and/or lead sheet. If seeking management, press kit should include photo and bio. SASE. Reports in 3 weeks.
Music: Mostly **modern rock**, **dance** and **pop**; also **techno** and **alternative**. Current acts include Mode to Joy (modern rock), Wolfgang-Wolfgang (dance) and Hakimashita (modern rock).
Tips: "Write daily, study successful writers."

MERRI-WEBB PRODUCTIONS, P.O. Box 5474, Stockton CA 95205. (209)948-8186. President: Nancy L. Merrihew. Management firm, music publisher (Kaupp's & Robert Publishing Co./BMI), record company (Kaupp Records). Represents regional (California) individual artists, groups and songwriters; currently handles 12 acts. Receives standard commission.
• See the listings for Kaupp's and Robert Publishing in the Music Publishers section and Kaupp Records in the Record Companies section.
How to Contact: Write first and obtain permission to submit. Prefers cassette (or VHS videocassette if available) with 3 songs maximum and lyric sheet. SASE. Reports in 3 months.
Music: Mostly **country**, **A/C rock** and **R&B**; also **pop**, **rock** and **gospel**. Works primarily with vocalists, bands and songwriters. Current acts include Rick Webb (singer/songwriter), Nanci Lynn (singer/songwriter) and Birmingham Country (country band).
Tips: "Know what you want, set a goal, focus in on your goals, be open to constructive criticism, polish tunes and keep polishing."

MID-EAST ENTERTAINMENT INC., P.O. Box 25027, Lexington KY 40524. (606)885-5507. Agent: Robert Moser. Represents artists and groups; currently handles 200 acts. Receives 15-20% commission. Reviews material for acts.
How to Contact: Submit demo tape by mail. Unsolicited submissions are OK. Prefers cassette with 3-6 songs, photo and songlist. Songs should have 1 verse, 1 bridge and 1 chorus. If seeking management, include tape, photo and playlist in press kit. SASE. Reports in 6 months.
Music: Mostly **top 40** and **R&B**; also **country**, **dance**, **easy listening**, **jazz**, **rock**, **soul** and **pop**. Works primarily with dance bands. Current acts include The Sensations (top 40/classics), The Marvells (top 40/oldies), Mixed Emotions (variety dance) and Nervous Melvin (college rock).

MIDNIGHT MUSIC MANAGEMENT, 8722½ W. Pico, Los Angeles CA 90035. (310)659-1784. Fax: (310)659-9347. Agent: Bob Diamond. Management firm. Estab. 1989. Represents individual artists, groups, songwriters and producers from anywhere; currently handles 10 acts. Receives 18% commission. Reviews material for acts.
How to Contact: Write first and obtain permission to submit a demo. Prefers cassette with 4 songs, lyric sheet and bios and press. If seeking management, press kit should include bio, press, tape and video (if available). Does not return material. Reports in 1 month.
Music: Mostly **alternative rock**, **R&B** and **country**; also **blues** and **worldbeat**. Works primarily with R&B/pop songwriters and producers, punk/alternative bands and acoustic rock bands. Current acts

include Brutal Juice (punk band from Texas, signed to Interscope) and Denise Rich (pop/R&B songwriter). Past cuts with Chaka Khan, Ce Ce Peniston and Jody Watley. Upcoming cuts with Toni Braxton, Celine Dion and Diana Ross and Evan and Jaron (folk/rock/pop acoustic duo).

*MIDNIGHT SPECIAL PRODUCTIONS, INC., P.O. Box 916, Hendersonville TN 37077. (615)822-6713. Fax: (615)824-3830. President: Marty Martel. Management firm, booking agency, music publisher (Brittkrisderon), record company (BAM) and record producer (Marty Martel). Estab. 1971. Represents Nashville individual artists and songwriters; currently handles 2 acts. Receives 10% commission. Reviews material for acts.
How to Contact: Submit demo tape by mail. Unsolicited submissions are OK. Prefers cassette with 3 songs and lyric sheet. If seeking management, press kit should include photo, tape and bio. SASE. Reports in 1 week.
Music: Mostly **country**. Works primarily with singers. Current acts include Johnny Paycheck (country), Teresa Langworthy (country) and Murl Allan (country).

*MIGHTY OAK MANAGEMENT, 473 Valley Rd., Port Stanley, Ontario N5L I6S **Canada**. (519)782-3334. Fax: (519)782-4618. President: Sid Steward. Management firm. Estab. 1990. Represents groups and songwriters from anywhere; currently handles 2 acts. Receives 10% commission. Reviews material for acts.
How to Contact: Submit demo tape by mail. Unsolicited submissions are OK. Prefers cassette, VHS videocassette or CD and lyric sheet. Does not return material. Reports in 2 weeks.
Music: Mostly **country rock** and **country**. Current acts include Harmony Road (electronic backed duo, country rock) and Rebecca Kickin' Horse (4 piece country).

MILESTONE MEDIA, P.O. Box 869, Venice CA 90291. (310)396-1234. Co-President: Mr. Sverdlin. Management firm. Estab. 1985. Represents individual artists, groups and songwriters from anywhere; currently handles 12 acts. Receives 20% commission.
How to Contact: Submit demo tape by mail. Unsolicited submissions are OK. Prefers cassette (or videocassette) with 3 songs. If seeking management, press kit should include credits and photo. Does not return material. Reports in 2 weeks.
Music: Mostly **rap**, **rock** and **dance**; also **country**, **house** and **movie**. Works primarily with singers, producers and composers. Current acts include Ray Goldman, Lori Lane and Feed.

THOMAS J. MILLER & COMPANY, 1802 Laurel Canyon Blvd., Los Angeles CA 90046. (213)656-7212. Fax: (213)656-7757. Artist Relations: Karen Deming. Management firm, music publisher and record company (Wilshire Park Records). Estab. 1975. Represents individual artists, groups and songwriters from anywhere; currently handles 12 acts. Reviews material for acts.
How to Contact: Submit demo tape by mail. Unsolicited submissions are OK. Prefers cassette (or NTSC videocassette) and lyric sheet. If seeking management, press kit should include photos, bio and video. Does not return material. Reports in 2-3 weeks.
Music: Mostly **rock**, **pop** and **jazz**; also **stage** and **country**. Current acts include Manowar, Fury in the Slaughterhouse and Champaign.

MIRKIN MANAGEMENT, 906½ Congress Ave., Austin TX 78701. (512)472-1818. Fax: (512)472-6915. Administrative Assistant: Robin Sullivan. Management firm. Estab. 1986. Represents individual artists, groups and songwriters from anywhere; currently handles 2 acts. Reviews material for acts.
How to Contact: Write or call first and obtain permission to submit a demo. Prefers cassette with 4 songs. If seeking management, press kit should include photo, press clippings and tape. SASE.
Music: All types. Current acts include Ian Moore Band (blues/rock) and Rocket Baby (pop).

MISTY INTERNATIONAL (formerly Misty Records), Route 1, Box 70-G, Dale TX 78616. Phone/fax: (512)398-7519. Vice President: Frank D. Jones Jr. Management firm, booking agency, music publisher (Motex Music, Misty Haze Music) and record producer (Don Jones). Estab. 1967. Represents individual artists and groups from anywhere; currently handles 8 acts. Receives 15-30% commission. Reviews material for acts.
● Misty International's publishing affiliate, Motex Music, is listed in the Music Publishers section and their record label, MCR, is in the Record Companies section.
How to Contact: Submit demo tape by mail. Unsolicited submissions are OK. Prefers cassette with 4 songs and lyric sheet. "If seeking management, include 8 × 10 photo, cassette with at least 4 songs,

THE TYPES OF MUSIC each listing is interested in are printed in boldface.

bio, photocopies of news articles and samples of products that have been previously released." SASE. Reports in 6 weeks.

Music: Mostly **country**, **Christian country** and **gospel**. Works primarily with bands and singers. Current acts include Sandy Samples (country-gospel), Toma (country) and Bud Robbins (country).

MONOPOLY MANAGEMENT, 162 N. Milford, Highland MI 48357. Vice President: Bob Zilli. Management firm. Estab. 1984. Represents songwriters from anywhere; currently handles 1 act. Receives 15% commission. Reviews material for acts.

How to Contact: Submit demo tape by mail. Unsolicited submissions are OK. Prefers cassette or VHS videocassette with 4 songs and lyric sheet. If seeking management, press kit should include tape, photo, bio, résumé of live performances. SASE. Reports in 1 month.

Music: Mostly **country**, **alternative** and **top 40**. Works primarily with singer/songwriters. Current acts include Robbie Richmond (songwriter).

*MONTEREY ARTISTS, INC., 901 18th Ave. S., Nashville TN 37212. (615)321-4444. Fax: (615)321-2446. Booking agency. Represents individual artists, groups and songwriters from anywhere; currently handles 37 acts. Receives 10% commission. Reviews material for acts.

How to Contact: Write or call first to arrange personal interview.

Music: Mostly **country**. Current acts include John Michael Montgomery, Lyle Lovett, The Mavericks, Hal Ketchum, Ricky Skaggs, Sawyer Brown and Junior Brown.

*GARY F. MONTGOMERY MANAGEMENT, P.O. Box 5106, Macon GA 31208. (912)749-7259. Fax: (912)757-0002. President: Gary F. Montgomery. Management firm, music publisher (g.f.m. Music/ASCAP, 12/31/49 Music/BMI) and production company. Estab. 1981. Represents individual artists, groups, songwriters, record producers and engineers from anywhere; currently handles 6 acts. Receives 10-25% commission (it varies depending on the act). Reviews material for acts.

How to Contact: Write or call first and obtain permission to submit a demo. Prefers cassette with 3-5 songs and lyric sheet. "Call first to see if we are accepting new clients." Does not return material. Reports in 1 month.

Music: All types. Works primarily with singer/songwriters. Current acts include Otis Redding III (singer/songwriter), Jan Krist (singer/songwriter folk, alterntive) and Carl Culpepper (instrumentalist/songwriter heavy rock).

Tips: "Write everyday—keep abreast of the new sounds and trends. Don't forget the sounds that went before, integrate the old with the new."

MOORE ENTERTAINMENT GROUP, 11 Possum Trail, Saddle River NJ 07458. (201)327-3698. President: Barbara Moore. Estab. 1984. Represents individual artists and groups; currently handles 4 acts. Receives 10% commission. Reviews material for acts.

How to Contact: Submit demo tape by mail. Unsolicited submissions are OK. Prefers cassette (or videocassette if available) and lyric sheet. "Include photo and bio." If seeking management, include tape, photo and bio in press kit. SASE. Reports in 6 weeks.

Music: Mostly **dance**, **rock**, **R&B** and **pop**. Works primarily with vocalists. Current acts include 4 Play (R&B), Paradise (dance/R&B) and Rene Rollins (country/pop).

Tips: "Have dedication, drive and determination and you will succeed."

THOMAS MORELLI ENTERPRISES, 15 Brimmer St., Brewer ME 04412. (207)989-2577. Owner: Thomas Morelli. Management firm and booking agency. Estab. 1980. Represents individual artists, groups, models from anywhere; currently handles 5 acts. Receives 2-10% commission.

How to Contact: Submit demo tape by mail. Unsolicited submissions are OK. Prefers cassette. If seeking management, press kit should include tape, bio and photo. SASE. Reports in 1 month.

Music: Mostly **country** and **rock**; also, single entertainer acts, for comedy/small bar circuit in New England. 90% bands, some duets, some single. Current acts include Allison Ames (country singer/songwriter), The Choice (high energy rock band) and Bootleg (modern country band).

Tips: "Since our main function is booking acts into club venues, we need quality country and rock acts who are honest and willing to work hard. The proof is in the performance!"

MUSIC MAN PROMOTIONS, 1/76 Mill Point Rd., South Perth 6151 **Western Australia**. (619)474-2300. Fax: (619)474-1779. Manager: Eddie Robertson. Booking agency. Estab. 1991. Represents individual artists and/or groups; currently handles 20 acts. Receives 10-15% commission. Reviews material for acts.

How to Contact: Submit demo tape by mail. Unsolicited submissions are OK. Prefers cassette or videocassette with photo, information on style and bio. If seeking management, press kit should include photos, bio, demo, song sheet and any other useful information. Does not return material. Reports in 1-2 month.

Music: Mostly **top 40/pop**, **jazz** and **'60s-'90s punk**; also **reggae** and **blues**. Works primarily with show bands and solo performers. Current acts include Faces (top 40/pop), Elizabeth Sanderson (jazz) and Maiden America (top 40/dance).
Tips: "Send as much information as possible. If you do not receive a call after four to five weeks, follow up with letter or phone call."

MUSIC MATTERS, P.O. Box 3773, San Rafael CA 94912-3773. (415)457-0700. Management firm. Estab. 1990. Represents local, regional or international individual artists, groups and songwriters; currently handles 8 acts. Reviews material for acts.
How to Contact: Submit demo tape by mail. Unsolicited submissions are OK. Prefers cassette (or VHS videocassette if available) with lyric sheet. If seeking management, include lyric sheets, demo tape, and bio. Does not return material.
Music: Mostly **rock**, **blues** and **pop**; also **jazz** and **R&B**. Works primarily with songwriting performers/bands (rock). Current acts include Canned Heat (rock/blues group), Olivia Rosestone (singer/songwriter), Sam Andrew (singer/songwriter from Big Brother and The Holding Company), Zero, Zakiya Hooker, Walter Trout, Mud Hut and New Riders.
Tips: "Write great *radio-friendly* songs."

*MUSICA MODERNA MANAGEMENT, 5626 Brock St., Houston TX 77023. (713)926-4436. Fax: (713)926-2253. President: Max Silva. Management firm and booking agency. Represents individual artists and/or groups from anywhere; currently handles 6 acts. Receives 20% commission. Reviews material for acts.
How to Contact: Call first to arrange personal interview or submit demo tape by mail. Unsolicited submissions are OK. Prefers cassette or VHS videocassette with 3 songs and lyric sheet. If seeking management, press kit should include bio, photo and demo tape. Does not return material. Reports in 4-5 weeks.
Music: Mostly **Tejano**. Works primarily with bands. Current acts include The Hometown Boys, Los Pekadorez and Annette y Axxion.

*JAMES E. MYERS ENTERPRISES, 1607 E. Cheltenham Ave., Philadelphia PA 19124. (215)288-7824. Owner: James E. Myers. Music publisher, record company and record producer. Estab. 1946. Represents individual artists and songwriters from anywhere; currently handles 2 acts.
How to Contact: Call first to arrange personal interview. If seeking management, press kit should include cassette, photo and bio. Does not return material.
Music: Mostly **country** and **rock**. Current acts include Joey Welz (singer) and Ed Gallagher (songwriter).

THE NASHVILLE CONNECTION, P.O. Box 4111, Lago Vista TX 78645. (512)267-4488. Contact: John Milam. Management firm, booking agency and music publisher. Estab. 1973. Represents individual artists and/or groups, songwriters from anywhere; currently handles 2 acts. Receives 15% commission. Reviews material for acts.
How to Contact: Submit demo tape by mail. Unsolicited submissions are OK. Prefers cassette or videocassette with 5 songs maximum and lyric sheet. If seeking management, press kit should include photo, tape, bio and work references. Does not return material. Reports in 2 weeks.
Music: **Country** only. Works primarily with groups that have potential of being national acts—no one that doesn't currently work. Current acts include Savannah Rose, Smokin' and Shameless. National artists who have previously worked through agency include Clay Walker, Doug Supernaw, Ty Herndon, Lonestar, Ricochette and Toby Keith.

BRIAN NELSON ENTERTAINMENT INC., P.O. Box 3008, Long Branch NJ 07740. (908)870-6911. Fax: (908)870-9664. President: Brian Nelson. Management firm. Estab. 1991. Represents individual artists, groups and songwriters from anywhere (specializes in local artists); currently handles 3 acts. Receives 15-25% commission. Reviews material for acts.
How to Contact: Submit demo tape by mail. Unsolicited submissions are OK. Prefers cassette or VHS videocassette with 3 or less songs and lyric sheet. If seeking management, press kit should include cassette or CD, bio, photo, letter stating what artist is looking for in mgmt. company, contact name and number. Artist will only be contacted if accepted. Does not return material. Reports in 1-2 months only if interested.
Music: Mostly **rock**, **alternative** and **A/C**. Works primarily with bands. Current acts include Mr. Reality (acoustic rock band), Sal Marra (blues guitarist) and Mars Needs Women (aggropop band).
Tips: "Be professionally minded. Don't play rock star. We're here to work together for the advancement of your career. We're not here to cater to your whims. There's no room in the music business for people not willing to work for their success."

J.P. NEWBY MANAGEMENT, P.O. Box 120725, Nashville TN 37212. (615)383-0889. Fax: (615)320-0889. President: Judith Newby. Management firm and public relations. Estab. 1975. Represents individual artists and groups from anywhere; currently handles 4 acts. Commission is individually negotiated. Reviews material for acts.

How to Contact: Submit demo tape by mail. Unsolicited submissions are OK. Prefers cassette with lyric sheet. If seeking management, press kit should include photo, bio and tape. Does not return material. Reports in 2 weeks.

Music: Mostly **country** and **rock**. Current acts include Everly Bros. (rock), RhymShot (country), Laura Sheridan (country) and Joe Dalton (country).

NIC OF TYME PRODUCTIONS, INC., P.O. Box 2114, Valparaiso IN 46384. (219)477-2083. Fax: (219)477-4075. President: Tony Nicoletto. Management firm, record promoter, music publisher (Twin Spin Publishing/BMI) and record company (KNG Records). Estab. 1990. Represents individual artists, groups and songwriters from anywhere; currently represents 12 acts. Receives 15-20% commission. Reviews material for acts.

• Nic Of Tyme's publishing affiliate, Twin Spin Publishing, is listed in the Music Publishers section.

How to Contact: Write or call first and obtain permission to submit. Prefers cassette (or videocassette) with 3 songs and lyric sheet. If seeking management, press kit should include picture, demo tape, words and autobiography of the artist. "Must be original and copyright material." Does not return material. Reports in 1-3 months.

Music: Mostly **country, R&B** and **pop**; also **rock, jazz, contemporary** and **gospel**. Works primarily with singers, bands and songwriters. Current acts include Bobby Lewis (R&B singer/songwriter), John Kontol (pop singer/songwriter), Neotone (adult alternative), Alison's Mailbox (alternative) and Jokers Death & Taxes (rock group).

Tips: "Review your material for clean-cut vocals. Keep trying hard and don't give up. We work primarily as a record promoter for the artist in mind. We pre-solicit labels that are interested in your style of music."

NIK ENTERTAINMENT COMPANY, 274 N. Goodman St., Rochester NY 14607. (716)244-0331. Fax: (716)244-0356. Owner/President: Gary Webb. Management firm and booking agency. Estab. 1988. Represents groups from anywhere; currently handles 5 acts. Receives 10-20% commission. Reviews material for acts.

How to Contact: Submit demo tape by mail. Unsolicited submissions are OK. Prefers cassette or VHS videocassette with lyric or lead sheet. SASE. Reports in 2 months.

Music: Mostly **mainstream rock** and **country**; also **pop**. Works primarily with bands. Current acts include Nik and the Nice Guys, Wild Nik West and The Bedrock Band.

CHRISTINA NILSSON PRODUCTION, Rörstrandsgatan 21, Stockholm 11340 **Sweden**. Phone: (08)317-277. Managing Director: Christina Nilsson. Management firm and booking agency. Estab. 1972. Represents individual artists, groups and songwriters; currently handles 3 acts. Receives 15% commission. Reviews material for acts.

How to Contact: Submit demo tape by mail. Unsolicited submissions are OK. Prefers cassette (or VHS videocassette if available) with 4-6 songs and lyric or lead sheet. If seeking management, include photo, bio and cassette tape. Does not return material. Reports in 1 month.

Music: Mostly **R&B, rock** and **gospel**; also "texts for stand-up comedians." Works primarily with concert bands. Current acts include Jan Schaffer (lead guitar, songwriter), Ted Astrom (singer, actor) and Malou Berg (gospel singer).

NORTHSTAR ARTIST MANAGEMENT, P.O. Box 2627, Dearborn MI 48123. (313)274-7000. President: Angel Gomez. Management firm. Estab. 1979. Represents local and international individual artists, groups and songwriters; currently handles 14 acts. Receives 10-20% commission. Reviews material for acts.

How to Contact: Write first and obtain permission to submit. Prefers cassette (or videocassette of performance) with 3-5 songs. If seeking management, include photo, tape, bio and itinerary of dates. Does not return material. Reports in 6-8 weeks.

Music: Mostly **rock, pop** and **top 40**; also **metal**. Works primarily with individual artists, groups (bar bands) and songwriters. Current artists include Craig Elliott (new music), Slyboy (rock), RH Factor (rock), Hunter Brucks (modern country), Reckless Youth (rock), Beggars Can't Be Choosers (rock), Planet Of Fun (rock) and Yardboss (alternative grunge).

Tips: "Listen to your tape before sending. Is it special?"

NOTEWORTHY PRODUCTIONS, 124½ Archwood Ave., Annapolis MD 21401. (410)268-8232. Fax: (410)268-2167. President: McShane Glover. Management firm, booking agency. Estab. 1985. Represents individual artists, groups and songwriters from everywhere; currently handles 13 acts. Receives 15-20% commission. Reviews material for acts.

How to Handle: Write first and obtain permission to submit. Prefers cassette with lyric sheet. If seeking management, press kit should include cassette or CD, photo, bio, venues played and press clippings (preferably reviews). "Follow up with a phone call 3-5 weeks after submission." Does not return material. Reports in 3 weeks.
Music: Mostly **country**, **folk**, and **bluegrass**; also **pop**. Works primarily with performing singer/ songwriters. Current acts include Travelers (acoustic folk/country), Catfish Hodge (blues) and Fred Koller (singer/songwriter).
Tips: "Honesty is the most important ingredient in any song—you cannot expect to touch other people's hearts if you do not write from your own. Don't become insular—write with other people, attend songwriting seminars, analyze songs by writers you admire and read copiously."

NOVA PRODUCTIONS & MANAGEMENT, P.O. Box 7892, Tampa FL 33605. (813)273-8796. CEO/A&R: A. Howard. Management firm, booking agency, record company (Quantum Records) and record producer. Estab. 1957. Represents individual artists, groups and songwriters from anywhere; currently handles 16 acts. Receives 18% commission. Reviews material for acts.
How to Contact: Submit demo tape by mail. Unsolicited submissions are OK. Prefers cassette with lyric or lead sheet. If seeking management, press kit should include demo, photo, musical goals and bio. SASE. Reports in 2 months.
Music: Mostly **jazz**, **blues** and **new country**. Works primarily with vocalists, singer/songwriters and bands. Current acts include Gypsy Eden (singer), Tory Thimes (singer) and Ben Vernon (singer).
Tips: "Send professional looking promo kit—professionally recorded demo—I want to take you seriously."

CRAIG NOWAG'S NATIONAL ATTRACTIONS, 6037 Haddington Drive, Memphis TN 38119-7423. (901)767-1990. Owner/President: Craig Nowag. Booking agency. Estab. 1958. Represents local, regional and international individual artists and groups; currently handles 21 acts. Receives 20-25% commission. Reviews material for acts.
How to Contact: Submit demo tape by mail. Unsolicited submissions are OK. Prefers cassette (or VHS videocassette if available) with 3-5 songs. Does not return material. Reports in 4-6 weeks.
Music: Mostly **R&B**, **pop** and **blues**; also **pop/rock**, **crossover country** and **re-makes**. Works primarily with oldies record acts, dance bands, blues bands, rock groups, R&B dance bands and nostalgia groups. Current acts include Famous Unknowns, Dianne Price and The Coasters.
Tips: "If the buying public won't buy your song, live act or record you have no saleability, and no agent or manager can do anything for you."

OB-1 ENTERTAINMENT, P.O. Box 22552, Nashville TN 37202. (615)672-0307. Partners: Jim O'Baid and Karen Hillebrand. Management firm, artist development and songplugging. Estab. 1990. Represents local, regional and international individual artists, groups and songwriters; currently handles 1 act. Receives 15-20% commission. Reviews material for acts.
How to Contact: Submit demo tape by mail. Unsolicited submissions are OK. Prefers cassette (or VHS videocassette if available) with 3 songs. If seeking management, include 8×10 photo, tape, bio and videocassette (if possible) in press kit. Does not return material. Reports in 2 months.
Music: Primarily **country**, but **pop** and **rock** also. Current acts include Amanda Thomas (singer).
Tips: "Don't spend a lot of money on demos until you really know the song is good enough to warrant the expenses."

*ODOM-MEADERS MANAGEMENT, 449½ Moreland Ave., Atlanta GA 30307. (404)521-9747. Fax: (404)521-0990. E-mail: odommeader@aol.com. Co-President: Kevin Meaders. Management firm. Estab. 1994. Represents groups from the Southeast mainly; currently handles 4 acts. Reviews material for acts.
How to Contact: Submit demo tape by mail. Unsolicited submissions are OK. Prefers cassette or CD. If seeking management, press kit should include bio, any available press, and audible CD or tape. SASE. Reports in 4-6 weeks.
Music: Mostly **rock** and **blues**. Works primarily with national and regional acts with a variety of styles and influences. Current acts include The Derek Trucks Band (nationally recognized guitar player),The Urban Shakedancers (straight ahead rock), Fiji Mariners (featuring Col. Bruce Hampton, eclectic mix of rock, blues, jazz and everything else/Capricorn Records) and Grapes (hippie jam band).

THE OFFICE, INC., 54 Skyline Ridge Rd., Bridgewater CT 06752-1727. President: John Luongo. Management firm, music publisher and production company. Estab. 1983. Represents local, regional and international individual artists, groups, songwriters and producer/engineers; currently handles 5 acts. Receives 25% commission. Reviews material for acts.
How to Contact: Submit demo tape by mail. Unsolicited submissions are OK. Prefers cassette (or VHS videocassette if available) with 2 songs and lyric sheet. If seeking management, press kit should include photo, bio, 2 songs on tape or video. SASE. Reports in 2 months.

Music: Mostly **hard rock/pop**, **R&B** and **CHR/top 40**; also **dance**. Works primarily with groups—female vocalists; solo R&B, male or female. Current acts include Joy Winter (pop), Traci Greene (country) and Oliver Who? (R&B).

Tips: "Do your homework before you submit. I am not your guidance counselor. If it's not great I don't want it!"

SCOTT O'MALLEY AND ASSOCIATES AGENCY, P.O. Box 9188, Colorado Springs CO 80932. (719)635-7776. Fax: (719)635-9789. Partner: Steve Weaver. Management firm, booking agency and music publisher (Monitor Publishing). Estab. 1993. Represents individual artists and songwriters from anywhere; currently handles 12 acts. Receives variable commission. Reviews material for acts.

How to Contact: Submit demo tape by mail. Unsolicited submissions are OK. Prefers cassette or VHS videocassette with lyric or lead sheet. If seeking management, press kit should include all current press. Does not return material. Reports in 1-2 months.

Music: Mostly **western**, **folk** and **country/western**. "No hard rock or rap." Current acts include Flash Cadillac (rock '60s-'70s with symphonies), Son of the San Joaquin (western) and The Bobs (a cappella).

*O'MALLEY ARTIST MANAGEMENT, INC., 160 W. Evergreen Ave., Suite 120, Longwood FL 32750. (407)339-9088. Fax: (407)339-5898. E-mail: observer80@aol.com. President: Kevin O'Malley. Management firm. Estab. 1992. Represents individual artists and groups from anywhere; currently handles 2 acts. Receives 15% of gross commission.

How to Contact: Submit demo tape by mail. Unsolicited submissions are OK. Prefers cassette or CD. If seeking management, press kit should include bio, photo, touring history and press. Does not return material. Reports in 1 month.

Music: Mostly **alternative pop**, **alternative rock** and **rock**. Works primarily with bands. Current acts include Spider Monkey (hard-edged pop band, Ambassador Records), Tabitha's Secret (light rock band) and Lather, Rinse, Repeat (alternative rock band).

ON STAGE MANAGEMENT, P.O. Box 679, Bronx NY 10469. (718)798-6980. E-mail: onstagemg t@aol.com. President: Paul M. Carigliano. Management firm and record producer. Estab. 1988. Represents individual artists and/or groups, songwriters from anywhere; currently handles 10 acts. Receives 15-25% commission. Reviews material for acts.

How to Contact: Submit demo tape by mail. Unsolicited submissions are OK. Prefers cassette or VHS videocassette with at least 2 songs, "the more the better." If seeking management, press kit should include cassette or VHS video tape, picture and bio. Does not return material. Reports in 2 weeks.

Music: Mostly **dance music**, **rock**, and **pop**; also **R&B**. Current acts include Lil' Suzy (dance artist), Eclipz and Strings of Time (rock group).

Tips: "Our artists sing songs with positive messages. We don't want songs that glorify violence or are too risque."

OPERATION MUSIC ENTERPRISES, 1400 E. Court St., Ottumwa IA 52501. (515)682-8283. President: Nada C. Jones. Management firm and booking agency. Represents artists, groups and songwriters; currently handles 4 acts. Receives 15% commission. Reviews material for acts.

How to Contact: Submit demo tape by mail. Unsolicited submissions are OK. Prefers cassette (or VHS videocassette if available) and lyric sheet. "Keep material simple. Groups—use *only group* members—don't add extras. Artists should include references." Does not return material. Reports in 6-8 weeks.

Music: Mostly **country**; also **blues**. Works primarily with vocalists and show and dance groups. Current acts include Reesa Kay Jones (country vocalist and recording artist), Chaperell Show and White River Country (country/bluegrass).

*THE OTHER ROAD, 1337 Forest Glen, Cuyahoga Falls OH 44221. Phone/fax: (216)945-4923. E-mail: otherroad@aol.com. Director: Gary Davis. Management firm and record producer. Estab. 1992. Represents individual artists from anywhere; currently handles 5 acts. Receives 15% commission. Reviews material for acts.

How to Contact: Call first and obtain permission to submit a demo. Prefers cassette or DAT, VHS videocassette or CD with 4 or more songs and lyric and/or lead sheet. If seeking management, press kit should include recording (CD preferable, but other formats accepted), photo(s), bio, reviews, etc. "Remember, you're selling yourself." SASE. Reports in 1 month.

Music: Mostly **progressive**, **New Age** and **jazz**; also **classical** and **avante garde**. Works primarily with individual artists who are virtuosos at their instrument. Current acts include Peter Banks (progressive guitarist formerly of Yes and Flash), Rhonda Larson (classical, folk, jazz flutist from Paul Winter Consort) and Richard Johnson (acoustic guitarist combining many styles).

*TOMMY OVERSTREET MUSIC COMPANIES, 3555 S. Mentor Ave., Springfield MO 65804. (417)889-8080. Fax: (417)889-8090. Owner: Tommy Overstreet. Management firm, booking agency

(On Stage Productions), music publisher (Tommy Overstreet Music/BMI) and record company (Tommy Overstreet). Estab. 1969. Represents individual artists, groups and songwriters from anywhere; currently handles 3 acts. Receives 15% commission. Reviews material for acts.

How to Contact: Submit demo tape by mail. Unsolicited submissions are OK. Prefers cassette with 3 songs and lyric sheet. If seeking management, press kit should include pictures (8×10 or 5×7), short biography and tape (no more than 5 songs). SASE. Reports "as soon as it's reasonably possible."

Music: Mostly **country** and **gospel**; also **light rock**. Current acts include Tommy Overstreet (country singer), Ken Fowler (country) and Rick Thompson (country).

Tips: "What you hear on the radio is your competition. If your song or songs don't compete with what you hear, don't send it! No one can 're-write' the amount of material submitted, so it must be professional in content, style and composition."

*PAQUIN ENTERTAINMENT GROUP, 1067 Sherwin Rd., Winnipeg, Manitoba R3H 0T8 **Canada**. (204)694-3104. Contact: Artist Relations. Management firm and booking agency. Estab. 1984. Represents local, regional and international individual artists; currently handles 4 acts. Reviews material for acts.

• See the listing for Branch Group Music in the Music Publishers section.

How to Contact: Submit demo tape by mail. Unsolicited submissions are OK. Prefers cassette or VHS videocassette with 3 songs and lyric sheet. Does not return material. Reports in 4-6 months.

Music: Mostly **children's**, **folk** and **comedy**; also **New Age** and **classical**. Works primarily with family performers. Current acts include Fred Penner (family entertainer/songwriter), Marc Jordan (singer/songwriter), Valdy (entertainer/songwriter) and Al Simmons (family entertainer/songwriter).

JACKIE PAUL ENTERTAINMENT GROUP, INC., 559 Wanamaker Rd., Jenkintown PA 19046. (215)884-3308. Fax: (215)884-1083. President: Jackie Paul. Management and promotion firm (East 2 West Marketing, Promotion and Publicity). Estab. 1985. Represents local and national artists, groups, producers and musicians; currently handles 1 act. Commission varies. Reviews material for acts.

How to Contact: Call first and obtain permission to submit. "Do not write—calls only." Prefers CD or cassette (or VHS videocassette if available) with 1-3 songs and lyric or lead sheets. "It's not mandatory but if possible, I would prefer a videocassette. A video simply helps get the song across visually. Do the best to help portray the image you represent, with whatever resources possible." If seeking management, include no more than 3 copyrighted songs, photo, bio (short and to the point), video (if possible), contact name, telephone number and address in press kit. SASE. Reports in 4-12 weeks.

Music: All types. Works primarily with vocalists (all original acts). Current acts include Blue Eagle (mainstream).

Tips: "If your song is custom-tailored for a particular performer, indicate who it is intended for. Always include lyric sheet with copyrighted material."

THE PERCEPTION WORKS INC., 615 Starkey Rd., Zionsville IN 46077. (317)873-5455. President: Lawrence Klein. Management firm. Estab. 1986. Deals with local, regional or international individual artists and groups; currently handles 4 acts. Receives 10-15% commission. Reviews material for acts.

How to Contact: Write first and obtain permission to submit. Prefers cassette (or VHS videocassette if available) with 4 songs and lyric sheet. If seeking management, include write-up on band, song list, lyrics and demo (CD or tape). Does not return material. Reports in 2 months.

Music: Mostly **rock**, **R&B** and **pop**; also **country** and **blues**. Works primarily with rock bands, R&B bands, blues bands, jazz bands and pop bands. Current acts include Michael Brown Group (jazz), JD and The Ol' #7 Band (country), Hail Mary (rock) and Red Beans and Rice (blues).

PERFORMERS OF THE WORLD INC. (P.O.W.), 8901 Melrose Ave., 2nd Floor, Los Angeles CA 90069-5605. President: Terry Rindal. Agents: Nita Scott, Bruce Eisenberg, Bob Ringe. Booking agency. Estab. 1987. Represents national and international individual artists and groups; currently handles 75 acts. Receives 10-15% commission.

How to Contact: Write first and obtain permission to submit. Prefers cassette (or VHS videocassette if available) with several songs and lyric sheet. If seeking management, include photo, bio, press clippings and recorded material in press kit. Does not return material. Reports in 1 month. "Send SASE for reply."

REFER TO THE CATEGORY INDEX (at the end of this section) to find exactly which companies are interested in the type of music you write.

Music: Mostly **rock**, **world music**, **alternative**, **jazz**, **R&B**, **folk** and **pop**. Current acts include John Cale, David Wilcox, Bryndle, Phoebe Snow, Bootsy Collins and Lydia Lunch.
Tips: "Don't harrass us after you submit—we are looking for artistry and quality—if you're not really prepared please don't waste your time (or ours)."

*PEROM INTERNATIONAL, 2461 Santa Monica Blvd., #C331, Santa Monica CA 90404. (310)450-3677. President: Stephanie Perom. Management firm and music publisher (Pretty Shayna Music/BMI). Estab. 1992. Represents individual artists and songwriters from anywhere; currently handles 4-5 acts. Receives 15% commission. Reviews material for acts.
- Perom International's publishing company, Pretty Shayna Music, is listed in the Music Publishers section.
How to Contact: Submit demo tape by mail. Unsolicited submissions are OK. Prefers cassette with 1-2 songs and lyric sheet. If seeking management, press kit should include photo, bio, any recent press clips and 2 song demo. SASE. Reports in 6-8 weeks.
Music: Mostly **pop**, **dance** and **R&B**; also **pop/rock**. Works primarily with singers, singer/songwriters and songwriter/producers. Current acts include Josie Aiello-Warnell (pop vocalist), Tim Tobias (jazz pop pianist-producer) and Howard Wright (singer/songwriter).

PHIL'S ENTERTAINMENT AGENCY LIMITED, 889 Smyth Rd., Ottawa Ontario K1G 1P4 **Canada**. (613)731-8983. President: Phyllis Woodstock. Booking agency. Estab. 1979. Represents artists and groups; currently handles 50 acts. Receives 10-15% commission. Reviews material for acts.
How to Contact: Submit demo tape by mail. Unsolicited submissions are OK. Prefers cassette (or videocassette) with 4-7 songs. "Be sure the name of artist and date of completion are on the video." Does not return material. Reports in 2-3 weeks.
Music: Mostly **country**; also **country/rock**, **MOR jazz**, **Dixieland** and **old rock 'n' roll**. "We work with show bands, male and female vocalists, bar bands and dance bands on a regular basis." Current acts include Elvis Aaron Presley Jr., The Valley Legends (country) and Eddy & The Stingrays ('50s and '60s dance band).
Tips: "Be professional and business-like. Keep agency supplied with up-to-date promo material and develop entertainment ability. Videotape your live performance, then give yourself an honest review."

*PILLAR RECORDS, P.O. Box 858, Carlisle PA 17013-0858. Phone/fax: (717)249-2536. E-mail: ckelley1@epix.net. Contact: A&R Department. Management firm, music publisher and record company. Estab. 1994. Represents individual artists, groups and songwriters from anywhere; currently handles 2 acts. Receives variable commission. Reviews material for acts.
How to Contact: Submit demo tape by mail. Unsolicited submissions are OK. Prefers cassette or CD with 3 songs and lyric sheet. If seeking management, press kit should include bio, photo, reviews, mailing list, tape or CD. "Please be neat and as professional as possible." Does not return material. Reports in 2-4 weeks.
Music: Mostly **pop/rock**, **rock** and **alternative rock**; also **country**, **blues** and **instrumental**. Works primarily with solo artists and bands. Current acts include Craig Kelley (solo artist, pop/rock).
Tips: "Never give up. Believe in yourself and your songs. If you don't feel good about something you've written, rewrite it! A positive attitude means everything."

PLATINUM EARS LTD., 285 Chestnut St., West Hempstead NY 11552. (516)489-0738. Fax: (516)565-9425. E-mail: platear1@aol.com. President: Mike Siskind. Vice President: Rick Olarsch. Management firm, music publisher (Siskatune Music Publishing Co./BMI). Estab. 1988. Represents national and international individual artists, groups and songwriters; currently handles 2 acts. Receives 20% commission.
- Platinum Ears' publishing company, Siskatune Music Publishing, is listed in the Music Publishers section.
How to Contact: Write first and obtain permission to submit. "No calls!" Prefers cassette with 1-3 songs and lyric sheet. If seeking management, include photo, press, who you've opened for, radio airplay in press kit. SASE. Reports in 3 months.
Music: **Rock** and **pop**. Current acts include Georgi Smith (rock) and Michael Ellis (songwriter).
Tips: "Send us your stuff only if it is *realistically* ready to submit to major label. Otherwise, we'll pass."

*PLATINUM GOLD MUSIC, Suite 1220, 9200 Sunset Blvd., Los Angeles CA 90069. Managers: Steve Cohen/David Cook. Management firm, production company and music publisher. Estab. 1978. Represents local or regional (East or West coasts) individual artists, groups and songwriters; currently handles 4 acts. Receives 20% commission. Reviews material for acts.
How to Contact: Write or call first and obtain permission to submit. Prefers cassette (or VHS videocassette if available) with 3 songs and lyric sheets. If seeking management, include photo, cassette

or videocassette, bio and press clip if available in press kit. Does not return material. Reports in 1-2 months.

Tips: "No ballads. We do not look for potential; be prepared and professional before coming to us—and ready to relocate to West Coast if necessary."

*PLATINUM TRACKS PRODUCTIONS, P.O. Box 5551, Wilmington DE 19808-0551. (302)456-3331. Fax: (302)456-3556. E-mail: plati5267@aol.com. Producer: Dean A. Banks. Management firm, music publisher (Pisces-Leo Music/BMI) and record producer. Estab. 1979. Represents individual artists, groups and songwriters from anywhere; currently handles 3 acts. Receives 20% commission.

How to Contact: Write first and obtain permission to submit a demo. Prefers cassette, or DAT, VHS videocassette or CD with 3 songs and lyric sheet. If seeking management, press kit should include cover letter, newsletter, bio, picture and press clippings. "Send query letters with bounce-back postcards." SASE. Reports in 2 months.

Music: Mostly **pop**, **rock** and **blues**; also **soundtracks**, **country** and **zydeco**. Works primarily with singer/songwriters, solo acts, bands and songwriters. Current acts include Joe Grant (blues-rock guitarist/singer/songwriter), Suzanne Oliver (pop-rock/vocalist/songwriter) and Vic Sadot (cajun/zydeco singer/songwriter).

Tips: "Don't reinvent the wheel, or argue with what works. Send material that is thought provoking and well produced. What's most important to me is the quality of the song, not lavish production. Please keep song length under four minutes."

*PRAIRIE FIRE MUSIC COMPANY, P.O. Box 9411, Mission KS 66201. (913)362-3084. President: Chris Stout. Management firm, booking agency, music publisher (Wild Prairie Publishing/BMI), record company (Prairie Fire Records) and record producer (Chris Stout). Estab. 1991. Represents midwest and southwest individual artists, groups and songwriters; currently handles 10-20 acts. Receives 15% commission. Reviews material for acts.

How to Contact: Submit demo tape by mail. Unsolicited submissions are OK. Prefers cassette with 3-15 songs and lyric and/or lead sheet. If seeking management, press kit should include bio, press releases, promotional materials, photograph and cassette/CD. "If SASE enclosed material will be returned if we have no interest." Reports in 4-6 weeks.

Music: Mostly **country**, **alternative** and **rock**; also **folk**, **New Age** and **crossover**. Works primarily with singer/songwriters and bands. Current acts include Jim Booth (original music, story, singer/songwriter), Matt Pollock (original folk/country/blues singer/songwriter) and Duane Woner (original folk/rock singer/songwriter, bass guitarist).

Tips: "We consider all materials submitted. Don't be afraid to submit a low quality demo. Let us decide."

PRECISION MANAGEMENT, 825 N. King St., #A-1, Hampton VA 23669-2814. (804)728-0046. Fax: (804)728-9144. Representative: Cappriccieo Scates. Management firm, music publisher (Mytrell/BMI). Estab. 1990. Represents individual artists and/or groups, songwriters from anywhere; currently handles 2 acts. Receives 20% commission. Reviews material for acts.

How to Contact: Write first and obtain permission to submit. Prefers cassette or VHS videocassette with 3-4 songs and lyric sheet. If seeking management, press kit should include photo, bio and all relevant press information. SASE. Reports in 4-6 weeks.

Music: Mostly **R&B**, **rap** and **gospel**; also **all types**. Current acts include Mi-L (R&B vocal act) and Different Flavor (R&B vocal act).

Tips: "Send us what you have and we will determine if it is marketable or not. Just put your best foot forward, and we will help you the rest of the way."

*PRESTIGE ARTISTES, "Foxhollow," West End, Nailsea Bristol BS19 2DB **United Kingdom**. Proprietor: David Rees. Management firm and booking agency. Associate company: Lintern Rees Organisation. Estab. 1983. Represents individual artists, groups, songwriters, comedians and specialty acts; currently handles over 200 acts. Receives 15% commission. Reviews material for acts.

How to Contact: Submit demo tape by mail. Unsolicited submissions are OK. Prefers cassette with 3 songs and lyric sheet. If seeking management, press kit should include good demo tape, bio, publicity photos and video if available (UK format). Artist should be based in the UK. Does not return material. Reports in 1 month.

Music: Mostly **MOR**, **pop**, **60s style**, **country** and **rock**. Works primarily with vocal guitarists/keyboards, pop groups, pub/club acts and guitar or keyboard duos. Current acts include Legend (duo), Ocean (four-piece group), Elvis Presley JNR (American artist), Andy Claridge (keyboard/vocalist), The Honeycombs and Mickie Freedom.

Tips: "Do not send more than three songs, your best available. Tell us what you want in the UK—be realistic."

PRO STAR TALENT AGENCY, P.O. Box 290 186, Nashville TN 37229. (615)754-2950. President: Ralph Johnson. Booking agency. Estab. 1960. Represents individual artists and/or groups. Currently handles 10 acts. Receives 15% commission. Reviews material for acts.
How to Contact: Write first and obtain permission to submit. If seeking management, press kit should include photo, demo and bio. SASE. Reports in 2 weeks.
Music: All types. Works primarily with vocalists and bands. Current acts include Stacy Edwards (country pop), Keith Bryant (country singer) and Kristena Crowley (country).

PRO TALENT CONSULTANTS, P.O. Box 1192, Clearlake Oak CA 95423. (707)998-3587. Coordinator: John Eckert. Assistant General Manager: Bryan Hyland. Management firm and booking agency. Estab. 1979. Represents individual artists and groups; currently handles 11 acts. Receives 9-13% commission. Reviews material for acts.
How to Contact: Submit demo tape by mail. Unsolicited submissions are OK. Prefers cassette (or VHS videocassette if available) with at least 4 songs and lyric sheet. "We prefer audio cassette (4 songs). Submit videocassette with live performance only." If seeking management, include an 8 × 10 photo, a cassette or CD of at least 4-6 songs, a bio on group/artist, references and business card or a phone number with address to contact in press kit. Does not return material. Reports in 3-4 weeks.
Music: Mostly **country**, **country/pop** and **rock**. Works primarily with vocalists, show bands, dance bands and bar bands. Current acts include Jon Richard (country singer), The Classics IV featuring Dennis Yost (pop group) and Jack Tatum's Swing Shift (big band).
Tips: "Keep working hard and place yourself with as many contacts as you can—you will succeed with strong determination!"

*PROCESS TALENT, P.O. Box 569, Franklin PA 16323. (814)432-4633. Management firm. Estab. 1970. Represents individual artists and groups from anywhere; currently handles 5-7 acts. Receives 10% commission. Reviews material for acts.
How to Contact: Submit demo tape by mail. Unsolicited submissions are OK. Prefers cassette or DAT with 2-4 songs and lyric and/or lead sheet. If seeking management, press kit should include demo, photo and bio. SASE. Reports in 1 week.
Music: Mostly **country**. Works primarily with country singers and bands. Current acts include the Junie Lou Show, Debbie Sue and Larry and Joan Pieper and the Hoe Down Country Band.

*PRODUCTIONS UNLIMITED, 6107 Elmendorf Dr., Suitland MD 20746. (301)568-1100. Fax: (301)736-6290. Managers: David J. Galinsky and Jennie Souder. Management firm and booking agency. Represents individual artists, groups and songwriters from anywhere. Receives 15% commission. Reviews material for acts.
How to Contact: Call first and obtain permission to submit a demo. Prefers cassette or CD. If seeking management, press kit should include tape or CD, picture, promo songlist and list of recent performances. Does not return material. Reports in 6 weeks.
Music: Mostly **rock (alternative, college), blues/R&B** and **country**; also **jazz** and **dance companies**. Works primarily with bands, soloists and singer/songwriters. Current acts include Genghis Angus (alternative rock band), Bobby Rush (blues/R&B), A La Carte Brass & Percussion (jazz) and Tommy Lepson & The Lazyboys (R&B).

*PROFESSIONAL ARTIST MANAGEMENT, LTD., P.O. Box 755, Shelburne VT 05482. (800)610-7625. Fax: (802)862-2899. E-mail: profartist@aol.com. General Manager: Tom Hughes. Management firm. Estab. 1994. Represents northeast and New York individual artists and groups; currently handles 10 acts. Receives 10-20% sliding commission. Reviews material for acts.
How to Contact: Submit demo tape by mail. Unsolicited submissions are OK. Prefers cassette, DAT, VHS videocassette or CD with 4 or more songs. If seeking management, press kit should include any commercial releases, reviews and airplay. Artist's background—other bands/acts, credits etc. SASE. Reports in 2 weeks.
Music: Mostly **alternative metal** and **acoustic blues/folk**.
Tips: "Be as serious and dedicated to pursuing the creative side of your career as we will be about managing the business side."

*RADIOACTIVE, 245 E. 54th St., New York NY 10022. (212)315-1919. Agent: Kenjamin Franklin. Booking and talent agency. Estab. 1983. Represents individual artists, groups and broadcasters from anywhere; currently handles 10 acts. Receives 10% commission. Reviews material for acts.
How to Contact: Submit demo tape by mail. Unsolicited submissions are OK. "Please do not phone." Prefers cassette or video with 3 songs and lyric sheet. If seeking management, press kit should include bio, press clippings, photo and 3 radio-friendly original songs. "Label all cassettes with phone number." Does not return material. Reports in 3 weeks. "We only call upon further interest."
Music: Mostly **modern rock**, **ballads** and **AAA**; also **A/C** and **pop/CHR**. Current acts include Ambrosia.

RAINBOW COLLECTION LTD., 4501 Spring Creek Rd., Bonita Springs FL 33923. (914)947-6978. Executive Producer: Richard (Dick) O'Bitts. Management firm, record company (Happy Man Records) and music publisher (Rocker Music, Happy Man Music). Represents individual artists, groups, songwriters and producers; currently handles 3 acts. Receives 10-20% commission. Reviews material for acts.

● Rainbow Collection's publishing affiliate, Rocker Music/Happy Man Music, is listed in the Music Publishers section, and their record label, Happy Man Records, is listed in the Record Companies section.

How to Contact: Submit demo tape by mail. Unsolicited submissions are OK. Prefers cassette (or VHS videocassette of live performance, if available) with 4 songs and lyric sheet. If seeking management, include photos, bio and tapes in press kit. SASE. Reports in 1 month.

Music: Mostly **country**, **pop** and **rock**. Works primarily with writer/artists and groups of all kinds. Current acts include Holly Ronick, Colt Gipson (traditional country), Overdue (rock), Flo Carter and the Bengter Sisters (gospel), The Challengers (country pop), Carl Hausman (instrumental) and Crosswinds (rock).

RANA INTERNATIONAL AFFILIATES, INC., P.O. Box 934273, Margate FL 33442-8034. Fax: (954)427-1819. President: Raffaele A. Nudo. Vice President: John Gaglione. Creative Director: John Dayton. Management firm, music publisher and record company (Chrismarie Records). Estab. 1990. Represents individual artists, groups and songwriters from anywhere; currently represents 7 acts. Receives 10-15% commission. Reviews material for acts.

● See their listing in the Music Publishers section, as well as the listing for Chrismarie Records in the Record Companies section.

How to Contact: Submit demo tape by mail. Unsolicited submissions are OK. Prefers cassette (or VHS videocassette) with 3-4 songs and lyric sheet. If seeking management, press kit should include bio and photos. Include SASE. Does not return material. Reports in 12-16 weeks.

Music: Mostly **pop**, **rock** and **ballads**; also **country**, **R&B** and **new music**. Primarily works with singer/songwriters, bands and performance artists. Current acts include Niko (singer/songwriter), Festa (pop), Xavier (singer/songwriter) and Adamos (singer/songwriter).

Tips: "We are working both in the USA and Europe. Our European offices and Reggio Emilia, in Milan Italy, have featured our clients on regional/national radio and television. So if you are serious about this business and want to pursue your dream, send in the material as we've requested, stay positive and have faith in your talent. All submissions must include name, phone number, etc. on all items. Ciao!"

*RAZ MANAGEMENT CO., Suite 1203, 161 West 54 St., New York NY 10019. (212)757-1289. Fax: (212)265-5726. E-mail: zeevon@aol.com. President: Ron Zeelens. Management firm. Estab. 1983. Represents individual artists and/or groups from anywhere; currently handles 4 acts. Receives 20% commission. Reviews material for acts.

How to Contact: Submit demo tape by mail. Unsolicited submissions are OK. Prefers cassette. If seeking management, press kit should include demo, photo, bio, press. SASE. Reports in 1-2 months.

Music: Mostly **rock**, **pop** and **metal**. Works primarily with bands and singer/songwriters. Current acts include Tom Lavin (blues singer/songwriter), Kim Masters (pop singer/songwriter), Mike Hickey (metal songwriter) and Andrew McIntyre (pop singer/songwriter).

*RDR MUSIC GROUP, 299 Lesmill Rd., Toronto, Ontario M3B 2V1 **Canada**. Phone/fax: (416)445-3077. E-mail: rdrmusic@interlog.com. Contact: Nancy Wilson. Management firm and record company (Rosedale Records). Represents local and regional individual artists; currently handles 1 act.

How to Contact: Write or call first and obtain permission to submit a demo. Does not return material.

Music: Mostly **alternative**, also **country**. Current acts includ Rena Gaile (country).

RICHARD REITER PRODUCTIONS, P.O. Box 43135, Upper Montclair NJ 07043. (201)857-2935. President: Richard Reiter. Management firm, booking agency, music publisher (Marchael Music/ASCAP) and record company (City Pigeon Records). Estab. 1974. Represents local individual artists, groups and songwriters; currently handles 4 acts. Receives 15% commission. Reviews material for acts.

How to Contact: Write first and obtain permission to submit. Prefers cassette with 3-6 songs and lyric sheet. If seeking management, "include nice folder with logo, 8×10 glossy photos (that print media will find exciting and print), enticing description of music act, reviews (don't pad it) and performing credits in press kit." Does not return material. Reports in 2 weeks.

Music: Mostly **jazz**, **R&B** and **pop**. Works primarily with instrumental jazz groups/artists, vocalists of jazz/swing. Current acts include Crossing Point (fusion), Richard Reiter Swing Band and Tricia Slafta (swing jazz vocalist).

*RELAX PRODUCTIONS, 7 Old Highway 63 South #20, P.O. Box 10154, Columbia MO 65205-4002. (573)442-2631. Fax: (573-875-6189. E-mail: relax@thoughtport.com. Website: http://www.thoughtport.com/cds/relax.html. Owner: Patrick Rule. Management firm, college radio/Internet promotions. Estab. 1983. Represents groups from anywhere; currently handles 2-3 acts. Receives 25% commission. Reviews material for acts.
How to Contact: Write first and obtain permission to submit a demo. Prefers DAT, videocassette or CD. If seeking management, press kit should include DAT, bio and photo. SASE. Reports in 3 months.
Music: Mostly **alternative**; also **reggae**. Current acts include Fears For Art (alternative band), If 6 Were 9 (alternative band) and Jimmy's New Wheelchair (punk band).
Tips: "Be unique, creative, and have an original sound. Don't try to imitate, try to innovate. Finished product is always a plus."

RENAISSANCE ENTERTAINMENT GROUP, P.O. Box 1222, Mountainside NJ 07092-1222. Director: Kevin A. Joy. Management firm, booking agency, record company (Suburan Records) record producer (Onyx Music, Bo²Legg Productions). Estab. 1992. Represents local and regional individual artists, groups, songwriters. Currently handles 3 acts. Receives 20% commission. Reviews material for acts.
How to Contact: Submit demo tape by mail. Unsolicited submissions are OK. Prefers cassette with 3 songs and lyric or lead sheet. If seeking management, press kit should include pictures and bio. Does not return material. Reports in 5 weeks.
Music: Mostly **R&B**, **rap** and **club**. Works primarily with R&B groups, rap and vocalists. Current acts include Hillside Stranglers (rap), Kendall Johnson (R&B) and Mark Charlie (rap).
Tips: "Hard work doesn't guarantee success, but without it you don't have a chance."

RGK ENTERTAINMENT GROUP, P.O. Box 243, Station C, Toronto Ontario M6J 3P4 **Canada**. (416)516-8267. Fax: (416)516-3557. Contact: Ron Kitchener. Management firm and booking agency. Estab. 1988. Represents individual artists, groups and songwriters from anywhere; currently handles 2 acts. Receives 15% commission. Reviews material for acts.
How to Contact: Submit demo tape by mail. Unsolicited submissions are OK. Prefers cassette or VHS videocassette with 2-4 songs and lyric sheet. If seeking management, press kit should include cassette of recent material, photos, recent press and bio. Does not return material. Reports in 1 month.
Music: Mostly **country**, **rock** and **folk**; also **roots**. Works primarily with singer/songwriters. Current acts include James Owen Bush and Jason McCoy (country singer/songwriters).
Tips: "Submit a cross section of tempos within your style of music."

*RHYME SYNDICATE MANAGEMENT, 451 N. Reese Place, Burbank CA 91506. (818)563-1030. Fax: (818)563-2826. Contact: Paul Filippone. Management firm. Represents individual artists, groups and songwriters from anywhere; currently handles 7 acts. Receives 15-20% commission.
How to Contact: Submit demo tape by mail. Unsolicited submissions are OK. Prefers cassette, DAT or VHS videocassette with 4 songs. If seeking management, press kit should include photo, bio, press ("although none of this is very important compared to the tape"). Does not return material. Reports in 1-2 months (artist should call).
Music: Mostly **alternative rock**, **rock**, **folk/acoustic**; also **all types**. Works primarily with bands. Current acts include Ice-T (rapper, Rhyme Syndicate Records), Body Count (hard rock band, Virgin Records) and Silver Jet (rock/pop band, Virgin Records).

JOEY RICCA, JR.'S ENTERTAINMENT AGENCY, 408 S. Main St., Milltown NJ 08850. (201)287-1230. Owner/President: Joseph Frank Ricca, Jr. Management firm and booking agency. Estab. 1985. Represents individual artists, groups and songwriters; currently handles 80 acts. Receives 10-15% commission. Reviews material for acts.
How to Contact: Write or call for permission to submit. "We prefer that all material be copyrighted and that a letter be sent right before submitting material, but neither of these is essential." Prefers cassette (or videocassette if available) with 3-4 songs and lyric or lead sheets. If seeking management, press kit should include tape (cassette or video) 8 × 10 promo photo, bios, photocopy news clippings of performances. SASE. Reports in 6-8 weeks.
Music: Mostly **love songs/ballads**, **songs for big band vocalists**, and **soft jazz/Latin**; also **good commercial material**. Works with show bands, dance bands and bar bands. Current acts include Maria Angela, Donny "Z," Anthony Paccone, One Trak Mind and Diamond.

 THE ASTERISK before a listing indicates that the listing is new in this edition. New markets are often the most receptive to unsolicited submissions.

Tips: "Good lyrics and strong musical arrangements are essential if our vocalists are to select a song they would like to sing. No matter what others may think of your work submit the songs you like best that you wrote. I look for good love songs, ballads and Broadway play type compositions. No metal."

DIANE RICHARDS WORLD MANAGEMENT, INC., 530 Manhattan Ave., New York NY 10027. Phone/fax: (212)663-6730. E-mail: drworldmgm@aol.com. President: Diane Richards. Management firm and record company (Third Eye Records, Inc.). Estab. 1994. Represents individual artists, groups, songwriters and producers from anywhere. Currently handles 5 acts. Receives 20-25% commission. Reviews material for acts.
How to Contact: Submit demo tape by mail. Unsolicited submissions are OK. Prefers cassette. If seeking management, press kit should include photograph, biography, cassette tape, telephone number and address. Does not return material. Reports in 4-6 weeks.
Music: Mostly **dance**, **pop** and **rap**; also **New Age**, **A/C** and **jazz**. Works primarily with pop and dance acts, and songwriters who also are recording artists. Current acts include Carlton Singer (R&B/pop-Sony) Myquan (hip hop/R&B), Sister Moon (5 piece self-contained band) and Big L (single rap artist on Columbia Records).

RIOHCAT MUSIC, P.O. Box 764, Hendersonville TN 37077-0764. (615)824-1435. Contact: Robert Kayne. Management firm, booking agency, record company (Avita Records) and music publisher. Estab. 1975. Represents individual artists and groups; currently handles 4 acts. Receives 20% commission. Reviews material for acts.
How to Contact: Submit demo tape by mail. Unsolicited submissions are OK. Prefers cassette and lead sheet. Does not return material. Reports in 1 month.
Music: Mostly **contemporary jazz** and **fusion**. Works primarily with jazz ensembles. Current acts include Group Tachoir (jazz), Tachoir Duo (jazz) and Tachoir/Manakes Duo (jazz).
Tips: "Be organized, neat and professional."

A.F. RISAVY, INC., 1312 Vandalia, Collinsville IL 62234. (618)345-6700. Divisions include Artco Enterprises, Golden Eagle Records, Swing City Music and Swing City Sound. Contact: Art Risavy. Management firm and booking agency. Estab. 1960. Represents artists, groups and songwriters; currently handles 50 acts. Receives 10% commission. Reviews material for acts.
How to Contact: Submit demo tape by mail. Unsolicited submissions are OK. Prefers 7½ ips reel-to-reel or cassette (or VHS videocassette if available) with 2-6 songs and lyric sheet. If seeking management, include pictures, bio and VHS videocassette in press kit. SASE. Reports in 2 weeks.
Music: Mostly **rock**, **country**, **MOR** and **top 40**.

ROCK OF AGES PRODUCTIONS, 517 Northlake Blvd. #4, N. Palm Beach FL 33408. (407)848-1500. Fax: (407)848-2400. President/Agency Director: Joe Larson. Booking agent. Estab. 1980. Represents individual artists and groups from anywhere. Currently handles 500 acts. Receives 15-25% commission. Reviews material for acts.
How to Contact: Submit demo tape by mail. Unsolicited submissions are OK. Prefers cassette or VHS videocassette with 3 or more songs and lead sheet. If seeking management, press kit should include videocassette and/or audio cassette, relevant press and bio, including recent photo. SASE. Reports in 3 months.
Music: Mostly **top 40**, **country/western** and **rock**; also **gospel** and **opera**. Works primarily with bands, singers, singer/songwriters. Current acts include Andrew Epps (ballad singer/songwriter), John Michael Ferrari (singer/songwriter) and Paola Semprini (opera star).

*ROCK WHIRLED MUSIC MANAGEMENT, 1423 N. Front St., Harrisburg PA 17102. (717)236-2386. E-mail: eclark@epix.net. Director: Philip Clark. Management firm, booking agency, publicists. Estab. 1987. Represents individual artists and/or groups from anywhere; currently handles 10 acts. Receives 10-25% commission. Reviews material for acts.
How to Contact: Submit demo tape by mail. Unsolicited submissions are OK. Prefers cassette. If seeking management, press kit should include bio, photo, song list, venue list, description of performance frequency, equipment needed, goals. SASE. Reports in 3 weeks.
Music: Mostly **rock**, **alternative** and **folk**. Works primarily with soloist singer/instrumentalists, duo acoustic acts, bands. Current acts include Every Day @ Six (alternative fusion), Cameron Molloy (country fusion) and Diane Diachishin (folk).
Tips: "Be brief, clear, focused in approach. Approach a variety of other agents and managers to get a feel for which companies make the best match. We look for clients who wish to work specifically with us, not just any firm."

ROCKY MOUNTAIN MANAGEMENT, Box 3660, Station B, Calgary Alberta T2M 4M4 **Canada**. (403)247-9100. Fax: (403)286-9708. E-mail: rockymtn@canuck.com. Website: http://www.rocky mtncd.com. President: Bryan Taylor. Management firm, booking agency and music publisher (Wordworks Publishing Inc.). Estab. 1990. Represents individual artists, groups, songwriters from anywhere; currently handles 7 acts. Receives 10-25% commission (depending on services required). Reviews material for acts.

How to Contact: Submit demo tape by mail. Unsolicited submissions are OK. Prefers cassette or CD with 3 songs and lyric sheet. If seeking management, press kit should include bio, recorded material, picture. SAE and IRC. Reports in 2 months.

Music: Mostly **country**, **roots** and **acoustic**; also **First Nations**. Works primarily with groups, singer/songwriters, songwriters. Current acts include Laura Vinson (folk), Danielle French (folk/pop), The Delevantes (roots/rock) and Brian Levi (songwriter).

Tips: "We are very open and easy to work with and are generally interested in performers who write their own songs."

CHARLES R. ROTHSCHILD PRODUCTIONS INC., 330 E. 48th St., New York NY 10017. (212)421-0592. President: Charles R. Rothschild. Booking agency. Estab. 1971. Represents local, regional and international individual artists, groups and songwriters; currently handles 17 acts. Receives 25% commission. Reviews material for acts.

How to Contact: Call first and obtain permission to submit. Prefers cassette or CD (or VHS videocassette if available) with 1 song and lyric and lead sheet. If seeking management, include cassette, photo, bio and reviews. SASE. Reports in 2 months.

Music: Mostly **rock**, **pop** and **folk**; also **country** and **jazz**. Current acts include Judy Collins (pop singer/songwriter), Leo Kottke (guitarist/composer) and Emmylou Harris (country songwriter).

*JIMMY RUFF PRODUCTION, 1921 Union 2D, Benton Harbor MI 49022. (616)925-9111. President: James Ruff. Management firm and record producer (JRP Records). Estab. 1966. Represents individual artists, groups and songwriters from artists anywhere; currently handles 1 act. Receives 10% commission. Reviews material for acts.

How to Contact: Submit demo tape by mail. Unsolicited submissions are OK. Prefers cassette with 2 songs and lyric sheet. SASE. Reports in 3 weeks.

Music: Mostly **gospel**, **pop**, **rock**; also **blues**, **rap**, **country**. Works primarily with singers. Current acts include Shadow Casters (rock group).

T. RUSSELL PRODUCTIONS, P.O. Box 36155, Houston TX 77236. (713)981-7278. Fax: (713)988-2324. Manager: Damon Russell. Management firm and music publisher. Estab. 1994. Represents local individual artists; currently handles 3 acts. Receives 25% commission. Reviews material for acts.

How to Contact: Submit demo tape by mail. Unsolicited submissions are OK. Prefers cassette or DAT with 2-4 songs and lyric sheet. If seeking management, press kit should include "8 × 10 black and white photos, demo tape with at least 2 songs (1 mid-tempo or fast and one ballad), a brief handwritten or typed bio on why you want to be an artist and other personal information and goals. Please state if you are currently under a management contract at present date." SASE. Reports in 2 weeks.

Music: Mostly **R&B**, **rap** and **jazz/blues**; also **Tejano**, **pop** and **rock**.

RUSTRON MUSIC PRODUCTIONS, Send all artist song submissions to: 1156 Park Lane, West Palm Beach FL 33417-5957. (407)686-1354. E-mail: p0086476@pbfreenet.seflin.lib.fl.us. Main Office: 42 Barrack Hill Rd., Ridgefield CT 06877. ("Main office does not review new material—only South Florida Branch office does.") Artist Consultants: Rusty Gordon and Davilyn Whims. Composition Management: Ron Caruso. Management firm, booking agency, music publisher (Rustron Music Publishers/BMI and Whimsong Publishing/ASCAP) and record producer (Rustron Music Productions). Estab. 1970. Represents individuals, groups and songwriters; currently handles 25 acts. Receives 10-25% commission. Reviews material for acts.

• See Rustron's listings in the Music Publishers, Record Companies and Record Producers sections.

How to Contact: Submit demo tape by mail. Unsolicited submissions are OK. Send cassette with 3-6 songs (CD/cassette produced for sale preferred). Provide lyric or lead sheet for every song in the submission. "SASE required for all correspondence." Reports in 2-4 months.

Music: Blues (**country folk/urban**, **Southern**), **country** (**rock**, **blues**, **progressive**), **easy listening**, **soft rock** (**ballads**), **women's music**, **R&B**, **folk/rock**, **New Age instrumentals** and **New Age folk fusion**. Current acts include Gary Jess (New Age fusion), Jayne Margo-Reby (adult contemporary fusions) and Boom Slang Swampsinger (country/folk, road house music).

Tips: "Send cover letter, typed lyric sheets for all songs. Carefully mix demo, don't drown the vocals, three to six songs in a submission. Prefer independent CD/cassette (store-ready product). Send photo if artist is seeking marketing and/or production assistance. Very strong hooks, definitive melody, evolved concepts, unique and unpredictable themes. Flesh out a performing sound unique to the artist."

MIKE RYMKUS MANAGEMENT AND PROMOTIONS, 21610 Park Wick Lane, Katy TX 77450. (713)492-0423. President: Mike Rymkus. Management firm. Estab. 1970. Represents local and regional (Texas) individual artists and songwriters; currently handles 1 act. Receives 20% commission. Reviews material for acts.
How to Contact: Submit demo tape by mail. Unsolicited submissions are OK. Prefers cassette. If seeking management, press kit should include a good bio, a good picture, 3 of your best songs on cassette. "Can not have any management ties or record deals." SASE "and I reserve the right to keep anything I receive." Reports in 2 months.
Music: Mostly **country**. Works primarily with singer/songwriters. Current acts include Tommy Lee (country singer/songwriter).

S.T.A.R.S. PRODUCTIONS, 1 Professional Quadrangle, 2nd Floor, Sparta NJ 07871. (201)729-7242. Fax: (201)729-2979. President: Steve Tarkanish. Booking agency. Estab. 1983. Represents individual artists, groups, songwriters from anywhere; currently handles 35-40 acts. Receives 15-20% commission. Reviews material for acts.
How to Contact: Submit demo tape by mail. Unsolicited submissions are OK. Prefers cassette with lyric or lead sheet. If seeking management, press kit should include biography, photo, cassette, calendar and song list. Does not return material. Reports in 2 months.
Music: Mostly **rock**, **alternative** and **country**; also **singles/duos** and **folk**. Primarily works with bands. Current acts include The Nerds (classic/party rock), Dog Voices (classic/alternative rock) and Soft Parade (Doors tribute).

SAFFYRE MANAGEMENT, 1200 Riverside Dr., Suite 371, Burbank CA 91506. (818)842-4368. Fax: (310)453-4478. President: Esta G. Bernstein. Management firm and booking agent. Estab. 1990. Represents individual artists, groups and songwriters from anywhere. Currently handles 1 act. Receives 10% commission. Reviews material for acts.
How to Contact: Submit demo tape by mail. Unsolicited submissions are OK. Prefers cassette, bio and photos with 3 songs and lyric sheet. Does not return material. Reports in 2 weeks (only if interested).
Music: Mostly **rock**, **top 40** and **jazz**; also **new wave** and **metal**. "We work mostly with bands and solo artists; our main objective is to obtain recording deals and contracts, while advising our artists on their careers and business relationships." Current artists include Jow (top 40 funk/rock).
Tips: "If you will have a better chance breaking into the music industry if your material sounds like no one else's."

SA'MALL MANAGEMENT, P.O. Box 8442, Universal City CA 91608. (818)506-8533. Fax: (818)506-8534. Manager: Nikki Ray. Management firm. Estab. 1990. Represents local, regional and international individual artists, groups and songwriters; currently handles 5 acts. Receives 25% commission. Reviews material for acts.
 • See the listings for Pollybyrd Publications in the Music Publishers section and MCI Entertainment Group in the Record Companies section.
How to Contact: Write or call first and obtain permission to submit. Prefers cassette with 2 songs and lyric and lead sheet. If seeking management, press kit should include picture, bio and tape. SASE. Reports in 2 months.
Music: **All types**. Current acts include I.B. Phyne, Suzette Cuseo, The Band Aka and LeJenz.
Tips: "Do your homework and learn your craft. Be realistic—are you any good?"

*SANDCASTLE PRODUCTIONS, 236 Sebert Road, Forest Gate, London E7 ONP **United Kingdom**. Phone: (0181)534-8500. Senior Partner: Simon Law. Management firm, music publisher (Sea Dream Music/PRS, Scarf Music Publishing and Really Free Music/PRS, Chain of Love Music, Crimson Flame) and record company (Plankton Records, Embryo Arts/Belgium and Gutta/Sweden) and record producers. Estab. 1980. Represents individual artists, groups and songwriters; currently handles 5 acts. Receives 10% commission. Reviews material for acts.
 • See the listings for Sea Dream Music in the Music Publishers and Music Print Publishers sections, and Plankton Records in the Record Companies section.
How to Contact: Write first and obtain permission to submit demo. Prefers cassette with 3 songs and lyric sheet. SAE and IRC. Reports in 3 months.
Music: Mostly **funk/rock**, **blues** and **rock**. Works primarily with bands or artists with a Christian bias to their material. Current acts include Fresh Claim (funk rock), Asylum (pop) and Marc Catley (folk).
Tips: "Have a commitment to communication of something real and honest in 'live' work."

*LONNY SCHONFELD PRODUCTIONS, P.O. Box 460086, Garland TX 75046. (214)497-1616. President: Lonny Schonfeld. Management firm (G-Town Entertainment), promotions, public relations and music publisher (Lonny Tunes/BMI). Estab. 1988. Represents local, regional or interna-

tional individual artists, groups and songwriters; currently handles 5 acts. Receives 15% commission. Reviews material for acts.
 • Lonny Schonfeld's publishing company, Lonny Tunes, is listed in the Music Publishers section, and his record label, Lonny Tunes Records, is in the Record Companies section.
How to Contact: Submit demo tape—unsolicited submissions are OK. Prefers cassette with 3-5 songs and lyric sheet. If seeking management, include 8 × 10 head shot, bio, studio demo, live demo. Does not return unsolicited material. Reports in 6-8 weeks.
Music: Mostly **country, pop**, and **rock**. Works primarily with vocal groups and comedians. Current acts include Randy Stout (singer/songwriter), Pauper (pop) and Doug Richardson (comedian).
Tips: "Make sure your songs are commercial. Listen to the current 'hits' to see how your song stacks up, because that's what you're competing with. Also, be as professional as possible—do not send garage tapes."

CRAIG SCOTT ENTERTAINMENT, P.O. Box 1722, Paramus NJ 07653-1722. (201)587-1066. Fax: (201)587-0481. E-mail: chornak@aol.com. Management firm. Estab. 1985. Represents individual artists and/or groups from anywhere; currently handles 3 acts. Commission varies. Reviews material for acts.
How to Contact: Call first and obtain permission to submit. Prefers cassette. If seeking management, press kit should include tape/CD, bio, picture, relevant press. Does not return material. Reports in 3-4 weeks.
Music: Mostly **jazz**. Current acts include Resolve (alternative), Poole (alternative) and Tom Gioia (songwriter/artist).
Tips: "Remember, if it was easy everybody would be successful!"

SECRET AGENT MEDIA ENTERTAINMENT GROUP, LTD., 6351 W. Montrose, Suite 333, Chicago IL 60634. (312)725-2525. Fax: (312)789-6601. E-mail: agent@ripro.com. Contact: Agent. Management firm. Estab. 1994. Represents individual artists, groups and songwriters from anywhere. Currently handles 5 acts. Receives 20% commission.
How to Contact: Submit demo tape by mail. Unsolicited submissions are OK. Prefers cassette or DAT with 2 songs and lyric sheet. If seeking management, press kit should include history of act. Does not return material. Reports in 1 month.
Music: All types. Current acts include Pete Special (pop/R&B) and Batteries Not Included (pop).

WILLIAM SEIP MANAGEMENT, INC., 1615 Highland Rd., Kitchener, Ontario N2G 3W5 **Canada**. (519)741-1252. Fax: (519)742-3398. Manager: William Seip. Management firm. Estab. 1978. Represents individual artists, groups, songwriters from anywhere; currently handles 3 acts. Receives 15-20% commission. Reviews material for acts.
How to Contact: Submit demo tape by mail. Unsolicited submissions are OK. Prefers cassette (or videocassette) and lyric sheet. If seeking management, press kit should include tape, lyric sheet, bio and photo. Does not return material. Reports in 2 months.
Music: Mostly **rock** and **country**. Current acts include Helix, Ray Lyell and The Result.

*SELLOUT! MANAGEMENT, P.O. Box 4160, Los Angeles CA 90078. (213)644-1595. Fax: (213)644-1596. E-mail: sellout@earthlink.net. Manager: J. Scavo. Management firm. Estab. 1993. Represents local groups and artists from anywhere; currently handles 5 acts. Receives variable commission. Reviews material for acts.
How to Contact: Submit demo tape by mail. Unsolicited submissions are OK. Prefers cassette or VHS videocassette. If seeking management, press kit should include photo, music, video, press and itinerary. Does not return material. Reports in 1 month.
Music: Mostly **alternative rock, death metal/rock** and **disco**. Works primarily with bands. Current acts include Possum Dixon (alternative band specializing in science fiction themes), Red 5 (punk/pop specializing in yelping) and Down By Law (get-your-ass-out-of-the-way punk).
Tips: "Trust no one."

*SEPETYS ENTERTAINMENT GROUP, 1223 Wilshire Blvd., Suite 804, Santa Monica CA 90403. Fax: (310)581-9353. E-mail: sepetys@aol.com. President: Ruta E. Sepetys. Management firm. Estab. 1994. Represents individual artists, groups and songwriters from anywhere; currently handles 4 acts. Receives 15% commission. Reviews material for acts.
How to Contact: Submit demo tape by mail. Unsolicited submissions are OK. Prefers cassette with lyric sheet. If seeking management, press kit should include press clips, tape, lyrics, bio and photo. "No phone calls please." SASE. Reports in 1 month.
Music: All types. Works primarily with bands, singer/songwriters and individual artists. Current acts include Steve Vai (guitarist on Relativity/Sony), Stain (band on Malicious Vinyl/Capitol), Danny Peck (singer/songwriter) and Hair of the Dog (rock band).

*SERGE ENTERTAINMENT GROUP, P.O. Box 672216, Marietta GA 30067-0037. (770)850-9560. Fax: (770)850-9646. E-mail: musmorsels@aol.com. President: Sandy Serge. Management firm and shopping firm/songplugger. Estab. 1987. Represents individual artists, groups, songwriters from anywhere. Currently handles 16 acts. Receives 15-25% commission.

How to Contact: Submit demo tape by mail. Unsolicited submissions are OK. Prefers cassette, VHS videocassette (press kit optional) with 4 songs and lyric sheet. If seeking management, press kit should include 8×10 photo, bio, max of 4 press clips, VHS videocassette, performance schedule and demo tape. "All information submitted must include name, address and phone number on each item." Does not return submissions. Reports in 4-6 weeks.

Music: Mostly **rock**, **pop** and **country**; also **R&B** and **instrumental**. Works primarily with singer/songwriters, bands. Current acts include The Steve Grimm Band (rock), Masino (hard rock band) and Marty Gassner (singer/songwriter).

Tips: "Send only your best material; songs that are catchy, but different with lyrics that tell a story and paint word pictures. We have acquired numerous publishing deals for all clients. Member of WMBA, NARAS, Atlanta Songwriters Association, Songwriters of Wisconsin. We have professional relationships with over 300 publishers and have connections at all the major labels."

*THE SEWITT GROUP, 9 Ash Court, Highland Mills NY 10930. (914)928-8481. Fax: (914)928-8463. President: George Sewitt. Management and consulting firm. Estab. 1983. Represents individual artists, groups and songwriters from anywhere; currently handles 2 acts. Receives 20-25% commission. Reviews material for acts.

How to Contact: Call first and obtain permission to submit demo. Prefers cassette or VHS videocassette with 3 songs and lyric sheet, and photo. "Quality of material is far more important than production values." Does not return material. Reports in 6 weeks.

Music: Mostly **rock**, **pop** and **country**; also **soul/R&B**, **rap** and **heavy metal**. Works primarily with solo artists, bands, singer/songwriters. Current acts include Ace Frehley (singer/guitarist) and Peter Criss (singer/drummer).

Tips: "Take your time putting the song together. Keep your ideas to the point. There is nothing wrong with being artistic as well as commercial. The song must have a good feel."

*SHANKMAN DEBLASIO MELINA, INC./SUNSET BLVD. ENTERTAINMENT, 740 N. La Brea Ave., 1st Floor, Los Angeles CA 90038. (213)933-9977. Fax: (213)933-0633. E-mail: sbe740 @aol.com. Contact: A&R Manager. Management firm, music publisher, record company. Estab. 1979. Represents individual artists, groups, songwriters from anywhere. Reviews material for acts.

How to Contact: Write first and obtain permission to submit demo. Prefers cassette with lyric sheet. Does not return material. Reports in 3 months.

SHAPIRO & COMPANY, C.P.A. (A Professional Corporation), 9229 Sunset Blvd., Suite 607, Los Angeles CA 90069. (310)278-2303. Certified Public Accountant: Charles H. Shapiro. Business management firm. Estab. 1979. Represents individual recording artists, groups and songwriters. Fee varies.

How to Contact: Write or call first to arrange personal interview.

Music: Mostly **rock** and **pop**. Works primarily with recording artists as business manager.

Tips: "We assist songwriters with administration of publishing."

*JIM SHARP MANAGEMENT, 121 17th Ave. South, Nashville TN 37203. (615)256-6848. Fax: (615)742-1123. Owner: Jim Sharp. Management firm. Estab. 1992. Represents individual artists and songwriters from anywhere. Currently handles 4 acts. Receives 15% commission. Reviews material for acts.

How to Contact: Call first and obtain permission to submit. Prefers cassette with 4 songs and lyric sheet. If seeking management, press kit should include photo and bio. Does not return material. Reports in 2 months.

Music: Mostly **country**, **Christian** and **blues**. Works primarily with country singer/songwriters. Current acts include Blake Shelton (country singer/songwriter), Mark Acan (country singer/songwriter) and Debra Dudley (country singer).

MICKEY SHERMAN ARTIST MANAGEMENT & DEVELOPMENT, P.O. Box 20814, Oklahoma City OK 73156. (405)755-0315. President: Mickey Sherman. Management firm. Estab. 1974. Represents individual artists and songwriters; currently handles 4 acts. Receives 10% commission. Reviews material for acts.

● Mickey Sherman's publishing company, Okisher Music, can be found in the Music Publishers section.

How to Contact: Submit demo tape by mail. Unsolicited submissions are OK. Prefers cassette (or VHS videocassette of live performance, if available) with 3 songs and lyric sheet or lead sheet. If seeking management, include thumbnail biography/picture/press clippings and résumé in press kit.

"Keep videos simple. Use good lighting." Does not return material. Reports in 3 months.
Music: Mostly **blues**, **pop** and **country**; also **R&B**, **rock** and **easy listening**. Works primarily with vocalists and showbands. Current acts include Jan Jo (singer/harmonica), Benny Kubiak (fiddler) and Burton Band.
Tips: "Send no more than three demos, lead sheet or legible lyric sheet. Record demos on good quality tape. If you're a performer as well, let us see a video."

SHOWCANA CORPORATION, P.O. Box 4689, Station 'C', Calgary Alberta T2T 5P1 **Canada**. (403)232-1111. Fax: (403)269-4119. E-mail: showcana@cia.com. President: Robert J. Chin. Management firm and production company. Estab. 1980. Represents individual artists, groups and songwriters from anywhere. Currently handles 7 acts. Reviews material for acts.
How to Contact: Submit demo tape by mail. Unsolicited submissions are OK. Prefers cassette, VHS videocassette or CD with 3 songs and lyric or lead sheet. If seeking management, press kit should include current pictures—8 × 10's only, bio info, demo of songs/performance, references. "We've taken on acts that have given us tapes done on a ghetto-blaster. If the songs are good, you know the rest." Does not return material. Reports in 2-6 months.
Music: Mostly **rock**, **country** and **various**; also **New Age**, **rockabilly** and **specialty**. Works primarily with singer/songwriters. Current acts include Rudy Rhodes, Little Tough Guy (rock singer/songwriter), Storm Warning (rock group), Mike Shields (country/rock singer/songwriter) and Calvin Wiggett (country singer).
Tips: "Prepare yourself for the life you've chosen and the highs and lows, which can be extreme. You're dealing with your passion and not just a job to buy time for your passion."

PHILL SHUTE MANAGEMENT PTY. LTD., Box 273, Dulwich Hill NSW 2203 **Australia**. Phone: (02)5692152. Managing Director: Phill Shute. Management firm, booking agency and record company (Big Rock Records). Estab. 1979. Represents local individual artists and groups; currently handles 3 acts. Receives 25% commission. Reviews material for acts.
How to Contact: Submit demo tape by mail—unsolicited submissions are OK. Prefers cassette with 4 songs and lyric sheet. SASE. Reports in 2 months.
Music: Mostly **rock**, **pop** and **R&B**; also **country rock**. Works primarily with rock bands, pop vocalists and blues acts (band and vocalists). Current acts include Chris Turner (blues/guitarist/vocalist), Collage (pop/rock band) and Big Rock Band (rock).
Tips: "Make all submissions well organized (e.g. bio, photo and experience of the act). List areas in which the act would like to work, complete details for contact."

SIDDONS & ASSOCIATES, 584 N. Larchmont Blvd., Hollywood CA 90004. (213)462-6156. Fax: (213)462-2076. President: Bill Siddons. Management firm. Estab. 1972. Represents individual artists and groups from anywhere; currently handles 4 acts. Reviews material for acts.
How to Contact: Write first and obtain permission to submit a demo. Prefers cassette or VHS videocassette with 3 songs and lyric sheet. If seeking management, press kit should include cassette of 3 songs, lyric sheet, VHS videocassette if available, biography, past credits and discography. Does not return material. Reports in 2 months.
Music: All styles. Current acts include David Crosby, Graham Nash and David Lanz (New Age pianist).

SIEGEL ENTERTAINMENT LTD., 101-1648 W. Seventh Ave., Vancouver British Columbia V6J 1S5 **Canada**. (604)736-3896. Fax: (604)736-3464. President: Robert Siegel. Management firm and booking agent. Estab. 1975. Represents individual artists, groups, songwriters from anywhere; currently handles 100 acts (for bookings). Receives 15-20% commission. Reviews material for acts.
How to Contact: Submit demo tape by mail. Unsolicited submissions are OK. Prefers cassette or VHS videocassette with 3 songs and lyric sheet. If seeking management, press kit should include 8 × 10 and cassette and/or video. Does not return material. Reports in 1 month.
Music: Mostly **rock**, **pop** and **country**; also **children's**. Current acts include Falcon Scream (rock group), Michael Behm (rock/pop) and Tim Brecht (pop/children's).

*SILVER BOW MANAGEMENT, 6260 130 St., Surrey, British Columbia V3X 1R6 **Canada**. (604)572-4232. Fax: (604)572-4252. E-mail: 75321.3576@compuserve.com. CEO: Candice James. Management firm, music publisher (Silver Bow Publishing), record company (Saddlestone Records) and record producer (Krazy Cat Productions). Estab. 1988. Represents individual artists, groups, songwriters from anywhere; currently handles 5 acts. Receives 10-20% commission. Reviews material for acts.
   ● See the listings for Saddlestone Publishing in the Music Publishers section; Saddlestone Records in the Record Companies section; and Silver Bow Productions in the Record Producers section.

How to Contact: Submit demo tape by mail. Unsolicited submissions are OK. Prefers cassette with 3 songs and lyric sheet. If seeking management, press kit should include 8 × 10 photo, bio, demo tape or CD with lyric sheets, current itinerary. "Visuals are everything—submit accordingly." SASE. Reports in 3 months.
Music: Mostly **country**, **MOR** and **rock**; also **R&B**, **Christian** and **alternative**. Works primarily with bands, vocalists, singer/songwriters. Current acts include Clancy Wright, Gerry King and Stan Giles.

*SILVER MOON PRODUCTIONS, 2770 S. Maryland Pkwy., Las Vegas NV 89109. (702)735-1444. Fax: (702)735-6166. Owner: Charles Cagiao. Management firm and booking agency. Estab. 1993. Represents individual artists and groups from anywhere; currently handles 4 acts. Receives 10-15% commission. Reviews material for acts.
How to Contact: Submit demo tape by mail. Unsolicited submissions are OK. Prefers cassette or VHS videocassette with 6 songs and lyric sheet. If seeking management, press kit should include photo, video and bio. SASE. Reports in 2-3 weeks.
Music: Mostly **rock**, **nostalgia** ('50s '60s) and **country rock**; also **magic**. Works primarily with bands. Current acts include The Platters featuring Monroe Powell, The Deadwood Dolls, The Magic of Craig Armes and Bobby Day's Satellites (aka The Hollywood Flames).

SIMMONS MANAGEMENT GROUP, Box 18711, Raleigh NC 27619. (919)832-2090. Fax: (919)832-0690. President: Harry Simmons. Management firm and music publisher. Represents producers, artists, groups and songwriters; currently handles 8 acts. Receives 15-20% commission. Reviews material for acts.
How to Contact: Submit demo tape by mail. Unsolicited submissions are OK. Prefers cassette or DAT (or VHS videocassette of performance) with 3-6 songs and lyric sheet; also submit promotional material, photos and clippings. "Videocassette does not have to be professional. Any information helps." If seeking management, include 3-song demo (tape or DAT), photos, bio and lyric sheet in press kit. Does not return material. Reports in 6 weeks.
Music: Mostly **modern pop**; also **modern rock**, **rock**, **metal**, **R&B**, **industrial** and **top 40/pop**. Works primarily with "original music recording acts or those that aspire to be." Current acts include Don Dixon (producer, songwriter and recording artist), Marti Jones (recording artist), Jim Brock (recording artist), Terry Anderson (songwriter, recording artist), PERALTA (original music band), The Veldt (recording artists), The Lincolns and Apparatus (recording artists).

SINGERMANAGEMENT, INC., 161 W. 54th St., Suite 1403, New York NY 10019. (212)757-1217. President: Robert Singerman. Management consulting firm. Estab. 1982. Represents local, regional or international individual artists and groups; currently handles 10-15 acts. Receives 5% commission. Reviews material for acts.
How to Contact: Submit demo tape by mail. Unsolicited submissions are OK. Prefers cassette (or VHS videocassette if available). If seeking management consultation, include tape, lyric sheet and bio in press kit. Does not return material. Reports in 3 weeks.
Music: Current acts include Kraze (world/dance/house), Black Rain (cyber punk) and The Young Gods (industrial).
Tips: "Be clear on the direction you are taking and your goals and resources."

SIRIUS ENTERTAINMENT, P.O. Box 5450, Oregon City OR 97045-8450. (503)657-1813. Fax: (503)656-1476. Owners: Dan Blair, Rhonda Ellis. Management firm and booking agency. Estab. 1991. Represents individual artists and/or groups and songwriters from anywhere; currently handles 10 acts. Receives 10-15% commission. Reviews material for acts.
How to Contact: Submit demo tape by mail. Unsolicited submissions are OK. Prefers cassette with 3 songs and lyric sheet. If seeking management, press kit should include 8 × 10 photo, résumé, cassette, video if available. "Résumé should include total career progress from beginning with all schooling listed." SASE. Reports in 2-3 weeks.
Music: Mostly **R&B** and **rock**; also **jazz**, **blues** and **classical**. Current acts include Dorothy Moore (R&B/blues), James Van Buren (jazz/blues), Linda Hornbuckle (R&B, blues, jazz) and Ernie Johnson (R&B, blues).
Tips: "If you can't afford the services of a good studio and good studio musicians to play your material, then use one acoustic instrument (guitar or piano)."

SIROCCO PRODUCTIONS, INC., 5660 E. Virgina Beach Blvd., #104, Norfolk VA 23502. (804)461-8987. Fax: (804)461-4669. Contact: Leonard A. Swann, Jr.. Management firm. Estab. 1991. Represents groups from anywhere; currently handles 4 acts. Commission varies. Reviews material for acts.
  ● See the listings for Pen Cob Publishing in the Music Publishers section and Trumpeter Records in the Record Companies section.

How to Contact: Write first to obtain permission to submit and arrange personal interview. Prefers VHS videocassette. If seeking management, press kit should include video, audio cassette, bio, songlist, publicity material, photos and reviews. SASE.

Music: Mostly **alternative**. Current acts include On Beyond Zee, Sea of Souls, The Mundahs and Egypt.

T. SKORMAN PRODUCTIONS, INC., 3660 Maguire Blvd., Suite 250, Orlando FL 32803. (407)895-3000. Fax: (407)895-1422. President: Ted Skorman. Management firm and booking agency. Estab. 1983. Represents groups; currently handles 40 acts. Receives 10-25% commission. Reviews material for acts.

How to Contact: Call first for permission to send tape. Prefers cassette with 3 songs (or videocassette of no more than 15 minutes). "Live performance—no trick shots or editing tricks. We want to be able to view act as if we were there for a live show." SASE. Reports in 6 weeks.

Music: **Top 40**, **techno**, **dance**, **MOR** and **pop**. Works primarily with high-energy dance acts, recording acts, and top 40 bands. Current acts include Ravyn (country), Tim Mikus (rock), Herb Williams and Gibralter (R&B), Dana Kamide (rock) and Big Daddy (R&B).

Tips: "We have many pop recording acts, and are looking for commercial material for their next albums."

GARY SMELTZER PRODUCTIONS, 603 W. 13th #2A, Austin TX 78701. (512)478-6020. Fax: (512)472-3850. Contacts: Gary Smeltzer/James Cruz/Don Torosian/DAX Robertson. Management firm and booking agent. Estab. 1967. Represents individual artists and groups from anywhere. "We book about 100 different bands each year—none are exclusive." Receives 20% commission. Reviews material for acts.

How to Contact: Submit demo tape by mail. Unsolicited submissions are OK. Prefers cassette, videocassette or CD. If seeking management, press kit should include cassette or CD, bio, picture. Does not return material. Reports in 2 weeks.

Music: Mostly **alternative**, **R&B** and **country**. Current acts include Ro Tel & the Hot Tomatoes (nostalgic 60's showband), Hot Wax (nostalgic 60's-90's showband) and Executives.

Tips: "We prefer performing songwriters that can gig their music as a solo or group."

MICHAEL SMITH AND ASSOCIATES, 1024 17th Ave. S., Nashville TN 37212. (615)327-1372. Fax: (615)329-1433. President: Mike Smith. Management firm. Estab. 1989. Represents individual artists and/or groups from anywhere; currently handles 4 acts. Receives 15-20% commission. Reviews material for acts.

How to Contact: Call first and obtain permission to submit. Prefers cassette or VHS videocassette with 3-4 songs and lyric sheet. If seeking management, press kit should include cassette, picture, bio. Does not return material. Reports in 2-3 months.

Music: Mostly **positive country** and **Christian country**. Works primarily with singer/songwriters. Current acts include Mid South (positive country group), Brian Barrett (Christian country, A/C), Ken Holloway (positive country) and Chonda Pierce (Christian comedian).

Tips: "Submissions should include original songs, not cover tunes. Positive country/Christian country is a new developing music."

***SOUND AND SERENITY MANAGEMENT**, P.O. Box 22105, Nashville TN 37202. (615)731-3100. Fax: (615)731-3005. E-mail: jyoke@edge.net. Management firm. Represents individual artists from anywhere; currently handles 3 acts. Receives standard commission.

How to Contact: Call first and obtain permission to submit a demo. Prefers cassette with lyric sheet. If seeking management, press kit should include photo, bio, press clippings and cassette. Does not return material; will reply with SASE. Reports in 3 months.

Music: Mostly **country**, **Americana**. Works primarily with individual artists. Current acts include Ken Mellons (traditional country singer/songwriter), Gene Watson (country singer/songwriter) and Jo'el Sonnier.

SOUND '86 TALENT MANAGEMENT, P.O. Box 222, Black Hawk SD 57718. Management firm. Estab. 1974. Represents 10 artists and groups. Receives 20% commission. Reviews material for acts.

HOW TO GET THE MOST out of *Songwriter's Market* (at the front of this book) contains comments and suggestions to help you understand and use the information in these listings.

How to Contact: Submit demo tape by mail. Unsolicited submissions are OK. Prefers cassette (or VHS videocassette-professional) with 3-8 songs and lyric sheet. If seeking management, press kit should include tape, publicity, picture, any other promo information. SASE. Reports in 1 month.
Music: Rock (all types); also **bluegrass, country, dance, easy listening** and **top 40/pop**. Works primarily with single artists. Current artists include Mountain Rose (band), Dr. K. (band) and Fancy (duo).

SP TALENT ASSOCIATES, P.O. Box 475184, Garland TX 75047. Talent Coordinator: Richard Park. Management firm and booking agency. Represents individual artists and groups; currently handles 7 acts. Receives 15% commission. Reviews material for acts.
How to Contact: Submit demo tape by mail. Unsolicited submissions are OK. Prefers VHS videocassette with several songs. Also, send photo and bio with material submitted. Does not return material. Reports back as soon as possible.
Music: Mostly **rock, nostalgia rock** and **country**; also **specialty acts** and **folk/blues**. Works primarily with vocalists and self-contained groups. Current acts include Joe Hardin Brown (country), Rock It! (nostalgia), Renewal (rock group), Juan Madera and the Supple Grain Seeds.
Tips: "Appearance and professionalism are *musts*!"

*THE SPHERE ORGANIZATION, 835 Pennant Hills Rd., Suite 21, Carlingford, NSW 2118 **Australia**. (02)872-4144. Fax: (02)872-3992. Principal/Director: Eric Carlini. Booking agency. Estab. 1978. Represents artists from anywhere; currently handles 70 acts. Receives 10% commission.
How to Contact: Submit demo tape by mail. Unsolicited submissions are OK. Prefers cassette or live or studio videocassette with 5 songs. Does not return material. Reports in 2 weeks.
Music: Mostly **cover bands, concept bands** and **recording acts**; also **specialty acts** (solos, duos and trios) and **reggae/funk**. Current acts include Renee Geyer (recording artist), The Beatnix (captures the excitement and atmosphere of the Beatles) and Andrew Sisters Sisters.

SPHERE PRODUCTIONS, P.O. Box 991, Far Hills NJ 07931-0991. (908)781-1650. Fax: (908)781-1693. President: Tony Zarrella. Talent Manager: Louisa Pazienza. Management firm and record producer. Estab. 1987. Represents individual artists and/or groups and songwriters internationally; currently handles 5 acts. Receives 20-25% commission. Reviews material for acts.
How to Contact: Submit demo tape by mail. Unsolicited submissions are OK. Prefers cassette or VHS videocassette with 3-5 songs. If seeking management, press kit should include tape, photo a must, bio, all press and video if available. SASE. Reports in 10-12 weeks.
Music: Mostly **pop/rock, pop/country** and **New Age**; also **R&B**. Works primarily with bands and solo singer/songwriters. Current acts include 4 of Hearts (pop/rock), Oona Falcon (pop/rock), Elexus Quinn and Ziggy Troe and the Nothing Is Meaningless Project.
Tips: "Develop and create your own style, focus on goals and work as a team and maintain good chemistry with all artists and business relationships. All work together toward success."

SQUAD 16, P.O. Box 65, Wilbraham MA 01095. (413)599-1456. E-mail: 103473.2344@compuserve .com. President: Tom Najemy. Booking agency. Estab. 1990. Represents individual artists, groups and songwriters; currently handles 21 acts. Specializes in the college marketplace. Receives 15-20% commission. Reviews material for acts.
How to Contact: Submit demo tape by mail. Unsolicited submissions are OK. Prefers CD. SASE. Reports in 2 months.
Music: Mostly **contemporary, funk/hiphop** and **rock**; also **reggae, world beat** and **jazz & blues**; also **contemporary rock, funk,** or **dance bands** and **acoustic performers**. Current acts include Chuck (funk/hip hop/rap), Letters to Cleo (alternative), 22 Brides (rock), The Mighty Charge (reggae), Waiting Rates (rock), and The Lucky Charms (rock).
Tips: "Do as much on your own so as to impress and put a buzz in the ears of those who can help you go further in the business."

BERNIE STAHL ENTERTAINMENTS, 5th Floor, Suite 17, Parkrise, Three Alison St., Surfers Paradise 4217 **Old Australia**. 07 55 388911. Fax: 07 55 703434. Managing Director: Bernie Stahl. Director: Suzanne Stahl. Management firm, booking agency, music publisher. Estab. 1963. Represents individual artists (including comedy) and/or groups, songwriters from anywhere; currently handles 6 acts. Commission varies. Reviews material for acts.
How to Contact: Submit demo tape by mail. Unsolicited submissions are OK. Prefers cassette or VHS videocassette with lyric sheet. If seeking management, press kit should include VHS video, photos, bio, posters, cassette-audio. Does not return material.
Music: Mostly **country** and **comedy**. Works primarily with comedians, bands, solo artists. Current acts include Bruno Lucia (comedian/actor), Chunky Custard (show band) and Col Elliott (comedian/country).

*STAIRCASE PROMOTION, P.O. Box 211, East Prairie MO 63845. (573)649-2211. President: Tommy Loomas. Vice President: Joe Silver. Management firm. Estab. 1975. Represents individual artists and groups from anywhere; currently handles 6 acts. Receives 25% commission. Reviews material for acts.
* See the listings for Lineage Publishing in the Music Publishers section and Capstan Record Production in the Record Companies section.
How to Contact: Submit demo tape by mail. Unsolicited submissions are OK. Prefers cassette with 3 songs and lyric sheet. If seeking management, press kit should include bio, photo, audio cassette and/or video and press reviews, if any. "Be as professional as you can." SASE. Reports in 2 months.
Music: Mostly **country**, **pop** and **easy listening**; also **rock**, **gospel** and **alternative**. Current acts include Skidrow Joe (country comedian, on Capstan Records), Vicarie Arcoleo (pop singer, on Treasure Coast Records) and Bobby Lee Morgan (rock singer, on Capstan Records).

*STANDER ENTERTAINMENT, 13834 Magnolia Blvd., Sherman Oaks CA 91423. Phone/fax: (818)905-6365. Manager: Jacqueline Stander. Management firm, music publisher (DocRon Publishing), record company (Soaring Records) and consulting firm. Estab. 1970. Represents local individual artists, groups and songwriters; currently handles 5 acts. Receives 15-20% commission. Reviews material for acts.
How to Contact: Call first and obtain permission to submit demo. Prefers cassette or VHS videocassette with 3-5 songs and lyric sheet. If seeking management, press kit should include photo, bio, press publicity, CD or cassette. SASE. Reports in 3 weeks.
Music: Mostly **jazz**, **pop** and **R&B** (no rap); also **world music** and **Broadway**. Works primarily with national recording artists, film composers and singer/songwriters. Current acts include Bill Cunliffe (jazz pianist/producer), Jazz at the Movies Band (jazz group), Gregg Karukas (NAC jazz keyboardist/producer), Lauren Wood (vocalist/songwriter) and Ruby (blues singer).
Tips: "Always looking for long term professionals who have worked to establish themselves in their market, yet want to go to the next level. For those who have something to offer and are just starting out, I am available for consulting by phone or in person. Please call for submission request."

STAR ARTIST MANAGEMENT INC., 17580 Frazho, Roseville MI 48066. (810)778-6469. Fax: 810-979-5115. E-mail: gaxman@aol.com. Website: http://ourworld.compuserve.com/homepages/GTA XMAN. Director of Canadian Operations: Brian Courtis. Director of West Coast Operations: Lindsey Feldman. Director of East Coast Operations: Nat Weiss. Management firm (business and personal). Estab. 1972. Represents solo acts and groups; currently handles 10 acts. Receives 5% (business management), 15-25% (personal management). Reviews material for acts.
How to Contact: Submit demo tape by mail. Unsolicited submissions are OK. Prefers cassette or CD (and videocassette if available) with 2-3 songs. If seeking management, press kit should include photo, video (if available), press clippings. Does not return material. Reports in 1 month.
Music: Rock, **pop** and **alternative (pop, metal, college)**. Current acts include Elvis Hitler (Sector 2 Records), Frank Turner (Track Records), His Name Is Alive (4AD/Warner Bros. Records), Insane Clown Posse (Jive Records), Jimmy Marinos (EMI Music Publishing), Playgrind (Track Records), The Publicans (Track Records) and Speedball (Energy Records).

STAR VEST MANAGEMENT ASSOCIATES INC., 102 Ryders Ave., East Brunswick NJ 08816. (908)846-0077. Fax: (908)846-7205. Vice President: Bob Knight. Management firm. Estab. 1984. Represents individual artists and/or groups, songwriters from anywhere; currently handles 4 acts. Receives 15-20% commission. Reviews material for acts.
How to Contact: Submit demo tape by mail. Unsolicited submissions are OK. Prefers cassette with 4 songs. If seeking management, press kit should include videocassette, audio cassette, bio, pictures and songlist. SASE. Reports in 6 weeks.
Music: Mostly **top 40**, **R&B** and **rock**; also **country** and **gospel**. Works primarily with bands. Current acts include The Delfonics (vocal), Big Smoothies (vocal/band) and The New Supremes.

STEELE MANAGEMENT, 7002 124th Terrace N., Largo FL 34643. (813)524-3006. President: Brett R. Steele. Management firm. Estab. 1987. Represents local, regional or international individual artists, groups and songwriters; currently handles 1 act. Receives 20% commission. Reviews material for acts.
How to Contact: Call first and obtain permission to submit. Prefers cassette (or VHS videocassette if available) with 5 songs and lyric sheet. If seeking management, include bio and photo. SASE. Reports in 2 months.
Music: Mostly **rock** and **pop**. Works primarily with rock bands, songwriters. Current acts include Roxx Gang (glam rock) and Kevin Steele (songwriter).
Tips: "Send only your best songs, make a *quality* recording and include a lyric sheet."

HARRIET STERNBERG MANAGEMENT, 15250 Ventura Blvd., #1215, Sherman Oaks CA 91403. (818)906-9600. Fax: (818)906-1723. President: Harriet Sternberg. Management firm. Estab. 1987. Represents individual artists and/or groups, songwriters from anywhere; currently handles 5 acts. Receives 15% commission. Reviews material for acts.
How to Contact: Write first and obtain permission to submit. Prefers cassette or VHS videocassette with 3 songs and lyric sheet. If seeking management, press kit should include detailed history of the artist and professional experience. "Industry referrals are crucial." SASE. Reports in 1 month.
Music: "Great songs." Works primarily with signed acts. Current acts include Delbert McClinton, Spinal Tap, Dan Zanes, Judith Owen and The Folksmen.
Tips: "Be knowledgeable about my artists and/or roster."

STEVE STEWART MANAGEMENT, 6161 Santa Monica Blvd., #303, Los Angeles CA 90038. (213)468-0250. Fax: (213)468-0255. President: Steve Stewart. Management firm. Estab. 1993. Represents individual artists and/or groups from anywhere; currently handles 3 acts. Receives 20% commission.
How to Contact: Submit demo tape by mail. Unsolicited submissions are OK. Prefers cassette. If seeking management, press kit should include tape, photo, bio and video if available. "Mail first, call 4-6 weeks later. Cannot return any material." Reports in 2 months.
Music: Mostly **alternative** and **rock**. Works primarily with bands. Current acts include Stone Temple Pilots, Wiskey Biscuit and Eleven.

*STORMIN' NORMAN PRODUCTIONS, 27 Broad St., Red Bank NJ 07701. (908)741-8733. (908)747-3516. Owner: Norman Seldin. Management firm, booking agency, music publisher (Noisy Joy Music/BMI) and record company (Ivory Records). Estab. 1967. Represents individual artists, groups and songwriters from anywhere; currently handles 10 acts. Receives 15% commission. Reviews material for acts.
How to Contact: Submit demo tape by mail. Unsolicited submissions are OK. Prefers cassette with 2-4 songs and lyric sheet. If seeking management, press kit should include demo cassette with cover and original songs, photo, song list, appearance credits, home base area, phone and address. SASE. Reports in 3-5 weeks.
Music: Mostly **country, rock** and **reggae**; also **soft rock, dynamic blues** and **folk**. Current acts include Stormin' Norman Band, Ronnie Dove and Darrell Norman.

STRICTLEY BIZINESS MUSIC MANAGEMENT, 691½ N. 13th St., Philadelphia PA 19123. (215)281-6514. CEO: Justus. President: Corey Hicks. Management and consulting firm. Estab. 1989. Represents local, regional and international individual artists, groups, songwriters and producers; currently handles 15 acts. Receives 25% commission. Reviews material for acts.
How to Contact: Submit demo tape by mail—unsolicited submissions are OK. Prefers cassette or VHS videocassette with 3-5 songs, lyric sheet, information on the artist and photo. Does not return material. Reports in 1 month.
Music: Mostly **R&B, pop, rock** and **rap**; also **gospel**. Current acts include Phoenix (rapper), Rich Tucker (producer/writer) and ASIS (rap group).

STRICTLY FORBIDDEN ARTISTS, 595 St. Clair West, Toronto M6C 1A3 **Canada**. (416)656-0085. Fax: (905)566-8442. A&R Director: Brad Black. Management firm, booking agent and record company. Estab. 1986. Represents individual artists and groups from anywhere; currently handles 6 acts. Receives 35% commission. Reviews material for acts.
How to Contact: Submit demo tape by mail. Unsolicited submissions are OK. Prefers cassette with 3-6 songs and lyric sheet. If seeking management, press kit should include biography, press clippings, 8×10, promo materials. "Once you've sent material, don't call us, we'll call you." Does not return material. Reports in 4-6 weeks.
Music: Mostly **alternative rock, art rock** and **grindcore**; also **electronic, hip hop** and **experimental**. Works primarily with performing bands, studio acts and performance artists. Current acts include Squidhead (alternative rock/metal), Rigid Wonzer (low-fi noise rock) and Severflesh (grindcore/electronic/industrial).
Tips: "As long as you have faith in your music, we'll have faith in promoting you and your career."

*SUNNYDAYS RECORDS, 6263 28th Ave., Montreal, Quebec PQ H1T 3H8 **Canada**. A&R Director: Fadel Chidiac. Management firm, music publisher and record company. Estab. 1990. Represents individual artists, groups and songwriters from anywhere; currently represents 10 acts. Receives 25% commission. Reviews material for acts.
How to Contact: Submit demo tape by mail. Unsolicited submissions are OK. Prefers cassette, VHS videocassette or CD with a full album of songs, photo and lyric sheet. If seeking management, press kit should include photos, videos, history, support staff/members, budget and touring experience. Does not return material. "Submissions are kept on file, not destroyed." Reports in 1-2 months.

Music: Mostly **rock, alternative** and **dance**; also **reggae, '70s style hard rock** and **'50s style rock** (no covers). Works primarily with bands and songwriters, with special attention to female performers. Current acts include F.U. (Australian rock), Forever Unholy ('70s hard rock) and Power Dreams (hard rock).

SUNSET PROMOTIONS OF CHICAGO, INC., 9359 S. Kedzie Ave., P.O. Box 42877, Evergreen Park IL 60805. (312)581-9009. Fax: (312)581-8869. President/CEO: Neil J. Cacciottolo. Management firm, music publisher (Sunset Publishing Division/ASCAP), record company (Sunset Records-America). Estab. 1981. Represents individual artists and/or groups, songwriters from anywhere; currently handles 10 acts. Receives 15% commission. Reviews material for acts.
How to Contact: Write or call first and obtain permission to submit. Prefers cassette or videocassette with 1 song and lyric or lead sheet. If seeking management, press kit should include bio, 5×7 or 8×10 b&w photo, general information, clippings. "All submissions are non returnable." Reports in 1 month.
Music: Mostly **traditional, country, gospel, classical, traditional blues, easy listening** and **New Age**. Current acts include Howard Burke (pop/jazz artist), Sally Holmes (gospel artist), Neil (Guitar Man) Cacci (country artist), Sheri Carlisle (country).
Tips: "Make absolutely sure that material is first quality."

*SUNSHADOW PRODUCTIONS, P.O. Box 1239, Wickenburg AZ 85358. (520)684-3075. Fax: (520)684-7010. Talent Manager: Travis Cole. Management firm, booking agency, music publisher (Sunshadow Music Publishers), record company (Silver Saddle Records) and record producer. Estab. 1991. Represents individual artists, groups and songwriters from anywhere; currently handles 10 acts. Receives 10-15% commission. Reviews material for acts.
How to Contact: Write or call first and obtain permission to submit a demo. Prefers cassette or VHS videocassette with 1-3 songs and lyric and/or lead sheet. "No B.S.—say what you mean and mean what you say. No long rambling life stories!" Does not return material. Reports in 2-3 weeks.
Music: Mostly **western** (cowboy). Works primarily with western singers, songwriters, bands, variety artists, animals acts and comedians. Current acts include Tex Hill (singing cowboy/songwriter), Jack Alan (singing cowboy/songwriter) and Rhythm Ranch Show (western stage show).

*SURFACE MANAGEMENT INC., 2935 Church St. Station, New York NY 10008. Phone/fax: (212)468-2828. President: Patti Beninoti. Management firm. Estab. 1990. Represents local individual artists and groups; currently handles 5 acts. Receives 20% commission. Reviews material for acts.
How to Contact: Write or call first and obtain permission to submit. Prefers cassette with 5 songs and lyric sheet. SASE. Reports in 6 weeks.
Music: Mostly **alternative** and **heavy rock**. Current acts include The Geflens, Daisy's Red Gravy Train and Big Stupid Guitars.

*SWEET PEA ARTIST MANAGEMENT, 7132 Cabot Dr., Nashville TN 37209. (615)356-7066. Fax: (615)370-1179. President: Julie Devereux. Management firm. Estab. 1995. Represents individual artists and groups from anywhere; currently handles 2 acts. Receives 20% commission. Reviews material for acts.
How to Contact: Call first and obtain permission to submit a demo. Prefers cassette with no more than 3 songs and lyric sheet. If seeking management, press kit should include bio, photo and 3 song demo. Does not return material. Reports in 1 month.
Music: Mostly **alternative, blues** and **country**. Works primarily with bands, lead vocalists and songwriters. Current acts include Custer & Logan (alternative folk).
Tips: "You only need to submit around the time an artist/group is working new project. Do not be a pest."

T.J. BOOKER LTD., P.O. Box 969, Rossland, B.C. V0G 1Y0 **Canada**. (604)362-7795. Contact: Tom Jones. Management firm, booking agency and music publisher. Estab. 1976. Represents local, regional or international individual artists, groups and songwriters; currently handles 25 acts. Receives 10-15% commission. Reviews material for acts.
How to Contact: Submit demo tape by mail. Unsolicited submissions are OK. Prefers cassette (or videocassette if available) with 3 songs. If seeking management, include demo tape, picture and bio in press kit. Does not return material.
Music: Mostly **MOR, crossover, rock, pop** and **country**. Works primarily with vocalists, show bands, dance bands and bar bands. Current acts include Kirk Orr (comedian), Tommy and T Birds (50s show band), Zunzee (top 40/pop), Mike Hamilton and Eclipse.
Tips: "There is always a market for excellence."

*T.L.C. BOOKING AGENCY, 37311 N. Valley Rd., Chattaroy WA 99003. (509)292-2201. Fax: (509)292-2205. Agent/Owners: Tom or Carrie Lapsansky. Booking agency. Estab. 1970. Represents individual artists and groups from anywhere; currently handles 17 acts. Receives 10-15% commission. Reviews material for acts.

How to Contact: Submit demo tape by mail. Unsolicited submissions are OK. Prefers cassette with 3-4 songs. Does not return material. Reports in 2-3 weeks.

Music: Mostly **rock**, **country** and **variety**; also **comedians** and **magicians**. Works primarily with bands, singles and duos. Current acts include Nobody Famous (variety/rock/country), Rope Trick (country) and Stronghold (rock).

*T 'n T ENTERPRISES, 3131 S. Dixie Dr., Suite 111, Dayton OH 45439-2223. (800)455-4332. Fax: (513)643-5559. E-mail: tominoh@aol.com. President: Tommy Collins. Booking agency. Estab. 1987. Represents groups from anywhere; currently handles 2 acts. Receives 15% commission. Reviews material for acts.

How to Contact: Write first and obtain permission to submit a demo. Prefers cassette with 1 song and lyric sheet. If seeking management, press kit should include picture, bio, experience, reviews. "Best quality possible on audio cassette." Does not return material. Reports in 1 month.

Music: Mostly **pop rock**, **nostalgia sounding** and **country**; also **rewrites of '50s and '60s**. Works primarily with nostalgia and classic country groups. Current acts include Sh-Boom (rock 'n roll oldies show) and Hazzard Brothers (classic country music show).

Tips: "Professionalism. It takes more than just songwriting to make it in the music business. Presentation, professionalism is key to getting your foot in the door."

T.S.J. PRODUCTIONS, 422 Pierce St. NE, Minneapolis MN 55413-2514. (612)331-8580. President/Artist Manager: Katherine J. Lange. Management firm and booking agency. Estab. 1974. Represents artists, groups and songwriters; currently handles 1 international act. Receives 20% commission. Reviews material for acts.

How to Contact: Submit demo tape by mail—unsolicited submissions are OK. Prefers "cassette tapes only for music audio with 4-6 songs and lyric sheets." SASE. Reports in 1 month.

Music: Mostly **country rock**, **symphonic rock**, **easy listening** and **MOR**; also **blues**, **country**, **folk**, **jazz**, **progressive**, **R&B** and **top 40/pop**. Currently represents Thomas St. James (songwriter/vocalist).

Tips: "We will view anyone that fits into our areas of music. However, keep in mind we work only with national and international markets. We handle those starting out as well as professionals, but all must be marketed on a professional level, if we work with you."

TALENT ASSOCIATES OF WISCONSIN, INC., P.O. Box 588, Brookfield WI 53008. (414)786-8500. President: John A. Mangold. Booking agency. Estab. 1971. Represents local groups; currently handles 25 acts. Receives 15-20% commission. Reviews material for acts.

How to Contact: Submit demo tape by mail. Unsolicited submissions are OK. Prefers cassette (or VHS videocassette if available) with 3 songs. If seeking management, press kit should include video, songlist, bio and picture poster. Does not return material. Reports in 1 month.

Music: Mostly **variety shows**, **rock/pop** and **dance**; also **R&B** and **jazz**. Works primarily with variety, rock and dance bands. Current acts include Temperament (R&B '90s style), Booze Bros. (take-off of Blues Bros.) and Brian McLaughlin Band (top dance hits from '80s-'90s).

Tips: "We're always looking for bands with high energy and a good stage presence, who enjoy what they're doing and radiate that through the audience, leaving all parties involved with a good feeling."

THE TANGLEWOOD GROUP INC., 2 Sheppard Ave. E., #900, Willowdale, Ontario M2N 5Y7 **Canada**. (416)787-8687. Fax: (416)322-0977. President: Bruce Davidson. Management firm, music publisher (William James Music Publishing Co.) and record company (Tanglewood Records). Estab. 1975. Represents individual artists, groups and songwriters from anywhere; currently handles 5 acts. Receives 20% commission. Reviews material for acts.

• One of Tanglewood's clients, Eric Nagler, has won two Juno Awards (the Canadian equivalent of the Grammy Awards).

How to Contact: Write or call first and obtain permission to submit a demo or write to arrange personal interview. Prefers cassette. Does not return material.

Music: Mostly **family**, **children's** and **country**. Works primarily with family/children's entertainers. Current acts include Eric Nagler, Glenn Bennett and Carmen Campagne.

Tips: "Remember to *never* talk/write down to children!"

LISTINGS OF COMPANIES in countries other than the U.S. have the name of the country in boldface type.

TANNER ENTERTAINMENT, 509 Summit Ave. South, Park Ridge IL 60068. (312)320-1940. E-mail: margaret.a.glover@al.com@internet. President: Margaret Glover. Management firm, booking agent and record company (Lunch Box). Estab. 1992. Represents groups from anywhere. Currently handles 1 act. Receives 20% commission. Reviews material for acts.
How to Contact: Write or call first and obtain permission to submit. Prefers cassette or vinyl/CD with 3 songs. If seeking management, press kit should include picture, bio, press releases, upcoming shows, tape/CD/vinyl. "Tell me what you are looking for in a manager/label/booker." Does not return material. Reports in 1 month.
Music: Mostly **college alternative**, **garage rock** and **punk**; also **country alternative** and **pop**. Current acts include Rockin' Billy (rockabilly/jazz/blues).
Tips: "Have songs with a hook. A person should come away from your tape or performance humming your song. Be professional to everyone you encounter—you never know who you may be talking to."

TAS MUSIC CO./DAVE TASSE ENTERTAINMENT, N2467 Knollwood Dr., Lake Geneva WI 53147-9731. Contact: David Tasse. Booking agency, record company and music publisher. Represents artists, groups and songwriters; currently handles 21 acts. Receives 10-20% commission. Reviews material for acts.
How to Contact: Submit demo tape by mail. Unsolicited submissions are OK. Prefers cassette with 2-4 songs and lyric sheet. Include performance videocassette if available. If seeking management, include tape, bio, photo. Does not return material. Reports in 3 weeks.
Music: Mostly **pop** and **jazz**; also **dance**, **MOR**, **rock**, **soul** and **top 40**. Works primarily with show and dance bands. Current acts include Dave Hulburt (blues), David Tasse (jazz) and Major Hamberlin (jazz).

*TCG MANAGEMENT, 1018 Wildrose Dr., Lutz FL 33549. (813)282-1449. Fax: (813)949-8101. Owner/Personal Manager: Susan Walls. Management firm. Estab. 1980. Represents individual artists (who also write) and groups from anywhere; currently handles 6 acts. Receives 15% commission. Reviews material for acts.
How to Contact: Submit demo tape by mail. Unsolicited submissions are OK. Prefers cassette or VHS or super 8 videocassette with at least 4 songs and lyric sheet. If seeking management, press kit should include bio/listing of appearance venues, photos, tape, video (if available) and references from industry, if possible. "Be sure artist indicates how they heard of TCG in a cover letter." SASE. Reports in 2 weeks.
Music: Mostly **country**, **contemporary Christian** and **jazz**. Works primarily with individual artists with or without band and country bands. Current acts include Tommy Townsend (country singer/writer), Pharis Browning (country singer/songwriter) and Kim Phoenix (country singer).
Tips: "Approach management as a necessity to achieve goals by teamwork between manager and artist."

*WILLIAM TENN ARTIST MANAGEMENT, #431-67 Mowat Ave., Toronto, Ontario M6K 3E3 Canada. (416)534-7763. Fax: (416)534-9726. E-mail: pmwtm@io.org. Management Assistant: Anna Marie. Management firm. Estab. 1981. Represents individual artists and groups in Canada, but not limited to that; currently handles 3 acts. Receives variable commission. Reviews material for acts.
How to Contact: Submit demo tape by mail. Unsolicited submissions are OK. Prefers cassette or CD with at least 3 songs, lyric sheet optional. If seeking management, press kit should include cassette with minimum 3 songs; recent press, reviews (live and/or album); photo (either b&w, color copied—to your discretion); contact info and return address. "Please do not call for at least two weeks to check on your submission. You will receive a response in the mail." SASE. Reports in 2 months.
Music: Mostly **rock/pop** and **alternative rock**. "We work with what we like. You don't need to be a certain type of artist." Current acts include Waltons (Sire/Elektra-Warner, pop), Barstool Prophets (Mercury/Polygram, rock) and Hayden (hardwood, solo alternative rock).
Tips: "Don't be pushy. If it's going to happen it will. Don't turn people off by being in their face. They'll call you if they want you. But don't disappear after sending them something, either."

*TEXAS MUSIC MASTERS, 11231 State Hwy. 64 E., Tyler TX 75707-9587. (903)566-5653. Fax: (903)566-5750. Vice President: Lonnie Wright. Management firm, music publisher and record company (TMM, Juke Box, Quazar). Estab. 1970. Represents international individual artists, groups and songwriters; currently handles 3 acts. Receives 20% commission. Reviews material for acts.
  • See their listing in the Record Producers section.
How to Contact: Write first and obtain permission to submit a demo. Prefers cassette with 3 songs. If seeking management, include short bio and photo with press kit. SASE. Reports in 1 month.
Music: Mostly **country**, **gospel** and **blues**. Works primarily with vocalists, writers and dance bands. Current acts include Seven Signs (rap), Steve Carpenter (country) and David Darst (country/Christian).

*TEXAS SOUNDS ENTERTAINMENT, 1851 Gulf Freeway South, Suite 3, League City TX 77573. (713)338-4033. Fax: (713)554-4114. Co-Owner: Mike Sandberg. Management firm, booking agency. Estab. 1980. Represents individual artists, groups and songwriters from anywhere. Receives 10% commission.
How to Contact: Write first and obtain permission to submit a demo. Prefers cassette with 3-4 songs and lyric and/or lead sheet. If seeking management, press kit should include bio, photo, accomplishments, demo tape. Does not return material.
Music: Mostly **country**, **R&B**. Works primarily with bands, orchestras, singer/songwriters. Current acts include Jim Rice (country singer/songwriter), Christine Albert (country singer/songwriter) and Hamilton Loomis (R&B singer/musician).

*THEATER ARTS NETWORK/STEPHEN PRODUCTIONS, 15 Pleasant Dr., Lancaster PA 17602. (717)394-0970. Fax: (717)394-2783. Promotions: Stephanie Lynn Brubaker. Management firm and booking agency. Estab. 1977. Represents East Coast individual artists and groups; currently handles 3 acts. Receives 10-20% commission. Reviews material for acts.
How to Contact: Submit demo tape by mail. Unsolicited submissions are OK. Prefers cassette (or VHS videocassette if available). If seeking management, press kit should include 8 × 10 photo, tape, video and tour schedule. Does not return material. Reports in 2 weeks if interested.
Music: Mostly **comedy/music**, **Christian contemporary** and **rock**. Current acts include Stephen and Other Dummies (comedy/music/ventriloquism), John Westford (magic) and Pete Geist (comedy).
Tips: "We book live acts only."

315 BEALE STUDIOS/TALIESYN ENTERTAINMENT, 2087 Monroe St., Memphis TN 38104. (901)276-0056. President: Eddie Scruggs. Management firm and music publisher. Estab. 1972. Represents individual artists and/or groups and songwriters from anywhere; currently handles 6 acts. Receives 20% commission. Reviews material for acts.
How to Contact: Submit demo tape by mail. Unsolicited submissions are OK. Prefers cassette. If seeking management, press kit should include bio, picture, tape and clippings. Does not return material. Reports in 3 weeks.
Music: Mostly **rock**, **urban** and **country**.

TIGER'S EYE ENTERTAINMENT MANAGEMENT & CONSULTING, 1876 Memorial Drive, Green Bay WI 54303. (414)494-1588. Manager/CEO: Thomas C. Berndt. Management firm and record producer. Estab. 1992. Represents individual artists, groups and songwriters from anywhere. Currently handles 4 acts. Receives 20% commission. Reviews material for acts.
How to Contact: Submit demo tape by mail. Unsolicited submissions are OK. Prefers cassette (or VHS videocassette) with 3-4 songs and lyric sheet. If seeking management, press kit should include tape, photo, relevant press and bio. "Artist should follow up with a call after 2 weeks." Does not return material. Reports in 2 weeks.
Music: Mostly **alternative**, **hard rock** and **folk-blues**; also **classical**, **funk** and **jazz**. Works primarily with vocalists, singer/songwriters, fresh alternative grunge. Current acts include B.B. Shine (variety act), Spastic Mime (hard rock) and Ugly Stick (alternative/hard rock).

TERRI TILTON MANAGEMENT, 7135 Hollywood, Suite 601, Los Angeles CA 90046. (213)851-8552. Fax: (213)850-1467. Personal Manager: Terri Tilton Stewart. Management firm. Estab. 1984. Represents individual artists and groups from anywhere; currently handles 3 acts. Receives 20% commission. Reviews material for acts.
How to Contact: Write or call first and obtain permission to submit. Prefers cassette. SASE. If seeking management, include bio, letter, tape, photo and résumé. Reports in 2 months.
Music: Mostly **jazz**, **pop**, **blues** and **R&B**. Current acts include Jimmy Stewart (guitarist/producer/composer), Kal David (guitarist/singer/songwriter), Toni Lee Scott (singer) and Allison Whyte (journalist).

*TONE ZONE BOOKING AGENCY, 939 W. Wilson Ave., Chicago IL 60640. (312)561-2450 ext. 2351. Fax: (312)989-2076. Website: http://www.mes.net/~stu. Submissions: Diane Borden and Colleen Davick. Management firm, booking agency and record company (Grrr Records). Represents local individual artists and groups; currently handles 6 acts. Reviews material for acts.
How to Contact: Submit demo tape by mail. Unsolicited submissions are OK. Prefers cassette with lyric sheet. If seeking management, press kit should include news clippings, bio information on band and individual members of the group, photo and lyric sheets. SASE.
Music: Mostly **rock**, **Celtic** and **hardcore**; also **contemporary gospel**, **rap/rave** and **blues**. Works primarily with bands. Current acts include Resurrection Band (rock), Glenn Kaiser (blues) and The Crossing (Celtic), Crash Dog (hardcore), Grace & Glory (gospel choir) and Cauzin Efekt (rap).

*TOPNOTCH® MUSIC & RECORDS, Box 1515, Sanibel Island FL 33957-1515. (941)982-1515. Fax: (941)472-5033. President/CEO/Producer: Vincent M. Wolanin. Management firm, merchandising company, music publisher (Topnotch® Publishing), record company and record producer (Vincent M. Wolanin). Estab. 1990. Represents individual artists, groups and songwriters from anywhere; currently handles 3 acts. Receives 20% commission. Reviews material for acts.

How to Contact: Submit demo tape by mail. Unsolicited submissions are OK. Prefers cassette or DAT or VHS videocassette with 3 songs and lyric and/or lead sheet. If seeking management, press kit should include picture, news clippings (if any), list of gigs played, résumé of education and touring (if applicable). Does not return material. Reports in 2 months.

Music: Mostly **alternative rock**, **pop-dance** and **modern rock**; also **blues-rock**. "Prefer groups that are cutting edge where all members are accomplished musicians, are sober, hard working and original in their musical and lyrical tastes." Current acts include Lyndal's Burning (alternative rock), Natalia (pop/dance) and Brian Fox (modern rock).

Tips: "It has got to be a slammin' tune in all respects. If it has a great melody, memorable lyrics and music, with at least one major hook (but preferably two) with potential for crossover to Top 40 as well as rock, Topnotch® is interested."

A TOTAL ACTING EXPERIENCE, Dept. Rhymes-1, 20501 Ventura Blvd., Suite 399, Woodland Hills CA 91364. Agent: Dan A. Bellacicco. Talent agency. Estab. 1984. Represents vocalists, lyricists, composers and groups; currently handles 30 acts. Receives 10% commission. Reviews material for acts. Agency License: TA-0698.

How to Contact: Submit demo tape by mail. Unsolicited submissions are OK. Prefers cassette (or VHS videocassette if available) with 3-5 songs and lyric or lead sheets. Please include a revealing "self talk" at the end of your tape. "Singers or groups who write their own material must submit a VHS videocassette with photo and resume." If seeking management, include VHS videotape, 5 8×10 photos, cover letter, professional typeset resume and business card in press kit. Does not return material. Reports in 3 months only if interested.

Music: Mostly **top 40/pop**, **jazz**, **blues**, **country**, **R&B**, **dance** and **MOR**; also "theme songs for new films, TV shows and special projects."

Tips: "No calls please. We will respond via your SASE. Your business skills must be strong. Please use a new tape and keep vocals up front. We welcome young, sincere talent who can give total commitment, and most important, *loyalty*, for a long-term relationship. We are seeking female vocalists (a la Streisand or Whitney Houston) who can write their own material, for a major label recording contract. Your song's story line must be as refreshing as the words you skillfully employ in preparing to build your well-balanced, orchestrated, climactic last note! Try to eliminate old, worn-out, dull, trite rhymes. A new way to write/compose or sing an old song/tune will qualify your originality and professional standing."

TRIANGLE TALENT, INC., 10424 Watterson, Louisville KY 40299. (502)267-5466. President: David H. Snowden. Booking agency. Represents artists and groups; currently handles 70 acts. Receives 10-20% commission. Reviews material for acts.

How to Contact: Submit demo tape by mail. Unsolicited submissions are OK. Prefers cassette (or VHS videocassette) with 2-4 songs and lyric sheet. If seeking management, include photo, audio cassette of at least 3 songs, and video if possible in press kit. Does not return material. Reports in 3-4 weeks.

Music: **Rock/top 40** and **country**. Current acts include Lee Bradley (contemporary country), Karen Kraft (country) and Four Kinsmen (Australian group).

TSMB PRODUCTIONS, 5248 Cedar Lane, Studio 158, Columbia MD 21044. (800)987-8762. Chief Executive Officer: Terry Tombosi. Management firm, booking agent, music publisher (BMI) and record company (TSMB Records). Estab. 1983. Represents local, regional or international individual artists, groups and songwriters; currently handles 25 acts. Receives 10% commission. Reviews material for acts.

How to Contact: Submit demo tape by mail—unsolicited submissions are OK. Prefers cassette (or VHS videocassette if available) with 3 songs and lyric or lead sheets. SASE. If seeking management, include photo, demo, newspaper articles, schedule. Reports in 2-3 weeks.

Music: Mostly **rock**, **blues** and **country**; also **Xmas songs**. Works primarily with show bands and bands with 3 year longevity. Current acts include The Hubcaps, The Roadsters and Jim Purdy.

Tips: "Put your best foot forward, know what you want, ask yourself, are you ready for management and advice?"

*TUTTA FORZA MUSIC, 30 Nurney St., Stamford CT 06902. (203)353-3397. Proprietor: Andrew Anello. Management firm, booking agency, music publisher (Tutta Forza Publishing/ASCAP) and record company. Estab. 1990. Represents New York Metro Area artists; currently handles 6 acts. Reviews material for acts.

How to Contact: Submit demo tape by mail. Unsolicited submissions are OK. Prefers cassette, VHS videocassette or CD with 3 songs. If seeking management, press kit should include recent press releases, music reviews, biography and cover letter. SASE. Reports in 2 weeks.
Music: Mostly **jazz fusion**, **classical** and **mordal combat jazz**; also **instrumentalists**, **composers** and **improvisors**. Works primarily with single artists, composers, improvisors and instrumentalists. Current acts include Andrew Anello (clarinetist/composer) and The Jazz X-Centrix.
Tips: "Looking for self-sufficient individualists; musicians who bring their own unique artistic qualities to work with. Genre of music not nearly as important as quality and taste in their style!"

UMBRELLA ARTISTS MANAGEMENT, INC., 2612 Erie Ave., P.O. Box 8385, Cincinnati OH 45208. (513)871-1500. Fax: (513)871-1510. President: Stan Hertzman. Management firm. Represents artists, groups and songwriters; currently handles 4 acts.
• See the listings for Hal Bernard Enterprises in the Record Producers and Music Publishers sections, and for Strugglebaby Recording Co. in the Record Companies section.
How to Contact: Submit demo tape by mail—unsolicited submissions are OK. Prefers cassette with 3 songs and lyric sheet. SASE. If seeking management, press kit should include a short bio, reviews, photo and cassette. Reports in 2 months.
Music: Progressive, **rock** and **top 40/pop**. Works with contemporary/progressive pop/rock artists and writers. Current acts include The Blue Birds (R&B/rock band), America Smith (rock), The Spanic Boys (modern band) and Adrian Belew.

*UMPIRE ENTERTAINMENT ENTERPRIZES, 1507 Scenic Dr., Longview TX 75604. (903)759-0300. Owner/President: Jerry Haymes. Management firm, music publisher (Golden Guitar, Umpire Music) and record company (Enterprize Records). Estab. 1974. Represents individual artists, groups, songwriters and rodeo performers from anywhere; currently handles 5 acts.
How to Contact: Write first and obtain permission to submit. Prefers cassette with lyric and lead sheets. If seeking management, press kit should include bio, picture and any recordings. Does not return material. "Submissions become part of files for two years, then disposed of." Reports in 1 month.
Music: Mostly **country, pop** and **gospel**.

UNIVERSAL MUSIC MARKETING, P.O. Box 2297, Universal City TX 78148. (210)659-2557. Contact: Frank Willson. Management firm, booking agency, music publisher, record producer. Estab. 1987. Represents individual artists, groups from anywhere. Currently handles 18 acts. Receives 21% commission. Reviews material for acts.
• See the listings for BSW Records in the Record Companies section and Frank Willson in the Record Producers section.
How to Contact: Submit demo tape by mail. Unsolicited submissions are OK. Prefers cassette (or ¾" videocassette) with 3 songs and lyric sheet. If seeking management, include tape/CD, bio, photo, current activities. SASE. Reports in 3-5 weeks.
Music: Mostly **country** and **light rock**; also **blues**. Works primarily with vocalists, singer/songwriters and bands. Current acts include Paradise Canyon, Patty David, Maria Rose, Candee Land, Harold Dean, Craig Robbins and Rusty Doherty.

UP FRONT MANAGEMENT, 1906 Seward Dr., Pittsburg CA 94565. Phone and fax: (510)427-7210. CEO/President: Charles Coke. Management firm, record company (Man Network) and record producer (Heavyweight Productions). Estab. 1977. Represents individual artists, groups, songwriters and producers from anywhere. Currently handles 3 acts. Receives 10-15% commission. Reviews material for acts.
• See their listing in the Record Producers section.
How to Contact: Submit demo tape by mail. Unsolicited submissions are OK. Prefers cassette, videocassette or CD's with 3-5 songs and lyric sheet. If seeking management, press kit should include bio, CD or cassette and picture. Does not return material. Reports in 1-3 weeks.
Music: Mostly **rock**, **country** and **R&B**. Works primarily with bands and singers. Current acts include John Payne, Psycho Betty (rock), Uncle Yazz (pop) and Van Zen (rock).

*VALIANT RECORDS & MANAGEMENT, P.O. Box 180099, Dallas TX 75218. (214)327-5477. Fax: (214)327-4888. E-mail: valiant@master.net. President: Andy Stone. Booking agency, music publisher (Brightstone Publishing Co.), record company and record producer (Ed Loftus). Estab. 1971. Represents individual artists, groups and songwriters from anywhere; currently handles 1 act. Receives 10-20% commission. Reviews material for acts.
How to Contact: Submit demo tape by mail. Unsolicited submissions are OK. Prefers cassette or VHS videocassette with 4 songs, lyric and/or lead sheet, if possible, and bio. "No more than four songs at a time, recorded clearly and professionally, with lyric sheets. I must be able to hear the words and melody. No arty mixes." SASE (no guarantees). Reports in 4-6 weeks.

Music: Mostly **top 40** and **top 40 country**; also **children's songs** and **novelty**. Works primarily with show groups for booking/managing, songwriters for placing songs and artists for release of new product. Current acts include Vince Vance & The Valiants (pop/pop country), Ed Loftus (A/C, singer/songwriter) and Mike Boyd (country/pop singer).
Tips: "The secret of becoming a great songwriter is to write a lot of songs. I don't like receiving one song from a first-time writer. It's a waste of time. If I can't hear the vocal lead upfront, I throw it in the garbage. For seasoned writers, don't force topics. Write what you feel and are familiar with."

HANS VAN POL MANAGEMENT, P.O. Box 9010, Amsterdam HOL 1006AA **Netherlands**. Phone: (31)20610-8281. Fax: (31)20610-6941. Managing Director: Hans Van Pol. Management firm, booking agency, consultant (Hans Van Pol Music Consultancy), record company (J.E.A.H.! Records) and music publisher (Blue & White Music). Estab. 1984. Represents regional (Holland/Belgium) individual artists and groups; currently handles 7 acts. Receives 20-30% commission. Reviews material for acts.
How to Contact: Submit demo tape by mail. Unsolicited submissions are OK. Prefers cassette or VHS videocassette with 3 songs and lyric sheets. If seeking management, include demo, possible video (VHS/PAL), bio, photo, release information. Does not return material. Reports in 1 month.
Music: Mostly **dance**: **rap/swing beat/hip house/R&B/soul/c.a.r.** Current acts include Tony Scott (rap), Erica (house/pop), Roxanna (R&B female singer), King Bee (rap/hard-core), All Star Fresh (producer/D.J.), Mc. Fixx-it (Euro house), Stereo Explosion and Anoir (Euro/house).

*RICHARD VARRASSO MANAGEMENT, P.O. Box 387, Fremont CA 94537. (510)792-8910. Fax: (510)792-0891. E-mail: rvarrasso@aol.com. President: Richard Varrasso. A&R: Saul Vigil. Management firm. Estab. 1976. Represents individual artists, groups and songwriters from anywhere; currently handles 10 acts. Receives 20% commission. Reviews material for acts.
How to Contact: Submit demo tape by mail. Unsolicited submissions are OK. Prefers cassette. If seeking management, press kit should include photos, bios, song lists, gig dates, cassette, press, references. Does not return material. Reports in 3 months.
Music: Mostly **rock** and **young country**. Works primarily with concert headliners and singers.

VICTORY ARTISTS, 55 Maria Dr., Suite 847, Petaluma CA 94954. (707)769-1210. Contact: Shelly Trumbo. Management firm, music publisher (ASCAP) and record company (Victory Label/Bay City). Estab. 1985. Represents individual artists and groups; currently handles 5 acts. Receives 15% commission. Reviews material for acts.
How to Contact: Write first and obtain permission to submit. Prefers cassette (or VHS videocassette if available) with 3 songs and lyric sheets. If seeking management, include photo, 3-song tape (video preferred), press clippings, cover letter. Does not return material. Reports in 1 month.
Music: Mostly **alternative**, **rock**, **pop** and **country**. Current acts include Freudian Slip (alternative), Este (rock) and Mark Allan (songwriter).
Tips: "We listen to all submissions. If we work with you we will make a difference in your career. Drive and talent is more important to us than past success or slick presentations. Send us your stuff."

VINTAGE CRIME MANAGEMENT, 35 Linden Ave., Suite #509, Long Beach CA 90802. (310)436-1713. Fax: (310)436-1473. President: Rich Modica. Management firm and record company (Blackwater Records). Estab. 1990. Represents individual artists, groups and songwriters from anywhere; currently handles 2 acts. Commission varies. Reviews material for acts.
How to Contact: Call first and obtain permission to submit a demo. Prefers cassette or videocassette with 3-5 songs. If seeking management, press kit should include bio, tear sheet, photo and 3-5 song tape. Does not return material. Reports in 1 month.
Music: Mostly **rock**, **roots rock** and **alternative**; also **country rock** and **punk**. Works primarily with bands and singer/songwriters. Current acts include Mystery Train (rock band), Michael Ubaldini (singer/songwriter) and Rambelins (folk rock band).

VOKES BOOKING AGENCY, P.O. Box 12, New Kensington PA 15068-0012. (412)335-2775. President: Howard Vokes. Represents individual traditional country and bluegrass artists. Books name acts in on special occasions. For special occasions books nationally known acts from Grand Ole Op'ry, Jamboree U.S.A., Appalachian Jubliee, etc. Receives 10-20% commission.
    • See the listings for Vokes Music Publishing in the Music Publishers section and Vokes Record Co. in the Record Companies section.
How to Contact: New artists send 45 rpm record, cassette, LP or CD. Reports back within a week.
Music: Traditional **country**, **bluegrass**, **old time** and **gospel**; definitely no rock or country rock. Current acts include Howard Vokes & His Country Boys (country) and Mel Anderson.
Tips: "We work mostly with traditional country bands and bluegrass groups that play various bars, hotels, clubs, high schools, malls, fairs, lounges, or fundraising projects. We work at times with other booking agencies in bringing acts in for special occasions. Also we work directly with well-known

and newer country, bluegrass and country gospel acts not only to possibly get them bookings in our area, but in other states as well. We also help 'certain artists' get bookings in the overseas marketplace."

*VTC ENTERTAINMENT MANAGEMENT, 20186-1395 Lawrence Ave. W., Toronto, Ontario M6L IA7 **Canada**. (416)241-3534. Fax: (416)248-2682. Owner: Vickie Theofanous. Management firm. Estab. 1994. Represents local groups; currently handles 1 act. Receives 20% commission.
How to Contact: Submit demo tape by mail. Unsolicited submissions are OK. Prefers cassette or CD with 4 songs and lyric sheet. If seeking management, press kit should include bio, photo, tearsheets, reviews, fact sheets and cassette/CD. "Be sure to include contact numbers/names and a return address." Does not return material. Reports in 1-2 months.
Music: Mostly **hard rock**, **metal** and **pop**. Works primarily with bands in the hard rock genre who are visually and musically interesting. Current acts include Sinisteria (hard rock 4 piece band).
Tips: "Be confident in your product, and be sincere with your sales pitch. Believe in yourself and the music that you write."

*W.E. (WHITMAN ENTERPRISES), P.O. Box 452, Sun Valley CA 91352. (818)759-7729. Vice President of A&R: Jyna Douglass. Management firm, music publisher (Polaris, Citcynsongs), record company (W.E., 3rds/X), record producer (R. Whitman, B. Paul, J. Martin) and festival production. Estab. 1988. Represents local and western US individual artists, groups, songwriters, CG artists and fine artists; currently handles 6 acts. Receives 8-25% commission. Reviews material for acts.
How to Contact: Submit demo tape by mail. Unsolicited submissions are OK. Prefers cassette or VHS videocassette, LP, CD, art samples with 3-6 songs and lyric sheet. If seeking management, press kit should include bio, photo(s), press releases and reviews, intro letter. "Photocopies OK, PC diskette submissions OK, tape with only intro letter is OK." Does not return material. Reports in 6-12 weeks.
Music: Mostly **progressive rock**, **acoustic only** and **children's genre**; also **computer and fine artists**, **visual producers** and **story writers**. Works primarily with bands, solo artists, lyricists, story writers, computer and fine artists, visual producers, crafts people, engineers and producers. Current acts include CITADEL® (progressive rock show), Ambesextrious (New Age Acoustic), R.U.1.2.? (folk duo) and Jazmyn (R&B/pop).
Tips: "State a clear goal in your intro letter. Worry more about your reasons for entering this market than about flashy promo kits. Have a message to share, study the masters. Don't wait for anyone to help you—do it. Be prepared for a long commitment. Our percentage is based on how much work the artist will take responsibility for versus what level of our services is required. Most of the artists we work with just need simple advice and follow-ups. We prefer to educate instead of fostering dependence. Our specialization is not mainstream and will not make you, or us, millionaires."

WESTWOOD ENTERTAINMENT GROUP, 1115 Inman Ave., Suite 330, Edison NJ 08820. (908)548-6700. Fax: (908)548-6748. President: Victor Kaply. General Manager: Elena Petillo. Artist management agency (Westunes Music/ASCAP). Estab. 1985. Represents regional artists and groups; currently handles 4 acts. Receives 15% commission. Reviews material for acts.
   • Westwood Entertainment's publishing affiliate, Westunes Music, is listed in the Music Publishers section.
How to Contact: Write first and obtain permission to submit. Prefers cassette with 3 songs, lyric sheet, bio, press clippings, and photo. SASE. Reports in 6 weeks.
Music: Mostly **rock**; also **pop**. Works primarily with singer/songwriters, show bands and rock groups. Current acts include Ground Zero (rock), Kidd Skruff (rock) and Tradia (rock).
Tips: "Present a professional promotional/press package with three song limit."

SHANE WILDER ARTISTS' MANAGEMENT, P.O. Box 3503, Hollywood CA 90078. (805)251-7526. President: Shane Wilder. Management firm, music publisher (Shane Wilder Music/BMI) and record producer (Shane Wilder Productions). Represents artists and groups; currently handles 2 acts. Receives 15% commission. Reviews material for acts.
   • See the listing for Shane Wilder Music in the Music Publishers section.
How to Contact: Submit demo tape by mail. Unsolicited submissions are OK. Prefers cassette (or videocassette of performance if available) with 4-10 songs and lyric sheet. If seeking management, send cassette with 4-10 songs, photos of individuals or groups, video if possible and any press releases. "Submissions should be highly commercial." SASE. Reports in 1 month.
Music: Country. Works primarily with single artists and groups. Current acts include Inez Polizzi, Billy O'Hara, Melanie Ray and Kimber Cunningham.
Tips: "Only submit your strongest material. We publish only country for Nashville artists and we are BMI. No ASCAP material will be considered. We do not publish songs with a reversion clause due to so many artists writing their own material, it takes longer to place the song."

*YVONNE WILLIAMS MANAGEMENT, 6433 Topanga Blvd. #142, Canoga Park CA 91303. (818)831-3426. Fax: (818)831-3427. President: Yvonne Williams. Management firm, music publisher

(Jerry Williams Music), record company (S.D.E.G.) and record producer (Jerry Williams). Estab. 1978. Represents individual artists and songwriters from anywhere; currently handles 5 acts. Receives 10-20% commission. Reviews material for acts.
How to Contact: Write first and obtain permission to submit a demo. Prefers cassette or DAT with any number of songs and lyric sheet. Include SASE, name, phone and any background in songs placed. Reports in 1-2 weeks.
Music: Mostly **R&B**, **rock** and **country**; also **gospel**. Works primarily with singer/songwriters and singers. Current acts include Swamp Dogg (rock), Ndesecent Xposure (X-rated rap) and Ruby Andrews (blues).
Tips: "Make a good clean dub, with a simple pilot vocal that is understandable."

WILLIS ENTERTAINMENT, INC., (formerly New Sound Atlanta, Inc.), 1007 Winston Way, Acworth GA 30102. (770)590-7990. Fax: (770)421-8852. E-mail: stuckmojo0@aol.com. Vice President/Management-Promotions: Mark Willis. Management firm. Estab. 1987. Represents international groups; currently handles 2 acts. Receives 20% commission. Reviews material for acts.
How to Contact: Submit demo tape by mail. Unsolicited submissions are OK. Prefers cassette or CD. If seeking management, press kit should include picture, bio, 3 song tape or CD, a list of upcoming performance dates. Does not return material. Reports in 2 months.
Music: Mostly **rock** and **alternative rock**. Works primarily with rock bands, all original, able to tour. Current acts include Stuck Mojo (metal) and Redrum (industrial).

*RICHARD WOOD ARTIST MANAGEMENT, 69 North Randall Ave., Staten Island NY 10301. (718)981-0641. Contact: Richard Wood. Management firm. Estab. 1974. Represents musical groups; currently handles 3 acts. Receives 20% commission. Reviews material for acts.
How to Contact: Submit demo tape by mail. Unsolicited submissions are OK. Prefers cassette and lead sheet. If seeking management, press kit should include demo tape, photo and bio. SASE. Reports in 3-4 weeks.
Music: Mostly **dance**, **R&B** and **top 40/pop**; also **MOR**. Works primarily with "high energy" show bands, bar bands and dance bands. Current acts include F.O.N. (rap), Salsa Gang (Latin) and Romero (dance).

*DEBORAH WOOD PUBLICITY & MANAGEMENT, 155 James St. E., Cobourg, Ontario K9A 1H4 **Canada**. (905)372-9339. Fax: (905)372-2011. Chief Executive: Debbie Wood. Management firm, publicist. Estab. 1989. Represents individual artists from anywhere; currently handles 1 act. Receives 5% commission. Reviews material for acts.
How to Contact: Submit demo tape by mail. Unsolicited submissions are OK. Prefers cassette with 3 songs and lyric sheet. "Not taking on new management clients." SASE. Reports in 3 weeks.
Music: **Country** only. Current acts include Susan Graham (country).

*WORLD BEYOND TALENT & PUBLICITY NETWORK, 73A Crawford St., Eatontown NJ 07724. (908)935-7218. Fax: (908)219-9548. Director/Management Consultant: Christopher Barry. Management firm, booking agency and publicity/public relations. Estab. 1986. Represents Jersey Shore/Northeast individual artists, songwriters and spoken word artists. Receives variable commission. Reviews material for acts.
How to Contact: Submit demo tape by mail. Unsolicited submissions are OK. Prefers cassette or VHS videocassette. If seeking management, press kit should include photographs and any pertinent news or magazine clippings. SASE. Reports in 6 weeks.
Music: Mostly **alternative**, **folk/'new folk'** and **experimental performance art**. Works primarily with singer/songwriters and spoken word artists. Current acts include R.W. Kingbird (singer/songwriter), The Lone Paranoid (spoken word artist) and Not For Nothing (grunge/pop alternative band).
Tips: "Do 'all the right things'; by that I mean don't overlook the obvious moves, but look into anything that looks or sounds as if it could be of potential help to you. Don't be afraid of wasting time."

WORLD WIDE MANAGEMENT, Box 599, Yorktown Heights NY 10598. (914)245-1156. Director: Steve Rosenfeld. Management firm and music publisher (Neighborhood Music/ASCAP). Estab. 1971. Represents artists, groups, songwriters and actors; currently handles 2 acts. Receives 15-25% commission. Reviews material for acts.
How to Contact: Write or call first and obtain permission to submit or to arrange personal interview. Prefers CD or cassette (or videocassete of performance) with 3-4 songs. If seeking management, press kit should include bio, photo and demo. Does not return material. Reports in 1 month.
Music: Mostly **contemporary pop**, **folk**, **folk/rock** and **New Age**; also **A/C**, **rock**, **jazz**, **bluegrass**, **blues**, **country** and **R&B**. Works primarily with self-contained bands and vocalists. Current acts include Small Things Big and Anya Block.

WYATT MANAGEMENT WORLDWIDE, INC., 10797 Onyx Circle, Fountain Valley CA 92708. (714)839-7700; Fax: (714)775-4300. E-mail: warren@wyattworld.com. Website: http://www.w yattworld.com. President: Warren Wyatt and Julie Hines. Management firm. Estab. 1976. Represents regional and international individual artists, groups and songwriters; currently handles 8 acts. Receives 15-20% commission. Reviews material for acts.
How to Contact: Submit demo tape by mail. Unsolicited submissions are OK. Prefers cassette (or VHS videocassette) with 2-10 songs and lyric sheet. If seeking management, include band biography, photos, video, members' history, press and demo reviews in press kit. SASE. Reports in 4 weeks.
Music: Mostly **rock**, **pop** and **R&B**; also **heavy metal**, **hard rock** and **top 40**. Works primarily with pop/rock groups. Current acts include Saigon Kick (hard rock), Carmine Appice (rock) and Mike Tramp (pop/rock).
Tips: "Always submit new songs/material, even if you have sent material that was previously rejected; the music biz is always changing."

Y-NOT PRODUCTIONS, P.O. Box 902, Mill Valley CA 94942. (415)561-9760. Administrative Asst.: Anthony Washington. Management firm and music publisher (Lindy Lane Music/BMI, LaPorte Ave. Music/BMI). Estab. 1989. Represents West Coast-USA individual artists, groups and songwriters; currently handles 4 acts. Receives 20% commission. Reviews material for acts.
How to Contact: Submit demo tape by mail. Unsolicited submissions are OK. Prefers cassette (or VHS videocassette if available) with 3 songs. Send tapes to the attention of Susan Korzela. If seeking management, press kit should include photo, video or DAT or cassette. SASE. Reports in 2 months.
Music: Mostly **contemporary jazz**, **pop** and **R&B/rock**. Works primarily with instrumental groups/ vocalists. Current acts include Tony Saunders (bassist/songwriter), Paradize (R&B), Essence (alternative) and Ken Phlow (rap).

ZANE MANAGEMENT, INC., 1608 Walnut St., Suite 703, Philadelphia PA 19103. (215)772-3010. Fax: (215)772-3717. President: Lloyd Zane Remick. Entertainment/sports consultants and managers. Represents artists, songwriters, producers and athletes; currently handles 5 acts. Receives variable commission.
How to Contact: Prefers cassette and lyric sheet. SASE. Reports in 1 month.
Music: **Dance**, **easy listening**, **folk**, **jazz** (fusion), **MOR**, **rock** (hard and country), **soul** and **top 40/pop**. Current acts include Bunny Sigler (disco/funk), Pieces of a Dream (consultant), Grover Washington, Jr. (management), Kevin Roth (singer/songwriter) and Christian Jos (singer).

Category Index

The Category Index is a good place to begin searching for a market for your songs. Below is an alphabetical list of 19 general music categories. If you write pop songs and are looking for a manager or booking agent to submit your songs to, check the Pop section in this index. There you will find a list of managers and booking agents who work with pop performers. Once you locate the entries for those managers and booking agents, read the Music subheading *carefully* to determine which companies are most interested in the type of pop music you write. Some of the markets in this section do not appear in the Category Index because they have not indicated a specific preference. Most of these said they are interested in "all types" of music. Listings that were very specific, or whose description of the music they're interested in doesn't quite fit into these categories, also do not appear here.

Adult Contemporary

All Star Talent Agency; *Anderson Associates Communications Group; Black Stallion Country Productions, Inc.; Bojo Productions Inc.; Brothers Management Associates; *Clugston Organization Pty. Ltd., The Neil; Five Star Entertainment; Flash Attractions Agency; *Glo Gem Productions, Inc.; Gueststar Entertainment Agency; Hale Enterprises; *Hill Entertainment Management, Steve; Insinna Management, Paul; *International Entertainment Bureau; *Jackson Artists Corp.; Junquera Productions, C.; *Kaufman Hill Management; Knight Agency, Bob; Landslide Management; Levinson

Entertainment Ventures International, Inc.; LMP Management Firm; Lutz Entertainment Agency, Richard; M.B.H. Music Management; Manapro Entertainment; Martin Productions, Rick; Merri-Webb Productions; Mid-East Entertainment Inc.; Nelson Entertainment Inc., Brian; Phil's Entertainment Agency Limited; *Prestige Artistes; *RadioActive; Richards World Management, Inc., Diane; Risavy, Inc., A.F.; Rustron Music Productions; Sherman Artist Management & Development, Mickey; *Silver Bow Management; Skorman Productions, Inc., T.; Sound '86 Talent Management; *Staircase Promotion; Sunset Promotions of Chicago Inc.; T.J. Booker Ltd.; T.S.J. Productions; Tas Music Co./Dave Tasse Entertainment; Total Acting Experience, A; World Wide Management; Zane Management, Inc.

Alternative

Alan Agency, Mark; All Access Entertainment Management Group, Inc.; *Aquila Entertainment; Arimte Entertainment Ltd.; *Arrived Alive Management Inc.; Arslanian & Associates, Inc.; babysue; Beacon Kendall Entertainment; Biscuit Productions Inc.; *Bohemia Entertainment Group; Class Act Productions/Management; Classic Rock Entertainment Agency; Countdown Entertainment; Courtright Management Inc.; Cranium Management; *Creative Management Group; *Crossfire Entertainment; *Crossover Entertainment; Cycle Of Fifths Management, Inc.; DAS Communications, Ltd.; *Debutante Management; *Depth Of Field Management; Direct Management; *Dr. Shay's; *Drastic Measures, Inc.; DSM Management; Earth Tracks Artists Agency; *EBI Inc.; Entercom; Entertainment Resource Management; Entertainment Services International; Eternal Records/Squigmonster Management; Eve's Cradle; Fat City Artists; FCC Management; Federici's Shark River Music, Danny; Foley Entertainment; Freedman Entertainment, Peter; Fritz Management, Ken; Hardman Management, Dustin; Hardway Music Management; *Headline Management; *Hill Entertainment Management, Steve; hm Management; Hologram Entertainment; James Gang Management; *Jerifka Productions, Inc.; *Kriete, Kincaid & Faith; Kuper Personal Management; Lazy Bones Recordings/Productions, Inc.; *Little Big Man Booking; Long Arm Talent; *Long Distance Entertainment; M.B.H. Music Management; Manapro Entertainment; *Merlin Management Corp.; Midnight Music Management; Monopoly Management; Music Man Promotions; Nelson Entertainment Inc., Brian; *O'Malley Artist Management, Inc.; Performers of the World Inc. (P.O.W.); *Pillar Records; *Prairie Fire Music Company; *Productions Unlimited; *Professional Artist Management, Ltd.; *RadioActive; *RDR Music Group; *Relax Productions; *Rhyme Syndicate Management; *Rock Whirled Music Management; S.T.A.R.S. Productions; *Sellout! Management; *Silver Bow Management; Simmons Management Group; Sirocco Productions, Inc.; Smeltzer Productions, Gary; *Staircase Promotion; Star Artist Management Inc.; Stewart Management, Steve; Strictly Forbidden Artists; *Sunnydays Records; *Surface Management Inc.; *Sweet Pea Artist Management; Tanner Entertainment; *Tenn Artist Management, William; Tiger's Eye Entertainment Management & Consulting; *Topnotch® Music & Records; Victory Artists; Vintage Crime Management; Willis Entertainment, Inc.; *World Beyond Talent & Publicity Network

Blues

*All Star Promotions; *Arrived Alive Management Inc.; *Barnard Management Services (BMS); *Big Boy Records & Artist Management; *Big Hand; Blowin' Smoke Productions; *Blue Sky Artist Management; Blumenauer Artists, Geoffrey; *Cash Productions, Inc; Classic Rock Entertainment Agency; Community Music Center of Houston; Courtright Management Inc.; DMR Agency; *Dr. Shay's; Empry Entertainment, Gino; *Faith Entertainment, James; Fat City Artists; Flash Attractions Agency; Foggy

---

 THE ASTERISK before a listing indicates that the listing is new in this edition. New markets are often the most receptive to unsolicited submissions.

Day Music; Golden Bull Productions; *Headline Talent Inc.; Hit City Records; Jam Entertainment & Events; James Gang Management; *Jazz-One Productions; *Living Eye Productions Ltd.; Mayo & Company, Phil; Midnight Music Management; Music Man Promotions; Music Matters; Nova Productions & Management; Nowag's National Attractions, Craig; *Odom-Meaders Management; Operation Music Enterprises; Perception Works Inc., The; *Pillar Records; *Platinum Tracks Productions; *Productions Unlimited; *Professional Artist Management, Ltd.; *Ruff Production, Jimmy; Russell Productions, T.; Rustron Music Productions; *Sandcastle Productions; *Sharp Management, Jim; Sirius Entertainment; Squad 16; *Stormin' Norman Productions; Sunset Promotions of Chicago Inc.; *Sweet Pea Artist Management; T.S.J. Productions; *Texas Music Masters; Tiger's Eye Entertainment Management & Consulting; *Tone Zone Booking Agency; *Topnotch® Music & Records; Total Acting Experience, A; TSMB Productions; Universal Music Marketing; *W.E. (Whitman Enterprises)

Children's

Brasswind Artist Management; Direct Management; Fritz Management, Ken; *Paquin Entertainment Group; Siegel Entertainment Ltd.; Tanglewood Group Inc., The; *Valiant Records & Management

Classical

*Aquila Entertainment; *Clousher Productions; Colwell Arts Management; Countrywide Producers; *Faith Entertainment, James; *Fiedler Management, B.C.; Its Happening Present Entertainment; Jana Jae Enterprises; *Other Road, The; *Paquin Entertainment Group; Rock Of Ages Productions; Sirius Entertainment; Sunset Promotions of Chicago Inc.; Tiger's Eye Entertainment Management & Consulting; *Tutta Forza Music

Country

Afterschool Publishing Company; Air Tight Management; Alexas Music Productions; All Access Entertainment Management Group, Inc.; All Star Management; All Star Talent Agency; Allen Entertainment Development, Michael; American Family Talent; Ardenne Int'l Inc.; *Arrived Alive Management Inc.; Atch Records and Productions; ATI Music; babysue; Bandstand (International) Entertainment Agency; *Barnard Management Services (BMS); Baxter Management, Dick; *Big Beat Productions, Inc.; *Bird Entertainment Agency, J.; Black Stallion Country Productions, Inc.; *Blue Sky Artist Management; Blumenauer Artists, Geoffrey; Bojo Productions Inc.; Bouquet-Orchid Enterprises; Brasswind Artist Management; Bullseye Entertainment; Burns Talent Agency, Dott; C & M Productions Management Group; Capitol Management & Talent; *Carlyle Management; *Cash Productions, Inc.; Cavalry Productions; Cedar Creek Productions and Management and Cedar Cove Music; Circuit Rider Talent & Management Co.; Class Act Productions/Management; Classic Rock Entertainment Agency; *Clousher Productions; Concept 2000 Inc.; Cool Records; Country Star Attractions; Countrywide Producers; Cranium Management; Crash Productions; Crawfish Productions; Creative Star Management; *Crossfire Entertainment; *Crowe Entertainment Inc.; De Miles Company, The Edward; Dinwoodie Management, Andrew; *Doran, P.C., James R.; Doss Presents, Col. Buster; EAO Music Corporation Of Canada; *EBI Inc.; Empry Entertainment, Gino; Entertainment Resource Management; Entertainment Services International; Eve's Cradle; Fame International; Fat City Artists; FCC Management; Federici's Shark River Music, Danny; Fenchel Entertainment Agency, Fred T.; *Fiedler Management, B.C.; First Time Management; Five Star Entertainment; *5 Star Music Group/Mike Waddell & Associates; Flash Attractions Agency; Foggy Day Music; Foley Entertainment; *Fox Management, Inc., Mitchell; Frick Enterprises, Bob Scott; Fudpucker Entertainment; Gallup Entertainment; *Glo Gem Productions, Inc.; GMI Entertainment Inc.; Grass Management; Great Lakes Country Talent Agency; Greeley Entertainment, Chris; Gueststar Entertainment Agency; Hale Enterprises; M. Harrell & Associates; Hawkeye Attractions; *Headline Talent Inc.; *Hill Entertainment Management, Steve; Hit City Records; Holiday Productions, Doc; Image

Promotions Inc.; Intermountain Talent; *International Entertainment Bureau; Its Happening Present Entertainment; J & V Management; *Jackson Artists Corp.; Jam Entertainment & Events; James Gang Management; James Management, Roger; Jana Jae Enterprises; Johnson Agency, Little Richie; Junquera Productions, C.; *Kaleidoscope Music; *KRC Records & Productions; Landslide Management; Lari-Jon Promotions; Lenthall & Associates; Levinson Entertainment Ventures International, Inc.; Levy Mgt, Rick; *Live-Wire Management; *Long Distance Entertainment; *Lowell Agency; Lutz Entertainment Agency, Richard; *M. & G. Entertainment Consortiums, Inc.; M.B.H. Music Management; McDonnell Group, The; Magnum Music Corporation Ltd.; Management Plus; Mayo & Company, Phil; MC Promotions & Public Relations; Merri-Webb Productions; Mid-East Entertainment Inc.; Midnight Music Management; *Midnight Special Productions, Inc.; *Mighty Oak Management; Milestone Media; Miller & Company, Thomas J.; Misty International; Monopoly Management; *Monterey Artists, Inc.; Morelli Enterprises, Thomas; *Myers Enterprises, James E.; Nashville Connection, The; Newby Management, J.P.; NIC Of Tyme Productions, Inc.; Nik Entertainment Company; Noteworthy Productions; Nova Productions & Management; Nowag's National Attractions, Craig; OB-1 Entertainment; O'Malley And Associates Agency, Scott; Operation Music Enterprises; *Overstreet Music Companies, Tommy; Perception Works Inc., The; Phil's Entertainment Agency Limited; *Pillar Records; *Platinum Tracks Productions; *Prairie Fire Music Company; *Prestige Artistes; Pro Talent Consultants; *Process Talent; *Productions Unlimited; Rainbow Collection Ltd.; RANA International Affiliates, Inc.; *RDR Music Group; RGK Entertainment Group; Risavy, Inc., A.F.; Rock Of Ages Productions; Rocky Mountain Management; Rothschild Productions Inc., Charles R.; *Ruff Production, Jimmy; Rustron Music Productions; Rymkus Management and Promotions, Mike; S.T.A.R.S. Productions; *Schonfeld Productions, Lonny; Seip Management, Inc., William; *Serge Entertainment Group; *Sewitt Group, The; *Sharp Management, Jim; Sherman Artist Management & Development, Mickey; Showcana Corporation; Shute Management Pty. Ltd., Phill; Siegel Entertainment Ltd.; *Silver Bow Management; *Silver Moon Productions; Smeltzer Productions, Gary; Smith and Associates, Michael; *Sound and Serenity Management; Sound '86 Talent Management; SP Talent Associates; Sphere Productions; Stahl Entertainments, Bernie; *Staircase Promotion; Star Vest Management Associates Inc.; *Stormin' Norman Productions; Sunset Promotions of Chicago Inc.; *Sunshadow Productions; *Sweet Pea Artist Management; T.J. Booker Ltd.; *T.L.C. Booking Agency; *T 'n T Enterprises; T.S.J. Productions; Tanglewood Group Inc., The; Tanner Entertainment; *TCG Management; *Texas Music Masters; *Texas Sounds Entertainment; 315 Beale Studios/Taliesyn Entertainment; Total Acting Experience, A; Triangle Talent, Inc.; TSMB Productions; *Umpire Entertainment Enterprizes; Universal Music Marketing; Up Front Management; *Valiant Records & Management; *Varrasso Management, Richard; Victory Artists; Vintage Crime Management; Vokes Booking Agency; Wilder Artists' Management, Shane; *Williams Management, Yvonne; *Wood Publicity & Management, Deborah; World Wide Management

Dance

*Anderson Associates Communications Group; *Arrived Alive Management Inc.; Artists Only, Inc.; Atlantic Entertainment Group; *Bassline Entertainment, Inc.; Biscuit Productions Inc.; Classic Rock Entertainment Agency; *Clousher Productions; *Clugston Organization Pty. Ltd., The Neil; Countdown Entertainment; Countrywide Producers; De Miles Company, The Edward; *Dr. Shay's; Earth Tracks Artists Agency; Ellipse Personal Management; First Time Management; Flash Attractions Agency; Freedman Entertainment, Peter; *Golden City International; Hardman Management, Dustin; Hardway Music Management; *Hill Entertainment Management, Steve; Insinna Management, Paul; *Jackson Artists Corp.; *Kaufman Hill Management; Landslide Management; Lutz Entertainment Agency, Richard; M.B.H. Music Management; *McGillis Music Publishing Co.; Manapro Entertainment; *Mark One-The Agency; Martin Productions, Rick; *Merlin Management Corp.; Mid-East Entertainment Inc.; Milestone Media; Moore Entertainment Group; Office, Inc., The; On Stage Management Inc.; *Perom International; *Productions Unlimited; Renaissance Entertainment Group;

Richards World Management, Inc., Diane; *Sellout! Management; *Silver Bow Management; Skorman Productions, Inc., T.; Sound '86 Talent Management; Squad 16; *Sunnydays Records; Talent Associates of Wisconsin, Inc.; Tas Music Co./Dave Tasse Entertainment; *Topnotch® Music & Records; Total Acting Experience, A; Van Pol Management, Hans; *Wood Artist Management, Richard; Zane Management, Inc.

Folk

Afterschool Publishing Company; Amok Inc.; ArkLight Management Co.; Blumenauer Artists, Geoffrey; Classic Rock Entertainment Agency; Community Music Center of Houston; Countrywide Producers; Dinwoodie Management, Andrew; DSM Management; Duckworthy/Atlantica; EAO Music Corporation Of Canada; *Faith Entertainment, James; Five Star Entertainment; Foggy Day Music; Hit City Records; Image Promotions Inc.; *Immigrant Music Inc.; *Living Eye Productions Ltd.; Ltd.; Noteworthy Productions; O'Malley and Associates Agency, Scott; *Paquin Entertainment Group; Performers of the World Inc. (P.O.W.); *Prairie Fire Music Company; *Professional Artist Management; RGK Entertainment Group; *Rhyme Syndicate Management; *Rock Whirled Music Management; Rothschild Productions Inc., Charles R.; Rustron Music Productions; S.T.A.R.S. Productions; SP Talent Associates; *Stormin' Norman Productions; T.S.J. Productions; Tiger's Eye Entertainment Management & Consulting; *World Beyond Talent & Publicity Network; World Wide Management; Zane Management, Inc.

Jazz

Afterschool Publishing Company; Air Tight Management; All Musicmatters; Arimte Entertainment Ltd.; *Arrived Alive Management Inc.; *Big Beat Productions, Inc.; *Big Hand; Blue Cat Agency/El Gato Azul Agency, The; Blumenauer Artists, Geoffrey; Burns Talent Agency, Dott; Cedar Creek Productions and Management and Cedar Cove Music; Classic Rock Entertainment Agency; Community Music Center of Houston; Concept 2000 Inc.; Countrywide Producers; D&D Talent Associates; *Dr. Shay's; Empry Entertainment, Gino; Entertainment Resource Management; *Faith Entertainment, James; Fame International; Fat City Artists; Flash Attractions Agency; *Fox Management, Inc., Mitchell; Fritz Management, Ken; *Glo Gem Productions, Inc.; Golden Bull Productions; *GSI Inc.; *International Entertainment Bureau; Its Happening Present Entertainment; Jae Enterprises, Jana; Jam Entertainment & Events; *Jazz-One Productions; *KenWan's Productions; L.D.F. Productions; *Live-Wire Management; *M. & G. Entertainment Consortiums, Inc.; McDonnell Group, The; *Melody's Music; Mid-East Entertainment Inc.; Miller & Company, Thomas J.; Music Man Promotions; Music Matters; NIC Of Tyme Productions, Inc.; Nova Productions & Management; *Other Road, The; Performers of the World Inc. (P.O.W.); Phil's Entertainment Agency Limited; *Productions Unlimited; Ricca, Jr.'s Entertainment Agency, Joey; Richards World Management, Inc., Diane; Riohcat Music; Rothschild Productions Inc., Charles R.; Russell Productions, T.; Saffyre Management; Scott Entertainment, Craig; Sirius Entertainment; Squad 16; *Stander Entertainment; T.S.J. Productions; Talent Associates of Wisconsin, Inc.; Tas Music Co./Dave Tasse Entertainment; *TCG Management; Tiger's Eye Entertainment Management & Consulting; Tilton Management, Terri; Total Acting Experience, A; *Tutta Forza Music; World Wide Management; Y-Not Productions; Zane Management, Inc.

Latin

African Diaspora Project, The; *Aquila Entertainment; Artists Only, Inc.; *Bassline Entertainment, Inc.; Blue Cat Agency/El Gato Azul Agency, The; Cavalry Productions; *Chabu Productions; *Cookman International; Corvalan-Condliffe Management; DiLeo Management, Liesa; *Fast Lane Productions; Flash Attractions Agency; Johnson Agency, Little Richie; *Long Distance Entertainment; *McGillis Music Publishing Co.; Management Plus; *Musica Moderna Management; Ricca, Jr.'s Entertainment Agency, Joey; Russell Productions, T.

Metal

Artist Representation and Management; Courtright Management Inc.; *Drastic Measures, Inc.; Entercom; Eternal Records/Squigmonster Management; H.L.A. Music; *Hill Entertainment Management, Steve; Jupiter Productions; Northstar Artist Management; *Professional Artist Management, Ltd.; *Raz Management Co.; Saffyre Management; *Sellout! Management; *Sewitt Group, The; Simmons Management Group; *Surface Management Inc.; *VTC Entertainment Management; Wyatt Management Worldwide, Inc.

New Age

Alexas Music Productions; *Aquila Entertainment; *Fast Lane Productions; Federici's Shark River Music, Danny; Firestar Promotions Inc.; *Hooker Enterprises; *Jerifka Productions, Inc.; *Live-Wire Management; *Other Road, The; *Paquin Entertainment Group; *Prairie Fire Music Company; Richards World Management, Inc., Diane; Rustron Music Productions; Saffyre Management; Showcana Corporation; Sphere Productions; Sunset Promotions of Chicago Inc.; World Wide Management

Novelty

Bandstand (International) Entertainment Agency; Cavalry Productions; Circuit Rider Talent & Management Co.; *Dr. Shay's; Eternal Records/Squigmonster Management; Fudpucker Entertainment; Hall Entertainment & Events, Bill; *Paquin Entertainment Group; Stahl Entertainments, Bernie; *Valiant Records & Management

Pop

Adelaide Rock Exchange; Afterschool Publishing Company; AKO Productions; Alan Agency, Mark; *Alert Music, Inc.; Alexas Music Productions; All Access Entertainment Management Group, Inc.; All Star Talent Agency; Allen Entertainment Development, Michael; American Artist, Inc.; American Family Talent; *Anderson Associates Communications Group; Ardenne Int'l Inc.; Arimte Entertainment Ltd.; ArkLight Management Co.; Artist Representation and Management; Artists Only, Inc.; Atch Records and Productions; babysue; *Bassline Entertainment, Inc.; Baxter Management, Dick; *Big Beat Productions, Inc.; *Big Hand; Big J Productions; *Bird Entertainment Agency, J.; Biscuit Productions Inc.; Blue Cat Agency/El Gato Azul Agency, The; Blumenauer Artists, Geoffrey; Bouquet-Orchid Enterprises; Brothers Management Associates; Burns Talent Agency, Dott; C & M Productions Management Group; Capitol Management & Talent; *Cash Productions, Inc; Cedar Creek Productions and Management and Cedar Cove Music; *Chabu Productions; Circuit Rider Talent & Management Co.; Class Act Productions/Management; Clockwork Entertainment Management Agency; *Clugston Organization Pty. Ltd., The Neil; Coffer Management, Raymond; Concept 2000 Inc.; Conscience Music; Corvalan-Condliffe Management; Countdown Entertainment; Countrywide Producers; Courtright Management Inc.; Cranium Management; Creative Star Management; Criss-Cross Industries; D & M Entertainment Agency; DAS Communications, Ltd.; De Miles Company, The Edward; DiLeo Management, Liesa; Dinwoodie Management, Andrew; DMR Agency; DSM Management; Earth Tracks Artists Agency; Ellipse Personal Management; Empry Entertainment, Gino; Entercom; Entertainment Resource Management; Eternal Records/Squigmonster Management; Evans Productions, Scott; Fat City Artists; Fenchel Entertainment Agency, Fred T.; *Fiedler Management, B.C.; First Time Management; Foley Entertainment; Freedman Entertainment, Peter; Fritz Management, Ken; Future Star Entertainment; *Glo Gem Productions, Inc.; GMI Entertainment Inc.; Golden Bull Productions; *Golden City International; Golden Guru Entertainment; Grass Management; Great Lakes Country Talent Agency; Greeley Entertainment, Chris; Hale Enterprises; *Harbour Agency Pty. Ltd., The; Hardman Management, Dustin; *Headline Management; High Energy Management; *Hill Entertainment Management, Steve; Holiday Productions, Doc; Its Happening Present Entertainment; *Jackson Artists Corp.; Jae Enterprises, Jana; Jam Entertainment & Events; James Gang Management; James Management, Roger; Kagan Productions, Sheldon; *Kaufman Hill Management; Knight Agency, Bob; L.D.F. Productions; Landslide Management; Lenthall & Associates; Levy Mgt, Rick; *Live-Wire Management; LMP Management Firm; Long Arm Talent; *Long Distance Entertainment; Lutz Entertainment Agency, Richard; McDonnell Group, The; *McGillis Music Publishing Co.; Manapro Entertainment; *Mark One-The Agency; Martin Productions, Rick; Mayo & Company, Phil; *Merlin Management Corp.; Merri-Webb Productions; Mid-East Entertainment Inc.; Miller & Company, Thomas J.; Monopoly Management; Moore Entertainment Group; Music Man Promotions; Music Matters; NIC Of Tyme Productions, Inc.; Nik Entertainment Company; Northstar Artist Management; Noteworthy Productions; Nowag's National Attractions, Craig; OB-1 Entertainment; Office, Inc., The; *O'Malley Artist Management, Inc.; On Stage Management Inc.; Perception Works Inc., The; Performers of the World Inc. (P.O.W.); *Perom International; *Pillar Records; Platinum Ears Ltd.; *Platinum Tracks Productions; *Prestige Artistes; Pro Talent Consultants; *RadioActive; Rainbow Collection Ltd.; RANA International Affiliates, Inc.; *Raz Management Co.; Reiter Productions, Richard; Richards World Management, Inc., Diane; Risavy, Inc., A.F.; Rock Of Ages Productions; Rothschild Productions Inc., Charles R.; *Ruff Production, Jimmy; Russell Productions, T.; Saffyre Management; *Schonfeld Productions, Lonny; *Serge Entertainment Group; Shapiro & Company, C.P.A.; Sherman Artist Management & Development, Mickey; Shute Management Pty. Ltd., Phill; Siegel Entertainment Ltd.; Simmons Management Group; Skorman Productions, Inc., T.; Sound '86 Talent Management; Sphere Productions; *Staircase Promotion; *Stander Entertainment; Star Artist Management Inc.; Star Vest Management Associates Inc.; Steele Management; Strictley Biziness Music Management; *Surface Management Inc.; T.J. Booker Ltd.; *T 'n T Enterprises; T.S.J. Productions; Talent Associates of Wisconsin, Inc.; Tanner Entertainment; Tas Music Co./Dave Tasse Entertainment; *Tenn Artist Management, William; Tilton Management, Terri; *Topnotch® Music & Records; Total Acting Experience, A; Triangle Talent, Inc.; Umbrella Artists Management, Inc.; *Umpire Entertainment Enterprizes; *Valiant Records & Management; Victory Artists; *VTC Entertainment Management; Westwood Entertainment Group; *Wood Artist Management, Richard; World Wide Management; Wyatt Management Worldwide, Inc.; Y-Not Productions; Zane Management, Inc.

R&B

Adelaide Rock Exchange; Alan Agency, Mark; *All Star Promotions; Allen Entertainment Development, Michael; American Artist, Inc.; *Anderson Associates Communications Group; Arimte Entertainment Ltd.; Artist Representation and Management; Atch Records and Productions; Atlantic Entertainment Group; *Barnard Management Services (BMS); *Bassline Entertainment, Inc.; Beacon Kendall Entertainment; *Big Boy Records & Artist Management; *Big Hand; Big J Productions; Biscuit Productions Inc.; Black Stallion Country Productions, Inc.; *Blackground; Blowin' Smoke Productions; Bojo Productions Inc.; Bouquet-Orchid Enterprises; Brothers Management Associates; Capitol Management & Talent; Cedar Creek Productions and Management and Cedar Cove Music; Circuit Rider Talent & Management Co.; Class Act Productions/ Management; Classic Rock Entertainment Agency; Community Music Center of Houston; Concept 2000 Inc.; Corvalan-Condliffe Management; Countdown Entertainment; Country Star Attractions; Countrywide Producers; Creative Star Management; Criss-Cross Industries; D & M Entertainment Agency; DAS Communications, Ltd.; De Miles Company, The Edward; DiLeo Management, Liesa; Dinwoodie Management, Andrew; Ellipse Personal Management; Entertainment Group, The; Entertainment Services International; Evans Productions, Scott; Federici's Shark River Music, Danny; Foley Entertainment; Freedman Entertainment, Peter; Frick Enterprises, Bob Scott; Future Star Entertainment; GMI Entertainment Inc.; Golden Bull Productions; *Golden City International; Grass Management; Greene Entertainment, Tim; Harrell & Associates, M.; *Headline Talent Inc.; High Energy Management; *Hill Entertainment Management, Steve; Holiday Productions, Doc; Hologram Entertainment; Image Promotions Inc.; Imani Entertainment Inc.; Insinna Management, Paul; Its Happening Present Entertainment; *Jackson Artists Corp.; *Jacobs Management; Jam Entertainment & Events;

James Gang Management; JAS Management; *KenWan's Productions; KKR Entertainment Group; Knight Agency, Bob; Landslide Management; Lenthall & Associates; Levinson Entertainment Ventures International, Inc.; Levy Mgt, Rick; *Live-Wire Management; LMP Management Firm; M & M Talent Agency Inc.; McDonnell Group, The; *Madstorm Production Company; Manapro Entertainment; *Melody's Music; Merri-Webb Productions; Mid-East Entertainment Inc.; Midnight Music Management; Moore Entertainment Group; Music Matters; NIC Of Tyme Productions, Inc.; Nilsson Production, Christina; Nowag's National Attractions, Craig; Office, Inc., The; On Stage Management Inc.; Perception Works Inc., The; Performers of the World Inc. (P.O.W.); *Perom International; Precision Management; *Productions Unlimited; RANA International Affiliates, Inc.; Reiter Productions, Richard; Renaissance Entertainment Group; Russell Productions, T.; Rustron Music Productions; *Serge Entertainment Group; *Sewitt Group, The; Sherman Artist Management & Development, Mickey; Shute Management Pty. Ltd., Phill; *Silver Bow Management; Simmons Management Group; Sirius Entertainment; Smeltzer Productions, Gary; Sphere Productions; *Stander Entertainment; Star Vest Management Associates Inc.; Strictley Biziness Music Management; T.S.J. Productions; Talent Associates of Wisconsin, Inc.; Tas Music Co./Dave Tasse Entertainment; *Texas Sounds Entertainment; 315 Beale Studios/Taliesyn Entertainment; Tilton Management, Terri; Total Acting Experience, A; Up Front Management; Van Pol Management, Hans; *Williams Management, Yvonne; *Wood Artist Management, Richard; World Wide Management; Wyatt Management Worldwide, Inc.; Y-Not Productions; Zane Management, Inc.

Rap

Afterschool Publishing Company; American Artist, Inc.; Arimte Entertainment Ltd.; Artists Only, Inc.; Atch Records and Productions; *Bassline Entertainment, Inc.; Biscuit Productions Inc.; *Blackground; Classic Rock Entertainment Agency; Creative Star Management; Cycle Of Fifths Management, Inc.; DME Management; First Time Management; *Golden City International; Greene Entertainment, Tim; H.L.A. Music; High Energy Management; Holiday Productions, Doc; Imani Entertainment Inc.; Insinna Management, Paul; Its Happening Present Entertainment; JAS Management; Jupiter Productions; KKR Entertainment Group; Lazy Bones Recordings/Productions, Inc.; Lenthall & Associates; *M. & G. Entertainment Consortiums, Inc.; *Madstorm Production Company; Milestone Media; Precision Management; Renaissance Entertainment Group; Richards World Management, Inc., Diane; *Ruff Production, Jimmy; Russell Productions, T.; *Sewitt Group, The; Strictley Biziness Music Management; Strictly Forbidden Artists; *Tone Zone Booking Agency; Van Pol Management, Hans

Religious

Alexas Music Productions; All Star Management; All Star Talent Agency; Allen Entertainment Development, Michael; Atch Records and Productions; ATI Music; babysue; Baxter Management, Dick; *Blackground; Bojo Productions Inc.; Bouquet-Orchid Enterprises; Brasswind Artist Management; Bullseye Entertainment; C & M Productions Management Group; Capitol Management & Talent; *Cash Productions, Inc.; Cavalry Productions; Cedar Creek Productions and Management and Cedar Cove Music; Circuit Rider Talent & Management Co.; Community Music Center of Houston; Concept 2000 Inc.; Country Star Attractions; Countrywide Producers; Crawfish Productions; Creative Star Management; Direct Management; Doss Presents, Col. Buster; *Exclesisa Booking Agency; Fenchel Entertainment Agency, Fred T.; First Time Management; *5 Star Music Group/Mike Waddell & Associates; Frick Enterprises, Bob Scott; *Glad Productions; Golden Bull Productions; *Golden City International; Great Lakes Country Talent Agency; Gueststar Entertainment Agency; Hit City Records; Holiday Productions, Doc; *Jackson Artists Corp.; James Gang Management; JAS Management; *Joy Artist Management, Inc.; *KenWan's Productions; *KRC Records & Productions; L.D.F. Productions; Lari-Jon Promotions; Lenthall & Associates; *M. & G. Entertainment Consortiums, Inc.; Magnum Music Corporation Ltd.; Mayo & Company, Phil; *Melody's Music; Merri-Webb Productions; Misty International; NIC Of Tyme Productions, Inc.;

Nilsson Production, Christina; *Overstreet Music Companies, Tommy; Precision Management; Rock Of Ages Productions; *Ruff Production, Jimmy; *Sharp Management, Jim; *Silver Bow Management; Smith and Associates, Michael; *Staircase Promotion; Star Vest Management Associates Inc.; Strictley Biziness Music Management; Sunset Promotions of Chicago Inc.; *TCG Management; *Texas Music Masters; *Theater Arts Network/Stephen Productions; *Tone Zone Booking Agency; *Umpire Entertainment Enterprizes; Vokes Booking Agency; *Williams Management, Yvonne

Rock

*W.E. (Whitman Enterprises); Adelaide Rock Exchange; Air Tight Management; AKO Productions; Alan Agency, Mark; *Alert Music, Inc.; All Access Entertainment Management Group, Inc.; All Star Management; *All Star Promotions; All Star Talent Agency; Allen Entertainment Development, Michael; *Anderson Associates Communications Group; *Aquila Entertainment; Ardenne Int'l Inc.; Arimte Entertainment Ltd.; ArkLight Management Co.; *Arrived Alive Management Inc.; Arslanian & Associates, Inc.; Artist Representation and Management; Artists Only, Inc.; Atch Records and Productions; Atlantic Entertainment Group; babysue; Bandstand (International) Entertainment Agency; *Barnard Management Services (BMS); *Bassline Entertainment, Inc.; Beacon Kendall Entertainment; *Big Beat Productions, Inc.; *Big Hand; Big J Productions; *Bird Entertainment Agency, J.; Blaze Productions; Blowin' Smoke Productions; Blue Cat Agency/El Gato Azul Agency, The; *Blue Sky Artist Management; Blumenauer Artists, Geoffrey; Bouquet-Orchid Enterprises; Brothers Management Associates; Capitol Management & Talent; *Carlyle Management; *Cash Productions, Inc; Cedar Creek Productions and Management and Cedar Cove Music; *Chabu Productions; Class Act Productions/Management; Classic Rock Entertainment Agency; Clockwork Entertainment Management Agency; *Clousher Productions; *Clugston Organization Pty. Ltd., The Neil; Coffer Management, Raymond; Conscience Music; Corvalan-Condliffe Management; Countdown Entertainment; Country Star Attractions; Countrywide Producers; Courtright Management Inc.; Crash Productions; *Creative Management Group; *Crossfire Entertainment; Cycle Of Fifths Management, Inc.; D & M Entertainment Agency; DAS Communications, Ltd.; *DCA Productions; De Miles Company, The Edward; *Debutante Management; *Depth Of Field Management; DiLeo Management, Liesa; Dinwoodie Management, Andrew; DME Management; DMR Agency; *Dr. Shay's; *Doran, P.C., James R.; DSM Management; EAO Music Corporation Of Canada; Earth Tracks Artists Agency; Ellipse Personal Management; Entercom; Entertainment Group, The; Entertainment Resource Management; Entertainment Services International; Eternal Records/Squigmonster Management; Eve's Cradle; *Faith Entertainment, James; Fat City Artists; Federici's Shark River Music, Danny; *5 Star Music Group/Mike Waddell & Associates; Flash Attractions Agency; Foggy Day Music; Foley Entertainment; *Fox Management, Inc., Mitchell; Fritz Management, Ken; Future Star Entertainment; Gallup Entertainment; Golden Bull Productions; Golden Guru Entertainment; Grass Management; Greeley Entertainment, Chris; H.L.A. Music; Hale Enterprises; *Harbour Agency Pty. Ltd., The; Hardman Management, Dustin; Hardway Music Management; *Headline Talent Inc.; *Hooker Enterprises; Image Promotions Inc.; Intermountain Talent; *International Entertainment Bureau; *Jackson Artists Corp.; *Jacobs Management; Jam Entertainment & Events; *Jerifka Productions, Inc.; Jupiter Productions; *Kaleidoscope Music; *Kaufman Hill Management; KKR Entertainment Group; Knight Agency, Bob; L.D.F. Productions; Landslide Management; Lari-Jon Promotions; Lenthall & Associates; Levinson Entertainment Ventures International, Inc.; *Living Eye Productions Ltd.; LMP Management Firm; Long Arm Talent; *Long Distance Entertainment; *M. & G. Entertainment Consortiums, Inc.; M & M Talent Agency Inc.; M.B.H. Music Management; McDonnell Group, The; *Mark One-The Agency; Mayo & Company, Phil; Merri-Webb Productions; Mid-East Entertainment Inc.; Milestone Media; Miller & Company, Thomas J.; Moore Entertainment Group; Morelli Enterprises, Thomas; Music Matters; *Myers Enterprises, James E.; Nelson Entertainment Inc., Brian; Newby Management, J.P.; NIC Of Tyme Productions, Inc.; Nik Entertainment Company; Nilsson Production, Christina; Northstar Artist Management; Nowag's National Attractions, Craig; OB-1 Entertainment; *Odom-Meaders

Management; Office, Inc., The; *O'Malley Artist Management, Inc.; On Stage Management Inc.; *Overstreet Music Companies, Tommy; Perception Works Inc., The; Performers of the World Inc. (P.O.W.); *Perom International; Phil's Entertainment Agency Limited; *Pillar Records; Platinum Ears Ltd.; *Platinum Tracks Productions; *Prairie Fire Music Company; *Prestige Artistes; Pro Talent Consultants; *Productions Unlimited; *RadioActive; Rainbow Collection Ltd.; RANA International Affiliates, Inc.; *Raz Management Co.; RGK Entertainment Group; *Rhyme Syndicate Management; Risavy, Inc., A.F.; Rock Of Ages Productions; *Rock Whirled Music Management; Rothschild Productions Inc., Charles R.; *Ruff Production, Jimmy; Russell Productions, T.; Rustron Music Productions; S.T.A.R.S. Productions; Saffyre Management; *Sandcastle Productions; *Schonfeld Productions, Lonny; Seip Management, Inc., William; *Serge Entertainment Group; *Sewitt Group, The; Shapiro & Company, C.P.A.; Sherman Artist Management & Development, Mickey; Showcana Corporation; Shute Management Pty. Ltd., Phill; Siegel Entertainment Ltd.; *Silver Bow Management; *Silver Moon Productions; Simmons Management Group; Sirius Entertainment; Sound '86 Talent Management; SP Talent Associates; Sphere Productions; Squad 16; *Staircase Promotion; Star Artist Management Inc.; Star Vest Management Associates Inc.; Steele Management; Stewart Management, Steve; *Stormin' Norman Productions; Strictley Biziness Music Management; Strictly Forbidden Artists; *Sunnydays Records; *Surface Management Inc.; T.J. Booker Ltd.; *T.L.C. Booking Agency; *T 'n T Enterprises; T.S.J. Productions; Talent Associates of Wisconsin, Inc.; Tanner Entertainment; Tas Music Co./Dave Tasse Entertainment; *Tenn Artist Management, William; *Theater Arts Network/Stephen Productions; 315 Beale Studios/Taliesyn Entertainment; Tiger's Eye Entertainment Management & Consulting; *Tone Zone Booking Agency; *Topnotch® Music & Records; Triangle Talent, Inc.; TSMB Productions; Umbrella Artists Management, Inc.; Universal Music Marketing; Up Front Management; *Varrasso Management, Richard; Victory Artists; Vintage Crime Management; *VTC Entertainment Management; Westwood Entertainment Group; *Williams Management, Yvonne; Willis Entertainment, Inc.; World Wide Management; Wyatt Management Worldwide, Inc.; Y-Not Productions; Zane Management, Inc.

World Music

African Diaspora Project, The; Amok Inc.; *Clousher Productions; Entertainment Works; *Faith Entertainment, James; *Fast Lane Productions; FCC Management; Flash Attractions Agency; Flinter Music; Foggy Day Music; *Fox Management, Inc., Mitchell; Grass Management; Hit City Records; *Immigrant Music Inc.; *International Entertainment Bureau; *Madstorm Production Company; Management Plus; Midnight Music Management; Music Man Promotions; Performers of the World Inc. (P.O.W.); *Relax Productions; *Sphere Organization, The; Squad 16; *Stander Entertainment; *Stormin' Norman Productions; *Sunnydays Records; *Tone Zone Booking Agency

---

✱ THE ASTERISK before a listing indicates that the listing is new in this edition. New markets are often the most receptive to unsolicited submissions.

Advertising, Audiovisual and Commercial Music Firms

The music used in commercial and audiovisual presentations is secondary to the picture (for TV, film or video) or the message being conveyed. Commercial music must enhance the product being sold. It must get consumers' attention, move them in some way and, finally, motivate them—all without overpowering the message or product it accompanies. Songwriters in this area are usually strong composers, arrangers and, sometimes, producers.

More than any other market listed in this book, the commercial music market expects composers to have made an investment in their material before beginning to submit. When dealing with commercial music firms, especially audiovisual firms and music libraries, high quality production is very important. Your demo may be kept on file at one of these companies and used or sold as you sent it. Also, a list of your credits should be part of your submission to give the company an idea of your experience in this field. In general, it's important to be as professional as you can in your submissions to these markets. Fully produced demo tapes and complete press kits will get your product recognized and heard.

Commercial music and jingle writing can be a lucrative field for the composer/songwriter with a gift for strong hook melodies and the ability to write in many different styles. The problem is, there are many writers and few jobs—it's a very competitive field.

ADVERTISING AGENCIES

Ad agencies work on assignment as their clients' needs arise. They work closely with their clients on radio and TV broadcast campaigns. Through consultation and input from the creative staff, ad agencies seek jingles and music to stimulate the consumer to identify with a product or service.

When contacting ad agencies, keep in mind they are searching for music that can capture and then hold an audience's attention. Most jingles are quick, with a strong, memorable hook that the listener will easily identify with. Remember, though, that when an agency listens to a demo, it is not necessarily looking for a finished product so much as for an indication of creativity and diversity. Most composers put together a reel of excerpts of work from previous projects, or short pieces of music which show they can write in a variety of styles.

AUDIOVISUAL FIRMS

Audiovisual firms create a variety of products. Their services may range from creating film and video shows for sales meetings (and other corporate gatherings) and educational markets, to making motion pictures and TV shows. With the increase of home video use, how-to videos are a big market now for audiovisual firms, as are spoken word educational videos.

Like advertising firms, AV firms look for versatile, well-rounded songwriters. The key to submitting demos to these firms is to demonstrate your versatility in writing specialized background music and themes. Listings for companies will tell what facet(s) of the audiovisual field they are involved in and what types of clients they serve.

COMMERCIAL MUSIC HOUSES AND MUSIC LIBRARIES

Commercial music houses are companies which are contracted (either by an advertising agency or the advertiser himself) to compose custom jingles. Since they are neither an ad agency nor an audiovisual firm, their main concern is music. And they use a lot of it—some composed by inhouse songwriters and some contributed by outside writers.

Music libraries are a bit different in that their music is not custom composed for a specific client. They provide a collection of instrumental music in many different styles that, for an annual fee or on a per-use basis, the customer can use however he chooses (most often in audiovisual and multi-media applications).

Commercial music houses and music libraries are identified as such in the following listings by **bold** typeface.

The commercial music market is similar to most other businesses in one aspect: experience is important. Until you develop a list of credits, pay for your work may not be high. Don't pass up work opportunities if the job is non- or low paying. These assignments will help make contacts, add to your experience and improve your marketability.

Many of the companies listed in this section pay by the job, but there may be some situations where the company asks you to sign a contract that will specify royalty payments. If this happens, research the contract thoroughly, and know exactly what is expected of you and how much you'll be paid.

Sometimes, depending on the particular job and the company, a composer/songwriter will be asked to sell one-time rights or all rights. One-time rights entail using your material for one presentation only. All rights means that the buyer can use your work any way he chooses for as long as he likes. Again, be sure you know exactly what you're giving up, and how the company may use your music in the future.

For additional names and addresses of advertising agencies who may use jingles and/ or commercial music, refer to the *Standard Directory of Advertising Agencies* (National Register Publishing). For a list of audiovisual firms, check out the latest edition of *Audiovisual Marketplace* (published by R.R. Bowker). To contact companies in your area, see the Geographic Index at the back of this book.

THE AD AGENCY, P.O. Box 470572, San Francisco CA 94147. Creative Director: Michael Carden. Advertising agency and **jingle/commercial music production house**. Clients include business, industry and retail. Estab. 1971. Uses the services of music houses, independent songwriter/composers and lyricists for scoring of videos and commercials, background music for commercials and videos, jingles for radio and TV commercials. Commissions 20 composers and 15 lyricists/year. Pays by the job or by the hour. Buys all rights.
How to Contact: Submit demo tape of previous work. Prefers cassette with 5-8 songs and lyric sheet. Does not return material. Reports in 2 weeks.
Music: Uses variety of musical styles for commercials, promotion, TV, video presentations.
Tips: "Our clients and our needs change frequently."

ADVANCE ADVERTISING AGENCY, 606 E. Belmont, #202, Fresno CA 93701. (209)445-0383. Manager: Martin Nissen. Advertising agency. Clients include various retail, general services. Estab. 1952. Uses the services of music houses and independent songwriters/composers for background music and jingles for radio and TV commercials. Pays by the job. Buys all rights.
How to Contact: Submit demo tape of previous work. Prefers cassette with any number of songs. Does not return material, but prefers to keep on file. Include business card.
Music: Uses nostalgic, Dixieland and traditional jazz for commercials. Does not use electronically created music (e.g. electric keyboard).
Tips: "Listen carefully to the assignment. Don't be too sophisticated or abstract. Stay simple and translatable. Aim toward individual listener."

AGA COMMUNICATIONS, (formerly Greinke, Eiers and Associates), 2557C North Terrace Ave., Milwaukee WI 53211-3822. (414)962-9810. Fax: (414)352-3233. CEO: Arthur Greinke. Advertising

INSIDER REPORT

Think "generic" when writing songs for films

Barbara Jordan vividly recalls her first encounter with the movie business. "I went with my hands and legs shaking to a movie producer's office and handed him a demo of my songs. He quickly listened to three or four songs, said which ones he liked, and asked if he could hold onto the tape. I thought I'd never hear from him again." As it turned out, one of the songs was perfect for a scene in the producer's movie. One week later, Jordan was in that office again, looking at a contract and making her first film deal.

Barbara Jordan

Today, Jordan works as an independent music supervisor for feature films and as a writer and producer of songs for MGM, HBO and Columbia Pictures, among others. She is also an assistant professor of music at the Berklee College of Music in Boston, author of *Songwriter's Playground, Innovative Exercises in Creative Songwriting*, and is a nationwide lecturer on songwriting. "I'm an educator," says Jordan, "because I've always felt it was important, once I learned the ropes, to teach others the reality, rather than the fantasy, of writing for film."

Jordan's reality of writing for film begins by pointing out the kinds of songs movie producers and music supervisors need. The most obvious are those songs that become part of the soundtracks of feature films. "These are the hardest cuts for any songwriter, especially beginners, to get. There are about 25 top-level music supervisors who put together movie soundtracks, and they work to get the highest ranking talent on the current pop charts to write and perform these songs."

The songs music supervisors look for from unknown songwriters, says Jordan, are songs that are not featured on the movie soundtracks. Rather, they are songs heard in the background of a film scene, playing on a jukebox or radio. This "atmospheric" music is made up of songs that are generic in nature, that sound familiar but don't draw attention to themselves. "These songs are part of the background, which means they should not distract from the dialogue or the images on screen. They have to have neutral content, but still say something that relates to the scene. This is not easy and is a craft that must be learned."

Jordan says there are many more opportunities for beginners writing these generic background songs for movies than in getting songs cut by top recording artists. "For consideration by a Dolly Parton or a Whitney Houston, you need to have a song that is nearly perfect because you're competing with top-notch songwriters for a limited number of cuts. But there are many more opportunities

INSIDER REPORT, *continued*

for placement of songs in film and TV, and it's not as critical that these songs be 'perfect.' They just have to set the right mood."

If you're lucky, says Jordan, you may already have a song that would be perfect as a background song in a movie scene. Or, a film producer or music supervisor will ask you to custom-write songs with a specific tempo, lyrical content and style for particular scenes in a film.

Custom writing background songs for films can "improve your songwriting chops," says Jordan. "In a film, when you are at the stage called post production, it's a rush to the finish. In television, the schedule is even tighter. You have to know how to write quickly." Jordan uses an experience of her own to demonstrate the time constraints of writing songs for television. "I was called on a Thursday morning to write a song for the following week's episode of a popular Thursday night show. I had to write the song that morning, demo it that afternoon, and Federal Express it that night so the director could hear it and dub it in on Tuesday. It was cut into the film and aired on Thursday night."

Jordan says songwriters wanting to write songs for film and TV must network and make industry contacts. Living near the action is a good way to start. When Jordan first moved to Los Angeles, "I was in the center of the film and entertainment business," she says, "so I just naturally socialized with people in the film industry. When it came up that I was a songwriter, some people asked to hear my songs. That was my first networking experience with the film and TV song world." She also suggests that beginning writers "concentrate their efforts on placing songs in smaller, independent film productions. Films currently in production are regularly listed in the film industry trades. Approach those productions with a telephone call inquiring about their needs. You may get the brush-off, but if you're nice enough and you practice your phone etiquette, you will eventually speak to someone who will allow you to send something and then give you some feedback. And you don't learn anything unless you get feedback."

Jordan advises songwriters to "always carry cassettes or CDs of your material. Mention to everyone what it is you do and what your goals are. If you meet someone in the film business who asks to hear something you've done, you'll have it right there with you, with your name and your phone number on it."

She also recommends joining songwriters' organizations like the Songwriters Guild and the National Academy of Songwriters. "These are networking organizations; publishers, music supervisors and recording artists show up at their meetings looking for material. And you don't have to live in Los Angeles, Nashville or New York to join these groups. If you are a member, you will receive their newsletters filled with valuable industry information for songwriters. Publications like *Performing Songwriter* and *American Songwriter* are also wonderfully informational.

"The most important thing to remember is that writing for film is not a part-time activity; it can't be a supplement to your other songwriting. Writing music for film is a specialized craft, and it's not learned overnight. But any songwriter with enough motivation can learn the basics. When a song is needed for film, if your song is well-crafted and appropriate for a scene, there's a good chance it will be accepted. It's that simple."

—Barbara Kuroff

agency, public relations/music artist management and media relations. Clients include small business, original music groups, special events. Estab. 1984. Uses the services of independent songwriters/composers and lyricists. Commissions 4-6 composers and 4-6 lyricists/year. Pays on a per job basis.
How to Contact: Submit demo tape of previous work. Prefers CD, cassette, DAT or VHS videocassette with any number of songs and lyric sheet. "We will contact only when job is open—but will keep submissions on file." Does not return material.
Music: Uses original rock, pop and heavy rock for recording groups, commercials and video projects.
Tips: "Try to give as complete a work as possible without allowing us to fill in the holes. High energy, unusual arrangements, be creative, different and use strong hooks!"

ALLEGRO MUSIC, 6500-4 Vanalden Ave., Reseda CA 91335. E-mail: dannymuse@aol.com. Owner: Daniel O'Brien. Scoring service, **jingle/commercial music production house**. Clients include film-makers, advertisers, network promotions and aerobics. Estab. 1991. Uses the services of independent songwriters/composers and lyricists for scoring of films, jingles for ad agencies and promotions, and commercials for radio and TV. Commissions 3 composers and 1 lyricist/year. Pays $500-2,000/job. Buys all rights.
How to Contact: Query with résumé of credits or submit demo tape of previous work. Prefers cassette and lyric sheet. Does not return material. Reports in 4-6 weeks (if interested).
Music: Varied: Contemporary pop to orchestral.
Tips: "Don't make claims which you can't deliver. Accept responsibility for your success."

ANDERSON COMMUNICATIONS, Dept. SM, 2245 Godby Rd., Atlanta GA 30349. (404)766-8000. President: Al Anderson. Producer: Vanessa Vaughn. Advertising agency and syndication operation. Estab. 1971. Clients include major corporations, institutions and media. Uses the services of independent songwriters/composers for background music for commercials and jingles for syndicated radio programs. Commissions 5-6 songwriters or composers and 6-7 lyricists/year. Pays by the job. Buys all rights.
How to Contact: Write first to arrange personal interview. Prefers cassette. Does not return material. Reports in 2 weeks or "when we have projects requiring their services."
Music: Uses a variety of music for music beds for commercials and jingles for nationally syndicated radio programs and commercials targeted at the black consumer market.
Tips: "Be sure that the composition plays well in a 60-second format."

ANGEL FILMS COMPANY, 967 Hwy. 40, New Franklin MO 65274-9778. Phone/fax: (573)698-3900. President: Arlene Hulse. Motion picture and record production company (Angel One Records). Estab. 1980. Uses the services of music houses, independent songwriters/composers and lyricists for scoring of feature films, animation, TV programs and commercials, background music for TV and radio commercials and jingles. Commissions 12-20 composers and 12-20 lyricists/year. Payment depends upon budget; each project has a different pay scale. Buys all rights.
• See their listing in the Record Producers section.
How to Contact: Submit demo tape of previous work or query with resume of credits. Prefers cassette (or VHS videocassette) with 3 pieces and lyric and lead sheet. "Do not send originals." SASE, but prefers to keep material on file. Reports in 1-2 months.
Music: Uses basically MOR, but will use anything (except C&W and religious) for record production, film, television and cartoon scores.
Tips: "Don't copy others, just do the best that you can. We freelance all our work for our film and television production company, plus we are always looking for that one break-through artist for Angel One Records."

AUGUSTUS BARNETT ADVERTISING/DESIGN, Dept. SM, 632 St. Helens Ave., Tacoma WA 98402. (206)627-8508. President/Creative Director: Augustus Barnett. Advertising agency/design firm. Clients include food and service, business to business and retail advertisers. Estab. 1981. Uses the services of independent songwriters/composers for scoring of and background music for corporate video work, and commercials for radio. Commissions 1-2 composers and 0-1 lyricist/year. Buys all rights, one-time rights or for multiple use.
How to Contact: Query with résumé of credits; write first to arrange personal interview. Prefers cassette. Does not return material; prefers to keep on file. Reports in 4 months.
Music: Uses up-tempo, pop and jazz for educational films and slide presentations.

*BEVERLY HILLS VIDEO GROUP, 2046 Armacost, West Los Angeles CA 90025. (310)207-3319. Fax: (310)207-2798. E-mail: orsi@aol.com. Senior VP: Thomas W. Orsi. Motion picture production company, **music sound effect library** and 10 bay production studio. Clients include Fox, UPN, Warner, A&E, Discovery. Estab. 1990. Uses the services of music houses and independent songwriters/composers for scoring of TV series and movies, background music for commercials and infomercials for TV. Commissions 6 composers/year. Pays per job. Rights purchased varies per job.

How to Contact: Submit demo tape of previous work. Prefers cassette, DAT or videocassette. SASE, but prefers to keep submitted material on file. "We will contact when client match is established."
Music: Uses all types for all assignments.
Tips: "Create a demo that has the most variety—no one type need be more than 90 seconds. Use only the 'best' sections of the material you have at hand, and be prepared—by being concise and to-the-point—for a phone call from us inquiring of your modus operandi. References are a must and will be contacted."

*BGM, 8501 Wilshire Blvd., Beverly Hills CA 90211. (310)657-5050. Fax: (310)659-1251. Creative Director: Robert Brown. Advertising agency. Clients include health care companies. Estab. 1970. Uses the services of music houses, independent songwriters/composers and lyricists for commercials for radio and TV and educational videos. Commissions 6 composers and 4 lyricists/year. Payment varies with each project. Rights vary with each project.
How to Contact: Query with résumé of credits, or submit demo tape of previous work. Prefers cassette or VHS videocassette with 2 songs and lyric sheet. Prefers to keep submitted material on file. SASE. Reports in 3-4 weeks.
Music: Uses up-tempo, pop, easy listening for educational videos and commercials.
Tips: "Be open to any type of project, be flexible with regard to requested changes from our agency and/or clients. Be fast and reliable."

*BIG EARS MUSIC/DUCKTAPE STUDIO, 435 Dorset #51, South Burlington VT 05403. (802)864-9871. Fax: (802)864-9869. Producer: Martin Guigui. **Commercial music production house** and publisher/album production. Clients include record labels, film and television. Estab. 1992. Uses the services of independent songwriters/composers and musicians for sessions and to record and place songs with established artists. Commissions 2 composers and 2 lyricists/year. Pay varies depending on projects and clients. Buys between 0-50% of rights.
How to Contact: Submit demo tape of previous and current work. Prefers cassette with lyric sheet. "No more than 3 songs per tape. Make sure they are your best songs." SASE. Reports in 2-3 weeks.
Music: Uses all styles but mostly a concentration on pop and R&B for film and TV (mostly children's).
Tips: "Write, write, write! It's a muscle—exercise it! Use the phone; cultivate your connections. Only do it if you truly love it. Keep the writing simple—never over-intellectualize the lyrical content. Be objective as possible all the time. Keep your demos raw and stripped down. Always use emotion, attitude and groove."

BLATTNER/BRUNNER INC., 1 Oxford Center, 6th Floor, Pittsburgh PA 15219. (412)263-2979. Broadcast Production Coordinator: Karen Smith. Clients include retail/consumer, service, high-tech/industrial/medical. Estab. 1975. Uses the services of music houses and independent songwriters/composers for background music for TV and radio spots and jingles for TV and radio spots. Commissions 2-3 composers/year. Pays by the job. Buys all rights or one-time rights, depending on the job.
How to Contact: Submit demo tape of previous work demonstrating background music or jingle skills. Prefers clearly labeled cassette (or VHS or ¾" videocassette) with 3-5 songs. Does not return material. Reports in 1-2 months.
Music: Uses up-beat, "unique-sounding music that stands out" for commercials and industrial videos.
Tips: "Send relevant work in conjunction to the advertising business—i.e., jingles."

*DAVID BOWMAN PRODUCTIONS, 20 Valley View Dr., Langhorne PA 19053. (215)702-7613 or (215)322-8078. Fax: (215)396-8693. President/Artistic Director: W. David Bowman. Scoring service, **jingle/commercial music production house**, music library producers/music production house and music publisher. Clients include television, radio, video production houses, computer/video game manufacturers, music production houses and multimedia developers. Estab. 1989. Uses the services of independent songwriters/composers and own team of music staff writers for scoring of films, documentaries and video productions, background music for television, radio, video productions and all multimedia applications, commercials for radio and TV and background instrumental works for use in their music library. Commissions 5-10 composers/year. Pays by the job. Buys all rights or one-time rights.
  • See their listing in the Music Publishers section.

LISTINGS OF COMPANIES within this section which are either commercial music production houses or music libraries will have that information printed in boldface type.

How to Contact: Submit demo tape of previous work. Prefers cassette with 3-5 songs. "We are looking for instrumental pieces of any length not exceeding three minutes for use in their music library." Does not return material. Reports in 1-2 months.
Music: Uses all styles for television and radio commercials, video productions, various multimedia applications.
Tips: "Network. Get your name and your work out there. Let everyone know what you are all about and what you are doing. Be patient, persistent and professional. What are you waiting for? Do it!"

CALDWELL VANRIPER, 1314 N. Meridian, Indianapolis IN 46202. (317)632-6501. Vice President/Executive Producer: Sherry Boyle. Advertising agency and public relations firm. Clients include industrial, financial and consumer/trade firms. Uses the services of music houses for scoring of radio, TV and A/V projects, jingles and commercials for radio and TV.
How to Contact: Submit demo tape of previously aired work. Prefers standard audio cassette. Does not return material. Prefers to keep materials on file. "Sender should follow up on submission. Periodic inquiry or reel update is fine."
Tips: "We do not work directly with composers, we work with music production companies. There are companies we work with locally in our market, and when we do use outside market companies, they are usually established production companies. I would suggest that composers contact the production companies directly."

CANARY PRODUCTIONS, Box 202, Bryn Mawr PA 19010. (215)825-1254. President: Ken Gross. **Music library.** Estab. 1984. Uses the services of music houses and independent songwriters for background music for AV use, jingles for all purposes, and commercials for radio and TV. Commissions 10 composers/year. Pays $100 per job. Buys all rights.
How to Contact: Submit demo tape of previous work. Prefers cassette with 5-10 pieces. Does not return material. Reports in 1 month.
Music: All styles, but concentrates on industrial. "We pay cash for produced tracks of all styles and lengths. Production value is imperative. No scratch tracks accepted."
Tips: "Be persistent and considerate of people's time."

CANTRAX RECORDERS, Dept. SM, 2119 Fidler Ave., Long Beach CA 90815. (310)498-6492. Owner: Richard Cannata. Recording studio. Clients include anyone needing recording services (i.e. industrial, radio, commercial). Estab. 1980. Uses the services of independent songwriters/composers for scoring of and background music for commercials for radio and TV. Commissions 10 composers/year. Pays by the job.
How to Contact: Query with résumé of credits or submit demo tape of previous work. Prefers cassette, 7½/15 ips reel-to-reel or DAT with lyric sheets. "Indicate noise reduction if used." SASE, but prefers to keep material on file. Reports in 3 weeks.
Music: Uses jazz, New Age, rock, easy listening and classical for slide shows, jingles and soundtracks.
Tips: "Send a 7½ or 15 ips reel, cassette or DAT tape for us to audition; you must have a serious, professional attitude."

CASANOVA-PENDRILL PUBLICIDAD, 3333 Michelson, Suite 300, Irvine CA 92715. (714)474-5001. Production: Kevan Wilkinson. Advertising agency. Clients include consumer and corporate advertising—Hispanic markets. Estab. 1985. Uses the services of music houses, independent songwriters/composers and lyricists for radio, TV and promotions. Pays by the job or per hour. Buys all rights or one-time rights.
How to Contact: Submit demo tape of previous work, tape demonstrating composition skills and manuscript showing music scoring skills. Prefers cassette (or ¾ videocassette). "Include a log indicating spot(s) titles." Does not return material; prefers to keep on file.
Music: All types of Hispanic music (e.g., salsa, merengue, flamenco, etc.) for TV/radio advertising.

*CINÉPOST FILM & VIDEO, 1937 Ontario Ave., Saskatoon, Saskatchewan S7K 1T5 **Canada**. (306)244-7788. Fax: (306)244-7799. President: Bill Stampe. Motion picture production company. Clients include broadcasting, corporate and retail. Estab. 1983. Uses the services of music houses, independent songwriter/composers and lyricists for scoring of corporate video/documentaries, background music for corporate videos and jingles for retail accounts. Commissions 6-10 composers and 3-4 lyricists/year. Pays negotiable fee per job. Buys all rights.
How to Contact: Query with résumé of credits, or submit demo tape of previous work. Prefers cassette or VHS/¾/BETA with 3 songs. SASE. Reports in 3 weeks.
Music: Uses modern contemporary, dramatic and uptempo for corporate, video, drama and educational films.
Tips: "Show me a creative style that doesn't sound like canned music and is up to speed with today's music."

CINEVUE, P.O. Box 428, Bostwick FL 32007. (904)325-5254. Director/Producer: Steve Postal. Motion picture production company. Estab. 1955. Serves all types of film distributors. Uses the services of music houses, independent songwriters, composers and lyricists for scoring and background music for films. Commissions 10 composers and 5 lyricists/year. Pays by the job. Buys all rights.
How to Contact: Query with résumé of credits or submit demo tape of previous work ("good tape only!"). Submit manuscript showing music scoring skills. Prefers cassette with 10 pieces and lyric or lead sheet. Does not return material. "Send good audio-cassette, then call me in a week." Reports in 2 weeks.
Music: Uses all styles of music for features (educational films and slide presentations). "Need horror film music on traditional instruments—no electronic music."
Tips: "Be flexible, fast—do first job free to ingratiate yourself and demonstrate your style. Follow up with two phone calls."

COAKLEY HEAGERTY, 1155 N. First St., San Jose CA 95112. (408)275-9400. Creative Director: Susann Rivera. Advertising agency. Clients include consumer, business to business and high tech firms. Estab. 1966. Uses the services of music houses for jingles for commercials for radio and TV. Commissions 15-20 songwriters/year. Pays by the job. Buys all rights.
How to Contact: Submit demo tape of previously aired work. Prefers cassette or 7½ ips reel-to-reel with 8-10 pieces. Does not return material; prefers to keep on file. Reports in 6 months.
Music: All kinds of music for jingles and music beds.
Tips: "Send only commercials of past clients. Please don't be pushy and call over and over again. I'll call when I have something I like. Please include costs for creative and final production in a cover letter, address issues of talent availability if you are not located in a major ad market."

COMMUNICATIONS FOR LEARNING, 395 Massachusetts Ave., Arlington MA 02174. (617)641-2350. E-mail: commlearn@aol.com. Executive Producer/Director: Jonathan L. Barkan. Audiovisual and design firm. Clients include multi-nationals, industry, government, institutions, local, national and international nonprofits. Uses services of music houses and independent songwriters/composers for background music for videos and multimedia. Commissions 1-2 composers/year. Pays $2,000-3,000/job and one-time fees.
How to Contact: Submit demo tape of previous work. Prefers cassette, CD or 7½ or 15 ips reel-to-reel (or ½" or ¾" videocassette). Does not return material; prefers to keep on file. "For each job we consider our entire collection." Reports in 2-3 months.
Music: Uses all styles of music for all sorts of assignments.
Tips: "Please don't call. Just send good material and when we're interested, we'll be in touch. Make certain name and phone number is on all submitted work, not only cover letter."

COMPOSITIONS, INC., 36 E. 22nd St., 2nd Floor, New York NY 10010. (212)677-8300. (212)677-3405. President/Creative Director: Steven M. Gold. **Jingle/commercial and television music production house**. Clients include advertising agencies and television and film producers. Estab. 1990. Uses the services of independent songwriters/composers for scoring of TV/radio commercials, TV theme and cue music, corporate videos and independent feature films. Commissions 6-8 composers and 1-3 lyricists/year. Pays $200-2,000/job. Buys-outs and royalty deals.
How to Contact: Submit demo tape of previous work. Prefers cassette, DAT or 3/4" videocassette. Prefers to keep material on file. Reports in 3 weeks.
Music: Uses all styles for TV series, specials, movies of the week, commercials and corporate videos.
Tips: "Submit great music in any format. It is not necessary to have :15 and :30 pieces or completed 'score to picture' works."

CREATIVE ASSOCIATES, Dept. SM, 44 Park Ave., Madison NJ 07940. (201)377-4440. Production Coordinator: Susan Graham. Audiovisual/multimedia firm. Clients include commercial, industrial firms. Estab. 1975. Uses the services of music houses and independent songwriters/composers for scoring of video programs, background music for press tours and jingles for new products. Pays $300-5,000/job. Buys all or one-time rights.
How to Contact: Submit demo tape of previous work demonstrating composition skills or query with résumé of credits. Prefers cassette or ½" or ¾" VHS videocassette. Prefers to keep material on file.
Music: Uses all styles for many different assignments.

CREATIVE HOUSE ADVERTISING, INC., 30777 Northwestern Hwy., Suite 301, Farmington Hills MI 48334. (810)737-7077. Senior Vice President/Executive Creative Director: Robert G. Washburn. Advertising agency and graphics studio. Serves commercial, retail, consumer, industrial, medical and financial clients. Uses the services of songwriters and lyricists for jingles, background music for radio and TV commercials and corporate sales meeting films and videos. Commissions 3-4 songwriters/year. Pays $1,500-10,000/job depending on job involvement. Buys all rights.

How to Contact: Query with résumé of credits or submit tape demo showing jingle/composition skills. Submit cassette (or ¾″ videocassette) with 6-12 songs. SASE, but would prefer to keep material on file. "When an appropriate job comes up associated with the talents/ability of the songwriters/musicians, then they will be contacted."
Music: "The type of music we need depends on clients. The range is multi: contemporary, disco, rock, MOR and traditional."
Tips: "Be fresh, innovative and creative. Provide good service and costs."

CREATIVE SUPPORT SERVICES, 1950 Riverside Dr., Los Angeles CA 90039. (213)666-7968. Contact: Michael M. Fuller. **Music/sound effects library**. Clients include audiovisual production houses. Estab. 1978. Uses the services of independent songwriters and musicians for production library. Commissions 3-5 songwriters and 1-2 lyricists/year. Buys all rights.
How to Contact: Submit demo tape of previous work. Prefers cassette ("chrome or metal only") or 7½ ips reel-to-reel with 3 or more pieces. Does not return material; prefers to keep on file. "Will call if interested."
Music: Uses "industrial music predominantly, but all other kinds or types to a lesser degree."
Tips: "Don't assume the reviewer can extrapolate beyond what is actually on the demo."

D.S.M. PRODUCERS INC., 161 W. 54th St., Suite 803, New York NY 10019. (212)245-0006. President, CEO: Suzan Bader. CFO, CPA: Kenneth R. Wiseman. Submit to: Jannell McBride, Director A&R. Vice President, National Sales Director: Doris Kaufman. Scoring service, **jingle/commercial music production house** and original stock library called "All American Composers Library (administered world wide except USA by Warner/Chappell Music, Inc.)" Clients include networks, corporate, advertising firms, film and video, book publishers (music only). Estab. 1979. Uses the services of independent songwriters/composers for scoring of TV and feature films, background music for feature films and TV, jingles for major products and commercials for radio and TV. Pays 50% royalty. Buys all rights.
• See their listings in the Music Publishers and Record Producers sections.
How to Contact: Write first and enclose SASE for return permission. Prefers cassette (or VHS videocassette) with 2 songs and lyric or lead sheet. "Use a large enough return envelope to put in a standard business reply letter." Reports in 3 months.
Music: Uses dance, New Age, country and rock for adventure films and sports programs.
Tips: "Carefully label your submissions. Include a short bio/resume of your works. Lyric sheets are very helpful to A&R. Only send your best tapes and tunes. Invest in your profession and get a local professional to help you produce your works. A master quality tape is the standard today. This is your competition so if you really want to be a songwriter, act like the ones who are successful—get a good tape of your tune. This makes it easier to sell overall."

dbF A MEDIA COMPANY, P.O. Box 2458, Waldorf MD 20604. (301)843-7110. President: Randy Runyon. Advertising agency, audiovisual and media firm and audio and video production company. Clients include business and industry. Estab. 1981. Uses the services of music houses, independent songwriters/composers and lyricists for background music for industrial videos, jingles and commercials for radio and TV. Commissions 5-12 composers and 5-12 lyricists/year. Pays by the job. Buys all rights.
How to Contact: Submit demo tape of previous work. Prefers cassette or 7½ ips reel-to-reel (or VHS videocassette) with 5-8 songs and lead sheet. SASE, but prefers to keep material on file. Reports in 1 month.
Music: Uses up-tempo contemporary for industrial videos, slide presentations and commercials.
Tips: "We're looking for commercial music, primarily A/C."

DELTA DESIGN GROUP, INC., Dept. SM, 409 Washington Ave., Greenville MS 38701. (601)335-6148. President: Noel Workman. Advertising agency. Serves industrial, health care, agricultural, casino and retail commercial clients. Uses the services of music houses for jingles and commercials for radio and TV. Commissions 3-6 pieces/year. Pays by the job. Buys "rights which vary geographically according to client. Some are all rights; others are rights for a specified market only. Buy out only. No annual licensing."
How to Contact: Submit demo tape showing jingle/composition skills. Prefers 7½ ips reel-to-reel with 3-6 songs. "Include typed sequence of cuts on tape on the outside of the reel box." Does not return material. Reports in 2 weeks.
Music: Needs "30- and 60-second jingles for agricultural, health care, gambling casinos, vacation destinations, auto dealers and chambers of commerce."

DISK PRODUCTIONS, 1100 Perkins Rd., Baton Rouge LA 70802. (504)343-5438. Director: Joey Decker. **Jingle/production house.** Clients include advertising agencies, slide production houses and film companies. Estab. 1982. Uses the services of music houses, independent songwriters/composers

and lyricists for scoring of TV spots and films and jingles for radio and TV. Commissions 7 songwriters/composers and 7 lyricists/year. Pays by the job. Buys all rights.
How to Contact: Submit demo tape of previous work. Prefers cassette or DAT (or ½″ videocassette) and lead sheet. Does not return material. Reports in 2 weeks.
Music: Needs all types of music for jingles, music beds or background music for TV and radio, etc.
Tips: "Advertising techniques change with time. Don't be locked in a certain style of writing. Give me music that I can't get from pay needle-drop."

eclectic MUSIC, 585 Warwick St., St. Paul MN 55116. Phone/fax: (612)690-4999. Creative Director: Don Wozniak. **Music sound effect library**. Clients include educational audio production houses, audiovisual, advertising agencies, corporate communication and marketing. Estab. 1994. Uses the services of independent songwriter/composers for non-broadcast industrial programs, co-op communication, educational and trade books on tape. Pays by buy-out. Buys all rights.
How to Contact: Submit demo tape of previous work. Prefers DAT or cassette. "Demonstrate all writing styles. Samples no longer than 2 minutes. Present one 5 sec, 10 sec and 15 sec piece. A variety of musical styles are preferred." Prefers to keep submitted material on file. Reports in 4-6 weeks.
Music: "We represent a broad portfolio of style—all genres will be reviewed. All assignments are published as cue music library CDs and are marketed to studios, production houses and audiovisual firms."
Tips: "eclectic music seeks professional project studio, competitively priced quotations, fast turnaround and a flexible creative nature—must write music to order. Quality material will be strongly considered and probably adopted."

ENSEMBLE PRODUCTIONS, Box 2332, Auburn AL 36831. (205)826-3045. E-mail: mcconbj@mail.auburn.edu. Owner: Barry J. McConatha. Interactive multimedia and video production/post production. Clients include corporate, governmental and educational. Estab. 1984. Uses services of music houses and independent songwriters/composers for background music for corporate public relations and training videos. Commissions 0-5 composers/year. Pays $25-250/job depending upon project. Buys all or one one-time rights.
How to Contact: Submit demo tape of previous work demonstrating composition skills. "Needs are sporadic, write first if submission to be returned." Prefers cassette or 7½ or 15 ips reel-to-reel (or VHS videocassette) with 3-5 songs. "Most needs are up-beat industrial sound but occasional mood setting music also. Inquire for details." Does not return material; prefers to keep on file. Reports in 3 months if interested."
Music: Uses up-beat, industrial, New Age, and mood for training, film, PR, education and multimedia.
Tips: "Provide a wide range of sounds."

ENTERTAINMENT PRODUCTIONS, INC., 2118 Wilshire Blvd., #744, Santa Monica CA 90403. (310)456-3143. President/Producer: Edward Coe. Motion picture and television production company. Clients include motion picture and TV distributors. Estab. 1972. Uses the services of music houses and songwriters for scores, production numbers, background and theme music for films and TV and jingles for promotion of films. Commissions/year vary. Pays by the job or by royalty. Buys motion picture and video rights.
How to Contact: Query with resume of credits. Demo should show flexibility of composition skills. "Demo records/tapes sent at own risk—returned if SASE included." Reports by letter in 1 month, "but only if SASE is included."
Tips: "Have resume on file. Develop self-contained capability."

ESTILO COMMUNICATIONS, 2700 S. First St., Austin TX 78704. (512)440-7014. Fax: (512)440-7124. E-mail: estilo@bizpro.com. President: Marion Sanchez. Advertising agency. Clients include Hispanic and general. Estab. 1989. Uses the services of independent songwriter/composers for background music for radio, jingles for radio and commercials for radio and TV. Commissions 1 composer and 2 lyricists/year. Pays by the job. Buys all rights.
How to Contact: Query with resumé of credits. Submit demo tape of previous work. Prefers cassette. SASE. Reports in 2 weeks.

FILM CLASSIC EXCHANGE, 143 Hickory Hill Circle, Osterville MA 02655-1322. (508)428-7198. Vice President: Elsie Aikman. Motion picture production company. Clients include motion picture industry/TV networks and affiliates. Estab. 1916. Uses the services of music houses, independent songwriters/composers and lyricists for scoring and background music for motion pictures, TV and video projects. Commissions 10-20 composers and 10-20 lyricists/year. Pays by the job. Buys all rights.
How to Contact: Submit demo tape of previous work. Prefers cassette (or VHS videocassette). SASE, but prefers to keep material on file. Reports in 3 weeks to 2 months.

Music: Uses pop and up-tempo for theatrical films/TV movies.
Tips: "Be persistent."

FINE ART PRODUCTIONS, 67 Maple St., Newburgh NY 12550-4034. Phone/fax: (914)561-5866. E-mail: richie.suraci@bbs.mhv.net. Website: http://www.geopages.com/Hollywood/1077. Producer/Researcher: Richard Suraci. Advertising agency, audiovisual firm, scoring service, **jingle/commercial music production house**, motion picture production company and **music sound effect library**. Clients include corporate, industrial, motion picture and broadcast firms. Estab. 1987. Uses services of music houses, lyricists and independent songwriters/composers for scoring, background music and jingles for various projects and commercials for radio and TV. Commissions 1-10 songwriters or composers and 1-10 lyricists/year. Pays by the job. Buys all or one-time rights.
How to Contact: Submit demo tape of previous work or tape demonstrating composition skills or query with resume of credits. Prefers cassette (or ½", ¾", or 1" videocassette) with as many songs as possible and lyric or lead sheets. SASE, but prefers to keep material on file. Reports in 3-9 months.
Music: Uses all types of music for all types of assignments.

FITZMUSIC, 37-75 63rd St., Suite B29, Woodside NY 11377. (718)446-3857. Producer: Gary Fitzgerald. Scoring service, **commercial music production house and music/sound effects library**. "We service the advertising, film and television community." Estab. 1987. Uses the services of independent songwriters, vocalists, lyricists and voice-over talent for scoring of TV, radio and industrials, background music for movies and jingles and commercials for radio and TV. Commissions 4-5 composers and 2 lyricists/year. "*New York talent only.*" Pays per project. Buys all rights.
How to Contact: Call first to obtain permission to submit demo tape of previous work. Will not open unsolicited submissions. Prefers cassette. Does not return material; prefers to keep on file. "A follow-up call must follow submission."
Music: Uses all styles of music.
Tips: "Complete knowledge of how the advertising business works is essential."

THE FRANKLYN AGENCY, 1010 Hammond St., #312, Los Angeles CA 90069. (213)272-6080. President: Audrey Franklyn. Advertising agency, public relations, audiovisual firm and cable production company. Clients include "everything from holistic health companies to singers." Estab. 1960. Uses the services of independent songwriters/composers and music houses for our cable TV show. Commissions 4 composers and 2 lyricists/year. Pays flat fee per job. Buys all rights.
How to Contact: Submit demo tape of previous work. Prefers cassette or videocassette. Does not return material. Reports in 3 months.
Music: Uses all types for cable background, live performance.

FREDRICK, LEE & LLOYD, 235 Elizabeth St., Landisville PA 17538. (717)898-6092. Vice President: Dusty Rees. **Jingle/commercial music production house**. Clients include advertising agencies. Estab. 1976. Uses the services of independent songwriters/composers and staff writers for jingles. Commissions 2 composers/year. Pays $650/job. Buys all rights.
How to Contact: Submit tape demonstrating composition skills. Prefers cassette or 7½ ips reel-to-reel with 5 jingles. "Submissions may be samples of published work or original material." SASE. Reports in 3 weeks.
Music: Uses pop, rock, country and MOR.
Tips: "The more completely orchestrated the demos are, the better."

GAFFE MARKETING, 2127 University Park Dr., Okemos MI 48864. (517)349-6770. Production Manager: Steven Gaffe. Advertising agency. Estab. 1979. Clients include financial and package goods firms. Uses services of music houses for scoring of commercials and training films, background music for slide productions, jingles for clients and commercials for radio and TV. Commissions 3 composers/year. Pays by the job. Buys all rights.
How to Contact: Submit demo tape of previous work. Prefers cassette (or ¾" videocassette) with 6-10 songs. SASE, but prefers to keep material on file.
Tips: "Give us good demo work."

LISTINGS OF COMPANIES within this section which are either commercial music production houses or music libraries will have that information printed in boldface type.

GK & A ADVERTISING, INC., 8200 Brookriver Dr., Suite 510, Dallas TX 75247. (214)634-9486. Advertising agency. Clients include retail. Estab. 1982. Uses the services of music houses, independent songwriters/composers and lyricists for jingles for commercials for radio and TV. Commissions 1 composer and 1 lyricist/year. Buys all rights.
How to Contact: Submit demo tape of previous work. Prefers cassette (or VHS videocassette). Does not return material; prefers to keep on file. Reports in 2 weeks.
Music: Uses all types for commercials.

GOLD COAST ADVERTISING ASSOCIATION INC., 4141 N.E. Second Ave., Suite 205, Miami FL 33137. (305)592-1192. President/Creative Director: Stuart Dornfield. Advertising agency. Clients include retail/beer/financial/automotive/business-to-business/package goods. Estab. 1982. Uses the services of music houses and independent songwriters/composers for scoring of TV and radio commercials, background music, jingles and commercials for radio and TV. Commissions 5 composers/year. Pays by the job. Buys all rights or 1 year licenses and/or buyouts.
How to Contact: Submit demo tape of previous work. Prefers cassette. "Include approximate cost of music pieces." Does not return material; prefers to keep on file. Reports "when the need of a project arises."
Music: Uses all for commercials.
Tips: "Know advertising, write great melodies, be versatile and cost-effective."

GROUP X, INC., P.O. Box 65, Reynoldsburg OH 43068-0065. (614)755-9565. Fax: (614)866-2636. President: Eddie Powell. Advertising agency. Clients include retail accounts. Estab. 1990. Uses the services of independent songwriters/composers for background music, jingles and commercials for radio and TV. Pays by the job. Buys all rights.
How to Contact: Submit demo tape of previous work. Prefers cassette, IPS reel-to-reel or VHS videocassette with lyric or lead sheet. SASE. Reports in 3 months.
Music: Uses country and contemporary for jingles and educational projects.
Tips: "Be patient—work available on an 'as needed' basis only!"

HAMMOND & ASSOCIATES, 11307 Tawinee, Houston TX 77065. (713)955-5029. Fax: (713)890-8784. Owner: Michael Hammond. Audiovisual firm, **jingle/commercial music production house**, motion picture production company. Clients include food store chains, land development, auto dealers, television stations. Estab. 1985. Uses the services of independent songwriters/composers and lyricists for jingles for TV, auto dealers, commercials for radio and TV. Pays per job. Buys one-time rights.
How to Contact: Query with résumé of credits. Prefers cassette (or VHS videocassette) with 3 songs and lyric sheet. SASE. Prefers to keep submitted material on file. Reports in 3 weeks.
Music: Uses up tempo, R&B, country and gospel for jingles, educational and commercial songs.

HEPWORTH ADVERTISING CO., 3403 McKinney Ave., Dallas TX 75204. (214)526-7785. President: S.W. Hepworth. Advertising agency. Clients include financial, industrial and food firms. Estab. 1952. Uses services of songwriters for jingles for commercials for radio and TV. Pays by the job. Buys all rights.
How to Contact: Query with résumé of credits. Prefers cassette. SASE. Reports as need arises.

*HEYWOOD FORMATICS & SYNDICATION, 1103 Colonial Blvd., Canton OH 44714. (216)456-2592. Owner: Max Heywood. Advertising agency and consultant. Clients include radio, TV, restaurants/lounges. Uses the services of independent songwriters/composers for jingles and commercials for radio and TV. Payment varies per project. Buys all rights.
How to Contact: Submit demo tape of previous work. Prefers cassette or 7½ or 15 ips reel-to-reel (or VHS/Beta videocassette). Does not return material.
Music: Uses pop, easy listening and CHR for educational films, slide presentations and commercials.

HILLMANN & CARR INC., 2121 Wisconsin Ave. NW, Washington DC 20007. (202)342-0001. E-mail: hillman@aol.com. President: Alfred Hillmann. Vice President/Treasurer: Ms. Michal Carr. Audiovisual firm and motion picture production company. Estab. 1975. Clients include corporate, government, associations and museums. Uses the services of independent songwriters/composers for scoring of film and video documentaries (mostly informational). Commissions 2-3 composers/year. Payment negotiable. Buys all rights.
How to Contact: Submit demo tape of previous work. Prefers cassette (or ¾″ VHS or Beta videocassette) with 5-10 pieces. Does not return material; prefers to keep on file. Reports only when interested.
Music: Uses contemporary, classical, up-tempo and thematic music for documentary film and video productions, multi-media exposition productions, public service announcements.

THE HITCHINS COMPANY, 22756 Hartland St., Canoga Park CA 91307. (818)715-0510. E-mail: whitchins@aol.com. President: W.E. Hitchins. Advertising agency. Estab. 1985. Uses the services independent songwriters/composers for commercials for radio and TV. Commissions 1-2 composers and 1-2 lyricists/year. Will negotiate pay.
How to Contact: Query with résumé of credits. Prefers cassette or VHS videocassette. "Check first to see if we have a job." Does not return material; prefers to keep on file.
Music: Uses variety of musical styles for commercials.

HODGES ASSOCIATES, INC., P.O. Box 53805, 912 Hay St., Fayetteville NC 28305. (910)483-8489. President/Production Manager: Chuck Smith. Advertising agency. Clients include industrial, retail and consumer ("We handle a full array of clientele."). Estab. 1974. Uses the services of music houses and independent songwriters/composers for background music for industrial films and slide presentations, and commercials for radio and TV. Commissions 1-2 composers/year. Pays by the job. Buys all rights.
How to Contact: Submit demo tape of previous work. Prefers cassette. Does not return material; prefers to keep on file. Reports in 2-3 months.
Music: Uses all styles for industrial videos, slide presentations and TV commercials.

HOME, INC., 731 Harrison Ave., Boston MA 02118. (617)266-1386. Director: Alan Michel. Audio-visual firm and video production company. Clients include cable television, nonprofit organizations, pilot programs, entertainment companies and industrial. Uses the services of music houses and independent songwriters/composers for scoring of music videos, background music and commercials for TV. Commissions 2-5 songwriters/year. Pays up to $200-600/job. Buys all rights and one-time rights.
How to Contact: Submit demo tape of previous work. Prefers cassette with 6 pieces. Does not return material; prefers to keep on file. Reports as projects require.
Music: Mostly synthesizer. Uses all styles of music for educational videos.
Tips: "Have a variety of products available and be willing to match your skills to the project and the budget."

IZEN ENTERPRISES, INC., Dept. SM, 26 Abby Dr., East Northport NY 11731. (516)368-4386. President: Ray Izen. Video services. Estab. 1980. Uses the services of music houses and independent songwriters/composers. Commissions 2 composers and 2 lyricists/year. Pays by the job. Buys all rights.
How to Contact: Submit demo tape of previous work. Prefers cassette or VHS videocassette. Does not return material; prefers to keep on file.

KAMSTRA COMMUNICATIONS, INC., 5914 W. Courtyard, Suite 320, Austin TX 78730. (512)343-8484. Fax: (512)343-6010. Contact: Broadcast Producer. Advertising agency. Estab. 1963. Uses the services of music houses for jingles for radio and TV. Pays by the job. Buys all rights and one-time rights.
How to Contact: Submit demo tape of previous work. Prefers cassette. Does not return material.

K&R'S RECORDING STUDIOS, 28533 Greenfield, Southfield MI 48076. (313)557-8276. Contact: Ken Glaza. Scoring service and **jingle/commercial music production house**. Clients include commercial, industrial firms. Services include sound for pictures (music, dialogue). Uses the services of independent songwriters/composers for scoring of industrial films and jingles and commercials for radio and TV. Commissions 1 composer/month. Pays by the job. Buys all rights.
How to Contact: Submit demo tape of previous work. Prefers cassette (or ¾" or VHS videocassette) with 5-7 pieces minimum. "Show me what you can do in 5 to 7 minutes."
Music: "Give me that hook. Your cassette as provided will be included in the client choice library."

*KATSIN/LOEB ADVERTISING INC., 825 Battery St., San Francisco CA 94111. (415)399-9960. Fax: (415)399-9264. Head of Production: Pam Zellers. Advertising agency. Clients include travel, health care, entertainment and retail. Estab. 1989. Uses the services of music houses and independent songwriters/composers for commercials for radio and TV. Commissions 3-6 composers/year. Pays by the job. Buys all rights.
How to Contact: Submit demo tape of previous work. Prefers cassette or ¾" videocassette. Prefers to keep submitted material on file.
Music: Uses all kinds for commercials.
Tips: "We look for great musical ideas that work in harmony with the commercials we produce. If you've got a reel filled with same, we may be able to do business."

KEATING MAGEE LONG ADVERTISING, 2223 Magazine, New Orleans LA 70130. (504)523-2121. President: Thomas J. Long. Advertising agency. Clients include retail, consumer products and services, business-to-business. Estab. 1981. Uses the services of music houses and independent song-writers/composers and lyricists for scoring of, background music and jingles for radio and TV commer-

cials. Commissions 4 composers/year. Pays by the job. Buys all or one time rights.
How to Contact: Submit demo tape of previous work. Prefers cassette (or VHS videocassette). Does not return material; prefers to keep on file. Reports in 2 weeks.
Music: Uses all types for commercials, presentations.
Tips: "Send reel of actual work and references."

KEN-DEL PRODUCTIONS INC., First State Production Center, 1500 First State Blvd., Wilmington DE 19804-3596. (302)999-1164. Estab. 1950. A&R Director: Shirl Lotz. General Manager: Edwin Kennedy. Clients include publishers, industrial firms and advertising agencies, how-to's and radio/TV. Uses services of songwriters for radio/TV commercials, jingles and multimedia. Pays by the job. Buys all rights.
How to Contact: "Submit all inquiries and demos in any format to general manager." Does not return material. Will keep on file for three years. Generally reports in 1 month.

SID KLEINER MUSIC ENTERPRISES, 10188 Winter View Dr., Naples FL 33942. (813)566-7701 or (813)566-7702. Managing Director: Sid Kleiner. Audiovisual firm. Serves the music industry and various small industries. Uses the services of music houses, songwriters and in-house writers for background music; lyricists for special material. Commissions 5-10 composers and 2-3 lyricists/year. Pays $25 minimum/job. Buys all rights.
  • Sid Kleiner's booking agency, Five Star Entertainment, is listed in the Managers and Booking Agents section.
How to Contact: Query with résumé of credits or submit demo tape of previously aired work. Prefers cassette with 1-4 songs. SASE. Reports in 5 weeks.
Music: "We generally need soft background music with some special lyrics to fit a particular project. Uses catchy, contemporary, special assignments for commercial/industrial accounts. We also assign country, pop, mystical and metaphysical. Submit samples—give us your very best demos, your best prices and we'll try our best to use your services."

LAPRIORE VIDEOGRAPHY, 86 Allston Ave., Worcester MA 01604. (508)755-9010. Owner: Peter Lapriore. Video production company. Clients include corporations, retail stores, educational and sports. Estab. 1985. Uses the services of music houses, independent songwriters/composers for background music for marketing, training and educational films. "We also own several music libraries." Commissions 2 composers/year. Pays $150-1,000/job. Buys all rights.
How to Contact: Submit demo tape of previous work. Prefers cassette or VHS videocassette with 5 songs and lyric sheet. Does not return material; prefers to keep on file. Reports in 3 weeks.
Music: Uses slow, medium, up-tempo, jazz and classical for marketing, educational films and commercials.
Tips: "Be very creative and willing to work on all size budgets."

LYONS PRESENTATIONS, 715 Orange St., Wilmington DE 19801. (302)654-6146. Creative Director: Dave Swajeski. Audiovisual firm. Clients include mostly large corporations: Dupont, ICI, FILA U.S.A., Corestates Bank of Delaware N.A. and Alco Standard. Estab. 1954. Uses the services of independent songwriters/composers and lyricists for scoring of multi-image, film and video. Commissions 8-12 composers/year. Pays by the job. Buys all rights.
How to Contact: Submit demo tape of previous work. Prefers cassette, 15 IPS reel-to-reel, (or VHS or ¾" videocassette) with 3-4 songs. "No phone calls please, unless composers are in local area." SASE, but prefers to keep submitted materials on file.
Music: Usually uses up-tempo motivational pieces for multi-image, video or film for corporate use.
Tips: "Pay close attention to the type of music that is used for current TV spots."

McCANN-ERICKSON WORLDWIDE, Dept. SM, 1360 Post Oak Blvd., Suite 1900, Houston TX 77056. (713)965-0303. Creative Director: Jesse Caesar. Advertising agency. Serves all types of clients. Uses services of songwriters for jingles and background music in commercials. Commissions 10 songwriters/year. Pays production cost and registrated creative fee. Arrangement fee and creative fee depend on size of client and size of market. "If song is for a big market, a big fee is paid; if for a small market, a small fee is paid." Buys all rights.
How to Contact: Submit demo tape of previously aired work. Prefers 7½ ips reel-to-reel. "There is no minimum or maximum length for tapes. Tapes may be of a variety of work or a specialization. We are very open to tape content; agency does own lyrics." SASE, but prefers to keep material on file. Responds by phone when need arises.
Music: All types.

MALLOF, ABRUZINO & NASH MARKETING, 477 E. Butterfield Rd., Lombard IL 60148. (708)964-7722. President: Ed Mallof. Advertising agency. Works primarily with auto dealer jingles.

Estab. 1980. Uses music houses for jingles for radio and TV and commercials for radio. Commissions 5-6 songwriters/year. Pays $600-2,000/job. Buys all rights.
How to Contact: Submit demo tape of previous work. Prefers cassette with 4-12 songs. SASE. Reports in 1 month.
Tips: "Send samples that are already produced and can be relyricized. Tracks should be upbeat, driving music."

*MANGA ENTERTAINMENT, 727 N. Hudson, #100, Chicago IL 60610. (312)751-0020. Fax: (312)751-2483. E-mail: manga@manga.com. Website: http://www.manga.com/manga. Talent Scout/A&R: Danielle Opyt. Film company (Japanese animation). "We are owned by Island International/Polygram." Estab. 1994 (in US). Uses the services of independent songwriters/composers for home videos and theatrical movies.
 • Manga Entertainment's theatrical movie, *The Secret Adventures of Tom Thumb* (soundtrack by John Paul Jones of Led Zeppelin), has won numerous awards, including the 1995 Best Animated Film Award by the Atlanta Film & Video Festival and the Grand Prix and Audience Prize Awards at Mediawave in Hungary.
How to Contact: Submit demo tape of previous work. "No calls unless we contact you with a yes." Prefers cassette and lead sheet. SASE. Reports in 1 month.
Music: Uses alternative, industrial rock (not metal), hip hop/rap and ethereal ("music that has action") for home videos and theatrical movies.
Tips: "We are looking to license music that fits the style of 'anime'—soundtrack material or single cuts, 10-30 seconds. This music must work well with action, cutting edge or ethereal sounds. We prefer major artists and/or new talent that is signed and looking to have great visuals for their music videos. We will work both ways and let them use some of our wild cartoon clips. We would prefer working with professionals in the music business."

MARK CUSTOM RECORDING SERVICE, INC., 10815 Bodine Rd., Clarence NY 14031-0406. (716)759-2600. Vice President: Mark J. Morette. **Jingle/commercial music production house**. Clients include ad agencies. Estab. 1962. Uses the services of independent songwriters/composers for commercials for radio and TV.
How to Contact: Write. Prefers cassette with 3 songs. Does not return material; prefers to keep on file.
Music: Uses pop and jazz for radio commercials.

MEDIA CONSULTANTS, INC., P.O. Box 130, Sikeston MO 63801. (573)472-1116. Owner: Richard Wrather. Advertising agency. Clients are varied. Estab. 1979. Uses the services of music houses, independent songwriters/composers and lyricists for background music for videos, jingles for clients and commercials for radio and TV. Commissions 10-15 composers and 10-15 lyricists/year. Pays varying amount/job. Buys all rights.
How to Contact: Submit a demo tape or CD of previous work demonstrating composition skills. Prefers cassette (or ½" or ¾" videocassette). Does not return material; prefers to keep on file. Reports in 6 weeks.
Music: Uses all styles of music for varied assignments.

MITCHELL & ASSOCIATES, Dept. SM, 7830 Old Georgetown Rd., Bethesda MD 20814. (301)986-1772. President: Ronald Mitchell. Advertising agency. Serves food, high-tech, transportation, financial, real estate, professional services, automotive and retail clients. Uses independent songwriters, lyricists and music houses for background music for commercials, jingles and post-TV scores for commercials. Commissions 3-5 songwriters and 3-5 lyricists/year. Pays by the job. Buys all rights.
How to Contact: Submit demo tape of previously aired work. Prefers cassette or 7½ ips reel-to-reel. Does not return material; prefers to keep on file.
Music: "Depends upon client, audience, etc."

*PATRICK MOORE COMPOSITIONS, 91 Cambermere Dr., North York, Ontario M3A 2W4 Canada. (416)446-2974. Owner/President: Patrick Moore. Scoring service and **jingle/commercial music production house**. Clients include producers of documentaries/films (educational). Estab. 1988. Uses the services of orchestrators for scoring of orchestral scores. Commissions 1 composer/year. Pays by royalty. Buys synchronization rights.
How to Contact: Write first to arrange personal interview. Prefers cassette. Does not return material. Prefers to keep submitted material on file. Reports in 4 weeks.
Music: "I specialize in combining ethnic music with current music for educational films/documentaries."
Tips: "My needs are very specific and must meet the requirements of the producer and music editor on each project. It is not unusual for me to work with film producers and music writers from all over

the world. I do a great deal of work by mailing video tapes and cassette tapes of rough drafts to producers and other professionals involved in a film production."

MOTIVATION MEDIA, INC., 1245 Milwaukee Ave., Glenview IL 60025. (708)297-4740. Production Manager: Glen Peterson. Audiovisual firm, video, multi-media production company and business meeting planner. Clients include business and industry. Estab. 1969. Uses the services of independent songwriters/composers for business meeting videos, multi-image production and motivational pieces. Commissions 3-5 composers/year. Payment varies. Buys one-time rights.
How to Contact: Submit demo tape of previous work. Prefers cassette with 5-7 songs. Does not return material. Responds in 1 month.
Music: Uses "up-beat contemporary music that motivates an audience of sales people."
Tips: "Be contemporary."

MULTI IMAGE PRODUCTIONS, Dept. SM, 8849 Complex Dr., San Diego CA 92123. (619)560-8383. Sound Editor/Engineer: Tim O'Keefe. Audiovisual firm and motion picture production company. Serves business, corporate, industrial, commercial, military and cultural clients. Uses the services of music houses, independent songwriters/composers and lyricists for scoring of corporate films and videos. Commissions 2-10 composers and 2-5 lyricists/year. Pays per job. Buys all rights.
How to Contact: Submit demo tape of previous work. Prefers DAT with 2-5 pieces. SASE. Reports "on same day if SASE."
Music: Uses "contemporary, pop, specialty, regional, ethnic, national and international" styles of music for background "scores written against script describing locales, action, etc. We try to stay clear of stereotypical 'canned' music and prefer a more commercial and dramatic (film-like) approach."
Tips: "We have established an ongoing relationship with a local music production/scoring house with whom songwriters would be in competition for every project; but an ability to score clean, full, broad, contemporary commercial and often 'film score' type music, in a variety of styles, would be a benefit."

NEW & UNIQUE VIDEOS, 2336 Sumac Dr., San Diego CA 92105. (619)282-6126. Contact: Candace Love. Production and worldwide distribution of special interest videotapes to varied markets. Estab. 1981. Uses the services of independent songwriters for background music in videos. Commissions 2-3 composers/year. Pays by the job. Buys all rights.
How to Contact: Query with resume of credits or submit demo tape of previous work. Prefers cassette. SASE. Reports in 1-2 months.
Music: Uses up-tempo, easy listening and jazz for educational film and action/adventure, nature and love stories.
Tips: "We are seeking upbeat, versatile music, especially for fast action sports videos (among others)."

NORTON RUBBLE & MERTZ, INC. ADVERTISING, 150 N. Wacker St., Suite 2900, Chicago IL 60606. (312)422-9500. Fax: (312)422-9501. President: Sue Gehrke. Advertising agency. Clients include consumer products, retail, business to business. Estab. 1987. Uses the services of music houses and independent songwriters/composers for jingles and background music for radio/TV commercials. Commissions 2 composers/year. Pays by the job.
How to Contact: Submit tape of previous work; query with résumé of credits. Prefers cassette. Does not return materials; prefers to keep on file.
Music: Uses up-tempo and pop for commercials.

OMNI COMMUNICATIONS, Dept. SM, 12955 Old Meridian St., P.O. Box 302, Carmel IN 46032-0302. (317)844-6664. President: W. H. Long. Television production and audiovisual firm. Estab. 1978. Serves industrial, commercial and educational clients. Uses the services of music houses and songwriters for scoring of films and television productions; background music for voice overs; lyricists for original music and themes. Pays by the job. Buys all rights.
How to Contact: Query with resume of credits. Prefers reel-to-reel, cassette (or videocassette). Does not return material. Reports in 2 weeks.
Music: Varies with each and every project; from classical, contemporary to commercial industrial.
Tips: "Submit good demo tape with examples of your range to command the attention of our producers."

ON-Q PRODUCTIONS, INC., 618 Gutierrez St., Santa Barbara CA 93103. (805)963-1331. President: Vincent Quaranta. Audiovisual firm. Clients include corporate accounts/sales conventions. Uses the services of music houses, independent songwriters/composers and lyricists for scoring, background music and jingles for AV shows. Commissions 1-5 composers and 1-5 lyricists/year. Buys all or one-time rights.
How to Contact: Query with résumé of credits. Prefers cassette or 15 ips reel-to-reel (or VHS videocassette). Prefers to keep material on file.
Music: Uses up-tempo music for slide, video and interactive presentations.

*OPULENT MUSIC GROUP, P.O. Box 15834, West Palm Beach FL 33416. (407)754-7914. Contact: Shah Crime. **Jingle/commercial production house**. Estab. 1993. Uses the services of independent songwriters/composers and lyricists for background music and jingles for commercials. Pays varying royalty. Buys all rights.
How to Contact: Call first to arrange personal interview, or submit demo tape of previous work. Prefers cassette, DAT or VHS videocassette with lyric sheet. SASE. Reports in 1 week.
Music: Uses pop, house, dance, R&B, rap, bass, freestyle and gangsta music for jingles, commercials, motion pictures and artists needing music.

PHILADELPHIA MUSIC WORKS, INC., P.O. Box 947, Bryn Mawr PA 19010. (610)825-5656. Vice President Production: Jim Andron. **Jingle producers/music library producers**. Uses independent composers and music houses for background music for commercials and jingles. Commissions 20 songwriters/year. Pays $100-300/job. Buys all rights.
How to Contact: Submit demo tape of previous work. Prefers cassette. "We are looking for quality jingle tracks already produced, as well as instrumental pieces between 2 and 3 minutes in length for use in AV music library." Does not return material; prefers to keep on file. Reports in 4 weeks.
Music: All types.
Tips: "Send your best and put your strongest work at the front of your demo tape."

PHOTO COMMUNICATION SERVICES, INC., 6055 Robert Dr., Traverse City MI 49684. (616)943-8800. President: M'Lynn Hartwell. Audiovisual firm and motion picture production company. Serves commercial, industrial and nonprofit clients. Uses services of music houses, independent songwriters, and lyricists for jingles and scoring of and background music for multi-image, film and video. Negotiates pay. Buys all or one-time rights.
How to Contact: Submit demo tape of previous work, tape demonstrating composition skills or query with resume of credits. Prefers cassette. Does not return material; prefers to keep on file. Reports in 6 weeks.
Music: Uses mostly industrial/commercial themes.

POPPE TYSON, (formerly the Jayme Organization), Erieview Tower, 1301 E. Ninth St., Suite 3400, Cleveland OH 44114. (216)623-1511. Creative Director: Ray Bethea. Advertising agency. Uses the services of songwriters and lyricists for jingles and background music. Pays by the job. Buys all rights.
How to Contact: Query first; submit demo tape of previous work. Prefers cassette with 4-8 songs. SASE. Responds by phone as needs arise.
Music: Jingles.

PREMIER RECORDING STUDIOS, (formerly Premier Video, Film and Recording Corp.), Dept. SM, 3033 Locust St., St. Louis MO 63103. (314)531-3555. Fax: (314)531-9588. President: Dan Thompson. Audio/visual production facility. Estab. 1931. Uses the services of music houses and independent songwriters and lyricists for scoring of commercial productions for retail sales, background music for video productions and commercials for radio/TV. Commissions 6-10 pieces and 5-10 lyricists/year. Pays by royalty or by contracted services. Buys all or one-time rights.
How to Contact: Query with résumé or credits, submit ms showing music scoring skills, or submit demo tape of previous work. Prefers VHS or cassette with any number of songs. Does not return material. Reports in 3 weeks.
Music: "As we serve every area of human development, all musical art forms are occasionally used."
Tips: "Send us your best work but show diversification."

PRICE WEBER MARKETING COMMUNICATIONS, INC., Dept. SM, P.O. Box 99337, Louisville KY 40223. (502)499-9220. Producer/Director: Kelly McKnight. Advertising agency and audiovisual firm. Estab. 1968. Clients include Fortune 500, consumer durables, light/heavy industrials and package goods. Uses services of music houses and independent songwriters/composer for scoring, background music and jingles for industrial and corporate image films and commercials for radio and TV. Commissions 6-8 composers/year. Pays by the job ($500-2,000). Buys all or one-time rights.
How to Contact: Submit demo tape of previous work demonstrating composition skills. Prefers cassette with 10 pieces. "Enclose data sheet on budgets per selection on demo tape." Does not return material; prefers to keep on file. "We report back only if we use it."

LISTINGS OF COMPANIES within this section which are either commercial music production houses or music libraries will have that information printed in boldface type.

Music: Uses easy listening, up-tempo, pop, jazz, rock and classical for corporate image industrials and commercials.
Tips: "Keep us updated on new works or special accomplishments. Work with tight budgets of $500-2,000. Show me what you're best at—show me costs."

QUALLY & COMPANY INC., 2238 Central St., #3, Evanston IL 60201-1457. (708)864-6316. Creative Director: Robert Qually. Advertising agency. Uses the services of music houses, independent songwriters/composers and lyricists for scoring, background music and jingles for radio and TV commercials. Commissions 2-4 composers and 2-4 lyricists/year. Pays by the job or by royalty. Buys various rights depending on deal.
How to Contact: Submit demo tape of previous work or query with resume of credits. Prefers cassette (or ¾" Beta videocassette). SASE, but prefers to keep material on file. Reports in 2 weeks.
Music: Uses all kinds of music for commercials.

RAMPION VISUAL PRODUCTIONS, 316 Stuart St., Boston MA 02116. (617)574-9601. Director/Camera: Steven V. Tringali. Motion picture multi media production company. Clients include educational, independent producers, corporate clients and TV producers. Estab. 1982. Uses the services of independent songwriters/composers for jingles, background music and scoring to longer form programming. Commissions 4-6 composers/year. Pays by the job. Buys all rights.
How to Contact: Submit demo tape of previous work or query with résumé of credits. Prefers cassette with variety of pieces. Does not return material; prefers to keep on file.
Music: Uses all styles for corporate, educational and original programming.
Tips: "Submit a varied demo reel showing style and client base."

RS MUSIC PRODUCTIONS, 378 Brooke Ave., Toronto, Ontario M5M 2L6 **Canada**. (416)787-1510. President: Richard Samuels. Scoring service, **jingle/commercial music production house**. Clients include songwriters (private sector), ad agencies, direct retailers, communications companies. Estab. 1989. Uses the services of music houses and independent songwriters/composers and lyricists for background music for film and commercials for radio and TV. Commissions 2-3 composers and 4-6 lyricists/year. Buys all or one-time rights.
How to Contact: Write first to arrange personal interview or submit demo tape of previous work. Prefers cassette (or VHS videocassette) with 4 songs and lyric sheet. Does not return material; prefers to keep on file. Reports in 1 month.
Music: Uses up-tempo and pop for jingles, corporate video underscore.
Tips: "Be exact in what you want to accomplish by contacting our company, i.e., what area of composition your forté is."

*THE SANDBOX, 11684 Ventura Blvd., Suite 134, Studio City CA 91604. (818)386-9135. Fax: (818)386-2862. Producer/writer: Mark Wolfson. Scoring service and record production. Clients include film and record companies. Estab. 1984. Uses the services of independent songwriters/composers for scoring of films. Commissions 1 composer and 10 lyricists/year. Pays by royalty; each project is different. Buys assorted rights.
   • See the listing for Sandbox Productions in the Record Producers section.
How to Contact: Submit demo tape of previous work. Prefers cassette with 4 songs and lyric sheet. SASE. Reports in 2 weeks.
Music: Uses pop, R&B, new country, alternative for records, films, new artist packaging.
Tips: "Send your best work or a work in progress. No more than four songs (ever)."

SOLOMON FRIEDMAN ADVERTISING, (formerly Robert Solomon and Associates Advertising), Dept. SM, 2000 N. Woodward, Suite 300, Bloomfield Hills MI 48304. (810)540-0660. Creative Director: Chato Hill. Advertising agency. Clients include package goods, food service accounts, convenience stores, retail accounts and small service businesses. Uses independent songwriters, lyricists and music houses for jingles and special presentations. Commissions 1-10 songwriters and 1-10 lyricists/year. Pays by the job. Buys all rights.
How to Contact: Submit demo tape of previously aired work. Prefers cassette or 7½ ips reel-to-reel with 1-5 pieces and lyric or lead sheets. "Submissions must be up-to-date and up to industry standards." Does not return material; prefers to keep on file.
Music: MOR, pop or rock jingles describing specific products or services.
Tips: "Please make sure all information presented is CURRENT!"

SOTER ASSOCIATES INC., 209 N. 400 W., Provo UT 84601. (801)375-6200. President: N. Gregory Soter. Advertising agency. Clients include financial, health care, municipal, computer hardware and software. Estab. 1970. Uses services of music houses, independent songwriters/composers and lyricists for background music for audiovisual presentations and jingles for radio and TV commercials. Commissions 1 composer, 1 lyricist/year. Pays by the job. Buys all rights.

How to Contact: Submit tape demonstrating previous work and composition skills. Prefers cassette or VHS videocassette. Does not return material; prefers to keep materials on file.

NATE STEWART ADVERTISING, 401 S. Main St., Cleburne TX 76031. (817)641-4389. Fax: (817)641-7446. Owner: Nate Stewart. Advertising agency and recording studio. Clients include "top musicians for work on the projects we are involved in and songwriters." Estab. 1983. Uses the services of music houses and independent songwriters/composers for background music for videos, "music for release on CD and tapes for specific purposes such as spiritual, political, educational and romantic." Commissions 4 composers and 2 lyricists/year. Pays by the job or the hour.
How to Contact: Query with résumé of credits. "If the résumé of credits fits the needs of the project, then current material may be requested." Prefers cassette with 3 songs and lyric sheet. "Please send an introductory letter if no résumé is available. Please send both introductory letter and résumé if possible." Prefers to keep submitted material on file. Reports in 4-6 weeks.
Music: "The style of music cannot be contained by a description. It must properly convey the spirit of the message either with or without words. You must take me and others there."

SULLIVAN & FINDSEN ADVERTISING, Dept. SM, 2165 Gilbert Ave., Cincinnati OH 45206. (513)281-2700. Director of Broadcast Production: Kirby Sullivan. Advertising agency. Clients include consumer and business-to-business firms. Uses the services of music houses and independent songwriters/composers for jingles and commercials for radio and TV. Commissions 3 composers and 3 lyricists/year. Pays by the job. Buys all rights.
How to Contact: Submit demo tape of previous work. Prefers cassette. Does not return material; prefers to keep on file. "We report back when we need some work."
Music: Uses all styles for commercials.
Tips: "Don't call!"

TIERNEY & PARTNERS, (formerly F.C.B., Inc.), Dept. SM, 200 S. Broad St., Philadelphia PA 19102. (215)790-4100. Broadcast Business Manager: Gloria Anderson. Advertising agency. Serves industrial and consumer clients. Uses music houses for jingles and background music in commercials. Pays creative fee asked by music houses.
How to Contact: Submit demo tape of previously aired work, all types of music. "You must send in previously published work. We do not use original material." Prefers cassette. Will return with SASE if requested, but prefers to keep on file.

TRF PRODUCTION MUSIC LIBRARIES, Dept. SM, 747 Chestnut Ridge Rd., Chestnut Ridge NY 10977. (914)356-0800. President: Michael Nurko. **Music/sound effect libraries.** Estab. 1931. Uses the services of independent composers for jingles, background and theme music for all media including films, slide presentations, radio and TV commercials. Pays 50% royalty.
How to Contact: Submit demo tape of new compositions. Prefers cassette with 3-7 pieces.
Music: Primarily interested in instrumental music for assignments in all media.

27TH DIMENSION INC., P.O. Box 992, Newnan GA 30264. (800)634-0091. E-mail: 70711.103@ compuserve.com. President: John St. John. Scoring service, **jingle/commercial music production house** and **music sound effect library**. Clients include audiovisual producers, video houses, recording studios and radio and TV stations. Estab. 1986. Uses the services of independent songwriters/composers for background music for commercials, industrials and A/V and for scoring of library material. Commissions 10 composers/year. Pays $100-1,000/job. "We buy the right to use in our library exclusively." Buys all rights except writer's publishing. Writer gets all performance fees (ASCAP or BMI).
How to Contact: Submit demo tape of previous work. Prefers CDR or DAT. "Call before sending." SASE, but prefers to keep on file. Reports in 1 month.
Music: Uses industrial, pop jazz, sports, contemporary and New Age for music library.

UNITED ENTERTAINMENT PRODUCTIONS, 4050 Broadway, Suite 205, Kansas City MO 64111. (816)756-0288. Operations Manager: Dave Maygers. Recording studio, artist management, publishing company, booking agency and record company. Serves musical groups, songwriters and ad clients. Estab. 1972. Uses the services of independent songwriters, lyricists and self-contained groups for scoring of album projects, background music for ads and industrial films, jingles and commercials for radio and TV. Pays negotiable royalty. Buys all rights or one-time rights.
How to Contact: Submit demo tape of previous work. "Send cassette of material and lyric sheet when applicable." Does not return material; prefers to keep material on file.
Music: Rock, pop, R&B, jazz, country to be used in music projects.

VALLEY PRODUCTION CENTER, 7249 Airport Rd., Bath PA 18014. (610)837-7550. Executive Producer: Jon Miller. Audiovisual firm, **jingle/commercial music production house** and video production company. Clients include industrial, commercial, institutional and special interest. Estab. 1970.

Uses the services of independent songwriters/composers and lyricists for scoring of themes, background music for audio and video production and live presentations and commercials for radio and TV. Commissions 5-15 composers and 2-5 lyricists/year. Buys all rights or one-time rights.
How to Contact: Query with résumé of credits and references. Prefers cassette with 7 songs and lyric or lead sheets. SASE. Reports in 2-3 weeks.
Music: Uses up-tempo and title music, introduction music for industrial marketing and training videos.

VIDEO I-D, INC., Dept. SM, 105 Muller Rd., Washington IL 61571. (309)444-4323. Manager, Marketing Services: Gwen Wagner. Post production/teleproductions. Clients include industrial and business. Estab. 1977. Uses the services of music houses and independent songwriters/composers for background music for video productions. Pays per job. Buys one-time rights.
How to Contact: Submit demo tape of previous work. Prefers cassette or VHS videocassette with 5 songs and lyric sheet. SASE, but prefers to keep submitted materials on file. Reports in 3-4 weeks.

VIP VIDEO, Film House, 143 Hickory Hill Circle, Osterville MA 02655. (508)428-7198. President: Jeffrey H. Aikman. Audiovisual firm. Clients include business, industry and TV stations. Estab. 1983. Uses the services of music houses, independent songwriters/composers and lyricists for scoring and-background music for motion pictures and home video. Commissions 15-20 composers and 15-20 lyricists/year. Pays by the job, amounts vary depending on the length and complexity of each project. Buys all rights.
How to Contact: Submit demo tape of previous work. Prefers cassette with 1-2 songs. SASE, but prefers to keep material on file unless specifically stated. Reports in 6-8 weeks.
Music: Uses easy listening, pop and up-tempo for feature films, TV series, TV pilots and background for videotapes. Currently working on scoring series of 26 feature length silent films. If project is successful, this series will be added to at the rate of 13 per year.

VISION STUDIOS, 3765 Marwick Ave., Long Beach CA 90808. (310)429-1042. Proprietor: Arlan H. Boll. Audiovisual firm, scoring service, audio production for all media. Clients include ad agencies, film and video directors, producers, etc. Estab. 1989. Uses the services of independent songwriters/composers for scoring of background music for all media: film, radio and TV. Commissions 2-4 composers and 2-4 lyricists/year. "Payment is negotiable." Buys all rights or one-time rights.
How to Contact: Write first to arrange personal interview. SASE. Reports in 1 month.
Music: Uses all types of music for all types of assignments.

WARD AND AMES, 7500 San Felipe, #350, Houston TX 77063. (713)266-9696. Fax: (713)266-2481. Partners: Danny Ward or Nancy Ames. Scoring service, **jingle/commercial music production house**, event design and consultant. Clients include corporations, ad agencies, political entities, TV markets, production houses. Estab. 1982. Produces custom music packages and uses audio recording studios for scoring of background music, jingles and commercials for radio; also industrials. Pays per job. Buys all rights.
How to Contact: Submit demo tape of previous work. Prefers cassette with lead sheet. SASE. Reports in 3 weeks.
Music: Uses all types, excluding heavy metal, for custom show production, jingles and industrials.

EVANS WYATT ADVERTISING, 346 Mediterranean Dr., Suite 220, Corpus Christi TX 78418. (512)939-7200. Fax: (512)939-7999. Owner: E. Wyatt. Advertising agency. Clients are general/all types. Estab. 1975. Uses the services of music houses and independent songwriters/composers for background music for soundtracks, jingles for advertising and commercials for radio and TV. Commissions 10-12 composers/year. Pays by the job. Buys all rights.
How to Contact: Submit demo tape of previous work demonstrating composition skills, query with resume of credits or write first to arrange personal interview. Prefers cassette. SASE, but prefers to keep material on file. Reports in 2 months.
Music: Uses all types for commercials plus videos mostly.

GREG YOUNGMAN MUSIC, P.O. Box 381, Santa Ynez CA 93460. (805)688-1136. Advertising agency/audio production. Serves all types of clients. Local, regional and national levels. Uses the services of music houses and independent composers/lyricists for commercials, jingles and audiovisual projects. Commissions 12-20 composers/year. Pays $500-10,000/project. Buys all or one-time rights.
How to Contact: Submit demo tape of previously aired work. Prefers cassette, R-DAT or reel-to-reel. Does not return material; prefers to keep on file. Reports in 1 month.
Music: Uses all types for radio commercials, film cues.
Tips: "Keep demos to ten minutes."

Play Producers and Publishers

Writing music for the stage is a considerable challenge in today's theater. Conventional wisdom says that if a composer or playwright doesn't have a production to his credit, he will have a difficult time establishing himself. Play producers in the major markets, especially Broadway, won't often take a chance on unproven talent when productions routinely cost millions of dollars and a show must run for several years to break even. It's a classic catch-22; the aspiring playwright needs experience to get his work produced, but can't get that experience without production.

Fortunately, the conventional wisdom about musical theater may not be accurate. Many venues for new musical works do exist, and are listed here. Contained within are listings of theater companies, producers, dinner theaters, and publishers of musical theater works. We've separated this section into two subsections: one for producers and one for publishers. All these markets are interested in and actively seeking new musical theater works of all types for their stages or publications.

Many of these listings are for small theaters run on a nonprofit basis. Their budgets for production and rehearsal time are, by necessity, limited. Keep this in mind when preparing to submit your work. When submitting, ask about other opportunities available for your work. Some companies or theaters may like your work, but may wish to present it in revue form. Others may be looking for incidental music for a spoken word play. Research each company or theater carefully and learn about their past performances, the type of work they present, and the kinds of material they're looking for. The more knowledgeable you are about the workings of a particular company or theater, the easier it is to tailor your work to fit its style and the more responsive they will be to you and your work.

Use research and further education to help you enrich your personal experience and therefore your work. Attend as many performances as possible; know exactly what kind of work a particular theater presents. Volunteer to work at a theater, whether it be moving sets or selling tickets. This will give you valuable insight into the day to day workings of a theater and the building of a new show. Look into professional internships at theaters and attend any theater workshops in your area (for more information, see the Workshops and Conferences section of this book; to find theaters in your area, consult the Geographic Index at the end of this book). As a composer for the stage, you need to know as much as possible about the theater and how it works, its history and the different roles played by the people involved in it. Flexibility is a key to successful productions, and having a knowledge of how the theater works will only aid you in cooperating and collaborating with the director, producer, technical people and actors.

Read the following listings carefully for information on each market, the type of work being sought, and submission procedures. Research the markets that you believe will be interested in your work. And when you've decided on the best markets for your work, follow submission procedures meticulously.

INSIDER REPORT

Understanding kids is the key to writing for children's theater

TADA! is a perfect name for Janine Nina Trevens's New York City theater—what word better expresses the excitement and wonder of a children's theater featuring musical productions performed entirely by kids?

Trevens, artistic director of TADA!, began the theater in 1984 to bring together her two loves, musical theater and children. The full-scale musicals produced by TADA! are original and commissioned especially for the company, which is unusual in the world of children's theater. "I wanted to give writers a place to get their work seen, so they can have a long run with a big cast and a live band. They have all those opportunities at TADA!," Trevens says.

Janine Nina Trevens

photo: Taz Hadami

When writing material for young performers, Trevens advises playwrights "to write for kids' vocal ranges, which are different from adults, and really understand where kids are. You want them to have a good time and mix in humor that works for kids as well as for adults. You don't talk down to kids; it's not about that. It's about understanding what's going on with kids. And some adults just don't have that understanding."

Preferences for subject matter for children's theater vary from company to company. Trevens is open to most anything. "I like subjects kids can relate to. It doesn't have to be a heavy message play. A play can just be about working together, or about accepting people for who they are. It could just be entertaining and have a general message of 'togetherness.' But I wouldn't want anything that's about negativity—it should be entertaining and positive. It has to be something everyone can enjoy."

Small theaters like TADA! have small budgets, but artistic directors can often work closely with writers. "I get very involved with the writers who write for the mainstage productions and really help develop their pieces," Trevens says.

TADA! performs two or three mainstage musical productions a year, each running five to seven weeks for about 40 performances, with casts of about 20 multi-ethnic actors, ages 6-17, found through open auditions. The plays are written specifically for family audiences, "which means it has to have a wide range," Trevens says. "It needs to be a large ensemble cast in which children are playing children. It can have multiple settings. It must have good music. Different styles are fine—show tunes or jazz or rock—it all depends what that person wants to write."

INSIDER REPORT, *Trevens*

What Trevens does not want are fairy tales or revised versions of something already done. She rejects preachy plays and work that talks down to kids. "What I want are things that kids can relate to, plays in which kids are playing kids and dealing with stuff kids have to deal with."

Trevens asks that writers interested in working with TADA! submit a script, a tape of the music, and the score of at least one of the songs. A character breakdown and a set breakdown are useful as well. However, submissions of just music or just a script are welcome. "If somebody wanted to send something they thought wasn't really right for the company, but just a good example of their work, they should indicate that in the cover letter. It's great to find writers who haven't written for kids yet but are interested in doing that."

Trevens finds a number of writers through TADA!'s annual Staged Reading Contest, for which she receives about 100 scripts for one-act plays with small casts, usually geared toward specific age groups. "I look at the contest entries and if there are writers I'm interested in pursuing, I talk to them. I like to get involved in the process, and have writers bring an idea to me and so I can help them tailor it to the kind of work TADA! produces."

—Alice P. Buening

A.D. PLAYERS, 2710 W. Alabama, Houston TX 77098. (713)526-2721. Contact: Literary Manager. Play producer. Estab. 1967. Produces 5 full-length, 5 children's and approximately 20 1 acts in repertory and 1-2 musicals/year. General public tend to be conservative—main stage shows, children/families—children's shows; churches schools, business—repertory shows. Payment varies.
How to Contact: Query with synopsis, character breakdown and set description. SASE. Reports in 6-12 months.
Musical Theater: "We prefer musicals for family and/or children, comedy or drama, full-length, original or classic adaptations with stories that reflect God's relevence and importance in our lives. Any style. Maximum 10 actors. No fly space required. Minimum wing space required. No New Age; anything contradictory to a Christian perspective; operatic; avant garde cabaret. Music should be simple, easy to learn and perform, we utilize a broad range of musical ability; will consider musical revue to musical comedy, play with music."
Productions: *Narnia*, by Jules Tasca (children, family, fantasy, musical); *Smoke on the Mountain*, by Connie Ray and Alan Bailey (family gospel, hymn heritage); and *Myrtle: A Melodrama*, by Jeannette Clift George (old-fashioned melodrama based on story of Esther).
Tips: "Learn the craft, structure and format of scriptwriting before submitting. Then be flexible and open to learning from any producing theatre which takes an interest in your work."

THE ACTING COMPANY, Dept. SM, P.O. Box 898, Times Square Station, New York NY 10108. (212)564-3510. Play producer. Estab. 1972. Produces 2-3 plays/year. "Have done musicals in the past. We are a national touring company playing universities and booking houses." Pays by royalty or negotiated fee/commission.
How to Contact: Submit through agent only. SASE. Reports in 12 weeks.
Musical Theater: "We would consider a wide variety of styles—although we remain a young, classical ensemble. Most of our classical plays make use of a lot of incidental music. Our company consists of 17 actors. All productions must be able to tour easily. We have no resident musicians. Taped sound is essential. Actors tend to remain active touring members for 2-3 seasons. Turnover is considerable. Musical ability of the company tends to vary widely from season to season. We would avoid shows which require sophisticated musical abilities and/or training."

ALLEGHENY HIGHLANDS REGIONAL THEATRE, 526 W. Ogle St., Ebensburg PA 15931. (814)472-4333. Business Director: Terry Chelednik. Play producer. Estab. 1974. Produces 4 plays and 2 musicals/year. "Rural audience, many elderly, many families; 200 seat arena." Pays $40-50/performance.
How to Contact: Query with synopsis, character breakdown and set description. SASE. Reports in 6 months.
Musical Theater: "Small cast, full-length musicals, preferably orchestrated for no more than 6 musicians. Anything set in Pennsylvania about Pennsylvanians is of particular interest. Especially interested in musicals for children, up to 60 minutes in length. Roles for children are a plus. We have difficulty finding men to audition. Few men's roles are a plus. No more than 19-20 including chorus, no more than 2-3 settings. Perhaps some underscoring for a mystery would be fun. Also pieces for young performers."
Productions: *Meet Me In St. Louis*, by Benson/Martin/Blane; and *Waiting for the Parade*, by Murrell.

AMERICAN LIVING, History Theater, Box 752, Greybull WY 82426. (307)765-9449. President and Artistic Director: Dorene Ludwig. Play producer. Estab. 1975. Produces 1-2 plays/year. Performs all over U.S.—conventions, schools, museums, universities, libraries, etc. Pays by royalty.
How to Contact: Query first. SASE. Reports in 6-12 months.
Musical Theater: "We use only primary source, historically accurate material: in music—*Songs of the Civil War* or *Songs of the Labor Movement*, etc.—presented as a program rather than play would be the only use I could foresee. We need music historians more than composers."
Tips: "Do not send fictionalized historical material. We use primary source material only."

AMERICAN MUSIC THEATER FESTIVAL, 123 S. Broad St., Suite 1820, Philadelphia PA 19109. (215)893-1570. Fax: (215)893-1233. Artistic Director: Ben Levit. Play producer. Estab. 1984. Produces 4 new musicals/year. "Mixed audience, mostly forward-thinking intellectuals." Plays performed at "Plays and Players theater, an old turn-of-the-century vaudeville house. 320 seats in Center City, Philadelphia." Pays royalties.
How to Contact: Submit complete manuscript and tape of songs. SASE. Reports in 6 weeks.
Music: "We seek musicals ranging from the traditional to very experimental. We encourage multimedia and technological applications. Topics can range. We are interested in music theater/opera that comments on current life. Musical styles can vary from folk through opera. Orchestra generally limited to a maximum of 7 pieces; cast size maximum of 10-14."
Musical Theater: *Floyd Collins*, by Tina Landau (true story); *Mystery of Love*, by Seku Sundiata (passion and friendship); and *Chippy: Diaries of a West Texas Hooker*, by Jo Harvey and Terry Allen (the life of a depression era call girl).
Tips: "We look for pieces that are music/lyric driven, not merely plays with music."

AMERICAN STAGE FESTIVAL, P.O. Box 225, Milford NH 03055. (603)889-2330. Producing Director: Matthew Parent. Play producer. Estab. 1975. Produces 5 mainstage plays, 10 children's and 2-3 musicals/year. Plays are produced in 496 seat proscenium stage for a general audience. Pays 5-12% royalty.
How to Contact: Query with synopsis, character breakdown and set description. SASE. Reports in 3 months.
Musical Theater: "We seek stories about interesting people in compelling situations. Besides our adult audience we have an active children's theater. We will not do a large chorus musical if cast size is over 18. We use original music in plays on a regular basis, as incidental music, pre-show and between acts, or as moments in and of themselves."
Productions: *1776*, by Edwards/Stone (history); *Alice Revisited*, by Julianne Boyd and Joan Micklin Silver (women's issues); and *Forever Plaid*, by Stuart Ross (revue of 1950s songs).
Tips: "We need musicals with a strong, intelligent book. Send tape of music along with initial query. Our decisions regarding musicals are based heavily upon the quality of the score."

ARDEN THEATRE COMPANY, 40 N. Second St., Philadelphia PA 19106. (215)922-8900. Fax: (215)922-1122. Producing Artistic Director: Terrence J. Nolen. Play producer. Estab. 1988. Produces 5 plays and 1-2 musicals/year. Adult audience—diverse. 150-175 seats, flexible. Pays 5% royalty.
How to Contact: Submit complete manuscript, score and tape of songs. SASE. Reports in 6 months.
Musical Theater: Full length plays and musicals. Intimate theater space, maximum cast approximately 15, minimum can be smaller. Not interested in children's music. Will consider original music for use in developing or pre-existing play. Composers should send samples of music on cassette.
Productions: *Sweeney Todd*, by Sondheim/Wheeler (musical thriller); *Change Partners & Dance*, by Dennis Raymond Smeal (romantic comedy); and *The Tempest*, by Shakespeare (classic).

ARIZONA THEATRE COMPANY, P.O. Box 1631, Tucson AZ 85702. (602)884-8210. Artistic Director: David Goldstein. Professional regional theater company. Members are professionals. Per-

forms 6 productions/year, including 1 new work. Audience is middle and upper-middle class, well-educated, aged 35-64. "We are a two-city operation based in Tucson, where we perform in a 603-seat newly renovated, historic building, which also has a 100-seat flexible seating cabaret space. Our facility in Phoenix, the Herberger Theater Center, is a 712-seat, proscenium stage." Pays 4-10% royalty.
How to Contact: Query first. Reports in 5 months.
Musical Theater: Musicals or musical theater pieces. 15-16 performers maximum including chorus. Instrumental scores should not involve full orchestra. No classical or operatic.
Productions: *Quilters*, by Barbara Damashek (musical theater piece); *Candide*, by Sondheim/Bernstein (musical); and *Dreamers of the Day*, by Anita Ruth (musical theater piece).
Tips: "As a regional theater, we cannot afford to produce extravagant works. Plot line and suitability of music to further the plot are essential considerations."

ARKANSAS REPERTORY THEATRE, 601 Main, P.O. Box 110, Little Rock AR 72203. (501)378-0445. Contact: Brad Mooy. Play producer. Estab. 1976. Produces 8 plays and 4 musicals (1 new musical)/year. "We perform in a 354-seat house and also have a 99 seat blackbox." Pays 5-10% royalty or $75-150 per performance.
How to Contact: Query with synopsis, character breakdown and set description. SASE. Reports in 6 months.
Musical Theater: "Small casts are preferred, comedy or drama and prefer shows to run 1:45 to 2 hours maximum. Simple is better; small is better, but we do produce complex shows. We aren't interested in children's pieces, puppet shows or mime. We always like to receive a tape of the music with the book."
Productions: *Sing, Baby Sing*, by Don Jones/Jack Heifner (original swing musical); and *Always . . . Patsy Cline*, by Ted Swindley (bio-musical).
Tips: "Include a *good* cassette of your music, *sung well*, with the script."

ASHLAWN-HIGHLAND SUMMER FESTIVAL, Route 6, Box 37, Charlottesville VA 22902. (804)293-4500. General Manager: Judith H. Walker. Play producer. Estab. 1978. Produces 1 musical and 2 operas/year. "Our operas and musicals are performed in a casual setting. The audience is composed of people from the Charlottesville area."
How to Contact: Query first. SASE. "We try to return items after review but depending on the time of year response time may vary."
Musical Theater: "We are very open to new ideas and young artists. Included in our season is a summer Saturday program designed for children. We enjoy puppet shows, story tellers and children-related plays. We are a small company with a limited budget. Our cast is usually 12 performers and a volunteer local chorus. Minimal scenery is done. Our audience is composed of families with children and retired adults. Material should suit their tastes." Would consider original music for use in a play being developed.
Productions: *The Magic Flute*, by Mozart; *My Fair Lady*, by Lerner & Loewe; and *The Tender Land*, by Copland.

ASOLO THEATRE COMPANY, Dept. SM, 5555 N. Tamiami Trail, Sarasota FL 34243. (941)351-9010. Literary Manager: Bruce E. Rodgers. Play producer. Produces 7-8 plays (1 musical)/year. Plays are performed at the Asolo Mainstage (500-seat proscenium house). Pays 5% minimum royalty.
How to Contact: Query with synopsis, character breakdown, set description and one page of dialogue. SASE. Reports in 3 months.
Musical Theater: "We want small to mid-size non-chorus musicals only. They should be full-length, any subject. There are no restrictions on production demands; however, musicals with excessive scenic requirements or very large casts may be difficult to consider."
Productions: *Sweet and Hot*, by Julie Boyd; *Svengali*, by Boyd, Wildhorn and Bettis; and *Das Barbecü*, by Warrender and Luis.

BAILIWICK REPERTORY, Bailiwick Arts Center, 1229 W. Belmont, Chicago IL 60657. (312)883-1091. Executive Director: David Zak. Artistic Director: Cecilie D. Keenan. Play producer. Estab. 1982. Produces 5 mainstage, 5 one-act plays and 1-2 new musicals/year. "We do Chicago productions of new works on adaptations that are politically or thematically intriguing and relevant. We also do an annual director's festival which produces 50-75 new short works each year." Pays 5-8% royalty.
How to Contact: "Send SASE (business size) first to receive manuscript submission guidelines. Material returned if appropriate SASE attached." Reports in 6 months.
Musical Theater: "We want innovative, dangerous, exciting material."
Productions: *The Christmas Schooner*, by John Reeger and Julie Shannon (holiday musical); *Pope Joan*, by Christopher Moore (dark ages); and *In The Deep Heart's Core*, by Joseph Sobel (Yeats).
Tips: "Be creative. Be patient. Be persistent. Make me believe in your dream."

BARTER THEATRE, P.O. Box 867, Abingdon VA 24212. (540)628-2281. Fax: (540)628-4551. Artistic Director: Richard Rose. Play producer. Estab. 1933. Produces 15 plays and 2-3 musicals (1 new musical)/year. Audience "varies; middle American, middle age, tourist and local mix." 400 seat proscenium stage, 150 seat thrust stage. Pays by $2,500 fee or 5% royalty.
How to Contact: Query with synopsis, character breakdown and set description. SASE. Reports in 6 months.
Musical Theater: "We investigate all types. We are not looking for any particular standard. Prefer sellable titles with unique use of music. Prefer small cast musicals, although have done large scale projects with marketable titles or subject matter. We use original music in almost all of our plays." Does not wish to see "political or very urban material, or material with very strong language."
Productions: *Peter Pan*, by Stevan Jackson (J.M. Barrie story); *Man of LaMancha*, by Mitchell Leigh (Don Quixote story); and *To Kill a Mockingbird* (with original music by Robin Mullins).

BERKSHIRE PUBLIC THEATRE, P.O. Box 860, 30 Union St., Pittsfield MA 01202. (413)445-4631. Artistic Director: Frank Bessell. Play producer. Estab. 1976. Produces 9 plays and 2 musicals/year. "Plays are performed in a 285-seat proscenium thrust theatre for a general audience of all ages with wide-ranging tastes." Pays negotiable royalty or amount per performance.
How to Contact: Query with synopsis, character breakdown and set description. SASE. Reports in 3 months.
Musical Theater: Seeking musicals with "no more than 3 acts (2½ hours). We look for fresh musicals with something to say. Our company has a flexible vocal range. Cast size must be 2-50, with a small orchestra." Would also consider original music "for a play being developed and possibly for existing works."
Productions: *Jesus Christ Superstar*, by Rice/Lloyd-Webber (gospel/life of Christ); *The Fantasticks*, by Tom Jones/Harvey Schmidt (youth and love); and *You're Gonna Love Tom*, by Sondheim (revue of Sondheim).
Tips: "We are a small company. Patience is a must. Be yourself—open, honest. Experience is not necessary but is helpful. We don't have a lot of money but we are long on nurturing artists!"

*BIRMINGHAM CHILDREN'S THEATRE, P.O. Box 1362, Birmingham AL 35201. (205)324-0470. Fax: (205)324-0494. Executive Director: Charlotte Lane Dominick. Play producer. Estab. 1947. Produces 9 plays and 1-4 new musicals/year. "Wee Folks" Series: preschool-grade 1; Children's Series: K-6; Young Adult Series: junior and senior high. Performs in 1,072-seat flexible thrust mainstage, 250 seat black box (touring venues vary). Pay is negotiable.
How to Contact: Query with synopsis, character breakdown and set description, or submit complete manuscript, score and tape of songs. SASE. Reports in 2 months.
Musical Theater: "Typically, original adaptations of classic children's stories. 'Wee Folks' productions should be 40-45 minutes; Children's Series 55-60 minutes; Young Adult Series 85-95 minutes. 'Wee Folks' shows should be interactive; all others presentational. Most productions tour, so sets must be lightweight, simple and portable. 'Wee Folks' shows prefer cast of four. Touring Children's Series shows prefer cast of six. All others prefer cast of 12 or less. BCT traditionally ultilizes a great deal of music for underscoring, transitions, etc. We welcome submissions from prospective sound designers."
Productions: *The Secret Garden*, by Michael Price Nelson; *A Midsummer Night's Dream*, by Shakespeare; and *Froggie Went A-Courtin'*, by Jeanmarie Collins (adaptations of classics).

THE BLOWING ROCK STAGE COMPANY, P.O. Box 2170, Blowing Rock NC 28605. (704)295-9168. Fax: (704)295-9104. Producing Director: Mark Wilson. Play producer. Estab. 1986. Produces 2 plays, 2 musicals and 1 new musical/year. Performances take place in a 221 seat proscenium summer theater in the Blue Ridge Mountains. Pays 5-10% royalty.
How to Contact: Query with synopsis, character breakdown and set description. SASE. Reports in 6 months.
Musical Theater: "Casts of 10 or less are preferred, with ideal show running time of 2 hours, intermission included. Limit set changes to three or less; or unit concept. Some comic relief, please. Not producing children's theater or stark adult themes."
Productions: *Radio Gals*, by Craver/Hardwick (early 20th century actor/musician tour de force); *Cowboy Cafe*, by Phyllis MacBride (country); and *Last Of the Red Hot Mamas*, by Parise/Baker (the Sophie Tucker "revusical").
Tips: "We're looking for inspiration. We enjoy supporting projects which are soulful and uplifting. Not saccharine, though. There's a difference."

BRISTOL RIVERSIDE THEATRE, Dept. SM, P.O. Box 1250, Bristol PA 19007. (215)785-6664. Artistic Director: Susan D. Atkinson. Play producer. Estab. 1986. Produces 5 plays and 2 musicals/year (1 new musical every 2 years). "302-seat proscenium Equity theater with audience of all ages from small towns and metropolitan area." Pays 6-8% royalty.

How to Contact: Submit complete manuscript, score and tape of songs. SASE. Reports in 6 months.
Musical Theater: "No strictly children's musicals. All other types with small to medium casts and within reasonable artistic tastes. Prefer one-set; limited funds restrict. Do not wish to see anything catering to prurient interests."
Productions: *Sally Blane, World's Greatest Girl Detective*, by David Levy/Leslie Eberhard (spoof of teen detective genre); *Moby Dick*, by Mark St. Germain, music by Doug Katsarous; and *Alive and Well*, by Larry Gatlin.
Tips: "You should be willing to work with small staff, open to artistic suggestion, and aware of the limitations of newly developing theaters."

*BROADWAY ON SUNSET, 10800 Hesby St., North Hollywood CA 91601. (818)508-9270. Play producer. Estab. 1981. Executive Director: Kevin Kaufman. "Sponsored by the National Academy of Songwriters (NAS), Broadway on Sunset is devoted exclusively to developing original material through various classes, workshops and staging opportunities."
How to Contact: Submit 10 pages of dialogue, 3 songs and SASE. Reports in 2-3 months.
Musical Theater: "Seeking original, unproduced musicals only, for mainstream audience. This is not the place for experimental, controversial material, although challenging themes and concepts are encouraged."
Productions: *American Twistory* (satirical review); *Out* (comedy/drama); and *Little Witch of Wichita* (chidren's musical).

WILLIAM CAREY COLLEGE DINNER THEATRE, William Carey College, Hattiesburg MS 39401-5499. (601)582-6218. Managing Director: O.L. Quave. Play producer. Produces 2 plays and 2 musicals/year. "Our dinner theater operates only in summer and plays to family audiences." Payment negotiable.
How to Contact: Query with synopsis, character breakdown and set description. Does not return material. Reports in 1 month.
Musical Theater: "Plays should be simply-staged, have small casts (8-10 maximum), and be suitable for family viewing; two hours maximum length. Score should require piano only, or piano, synthesizer."
Productions: *Rodgers and Hart: A Musical Celebration*; and *Side by Side by Sondheim*.

CENTENARY COLLEGE, THEATRE DEPARTMENT, Shreveport LA 71134-1188. (318)869-5011. Chairman: Robert R. Buseick. Play producer. Produces 6 plays (1-2 new musicals)/year. Plays are presented in a 350-seat playhouse to college and community audiences.
How to Contact: Submit manuscript and score. SASE. Reports in 1 month.
Productions: *Into the Woods*; *Little Shop of Horrors*; and *Jerry's Girls*, by Todd Sweeney.

CENTER THEATER, 1346 W. Devon, Chicago IL 60660. (312)508-0200. Contact: Literary Manager. Play producer. Estab. 1984. Produces 6 plays and 1 musical (1 new musical)/year. "Our 80 seat modified thrust theater has produced 3 original musicals, based on novels or plays." Royalty negotiable.
How to Contact: Query with synopsis, character breakdown and set description. SASE. "Have a complete script and a demo tape with professional singers." Reports in 3 months.
Musical Theater: 12 person maximum.
Productions: *The Black Tulip*, by Tracy Friedman/Brian Lasser (adaptation of Dumas novel); *Two Many Bosses*, by Dan La Morte/Donald Coates (musical adaptation of *Servant of Two Masters*); and *Lysistrata 2411 A.D.*, by Dale Calandra/Donald Coates (futuristic musical adaptation).
Tips: "We also host an annual international play contest which includes plays/musicals of all genres and subject matter. SASE for contest guidelines."

*CIRCA' 21 DINNER PLAYHOUSE, Dept. SM, Box 3784, Rock Island IL 61204-3784. (309)786-2667. Producer: Dennis Hitchcock. Play producer. Estab. 1977. Produces 1-2 plays and 4-5 musicals (1 new musical)/year. Plays produced for a general audience. Two children's works/year, concurrent with major productions. Payment is negotiable.
How to Contact: Query with synopsis, character breakdown and set description or submit complete manuscript, score and tape of songs. SASE. Reports in 8 weeks.

 THE ASTERISK before a listing indicates that the listing is new in this edition. New markets are often the most receptive to unsolicited submissions.

Musical Theater: "We produce both full length and one act children's musicals. Folk or fairy tale themes. Works that do not condescend to a young audience yet are appropriate for entire family. We're also seeking full-length, small cast musicals suitable for a broad audience." Would also consider original music for use in a play being developed.
Productions: *Cowgirls*, by Mary Murfitt and Betsy Howie; *A Closer Walk with Patsy Cline*, by Dean Regan; and *Sleeping Beauty*, by Jim Eiler.
Tips: "Small, upbeat, tourable musicals (like *Pump Boys*) and bright musically-sharp children's productions (like those produced by Prince Street Players) work best. Keep an open mind. Stretch to encompass a musical variety—different keys, rhythms, musical ideas and textures."

CIRCLE IN THE SQUARE THEATRE, Dept. SM, 1633 Broadway, New York NY 10019. (212)307-2700. Contact: Literary Advisor. Play producer. Estab. 1951. Produces 3 plays/year; occasionally produces a musical. Pays by royalty.
How to Contact: Submit through agent only. Does not return material. Reports in 6 months.
Musical Theater: "We are looking for original material with small cast and orchestra requirements. We're not interested in traditional musical comedies."
Productions: *Pal Joey*, *Sweeney Todd* and *Anna Karenina*.
Tips: "The material has to be 'do-able' in our unique arena space."

*CITY THEATRE COMPANY, INC., 57 S. 13th St., Pittsburgh PA 15203. (412)431-4400. General Manager: Adrienne Keriotis. Play producer. Estab. 1974. Produces 5 plays/year. "Plays are performed in a 225 seat thrust-stage or proscenium configuration theater to an adventurous subscriber base consisting of a wide variety of urban professionals, elderly and college students looking for new and risky works." Pays negotiable royalty.
How to Contact: Query with synopsis, character breakdown and set description. "We select plays through Play Showcases (Louisville, Denver and Rochester), Summer Workshop Programs (Shenandoah, New Harmony and Carnegie Mellon University) and local playwright centers and organizations from new dramatists in New York, Chriog Dramatists Workshop and Southeast Playwrights project. Also various scriptshare and play catalogue newsletters." SASE. Reports in 2 months.
Musical Theater: "We want sophisticated plays with music. We prefer a small cast with no more than 10 (including musicians) and single set because we have small stage capabilities only. We don't want traditional, large cast musical comedies."
Productions: *American Song*, by Peter Glazer (folk music); and *Spunk*, by George C. Wolfe (African American).
Tips: "Unique material comes from a personal stake in the work."

COCKPIT IN COURT SUMMER THEATRE, 7201 Rossville Blvd., Baltimore MD 21237. (410)780-6534. Managing Director: F. Scott Black. Play producer. Estab. 1973. Produces 6-8 plays and 5-7 musicals/year. "Plays are produced at four locations: Mainstage (proscenium theater), Courtyard (outdoor theater), Cabaret (theater-in-the-round) and Lecture Hall (children's theater)."
How to Contact: Query with synopsis, character breakdown and set description. SASE. Reports in 1 month.
Musical Theater: "Seeking musical comedy and children's shows. We have the capacity to produce large musicals with up to 50 cast members."
Productions: *42nd Street*, *Kismet* and *Robin Hood*.
Tips: "We look for material that appeals to a community theater audience."

THE COTERIE, 2450 Grand Ave., Kansas City MO 64108. (816)474-6785. Artistic Director: Jeff Church. Play producer. Estab. 1979. Produces 7-8 plays/year. Plays produced at Hallmark's Crown Center in downtown Kansas City in The Coterie's resident theater (capacity 240). Musicals are produced for adventurous families and schools K-12. A typical performance run is one month in length. "We retain some rights on commissioned plays. Writers are paid a royalty for their work per performance or flat fee."
How to Contact: Query with synopsis and character breakdown. Submit complete manuscript and score "if established writer in theater for young audiences. We will consider musicals with smaller orchestration needs (3-5 pieces), or a taped score." SASE. Reports in 8 months.
Musical Theater: "Types of plays we produce: pieces which are universal in appeal; plays for all ages. They may be original or adaptations of classic or contemporary literature. Limitations: Typically not more than 12 in a cast—prefer 5-9 in size. No fly space or wing space. No couch plays. Prefer plays by seasoned writers who have established reputations. Groundbreaking and exciting scripts from the youth theater field welcome. It's perfectly fine if your musical is a little off center."
Productions: *I Can't Eat Goat Head*, by Sylvia Gonzales S. (Latino journey); *The Little Prince*, by Jeff Church (adaptation of classic literature); and *A Woman Called Truth*, by Sandra Asher (life of Sojourner Truth).

Tips: "Make certain your submitted musical is very theatrical and not cinematic. Writers need to see how far the field of youth and family theater has come—the interesting new areas we're doing—before sending us your query or manuscript. We like young protagonists in our plays, but make sure they're not romanticized or stereotyped good-and-bad like the children's theater playwrights of yesterday would have them."

CREATIVE PRODUCTIONS, INC., 2 Beaver Place, Aberdeen NJ 07747. (908)566-6985. Director: Walter L. Born. Play producer. Estab. 1970. Produces 2 musicals (1-2 new musicals)/year. "Our audience is the general community with emphasis on elderly and folks with disabilities. We use local public school theater facilities." Pays $2,000-3,000 for outright purchase.
How to Contact: Query with synopsis, character breakdown and set description, then submit complete manuscript and score. SASE. Reports in 1 month.
Musical Theater: "We want family type material (i.e. *Brigadoon*, *Charlie Brown*) with light rock to classical music and a maximum running time of two hours. We have no flying capability in facility; cast size is a maximum 10-12; the sets are mostly on small wagons, the orchestra is chamber size with standard instruments. We don't want pornographic material or children's shows. We want nothing trite and condescending in either the material or the treatment. We like the unusual treatment well-structured and thought out, with minimal sets and changes. We can't handle unusual vocal requirements. We prefer an integrated piece with music a structural part from the beginning."
Productions: *Reluctant Dragon*, by K. Grahame (myth); *For Love Or Money*, by M. Lombardo/J. Callis (based on O. Henry); and *Champion Kid's Foods*, by Don Tennent (abandoned kids).
Tips: "Prepare/send representative script and music based on above criteria and follow up with phone call after our response."

CREATIVE THEATRE, 102 Witherspoon St., Princeton NJ 08540. (609)924-3489. Artistic Director: Kenneth Harper-Mosley. Play producer. Estab. 1969. Produces 5 plays, all with music (1 new musical)/year. "Plays are performed for young audiences grades K-8. The plays are always audience participation and done in schools (45 minute format)." Pays a fee for writing and production and royalty for two seasons, then per performance royalty fee.
How to Contact: Query with synopsis, character breakdown and set description. SASE. Reports in 2 months.
Musical Theater: "Audience participation plays, 45 minutes in length, 4-6 performers, usually presentational style. Topics can range from original plots to adaptations of folk and fairytales. Staging is usually in the round with audience of no more than 300/seating on the floor. No lighting and usually piano accompaniment. Actor is focus with strong but very lean set and costume design." Does not wish to see plays without audience participation. "We are not doing as many 'heavy musicals,' but are looking for light plays with less music."
Productions: *The Bremen Town Musicians*, by Jean Prall (fairy tale); *Festival of Folktales*, by Barbara Ackerman/Eloise Bruce (multicultural); and *Sorcerer's Apprentice*, by Rita Asch (fairy tale).
Tips: "Give us a strong idea represented within the characters—'cute' is not acceptable. Humor flows naturally from character and circumstance. Audience participation is integral to plot and involves audience as community in play."

*CREEDE REPERTORY THEATRE, P.O. Box 269, Creede CO 81130. (719)658-2541. Producing/Artistic Director: Richard Baxter. Play producer. Estab. 1966. Produces 6 plays and 1 musical/year. Performs in 243-seat proscenium theatre; audience is ½ local support and ½ tourist base from Texas, Oklahoma, New Mexico and Colorado. Pays 7% royalty.
How to Contact: Query first. SASE. Reports in 1 year.
Musical Theater: "We prefer historical Western material with cast no larger than 11. Staging must be flexible as space is limited."
Productions: *Baby Doe Tabor*, by Kenton Kersting (Colorado history); *A Frog in His Throat*, by Feydeau, adapted by Eric Conger (French farce); and *Tommyknockers*, by Eric Engdahl, Mark Houston and Chris Thompson (mining).
Tips: "Songwriter must have the ability to accept criticism and must be flexible."

STEVE DOBBINS PRODUCTIONS, 650 Geary St., San Francisco CA 94102. Administrative Director: Alan Ramos. Play producer. Estab. 1978. Produces 4 plays and 1 new musical/year. Plays performed for San Francisco Bay Area avante garde, racially mixed audiences. Pays 6% royalty.
How to Contact: Query with synopsis, character breakdown and set description. SASE. Reports in 3 months.
Musical Theater: "We seek all types of material as long as the ideas are new. No formula scripts." Would consider original music for use in a play being developed.
Productions: *Hoagy*, by Billy Philadelphia (Hoagy Carmichael); *Doo Wop*, by David Glover ('50s black musical); and *A Slice of Saturday Night*, by Heather Brothers ('60s teen musical).
Tips: "Write to us explaining your idea."

GEOF ENGLISH, PRODUCER, SADDLEBACK CIVIC LIGHT OPERA, Saddleback College, 28000 Marguerite Pkwy., Mission Viejo CA 92692. (714)582-4763. Performing Arts Director: Geofrey English. Play producer for musical theater. Produces 4 musicals/year. Community audience of mostly senior citizens. Pays by royalty and performance.
How to Contact: Submit complete manuscript, score and tape of songs. Does not return material. Reports in 2-3 months.
Musical Theater: "Looking for mainly family musicals. No limitations, open to options. It is important that music must be sent along with scripts. Best not to call. Just send materials."
Productions: More than 50 musicals produced since company formed in 1978.
Tips: "Submit materials in a timely manner—usually at least one year in advance."

FOOLS COMPANY, INC., 311 W. 43rd St., New York NY 10036. (212)307-6000. Artistic Director: Martin Russell. Play producer. Estab. 1970. Produces 4-6 plays/year; produces 1-2 musicals (1-2 new musicals)/year. "Audience is comprised of general public and teens, ages 16-20. Plays are performed at our own mid-Manhattan theater."
How to Contact: Submit complete manuscript, score and tape of songs or query with synopsis, character breakdown and set description. SASE. Reports in 1 month.
Musical Theater: "We seek new and unusual, contemporary and experimental material. We would like small, easy-to-tour productions. Nothing classical, folkloric or previously produced." Would also consider original music for use in a play being developed.
Productions: *Zen Puppies Unleashed* (company collective); *No Dust*, by Fools Co. Collaborators (humanity); and *Relief*, by I. P. Daly (youth growth).
Tips: "Save your pennies and showcase in NYC."

THE FOOTHILL THEATRE COMPANY, P.O. Box 1812, Nevada City CA 95959. (916)265-9320. Artistic Director: Philip Charles Sneed. Play producer. Estab. 1977. Produces 6-10 plays and 1-2 musicals/year. Rural audience, with some urban visitors to the area. 250-seat historic proscenium house; built in 1865 (oldest in CA). "We haven't yet produced a new play, but will seriously consider it within the next 2 years; payment will be decided later." Payment negotiated.
How to Contact: Query with synopsis, character breakdown and set description. SASE. Reports in 6 months.
Musical Theater: "We're particularly interested in works which deal with the region's history or with issues relevant to the area today. We are also interested in one-act musicals and children's musicals. We have limited space backstage, especially in the wings. We also have very limited fly space. We're interested in original ideas, nothing derivative (except in an adaptation, of course). A good rock musical would be nice. Will consider original music for use in a play being developed, or for use in a pre-existing play. The use will depend upon the play: could be preshow, or underscoring, or scene change, or any combination."
Productions: *Quilters*, by Damaschek and Newman (pioneer story); *Jacques Brel*, by Herbert Blau (cabaret musical); and *Man of La Mancha*, by Dale Wasserman, Mitch Leigh and Joe Darion.
Tips: "Know something about our region and its history."

*THE WILL GEER THEATRICUM BOTANICUM, P.O. Box 1222, Topanga CA 90290. (310)455-2322. Artistic Director: Ellen Geer. Play producer. Produces 4 plays, 1 new musical/year. Plays are performed in "large outdoor amphitheater with 60′ x 25′ wooden stage. Rustic setting." Pays negotiable royalty.
How to Contact: Query with synopsis, tape, character breakdown and story description. SASE. Submit scripts in September for prompt reply.
Musical Theater: Seeking social or biographical works, children's works, full length musicals with cast of up to 10 equity actors (the rest non-equity). Requires "low budget set and costumes. We emphasize paying performers." Would also consider original music for use in a play being developed. Does not wish to see "anything promoting avarice, greed, violence or apathy."

*GEORGE STREET PLAYHOUSE, 9 Livingston Ave., New Brunswick NJ 08901. (908)846-2895. Fax: (908)247-9151. Literary Manager: Tricia Roche. Producing Artistic Director: Gregory Hurst. Play producer. Estab. 1974. Produces 7 plays, including 1-2 new musicals/year. "We are a 367-seat thrust theater working under a LORT C-contract with a 5,500 subscriber base." Fees vary. "Each situation is handled individually."
How to Contact: Query with synopsis, character breakdown and set description. SASE. Reports in 6-8 months.
Musical Theater: Seeking musical adaptations. "We are interested in a variety of themes and formats. We aren't seeking to limit the things we read. We prefer fewer than 9 actors."
Productions: *Off-Key*, by Bill C. Davis and Richard Adler; *Opal*, by Robert Nassif Lindsay; and *Love Comics*, by Sarah Schlesinger and David Evans.

GOLDEN FLEECE LTD., 204 W. 20th St., New York NY 10011. (212)691-6105. Producing Artistic Director: Lou Rodgers. Play producer. Estab. 1976. Produces 4 operas and 30 readings/year. Audience is general —"primarily an opera/music theater audience." Performance space holds 80 seats. Pays by an annual composers' commission.
How to Contact: Query with synopsis, character breakdown, set description and cassette tape of project sample. SASE.
Musical Theater: "We produce one act chamber operas and musical theater works. We do readings of opera/musical theater works in progress. The works we produce are small scale productions, casts from 3-7, simple scenery, small musical ensemble. We are a composer's theater company, so all our works involve music."
Productions: *Peace Canal*, by Lou Rodgers; *South and Easy*, by Memrie Innerarity; and *Pigs is Pigs*, by Linder Charson.
Tips: "Attend our performances if possible and see what we do."

GREAT AMERICAN HISTORY THEATRE, 30 E. Tenth St., St. Paul MN 55101. (612)292-4323. Artistic Director: Ron Peluso. Play producer. Estab. 1978. Produces 5-6 plays, 1 or 2 musicals (1 or 2 new musicals)/year. Pays 5-10% royalty or by commission.
How to Contact: Query first with synopsis, character breakdown and set description. SASE. Reports in 6 months.
Musical Theater: "Plays based on people, events, ideas in history. Preferably Midwestern or American history. However, must be *real* plays, we *do not* teach history. *No* pageants. No larger than cast of 10. Technical considerations must be simple. We like nonrealism."
Productions: *Mesabi Red*, by Lance S. Belville (iron range musical); *Inner-City Opera*, by J.D. & Fred Steele (growing up in the inner-city); and *Small Town Triumphs & Cowboy Colors*, by Bart Sutter/Paul Zarzyski (poetry adapted to stage about small towns and cowboys).

GREAT AMERICAN MELODRAMA & VAUDEVILLE, P.O. Box 1026, Oceano CA 93445. (805)481-4880, ext. 32. Fax: (805)489-5539. Owner/producer: John Schlenker. Play producer. Estab. 1976. Produces 7 plays and 2-3 musicals/year. "Family entertainment—all ages." Performances held in a 260 seat theater, cabaret-style seating with bench seats surrounding theater. Payment by outright purchase or percentage of royalty.
How to Contact: Query with synopsis, character breakdown and set description. "All plays are selected for the year July through September." Does not return material. Reports in 5 weeks.
Musical Theater: "Everything from Gilbert & Sullivan, Cinderella to Western shoot-'em-up spoofs play extremely well here. Must be shows suitable for families. Victorian melodramas are our bread and butter, therefore, musical adaptations of period melodramas would be great! Cast size 10-12, usually 6 men and 4 women." Does not wish to see "realistic hardcore contemporary dramatic literature. People do not come to our theater looking for a slice of their daily lives. All plays and/or musicals must play in 75 minutes actual playing time, since they are followed with a 35 minute musical revue. High style action-packed shows work like gangbusters. A little adult humor is okay as long as it is done with taste and adults get it but children don't."
Productions: *Dames at Sea*; *Once Upon A Mattress*; and *The Madman's Daughter*, by Gene Casey (original melodrama).
Tips: "Call me regarding our theatrical style and playbill. We do a lot of original plays (melodramas, thrillers, comedies and musicals). Everything is followed by a revue. We are a 20-year-old, well established fulltime, year-round theater and we produce a *lot* of original work. I am always looking."

HARTFORD STAGE COMPANY, 50 Church St., Hartford CT 06103. (203)525-5601. Fax: (203)525-4420. Director of New Play Development: Kim Euell. Play producer. Estab. 1963. Produces 6 plays and 1-2 musicals/year. "Mainly white-collar, upper middle-class audience; plays performed on a thrust stage, seats 489 people." Pays royalty.
How to Contact: Query with synopsis, character breakdown and set description, 10-page dialogue sample and tape if possible, or submit through agent. SASE. Reports in 3-6 months.
Musical Theater: Looking for "any kind of musicals except for children's theater. Musicals are preferred to be 2-2½ hours in length, but longer ones accepted also. We are mainly interested in small to medium-sized casts, up to 12 actors, although larger ones are also accepted." Does not wish to see "anything in the vein of the typical Broadway musical—*Phantom of the Opera*, *Miss Saigon*, etc."
Productions: *Herringbone*, by Tom Cone (one-man show); *Martin Gtuerre*, by Laura Harrington (adaptation of French film); and *March of the Falsettos and Falsettolands*, by William Finn (gay man's journey among friend's family).

HIP POCKET THEATRE, 1627 Fairmount Ave., Ft. Worth TX 76104-4237. (817)927-2833. Producer: Diane Simons. Play producer. Produces 7 plays/year (including new musicals). Estab. 1977. "Our audience is an eclectic mix of Ft. Worth/Dallas area residents with varying levels of incomes and backgrounds. Payment varies according to type of script, reputation of playwright, etc."

How to Contact: Query with synopsis, character breakdown and set description "with script portion and selected songs on tape." SASE. Reports in 5 weeks.

Musical Theater: "We are not interested in cabaret revues, but rather in full-length pieces that can be for adults and/or children. We tend to produce more fanciful, whimsical musicals (something not likely to be found anywhere else), but would also consider political pieces and other subjects. Basically, we're open for anything fresh and well-written. We prefer no more than 15 in a cast, and a staging adapted to an outdoor environmental thrust stage to be considered for summer season. Smaller cast shows are a requirement for the indoor, more intimate performance space."

Productions: *Swank City*, by Pete Gooch and Jim Toler (film noir); *Daughters of Zeeack*, by Johnny Simons with music arrangements by Michael Appleby (out-of-body experiences); and *A Bowl of Red*, by Johnny Simons and Douglas Balentine (the history of chili—the kind you eat).

Tips: "Think creative, complex thoughts and musical visions that can be transformed into reality by creative, visionary musicians in theaters that rarely have the huge Broadway dollar."

HORIZON THEATRE CO., P.O. Box 5376, Station E, Atlanta GA 30307. (404)523-1477. Artistic Directors: Lisa and Jeff Adler. Play producer. Estab. 1983. Produces 4 plays and 1 musical/year. "Our audience is comprised mostly of young professionals looking for contemporary comedy with some social commentary. Our theater features a 185-seat facility with flexible stage." Pays 6-8% royalty.

How to Contact: Query with synopsis, character breakdown, set description and résumé. SASE. Reports in 6 months.

Musical Theater: "We prefer musicals that have a significant book and a lot of wit (particularly satire). Our casts are restricted to 10 actors. We prefer plays with equal number of male and female roles, or more female than male roles. We have a limited number of musicians available. No musical revues and no dinner theater fluff. One type of play we are currently seeking is a country musical with women's themes. We generally contract with a musician or sound designer to provide sound for each play we produce. If interested send résumé, synopsis, references, tape with music or sound design samples."

Productions: *Angry Housewives*, by A.M. Collins/Chad Henry; *A. . . . My Name Is Still Alice*, conceived by Julianne Boyd/Joan Micklin Silver; and *The Good Times Are Killing Me*, by Lynda Barry.

Tips: "Have patience and use subtle persistence. Work with other theater artists to get a good grasp of the form."

JEWISH REPERTORY THEATRE, 1395 Lexington Ave., New York NY 10128. (212)415-5550. Director: Ran Avni. Play producer. Estab. 1974. Produces 4 new musicals/year. Pays royalty.

How to Contact: Submit complete manuscript, score and tape of songs. SASE. Reports in 6-12 weeks.

Musical Theater: Seeking "musicals in English relating to the Jewish experience. No more than 8 characters."

Productions: *That's Life!* (musical revue); *Theda Bara and the Frontier Rabbi* (musical comedy); and *The Shop on Main Street* (musical drama).

THE LAMB'S THEATRE CO., 130 W. 44th St., New York NY 10036. (212)997-0210. Literary Manager: James Masters. Play producer. Estab. 1984. Produces 2-3 plays and 1 musical (1 new musical)/year. Plays are performed for "family-oriented audiences." Pays by royalty.

How to Contact: Query with synopsis, character breakdowns, dialogue or lyric sample. SASE. Reports in 3 months.

Musical Theater: "We are looking for full length musicals that are entertaining, but moving, and deal with serious issues as well as comic situations. No one-act plays. Large-cast epics are out. Both our spaces are intimate theaters, one a 130-seat black box space and one a 349-seat proscenium. Material with sex and nudity and plays with obscene language are not appropriate for this theater. We require a small orchestra in a musical."

Productions: *Johnny Pye & The Foolkiller*, by R. Courts/M. St. Germain (original musical based on Stephen V. Benet short story); and *The Gifts of the Magi*, by R. Courts/M. St. Germain (original musical based on O. Henry short stories).

LOS ANGELES DESIGNERS' THEATRE, P.O. Box 1883, Studio City CA 91614-0883. (213)650-9600. Fax: (818)985-9200. E-mail: ladesigners'@mcimail.com. Artistic Director: Richard Niederberg. Play producer. Estab. 1970. Produces 20-25 plays, 8-10 new musicals/year. Plays are produced at several locations, primarily Studio City, California. Pay is negotiable.

  • See the interview with Artistic Director Richard Niederberg in the 1996 *Songwriter's Market*, and their listing in the Contests and Awards section.

How to Contact: Submit complete synopsis, score and tape of songs, character breakdown and set descriptions. Video tape submissions are also accepted. Does not return material. Reports in 4 months.

Musical Theater: "We seek out controversial material. Street language OK, nudity is fine, religious themes, social themes, political themes are encouraged. Our audience is very 'jaded' as it consists of

TV, motion picture and music publishing executives who have 'seen it all'." Does not wish to see bland, 'safe' material. "We like first productions. In the cover letter state in great detail the proposed involvement of the songwriter, other than as a writer (i.e. director, actor, singer, publicist, designer, etc.). Also, state if there are any liens on the material or if anything has been promised."
Productions: *Offenbach in the Underworld*, by Frederick Grab (musical with Can-Can); *St. Tim*, by Fred Grab (historical 60's musical); and *Slipper and the Rose* (gang musical).
Tips: "Make it very 'commercial' and inexpensive to produce. Allow for non-traditional casting. Be prepared with ideas as to how to transform your work to film or videotaped entertainment."

MANHATTAN THEATRE CLUB, 453 W. 16th St., New York NY 10011. (212)645-5590. Director of Musical Theater Program: Clifford Lee Johnson III. Associate Artistic Director: Michael Bush. Play producer. Estab. 1971. Produces 8 plays and sometimes 1 musical/year. Plays are performed at the Manhattan Theatre Club before varied audiences. Pays negotiated fee.
How to Contact: Query first. SASE. Reports in 6 months.
Musical Theater: "Original work."
Productions: *Groundhog*, by Elizabeth Swados; *1-2-3-4-5*, by Maury Yeston and Larry Gelbart; and *Putting It Together*, by Stephen Sondheim.
Tips: "Make sure your script is tightly and securely bound."

*MILL MOUNTAIN THEATRE, 1 Market Square, 2nd Floor, Roanoke VA 24011-1437. (540)342-5730. Fax: (540)342-5745. Literary Manager: Jo Weinstein. Play producer. Estab. 1964. Produces 11-14 plays and generally 3 established musicals (1-2 new musicals)/year. General theater audience on mainstage; a more open minded audience in Theatre B; also children's musicals. 400 seat proscenium mainstage; 125 seat alternate space. Pays variable royalty.
How to Contact: Query with synopsis, character breakdown and demo tape. SASE. Reports in 6 months.
Musical Theater: "We seek children's musicals (especially those adapted from recognizable children's works); we also accept contemporary musicals which explore new forms and themes, especially those which encourage diversity of life experiences. Smaller cast musicals with a minimum of technical requirements are encouraged. We have, in the past, used original music for existing plays (*Midsummer Night's Dream*, *To Kill A Mockingbird*), usually to set the production's mood and emphasize the action on stage."
Productions: *The Christmas Cup*, based on the book by Nancy Ruth Patterson, adapted by Jere Lee Hodgin (girl's coming of age); *Through The Picture Tube*, by Ed Sala, music by Michael Hirsch (TV's influence on one family); and *Everything I Need To Know I Learned in Kindergarten*, based on books by Robert Fulgum, adapted by Ernest Zulia (life and its everyday wonders).

MIXED BLOOD THEATRE CO., 1501 S. Fourth St., Minneapolis MN 55454. (612)338-0937. Script Czar: David Kunz. Play producer. Estab. 1976. Produces 4-5 plays a year and perhaps 1 new musical every 2 years. "We have a 200-seat theater in a converted firehouse. The audience spans the socio-economic spectrum."
   • See the listing for the Mixed Blood Versus America Playwriting Contest in the Contests and Awards section.
How to Contact: Query first. SASE. Reports in 3-6 weeks.
Musical Theater: "We want full-length, non-children's works with a message. Always query first. Never send unsolicited script or tape."
Productions: *Black Belts II*, musical revue (black female vocalists and their music).
Tips: "Always query first. Keep it professional, keep it concise, but make it interesting."

NATIONAL MUSIC THEATER NETWORK, INC., 1697 Broadway #902, New York NY 10019. President: Timothy Jerome. Co-artistic Directors: Gideon Y. Schein and John Margulis. Service to evaluate new musical works and publish a catalogue of recommended works to play producers. "Our catalogue of recommended works is targeted to regional theaters and musical producers interested in presenting new works. Our 'sampler' series concerts feature excerpts from recommended works for the NYC area. Producers contact us for creators' works. We contact creators and creators contact producers."

How to Contact: Query first. Writers are required to "fill out our submission form plus $45 fee." SASE. Reports in 6-12 months.
Musical Theater: "We accept musicals. Take the time to present your materials neatly. We accept only *completed* musicals, i.e. script/tape."
Productions: *Quilt*, by Morgan/Stochler (the AIDS memorial quilt); and *Bring in the Morning*, by Friedman (ghetto children).
Tips: "Use us as a resource to help you market your work. Submit a synopsis which captures the heart of your piece; inject your piece with a strong voice and intent and try to surprise and excite us."

*NEW YORK STATE THEATRE INSTITUTE, 155 River St., Troy NY 12180. (518)274-3200. Producing Artistic Director: Patricia Di Benedetto Snyder. Patricia B. Snyder. Play producer. Produces 5 plays (1 new musical)/year. Plays performed for student audiences grades K-12, family audiences and adult audiences. Theater seats 900 with full stage. Pay negotiable.
How to Contact: Query with synopsis, character breakdown and set description or submit complete manuscript, score and tape of songs. SASE. Reports in 2-3 weeks for synopsis, 3-4 months for manuscript.
Musical Theater: Looking for "intelligent and well-written book with substance, a score that enhances and supplements the book and is musically well-crafted and theatrical." Length: up to 2 hours. Could be play with music, musical comedy, musical drama. Excellence and substance in material is essential. Cast could be up to 12; orchestra size up to 8.
Productions: *A Tale of Cinderella*, by W.A. Frankonis/Will Severin/George David Weiss (adaptation of fairy tale); *The Silver*, by Lanie Robertson/Byron Janis/George David Weiss (adaptation of book); and *Big River*, by William Hauptman/Roger Miller (adapted from Mark Twain).
Tips: "There is a great need for musicals that are well-written with intelligence and substance which are suitable for family audiences."

*NEW YORK THEATRE WORKSHOP, 79 E. Fourth St., New York NY 10036. (212)780-9037. Artistic Director: James C. Nicola. Play producer. Produces 4 mainstage plays and approximately 50 readings/year. "Plays are performed in our theater on East Fourth St. Audiences include: subscription/single ticket buyers from New York area, theater professionals, and special interest groups." Pays by negotiable royalty.
How to Contact: Query with synopsis, character breakdown and set description. SASE. Reports in 5 months.
Musical Theater: "As with our nonmusicals, we seek musicals of intelligence and social consciousness that challenge our perceptions of the world and the events which shape our lives. We favor plays that possess a strong voice, distinctive and innovative use of language and visual imagery. Integration of text and music is particularly of interest. Musicals which require full orchestrations would generally be too big for us. We prefer 'musical theater pieces' rather than straightforward 'musicals' per-se. We often use original music for straight plays that we produce. This music may be employed as pre-show, post-show or interlude music. If the existing piece lends itself, music may also be incorporated within the play itself. Large casts (12 or more) are generally prohibitive and require soliciting of additional funds. Design elements for our productions are of the highest quality possible with our limited funds—approximately budgets of $10,000 are allotted for our productions."
Productions: *The Waves*, adapted from Virginia Woolf's novel, music and lyrics by David Bucknam and text and direction by Lisa Peterson; *My Children! My Africa*, by Athol Fugard; and *Mad Forest*, by Caryl Churchill.
Tips: "Submit a synopsis which captures the heart of your piece; inject your piece with a strong voice and intent and try to surprise and excite us."

ODYSSEY THEATRE ENSEMBLE, Dept. SM, 2055 S. Sepulveda Blvd., Los Angeles CA 90025. (310)477-2055. Director of Literary Programs: Jan Lewis. Play producer. Estab. 1969. Produces 9 plays, 1 musical and 1-2 new musicals/year. "Our audience is predominantly over 35, upper middle-class audience interested in eclectic brand of theater which is challenging and experimental." Pays by royalty (percentage to be negotiated).
How to Contact: Query with synopsis, character breakdown, 8-10 pages of libretto, cassette of music and set description. Query should include résumé(s) of artist(s) and tape of music. SASE. "Unsolicited material is not read or screened at all." Reports on query in 1 month; manuscript in 6 months.
Musical Theater: "We want nontraditional forms and provocative, unusual, challenging subject matter. We are not looking for Broadway-style musicals. Comedies should be highly stylized or highly farcical. Works should be full-length only and not requiring a complete orchestra (small band preferred.) Political material and satire are great for us. We're seeking interesting musical concepts and approaches. The more traditional Broadway-style musicals will generally not be done by the Odyssey. If we have a work in development that needs music, original music will often be used. In such a case, the writer and composer would work together during the development phase. In the case of a pre-existing play,

the concept would originate with the director who would select the composer."

Productions: *Blue Corridor*, by Mimi Seton (abstract journey); *Eating Raoul*, by Paul Bartel (camp/sex); and *Frauleins In Underwear*, by various (Germany in the '30s).

Tips: "Stretch your work beyond the ordinary. Look for compelling themes or the enduring questions of human existence. If it's a comedy, go for broke, go all the way, be as inventive as you can be."

OFF CENTER THEATRE, 1501 Broadway, New York NY 10036. (212)768-3277. Producer: Abigail McGrath. Play producer. Estab. 1968. Produces varying number of plays and new musicals/year. The plays are performed Off Broadway. Pays percentage of box office receipts after initial expenses have been recouped.

How to Contact: Query first. SASE. Reports in 3 months.

Musical Theater: Socially relevant. Not for children/young audiences. Issue oriented, small cast.

Productions: *Biting the Apple*, by Tony McGrath and Stanley Seidman (revue); *In the Spirit*, by Abigail McGrath (ghosts); and *Hello, This Is Barbara, I'm Not in Right Now . . .*, by Barbara Schottenfeld (singles in New York City).

Tips: "Must be in New York City area for a length of time to work on a piece during readings and/or workshop—without guarantee of production."

OMAHA MAGIC THEATRE, 325 S. 16th St., Omaha NE 68102. (402)346-1227. Artistic Director: Jo Ann Schmidman. Play producer. Estab. 1968. Produces 8 performance events with music/year. "Plays are produced in our Omaha facility and on tour throughout the nation. Our audience is a cross-section of the community." Pays standard royalty, outright purchase ($500-1,500) or per performance ($20-25).

How to Contact: Query with synopsis, character breakdown and set description. SASE. Reports in 6 months.

Musical Theater: "We want the most avant of the avant garde—plays that never get written, or if written are buried deep in a chest because the writer feels there are not production possibilities in this nation's theaters. Plays must push form and/or content to new dimensions. The clarity of the playwright's voice must be strong and fresh. We do not produce standard naturalistic or realistic musicals. At the Omaha Magic Theatre original music is considered as sound structure and for lyrics."

Productions: *Body Leaks* (self-censorship) and *Sound Fields*, by Megan Terry, Jo Ann Schmidman and Sora Kimberlain (a new multi-dimensional performance event about acute listening); and *Belches on Couches*, by Megan Terry, Jo Ann Schmidman and Sora Kimberlain.

Tips: "Looking for alternative music."

THE OPEN EYE THEATER, P.O. Box 204, Denver NY 12421. (607)326-4986 or (607)326-3330. Artistic Director: Amie Brockway. Play producer. Estab. 1972. Produces approximately 3 full length or 3 new plays for multi-generational audiences. Pays on a fee basis.

How to Contact: Query first. "We deeply regret that we are forced to discontinue our policy of accepting unsolicited manuscripts. Until further notice, a manuscript will be accepted and read only if it is a play for multi-generational audiences and is: 1) Submitted by a recognized literary agent; 2) Requested or recommended by a staff or company member; or 3) Recommended by a professional colleague with whose work we are familiar. Playwrights may submit a one-page letter of inquiry including a very brief plot synopsis. Please enclose a self-addressed (but not stamped) envelope. We will reply only if we want you to submit the script."

Musical Theater: "The Open Eye Theater draws on the creative power of the theater arts—music, dance, drama and comedy—to mount innovative productions of excellence that appeal to people of all cultures and ages. Our commitment to the city's youth, and those from surrounding suburban and rural regions, is seen in programs that help foster a strong sense of community and emphasize the power of diverse cultures. Through timely original works, we seek to bring people together, communicate our shared heritage, and provide a fresh perspective on universal human experience."

Productions: *The Odyssey*, adapted by Amie Brockway, music by Elliot Sokolov; *The Wise Men of Chelm*, by Sandra Fenichel Asher; and *Freedom is My Middle Name*, by Lee Hunkins.

Tips: "Write to us. Come see our work."

*PAPER MILL PLAYHOUSE, Brookside Dr., Milburn NJ 07041. (201)379-3636. Contact: Angelo Del Rossi. Play producer. Equity theater producing 2 plays and 4 musicals/year. "Audience based on 42,000 subscribers; plays performed in 1,192-seat proscenium theater."

How to Contact: Query with synopsis and cassette (if applicable) only (no full scripts accepted!). SASE.

Musical Theater: "Paper Mill runs a Musical Theater Lab Project which develops 4-6 readings/season, 3 of which went on to fully staged productions. The theater runs an open submission policy, and is especially interested in large scale shows."

Productions: *Dreamgirls*; *You Never Know*, by Cole Porter; and *Comfortable Shoes*, by Clint Holmes.

PLAYHOUSE ON THE SQUARE, 51 S. Cooper, Memphis TN 38104. (901)725-0776. Executive Producer: Jackie Nichols. Play producer. Produces 12 plays (4 musicals)/year. Plays are produced in a 260-seat proscenium resident theater. Pays $500 for outright purchase.
How to Contact: Submit complete ms and score. Unsolicited submissions OK. SASE. Reports in 4 months.
Musical Theater: Seeking "any subject matter—adult and children's material. Small cast preferred. Stage is 26' deep by 43' wide with no fly system." Would also consider original music for use in a play being developed.
Productions: *Gypsy*, by Stein and Laurents; *The Spider Web*, by Agatha Christie; and *A Midsummer Night's Dream*, by William Shakespeare.

*PLAYWRIGHTS HORIZONS, 416 W. 42nd St., New York NY 10036. (212)564-1235. Artistic Director: Tim Sanford. Director, Musical Theater Program: Dana L. Williams. Play producer. Estab. 1971. Produces about 4 plays and 1 new musical/year. "A general New York City audience." Pays by fee/royalty.
How to Contact: Submit complete ms, score and tape of songs. SASE. Reports in 4-5 months.
Musical Theater: American writers. "No revivals or children's shows; otherwise we're flexible. We generally develop work from scratch; we're open to proposals for shows, and scripts in early stages of development."
Productions: *Once on This Island*, by Lynn Ahrens/Stephen Flaherty (comedy); *Avenue X*, by John Jiles/Ray Leslee (a cappella); and *Jack's Holiday*, by Randy Courts and Mark St. Germain.

PRIMARY STAGES COMPANY, 584 Ninth Ave., New York NY 10036. (212)333-7471. Fax: (212)333-2025. Literary Manager: Andrew Leynse. Play producer. Estab. 1984. Produces 4 plays and 1 musical/year. "New York theater-going audience representing a broad cross-section, in terms of age, ethnicity, and economic backgrounds. 99 seat, Off Broadway theater."
How to Contact: Query with synopsis, character breakdown and set description. SASE. Reports in 3-4 weeks.
Musical Theater: "We are looking for work of heightened theatricality, that challenges realism—musical plays that go beyond film and televisions standard fare. We are looking for small cast shows, with limited sets. We are interested in original works, that have not been produced in New York."
Productions: *Model Apartment*, by Donald Margulies; *Ancient History*, by David Ives; and *The Preservation Society*, by W.M. Levengood.

THE REPERTORY THEATRE OF ST. LOUIS, P.O. Box 191730, St. Louis MO 63119. (314)968-7340. Associate Artistic Director: Susan Gregg. Play producer. Estab. 1966. Produces 9 plays and 1 or 2 musicals/year. "Conservative regional theater audience. We produce all our work at the Loretto Hilton Theatre." Pays by royalty.
How to Contact: Query with synopsis, character breakdown and set description. Does not return material. Reports in 1 year.
Musical Theater: "We want plays with a small cast and simple setting. No children's shows or foul language. After a letter of inquiry we would prefer script and demo tape."
Productions: *Almost September* and *Esmeralda*, by David Schechter and Steve Lutvak; and *Jack*, by Barbara Field and Hiram Titus.

SECOND STAGE THEATRE, P.O. Box 1807, Ansonia Station, New York NY 10023. (212)787-8302. Dramaturg/Literary Manager: Mr. Erin Sanders. Play producer. Estab. 1979. Produces 4 plays and 1 musical (1 new musical)/year. Plays are performed in a small, 108-seat Off Broadway House. Pays per performance.
How to Contact: Query with synopsis, character breakdown and set description. No unsolicited manuscripts. Does not return material. Reports in 4-6 months.
Musical Theater: "We are looking for innovative, unconventional musicals that deal with sociopolitical themes."
Productions: *In a Pig's Valise*, by Eric Overmyer and Kid Creole (spoof on '40s film noir); *A . . . My Name Is Still Alice*, by various (song/sketch revue); and *The Good Times Are Killing Me*, by Lynda Barry (a play with music).
Tips: "Submit through agent; have strong references; show a sample of the best material."

SHENANDOAH INTERNATIONAL PLAYWRIGHTS RETREAT (A PROJECT OF SHENAN ARTS, INC.), Rt. 5, Box 167-F, Staunton VA 24401. (703)248-1868. Director of Playwriting and Screenwriting Programs: Robert Graham Small. Play producer. Estab. 1976. Develops 10-12 plays/year for family audience. Pays fellowships.
How to Contact: Query with synopsis, character breakdown tape of songs and set description. SASE. Reports in 4 months.

Productions: *Smoke On the Mountain, Joseph and the Amazing Technicolor Dreamcoat* and *Pump Boys and Dinettes*.
Tips: "Submit materials January-February 1. Submit synopsis and demo tape to Paul Hildebrand for touring and full production."

STAGE ONE, 425 W. Market St., Louisville KY 40202. (502)589-5946. Producing Director: Moses Goldberg. Play producer. Estab. 1946. Produces 7-8 plays and 0-2 musicals (0-2 new musicals)/year. "Audience is mainly young people ages 5-18." Pays 3-6% royalty, flat fee or $25-75 per performance.
How to Contact: Submit complete manuscript and tape of songs. SASE. Reports in 4 months.
Musical Theater: "We seek stageworthy and respectful dramatizations of the classic tales of childhood, both ancient and modern. Ideally, the plays are relevant to young people and their families, as well as related to school curriculum. Cast is rarely more than 12."
Productions: *Legend of Sleepy Hollow*, by Philip Hall; *Red Riding Hood*, by Goldberg/Cornett (fairytale); and *Tale of the Mandann Ducks*, by Paterson, Tolum and Liebman (Japanese fairytale).
Tips: "Stage One accepts unsolicited manuscripts that meet our artistic objectives. Please do not send plot summaries or reviews. Include author's résumé, if desired. In the case of musicals, a cassette tape is preferred. Cast size is not a factor, although, in practice, Stage One rarely employs casts of over 12. Scripts will be returned in approximately 3-4 months, if SASE is included. No materials can be returned without the inclusion of a SASE. Due to the volume of plays received, it is not possible to provide written evaluations."

TADA!, 120 W. 28th St., New York NY 10001. (212)627-1732. Artistic Director: Janine Nina Trevens. Play producer. Estab. 1984. Produces 4 staged readings and 2-4 new musicals/year. "TADA! is a company producing works performed by children ages 6-17 for family audiences in New York City. Performances run approximately 30-45 performances. Pays varying royalty.
• For more information, see the interview with Artistic Director Janine Nina Trevens in this section.
How to Contact: Submit complete ms with synopsis, character breakdown, score and tape of songs. SASE. Reports in 6 months.
Musical Theater: "We do not produce plays as full productions. At this point, we do staged readings of plays. We produce original commissioned musicals written specifically for the company."
Productions: *Sleepover*, by Phillip Freedman (music and lyrics by James Beloff); *The History Mystery*, book by Janine Nina Trevens, music by Eric Rockwell, lyrics by Margaret Rose; and *Flies in The Soup*, book, music, and lyrics by Dan Feigelson and Jon Agee.
Tips: "When writing for children don't condescend. The subject matter should be appropriate but the music/treatment can still be complex and interesting."

THE TEN-MINUTE MUSICALS PROJECT, Box 461194, West Hollywood CA 90046. (213)656-8751. Producer: Michael Koppy. Play producer. Estab. 1987. All pieces are new musicals. Pays equal share of 6-7% royalty.
• See their listings in the Workshops and Contests and Awards sections.
How to Contact: Submit complete manuscript, score and tape of songs. SASE. Reports in 3 months.
Musical Theater: Seeks complete short stage musicals of between 8 and 15 minutes in length. Maximum cast: 9. "No parodies—original music only."
Productions: *The Furnished Room*, by Saragail Katzman (the O. Henry story); *An Open Window*, by Enid Futterman and Sara Ackerman (the Saki story); and *Pulp's Big Favor*, by David Spencer and Bruce Peyton (an original detective mystery).
Tips: "Start with a *solid* story—either an adaptation or an original idea—but with a solid beginning, middle and end (probably with a plot twist at the climax)."

*THEATRE THREE, INC., 2800 Routh St., Dallas TX 75201. (214)871-2933. Fax: (214)871-3139. Musical Director: Terry Dobson. Play producer. Estab. 1961. Produces 10-12 plays and 3-4 musicals (1 or 2 new musicals)/year. "Subscription audience of 4,500 enjoys adventurous, sophisticated musicals." Performance space is an "arena stage (modified). Seats 250 per performance. Quite an intimate space." Pays varying royalty.
How to Contact: Query with synopsis, character breakdown and set description. SASE. Reports in 2-8 weeks.

HOW TO GET THE MOST out of *Songwriter's Market* (at the front of this book) contains comments and suggestions to help you understand and use the information in these listings.

Musical Theater: "Off the wall topics. We have, in the past, produced *Little Shop of Horrors*, *Angry Housewives*, *Sweeney Todd*, *Groucho*, *A Life in Revue*, *The Middle of Nowhere* (a Randy Newman revue) and *A . . . My Name Is Alice*. We prefer small cast shows, but have done shows with a cast as large as 15. Orchestrations can be problematic. We usually do keyboards and percussion or some variation. Some shows can be a design problem; we cannot do 'spectacle.' Our audiences generally like good, intelligent musical properties. Very contemporary language is about the only thing that sometimes causes 'angst' among our subscribers. We appreciate honesty and forthrightness . . . and good material done in an original and creative manner."
Productions: *Lucky Stiff*, by Flaherty/Ahrens (death and grand theft); *Pump Boys & Dinettes*, by Hardwick/Monk/Wann (C&W); and *The Cocoanuts*, by Haufman/Berlin (Marx Brothers in Florida).

THEATRE WEST VIRGINIA, P.O. Box 1205, Beckley WV 25802. (800)666-9142. Play producer. Estab. 1955. Produces 5 plays and 2 musicals/year. "Audience varies from mainstream summer stock to educational tours (ages K—high school)." Pays 5% royalty or $25/performance.
How to Contact: Query with synopsis, character breakdown and set description; should include cassette tape. SASE.
Musical Theater: "Theatre West Virginia is a year-round performing arts organization that presents a variety of productions including community performances and statewide educational programs on primary, elementary and secondary levels. This is in addition to our summer, outdoor dramas of *Hatfields & McCoys* and *Honey in the Rock*, now in their 36th year." Anything suitable for secondary school tours and/or dinner theater type shows. No more than 7 in cast. Play should be able to be accompanied by piano/synthesizer.
Productions: *Man In The Iron Mask*, adapted by Craig Johnson; and *The Three Little Pigs*.

*THEATREVIRGINIA, 2800 Grove Ave., Richmond VA 23221-2466. (804)353-6100. Artistic Director: George Black. Play producer. Estab. 1955. Produces 5-9 plays (2-5 musicals)/year. "Plays are performed in a 500-seat LORT-C house for the Richmond-area community." Payment negotiable.
How to Contact: "Please submit synopsis, sample of dialogue and sample of music (on cassette) along with a self-addressed, stamped letter-size envelope. If material seems to be of interest to us, we will reply with a solicitation for a complete manuscript and cassette. Response time for synopses is 4 weeks; response time for scripts once solicited is 5 months."
Musical Theater: "We do not deal in one-acts or in children's material. We would like to see full length, adult musicals. There are no official limitations. We would be unlikely to use original music as incidental/underscoring for existing plays, but there is potential for adapting existing plays into musicals."
Productions: *Dancing At Lughnasa*, by Brian Friel; *Sweeney Todd*, by Stephen Sondheim; and *The Pirates of Penzance*, by Gilbert and Sullivan.
Tips: "Read plays. Study structure. Study character. Learn how to concisely articulate the nature of your work. A beginning musical playwright, wishing to work for our company should begin by writing a wonderful, theatrically viable piece of musical theater. Then he should send us the material requested in our listing, and wait patiently."

THEATREWORKS/USA, 890 Broadway, New York NY 10003. (212)677-5959. Literary Manager: Barbara Pasternack. Play producer. Produces 10-13 plays, most are musicals (3-4 new musicals)/year. Audience consists of children and families. Pays 6% royalty and aggregate of $1,500 commission-advance against future royalties.
How to Contact: Query with synopsis, character breakdown and sample scene and song. SASE. Reports in 6 months.
Musical Theater: "One hour long, 5-6 adult actors, highly portable, good musical theater structure; adaptations of children's literature, historical or biographical musicals, issues, fairy tales—all must have something to say. We demand a certain level of literary sophistication. No kiddy shows, no camp, no fractured fables, no shows written for school or camp groups to perform. Approach your material, not as a writer writing for kids, but as a writer addressing any universal audience. You have 1 hour to entertain, say something, make them care—don't preach, condescend. Don't forget an antagonist. Don't waste the audience's time. We always use original music—but most of the time a project team comes complete with a composer in tow."
Productions: *Freaky Friday*, music by Mary Rodgers, book and lyrics by John Forster; *Little Prince*, by Jeff Linden and Art Perlman; and *Where's Waldo*, book by Michael Slade, music by David Evans, lyrics by Faye Greenberg.
Tips: "Write a good show! Make sure the topic is something we can market! Come see our work to find out our style."

13TH STREET REPERTORY COMPANY, 50 W. 13th St., New York NY 10011. (212)675-6677. Dramaturg: Ken Terrell. Play producer. Estab. 1974. Produces 6 plays/year including 2 new musicals. Audience comes from New York and surrounding area. Children's theater performs at 50 W. 13th in

NYC. "We do not pay. We are an off-off Broadway company and provide a stepping stone for writers, directors, actors."
How to Contact: Query with synopsis, character breakdown and set description. Does not return material. Reports in 6 months.
Musical Theater: Children's musicals and original musical shows. Small cast with limited musicians. Stagings are struck after each performance. Would consider original music for "pre-show music or incidental music."
Productions: *Journeys*, a collaborative effort about actors' work in New York City; *New York, Paris, Everywhere*, by Ken Terrell; and *The Smart Set*, by Enrico Garzilli.

*TUACAHN CENTER FOR THE ARTS, Heritage Arts Foundation, 1100 Tuacahn Dr., Ivins UT 84738. (801)674-0012. Fax: (801)674-0013. Managing Artistic Director: David Grapes. Play producer. Produces 3-5 musicals (1 new musical)/year. Educated, community/university audience. Pays $50-300/performance.
How to Contact: Submit complete ms, score and tape of songs. SASE. Reports in 6 months.
Musical Theater: "We look for outstanding works in all categories. Particular interest in scripts that deal with issues and topics of interest to LDS Church."
Productions: *Utah!*, by Robert Paxton; *Grapes of Wrath*; and *Seekers of the Light*, by Zinober.

UNIVERSITY OF ALABAMA NEW PLAYWRIGHTS' PROGRAM, P.O. Box 870239, Tuscaloosa AL 35487-0239. (205)348-9032. Fax: (205)348-9048. E-mail: pcastagn@rojoas.ua.edu. Director/Dramaturg: Dr. Paul Castagno. Play producer. Estab. 1982. Produces 8-10 plays and 1 musical/year; 1 new musical every other year. University audience. Pays by arrangement. Stipend is competitive. Also expenses and travel.
How to Contact: Submit complete manuscript, score and tape of songs. SASE. Reports in 4-6 months.
Musical Theater: Any style or subject (but no children's or puppet plays). No limitations—just solid lyrics and melodic line. Drama with music, musical theater workshops, and chamber musicals. "We love to produce a small-scale musical."
Productions: *Gospels According to Esther*, by John Erlanger.
Tips: "Take your demos seriously. We really want to do something small scale, for actors, often without the greatest singing ability. Use fresh sounds not derivative of the latest fare. While not ironclad by any means, musicals with Southern themes might stand a better chance."

WALNUT STREET THEATRE COMPANY, 825 Walnut St., Philadelphia PA 19107. (215)574-3584. Literary Manager: Beverly Elliott. Play producer. Estab. 1982. Produces 8 plays and 2 musicals (1 new musical)/year. Plays produced on a mainstage with seating for 1,052 to a family audience; and in studio theaters with seating for 79-99 to adult audiences. Pays by royalty or outright purchase.
How to Contact: Query with synopsis, character breakdown, set description, and ten pages. SASE. Reports in 6 months.
Musical Theater: "We seek musicals with lyrical non-operatic scores and a solid book. We are looking for a small musical for springtime and one for a family audience at Christmas time. We remain open on structure and subject matter and would expect a tape with the script. Cast size: around 20 equity members (10 for smaller musical); preferably one set with variations." Would consider original music for incidental music and/or underscore. This would be at each director's discretion.
Productions: *Cabaret*; *Wizard of Oz*; and *Lust*, by Heather Brothers.
Tips: "Send a good quality tape. Understand what the theater looks for before you submit."

WATERLOO COMMUNITY PLAYHOUSE, P.O. Box 433, Waterloo IA 50704. (319)235-0367. Managing Artistic Director: Charles Stilwill. Play producer. Estab. 1917. Produces 12 plays (1-2 musicals)/year. "Our audience prefers solid, wholesome entertainment, nothing risque or with strong language. We perform in Hope Martin Theatre, a 366-seat house." Pays $15-150/performance.
How to Contact: Submit complete manuscript, score and cassette tape of songs. SASE. Reports in 8-10 months.
Musical Theater: "Casts may vary from as few as 6 people to 54. We are producing children's theater as well. We're *especially* interested in new adaptations of classic children stories."
Productions: *Bridge to Terabithia* (children's); *A Christmas Carol* (holiday); and *Wizard of Oz* (traditional).
Tips: "The only 'new' musicals we are likely to produce are adaptations of name shows that would fit in our holiday slot or for our children's theater."

WEST COAST ENSEMBLE, Box 38728, Los Angeles CA 90038. (213)871-8673. Artistic Director: Les Hanson. Play producer. Estab. 1982. Produces 4-8 plays and 1 new musical/year. "Our audience is a wide variety of Southern Californians. Plays will be produced in one of our two theaters in Hollywood." Pays $35-50 per performance.

• See the listing for West Coast Ensemble Musical Stairs in the Contests and Awards section.
How to Contact: Submit complete manuscript, score and tape of songs. SASE. Reports in 6-8 months.
Musical Theater: "There are no limitations on subject matter or style. Cast size should be no more than 12 and sets should be simple. If music is required we would commission a composer, music would be used as a bridge between scenes or to underscore certain scenes in the play."
Productions: *The Human Comedy*, by Galt McDermott (adaptation of the Saroyan novel); *The Much Ado Musical*, by Tony Tanner (adaptation of Shakespeare); and *A Grand Night for Singing*.
Tips: "Submit work in good form and be patient. We look for musicals with a strong book and an engaging score with a variety of styles."

WEST END ARTISTS, 18034 Ventura Blvd., #291, Encino CA 91316. (818)996-0505. Artistic Director: Edmund Gaynes. Play producer. Estab. 1983. Produces 5 plays and 3 new musicals/year. Audience "covers a broad spectrum, from general public to heavy theater/film/TV industry crowds. Proscenium—83 seats, operating under A.E.A. 99-seat plan." Payment is negotiable.
How to Contact: Submit complete manuscript and score. SASE. Reports in 3 months.
Musical Theater: "Prefer small-cast musicals and revues. Full length preferred. Interested in children's shows also." Cast size: "Maximum 12; exceptional material with larger casts will be considered."
Productions: *Crazy Words, Crazy Tunes*, by Milt Larsen and Gene Casey (novelty songs of the '20s, '30s and '40s); *Starting Here, Starting Now*, by David Shire and Richard Maltby, Jr. (songs by Shire and Maltby); and *Broadway Sings Out!*, by Ray Malvani (Broadway songs of social significance).
Tips: "If you feel every word or note you have written is sacred and chiseled in stone, and are unwilling to work collaboratively with a professional director, don't bother to submit."

*WESTBETH THEATRE CENTER, 151 Bank St., New York NY 10014. (212)691-2272. Literary Manager: Steven Bloom. Play producer. Estab. 1978. Produces 1-2 musicals/year. Audience consists of New York theater professionals and Village neighborhood. "We have 5 performance spaces, including a music hall and cafe theater." Uses usual New York showcase contract.
How to Contact: Submit complete manuscript, score and tape of songs. SASE. Reports in 4-6 months. "Artists must be accessible to NYC."
Musical Theater: "Full length musicals, all Broadway styles. Small, ensemble casts the best." Does not wish to see "one character musicals, biographies and historical dramas. Musicals selected for development will undergo intense process. We look for strong collaborators."
Productions: *The Life*, by Cy Coleman (urban life); *The Taffetas*, by Rick Lewis ('50s girl group revue); and *Bodyshop*, by Walter Marks.
Tips: "Be open to the collaborative effort. We are a professional theater company, competing in the competitive world of Broadway and off-Broadway, so the work we present must reach for the highest standard of excellence."

WESTSIDE REPERTORY THEATRE, 252 W. 81st St., New York NY 10024. (212)874-7290. Artistic Director: David R. Zyla. Managing Director: Elizabeth Mahon. Play producer. Estab. 1969. Produces 6 plays/year. Intimate proscenium 40 seat theater. Pays stipend.
How to Contact: Query first. SASE. Reports in 4-6 weeks. "Please, no phone calls. Best time to apply: February."
Musical Theater: "Our repertory is comprised of classical and clasically based plays. We frequently commission composers to create original music. Our stage is not suitable for regular book musicals. We do not do new or contemporary plays as part of our mainstage season, but would consider such material for our Staged Reading series."
Productions: *Man & Superman*, by George B. Shaw (comedy); *The Learned Ladies*, by Moliere (satire); and *Ghosts*, by Henrik Ibsen (drama).

WILLOWS THEATRE COMPANY, (formerly Citiarts Theatre), 1975 Diamond Blvd., A-20, Concord CA 94520. (510)798-1300. Artistic Director: Richard H. Elliott. Play producer. Estab. 1973. Produces 8 plays and 4 musicals (0-4 new musicals)/year. "The 203-seat Willows Theatre is a proscenium stage in Concord, located in suburban San Francisco." Pays variable royalty.
How to Contact: Query first. SASE. Reports in 6 months.
Musical Theater: "Full-length musicals addressing contemporary themes or issues, small to mid-size cast (maximum 15 characters) with maximum 15 instruments. Topics which appeal to an educated suburban and liberal urban audience are best. Maximum 10 cast members, 9 musicians, prefer unit set (we have no fly loft or wing space)."
Productions: *Smoke On The Mountain*, by Ray/Bailey (white southern gospel); *Nunsense II*, by Goggin (religious satire); and *Grease*, by Jacobs/Casey ('50s rock).

*WINGS THEATRE CO., 154 Christopher St., New York NY 10014. (212)627-2960. Fax: (212)627-2961. Contact: Literary Director. Play producer. Estab. 1987. Produces 12-15 plays and 5 musicals/year. Performance space is a 74-seat O.O.B. proscenium; repertoire includes a mainstage series, a gay-play series and a children's series—we produce musicals in all three series. Pays $100 for limited rights to produce against 3% of gross box office receipts.
How to Contact: Submit complete manuscript, score and tape of songs (score is not essential). SASE. Reports in 8-12 months.
Musical Theater: "Eclectic. Entertaining. Enlightening. This is an O.O.B. theater. Funds are limited." Does not wish to see "movies posing as plays. Television theater."
Productions: *The Great American Backstage Musical*, by Bill Solly/Donald Ward (1940s WWII musical); *The Captain's Boy*, by Clint Jeffries (gay pirate musical); and *In a Darkened Theatre*, by Chris Jackson (gay musical drama).
Tips: "Book needs to have a well-developed plot line and interesting, fully-realized characters. We place emphasis on well-written scripts, as opposed to shows which rely exclusively on the quality of the music to carry the show. Also be patient—we often hold onto plays for a full year before making a final decision."

WOMEN'S PROJECT AND PRODUCTIONS, JULIA MILES, ARTISTIC DIRECTOR, 10 Columbus Circle #2270, New York NY 10019. (212)765-1706. Literary Manager: Sharon Ross. Estab. 1978. Produces 3 plays/year. Pays by outright purchase.
How to Contact: Submit synopsis, 10 sample pages of dialogue and sample tape. SASE. Reports in 1 month. "Adult audience. Plays by women only."
Musical Theater: "We usually prefer a small to medium cast of 3-6. We produce few musicals and produce *only* women playwrights."
Productions: *Ladies*, by Eve Ensler (homelessness); *O Pioneers!*, by Darrah Cloud (adapted from Willa Cather's novel); and *Skirting the Issues* (musical cabaret).
Tips: "Resist sending early drafts of work."

WOOLLY MAMMOTH THEATRE CO., M, 1401 Church St. NW, Washington DC 20005. (202)234-6130. Literary Manager: Jim Byrnes. Play producer. Estab. 1978. Produces 4 plays/year. Pay is negotiable.
How to Contact: Submit letter of inquiry with synopsis or full package (i.e., complete manuscript, score and tape of songs). SASE. Reports in 2 months.
Musical Theater: "We do unusual works. We have done 1 musical, the *Rocky Horror Show* (very successful). 8-10 in cast. We do not wish to see one-acts."
Productions: *The Artificial Jungle*, by Charles Ludlam.
Tips: "Know what we do. Read or see our plays."

Play Publishers

AMELIA MAGAZINE, 329 "E" St., Bakersfield CA 93304. (805)323-4064. Editor: Frederick A. Raborg, Jr. Play publisher. Estab. 1983. Publishes 1 play/year. General audience; one-act plays published in *Amelia Magazine*. Best play submitted is the winner of the annual Frank McClure One-Act Play Award.
How to Contact: Submit complete manuscript and score per contest rules by postmark deadline of May 15. SASE. Reports in 6-8 weeks. "We would consider publishing musical scores if submitted in clean, camera-ready copy—also single songs. Best bet is with single songs complete with clear, camera-ready scoresheets, for regular submissions. We use only first North American serial rights. All performance and recording rights remain with songwriter. Payment same as for poetry—$25 plus copies."
Tips: "Be polished, professional, and submit clear, clean copy."

*ARAN PRESS, 1320 S. Third St., Louisville KY 40208. (502)636-0115. Editor/Publisher: Tom Eagan. Play publisher. Estab. 1983. Publishes 40-50 plays, 1-2 musicals and 1-2 new musicals/year. Professional, college/university, community, summer stock and dinner theater audience. Pays 50% production royalty or 10% book royalty.
How to Contact: Submit manuscript, score and tape of songs. SASE. Reports in 2 weeks.
Musical Theater: "The musical should include a small cast, simple set for professional, community, college, university, summer stock and dinner theater production."
Publications: *Truck Stop*, by Jim Murphy; *Cleopatra And The Night*, by Bruce Feld; and *Desperation*, by Mart M. Troy.

ART CRAFT PUBLISHING CO., P.O. Box 1058, Cedar Rapids IA 52406. (319)364-6311. Editor: C. Emmett McMullen. Play publisher. Estab. 1928. Publishes 10-15 plays/year. "We publish plays and musicals for the amateur market including middle, junior and smaller senior high schools and church groups." Pays varying rate for outright purchase or varying royalty.

How to Contact: Query with synopsis, character breakdown and set description. SASE. Reports in 2 months.

Musical Theater: "Seeking material for high school productions. All writing within the scope of high school groups. No works with X-rated material or questionable taboos. Simplified staging and props. Currently seeking material with larger casts, preferably with more women than male roles."

Publications: *Brave Buckaroo*, by Renee J. Clark; *Rest Assured*, by Donald Payton; and *Murder At Coppersmith Inn*, by Dan Neidermyer.

Tips: "We are primarily interested in full length musical comedies, farces, and mysteries with a large number of characters. Since the vast majority of people who perform our plays have little or no theatrical experience, simplicity and ease of production are chief factors in the acceptance of a play. As our primary markets are junior and senior high schools, we are unable to publish works that are offensive or controversial in nature."

BAKER'S PLAYS, 100 Chauncy St., Boston MA 02111. (617)482-1280. Associate Editor: Raymond Pape. Play publisher. Estab. 1845. Publishes 15-22 plays and 0-3 new musicals/year. Plays are used by children's theaters, junior and senior high schools, colleges and community theaters. Pays negotiated royalty.

How to Contact: Submit complete manuscript, score and cassette tape of songs. SASE. Reports in 2-6 months.

Musical Theater: "Seeking musicals for teen production and children's theater production. We prefer large cast, contemporary musicals which are easy to stage and produce. Plot your shows strongly, keep your scenery and staging simple, your musical numbers and choreography easily explained and blocked out. We want innovative and tuneful shows but no X-rated material." Would consider original music for use in a play being developed or in a pre-existing play.

Tips: "As we publish musicals that can be produced by high school theater departments with high school talent, the writer should know if their play can be done on the high school stage. I recommend that the writer go to performances of original musicals whenever possible."

*I.E. CLARK PUBLICATIONS, P.O. Box 246, Schulenburg TX 78956. General Manager: Donna Cozzaglio. Play publisher. Estab. 1956. Publishes 10-15 new plays and 2-4 new musicals/year. Pays negotiable royalty.

How to Contact: Query with synopsis, character breakdown and set description. SASE. Reports in 2-4 months.

Musical Theater: "Musicals for children's theater and for high school and community theater, adaptations of well-known stories and novels. We do not publish puppet shows. We seek plays that appeal to a wide spectrum of producers—professional, community, college, high school, junior high, elementary schools, children's theater, etc. The more of these groups a play will appeal to, the better the sales—and the better the chance that we will accept the play for publication." Does not wish to see plays with obscenities or blasphemous material. "We feel that the songs and musical numbers in a play should advance the plot and action, rather than interrupting the flow of the play for the sake of the music."

Publications: *Peter Pan in Neverland*, by R. Eugene Jackson/David Ellis (a "non-flying" adaptation); *The Age of Discretion*, by Sharon Ferranti/Jay Ferranti (a play about AIDS); and *The Ghost Sonata*, by August Strindberg, translated by Joe Martin with music by Anna Larson.

Tips: "We demand originality and high literary quality. Avoid clichés, both in plot and music."

CONTEMPORARY DRAMA SERVICE, 885 Elkton Dr., Colorado Springs CO 80907. (719)594-4422. Executive Editor: Arthur Zapel. Assistant Editor: Rhonda Wray. Play publisher. Estab. 1979. Publishes 40-50 plays and 4-6 new musicals/year. "We publish for young children and teens in mainstream Christian churches and for teens and college level in the secular market. Our musicals are performed in churches, schools and colleges." Pays 10% royalty (for music books), 50% royalty for performance and "sometimes we pay royalty up to buy-out fee for minor works."

How to Contact: Submit complete manuscript, score and tape of songs. SASE. Reports in 2 months.

Musical Theater: "For churches we publish musical programs for children and teens to perform at Easter, Christmas or some special occasion. Our school musicals are for teens to perform as class plays or special entertainments. Cast size may vary from 5-25 depending on use. We prefer more parts for girls than boys. Music must be written in the vocal range of teens. Staging should be relatively simple but may vary as needed. We are not interested in elementary school material. Elementary level is OK for church music but not public school elementary. Music must have full piano accompaniment and be professionally scored for camera-ready publication."

Publications: *No Ordinary Night*, by Eleanor Miller and Roland A. Caire (Christmas musical for children); *Three Wishes*, by Ted Sod/Suzanne Grant (musical about teenage pregnancy); and *Christmas Is Coming!*, by Jarl K. Iverson (Christmas musical for children).

Tips: "Familiarize yourself with the type of musicals we publish. Note general categories, then give us something that would fit, yet differs from what we've already published. Religious Christmas musicals for church performance and classics or issues-oriented musicals for high school performance are your best bets."

THE DRAMATIC PUBLISHING COMPANY, 311 Washington St., Woodstock IL 60098. (815)338-7170. Music Editor: Dana Wolworth. Play publisher. Publishes 35 plays (3-5 musicals)/year. Estab. 1885. Plays used by community theaters, high schools, colleges, stock and professional theaters and churches. Pays negotiable royalty
How to Contact: Submit complete manuscript, score and tape of songs. SASE. Reports in 10-12 weeks.
Musical Theater: Seeking "children's musicals not over 1¼ hours, and adult musicals with 2 act format. No adaptations for which the rights to use the original work have not been cleared. If directed toward high school market, large casts with many female roles are preferred. For professional, stock and community theater small casts are better. Cost of producing a play is always a factor to consider in regard to costumes, scenery and special effects." Would also consider original music for use in a pre-existing play "if we or the composer hold the rights to the non-musical work."
Publications: *The Secret Garden*, by Sharon Burgett/Jim Crabtree; *Dream on Royal Street*, by Alan Menken/June Walker Rogers/David Rogers; and *Shakespeare and the Indians*, by Dale Wasserman/Allan Jay Friedman.
Tips: "It is best if the show tunes are written with catchy hooks—something people will go away humming. Also, good presentation of the music itself is a must."

ELDRIDGE PUBLISHING CO., INC., P.O. Box 1595, Venice FL 34284. (800)HI-STAGE. Editor: Nancy S. Vorhis. Play publisher. Estab. 1906. Publishes 40 plays and 2-3 musicals/year. Seeking "large cast musicals which appeal to students. We like variety and originality in the music, easy staging and costuming. Also looking for children's theater musicals which have smaller casts and are easy to tour. We serve the school and church market, 6th grade through 12th; also Christmas and Easter musicals for churches." Would also consider original music for use in a play being developed; "music that could make an ordinary play extraordinary." Pays 50% royalty and 10% copy sales in school market.
How to Contact: Submit manuscript, score and tape of songs. SASE. Reports in 2 months.
Publications: *I am a Star!*, by Billie St. John and Wendell Jimerson (high schoolers vying for movie roles); *The Wind in the Willows*, by Frumi Cohen (children's theater); and *Magnolia*, by Sodaro and Francoeur (a *Gone with the Wind* takeoff).
Tips: "We're always looking for talented composers but not through individual songs. We're only interested in complete school or church musicals. Lead sheets, cassette tape and script are best way to submit. Let us see your work!"

ENCORE PERFORMANCE PUBLISHING, P.O. Box 692, Orem UT 84059. (801)225-0605. Editor: Michael C. Perry. Play publisher. Estab. 1979. Publishes 20-30 plays (including musicals)/year. "We are interested in plays which emphasize strong family values and play to all ages." Pays 50% royalty.
How to Contact: Query with synopsis, character breakdown, set description and production history. SASE. Reports in 1-3 weeks on query, 1-2 months on submissions.
Musical Theater: Musicals of all types for all audiences. Can be original or adapted. "We tend to favor shows with at least an equal male/female cast." Do not wish to see works that can be termed offensive or vulgar. However, experimental theater forms are also of interest.
Publications: *The Secret Garden*, by Frumi Cohen; and *The Planemaker*, by Marvin Payne and Guy Randle.
Tips: "Always write with an audience in mind."

THE FREELANCE PRESS, P.O. Box 548, Dover MA 02030. (508)785-1260. Managing Editor: Narcissa Campion. Play publisher. Estab. 1979. Publishes 20 plays/year; 19 musicals (3 new musicals)/year. "Pieces are primarily for elementary to high school students; large casts (approximately 30); plays are produced by schools and children's theaters." Pays 10% of purchase price of script or score, 50% of collected royalty.
How to Contact: Query first. SASE. Reports in 6 months.
Musical Theater: "We publish previously produced musicals and plays for children in the primary grades through high school. Plays are for large casts (approximately 30 actors and speaking parts) and run between 45 minutes to 1 hour and 15 minutes. Subject matter should be contemporary issues (sibling rivalry, friendship, etc.) or adaptations of classic literature for children (*Alice in Wonderland*, *Treasure Island*, etc.). We do not accept any plays written for adults to perform for children."
Publications: *Tortoise vs. Hare*, by Stephen Murray (modern version of classic); *Tumbleweed*, by Sebastian Stuart (sleepy time western town turned upside down); and *Mything Links*, by Sam Abel (interweaving of Greek myths with a great pop score).

Tips: "We enjoy receiving material that does not condescend to children. They are capable of understanding many current issues, playing complex characters, handling unconventional material, and singing difficult music."

SAMUEL FRENCH, INC., 45 W. 25th St., New York NY 10010. (212)206-8990. President: Charles R. Van Nostrand. Play publisher. Estab. 1830. Publishes 40-50 plays and 2-4 new musicals/year. Amateur and professional theaters.
How to Contact: Query first. SASE. Reports in minimum 10 weeks.
Musical Theater: "We publish successful musicals from the NYC, London and regional stage."
Publications: *Eating Raoul*, by Paul Bartel; *Hello Muddah Hello Faddah*, by Bernstein/Krause; and *Love and Shrimp*, by Judith Viorst.

HEUER PUBLISHING CO., P.O. Box 248, Cedar Rapids IA 52406. (319)364-6311. Publisher: C. Emmett McMullen. Musical play publisher. Estab. 1928. Publishes plays and musicals for the amateur market including middle schools, junior and senior high schools and church groups. Pays by outright purchase or percentage royalty.
How to Contact: Query with synopsis, character breakdown and set description or submit complete manuscript, score and tape of songs. SASE. Reports in 2 months.
Musical Theater: "We prefer two or three act comedies or mystery-comedies with a large number of characters."
Publications: *Brave Buckaroo*, by Renee J. Clark (musical melodrama).
Tips: "We sell almost exclusively to junior and smaller senior high schools. Thus flexible casting is extremely important. In middle school, girls' voices are generally stronger than boys', so if you are writing musicals, we stress more choral numbers and more solos for girls than boys."

PIONEER DRAMA SERVICE, P.O. Box 4267, Englewood CO 80155. (303)779-4035. Play publisher. Estab. 1963. "Plays are performed by junior high and high school drama departments, church youth groups, college and university theaters, semi-professional and professional children's theaters, parks and recreation departments." Playwrights paid 50% royalty (10% sales).
How to Contact: Query with synopsis, character breakdown and set description. SASE. Reports in 3 months.
Musical Theater: "We seek full length children's musicals, high school musicals and one act children's musicals to be performed by children, secondary school students, and/or adults. We are seeking musicals easy to perform, simple sets, many female roles and very few solos. Must be appropriate for educational market. We are actively seeking musicals to be produced by elementary schools—20 to 30 minutes in length, with 2 to 3 songs and large choruses. We are not interested in profanity, themes with exclusively adult interest. Several of our full-length plays are being converted to musicals."
Publications: *Kilroy Was Here* and *Oz!*, by Tim Kelly/Bill Francoeur; and *Attack of the Killer Grasshoppers*, by R. Swift/G.V. Castle/M.Vigilant.

PLAYERS PRESS, INC., P.O. Box 1132, Studio City CA 91614. (818)789-4980. Associate Editor: Marjorie Clapper. Vice President: Robert W. Gordon. Play publisher. Estab. 1965. Publishes 20-70 plays and 1-3 new musicals/year. Plays are used primarily by general audience and children. Pays 10-50% royalty and 25-80% of performance.
How to Contact: Query first. SASE. Reports in 1 year (1 week on query).
Musical Theater: "We will consider all submitted works. Presently musicals for adults and high schools are in demand. When cast size can be flexible it sells better."
Publications: *The Deerstalker*, by Terrence Mustoo (Sherlock Holmes-musical); *The King of Escapes*, by Milton Polsky et. al.; and *The Revolution Machine*, by Donna Marie Swajeski (historical).
Tips: "Have your work produced at least twice. Be present for rehearsals and work with competent people. Then submit material asked for in good clear copy with good audio tapes."

*THIS MONTH ON STAGE, P.O. Box 62, Hewlett NY 11557-0062. (800)536-0099. E-mail: dlonstage@aol.com. Associate Editor: Eric Harris. Play publisher. Estab. 1991. Publishes 6-9 plays and 0-1 musicals/year. "Musical must read well on paper (we don't publish the score). TMOS readers are theater lovers and members of the professional theater industry." Pays for one-time purchase.
How to Contact: Submit complete manuscript. SASE. Reports in 18-24 months.
Musical Theater: "Open to various styles and themes, children's also. Short and one-act musicals especially welcome." No "non-linear, visual-oriented material or religious pageant plays."
Publications: *Truck Stop Parking Lot*, by Wm. S. Leavengood (drama); *Miracle Teller*, by Trisha L. Frankhart (comedy); and *When the Twain Met*, by Matt K. Miller (absurdist one-act).

Classical Performing Arts

For the aspiring composer it is vital to have his work performed for an interested audience. A résumé of performances aids in identifying a composer within the concert music community. One excellent, exciting performance may lead to others by different groups or commissions for new works.

All of the groups listed in this section are interested in hearing new music. From chamber groups to symphony orchestras, they are open to new talent and feel their audiences are progressive and interested enough to support new music.

Bear in mind the financial and artistic concerns as you submit material. Many classical music organizations are nonprofit, and may be understaffed. It could take a while for someone to get back to you, so it pays to be patient. Always follow submission instructions diligently. Be professional when you contact the music directors, and keep in mind the audience they are selecting music for. Chamber musicians and their audiences, for instance, are a good source for performance opportunities. Their repertoire is limited and most groups are enthusiastic about finding or commissioning new works. Furthermore, the chamber music audience is smaller and likewise enthusiastic enough to enjoy contemporary music.

Don't be disappointed if the payment offered by these groups is small or even nonexistent. Most classical music organizations are struggling economically and can't pay large fees to even the most established composers. Inquire into other opportunities to submit your work; many of these groups also offer periodic competitions for new works. See the Contests and Awards section for more information and possibilities. To locate performing arts organizations in your area, see the Geographic Index at the end of this book.

THE ABBEY SINGERS, St. Vincent College, Latrobe PA 15650. (412)532-6000, ext. 4539. Fax: (412)537-4554. Music Director: Dominic-Savio Rossi, OSB. Professional vocal sextet. Estab. 1993. Members are professionals. Performs 15 concerts/year including several new works. A professional vocal sextet specializing in jazz, Broadway and light classics accompanied by light instrumentation. In addition to their own series they perform in the tri-state area for recital and concert series, festivals and other special events.
How to Contact: Query first. SASE. Reports in 1 month.
Music: "SATB—light jazz, Broadway."
Performances: Waller/Brooks/Gritton's *Ain't Misbehavin'*; Hupfield/Raycroft's *As Time Goes By*; and Sanatamria/Nowak's *Baby Come Back To Me*.
Tips: "Use voicing to bring out all six parts."

ACADIANA SYMPHONY ORCHESTRA, P.O. Box 53632, Lafayette LA 70505. (318)232-4277. Fax: (318)237-4712. Music Director: Xiao-lu Li. Symphony orchestra. Estab. 1984. Members are amateurs and professionals. Performs 20 concerts/year, including 1 new work. Commissions 1 new work/year. Performs in 2,230-seat hall with "wonderful acoustics." Pays "according to the type of composition."
How to Contact: Query first. Does not return material.
Music: Full orchestra—10 minutes at most. Reduced orchestra, educational pieces—short, not more than 5 minutes.
Performances: Quincy Hilliard's *Universal Covenant* (orchestral suite); James Hanna's *In Memoriam* (strings/elegy); and Gregory Danner's *A New Beginning* (full orchestra fanfare).

ADRIAN SYMPHONY ORCHESTRA, 110 S. Madison St., Adrian MI 49221. (517)264-3121. Music Director: David Katz. Symphony orchestra and chamber music ensemble. Estab. 1981. Members are professionals. Performs 25 concerts/year including 2-3 new works. Commissions 1 new composer

INSIDER REPORT

Boychoirs not just for kids

James Litton

Writing music for boychoirs is much more challenging than you might think; even though you're writing for children, the work needs to be sophisticated. "There has been a marked improvement in repertoire over the last decade, so there are more and more things that we can do," says James Litton, music director of the American Boychoir. Yet much of what he hears is too basic for the choir's 11 to 14-year-old boys. "We need things that are both musically and textually a little bit sophisticated. Even though they're still young kids, they're very astute. If they think something's too young for them, they tend to be very critical."

The difficulty of finding such works is due in part to the American Boychoir's unique sonority. "As this choir has evolved," says Litton, "it has developed a special sound. We use a very expanded range. Some boychoirs are normally thought of as being three-part; soprano-soprano-alto or, at most, soprano-soprano-alto-alto. But we use changing voices for the altos, enabling them to move into a tenor/baritone range, as well."

Some keys work better than others for this range. "F sharp major and minor work very well. The key of A flat often is a pretty good key for us, and A major is a very good key. G is used a lot, but can sometimes be a problem in tuning. And obviously, D is an extremely good key."

No matter what key a piece is set in, it must cover the entire vocal range. "We want a full range," Litton says, "Basically, from C below middle C all the way up to the C two octaves above middle C." This is especially important for the first and second sopranos, which require "a part that explores the full range of that voice and doesn't just stay within a limited tessitura." At the same time, a composer must make sure that the spacing of the chords will produce the optimum vocal sonorities which boys can attain. "There is a distinctive brilliance to the sound. Certain keys work particularly well, and certainly the tessitura is a very big part. If they don't get the chance to sing a high G, at least occasionally, it might be kind of dull."

Depending on the season, the American Boychoir performs between 150 and 200 compositions. Of those, 10 to 20 are new or very recent works. So as you might imagine, Litton receives many submissions from composers. He and his assistant review the manuscripts when time allows. "Generally, I reserve that for the summertime, because the concert schedule here is so heavy. Between rehearsals and concerts during the regular season, there just isn't much time for manuscript review."

INSIDER REPORT, *Litton*

Litton also searches for new material in other ways. "I scan all of the reviews and ads in *Choral Journal* and other such publications," he says. "I try to keep up on new catalogs from publishers and I listen to recordings. Also, much of it is word-of-mouth; going to conventions and things of that nature. I try to keep open to music dealers and music stores, as well." The choir also commissions works. "We had a three-prong commission several years ago and we received three major works for Ned Rorem, Daniel Pinkham and Milton Babbitt," Litton explains. "We've also commissioned some arrangements of specific kinds of things; for example, medleys of the more popular Christmas songs. We have a very good arranger—Bill Holcum—who helps us on some of those medleys. And we've commissioned things from some New York composers, too. Specific arrangements usually of lighter things."

This may help to explain the choir's musical diversity. "Every concert has an extremely wide variety of music. We try to start each performance with classical music from the 15th through the 20th centuries. That tends to be mainly religious music, as that's what was written for boys' voices. Then the second part of the program is normally arrangements of folk songs, sometimes with some art songs or even an ensemble from an opera. We've done a trio from Mozart's *Cosi Fan Tutti* and several of the Dvořák duets, for example. And in the last part of the program, we try to do all American music, either original compositions by American composers or arrangements of spirituals and American folk songs. We've done Gershwin medleys, medleys of songs from the '40s, blues medleys and so forth."

Chances are you've heard the American Boychoir, even if you've never heard *of* them. They have performed with several symphony and pops orchestras, including the Boston Symphony Orchestra and the New York Pops. They performed on the soundtrack to the film *Interview with the Vampire* and in a Kodak film commercial in which they sang an adaptation of "True Colors," the song made popular by Cyndi Lauper.

In its 58-year history, the American Boychoir has toured throughout the world, visiting countries such as Latvia, France, Andorra, Taiwan, Korea, Poland, Canada and Guatemala. The choir has performed with the acclaimed a cappella group Chanticleer, participated in a musical celebration in honor of Nobel Prize winner Archbishop Desmond Tutu, and completed two recordings for Angel records (*Hymn* and *By Request*). The choir has also sung under the direction of Toscanini, Ormandy, Leinsdorf, Bernstein, Mehta, Previn, Ozawa and Masur.

Even with such an impressive history, the Princeton, New Jersey-based choir is always searching for new, innovative works. Litton advises anyone interested in composing for a particular choir to become familiar with their work before beginning to write. Go and see the choir in concert, or listen to any recordings it might have. This will help gain a clear perspective on the level of sophistication and difficulty they look for in the works they perform.

—*David Borcherding*

or new work/year. 1,200 seat hall—"Rural city with remarkably active cultural life." $100-2,500 for outright purchase or commission.

• See the interview with Music Director David Katz in the 1996 *Songwriter's Market*.

How to Contact: Submit complete score and tapes of piece(s). SASE. Reports in 6 months.

Music: Chamber ensemble to full orchestra. "Limited rehearsal time dictates difficulty of pieces selected." Does not wish to see "rock music or country—not at this time."

Performances: Michael Pratt's *Dancing on the Wall* (orchestral—some aleatoric); Sir Peter Maxwell Davies' *Orkney Wedding* (orchestral); and Gwyneth Walker's *Fanfare, Interlude, Finale* (orchestral).

THE AKRON CITY FAMILY MASS CHOIR, 429 Homestead St., Akron OH 44306. (216)773-8529. President: Walter E.L. Scrutchings. Vocal ensemble. Estab. 1984. Members are professionals. Performs 5-7 concerts/year, including 30-35 new works. Commissions 10-15 composers or new works/year. Audience mostly interested in new original black gospel music. Performs in various venues. Composers paid 50% royalty.

How to Contact: Submit complete score and tapes of piece(s). Does not return material. Reports in 2 months.

Music: Seeks "traditional music for SATB black gospel; also light contemporary. No rap or non-spiritual themes."

Performances: R.W. Hinton's *I Can't Stop Praising God*; W. Scrutchings' *A Better Place*; and Rev. A. Wright's *Christ In Your Life*.

THE AMERICAN BOYCHOIR, 19 Lambert Dr., Princeton NJ 08540. (609)924-5858. Music Director: James H. Litton. Professional boychoir. Estab. 1937. Members are highly skilled children. Performs 250 concerts/year, including 20 new works. Commissions 1 composer or new work/year. Performs community concerts, orchestral concerts, for local concert associations, church concert series and other bookings.

• See the interview with Music Director James H. Litton in this section.

How to Contact: Query first. SASE. Reports in 1 year.

Music: Dramatic works for boys voices (age 10-14); 15 to 20 minutes short opera to be staged and performed throughout the US. Choral pieces, either in unison, SSA, SA or SSAA division; unaccompanied and with piano or organ; occasional chamber orchestra accompaniment. Pieces are usually sung by 26 to 50 boys. Composers must know boychoir sonority.

Performances: Laurie Altman's *Band of Fire*; Anne Phillips' *Singing About the Blues*; and Benjamin Britton's *War Requiem*.

*AMERICAN JAZZ PHILHARMONIC, 6022 Wilshire Blvd., #200A, Los Angeles CA 90036. (213)937-4905. Fax: (213)937-4908. Executive Director: Mitchell Glickman. Symphonic jazz orchestra (72 piece). Estab. 1979. Members are professionals. Performs 3-4 concerts/year, all new works. Commissions 1-2 composers or new works/year. Performs in major concert halls nationwide: Avery Fisher (New York), Royce Hall (Los Angeles), Pick-Staiger (Chicago). Pays $2,500-5,000 for commission.

How to Contact: Query first then submit complete score and tape of piece(s) with résumé. SASE. "Newly commissioned composers are chosen each July. Submissions should be sent by June 15th, returned by August 15th."

Music: "The AJP commissions 1-2 new symphonic jazz works annually. Decisions to commission are based on composer's previous work in the symphonic jazz genre. The AJP is a 72-piece symphonic jazz ensemble that includes a rhythm section and woodwinds who double on saxophones, plus traditional symphonic orchestra."

Performances: John Clayton's *Three Shades of Blue* (solo tenor sax and orchestra); Lennie Niehaus' *Tribute to Bird* (solo alto sax and orchestra); and Eddie Karam's *Stay 'N See* (symphonic jazz overture).

Tips: "The AJP has been a recipient of a Reader's Digest/Meet the Composer grant and has received awards from ASCAP and the American Symphony Orchestra League for its programming. The ensemble has also received a Grammy Award nomination for its debut album on GRP Records featuring Ray Brown and Phil Woods."

AMHERST SAXOPHONE QUARTET, 137 Eagle St., Williamsville NY 14221-5721. (716)632-2445. Director: Steve Rosenthal. Chamber music ensemble. Estab. 1978. Performs 80-100 concerts/year including 10-20 new works. Commissions 1-2 composers or new works/year. "We are a touring ensemble." Payment varies.

How to Contact: Query first. SASE. Reports in 1 month.

Music: "Music for soprano, alto, tenor and baritone (low A) saxophone. We are interested in great music of many styles. Level of difficulty is commensurate with full-time touring ensembles."

Performances: Lukas Foss's *Saxophone Quartet* (classical); David Stock's *Sax Appeal* (New Age); and Chan Ka Nin's *Saxophone Quartet* (jazz).

Tips: "Professionally copied parts help! Write what you truly want to write."

ANDERSON SYMPHONY ORCHESTRA, P.O. Box 741, Anderson IN 46015. (317)644-2111. Conductor: Dr. Richard Sowers. Symphony orchestra. Estab. 1967. Members are professionals and amateurs. Performs 7 concerts/year including 1 new work. Performs for typical mid-western audience in a 1,500-seat restored Paramount Theatre. Pay negotiable.
How to Contact: Query first. SASE. Reports in several months.
Music: "Shorter lengths better; concerti OK; difficulty level: mod high; limited by typically 3 full service rehearsals."
Performances: Garland Anderson's *Piano Conterto #2* and Michael Wooden's *Brother? Man?*

ATLANTA POPS ORCHESTRA, P.O. Box 723172, Atlanta GA 31139-0172. (770)435-1222. Musical Director/Conductor: Albert Coleman. Pops orchestra. Estab. 1945. Members are professionals. Performs 10-20 concerts/year. Concerts are performed for audiences of 5,000-10,000, primarily middle-aged. Composers are paid by outright purchase or per performance.
How to Contact: Submit complete score and tape of piece(s). SASE. Reports in 1 week.
Performances: Vincent Montana, Jr.'s *Magic Bird of Fire*; Louis Alter's *Manhattan Serenade*; and Nelson Riddle's *It's Alright With Me*.
Tips: "My concerts are pops concerts—no deep classics."

THE ATLANTA YOUNG SINGERS OF CALLANWOLDE, (formerly The Young Singers of Callanwolde), 980 Briarcliff Rd. N.E., Atlanta GA 30306. (404)873-3365. Fax: (404)973-0756. Music Director: Stephen J. Ortlip. Community children's chorus. Estab. 1975. Members are amateurs. Performs 25 concerts/year including a few new works. Audience consists of community churches, retirement homes, schools. Performs most often at churches. Pay is negotiable.
How to Contact: Submit complete score and tape of piece(s). SASE. Reports in accordance with request.
Music: "Subjects and styles appealing to grammar and junior high boys and girls. Contemporary concerns of the world of interest. Unusual sacred, folk, classic style. Internationally and ethnically bonding. Medium difficulty preferred, with keyboard accompaniment."
minutes in length—full orchestra winds in threes; four trumpets; four trombones; tuba, six percussion, keyboard. No chamber pop."
Performances: Bill Hofelot's *Chaconne* (intermediate level).
Tips: "Look for exposure, very little money! Our budget for commissions is $0."

AUGSBURG CHOIR (AUGSBURG COLLEGE), 731 21st Ave. S., Minneapolis MN 55454. Director of Choral Activities: Peter A. Hendrickson. Vocal ensemble (SATB choir). Members are amateurs. Performs 30 concerts/year, including 2-5 new works. Commissions 1-3 composers or new works/year. Concerts are performed in churches, concert halls and schools. Pays by outright commission.
How to Contact: Submit complete score and tape of piece(s). SASE. Reports in 1-2 months.
Music: Seeking "sacred choral pieces, no more than 5-7 minutes long, to be sung a cappella or with obbligato instrument. Can contain vocal solos. We have 50-60 members in our choir."
Performances: Steve Heitzeg's *On This Night*; Conrad Susa's *Three Mystical Carols*; and Leland B. Sateren's *The Poor & Needy*.

AUREUS QUARTET, 22 Lois Ave., Demarest NJ 07627-2220. (201)767-8704. Artistic Director: James J. Seiler. Vocal ensemble (a cappella). Estab. 1979. Members are professionals. Performs 75 concerts/year, including 3 new works. Pays for outright purchase.
How to Contact: Query first. SASE. Reports in 2-3 weeks.
Music: "We perform anything from pop to classic—mixed repertoire so anything goes. Some pieces can be scored for orchestras as we do pops concerts. Up to now, we've only worked with a quartet. Could be expanded if the right piece came along. Level of difficulty—no piece has ever been too hard." Does not wish to see electronic or sacred pieces. "Electronic pieces would be hard to program. Sacred pieces not performed much. Classical/jazz arrangements of old standards are great!"
Tips: "We perform for a very diverse audience—luscious, four part writing that can showcase well-trained voices is a must. Also, clever arrangements of old hits from '20s through '50s are sure bets. (Some pieces could take optional accompaniment.)"

 THE ASTERISK before a listing indicates that the listing is new in this edition. New markets are often the most receptive to unsolicited submissions.

BALTIMORE OPERA COMPANY, INC., 1202 Maryland Ave., Baltimore MD 21201. (410)625-1600. Artistic Administrator: James Harp. Opera company. Estab. 1950. Members are professionals. Performs 16 concerts/year. "The opera audience is becoming increasingly diverse. Our performances are given in the 3,000-seat Lyric Opera House." Pays by outright purchase.
How to Contact: Submit complete score and tapes of piece(s). SASE. Reports in 2 months.
Music: "Our General Director, Mr. Michael Harrison, is very much interested in presenting new works. These works would be anything from Grand Opera with a large cast to chamber works suitable for school and concert performances. We would be interested in perusing all music written for an operatic audience."
Performances: Floyd's *Susannah*; Saint-Saëns' *Samson et Dalila*; and Puccini's *Manon Lescaut*.
Tips: "Opera is the most expensive art form to produce. Given the current economic outlook, opera companies cannot be too avant garde in their selection of repertoire. The modern operatic composer must give evidence of a fertile and illuminating imagination, while also keeping in mind that opera companies have to sell tickets."

BILLINGS SYMPHONY, 401 N. 31st St., Suite 530, Box 7055, Billings MT 59103. (406)252-3610. Fax: (406)252-3353. Music Director: Dr. Uri Barnea. Symphony orchestra, orchestra and chorale. Estab. 1950. Members are professionals and amateurs. Performs 15 concerts/year, including 6-7 new works. Traditional audience. Performs at Alberta Bair Theater (capacity 1,418). Pays by outright purchase (or rental).
How to Contact: Query first. SASE. Reports in 2-3 months.
Music: Any style. Traditional notation preferred.
Performances: Jerod S. Tate's *Winter Moons* (ballet suite); Alberto Ginastera's *Harp Concerto* (concerto); and Olga Victorova's *Compliments to American Audience* (orchestral piece).
Tips: "Write what you feel (be honest) and sharpen your compositional and craftsmanship skills."

BIRMINGHAM-BLOOMFIELD SYMPHONY ORCHESTRA, 1592 Buckingham, Birmingham MI 48009. (810)645-2276. Fax: (810)645-22760. Executive Director: Carla Lamphere. Symphony orchestra. Estab. 1975. Members are professionals. Performs 6 concerts including 1 new work/year. Performs for middle-to-upper class audience at Temple Beth El's Sanctuary. "Composers pay us to perform."
How to Contact: Query first. SASE. Reports in 1-2 months.
Music: "We are a symphony orchestra but also play pops. Usually 3 works on program (2 hrs.) Orchestra size 65-75. If pianist is involved, they must rent piano."
Performances: Shawn Wygant's *Piano Concerto No. 1* (classical).

BRAVO! L.A., (formerly Trio Of The Americas), 16823 Liggett St., North Hills CA 91343. (818)892-8737. Fax: (818)892-1227. Director: Dr. Janice Foy. An umbrella organization of recording/touring musicians, formed in 1994. Includes the following musical ensembles: Trio of the Americas (piano, clarinet, cello); the New American Quartet (string quartet); BRAVO! L.A. (string trio); Moonlight Serenaders (harp, violin, cello or harp/cello duo); and the New American Piano Ensemble (piano with strings).
How to Contact: Submit complete score and tape of piece(s). SASE. Reports in a few weeks.
Music: "Classical, Romantic, Baroque, Popular (including new arrangements done by Shelly Cohen, from the 'Tonight Show Band'), ethnic (including gypsy) and contemporary works (commissioned as well). The New American Quartet just finished a recording project which features music of Mozart, Eine Kleine Nachtmusik, Borodin Nocturne, Puccini Opera Suite (S. Cohen), Strauss Blue Danube Waltz, Trepak of Tschaikovsky, 'El Choclo' (Argentinian tango), Csardas! and arrangements of Cole Porter, Broadway show tunes and popular classics."
Performances: Miriam Gerberg's *Suite for Strings and Oud*, with John Bilezikjian.
Tips: "Please be open to criticism/suggestions about your music and try to appeal to mixed audiences."

BROWN UNIVERSITY ORCHESTRA, P.O. Box 1924, Providence RI 02912. (401)863-3234. Fax: (401)863-1256. Music Director: Paul Phillips. Symphony orchestra. Estab. 1918. Members are students. Performs 8-10 concerts including 3-4 new works/year. Commissions 0-1 composers or new works/year. Brown University community audience, performs in Sayles Hall (500 seats). Pay negotiable.
How to Contact: Submit complete score and tape of piece(s). SASE. Reports in 6 months.
Music: "We're seeking works for full orchestra, of any style or length, appropriate for performance by an outstanding university orchestra."
Performances: Steven Sunday's *Transparent Things* (orchestra piece); William Bolcom's *Violin Concerto in D* (concerto); and Elaine Bearer's *Seaselves* (work for narrator and orchestra).

BUFFALO GUITAR QUARTET, 402 Bird Ave., Buffalo NY 14213. (716)883-8429. Fax: (716)883-8429. Executive Director: James Piorkowski. Chamber music ensemble and classical guitar

quartet. Estab. 1976. Members are professionals. Performs 45 concerts/year including 2 new works. Commissions 1 composer or new work every 2 years. Pays for outright purchase.
How to Contact: Query first. SASE. Reports in 3-4 months.
Music: "Any style or length. 4 classical guitarists, high level of difficulty."
Performances: Buzz Gravelle's *They Go On Mumbling* (prepared guitars); Leo Broower's *Toccata* (mainstream); and Walter Hartley's *Quartet For Guitars* (neo-classical).
Tips: "Don't be afraid of trying new approaches, but know the instrument."

CALGARY BOYS CHOIR, 305-10 Ave. SE, Calgary T2G 0W9 **Canada**. (403)262-7742. Fax: (403)571-5049. Artistic Director: Gerald Wirth. Boys choir. Estab. 1973. Members are amateurs. Performs 70 concerts/year including 1-2 new works. Pay negotiable.
How to Contact: Query first. SASE. Reports in 1 month.
Music: "Style fitting for boys choir. Lengths depending on project. Orchestration preferable a cappella/for piano/sometimes orchestra."
Performances: G. Wirth's *Sadhaka* and *Our Normoste*; and Shri Mataji Nirmala Devi's *Binati Suniye*.

CANADIAN OPERA COMPANY, 227 Front St. E., Toronto, Ontario M5A 1E8 **Canada**. (416)363-6671. Associate Artistic Administrator: Sandra J. Gavinchuk. Opera company. Estab. 1950. Members are professionals. 50 performances, including a minimum of 1 new work/year. "New works are done in the DuMaurier Theatre, which seats approximately 250." Pays by contract.
How to Contact: Submit complete score and tapes of vocal and/or operatic works. "Vocal works please." SASE. Reports in 5 weeks.
Music: Vocal works, operatic in nature. 12 singers maximum, 1½ hour in duration and 18 orchestral players. "Do not submit works which are not for voice. Ask for requirements for the Composers-In-Residence program."
Performances: Gary Kulesha's *Red Emma* (1995-96); Bartok's *Bluebeard's Castle* (1995); and Schöenberg's *Erwartung*.
Tips: "We have a Composers-In-Residence program which is open to Canadian composers or landed immigrants."

CANTATA ACADEMY, 2441 Pinecrest Dr., Ferndale MI 48220. (810)546-0420. Music Director: Frederick Bellinger. Vocal ensemble. Estab. 1961. Members are professionals. Performs 10-12 concerts/year including 5-6 new works. Commissions 1-2 composers or new works/year. "We perform in churches and small auditoriums throughout the Metro Detroit area for audiences of about 500 people." Pays variable rate for outright purchase.
How to Contact: Submit complete score. SASE. Reports in 1-3 months.
Music: Four-part a cappella and keyboard accompanied works, two and three-part works for men's or women's voices. Some small instrumental ensemble accompaniments acceptable. Work must be suitable for forty voice choir. No works requiring orchestra or large ensemble accompaniment. No pop.
Performances: Charles S. Brown's *Five Spirituals* (concert spiritual); Kirke Mechem's *John Brown Cantata*; and Libby Larsen's *Ringeltanze* (Christmas choral with handbells & keyboard).
Tips: "Be patient. Would prefer to look at several different samples of work at one time."

*CARMEL SYMPHONY ORCHESTRA, P.O. Box 761, Carmel IN 46032. (317)844-9717. Music Director/Conductor: David Pickett. Symphony orchestra. Estab. 1976. Members are professionals and amateurs. Performs 15 concerts/year. Audience is "40% senior citizens, 85% white." Performs in a 1,500 seat high school performing arts center. Pay is negotiable.
How to Contact: Query first. SASE. Reports in 3-6 months.
Music: "Full orchestra works, 10-20 minutes in length. Can be geared toward 'children's' or 'Masterworks' programs. 65-70 piece orchestra, medium difficulty."
Performances: Kabelevsky's *Violin Concerto*; Stravinksy's *Firebird Suite*; and various selections by Andrew Lloyd Webber.

CARSON CITY CHAMBER ORCHESTRA, P.O. Box 2001, Carson City NV 89702-2001 or 191 Heidi Circle, Carson City NV 89701-6532. (702)883-4154. Fax: (702)883-4371. E-mail: dcbugli@ad.-com. Conductor: David C. Bugli. Amateur community orchestra. Estab. 1984. Members are amateurs. Performs 5 concerts, including 2-3 new works/year. "Most concerts are performed in the Carson City Community Center Auditorium, which seats 840. We pay composers on rare occasions."

LISTINGS OF COMPANIES in countries other than the U.S. have the name of the country in boldface type.

How to Contact: Query first. SASE. Reports in 2 months.
Music: "We want classical, pop orchestrations, orchestrations of early music for modern orchestras, concertos for violin or piano, holiday music for chorus and orchestra (children's choirs and handbell ensemble available), music by women, music for brass choir. Most performers are amateurs, but there are a few professionals who perform with us. Available winds and percussion: 2 flutes and flute/piccolo, 2 oboes (E.H. double), 2 clarinets, 1 bass clarinet, 2 bassoons, 3 or 4 horns, 3 trumpets, 3 trombones, 1 tuba, timpani, and some percussion. Harp and piano. Strings: 8-10-5-5-2. Avoid rhythmic complexity (except in pops) and music that lacks melodic appeal. Composers should contact us first. Each concert has a different emphasis. Note: Associated choral group, Carson Chamber Singers, performs several times a year with the orchestra and independently."
Performances: David Bugli's *State of Metamorphosis, Variations on "My Dancing Day"*; Gwyneth Walker's *A Concerto of Hymns and Spirituals for Trumpet and Orchestra*; and Ronald R. Williams' *Noah: Suite After Andre Obey*.
Tips: "It is better to write several short movements well than to write long, unimaginative pieces, especially when starting out. Be willing to revise after submitting the work, even if it was premiered elsewhere."

*CENTER FOR CONTEMPORARY OPERA, P.O. Box 1350, Gracie Station, New York NY 10028-0010. (212)308-6728. Fax: (212)308-6744. E-mail: conopera@ix.netcom.com. Director: Richard Marshall. Opera. Estab. 1982. Members are professionals. Performs 1-3 operas/year; including 1 or more new works. 650-seat theater. Pays royalties.
How to Contact: Query first. SASE. Reports in 1 year (with opera).
Music: "Looking for full-length operas. Limited orchestras and choruses. Orchestra—not over 25."
Performances: Beeson's *My Heart is in the Highlands* (stage premiere, opera); Susa's *Transformations*; and Kalmanoff's *Insect Comedy* (premiere).
Tips: "Make work practical to perform. Have an excellent libretto. Have contacts to raise money."

CHASPEN SYMPHONY ORCHESTRA, 27819 NE 49th St., Redmond WA 98053. Phone/fax: (206)880-6035. E-mail: chaspen@aol.com. Executive Director: Penny Orloff. Symphony orchestra, chamber music ensemble and opera/music theater ensemble. Estab. 1991. Members are professionals. Performs 6-10 concerts/year including 2 new works. Audience is generally upper-middle class families and seniors. Performs in space with 250-600 seats, depending upon space requirements. Pay negotiable.
How to Contact: Query first. SASE. Reports in 2 months.
Music: "Thematic revues for 6-8 singers, pianist, auxiliary keyboard; accessible symphonic pieces for voice and 40-50 piece symphony orchestra on contemporary themes; small chamber works for narrator/voice(s), and mixed chamber ensemble. 12-tone or serial pieces are NOT considered, nor are symphonic works using more players than a standard Mozart symphony orchestration. We do not wish to see any work which may not be performed for a family audience. Keep it clean!"
Performances: Charles Long's *Requiem* (oratorio); P. Orloff's *Atlanta Games* (opera) and *Broadway, Baby!* (revue).
Tips: "Flexibility, imagination, economy: If you are difficult to work with, and your piece requires a lot of extras, we won't be producing it. Have a heart. Have a sense of humor."

*CHEYENNE SYMPHONY ORCHESTRA, P.O. Box 851, Cheyenne WY 82003. (307)778-8561. CSO Music Director: Mark Russell Smith. Symphony orchestra. Estab. 1955. Members are professionals. Performs 6 concerts/year including 1-3 new works. "Orchestra performs for a conservative, mid-to-upper income audience of 1,200 season members." Pay varies.
How to Contact: Query first. Does not return material. Reports in 3-8 weeks.
Performances: Bill Hill's *Seven Abstract Miniatures* (orchestral).

THE CHICAGO STRING ENSEMBLE, 3524 W. Belmont Ave., Chicago IL 60618. (312)332-0567. Fax:(708)869-3925. Acting Executive Director: Virginia Graham. Professional string orchestra. Estab. 1977. Members are professionals. Performs 20 concerts/year, including 2-3 new works. Commissions 2-3 new works/year. Audience is a Chicago and suburban cross-section. Performance space: 3 large, acoustically favorable area churches. Composers are not paid.
How to Contact: Submit complete score and tape of piece. Does not return material. Reports in 6 months.
Music: "Open to any work for string orchestra, with or without a solo instrument. Additional instrumentation (e.g., harp, keyboard, percussion, a few winds) is possible but not encouraged. Must be possible to 6-6-4-4-2 or fewer strings. 10-15 minutes long. No electronics."
Performances: David Bernstein's *Sound Portraits* (string orchestra arrangement); Robert Lombardo's *Concertino for Mandolin* (string orchestra and mandolin arrangement); and Paul Seitz's *When Touched By Better Angels* (harp and strings).

*CIMARRON CIRCUIT OPERA COMPANY, P.O. Box 1085, Norman OK 73070. (405)364-8962. Music Director: Dr. Linda Wilds Beckman. Opera company. Estab. 1975. Members are professionals. Performs 100 concerts/year including 1-2 new works. Commissions 1 or less new works/year. "CCOC performs for children across the state of Oklahoma and for a dedicated audience in central Oklahoma. We do not have a permanent location. As a touring company, we adapt to the performance space provided, ranging from a classroom to a full raised stage." Pay is negotiable.
How to Contact: Submit complete score and tape of piece(s). SASE. Reports in 6-12 weeks ("time may vary depending on time of year.")
Music: "We are seeking operas or operettas in English only. We would like to begin including new, American works in our repertoire. Children's operas should be no longer than 45 minutes and require no more than a synthesizer for accompaniment. Adult operas should be appropriate for families, and may require either full orchestration or synthesizer. CCOC is a professional company whose members have varying degrees of experience, so any difficulty level is appropriate. There should be a small to moderate number of principals. Children's work should have no more than four principals. Our slogan is 'Opera is a family thing to do.' If we cannot market a work to families, we do not want to see it."
Performances: Mozart's *Die Fledermaus*; Barab's *Little Red Riding Hood*; and Gilbert & Sullivan's *The Mikado*.
Tips: "45-minute fairy tale-type children's operas with possibly a 'moral' work well for our market. Looking for works appealing to 8-12th grade students. No more than four principles."

COLORADO CHILDREN'S CHORALE, 910 15th St., Suite 1020, Denver CO 80202. (303)892-5600. Artistic Director: Duain Wolfe. Vocal ensemble and highly trained children's chorus. Estab. 1974. Members are professionals and amateurs. Performs 150 concerts/year including 3-5 new works. Commissions 2-5 composers or new works/year. "Our audiences' ages range from 5-80. We give school performances and tour (national, international). We give subscription concerts and sing with orchestras (symphonic and chamber). Halls: schools to symphony halls to arenas to outdoor theaters." Pays $100-500 outright purchase (more for extended works).
How to Contact: Submit complete score and tapes of piece(s). Does not return material. Reports in 1-3 months. "No guarantee of report on unsolicited material."
Music: "We want short pieces (3-5 minutes): novelty, folk arrangement, serious; longer works 5-20: serious; staged operas/musicals 30-45 minutes: piano accompaniment or small ensemble; or possible full orchestration if work is suitable for symphony concert. We are most interested in SA, SSA, SSAA. We look for a variety of difficulty ranges and encourage very challenging music for SSA-SSAA choruses (32 singers, unchanged voices). We don't want rock, charts without written accompaniments or texts that are inappropriate for children. We are accessible to all audiences. We like some of our repertoire to reflect a sense of humor, others to have a message. We're very interested in well crafted music that has a special mark of distinction."
Performances: John Kuzma's *O, Excellence* (virtuosit encore); Normand Lockwood's *Thought of Him I Love* (15-minute serious of chamber orchestra); and Samuel Lancaster's *Stocking Stuffer 1994* (8-minute comic number with full symphony orchestra).
Tips: "Submit score and tape with good cover letter, résumé and record of performance. Wait at least three weeks before a follow-up call or letter. Materials should be in excellent condition. We review a great quantity of material that goes through several channels. Please be patient. Sometimes excellent material simply doesn't fit our current needs and is put in a 'future consideration file.' "

COMMONWEALTH OPERA INC., P.O. Box 391, Northampton MA 01061-0391. (413)586-5026. Artistic Director: Richard R. Rescia. Opera company. Estab. 1977. Members are professionals and amateurs. Performs 4 concerts/year. "We perform at the Academy of Music at Northampton in an 800-seat opera house. Depending on opera, audience could be family oriented or adult."
How to Contact: Query first. Does not return material.
Music: "We are open to all styles of opera. We have the limitations of a regional opera company with local chorus. Principals come from a wide area. We look only at opera scores."
Performances: Leoncavallo's *I Pagliacci* (opera); Mozart's *Don Giovanni* (opera); and Menotti's *Amahl and the Night Visitors* (opera).
Tips: "We're looking for opera that is accessible to the general public and performable by a standard opera orchestra."

CONNECTICUT CHORAL ARTISTS/CONCORA, 90 Main St., New Britain CT 06051. (203)224-7500. Artistic Director: Richard Coffey. Professional concert choir. Estab. 1974. Members are professionals. Performs 15 concerts/year, including 3-5 new works. "Mixed audience in terms of age and background; performs in various halls and churches in the region." Payment "depends upon underwriting we can obtain for the project."
How to Contact: Query first. "No unsolicited submissions accepted." SASE. Reports in 6-12 months.

Music: Seeking "works for mixed chorus of 36 singers; unaccompanied or with keyboard and/or small instrumental ensemble; text sacred or secular/any language; prefers suites or cyclical works, total time not exceeding 15 minutes. Performance spaces and budgets prohibit large instrumental ensembles. Works suited for 750-seat halls are preferable. Substantial organ or piano parts acceptable. Scores should be very legible in every way."

Performances: Wm. Schuman's *Carols of Death* (choral SATB); Charles Ives' *Psalm 90* (choral SATB); and Frank Martin's *Mass for Double Chorus* (regional premiere).

Tips: "Use conventional notation and be sure manuscript is legible in every way. Recognize and respect the vocal range of each vocal part. Work should have an identifiable *rhythmic* structure."

*DESERT CHORALE, P.O. Box 2813, Santa Fe NM 87504-2813. (505)988-2282. Fax: (505)988-7522. Music Director: Lawrence Bandfield. Vocal ensemble. Members are professionals. Performs 35 concerts/year including 2 new works. Commissions 1 new composer or new work/year. "Highly sophisticated audiences who are eager for interesting musical experiences. We pay $5,000 to $2,000 for premieres, often as part of consortium."

How to Contact: Query first. Submit complete score and tape *after* query. Does not return material. Reports in 1-2 years.

Music: "Challenging chamber choir works 6 to 20 minutes in length. Accompanied works are sometimes limited by space—normally no more than 5 or 6 players. "We sing both a cappella and with chamber orchestra; size of choir varies accordingly (20-32). No short church anthem-type pieces."

Performances: Edwin London's *Jove's Nectar* (choral with 5 instruments); Lanham Deal's *Minituras de Sor Juana* (unaccompanied); and Steven Sametz's *Desert Voices* (choral with 4 instruments).

Tips: "Call me or see me and I'll be happy to tell you what I need and I will also put you in touch with other conductors in the growing professional choir movement."

DÚO CLÁSICO, 31-R Fayette St., Cambridge MA 02139-1111. (617)864-8524. Fax: (617)491-4696. Contact: David Witten. Chamber music ensemble. Estab. 1986. Members are professionals. Performs 14 concerts/year including 5 new works. Commissions 1 composer or new work/year. Performs in small recital halls. Pays 15% royalty.

How to Contact: Query first. SASE. Reports in 3 weeks.

Music: "We welcome scores for flute solo, piano solo or duo. Particular interest in Latin American composers."

Performances: Diego Luzuriaga's *La Múchica* (modern—with extended techniques); Robert Starer's *Yizkor & Anima Aeterna* (rhythmic); and Piazzolla's *Etudes Tanguistiques* (solo flute).

Tips: "Extended techniques, or with tape, are fine!"

EASTERN NEW MEXICO UNIVERSITY, Station 16, Portales NM 88130. (505)562-2736. Director of Orchestral Activities: Robert Radmer. Symphony orchestra, small college-level orchestra with possible choral collaboration. Estab. 1934. Members are students (with some faculty). Performs 12 concerts/year including 1-2 new works. "Our audiences are members of a college community and small town. We perform in a beautiful, acoustically fine 240-seat hall with a pipe organ." Payment is negotiable.

How to Contact: Query first. SASE. Reports in 3 months.

Music: "Pieces should be 12-15 minutes; winds by 2, full brass. Work shouldn't be technically difficult. Organ, harpsicord, piano(s) are available. We are a small college orchestra; normal instrumentation is represented but technical level is uneven throughout orchestra. We have faculty available to do special solo work. We like to see choral-orchestral combinations and writing at different technical levels within each family, i.e., 1st clarinet might be significantly more difficult than 2nd clarinet."

Performances: Stothart's *Wizard of Oz* (original film music).

Tips: "I'm looking for a 20-minute suite (four to five movements). Call us and discuss your work prior to submitting."

*EUROPEAN COMMUNITY CHAMBER ORCHESTRA, Fermain House, Dolphin St., Colyton EX13 6LU **United Kingdom**. Phone: (44)1297 552272. Fax: (44)1297 553744. E-mail: 101461.330@compuserve.com. General Manager: Ambrose Miller. Chamber orchestra. Members are professionals. Performs 70 concerts/year, including 2 new works. Commissions 2 composers or new works/year. Performs regular tours of Europe, Americas and Asia, including major venues. Pays per performance or for outright purchase, depending on work.

How to Contact: Query first. Does not return material. Reports in 6 weeks.

Music: Seeking compositions for strings, 2 oboes and 2 horns with a duration of about 10 minutes.

Performances: G. Sollima's *Angeli* (suite for strings); Taylor's *Banquet Invasion* (percussion and strings); and R. Orton's *Stellation* (strings).

Tips: "Keep the work to less than 15 minutes in duration, it should be sufficiently 'modern' to be interesting but not too difficult as this could take up rehearsal time. It should be possible to perform without a conductor."

FLORIDA SPACE COAST PHILHARMONIC, INC., P.O. Box 3344, Cocoa FL 32924 or 2150 Lake Dr., Cocoa FL 32926. (407)632-7445. General Manager: Alyce Christ. Music Director and Conductor: Dr. Candler Schaffer. Philharmonic orchestra and chamber music ensemble. Estab. 1986. Members are professionals. Performs 7-14 concerts/year. Concerts are performed for "average audience—they like familiar works and pops. Concert halls range from 600 to 2,000 seats." Pays 10% royalty (rental); outright purchase of $2,000; $50-600/performance; or by private arrangement.
How to Contact: Query first; submit complete score and tape of piece(s). SASE. Reports in 1-3 months. "Our conductor tours frequently thus we have to keep material until he can hear it."
Music: Seeks "pops and serious music for full symphony orchestra, but not an overly large orchestra with unusual instrumentation. We use about 60 musicians because of hall limitations. Works should be medium difficulty—not too easy and not too difficult—and not more than 10 minutes long." Does not wish to see avant-garde music.
Performances: Dr. Elaine Stone's *Cello Concerto* (cello solo with orchestra).
Tips: "If we would commission a work it would be to feature the space theme in our area."

FONTANA CONCERT SOCIETY, 821 W. South St., Kalamazoo MI 49007. (616)382-0826. Artistic Director: Paul Nitsch. Chamber music ensemble presenter. Estab. 1980. Members are professionals. Performs 20 concerts/year including 1-3 new works. Commissions 1-2 composers or new works/year. Audience consists of "well-educated people who expect to be challenged but like the traditional as well." Summer—180 seat hall; Fall/winter—various venues, from churches to libraries to 500-seat theaters.
How to Contact: Submit complete score and tapes of piece(s). SASE. Reports in 1 month.
Music: "Good chamber music—any combination of strings, winds, piano." No "pop" music, new age type. "We like to see enough interest for the composer to come for a premiere and talk to the audience."
Performances: Ramon Zupko's *Folksody* (piano trio-premiere); Sebastian Currier's *Vocalissimus* (soprano, 4 percussion, strings, winds, piano-premiere); and Mark Schultz's *Work for Horn & Piano*.
Tips: "Provide a résumé and clearly marked tape of a piece played by live performers."

GREAT FALLS SYMPHONY ASSOCIATION, P.O. Box 1078, Great Falls MT 59403. (406)453-4102. Music Director and Conductor: Gordon J. Johnson. Symphony orchestra. Estab. 1959. Members are professionals and amateurs. Performs 9 concerts (2 youth concerts)/year including 1-2 new works. Commissions 1-2 new works/year. "Our audience is conservative. Newer music is welcome; however, it might be more successful if it were programatic." Plays in Civic Center Auditorium seating 1,850. Negotiable payment.
How to Contact: Query first. SASE. Reports in 2 months.
Music: "Compositions should be for full orchestra. Should be composed idiomatically for instruments avoiding extended techniques. Duration 10-20 minutes. Avoid diverse instruments such as alto flute, saxophones, etc. Our orchestra carries 65 members, most of whom are talented amateurs. We have a resident string quartet and woodwind quintet that serve as principals. Would enjoy seeing a piece for quartet or quintet solo and orchestra. Send letter with clean score and tape (optional). We will reply within a few weeks."
Peformances: Bernstein's *Chichester Psalms* (choral and orchestra); Hodkinson's *Boogie, Tango and Grand Tarantella* (bass solo); and Stokes' *Native Dancer*.
Tips: "Music for orchestra and chorus is welcome. Cross cues will be helpful in places. Work should not require an undue amount of rehearsal time (remember that a concerto and symphony are probably on the program as well)."

HASTINGS SYMPHONY ORCHESTRA, Fuhr Hall, Ninth & Ash, Hastings NE 68901. (402)463-2402. Conductor/Music Director: Dr. James Johnson. Symphony orchestra. Estab. 1926. Members are professionals and amateurs. Performs 6-7 concerts/year including 1 new work. "Audience consists of conservative residents of mid-Nebraska who haven't heard most of the classics." Concert Hall: Masonic Temple Auditorium (950). Pays per performance.
How to Contact: Submit complete score and tapes of piece(s). SASE. Reports in 3-4 months.
Music: "We are looking for all types of music within the range of an accomplished community orchestra. Write first and follow with a phone call."
Performances: Richard Wilson's *Silhouette*; and James Oliverio's *Pilgrimage* (symphonic).
Tips: "Think about the size, ability and budgetary limits. Confer with our music director about audience taste. Think of music with special ties to locality."

HAWAII OPERA THEATRE, 987 Waimanu St., Honolulu HI 96814. (808)596-7372. Fax: (808)596-0379. General and Artistic Director: J. Mario Ramos. Opera Company. Estab. 1980. Members are professionals. Performs 20 concerts/year. Multicultural and multiethnic audience; performs in a 2,017 seat auditorium.

How to Contact: Query first. Does not return material. Reports in 6 months.
Music: Looking for children's operas, 45 minutes in length, with piano—melodic, please. Also full length operas, 2¼-3 hours in length.

*HELENA SYMPHONY, P.O. Box 1073, Helena MT 59624. (406)442-1860. Symphony orchestra. Estab. 1955. Members are professionals and amateurs. Performs 10-12 concerts/year including 2 new works. Performance space is an 1,800 seat concert hall. Payment varies.
How to Contact: Query first. SASE. Reports in 3 months.
Music: "Imaginative, collaborative, not too atonal. We want to appeal to an audience of all ages. We don't have a huge string complement. Medium to difficult okay—at frontiers of professional ability we cannot do."
Performances: Eric Funk's *A Christmas Overture* (orchestra); Donald O. Johnston's *A Christmas Processional* (orchestra/chorale); and Elizabeth Sellers' *Prairie* (orchestra/short ballet piece).
Tips: "Try to balance tension and repose in your works. New instrument combinations are appealing."

*HERMAN SONS GERMAN BAND, P.O. Box 162, Medina TX 78055. (210)589-2268. Music Director: Herbert Bilhartz. Community band with German instrumentation. Estab. 1990. Members are both professionals and amateurs. Performs 12 concerts/year including 6 new works. Commissions no new composers or new works/year. Performs for "mostly older people who like German polkas, waltzes, and marches. We normally play only published arrangements from Germany."
How to Contact: Query first; then submit full set of parts & score, condensed or full. SASE. Reports in 6 weeks.
Music: "We like European-style polkas or waltzes (Viennese or Missouri tempo), either original or arrangements of public domain tunes. Arrangements of traditional American folk tunes in this genre would be especially welcome. Also, polkas or waltzes featuring one or two solo instruments (from instrumentation below) would be great. OK for solo parts to be technically demanding. Although we have no funds to commission works, we will provide you with a cassette recording of our performance. Also, we would assist composers in submitting works to band music publishers in Germany for possible publication. Polkas and waltzes generally follow this format: Intro; 1st strain repeated; 2nd strain repeated; DS to 1 strain; Trio: Intro; 32 bar strain; 'break-up' strain; Trio DS. Much like military march form. Instrumentation: fl/picc, 3 clars in Bb, 2 Fluegelhorns in Bb; 3 tpts in Bb, 2 or 4 hns in F or Eb, 2 baritones (melody/countermelody parts; 1 in Bb TC, 1 in BC), 2 baritones in Bb TC (rhythm parts), 3 trombones, 2 tubas (in octaves, mostly), drum set, timpani optional. No saxes. Parts should be medium to medium difficult. All parts should be considered one player to the part. No concert type pieces; no modern popular or rock styles. However, a 'theme and variations' form with contrasting jazz, rock, country, modern variations would be clever, and our fans might go for such a piece (as might a German publisher)."
Performances: Siegfried Rundel's *Sounds of Friendship* (march); Pavel Stanek's *Folk Music Polonaise* (Polonaise); and Freek Mestrini's *Bohemian Serenade* (polka).
Tips: "German town bands love to play American tunes. There are many thousands of these bands over there and competition among band music publishers in Germany is keen. Few Americans are aware of this potential market, so few American arrangers get published over there. Simple harmony is best for this style, but good counterpoint helps a lot. Make use of the dark quality of the Fluegelhorns and the bright, fanfare quality of the trumpets. Give the two baritones (one in TC and one in BC) plenty of exposed melodic material. Keep them in harmony with each other (3rds and 6ths), unlike American band arrangements, which have only one Baritone line. If you want to write a piece in this style, give me a call, and I will send you some sample scores to give you a better idea."

HERSHEY SYMPHONY ORCHESTRA, P.O. Box 93, Hershey PA 17033. (800)533-3088. Music Director. Dr. Sandra Dackow. Symphony orchestra. Estab. 1969. Members are professionals and amateurs. Performs 6 concerts/year, including 1-3 new works. Performance space is a 1,900 seat grand old movie theater. Payment varies.
How to Contact: Submit complete score and tape of piece(s). SASE. Reports in 3 months.
Music: "Symphonic works of various lengths and types which can be performed by a non-professional orchestra. We are flexible but like to involve all our players."
Performances: Paul W. Whear's *Lyrical Dances* (suite); Scott Robinson's *Global Village Barn Dance* (premiere); and Katherine Hoover's *Summer Evening.*
Tips: "Please lay out rehearsal numbers/letter and rests according to phrases and other logical musical divisions rather than in groups of ten measures, etc., which is very unmusical and wastes time and causes a surprising number of problems. Also, please do not send a score written in concert pitch; use the usual transpositions so that the conductor sees what the players see; rehearsal is much more effective this way. Cross cue all important solos; this helps in rehearsal where instruments may be missing."

HIGH DESERT SYMPHONY ASSOCIATION, 18422 Bear Valley Rd., Victorville CA 92392. (619)245-4271, ext. 387. Music Director: Dr. K.C. Manji. Symphony orchestra. Estab. 1967. Members

are professionals and amateurs. Performs 2-4 concerts/year including 1-2 new works. 500 seat auditorium. Composers are not paid.
How to Contact: Submit complete score and tape of piece(s). SASE. Reports in 1 month.
Music: "Any type of music but for a smaller orchestra. 2222 2200 T strings."
Tips: "Make sure the work is legible and instrumentation is conservative."

*THE PAUL HILL CHORALE (AND) THE WASHINGTON SINGERS, 5630 Connecticut Ave. NW, Washington DC 20015. (202)364-4321. Music Director: Paul Hill. Vocal ensemble. Estab. 1967. Members are professionals and amateurs. Performs 7 concerts/year including 3-4 new works. Commissions one new composer or work every 2-3 years. "Audience covers a wide range of ages and economic levels drawn from the greater Washington DC metropolitan area. Kennedy Center Concert Hall seats 2,700." Pays by outright purchase.
How to Contact: Query first. SASE. Reports in 2-3 months.
Music: Seeks new works for: 1)large chorus with or without symphony orchestras; 2)chamber choir and small ensemble.
Performances: Daniel Gawthrop's *Lo, How a Rose E'er Blooming*; Samuel Adler's *A Prolific Source of Sorrow*; and Mark Adamo's *Three Appalachian Folk Songs* (all choral).

KENTUCKY OPERA, 101 S. Eighth St. at Main, Louisville KY 40202. (502)584-4500. Opera. Estab. 1952. Members are professionals. Performs 16 times/year. Performs at Whitney Hall, The Kentucky Center for the Arts, seating is 2,400; Bomhard Theatre, The Kentucky Center for the Arts, 620; Macauley Theatre, 1,400. Pays by royalty, outright purchase or per performance.
How to Contact: Submit complete score. SASE. Reports in 6 months.
Music: Seeks opera—1 to 3 acts with orchestrations. No limitations.
Performances: *Cinderella*; *Side by Side by Sondheim*; and *Cavalleria Rusticana/I Pagliacci*.

KITCHENER-WATERLOO CHAMBER ORCHESTRA, Box 34015, Highland Hills P.O., Kitchener, Ontario N2N 3G2 **Canada**. (519)744-3828. Music Director: Graham Coles. Chamber Orchestra. Estab. 1985. Members are professionals and amateurs. Performs 6 concerts/year including 2 new works. "We perform mainly baroque and classical repertoire, so any contemporary works must not be too dissonant, long or far fetched." Pays per performance.
How to Contact: "It's best to query first so we can outline what not to send. Include: complete CV—list of works, performances, sample reviews." Does not return material. Reports in 4 weeks.
Music: "Musical style must be accessible to our audience and players (3 rehearsals). Length should be under 20 minutes. Maximum orchestration 2/2/2/2 2/2/0/0 Timp/1 Percussion Harpsichord/organ String 5/5/3/4/2. We have limited rehearsal time, so keep technique close to that of Bach-Beethoven. We also play chamber ensemble works—octets, etc. We do not want choral or solo works."
Performances: Peter Jona Korn's *4 Pieces for Strings* (string orchestra); Graham Coles' *Variations on a Mozart Rondo* (string orchestra); and Alan Heard's *Sinfonietta* (orchestra).
Tips: "If you want a first-rate performance, keep the technical difficulties minimal."

KNOX-GALESBURG SYMPHONY, Box 31, Knox College, Galesburg IL 61401. (309)343-0112, ext. 208. Music Director: Bruce Polay. Symphony orchestra. Estab. 1951. Members are professionals and amateurs. Performs 7 concerts/year including 1-3 new works. High diverse audience; excellent, recently renovated historical theater. Pays is negotiable.
How to Contact: Submit complete score and tapes of piece(s). "Pops material also welcome." SASE. Reporting time varies.
Music: Moderate difficulty 3222/4331/T piano, harpsichord, celesta and full strings. No country.
Performances: Polay's *Bondi's Journey: An Orchestra Rhapsody on Jewish Themes* (orchestra); Finko's *Russia: A Symphony Poem*; and Wallace's *Introduction and Passacaglia*.
Tips: "Looking for moderately difficult, 8-10 minute pieces for standard orchestra."

LA STELLA FOUNDATION, 14323 64th Ave. W., Edmonds WA 98026. (206)743-5010. Managing Director: Thomas F. Chambers. Opera company. Estab. 1990. Members are professionals. Performs 10 concerts/year, including 2 new works. Produces operatic performances exclusively for recordings, video and television markets. Payment individually negotiated.

REMEMBER: Don't "shotgun" your demo tapes. Submit only to companies interested in the type of music you write. For more submission hints, refer to Getting Started on page 5.

How to Contact: Submit complete score and tape of piece(s). SASE. Reports in 3 months.

Music: "Music must have strong melodic value (Puccini-ish) with good harmonic chord structures and regular solid rhythms. Smaller casts with no chorus parts and smaller orchestras will get first consideration. Do not submit contemporary 'a-tonal,' non-harmonic, non-melodic, rhythmically weird garbage! Looking for pieces with romantic flavor like Puccini and dramatic movement like Verdi, written to showcase heavy lyric voices (i.e. soprano, tenor, baritone)."

Performances: Frank DeMiero's *Now You're Gone* and *I Want to Hold You In My Arms* (pop); and Hayden Wayne's *Dracula* (opera).

Tips: "Looking for hit tunes/melodies with good chord structures and strong rhythmic values."

LAKESIDE SUMMER SYMPHONY, 236 Walnut Ave., Lakeside OH 43440. (419)798-4461. Contact: G. Keith Addy. Conductor: Robert L. Cronquist. Symphony orchestra. Members are professionals. Performs 8 concerts/year. Performs "Chautauqua-type programs with an audience of all ages (2-102). Hoover Auditorium is a 3,000-seat auditorium."

How to Contact: Query first. SASE.

Music: Seeking "classical compositions for symphony composed of 50-55 musicians. The work needs to have substance and be a challenge to our symphony members. No modern jazz, popular music or hard rock."

Performances: Richard's Nanes' *Prelude, Canon & Fugue* (classical).

LAMARCA SINGERS, 2655 W. 230th Place, Torrance CA 90505. (310)325-8708. Director: Priscilla LaMarca Kandel. Vocal ensemble. Estab. 1979. Members are professionals and amateurs. Performs 20 concerts/year including 5 new works. Performs at major hotels, conventions, community theaters, fund raising events, cable TV, community fairs and Disneyland.

How to Contact: Query first or submit score and tape. SASE. Reports in 2 weeks.

Music: "Seeks 3-10 or 15 minute medleys; a variety of musical styles from Broadway—pop styles to humorous specialty songs. Top 40 dance music, Linda Ronstadt-style to Whitney Houston. Light rock and patriotic themes. Also interested in music for children. No heavy metal or anything not suitable for family audiences."

Performances: Priscilla LaMarca's *Hip Hop Alphabet* (upbeat educational); Mariah Carey's *Hero* (inspirational); and *Colors of the Wind* (ballad).

LEHIGH VALLEY CHAMBER ORCHESTRA, Box 20641, Lehigh Valley PA 18002-0641. (610)770-9666. Music Director: Donald Spieth. Symphony orchestra. Estab. 1979. Performs 25 concerts/year including 2-3 new works. Members are professionals. Commissions 1-2 composers or new works/year. Typical orchestral audience, also youth concerts. Pays commission for first 2 performances, first right for recording.

How to Contact: Submit complete score and tape of piece(s). SASE. Reports in 4 months.

Music: "Classical orchestral; works for youth and pops concerts. Duration 10-15 minutes. Chamber orchestra 2222-2210 percussion, strings (76442). No limit on difficulty."

Performances: David Stock's *String Set* (4 dances for strings); and John Scully's *Letters from Birmingham Jail* (soprano and orchestra).

Tips: "Send a sample tape and score of a work(s) written for the requested medium."

LEXINGTON PHILHARMONIC SOCIETY, 161 N. Mill St., Arts Place, Lexington KY 40507. (606) 233-4226. Music Director: George Zack. Symphony orchestra. Estab. 1961. Performs 50-60 concerts/year including 12-15 new works. Members are professionals. Commissions 1-2 composers or new works/year. Series includes "7 serious, classical subscription concerts (hall seats 1,500); 3 concerts called Unplugged and Untied; 30 outdoor pops concerts (from 1,500 to 5,000 tickets sold); 3-5 run-out concerts (½ serious/½ pops); and 10 children's concerts, 2 rock/pops concerts (hall seats 1,500)." Pays via ASCAP and BMI, rental purchase and private arrangements.

How to Contact: Submit complete score and tape of piece(s). SASE.

Music: Seeking "good current pops material and good serious classical works. No specific restrictions, but overly large orchestra requirements, unusual instruments and extra rentals help limit our interest."

Performances: Zwillich's *Celebration* (overture); Crumb's *A Haunted Landscape* (tone poem); and Corigliano's *Promenade* (overture).

Tips: "When working on large-format arrangement, use cross-cues so orchestra can be cut back if required. Submit good quality copy, scores and parts. Tape is helpful."

LIMA SYMPHONY ORCHESTRA, 67 Town Square, P.O. Box 1651, Lima OH 45802. (419)222-5701. Fax: (419)222-6587. Music Director Emeritus: Joseph Firszt. Symphony orchestra. Estab. 1952. Members are professionals. Performs 17-18 concerts including at least 1 new work/year. Commissions at least 1 composer or new work/year. Middle to older audience; also Young People's Series. Mixture for stage and summer productions. Performs in Veterans' Memorial Civic & Convention Center, a beautiful hall seating 1,670; Locomotive Erecting Shop (Pops At The Loco); various temporary shells

for summer outdoors events; churches; museums and libraries. Pays $2,500 for outright purchase (Anniversary commission) or grants $1,500-5,000.
How to Contact: Submit complete score if not performed; otherwise submit complete score and tape of piece(s). SASE. Reports in 3 months.
Music: "Good balance of incisive rhythm, lyricism, dynamic contrast and pacing. Chamber orchestra to full (85-member) symphony orchestra." Does not wish to see "excessive odd meter changes."
Performances: Frank Proto's *American Overture* (some original music and fantasy); Werner Tharichen's *Concerto for Timpani and Orchestra*; and James Oliverio's *Pilgrimage—Concerto for Brass* (interesting, dynamic writing for brass and the orchestra).
Tips: "Know your instruments, be willing to experiment with unconventional textures, be available for in depth analysis with conductor, be at more than one rehearsal. Be sure that individual parts are correctly matching the score and done in good, neat calligraphy."

LITHOPOLIS AREA FINE ARTS ASSOCIATION, 3825 Cedar Hill Rd., Canal Winchester OH 43110-9507. (614)837-8925. Series Director: Virginia E. Heffner. Performing Arts Series. Estab. 1973. Members are professionals and amateurs. Performs 6 concerts/year including 1 new work. "Our audience consists of couples and families 30-80 in age. Our hall is acoustically excellent and seats 400. It was designed as a lecture-recital hall in 1925." Composers "may apply for Ohio Arts Council Grant under the New Works category."
How to Contact: Query first. SASE. Reports in 1 month.
Music: "We prefer that a composer is also the performer and works in conjunction with another artist, so they could be one of the performers on our series. Piece should be musically pleasant and not too dissonant. It should be scored for small vocal or instrumental ensemble. Dance ensembles have difficulty with 15' high 15' deep and 27' wide stage. We do not want avant-garde or obscene dance routines. No ballet (space problem). We're interested in something historical—national or Ohio emphasis would be nice. Small ensembles or solo format is fine."
Performances: Alice Parker's *Lancaster Chorale* (folk song arrangement); and John McCutcheon's *Cut the Cake* (folk-family).
Tips: "Call in September of '96 for queries about our '96-'97 season. We do a varied program. We don't commission artists. Contemporary music is used by some of our artist or groups. By contacting these artists, you could offer your work for inclusion in their program."

*LYRIC OPERA OF CHICAGO, 20 N. Wacker Dr., Chicago IL 60606. (312)332-2244. Fax: (312)419-8345. Music Administrator: Philip Morehead. Opera company. Estab. 1953. Members are professionals. Performs 80 operas/year including 1 new work in some years. Commissions 1 new work every 4 or 5 years. "Performances are held in a 3,563 seat house for a sophisticated opera audience, predominantly 30+ years old." Pays by negotiated fee.
How to Contact: Query first. Does not return material. Reports in 6 months.
Music: "Full-length opera suitable for a large house with full orchestra. No musical comedy or Broadway musical style. We rarely perform one-act operas. We are only interested in works by composers and librettists with extensive theatrical experience. We have few openings for new works, so candidates must be of the highest quality. Do not send score or other materials without a prior contact."
Performances: William Bolcom's *McTeague*; John Lorigliano's *Ghosts of Versailles*; and Leonard Bernstein's *Candide*.
Tips: "Have extensive credentials and an international reputation."

MEASURED BREATHS THEATRE COMPANY, 193 Spring St., #3R, New York NY 10012. (212)334-8402. Artistic Director: Robert Press. Nonprofit music-theater producing organization. Estab. 1989. Members are professionals. Performs 2 concerts/year. "Performances in small (less than 100 seats) halls in downtown Manhattan; strongly interested in highly theatrical/political vocal works for avant-garde audiences." Pays $500 for outright purchase.
How to Contact: Query first. SASE. Reports in 3 months.
Music: "Traditionally, we have produced revivals of baroque or modern vocal works. We are interested in soliciting new works by theatrically adept composers. Typical orchestration should be 7 pieces or less. Would prefer full-length works." Chamber-size, full-length operas preferred. At most 10 performers. Difficult works encouraged.
Performances: Ramean's *Those Fabulous Americans* (opera, French, 1735); Monteverdi's *Madrigals of Love and War* (opera; Italian, 1638); and Lully's *Amadis* (opera; French, 1684).

MELROSE SYMPHONY ORCHESTRA, P.O. Box 175, Melrose MA 02176. (617)662-0641. President and CEO: Millie Rich. Symphony orchestra. Estab. 1918. Members are both professionals and amateurs. Performs 4 concerts/year. Audience covers all ages from children to senior citizens; performances take place in a 1,000 seat capacity auditorium. Pays through ASCAP.
How to Contact: Query first. SASE. "Reporting time varies depending on time of submission. We are all volunteers."

Music: Full orchestral pieces. 60 performers, all community level performers.

MESQUITE SYMPHONY ORCHESTRA, P.O. Box 0192, Mesquite TX 75185. Fax: (214)216-6397. Interim Music Director: Roger Gilliam. Symphony orchestra. Estab. 1987. Members are both professionals and amateurs. Performs 4-5 concerts/year including 0-1 new work. Commissions 0-1 new work/year. Audiences are of middle-high music literacy. Performances take place in church or school. Does not pay composers.
How to Contact: Query first. SASE. Reports in 3 months.
Music: "Full orchestra, tonal, average to above average technical ability, any style, 10-20 minutes. Any number of performers, average to above average level of difficulty, no concerto or featured soloist."

MILWAUKEE YOUTH SYMPHONY ORCHESTRA, 929 N. Water St., Milwaukee WI 53202. (414)272-8540. Executive Director: Frances Richman. Youth orchestra. "We also have a Junior Wind Ensemble." Estab. 1956. Members are students. Performs 12-15 concerts/year including 1-2 new works. "Our groups perform in Uihlein Hall at the Performing Arts Center in Milwaukee plus area sites. The audiences usually consist of parents, music teachers and other interested community members. We sometimes are reviewed in either the *Milwaukee Journal* or *Sentinel*."
How to Contact: Query first. Does not return material.
Performances: John Downey's *Ode to Freedom* (wind/brass).
Tips: "Be sure you realize you are working with students and (albeit many of the best in southeastern Wisconsin) not professional musicians. The music needs to be technically on a level students can handle. Our students are 8-18 years of age, in five different orchestras."

*THE MIRECOURT TRIO, 585 E. Second Ave. Apt. 9, Salt Lake City UT 84103-2920. (801)532-0469. Fax: (801)532-2533. Contact: Terry King. Chamber music ensemble; violin, cello, piano. Estab. 1973. Members are professionals. Performs 20 concerts/year including 2-6 new works. Commissions 2-6 composers or new works/year. Concerts are performed for university, concert series, schools, societies and "general chamber music audiences of 100-1,500."
How to Contact: Query first. SASE. Reports in 6 months.
Music: Seeks "music of short to moderate duration (5-20 minutes) that entertains, yet is not derivative or clichéd. Orchestration should be basically piano, violin, cello, occasionally adding voice or instrument. We do not wish to see academic or experimental works."
Performances: Lou Harrison's *Trio*; Otto Leuning's *Fantasia No. 2*; and Henry Cowell's *Scenario*.
Tips: "Submit works that engage the audience or relate to them, that reward the players as well."

MOHAWK TRAIL CONCERTS, P.O. Box 75, Shelburne Falls MA 01370. (413)625-9511. Executive Director: E. Lary Grossman. Artistic Director: Arnold Black. Chamber music presenter. Estab. 1970. Members are professionals. Performs 15 concerts/year including 3-5 new works. Conducts school performances. "Audience ranges from farmers to professors, children to elders. Concerts are performed in churches and town halls around rural Franklin County, MA." Pays by variable rate.
How to Contact: Query first. (Attention: Arnold Black, Artistic Director). SASE. Reports in months.
Music: "We want chamber music, generally not longer than 30 minutes. We are open to a variety of styles and orchestrations for a maximum of 8 performers. We don't want pop, rock or theater music."
Performances: Michael Cohen's *Fantasia for Flute, Piano and Strings* (chamber); William Bolcom's *Nes Songs* (piano/voice duo); and Arnold Black's *Laments & Dances* (string quartet and guitar duo).
Tips: "We are looking for artistic excellence, a committment to quality performances of new music, and music that is accessible to a fairly conservative (musically) audience."

MONTREAL CHAMBER ORCHESTRA, 1200 McGill College Ave., Suite 1100, Montreal Quebec H3B 4G7 **Canada**. (514)871-1224. Fax: (514)393-9069. Conductor and Music Director: Wanda Kaluzny. Chamber orchestra. Estab. 1974. Members are professionals. Performs 6 concerts including 1-3 new works/year. Commissions various new works/year (Canadian composers only). Audience is mixed ages, mixed income levels. Orchestra performs in a church, seating 800. Pays "through the composer's performing arts organization."
How to Contact: Submit complete score. Does not return material. Reports "only if performing the work."
Music: Works with string orchestra (6 / 4 / 2 / 2 / 1), 8-12 min. duration. Strings (6 / 4 / 2 / 2 / 1).
Performances: Alan Belkin's *Nocturne* (chamber orchestra); Hope Lee's *Chan Chan* (string orchestra); and David Eagle's *Waves Echo Upon Stone* (chamber orchestra).

*MOZART FESTIVAL ORCHESTRA, INC., 33 Greenwich Ave., New York NY 10014. (212)675-9127. Conductor: Baird Hastings. Symphony orchestra. Estab. 1960. Members are professionals. Performs 1-4 concerts/year including 2 new works. Audience members are Greenwich Village

professionals of all ages. Performances are held at the First Presbyterian Church, Fifth Ave. and 12th St., ("wonderful acoustics"). Pay varies.
How to Contact: Query first. SASE. Reports in 2 weeks.
Music: "We are an established chamber orchestra interested in *unusual* music of all periods, but not experimental. Orchestra size usually under 20 performers."

NATIONAL ASSOCIATION OF COMPOSERS/USA, P.O. Box 49256, Los Angeles CA 90049. (310)541-8213. President: Marshall Bialosky. Chamber music ensemble and composers' service organization. Estab. 1932. Members are professionals. Performs 3-4 concerts/year—all new works. Usually performed at universities in Los Angeles and at a mid-town church in New York City. Paid by ASCAP or BMI (NACUSA does not pay composers).
How to Contact: Query first. SASE.
Music: Chamber music for five or fewer players; usually in the 5 to 20 minute range. "Level of difficulty is not a problem; number of performers is solely for financial reasons. We deal in serious, contemporary concert hall music. No 'popular' music."
Performances: Bruce Taub's *Sonata for Solo Viola*; Tom Flaherty's *Quartet for Viola, Cello, and Digital Synthesizer*; and Maria Newman's *Sonata for Bass Trombone and Piano*.
Tips: "Send in modest-sized pieces—not symphonies and concertos."

*NEW JERSEY SYMPHONY ORCHESTRA/GREATER NEWARK YOUTH ORCHES-TRA, 2 Central Ave., Newark NJ 07102. (201)624-3713. Fax: (201)624-2115. Assistant Conductor: Mariusz Smolij. Symphony orchestra and youth orchestra. Estab. 1922. Members are professionals and students for youth orchestra. Performs 2-10 new works/year. Commissions 1-3 composers or new works/year.
How to Contact: Query first or submit complete score and tape of piece(s). SASE. Reports in 1-2 months.
Music: Classical with jazz, pop influence, or the fusion of the above. Compositions for young people's concerts.

THE NEW STAR-SCAPE SINGERS, P.O. Box 793, Station F, Toronto Ontario M4Y 2N7 **Canada**. (905)470-8634. Fax: (905)470-1632. Assistant to the Conductor: Ellen Mann. A cappella choir (10-12 voices). Estab. 1976. Members are professionals. Performs 15 concerts/year including over 170 original works. Audience is appreciative of extraordinary technical ability of the ensemble and recognize that "this music, this art opens up the soul." Performances take place in concert halls and churches. Does not pay composers.
How to Contact: Query first. SASE.
Performances: Kenneth G. Mills/Christopher Dedrick's *Hey There!* (a cappella); *He's Got The Whole World In His Hands* (spiritual); and Kenneth G. Mills/Jacek Sykulski's *Love Answers* (a cappella).

*NEW WORLD YOUTH SYMPHONY ORCHESTRA, 10815 Brenda Court, Fortville IN 46040. (317)485-6022. Fax: (317)485-5247. Music Director: Susan Kitterman. Youth orchestra. Estab. 1982. Members are amateurs. Performs 6 concerts/year including 1 or 2 new works. Commissions 1 composer or new work every other year. "Typically 500-1,500 in attendance, broad spectrum of arts patrons and educators." Performs at Circle Theatre, downtown Indianapolis, home of Indianapolis Symphony; also at the Warren Performing Arts Center. Pay variable for outright purchase.
How to Contact: Query first. SASE. Reports in 2 months.
Music: "Innovative, creative works for full or string orchestra, brass or woodwind or percussion ensemble—may be with vocal or instrumental soloist. Any length."
Performances: David Baker's *Alabama Landscape* (orchestral with narration); Robert Ward's *Jubilation* (orchestral overture); and Paul Hindemith's *Symphonic Metamorphases* (orchestral).
Tips "Come hear and meet our ensemble. Make the creative process highly individualized and one all can participate in."

THE NEW YORK CONCERT SINGERS, 75 East End Ave., Suite 9L, New York NY 10028. (212)879-4412. Music Director/Conductor: Judith Clurman. Chorus. Estab. 1988. Performs 4-5 concerts/year including new works. Frequently commissions new composers. "Audience is mixture of young and old classical music 'lovers.' Chorus performs primarily at Menkin Concert Hall and Lincoln Center, NYC." ASCAP, BMI fees paid.
How to Contact: Submit complete score with tape of piece(s). SASE. Reports in 2 months.
Music: Seeks music "for small professional ensemble, with or without solo parts, a cappella or small instrumental ensemble. Looking for pieces ranging from 7-20 minutes."
Performances: William Bolcom's *Alleluia* (a cappella); Arvo Part's *Summa and Magnificent* (a cappella); and Robert Bearer's *Psalm 150*.
Tips: "When choosing a piece for a program I study both the text and music. Both are equally important."

NORFOLK CHAMBER MUSIC FESTIVAL/YALE SUMMER SCHOOL OF MUSIC, 96 Wall St., New Haven CT 06520-8246. (203)432-1966. Summer music festival. Estab. 1941. Members are international faculty/artists plus young professionals. Performs 20 concerts, 15 recitals/year, including 3-6 new works. Commissions 1 composer or new work/year. Pays a commission fee. Also offers a Composition Search and Residency biennially. The Norfolk Chamber Music Festival-Yale Summer School of Music seeks new chamber music works from American composers under the age of 35. The goal of this search is to identify promising young composers and to provide a visible and high quality venue for the premiere of their work. A maximum of two winning compositions are selected. Winners are invited to the Norfolk Chamber Music Festival for a week-long residency.
* The Norfolk Chamber Music Festival/Yale Summer School of Music has won an ASCAP/ Chamber Music America award for adventurous programming.
How to Contact: Submit complete score and tapes of piece(s), SASE and completed application form (available by calling (203)432-1966). Reports in 6 months.
Music: "Chamber music of combinations, particularly for strings, woodwinds, brass and piano. There are 1-2 chamber orchestra concerts per season which include the students and feature the festival artists. Other than this, orchestra is not a featured medium, rather, chamber ensembles are the focus."
Performances: Betsy Jolas's *Music For Here* (trio); Scott Robbins' *Samba & Epilogue* (chamber ensemble); and Peter Schickele's *Bestiary* (Renaissance ensemble).

*THE NORFOLK SINGERS' CHORUS AND ORCHESTRA, P.O. Box 955, Simcoe, Ontario N0E 1Y0 **Canada**. (519)428-3185. Fax: (519)426-1573. Director: Ronald Beckett. Semi-professional chorus and orchestra. Estab. 1983. Members are both professionals and amateurs. Performs 3 concerts/ year including 1 new work. Commissions 1 commmposer or new work/year. Pay negotiable.
How to Contact: Submit complete score and tape of piece(s). SASE.
Music: "Compositions appropriate for ensemble accustomed to performance of chamber works, accompanied or unaccompanied, with independence of parts. Specialize in repetoire of 17th, 18th and 20th centuries. Number of singers does not exceed 45. Orchestra is limited to strings, supported by a professional quartet. No popular, commercial, or show music."
Performances: Benjamin Britten's *St. Nicholas Cantata* (cantata) and *Hymn to St. Cecilia* (SSATB unaccompanied); and Ronald A. Beckett's *Ruth* (drama).
Tips: "Write for conservative resources (i.e., small ensembles). Performance level must take into account the limited amount of time available for rehearsal. Small-scale is generally more effective than large-scale. Although the ensemble has been active for more than a decade, it is relatively new to the field of contemporary premieres. Would welcome, however, any inquiries from composers."

NORTH ARKANSAS SYMPHONY ORCHESTRA, P.O. Box 1243, Fayetteville AR 72702. (501)521-4166. Music Director: Carlton Woods. Symphony orchestra, chamber music ensemble, youth orchestra and community chorus. Estab. 1950. Members are professionals and amateurs. Performs 20 concerts/year including 4-5 new works. "General audiences—performs in Walton Arts Center (capacity 1,200)." Pays $500 for outright purchase.
How to Contact: Query first. Does not return material.
Music: Seeks "audience pleasers—rather short (10-15 minutes); and full orchestra pieces for subscription (classical) concerts. Orchestra is 80 members."
Performances: Kimo Williams' *Symphony for Sons of 'Nam* (orchestral); Michael Woods' *Brother Man* (orchestral and choral); and Corigliano's *Symphony No. 1* (orchestral).

OPERA FESTIVAL OF NEW JERSEY, 55 Princeton-Hightstown Rd., Suite 202, Princeton Junction NJ 08550. (609)936-1505. Fax: (609)936-0008. General Director: Ms. Deborah Sandler. Professional opera company. Estab. 1983. Members are professionals. Performs 3 productions/year. "Performances for mainstage season are held in the Allan P. Kirby Art Center, on the campus of The Lawrenceville School. Small proscenium stage with approximately 900 seats. Intimate hall with great acoustics."
How to Contact: Query first. Does not return material.
Performances: Peter Maxwell Davies' *The Lighthouse* (opera); Peter Westergaard's *The Tempest* (opera); and Benjamin Britten's *Turn of the Screw* (opera).

OPERA MEMPHIS, U of M South Campus #47, Memphis TN 38152. (901)678-2706. Fax: (901)678-3506. Artistic Director: Michael Ching. Opera company. Estab. 1965. Members are professionals. Performs 8-15 concerts/year including 1 new work. Commissions 1 composer or new work/year. Audience consists of older, wealthier patrons, along with many students and young professionals. Pay is negotiable.
How to Contact: Query first. SASE. Reports in 1 year.
Music: Accessible practical pieces for educational or main stage programs. Educational pieces should not exceed 90 minutes or 4-6 performers. We encourage songwriters to contact us with proposals or work samples for theatrical works. We are very interested in crossover work.

Performances: Mike Reid's *Different Fields* (one act opera); David Olney's *Light in August* (folk opera); and Sid Selvidge's *Riversongs* (one act opera).
Tips: "Spend many hours thinking about the synopsis (plot outline)."

OPERA ON THE GO, 184-61 Radnor Rd., Jamaica Estates NY 11432. (718)380-0665. Artistic Director: Jodi Rose. American opera chamber ensemble. Estab. 1985. Members are professionals. Performs about 60-80 operas/year including 1-2 new works. "We perform primarily in schools and community theaters. We perform only American contemporary opera. It must be lyrical in sound and quality as we perform for children as well as adults. We prefer pieces written for children based on fairy tales needing 4 to 6 singers." Pays $20-30 per performance. "We also help composers acquire a 'Meet the Composer' grant."
How to Contact: Query first, then submit complete score and tapes of piece(s). SASE. Reports in 2 months.
Music: Need works in all age groups including adults. For older ages the pieces can be up to 60 minutes. Rarely use orchestra. "Keep the music as short as possible since we do a prelude (spoken) and postlude involving the children's active participation and performance. If it is totally atonal it will never work in the schools we perform in."
Performances: Bob Miles' *Alice In Wonderland* (musical); Mark Bucci's *Sweet Betsy From Pike* (opera); and Seymour Barab's *Little Red Riding Hood* (opera).
Tips: "Be flexible. Through working with children we know what works best with different ages. If this means editing music to guarantee its performance, don't get offended or stubborn. All operas must have audience participatory sections."

OPERA ORA NOW CANADA, INC., 4 Woodthorpe Rd., Toronto Ontario M4A 1S4 **Canada**. (416)759-5424. Artistic Director: Julia Iacono. Opera company. Estab. 1989. Dedicated to producing 20th century opera/music theater. Artists are professionals. Performs 2 productions/year including 1 new work. "Very mixed audience—theater, dance, opera." Performs in "300 seat intimate theater with large stage." Pay is negotiable.
How to Contact: Query first. Does not return material. Reports in 2 months.
Music: "Sophisticated music in modern classical idioms which are accessible to a broad audience. One-act to three act operatic pieces. Casting—no more than 5 characters. Orchestration—nothing greater than 12 instruments." Does not wish to see "anything that is too avant-garde or esoteric."
Performances: Dominick Argento's *A Waterbird Talk* and *The Boor* (chamber opera); and Menotti's *The Consul* (chamber opera).
Tips: "I wish more opera composers would use famous '40s and '50s movies as a basis for their operas. This is so helpful in perking the interest of the public—familiar titles and familiar subjects really help publicity. Please write lyrical, beautiful music for the voice. Please write about exciting and dramatic things that hold the interest of the audience."

ORCHESTRA SEATTLE/SEATTLE CHAMBER SINGERS, 1305 Fourth Ave. #402, Seattle WA 98101. (206)682-5208. Fax: (206)628-3758. Managing Director: Dan Petersen. Symphony orchestra, chamber music ensemble and community chorus. Estab. 1969. Members are amateurs and professionals. Performs 8 concerts/year including 2 new works. Commissions 1-2 composers or new works/year. "Our audience is made up of both experienced and novice classical music patrons. The median age is 45 with an equal number of males and females in the upper income range. OS/SCS performs in a variety of locations to suit the composition and reach the broadest audience possible." Pays for outright purchase.
How to Contact: Query first. SASE. Reports in 6-12 months.
Performances: Frank Becker's *Five Canticles for Chorus and Orchestra*; Huntley Beyer's *Romantic Lines* and *The Passion According to St. Mark*.

OREGON SYMPHONY, 711 SW Alder, Portland OR 97205. (503)228-4294. Orchestra Manager: Peggie Schwarz. Symphony orchestra. Estab. 1896. Members are professionals. Performs 125 concerts/year including 3 new works. Commissions varying number of new works. "Classical concerts are attended predominantly by 35-60 year olds. Hall seats 2,776—renovated vaudeville house." Pay is negotiable.
How to Contact: Submit complete score and tapes of piece(s). SASE. Reports in 2 months.
Music: "Classical 10-20 min.: 3333-5331 3 perc, 1 tmp, 1 harp, 1 keyboard, strings: 16-14-12-10-8; pops, jazz: same, except strings 12-10-8-6-4. No country. Send a list of other orchestras with whom you have performed."
Performances: Primous Fountain III's *Symphony No. 1*; Hale Smith's *Innerflexions*; and Robert Rodriguez's *A Gathering of Angels*.

PACIFIC CHORALE, 1221 E. Dyer Rd., Suite 230, Santa Ana CA 92705. (714)662-2345. Fax: (714)662-2395. Artistic Director: John Alexander. Semi-professional, independent chorus. Estab. 1967.

Members are both professionals and amateurs. Performs 12-15 concerts/year including 10 new works. "Our audience includes all ages in the 3,000-seat Orange County Performing Arts Center in Costa Mesa." Pay is negotiable.

How to Contact: Submit complete score and tape of piece(s) if available. SASE. Reports in 6 months.

Music: "We seek a cappella pieces of any length. Voicings may be SSAA, TTBB, or SATB. We also want major choral works with orchestration for full symphony using significant texts—length may vary from 10-45 minutes. Music should be suitable for an SATB chorus of 180 (equal numbers men/women). No limit on difficulty."

Performances: Stephen Paulus' *Voices* (choral/orchestral secular); Dominic Argento's *Te Deum* (choral/orchestral); and Libby Larsen's *The Settling Years* ("Coplandesque" chamber work).

PICCOLO OPERA COMPANY, 24 Del Rio Blvd., Boca Raton FL 33432-4737. (800)282-3161. Executive Director: Marjorie Gordon. Opera company. Estab. 1962. Members are professionals. Performs 1-50 concerts/year including 1-2 new works. Commissions 1 composer or new work/year. Operas are performed for a mixed audience of children and adults. Pays by performance or outright purchase.

How to Contact: Query first and submit complete score and tape of piece(s). SASE.

Music: "Musical theater pieces, lasting about one hour, for adults to perform for adults and/or youngsters. Performers are mature singers with experience. The cast should have few performers (up to 10), no chorus or ballet, accompanied by piano or orchestra. Skeletal scenery. All in English."

Performances: *Hansel & Gretel; Cosi Fan Tutte;* and *Die Fledermaus.*

*PRINCETON CHAMBER SYMPHONY, P.O. Box 250, Princeton NJ 08542. (609)497-0020. (609)924-3935. Music Director: Mark Laycock. Symphony orchestra. Estab. 1980. Members are professionals. Performs 6-10 concerts/year including some new works. Commissions 1 composer or new work/year. Performs in a "beautiful, intimate 800-seat hall with amazing sound." Pays by arrangement.

How to Contact: Submit through agent only. SASE. Reports in 6 months.

Music: "Orchestra usually numbers 40-60 individuals."

PRISM SAXOPHONE QUARTET, 257 Harvey St., Philadelphia PA 19144. (215)438-5282. President, New Sounds Music Inc. Prism Quartet: Matthew Levy. Chamber music ensemble. Estab. 1984. Members are professionals. Performs 80 concerts/year including 10-15 new works. Commissions 5 composers or new works/year. "Ours are primarily traditional chamber music audiences." Pays royalty per performance from BMI or ASCAP or commission range from $100 to $15,000.

How to Contact: Submit complete score (with parts) and tape of piece(s). Does not return material. Reports in 3 months.

Music: "Orchestration—sax quartet, SATB. Lengths—5-60 minutes. Styles—contemporary, classical, jazz, crossover, ethnic, gospel, avant-garde. No limitations on level of difficulty. No more than 4 performers (SATB sax quartet). No transcriptions. The Prism Quartet places special emphasis on crossover works which integrate a variety of musical styles."

Performances: Franch Amsallem's *The Farewell* (jazz); Bradford Ellis's *Tooka-Ood Zasch* (ethnic-world music); and William Albright's *Fantasy Etudes* (contemporary classical).

QUEENS OPERA, P.O. Box 140066, Brooklyn NY 11214. (908)390-9472. General Director: Joe Messina. Opera company. Estab. 1961. Members are professionals. Performs 9 concerts/year including 1 new work.

How to Contact: SASE. Reports in 1 month.

Music: "Operatic scores and songs, small orchestra."

Performances: Rossini's *Il Barbiere di Siviglia;* Verdi's *Il Trovatore;* and Owen's *Tom Sawyer.*

RENO CHAMBER ORCHESTRA, P.O. Box 547, Reno NV 89504. (702)348-9413. Fax: (702)348-0643. Music Director: Vahe Khochayan. Chamber orchestra. Estab. 1974. Members are professionals. Performs 6-7 concerts/year including 1 new work every other year. Students and retirees are largest segment of audience. Nightingale concert hall, 615 seats with fine acoustics. Payment to be negotiated—depends if composer is also guest soloist.

How to Contact: Query first. Does not return material. Reports in 3 months.

Music: "Pieces of 10-15 minutes in length—can be longer if very accessible—for string orchestra or strings plus solo instrument, strings and winds. Preferably 35 players or less. Our professional orchestra can handle most anything." Not interested in stridently atonal compositions, pops, jazz.

Performances: Armin Schibler's *Concerto For Strings* (concerto); James Winn's *Concerto in E-flat Minor* (piano concerto); and Efrem Zimbalist Sr.'s *Suite in the Olden Style.*

Tips: "Take advantage of our strong viola and cello sections."

RIDGEWOOD SYMPHONY ORCHESTRA, P.O. Box 176, Ridgewood NJ 07451. (201)612-0118. Fax: (201)445-2762. Music Director: Dr. Sandra Dackow. Symphony orchestra. Estab. 1939.

Members are professionals and amateurs. Performs 6 concerts/year including 1-3 new works. Audience is "sophisticated." Performance space is 800-seat school auditorium. Payment varies.
How to Contact: Submit complete score and tape of piece(s). SASE. Reports in 3 months ("It depends on how busy we are.")
Music: "Symphonic works of various lengths and types which can be performed by a nonprofessional orchestra. We are flexible but would like to involve all of our players; very restrictive instrumentations do not suit our needs."
Performances: Paul W. Whear's *Fanfare for the Century*; Richard Lane's *Kaleidoscope Overture*; and Howard Hansen's *Rhythmic Variations on Two Ancient Hymns*.
Tips: "Please lay out rehearsal numbers/letters and rests according to phrases and other logical musical divisions rather than in groups of ten measures, etc., which is very unmusical, wastes time and causes a surprising number of problems. Also, please *do not* send a score written in concert pitch; use the usual transpositions so that the conductor sees what the players see. Rehearsal is much more effective this way. Cross cue all important solos; this helps in rehearsal where instruments may be missing."

ST. LOUIS CHAMBER CHORUS, P.O. Box 11558, Clayton MO 63105. (314)458-4343. Music Director: Philip Barnes. Vocal ensemble, chamber music ensemble. Estab. 1956. Members are professionals and amateurs. Performs 5-6 concerts/year including 5 new works. Commissions 1-3 new works/year. Performances take place at various auditoria noted for their excellent acoustics—churches, synagogues, schools and university halls. Pays by arrangement.
How to Contact: Query first. SASE. "Panel of 'readers' submit report to Artistic Director. Reports in 2-3 months. 'General Advice' leaflet available on request."
Music: "Only *a cappella* writing; no contemporary 'popular' works; historical editions welcomed. No improvisatory works. Our programs are tailored for specific acoustics—composers should indicate their preference."
Performances: Ronald Arnatt's *Music and Ceremonies* (commissioned partsong); Audrey Kooper Hammann's *Winter Celebration* (commissioned partsong); and Jon Leifs' *Requiem* (op.33b.).
Tips: "We only consider a cappella works which can be produced in five rehearsals. Therefore pieces of great complexity or duration are discouraged."

SALT LAKE SYMPHONIC CHOIR, P.O. Box 45, Salt Lake City UT 84110. (801)466-8701. Manager: Richard M. Taggart. Professional touring choir. Estab. 1949. Members are professionals and amateurs. Performs 3-15 concerts/year, including 1-3 new works. Commissions 1-3 new works or composers/year. "We tour throughout U.S. and Canada for community concert series, colleges and universities." Pay is negotiable.
How to Contact: Query first. Does not return material. Reports in 3-5 months.
Music: Seeking "4-8 part choral pieces for a 100-voice choir—from Bach to rock."
Performances: Howard Hanson's *Song of Democracy*.

SAN ANTONIO OPERA COMPANY, 10-100 Reunion Place, Suite 745, San Antonio TX 78216. (210)524-9665. Fax: (210)340-8019. President: Wilford Lee Stapp. Opera company. Estab. 1991. Members are professionals. Performs 6 events including 1 new work/year. High school and college level audiences. Performs at high school auditoriums and college stages. Pay is negotiable.
How to Contact: Query first. SASE. Reports in 5 weeks.
Music: "Currently our voices are tenor and soprano and string quartet (2 violins, viola and cello). Subject material should be appropriate for conservative high school. Can use one or both voices. Soprano range, tenor range (bass baritone range is also possible. Please write to consult)."
Performances: Alice Gomez's *Somewhere In Time* (wedding reception).

SAN FRANCISCO GIRLS CHORUS, P.O. Box 15397, San Francisco CA 94115-0397. (415)673-1511. Fax: (415)673-0639. Artistic Director: Dr. Sharon J. Paul. Vocal ensemble. Estab. 1978. Volunteer chorus with a core of paid professionals. Performs 8-10 concerts/year including 3-4 new works. Commissions 2-3 composers or new works/year. Concerts are performed for "choral/classical music lovers of all ages, plus family audiences; audiences interested in international repertoire. Season concerts are performed in a 900-seat church with excellent acoustics; one concert is performed in San Francisco's Davies Symphony Hall, a 2,800-seat state-of-the-art auditorium." Pay negotiable for outright purchase.
  • The San Francisco Girls Chorus was a featured guest performer on the San Francisco Symphony's recording of Carl Orff's *Carmina Burana*, which won a 1993 Grammy Award for best choral recording.
How to Contact: Submit complete score. SASE. Reports in 6 months.
Music: "Music for treble voices (SSAA); a cappella, piano accompaniment, or small orchestration; 3-10 minutes in length. Wide variety of styles; 45 singers; challenging music is encouraged."
Performances: Einojuhani Rautavaara's *Suite de Lorca*; Veljo Tormis' *Sügismaastikud (Autumn Landscapes)*; and József Karai's *Rhythmuse Gariali* (all a cappella).

Tips: "Choose excellent texts and write challenging and beautiful music! The San Francisco Girls Chorus has pioneered in establishing girls choral music as an art form in the United States. The Girls Chorus is praised for its 'stunning artistic standard' (*San Francisco Chronicle*) in performances in the San Francisco Bay Area on tour. SFGC's annual concert season showcases the organization's concert/touring ensembles, Chorissima and Virtuose, in performances of choral masterworks from around the world, commissioned works by contemporary composers, and 18th-century music from the Venetian Ospedali which SFGC has brought out of the archives and onto the concert stage. Chorissima and Virtuose tour through California with partial support provided by the California Arts Council Touring Program and have represented the U.S. and the City of San Francisco nationally and abroad. The choruses provide ensemble and solo singers for performances and recordings with the San Francisco Symphony and San Francisco Opera, Women's Philharmonic, and many other music ensembles. SFGC's discography includes music by Charles Davidson, Benjamin Britten, and a collection of Hungarian and American works for girls' voices."

SASKATOON SYMPHONY ORCHESTRA, P.O. Box 1361, Saskatoon, Saskatchewan S7K 3N9 **Canada**. (306)665-6414. Fax: (306)652-3364. Artistic Director: Dennis Simons. General Manager: Sigrid-Ann Thors. Symphony orchestra. Performs 20 full orchestra concerts/year including 3-4 new works.
How to Contact: Query first. Does not return material. Reports in 2-4 weeks.
Music: "We are a semi-professional orchestra with a full time core of ten artists-in-residence. Our season runs from September to May with classical concerts, chamber series and children's series."
Performances: Melissa Hui's *Inner Voices*; Stewart Grant's *Landscapes*; and David Scott's *Overture*.

*SAULT STE. MARIE SYMPHONY ORCHESTRA, 3128 Lakeshore Dr., Sault Ste. Marie MI 49783. (906)635-2265. Music Director: Dr. John Wilkinson. Symphony orchestra. Estab. 1972. Members are professionals and amateurs. Performs 8 full orchestra concerts/year including 1-2 new works. "Our audience is conservative. Our performance hall seats 964."
How to Contact: Query first. SASE.
Music: "We have traditional orchestra size 2222/4231/2, plus strings. String 88552. We want pieces of length (5-15 minutes) in approachable styles. We have 45-50 performers. Pieces should be of moderate difficulty (or less!). Engage the listener; make it playable."
Performances: Ridout-Quesnel's *Colas et Colinette* (light overture); S. Glick's *Elegy* (elegy); and J. Weinzweig's *The Red Ear of Corn* (ballet suite).

*SINGERS FORUM, 39 W. 19th St., New York NY 10011. (212)366-0541. Fax: (212)366-0546. Administrator: Denise Galon. Vocal school and presenting organization. Estab. 1978. Members are professionals and amateurs. Performs more than 50 concerts/year including 4 new works. Commissions 2 composers or new works/year. 75-seat performance space with varied audience. Pays through donations from patrons.
How to Contact: Query first. SASE. Reports in 2 months.
Music: "All popular music, art songs, full musicals and small operas with minimal orchestration. No rock. I'm always looking for works to fit our current voices, mainly new operas and musicals."
Performances: Maria Kildegaard and Valerie Osterwalder's *Angels Part I* (new music); *Women of a Certain Age Carrying On* (collection of women's music); and *Big Girls Don't Cry* (contemporary mixed cabaret).
Tips: "Think of the voice."

SINGING BOYS OF PENNSYLVANIA, P.O. Box 206, Wind Gap PA 18091. (610)759-6002. Director: K. Bernard Schade, Ed. D. Vocal ensemble. Estab. 1970. Members are professional children. Performs 100 concerts/year including 4-6 new works. "We attract general audiences: family, senior citizens, churches, concert associations, university concert series and schools." Pays $300-3,000 for outright purchase.
How to Contact: Query first. SASE. Reports in 3 months.
Music: "We want music for commercials, voices in the SSA or SSAA ranges, sacred works or arrangements of American folk music with accompaniment. Our range of voices are from G below middle C to A (13th above middle C). Reading ability of choir is good but works which require a lot of work with little possibility of more than one performance are of little value. We sing very few popular songs

---

MARKET CONDITIONS are constantly changing! If you're still using this book and it is 1998 or later, buy the newest edition of *Songwriter's Market* at your favorite bookstore or order directly from Writer's Digest Books.

except for special events. We perform music by composers who are well-known and works by living composers who are writing in traditional choral forms. Works which have a full orchestral score are of interest. The orchestration should be fairly light, so as not to cover the voices. Works for Christmas have more value than some other, since we perform with orchestras on an annual basis."

Performances: Don Locklair's *The Columbus Madrigals* (opera).

Tips: "It must be appropriate music and words for children. We do not deal in pop music. Folk music, classics and sacred are acceptable."

SOLI DEO GLORIA CANTORUM, 3402 Woolworth Ave., Omaha NE 68105. (402)341-9381. Music Director: Almeda Berkey. Professional choir. Estab. 1988. Members are professionals. Performs 5-7 concerts/year; several are new works. Commissions 1-2 new works/year. Performance space: "cathedral, symphony hall, smaller intimate recital halls as well." Payment is "dependent upon composition and composer."

How to Contact: Submit complete score and tape of piece(s). SASE. Reports in 1-2 months.

Music: "Generally a cappella compositions from very short to extended range (6-18 minutes) or multimovements. Concerts are of a formal length (approx. 75 minutes) with 5 rehearsals. Difficulty must be balanced within program in order to adequately prepare in a limited rehearsal time. 28 singers. Not seeking orchestral pieces, due to limited budget."

Performances: Jackson Berkey's *Native American Ambiances*; John Rutter's *Hymn to the Creator of Light*; and Arvo Part's *Magnificat*.

STAR WITHIN ENTERPRISES, 170 W. 73rd St., New York NY 10023. (212)873-9531. Artistic Director: David Leighton. Chamber music ensemble and chamber opera producers. Estab. 1994. Members are professionals. Performs 20 concerts including 5 new works/year. Commissions 2-3 new composers or new works/year. Diverse audience—classical music enthusiasts and avant-garde art scene. Spaces: 100-400 seat theaters, traditional and experimental. Pay is negotiable.

How to Contact: Submit complete score and tape of piece(s). SASE. Reports in 3-6 months.

Music: "Seeking innovative chamber opera and concert pieces for small-medium size groups, innovative use of synthesizers."

Performances: Wolfgang Fortner's *That Time* (music theater); George Crumb's *Ancient Voices of Children* (music theater); and Peter Maxwell Davis' *Martyrdom of St. Magnus* (chamber opera).

SUSQUEHANNA SYMPHONY ORCHESTRA, P.O. Box 485, Forest Hill MD 21050. (410)838-6465. Music Director: Sheldon Bair. Symphony orchestra. Estab. 1978. Members are amateurs. Performs 6 concerts/year including 2 new works. "We perform in 1 hall, 600 seats with fine acoustics. Our audience encompasses all ages."

How to Contact: Query first. SASE. Reports in 3-6 or more months.

Music: "We desire works for large orchestra any length, in a 'conservative 20th century' style. Seek fine music for large orchestra. We are a community orchestra, so the music must be within our grasp. Violin I to 7th position by step only; Violin II—stay within 5th position; English horn and harp are OK. Full orchestra pieces preferred."

Performances: William Grant Still's *Los Alnados de Espana* (orchestral); James McVoy's *Gulliver's Travels*; and Richard Yardumian's *To Mary in Heaven*.

TORONTO MENDELSSOHN CHOIR, 60 Simcoe St., Toronto, Ontario M5J 2H5 **Canada**. (416)598-0422. Manager: Ruth Kitchen. Vocal ensemble. Members are professionals and amateurs. Performs 25 concerts/year including 1-3 new works. "Most performances take place in Roy Thomson Hall. The audience is reasonably sophisticated, musically knowledgeable but with moderately conservative tastes." Pays by commission and ASCAP/SOCAN.

How to Contact: Query first or submit complete score and tapes of pieces. SASE. Reports in 6 months.

Music: All works must suit a large choir (180 voices) and standard orchestral forces or with some other not-too-exotic accompaniment. Length should be restricted to no longer than ½ of a nocturnal concert. The choir sings at a very professional level and can sight-read almost anything. "Works should fit naturally with the repertoire of a large choir which performs the standard choral orchestral repertoire."

Performances: Holman's *Jezebel*; Orff's *Catulli Carmina*; and Lambert's *Rio Grande*.

*TOURING CONCERT OPERA CO. INC., 228 E. 80th, New York NY 10021. (212)988-2542. Director: Anne DeFigols. Opera company. Estab. 1971. Members are professionals. Performs 30 concerts/year including 1 new work. Payment varies.

How to Contact: Submit complete score and tape of piece(s). Does not return material. Reporting time varies.

Music: "Operas or similar with small casts."
Tips: "We are a touring company which travels all over the world. Therefore, operas with casts that are not large and simple but effective sets are the most practical."

*TULSA OPERA INC., 1610 S. Boulder, Tulsa OK 74119-4479. (918)582-4035. Fax: (918)592-0380. Artistic Director: Carol I. Crawford. Opera company. Estab. 1948. Members are professionals. Performs 3 concerts/year including 1 new work. Commissions 1 composer or new work/year. "We have a contract with the Performing Arts Center. It holds approximately 2,300." Pays for outright purchase or by royalty (negotiable).
How to Contact: Query first. SASE. Reports in 2 months.
Music: "At the present time we are looking for new material for student operas. They need to be approximately 45-50 minutes in length, with piano accompaniment. For our main stage productions we use the Philharmonic Orchestra and our Artistic Director auditions our singers. Our student performances are sometimes done by young artists. The student materials need to be adapted for four to five singers. These young artists are usually just beginning their careers therefore they are limited in difficulty of the music. Our main stage artists are adept in doing more difficult roles and roles of the classic operas."
Performances: Seymour Barab's *Little Red Riding Hood* (children's 1-act opera).
Tips "Our Artistic Director is very open to ideas and materials. She is interested in new works to present for our opera season."

UNIVERSITY OF HOUSTON OPERA THEATRE, School of Music, Houston TX 77204-4893. (713)743-3162. Director of Opera: Buck Ross. Opera/music theater program. Members are professionals, amateurs and students. Performs 8-10 concerts/year including 1 new work. Performs in a proscenium theater which seats 1,100. Pit seats approximately 40 players. Audience covers wide spectrum, from first time opera-goers to very sophisticated." Pays by royalty.
How to Contact: Submit complete score and tapes of piece(s). SASE. Reports in 3 months.
Music: "We seek music that is feasible for high graduate level student singers. Chamber orchestras are very useful. No more than 2½ hours. No children's operas."
Performances: Mary Carol Warwick's *Twins* (opera); Robert Nelson's *Tickets, Please* (opera); and Robert Nelson's *A Room With A View.*

VANCOUVER YOUTH SYMPHONY ORCHESTRA SOCIETY, 3737 Oak St., #204, Vancouver, British Columbia V6H 2M4 **Canada**. Music Director: Arthur Polson. Youth orchestra. Estab. 1930. Members are amateurs. Performs 6-8 concerts/year. Performs in various venues from churches to major concert halls.
How to Contact: Query first. Does not return material.
Music: "The Senior Orchestra performs the standard symphony repertoire. Programs usually consist of an overture, a major symphony and perhaps a concerto or shorter work. The Christmas concert and tour programs are sometimes lighter works."
Performances: Victor Davies' *Dream Variations* (overture); Arthur Polson's *Peter & the Turkey*; and Glen Morley's *Christmas Overture.*

VENTUS MUSICUS, P.O. Box 141, Redlands CA 92373. (909)793-0513. Trumpet Player: Larry Johansen. Chamber music ensemble (organ/trumpet duo). Estab. 1978. Members are professionals. Performs 2-10 concerts/year including 1-4 new works (as available). Most performances done in churches. "Have paid $250/work."
How to Contact: Submit complete score. SASE. Reports in 4 months.
Music: "Most organ/trumpet material is church oriented (hymns, chants, stained glass, etc.); this is useful, but not mandatory—we play for college and A.G.O. Groups as well as church recital series. We are open to pretty much anything, except improvised jazz. We are interested in the composer's ideas, not ours. Go for it! And we'll try it."
Performances: O.D. Hall's *Crown Him*; Donald Grantham's *Ceremony*; and Daniel Pinknam's *Psalms.*
Tips: "Send a good piece and we'll try to perform it. We play in various situations—not all pieces work in all situations. Always looking for new stuff."

 THE ASTERISK before a listing indicates that the listing is new in this edition. New markets are often the most receptive to unsolicited submissions.

VIRGINIA OPERA, P.O. Box 2580, Norfolk VA 23501. (804)627-9545. Fax:(804)622-0058. Assistant Artistic Administrator: Jerome Shannon. General Director: Peter Mark. Opera company. Estab. 1974. Members are professionals. Performs 450 concerts/year. Concerts are performed for school children throughout Virginia, grades K-9 at the Harrison Opera House in Norfolk, and at public/private schools in Virginia. Pays for outright purchase or by royalty.
How to Contact: Submit complete score and tape of piece(s). SASE. Reports in 3 months.
Music: "Audience accessible style approximately 45 minutes in length. Limit cast list to three vocal artists of any combination. Accompanied by piano and/or keyboard. Works are performed before school children of all ages. Pieces must be age appropriate both aurally and dramatically. Musical styles are encouraged to be diverse, contemporary as well as traditional. Works are produced and presented with sets, costumes, etc." Limitations: "Three vocal performers (any combination). One keyboardist. Medium to difficult acceptable, but prefer easy to medium. Seeking only pieces which are suitable for presentation as part of an opera education program for Virginia Opera's education and outreach department. Subject matter must meet strict guidelines relative to Learning Objectives, etc. Musical idiom must be representative of current trends in opera, musical theater. Extreme dissonance, row systems not applicable to this environment."
Tips: "Theatricality is very important. New works should stimulate interest in musical theater as a legitimate art form for school children with no prior exposure to live theatrical entertainment. Composer should be willing to create a product which will find success within the educational system."

THE DALE WARLAND SINGERS, 119 N. Fourth St., Minneapolis MN 55401. (612)339-9707. Fax: (612)339-9826. Composer in Residence: Carol Barnett. Vocal ensemble. Estab. 1972. Members are professionals. Performs 20-25 concerts/year including 5-10 new works. Commissions 5 composers or new works/year. Performance spaces vary, including concert halls, high school/college auditoriums and churches. Pay varies, depending on published status, length, etc.
How to Contact: Submit complete score and tape of piece(s). SASE. Reports in 2-4 months.
Music: "A cappella or with small accompanying forces; texts primarily secular; works for concert choir or vocal jazz ensemble (a 'cabaret' subgroup); 5-15 minutes in length (semi-extended)." Does not wish to see "show choir material or gospel."
Performances: Brent Michael David's *Native American Suite*; Judith Lang Zaimont's *Miracle of Light—A Festival Piece*; and Jing Jing Luo's *An Huan—A Chinese Requiem*.
Tips: "Keep in mind that there will never be enough rehearsal time. Be clear and concise in notation, and write for the capabilities of the choral voice. We seek from our composers not only craft, but a certain 'magic' quality."

WESTMINSTER PRESBYTERIAN CHURCH, 724 Delaware Ave., Buffalo NY 14209-2294. (716)884-9437. Fax: (716)884-3450. Organist and Choirmaster: Thomas Swan. Vocal ensemble. Estab. 1976. Members are professionals and amateurs. Performs 10 concerts/year including 3 new works. Commissions 1 composer or new work/year. Performs in Kleinhans Music Hall (2,800) and church (1,000). Pays $1,500 for outright purchase.
How to Contact: Query first, or submit complete score. SASE. Reports in 2 months.
Music: Choral/orchestral-SATB, with or without soloists. A cappella SATB—sacred or secular. Chamber orchestra/choral. "My semi-professional church choir numbers 45."
Performances: Fred Thayer's *Gloria* (choral/orchestral SATB/soloist); Fred Thayer's *Three Motets* (a cappella); and Mack Wilberg's *Tres Cantus Laudeni* (SATB/large brass and percussion).
Tips: "Composers writing for the church should carefully consider text and instrumentation. Music written for a cappella singing is especially useful."

WHEATON SYMPHONY ORCHESTRA, 344 Spring Ave., Glen Ellyn IL 60137. (708)790-1430. Manager: Donald C. Mattison. Symphony orchestra. Estab. 1959. Members are professionals and amateurs. Performs 3 summer concerts/year including 1 new work. Pays $100/per performance.
How to Contact: Query first. SASE. Reports in 1 month.
Music: "This is a *good* amateur orchestra that wants pieces in a traditional idiom. Large scale works for orchestra only. No avant garde, 12-tone or atonal material. Pieces should be 20 minutes or less and must be prepared in 3 rehearsals. Instrumentation is woodwinds in 3s, full brass 4-3-3-1, 4-5 percussion and strings—maximum instrumentation only."
Performances: Jerry Bilik's *Aspects of Man* (4-section suite); Walton's *Variations on a Theme of Hindeminth's*; and Augusta Read Thomas' *A Crystal Planet*.

Resources

Organizations

Songwriter organizations are more than just groups of aspiring writers sitting around talking about their songs. Offering encouragement, instruction, contacts and feedback, a songwriting organization can help provide a songwriter with the skills needed in order to compete in today's music industry.

Most songwriter organizations are nonprofit groups with membership open to anyone interested in songwriting. They can be local groups with a membership of less than 100 people, or a large national organization with thousands of members from all over the country. Most of these organizations offer regular meetings of their membership and occasionally sponsor events such as seminars and workshops to which music industry people are invited—to talk about the business and perhaps listen to and critique demo tapes. If you are unable to locate an organization within an easy distance of your home (check bulletin boards at local music stores and your local newspaper), you may want to consider joining one of the national groups. These groups, based in New York, Los Angeles and Nashville, keep their members involved and informed through newsletters, magazines, regional workshops and large yearly conferences. They can help a writer who feels isolated in his hometown to keep up contacts and get his music heard in the major music centers.

Songwriting organizations can provide you with a myriad of opportunities, and the type of organization you choose to join depends on what you want to get out of it. Local groups can offer you a friendly, supportive environment where you can work on your songs and have them critiqued in a constructive way by other songwriters. They're also great places to meet collaborators, if you're looking for someone to write with in your hometown. Larger, national organizations can give you access to music business executives and other songwriters across the country.

In the following listings, organizations describe their purpose and activities. Before joining any organization, research carefully what they have to offer and how becoming a member will benefit you.

ACADEMY OF COUNTRY MUSIC, 6255 Sunset Blvd., #923, Hollywood CA 90028. (213)462-2351. Executive Director: Fran Boyd. Estab. 1964. Serves producers, artists, songwriters, talent buyers and others involved with the country music industry. Eligibility for professional members is limited to those individuals who derive some portion of their income directly from country music. Each member is classified by one of the following categories: artist/entertainer, club operator/employee, musician/trend leader, DJ, manager/booking agent, composer, music publisher, promotion, publications, radio, TV/motion picture, record company or affiliated (general). The purpose of ACM is to promote and enhance the image of country music. The Academy is involved year-round in activities important to the country music community. Some of these activities include charity fund-raisers, participation in country music seminars, talent contests, artist showcases, assistance to producers in placing country music on television and in motion pictures and backing legislation that benefits the interests of the country music community. The ACM is governed by directors and run by officers elected annually. Applications are accepted throughout the year. Membership is $60/year.

AMERICAN COMPOSERS FORUM, (formerly Minnesota Composers Forum), 332 Minnesota St., #E145, St. Paul MN 55101. (612)228-1407. Fax: (612)291-7978. E-mail: compfrm@maroon.t-

INSIDER REPORT

Regional workshops link songwriters with Nashville

As one of the world's largest songwriting organiza- tions, the Nashville Songwriters Association Inter- national (NSAI) has been devoted to educating songwriters about the craft of songwriting for al- most 30 years. With more than 4,500 members all over the world, ranging from up-and-coming writ- ers to professionals such as Susan Longacre, Hugh Prestwood, Pat Alger and Garth Brooks, NSAI of- fers its members guidance and information on the songwriting process through song evaluations, edu- cational seminars and conferences, and by lobbying for songwriter rights in Washington.

Jim Melko

NSAI reaches out to songwriters not living in Nashville through its regional workshops program. With more than 70 workshops in 33 states, as well as workshops in Germany, England and New Zealand, NSAI reaches far beyond the environs of Nashville.

Jim Melko, coordinator for the Dayton/Cincinnati workshop in Ohio, has been conducting his workshop for four years. He describes NSAI's goals as being more about the craft than the business of songwriting. "NSAI is not the place to develop your business connections," he says. "It's the place to develop your craft. If you're serious about being a songwriter, join NSAI. You'll find out what you're really worth, where your songs are, and learn that no matter how good you believe yourself to be as a writer, there's always something you can improve."

Melko sees NSAI's local workshops as great places for songwriters to begin developing new songs. "The workshops provide an environment for a writer to craft and improve upon a song before sending it in for NSAI's song evaluation service by mail," he says. "And unlike the NSAI service where you have to send in a complete song, you can bring in a lyric or a melody or a half-finished song to the workshop and get some good feedback." Song evaluations are one of the most valuable services NSAI has to offer, says Melko. "I constantly encourage the writers in my workshop to send their tapes in. The feedback one gets is incredible. You may not agree with what the critiquer says but he or she has at least pointed out an area for potential improvement."

Another benefit offered by local workshops is helping writers find collabora- tors. "If you can find somebody to write with, you've got somebody you can work with locally and who can provide additional support. In addition, local workshops are a way to test yourself against people in your area; you get immedi- ate feedback on a regular basis, and it provides you actual, regular instruction in the craft of songwriting. An enthusiastic workshop coordinator will support you and encourage you every step of the way."

When choosing a local workshop to join, Melko urges writers to "take a serious look at who the members are and whether they are there simply to find an audience who will appreciate them or whether they're really there to further their craft." With NSAI workshops, "everybody knows before they come to the workshop that we focus on well-crafted songwriting," Melko says. "The workshop's goal is to emphasize what it takes to turn your songs into commercial products and we assume that in coming to the meetings, a writer sincerely desires to improve his craft and can accept all types of feedback."

Melko's workshops, which meet twice a month, usually follow a set agenda. "The first hour is a lesson about the craft of songwriting." Then come the song evaluations, where members listen to each other's songs. "The first response to a song must always be positive. Criticisms should be constructive." Some workshops may take a different turn and feature a guest speaker. "Sometimes we'll bring in professional writers or have other guest speakers. Sometimes we'll have a taped session. NSAI tapes each monthly Nashville workshop guest speaker seminar held in Nashville. If the information's particularly applicable I'll play the tape or excerpts from it at our workshop meeting."

Melko also offers advice for someone wanting to start a workshop not affiliated with a larger organization. "Start with a core of sincere writers," he says. "It's important to offer them resource materials and encourage professionalism. Find a place to meet that's centrally located and has an atmosphere of professionalism." Many places such as church or civic organizations will not charge a fee for using their facilities. "Make sure your members are aware that they are competing with the music industry's top songwriters in getting their material heard. You should stress a sense of realism but also optimism.

"Any songwriting organization that gives you feedback on how to improve your song is better than nothing at all," Melko says, but he finds several advantages in belonging to a workshop associated with a national organization. "With NSAI, we get everything a local organization has plus we have the assistance of the national organization in bringing in speakers and being kept up to date with what's going on. The only difference is it might be more expensive to join a national organization. But NSAI allows members to attend a local workshop meeting once or twice before joining as a member."

Melko's advice to beginning songwriters? "Buy craft and business books and read them thoroughly to understand what you're getting into," he says. "Plan it out. Don't base your career on the idea that you're going to take off from where you are and get to the final stage all at once. Understand that it's the hardest, most frustrating thing you're ever going to do in your life." He sees his work as a volunteer NSAI coordinator as more a labor of love than anything else. "For me, I love teaching songwriting every bit as much as I love writing. It would mean almost as much to me if one of my writers were to be successful as it would for me to have that same success."

—*Cindy Laufenberg*

c.umn.edu. Website: http://www.umn.edu/nlhome/m111/compfrm. Contact: Larry Fuchsberg. Estab. 1973. "The American Composers Forum links communities with composers and performers, encouraging the making, playing and enjoying of new music. Building two-way relationships with artists and the public, the Forum develops programs that educate today's and tomorrow's audiences, energize composers' careers, stimulate entrepreneurship and collaboration, promote musical creativity, and serve as models for effective support for the arts. The Forum's members, more than a thousand strong, live in 45 states and 16 countries; membership is open to all."

AMERICAN MUSIC CENTER, INC., 30 W. 26th St., Suite 1001, New York NY 10010-2011. (212)366-5260. Fax: (212)366-5265. E-mail: center@amc.net. Website: http://www.amc.NET/AMC/. Executive Director: Nancy Clarke. Estab. 1939. For composers and performers. Members are American composers, performers, critics, publishers and others interested in contemporary concert music and jazz. Offers circulating library of contemporary music scores and advice on opportunities for composers and new music performers; disseminates information on American music. Purpose is to encourage the recognition and performance of contemporary American music. Members receive professional monthly "Opportunity Updates," eligibility for group health insurance and the right to vote in AMC elections. Members are eligible to apply to the Margaret Fairbank Jory Copying Assistance Program to support the copying of parts for premiere performances. Memebers are also eligible to link their artists' pages to the center's website.

AMERICAN SOCIETY OF COMPOSERS, AUTHORS AND PUBLISHERS (ASCAP), 1 Lincoln Plaza, New York NY 10023. (212)621-6000. Contact: Michael Kerker (Director, Musical Theatre/Cabaret), Ivan Alvarez (Latin Music) in New York office; or the following branch offices: Todd Brabec, Suite 300, 7920 Sunset Blvd., Los Angeles, CA 90046; Damon Booth, 2nd Floor, 3500 W. Hubbard St., Chicago, IL 60610; Connie Bradley, 2 Music Square W., Nashville, TN 37203, Michael Stack, 52 Haymarket, London SW1Y 4RP **England**. Members are songwriters, composers, lyricists and music publishers. Applicants must "have at least one song copyrighted for associate membership; have at least one song commercially available as sheet music, available on rental, commercially recorded, or performed in media licensed by the Society (e.g., performed in a nightclub or radio station) for full membership. ASCAP is a membership-owned, performing right licensing organization that licenses its members' nondramatic musical compositions for public performance and distributes the fees collected from such licensing to its members based on a scientific random sample survey of performances." Primary value is "as a clearinghouse, giving users a practical and economical bulk licensing system and its members a vehicle through which the many thousands of users can be licensed and the members paid royalties for the use of their material. All monies collected are distributed after deducting only the Society's cost of doing business."
Tips: "The Society sponsors a series of writers' workshops in Los Angeles, Nashville and New York open to members and nonmembers. Grants to composers available to members and nonmembers."

AMERICAN SONGWRITERS NETWORK, (formerly Alumni Songwriters Association), Dept ASA95, Box 15312, Boston MA 02215. E-mail: asn@tiac.net. Contact: Network Manager. Estab. 1995. Serves "professional level songwriters/composers with monthly tipsheet/newsletter. Songwriters/composers will use tipsheet/newsletter to pitch their songs to the most current listing of producers, A&R managers, record labels, entertainment attorneys and publishing companies. Any songwriter from any part of the country or world can be a member of this network. The purpose of this organization is to foster a better professional songwriting community by helping members to place their songs. Applications accepted year-round. Membership fee is $140.
Tips: "Please send SASE or e-mail for application form."

*ARKANSAS SONGWRITERS, 6817 Gingerbread, Little Rock AR 72204. (501)569-8889. President: Peggy Vining. Estab. 1979. Serves songwriters, musicians and lovers of music. Anyone interested may join. The purpose of this organization is to promote and encourage the art of songwriting. Offers competitions, instruction, lectures, newsletter, performance opportunities, social outings and workshops. Applications accepted year round. Membership fee is $15/year.
Tips: "We also contribute time, money and our energies to promoting our craft in other functions. Meetings are held on the first Tuesday of alternate months at 6:45 p.m."

ARTS MIDWEST, 528 Hennepin Ave., Suite 310, Minneapolis MN 55403. (612)341-0755. E-mail: bobbi@artsmidwest.org. Website: http://www.artswire.org/Artswire/artsmidwest/home.htm. Director of Funding Programs: Bobbi Kady. Estab. 1985. Serves composers, musicians, dancers, actors and visual artists. "Arts Midwest is a nonprofit arts organization which provides funding, training, and publications to artists and arts organizations in the Midwest. We are a resource for musicians, songwriters and other artists in the region which includes the states of Illinois, Indiana, Iowa, Michigan, Minnesota, North Dakota, Ohio, South Dakota and Wisconsin. Arts Midwest generates opportunities for artists and arts organizations, extending, enriching and complementing the programs and services of the member state arts agencies. Arts Midwest funding brings Midwest arts to Midwest audiences through funding programs like Meet The Composer/Midwest, Jazz Satellite Touring Fund and Performing Arts Touring Fund. We encourage performing artists to travel to stages and community centers throughout the Midwest. Our Jazz Master Awards honor outstanding life-long achievements as performers, educators and preservers of the jazz tradition deserve greater recognition. We also publish a free quarterly newsletter, *Midwest Jazz*; *Applause!*, an annual catalog of Midwest performing artists; and *Insights on Jazz*, a series of five informative booklets for jazz artists, presenters, and educators." Applications are accepted throughout the year; however, "there are specific deadline periods for all of our funding programs." Offers competitions, lectures, performance opportunities, fellowships, workshops, touring programs and newsletter.

ASSOCIATED MALE CHORUSES OF AMERICA, RR1, Box 106, Dunsford, Ontario K0M 1L0 **Canada**. Executive Secretary: William J. Bates. Estab. 1924. Serves musicians and male choruses of US and Canada. "Our members are people from all walks of life. Many of our directors and accompanists are professional musicians. Age ranges from high school students to members in their 70's and 80's. Potential members must be supportive of Male Chorus Singing. They do not have to belong to a chorus to join. We have both Associate and Affiliate memberships. Our purpose is to further the power of music, not only to entertain and instruct, but to uplift the spirit, arouse the finest instincts, and develop the soul of man. With so little male chorus music being written, we as a 1,500 member organization provide a vehicle for songwriters, so that the music can be performed." Offers competitions, instruction, lectures, library, newsletter, performance opportunities, social outings and workshops. Applications accepted year-round. Membership fees are Regular Members: $5; Affiliate Members: $10; Student Members: $2; Life Members: $125 (one time fee).

ATLANTIC CANADIAN COMPOSERS ASSOCIATION, 214 Jones St., Moncton, New Brunswick E1C 6K3 **Canada**. (506)388-4224. Member at Large: Richard Gibson. Estab. 1980. "Our membership consists of people who write 'serious' (as opposed to commercial, pop, jazz, industrial) music. An applicant must be resident in one of the four Atlantic Canadian provinces and must be able to demonstrate a fluency with a variety of genres of notated music. An applicant must be prepared to submit five completed scores." Offers performance opportunities. Applications accepted year round. Membership fee is 35 Canadian dollars.

AUSTIN SONGWRITERS GROUP, P.O. Box 2578, Austin TX 78768. (512)442-TUNE. Fax: (512)288-0793. President: Rob Carter. Estab. 1986. Serves all ages and all levels, from just beginning to advanced. Perspective members should have an interest in the field of songwriting, whether it be for profit or hobby. The main purpose of this organization is "to educate members in the craft and business of songwriting; to provide resources for growth and advancement in the area of songwriting; and to provide opportunities for performance and contact with the music industry." The primary benefit of membership to a songwriter is "exposure to music industry professionals, which increases contacts and furthers the songwriter's education in both craft and business aspects." Offers competitions, instruction, lectures, library, newsletter, performance opportunities, evaluation services, workshops and "contact with music industry professionals through special guest speakers at meetings, plus our yearly 'Summer Songwriters Series,' which includes instruction, song evaluations, and song pitching direct to those pros currently seeking material for their artists, publishing companies, etc." Applications accepted year round. $35 membership fee/year.
Tips: "Our newsletter is top-quality—packed with helpful information on all aspects of songwriting— craft, business, recording and producing tips, and industry networking opportunities. (Members also receive and are included in the ASG Directory, which aids networking among the membership.)"

*BERMUDA SONGWRITERS ASSOCIATION, P.O. Box 2857, Hamilton HM LX **Bermuda**. (441)291-1769. Fax: (441)234-0943. E-mail: rbassett@ibl.bm. President: Richard T. Bassett. Estab. 1995. "Ages range from 20 to approximately 60 years. Interest ranges from hobbyists to persons seeking publishing and record deals. Skill levels range from amateur to professional musician/recording artists. BSA is open to all writers at all skill levels. BSA's objectives are to provide local and international songwriting networking and collaborative opportunities and to provide education that will help develop songwriting skills through seminars and workshops. It was formed for the advancement of creative songwriting and to provide talent discovery opportunities for Bermuda-based songwriters." Offers lectures, performance opportunities, instruction, newsletter and workshops. Applications accepted year-round. Membership fee is $75/6 months, $150/full year.

THE BLACK ROCK COALITION, P.O. Box 1054, Cooper Station, New York NY 10276. (212)713-5097. E-mail: brc/ny@aol.com. Membership Manager: Joel Brockman. Estab. 1985. Serves musicians, songwriters—male and female ages 18-40 (average). Also engineers, entertainment attorneys and producers. Looking for members who are "mature and serious about music as an artist or activist willing to help fellow musicians. The BRC independently produces, promotes and distributes

Black alternative music acts as a collective and supportive voice for such musicians within the music and record business. The main purpose of this organization is to produce, promote and distribute the full spectrum of black music along with educating the public on what black music is." Offers instruction, newsletter, lectures, free seminars and workshops, monthly membership meeting, quarterly magazine, performing opportunities, evaluation services, business advice. Applications accepted year-round. Membership fee is $25 per individual/$100 per band.

*THE BOSTON SONGWRITERS WORKSHOP, 14 Skelton Rd., Burlington MA 01803. (617)499-6932. E-mail: elliott_a._jacobowitz@bcsmac.org. Executive Director: Elliott Jacobowitz. Estab. 1989. "The Boston Songwriters Workshop is made up of a very diverse group of people, ranging in age from late teens to people in their forties, fifties, and sixties. The interest areas are also diverse, running the gamut from folk, pop and rock to musical theater, jazz, R&B, dance, rap and classical. Skill levels within the group range from relative newcomers to established veterans that have had cuts and/or songs published. By virtue of group consensus, there are no eligibility requirements other than a serious desire to pursue one's songwriting ventures, and availability and interest in volunteering for the various activities required to run the organization. The purpose of the BSW is to establish a community of songwriters and composers within the greater Boston area, so that its members may better help each other to make further gains in their respective musical careers." Offers performance opportunities, instruction, newsletter, workshops and bi-weekly critique sessions. Applications accepted year-round. Full membership: $35/year; flyer (newsletter) membership: $17.50/year; guest (non-member) fees: $3/meeting.

BROADCAST MUSIC, INC. (BMI), 320 W. 57th St., New York NY 10019. (212)586-2000; 8730 Sunset Blvd., Los Angeles CA 90069, (310)659-9109; and 10 Music Square East, Nashville TN 37203, (615)291-6700. President and CEO: Frances W. Preston. Senior Vice President, Performing Rights: Del R. Bryant. Vice President, California: Rick Riccobono. Vice President, New York: Charlie Feldman. Vice President, Nashville: Roger Sovine. BMI is a performing rights organization representing over 160,000 songwriters, composers and music publishers in all genres of music, including pop, rock, country, R&B, rap, jazz, Latin, gospel and contemporary classical. "Applicants must have written a musical composition, alone or in collaboration with other writers, which is commercially published, recorded or otherwise likely to be performed." Purpose: BMI acts on behalf of its songwriters, composers and music publishers by insuring payment for performance of their works through the collection of licensing fees from radio stations, broadcast and cable TV stations, hotels, nightclubs, aerobics centers and other users of music. This income is distributed to the writers and publishers in the form of royalty payments, based on how the music is used. BMI also undertakes intensive lobbying efforts in Washington D.C. on behalf of its affiliates, seeking to protect their performing rights through the enactment of new legislation and enforcement of current copyright law. In addition, BMI helps aspiring songwriters develop their skills through various workshops, seminars and competitions it sponsors throughout the country. Applications accepted year round. There is no membership fee for songwriters; a one-time fee of $100 is required to affiliate a publishing company.

BROADWAY ON SUNSET, 10800 Hesby, Suite 9, North Hollywood CA 91601. (818)508-9270. Fax: (818)508-1806. E-mail: bosmt@aol.com. Website: http://members.aol.com/bosmt. Executive Director: Kevin Kaufman. Estab. 1981. Sponsored by the National Academy of Songwriters. Members are musical theater writers (composers, lyricists, librettists) at all skill levels. All styles of music and musicals accepted. Participants need to have access to the Los Angeles area to attend our programs. "We provide writers of new musicals with a structured development program that gives them a full understanding of the principles and standards of Broadway-level craft, and provides them with opportunities to test their material in front of an audience." Offers lectures, production opportunities, evaluation and consultation services, workshops and instruction. Co-produces full productions of developed original musicals in various local theaters. Applications accepted year round. No membership fee per se; writers pay nominal fees to participate in classes and workshops. Certain scholarships are available.

CANADA COUNCIL/CONSEIL DES ARTS DU CANADA, 350 Albert St., P.O. Box 1047, Ottawa, Ontario K1P 5V8 **Canada**. (613)566-4365 or (613)566-4366. Information Officers: Maria Martin and Lise Rochon. Estab. 1957. An independent agency that fosters and promotes the arts in Canada by providing grants and services to professional artists including songwriters and musicians. "Individual artists must be Canadian citizens or permanent residents of Canada, and must have completed basic training and/or have the recognition as professionals within their fields. The Canada Council offers grants to professional musicians to pursue their own personal and creative development. There are specific deadline dates for the various programs of assistance." Call or write for more details.

CANADIAN ACADEMY OF RECORDING ARTS & SCIENCES (CARAS), 124 Merton St., 3rd Floor, Toronto, Ontario M4S 2Z2 **Canada**. (416)485-3135. Fax: (416)485-4978. Executive Director: Daisy C. Falle. Membership is open to all employees (including support staff) in broadcasting and record companies, as well as producers, personal managers, recording artists, recording engineers, arrangers, composers, music publishers, album designers, promoters, talent and booking agents, record retailers, rack jobbers, distributors, recording studios and other music industry related professions (on approval). Applicants must be affliliated with the Canadian recording industry. Offers newsletter, Canadian artist record discount program, nomination and voting privileges for Juno Awards and discount tickets to Juno awards show. Also discount on trade magazines and complimentary Juno Awards CD. "CARAS strives to foster the development of the Canadian music and recording industries and to contribute toward higher artistic standards." Applications accepted year-round. Membership fee is $45/year. Applications accepted from individuals only, not from companies or organizations.

CANADIAN AMATEUR MUSICIANS/MUSICIENS AMATEURS DU CANADA (CAMMAC), 1751 Richardson, #2509, Montreal, Quebec H3K 1G6 **Canada**. (514)932-8755. Fax: (514)932-9811. Website: http://www.io.org/n cammac. Executive Director: Danièle Rhéaume. Estab. 1953. Serves amateur musicians of all ages and skill levels. "CAMMAC is a nonprofit organization that provides opportunities for amateur musicians of all ages and levels to develop their skills in a supportive and non-competitive environment, and to enjoy making music together. We provide contact with musicians of varying levels and interests—the perfect testing ground for any number of styles and challenges. We also offer a variety of musical workshops, including singing, playing and improvisation at our summer camp at Lake McDonald in the Laurentians." Offers performance opportunities, library, instruction, newsletter, workshops and summer camp (families and individuals). Applications accepted year-round. Regular membership fee is Adult: $35, Family: $50, Student and Senior: $20, Group $50 plus $2/member for library borrowing privileges.

CANADIAN COUNTRY MUSIC ASSOCIATION (CCMA), 3800 Steeles Ave. W., Suite 127, Woodbridge, Ontario L4L 4G9 **Canada**. (905)850-1144. Fax: (905)856-1633. Executive Director: Sheila Hamilton. Estab. 1976. Members are songwriters, musicians, producers, radio station personnel, managers, booking agents and others. Offers newsletter, workshops, performance opportunities and annual awards. "Through our newsletters and conventions we offer a means of meeting and associating with artists and others in the industry. During our workshops or seminars (Country Music Week), we include a songwriters' seminar. The CCMA is a federally chartered, nonprofit organization, dedicated to the promotion and development of Canadian country music throughout Canada and the world and to providing a unity of purpose for the Canadian country music industry." Send for application.

CENTRAL OREGON SONGWRITERS ASSOCIATION, 67055 Fryrear Rd., Bend OR 97701. (541)388-6985. President: Hal Worcester. Estab. 1993. "Our members range in age from their 20s into their 80s. Membership includes aspiring beginners, accomplished singer/songwriter performing artists and all in between. Anyone with an interest in songwriting (any style) is invited to and welcome at COSA. COSA is a nonprofit organization to promote, educate and motivate members in the skills of writing, marketing and improving their craft." Offers competitions, instruction, newsletter, lectures, library, workshops, performance opportunities, evaluation services and collaboration. Applications accepted year-round. Membership fee is $25.
Tips: "COSA enjoys a close association with other like associations, thereby increasing and expanding the benefits of association."

CHICAGO MUSIC ALLIANCE, 410 S. Michigan Ave., Suite 819, Chicago IL 60647. (312)987-9296. Fax: (312)987-1127. Executive Director: Matthew Brockmeier. Program Manager: Heidi Zwart. Estab. 1984. "Chicago Music Alliance is comprised of organizations and individuals involved in music of all styles at all levels of skill. Administrators, composers, students, performers, educators and others are members as well as groups from the smallest ensemble to full symphony orchestras. Ensembles should reside and perform in the Chicago area, as should individuals. Individuals across the country are CMA members, but they have a connection with Chicago in some way (want to stay in touch, are interested in moving to Chicago, their work is performed in Chicago, etc). Our mission is to celebrate and support all of the music produced in the Chicago area. As a service organization we are committed to meeting the needs of our members. We act as a center for the exchange of ideas and resources, maintain ties with the educational community, and develop programs to serve our members with their direct input. Our activities include workshops, radio broadcasts, events listings, music performance and merchandise discounts, and résumé/career counseling." Offers newsletter, lectures, workshops, performance opportunities, research and information finding services, information on auditions and competitions. Applications accepted year-round. Membership fee for individuals is $30. Fees for ensembles vary by budget size.

THE COLLEGE MUSIC SOCIETY, 202 W. Spruce St., Missoula MT 59802. (406)721-9616. Fax: (406)721-9419. E-mail: cms@music.org. Website: http://www.music.org. Estab. 1959. Serves college, university, and conservatory professors. CMS Publications, Inc. is the publications arm of The College Music Society. "It is dedicated to gathering, considering and disseminating ideas on the philosophy and practice of music as an integral part of higher education, and to developing and increasing communication among the various disciplines of music." The products and services offered by CMS Publications, Inc. which may be of interest to songwriters are outlined in a brochure that may be obtained by writing to the CMS. Offers journal, newsletter, lectures, workshops, performance opportunities, job listing service, directory of music faculty, mailing lists of music faculty. Applications accepted year-round. Membership fee is $60 (regular dues).

*COMPOSERS GUILD, 40 N. 100 West, Box 586, Farmington UT 84025. (801)451-2275. Resident: Ruth Gatrell. Estab. 1963. Serves all ages, including children. Musical skill varies from beginners to professionals. An interest in composing is the only requirement. The purpose of this organization is to "help composers in every way possible through classes, workshops and symposiums, concerts, composition contests and association with others of similar interests." Offers competitions, instruction, lectures, newsletter, performance opportunities, evaluation services and workshops. Applications accepted year-round. Membership fee is $25/year. Associate memberships for child, spouse, parent, grandchild or grandparent of member: $15. "Holds four concerts/year. January: Composer's Spectacular featuring contest winners; June: Farmington Composers Concert in the Park; July: Americana, Patriotic and American Scene compositions; and December: New Sounds for Christmas. Annual Composition Contest: Deadline August 31. Fees: Less than 7 minutes: $5/members, $15/non-dues-paying; 7 minutes or more, including multi-movement works: $10/members, $20/non-members. Comments from judges given on all compositions. Return of materials if mailers and postage furnished. Categories: Arrangements, Children's, Choral, Instrumental, Jazz/New Age, Keyboard, Orchestra/Band, Popular, Vocal Solo and Young Composer (18 or under on Aug. 31). Age groups: 16-18, 13-15, 10-12, 7-9, 6 or under. Awards in each category: First prize $100, 2nd prize $50, 3rd prize: $25. Best of Contest in lieu of 1st prize: $500. Honorable Mention and Best of Age Group awards also given."

CONNECTICUT SONGWRITERS ASSOCIATION, P.O. Box 1292, Glastonbury CT 06033. (860)659-8992. E-mail: wdpsongs@aol.com. Executive Director: Don Donegan. "We are an educational, nonprofit organization dedicated to improving the art and craft of original music. Founded in 1979 by Don Donegan, CSA has grown to over 250 active members and has become one of the best known songwriter's associations in the country. Membership in the CSA admits you to 12-18 seminars/workshops/song critique sessions per year at 5 locations throughout Connecticut. Out of state members may mail in songs for critique at our meetings. Noted professionals deal with all aspects of the craft and business of music including lyric writing, music theory, music technology, arrangement and production, legal and business aspects, performance techniques, song analysis and recording techniques. CSA also offers showcases and concerts which are open to the public and designed to give artists a venue for performing their original material for an attentive, listening audience. CSA benefits help local soup kitchens, group homes, hospice, world hunger, libraries, nature centers, community centers and more. CSA shows encompass ballads to bluegrass and Bach to rock. Our monthly newsletter, *Connecticut Songsmith*, offers free classified advertising for members, and has been edited and published by Bill Pere since 1980. Annual dues are $40; senior citizen and full time students $20; organizations $80. Memberships are tax-deductible as business expenses or as charitable contributions to the extent allowed by law."

COUNTRY MUSIC SHOWCASE INTERNATIONAL, INC., P.O. Box 368, Carlisle IA 50047. (515)989-3748. President: Harold L. Luick. Vice President: Barbara A. Luick. "We are a nonprofit, educational performing arts organization for songwriters, recording artists and entertainers. The organization showcases songwriters at different seminars and workshops held at the request of its members in many different states across the nation. It also showcases recording artists/entertainer members at many Fair Association showcases held across the United States. When a person becomes a member they receive a membership card, newsletters, an educational information packet (about songwriting/entertainment business), a question and answer service by mail or phone, a song evaluation and critique service, info on who's looking for song material, songwriters who are willing to collaborate, and songwriting contests. Members can submit 1 song per month for a critique. We offer good constructive criticism and honest opinions. We maintain that a songwriter, recording artist or entertainer should associate himself with professional people and educators that know more about the business of music than they do; otherwise, they cannot reach their musical goals." Supporting Songwriter membership donation is $40 per year and Supporting Recording Artist/Entertainer membership donation is $60/year; Supporting Band, Group or music related business membership donation is $100/year. For free information, brochure or membership application send SASE to the above address.

*CREATIVE ALLIANCE OF FLORIDA, P.O. Box 222306, Hollywood FL 33022. (954)920-5119. Fax: (954)962-9555. E-mail: mohawk6@aol.com. President: Rose Tucci. Membership Director: Lisa Hoffman. Estab. 1993. Membership consists of "a mixture of educators, students, performing artists, actors, managers, agents, club owners, publishers and performing rights organizations. Every facet of cultural arts." The only requirements are "a love, passion or interest in the worldwide entertainment community. We are a nonprofit organization whose vision is to become the ultimate network for resources and access in the cultural arts, music and entertainment community of Florida." Offers performance opportunities, library, newsletter, monthly picnics and other networking opportunities. Applications accepted year-round. Membership fee is $15 students; $20 individual; $50 performing artists; $100 organizations.

DALLAS SONGWRITERS ASSOCIATION, 7139 Azalea, Dallas TX 75230. (214)750-0916. E-mail: dashley@iadfw.net. President: Beverly Houston. Estab. 1988. Serves songwriters and lyricists of Dallas/Ft. Worth metroplex. Members are adults ages 18-65, Dallas/Ft. Worth area songwriters/ lyricists who aspire to be professionals. Purpose is to provide songwriters an opportunity to meet other songwriters, share information, find co-writers and support each other through group discussions at monthly meetings; to provide songwriters an opportunity to have their songs heard and critiqued by peers and professionals by playing cassettes and providing an open mike at monthly meetings and by offering contests judged by publishers; to provide songwriters opportunities to meet other music business professionals by inviting guest speakers to monthly meetings and the Dallas Songwriters Seminar (which will be held this year in November and feature industry professionals and songwriters from all over the country); and to provide songwriters opportunities to learn more about the craft of songwriting and the business of music by presenting mini-workshops at each monthly meeting. "We offer a chance for the songwriter to learn from peers and industry professionals and an opportunity to belong to a supportive group environment to encourage the individual to continue his/her songwriting endeavors." Offers competitions, field trips, instruction, lectures, newsletter, performance opportunities, social outings, workshops and seminars. "Our members are eligible to join the Southwest Community Credit Union and for discounts at several local music stores and seminars." Applications accepted year round. Membership fee is $35 US, $45 Foreign. When inquiring by phone, please leave complete mailing address and phone number where you can be reached day and night.

THE DRAMATISTS GUILD, INC., 234 W. 44th St., New York NY 10036. (212)398-9366. Executive Director: Richard Garmise. "Celebrating its 75th anniversary this year, The Dramatists Guild is the professional association of playwrights, composers and lyricists, with more than 6,000 members across the country. All theater writers, whether produced or not, are eligible for Associate membership ($75/year); those who are engaged in a drama-related field but are not a playwright are eligible for Subscribing membership ($50/year); students enrolled in writing degree programs at colleges or universities are eligible for Student membership ($35/year); writers who have been produced on Broadway, Off-Broadway or on the main stage of a resident theater are eligible for Active membership ($125/ year). The Guild offers its members the following activities and services: use of the Guild's contracts (including the Approved Production Contract for Broadway, the Off-Broadway contract, the LORT contract, the collaboration agreements for both musicals and drama, the 99 Seat Theatre Plan contract, the Small Theatre contract, commissioning agreements, and the Underlying Rights Agreements contract; advice on all theatrical contracts including Broadway, Off-Broadway, regional, showcase, Equity-waiver, dinner theater and collaboration contracts); a nationwide toll-free number for all members with business or contract questions or problems; advice and information on a wide spectrum of issues affecting writers; free and/or discounted ticket service; symposia led by experienced professionals in major cities nationwide; access to two health insurance programs and a group term life insurance plan; a reference library; a spacious and elegant meeting room which can accommodate up to 50 people for readings and auditions on a rental basis to members; and a Committee for Women. The Guild's publications are: *The Dramatists Guild Quarterly*, a journal containing articles on all aspects of the theater, an annual marketing directory with up-to-date information on agents, grants, producers, playwriting contests, conferences and workshops; and *The Dramatists Guild Newsletter*, issued 8 times a year, with announcements of all Guild activities and current information of interest to dramatists. Only subscribing members receive *The Dramatists Guild Quarterly*."

THE FOLK ALLIANCE, 1001 Connecticut Ave., NW, #501, Washington DC 20036. (202)835-3655. Fax: (202)835-3656. E-mail: fa@folk.org. Website: http://www.hidwater.com/folkalliance/. Contact: Phyliss Barney. Estab. 1989. Serves songwriters, musicians and folk music and dance organizations. Members are organizations and individuals involved in traditional and contemporary folk music and dance in the US and Canada. Members must be active in the field of folk music (singers/songwriters in any genre—blues, bluegrass, Celtic, Latino, old-time, etc.). The Folk Alliance serves members through education, advocacy, field development, professional development, networking and showcases. Offers newsletter, performance opportunities, social outings, workshops and "database of members, organizations, presenters, folk radio, etc." Applications accepted year round. Membership fee is $35/ year for individual (voting); $75-350/year for organizational. "The Folk Alliance hosts its annual conference in late February at different locations in the US and Canada. 1997 site: Toronto, Ontario; 1998: Memphis, TN; 1999: Albuquerque, NM. We *do not* offer songwriting contests. We are *not* a publisher—no demo tapes, please."

FORT BEND SONGWRITERS ASSOCIATION, P.O. Box 1273, Richmond TX 77406. (713)665-4676. Info line: 713-CONCERT (Access Code FBSA). Fax: (713)665-5576. Contact: Membership Director. Estab. 1991. Serves "any person, amateur or professional, interested in songwriting or music. Our members write pop, rock, country, rockabilly, gospel, R&B, children's music and musical plays." Open to all, regardless of geographic location or professional status. The FBSA provides its membership with help to perfect their songwriting crafts. The FBSA provides instruction for beginning writers and publishing and artist tips for the more accomplished writer. Offers competitions, field trips, instruction, lectures, newsletter, performance opportunities, workshops, mail-in critiques and collaboration opportunities. Applications accepted year-round. Membership fees are: Regular: $35; Renewals; $25; Family or Band: $45; Associate: $20; Business: $150; and Lifetime: $250. For more information send SASE.

THE GOOD ROAD NETWORK, 1201 First Ave. S., #304, Seattle WA 98134. (206)583-0838. Fax: (206)583-0842. E-mail: gdroad@aol.com. Website: http://www:GRN.net. Contact: Laura Freed. Estab. 1993. Serves "developing acts in the areas of modern rock, blues, heavy metal, AAA, alternative, country, C&W, rock, modern folk/acoustic and acid jazz/rap. The main purpose of this organization is to provide affordable resources to the music community for purposes of promotion, performance and distribution of innovative music. GRN is currently focusing on publishing guides and the 'Exposed!' television/Internet program."

GOSPEL MUSIC ASSOCIATION, 1205 Division St., Nashville TN 37203. (615)242-0303. E-mail: gmatoday@aol.com. Website: http://www.gospelmusic.org/. Membership Coordinator: Tim Marshall. Estab. 1964. Serves songwriters, musicians and anyone directly involved in or who supports gospel music. Professional members include advertising agencies, musicians, agents/managers, composers, retailers, music publishers, print and broadcast media, and other members of the recording industry. Associate members include supporters of gospel music and those whose involvement in the industry does not provide them with income. The primary purpose of the GMA is to promote the industry of gospel music, and provide professional development series for industry members. Offers library, newsletter, performance opportunities and workshops. Applications accepted year round. Membership fee is $50/year (professional) and $25/year (associate).

THE GUILD OF INTERNATIONAL SONGWRITERS & COMPOSERS, Sovereign House, 12 Trewartha Rd., Praa Sands, Penzance, Cornwall TR20 9ST **England**. Phone: (01736)762826. Fax: (01736)763328. Secretary: C.A. Jones. Serves songwriters, musicians, record companies, music publishers, etc. "Our members are amateur and professional songwriters and composers, musicians, publishers, studio owners and producers. Membership is open to all persons throughout the world of any age and ability, from amateur to professional. The Guild gives advice and services relating to the music industry. A free magazine is available upon request with an SAE or 3 IRC's. We provide contact information for artists, record companies, music publishers, industry organizations; free copyright service; *Songwriting & Composing Magazine*; and many additional free services." Applications accepted year round. Annual dues are £35 in the U.K.; £40 in E.E.C. countries; £40 overseas. (Subscriptions in pounds sterling only).

IMC TRENDSETTER, P.O. Box 201, Smyrna GA 30081. (770)432-2454. President: Tom Hodges. Estab. 1965. "Our members range from young to old, from interested listener to accomplished songwriter/performer. The IMC is a network sales organization dedicated to selling and promoting independent music product. We have international distributor set-up. Music is promoted via a radio program of pre-recorded tapes of artists. Our members help to promote and sell member tapes and CDs to friends, family and associates. Our goal is to create a mid-level market for the independent artist/songwriter. Songwriters will have new chances at release, as our independent artists finally have a market to sell their product. We are creating a 'middle class' in the music industry. More releases will translate into more songwriters being paid. Call or write for free information." Offers performance opportunities, newsletter and product distribution. Applications accepted year-round. Membership fee: $12/1st year (with free CD or cassette/album); $12 renewal.

INDEPENDENT COMPOSERS ASSOCIATION, P.O. Box 45134, Los Angeles CA 90045-5134. (310)828-3004. Fax: (310)829-5923. E-mail: drburt@aol.com. President: Burt Goldstein. Estab. 1978. "The ICA is a nonprofit arts organization suppporting new music in the Los Angeles area by sponsoring concerts, commissioning works, and providing information on grants and other opportunities to composers. Membership is open to all persons." Offers competitions, newsletter and performance opportunities. Applications accepted year-round. Membership fee is $35/year.

INDEPENDENT MUSIC ASSOCIATION, 10 Spruce Rd., Saddle River NJ 07458. (201)818-6789. Fax: (201)818-6996. President: Don Kulak. Estab. 1989. Serves independent record companies, distributors, musicians and songwriters. Members are those "serious about marketing their music."

The purpose of this organization is to market and distribute independently produced music. "We provide contact with record labels looking for new material as well as information on forming a record label and distributing your own material." Offers instruction, newsletter, workshops, CD and cassette manufacturing discounts, trade show representation, the IMA syndicated radio program and how-to books on marketing and distribution. Applications accepted year round. Membership fee: $85/year.

THE INDIANAPOLIS SONGWRITERS ASSOCIATION, INC., P.O. Box 44724, Indianapolis IN 46244-0724. (317)257-2046. President: Kathy Cancilla. Estab. 1983. Purpose is "to create an affiliation of serious-minded songwriters, promote the artistic value of the musical composition, the business of music and recognition for the songwriter and his craft." Sponsors quarterly newsletter, monthly meetings, periodic showcases and periodic seminars and workshops. "The monthly critiques are helpful for improving songwriting skills. The meetings offer opportunities to share information concerning publishing, demos, etc. Also offers discounts to recording studios and monthly tip sheets. In addition, it provides the opportunity for members to meet co-writers." Membership fee: $20/year.

INTERNATIONAL ALLIANCE FOR WOMEN IN MUSIC, George Washington University, Academic Center B144, Washington DC 20052. E-mail: reid@acuvax.acu.edu. Estab. 1975. Serves women composers of serious concert music. "Created in January 1995 through the uniting of the International Congress on Women in Music (ICWM), the American Women Composers (AWC) and the International League of Women Composers (ILWC), the IAWM is dedicated to fulfilling the purposes of the three organizations it unites, creating and expanding opportunities for women composers of serious music and documenting the contributions of women musicians, past, present and future. A coalition of professional composers, conductors, performers, musicologists, educators, librarians and lovers of music, men as well as women, the IAWM encourages the dissemination of music through its various projects, including publication of the IAWM Journal, the student Search for New Music, recording grants, broadcast series and the International Congresses on Women in Music. The IAWM has an electronic mailing list (send message "subscribe" to iawm-request@acuvax.acu.edu) and a web site archive (http://music.acu.edu/www/iawm/home.html). Annual dues are $40 for individuals; $25 for students and seniors; $75 for affiliates (organizations with affiliate board status) and $50 for institutions (libraries)."

INTERNATIONAL BLUEGRASS MUSIC ASSOCIATION (IBMA), 207 E. Second St., Owensboro KY 42303. (502)684-9025. Executive Director: Dan Hays. Estab. 1985. Serves songwriters, musicians and professionals in bluegrass music. "IBMA is a trade association composed of people and organizations involved professionally and semi-professionally in the bluegrass music industry, including performers, agents, songwriters, music publishers, promoters, print and broadcast media, local associations, recording manufacturers and distributors. Voting members must be currently or formerly involved in the bluegrass industry as full or part-time professionals. A songwriter attempting to become professionally involved in our field would be eligible. We promote the bluegrass music industry and unity within it. IBMA publishes bimonthly *International Bluegrass*, holds an annual trade show/convention during September in Owensboro, represents our field outside the bluegrass music community, and compiles and disseminates databases of bluegrass related resources and organizations. The primary value in this organization for a songwriter is having current information about the bluegrass music field and contacts with other songwriters, publishers, musicians, and record companies." Offers social outings, workshops, liability insurance, rental car discounts, consultation and databases of record companies, radio stations, press, organizations and gigs. Applications accepted year round. Membership fee for a non-voting patron $20/year; for an individual voting professional $40/year; for an organizational voting professional $110/year.

INTERNATIONAL SONGWRITERS ASSOCIATION LTD., 37b New Cavendish St., London WI **England**. (0171)486-5353. Membership Department: Anna M. Sinden. Serves songwriters and music publishers. "The ISA headquarters is in Limerick City, Ireland, and from there it provides its members with assessment services, copyright services, legal and other advisory services and an investigations service, plus a magazine for one yearly fee. Our members are songwriters in more than 50 countries worldwide, of all ages. There are no qualifications, but applicants under 18 are not accepted. We provide information and assistance to professional or semi-professional songwriters. Our publication, *Songwriter*, which was founded in 1967, features detailed exclusive interviews with songwriters and music publishers, as well as directory information of value to writers." Offers competitions, instruction, library and newsletter. Applications accepted year round. Membership fee for European writers is £19.95; for non-European writers, US $30.

*INTERNATIONAL SONGWRITERS CO-OP, 1719 West End Ave., Suite 214-E, Nashville TN 37203. (615)327-9977. Fax: (615)327-3408. E-mail: compuserve:go-songwriter. Director: Michael E. James. Estab. 1993. Serves all songwriters, 18-60 years old. Members must be music professionals. Offers instruction, newsletter, lectures, workshops, performance opportunities, evaluation services and

databank. Applications accepted year-round. Membership fee is $75/year.
Tips: "We are a grass roots organization for the education and advancement of the music professional world-wide, with members throughout the U.S., Canada and Europe."

KERRVILLE MUSIC FOUNDATION INC., P.O. Box 1466, Kerrville TX 78029-1466. (210)257-3600. Executive Director: Rod Kennedy. The Kerrville Music Foundation was "founded in 1975 for the recognition and promotion of original music and has awarded more than $27,000 to musicians over the last 24 years through open competitions designed to recognize and encourage excellence in songwriting. Annually, 32 new folk finalists are selected to sing their 2 songs entered and 6 new folk Award Winners receive $150 prize money each and are invited to share 20 minutes of their songs at the Kerrville Folk Festival with 1 or more selected to perform on the main stage the next year." Opportunities include: The New Folk Concerts for Emerging Songwriters at the Kerrville Folk Festival.

KNOXVILLE SONGWRITERS ASSOCIATION, P.O. Box 603, Knoxville TN 37901. Estab. 1982. Serves songwriters of all ages. "Some have been members since 1982, others are beginners. Members must be interested in learning the craft of songwriting. Not only a learning organization but a support group of songwriters who want to learn what to do with their song after it has been written. We open doors for aspiring writers. The primary benefit of membership is to supply information to the writer on how to write a song. Eight members have received major cuts." Offers video showcases, instruction, lectures, library, newsletter, performance opportunities, evaluation services and workshops. Applications accepted year-round. Membership fee is $40 per year ($30 for fulltime students and senior citizens).

THE LAS VEGAS SONGWRITERS ASSOCIATION, P.O. Box 42683, Las Vegas NV 89116-0683. (702)459-9107. President: Betty Kay Miller. Estab. 1980. "We are an educational, nonprofit organization dedicated to improving the art and craft of the songwriter. We offer quarterly newsletters, monthly information meetings, workshops three times a month and quarterly seminars with professionals in the music business." Dues are $20 per year. Members must be at least 18 years of age.

*LONG ISLAND SONGWRITERS ASSOCIATION, INC., P.O. Box 395, Holbrook NY 11741. (516)338-5154. Fax: (516)666-6478. President: Erwin Cochran. Estab. 1990. "For songwriters 21-60 years of age who are primarily interested in getting original compositions to publishers/artists. Many are professional but some need workshops, seminars and networking services. We have applicants from all over the nation and only require submission of 'good songs' of any type." The main purpose of this organization is "to assist members in marketing their work, to collect and disseminate information on issues affecting songwriters, and to promote communication among our members and enhance their professional competence." Offers competitions, newsletters, lectures, workshops and evaluation services. Applications accepted year-round. Membership fee is $52/year for services; $21/year for newsletter only.

*LOS ANGELES MUSIC NETWORK, P.O. Box 8934, Universal City CA 91618-8934. (818)769-6095. E-mail: lamnetwork@aol.com. Estab. 1988. "Ours is an association of record industry professionals, i.e., people who work at record companies, in publishing, management, entertainment law, etc. Members are ambitious and interested in advancing their careers. We prefer people who are employed full-time in some capacity in the record business, not so much singers and songwriters because there already exist so many organizations to meet and promote their needs. LAMN is an association created to promote career advancement, communication and continuing education among record industry professionals, and top executives. LAMN sponsors industry events and educational panels held bi-monthly at venues in the Hollywood area." Offers instruction, newsletter, lectures, seminars, record industry job listings. See our website for current job listings and a calendar of upcoming events at http://www.iuma.com/LAMN. Applications accepted year-round. Membership fee is $75.

THE LOS ANGELES SONGWRITERS SHOWCASE (LASS), now part of the National Academy of Songwriters. See their listing in this section.

LOUISIANA SONGWRITERS ASSOCIATION, P.O. Box 80425, Baton Rouge LA 70898-0425. (504)924-0804. Website: http://www.tyrell.net/~pvida.Chairman: Pete Cicero. Vice President of Membership: Martha Boutwell. Serves songwriters. "LSA has been organized to educate songwriters in all areas of their trade, and promote the art of songwriting in Louisiana. We are of course honored to have a growing number of songwriters from other states join LSA and fellowship with us. LSA membership is open to people interested in songwriting, regardless of age, musical ability, musical preference, ethnic background, etc. One of our goals is to work together as a group to establish a line of communication with industry professionals in order to develop a music center in our area of the country. LSA offers competitions, lectures, library, newsletter, directory, marketing, performance opportunities, workshops, discounts on various music related books and magazines, discounts on studio time, and we are developing a service manual that will contain information on music related topics, such as copyrighting, licensing, etc." Also offers regular showcases in Baton Rouge and New Orleans. General membership dues are $25/year.

*MANITOBA AUDIO RECORDING INDUSTRY ASSOCIATION (MARIA), 221B-100 Arthur St., Winnipeg Manitoba R3B 1H3 **Canada**. (204)942-8650. Fax: (204)956-5780. Executive Director: Gaylene Dempsey. Estab. 1987. Organization consists of "songwriters, producers, agents, musicians, managers, retailers, publicists, radio, talent buyers, media, record labels, etc. (no age limit, no skill level minimum). Must have interest in the future of Manitoba's sound recording industry." The main purpose of this organization is "to foster growth in all areas of Manitoba's sound recording industry." Offers newsletter, lectures, workshops, performance opportunities, evaluation services. Applications accepted year-round. Membership fee is $25 (Canadian funds).

*MEET THE COMPOSER, 2112 Broadway, Suite 505, New York NY 10023. (212)787-3601. Estab. 1974. "Meet the Composer serves all American composers working in all styles of music, at every career stage, through a variety of grant programs and information resources. A nonprofit organization, Meet The Composer raises money from foundations, corporations, individual patrons and government sources and designs programs that support all genres of music—from folk, ethnic, jazz, electronic, symphonic, and chamber to choral, music theater, opera and dance." This is not a membership organization. "Meet the Composer was founded in 1974 to foster the creation and performance of music by American composers and to broaden the audience for music of our time." Offers grant programs and information services. Deadlines vary for each grant program.

MEMPHIS SONGWRITERS' ASSOCIATION, 1494 Prescott St., Memphis TN 38111. (901)744-4121. Fax: (901)743-4987. President: David Edmaiston. Estab. 1973. "MSA is a nonprofit songwriters organization serving songwriters nationally. Our mission is to dedicate our services on a monthly basis to promote, advance, and help songwriters in the composition of music, lyrics and songs; to work for better conditions in our profession; and to secure and protect the rights of MSA songwriters. We offer a correspondence course for all members outside of Memphis. MSA provides a monthly Basic Lyric Writing Course for beginners with a focus on commercial songwriting. We also supply copyright forms, pitch sheets and a collaborator's guide. We offer critique sessions for advanced writers at our monthly meetings. We also have monthly jam sessions to encourage creativity, networking and co-writing. We host an annual songwriter's seminar and an annual songwriter's showcase, as well as a bi-monthly guest speaker series, which provide education, competition and entertainment for the songwriter. In addition, our members receive a monthly newsletter to keep them informed of MSA activities, demo services and opportunities in the songwriting field." Annual fee: $35.

MICHIGAN SONGWRITERS ASSOCIATION, 28935 Flanders Dr., Warren MI 48093. (810)831-1380. Estab. 1990. Serves songwriters, musicians, artists and beginners. "Members are from NY, IL, MI, OH, etc. with interests in country, pop, rock and R&B. The main purpose of this organization is to educate songwriters, artists and musicians in the business of music." MSA offers performance opportunities, evaluation services, instruction, quarterly newsletter and 3 workshops/year. Applications accepted year-round. Membership fee is $40/year. Newsletter subscription available for $15/year.
Tips: "Our purpose is to fully educate the songwriter to obtain his/her full success."

MIDWEST CHRISTIAN SONGWRITERS ASSOCIATION, 1715 Marty, Department 2130, Kansas City KS 66103. (913)384-3891. Director: Robert Thomas. Estab. 1994. "Our members range in age from 15 to 65. Some are high school students interested in the craft of songwriting. We also have some very good writers who have been published and have had songs released. Also we have several members who are artists. Anyone that is interested in the craft of Christian songwriting can join. Some of our members are from the United Kingdom, Germany, Ireland and Denmark. Our association is open to writers worldwide." The main purpose of this organization is "to give the writer a chance to get his music heard by the right people, the people who will listen." Offers competitions, newsletter, performance opportunities, evaluation services. Applications accepted year-round. Membership fee is $15/year.
Tips: "The Midwest Christian Songwriters Association has its own record label, Midwest Gospel Records. We have made lots of contacts with music publishers around the country that have given our members the OK to send them material."

MIDWESTERN SONGWRITERS ASSOCIATION, 238 Eldon Ave., Columbus OH 43204. (614)279-1892. President: Dean Martin. Estab. 1978. Serves songwriters. All interested songwriters are eligible—either amateur or professional residing in the midwestern region of US. Main purpose is the education of songwriters in the basics of their craft. Offers competitions, instruction, lectures, library, newsletter, monthly tip sheet, social outings and workshops. Applications accepted year-round. Membership fee is $20/year, pro-rated at $5 per calendar quarter (March, June, September, December).

Tips: "We do not refer songwriters to publishers or artists—we are strictly an educational organization."

*MINNESOTA ASSOCIATION OF SONGWRITERS, P.O. Box 581816, Minneapolis MN 55458. President: Joe Schreifels. "Includes a wide variety of members, ranging in age from 18 to 60; types of music are very diverse ranging from alternative rock to contemporary Christian; skill levels range from newcomers to songwriting to writers with published material and songs on CDs in various parts of the country. Main requirement is an interest in songwriting—although most members come from the Minneapolis-St. Paul area, others come in from surrounding cities and nearby Wisconsin. Some members are fulltime musicians, but most represent a wide variety of occupations. MAS is a nonprofit community of songwriters which informs, educates, inspires, and assists its members in the art and business of songwriting." Offers instruction, newsletter, lectures, library, workshops, performance opportunities, evaluation services, MAS compilation CDs and bimonthly meetings. Applications accepted year-round. Membership fee is $25.
Tips: "Through a monthly newsletter and announcements at bimonthly meetings, members are kept current on resources and opportunities. Original works are played at meetings and are critiqued by the group. Through this process, writers hone their skills and gain experience and confidence in submitting their works to others. Members vote to endorse the songs critiqued at meetings. The MAS assists writers of endorsed songs by selectively marketing the compositions and by providing access to an expanding pool of industry contacts."

MISSOURI SONGWRITERS ASSOCIATION, INC., 693 Green Forest Dr., Fenton MO 63026. (314)343-6661. President: John G. Nolan, Jr. Serves songwriters and musicians. No eligibility requirements. "The MSA (a non-profit organization founded in 1979) is a tremendously valuable resource for songwriting and music business information outside of the major music capitals. Only with the emphasis on education can the understanding of craft and the utilization of skill be fully realized and in turn become the foundation for the ultimate success of MSA members. Songwriters gain support from their fellow members when they join the MSA, and the organization provides 'strength in numbers' when approaching music industry professionals. As a means toward its goals the organization offers: (1) an extremely informative newsletter; (2) Annual Songwriting Contest; prizes include: CD and/or cassette release of winners, publishing contract, free musical merchandise and equipment, free recording studio time, plaque or certificate; (3) Annual St. Louis Original Music Celebration featuring live performances, recognition, showcase, radio simulcast, videotape for later broadcast and awards presentation; (4) seminars on such diverse topics as creativity, copyright law, brainstorming, publishing, recording the demo, craft and technique, songwriting business, collaborating, etc.; (5) workshops including song evaluation, establishing a relationship with publishers, hit song evaluations, the writer versus the writer/artist, the marriage of collaborators, the business side of songwriting, lyric craft, etc; (6) services such as collaborators referral, publisher contacts, consultation, recording discounts, musicians referral, library, etc. The Missouri Songwriters Association belongs to its members and what a member puts into the organization is returned dynamically in terms of information, education, recognition, support, camaraderie, contacts, tips, confidence, career development, friendships and professional growth." Applications accepted year round. Tax deductible dues are $50/year.

THE MUSIC NETWORK, 516 E. Front St., Traverse City MI 49686. (616)941-7868. Fax: (616)941-9577. E-mail: fcircle@gtii.com. Chairperson: Michael Curths/Kitty Gauss. Estab. 1993. Serves "all ages (currently 18-70), all interests (although we have currently mostly singer/songwriters) and all skill levels (novice to seasoned professionals). No special requirements needed—only a love of music and a desire to contribute ideas. The main purpose of this organization is to network with area musicians and songwriters, collaborate on material, sharpen musical and lyrical skills, and critique original songs from members." Offers newsletter, lectures, workshops, performance opportunities, evaluation services, jam sessions, guest artists and speakers, instrument clinics and new product seminars. Also offers CD replication and cassette duplication services at low prices. Call 1-800-341-7868. The Music Network's inhouse record label, Manitou Records, accepts unsolicited material. All styles accepted, with emphasis on folk, jazz and children's. Applications accepted year-round. Membership is $12/year.

*MUSICIANS CONTACT SERVICE, P.O. Box 788, Woodland Hills CA 91365. (818)347-8888. Estab. 1969. "A referral service for bands and musicians seeking each other. Job openings updated daily on 24-hour hotline. Bands and collaborators phone in to hear voice classified ads of available players, many with demo tapes."

NASHVILLE SONGWRITERS ASSOCIATION INTERNATIONAL (NSAI), 15 Music Square W., Nashville TN 37203. (615)256-3354. Executive Director: Carol Fox. Purpose: a not-for-profit service organization for both aspiring and professional songwriters in all fields of music. Membership: Spans the United States and several foreign countries. Songwriters may apply in one of four annual categories: Active ($70—for songwriters who have at least one song contractually signed to a publisher affiliated with ASCAP, BMI or SESAC); Associate ($70—for songwriters who are not yet published or for anyone wishing to support songwriters); Student ($35—for full-time college students or for students of an accredited senior high school); Professional ($100—for songwriters who derive their primary source of income from songwriting or who are generally recognized as such by the professional songwriting community). Membership benefits: music industry information and advice, song evaluations by mail, quarterly newsletter, access to industry professionals through weekly Nashville workshop and several annual events, regional workshops, use of office facilities, discounts on books and blank audio cassettes, discounts on NSAI's three annual instructional/awards events. There are also "branch" workshops of NSAI. Workshops must meet certain standards and are accountable to NSAI. Interested coordinators may apply to NSAI.

● For more information, see the interview with NSAI workshop coordinator Jim Melko in this section.

NATIONAL ACADEMY OF POPULAR MUSIC (NAPM), 30 W. 58th St., Suite 411, New York NY 10019-1827. (212)957-9230. Fax: (212)957-9227. Projects Director: Bob Leone. Estab. 1969. "The majority of our members are songwriters, but also on NAPM's rolls are music publishers, producers, record company executives, music attorneys, and lovers of popular music of all ages. Professional members are affiliated with ASCAP, BMI and/or SESAC; or are employed by music industry firms. Associate membership, however, merely requires a completed application and $25 dues. NAPM was formed to determine a variety of ways to celebrate the songwriter (e.g., induction into the Songwriters' Hall of Fame). We also provide educational and networking opportunities to our members through our workshop and showcase programs." Offers newsletter, workshops, performance opportunities and scholarships for excellence in songwriting. Applications accepted year-round. Membership fee is $25.
Tips: "Our priority at this time is to locate a site for the re-establishment of the Songwriters' Hall of Fame Museum in New York City."

NATIONAL ACADEMY OF SONGWRITERS (NAS), 6255 Sunset Blvd., Suite 1023, Hollywood CA 90028. (213)463-7178 or (800)826-7287. Executive Director: Brett W. Perkins. A nonprofit organization dedicated to the education and protection of songwriters. Estab. 1974. Offers group legal discount; toll free hotline; *SongTalk* newspaper with songwriter interviews; collaborators network and tipsheet; song evaluation workshops; song screening sessions; open mics; and more. Also produces the highly acclaimed "Acoustic Underground" Showcase, "Writers In The Round," "Noches Calientes" (Latin music), "A Hip-Hop Kinda Thang" (R&B/hip hop), "Nashville on Fairfax" (country), the annual "Songwriter's Expo" (international songwriters event) and the annual "Salute to the American Songwriter." "We offer services to all songwriter members from street-level to superstar: substantial discount on books and tapes, song evaluation through the mail, health insurance program and mail-in publisher pitches for members. Our services provide education in the craft and opportunities to market songs." Membership fees are $95 general; $125 professional; $200 gold.

*NATIONAL ASSOCIATION OF CHRISTIAN ARTISTS AND SONGWRITERS (NACAS), 200 Countryside Dr., Franklin TN 37069. (800)79-NACAS. Fax: (615)591-7408. E-mail: nacas@aol.com. President/Founder: Chuck Sugar. Executive Director: Bethany Harrell. Estab. 1990. "All ages and skill levels are welcome. You must be a Christian artist or songwriter." The main purpose of this organization is "to support Christian artists and songwriters by providing education, building relationships and offering exposure to the Christian music industry." Offers competitions, newsletter, lectures, workshops, evaluation services and internet activity. Applications accepted throughout the year. Fee: $25/year (individual), $45/year (groups).

THE NATIONAL ASSOCIATION OF COMPOSERS/USA, P.O. Box 49256, Barrington Station, Los Angeles CA 90049. (310)541-8213. President: Marshall Bialosky. Estab. 1932. Serves songwriters, musicians and classical composers. "We are of most value to the concert hall composer. Members are serious music composers of all ages and from all parts of the country, who have a real interest in composing, performing, and listening to modern concert hall music. The main purpose of our organization is to perform, publish, broadcast and write news about composers of serious concert hall music—mostly chamber and solo pieces. Composers may achieve national notice of their work through our newsletter and concerts, and the fairly rare feeling of supporting a non-commercial music enterprise dedicated to raising the musical and social position of the serious composer." Offers competitions, lectures, performance opportunities, library and newsletter. Applications accepted year round. $20 membership fee; $40 for Los Angeles and New York chapter members.
Tips: "99% of the money earned in music is earned, or so it seems, by popular songwriters who might feel they owe the art of music something, and this is one way they might help support that art. It's a chance to foster fraternal solidarity with their less prosperous, but wonderfully interesting classical

colleagues at a time when the very existence of serious art seems to be questioned by the general populace."

*NATIONAL DISC JOCKEY ASSOCIATION, P.O. Box 2888, San Diego CA 92112-2888. (619)531-0990. Executive Director: Bryan A. Rohrbach. Estab. 1994. "Our membership includes individuals and companies with an active interest in the disc jockey field as a profession, from high school and college students who are considering entering the field after graduation to individuals who are professional radio, club or mobile DJs. We also offer Associate memberships for companies who provide services in the music industry and carry a shared interest in advancing the field of professionalism of the individual DJ as a professional. The main purpose in founding our Association was to inspire excellence through education and advance the disc jockey profession overall. We encourage students and faculty members to apply. Professional disc jockeys are the driving force of our organization. NDJA is a nonprofit equal opportunity trade organization. We're dedicated to the field of education in all facets of the music industry. All members have access to the NDJA Scholarship Fund, which is supported by a portion of each members' dues being automatically directed to the Fund. Members receive many benefits including *Soundtrax* (our newsletter) and discounts to many services. We also have an International Referral Network, which is free for members." Offers newsletter, workshops and performance opportunities. Applications accepted year-round. Membership fee: Student/faculty $65/year; Affiliate (DJs) $150/year; Associate $200/year.

*NEW ENGLAND SONGWRITERS & MUSICIANS ASSOCIATION, Long Sands Rd., Center Ossipee NY 03814. (800)448-3621. Director: Peter C. Knickles. "Our organization serves all ages and all types of music. We focus primarily on networking opportunities, the business of songwriting and the music business. We have done various co-promotions of seminars with BMI and may continue to do so in the future. We are very open to and actively seeking individuals that are cheerfully driven to volunteer time into designing and administering any type of nonprofit programs, large and small, that would benefit our members. Funding and other resources are available for new programs. Membership is currently free. Call to be on our mailing list and receive a sample copy of *Basements To Backstage Magazine*.

NEW JERSEY AND PENNSYLVANIA SONGWRITERS ASSOC., 226 E. Lawnside Ave., Westmont NJ 08108. (609)858-3849. President and Founder: Bruce M. Weissberg. Estab. 1985. Serves songwriters and musicians. Members are ages 16-80, representing all types of music from Delaware, Philadelphia and North and South Jersey area. Must be serious about songwriting. Provides networking, information and promotional center for workshops and guest speakers. "Primary value is that it enables musicians to network with other songwriters in the area." Offers lectures, library, newsletter, performance opportunities and workshops. Applications accepted year round. Membership fee is $30/year (single), $35/year (band). "Our group is always interested in new ideas, new interested guest speakers and a true professional type of atmosphere."

NORTH FLORIDA CHRISTIAN MUSIC WRITERS ASSOCIATION, P.O. Box 61113, Jacksonville FL 32236. (904)786-2372. President: Jackie Hand. Estab. 1974. "People from all walks of life who promote Christian music—not just composers or performers, but anyone who wants to share today's message in song with the world. No age limit. Anyone interested in promoting Christian music is invited to join. If you are talented in several areas you might be asked to conduct a training session or workshop. Your expertise is wanted and needed by our group. The group's purpose is to serve God by using our God-given talents and abilities and to assist our fellow songwriters, getting their music in the best possible form to be ready for whatever door God chooses to open for them concerning their music. Members works are included in songbooks published by our organization—also biographies." Offers competitions, performance opportunities, field trips, instruction, newsletter, workshops and critiques. Applications accepted year-round. Membership fee is $15/year, $20 for husband/wife team. Make checks payable to Jackie Hand.
Tips: "If you are serious about your craft, you need fellowship with others who feel the same. A Christian songwriting organization is where you belong if you write Christian songs."

NORTHERN CALIFORNIA SONGWRITERS ASSOCIATION, 855 Oak Grove Ave., Suite 211, Menlo Park CA 94025. (415)327-8296. Fax: (415)327-0301, or (800)FORSONG (California and Nashville only). E-mail: ianncsa@aol.com. Executive Director: Ian Crombie. Serves songwriters and musicians. Estab. 1979. "Our 1,200 members are lyricists and composers from ages 16-80, from beginners to professional songwriters. No eligibility requirements. Our purpose is to provide the education and opportunities that will support our writers in creating and marketing outstanding songs. NCSA provides support and direction through local networking and input from Los Angeles and Nashville music industry leaders, as well as valuable marketing opportunities. Most songwriters need some form of collaboration, and by being a member they are exposed to other writers, ideas, critiquing, etc." Offers annual Northern California Songwriting Conference, "the largest event in northern California.

This 2-day event held in September features 16 seminars, 50 screening sessions (over 1,200 songs listened to by industry profesionals) and a sunset concert with hit songwriters performing their songs." Also offers monthly visits from major publishers, songwriting classes, seminars conducted by hit songwriters ("we sell audio tapes of our seminars—list of tapes available on request"), mail-in song-screening service for members who cannot attend due to time or location, a monthly newsletter, monthly performance opportunities and workshops. Applications accepted year round. Dues: $75/year; $30 extra for industry tipsheet (sent out on a quarterly basis).

Tips: "NCSA's functions draw local talent and nationally recognized names together. This is of a tremendous value to writers outside a major music center. We are developing a strong songwriting community in Northern California. We serve the San Jose, Monterey Bay, East Bay, San Francisco and Sacramento areas and we have the support of some outstanding writers and publishers from both Los Angeles and Nashville. They provide us with invaluable direction and inspiration."

OKLAHOMA SONGWRITERS & COMPOSERS ASSOCIATION, %Humanities Division, Rose State College, 6420 SE 15th St., Midwest City OK 73110. (405)949-9161. 24 hour info line: (405)949-2938. President: Ann Wilson. Estab. 1983. Serves songwriters and musicians, professional writers, amateur writers, college and university faculty, musicians, poets and others from labor force as well as retired individuals. "A nonprofit, all-volunteer organization sponsored by Rose State College and local music merchants. Providing educational and networking opportunities for songwriters, lyricists, composers and performing musicians. All styles of music. Each month we sponsor forums, open-mic nights, demo critiques and the *OSCA News*. Throughout the year we sponsor workshops, contests and original music showcases." Applications accepted year round. Membership fee is $25 for new members, $15 for renewal.

OPERA AMERICA, 1156 15th St., NW, Suite 810, Washington DC 20005-1704. (202)293-4466. Estab. 1970. Members are composers, musicians and opera/music theater producers. "OPERA America maintains an extensive library of reference books and domestic and foreign music periodicals, and the most comprehensive operatic archive in the United States. OPERA America draws on these unique resources to supply information to its members." Offers conferences. Publishes directories of opera/music theater companies in the US and Canada. Publishes directory of opera and musical performances world-wide and US. Applications accepted year round. Membership fee is on a sliding scale.

PACIFIC MUSIC INDUSTRY ASSOCIATION, 400-177 W. Seventh Ave., Vancouver, British Columbia V5Y 1L8 **Canada**. (604)873-1914. Fax: (604)876-4104. E-mail: ellie@pmia.org. Website: http://www.nextlevel.com. Executive Director: Ellie O'Day. Estab. 1990. Serves "mostly young adults and up from semi-pro to professional. Writers, composers, performers, publishers, engineers, producers, broadcasters, studios, retailers, manufacturers, managers, publicists, entertainment lawyers and accountants, etc. Must work in some area of music industry." The main purpose of this organization is "to promote B.C. music and music industry; stimulate activity in B.C industry; promote communication and address key issues." Offers competitions, newsletters, library and workshops. Applications accepted year-round. Membership fee is $40 Canadian.

Tips: "We also administer the Pacific Music/Fraser MacPherson Music Scholarship Fund for young B.C. instrumentalists (up to age 25). The fund awards $2,000 bursaries to further their music education."

PACIFIC NORTHWEST SONGWRITERS ASSOCIATION, Box 98564, Seattle WA 98198. (206)824-1568. "PNSA is a nonprofit organization, serving the songwriters of the Puget Sound area since 1977. Members have had songs recorded by national artists on singles, albums, videos and network television specials. Several have released their own albums and the group has done an album together. For only $35 per year, PNSA offers monthly workshops, a quarterly newsletter, free legal advice and direct contact with national artists, publishers, producers and record companies. New members are welcome and good times are guaranteed. And remember, the world always needs another great song!"

PACIFIC SONGWRITERS' ASSOCIATION (PSA), P.O. Box 15453, 349 W. Georgia St., Vancouver, British Columbia V6B-5B2 **Canada**. (604)876-SONG. Fax: (604)685-5844. Vice President: Terry Tarapacki. Estab. 1983. "Our organization mainly deals with emerging songwriters to semi-professional to professional. PSA is not geared for any specific style of music, we feel that songwriting should include all styles. Members range in age from 13-60 plus. PSA has no eligibility requirements. All we ask of a songwriter is that they are willing to learn, promote and have fun writing songs." The main purpose of this organization is to "assist, develop, encourage, promote, serve and support emerging and professional songwriters; and to enhance and elevate the art and state of songwriting." Offers newsletter, lectures, workshops, performance opportunities and evaluation services. Applications accepted year-round. Membership fee is $40 Canadian.

PITTSBURGH SONGWRITERS ASSOCIATION, 408 Greenside Ave., Canonsburg PA 15317. President: Deborah J. Berwyn. Estab. 1983. Serves songwriters. "Any age group is welcome. Current members are from mid-20s to mid-50s. All musical styles and interests are welcome. Country and pop predominate the current group; some instrumental, dance, rock and R&B also. Our organization wants to serve as a source of quality material for publishers and other industry professionals. We assist members in developing their songs. Also, we provide a support group for area songwriters, collaboration opportunities, instruction, lectures, library and social outings. Annual dues are $30. We have no initiation fee." Interested parties please contact membership coordinator: Roger Horne, 175 Melody Lane, Washington PA 15301.

POP RECORD RESEARCH, 10 Glen Ave., Norwalk CT 06850. Director: Gary Theroux. Estab. 1962. Serves songwriters, musicians, writers, researchers and media. "We maintain archives of materials relating to music, TV and film, with special emphasis on recorded music (the hits and hitmakers 1877-present): bios, photos, reviews, interviews, discographies, chart data, clippings, films, videos, etc." Offers library and clearinghouse for accurate promotion/publicity to biographers, writers, reviewers, the media. Offers programming, annotation and photo source for reissues or retrospective album collections on any artist (singers, songwriters, musicians, etc.), also music consultation services for film or television projects. "There is no charge to include publicity, promotional or biographical materials in our archives. Artists, writers, composers, performers, producers, labels and publicists are always invited to add or keep us on their publicity/promotion mailing list with career data, updates, new releases and reissues of recorded performances, etc. Fees are assessed only for reference use by researchers, writers, biographers, reviewers, etc. Songwriters and composers (or their publicists) should keep or put us on their publicity mailing lists to ensure that the information we supply others on their careers, accomplishments, etc. is accurate and up-to-date."

PORTLAND SONGWRITERS ASSOCIATION, 1920 N. Vancouver, Portland OR 97227. (503)727-9072. President: Steve Cahill. "The P.S.A. is a nonprofit organization dedicted to providing educational and networking opportunities for songwriters. All songwriters, lyricists, and musicians are welcome. The association offers a yearly national songwriting contest, monthly workshops, a Songwriters Showcase, weekly open mikes, discounted legal services and seminars by industry pros for all members and non-members. Our goal is to provide you with the knowledge and contacts you need to continue your growth as a songwriter and gain access to publishing, recording and related music markets. For more information please write or call."

RED RIVER SONGWRITERS ASSOCIATION, P.O. Box 412, Ft. Towson OK 74735. President: Dan Dee Beal. Estab. 1991. Members range from beginners to accomplished writers of all ages. Primarily country music. "The main purpose of this organization is to help songwriters get record cuts, obtain information and continually learn more about songwriting. Some of our members now have commercial releases and are getting U.S. and foreign radio airplay." Offers lectures, performance opportunities, library, evaluation services, instruction, newsletter and workshops. Also has recording studios available at reasonable rates—can make demos to full-production masters. Applications accepted year round. Membership fee is $10/(one-time fee); $2/month dues (voluntary).

RHODE ISLAND SONGWRITERS' ASSOCIATION (RISA), P.O. Box 1149, Providence RI 02901-1149. (401)245-6472. Co-Chairs: Jeff Olson and Steve Valentine. Founder: Mary Wheelan. Estab. 1993. "Membership consists of novice songwriters who may have only written a couple of songs and who may or may not perform to established regional artists/writers who have recordings, are published and perform regularly. The only eligibility requirement is an interest in the group and the group's goals. Non-writers are welcome as well." The main purpose is to "encourage, foster and conduct the art and craft of original musical and/or lyrical composition by educating and encouraging songwriters, and to provide opportunities for the performance of original compositions in the broadest geographical area possible." Offers instruction, newsletter, lectures, workshops, performance opportunities and evaluation services. Applications accepted year-round. Membership fee is $25 annually. "The group holds twice monthly critique sessions; twice monthly performer showcases (one performer featured) at a local coffeehouse; songwriter showcases (usually 6-8 performers); weekly open mikes; and a yearly songwriter festival called 'Hear In Rhode Island,' featuring approximately 50 acts, over two days. Group is also a member group of The North American Folk Alliance."

*SAN DIEGO SONGWRITERS GUILD, 3368 Governor Dr., Suite F-326, San Diego CA 92122. (619)225-2131. Secretary: Randy Fischer. President: Mark Hattersley. Estab. 1982. "Members range from their early 20's to senior citizens with a variety of skill levels. Several members perform and work full time in music. Many are published and have songs recorded. Some are getting major artist record cuts. Most members are from San Diego county. New writers are encouraged to participate and meet others. All musical styles are represented." The purpose of this organization is to "serve the needs of songwriters, especially helping them in the business and craft of songwriting through industry guest appearances." Offers competitions, newsletter, workshops, performance opportunities, in-person song pitches and evaluations by publishers, producers and A&R executives. Applications accepted year-round. Membership dues are $45.

Tips: "Members benefit most from participation in meetings and concerts. Generally, one major meeting held monthly on a Monday evening, at the Red Lion Hotel, Mission Valley, San Diego. Call for meeting details. Can join at meetings."

SAN FRANCISCO FOLK MUSIC CLUB, 885 Clayton, San Francisco CA 94117. (415)661-2217. Serves songwriters, musicians and anyone who enjoys folk music. "Our members range from age 2 to 80. The only requirement is that members enjoy, appreciate and be interested in sharing folk music. As a focal point for the San Francisco Bay Area folk music community, the SFFMC provides opportunities for people to get together to share folk music, and the newsletter *The Folknik* disseminates information. We publish 2 songs by our members an issue (6 times a year) in our newsletter, our meetings provide an opportunity to share new songs, and at our camp-outs there are almost always songwriter workshops." Offers library, newsletter, informal performance opportunities, annual free folk festival, social outings and workshops. Applications accepted year round. Membership fee is $5/year.

SESAC INC., 421 W. 54th St., New York NY 10019. (212)586-3450; 55 Music Square East, Nashville TN 37203. (615)320-0055. Website: http://sesac.com. President and Chief Operating Officer: Bill Velez. Serves writers and publishers in all types of music who have their works performed by radio, television, nightclubs, cable TV, etc. Purpose of organization is to collect and distribute performance royalties to all active affiliates. "Prospective affiliates are requested to present a demo tape of their works which is reviewed by our Screening Committee." For possible affiliation, call Nashville or New York for appointment.

SOCIETY OF COMPOSERS, AUTHORS AND MUSIC PUBLISHERS OF CANADA (SO-CAN), Head Office: 41 Valleybrook Dr., Don Mills, Ontario M3B 2S6 **Canada**. (416)445-8700, (800)55 SOCAN. Fax: (416)445-7108. General Manager: Michael Rock. The purpose of the society is to collect music user license fees and distribute performance royalties to composers, lyricists, authors and music publishers. The SOCAN catalogue is licensed by ASCAP, BMI and SESAC in the US.

SODRAC INC., Victoria Square, Suite 420, 759, Montreal, Quebec H2Y 2J7 **Canada**. (514)845-3268. Fax: (514)845-3401. E-mail: sodrac@login.net. Membership Department: George Vuotto. Estab. 1985. Serves those with an interest in songwriting and music publishing no matter what their age or skill level is. "Members must have written or published at least one musical work that has been reproduced on an audio (CD, cassettte, LP) or audio-visual support (TV, video). The main purpose of this organization is to administer the reproduction rights of its members: author/composers and publishers. The new member will benefit of a society working to secure his reproduction rights (mechanicals)." Applications accepted year-round. "There is no membership fee or annual dues. SODRAC retains a commission currently set at 10% for amounts collected in Canada and 5% for amounts collected abroad." SODRAC is the only Reproduction Rights Society in Canada where both songwriters and music publishers are represented, directly and equally.

THE SONGWRITERS ADVOCATE (TSA), 47 Maplehurst Rd., Rochester NY 14617. (716)266-0679. E-mail: jerrycme@aol.com. Director: Jerry Englerth. "TSA is a nonprofit educational organization that is striving to fulfill the needs of the songwriter. We offer opportunities for songwriters which include song evaluation workshops to help songwriters receive an objective critique of their craft. TSA evaluates tapes and lyric sheets via the mail. We do not measure success on a monetary scale, ever. It is the craft of songwriting that is the primary objective. If a songwriter can arm himself with knowledge about the craft and the business, it will increase his confidence and effectiveness in all his dealings. However, we feel that the songwriter should be willing to pay for professional help that will ultimately improve his craft and attitude." Membership dues are $10/year. Must be member to receive discounts or services provided.

SONGWRITERS & LYRICISTS CLUB, %Robert Makinson, Box 23304, Brooklyn NY 11202-0066. Director: Robert Makinson. Estab. 1984. Serves songwriters and lyricists. Gives information regarding songwriting: creation of songs, reality of market, collaboration, disc jockeys and other contacts. Only requirement is ability to write lyrics or melodies. Beginners are welcome. The primary benefits of membership for the songwriter are opportunities to collaborate and assistance with creative aspects and marketing of songs through publications and advice. Offers newsletter and assistance with lead sheets and demos. Songwriters & Lyricists Club Newsletter will be mailed semi-annually to members. Other publications, such as "Climbing the Songwriting Ladder" and "Roster of Songs by Members," are mailed to new members upon joining. Applications accepted year-round. Dues are $35/year, remit to Robert Makinson. Write with SASE for more information. "Plan and achieve realistic goals. If you have a great song, we'll make every effort to help promote it."

SONGWRITERS AND POETS CRITIQUE, 11599 Coontz Rd., Orient OH 43146. (614)877-1727. Founder/Publicity Director: Ellis Cordle. Estab. 1985. Serves songwriters, musicians, poets, lyricists and performers. Meets second and fourth Friday of every month to discuss club events and critique one another's work. Offers seminars and workshops with professionals in the music industry. Has established Nashville contacts. We critique mail-in submissions from long-distance members. We have over 200 members from the local area, 16 states, and Canada. "Our goal is to provide support, opportunity and community to anyone interested in creating songs or poetry." Applications are accepted year-round. Call or write (please include legal size SASE) for more information. Annual dues are $25.

SONGWRITERS ASSOCIATION OF WASHINGTON, 1413 K St. NW, 1st Floor, Washington DC 20005. (301)654-8434. President: Jordan Musen. Estab. 1979. "S.A.W. is a nonprofit organization committed to providing its members with the means to improve their songwriting skills, learn more about the music business and gain exposure in the industry. S.A.W. sponsors various events to achieve this goal, such as workshops, open mikes, song swaps, seminars, meetings, showcases and the Mid-Atlantic song contest. S.A.W. publishes *S.A.W. Notes*, a quarterly newsletter containing information on the music business, upcoming events around the country, tip sheets and provides free classifieds to its members. Joint membership is available with the Washington Area Music Association. For more information regarding membership write or call."

THE SONGWRITERS GUILD OF AMERICA, 1500 Harbor Blvd, Weehawken NJ 07087-6732. (201)867-7603. E-mail: songnews@aol.com. West Coast: Suite 317, 6430 Sunset Blvd., Hollywood CA 90028. (213)462-1108. Nashville: 1222 16th Ave. S., Nashville TN 37203. (615)329-1782. "The Songwriters Guild of America is the nation's largest, oldest, most respected and most experienced songwriters' association devoted exclusively to providing songwriters with the services, activities and protection they need to succeed in the business of music." President: George David Weiss. Executive Director: Lewis M. Bachman. National Projects Director: George Wurzbach. West Coast Regional Director: Aaron Meza. Nashville Regional Director: Debbie McClure. "A full member must be a published songwriter. An associate member is any unpublished songwriter with a desire to learn more about the business and craft of songwriting. The third class of membership comprises estates of deceased writers. The Guild contract is considered to be the best available in the industry, having the greatest number of built-in protections for the songwriter. The Guild's Royalty Collection Plan makes certain that prompt and accurate payments are made to writers. The ongoing Audit Program makes periodic checks of publishers' books. For the self-publisher, the Catalogue Administration Program (CAP) relieves a writer of the paperwork of publishing for a fee lower than the prevailing industry rates. The Copyright Renewal Service informs members a year in advance of a song's renewal date. Other services include workshops in New York and Los Angeles, free Ask-A-Pro rap sessions with industry pros, critique sessions, collaborator service and newsletters. In addition, the Guild reviews your songwriter contract on request (Guild or otherwise); fights to strengthen songwriters' rights and to increase writers' royalties by supporting legislation which directly affects copyright; offers a group medical and life insurance plan; issues news bulletins with essential information for songwriters; provides a songwriter collaboration service for younger writers; financially evaluates catalogues of copyrights in connection with possible sale and estate planning; operates an estates administration service; and maintains a nonprofit educational foundation (The Songwriters Guild Foundation)."

SONGWRITERS OF OKLAHOMA, P.O. Box 4121, Edmond OK 73083-4121. (405)348-6534. President: Harvey Derrick. Offers information on the music industry: reviews publishing/artist contracts, where and how to get demo tapes produced, presentation of material to publishers or record companies, royalties and copyrights. Also offers information on the craft of songwriting: co-writers, local songwriting organizations, a written critique of lyrics, songs and compositions on tapes as long as a SASE is provided for return of critique. A phone service is available to answer any questions writers, composers or artists may have. All of these services are provided at no cost; there is no membership fee.

SONGWRITERS OF WISCONSIN, P.O. Box 874, Neenah WI 54957-0874. (414)725-1609. E-mail: sowtoner@aol.com. Director: Tony Ansems. Estab. 1983. Serves songwriters. "Membership is open to songwriters writing all styles of music. Residency in Wisconsin is recommended but not required. Members are encouraged to bring tapes and lyric sheets of their songs to the meetings, but it is not required. We are striving to improve the craft of songwriting in Wisconsin. Living in Wisconsin, a songwriter would be close to any of the workshops and showcases offered each month at different towns. The primary value of membership for a songwriter is in sharing ideas with other songwriters, being critiqued and helping other songwriters." Offers competitions, field trips, instruction, lectures, newsletter, performance opportunities, social outings, workshops and critique sessions. Applications accepted year round. $15 subscription fee for newsletter.

Tips: "Songwriters of Wisconsin now offers four critique meetings each month. For information call: Fox Valley chapter, Dana Erlandson (414)435-9052; Milwaukee chapter, Joe Warren (414)475-0314; La Crosse chapter, Jeff Cozy (608)781-4391."

*SONGWRITERS' TELEPHONE SHOWCASE, 906 Sycamore Rd., Richmond TX 77469-9411. (713)342-2404. Estab. 1992. "Songwriters' Telephone Showcase is a song preview service for published songs and new unpublished works from songwriters. Anyone looking for songs can pick from our categorized catalog of lyrics and then preview the song over the telephone by using our automatic playback system that is operated by touch-tone buttons. Our system allows the caller to play back all or just a portion of a song. After the preview, if the caller is interested in contacting the songwriter, a message can be left on our recorder. Contact information will be supplied by mail. We extend an invitation to anyone (songwriters, publishers, artists) to call 1-800-769-0269 about prices and to request application forms."

*THE SONGWRITERS WORKSHOP, P.O. Box 238, Babylon NY 11702-0238. (516)969-0375. President: Sal Rainone. Estab. 1975. "Members are all ages (18 and up) with an interest in writing songs (music or lyrics) and production of demos and professional recordings." The main purpose of this organization is to help songwriters (and lyric writers) to perfect songs and introducing lyric writers to music writers to form collaborations. Assistance at no charge for copyright information, free evaluation of lyrics/music and lyrics and introduction to publishers. Offers newsletter, lectures, workshops, evaluation services and production of demo recordings. Applications accepted year-round. No dues required—only SASE for assistance.
Tips: "We have assisted many songwriters in perfecting and having songs accepted and recorded by publishers and record companies."

SOUTHWEST VIRGINIA SONGWRITERS ASSOCIATION, P.O. Box 698, Salem VA 24153. (703)864-7043. President: Sidney V. Crosswhite. Estab. 1981. 80 members—all ages—all levels—mainly country and gospel and rock but other musical interests too. "Prospective members are subject to approval by SVSA Board of Directors. The purpose of SVSA is to increase, broaden and expand the knowledge of each member and to support, better and further the progress and success of each member in songwriting and related fields of endeavor." Offers performance opportunities, evaluation services, instruction, newsletter, workshops, monthly meetings, monthly newsletter. Application accepted year-round. Membership fee is $15 one time fee (initiation); $12/year—due in January.

THE TENNESSEE SONGWRITERS INTERNATIONAL, P.O. Box 2664, Hendersonville TN 37077-2664. TSA Hotline: (615)969-5967. (615)824-4555. Executive Director: Jim Sylvis. Serves songwriters. "Our membership is open to all ages and consists of both novice and experienced professional songwriters. The only requirement for membership is a serious interest in the craft and business of songwriting. Our main purpose and function is to educate and assist the songwriter, both in the art/craft of songwriting and in the business of songwriting. In addition to education, we also provide an opportunity for camaraderie, support and encouragement, as well a chance to meet co-writers. We also critique each others' material and offer suggestions for improvement, if needed. We offer the following to our members: Informative monthly newsletters; 'Pro-Rap'—once or twice a month a key person from the music industry addresses our membership on their field of specialty. They may be writers, publishers, producers and sometimes even the recording artists themselves; 'Pitch-A-Pro'—we schedule a publisher, producer or artist who is currently looking for material to come to our meeting and listen to songs pitched by our members; Annual Awards Dinner—honoring the most accomplished of our TSAI membership during the past year; Tips—letting our members know who is recording and how to get their songs to the right people. Other activities—a TSAI summer picnic, parties throughout the year, and opportunities to participate in music industry-related charitable events, such as the annual Christmas For Kids, which the TSAI proudly supports." Applications accepted year round. Membership runs for one year from the date you join. Membership fee is $35/year.

TORONTO MUSICIANS' ASSOCIATION, 101 Thorncliffe Park Dr., Toronto Ontario M4H 1M2 **Canada**. (416)421-1020. Fax: (416)421-7011. Executive Assistant: Nancy. Estab. 1887. Serves musicians—*All* musical styles, background, areas of the industry. "Must provide two letters of recommendation from people within the music industry, and be a Canadian citizen (or show proof of immigrant status)." The purpose of this organization is "to unite musicians into one organization, in order that they may, individually and collectively, secure, maintain and profit from improved economic, working and artistic conditions." Offers newsletter. Applications accepted year-round. Membership fee is $235.

TREASURE COAST SONGWRITERS ASSN. (TCSA), P.O. Box 7066, Port St. Lucie FL 34985-7066. Co-Directors: George Boley and Bill Powers. Founder/Advisor: Judy Welden. Estab. 1993. A service organization for and about songwriters. Age range of members, 20-85; varying levels of ability, from beginning writer to professional writers with substantial catalogs, publishing track records, radio airplay and releases. General Members—no requirement except desire to write and learn. Professional Members—at least 1 commercially released song, or a substantial marketable catalog, but no commercial releases. Gold Members—at least 1 song on RIAA-certified gold release. Offers competitions, lectures, performance opportunities, evaluation services, instruction, newsletter, workshops and local radio airplay through station-sponsored contests. Applications accepted year round. Membership fee is $45 general, $60 professional, $100 gold. Those with financial hardship can work as volunteers to entitle them to membership (except for Gold status.)

TULSA SONGWRITERS ASSOCIATION, INC., P.O. Box 254, Tulsa OK 74101-0254. (918)665-3334. President: Jeff Johnson. Estab. 1983. Serves songwriters and musicians. Members are age 18-65 and have interests in all types of music. Main purpose of the organization is "to create a forum to educate, develop, improve, discover and encourage songwriting in the Tulsa area." Offers competitions, lectures, performance opportunities, field trips, social outings, instruction, newsletter and workshops. Applications accepted year-round. Dues are $30/year.
Tips: "We hold a monthly 'Writer's Night' open to the public for performance of original songs to expose the many talented writers in Tulsa."

UTAH SONGWRITERS ASSOCIATION (USA), P.O. Box 571325, Salt Lake City UT 84157. (801)596-3058. Secretary/Treasurer: Marie Vosgerau. Estab. 1984. "Anyone who is interested in songwriting may join. Primarily we want to promote the craft of songwriting. USA is a support group for songwriters. We distribute information; teach workshops on how to write better songs; showcase members original material. Provides song analyses, contest opportunities, seminars with professional music business people. The newsletter, *The Melody Line*, gives valuable information on contests, publishers looking for material, tips, etc. Workshops and showcases build confidence. Annual seminar with publishers, etc." Offers a songwriting contest, performance opportunities, evaluation services, instruction, newsletter, workshops. "For a copy of our book of songwriting tips, *Tricks of The Trade*, send $8." Applications accepted year-round. Membership fee is $25 per member/year or $30 for a family membership/year. For information send SASE.
Tips: "The USA exchanges newsletters with many songwriting associations across the United States. We welcome any exchange of ideas with other songwriting associations."

VERMONT SONGWRITERS ASSOCIATION, RD 2 Box 277, Underhill VT 05489. (802)899-3787. President: Bobby Hackney. Estab. 1991. "Membership open to anyone desiring a career in songwriting, or anyone who seeks a supportive group to encourage co-writing, meeting other songwriters, or to continue their songwriting endeavors." Purpose is to give songwriters an opportunity to meet industry professionals at monthly meetings and seminars, to have their works critiqued by peers and to help learn more about the craft and the complete business of songwriting. Offers competitions, instruction, lectures, library, newsletter, performance opportunities and workshops. Applications accepted year-round. Membership fee is $30/year.
Tips: "We are a nonprofit association dedicated to creating opportunities for songwriters. Even though our office address is Underhill, Vermont, our primary place of business is in Burlington, Vermont, where monthly meetings and seminars are held."

VICTORY MUSIC, P.O. Box 7515, Bonney Lake WA 98390. (206)863-6617. Estab. 1969. Serves songwriters, audiences and local acoustic musicians of all music styles. Victory Music provides places to play, showcases, opportunities to read about the business and other songwriters, referrals and seminars. Produced 5 albums of NW songwriters. Offers library, magazine, newsletter, performance opportunities, business workshops and music business books. Applications accepted year round. Membership fee is $20/year single; $50/year business; $28/year couple; $175 lifetime.

VOLUNTEER LAWYERS FOR THE ARTS, 1 E. 53rd St., 6th Floor, New York NY 10022. (212)319-2910 (Monday-Friday 9:30-4:30 EST). Estab. 1969. Serves songwriters, musicians and all performing, visual, literary and fine arts artists and groups. Offers legal assistance and representation to eligible individual artists and arts organizations who cannot afford private counsel. Also sells publications on arts-related issues. In addition, there are affiliates nationwide who assist local arts organizations and artists. Offers conferences, lectures, seminars and workshops. Call for information.
Tips: VLA now offers a monthly copyright seminar—"Copyright Basics," for songwriters and musicians as well as artists in other creative fields.

Workshops and Conferences

Conferences and workshops are great places for songwriters to discover exactly how marketable and viable their songs are in the competitive music industry. Conferences can provide opportunities for writers to have their songs evaluated, hear suggestions for further improvement and receive feedback from industry experts. They are also excellent places to make valuable industry contacts. Workshops can help a songwriter improve his craft and learn more about the business of songwriting. They may involve classes on songwriting and the business, as well as lectures and seminars by industry professionals.

Hundreds of workshops and conferences take place all over the country, from small regional workshops held in local churches to large national conferences such as South by Southwest in Austin, Texas, which hosts more than 5,000 industry people, songwriters and performers each year. Many songwriting organizations host workshops that offer instruction on just about every songwriting topic imaginable, from lyric writing and marketing strategy to contract negotiation. Conferences offer songwriters the chance to meet one on one with publishing and record company professionals as well as give performers the chance to showcase their work for a live audience (usually consisting of industry people) during the conference.

A workshop exists to address almost every type of music. There are programs for songwriters, performers, musical playwrights and much more. This section includes national and local workshops and conferences with a brief description of what each offers. Write or call any that interest you for further information.

APPEL FARM ARTS AND MUSIC FESTIVAL, P.O. Box 888, Elmer NJ 08318. (609)358-2472. E-mail: appelarts@aol.com. Website: http://www.ROWAN.edu/~APPEL. Artistic Director: Sean Timmons. Estab. Festival: 1989; Series: 1970. "Our annual open air festival is the highlight of our year-round Performing Arts Series which was established to bring high quality arts programs to the people of South Jersey. Festival includes acoustic and folk music, blues, etc." Past performers have included Randy Newman, Nanci Griffith, Shawn Colvin, Arlo Guthrie, Patty Larkin and John Gorka. Programs for songwriters and musicians include performance opportunities as part of Festival and Performing Arts Series. Programs for musical playwrights also include performance opportunities as part of Performing Arts Series. Festival is a one-day event held in June, and Performing Arts Series is held year-round. Both are held at the Appel Farm Arts and Music Center, a 176-acre farm in Southern New Jersey. Up to 20 songwriters/musicians participate in each event. Participants are songwriters, individual vocalists, bands, ensembles, vocal groups, composers, individual instrumentalists and dance/mime/movement. Participants are selected by demo tape submissions. Applicants should send a press packet, demonstration tape and biographical information. Application materials accepted year round. Faculty opportunities are available as part of residential Summer Arts Program for children, July/August.

*ARCADY MUSIC FESTIVAL, P.O. Box 780, Bar Harbor ME 04609. (207)288-3151. Executive Director: Dr. Melba Wilson. Estab. 1980. Promotes classical chamber music, chamber orchestra concerts, master classes and a youth competition in Maine. Offers programs for performers. Workshops take place year round in several towns in Eastern Maine. 30-50 professional, individual instrumentalists participate each year. Performers selected by invitation. "Sometimes we premiere new music by songwriters but usually at request of visiting musician."

ASH LAWN-HIGHLAND SUMMER FESTIVAL, Rt. 6, Box 37, Charlottesville VA 22902. (804)293-4500. General Manager: Judy Walker. Estab. 1978. Five Music At Twilight programs—classical or contemporary concerts. Opera series in repertoire with orchestra. Summer only. June, July and August. 12 songwriters/musicians participate in each festival. Participants are amateur and professional individual vocalists, ensembles, individual instrumentalists and orchestras. Participants are chosen by audition.

*ASPEN MUSIC FESTIVAL AND SCHOOL, 2 Music School Rd., Aspen CO 81611. (970)925-3254. Fax: (970)925-3802. E-mail: festival@aspenmusic.org. Website: http://www.csn.net/aspenmusic. Estab. 1949. Promotes classical music by offering programs for composers. Offers several other music programs as well. Master classes in composition offered 3 times/week. School and Festival run June to August in Aspen CO. Participants are amateur and professional composers, individual instrumentalists and ensembles. Send for application. Charges $2,000 for full 9 weeks, $1,350 for one of two 4½ week sessions. Advanced Master Class in composition offered 1st half session only. Scholarship assistance is available.

BMI-LEHMAN ENGEL MUSICAL THEATRE WORKSHOP, 320 W. 57th St., New York NY 10019. (212)830-2515. Website: http://bmi.com. Director of Musical Theatre: Norma Grossman. Estab. 1961. "BMI is a music licensing company, which collects royalties for affiliated writers. We have departments to help writers in jazz, concert, Latin, pop and musical theater writing." Offers programs "to musical theater composers and lyricists. The BMI-Lehman Engel Musical Theatre Workshops were formed in an effort to refresh and stimulate professional writers, as well as to encourage and develop new creative talent for the musical theater." Each workshop meets one afternoon a week for two hours at BMI, New York. Participants are professional songwriters, composers and playwrights. "BMI-Lehman Engel Musical Theatre Workshop Showcase presents the best of the workshop to producers, agents, record and publishing company execs, press and directors for possible option and production." Call for application. Tape and lyrics of 3 compositions required with application. "BMI nows sponsors a jazz composers workshop. For more information call Burt Korall at (212)586-2000."

BROADWAY TOMORROW PREVIEWS, % Broadway Tomorrow Musical Theatre, 191 Claremont Ave., Suite 53, New York NY 10027. Artistic Director: Elyse Curtis. Estab. 1983. Purpose is the enrichment of American theater by nurturing new musicals. Offers series in which composers living in New York City area present scores of their new musicals in concert. 2-3 composers/librettists/lyricists of same musical and 1 musical director/pianist participate. Participants are professional singers, composers and opera/musical theater writers. Submission by recommendation of past participants only. Submission is by audio cassette of music, script if completed, synopsis, cast breakdown, résumé, reviews, if any, acknowledgement postcard and SASE. Participants selected by screening of submissions. Programs are presented in fall and spring with possibility of full production of works presented in concert. No entry fee.

CANADIAN MUSIC WEEK, 5399 Eglinton Ave. W., Suite 301, Toronto Ontario M9C 5K6 **Canada**. (416)695-9236. Fax: (416)695-9239. President: Neill Dixon. Estab. 1985. Offers annual programs for songwriters, composers and performers. Event takes place mid-March in Toronto. 100,000 public, 400 bands and 1,200 delegates participate in each event. Participants are amateur and professional songwriters, vocalists, composers, bands and instrumentalists. Participants are selected by submitting demonstration tape. Send for application and more information. Concerts take place in 25 clubs and 5 concert halls, and 3 days of seminars and exhibits are provided. Fee: $375 (Canadian).

*CANADIAN MUSICIAN SEMINARS, 23 Hannover Dr., #7, St. Catharines, Ontario L2W 1A3 **Canada**. (905)641-3471. Fax: (905)641-1648. E-mail: mail@nor.com. Special Events Coordinator: Sue Grierson. Estab. 1980. Offers programs for songwriters, composers and performers. Offers programs year-round. Held in different locations across Canada and the US. 100-300 songwriters/musicians participate in each event. Participants are amateur and professional songwriters, composers, vocalists, bands and instrumentalists. Contact via phone, fax or e-mail. Fee varies. Offers workshops, roundtables, networking areas and demo critiques.

*CROSSROADS MUSIC EXPO, P.O. Box 41858, Memphis TN 38174-1858. (901)526-4280. Fax: (901)527-8326. E-mail: XroadsExpo@aol.com. Managing Director: Terron Shoemaker. Event Coordinator: Pam McGaha. Estab. 1990. "Crossroads' main purpose is to showcase unsigned music (rock, pop, alternative, country, gospel, singer/songwriter, etc.) to a host of industry executives and reps. In addition to showcasing over 200 acts, Crossroads offers panels, clinics, workshops and networking opportunities. Offers programs for songwriters and performers. Event takes place annually on historic Beale St. in Memphis, TN, in April. Call for dates. Approximately 200 bands are showcased. Participants are songwriters, vocalists, bands and instrumentalists. Participants are selected by demo tape audition. Send for application. Fee: $20.

CUTTING EDGE MUSIC BUSINESS CONFERENCE, 710 S. Broad St., New Orleans LA 70119. (504)827-5700. Fax: (504)827-1115. E-mail: 74777.754@compuserve.com. Website: http://www.satchmo.com/cuttingedge/. Director: Eric L. Coger. Estab. 1993. "The conference is a five-day international conference which covers the business and educational aspects of the music industry. As part of the conference, the New Works showcase features over 200 bands and artists from around the country and Canada in showcases of original music. All music genres are represented." Offers programs for songwriters and performers. "Bands and artists should submit material for consideration of entry into the New Works showcase." Event takes place late August, 1997, in New Orleans. 1,000 songwriters/musicians participate in each event. Participants are songwriters, vocalists and bands. Send for application. Deadline: June 1, 1997. Fee: $15. "The Music Business Institute offers a month-long series of free educational workshops for those involved in the music industry. The workshops take place each October."

PETER DAVIDSON'S WRITER'S SEMINAR, 12 Orchard Lane, Estherville IA 51334. Seminar Presenter: Peter Davidson. Estab. 1985. "Peter Davidson's Writer's Seminar is for persons interested in writing all sorts of materials, including songs. Emphasis is placed on developing salable ideas, locating potential markets for your work, copyrighting, etc. The seminar is not specifically for writers of songs, but is very valuable to them, nevertheless." Offers programs for songwriters and musical playwrights. Offers programs year-round. One-day seminar, 9:00 a.m.-4:00 p.m. Event takes place on various college campuses in Minnesota, Iowa, South Dakota, Nebraska, Kansas, Colorado and Wyoming. Up to one hundred songwriters/musicians participate in each event. Participants are both amateur and professional songwriters and musical playwrights. Anyone can participate. Send SASE for schedule. Deadline: day of the seminar. Fee: $40-59. "All seminars are held on college campuses in college facilities—various colleges sponsor and promote the seminars."

*DOING MUSIC & NOTHING ELSE: THE MUSIC BUSINESS WEEKEND SEMINAR, Music Business Seminars, Long Sands Rd., Center Ossipee NH 03814. (800)448-3621. Instructor: Peter C. Knickles. Estab. 1986. "This program has taught over 25,000 musicians, songwriters, and industry VIPs the true inner workings of the music business. Seminar is presented in 24 major cities each year. DM&NE is for all styles of music, bands and soloists who are pursuing a career in original music songwriting, recording, and performing. Topics include establishing the right goals, attracting a publishing or recording contract, booking profitable gigs, raising capital, and more. Opportunities for alumni include toll-free counseling with instructor, eligibility for A&R Bridge Charts, Inner Circle Cash Awards and lifetime subscription to *Basements To Backstage Magazine*. Seminar is also available on 16 audio tapes with workbook. Call to receive brochure with dates and locations.

FOLK ALLIANCE ANNUAL CONFERENCE, 1001 Connecticiut Ave. NW, #501, Washington DC 20036. (202)835-3655. Fax: (202)835-3656. E-mail: fa@folk.org. Website: http://www.hidwater. com/folkalliance/. Contact: Phyllis Barney. Estab. 1989. Conference/workshop topics change each year. Conference takes place mid-February and lasts 4 days at a different location each year. 1,000 amateur and professional musicians participate. Offers songwriter critique sessions. Artist showcase participants are songwriters, individual vocalists, bands, ensembles, vocal groups and individual instrumentalists. Participants are selected by demo tape submission. Applicants should write for application form. Closing date for application is May 31. Application fee $15 for members, $50 for non-members. Charges $75 on acceptance. Additional costs vary from year to year. For 1996 the cost was $165 in advance, which coverd 2 meals, a dance, workshops and showcase. Performers' housing is separate for the event, which is usually held in Convention hotel. 1997: Toronto, Ontario; 1998: Memphis, TN; 1999: Albuquerue, NM.

FOUNDATIONS FORUM, 1133 Broadway, #1220, New York NY 10010. (212)645-1360. Fax: (212)645-2607. E-mail: concrete@aol.com. Website: http://www.com/concrete.html. Vice President: Kevin Keenan. Estab. 1988. "We showcase unsigned/signed bands. The focus is on hard and alternative music. FF brings together the music community from around the world. We have have plenty of opportunities for unsigned artists to be involved through our CD compilation, directory and video channels." Offers programs annually. Event takes place in California. 4,000 songwriters/musicians participate in each event. Participants are both amateur and professional bands, industry/non-industry managers, booking agents, record company execs, just about every facet. Participants are selected by submitting demonstration tape (for unsigned stage). Call for information. Fee: registration for 3 days: $195. No fee for unsigned bands to submit tapes for showcase consideration. "There are music publishing workshops, as well as A&R and management panels."

ICEBREAKER, P.O. Box 2823, Minneapolis MN 55402. (612)341-1777. E-mail: mma@bitstream.net .mplf.mn.us. Event Producer: Lynne Bengtson. Estab. 1985. "A weekend of educational seminars, showcases and music events (including Minnesota Music Awards) that educate, promote and recognize musicians from Minnesota or with a Minnesota connection." Offers programs for songwriters, composers and performers. Offers programs annually. Event takes place second weekend in July in Minneapolis. Over 180 songwriters/musicians participate in each event. Participants are both amateur and professional songwriters, vocalists, composers, bands, instrumentalists, music critics, booking agents, managers and industry professionals. Participants are selected by submitting demo tape. Send for application. Fees vary per event; membership is $11/year. Deadline: February 1.

INDEPENDENT LABEL FESTIVAL, 600 S. Michigan Ave., Chicago IL 60605. (312)341-9112. E-mail: indiefest@aol.com. Executive Director: Leopoldo Lastre. Estab. 1993. An annual conference promoting all types of independent music. Offers programs for songwriters, composers and performers, such as seminars, workshops and showcases. Offers showcases year-round. "Workshops take place in the summer, generally July in downtown Chicago (usually in or around Columbia College)." Participants are professional songwriters, bands, composers, individual vocalists and instrumentalists, managers, promoters and professionals in the music industry. Participants are selected by demo tape audition or invitation. Call for submission and registration information. Closing date for submissions is March 29. Fee: $75 until March 29, $100 until May 10, $125 until June 14, $150 after July 1.

JAZZTIMES CONVENTION, 7961 Eastern Ave. #303, Silver Spring MD 20910. (301)588-4114. Fax: (301)588-5531. E-mail: jtimes@aol.com. Website: jazzcentralstation.com. Convention Director: Lee Mergner. Estab. 1979. "Brings together entire jazz industry in a series of workshops, panels and showcase performances." Offers programs for performers. Offers programs annually. Event takes place mid-November in New York City. 800-1,000 industry professionals participate in each event. Participants are professional vocalists, bands, instrumentalists and industry professionals. Showcase performers are selected by invitation.

KERRVILLE FOLK FESTIVAL, Kerrville Festivals, Inc., P.O. Box 1466, Kerrville TX 78029. (210)257-3600. E-mail: kfest@hilconet.com. Website: http://www.fmp.com/~kerrfest. Founder/President: Rod Kennedy. Estab. 1972. Hosts 3-day songwriters' school and New Folk concert competition sponsored by the Kerrville Music Foundation. Programs held in late spring and late summer. Spring festival lasts 25 days and is held outdoors at Quiet Valley Ranch. Around 150 acts participate. Performers are professional songwriters and bands. "Now hosting an annual 'house concert' seminar to encourage the establishment and promotion of monthly house concerts for traveling singers/songwriters to provide additional dates and income for touring." Participants selected by submitting demo, by invitation only. Send cassette, or CD, promotional material and list of upcoming appearances. "Songwriter schools are $144 and include lunch, experienced professional instructors, camping on ranch and concerts. Rustic facilities—no electrical hookups. Food available at reasonable cost. Audition materials accepted at above address."

*KLASSIK KOMM, Rottscheideter Str. 6, 42329 Wuppertal **Germany**. (0202)278310. Fax: (0202)789161. E-mail: popkomm@wildpark.com. Head PR: Andrea Zech. Estab. 1994. Offers programs for songwriters, composers, musical playwrights and performers. Offers programs annually. Events take place in September in Cologne, Germany. 1,600 songwriters/musicians participate in each event. Participants are amateur and professional songwriters, composers, musical playwrights, vocalists, bands and instrumentalists. Anyone can participate. Send for application or call + +48-202-278310. Charges fee.

MUSIC BUSINESS FILE/CAREER BUILDING WORKSHOPS, P.O. Box 266, Astor Station, Boston MA 02123-0266. (617)577-8585. E-mail: Peter@arts-online.com. Website: http://muguru.com. Director: Peter Spellman. Estab. 1991. Workshop titles include "How to Succeed in Music Without Overpaying Your Dues," "How to Start and Grow Your Own Record Label or Music Production Company" and "Promoting and Marketing Music Toward the Year 2000." Offers programs for music entrepreneurs, songwriters, musical playwrights, composers and performers. Offers programs year-round, annually and bi-annually. Event takes place at various colleges, recording studios, hotels, conferences. 10-100 songwriters/musicians participate in each event. Participants are both amateur and professional songwriters, vocalists, music business professionals, composers, bands, musical playwrights and instrumentalists. Anyone can participate. Call or write (regular or e-mail) for application. Fee: $50-125. "Music Business File offers a number of other services and programs for both songwriters and musicians including: Promotion over the Internet through 'Music House,' an online 'cyberservice' where artists and songwriters can post their press kits in multi-media fashion and be actively promoted to the music industry; and publication of *Music Biz Insight: Power Reading for Busy Music Professionals*, a quarterly infoletter chock full of music management and marketing tips and resources."

*MUSIC FACTORY, Rottscheidter Str. 6, 42329 Wuppertal **Germany**. (0202)278310. Fax: (0202)789161. E-mail: popkomm@wildpark.com. Head PR: Andrea Zech. Estab. 1996. Promotes rock, pop and techno music. Offers programs for songwriters, composers, musical playwrights and performers. Events take place in October in Cologne, Germany. Participants are amateur and professional songwriters, composers, musical playwrights, vocalists, bands and instrumentalists. Anyone can participate. Send for application or call + +49-202-278310. Charges fee.

*MUSIC WEST, 306-21 Water St., Vancouver B.C. V6B 1A1 **Canada**. (604)684-9338. Fax: (604)684-9337. E-mail: festival@musicwest.com. Website: http://www.musicwest.com/. Producers: Maureen Jack/Laurie Mercer. Estab. 1990. A four day music festival and conference held May each year in Vancouver, B.C. Festival: indie original artists selected by tape submissions. Showcases held at 25 live music venues. Conferences: panels/workshops for songwriters, composers, performers, producers and managers, attended by international music industry reps. Largest music industry event in the North Pacific Rim. Fee varies pending on conference/festival options preference.

*MUSICAL THEATRE WORKS, INC., 440 Lafayette St., New York NY 10003. (212)677-0040. Literary Manager: Pam Klappas. Estab. 1983. "We develop and produce new works for the musical theater: informal readings, staged readings and workshops of new musicals." Functions year-round. Participants are amateur and professional composers and songwriters and opera/musical theater writers. Participants are selected through a critique/evaluation of each musical by the Literary Manager and his staff. To contact, send complete script, cassette and SASE to the above address.

NORTHERN CALIFORNIA SONGWRITERS ASSOCIATION CONFERENCE, 855 Oak Grove Ave. #211, Menlo Park CA 94025. (415)327-8926 or (800)FOR-SONG. Fax: (415)327-0301. E-mail: ianncsa@aol.com. Executive Director: Ian Crombie. Estab. 1980. "Conference offers opportunity and education. 16 seminars, 50 song screening sessions (1,500 songs reviewed), performance showcases, one on one sessions and concerts." Offers programs for songwriters, composers and performers. "During the year we have competitive open mics. Winners go into the playoffs. Winners of the playoffs perform at the sunset concert at the conference." Event takes place second weekend in September at Foothill College, Los Altos Hills, CA. Over 500 songwriters/musicians participate in this event. Participants are songwriters, composers, musical playwrights, vocalists, bands, instrumentalists and those interested in a career in the music business. Send for application. Deadline: September 1. Fee: $90-175. "See our listing in the Organizations section."

ORFORD FESTIVAL, Orford Arts Centre, 3165 Chemim DuTarc, Canton D'orford Quebec J1X 3W3 **Canada**. (819)843-3981. Artistic Director: Agnès Grossman. Estab. 1951. "Each year, the Centre d'Arts Orford produces up to 30 concerts in the context of its Music Festival. It receives artists from all over the world in classical and chamber music." Offers master classes for young music students, young professional classical musicians and chamber music ensembles. Master classes last 7-8 weeks and take place at Orford Arts Centre during July and August. 350 students participate each year. Participants are selected by demo tape submissions. Send for application. Closing date for application is March 31st. Scholarships for qualified students. Registration fees $45 (Canadian). Tuition fees $235 (Canadian)/week. Accommodations $250 (Canadian).

PHILADELPHIA MUSIC CONFERENCE, P.O. Box 29363, Philadelphia PA 19125. (215)426-4109. Fax: (215)426-4138. E-mail: gopmc@aol.com. Showcase Director: Joe Boucher. Estab. 1992. "The purpose of the PMC is to bring together rock, hip hop and acoustic music for three days of panels and four nights of showcases. Offers programs for songwriters, composers and performers, including one-on-one sessions to meet with panelists and song evaluation sessions to have your music heard. We present 45 panels on topics of all facets of the music industry; 350 showcases at clubs around the city. Also offer a DJ cutting contest." Held annually at the Doubletree Hotel in Philadelphia in October. 3,000 amateur and professional songwriters, composers, individual vocalists, bands, individual instrumentalists, attorneys, managers, agents, publishers, A&R, promotions, club owners, etc. participate each year. "As per showcase application, participants are selected by independent panel of press, radio and performing rights organizations." Send for application. Deadline: July 1. Fee: $15 showcase application fee. "The Philadelphia Music Conference is one of the fastest-growing and exciting events around. Our goal is not just to make the Philadelphia Music Conference one of the biggest in America, but to make it one of the best. 15 artists were signed to major label deals in the first three years of the conference. We will continue to build upon our ideas to keep this an event that is innovative, informative and fun."

*POPKOMM, Rottscheidter Str. 6, 42329 Wuppertal **Germany**. (0202)278310. Fax: (0202)789161. E-mail: popkomm@wildpark.com. Head PR: Andrea Zech. Estab. 1989. Offers programs for songwriters, composers, musical playwrights and performers. Offers programs annually. Events take place in August in Cologne, Germany. 12,000 amateur and professional songwriters, composers, musical playwrights, vocalists, bands, instrumentalists, record companies and media participate each year. Anyone can participate. Send for application or call + +49-202-278310. Charges fee.

*RECORDING INDUSTRY SEMINARS INTERNATIONAL, 1300 Division St., #206, Nashville TN 37203. Phone/fax: (615)259-0103. Presidents: John Edman and Raynee Steele. Estab. 1992. Offers programs for songwriters and performers. Offers programs 4 times/year. Event takes place every 3 months at the Stadium Club, Nashville; sometimes, California and New York. 1,000 songwriters/musicians participate in each event. Participants are amateur and professional songwriters, vocalists, instrumentalists, personal managers and booking agents. Anyone can participate. Write or call for application. Fee varies depending upon the status of the speakers and the length of seminar.

*SFO3 (a Gavin Event), 140 Second St., San Francisco CA 94105. (415)495-1990. Fax: (415)495-2580. Website: http://www.iuma.com/gavin/. Director, Convention Services: Natalie Duitsman. Estab. 1994. For new artists and unsigned bands. Offers programs for songwriters, composers and performers. Offers programs annually. Event takes place in San Francisco. Participants are amateur and professional songwriters, composers, vocalists, bands, instrumentalists, industry professionals and record company executives. Participants are selected by demo tape audition. Call (415)495-1990, x633. Fee: $10 to submit tape, plus registration fee (call for latest information). Three day seminar with educational workshops, live performances and cocktail party.

SONGCRAFT SEMINARS, 441 E. 20th St., Suite 11B, New York NY 10010-7515. (212)674-1143. Estab. 1986. Year-round classes for composers and lyricists conducted by teacher/consultant Sheila Davis, author of *The Craft of Lyric Writing*, *Successful Lyric Writing* and *The Songwriter's Idea Book*. The teaching method, grounded in fundamental principles, incorporates whole-brain writing techniques. The objective: To express your unique voice. All courses emphasize craftsmanship and teach principles that apply to every musical idiom—pop, theater, or cabaret. For details on starting dates, fees and location of classes, write or call for current listing.
Successful Lyric Writing: A 3-Saturday course. Three 6-hour classes on the fundamental principles of writing words for and to music. Required text: *Successful Lyric Writing*. Held 3 times a year at The New School. Limited to 12.
Beyond the Basics: An 8-week workshop open to all "grads" of the *Successful Lyric Writing* Basics Course. It features weekly assignments and in-depth criticism to help writers turn first drafts into "music-ready" lyrics. Held four times a year at The Songwriters Guild of America (SGA).
Song by Song by Sondheim: A one-day seminar focused on the elements of fine craftsmanship exemplified in the words and music of Stephen Sondheim, America's pre-eminent theater writer. Significant songs are played and analyzed from the standpoint of form, meter, rhyme, literary devices and thematic development. Attendees are helped to apply these elements to their own writing. Held twice a year at The New School.
The Figurative Language Master Class: An 8-week intensive course/workshop that expands your usual ways of thinking and expressing ideas through the practice of figurative language. You'll learn to identify, define and use with competence the four master figures of speech—metaphor, synecdoche, metonymy and irony—and their many subtypes. And you'll acquire new skills in structuring your thoughts to make your songs more memorable and thus, more marketable. Held twice a year at the Songwriters Guild.
Successful Lyric Writing Consultation Course: This course, an outgrowth of the instructor's book, covers the same theory and assignments as The Basics Course. Participants receive critiques of their work by the book's author via 1-hour phone sessions.

THE SONGWRITERS GUILD FOUNDATION, 6430 Sunset Blvd., Suite 1002, Hollywood CA 90028. (213)462-1108. West Coast Director: B. Aaron Meza.
Ask-A-Pro/Song Critique: SGA members are given the opportunity to present their songs and receive constructive feedback from industry professionals. A great chance to meet industry people, make contacts, ask questions and get your song heard! Free to SGA members. Reservations required. Call for schedule. Members outside regional area send tape with lyric and SASE for tape return.
Jack Segal's Songshop: This very successful 9-week workshop focuses on working a song through to perfection, including title, idea, rewrites and pitching your songs. Please call for more information regarding this very informative workshop. Dates to be announced. Fee.
Phil Swan Country Music Workshop: Held each Monday from 7-10 p.m., this shop is perfect for those writers who want an inside look into the world of country music. Fee.
Special Seminars and Workshops: Held through the year. Past workshops included Sheila Davis on lyrics, tax workshops for songwriters, MIDI workshops, etc. Call for schedule.

THE SONGWRITERS GUILD OF AMERICA, 1560 Broadway #1306, New York NY 10036. (212)768-7902. E-mail: songnews@aol.com. National Projects Director: George Wurzbach. Estab. 1931.
Ask-A-Pro: "2-hour biweekly music business forum to which all writers are welcome. It features industry professionals—publishers, producers, A&R people, record company executives, entertainment lawyers, artists—fielding questions from new songwriters." Offered year-round, except during summer. Charge: free to members, $2 for nonmembers.
Song Critique: New York's oldest ongoing song critique. Guild songwriters are invited to either perform their song live or present a cassette demo for feedback. A Guild moderator is on hand to direct comments. Nonmembers may attend and offer comments. Free to members, $2 charge for nonmembers.
The Practical Songwriter: This is a 4-hour nuts and bolts seminar dealing with industry networking, song marketing, contracts and publishing. Sessions are highlighted by visits from industry profession-

als. Instructor is songwriter/musician George Wurzbach. Fee: free for SGA members, $10 for non-members.

Pro-Shop: For each of 6 sessions an active publisher, producer or A&R person is invited to personally screen material from professional Guild writers. Participation is limited to 10 writers. Audition of material is required. Coordinator is producer/musician/award winning singer, Ann Johns Ruckert. Fee: $75 (SGA members only).

SGA Week: Held in April and September of each year, this is a week of scheduled events and seminars of interest to songwriters. Events include workshops, seminars and showcases. For schedule and details contact the SGA office beginning several weeks prior to SGA Week.

Inside Track: This is a 4-hour workshop designed to introduce the songwriter to the mechanics of the recording studio environment. Various aspects of recording techniques, signal processing, drum and sequencer programing, etc., are examined in order to prepare a songwriter to clearly communicate with an engineer or session musician thereby ensuring a demo closer to the writer's design. Call SGA for more details.

*SONGWRITERS PLAYGROUND®, 1085 Commonwealth Ave., #323, Boston MA 02215. (617)424-9490. Director: Barbara Jordan. Estab. 1990. "To help songwriters, performers and composers develop creative and business skills through the critically acclaimed programs *Songwriters Playground®, The 'Reel' Deal on Getting Songs Placed in Film and Television*, and the *Mind Your Own Business* Seminars. We offer programs year-round. Workshops last anywhere from 2-15 hours. Workshops are held at various venues throughout the United States. Prices vary according to the length of the workshop." Participants are amateur and professionals. Anyone can participate. Send or call for application.
  • See the interview with Director Barbara Jordan in the Advertising, AV and Commercial Music Firms section.

*SOUTH BY SOUTHWEST MUSIC AND MEDIA CONFERENCE, P.O. Box 4999, Austin TX 78765. (512)467-7979. Fax: (512)451-0754. E-mail: 72662.2465@compuserve.com. Estab. 1987. "We have over 575 bands perform in over 30 venues over 4 nights featuring every genre of alternative-based music." Offers programs for songwriters and performers. Annual event takes place the third weekend in March at the Austin Convention Center, Austin, TX. Participants are songwriters, vocalists, bands and instrumentalists. Participants are selected by demo tape audition. Deadline: November 15. Fee: $10 early fee; $15 late fee. "We have a mentor program during the conference where participants can have a one-on-one with professionals in the music business."

*SOUTHEASTERN MUSIC CENTER, P.O. Box 8348, Columbus GA 31907. (706)568-2465. Artistic Director: Dr. Ronald Wirt. Estab. 1983. Orchestral and chamber music experience for high school and college musicians. Offers lessons for guitar and orchestral instruments, beginning music theory, repertoire, rehearsals and concerts of chamber and orchestral ensembles for performers. Concerto competition open to registered students. Prize is a performance with orchestra. Offers other programs summer only at Columbus College. Participants are selected by demo tape audition. Send for application. Deadline: May 1st. Fee: $25 application; Day Student: $350; Resident: $625. Two concert halls, several rehearsal rooms and classrooms, MIDI lab.

SUMMER LIGHTS IN MUSIC CITY, %Greater Nashville Arts Foundation, 209 10th Ave., South, Suite 347, Nashville TN 37203. (615)256-7333. Program Coordinator: Erika Wollam. (615)259-0900. Estab. 1981. Goal is to present the arts of Nashville to the world. Featured music is the music of Nashville: jazz, bluegrass, country, rock and gospel. Nashville Songwriters Association International involvement. Festival presents specific segments designed to showcase songwriters and songwriting. Offers programs year-round; music programs all year; festival lasts 4 days. Approximately 2,000 performers participate in festival. Participants are amateur and professional individual vocalists, bands, ensembles, vocal groups, composers, individual instrumentalists, orchestras and opera/musical theater writers. Performers selected by invitation only. Performers work outside on stages and in the street of the city; those from out of town stay in hotels and motels.

THE SWANNANOA GATHERING—CONTEMPORARY FOLK WEEK, Warren Wilson College, P.O. Box 9000, Asheville NC 28815-9000. (704)298-3325, ext. 426. Fax: (704)299-3326. E-mail: gathering@warren-wilson.edu. Website: http://www.hidwater.com/gathering/. Director: Jim Magill. "For anyone who ever wanted to make music for an audience, we offer a comprehensive week in artist development, divided into four major subject areas: Songwriting, Performance, Sound & Recording and Vocal Coaching, along with daily panel discussions of other business matters such as promotion, agents and managers, logistics of touring, etc. 1996 staff includes Tom Paxton, Catie Curtis, David Massengill, Leslie Ritter, Scott Petito, Bridget Ball, Christopher Shaw, Paul Reisler, Rex Fowler, Bob Franke, Freyda Epstein and Eric Garrison. For a brochure or other info contact Jim Magill, Director, The Swannanoa Gathering, at the phone number/address above. Tuition: $275. Takes place last week in July. Housing (including all meals): $195. Annual program of The Swannanoa Gathering Folk Arts Workshops."

THE TEN-MINUTE MUSICALS PROJECT, P.O. Box 461194, West Hollywood CA 90046. (213)656-8751. Producer: Michael Koppy. Estab. 1986. Promotes short complete stage musicals. Offers programs for songwriters, composers and musical playwrights. "Works selected are generally included in full-length 'anthology musical'—11 of the first 16 selected works are now in the show *Stories*, for instance." Awards a $250 royalty advance for each work selected. Participants are amateur and professional songwriters, composers and musical playwrights. Participants are selected by demonstration tape, script, lead sheets. Send for application. Deadline: August 31st annually.

UNDERCURRENTS, P.O. Box 94040, Cleveland OH 44101-6040. Phone/fax: (216)463-3595. E-mail: undercurrent@msn.com. Website: http://www.undercurrents.com. Director: John Latimer. Estab. 1989. A yearly music industry expo featuring seminars, trade show, media center and showcases of rock, alternative, metal, folk, jazz and blues music. Offers programs for songwriters, composers, music industry professionals and performers. Dates for Undercurrents '97 are May 15-17. Deadline for showcase consideration is February 1, 1997. Participants are selected by demo tape, biography and 8 × 10 photo audition. Send for application. Fee: $10.

*WINTER MUSIC CONFERENCE INC., 3450 NE 12 Terrace, Ft. Lauderdale FL 33334. (305)563-4444. Fax: (305)563-6889. President: Louis Possenti. Estab. 1985. Features educational seminars and showcases for dance, hip hop, alternative and rap. Offers programs for songwriters and performers. Offers programs annually. Event takes place March of each year in Miami, Florida. 1,500 songwriters/musicians participate in each event. Participants are amateur and professional songwriters, composers, musical playwrights, vocalists, bands and instrumentalists. Participants are selected by submitting demo tape. Send or call for application. Deadline: February. Event held at either nightclubs or hotel with complete staging, lights and sound.

Contests and Awards

Participation in contests is a great way to gain exposure for your music. Winners may receive cash prizes, musical merchandise, studio time and even publishing and recording deals. For musical theater and classical composers, the winning work may be performed for an audience. Even if you don't win a prize, valuable contacts can be made through contests. Many times, contests are judged by music publishers and other industry professionals, so your music may find its way into the hands of key industry people who can help further your career.

It's important to remember when entering any contest to do proper research before signing anything or sending any money. We have confidence in the contests listed in *Songwriter's Market*, but it pays to be aware of several things. Be sure you understand the contest rules and stipulations once you receive the entry forms and guidelines. You need to weigh what you will gain against what they're asking you to give up. If a publishing contract is involved as a prize, don't give away your publishing rights. If you do, you're endangering possible future royalties from the song, which is clearly not in your best interest. Be wary of exorbitant entry fees, and if you have any doubts whatsoever as to the legitimacy of a contest, it's best to stay away. Songwriters need to approach a contest, award or grant in the same manner as they would a record or publishing company. Make sure your submission is as professional as possible; follow directions and submit material exactly as stated on the entry form.

Contests in this section encompass all types of music and levels of competition. Read each listing carefully and contact them if the contest interests you. Be sure to read the rules carefully and be sure you understand them before entering.

*AGO/ECS PUBLISHING AWARD IN CHORAL COMPOSITION, American Guild of Organists, 475 Riverside Dr., Suite 1260, New York NY 10115. (212)870-2310. Fax: (212)870-2163. E-mail: ago@walrus.com. For composers. Biannual award.
Requirements: One work for SATB chorus and organ in which the organ plays a distinctive and significant role. Specifics vary from year to year. Work submitted must be unpublished. Competitors must be citizens of the United States, Canada or Mexico. There is no age restriction. Deadline: July 31. Send for application.
Awards: $2,000; performances at Regional Convention and National Convention; publication of winning composition by ECS Publishing.

ALEA III INTERNATIONAL COMPOSITION PRIZE, 855 Commonwealth Ave., Boston MA 02215. (617)353-3340. Executive Administrator: Synneve Carlino. For composers. Annual award.
Purpose: To promote and encourage young composers in the composition of new music.
Requirements: Composers 40 years of age and younger may apply; one score per composer. Works may be for solo voice or instrument or for chamber ensemble up to 15 members lasting between 6 and 15 minutes. All works must be unpublished. Deadline: March 15. Send for application. Samples of work required with application. "Real name should not appear on score; a nome de plume should be signed instead. Sealed envelope with entry form should be attached to each score."
Awards: ALEA III International Composition Prize: $2,500. Awarded once annually. Between 8-10 finalists are chosen and their works are performed in a competition concert by the ALEA III contemporary music ensemble. One grand prize winner is selected by a panel of judges.
Tips: "Emphasis placed on works written in 20th century compositional idioms."

AMERICAN ACCORDIAN MUSICOLOGICAL SOCIETY COMPOSITION FOR CLASSICAL ACCORDIAN, 334 S. Broadway, Pitman NJ 08071. (609)854-6628. Secretary: Stanley Darrow. Estab. 1971. Serves songwriters and composers. Annual award.

GET YOUR WORK INTO THE RIGHT BUYERS' HANDS!

You work hard... and your hard work deserves to be seen by the right buyers. But with the constant changes in the industry, it's not always easy to know who those buyers are. That's why you'll want to keep up-to-date and on top with the most current edition of this indispensable market guide.

Totally Updated Each Year

Keep ahead of the changes by ordering *1998 Songwriter's Market* today. You'll save the frustration of getting your songs returned in the mail, stamped MOVED: ADDRESS UNKNOWN. And of NOT submitting your work to new listings because you don't know they exist. All you have to do to order the upcoming 1998 edition is complete the attached order card and return it with your payment or credit card information. Order now and you'll get the 1998 edition at the 1997 price—just $22.99—no matter how much the regular price may increase! *1998 Songwriter's Market* will be published and ready for shipment in September 1997.

Keep on top of the changing industry and get a jump on selling your work with help from the *1998 Songwriter's Market*. Order today! You deserve it!

1998 SONGWRITER'S MARKET

WHERE & HOW TO PUBLISH YOUR SONGS

2,500 listings of music publishers, record companies, producers, AV firms, managers, classical groups, theater companies!

Totally Updated! Plus 400 New Markets!

Turn over for more books to help you write and sell your songs ➡

☐ **Yes!** I want the most current edition of *Songwriter's Market*. Please send me the 1998 edition at the 1997 price – $22.99.* (NOTE: *1998 Songwriter's Market* will be ready for shipment in September 1997.) #10515

I also want:

Book # _____ Price $_____

Book # _____ Price $_____

Book # _____ Price $_____

Book # _____ Price $_____

Subtotal $_____

*Add $3.50 postage and handling for one book; $1.00 for each additional book.

Postage and handling $_____

Payment must accompany order.
Ohioans add 6% sales tax.

Total $_____

☐ **FREE CATALOG.** Ask your bookstore about other fine Writer's Digest Books, or mail this card today for a complete catalog.

VISA/MasterCard orders call
TOLL-FREE 1-800-289-0963

☐ Payment enclosed $_____ (or)

Charge my: ☐ Visa ☐ MasterCard Exp._____

Account # _____

Signature_____

Name_____

Address _____

City_____ State _____ Zip _____

Phone Number _____
(will be used only if we must contact you regarding this order.)

30-Day Money Back Guarantee
on every book you buy!

 Mail to:

Writer's Digest Books
1507 Dana Avenue
Cincinnati, OH 45207

6898

More Great Books to Help You Sell Your Songs!

Creating Melodies
by Dick Weissman
You'll be singing all the way to the bank when you discover the secrets of creating memorable melodies—from love ballads to commercial jingles!
#10400/$18.95/144 pages

Hot Tips for Home Recording
by Hank Linderman
Discover the tricks to recording a tight, polished, professional demo! Musicians acquainted with recording technology will learn how to lay down basic tracks, add vocals, and mix to get exactly the sound they want.
#10415/$18.99/160 pages

Essential!
Songwriter's Market Guide to Song and Demo Submission Formats
Get your foot in the door with knock-out query letters, slick demo presentation, and the best advice for dealing with every player in the industry!
#10401/$19.99/160 pages

The Craft and Business of Songwriting
by John Braheny
From generating a song idea to signing a record deal, you'll discover how to create and market artistically and commercially successful songs in today's market.
#10429/$21.99/322 pages/paperback

Writing Better Lyrics
Make every song sizzle using this unique, in-depth approach to lyric writing. You'll examine extraordinary songs to determine what makes them so effective; work through more than 30 language exercises to find snappy rhymes and create meaningful metaphors and similes.
#10453/$19.99/192 pages

Making Money Teaching Music
Discover lucrative teaching opportunities. This guide shows you how to market yourself as a professional, recruit students, manage time and work schedules, and more!
#10428/$18.99/240 pages/paperback

Beginning Songwriter's Answer Book
This revised resource answers all of your questions about getting started as a songwriter, then gives professional advice to help you succeed in the lucrative music industry.
#10376/$16.99/128 pages/paperback

Order these helpful references today from your local bookstore, or use the handy order card on the reverse.

Purpose: "To write a 4 or 5 minute composition in a serious style for accordion."
Requirements: Deadline: September. Samples are not required.
Awards: Amateur: $300. Professional: $600. Each award good for 1 year. Applications judged by professional composers.
Tips: "Get to understand or listen to some serious performers of classical accordion."

AMERICAN SONGWRITER LYRIC CONTEST, 121 17th Ave. S., Nashville TN 37203-2707. (615)244-6065. Fax: (615)742-1123. Editor: Vernell Hackett. Estab. 1984. For songwriters and performing artists. Award for each bimonthly issue of *American Songwriter* magazine, plus grand prize at year-end.
Purpose: To promote the art of songwriting and to allow readers the opportunity to be actively involved.
Requirements: Lyrics must be typed and check for $10 must be enclosed. Deadlines: January 26, March 29, May 24, July 26, September 27, November 22. Samples are not required. Call for required official form.
Awards: A guitar, with different sponsors each year. Good for 3 months. Lyrics judged by 5-6 industry people—songwriters, publishers, journalists.
Tips: "Pick your best lyric, don't just send them at random."

ARTISTS' FELLOWSHIPS, New York Foundation for the Arts, 155 Avenue of Americas, 14th Floor, New York NY 10013. To receive an application, or contact the fellowship's department, call: (212)366-6900, ext. 217. Fax: (212)366-1778. E-mail: nyfaafp@tmn.com. Website: http://www.tmn. com/Artswire/www/nyfa.html. Director, Artists' Programs and Services: Penelope Dannenberg. For songwriters, composers and musical playwrights. Annual award, but each category funded biennially. Estab. 1984.
Purpose: "Artists' Fellowships are $7,000 grants awarded by the New York Foundation for the Arts to individual originating artists living in New York State. The Foundation is committed to supporting artists from all over New York State at all stages of their professional careers. Fellows may use the grant according to their own needs; it should not be confused with project support."
Requirements: Must be 18 years of age or older; resident in New York State for 2 years prior to application; and cannot be enrolled in any graduate or undergraduate degree program. Applications will be available in July. Deadline: October. Samples of work are required with application. 1 or 2 original compositions on separate audiotapes and at least 2 copies of corresponding scores or fully harmonized lead sheets.
Awards: All Artists' Fellowships awards are for $7,000. Payment of $6,500 upon verification of NY State residency, and remainder upon completion of a mutually agreed upon public service activity. Nonrenewable. "Fellowships are awarded on the basis of the quality of work submitted and the evolving professional accomplishments of the applicant. Applications are reviewed by a panel of 5 composers representing the aesthetic, ethnic, sexual and geographic diversity within New York State. The panelists change each year and review all allowable material submitted."
Tips: "Please note that musical playwrights may submit only if they write the music for their plays— librettists must submit in our playwrighting category."

ASCAP FOUNDATION GRANTS TO YOUNG COMPOSERS, ASCAP Bldg., 1 Lincoln Plaza, New York NY 10023. (212)621-6327. Fax: (212)721-0956. Contact: Frances Richard.
Purpose: To provide grants to young composers to encourage the development of talented young American composers.
Requirements: Applicants must be citizens or permanent residents of the United States of America who have not reached their 30th birthday by March 15. Original music of any style will be considered. However, works which have earned awards or prizes in any other national competition or grant giving program are ineligible. Arrangements are ineligible. Each applicant must submit a completed application form; one reproduction of a manuscript or score; biographical information listing prior music studies, background and experience; a list of compositions to date; and one professional recommendation to be mailed by the referee directly to ASCAP under separate cover. A cassette tape of the composition submitted for the competition may be included if it is marked with the composer's name, the title of the work and the names of the performers. Tapes of electronic music must also be accompanied by written information concerning source material and electronic equipment used. A composition that involves a text must be accompanied by information about the source of the text with evidence that it is in the public domain or by written permission from the copyright proprietor. Deadline: All materials must be postmarked no later than March 15.
Awards: ASCAP Foundation awards total $20,000 and grants range from $500-2,500. Length: 1 year. Applications judged by screening-panel of composers.

*BAKER'S PLAYS HIGH SCHOOL PLAYWRITING CONTEST, Baker's Plays 100 Chauncy St., Boston MA 02111. (617)482-1280. Fax: (617)482-7613. Associate Editor: Raymond Pape. Estab. 1990. For musical playwrights. Annual award.

Requirements: Plays should be about the "high school experience," but may also be about any subject and of any length, so long as the play can be reasonably produced on the high school stage. Plays must be accompanied by the signature of a sponsoring high school drama or English teacher, and it is recommended that the play receive a production or a public reading prior to the submission. Multiple submissions and co-authored scripts are welcome. Teachers may not submit a student's work. The ms must be firmly bound, typed and come with a SASE. Include enough postage to cover the return of the ms. Plays that do not come with an SASE will not be returned. Do not send originals; copies only. Deadline: January 31st. Send for guidelines.

Awards: First Place: $500 and the play will be published by Baker's Plays; Second Place: $250 and an Honorable Mention; Third Place: $100 and an Honorable Mention.

BILLBOARD SONG CONTEST, P.O. Box 35346, Tulsa OK 74153-0346. (918)627-0351. Fax: (918)627-6681. Administrator: Kathy Purple. Estab. 1988. For songwriters. Annual contest.

Purpose: "To award cash, merchandise and press to the unknown but deserving songwriter."

Requirements: Entry form, audio cassette, lyric sheet and $15 fee. Deadline: Late fall. Send for application. Samples are not required.

Awards: Grand prize of $5,000 plus merchandise. 1st Place in each category (excluding grand prize category) of $1,000 plus merchandise. Entries accepted in pop, rock, country, Latin, R&B, jazz and gospel. "Songs are judged on lyrics, originality, melody and composition. Production and/or voice quality is not a consideration in judging."

BUSH ARTIST FELLOWSHIPS, E-900 First National Bank Bldg., 332 Minnesota St., St. Paul MN 55101. (612)227-5222. Director, Bush Artist Fellowships: Sally Dixon. Estab. 1976. For songwriters, composers, and musical playwrights. Annual award. Applications in music composition are accepted in alternate years.

Purpose: "To provide uninterrupted time (12-18 months) for artists to pursue their creative development—do their own work."

Requirements: Applicant must be a Minnesota, North Dakota, South Dakota or western Wisconsin resident for 12 of preceeding 36 months, 25 years or older, not a student. Deadline: late October. Send for application. Samples of work on cassette required with application. "Music composition applications will not be taken again until the fall of 1996. Applications will be taken in the fall of 1996 in the following areas: music composition and scriptworks (screenwriting and playwriting)."

Awards: Fellowships: $36,000 each. Award is good for 12-18 months. "Five years after completion of preceeding fellowship, one may apply again." Applications are judged by peer review panels.

CINTAS FELLOWSHIP, I.I.E 809 UN Plaza, New York NY 10017. (212)984-5370. Fax: (212)984-5574. Program Officer: Miriam Gonzalez Acosta. For composers and musical playwrights. Annual award. Estab. 1964.

Requirements: "Fellowships awarded to persons of Cuban citizenship or lineage for achievement in music composition (architecture, painting, sculpture, printmaking, photography and literature); students wishing to pursue academic programs are not eligible, nor are performing artists. Applicants must be creative artists of Cuban descent who have completed their academic and technical training." For next deadline, please call. Send for application. Samples of work required with application. "Send complete score and a cassette tape. Compositions submitted must be serious contemporary works. Popular songs and ballads will not be accepted."

Awards: Cintas Fellowship: $10,000 per grantee. Fellowship is good for 12 months. Applicant may receive an award no more than twice. Selection committee reviews applications.

COLUMBIA ENTERTAINMENT COMPANY'S JACKIE WHITE MEMORIAL PLAYWRITING CONTEST, 309 Parkade Blvd., Columbia MO 65202. (314)874-5628. Chairperson, CEC Contest: Betsy Phillips. For musical playwrights. Annual award.

Purpose: "We are looking for top-notch scripts for theater school use, to challenge and expand the talents of our students, ages 10-15. We want good plays with large casts (20-30 characters) suitable for use with our theater school students. Full production of the winning script will be done by the students. A portion of travel expenses, room and board offered to winner for production of show."

Requirements: "Must be large cast plays, original story lines and cannot have been previously published. Please write for complete rules." Send SASE for application; then send scripts to address above. Full-length play, neatly typed. No name on title page, but name, address and name of play on a 3×5 index card. Cassette tape of musical numbers required. $10 entry fee. SASE for entry form."

Awards: $250 first prize and partial travel expenses to see play produced. Second place winner gets no prize money but receives production of the play by the theater school plus partial travel expenses. This is a one-time cash award, given after any revisions required are completed. "The judging committee is taken from members of Columbia Entertainment Company's Executive and Advisory boards. At least eight members, with at least three readings of all entries, and winning entries being read by entire committee. We are looking for plays that will work with our theater school students."

Tips: "Remember the play we are looking for will be performed by 10-15 year old students with normal talents—difficult vocal ranges, a lot of expert dancing and so forth will eliminate the play. We especially like plays that deal with current day problems and concerns. However, if the play is good enough, any suitable subject matter is fine. It should be fun for the audience to watch."

COMPOSERS COMMISSIONING PROGRAM, ACF, 332 Minnesota St., #E-145, St. Paul MN 55101. (612)228-1407. Fax: (612)291-7978. E-mail: compfrm@maroon.tc.umn.edu. E-mail: http://www.umn.edu/nlhome/m111/compfrm. Program Director: Philip Blackburn. Estab. 1979. For songwriters, musical playwrights, composers and performers. Annual award.

Purpose: "CCP provides grants to support the commissioning of new works by emerging composers."

Requirements: Membership of Minnesota Composers Forum (not for students). Deadline: end of July. Send for application. Samples of work are required with application. Send score/tape.

Awards: 18-22 commissioning grants of $500-6,000; each grant good for 5 years. Applications are judged by peer review panel (anonymous).

Tips: "Composers pair up with performers: one party must be based in Minnesota or New York City."

CRS NATIONAL COMPOSERS COMPETITION, 724 Winchester Rd., Broomall PA 19008. (215)544-5920. Fax: (215)544-5921. Administrative Assistant: Caroline Hunt. For songwriters, composers and performing artists. Annual award.

Requirements: Write or fax for application with SASE. Send a detailed résumé with application form. Samples of work required with application. Application fee $50.

Awards: 1st Prize: Commercial recording grant. Applications are judged by panel of judges determined each year.

*CUNNINGHAM PRIZE FOR PLAYWRITING, The Theatre School, DePaul University, 2135 N. Kenmore Ave., Chicago IL 60614. (312)325-7938. Fax: (312)325-7920. Public Relations Director: Lara Goetsch. Estab. 1990. For musical playwrights. Annual award.

Purpose: "The purpose of the prize is to recognize and encourage the writing of dramatic works which affirm the centrality of religion, broadly defined, and the human quest for meaning, truth and community. It is the intent of the endowment to consider submissions of new dramatic writing in all genres, including works for children and young people."

Requirements: "The focus for the awarding of the prize is metropolitan Chicago. The candidates for the award must be writers whose residence is in the Chicago area, defined as within 100 miles of the Loop." Deadline: December 1. Send for application with SASE.

Awards: $5,000. "Winners may submit other work for subsequent prize year. The Selection Committee is composed of distinguished citizens including members of DePaul University, representatives of the Cunningham Prize Advisory Committee, critics and others from the theater professions, and is chaired by John Ransford Watts, dean of The Theatre School."

*DELTA OMICRON INTERNATIONAL COMPOSITION COMPETITION, 12297 W. Tennessee Place, Lakewood CO 80228. (303)989-2871. Composition Competition Chairman: Judith L. Eidson. For composers. Triennial award.

Purpose: "To encourage composers worldwide to continually add to our wonderful heritage of musical creativity instrumentally and/or vocally."

Requirements: People from college age on (or someone younger who is enrolled in college). Work must be unpublished and unperformed in public. Deadline: mid-March of 2nd year of triennium. Send for application. Samples of work are required with application.

Awards: 1st place: $500 and world premiere at Delta Omicron Triennal Conference. Judged by 2-3 judges (performers and/or composers).

FORT BEND SONGWRITER'S ASSOCIATION ANNUAL SONG & LYRIC CONTEST, P.O. Box 1273, Richmond TX 77406-1273. Chairman: Dave Davidson. For songwriters, composers and lyricists. Annual award.

• See the listing for the Fort Bend Songwriter's Association in the Organizations section.

Purpose: To promote song and lyric writing from the first attempt to becoming a recorded composer.

Requirements: Any songwriter who wishes to enter may do so. It is our belief that songwriters must learn to compete with the best in order to reach their goals. Deadline: April 30. Send for application. Must send SASE with request. Send one song per entry on a cassette with plainly written or typed label and lyric sheet. Lyric sheet only for lyric contest.

Awards: "Each year the prizes are based on the number of entries; we give back at least half of the entry money after expenses plus merchandise and studio time donated by our supporters."

*FREE STAGED READING SERIES PLAYWRITING COMPETITION, 120 W. 28th St., New York NY 10001. (212)627-1732. Fax: (212)243-6736. Assistant to the Artistic Director: Tara Bahna-James. Estab. 1984. For musical playwrights or anyone wanting to write a play.
Purpose: "The series, now entering its sixth year, was initiated to encourage playwrights, composers, and lyricists to write for family audiences and to involve children and their parents in the excitement of the play development process."
Requirements: "Script must be original, unproduced and unpublished. Any age may apply. One act musical or non-musical cast must be primarily youth ages 7-18; children do not play adults—adult actors can be hired. Script must be typed, include character breakdown, set and costume description." Deadline: February 1. Send for guidelines.
Tips: "Issues having to do with children and what they are going through in life and good teen issues are especially relevant."

FULBRIGHT SCHOLAR PROGRAM, COUNCIL FOR INTERNATIONAL EXCHANGE OF SCHOLARS, 3007 Tilden St. NW, Suite 5M, Box News, Washington DC 20008-3009. (202)686-7877. E-mail: ciesl@ciesnet.cies.org. Website: http://www.cies.org. Estab. 1946. For songwriters, composers, performing artists, musical playwrights and faculty and professionals with PhD or MFA. Annual award.
Purpose: "Awards for university lecturing and advanced research abroad are offered annually in virtually all academic disciplines including musical composition."
Requirements: "U.S. citizenship at time of application; M.F.A., Ph.D. or equivalent professional qualifications; for lecturing awards, university teaching experience." Applications become available in March each year, for grants to be taken up 1½ years later. Application deadlines: August 1, all world areas. Write or call for application. Samples of work are required with application.
Awards: "Benefits vary by country, but generally include round-trip travel for the grantee and for most full academic-year awards, one dependent; stipend in U.S. dollars and/or local currency; in many countries, tuition allowance for school age children; and book and baggage allowance. Grant duration ranges from two months-one academic year."

*FUTURE CHARTERS, 332 Eastwood Ave., Feasterville PA 19053. (800)574-2986. Phone/fax: (215)953-0952. E-mail: a1foster@aol.com. Editor/Publisher: Allen Foster. Estab. 1993. For songwriters. Quarterly award.
Requirements: To enter, send a clean demo tape of one song with vocals up front, a photo, a bio, lyric sheet, contact information and a SASE (if you'd like your tape returned).
Awards: Winners will receive a writeup in an upcoming issue of *Songwriter's Monthly*, plus your song will be placed on the Songwriter's Telephone Showcase so interested parties will be able to call up and listen to your song.
Tips: "Send your best song. It doesn't have to be an expensive demo, but it does have to sound clean."

HARVEY GAUL COMPOSITION CONTEST, The Pittsburgh New Music Ensemble, Inc., School of Music, Duquesne University, Pittsburgh PA 15282. (412)261-0554. Fax: (412)396-5479. Conductor/Executive Director: David Stock/Eva Tumiel-Kozak. For composers. Biennial.
Purpose: Objective is to encourage composition of new music. Winning piece to be premiered by the PNME.
Requirements: "Must be citizen of the US. New works scored for 6 to 16 instruments drawn from the following: flute, oboe, 2 clarinets, bassoon, horn, trumpet, trombone, tuba, 2 violins, cello, bass, 2 percussion, piano, harp, electronic tape." Deadline: April 15. Send SASE for application. Samples of work are required with application. "Real name must not appear on score—must be signed with a 'nom de plume'." Entry fee: $15.
Awards: Harvey Gaul Composition Contest: $3,000.

GILMAN & GONZALEZ-FALLA THEATRE FOUNDATION MUSICAL THEATER AWARDS, 109 E. 64th St., New York NY 10021. (212)734-8001. Contact: J. Weiss. For composers, musical playwrights, any composer/lyricist/creative team with a produced musical to his/her/their credit. Annual award.
Requirements: Send for application. Deadline: August.
Awards: $25,000.

HENRICO THEATRE COMPANY ONE-ACT PLAYWRITING COMPETITION, P.O. Box 27032, Richmond VA 23273. (804)672-5100. Cultural Arts Coordinator: J. Larkin Brown. For musical playwrights. Annual award.
Purpose: Original one-act musicals for a community theater organization.
Requirements: "Only one-act plays or musicals will be considered. The manuscript should be a one-act original (not an adaptation), unpublished, and unproduced, free of royalty and copyright restrictions. Scripts with smaller casts and simpler sets may be given preference. Controversial themes should be

avoided. Standard play script form should be used. All plays will be judged anonymously, therefore, there should be two title pages; the first must contain the play's title and the author's complete address and telephone number. The second title page must contain only the play's title. The playwright must submit two excellent quality copies. Receipt of all scripts will be acknowledged by mail. Scripts will be returned if SASE is included. No scripts will be returned until after the winner is announced. The HTC does not assume responsibility for loss, damage or return of scripts. All reasonable care will be taken." Deadline: July 1st. Send for application first.
Awards: 1st prize $250; 2nd prize $125; 3rd prize $125.

*HOLTKAMP-AGO AWARD IN ORGAN COMPOSITION, American Guild of Organists, 475 Riverside Dr., Suite 1260, New York NY 10115. E-mail: ago@walrus.com. Biannual award.
Requirements: Organ solo, no longer than eight minutes in duration. Specifics vary from year to year. Composer must be a citizen of the United States, Canada or Mexico. Deadline: June 1. Send for application.
Award: $2,000 provided by the Holtkamp Organ Company; publication by Hinshaw Music Inc.; performance at the biennial National Convention of the American Guild of Organists.

*INDIANA OPERA THEATRE MACALLISTER AWARDS, 2825 E. 56th St., Indianapolis IN 46220. (317)253-1001. Fax: (317)253-2008. Artister/General Director: E. Bookwahter. Estab. 1980. For composers.
Requirements: For professional and amateurs. New works for high school/college students; small cast; contemporary, dealing with issues. Also one or two person works. Send for application.

INTERMOUNTAIN SONGWRITING COMPETITION, Box 571325, Salt Lake City UT 84157. Estab. 1987. For songwriters. Annual award by Utah Songwriters Association.
Requirements: For information send SASE. All amateur songwriters may enter. Deadline: January 31. One song per tape. Contest runs from October 15 to January 31 each year. Entry must be postmarked by January 31. Winners announced April 30. Entry fee: $10 for first song, $5 each additional song.
Awards: First place winner receives $500 cash, $100 for each category winner. Judging sheets returned to entrant.
Tips: "Submit a well-written song with a good vocal and instruments well in tune. Have the vocals out front and the words clear. Remember, this is a competition so make your song competitive by having a good recording. Type lyric sheets neatly and *please* have your lyrics match the words on your recording. We look for songs that say something important and have a good hook. Enter as many tapes as you wish, from anywhere in the world—offensive material will be disqualified with no refund. For additional information, call Marie at (801)596-3058."

*INTERNATIONAL AWARD OF MUSICAL COMPOSITIONS CIUTAT DE TARRA-GONA, Ajuntament de Tarragona, Placa de la Font 1, E43003 Tarragona **Spain**. Contact: Registre General. For composers. Annual award.
Requirements: "Any symphonic composition may be submitted for this award, either with or without soloists and with or without electro-acoustics. The composition must be unpublished, never have been performed in public nor been awarded a prize." Deadline: November 15. Send for application.
Awards: First prize: 1.000.000 pesetas and performance of the composition; Second prize: 500.000 pesetas.

KATE NEAL KINLEY MEMORIAL FELLOWSHIP, 608 E. Lorado Taft Dr., #110, Champaign IL 61820. (217)333-1661. Secretary: Ruth Wilcoxon. Estab. 1931. For students of architecture, art or music. Annual award.
Purpose: The advancement of study in the Fine Arts.
Requirements: "The Fellowship will be awarded upon the basis of unusual promise in the Fine Arts." Deadline: February 15. Send for application or call. Samples of work are required with application.
Awards: "Two or three major Fellowships which yield the sum of $7,000 each which is to be used by the recipients toward defraying the expenses of advanced study of the Fine Arts in America or abroad." Good for 1 year. Grant is nonrenewable.

LEE KORF PLAYWRITING AWARD, Cerritos College, 11110 Alondra Blvd., Dept. of Theatre, Norwalk CA 90650. (310)860-2451, ext. 2638. Fax: (310)467-5005. Theatre Production: Gloria Manriquez. For musical playwrights and playwrights. Annual award.
Purpose: "We look for promising playwrights who have something exciting to say with a fresh innovative way of saying it."
Requirements: "Submit two firmly bound manuscripts and entry fee of $5 with SASE for return." Deadline: September 1 postmark. Send for complete guidelines and application.

Awards: Lee Korf Playwriting Award: Prizes range from $250 for workshop to $750 for full scale production. Award is one time only. Award is nonrenewable. "Submissions are read by faculty. Recommended scripts are discussed by directors."
Tips: "We are looking for previously unproduced works."

L.A. DESIGNERS' THEATRE MUSIC AWARDS, P.O. Box 1883, Studio City CA 91614-0883. (213)650-9600. (818)769-9000 (T.D.D.). Fax: (818)985-9200. E-mail: ladesigners'@mcimail.com. Artistic Director: Richard Niederberg. For songwriters, composers, performing artists, musical playwrights and rights holders of music.
Purpose: To produce new musicals, operettas, opera-boufes and plays with music, as well as new dance pieces with new music scores.
Requirements: Submit nonreturnable cassette, tape, CD or other medium by first or 4th class mail. Acceptance: continuous. Submit nonreturnable materials with cover letter. No application form or fee is necessary.
Awards: Music is commissioned for a particular project. Amounts are negotiable. Applications judged by our artistic staff.
Tips: "Make the material 'classic, yet commercial' and easy to record/re-record/edit. Make sure rights are totally free of all 'strings,' 'understandings,' 'promises,' etc. ASCAP/BMI/SESAC registration is OK, as long as 'grand' or 'performing rights' are available."

MCKNIGHT VISITING COMPOSER PROGRAM, ACF, 332 Minnesota St., #E 145, St. Paul MN 55101. (612)228-1407. Fax: (612)291-7978. E-mail: compfrm@maroon.tc.umn.edu. Program Director: Philip Blackburn. Estab. 1994. For songwriters, musical playwrights and composers. Annual award.
Purpose: "Up to 2 annual awards for non-Minnesota composers to come to Minnesota for a self-designed residency of at least 3 months."
Requirements: Not for Minnesota residents or students. American Composers Forum membership required. Deadline: March. Send for application. Samples of work are required with application. Send score/tape.
Awards: McKnight Visiting Composer $10,000 stipend. Each award good for 1 year. Applications are judged by peer review panel.
Tips: "Find committed partners in Minnesota with whom to work, and explore diverse communities."

*McLAREN COMEDY PLAYWRITING COMPETITION, 2000 W. Wadley, Midland TX 79705. (915)682-2544. Fax: (915)682-6136. Coordinator: Mary Lou Cassidy. Estab. 1990. For musical playwrights. Annual award.
Purpose: "The purpose of The McLaren Competition is to develop new comedy scripts suitable for production by community theaters and other nonprofit theaters. The competition honors Mike McLaren, a writer, actor and radio personality, who often appeared in Midland Community Theatre productions."
Requirements: "We are seeking comedy scripts only. Plays submitted should be unproduced. We do not count previous 'readings' as productions; we will consider plays produced once in a nonprofit setting. Length, number of characters, setting is not limited. The playwright retains all rights to the work submitted." Deadline: January 31. Send for application. Scripts should be submitted between December 1 and January 31 with a $5 entry fee.
Awards: "The winning play will be presented in a staged reading at Theatre Midland in July or August of the year selected. The winning playwright will receive a $400 cash prize and accommodations in Midland during the rehearsal and production period of his or her play. The winning play will be considered for inclusion in the membership season at MCT." Scripts are judged by a committee.

MAXIM MAZUMDAR NEW PLAY COMPETITION, One Curtain Up Alley, Buffalo NY 14202-1911. (716)852-2600. Dramaturg: Joyce Stilson. For musical playwrights. Annual award.
Purpose: Alleyway Theatre is dedicated to the development and production of new works. Winners of the competition will receive production and royalties.
Requirements: Unproduced full-length work not less than 90 minutes long with cast limit of 10 and unit or simple set, or unproduced one-act work less than 60 minutes long with cast limit of 6 and simple set; prefers work with unconventional setting that explores the boundaries of theatricality; limit of submission in each category; guidelines available, no entry form. $5 playwright entry fee. Script, résumé, SASE optional. Cassette preferred, but not mandatory. Deadline: Sept. 1.
Awards: $400, production with royalty and travel and housing to attend rehearsals for full-length play or musical; $100 and production for one-act play or musical.
Tips: "Entries may be of any style, but preference will be given to those scripts which take place in unconventional settings and explore the boundaries of theatricality. No more than 10 performers is a definite, unchangeable requirement."

MID-ATLANTIC SONG CONTEST, 1413 K St. NW, 1st Floor, Washington DC 20005. (301)654-8434. Contact: Director. Estab. 1982. Sponsored by BMI and the Songwriters of Washington. Annual award.

Purpose: "Contest is designed to afford *amateurs* the opportunity of receiving awards/exposure/feedback of critical nature in an environment of peer competition." Applicants must send for application to: Mid-Atlantic Song Contest, P.O. Box 10703, McClean, VA 22102. Rules and regulations explained—amateur status is most important requirement. Samples of work are required with application: cassette, entry form and 3 copies of lyrics.

Awards: "Awards usually include free recording time, merchandise and cash. Awards vary from year to year. Awards must be used within one calendar year. Winning songs will be placed on a winners CD, which will be distributed to major music publishers."

Requirements: Applications are judged by a panel of 3 judges per category, for 3 levels, to determine top winners in each category and to arrive at the Grand Prize winner. Grand Prize winner will be determined by a panel of representatives from music publishers and performing rights organizations specifically selected by BMI. Reduced entry fees are offered for SAW members. Membership also entitles one to a newsletter and reduced rates for special events/seminars.

Tips: "Keep intros short; avoid instrumental solos; get to the chorus quickly and; don't bury vocals."

MIXED BLOOD VERSUS AMERICA PLAYWRITING CONTEST, 1501 S. Fourth St., Minneapolis MN 55454. (612)338-0937. Script Czar: Dave Kunz. For musical playwrights. Annual award. Estab. 1983.

Purpose: To encourage emerging musical playwrights.

Requirements: "Send previously unproduced play (musical,) résumé, query letter and short, 1-page synopsis." Deadline March 15. Send SASE for copy of contest guidelines. Samples are not required.

Awards: Winner: $2,000 and full production of winning play/musical.

Tips: "Professionalism is always a plus. Surprise us. All subject matter accepted. Political satires and shows involving sports (baseball, golf, etc.) always of interest."

MUSEUM IN THE COMMUNITY COMPOSER'S AWARD, P.O. Box 251, Scott Depot WV 25560. (304)562-0484. Fax: (304)562-5375. Competition Administrator: Patricia Fisher. For composers. Biennial award.

Purpose: The Composer's Competition is to promote the writing of new works. "Specific type of competition changes. Past competitions have included string quartet, full orchestra and nonet."

Requirements: Work must not have won any previous awards nor have been published, publicly performed or used commercially. Requires 3 copies of the original score, clearly legible and bound. Title to appear at the top of each composition, but the composer's name must not appear. Entry forms must be filled out and a SASE of the proper size enclosed for return of entry. Enclose $25 entry fee (non-refundable). Send for application.

Awards: "Next competition will open in winter 1998. Contest format undecided at present. Winning composition announced January 1999 with concert in Spring 1999. Prize will be from $2,500 to $5,000 depending on type of competition." Jurors will be 3 nationally known musicologists. Winning composer will be awarded a cash prize and a premiere concert of the composition. Transportation to the premiere from anywhere in the continental United States will be provided by the Museum.

Tips: "Read *and* follow rules listed in Prospectus. Neatness still counts!"

*NEW FOLK CONCERTS FOR EMERGING SONGWRITERS, P.O. Box 1466, Kerrville TX 78029. (210)257-3600. E-mail: kfest@hilconet.com. Website: http://www.com/~kerrfest. Attn: New Folk. For songwriters and composers. Annual award.

Purpose: "Our objective is to provide an opportunity for unknown songwriters to be heard and rewarded for excellence."

Requirements: Songwriter enters 2 previously unrecorded songs on same side of cassette tape—$8 entry fee; no more than one tape may be entered; 6-8 minutes total for 2 songs. No written application necessary; no lyric sheets or press material needed. Deadline: April 1st. Call for detailed information.

Awards: New Folk Award Winner. 32 finalists invited to sing the 2 songs entered during The Kerrville Folk Festival. 6 writers are chosen as award winners. Each of the 6 receives a cash award of $150 and performs at a winner's concert during the Kerrville Folk Festival. Initial round of entries judged by the Festival Producer. 40 finalists judged by panel of 3 performer/songwriters.

Tips: "Make certain cassette is rewound and ready to play. Do not allow instrumental accompaniment to drown out lyric content. Don't enter without complete copy of the rules. Former winners include Lyle Lovett, Nanci Griffith, Hal Ketchum, John Gorka, David Wilcox, Lucinda Williams and Robert Earl Keen."

OMAHA SYMPHONY GUILD NEW MUSIC COMPETITION, 1605 Howard St., Omaha NE 68102-2705. (402)342-3836. Contact: Chairman, New Music Competition. For composers with an annual award. Estab. 1976.

Purpose: "The objective of the competition is to promote new music scored for chamber orchestra."
Requirements: "Follow competition guidelines including orchestration and length of composition."
Deadline: usually May 15. Send for application or call (402)342-3836. Each fall new guidelines and application forms are printed.
Awards: "Monetary award is $2,000. Winner has an optional premiere performance by the Omaha Symphony Chamber Orchestra. Applications are screened by Omaha Symphony music director. Finalists are judged by a national panel of judges."
Tips: "This is an annual competition and each year has a new Symphony Guild chairman; all requests for extra information sent to the Omaha Symphony office will be forwarded. Also, 1,700-1,800 application information brochures are sent to colleges, universities and music publications each fall."

PLAYHOUSE ON THE SQUARE NEW PLAY COMPETITION, 51 S. Cooper, Memphis TN 38104. (901)725-0776. Executive Director: Jackie Nichols. For musical playwrights. Annual award. Estab. 1983.
Requirements: Send script, tape and SASE. "Playwrights from the South will be given preference." Open to full-length, unproduced plays. Musicals must be fully arranged for piano when received. Deadline: April 1.
Awards: Grants may be renewed. Applications judged by 3 readers.

*PULITZER PRIZE IN MUSIC, 702 Journalism, Columbia University, New York NY 10027. (212)854-3841. Website: http://www.pulitzer.org/. Music Secretary: Elizabeth Mahaffey. For composers and musical playwrights. Annual award.
Requirements: "For distinguished musical composition by an American in any of the larger forms including chamber, orchestral, choral, opera, song, dance or other forms of musical theater. The piece must have its American premiere between March 2 and March 1 of the one-year period in which it is submitted for consideration." Deadline: March 1. Samples of work are required with application, entry form and $20 entry fee. "Send tape and score."
Awards: "One award: $3,000. Applications are judged first by a nominating jury, then by the Pulitzer Prize Board."

*RIVER POETS MUSIC SONG CONTEST, 9 Music Square S., Suite 382, Nashville TN 37203. (615)370-4331. Co-Director of Operations: Pamela D. Stevenson. Estab. 1995. For songwriters and composers. Annual award.
Purpose: "Our objective is to provide an outlet for songs from writers all over the nation to be heard by the people who need to hear them. We provide the opportunity for the music to be analyzed by top industry professionals. The goals of the artists should never be forgotten."
Requirements: "No more than 2 copyrighted songs (any style), with lyric sheets, composer/writer names and addresses, contact phone, and $5 entry fee per song. Songs should be no more than 5 minutes in length." Deadline: October 30. Send for application or call (800)484-8470, ext. 7456. Samples of work are not required.
Awards: 1st: $100, single song contract and certificate; 2nd: $50 and certificate; 3rd: $25 and certificate; 5 Honorable Mentions. All are published in the January Issue of *The River Poet* Magazine. Applications judged on lyrics, musicality, commercial and overall appeal.

RICHARD RODGERS AWARDS, American Academy of Arts and Letters, 633 W. 155th St., New York NY 10032. (212)368-5900. Estab. 1978. "The Richard Rodgers Awards subsidize full productions, studio productions, and staged readings by nonprofit theaters in New York City of works by composers and writers who are not already established in the field of musical theater. The awards are only for musicals—songs by themselves are not eligible. The authors must be citizens or permanent residents of the United States." (Guidelines for this award may be obtained by sending a SASE to above address.)

LOIS AND RICHARD ROSENTHAL NEW PLAY PRIZE, % Cincinnati Playhouse, P.O. Box 6537, Cincinnati OH 45206. (513)345-2242. E-mail: theater1@tso.cin.ix.net. Website: http://www.cinc yplay.com. Contact: Artistic Associate. For playwrights and musical playwrights. Annual award.
Purpose: The Lois and Richard Rosenthal New Play Prize was established in 1987 to encourage the development of new plays that are original, theatrical, strong in character and dialogue and that are a significant contribution to the literature of American theater. Lois Rosenthal is the author of books in the consumer information field and is the editor of *Story* magazine, the classic literary quarterly. Richard Rosenthal operates F&W Publications, a family company founded in 1910, which publishes books and magazines for writers and artists. Residents of Cincinnati, the Rosenthals are committed to supporting arts organizations and social agencies that are innovative and that foster social change.
Requirements: "The play must be full-length and can be of any style: comedy, drama, musical, etc. Individual one-acts are not acceptable. Collaborations are welcome, in which case the prize benefits are shared. The play must not have received a full-scale, professional production, and it must be

unpublished prior to submission. A play that has had a workshop, reading or non-professional production is eligible. Playwrights with past production experience are especially encouraged to submit new work. Any play previously submitted for the Rosenthal Prize is ineligible. Only one submission per playwright. Submit a two-page maximum abstract of the play including title, playwright, character breakdown, story synopsis, a short bio of the playwright and any other information you wish to provide. Also send up to five pages of sample dialogue. All abstracts will be read. From these, selected manuscripts will be solicited. Do not send a manuscript with or instead of the abstract. All unsolicited manuscripts will be returned unread. The Rosenthal Prize is open for submission from October 15th to February 1st."

Awards: The Rosenthal Prize play is produced at the Cincinnati Playhouse in the Park as part of the theater's annual season, and it is given regional and national promotion. The playwright receives a $10,000 prize plus travel expenses and residency in Cincinnati during production. In addition to the prize-winning play, a number of plays are selected to be given a workshop at the Playhouse with a professional director and actors. Playwrights are provided travel expenses and residency in Cincinnati for these workshops. It is possible for a play that has been given a workshop to be chosen as the Rosenthal Prize recipient for the following season with complete prize benefits.

*SALOP/SLATES MEMORIAL COMPOSITION CONTEST, P.O. Box 6968, Radford VA 24142. Vice President-Southeastern Composers League: Bruce Mahin. For composers. Annual award.
Requirements: Undergraduate or graduate students in Maryland, Delaware, Washington D.C., Virginia, West Virginia, North and South Carolina, Tennessee, Kentucky, Georgia, Florida, Alabama, Louisiana, Mississippi and Arkansas are eligible. Deadline: October 31. Send for application. Samples of work are required with application. Send clean, legible score.
Awards: 1st Place $150; 2nd Place $100 (for both undergraduate and graduate competitions). Applications judged by officers of the Southeastern Composers League.

*REVA SHINER FULL-LENGTH CONTEST, Bloomington Playwrights Project, 308 S. Washington St., Bloomington IN 47401. (812)334-1188. Literary Manager: Gretchen Baer. For musical playwrights. Annual award.
Purpose: "The Bloomington Playwrights Project is a script-developing organization. Winning playwrights are expected to become part of the development process, working with the director in person or via long-distance. The Reva Shiner contest is intended to encourage production and development of new plays."
Requirements: "Plays must be unpublished and unproduced. Must be full-length (75-150 minutes). Submissions must include a cover letter, a SASE for the script to be returned, and a $5 reader's fee." Deadline: January 15. Send for application. Samples of work are required with application. Submit complete script with tape.
Awards: $500 and production of play in following season. Applications are judged by a committee of readers, including the Artistic Director and Literary Manager.

SONG SPREE SONGWRITER COMPETITION, 2417 Pinewood Rd. W., Dept. 97, Nunnelly TN 37137. E-mail: spree@mixcom.com. President: Lynda Bostwick. Estab. 1995. For songwriters. Annual award.
Purpose: "Seeking best songs in 4 categories: rock, country, blues and R&B, and soft alternatives. (Note: gospel accepted in all categories.) Winners to be recorded and released on CD."
Requirements: Send lyric and (separate) cassette for each song along with entry fee ($20 first song, $15 each additional song). Deadline: March 15,1997. For complete rules and prize list send #10 SASE.
Awards: "Winners receive trip to Nashville, get recorded on CD and earn royalties. Publishing contracts offered if desired. *All* entrants receive free CD of winning songs."

*THE SOUTH PACIFIC SONG CONTEST, P.O. Box 349, Surfers Paradise Queensland 4217 **Australia**. Phone/fax: (07)55922318. Chief Executive: James Haddleton. Estab. 1994. For songwriters and composers. Annual award.
Purpose: "To provide an international platform to give recognition for excellence to songwriters of popular music and in so doing bring them to the attention of the music industry and the general public."
Requirements: "The contest is open to all songwriters. Songs entered must not be released on major record label prior to March 29, 1997." Deadline: Entries must be received by January 31. Samples of work are required with entry form and fee. Songs should be submitted on cassette.
Awards: First prize: $3,000 cash plus record and publishing contract with guarantee of release. Entries are judged by a panel of music industry professionals.

*MARVIN TAYLOR PLAYWRIGHTING AWARD, P.O. Box 3030, Sonora CA 95370. (209)532-3120. Fax: (209)532-7270. Producing Director: Dennis Jones. Estab. 1981. For all playwrights (comedy, drama, musical). Annual award.

Purpose: "To encourage new voices in American theater."
Requirements: "Any new plays and unpublished scripts with no more than 2 previous productions are eligible." Deadline: August 31. Send for application. Samples of work are required with application. Scripts should be typed.
Awards: $500. "Applications are read by our Dramaturg and the Producing Director."

THE TEN-MINUTE MUSICALS PROJECT, P.O. Box 461194, West Hollywood CA 90046. (213)656-8751. Producer: Michael Koppy. For songwriters, composers, musical playwrights. Annual award.
Purpose: "We are building a full-length stage musical comprised of complete short musicals, each of which play for between 8-14 minutes. Award is $250 for each work chosen for development towards inclusion in the project, plus a share of royalties when produced."
Requirements: Deadline: August 31, annually. For guidelines, write or phone. Final submission should include script, cassette and lead sheets.
Awards: $250 for each work selected. "Works should have complete stories, with a definite beginning, middle and end."

*THEATER AT LIME KILN REGIONAL PLAYWRITING CONTEST, 14 S. Randolph St., Lexington VA 24450. (540)463-7088. Fax: (540)463-1082. E-mail: limekiln@cfw.com. Community Liaison/Dramaturg: Eleanor Connor. For musical playwrights. Annual award.
Purpose: "This contest was created to encourage writers to celebrate the culture, history and events of the Appalachian Region."
Requirements: Deadline: August 1-September 30. Send for application. Samples of work are required only upon submission in contest.
Awards: 1st place: $1,000; 2nd place: $500, with possibility of staged readings. Applications are judged by a reading panel of professionals and lay people.
Tips: "Theater at Lime Kiln is an outdoor theater with a summer season. We prefer smaller cast shows and are always looking for new musicals or plays with music."

U.S.A. SONGWRITING COMPETITION, Dept A.W. 97, Box 15312, Boston MA 02215-5312. Fax: (617)738-7292. E-mail: bliss@tiac.net. Contact: Contest Manager. Estab. 1994. For songwriters. Annual award.
Purpose: "To honor good songwriters all over the country (or foreign countries), especially the unknown ones."
Requirements: Contest runs from October 1st to February 28 each year. All amateur/professional songwriters may enter. You may submit as many entries as you wish. Each entry must include an entry fee of $10 per song, a cassette tape of song(s) and lyric sheet(s). Judging/critique sheets will be returned to entrant. Winners will be announced on May 1st. Judged by industry people—publishers, etc. Deadline: March 1, 1997. Send or e-mail for application. Samples of work are not required.
Awards: Grand prize winner receives $500 cash. 1st Prizes: pop $100; country $100; rock/metal/alternative $100; R&B/jazz $100. 20 consolation prizes.
Tips: "Clear vocals and instruments in tune. Please have the lyric written or typed neatly. All genres are acceptable."

*U.S.-MEXICO FUND FOR CULTURE, Londres 16-PB, Col. Juarez Mexico City **Mexico** 06600. (525)592-5386. Fax: (525)208-8943. Assistant Program Coordinator: Beatriz E. Nava. Estab. 1991. For songwriters, composers, musical playwrights and performers. Annual award.
Purpose: "The U.S.-Mexico Fund for Culture, an independent body created through a joint initiative of the Bancomer Cultural Foundation, The Rockefeller Foundation and Mexico's National Fund for Culture and the Arts, provides financial support for the development of cultural binational projects in music, theater, visual arts, cultural studies, literary and cultural publications and interdisciplinary."
Requirements: Deadline: April 19. Send for application with SASE ($9\frac{1}{2} \times 6\frac{1}{2}$ envelope). Samples of work are required with application in duplicate.
Awards: Range from $2,500-25,000. Award is good for 1 year. Judged by binational panel of experts in each of the disciplines, one from Mexico and one from the USA.
Tips: "Proposals must be bi-national in character and have a close and active collaboration with artist from Mexico. The creation of new works is highly recommendable."

V.O.C.A.L. SONGWRITER'S CONTEST, P.O. Box 34606, Richmond VA 23234-0606. (804)796-1444 or (804)342-0662. E-mail: vocal10@aol.com. Website: http://members.aol.com/vocal 10/. President: Gary Shaver. Song Contest Director: Matthew Costello. For songwriters, lyricists and composers. Annual award with up to 11 categories.
Purpose: "To recognize good songs and lyrics as well as the writers of same."
Requirements: "Original songs/lyrics/compositions only." Postal deadline: March 31 of the contest year. Send for entry forms and information. Song entries must be on cassette tape. Lyric entries should

be typed or neatly printed on white paper." Contest entries and inquiries should be sent to the above address. Include SASE.

Awards: Prizes for first, second, third places awarded for best song overall, the lyric competition, and category competitions. Prizes include: Cash, merchandise, T-shirts, certificates and more.

Tips: "Be sure to use a fresh tape to record your entry. Listen to the entry to be sure it's not distorted or too low in volume. A clean sounding tape stands a much better chance. The judges can only grade based on what they hear. Don't overproduce your entry. That will take away from the song itself. Fill out the entry form completely and follow all rules of the contest. The contest begins January 1st and entries must be postmarked no later than March 31 of that contest year. Mail your entry early."

WEST COAST ENSEMBLE–MUSICAL STAIRS, P.O. Box 38728, Los Angeles CA 90038. (213)871-8673. Artistic Director: Les Hanson. For musical playwrights. Annual award.

Purpose: To provide an arena and encouragement for the development of new musicals for the theater.

Requirements: Submit book and a cassette of the score to the above address.

Awards: The West Coast Ensemble Musical Stairs Competition Award includes a production of the selected musical and $500 prize. The selected musical will be part of the 1997 season. Panel of judges reads script and listen to cassette. Final selection is made by Artistic Director.

Tips: "Submit libretto in standard playscript format along with professional sounding cassette of songs."

*WORDS BY, 332 Eastwood Ave,. Feasterville PA 19053. (800)574-2986. Phone/fax: (215)953-0952. E-mail: a1foster@aol.com. Editor/Publisher: Allen Foster. Estab. 1992. For lyricists. Monthly contest.

Requirements: "To enter, send your best lyrics and contact information."

Awards: Winning lyrics will be published along with your address so interested parties may contact you directly.

Tips: "Send only one set of your best lyrics."

*Y.E.S. FESTIVAL OF NEW PLAYS, Northern Kentucky University Dept. of Theatre, FA-206, Highland Heights KY 41099-1007. (606)572-6362. E-mail: mking@nku.edu. Project Director: Mike King. Estab. 1983. For composers and musical playwrights. Biennial award.

Purpose: "The festival seeks to encourage new playwrights and develop new plays and musicals. Three plays or musicals are given full productions and one is given a staged reading."

Requirements: "Submit a script with a completed entry form. Musicals should be submitted with a piano/conductor's score and a vocal parts score." Deadline: October 15. Send for application. Samples of work are required with application. Submit complete script and score.

Awards: Four awards of $400. "The four winners are brought to NKU at our expense to view late rehearsals and opening night." Applications are judged by a panel of readers.

Tips: "Plays/musicals which have heavy demands for mature actors are not as likely to be selected as an equally good script with roles for 18-25 year olds."

YOUNG COMPOSERS AWARDS, % NGCSA, 40 North Van Brunt St., Suite 32, Box 8018, Englewood NJ 07631. (201)871-3337. Executive Director: Lolita Mayadas. For composers. Open to students age 13-18. Annual award.

Purpose: "To encourage young students to write music, so that the art of composition—with no restrictions as to the category of music in which the works are written—will once again occupy the place in the center of music education where it belongs. It takes tons of ore to extract one ounce of gold: by focusing on the inventiveness of many students, the Awards may lead to the discovery of genuine creative talents—that is the eventual goal."

Requirements: "Applicants must be enrolled in a public or private secondary school, in a recognized musical institution, or be engaged in the private study of music with an established teacher. No compositions will be considered without certification by the applicant's teacher. Each applicant may submit only one work. Deadline: May 1. Send for application. Samples of work are required with application. Four photocopies of the work must be submitted and, if available, a cassette recording. All manuscripts must be in legible form and may be submitted on usual score paper or reduced under a generally accepted process. The composer's name must not appear on the composition submitted. The composition must be marked with a pseudonym on the manuscript as well as on the optional accompanying cassette recording."

Awards: Herbert Zipper Prizes: First Prize, $1,000; Second Prize, $750; Third Prize, $500; Fourth Prize, $250. "Announcement of the Awards are made no later than May 15 each year. In the event that no entry is found to be worthy of the $1,000 Prize, the jury may award one or both of the other Prizes or none at all. NGCSA appoints an independent jury to review all entries submitted. The jury consists of not less than three qualified judges."

Tips: "Paramount would be neatness and legibility of the manuscript submitted. The application must be complete in all respects."

Publications of Interest

Knowledge about the music industry is essential for both creative and business success. Staying informed requires keeping up with constantly changing information. Updates on the changing trends in the music business are available to you in the form of music magazines, music trade papers and books. There is a publication aimed at almost every type of musician, songwriter and music fan, from the most technical knowledge of amplification systems to gossip about your favorite singer. These publications can enlighten and inspire you and provide information vital in helping you become a more well-rounded, educated, and, ultimately, successful musical artist.

This sections lists all types of magazines and books you may find interesting. From home-grown fanzines and glossy music magazines to tip sheets and how-to books, there should be something listed here that you'll enjoy and benefit from.

PERIODICALS

THE ALBUM NETWORK, 120 N. Victory Blvd., Burbank CA 91502. (818)955-4000. *Weekly music industry trade magazine.*

AMERICAN SONGWRITER MAGAZINE, 121 17th Ave. S., Nashville TN 37203. (615)244-6065. E-mail: asongmag@aol.com. Website: http://www.nol.com/nol. *Bimonthly publication for and about songwriters.*

AUDIO IMAGES 2000, P.O. Box 250806, Holly Hill, FL 32125-0806. (904)238-3820. E-mail: bjsrecords@aol.com. *Bimonthly songwriters' newsletter.*

BILLBOARD, 1515 Broadway, New York NY 10036. (800)247-2160. Website: http://www/billboard-online.com. *Weekly industry trade magazine.*

CANADIAN MUSICIAN, 23 Hannover Dr., Suite 7, St. Catharines, Ontario L2W 1A3 Canada. (905)641-1512. Website: http://www.nor.com/nwc. *Bimonthly publication for Canadian songwriters.*

CASH BOX MAGAZINE, 6464 Sunset Blvd., Suite 605, Hollywood CA 90028. (213)464-8241. *Weekly music industry trade publication.*

CMJ NEW MUSIC REPORT, 11 Middle Neck Rd., Suite 400, Great Neck NY 11021-2301. (516)466-6000. E-mail: cmj@cmjmusic.com. *Weekly college radio and alternative music tip sheet.*

DAILY VARIETY, 5700 Wilshire Blvd., Suite 120, Los Angeles CA 90036. (213)857-6600. *Daily entertainment trade newspaper.*

THE DRAMATISTS GUILD QUARTERLY, 234 W. 44th St., 11th Floor, New York NY 10036. (212)398-9366. *The quarterly journal of the Dramatists Guild, the professional association of playwrights, composers and lyricists.*

ENTERTAINMENT LAW & FINANCE, New York Law Publishing Co., 345 Park Ave. S., 8th Floor, New York NY 10010. (212)545-6220. *Monthly newsletter covering music industry contracts, lawsuit filings, court rulings and legislation.*

FAST FORWARD, Disc Makers, 7905 N. Rt. 130, Pennsauken NJ 08110. (800)468-9353. E-mail: webmaster@discmakers.com. *Quarterly newsletter featuring companies and products for performing and recording artists.*

THE GAVIN REPORT, 140 Second St., San Francisco CA 94105. (415)495-1990. E-mail: editorial @gavin.com. Website: http://www/gavin.com. *Weekly listing of radio charts.*

HITS MAGAZINE, 14958 Ventura Blvd., Sherman Oaks CA 91403. (818)501-7900. *Weekly music industry trade publication.*

JAZZTIMES, 7961 Eastern Ave. #303, Silver Spring MD 20910. (301)588-4114. E-mail: jtimes@aol. com. *10 issues/year magazine covering the American jazz scene.*

THE LEADS SHEET, Allegheny Music Works, 306 Cypress Ave., Johnstown PA 15902. (814)535-3373. *Monthly tip sheet.*

MIX BOOKSHELF, 100 Newfield Ave., Edison NJ 08837. (800)233-9604. *Catalog of information resources for music professionals.*

MUSIC BUSINESS INTERNATIONAL MAGAZINE, 2 Park Ave., Suite 1820, New York NY 10016. (212)779-1212, ext. 126. *Bimonthly magazine for senior executives in the music industry.*

MUSIC CONNECTION MAGAZINE, 4731 Laurel Canyon Blvd., N. Hollywood CA 91607. (818)755-0101. E-mail: muscon@earthlink.net. *Biweekly music industry trade publication.*

THE MUSIC PAPER, Sound Resources Ltd., P.O. Box 304, Manhasset NY 11030. (516)883-8898. *Monthly music magazine for musicians.*

MUSIC ROW MAGAZINE, Music Row Publications, Inc., 1231 17th Ave. S., Nashville TN 37212. (615)321-3617. E-mail: news@musicrow.com. *Biweekly Nashville industry publication.*

MUSICIAN MAGAZINE, Billboard Publications, 1515 Broadway, 11th Floor, New York NY 10036. (212)536-5208. E-mail: musicianmag@sonicnet.com. *Monthly music magazine.*

THE NETWORK NEWS The Los Angeles Music Network, P.O. Box 8934, Universal City CA 91618-8934. (818)769-6095. E-mail: lamnetwork@aol.com. *Bimonthly publication of the Los Angeles Music Network.*

OFFBEAT MAGAZINE, OffBeat, Inc., 333 St. Charles Ave. #614, New Orleans LA 70130. (504)522-45533. E-mail: offbeat@neosoft.com. *Monthly magazine covering Louisiana music and artists.*

THE PERFORMING SONGWRITER, P.O. Box 158159, Nashville TN 37215-9998. (800)883-7664. E-mail: perfsong@aol.com. *Bimonthly songwriters' magazine.*

PRODUCER REPORT, Mojave Music, Inc., 115 S. Topanga Canyon Blvd., Suite 114, Topanga CA 90290. (310)455-0888. E-mail: 72570.440@compuserve.com. *22 times/year publication dealing with record producers, published via fax or modem.*

PUBLIC DOMAIN REPORT, P.O. Box 3102, Margate NJ 08402. (609)822-9401. E-mail: pdrcpub @aol.com. *Monthly guide to significant titles entering the public domain.*

RADIO AND RECORDS, 10100 Santa Monica Blvd., 5th Floor, Los Angeles CA 90067. (310)553-4330. *Weekly newspaper covering the radio and record industries.*

RADIR, BBH Software, Inc., 15072 E. Mississippi Ave. Suite 33, Aurora CO 80012. (800)277-8224. *Quarterly radio station database on disk.*

SING OUT!, P.O. Box 5253, Bethlehem PA 18015-0253. (610)865-5366. *Quarterly folk music magazine.*

SONGWRITER ALERT, 1719 West End Ave., Suite 214E, Nashville TN 37203. (615)327-9977. *Professional newsletter for songwriters.*

SONGWRITER PRODUCTS, IDEAS AND NECESSITIES, NSP Music Publishing, 345 Sprucewood Rd., Lake Mary FL 32746-5917. (407)321-3702. *Semi-annual catalog of songwriting tips, tools and accessories.*

SONGWRITER'S MONTHLY, 332 Eastwood Ave., Feasterville PA 19053. Phone/fax: (215)953-0952. (800)574-2986. E-mail: a1foster@aol.com. *Monthly songwriters' magazine.*

TOURNEE INTERNATIONAL,via Orti 24, 20122 Milano Italy. 0039 (2) 55184004. E-mail: fr.fontana@agora.stm.it. *Bimonthly international music magazine.*

WORDS AND MUSIC, 41 Valleybrook Dr., Don Mills, Ontario M3B 2S6 Canada. (416)445-8700. E-mail: rmacmillan@socan.ca. *Monthly songwriters' magazine.*

BOOKS AND DIRECTORIES

THE A&R REGISTRY, by Ritch Esra, SRS Publishing, 7510 Sunset Blvd. #1041, Los Angeles CA 90046-3418. (800)377-7411. Fax: (213)882-6813. E-mail: 76513.3543@compuserve.com or srs publ@aol.com.

ATTENTION: A&R, second edition, by Teri Muench and Susan Pomerantz, Alfred Publishing Co. Inc., Box 10003, Van Nuys CA 91410-0003. (800)292-6122.

BEGINNING SONGWRITER'S ANSWER BOOK, by Paul Zollo, Writer's Digest Books, 1507 Dana Ave., Cincinnati OH 45207. (800)289-0963. E-mail: wdigest@aol.com.

CMJ DIRECTORY, 11 Middle Neck Rd., Suite 400, Great Neck NY 11021-2301. (516)466-6000.

THE CRAFT AND BUSINESS OF SONGWRITING, by John Braheny, Writer's Digest Books, 1507 Dana Ave., Cincinnati OH 45207. (800)289-0963. E-mail: wdigest@aol.com.

DIRECTORY OF INDEPENDENT MUSIC DISTRIBUTORS, by Jason Ojalvo, Disc Makers, 7905 N. Rt. 130, Pennsauken NJ 08110. (800)468-9353. E-mail: webmaster@discmakers.com.

FILM/TV MUSIC GUIDE, by Ritch Esra, SRS Publishing, 7510 Sunset Blvd. #1041, Los Angeles CA 90046-3418. (800)377-7411. Fax: (213)882-6813. E-mail: 76513.3543@compuserve.com or srs publ@aol.com.

GUIDE TO INDEPENDENT MUSIC PUBLICITY, by Veronique Berry, Disc Makers, 7905 N. Rt. 130, Pennsauken NJ 08110. (800)468-9353. E-mail: webmaster@discmakers.com.

GUIDE TO MASTER TAPE PREPARATION, by Dave Moyssiadis, Disk Makers, 7905 N. Rt. 130, Pennsauken NJ 08110. (800)468-9353. E-mail: webmaster@discmakers.com.

HOW YOU CAN BREAK INTO THE MUSIC BUSINESS, by Marty Garrett, Lonesome Wind Corporation, P.O. Box 2143, Broken Arrow OK 74013-2143. (800)210-4416.

THE INTERNATIONAL SONGWRITER, by Dennis R. Sinnott, Christel Music Ltd., Fleet House, 173 Haydons Rd., Wimbledon London SW19 8TB England. (0181)679-5010.

LOUISIANA MUSIC DIRECTORY, OffBeat, Inc., 333 St. Charles Ave., Suite 614, New Orleans, LA 70130. (504)522-5533. E-mail: offbeat eosoft.com.

MUSIC DIRECTORY CANADA, sixth edition, Norris-Whitney Communications Inc., 23 Hannover Dr., Suite 7, St. Catherines, Ontario L2W 1A3 Canada. (905)641-3471.

THE MUSIC PUBLISHER REGISTRY, by Ritch Esra, SRS Publishing, 7510 Sunset Blvd. #1041, Los Angeles CA 90046-3418. (800)377-7411. Fax: (213)882-6813. E-mail: 76513.3543@compuser ve.com or srspubl@aol.com.

NATIONAL DIRECTORY OF RECORD LABELS AND MUSIC PUBLISHERS, fifth edition, Rising Star Music Publishers, 52 Executive Park S., Suite 5203, Atlanta GA 30329. (800)247-3108. E-mail: ristar@mindspring.com.

OFFICIAL COUNTRY MUSIC DIRECTORY, Entertainment Media, P.O. Box 700, Rancho Mirage CA 92270. (800)395-6736.

RECORDING INDUSTRY SOURCEBOOK, Cardinal Business Media, 100 Newfield Ave., Edison NJ 08837. (800)233-9604.

THE SONGWRITER'S MARKET GUIDE TO SONG & DEMO SUBMISSION FORMATS, Writer's Digest Books, 1507 Dana Ave., Cincinnati OH 45207. (800)289-0963. E-mail: wdigest@aol. com.

SONGWRITER'S PLAYGROUND - INNOVATIVE EXERCISES IN CREATIVE SONG-WRITING, by Barbara L. Jordan, Creative Music Marketing, 1085 Commwealth Ave., Suite 323, Boston MA 02215. (617)424-9490.

SONGWRITING AND THE CREATIVE PROCESS, by Steve Gillette, Sing Out! Publications, P.O. Box 5253, Bethlehem PA 18015-0253. (800)4-WE-SING.

TIM SWEENEY'S GUIDE TO RELEASING INDEPENDENT RECORDS, by Tim Sweeney, TSA Books, 21213-B Hawthorne Blvd. #5255, Torrance CA 90503. (310)542-6430. E-mail: tsah q@aol.com.

TEXAS MUSIC INDUSTRY DIRECTORY, Texas Music Office, Office of the Governor, P.O. Box 13246, Austin TX 78711. (512)463-6666. Fax: (512)463-4114. E-mail: music@governor.texas.gov. Website: http://link.tsl.texas.gov.

WOMEN'S MUSIC PLUS: DIRECTORY OF RESOURCES IN WOMEN'S MUSIC & CUL-TURE, by Toni Armstrong Jr., Empty Closet Enterprises Inc., 5210 N. Wayne, Chicago IL 60640-2223. (312)769-9009. E-mail: tonijr@aol.com.

THE YELLOW PAGES OF ROCK, The Album Network, 120 N. Victory Blvd., Burbank CA 91502. (818)955-4000.

Websites of Interest

The Internet can provide a wealth of information for songwriters and performers, and the number of sites devoted to music grows each day. Below is a list of some websites that can offer you information, links to other music sites, contact with other songwriters and places to showcase your songs. Since the online world is changing and expanding at such a rapid pace, this is hardly a comprehensive list, and some of these addresses may be obsolete by the time this book goes to print. But it gives you a place to start on your journey through the Internet to search for opportunities to get your music heard.

AMERICAN MUSIC CENTER: http://www.amc.net/amc/index.html
Classical/jazz archives, includes a list of composer organizations and contacts.

ARTIST UNDERGROUND: http://www.aumusic.com
A place for artists to place songs and information on the Internet, along with the capability to sell their CDs and tapes online.

COUNTRY CONNECTION: http://digiserve.com/country
Country music archive, provides links to other country music sites.

INTERNET UNDERGROUND MUSIC ARCHIVE (IUMA): http://www.iuma.com
Features unsigned bands, news and zines, as well as record label sites, a record store and more.

JAZZ CENTRAL STATION: http://~jazzcentralstation.com
Jazz-related information, including reviews, magazines, a listing of jazz record labels and contacts, managers and more.

KALEIDOSPACE: http://kspace.com. *Website for independent artists to place their material online, along with the capability to contact the artists and purchase their work.*

LIBRARY OF MUSICAL LINKS: http://www-scf.usc.edu/~jrush/music
A link to music-related websites with search capabilities.

LOS ANGELES MUSIC ACCESS (LAMA): http://com.primenet.com/home
Database of Los Angeles bands, clubs and resources sponsored by a group that promotes independent artists.

MARKETING MUSIC ON THE WEB: http://www.magicnet.net/rz/web_music
Virtual report of music marketing opportunities on the web.

METAVERSE: http://www.metaverse.com
Provides a forum for unsigned bands to showcase their work.

MUSIC PUBLISHERS ASSOCIATION: http://host.mpa.org
Provides a copyright resource center, directory of member publishers and information on the organization.

MUSIC WORLD: http://music-world.co
A directory of music industry resources.

MUSICPRO, THE MUSIC INDUSTRY'S INTERNET CONNECTION: http://www.music-pro.com
Provides links to other music sites on the Web.

NATIONAL MUSIC PUBLISHERS ASSOCIATION: http://www.nmpa.org/nmpa.html
The organization's online site with information about copyright, legislation and other concerns of the music publishing world.

THE NATIONAL ONLINE MUSIC ALLIANCE: http://songs.com/noma
Forum for indie artists and labels to showcase and sell their work online.

ROCKTROPOLIS: http://underground.net/Rocktropolis
Music-based virtual "city" featuring the work of established and new artists.

SONGWRITER'S COLLABORATION NETWORK: http://www.earthlink.net/~songmd
Songwriter Molly-Ann Leiken's website of songwriting articles and books.

SONGSCAPE: http://www.genoagrp.com/genoagrp
Music database and music industry news service.

Glossary

A&R Director. Record company executive in charge of the Artists and Repertoire Department who is responsible for finding and developing new artists and matching songs with artists.

A/C. Adult contemporary music.

Advance. Money paid to the songwriter or recording artist before regular royalty payment begins. Sometimes called "up front" money, advances are deducted from royalties.

AFM. American Federation of Musicians. A union for musicians and arrangers.

AFTRA. American Federation of Television and Radio Artists. A union for performers.

AIMP. Association of Independent Music Publishers.

Airplay. The radio broadcast of a recording.

AOR. Album-Oriented Rock. A radio format which primarily plays selections from rock albums as opposed to hit singles.

Arrangement. An adaptation of a composition for a recording or performance, with consideration for the melody, harmony, instrumentation, tempo, style, etc.

ASCAP. American Society of Composers, Authors and Publishers. A performing rights society.

Assignment. Transfer of rights of a song from writer to publisher.

Audiovisual. Refers to presentations which use audio backup for visual material.

Bed. Prerecorded music used as background material in commercials.

BMI. Broadcast Music, Inc. A performing rights society.

Booking agent. Person who schedules performances for entertainers.

Business manager. Person who handles the financial aspects of artistic careers.

b/w. Backed with. Usually refers to the B-side of a single.

C&W. Country and western.

Catalog. The collected songs of one writer, or all songs handled by one publisher.

CD. Compact Disc (see below).

CD-ROM. Compact Disc-Read Only Memory. A computer information storage medium capable of holding enormous amounts of data. Information on a CD-ROM cannot be deleted. A computer user must have a CD-ROM drive to access a CD-ROM.

Chart. The written arrangement of a song.

Charts. The trade magazines' lists of the best selling records.

CHR. Comtemporary Hit Radio. Top 40 pop music.

Compact disc. A small disc (about 4.7 inches in diameter) holding digitally encoded music that is read by a laser beam in a CD player.

Co-publish. Two or more parties own publishing rights to the same song.

Copyright. The exclusive legal right giving the creator of a work the power to control the publishing, reproduction and selling of the work.

Cover recording. A new version of a previously recorded song.

Crossover. A song that becomes popular in two or more musical categories (e.g., country and pop).

Cut. Any finished recording; a selection from a LP. Also to record.

DAT. Digital Audio Tape. A professional and consumer audio cassette format for recording and playing back digitally-encoded material. DAT cassettes are approximately one-third smaller than conventional audio cassettes.

DCC. Digital Compact Cassette. A consumer audio cassette format for recording and playing back digitally-encoded tape. DCC tapes are the same size as analog cassettes.

Demo. A recording of a song submitted as a demonstration of writer's or artist's skills.

Distributor. Marketing agent responsible for getting records from manufacturers to retailers.

Donut. A jingle with singing at the beginning and end and instrumental background in the middle. Ad copy is recorded over the middle section.

E-mail. Electronic mail. Computer address where a company or individual can be reached via modem.

Engineer. A specially trained individual who operates all recording studio equipment.

Enhanced CD. General term for an audio CD that also contains multimedia computer information. It is playable in both standard CD players and CD-ROM drives.

EP. Extended play record or cassette containing more selections than a standard single, but fewer than a standard album.

Exploit. To seek legitimate uses of a song for income.

Folio. A softcover collection of printed music prepared for sale.

Harry Fox Agency. Organization that collects mechanical royalties.

Hip-hop. A dance oriented musical style derived from a combination of disco, rap and R&B.

Hit. A song or record that achieves top 40 status.

Hook. A memorable "catch" phrase or melody line which is repeated in a song.

House. Dance music created by remixing samples from other songs.

Hypertext. Words or groups of words in an electronic document that are linked to other text, such as a definition or a related document. Hypertext can also be linked to illustrations.

Indie. An independent record label, music publisher or producer.

Internet. A worldwide network of computers that offers access to a wide variety of electronic resources.

ips. Inches per second; a speed designation for tape recording.

IRC. International reply coupon, necessary for the return of materials sent out of the country. Available at most post offices.

Jingle. Usually a short verse set to music designed as a commercial message.

Lead sheet. Written version (melody, chord symbols and lyric) of a song.

Leader. Plastic (non-recordable) tape at the beginning and between songs for ease in selection.

LP. Designation for long-playing record played at 33⅓ rpm.

Lyric sheet. A typed or written copy of a song's lyrics.

Market. A potential song or music buyer; also a demographic division of the record-buying public.

Master. Edited and mixed tape used in the production of records; the best or original copy of a recording from which copies are made.

MD. MiniDisc. A 2.5 inch disk for recording and playing back digitally-encoded music.

Mechanical right. The right to profit from the physical reproduction of a song.

Mechanical royalty. Money earned from record, tape and CD sales.

MIDI. Musical instrument digital interface. Universal standard interface which allows musical instruments to communicate with each other and computers.

Mix. To blend a multi-track recording into the desired balance of sound.

Modem. MOdulator/DEModulator. A computer device used to send data from one computer to another via telephone line.

MOR. Middle of the road. Easy-listening popular music.

Ms. Manuscript.

Multimedia. Computers and software capable of integrating text, sound, photographic-quality images, animation and video.

Music jobber. A wholesale distributor of printed music.

Music publisher. A company that evaluates songs for commercial potential, finds artists to record them, finds other uses (such as TV or film) for the songs, collects income generated by the songs and protects copyrights from infringement.

NARAS. National Academy of Recording Arts and Sciences.

Needle-drop. Use of a prerecorded cut from a stock music house in an audiovisual soundtrack.

Network. A group of computers electronically linked to share information and resources.

NMPA. National Music Publishers Association.

One-off. A deal between songwriter and publisher which includes only one song or project at a time. No future involvement is implicated. Many times a single song contract accompanies a one-off deal.

One-stop. A wholesale distributor of records representing several manufacturers to record stores, retailers and jukebox operators.

Overdub. To record an additional part (vocal or instrumental) onto a basic multi-track recording.

Payola. Dishonest payment to broadcasters in exchange for airplay.

Performing rights. A specific right granted by US copyright law that protects a composition from being publicly performed without the owner's permission.

Performing rights organization. An organization that collects income from the public performance of songs written by its members and then proportionally distributes this income to the individual copyright holder based on the number of performances of each song.

Personal manager. A person who represents artists to develop and enhance their careers. Personal managers may negotiate contracts, hire and dismiss other agencies and personnel relating to the artist's career, review material, help with artist promotions and perform many services.

Piracy. The unauthorized reproduction and selling of printed or recorded music.

Pitch. To attempt to sell a song by audition.

Playlist. List of songs that a radio station will play.

Points. A negotiable percentage paid to producers and artists for records sold.

Producer. Person who supervises every aspect of a recording project.

Production company. Company that specializes in producing jingle packages for advertising agencies. May also refer to companies that specialize in audiovisual programs.

Professional manager. Member of a music publisher's staff who screens submitted material and tries to get the company's catalog of songs recorded.

Public domain. Any composition with an expired, lapsed or invalid copyright.

Purchase license. Fee paid for music used from a stock music library.

Query. A letter of inquiry to an industry professional soliciting his interest.

R&B. Rhythm and blues.

Rate. The percentage of royalty as specified by contract.

Release. Any record issued by a record company.

Residuals. In advertising or television, payments to singers and musicians for use of a performance.

RIAA. Recording Industry Association of America.

Royalty. Percentage of money earned from the sale of records or use of a song.

RPM. Revolutions per minute. Refers to phonograph turntable speed.

SAE. Self-addressed envelope (with no postage attached).

SASE. Self-addressed stamped envelope.

Self-contained. A band or recording act that writes all their own material.

SESAC. A performing rights organization.

SFX. Sound effects.

Shop. To pitch songs to a number of companies or publishers.

Single. 45 rpm record with only one song per side. A 12″ single refers to a long version of one song on a 12″ disc, usually used for dance music.

SOCAN. A Canadian performing rights organization.

Solicited. Songs or materials that have been requested.

Song plugger. A songwriter representative whose main responsibility is promoting uncut songs to music publishers, record companies, artists and producers.

Song shark. Person who deals with songwriters deceptively for his own profit.

Soundtrack. The audio, including music and narration, of a film, videotape or audiovisual program.

Split publishing. To divide publishing rights between two or more publishers.

Statutory royalty rate. The maximum payment for mechanical rights guaranteed by law that a record company may pay the songwriter and his publisher for each record or tape sold.

Subpublishing. Certain rights granted by a US publisher to a foreign publisher in exchange for promoting the US catalog in his territory.

Synchronization. Technique of timing a musical soundtrack to action on film or video.

Take. Either an attempt to record a vocal or instrument part, or an acceptable recording of a performance.

Top 40. The first forty songs on the pop music charts at any given time. Also refers to a style of music which emulates that heard on the current top 40.

Track. Divisions of a recording tape (e.g., 24-track tape) that can be individually recorded in the studio, then mixed into a finished master.

Trades. Publications that cover the music industry.

12″ Single. A twelve inch record containing one or more remixes of a song, originally intended for dance club play.

Unsolicited. Songs or materials that were not requested and are not expected.

VHS. ½″ videocassette format.

Website. An address on the World Wide Web that can be accessed by computer modem. It may contain text, graphics and sound.

World Wide Web (WWW). An internet resource that utilizes hypertext to access information. It also supports formatted text, illustrations and sounds, depending on the user's computer capabilities.

Geographic Index

ALABAMA

Music Publishers
Cheavoria Music Co.
Nebo Ridge Publishing
   Company
Woodrich Publishing Co.

Record Companies
Bolivia Records
Woodrich Records

Record Producers
Airwave Production Group
   Inc.
Known Artist Productions
Nebo Record Company
Sound Cell

AD, AV, Commercial Music Firms
Ensemble Productions

Play Producers and Publishers
*Birmingham Children's
   Theatre
University of Alabama New
   Playwrights' Program

ALASKA

Record Producers
Nightwork Records

ARIZONA

Music Publishers
Blue Spur Entertainment,
   Inc./Git A Rope
   Publishing
*Funzalo Music
Ho-hum Music
Myko Music
Spradlin/Gleich Publishing
White Cat Music

Music Print Publishers
Still Music, William Grant

Record Companies
*Ariana Records
Canyon Records and Indian
   Arts
Care Free Records Group
Comstock Records Ltd.
*Lyra House, Ltd.

Record Producers
Care Free Records Group
Parker, Patty
Talent Recognition Services

Managers and Booking Agents
*Kaleidoscope Music
Reiter Productions, Richard
*Sunshadow Productions

Classical
Arizona Theatre Company

ARKANSAS

Music Publishers
Delpha's Music Publishers

Play Producers and Publishers
Arkansas Repertory
   Theatre

Classical
North Arkansas Symphony
   Orchestra

CALIFORNIA

Music Publishers
Alexis
Amiron Music
Audio Music Publishers
Bal & Bal Music Publishing
   Co.
Beecher Publishing, Earl
Big Fish Music Publishing

Black Stallion Country
   Publishing
Bonnfire Publishing
Bronx Flash Music, Inc.
Bug Music, Inc.
California Country Music
Centium Entertainment,
   Inc.
*Chicago Kid Productions
Christmas & Holiday Music
Dagene Music
Dean Enterprises Music
   Group
Doré Records
Duane Music, Inc.
Emandell Tunes
Famous Music Publishing
*Fingerprint Songs
First Release Music
   Publishing
Frontline Music Group
*GFI West Music
   Publishing
Happy Hour Music
Interscope Music
   Publishing
Josena Music
Kaupps & Robert
   Publishing
Kingsport Creek Music
   Publishing
*Magic Message Music
MCA Music Publishing
Merry Marilyn Music
   Publishing
*Motor Music Co.
Music Room Publishing
   Group, The
Operation Perfection
peermusic
Philippopolis Music
*Platinum Gold Music
Pollybyrd Publications
   Limited
*Pretty Shayna Music
Primal Visions Music
Rent-A-Song
Rhythms Productions

Managers and Booking Agents
O'Malley and Associates
    Agency, Scott

Play Producers and Publishers
Contemporary Drama
    Service
*Creede Repertory Theatre
Pioneer Drama Service

Classical
Colorado Children's
    Chorale

CONNECTICUT
Music Publishers
Blue Hill Music/Tutch
    Music
Ridge Music Corp.

Record Companies
Backstreet Records
*BMX Entertainment
Generic Records, Inc.
Pop Records Research
Target Records
Wonderland Records

Record Producers
Creative Music Services
*Perennial Productions
Person to Person
    Productions
Red Kastle Productions
Wytas Productions, Steve

Managers and Booking Agents
Air Tight Management
Martin Productions, Rick
Office, Inc., The
*Tutta Forza Music

Play Producers and Publishers
Hartford Stage Company

Classical
Connecticut Choral Artists/
    Concora
Norfolk Chamber Music
    Festival/Yale Summer
    School of Music

DELAWARE
Managers and Booking Agents
*Platinum Tracks
    Productions

AD, AV, Commercial Music Firms
Ken-Del Productions Inc.
Lyons Presentations

DISTRICT OF COLUMBIA
Music Publishers
Wheelerboy Entertainment

Record Companies
EMA Music Inc.
*Smithsonian/Folkways
    Recordings

AD, AV, Commercial Music Firms
Hillmann & Carr Inc.

Play Producers and Publishers
Woolly Mammoth Theatre
    Co.

Classical
*Hill Chorale (and) The
    Washington Singers,
    The Paul

FLORIDA
Music Publishers
Aljoni Music Co.
Audio Images Two
    Thousand Music
    Publishing
Cowboy Junction Flea
    Market and Publishing
    Co.
Joey Boy Publishing Co.
*Last Brain Cell
Lovey Music, Inc.
NSP Music Publishing Inc.
Otto Publishing Co.
Pine Island Music
*Power Voltage Music
Pritchett Publications
Rana International &
    Affiliates
*Rob-Lee Music
Rocker Music/Happy Man
    Music

Rustron Music Publishers
Stuart Music Co., Jeb
Unimusica Inc.
*Wize World of Muzic

Music Print Publishers
Plymouth Music Co.

Record Companies
*All Star Promotions
Black Dog Records
CHRISMARIE Records
Hallway International
    Records/1st Coast Posse
    Mixes
Happy Man Records
Joey Boy Records Inc.
*Live Oak Records
Loconto Productions/
    Sunrise Studio
*Phisst Records
    Corporation
Pinecastle/WEBCO
    Records
Playback Records
Rustron Music Productions
*Shang Records
*Sunset Records
Top Ten Hits Records Inc.
*28 Records

Record Producers
Eight Ball MIDI & Vocal
    Recording
Esquire International
Fera Productions, Vito
Gale, Jack
GoodKnight Productions
*Jay Jay Publishing and
    Record
Leavell, John
Loconto Productions
Musicland Productions
*Omari Productions
Pine Island Music
Rustron Music Productions
Vickers Music Association,
    Charles

Managers and Booking Agents
*All Star Promotions
*Big Beat Productions, Inc.
*Bird Entertainment
    Agency, J.
Burns Talent Agency, Dott
DiLeo Management, Liesa
Evans Productions, Scott

Five Star Entertainment
Hardman Management,
   Dustin
Levy Mgt, Rick
*Long Distance
   Entertainment
*McGillis Music Publishing
   Co.
Nova Productions &
   Management
*O'Malley Artist
   Management
Rana International
   Affiliates, Inc.
Rainbow Collection Ltd.
Rock of Ages Productions
Rustron Music Productions
Skorman Productions, Inc.,
   T.
Steele Management
*TCG Management
*Topnotch® Music &
   Records

AD, AV, Commercial Music Firms
Cinevue
Gold Coast Advertising
   Association Inc.
Kleiner Music Enterprises,
   Sid
*Opulent Music Group

Play Producers and Publishers
Asolo Theatre Company
Eldridge Publishing Co.,
   Inc.

Classical
Florida Space Coast
   Philharmonic, Inc.
Piccolo Opera Company

GEORGIA
Music Publishers
*Bartow Music
BOAM
Flea Circus Music
Focal Point Music
   Publishers
*Fresh Entertainment
Frozen Inca Music
Giftness Enterprise
McGibony Publishing
Orchid Publishing
Rising Star Records and
   Publishers

Record Companies
American Music Network,
   Inc.
babysue
Bouquet Records
Fresh Entertainment
Intersound Inc.
Landslide Records
*Peachtown Record Co. Inc.
Rising Star Records And
   Publishers Inc.
Trend Records®

Record Producers
Janoulis Productions,
   Alexander
Kovach, Robert R.

Managers and Booking Agents
Bojo Productions Inc.
Bouquet-Orchid
   Enterprises
babysue
*Drastic Measures, Inc.
*Hill Entertainment
   Management, Steve
*Montgomery
   Management, Gary F.
*Odom-Meaders
   Management
*Serge Entertainment
   Group
Willis Entertainment, Inc.

AD, AV, Commercial Music Firms
Anderson Communications
27th Dimension Inc.

Play Producers and Publishers
Horizon Theatre Co.

Classical
Atlanta Pops Orchestra
Atlanta Young Singers of
   Callanwolde, The

HAWAII
Music Publishers
Martin's Music Publishing,
   Rod

Record Companies
Maui Arts & Music
   Association

Record Producers
Sanders Company, Ray

Classical
Hawaii Opera Theatre

IDAHO
Music Publishers
*Kelly Entertainment,
   Robert

ILLINOIS
Music Publishers
*Baylor-Eselby Music
Foster Music Company,
   Mark
Jerjoy Music
*Kidsource Publishing
Mack Music, Danny
Mighty Twinns Music
Music In the Right Keys
   Publishing Company
Paluch Company, J. S./
   World Library
   Publications, Inc.
Sound Cellar Music
World Famous Music Co.

Music Print Publishers
Foster Music Company,
   Mark
Shelley Music

Record Companies
Briarhill Records
Bright Green Records
Broken Records
Cellar Records
*Direct Records, Inc.
Drag City, Inc.
Green Valley Records
Hammerhead Records, Inc.
*IMI Records
Jabala Music
Old School Records
Pravda Records
*Thick Records
Universal-Athena Records
Victory Records
*Whitehouse Records
Widely Distributed Records
Young Star Productions,
   Inc.

Record Producers
Coachouse Music
JGM Recording Studio

Neu Electro Productions
Pegasus Recording
Vector Sound

Managers and Booking Agents
*Big Boy Records & Artist
 Management
Conscience Music
H.L.A. Music
*Kaufman Hill
 Management
Risavy, Inc., A.F.
Secret Agent Media
 Entertainment Group,
 Ltd.
Sunset Promotions of
 Chicago
Tanner Entertainment
*Tone Zone Booking
 Agency

AD, AV, Commercial Music Firms
Mallof, Abruzino & Nash
 Marketing
*Manga Entertainment
Motivation Media, Inc.
Norton Rubble & Mertz,
 Inc. Advertising
Qually & Company Inc.
Video I-D, Inc.

Play Producers and Publishers
Bailiwick Repertory
Center Theater
*Circa' 21 Dinner
 Playhouse
Dramatic Publishing
 Company

Classical
Chicago String Ensemble,
 The
Knox-Galesburg Symphony
Lyric Opera of Chicago
Wheaton Symphony
 Orchestra

INDIANA
Music Publishers
De Miles Music Company,
 The Edward
*Dream Seekers Publishing
Hammel Associates, Inc.,
 R.L.
Hickory Valley Music

Interplanetary Music
*Ontrax Companies
*Twin Spin Publishing

Record Companies
Dale Productions, Alan
LBJ Productions
Sahara Records and
 Filmworks
 Entertainment
Yellow Jacket Records

Record Producers
De Miles, Edward

Managers and Booking Agents
De Miles Company, The
 Edward
Entertainment Group, The
Hale Enterprises
Hawkeye Attractions
*International
 Entertainment Bureau
M. Harrell & Associates
NIC Of Tyme Productions,
 Inc.
Perception Works Inc., The

AD, AV, Commercial Music Firms
Caldwell Vanriper
Omni Communications

Classical
Anderson Symphony
 Orchestra
*Carmel Symphony
 Orchestra
*New World Youth
 Symphony Orchestra

IOWA
Music Publishers
*JoDa Music
Luick & Associates Music
 Publisher, Harold
This Here Music

Music Print Publishers
Luick & Associates, Harold

Record Producers
Heart Consort Music
Luick & Associates, Harold

Managers and Booking Agents
Fenchel Entertainment
 Agency, Fred T.
Operation Music
 Enterprises

Play Producers and Publishers
Art Craft Publishing Co.
Heuer Publishing Co.
Waterloo Community
 Playhouse

KANSAS
Music Publishers
Cisum
Country Breeze Music

Record Companies
Country Breeze Records
*The Man On Page 602

Record Producers
Masterpiece Productions &
 Studios

Managers and Booking Agents
*Jackson Artists Corp.
*Prairie Fire Music
 Company

KENTUCKY
Music Publishers
Green Meadows Publishing
Holy Spirit Music
*Just a Note
Steel Rain Publishing
Trusty Publications

Music Print Publishers
Willis Music Company

Record Companies
*Heath & Associates
Trusty Records

Record Producers
Mr. Wonderful Productions

Managers and Booking Agents
*KRC Records &
 Productions

Mid-East Entertainment
   Inc.
Triangle Talent, Inc.

*AD, AV, Commercial
Music Firms*
Price Weber Marketing
   Communications, Inc.

*Play Producers and
Publishers*
*Aran Press
Stage One

Classical
Lexington Philharmonic
   Society

LOUISIANA
Music Publishers
Darbonne Publishing Co.
EMF Productions
Jon Music
*Snowcliff Publishing
Whitewing Music

Record Companies
*EMF Productions
Lanor Records
Master-Trak Enterprises
White Car Records

Record Producers
Miller Productions, Jay

*Managers and Booking
Agents*
Big J Productions
*GSI Inc.
Hit City Records

*AD, AV, Commercial
Music Firms*
Disk Productions
Keating Magee Long
   Advertising

*Play Producers and
Publishers*
Centenary College, Theatre
   Department

Classical
Acadiana Symphony
   Orchestra

MAINE
Music Publishers
Gowell Music, Richard E.

Record Companies
Cat's Voice Productions

Record Producers
Stuart Audio Services

*Managers and Booking
Agents*
Crash Productions
Greeley Entertainment,
   Chris
Morelli Enterprises,
   Thomas

MARYLAND
Music Publishers
Cash Productions, Inc.
Country Showcase America
*Orderlottsa Music

Record Companies
Continental Records
Merkin Records Inc.
Order Records
Spiritual Walk Records
Startrak Records, Inc.

Record Producers
Basement Boys, Inc.

*Managers and Booking
Agents*
*Cash Productions, Inc
Entertainment Works
Noteworthy Productions
*Productions Unlimited
TSMB Productions

*AD, AV, Commercial
Music Firms*
Mitchell & Associates

*Play Producers and
Publishers*
Cockpit in Court Summer
   Theatre

Classical
Baltimore Opera Company,
   Inc.
Susquehanna Symphony
   Orchestra

MASSACHUSETTS
Music Publishers
Halo International
Henly Music Associates
Scott Music Group, Tim
Segal's Publications

Music Print Publishers
Boston Music Co.
ECS Publishing
Warren Music Service,
   Frank E.

Record Companies
*BCN/Beacon Records
Belmont Records
*Castle von Buhler Records
*Critique Records, Inc.
Eastern Front Records, Inc.
Keeping It Simple And Safe
MSM Records
Stargard Records

Record Producers
Mona Lisa Records/Bristol
   Studios
Nelson, Bill
Segal's Productions
*Willow Shade Records

*Managers and Booking
Agents*
*Arrived Alive Management
Beacon Kendall
   Entertainment
Clockwork Entertainment
   Management Agency
Foggy Day Music
*Madstorm Production
   Company
Squad 16

*AD, AV, Commercial
Music Firms*
Communications for
   Learning
Film Classic Exchange
Home, Inc.
Lapriore Videography
Rampion Visual
   Productions
VIP Video

*Play Producers and
Publishers*
Baker's Plays
Berkshire Public Theatre
Freelance Press, The

Classical
Commonwealth Opera, Inc.
Dúo Clásico
Melrose Symphony
  Orchestra
Mohawk Trail Concerts

MICHIGAN
Music Publishers
Abalone Publishing
Betty Jane/Josie Jane
  Music
*Cunningham Music
National Talent
Prejippie Music Group

Record Companies
Gueststar Records
L.A. Records
Nocturnal Records
PMG Records
RAVE Records, Inc.
Rosebud Records
Ruffcut Productions
Wall Street Music

Record Producers
Aurora Productions
Dudick, J.D.
*Modern Tribe Records
Prejippie Music Group
Wall Street Productions

*Managers and Booking
Agents*
Afterschool Publishing
*Glo Gem Productions, Inc.
Gueststar Entertainment
  Agency
Hardway Music
  Management
J & V Management
*Joy Artist Management,
  Inc.
Monopoly Management
Northstar Artist
  Management
*Ruff Production, Jimmy
Star Artist Management
  Inc.

*AD, AV, Commercial
Music Firms*
Creative House Advertising
Gaffe Marketing
K&R's Recording Studios
Photo Communication
  Services, Inc.

Solomon Friedman
  Advertising

Classical
Adrian Symphony
  Orchestra
Birmingham-Bloomfield
  Symphony Orchestra
Cantata Academy
Fontana Concert Society
*Sault Ste. Marie Symphony
  Orchestra

MINNESOTA
Music Publishers
Big Snow Music
Dell Music, Frank
Portage Music

Record Companies
Music Services &
  Marketing
Oar Fin Records

Record Producers
Rainbow Recording

*Managers and Booking
Agents*
Alan Agency, Mark
Artist Representation and
  Management
*Blue Sky Artist
  Management
Entertainment Services
  International
Eternal Records/
  Squigmonster
  Management
Golden Bull Productions
Hologram Entertainment
Jupiter Productions
T.S.J. Productions

*AD, AV, Commercial
Music Firms*
eclectic Music

*Play Producers and
Publishers*
Great American History
  Theatre
Mixed Blood Theatre Co.

Classical
Augsburg Choir
Warland Singers, The Dale

MISSISSIPPI
Music Publishers
*Bay Ridge Publishing Co.
Stylecraft Music Co.

Record Companies
Malaco Records
Missile Records
New Beginning Record
  Productions

*Managers and Booking
Agents*
*Exclesisa Booking Agency

*AD, AV, Commercial
Music Firms*
Delta Design Group, Inc.

*Play Producers and
Publishers*
Carey College Dinner
  Theatre, William

MISSOURI
Music Publishers
Green One Music
Lineage Publishing Co.
Radiant Music
Southern Most Publishing
  Company

Music Print Publishers
Bay Publications, Inc., Mel

Record Companies
Capstan Record Production
Green Bear Records
Inferno Records
*M.E.G. Records Co.
RBW, Inc.
Teeter-Tot Records

Record Producers
Angel Films Company
Haworth Productions

*Managers and Booking
Agents*
American Family Talent
*Doran, P.C., James R.
Fudpucker Entertainment
*Overstreet Music
  Companies, Tommy
*Relax Productions
*Staircase Promotion

*AD, AV, Commercial
Music Firms*
Media Consultants, Inc.
United Entertainment
   Productions

*Play Producers and
Publishers*
Coterie, The
Repertory Theatre of St.
   Louis, The

Classical
St. Louis Chamber Chorus

MONTANA
Classical
Billings Symphony
Great Falls Symphony
*Helena Symphony

NEBRASKA
Music Publishers
*Lari-Jon Publishing

Record Companies
Lari-Jon Records
*Redemption Records

Record Producers
Lari-Jon Productions

*Managers and Booking
Agents*
Lari-Jon Promotions
Lutz Entertainment Agency,
   Richard

*Play Producers and
Publishers*
Omaha Magic Theatre

Classical
Hastings Symphony
   Orchestra
Soli Deo Gloria Cantorum

NEVADA
Music Publishers
*Flaming Star West Music
Platinum Boulevard
   Publishing
Watchesgro Music

Record Companies
Interstate 40 Records
Platinum Boulevard
   Records

Record Producers
New Horizon Records
Triplane Production

*Managers and Booking
Agents*
Biscuit Productions Inc.
*Jerifka Productions, Inc.
*Silver Moon Productions

Classical
Carson City Chamber
   Orchestra
Reno Chamber Orchestra

NEW HAMPSHIRE
Record Companies
Kingston Records

Record Producers
Kingston Records and
   Talent
Reel Adventures

*Play Producers and
Publishers*
American Stage Festival

NEW JERSEY
Music Publishers
Baby Raquel Music
Gary Music, Alan
Genetic Music Publishing
Omni 2000, Inc.
PPI/Peter Pan Industries
*Rachel Marie Music Ltd.
Roots Music
Sha-La Music, Inc.
*T.C. Productions/Etude
   Publishing Co.
Westunes Music Publishing
Yorgo Music

Record Companies
*Antiphon International
Digitalia Records
Jamoté Music Group
Lucifer Records, Inc.
Megaforce Worldwide
   Entertainment
Nucleus Records
*Omni 2000 Inc.
Presence Records
Sonic Group, Ltd.
VAI Distribution

Record Producers
Blaze Productions
Bowden, Robert
Omni 2000 Inc.
Soundboard Studios
Sphere Productions

*Managers and Booking
Agents*
Amazing Maze Productions
American Artist, Inc.
Atlantic Entertainment
   Group
Blaze Productions
Brothers Management
   Associates
Foley Entertainment
hm Management
*Jazz-One Productions
Manapro Entertainment
Moore Entertainment
   Group
Nelson Entertainment Inc.,
   Brian
Reiter Productions, Richard
Renaissance Entertainment
Ricca, Jr.'s Entertainment
   Agency, Joey
Scott Entertainment, Craig
Sphere Productions
S.T.A.R.S. Productions
Star Vest Management
   Associates Inc.
*Stormin' Norman
   Productions
Westwood Entertainment
*World Beyond Talent &
   Publicity Network

*AD, AV, Commercial
Music Firms*
Creative Associates

*Play Producers and
Publishers*
Creative Productions, Inc.
Creative Theatre
*George Street Playhouse
*Paper Mill Playhouse

Classical
American Boychoir, The
Aureus Quartet
*New Jersey Symphony
   Orchestra/Greater
   Newark Youth
   Orchestra

Opera Festival of New
  Jersey
*Princeton Chamber
  Symphony
Ridgewood Symphony
  Orchestra

NEW MEXICO
Music Publishers
Johnson Music, Little
  Richie
Pecos Valley Music

Record Companies
LRJ
SunCountry Records

Record Producers
Johnson, Little Richie

*Managers and Booking
Agents*
*Aquila Entertainment
Johnson Agency, Little
  Richie

Classical
*Desert Chorale
Eastern New Mexico
  University

NEW YORK
Music Publishers
Alpha Music Inc.
*Bahoomba Music
Bourne Co. Music
  Publishers
Camex Music
*Colton Shows, Glenn
D.S.M. Producers Inc.
EMI Music Publishing
Glass Songs/EMI, Seymour
GlobeArt Inc.
Gold Music Publishing, Jay
*Gold Music, S.M.
*High Pockets Publishing
  Inc.
Hit & Run Music Publishing
Jasper Stone Music/JSM
  Songs
*JK Jam Music
Kozkeeozko Music
*Largo Music Publishing
Laurmack Music
Lin's Lines
Loux Music Co. &
  Dovehouse Editions.

Majestic Control
One Hot Note Music Inc.
Phaja Music
Prescription Company
Quark, Inc.
Ren Maur Music Corp.
Rockford Music Co.
Rose Hill Group
Siskatune Music Publishing
  Co.
Spring Rose Music
Sunfrost Music
Sunsongs Music/
  Hollywood East
  Entertainment
Tops And Bottoms Music
Worship Music
*Zomba Music Publishing

Music Print Publishers
Bourne Company
Fischer, Inc., Carl
Transcontinental Music
  Publications

Record Companies
Alyssa Records
*Arista Records
*Arkadia Entertainment
  Corp.
*Atlantic Records
audiofile Tapes
Blue Wave
*Caroline Records, Inc.
*Columbia Records
Com-Four
*CTI Records
*Earth Flight Productions
*Epic Records
Factory Beat Records, Inc.
Fiction Songs
*Flip Records
Gold City Records, Inc.
Guitar Recordings
Hot Wings Entertainment
J&J Musical Enterprises
  Ltd.
*Jive Records
Kept In The Dark Records
Lamar Music Group
*Lotus Records
MCA Records
*Metal Blade Records
Mighty Records
Mirror Records, Inc.
Modern Blues Recordings
Modern Voices
  Entertainment, Ltd.

*Musikus Productions, Inc.
Paint Chip Records
Pirate Records
*Provocative Entertainment
  Group Inc. Recordings
*Quark Records
*Radical Records
Round Flat Records
Royalty Records
*Shimmy-Disc
Sky-Child Records
Source Unlimited Records
*Strictly Rhythm Records
TVT Records
Wizmak Productions
*Worship & Praise Records
Xemu Records
Zero Hour Records

Record Producers
Allyn, Stuart J.
Carlock Productions
*Casale Music, Inc., Don
Chucker Music, Inc.
D.S.M. Producers, Inc.
Darrow, Danny
Guess Who?? Productions
Jazzand
JK Jam Productions
KMA
Must Rock Productionz
  Worldwide
Prescription Co., The
Richmond St. Recordings,
  Inc.
Rosenman, Mike
SAS Corporation/Special
  Audio Services
*Siskind Productions, Mike
12 Meter Productions

*Managers and Booking
Agents*
All Access Entertainment
  Management Group,
  Inc.
*Anderson Associates
  Communications Group
Artists Only, Inc.
*Bassline Entertainment,
  Inc.
*Casale Music, Inc., Don
Countdown Entertainment
Courtright Management
  Inc.
*Crossfire Entertainment
*Crossover Entertainment

Cycle Of Fifths
   Management
DAS Communications, Ltd.
*DCA Productions
*Debutante Management
*Depth Of Field
   Management
DMR Agency
*Dr. Shay's
Earth Tracks Artists
   Agency
*EBI Inc.
*Faith Entertainment,
   James
Flash Attractions Agency
Freedman Entertainment,
   Peter
Gallup Entertainment
GMI Entertainment Inc.
Great Lakes Country Talent
   Agency
*Headline Management
*Headline Talent Inc.
Horizon Management Inc.
Imani Entertainment Inc.
Insinna Management, Paul
Knight Agency, Bob
*Kriete, Kincaid & Faith
Landslide Management
L.D.F. Productions
*Little Big Man Booking
*Living Eye Productions
   Ltd.
M & M Talent Agency Inc.
Nik Entertainment
   Company
On Stage Management Inc.
Platinum Ears Ltd.
*Radioactive
*Raz Management Co.
Richards World
   Management, Inc.,
   Diane
Rothschild Productions
   Inc., Charles R.
*Sewitt Group, The
Singermanagment, Inc.
*Surface Management Inc.
*Wood Artist Management,
   Richard
World Wide Management

*AD, AV, Commercial
Music Firms*
Compositions, Inc.
D.S.M. Producers Inc.
Fine Art Productions
Fitzmusic

Izen Enterprises, Inc.
Mark Custom Recording
   Service, Inc.
TRF Production Music
   Libraries

*Play Producers and
Publishers*
Acting Company, The
Circle in the Square Theatre
Fools Company, Inc.
French, Inc., Samuel
Golden Fleece Ltd.
Jewish Repertory Theatre
Lamb's Theatre Co., The
Manhattan Theatre Club
National Music Theater
   Network, Inc.
*New York State Theatre
   Institute
*New York Theatre
   Workshop
Off Center Theatre
Open Eye Theater, The
*Playwrights Horizons
Primary Stages Company
Second Stage Theatre
TADA!
Theatreworks/USA
13th Street Repertory
   Company
*This Month On Stage
*Westbeth Theatre Centre
Westside Repertory
   Theatre
*Wings Theatre Co.
Women's Project and
   Productions, Julia Miles,
   Artistic Director

Classical
Amherst Saxophone
   Quartet
Buffalo Guitar Quartet
*Center for Contemporary
   Opera
Measured Breaths Theatre
   Company
*Mozart Festival Orchestra
New York Concert Singers,
   The
Opera on the Go
Queens Opera
*Singers Forum
Star Within Enterprises
*Touring Concert Opera
   Co.

Westminster Presbyterian
   Church

NORTH CAROLINA

Music Publishers
Davis & Davis Music
Lindsay Publishing, Doris

Music Print Publishers
Alry Publications
Hinshaw Music
*TPM/Studio

Record Companies
*Fireant
Fountain Records
*Lamon Records
Salexo Music
Sheffield Lab Recording

Record Producers
*Jag Studio, Ltd.
WLM Music/Recording

*Managers and Booking
Agents*
*KenWan's Productions
*M. & G. Entertainment
   Consortiums, Inc.

*AD, AV, Commercial
Music Firms*
Hodges Associates, Inc.

*Play Producers and
Publishers*
Blowing Rock Stage
   Company, The

NORTH DAKOTA
Record Companies
Starcrest Productions, Inc.

OHIO
Music Publishers
*A.A.A. Audio Management
Accent Publishing Co.
Alexander Sr., Music
Barkin' Foe The Master's
   Bone
Barren Wood Publishing
Bernard Enterprises, Inc.,
   Hal
Bradley Music, Allan
Faiella Publishing, Doug

*Harbor Gospel Music
  Production
Heartbeat Music
*Jacksongs Music
  Publishing, d.t.
New Rap Jam Publishing, A
Oyster Bay Music
Scrutchings Music
Without Papers Music
  Publishing Inc.

Music Print Publishers
Lorenz Corporation

Record Companies
Bold 1 Records
Emerald City Records
New Experience Records/
  Grand Slam Records
*Paul Records, J.
Strugglebaby Recording
  Co.
Twin Sisters Productions,
  Inc.

Record Producers
Bernard Enterprises, Inc.,
  Hal
Eternal Song Agency, The
Faiella Productions, Doug
Flair Productions
Nemesis Media Labs
New Experience Records
Realworld Entertainment
  Corp.
Syndicate Sound, Inc.
Tomsick Brothers
  Productions

**Managers and Booking
Agents**
All Star Management
Concept 2000 Inc.
Creative Star Management
Entertainment International
*Other Road, The
*T 'n T Enterprises
Umbrella Artists
  Management

**AD, AV, Commercial
Music Firms**
Group X, Inc.
*Heywood Formatics &
  Syndication
Poppe Tyson
Sullivan & Findsen
  Advertising

Classical
Akron City Family Mass
  Choir
Lakeside Summer
  Symphony
Lima Symphony Orchestra
Lithopolis Area Fine Arts
  Association

OKLAHOMA
Music Publishers
*Enid, Oklahoma Music
  Publishing
Furrow Music
Jae Music, Jana
*Miller Music, Jody
Okisher Music
Old Slowpoke Music

Record Companies
Cherry Street Records
*Country Style Records
Lark Record Productions,
  Inc.
Lonesome Wind
  Corporation
*Traveler Enterprises

Record Producers
Lark Talent & Advertising

**Managers and Booking
Agents**
Jae Enterprises, Jana
Sherman Artist
  Management &
  Development, Mickey

Classical
*Cimarron Circuit Opera
  Company
*Tulsa Opera Inc.

OREGON
Music Publishers
Earritating Music
  Publishing
High-Minded Moma
  Publishing &
  Productions
Macman Music, Inc.
Moon June Music

Record Companies
Flying Heart Records
OCP Publications

Record Producers
Celt, Jan

**Managers and Booking
Agents**
Sirius Entertainment

Classical
Oregon Symphony

PENNSYLVANIA
Music Publishers
Allegheny Music Works
Bowman Productions & W.
  David Music, David
Coffee and Cream
  Publishing Company
Country Star Music
Delev Music Company
*Flammer Music, Harold
Kaylee Music Group, Karen
Kommunication Koncepts
Krude Toonz Music
Makers Mark Gold
*RNR Publishing
Shu'Baby Montez Music
Vokes Music Publishing

Music Print Publishers
Kallisti Musici Press
Presser Co., Theodore

Record Companies
Allegheny Music Works
Big Pop
CITA Communications Inc.
Country Star International
Golden Triangle Records
*Mountain Records
Rage-N-Records
*Reiter Records Ltd.
*Saturn Records
Sirr Rodd Record &
  Publishing
Surprize Records, Inc.
Vokes Music Record Co.

Record Producers
Big Sky Audio Productions
Coffee and Cream
  Productions
Country Star Productions
Ivory Productions, Inc.
James, Sunny
London Brijj Productions
Makers Mark Music
Philly Breakdown
Rockstar Productions

Shu'Baby Montez Music
Westwires Digital USA

Managers and Booking Agents
Blank & Blank
*Clousher Productions
Country Star Attractions
Countrywide Producers
DSM Management
Fame International
Golden Guru Entertainment
Hall Entertainment & Events, Bill
High Energy Management
McDonnell Group, The
*Myers Enterprises, James E.
Paul Entertainment Group, Inc., Jackie
*Pillar Records
*Process Talent
*Rock Whirled Music Management
Strictley Biziness Music Management
*Theater Arts Network/ Stephen Productions
Vokes Booking Agency
Zane Management, Inc.

AD, AV, Commercial Music Firms
Blattner/Brunner
*Bowman Productions, David
Canary Productions
Fredrick, Lee & Lloyd
Philadelphia Music Works, Inc.
Tierney & Partners
Valley Production Center

Play Producers and Publishers
Allegheny Highlands Regional Theatre
American Music Theater Festival
Arden Theatre Company
Bristol Riverside Theatre
*City Theatre Company, Inc.
Walnut Street Theatre Company

Classical
Abbey Singers, The
Hershey Symphony Orchestra
Lehigh Valley Chamber Orchestra
Prism Saxophone Quartet
Singing Boys of Pennsylvania

RHODE ISLAND
Music Publishers
Parravano Music

Record Companies
Black & Blue
Marks Records, John
North Star Music
*Peridot Records

Managers and Booking Agents
D & M Entertainment Agency

Classical
Brown University Orchestra

SOUTH CAROLINA
Music Publishers
Riverhawk Music

Record Companies
Wanstar Group, The

SOUTH DAKOTA
Managers and Booking Agents
Intermountain Talent
Sound '86 Talent Management

TENNESSEE
Music Publishers
Aim High Music Company
*Aladdin Music Group
AlliSongs Inc.
*Beaverwood Audio-Video
Best Buddies, Inc.
Buried Treasure Music
Calinoh Music Group
Castle Music Group
Chestnut Mound Music Group
*Copperfield Music Group
Cornelius Companies, The
Cottage Blue Music
*Country Rainbow Music
Craig Music, Loman
Cupit Music
Denny Music Group
Doss Music, Buster
EMI Christian Music
ESI Music Group
Farr-Away Music
Fat City Publishing
Fox Farm Recording
Frick Music Publishing Co.
Goodland Music Group Inc.
Hitsburgh Music Co.
Holton Music
Humanform Publishing
Hutchins Music, Gregg
*Immortal Beloved Music
Iron Skillet Music
Jaclyn Music
Jolson Black & White Music, Al
Joseph Music Inc., Patrick
JW One Music Publishing Co.
Lion Hill Music Publishing Co.
McCartney Music
Mathes Company, The
Nautical Music Co.
Newcreature Music
Oh My Gosh Music
Panchatantra Music Enterprises
Peters Music, Justin
Silver Thunder Music Group
Simply Grand Music, Inc.
Sizemore Music
Song Farm Music
*Sony/ATV Music Publishing
Sun Star Songs
*Sunapee Music Group
*Surespin Songs
Tooth and Nail Music
Ultimate Peak Music

Music Print Publishers
Abingdon Press
Genevox Music Group

Record Companies
A & R Records
Arion Records
Bandit Records
BNA Records
*Breeden Music Group
Brentwood Music
Carlyle Records, Inc.
Cedar Creek Records™

Fame and Fortune
Enterprises
Fat City Artists
General Broadcasting
Service
Jalyn Recording Co.
*K-Ark Records
Kottage Records
Landmark Communications
Mathes Company, The
Orbit Records
Paragold Records & Tapes
PBM Records
Phoenix Records, Inc.
*Plateau Music
Platinum Plus Records
International
R.E.F. Records
Rejoice Records of
Nashville
Richway Records
International
*Silver Wing Records
Sound Achievement Group
Stardust
Wedge Records
Wence Sense Music/Bill
Wence Promotions

Record Producers
*Aladdin Productions
Capitol Ad, Management &
Talent Group
Cedar Creek Productions
Cupit Productions, Jerry
DeLory and Music Makers,
Al
Doss Presents, Col. Buster
*Double K Entertainment
Frick, Bob Scott
James Productions, Neal
Johnson, Ralph D.
Kennedy Enterprises, Inc.,
Gene
Landmark Communications
Lloyd Productions, Mick
Mathes Productions, David
Nashville Country
Productions
Pierce, Jim
Sharpe Sound Productions
*Silver Thunder Music
Group
Sound Control Productions
Soundstage South
Sullivan Enterprises,
Preston
*Walton Record
Productions

Managers and Booking Agents
All Star Talent Agency
Allen Entertainment
Development, Michael
C & M Productions
Management Group
Capitol Management &
Talent
*Carlyle Management
Cedar Creek Productions
and Management and
Cedar Cove Music
Circuit Rider Talent &
Management Co.
*Crowe Entertainment Inc.
Doss Presents, Col. Buster
Fat City Artists
FCC Management
*5 Star Music Group/Mike
Waddell & Associates
*Fox Management, Inc.,
Mitchell
Frick Enterprises, Bob
Scott
James Gang Management
*Midnight Special
Productions
*Monterey Artists, Inc.
Newby Management, J.P.
Nowag's National
Attractions, Craig
OB-1 Entertainment
Pro Star Talent Agency
Riohcat Music
*Sharp Management, Jim
Smith and Associates,
Michael
*Sound and Serenity
Management
*Sweet Pea Artist
Management
315 Beale Studios/Taliesyn
Entertainment

Play Producers and Publishers
Playhouse on the Square

Classical
Opera Memphis

TEXAS
Music Publishers
Axbar Productions
Bagatelle Music Publishing
Co.
Cherie Music

Christopher Publishing,
Sonny
De Leon Publishing
*Earthscream Music
Flash International
Flying Red Horse
Publishing
Hinds Feet Music
Jaelius Enterprises
Kansa Records Corporation
Keno Publishing
Kilowatt Music
*LCS Music Group, Inc.
Lonny Tunes Music
Manny Music, Inc.
Motex Music
Padrino Music Publishing
Paradise Publications
Planet Dallas Recording
Studios
Pollard Sound World
Prospector Three D
Publishing
Raving Cleric Music
Publishing/Euro Export
Entertainment
Ryan Music, Joshua
Samuel Three Productions
Silicon Music Publishing
Co.
*Smokey Lane Music
Spacek Co., The
Stable Music Co.
Starbound Publishing Co.
Sweet June Music
Tentex Music Publishing
Velocity Productions
*Watonka Records Co.

Record Companies
Albatross Records
*Alpha Recording Co.
Bagatelle Record Company
Bodarc Productions
BSW Records
*Christian Media
Enterprises
Dejadisc, Inc.
Howdy Records
Jamaka Record Co.
JAV Records
*Lonny Tunes
Manny Music, Inc.
Maverick Group, The
MCR
*Powerhouse Records
Red Dot/Puzzle Records
*Rockadelic Records
Sabre Productions

Scratched Records
*Urgent Music, Inc.
Watusi Productions
*Wolftrax Records

Record Producers
ACR Productions
Austin Recording Studio
Corwin, Dano
Mittelstedt, A.V.
Planet Dallas
Slavesong Corporation, Inc.
Texas Fantasy Music
*Texas Music Masters
TMC Productions
Trinity Studio, The
Twist Tunes
Willson, Frank

Managers and Booking Agents
All Musicmatters
Atch Records and
    Productions
Brasswind Artist
    Management
Bullseye Entertainment
Cavalry Productions
*Chabu Productions
Classic Rock Entertainment
Community Music Center
    of Houston
Direct Management
Eve's Cradle
JAS Management
Kuper Personal
    Management
Management Plus
Mirkin Management
Misty International
*Musica Moderna
    Management
Nashville Connection, The
Russell Productions, T.
Rymkus Management and
    Promotions, Mike
Smeltzer Productions, Gary
SP Talent Associates
*Texas Music Masters
*Texas Sounds
    Entertainment
*Umpire Entertainment
    Enterprizes
Universal Music Marketing
*Valiant Records &
    Management

AD, AV, Commercial Music Firms
Estilo Communications
GK & A Advertising, Inc.
Hammond & Associates
Hepworth Advertising Co.
Kamstra Communications,
    Inc.
McCann-Erickson
    Worldwide
Stewart Advertising, Nate
Ward and Ames
Wyatt Advertising, Evans

Play Producers and Publishers
A.D. Players
*Clark Publications, I.E.
Hip Pocket Theatre
*Theatre Three, Inc.

Classical
*Hermann Sons German
    Band
Mesquite Symphony
    Orchestra
San Antonio Opera
    Company
University of Houston
    Opera Theatre

UTAH
Music Publishers
Non-Stop Music Publishing
Shaolin Music

Record Companies
Shaolin Film & Records

Managers and Booking Agents
Alexas Music Productions

AD, AV, Commercial Music Firms
Soter Associates, Inc.

Play Producers and Publishers
Encore Performance
    Publishing
*Tuacahn Center For The
    Arts

Classical
*Mirecourt Trio, The
Salt Lake Symphonic Choir

VERMONT
Music Publishers
Elect Music Publishing

Music Print Publishers
Trillenium Music

Record Companies
*LBI Records

Record Producers
Jericho Sound Lab

Managers and Booking Agents
*Management, Ltd.
Mayo & Company, Phil

AD, AV, Commercial Music Firms
*Big Ears Music/Ducktape
    Studio

VIRGINIA
Music Publishers
Cimirron Music
*Coast Line Events, Inc.
Doc Publishing
Hawksbill Music
Namax Music Publishing
Pen Cob Publishing Inc.
Slanted Circle Music
Soundbyte Corporation
*Weaver Words of Music

Record Companies
Cimirron/Rainbird Records
*Fink-Pinewood Records
Trumpeter Records Inc.

Record Producers
Bonta, Peter L.

Managers and Booking Agents
ArkLight Management Co.
*Cody Entertainment
    Group
D&D Talent Associates
*Glad Productions
Holiday Productions, Doc
Image Promotions Inc.
Precision Management
Sirocco Productions, Inc.

Play Producers and Publishers
Ashlawn-Highland Summer
    Festival

Barter Theatre
*Mill Mountain Theatre
Shenandoah International
 Playwrights Retreat (A
 Project of Shenan Arts,
 Inc.)
*Theatrevirginia

Classical
Virginia Opera

WASHINGTON
Music Publishers
Saddlestone Publishing
Sounds of Aicram
Valet Publishing Co.
Your Best Songs Publishing

Music Print Publishers
Vivace Press

Record Companies
*L. P. S. Records, Inc.
RR&R Records
Saddlestone Records
*Satin Records
*World Disc Productions

Record Producers
Around Sounds Publishing
Earmark Audio
Ormsby, John "Buck"/
 Etiquette Productions
RR & R Music Productions
 Inc.
Sound Sound/Savage
 Fruitarian

*Managers and Booking
Agents*
Lazy Bones Recordings/
 Productions, Inc.
*T.L.C. Booking Agency

*AD, AV, Commercial
Music Firms*
Barnett Advertising/
 Design, Augustus

Classical
Chaspen Symphony
 Orchestra
La Stella Foundation
Orchestra Seattle/Seattle
 Chamber Singers

WEST VIRGINIA
Music Publishers
McCoy Music, Jim
Purple Haze Music

Record Companies
Scene Productions
Winchester Records

Record Producers
McCoy Productions, Jim

*Play Producers and
Publishers*
Theatre West Virginia

WISCONSIN
Music Publishers
Cactus Music and
 Winnebago Publishing
Don Del Music
*Kirchstein Publishing Co.
M & T Waldoch Publishing,
 Inc.

Record Companies
Cha Cha Records
*decibel
*Don't Records
Zerobudget Records

*Managers and Booking
Agents*
Talent Associates of
 Wisconsin
Tas Music Co./Dave Tasse
 Entertainment
Tiger's Eye Entertainment
 Management &
 Consulting

Classical
Milwaukee Youth
 Symphony Orchestra

WYOMING
Music Publishers
Kel-Cres Publishing

*Play Producers and
Publishers*
American Living

Classical
Cheyenne Symphony
 Orchestra

CANADA
Music Publishers
Alleged Iguana Music
Arylis Corporation
Berandol Music Ltd.
Branch Group Music
Corporate Music
G-String Publishing
Hickory Lane Publishing
 And Recording
ISBA Music Publishing Inc.
Kwaz Song Music
Lilly Music Publishing
Montina Music
Nashville Sound Music
S.M.C.L. Productions, Inc.
*Sci-Fi Music
*Third Wave Productions
Warner/Chappell Music
 Canada Ltd.
Zauber Music Publishing

Music Print Publishers
Music Box Dancer
 Publications

Record Companies
*Arial Records
Berandol Music
Dancer Publishing Co.
*Def Beat Records
DMT Records
Justin Time Records Inc.
KSM Records
L.A. Records
Magnum Music Corp. Ltd.
Monticana Records
P. & N. Records
Rammit Records
Random Records
Reveal
*Shaky Records
Sunshine Group, The
*Third Wave Productions
 Ltd.

Record Producers
"A" Major Sound
 Corporation
*Cousins Proudctions,
 Randall
*Harlow Sound
Hickory Lane Publishing
 and Recording
I.V.M. Communications
*Janus Management
*Jay Bird Productions

Kane Producer/Engineer,
  Karen
*Merlin Productions
Moffet, Gary
Monticana Productions
Musicom Music
  Productions
Panio Brothers Label
Poku Productions
Rammit Records
Silver Bow Productions
*Szawlowski Productions &
  Ventura Music
  Publishing, William

**Managers and Booking
Agents**
*Alert Music, Inc.
Amok Inc.
Ardenne Int'l Inc.
Arimte Entertainment Ltd.
ATI Music
Bandstand (International)
  Entertainment Agency
*Big Hand
Colwell Arts Management
Duckworthy/Atlantica
EAO Music Corporation of
  Canada
Empry Entertainment, Gino
Entercom
Entertainment Resource
  Management
Feldman & Associates, S.L.
*Fiedler Management, B.C.
Firestar Promotions Inc.
*Immigrant Music Inc.
Kagan Productions,
  Sheldon
Lenthall & Associates
Magnum Music
  Corporation
Management Trust Ltd.,
  The
M.B.H. Music Management
*Merlin Management Corp.
*Mighty Oak Management
*Paquin Entertainment
  Group
Phil's Entertainment
  Agency
*RDR Music Group
RGK Entertainment Group
Rocky Mountain
  Management
Seip Management, Inc.,
  William
Showcana Corporation

Siddons & Associates
Siegel Entertainment Ltd.
*Silver Bow Management
Strictly Forbidden Artists
*Sunnydays Records
Tanglewood Group Inc.,
  The
*Tenn Artist Management,
  William
T.J. Booker Ltd.
*VTC Entertainment
  Management
*Wood Publicity &
  Management, Deborah

**AD, AV, Commercial
Music Firms**
*Cinépost Film & Video
*Moore Compositions,
  Patrick
RS Music Productions

Classical
Calgary Boys Choir
Canadian Opera Company
Kitchener-Waterloo
  Chamber Orchestra
Montreal Chamber
  Orchestra
New Star-Scape Singers,
  The
*Norfolk Singers' Chorus
  and Orchestra, The
Opera Ora Now Canada,
  Inc.
Saskatoon Symphony
  Orchestra
Toronto Mendelssohn
  Choir
Vancouver Youth
  Symphony Orchestra
  Society

AUSTRALIA
Music Publishers
Colstal Music

Record Companies
Big Rock Pty. Ltd.
Makeshift Music

**Managers and Booking
Agents**
Adb Management Group
Adelaide Rock Exchange
*Clugston Organization
  Pty. Ltd., The Neil
Cranium Management

Dinwoodie Management,
  Andrew
*Harbour Agency Pty. Ltd.,
  The
*Mark One-The Agency
Music Man Promotions
Shute Management Pty.
  Ltd., Phill
*Sphere Organization, The
Stahl Entertainments,
  Bernie

AUSTRIA
Music Publishers
Aquarius Publishing
Hit-Fabrik Musikverlag
Honk Music —
  Musikverlag H.
  Gebetsroither
*Musikverlag K. Urbanek
*Musikverlag Rossori
West & East Music

BELGIUM
Music Publishers
Inside Records/OK Songs
Jump Music
*Promo
Succes

Music Print Publishers
Jump Music

**Managers and Booking
Agents**
Flinter Music

DENMARK
Record Companies
Modal Music, Inc.™

FRANCE
Music Publishers
Editions Scipion
*Pas Mal Publishing Sarl

GERMANY
Music Publishers
AUM Circle Publishing
Clevère Musikverlag, R.D.
Heupferd MusikVerlag
  GmbH
Ja/Nein Musikverlag
  GmbH
Mento Music Group
Siegel Music Companies

Transamerika Musikverlag
KG
UBM
Wengert, Berthold
(Musikverlag)

Record Companies
Alpha-Beat
Comma Records & Tapes
*Mons Records
Playbones Records
Westpark Music - Records,
Production & Publishing

ITALY
Music Publishers
Dingo Music

Record Companies
*Top Records

NEW ZEALAND
Music Publishers
Pegasus Music

SCOTLAND
Music Publishers
Brewster Songs, Kitty
Jammy Music Publishers
Ltd.

SWEDEN
Record Companies
*Megarock Records

**Managers and Booking
Agents**
Nilsson Production,
Christina

UNITED
KINGDOM
Music Publishers
Bad Habits Music
Publishing
Bearsongs
Brothers Organisation, The
Christel Music Limited
CTV Music (Great Britain)
Demi Monde Records &
Publishing Ltd.
Ever-Open-Eye Music
First Time Music
(Publishing)
Go! Discs Music
Havasong Music

Music Print Publishers
R.T.F.M.
*Sea Dream Music

Record Companies
Big Bear Records
Demi Monde Records and
Publishing, Ltd.
First Time Records
Le Matt Music Ltd.
Nervous Records
*Plankton Records
Red Sky Records
Red-Eye Records

Record Producers
Big Bear
Coppin, Johnny/Red Sky
Records
E.S.R. Productions
June Productions Ltd.

**Managers and Booking
Agents**
Coffer Management,
Raymond
First Time Management
James Management, Roger
Marsupial Ltd.
*Prestige Artistes
*Sandcastle Productions

Classical
*European Community
Chamber Orchestra

General Index

You'll notice as you flip through this index that more than 475 asterisks (*) appear. This symbol appears for the first time in this index, and it denotes markets that are new to this edition. Also for the first time in this index, we list companies that appeared in the 1996 edition of *Songwriter's Market*, but do not appear this year. Instead of page numbers beside these markets you will find two-letter codes in parentheses that explain why these markets no longer appear. The codes are: **(ED)**—Editorial Decision, **(NS)**—Not Accepting Submissions, **(NR)**—No (or late) Response to Listing Request, **(UC)**—Unable to Contact.

Bouquet-Orchid Enterprises 296
Bourne Company 135
Bourne Co. Music Publishers 51
Bovine International Record Company (NR)
Bowden, Robert 238
Bowman Productions & W. David Music, David 51
*Bowman Productions, David 380
Bradley Music, Allan 51
*BrainChild Records 155
Branch Group Music 51
Brasswind Artist Management 296
BRAVO! L.A. 424
*Breeden Music Group 155
Brentwood Music 156
Brewster Songs, Kitty 51
Briarhill Records 156
Bridges Productions 238
Bright Green Records 156
Bristol Riverside Theatre 400
Bristol Studios (see Mona Lisa Records/Bristol Studios 260)
Broadcast Music, Inc. 449
Broadway On Sunset 449
*Broadway on Sunset (Play Producers) 401
Broadway Tomorrow Previews 467
Broken Records 156
Broken Rekids (UC)
Bronx Flash Music, Inc. 52
Brothers Management Associates 296
Brothers Organisation, The 52
Brown University Orchestra 424
BSA Inc. (see Bill Stein Associates)
BSW Records 156
Buffalo Guitar Quartet 424
Bug Music, Inc. 52
Bullet Proof Management (ED)
Bullseye Entertainment 296
Buried Treasure Music 52
Burns Talent Agency, Dott 296
Bush Artist Fellowships 476
Butler Music, Bill (UC)
Butwin & Associates (OB)
Buy or Die CDs and LPs (NS)
Buzz Factory Records (NR)

C

C & M Productions Management Group 297
*C.E.G. Records, Inc. 157
C.S.B. Mix Inc. (RR)
Cactus Music and Winnebago Publishing 52
Cactus Records (NR)
Caffeine Disk 157
Cahn-Man (NS)
Caldwell Vanriper 381
Caledonia Folk Club (NR)
Calgary Boys Choir 425
Caliber Records (UC)
California Country Music 53
Calinoh Music Group 53
Cambria Records & Publishing 157
Camex Music 53
Campbell Group, The (NR)
Canaberry Music (RR)
Canada Council/Conseil des Arts du Canada 449
Canadian Academy of Recording Arts & Sciences (CARAS) 449
Canadian Amateur Musicians/Musiciens Amateurs du Canada (CAMMAC) 450
Canadian Children's Opera Chorus (UC)
Canadian Country Music Association (CCMA) 450
Canadian Music Week 467
Canadian Musician 486
*Canadian Musician Seminars 467
Canadian Opera Company 425
Canary Productions 381
'Cane Records (UC)
Cantata Academy 425
Cantata Singers of Ottawa (NR)
Cantilena Records (NR)
Cantrax Recorders 381
Canyon Records and Indian Arts 157
Capitol Ad, Management & Talent Group 238
Capitol Management & Talent 297
Capitol Records 157
Capstan Record Production 157
Care Free Records Group 158, 238

Carey College Dinner Theatre, William 401
Carlock Productions 239
*Carlyle Management 297
*Carlyle Productions 239
Carlyle Records, Inc. 158
Carmel Records (NR)
*Carmel Symphony Orchestra 425
*Caroline Records, Inc. 158
Carousel Records, Inc. (NR)
Carson City Chamber Orchestra 425
*Casale Music, Inc., Don 239, 297
Casanova-Pendrill Publicidad 381
Casaro Records 158
Cash Box Magazine 486
*Cash Productions, Inc. (Managers and Booking Agents) 297
Cash Productions, Inc. 53
Castle Music Group 53
*Castle von Buhler Records 158
Caterwaul Records (NR)
Cat's Voice Productions 159
Cavalry Productions 298
Cedar Creek Music (UC)
Cedar Creek Productions 239
Cedar Creek Productions and Management/Cedar Cove Music 298
Cedar Creek Records™ 159
Cellar Records 159
Celt, Jan 239
Centenary College, Theatre Department 401
*Center for Contemporary Opera 426
Center Theater 401
Centium Entertainment, Inc. 53, 159
Central Oregon Songwriters Association 450
Cerebral Records 160
Cha Cha Records 160
*Chabu Productions 298
Chapie Music (RR)
Chapman, Chuck (RR)
Chapman Recording Studios (NS)
Charis Music (NR)
Chaspen Symphony Orchestra 426
Chattahoochee Records 160
Cheavoria Music Co. 54

Discover How to Make More Money Making Music!

Writing Better Lyrics—Make every song sizzle using this unique, in-depth approach to lyric writing. You'll examine 17 extraordinary songs to discover what makes them so effective. Plus, you'll work through more than 30 language exercises as you learn to find snappy themes, avoid clichés and create meaningful metaphors and similes. *#10453/$19.99/192 pages*

The Craft and Business of Songwriting—From generating a song idea to signing a record deal, you'll discover how to create and market artistically and commercially successful songs in today's tough market. *#10429/$21.99/322 pages/paperback*

Hot Tips for the Home Recording Studio—Discover the tricks to recording a tight, polished, professional demo! Musicians acquainted with recording technology will learn how to lay down basic tracks, add vocals and mix to get exactly the sound they want. *#10415/$18.99/160 pages*

Creating Melodies—You'll be singing all the way to the bank when you discover the secrets of creating memorable melodies—from love ballads to commercial jingles! *#10400/$18.95/144 pages*

The Songwriter's Market Guide to Song & Demo Submission Formats—Get your foot in the door with knock-out query letters, slick demo presentations and the best advice for dealing with every player in the industry. *#10401/$19.99/160 pages*

Making Money Teaching Music—Discover how to find lucrative teaching opportunities. This guide shows you how to market yourself as a professional, recruit students of all ages, manage time and work schedules and much more! *#10428/$18.99/240 pages/44 b&w illus./paperback*

Who Wrote That Song?—If you're a music buff, you'll love the 12,000 songs listed here! Find everything from mid-nineteenth century ballads to today's Top Forty hits, with an emphasis on the last 40 years. Each listing includes the title, composer, lyricist and publication year. Where appropriate, listings also reveal who made the song popular, others who recorded it and who sang it on Broadway or in the movies. *#10403/$19.99/448 pages/paperback*

Making Money Making Music (No Matter Where You Live)—Cash in on scores of ways to make a profitable living with your musical talent—no matter where you live. This guide covers performing as a soloist or in a group, writing music for the radio, jingles and more! *#10174/$18.95/180 pages/paperback*

Networking in the Music Business—Who you know can either make—or break—your music career. Discover how to make and capitalize on the contacts you need to succeed. *#10365/$17.99/128 pages/paperback*

Beginning Songwriter's Answer Book—This newly revised and updated resource answers the questions most asked by beginning songwriters and gives you the know-how to get started in the music business. *#10376/$16.99/128 pages/paperback*

The Songwriter's Idea Book—You'll find 40 proven songwriting strategies sure to spark your creativity in this innovative handbook. Plus, learn how to use your unique personality to develop a strong writing style. *#10320/$18.99/240 pages*

The Craft of Lyric Writing—You'll get a complete guide on writing words for and to music, choosing song formats and creating lyrics with universal appeal from bestselling author and songwriter, Sheila Davis. *#01148/$23.99/350 pages*

88 Songwriting Wrongs & How to Right Them—88 ways to spot what's wrong with a song—along with expert instruction on how to fix it! Songwriters Pat & Pete Luboff cover it all, pointing out pitfalls and supplying concrete ways to improve your songwriting and make your songs more marketable. *#10287/$17.99/144 pages/paperback*

Music Publishing: A Songwriter's Guide—An insider in the music publishing game gives you all the information you need to make the best publishing deals for you and your songs. *#10195/$18.99/144 pages/paperback*

Successful Lyric Writing: A Step-by-Step Course & Workbook—This companion to Davis' *The Craft of Lyric Writing* is the first complete textbook on writing professional lyrics for every genre—from country to cabaret. Includes a series of 45 warm-up exercises, 10 graduated assignments, a 10-point guideline for figurative language, and a primer on right brain/left brain writing. *#10015/$19.99/292 pages/paperback*

Success Without a Record Deal

Getting a record deal isn't the only way to make a living through your music. Roger Day, Jana Stanfield and John Tirro are three successful singer/songwriters who enjoy the freedom of writing their own songs, performing live and selling their own CDs and tapes.

- "I'm doing better than most people I know with record deals, because I've been able to maintain total artistic independence and it has given me the financial resources to do independent projects." —**Roger Day**

- "In Nashville singer/songwriters have a lot more clout than someone who just sings. So I started writing songs to help me get a record deal, not realizing that songwriting was my true calling." —**Jana Stanfield**

- "The best thing to do is to go everywhere you can and at some point you'll be at the right place at the right time." —**John Tirro**